Critics Praise Bhagavad-gītā As It Is

With over ten million hardbound copies in print in over fifty languages, *Bhagavad-gītā As It Is,* by His Divine Grace A.C. Bhaktivedanta Swami Prabhupāda, is the best-selling and most authoritative edition of this classic of world literature. Here are some comments on *Bhagavad-gītā As It Is* from some of the world's leading scholars.

"There is little question that this edition is one of the best books available on the *Gītā* and on devotion. Prabhupāda's translation is an ideal blend of literal accuracy and religious insight."

Dr. Thomas J. Hopkins
Emeritus Chairman, Dept. of Religious Studies
Franklin and Marshall College

"The *Gītā* can be seen as the main literary support for the great religious civilization of India, the oldest surviving culture in the world. The present translation and commentary is another manifestation of the permanent living importance of the *Gītā.* Swami Bhaktivedanta brings to the West a salutary reminder that our highly activistic and one-sided culture is faced with a crisis that may end in self-destruction because it lacks the inner depth of an authentic metaphysical consciousness. Without such depth, our moral and political protestations are just so much verbiage."

Thomas Merton
Catholic theologian, monk, author

"No work in all Indian literature is more quoted, because none is better loved in the West than *Bhagavad-gītā.* Translation of such a work demands not only knowledge of Sanskrit but an inward sympathy with the theme and a verbal artistry. For the poem is a symphony in which God is seen in all things.

"His Divine Grace A.C. Bhaktivedanta Swami Prabhupāda is, of course, profoundly sympathetic to the theme. He brings to it, moreover, a special interpretive insight, a powerful and persuasive presentation in the *bhakti* [devotional] tradition.... The Swami does a real service for students by investing the beloved Indian epic with fresh meaning. Whatever our outlook may be, we should all be grateful for the labor that has led to this illuminating work."

Dr. Geddes MacGregor
Emeritus Distinguished Professor of Philosophy
University of Southern California

"In this beautiful translation, Śrīla Prabhupāda has caught the deep devotional spirit of the *Gītā* and has supplied the text with an elaborate commentary in the truly authentic tradition of Śrī Kṛṣṇa Caitanya, one of India's most important and influential saints."

Dr. J. Stillson Judah
Emeritus Professor of the History of Religions
and Director of the Library
Graduate Theological Union, Berkeley

"If truth is what works, as Pierce and the pragmatists insist, there must be a kind of truth in the *Bhagavad-gītā As It Is,* since those who follow its teachings display a joyous serenity usually missing in the bleak and strident lives of contemporary people."

Dr. Elwin H. Powell
Professor of Sociology
State University of New York

"Whether the reader be an adept of Indian spirituality or not, a reading of *Bhagavad-gītā As It Is* will be extremely profitable, for it will allow him to understand the *Gītā* as still today the majority of Hindus do. For many, this will be the first contact with the true India, the ancient India, the eternal India."

Dr. Francois Chenique
Doctor of Religious Sciences
Institute of Political Studies, Paris

"*Bhagavad-gītā As It Is* is a deeply felt, powerfully conceived and beautifully explained work.... I have never seen any other work on the *Gītā* with such an important voice and style. It is a work of undoubted integrity.... It will occupy a significant place in the intellectual and ethical life of modern man for a long time to come."

Dr. S. Shukla
Assistant Professor of Linguistics
Georgetown University

"The scholar, the student of Gauḍīya Vaiṣṇavism, and the increasing number of Western readers interested in classical Vedic thought have been done a service by Swami Bhaktivedanta. By bringing us a new and living interpretation of a text already known to many, he has increased our understanding manifold."

Dr. Edward C. Dimock, Jr.
Dept. of Sanskrit and Indian Studies
University of Chicago

Books by His Divine Grace
A. C. Bhaktivedanta Swami Prabhupāda

Bhagavad-gītā As It Is
Śrīmad-Bhāgavatam (*completed by disciples*)
Śrī Caitanya-caritāmṛta
Kṛṣṇa, the Supreme Personality of Godhead
Teachings of Lord Caitanya
The Nectar of Devotion
The Nectar of Instruction
Śrī Īśopaniṣad
Light of the Bhāgavata
Easy Journey to Other Planets
Teachings of Lord Kapila, the Son of Devahūti
Teachings of Queen Kuntī
Message of Godhead
The Science of Self-Realization
The Perfection of Yoga
Beyond Birth and Death
On the Way to Kṛṣṇa
Rāja-vidyā: The King of Knowledge
Elevation to Kṛṣṇa Consciousness
Kṛṣṇa Consciousness: The Matchless Gift
Kṛṣṇa Consciousness: The Topmost Yoga System
Perfect Questions, Perfect Answers
The Nārada-bhakti-sūtra (*completed by disciples*)
The Mukunda-mālā-stotra (*completed by disciples*)
Back to Godhead magazine (*founder*)

Books compiled from the teachings
of Śrīla Prabhupāda after his lifetime

The Journey of Self-Discovery
Civilization and Transcendence
The Laws of Nature
Renunciation Through Wisdom
Life Comes from Life
Beyond Illusion and Doubt
Veda: Secrets from the East
The Hare Kṛṣṇa Challenge
Chanting Hare Kṛṣṇa

गीतोपनिषद्

BHAGAVAD-GĪTĀ AS IT IS

Second Edition

Revised and Enlarged

with the original Sanskrit text,
roman transliteration, English equivalents,
translation and elaborate purports

by

His Divine Grace
A. C. Bhaktivedanta Swami Prabhupāda
Founder-*Ācārya* of the International Society for Krishna Consciousness

THE BHAKTIVEDANTA BOOK TRUST

Readers interested in the subject matter of this book are invited to contact the International Society for Krishna Consciousness (see address list in back of book) or the following information centers:

ISKCON Reader Services UK
• Tel. +44 (0)1923 851000
readerservices@pamho.net

ISKCON Reader Services Ireland
Tel. +44 (0)28 6772 3878
tp@krishnaisland.com

ISKCON Reader Services Hungary
Tel. +36-1-212-6270
info@krisna.hu

"A Summary of the *Bhagavad-gītā,*" reprinted with permission from *Surrender Unto Me: An Overview of the Bhagavad-gītā,* © Warren Weinstein (Bhūrijana Dāsa). Special thanks also for his "Yoga Ladder" notes from *Surrender Unto Me,* which served as the inspiration for the "Notes on the Stages of Yoga" that appears in this book.

www.krishna.com
www.bbt.se
www.bbtmedia.com

ISBN 978-91-7149-854-0

Printed in 2015

The ebook version of this title
is available for free at
www.bbtmedia.com/en
Code: **EB16EN44368P**

To
Śrīla Baladeva Vidyābhūṣaṇa,
who presented so nicely
the *Govinda-bhāṣya* commentary
on Vedānta philosophy

About Bhagavad-gītā

The *Bhagavad-gītā,* in 700 concise verses, presents a distillation of India's spiritual philosophy. Set as eighteen chapters in the epic *Mahābhārata,* the *Gītā's* teachings cross cultural and religious divides to present a universal spiritual truth as relevant today as when first spoken five thousand years ago.

That universal truth is presented through a conversation between God in the form of Krishna and His warrior friend Arjuna. Arjuna faced a dilemma most of us will never face, and yet dilemmas are integral to the human experience. While we may not hear the *Bhagavad-gītā's* teachings at the dawn of a literal battle as Arjuna did, the figurative battles in our own lives often force us to face the same unsolvable problem: if we win, we lose, and if we lose, we lose. Such moments can force us to reexamine everything we thought we knew about ourselves, the world, and spirituality, and we find ourselves becoming spiritual seekers.

The *Gītā* speaks to seekers of all faiths and creeds as well as those on no particular path. Whatever our frame of reference, the universal principles taught in the *Gītā* resonate with a seeker's heart.

The *Gītā* discusses such questions as

- Who am I?
- Is there life after death?
- How can I balance the material and spiritual aspects of my life?
- Why would a kind and just God allow suffering?
- How can I help this troubled world?
- Does my life run a predestined course or do I have choices?

About This Edition

There are already hundreds of editions of the *Bhagavad-gītā* in English, but few focus on the *Gītā's* real heart: devotional service (*bhakti-yoga*) as the culmination of all spiritual practice. This conclusive theme is transparently clear in *Bhagavad-gītā As It Is*. In this edition, first published in

1968, A.C. Bhaktivedanta Swami Prabhupāda, a consummate Sanskrit scholar and lifelong practitioner of *bhakti-yoga,* presents Kṛṣṇa's unfiltered teachings directly and without interpretation. Śrīla Prabhupāda's straightforward approach has made *Bhagavad-gītā As It Is*, with sixteen million copies in print in fifty-seven languages, the world's most widely read edition.

Selected Verses

As the embodied soul continuously passes, in this body, from boyhood to youth to old age, the soul similarly passes into another body at death. A sober person is not bewildered by such a change. (Chapter 2, text 13)

As a person puts on new garments, giving up old ones, the soul similarly accepts new material bodies, giving up the old and useless ones. (Chapter 2, text 22)

As all surrender unto Me, I reward them accordingly. Everyone follows My path in all respects, O son of Pṛthā. (Chapter 4, text 11)

In this world, there is nothing so sublime and pure as transcendental knowledge. Such knowledge is the mature fruit of all mysticism. And one who has become accomplished in the practice of devotional service enjoys this knowledge within himself in due course of time. (Chapter 4, text 38)

When one is enlightened with the knowledge by which nescience is destroyed, then his knowledge reveals everything, as the sun lights up everything in the daytime. (Chapter 5, text 16)

An intelligent person does not take part in the sources of misery, which are due to contact with the material senses. O son of Kuntī, such pleasures have a beginning and an end, and so the wise man does not delight in them. (Chapter 5, text 22)

In the stage of perfection called trance, or *samādhi,* one's mind is completely restrained from material mental activities by practice of yoga. This perfection is characterized by one's ability to see the self by the pure mind and to relish and rejoice in the self. In that joyous state, one is situated in boundless transcendental happiness, realized through transcendental senses. Established thus, one never departs from the truth, and upon gaining this he thinks there is no greater gain. Being situated in such a position, one is never shaken, even in the midst of greatest difficulty. This indeed is actual freedom from al miseries arising from material contact. (Chapter 6, texts 20–23)

For one who sees Me everywhere and sees everything in Me, I am never lost, nor is he ever lost to Me. (Chapter 6, text 30)

Of all yogis the one with great faith who always abides in Me, thinks of Me within, and renders transcendental loving service to Me – he is the most intimately united with Me in yoga and is the highest of all. That is My opinion. (Chapter 6, text 47)

O Arjuna, there is no truth superior to Me. Everything rests upon Me, as pearls are strung on a thread. (Chapter 7, text 7)

O son of Kuntī, I am the taste of water, the light of the sun and the moon, the syllable *om* in the Vedic mantras; I am the sound in ether and ability in man. I am the original fragrance of the earth, and I am the heat in fire. I am the life of all that lives, and I am the penances of all ascetics. (Chapter 7, texts 8–9)

The Supreme Personality of Godhead said: Time I am, the great destroyer of the worlds. (Chapter 11, text 32)

Only by undivided devotional service can I be understood as I am, standing before you, and can thus be seen directly. Only in this way can you enter into the mysteries of My understanding. (Chapter 11, text 54)

Those with the vision of eternity can see that the imperishable soul is transcendental, eternal, and beyond the modes of nature. Despite contact with the material body, O Arjuna, the soul neither does anything nor is entangled. (Chapter 13, text 32)

The demoniac, who are lost to themselves and who have no intelligence, engage in unbeneficial, horrible works meant to destroy the world. (Chapter 16, text 9)

If you become conscious of Me, you will pass over all the obstacles of conditioned life by My grace. If, however, you do not work in such consciousness but act through false ego, not hearing Me, you will be lost. (Chapter 18, text 58)

Answers from the Bhagavad-gītā

The tradition in which the *Bhagavad-gītā* appears recognizes the value of both the original text and the commentaries in Sanskrit, *ṭīkās* written by learned and spiritually astute practitioners. This edition of the *Bhagavad-gītā* is exceptional in that for almost every verse it offers extensive "purports," or explanations, drawn from such authentic commentaries, to provide spiritual, scriptural, and philosophical understandings. These purports form a treasury of spiritual wisdom in themselves.

Here are some markers to places where both verses and purports speak to questions about the soul, reincarnation, *yoga,* peace, and the Supreme.

The Soul

What is our real identity?

Chapter 2, text 13, purport, paragraph 1

What is the soul like?

Chapter 2, text 17

Chapter 2, text 20 and purport, paragraph 1

Chapter 2, texts 23–25

Is it possible to see the soul?

Chapter 2, text 25, purport

Why is it so hard to understand the soul?

Chapter 2, text 29 and purport

Where did we come from?

Chapter 7, text 6 and purport

I've heard that the Vedas say all living things have souls. Can you explain how it is that animals have souls?

Chapter 2, text 20, purport, paragraph 4

Reincarnation

Is there life after death?

Chapter 2, text 22

Chapter 15, text 8, paragraph 1

How do you end the cycle of birth and death once and for all?

Chapter 2, text 51 and its purport

Chapter 15, text 6, paragraphs 2 and 3

Yoga

What is yoga?

Chapter 6, text 3, purport, pararaph 1

Chapter 6, text 46, purport

What are aṣṭāṅga-yoga & prāṇāyāma?

Chapter 4, text 29, purport, paragraph 1

Chapter 5, text 27–28, purport, paragraphs 2–3

Chapter 6, texts 11–15

What is the ultimate goal of yoga practice?

Chapter 6, text 15, purport, paragraph 1

What lifestyle would enhance my yoga practice?

Chapter 6, texts 16 and 17 and their purports

What is bhakti-yoga Kṛṣṇa consciousness and how do I practice it?

Chapter 4, text 24 and its purport

Chapter 12, text 9, purport, paragraphs 2–4

Vegetarianism

What's wrong with killing animals?

Chapter 14, text 16, purport, paragraph 2

What's the best diet for a spiritualist?

Chapter 17, text 10, purport, paragraph 1

Peace

How can I achieve inner peace?

Chapter 2, text 66, purport, paragraph 1

Chapter 5, text 29 and its purport, paragraph 1

Why am I suffering and how can I mitigate it?

Chapter 5, text 14, purport

Chapter 15, text 9, purport

How can I deal with the ups and downs of life?

Chapter 2, text 14 and its purport, paragraph 1

Chapter 2, text 57, purport, paragraph 1

Can sex be a part of our spirituality?

Chapter 3, text 34, purport, paragraph 1

The Supreme

Is God an energy or a person?

Chapter 2, text 2, purport, paragraphs 1–5

What does God look like?

Chapter 4, text 6 and purport

Why does God appear in this world?

Chapter 4, texts 7 and 8, and the purport to text 7, paragraph 1

Why did God create the universe?

Chapter 3, text 37, purport, paragraph 2

Matter and Spirit

What is the spiritual world and how can I go there?

Chapter 15, text 6 and its purport

How does spiritual knowledge help us solve life's material dilemmas?

Chapter 2, text 8, paragraphs 4–6

Is it true that spiritual topics cannot be understood without the help of a guru?

Chapter 2, text 7 and its purport

What's the best way to approach a spiritual master?

Chapter 4, text 34 and its purport

Why was the material world created in the first place?

Chapter 3, text 10, paragraph 1

Understanding the Gītā

How can I get the most of my reading of the Gītā?

Chapter 1, text 1, paragraph 1

I've heard the Gītā propounds violence, which is immoral.

Chapter 18, text 78, paragraph 3

Contents

Appendixes

Setting the Scene

Although widely published and read by itself, *Bhagavad-gītā* originally appears as an episode in the *Mahābhārata,* the epic Sanskrit history of the ancient world. The *Mahābhārata* tells of events leading up to the present Age of Kali. It was at the beginning of this age, some fifty centuries ago, that Lord Kṛṣṇa spoke *Bhagavad-gītā* to His friend and devotee Arjuna.

Their discourse – one of the greatest philosophical and religious dialogues known to man – took place just before the onset of war, a great fratricidal conflict between the hundred sons of Dhṛtarāṣṭra and on the opposing side their cousins the Pāṇḍavas, or sons of Pāṇḍu.

Dhṛtarāṣṭra and Pāṇḍu were brothers born in the Kuru dynasty, descending from King Bharata, a former ruler of the earth, from whom the name *Mahābhārata* derives. Because Dhṛtarāṣṭra, the elder brother, was born blind, the throne that otherwise would have been his was passed down to the younger brother, Pāṇḍu.

When Pāṇḍu died at an early age, his five children – Yudhiṣṭhira, Bhīma, Arjuna, Nakula and Sahadeva – came under the care of Dhṛtarāṣṭra, who in effect became, for the time being, the king. Thus the sons of Dhṛtarāṣṭra and those of Pāṇḍu grew up in the same royal household. Both were trained in the military arts by the expert Droṇa and counseled by the revered "grandfather" of the clan, Bhīṣma.

Yet the sons of Dhṛtarāṣṭra, especially the eldest, Duryodhana, hated and envied the Pāṇḍavas. And the blind and weak-minded Dhṛtarāṣṭra wanted his own sons, not those of Pāṇḍu, to inherit the kingdom.

Thus Duryodhana, with Dhṛtarāṣṭra's consent, plotted to kill the young sons of Pāṇḍu, and it was only by the careful protection of their uncle Vidura and their cousin Lord Kṛṣṇa that the Pāṇḍavas escaped the many attempts against their lives.

Now, Lord Kṛṣṇa was not an ordinary man but the Supreme Godhead Himself, who had descended to earth and was playing the role of a prince in a contemporary dynasty. In this role He was also the nephew of Pāṇḍu's wife Kuntī, or Pṛthā, the mother of the Pāṇḍavas. So both as a relative and as the eternal upholder of religion, Kṛṣṇa favored the righteous sons of Pāṇḍu and protected them.

Ultimately, however, the clever Duryodhana challenged the Pāṇḍavas to a gambling match. In the course of that fateful tournament, Duryodhana and his brothers took possession of Draupadī, the chaste and devoted wife of the Pāṇḍavas, and insultingly tried to strip her naked before the entire assembly of princes and kings. Kṛṣṇa's divine intervention saved her, but the gambling, which was rigged, cheated the Pāṇḍavas of their kingdom and forced them into thirteen years of exile.

Upon returning from exile, the Pāṇḍavas rightfully requested their kingdom from Duryodhana, who bluntly refused to yield it. Duty-bound as princes to serve in public administration, the five Pāṇḍavas reduced their request to a mere five villages. But Duryodhana arrogantly replied that he wouldn't spare them enough land into which to drive a pin.

Throughout all this, the Pāṇḍavas had been consistently tolerant and forbearing. But now war seemed inevitable.

Nonetheless, as the princes of the world divided, some siding with the sons of Dhṛtarāṣṭra, others with the Pāṇḍavas, Kṛṣṇa Himself took the role of messenger for the sons of Pāṇḍu and went to the court of Dhṛtarāṣṭra to plead for peace. When His pleas were refused, war was now certain.

The Pāṇḍavas, men of the highest moral stature, recognized Kṛṣṇa to be the Supreme Personality of Godhead, whereas the impious sons of Dhṛtarāṣṭra did not. Yet Kṛṣṇa offered to enter the war according to the desire of the antagonists. As God, He would not personally fight; but whoever so desired might avail himself of Kṛṣṇa's army – and the other side could have Kṛṣṇa Himself, as an advisor and helper. Duryodhana, the political genius, snatched at Kṛṣṇa's armed forces, while the Pāṇḍavas were equally eager to have Kṛṣṇa Himself.

In this way, Kṛṣṇa became the charioteer of Arjuna, taking it upon Himself to drive the fabled bowman's chariot. This brings us to the point at which *Bhagavad-gītā* begins, with the two armies arrayed, ready for combat, and Dhṛtarāṣṭra anxiously inquiring of his secretary Sañjaya, "What did they do?"

The scene is set, with only the need for a brief note regarding this translation and commentary.

The general pattern translators have followed in rendering *Bhagavad-gītā* into English has been to brush aside the person Kṛṣṇa to make room for their own concepts and philosophies. The history of the *Mahābhārata* is taken as quaint mythology, and Kṛṣṇa becomes a poetic device for presenting the ideas of some anonymous genius, or at best He becomes a minor historical personage.

But the person Kṛṣṇa is both the goal and the substance of *Bhagavad-gītā,* so far as the *Gītā* speaks of itself.

This translation, then, and the commentary that accompanies it propose to direct the reader *to* Kṛṣṇa rather than away from Him. The *Bhagavad-gītā* thus becomes wholly consistent and comprehensible. Since Kṛṣṇa is the speaker of the *Gītā,* and its ultimate goal as well, *Bhagavad-gītā As It Is* presents this great scripture in its true terms.

The Publishers

But the person of Kṛṣṇa is both the goal and the substance of *Bhagavad-gītā As It Is*, as the *Gītā* speaks of itself.

This translation, then, and the commentary that accompanies it propose to direct the reader to Kṛṣṇa rather than away from Him. The *Bhagavad-gītā* thus becomes wholly consistent and comprehensible. Since Kṛṣṇa is the speaker of the *Gītā* and its ultimate goal as well, *Bhagavad-gītā As It Is* presents this great scripture in its true terms.

The Publishers

Preface

Originally I wrote *Bhagavad-gītā As It Is* in the form in which it is presented now. When this book was first published, the original manuscript was, unfortunately, cut short to less than 400 pages, without illustrations and without explanations for most of the original verses of the *Śrīmad Bhagavad-gītā*. In all of my other books – *Śrīmad-Bhāgavatam, Śrī Īśopaniṣad,* etc. – the system is that I give the original verse, its English transliteration, word-for-word Sanskrit-English equivalents, translations and purports. This makes the book very authentic and scholarly and makes the meaning self-evident. I was not very happy, therefore, when I had to minimize my original manuscript. But later on, when the demand for *Bhagavad-gītā As It Is* considerably increased, I was requested by many scholars and devotees to present the book in its original form. Thus the present attempt is to offer the original manuscript of this great book of knowledge with full *paramparā* explanation in order to establish the Kṛṣṇa consciousness movement more soundly and progressively.

Our Kṛṣṇa consciousness movement is genuine, historically authorized, natural and transcendental due to its being based on *Bhagavad-gītā As It Is*. It is gradually becoming the most popular movement in the entire world, especially amongst the younger generation. It is becoming more and more interesting to the older generation also. Older gentlemen are becoming interested, so much so that the fathers and grandfathers of my disciples are encouraging us by becoming life members of our great society, the International Society for Krishna Consciousness. In Los Angeles many fathers and mothers used to come to see me to express their feelings of gratitude for my leading the Kṛṣṇa consciousness movement throughout the entire world. Some of them said that it is greatly fortunate for the Americans that I have started the Kṛṣṇa consciousness movement in America. But actually the original father of this movement is Lord Kṛṣṇa Himself, since it was started a very long time ago but is coming down to human society by disciplic succession. If I have any credit in this connection, it does not belong to me personally, but it is due to my eternal spiritual master, His Divine Grace Oṁ Viṣṇupāda Paramahaṁsa Parivrājakācārya 108 Śrī Śrīmad Bhaktisiddhānta Sarasvatī Gosvāmī Mahārāja Prabhupāda.

If personally I have any credit in this matter, it is only that I have tried to present *Bhagavad-gītā* as it is, without any adulteration. Before my presentation of *Bhagavad-gītā As It Is,* almost all the English editions of *Bhagavad-gītā* were introduced to fulfill someone's personal ambition. But our attempt, in presenting *Bhagavad-gītā As It Is,* is to present the mission of the Supreme Personality of Godhead, Kṛṣṇa. Our business is to present the will of Kṛṣṇa, not that of any mundane speculator like the politician, philosopher or scientist, for they have very little knowledge of Kṛṣṇa, despite all their other knowledge. When Kṛṣṇa says, *man-manā bhava mad-bhakto mad-yājī māṁ namaskuru,* etc., we, unlike the so-called scholars, do not say that Kṛṣṇa and His inner spirit are different. Kṛṣṇa is absolute, and there is no difference between Kṛṣṇa's name, Kṛṣṇa's form, Kṛṣṇa's qualities, Kṛṣṇa's pastimes, etc. This absolute position of Kṛṣṇa is difficult to understand for any person who is not a devotee of Kṛṣṇa in the system of *paramparā* (disciplic succession). Generally the so-called scholars, politicians, philosophers, and *svāmīs,* without perfect knowledge of Kṛṣṇa, try to banish or kill Kṛṣṇa when writing commentary on *Bhagavad-gītā*. Such unauthorized commentary upon *Bhagavad-gītā* is known as *māyāvāda-bhāṣya,* and Lord Caitanya has warned us about these unauthorized men. Lord Caitanya clearly says that anyone who tries to understand *Bhagavad-gītā* from the Māyāvādī point of view will commit a great blunder. The result of such a blunder will be that the misguided student of *Bhagavad-gītā* will certainly be bewildered on the path of spiritual guidance and will not be able to go back to home, back to Godhead.

Our only purpose is to present this *Bhagavad-gītā As It Is* in order to guide the conditioned student to the same purpose for which Kṛṣṇa descends to this planet once in a day of Brahmā, or every 8,600,000,000 years. This purpose is stated in *Bhagavad-gītā,* and we have to accept it as it is; otherwise there is no point in trying to understand the *Bhagavad-gītā* and its speaker, Lord Kṛṣṇa. Lord Kṛṣṇa first spoke *Bhagavad-gītā* to the sun-god some hundreds of millions of years ago. We have to accept this fact and thus understand the historical significance of *Bhagavad-gītā,* without misinterpretation, on the authority of Kṛṣṇa. To interpret *Bhagavad-gītā* without any reference to the will of Kṛṣṇa is the greatest offense. In order to save oneself from this offense, one has to understand the Lord as the Supreme Personality of Godhead, as He was directly understood by Arjuna, Lord Kṛṣṇa's first disciple. Such understanding of *Bhagavad-gītā* is really profitable and authorized for the welfare of human society in fulfilling the mission of life.

The Kṛṣṇa consciousness movement is essential in human society, for it offers the highest perfection of life. How this is so is explained fully in the *Bhagavad-gītā*. Unfortunately, mundane wranglers have taken advantage of *Bhagavad-gītā* to push forward their demonic propensities and mislead people regarding right understanding of the simple principles of life. Everyone should know how God, or Kṛṣṇa, is great, and everyone should know the factual position of the living entities. Everyone should know that a living entity is eternally a servant and that unless one serves Kṛṣṇa one has to serve illusion in different varieties of the three modes of material nature and thus wander perpetually within the cycle of birth and death; even the so-called liberated Māyāvādī speculator has to undergo this process. This knowledge constitutes a great science, and each and every living being has to hear it for his own interest.

People in general, especially in this Age of Kali, are enamored by the external energy of Kṛṣṇa, and they wrongly think that by advancement of material comforts every man will be happy. They have no knowledge that the material or external nature is very strong, for everyone is strongly bound by the stringent laws of material nature. A living entity is happily the part and parcel of the Lord, and thus his natural function is to render immediate service to the Lord. By the spell of illusion one tries to be happy by serving his personal sense gratification in different forms which will never make him happy. Instead of satisfying his own personal material senses, he has to satisfy the senses of the Lord. That is the highest perfection of life. The Lord wants this, and He demands it. One has to understand this central point of *Bhagavad-gītā*. Our Kṛṣṇa consciousness movement is teaching the whole world this central point, and because we are not polluting the theme of *Bhagavad-gītā As It Is,* anyone seriously interested in deriving benefit by studying the *Bhagavad-gītā* must take help from the Kṛṣṇa consciousness movement for practical understanding of *Bhagavad-gītā* under the direct guidance of the Lord. We hope, therefore, that people will derive the greatest benefit by studying *Bhagavad-gītā As It Is* as we have presented it here, and if even one man becomes a pure devotee of the Lord, we shall consider our attempt a success.

A.C. Bhaktivedanta Swami, 12 May 1971, Sydney, Australia

The Kṛṣṇa consciousness movement is essential in human society, for it offers the highest perfection of life. How this is so is explained fully in the *Bhagavad-gītā*. Unfortunately, mundane wranglers have taken advantage of *Bhagavad-gītā* to push forward their demonic propensities and mislead people regarding right understanding of the simple principles of life. Everyone should know how God, or Kṛṣṇa, is great, and everyone should know the factual position of the living entities. Everyone should know that a living entity is eternally a servant and that unless one serves Kṛṣṇa, one has to serve illusion in different varieties of the three modes of material nature, and thus wander perpetually within the cycle of birth and death; even the so-called liberated Māyāvādī speculator has to undergo this process. This knowledge constitutes a great science, and each and every living being has to hear it for his own interest.

People in general, especially in this Age of Kali, are enamored by the external energy of Kṛṣṇa, and they wrongly think that by advancement of material comforts every man will be happy. They have no knowledge that the material or external nature is very strong, for everyone is strongly bound by the stringent laws of material nature. A living entity is happily the part and parcel of the Lord, and thus his natural function is to render immediate service to the Lord. By the spell of illusion one tries to be happy by serving his personal sense gratification in different forms which will never make him happy. Instead of satisfying his own personal material senses, he has to satisfy the senses of the Lord. That is the highest perfection of life. The Lord wants this, and He demands it. One has to understand this central point of *Bhagavad-gītā*. Our Kṛṣṇa consciousness movement is teaching the whole world this central point, and because we are not polluting the theme of *Bhagavad-gītā As It Is*, anyone seriously interested in deriving benefit by studying the *Bhagavad-gītā* must take help from the Kṛṣṇa consciousness movement for practical understanding of *Bhagavad-gītā* under the direct guidance of the Lord. We hope, therefore, that people will derive the greatest benefit by studying *Bhagavad-gītā As It Is* as we have presented it here, and if even one man becomes a pure devotee of the Lord, we shall consider our attempt a success.

A. C. Bhaktivedanta Swami 12 May 1971 Sydney, Australia

Introduction

oṁ ajñāna-timirāndhasya, jñānāñjana-śalākayā
cakṣur unmīlitaṁ yena, tasmai śrī-gurave namaḥ

śrī-caitanya-mano-'bhīṣṭaṁ, sthāpitaṁ yena bhū-tale
svayaṁ rūpaḥ kadā mahyaṁ, dadāti sva-padāntikam

I was born in the darkest ignorance, and my spiritual master opened my eyes with the torch of knowledge. I offer my respectful obeisances unto him.

When will Śrīla Rūpa Gosvāmī Prabhupāda, who has established within this material world the mission to fulfill the desire of Lord Caitanya, give me shelter under his lotus feet?

vande 'haṁ śrī-guroḥ śrī-yuta-pada-kamalaṁ śrī-gurūn vaiṣṇavāṁś ca
śrī-rūpaṁ sāgrajātaṁ saha-gaṇa-raghunāthānvitaṁ taṁ sa-jīvam
sādvaitaṁ sāvadhūtaṁ parijana-sahitaṁ kṛṣṇa-caitanya-devaṁ
śrī-rādhā-kṛṣṇa-pādān saha-gaṇa-lalitā-śrī-viśākhānvitāṁś ca

I offer my respectful obeisances unto the lotus feet of my spiritual master and unto the feet of all Vaiṣṇavas. I offer my respectful obeisances unto the lotus feet of Śrīla Rūpa Gosvāmī along with his elder brother Sanātana Gosvāmī, as well as Raghunātha Dāsa and Raghunātha Bhaṭṭa, Gopāla Bhaṭṭa, and Śrīla Jīva Gosvāmī. I offer my respectful obeisances to Lord Kṛṣṇa Caitanya and Lord Nityānanda along with Advaita Ācārya, Gadādhara, Śrīvāsa, and other associates. I offer my respectful obeisances to Śrīmatī Rādhārāṇī and Śrī Kṛṣṇa along with Their associates Śrī Lalitā and Viśākhā.

he kṛṣṇa karuṇā-sindho, dīna-bandho jagat-pate
gopeśa gopikā-kānta, rādhā-kānta namo 'stu te

O my dear Kṛṣṇa, You are the friend of the distressed and the source of creation. You are the master of the *gopīs* and the lover of Rādhārāṇī. I offer my respectful obeisances unto You.

tapta-kāñcana-gaurāṅgi, rādhe vṛndāvaneśvari
vṛṣabhānu-sute devi, praṇamāmi hari-priye

I offer my respects to Rādhārāṇī, whose bodily complexion is like molten gold and who is the Queen of Vṛndāvana. You are the daughter of King Vṛṣabhānu, and You are very dear to Lord Kṛṣṇa.

vāñchā-kalpa-tarubhyaś ca, kṛpā-sindhubhya eva ca
patitānāṁ pāvanebhyo, vaiṣṇavebhyo namo namaḥ

I offer my respectful obeisances unto all the Vaiṣṇava devotees of the Lord. They can fulfill the desires of everyone, just like desire trees, and they are full of compassion for the fallen souls.

śrī-kṛṣṇa-caitanya prabhu-nityānanda
śrī-advaita gadādhara śrīvāsādi-gaura-bhakta-vṛnda

I offer my obeisances to Śrī Kṛṣṇa Caitanya, Prabhu Nityānanda, Śrī Advaita, Gadādhara, Śrīvāsa and all others in the line of devotion.

hare kṛṣṇa hare kṛṣṇa kṛṣṇa kṛṣṇa hare hare
hare rāma hare rāma rāma rāma hare hare

Bhagavad-gītā is also known as *Gītopaniṣad.* It is the essence of Vedic knowledge and one of the most important *Upaniṣads* in Vedic literature. Of course there are many commentaries in English on the *Bhagavad-gītā,* and one may question the necessity for another one. This present edition can be explained in the following way. Recently an American lady asked me to recommend an English translation of *Bhagavad-gītā.* Of course in America there are so many editions of *Bhagavad-gītā* available in English, but as far as I have seen, not only in America but also in India, none of them can be strictly said to be authoritative because in almost every one of them the commentator has expressed his own opinions without touching the spirit of *Bhagavad-gītā* as it is.

The spirit of *Bhagavad-gītā* is mentioned in *Bhagavad-gītā* itself. It is just like this: If we want to take a particular medicine, then we have to follow the directions written on the label. We cannot take the medicine according to our own whim or the direction of a friend. It must be taken according to the directions on the label or the directions given by a physician. Similarly, *Bhagavad-gītā* should be taken or accepted as it is directed by the speaker Himself. The speaker of *Bhagavad-gītā* is Lord Śrī Kṛṣṇa. He is mentioned on every page of *Bhagavad-gītā* as the Supreme Personality of Godhead, Bhagavān. Of course the word *bhagavān* sometimes refers to any powerful person or any powerful demigod, and certainly here *bhagavān* designates Lord Śrī Kṛṣṇa as a great personality, but at the same time we should know that Lord Śrī Kṛṣṇa is the Supreme Personality of Godhead, as is confirmed by all great *ācāryas* (spiritual masters) like Śaṅkarācārya, Rāmānujācārya, Madhvācārya, Nimbārka Svāmī, Śrī Caitanya Mahāprabhu and many other authorities of Vedic knowledge in India. The Lord Himself also establishes Himself as the Supreme Personality of Godhead in the *Bhagavad-gītā,* and He is accepted as such in the *Brahma-saṁhitā* and all the *Purāṇas,* especially the *Śrīmad-Bhāgavatam,* known as the *Bhāgavata Purāṇa* (*kṛṣṇas tu bhagavān svayam*). Therefore we should take *Bhagavad-gītā* as it is directed by the Personality of Godhead Himself. In the Fourth Chapter of the *Gītā* (4.1–3) the Lord says:

imaṁ vivasvate yogaṁ, proktavān aham avyayam
vivasvān manave prāha, manur ikṣvākave 'bravīt

evaṁ paramparā-prāptam, imaṁ rājarṣayo viduḥ
sa kāleneha mahatā, yogo naṣṭaḥ paran-tapa

sa evāyaṁ mayā te 'dya, yogaḥ proktaḥ purātanaḥ
bhakto 'si me sakhā ceti, rahasyaṁ hy etad uttamam

Here the Lord informs Arjuna that this system of *yoga,* the *Bhagavad-gītā,* was first spoken to the sun-god, and the sun-god explained it to Manu, and Manu explained it to Ikṣvāku, and in that way, by disciplic succession, one speaker after another, this *yoga* system has been coming down. But in the course of time it has become lost. Consequently the Lord has to speak it again, this time to Arjuna on the Battlefield of Kurukṣetra.

He tells Arjuna that He is relating this supreme secret to him because Arjuna is His devotee and His friend. The purport of this is that *Bhagavad-gītā* is a treatise which is especially meant for the devotee of the Lord. There are three classes of transcendentalists, namely the *jñānī,* the *yogī* and the *bhakta,* or the impersonalist, the meditator and the devotee. Here the Lord clearly tells Arjuna that He is making him the first receiver of a new *paramparā* (disciplic succession) because the old succession was broken. It was the Lord's wish, therefore, to establish another *paramparā* in the same line of thought that was coming down from the sun-god to others, and it was His wish that His teaching be distributed anew by Arjuna. He wanted Arjuna to become the authority in understanding the *Bhagavad-gītā.* So we see that *Bhagavad-gītā* is instructed to Arjuna especially because Arjuna was a devotee of the Lord, a direct student of Kṛṣṇa, and His intimate friend. Therefore *Bhagavad-gītā* is best understood by a person who has qualities similar to Arjuna's. That is to say he must be a devotee in a direct relationship with the Lord. As soon as one becomes a devotee of the Lord, he also has a direct relationship with the Lord. That is a very elaborate subject matter, but briefly it can be stated that a devotee is in a relationship with the Supreme Personality of Godhead in one of five different ways:

1. One may be a devotee in a passive state;
2. One may be a devotee in an active state;
3. One may be a devotee as a friend;
4. One may be a devotee as a parent;
5. One may be a devotee as a conjugal lover.

Arjuna was in a relationship with the Lord as friend. Of course there is a gulf of difference between this friendship and the friendship found in the material world. This is transcendental friendship, which cannot be had by everyone. Of course everyone has a particular relationship with the Lord, and that relationship is evoked by the perfection of devotional service. But in the present status of our life, not only have we forgotten the Supreme Lord, but we have forgotten our eternal relationship with the Lord. Every living being, out of the many, many billions and trillions of living beings, has a particular relationship with the Lord eternally. That is called *svarūpa.* By the process of devotional service, one can revive that *svarūpa,* and that stage is called *svarūpa-siddhi* – perfection of one's constitutional position. So Arjuna was a devotee, and he was in touch with the Supreme Lord in friendship.

How Arjuna accepted this *Bhagavad-gītā* should be noted. His manner of acceptance is given in the Tenth Chapter (10.12–14):

arjuna uvāca
paraṁ brahma paraṁ dhāma, pavitraṁ paramaṁ bhavān
puruṣaṁ śāśvataṁ divyam, ādi-devam ajaṁ vibhum

āhus tvām ṛṣayaḥ sarve, devarṣir nāradas tathā
asito devalo vyāsaḥ, svayaṁ caiva bravīṣi me

sarvam etad ṛtaṁ manye, yan māṁ vadasi keśava
na hi te bhagavan vyaktiṁ, vidur devā na dānavāḥ

"Arjuna said: You are the Supreme Personality of Godhead, the ultimate abode, the purest, the Absolute Truth. You are the eternal, transcendental, original person, the unborn, the greatest. All the great sages such as Nārada, Asita, Devala and Vyāsa confirm this truth about You, and now You Yourself are declaring it to me. O Kṛṣṇa, I totally accept as truth all that You have told me. Neither the demigods nor the demons, O Lord, can understand Your personality."

After hearing *Bhagavad-gītā* from the Supreme Personality of Godhead, Arjuna accepted Kṛṣṇa as *paraṁ brahma,* the Supreme Brahman. Every living being is Brahman, but the supreme living being, or the Supreme Personality of Godhead, is the Supreme Brahman. *Paraṁ dhāma* means that He is the supreme rest or abode of everything; *pavitram* means that He is pure, untainted by material contamination; *puruṣam* means that He is the supreme enjoyer; *śāśvatam,* eternal; *divyam,* transcendental; *ādi-devam,* the original Supreme Personality of Godhead; *ajam,* the unborn; and *vibhum,* the greatest.

Now one may think that because Kṛṣṇa was the friend of Arjuna, Arjuna was telling Him all this by way of flattery, but Arjuna, just to drive out this kind of doubt from the minds of the readers of *Bhagavad-gītā,* substantiates these praises in the next verse when he says that Kṛṣṇa is accepted as the Supreme Personality of Godhead not only by himself but by authorities like Nārada, Asita, Devala and Vyāsadeva. These are great personalities who distribute the Vedic knowledge as it is accepted by all *ācāryas.* Therefore Arjuna tells Kṛṣṇa that he accepts whatever He says to be completely perfect. *Sarvam etad ṛtaṁ manye:* "I accept everything You say to be true." Arjuna also says that the personality of the Lord is very difficult to understand and that He cannot be known even by the great demigods. This means that the Lord cannot even be known by personalities greater than human beings. So how can a human being understand Lord Śrī Kṛṣṇa without becoming His devotee?

Therefore *Bhagavad-gītā* should be taken up in a spirit of devotion. One should not think that he is equal to Kṛṣṇa, nor should he think that Kṛṣṇa is an ordinary personality or even a very great personality. Lord Śrī Kṛṣṇa is the Supreme Personality of Godhead. So according to the statements of *Bhagavad-gītā* or the statements of Arjuna, the person who is trying to understand the *Bhagavad-gītā,* we should at least theoretically accept Śrī Kṛṣṇa as the Supreme Personality of Godhead, and with that submissive spirit we can understand the *Bhagavad-gītā.* Unless one reads the *Bhagavad-gītā* in a submissive spirit, it is very difficult to understand *Bhagavad-gītā,* because it is a great mystery.

Just what is the *Bhagavad-gītā*? The purpose of *Bhagavad-gītā* is to deliver mankind from the nescience of material existence. Every man is in difficulty in so many ways, as Arjuna also was in difficulty in having to fight the Battle of Kurukṣetra. Arjuna surrendered unto Śrī Kṛṣṇa, and consequently this *Bhagavad-gītā* was spoken. Not only Arjuna, but every one of us is full of anxieties because of this material existence. Our very existence is in the atmosphere of nonexistence. Actually we are not meant to be threatened by nonexistence. Our existence is eternal. But somehow or other we are put into *asat. Asat* refers to that which does not exist.

Out of so many human beings who are suffering, there are a few who are actually inquiring about their position, as to what they are, why they are put into this awkward position and so on. Unless one is awakened to this position of questioning his suffering, unless he realizes that he doesn't want suffering but rather wants to make a solution to all suffering, then one is not to be considered a perfect human being. Humanity begins when this sort of inquiry is awakened in one's mind. In the *Brahma-sūtra* this inquiry is called *brahma-jijñāsā. Athāto brahma-jijñāsā.* Every activity of the human being is to be considered a failure unless he inquires about the nature of the Absolute. Therefore those who begin to question why they are suffering or where they came from and where they shall go after death are proper students for understanding *Bhagavad-gītā.* The sincere student should also have a firm respect for the Supreme Personality of Godhead. Such a student was Arjuna.

Lord Kṛṣṇa descends specifically to reestablish the real purpose of life when man forgets that purpose. Even then, out of many, many human beings who awaken, there may be one who actually enters the spirit of understanding his position, and for him this *Bhagavad-gītā* is spoken. Actually we are all swallowed by the tigress of nescience, but the Lord is very merciful upon living entities, especially human beings. To this end He spoke the *Bhagavad-gītā,* making His friend Arjuna His student.

Being an associate of Lord Kṛṣṇa, Arjuna was above all ignorance, but Arjuna was put into ignorance on the Battlefield of Kurukṣetra just to question Lord Kṛṣṇa about the problems of life so that the Lord could explain them for the benefit of future generations of human beings and chalk out the plan of life. Then man could act accordingly and perfect the mission of human life.

The subject of the *Bhagavad-gītā* entails the comprehension of five basic truths. First of all, the science of God is explained and then the constitutional position of the living entities, *jīvas.* There is *īśvara,* which means the controller, and there are *jīvas,* the living entities which are controlled. If a living entity says that he is not controlled but that he is free, then he is insane. The living being is controlled in every respect, at least in his conditioned life. So in the *Bhagavad-gītā* the subject matter deals with the *īśvara,* the supreme controller, and the *jīvas,* the controlled living entities. *Prakṛti* (material nature) and time (the duration of existence of the whole universe or the manifestation of material nature) and *karma* (activity) are also discussed. The cosmic manifestation is full of different activities. All living entities are engaged in different activities. From *Bhagavad-gītā* we must learn what God is, what the living entities are, what *prakṛti* is, what the cosmic manifestation is, how it is controlled by time, and what the activities of the living entities are.

Out of these five basic subject matters in *Bhagavad-gītā* it is established that the Supreme Godhead, or Kṛṣṇa, or Brahman, or the supreme controller, or Paramātmā – you may use whatever name you like – is the greatest of all. The living beings are in quality like the supreme controller. For instance, the Lord has control over the universal affairs of material nature, as will be explained in the later chapters of *Bhagavad-gītā.* Material nature is not independent. She is acting under the directions of the Supreme Lord. As Lord Kṛṣṇa says, *mayādhyakṣeṇa prakṛtiḥ sūyate sa-carācaram:* "This material nature is working under My direction." When we see wonderful things happening in the cosmic nature, we should know that behind this cosmic manifestation there is a controller. Nothing could be manifested without being controlled. It is childish not to consider the controller. For instance, a child may think that an automobile is quite wonderful to be able to run without a horse or other animal pulling it, but a sane man knows the nature of the automobile's engineering arrangement. He always knows that behind the machinery there is a man, a driver. Similarly, the Supreme Lord is the driver under whose direction everything is working. Now the *jīvas,* or the living entities, have been accepted by the Lord, as we will note in the later chapters, as His parts and parcels. A particle of gold is also gold, a drop of water from the ocean is also salty, and similarly we the living entities, being part and parcel of the supreme controller, *īśvara,* or Bhagavān, Lord Śrī Kṛṣṇa, have all the qualities of the Supreme Lord in minute quantity because we are minute *īśvaras,* subordinate *īśvaras.* We are trying to control nature, as presently we are trying to control space or planets, and this tendency to control is there because it is in Kṛṣṇa. But although we have a tendency to lord it over material nature, we should know that we are not the supreme controller. This is explained in *Bhagavad-gītā.*

What is material nature? This is also explained in the *Gītā* as inferior *prakṛti,* inferior nature. The living entity is explained as the superior *prakṛti. Prakṛti* is always under control, whether inferior or superior. *Prakṛti* is female, and she is controlled by the Lord just as the activities of a wife are controlled by the husband. *Prakṛti* is always subordinate, predominated by the Lord, who is the predominator. The living entities and material nature are both predominated, controlled by the Supreme Lord. According to the *Gītā,* the living entities, although parts and parcels of the Supreme Lord, are to be considered *prakṛti.* This is clearly mentioned in the Seventh Chapter of *Bhagavad-gītā. Apareyam itas tv anyāṁ prakṛtiṁ viddhi me parām/ jīva-bhūtām:* "This material nature is My inferior *prakṛti,* but beyond this is another *prakṛti – jīva-bhūtām,* the living entities."

Material nature itself is constituted by three qualities: the mode of goodness, the mode of passion and the mode of ignorance. Above these modes there is eternal time, and by a combination of these modes of nature and under the control and purview of eternal time there are activities, which are called *karma.* These activities are being carried out from time immemorial, and we are suffering or enjoying the fruits of our activities. For instance, suppose I am a businessman and have worked very hard with intelligence and have amassed a great bank balance. Then I am an enjoyer. But then say I have lost all my money in business; then I am a sufferer. Similarly, in every field of life we enjoy the results of our work, or we suffer the results. This is called *karma.*

Īśvara (the Supreme Lord), *jīva* (the living entity), *prakṛti* (nature), *kāla* (eternal time) and *karma* (activity) are all explained in the *Bhagavad-gītā.* Out of these five, the Lord, the living entities, material nature and time are eternal. The manifestation of *prakṛti* may be temporary, but it is not false. Some philosophers say that the manifestation of material nature is false, but according to the philosophy of *Bhagavad-gītā* or according to the philosophy of the Vaiṣṇavas, this is not so. The manifestation of the world is not accepted as false; it is accepted as real, but temporary. It is likened unto a cloud which moves across the sky, or the coming of the rainy season, which nourishes grains. As soon as the rainy season is over and as soon as the cloud goes away, all the crops which were nourished by the rain dry up. Similarly, this material manifestation takes place at a certain interval, stays for a while and then disappears. Such are the workings of *prakṛti.* But this cycle is working eternally. Therefore *prakṛti* is eternal; it is not false. The Lord refers to this as "My *prakṛti.*" This material nature is the separated energy of the Supreme

Lord, and similarly the living entities are also the energy of the Supreme Lord, although they are not separated but eternally related. So the Lord, the living entity, material nature and time are all interrelated and are all eternal. However, the other item, *karma,* is not eternal. The effects of *karma* may be very old indeed. We are suffering or enjoying the results of our activities from time immemorial, but we can change the results of our *karma,* or our activity, and this change depends on the perfection of our knowledge. We are engaged in various activities. Undoubtedly we do not know what sort of activities we should adopt to gain relief from the actions and reactions of all these activities, but this is also explained in the *Bhagavad-gītā.*

The position of *īśvara,* the Supreme Lord, is that of supreme consciousness. The *jīvas,* or the living entities, being parts and parcels of the Supreme Lord, are also conscious. Both the living entity and material nature are explained as *prakṛti,* the energy of the Supreme Lord, but one of the two, the *jīva,* is conscious. The other *prakṛti* is not conscious. That is the difference. Therefore the *jīva-prakṛti* is called superior because the *jīva* has consciousness which is similar to the Lord's. The Lord's is supreme consciousness, however, and one should not claim that the *jīva,* the living entity, is also supremely conscious. The living being cannot be supremely conscious at any stage of his perfection, and the theory that he can be so is a misleading theory. Conscious he may be, but he is not perfectly or supremely conscious.

The distinction between the *jīva* and the *īśvara* will be explained in the Thirteenth Chapter of *Bhagavad-gītā.* The Lord is *kṣetra-jña,* conscious, as is the living being, but the living being is conscious of his particular body, whereas the Lord is conscious of all bodies. Because He lives in the heart of every living being, He is conscious of the psychic movements of the particular *jīvas.* We should not forget this. It is also explained that the Paramātmā, the Supreme Personality of Godhead, is living in everyone's heart as *īśvara,* as the controller, and that He is giving directions for the living entity to act as he desires. The living entity forgets what to do. First of all he makes a determination to act in a certain way, and then he is entangled in the actions and reactions of his own *karma.* After giving up one type of body, he enters another type of body, as we take off and put on clothes. As the soul thus migrates, he suffers the actions and reactions of his past activities. These activities can be changed when the living being is in the mode of goodness, in sanity, and understands what sort of activities he should adopt. If he does so, then all the actions and reactions of his past activities can be changed. Consequently, *karma* is not eternal.

Therefore we stated that of the five items (*īśvara, jīva, prakṛti,* time and *karma*) four are eternal, whereas *karma* is not eternal.

The supreme conscious *īśvara* is similar to the living entity in this way: both the consciousness of the Lord and that of the living entity are transcendental. It is not that consciousness is generated by the association of matter. That is a mistaken idea. The theory that consciousness develops under certain circumstances of material combination is not accepted in the *Bhagavad-gītā.* Consciousness may be pervertedly reflected by the covering of material circumstances, just as light reflected through colored glass may appear to be a certain color, but the consciousness of the Lord is not materially affected. Lord Kṛṣṇa says, *mayādhyakṣeṇa prakṛtiḥ.* When He descends into the material universe, His consciousness is not materially affected. If He were so affected, He would be unfit to speak on transcendental matters as He does in the *Bhagavad-gītā.* One cannot say anything about the transcendental world without being free from materially contaminated consciousness. So the Lord is not materially contaminated. Our consciousness, at the present moment, however, *is* materially contaminated. The *Bhagavad-gītā* teaches that we have to purify this materially contaminated consciousness. In pure consciousness, our actions will be dovetailed to the will of the *īśvara,* and that will make us happy. It is not that we have to cease all activities. Rather, our activities are to be purified, and purified activities are called *bhakti.* Activities in *bhakti* appear to be like ordinary activities, but they are not contaminated. An ignorant person may see that a devotee is acting or working like an ordinary man, but such a person with a poor fund of knowledge does not know that the activities of the devotee or of the Lord are not contaminated by impure consciousness or matter. They are transcendental to the three modes of nature. We should know, however, that at this point our consciousness is contaminated.

When we are materially contaminated, we are called conditioned. False consciousness is exhibited under the impression that I am a product of material nature. This is called false ego. One who is absorbed in the thought of bodily conceptions cannot understand his situation. *Bhagavad-gītā* was spoken to liberate one from the bodily conception of life, and Arjuna put himself in this position in order to receive this information from the Lord. One must become free from the bodily conception of life; that is the preliminary activity for the transcendentalist. One who wants to become free, who wants to become liberated, must first of all learn that he is not this material body. *Mukti,* or liberation, means freedom from material consciousness. In the *Śrīmad-Bhāgavatam* also the definition of liberation is given. *Muktir hitvānyathā-rūpaṁ svarūpeṇa vyavasthitiḥ: mukti* means liberation from the contaminated consciousness of this material world and situation in pure consciousness. All the instructions of *Bhagavad-gītā* are intended to awaken this pure consciousness, and therefore we find at the last stage of the *Gītā's* instructions that Kṛṣṇa is asking Arjuna whether he is now in purified consciousness. Purified consciousness means acting in accordance with the instructions of the Lord. This is the whole sum and substance of purified consciousness. Consciousness is already there because we are part and parcel of the Lord, but for us there is the affinity of being affected by the inferior modes. But the Lord, being the Supreme, is never affected. That is the difference between the Supreme Lord and the small individual souls.

What is this consciousness? This consciousness is "I am." Then what am I? In contaminated consciousness "I am" means "I am the lord of all I survey. I am the enjoyer." The world revolves because every living being thinks that he is the lord and creator of the material world. Material consciousness has two psychic divisions. One is that I am the creator, and the other is that I am the enjoyer. But actually the Supreme Lord is both the creator and the enjoyer, and the living entity, being part and parcel of the Supreme Lord, is neither the creator nor the enjoyer, but a cooperator. He is the created and the enjoyed. For instance, a part of a machine cooperates with the whole machine; a part of the body cooperates with the whole body. The hands, legs, eyes and so on are all parts of the body, but they are not actually the enjoyers. The stomach is the enjoyer. The legs move, the hands supply food, the teeth chew, and all parts of the body are engaged in satisfying the stomach because the stomach is the principal factor that nourishes the body's organization. Therefore everything is given to the stomach. One nourishes the tree by watering its root, and one nourishes the body by feeding the stomach, for if the body is to be kept in a healthy state, then the parts of the body must cooperate to feed the stomach. Similarly, the Supreme Lord is the enjoyer and the creator, and we, as subordinate living beings, are meant to cooperate to satisfy Him. This cooperation will actually help us, just as food taken by the stomach will help all other parts of the body. If the fingers of the hand think that they should take the food themselves instead of giving it to the stomach, then they will be frustrated. The central figure of creation and of enjoyment is the Supreme Lord, and the living entities are cooperators. By cooperation they enjoy. The relation is also like that of the master and the servant. If the master is fully satisfied, then the servant is satisfied. Similarly, the Supreme Lord should be satisfied, although the tendency to become the creator and the tendency to enjoy the material world are there also in the living entities because these tendencies are there in the Supreme Lord who has created the manifested cosmic world.

We shall find, therefore, in this *Bhagavad-gītā* that the complete whole is comprised of the supreme controller, the controlled living entities, the cosmic manifestation, eternal time and *karma,* or activities, and all of these are explained in this text. All of these taken completely form the complete whole, and the complete whole is called the Supreme Absolute Truth. The complete whole and the complete Absolute Truth are the complete Personality of Godhead, Śrī Kṛṣṇa. All manifestations are due to His different energies. He *is* the complete whole.

It is also explained in the *Gītā* that impersonal Brahman is also subordinate to the complete Supreme Person (*brahmaṇo hi pratiṣṭhāham*). Brahman is more explicitly explained in the *Brahma-sūtra* to be like the rays of the sunshine. The impersonal Brahman is the shining rays of the Supreme Personality of Godhead. Impersonal Brahman is incomplete realization of the absolute whole, and so also is the conception of Paramātmā. In the Fifteenth Chapter it shall be seen that the Supreme Personality of Godhead, Puruṣottama, is above both impersonal Brahman and the partial realization of Paramātmā. The Supreme Personality of Godhead is called *sac-cid-ānanda-vigraha.* The *Brahma-saṁhitā* begins in this way: *īśvaraḥ paramaḥ kṛṣṇaḥ sac-cid-ānanda-vigrahaḥ/ anādir ādir govindaḥ sarva-kāraṇa-kāraṇam.* "Govinda, Kṛṣṇa, is the cause of all causes. He is the primal cause, and He is the very form of eternity, knowledge and bliss." Impersonal Brahman realization is the realization of His *sat* (eternity) feature. Paramātmā realization is the realization of *sat-cit* (eternal knowledge). But realization of the Personality of Godhead, Kṛṣṇa, is realization of all the transcendental features: *sat, cit* and *ānanda* (eternity, knowledge and bliss) in complete *vigraha* (form).

People with less intelligence consider the Supreme Truth to be impersonal, but He is a transcendental person, and this is confirmed in all Vedic literatures. *Nityo nityānāṁ cetanaś cetanānām.* (*Kaṭha Upaniṣad* 2.2.13) As we are all individual living beings and have our individuality, the Supreme Absolute Truth is also, in the ultimate issue, a person, and realization of the Personality of Godhead is realization of all of the transcendental features in His complete form. The complete whole is not formless. If He is formless, or if He is less than any other thing, then He cannot be the complete whole. The complete whole must have everything within our experience and beyond our experience, otherwise it cannot be complete.

The complete whole, the Personality of Godhead, has immense potencies (*parāsya śaktir vividhaiva śrūyate*). How Kṛṣṇa is acting in different potencies is also explained in *Bhagavad-gītā.* This phenomenal world or material world in which we are placed is also complete in itself because the twenty-four elements of which this material universe is a temporary manifestation, according to Sāṅkhya philosophy, are completely adjusted to produce complete resources which are necessary for the maintenance and subsistence of this universe. There is nothing extraneous, nor is there anything needed. This manifestation has its own time fixed by the energy of the supreme whole, and when its time is complete, these temporary manifestations will be annihilated by the complete arrangement of the complete. There is complete facility for the small complete units, namely the living entities, to realize the complete, and all sorts of incompleteness are experienced due to incomplete knowledge of the complete. So *Bhagavad-gītā* contains the complete knowledge of Vedic wisdom.

All Vedic knowledge is infallible, and Hindus accept Vedic knowledge to be complete and infallible. For example, cow dung is the stool of an animal, and according to *smṛti,* or Vedic injunction, if one touches the stool of an animal he has to take a bath to purify himself. But in the Vedic scriptures cow dung is considered to be a purifying agent. One might consider this to be contradictory, but it is accepted because it is Vedic injunction, and indeed by accepting this, one will not commit a mistake; subsequently it has been proved by modern science that cow dung contains all antiseptic properties. So Vedic knowledge is complete because it is above all doubts and mistakes, and *Bhagavad-gītā* is the essence of all Vedic knowledge.

Vedic knowledge is not a question of research. Our research work is imperfect because we are researching things with imperfect senses. We have to accept perfect knowledge which comes down, as is stated in *Bhagavad-gītā,* by the *paramparā* (disciplic succession). We have to receive knowledge from the proper source in disciplic succession beginning with the supreme spiritual master, the Lord Himself, and handed down to a succession of spiritual masters. Arjuna, the student who took lessons from Lord Śrī Kṛṣṇa, accepts everything that He says without contradicting Him. One is not allowed to accept one portion of *Bhagavad-gītā* and not another. No. We must accept *Bhagavad-gītā* without interpretation, without deletion and without our own whimsical participation in the matter. The *Gītā* should be taken as the most perfect presentation of Vedic knowledge. Vedic knowledge is received from transcendental sources, and the first words were spoken by the Lord Himself. The words spoken by the Lord are called *apauruṣeya,* meaning that they are different from words spoken by a person of the mundane world who is infected with four defects. A mundaner (1) is sure to commit mistakes, (2) is invariably illusioned, (3) has the tendency to cheat others and (4) is limited by imperfect senses. With these four imperfections, one cannot deliver perfect information of all-pervading knowledge.

Vedic knowledge is not imparted by such defective living entities. It was imparted unto the heart of Brahmā, the first created living being, and Brahmā in his turn disseminated this knowledge to his sons and disciples, as he originally received it from the Lord. The Lord is *pūrṇam,* all-perfect, and there is no possibility of His becoming subjected to the laws of material nature. One should therefore be intelligent enough to know that the Lord is the only proprietor of everything in the universe and that He is the original creator, the creator of Brahmā. In the Eleventh Chapter the Lord is addressed as *prapitāmaha* because Brahmā is addressed as *pitāmaha,* the grandfather, and He is the creator of the grandfather. So no one should claim to be the proprietor of anything; one should accept only things set aside for him by the Lord as his quota for his maintenance.

There are many examples given of how we are to utilize those things which are set aside for us by the Lord. This is also explained in *Bhagavad-gītā.* In the beginning, Arjuna decided that he should not fight in the Battle of Kurukṣetra. This was his own decision. Arjuna told the Lord that it was not possible for him to enjoy the kingdom after killing his own kinsmen. This decision was based on the body because he was thinking that the body was himself and that his bodily relations or expansions were his brothers, nephews, brothers-in-law, grandfathers and so on. Therefore he wanted to satisfy his bodily demands. *Bhagavad-gītā* was spoken by the Lord just to change this view, and at the end Arjuna decides to fight under the directions of the Lord when he says, *kariṣye vacanaṁ tava:* "I shall act according to Your word."

In this world men are not meant for quarreling like cats and dogs. Men must be intelligent to realize the importance of human life and refuse to act like ordinary animals. A human being should realize the aim of his life, and this direction is given in all Vedic literatures, and the essence is given in *Bhagavad-gītā.* Vedic literature is meant for human beings, not for animals. Animals can kill other living animals, and there is no question of sin on their part, but if a man kills an animal for the satisfaction of his uncontrolled taste, he must be responsible for breaking the laws of nature. In the *Bhagavad-gītā* it is clearly explained that there are three kinds of activities according to the different modes of nature: the activities of goodness, of passion and of ignorance. Similarly, there are three kinds of eatables also: eatables in goodness, passion and ignorance. All of this is clearly described, and if we properly utilize the instructions of *Bhagavad-gītā,* then our whole life will become purified, and ultimately we will be able to reach the destination which is beyond this material sky.

That destination is called the *sanātana* sky, the eternal, spiritual sky (*yad gatvā na nivartante tad dhāma paramaṁ mama*). In this material world we find that everything is temporary. It comes into being, stays for some time, produces some by-products, dwindles and then vanishes. That is the law of the material world, whether we use as an example this body, or a piece of fruit or anything. But beyond this temporary world there is another world of which we have information. That world consists of another nature, which is *sanātana,* eternal. The *jīva* is also described as *sanātana,* eternal, and the Lord is also described as *sanātana* in the Eleventh Chapter. We have an intimate relationship with the Lord, and because we are all qualitatively one – the *sanātana-dhāma,* or sky, the *sanātana* Supreme Personality and the *sanātana* living entities – the whole purpose of *Bhagavad-gītā* is to revive our *sanātana* occupation, or *sanātana-dharma,* which is the eternal occupation of the living entity. We are temporarily engaged in different activities, but all of these activities can be purified when we give up all these temporary activities and take up the activities which are prescribed by the Supreme Lord. That is called our pure life.

The Supreme Lord and His transcendental abode are both *sanātana,* as are the living entities, and the combined association of the Supreme Lord and the living entities in the *sanātana* abode is the perfection of human life. The Lord is very kind to the living entities because they are His sons. Lord Kṛṣṇa declares in *Bhagavad-gītā, sarva-yoniṣu . . . ahaṁ bīja-pradaḥ pitā:* "I am the father of all." Of course there are all types of living entities according to their various *karmas,* but here the Lord claims that He is the father of all of them. Therefore the Lord descends to reclaim all of these fallen, conditioned souls, to call them back to the *sanātana* eternal sky so that the *sanātana* living entities may regain their eternal *sanātana* positions in eternal association with the Lord. The Lord comes Himself in different incarnations, or He sends His confidential servants as sons or His associates or *ācāryas* to reclaim the conditioned souls.

Therefore, *sanātana-dharma* does not refer to any sectarian process of religion. It is the eternal function of the eternal living entities in relationship with the eternal Supreme Lord. *Sanātana-dharma* refers, as stated previously, to the eternal occupation of the living entity. Śrīpāda Rāmānujācārya has explained the word *sanātana* as "that which has neither beginning nor end," so when we speak of *sanātana-dharma,* we must take it for granted on the authority of Śrīpāda Rāmānujācārya that it has neither beginning nor end.

The English word *religion* is a little different from *sanātana-dharma. Religion* conveys the idea of faith, and faith may change. One may have faith in a particular process, and he may change this faith and adopt another, but *sanātana-dharma* refers to that activity which cannot be changed. For instance, liquidity cannot be taken from water, nor can heat be taken from fire. Similarly, the eternal function of the eternal living entity cannot be taken from the living entity. *Sanātana-dharma* is eternally integral with the living entity. When we speak of *sanātana-dharma,* therefore, we must take it for granted on the authority of Śrīpāda Rāmānujācārya that it has neither beginning nor end. That which has neither end nor beginning must not be sectarian, for it cannot be limited by any boundaries. Those belonging to some sectarian faith will wrongly consider that *sanātana-dharma* is also sectarian, but if we go deeply into the matter and consider it in the light of modern science, it is possible for us to see that *sanātana-dharma* is the business of all the people of the world – nay, of all the living entities of the universe.

Non-*sanātana* religious faith may have some beginning in the annals of human history, but there is no beginning to the history of *sanātana-dharma,* because it remains eternally with the living entities. Insofar as the living entities are concerned, the authoritative *śāstras* state that the living entity has neither birth nor death. In the *Gītā* it is stated that the living entity is never born and he never dies. He is eternal and indestructible, and he continues to live after the destruction of his temporary material body. In reference to the concept of *sanātana-dharma,* we must try to understand the concept of religion from the Sanskrit root meaning of the word. *Dharma* refers to that which is constantly existing with a particular object. We conclude that there is heat and light along with the fire; without heat and light, there is no meaning to the word fire. Similarly, we must discover the essential part of the living being, that part which is his constant companion. That constant companion is his eternal quality, and that eternal quality is his eternal religion.

When Sanātana Gosvāmī asked Śrī Caitanya Mahāprabhu about the *svarūpa* of every living being, the Lord replied that the *svarūpa,* or constitutional position, of the living being is the rendering of service to the Supreme Personality of Godhead. If we analyze this statement of Lord

Caitanya's, we can easily see that every living being is constantly engaged in rendering service to another living being. A living being serves other living beings in various capacities. By doing so, the living entity enjoys life. The lower animals serve human beings as servants serve their master. A serves B master, B serves C master, and C serves D master and so on. Under these circumstances, we can see that one friend serves another friend, the mother serves the son, the wife serves the husband, the husband serves the wife and so on. If we go on searching in this spirit, it will be seen that there is no exception in the society of living beings to the activity of service. The politician presents his manifesto for the public to convince them of his capacity for service. The voters therefore give the politician their valuable votes, thinking that he will render valuable service to society. The shopkeeper serves the customer, and the artisan serves the capitalist. The capitalist serves the family, and the family serves the state in the terms of the eternal capacity of the eternal living being. In this way we can see that no living being is exempt from rendering service to other living beings, and therefore we can safely conclude that service is the constant companion of the living being and that the rendering of service is the eternal religion of the living being.

Yet man professes to belong to a particular type of faith with reference to a particular time and circumstance and thus claims to be a Hindu, Muslim, Christian, Buddhist or an adherent of any other sect. Such designations are non–*sanātana-dharma.* A Hindu may change his faith to become a Muslim, or a Muslim may change his faith to become a Hindu, or a Christian may change his faith and so on. But in all circumstances the change of religious faith does not affect the eternal occupation of rendering service to others. The Hindu, Muslim or Christian in all circumstances is a servant of someone. Thus, to profess a particular type of faith is not to profess one's *sanātana-dharma.* The rendering of service is *sanātana-dharma.*

Factually we are related to the Supreme Lord in service. The Supreme Lord is the supreme enjoyer, and we living entities are His servitors. We are created for His enjoyment, and if we participate in that eternal enjoyment with the Supreme Personality of Godhead, we become happy. We cannot become happy otherwise. It is not possible to be happy independently, just as no one part of the body can be happy without cooperating with the stomach. It is not possible for the living entity to be happy without rendering transcendental loving service unto the Supreme Lord.

In the *Bhagavad-gītā,* worship of different demigods or rendering service to them is not approved. It is stated in the Seventh Chapter, twentieth verse:

kāmais tais tair hṛta-jñānāḥ, prapadyante 'nya-devatāḥ
taṁ taṁ niyamam āsthāya, prakṛtyā niyatāḥ svayā

"Those whose intelligence has been stolen by material desires surrender unto demigods and follow the particular rules and regulations of worship according to their own natures." Here it is plainly said that those who are directed by lust worship the demigods and not the Supreme Lord Kṛṣṇa. When we mention the name Kṛṣṇa, we do not refer to any sectarian name. *Kṛṣṇa* means the highest pleasure, and it is confirmed that the Supreme Lord is the reservoir or storehouse of all pleasure. We are all hankering after pleasure. *Ānanda-mayo 'bhyāsāt* (*Vedānta-sūtra* 1.1.12). The living entities, like the Lord, are full of consciousness, and they are after happiness. The Lord is perpetually happy, and if the living entities associate with the Lord, cooperate with Him and take part in His association, then they also become happy.

The Lord descends to this mortal world to show His pastimes in Vṛndāvana, which are full of happiness. When Lord Śrī Kṛṣṇa was in Vṛndāvana, His activities with His cowherd boyfriends, with His damsel friends, with the other inhabitants of Vṛndāvana and with the cows were all full of happiness. The total population of Vṛndāvana knew nothing but Kṛṣṇa. But Lord Kṛṣṇa even discouraged His father Nanda Mahārāja from worshiping the demigod Indra, because He wanted to establish the fact that people need not worship any demigod. They need only worship the Supreme Lord, because their ultimate goal is to return to His abode.

The abode of Lord Śrī Kṛṣṇa is described in the *Bhagavad-gītā,* Fifteenth Chapter, sixth verse:

na tad bhāsayate sūryo, na śaśāṅko na pāvakaḥ
yad gatvā na nivartante, tad dhāma paramaṁ mama

"That supreme abode of Mine is not illumined by the sun or moon, nor by fire or electricity. Those who reach it never return to this material world."

This verse gives a description of that eternal sky. Of course we have a material conception of the sky, and we think of it in relationship to the sun, moon, stars and so on, but in this verse the Lord states that in the eternal sky there is no need for the sun nor for the moon nor electricity or fire of any kind because the spiritual sky is already illuminated by the *brahma-jyotir,* the rays emanating from the Supreme Lord. We are trying with difficulty to reach other planets, but it is not difficult to understand the abode of the Supreme Lord. This abode is referred to as Goloka. In the *Brahma-saṁhitā* (5.37) it is beautifully described: *goloka eva nivasaty akhilātma-bhūtaḥ.* The Lord resides eternally in His abode Goloka, yet He can be approached from this world, and to this end the Lord comes to manifest His real form, *sac-cid-ānanda-vigraha.* When He manifests this form, there is no need for our imagining what He looks like. To discourage such imaginative speculation, He descends and exhibits Himself as He is, as Śyāmasundara. Unfortunately, the less intelligent deride Him because He comes as one of us and plays with us as a human being. But because of this we should not consider the Lord one of us. It is by His omnipotency that He presents Himself in His real form before us and displays His pastimes, which are replicas of those pastimes found in His abode.

In the effulgent rays of the spiritual sky there are innumerable planets floating. The *brahma-jyotir* emanates from the supreme abode, Kṛṣṇaloka, and the *ānanda-maya, cin-maya* planets, which are not material, float in those rays. The Lord says, *na tad bhāsayate sūryo na śaśāṅko na pāvakaḥ/ yad gatvā na nivartante tad dhāma paramaṁ mama.* One who can approach that spiritual sky is not required to descend again to the material sky. In the material sky, even if we approach the highest planet (Brahmaloka), what to speak of the moon, we will find the same conditions of life, namely birth, death, disease and old age. No planet in the material universe is free from these four principles of material existence.

The living entities are traveling from one planet to another, but it is not that we can go to any planet we like merely by a mechanical arrangement. If we desire to go to other planets, there is a process for going there. This is also mentioned: *yānti deva-vratā devān pitṝn yānti pitṛ-vratāḥ.* No mechanical arrangement is necessary if we want interplanetary travel. The *Gītā* instructs: *yānti deva-vratā devān.* The moon, the sun and higher planets are called Svargaloka. There are three different statuses of planets: higher, middle and lower planetary systems. The earth belongs to the middle planetary system. *Bhagavad-gītā* informs us how to travel to the higher planetary systems (Devaloka) with a very simple formula: *yānti deva-vratā devān.* One need only worship the particular demigod of that particular planet and in that way go to the moon, the sun or any of the higher planetary systems.

Yet *Bhagavad-gītā* does not advise us to go to any of the planets in this material world, because even if we go to Brahmaloka, the highest planet, through some sort of mechanical contrivance by maybe traveling for forty thousand years (and who would live that long?), we will still find the material inconveniences of birth, death, disease and old age. But one who wants to approach the supreme planet, Kṛṣṇaloka, or any other planet within the spiritual sky, will not meet with these material inconveniences. Amongst all of the planets in the spiritual sky there is one supreme planet called Goloka Vṛndāvana, the original planet in the abode of the original Personality of Godhead Śrī Kṛṣṇa. All of this information is given in *Bhagavad-gītā,* and we are given through its instruction information how to leave the material world and begin a truly blissful life in the spiritual sky.

In the Fifteenth Chapter of the *Bhagavad-gītā,* the real picture of the material world is given. It is said there:

ūrdhva-mūlam adhaḥ-śākham, aśvatthaṁ prāhur avyayam
chandāṁsi yasya parṇāni, yas taṁ veda sa veda-vit

Here the material world is described as a tree whose roots are upwards and branches are below. We have experience of a tree whose roots are upward: if one stands on the bank of a river or any reservoir of water, he can see that the trees reflected in the water are upside down. The branches go downward and the roots upward. Similarly, this material world is a reflection of the spiritual world. The material world is but a shadow of reality. In the shadow there is no reality or substantiality, but from the shadow we can understand that there are substance and reality. In the desert there is no water, but the mirage suggests that there is such a thing as water. In the material world there is no water, there is no happiness, but the real water of actual happiness is there in the spiritual world.

The Lord suggests that we attain the spiritual world in the following manner (*Bhagavad-gītā* 15.5):

nirmāna-mohā jita-saṅga-doṣā
adhyātma-nityā vinivṛtta-kāmāḥ
dvandvair vimuktāḥ sukha-duḥkha-saṁjñair
gacchanty amūḍhāḥ padam avyayaṁ tat

That *padam avyayam,* or eternal kingdom, can be reached by one who is *nirmāna-moha.* What does this mean? We are after designations. Someone wants to become "sir," someone wants to become "lord," someone wants to become the president or a rich man or a king or something else. As long as we are attached to these designations, we are attached to the body, because designations belong to the body. But we are not these bodies, and realizing this is the first stage in spiritual realization. We are associated with the three modes of material nature, but we must become detached through devotional service to the Lord. If we are not attached to devotional service to the Lord, then we cannot become detached from the modes of material nature. Designations and attachments are due to our lust and desire, our wanting to lord it over the material nature. As long as we do not give up this propensity of lording it over material nature, there is no possibility of returning to the kingdom of the Supreme, the *sanātana-dhāma.* That eternal kingdom, which is never destroyed, can be approached by one who is not bewildered by the attractions of false material enjoyments, who is situated in the service of the Supreme Lord. One so situated can easily approach that supreme abode.

Elsewhere in the *Gītā* (8.21) it is stated:

avyakto 'kṣara ity uktas, tam āhuḥ paramāṁ gatim
yaṁ prāpya na nivartante, tad dhāma paramaṁ mama

Avyakta means unmanifested. Not even all of the material world is manifested before us. Our senses are so imperfect that we cannot even see all of the stars within this material universe. In the Vedic literature we can receive much information about all the planets, and we can believe it or not believe it. All of the important planets are described in the Vedic literatures, especially *Śrīmad-Bhāgavatam,* and the spiritual world, which is beyond this material sky, is described as *avyakta,* unmanifested. One should desire and hanker after that supreme kingdom, for when one attains that kingdom, he does not have to return to this material world.

Next, one may raise the question of how one goes about approaching that abode of the Supreme Lord. Information of this is given in the Eighth Chapter. It is said there:

anta-kāle ca mām eva, smaran muktvā kalevaram
yaḥ prayāti sa mad-bhāvaṁ, yāti nāsty atra saṁśayaḥ

"And whoever, at the end of his life, quits his body remembering Me alone at once attains My nature. Of this there is no doubt." (*Bhagavad-gītā* 8.5) One who thinks of Kṛṣṇa at the time of his death goes to Kṛṣṇa. One must remember the form of Kṛṣṇa; if he quits his body thinking of this form, he surely approaches the spiritual kingdom. *Mad-bhāvam* refers to the supreme nature of the Supreme Being. The Supreme Being is *sac-cid-ānanda-vigraha* – that is, His form is eternal, full of knowledge and bliss. Our present body is not *sac-cid-ānanda.* It is *asat,* not *sat.* It is not eternal; it is perishable. It is not *cit,* full of knowledge, but it is full of ignorance. We have no knowledge of the spiritual kingdom, nor do we even have perfect knowledge of this material world, where there are so many things unknown to us. The body is also *nirānanda;* instead of being full of bliss it is full of misery. All of the miseries we experience in the material world arise from the body, but one who leaves this body thinking of Lord Kṛṣṇa, the Supreme Personality of Godhead, at once attains a *sac-cid-ānanda* body.

The process of quitting this body and getting another body in the material world is also organized. A man dies after it has been decided what form of body he will have in the next life. Higher authorities, not the living entity himself, make this decision. According to our activities in this life, we either rise or sink. This life is a preparation for the next life. If we can prepare, therefore, in this life to get promotion to the kingdom of God, then surely, after quitting this material body, we will attain a spiritual body just like the Lord's.

As explained before, there are different kinds of transcendentalists – the *brahma-vādī, paramātma-vādī* and the devotee – and, as mentioned, in the *brahma-jyotir* (spiritual sky) there are innumerable spiritual planets. The number of these planets is far, far greater than all of the planets of this material world. This material world has been approximated as only one quarter of the creation (*ekāṁśena sthito jagat*). In this material segment there are millions and billions of universes with trillions of planets and suns, stars and moons. But this whole material creation is only a fragment of the total creation. Most of the creation is in the spiritual sky. One who desires to merge into the existence of the Supreme Brahman is at once transferred to the *brahma-jyotir* of the Supreme Lord and thus attains the spiritual sky. The devotee, who wants to enjoy the association of the Lord, enters into the Vaikuṇṭha planets, which are innumerable, and the Supreme Lord by His plenary expansions as Nārāyaṇa with four hands and with different names like Pradyumna, Aniruddha and Govinda associates with him there. Therefore at the end of life the transcendentalists think either of the *brahma-jyotir,* the Paramātmā or the Supreme Personality of Godhead Śrī Kṛṣṇa. In all cases they enter into the spiritual sky, but only the devotee, or he who is in personal touch with the Supreme Lord, enters into the Vaikuṇṭha planets or the Goloka Vṛndāvana planet. The Lord further adds that of this "there is no doubt." This must be believed firmly. We should not reject that which does not tally with our imagination; our attitude should be that of Arjuna: "I believe everything that You have said." Therefore when the Lord says that at the time of death whoever thinks of Him as Brahman or Paramātmā or as the Personality of Godhead certainly enters into the spiritual sky, there is no doubt about it. There is no question of disbelieving it.

The *Bhagavad-gītā* (8.6) also explains the general principle that makes it possible to enter the spiritual kingdom simply by thinking of the Supreme at the time of death:

yaṁ yaṁ vāpi smaran bhāvaṁ, tyajaty ante kalevaram
taṁ tam evaiti kaunteya, sadā tad-bhāva-bhāvitaḥ

"Whatever state of being one remembers when he quits his present body, in his next life he will attain to that state without fail." Now, first we must understand that material nature is a display of one of the energies of the Supreme Lord. In the *Viṣṇu Purāṇa* (6.7.61) the total energies of the Supreme Lord are delineated:

viṣṇu-śaktiḥ parā proktā, kṣetra-jñākhyā tathā parā
avidyā-karma-saṁjñānyā, tṛtīyā śaktir iṣyate

The Supreme Lord has diverse and innumerable energies which are beyond our conception; however, great learned sages or liberated souls have studied these energies and have analyzed them into three parts. All of the energies are of *viṣṇu-śakti,* that is to say they are different potencies of Lord Viṣṇu. The first energy is *parā,* transcendental. Living entities also belong to the superior energy, as has already been explained. The other energies, or material energies, are in the mode of ignorance. At the time of death either we can remain in the inferior energy of this material world, or we can transfer to the energy of the spiritual world. So the *Bhagavad-gītā* (8.6) says:

yaṁ yaṁ vāpi smaran bhāvaṁ, tyajaty ante kalevaram
taṁ tam evaiti kaunteya, sadā tad-bhāva-bhāvitaḥ

"Whatever state of being one remembers when he quits his present body, in his next life he will attain to that state without fail."

In life we are accustomed to thinking either of the material or of the spiritual energy. Now, how can we transfer our thoughts from the material energy to the spiritual energy? There are so many literatures which fill our thoughts with the material energy – newspapers, magazines, novels, etc. Our thinking, which is now absorbed in these literatures, must be transferred to the Vedic literatures. The great sages, therefore, have written so many Vedic literatures, such as the *Purāṇas.* The *Purāṇas* are not imaginative; they are historical records. In the *Caitanya-caritāmṛta* (*Madhya* 20.122) there is the following verse:

māyā-mugdha jīvera nāhi svataḥ kṛṣṇa-jñāna
jīvere kṛpāya kailā kṛṣṇa veda-purāṇa

The forgetful living entities or conditioned souls have forgotten their relationship with the Supreme Lord, and they are engrossed in thinking of material activities. Just to transfer their thinking power to the spiritual sky, Kṛṣṇa-dvaipāyana Vyāsa has given a great number of Vedic literatures. First he divided the *Vedas* into four, then he explained them in the *Purāṇas,* and for less capable people he wrote the *Mahābhārata.* In the *Mahābhārata* there is given the *Bhagavad-gītā.* Then all Vedic literature is summarized in the *Vedānta-sūtra,* and for future guidance he gave a natural commentation on the *Vedānta-sūtra,* called *Śrīmad-Bhāgavatam.* We must always engage our minds in reading these Vedic literatures. Just as materialists engage their minds in reading newspapers, magazines and so many materialistic literatures, we must transfer our reading to these literatures which are given to us by Vyāsadeva; in that way it will be possible for us to remember the Supreme Lord at the time of death. That is the only way suggested by the Lord, and He guarantees the result: "There is no doubt."

tasmāt sarveṣu kāleṣu, mām anusmara yudhya ca
mayy arpita-mano-buddhir, mām evaiṣyasy asaṁśayaḥ

"Therefore, Arjuna, you should always think of Me in the form of Kṛṣṇa and at the same time continue your prescribed duty of fighting. With your activities dedicated to Me and your mind and intelligence fixed on Me, you will attain Me without doubt." (*Bhagavad-gītā* 8.7)

He does not advise Arjuna simply to remember Him and give up his occupation. No, the Lord never suggests anything impractical. In this material world, in order to maintain the body one has to work. Human society is divided, according to work, into four divisions of social order – *brāhmaṇa, kṣatriya, vaiśya* and *śūdra.* The *brāhmaṇa* class or intelligent class is working in one way, the *kṣatriya* or administrative class is working in another way, and the mercantile class and the laborers are all tending to their specific duties. In the human society, whether one is a laborer, merchant, administrator or farmer, or even if one belongs to the highest class and is a literary man, a scientist or a theologian, he has to work in order to maintain his existence. The Lord therefore tells Arjuna that he need not give up his occupation, but while he is engaged in his occupation he should remember Kṛṣṇa (*mām anusmara*). If he doesn't practice remembering Kṛṣṇa while he is struggling for existence, then it will not be possible for him to remember Kṛṣṇa at the time of death. Lord Caitanya also advises this. He says, *kīrtanīyaḥ sadā hariḥ:* one should practice chanting the names of the Lord always. The names of the Lord and the Lord are nondifferent. So Lord Kṛṣṇa's instruction to Arjuna to "remember Me" and Lord Caitanya's injunction to "always chant the names of Lord Kṛṣṇa" are the same instruction. There is no difference, because Kṛṣṇa and Kṛṣṇa's name are nondifferent. In the absolute status there is no difference between reference and referrent. Therefore we have to practice remembering the Lord always, twenty-four hours a day, by chanting His names and molding our life's activities in such a way that we can remember Him always.

How is this possible? The *ācāryas* give the following example. If a married woman is attached to another man, or if a man has an attachment for a woman other than his wife, then the attachment is to be considered very strong. One with such an attachment is always thinking of the loved one. The wife who is thinking of her lover is always thinking of meeting him, even while she is carrying out her household chores. In fact, she carries out her household work even more carefully so her husband will not suspect her attachment. Similarly, we should always remember the supreme lover, Śrī Kṛṣṇa, and at the same time perform our material duties very nicely. A strong sense of love is required here. If we have a strong sense of love for the Supreme Lord, then we can discharge our duty and at the same time remember Him. But we have to develop that sense of love. Arjuna, for instance, was always thinking of Kṛṣṇa; he was the constant companion of Kṛṣṇa, and at the same time he was a warrior. Kṛṣṇa did not advise him to give up fighting and go to the forest to meditate. When Lord Kṛṣṇa delineates the *yoga* system to Arjuna, Arjuna says that the practice of this system is not possible for him.

arjuna uvāca
yo 'yaṁ yogas tvayā proktaḥ, sāmyena madhusūdana
etasyāhaṁ na paśyāmi, cañcalatvāt sthitiṁ sthirām

"Arjuna said: O Madhusūdana, the system of *yoga* which You have summarized appears impractical and unendurable to me, for the mind is restless and unsteady." (*Bhagavad-gītā* 6.33)

But the Lord says:

yoginām api sarveṣāṁ, mad-gatenāntar-ātmanā
śraddhāvān bhajate yo māṁ, sa me yukta-tamo mataḥ

"Of all *yogīs,* the one with great faith who always abides in Me, thinks of Me within himself, and renders transcendental loving service to Me is the most intimately united with Me in *yoga* and is the highest of all. That is My opinion." (*Bhagavad-gītā* 6.47) So one who thinks of the Supreme Lord always is the greatest *yogī,* the supermost *jñānī,* and the greatest devotee at the same time. The Lord further tells Arjuna that as a *kṣatriya* he cannot give up his fighting, but if Arjuna fights remembering Kṛṣṇa, then he will be able to remember Kṛṣṇa at the time of death. But one must be completely surrendered in the transcendental loving service of the Lord.

We work not with our body, actually, but with our mind and intelligence. So if the intelligence and the mind are always engaged in the thought of the Supreme Lord, then naturally the senses are also engaged in His service. Superficially, at least, the activities of the senses remain the same, but the consciousness is changed. The *Bhagavad-gītā* teaches one how to absorb the mind and intelligence in the thought of the Lord. Such absorption will enable one to transfer himself to the kingdom of the Lord. If the mind is engaged in Kṛṣṇa's service, then the senses are automatically engaged in His service. This is the art, and this is also the secret of *Bhagavad-gītā:* total absorption in the thought of Śrī Kṛṣṇa.

Modern man has struggled very hard to reach the moon, but he has not tried very hard to elevate himself spiritually. If one has fifty years of life ahead of him, he should engage that brief time in cultivating this practice of remembering the Supreme Personality of Godhead. This practice is the devotional process:

śravaṇaṁ kīrtanaṁ viṣṇoḥ, smaraṇaṁ pāda-sevanam
arcanaṁ vandanaṁ dāsyaṁ, sakhyam ātma-nivedanam
(*Śrīmad-Bhāgavatam* 7.5.23)

These nine processes, of which the easiest is *śravaṇam,* hearing the *Bhagavad-gītā* from the realized person, will turn one to the thought of the Supreme Being. This will lead to remembering the Supreme Lord and will enable one, upon leaving the body, to attain a spiritual body which is just fit for association with the Supreme Lord.

The Lord further says:

abhyāsa-yoga-yuktena, cetasā nānya-gāminā
paramaṁ puruṣaṁ divyaṁ, yāti pārthānucintayan

"He who meditates on Me as the Supreme Personality of Godhead, his mind constantly engaged in remembering Me, undeviated from the path, he, O Arjuna, is sure to reach Me." (*Bhagavad-gītā* 8.8)

This is not a very difficult process. However, one must learn it from an experienced person. *Tad-vijñānārthaṁ sa gurum evābhigacchet:* one must approach a person who is already in the practice. The mind is always flying to this and that, but one must practice concentrating the mind always on the form of the Supreme Lord, Śrī Kṛṣṇa, or on the sound of His name. The mind is naturally restless, going hither and thither, but it can rest in the sound vibration of Kṛṣṇa. One must thus meditate on *paramaṁ puruṣam,* the Supreme Personality of Godhead in the spiritual kingdom, the spiritual sky, and thus attain Him. The ways and the means for ultimate realization, ultimate attainment, are stated in the *Bhagavad-gītā,* and the doors of this knowledge are open for everyone. No one is barred out. All classes of men can approach Lord Kṛṣṇa by thinking of Him, for hearing and thinking of Him are possible for everyone.

The Lord further says (*Bhagavad-gītā* 9.32–33):

māṁ hi pārtha vyapāśritya, ye 'pi syuḥ pāpa-yonayaḥ
striyo vaiśyās tathā śūdrās, te 'pi yānti parāṁ gatim

kiṁ punar brāhmaṇāḥ puṇyā, bhaktā rājarṣayas tathā
anityam asukhaṁ lokam, imaṁ prāpya bhajasva mām

Thus the Lord says that even a merchant, a fallen woman or a laborer or even human beings in the lowest status of life can attain the Supreme. One does not need highly developed intelligence. The point is that anyone who accepts the principle of *bhakti-yoga* and accepts the Supreme Lord as the *summum bonum* of life, as the highest target, the ultimate goal, can approach the Lord in the spiritual sky. If one adopts the principles enunciated in *Bhagavad-gītā,* he can make his life perfect and make a permanent solution to all the problems of life. This is the sum and substance of the entire *Bhagavad-gītā.*

In conclusion, *Bhagavad-gītā* is a transcendental literature which one should read very carefully. *Gītā-śāstram idaṁ puṇyaṁ yaḥ paṭhet prayataḥ pumān:* if one properly follows the instructions of *Bhagavad-gītā,* one can be freed from all the miseries and anxieties of life. *Bhaya-śokādi-varjitaḥ.* One will be freed from all fears in this life, and one's next life will be spiritual. (*Gītā-māhātmya* 1)

There is also a further advantage:

gītādhyāyana-śīlasya, prāṇāyāma-parasya ca
naiva santi hi pāpāni, pūrva-janma-kṛtāni ca

"If one reads *Bhagavad-gītā* very sincerely and with all seriousness, then by the grace of the Lord the reactions of his past misdeeds will not act upon him." (*Gītā-māhātmya* 2) The Lord says very loudly in the last portion of *Bhagavad-gītā* (18.66):

sarva-dharmān parityajya, mām ekaṁ śaraṇaṁ vraja
ahaṁ tvāṁ sarva-pāpebhyo, mokṣayiṣyāmi mā śucaḥ

"Abandon all varieties of religion and just surrender unto Me. I shall deliver you from all sinful reactions. Do not fear." Thus the Lord takes all responsibility for one who surrenders unto Him, and He indemnifies such a person against all reactions of sins.

mala-nirmocanaṁ puṁsāṁ, jala-snānaṁ dine dine
sakṛd gītāmṛta-snānaṁ, saṁsāra-mala-nāśanam

"One may cleanse himself daily by taking a bath in water, but if one takes a bath even once in the sacred Ganges water of *Bhagavad-gītā,* for him the dirt of material life is altogether vanquished." (*Gītā-māhātmya* 3)

gītā su-gītā kartavyā, kim anyaiḥ śāstra-vistaraiḥ
yā svayaṁ padmanābhasya, mukha-padmād viniḥsṛtā

Because *Bhagavad-gītā* is spoken by the Supreme Personality of Godhead, one need not read any other Vedic literature. One need only attentively and regularly hear and read *Bhagavad-gītā.* In the present age, people are so absorbed in mundane activities that it is not possible for them to read all the Vedic literatures. But this is not necessary. This one book, *Bhagavad-gītā,* will suffice, because it is the essence of all Vedic literatures and especially because it is spoken by the Supreme Personality of Godhead. (*Gītā-māhātmya* 4)

As it is said:

bhāratāmṛta-sarvasvaṁ, viṣṇu-vaktrād viniḥsṛtam
gītā-gaṅgodakaṁ pītvā, punar janma na vidyate

"One who drinks the water of the Ganges attains salvation, so what to speak of one who drinks the nectar of *Bhagavad-gītā*? *Bhagavad-gītā* is the essential nectar of the *Mahābhārata,* and it is spoken by Lord Kṛṣṇa

Himself, the original Viṣṇu." (*Gītā-māhātmya* 5) *Bhagavad-gītā* comes from the mouth of the Supreme Personality of Godhead, and the Ganges is said to emanate from the lotus feet of the Lord. Of course, there is no difference between the mouth and the feet of the Supreme Lord, but from an impartial study we can appreciate that *Bhagavad-gītā* is even more important than the water of the Ganges.

sarvopaniṣado gāvo, dogdhā gopāla-nandanaḥ
pārtho vatsaḥ su-dhīr bhoktā, dugdhaṁ gītāmṛtaṁ mahat

"This *Gītopaniṣad, Bhagavad-gītā,* the essence of all the *Upaniṣads,* is just like a cow, and Lord Kṛṣṇa, who is famous as a cowherd boy, is milking this cow. Arjuna is just like a calf, and learned scholars and pure devotees are to drink the nectarean milk of *Bhagavad-gītā*." (*Gītā-māhātmya* 6)

ekaṁ śāstraṁ devakī-putra-gītam, eko devo devakī-putra eva
eko mantras tasya nāmāni yāni, karmāpy ekaṁ tasya devasya sevā
(*Gītā-māhātmya* 7)

In this present day, people are very much eager to have one scripture, one God, one religion, and one occupation. Therefore, *ekaṁ śāstraṁ devakī-putra-gītam:* let there be one scripture only, one common scripture for the whole world – *Bhagavad-gītā. Eko devo devakī-putra eva:* let there be one God for the whole world – Śrī Kṛṣṇa. *Eko mantras tasya nāmāni:* and one hymn, one mantra, one prayer – the chanting of His name: Hare Kṛṣṇa, Hare Kṛṣṇa, Kṛṣṇa Kṛṣṇa, Hare Hare/ Hare Rāma, Hare Rāma, Rāma Rāma, Hare Hare. *Karmāpy ekaṁ tasya devasya sevā:* and let there be one work only – the service of the Supreme Personality of Godhead.

THE DISCIPLIC SUCCESSION

Evaṁ paramparā-prāptam imaṁ rājarṣayo viduḥ (*Bhagavad-gītā* 4.2). This *Bhagavad-gītā As It Is* is received through this disciplic succession:

1. Kṛṣṇa
2. Brahmā
3. Nārada
4. Vyāsa
5. Madhva
6. Padmanābha
7. Nṛhari
8. Mādhava
9. Akṣobhya
10. Jaya Tīrtha
11. Jñānasindhu
12. Dayānidhi
13. Vidyānidhi
14. Rājendra
15. Jayadharma
16. Puruṣottama
17. Brahmaṇya Tīrtha
18. Vyāsa Tīrtha
19. Lakṣmīpati
20. Mādhavendra Purī
21. Īśvara Purī, (Nityānanda, Advaita)
22. Lord Caitanya
23. Rūpa, (Svarūpa, Sanātana)
24. Raghunātha, Jīva
25. Kṛṣṇadāsa
26. Narottama
27. Viśvanātha
28. (Baladeva), Jagannātha
29. Bhaktivinoda
30. Gaurakiśora
31. Bhaktisiddhānta Sarasvatī
32. A. C. Bhaktivedanta Swami Prabhupāda

CHAPTER ONE

Observing the Armies on the Battlefield of Kurukṣetra

Text 1 धृतराष्ट्र उवाच
धर्मक्षेत्रे कुरुक्षेत्रे समवेता युयुत्सवः ।
मामकाः पाण्डवाश्चैव किमकुर्वत सञ्जय ॥१॥

dhṛtarāṣṭra uvāca
dharma-kṣetre kuru-kṣetre, samavetā yuyutsavaḥ
māmakāḥ pāṇḍavāś caiva, kim akurvata sañjaya

dhṛtarāṣṭraḥ uvāca – King Dhṛtarāṣṭra said; *dharma-kṣetre* – in the place of pilgrimage; *kuru-kṣetre* – in the place named Kurukṣetra; *samavetāḥ* – assembled; *yuyutsavaḥ* – desiring to fight; *māmakāḥ* – my party (sons); *pāṇḍavāḥ* – the sons of Pāṇḍu; *ca* – and; *eva* – certainly; *kim* – what; *akurvata* – did they do; *sañjaya* – O Sañjaya.

Dhṛtarāṣṭra said: O Sañjaya, after my sons and the sons of Pāṇḍu assembled in the place of pilgrimage at Kurukṣetra, desiring to fight, what did they do?

PURPORT: *Bhagavad-gītā* is the widely read theistic science summarized in the *Gītā-māhātmya* (*Glorification of the Gītā*). There it says that one should read *Bhagavad-gītā* very scrutinizingly with the help of a person who is a devotee of Śrī Kṛṣṇa and try to understand it without personally motivated interpretations. The example of clear understanding is there in the *Bhagavad-gītā* itself, in the way the teaching is understood by Arjuna, who heard the *Gītā* directly from the Lord. If someone is fortunate enough to understand the *Bhagavad-gītā* in that line of disciplic succession, without motivated interpretation, then he surpasses all studies of Vedic wisdom, and all scriptures of the world. One will find in the *Bhagavad-gītā* all that is contained in other scriptures, but the reader will also find things which are not to be found elsewhere. That is the specific standard of the *Gītā*. It is the perfect theistic science because it is directly spoken by the Supreme Personality of Godhead, Lord Śrī Kṛṣṇa.

The topics discussed by Dhṛtarāṣṭra and Sañjaya, as described in the *Mahābhārata,* form the basic principle for this great philosophy. It is understood that this philosophy evolved on the Battlefield of Kurukṣetra, which is a sacred place of pilgrimage from the immemorial time of the Vedic age. It was spoken by the Lord when He was present personally on this planet for the guidance of mankind.

The word *dharma-kṣetra* (a place where religious rituals are performed) is significant because, on the Battlefield of Kurukṣetra, the Supreme Personality of Godhead was present on the side of Arjuna. Dhṛtarāṣṭra, the father of the Kurus, was highly doubtful about the possibility of his sons' ultimate victory. In his doubt, he inquired from his secretary Sañjaya, "What did they do?" He was confident that both his sons and the sons of his younger brother Pāṇḍu were assembled in that Field of Kurukṣetra for a determined engagement of the war. Still, his inquiry is significant. He did not want a compromise between the cousins and brothers, and he wanted to be sure of the fate of his sons on the battlefield. Because the battle was arranged to be fought at Kurukṣetra, which is mentioned elsewhere in the *Vedas* as a place of worship – even for the denizens of heaven – Dhṛtarāṣṭra became very fearful about the influence of the holy place on the outcome of the battle. He knew very well that this would influence Arjuna and the sons of Pāṇḍu favorably, because by nature they were all virtuous. Sañjaya was a student of Vyāsa, and therefore, by the mercy of Vyāsa, Sañjaya was able to envision the Battlefield of Kurukṣetra even while he was in the room of Dhṛtarāṣṭra. And so, Dhṛtarāṣṭra asked him about the situation on the battlefield.

Both the Pāṇḍavas and the sons of Dhṛtarāṣṭra belong to the same family, but Dhṛtarāṣṭra's mind is disclosed herein. He deliberately claimed only his sons as Kurus, and he separated the sons of Pāṇḍu from the family heritage. One can thus understand the specific position of Dhṛtarāṣṭra in his relationship with his nephews, the sons of Pāṇḍu. As in the paddy field the unnecessary plants are taken out, so it is expected from the very beginning of these topics that in the religious field of Kurukṣetra, where the father of religion, Śrī Kṛṣṇa, was present, the unwanted plants like Dhṛtarāṣṭra's son Duryodhana and others would be wiped out and the thoroughly religious persons, headed by Yudhiṣṭhira, would be established by the Lord. This is the significance of the words *dharma-kṣetre* and *kuru-kṣetre,* apart from their historical and Vedic importance.

Text 2 सञ्जय उवाच
दृष्ट्वा तु पाण्डवानीकं व्यूढं दुर्योधनस्तदा ।
आचार्यमुपसङ्गम्य राजा वचनमब्रवीत् ॥ २ ॥

sañjaya uvāca
dṛṣṭvā tu pāṇḍavānīkaṁ, vyūḍhaṁ duryodhanas tadā
ācāryam upasaṅgamya, rājā vacanam abravīt

sañjayaḥ uvāca – Sañjaya said; *dṛṣṭvā* – after seeing; *tu* – but; *pāṇḍava-anīkam* – the soldiers of the Pāṇḍavas; *vyūḍham* – arranged in a military phalanx; *duryodhanaḥ* – King Duryodhana; *tadā* – at that time; *ācāryam* – the teacher; *upasaṅgamya* – approaching; *rājā* – the king; *vacanam* – words; *abravīt* – spoke.

Sañjaya said: O King, after looking over the army arranged in military formation by the sons of Pāṇḍu, King Duryodhana went to his teacher and spoke the following words.

PURPORT: Dhṛtarāṣṭra was blind from birth. Unfortunately, he was also bereft of spiritual vision. He knew very well that his sons were equally blind in the matter of religion, and he was sure that they could never reach an understanding with the Pāṇḍavas, who were all pious since birth. Still he was doubtful about the influence of the place of pilgrimage, and Sañjaya could understand his motive in asking about the situation on the battlefield. Sañjaya wanted, therefore, to encourage the despondent king and thus assured him that his sons were not going to make any sort of compromise under the influence of the holy place. Sañjaya therefore informed the king that his son, Duryodhana, after seeing the military force of the Pāṇḍavas, at once went to the commander in chief, Droṇācārya, to inform him of the real position. Although Duryodhana is mentioned as the king, he still had to go to the commander on account of the seriousness of the situation. He was therefore quite fit to be a politician. But Duryodhana's diplomatic veneer could not disguise the fear he felt when he saw the military arrangement of the Pāṇḍavas.

Text 3 पश्यैतां पाण्डुपुत्राणामाचार्य महतीं चमूम् ।
व्यूढां द्रुपदपुत्रेण तव शिष्येण धीमता ॥ ३ ॥

paśyaitāṁ pāṇḍu-putrāṇām, ācārya mahatīṁ camūm
vyūḍhāṁ drupada-putreṇa, tava śiṣyeṇa dhīmatā

paśya – behold; *etām* – this; *pāṇḍu-putrāṇām* – of the sons of Pāṇḍu; *ācārya* – O teacher; *mahatīm* – great; *camūm* – military force; *vyūḍhām* – arranged; *drupada-putreṇa* – by the son of Drupada; *tava* – your; *śiṣyeṇa* – disciple; *dhī-matā* – very intelligent.

O my teacher, behold the great army of the sons of Pāṇḍu, so expertly arranged by your intelligent disciple the son of Drupada.

PURPORT: Duryodhana, a great diplomat, wanted to point out the defects of Droṇācārya, the great *brāhmaṇa* commander in chief. Droṇācārya had some political quarrel with King Drupada, the father of Draupadī, who was Arjuna's wife. As a result of this quarrel, Drupada performed a great sacrifice, by which he received the benediction of having a son who would be able to kill Droṇācārya. Droṇācārya knew this perfectly well, and yet as a liberal *brāhmaṇa* he did not hesitate to impart all his military secrets when the son of Drupada, Dhṛṣṭadyumna, was entrusted to him for military education. Now, on the Battlefield of Kurukṣetra, Dhṛṣṭadyumna took the side of the Pāṇḍavas, and it was he who arranged for their military phalanx, after having learned the art from Droṇācārya. Duryodhana pointed out this mistake of Droṇācārya's so that he might be alert and uncompromising in the fighting. By this he wanted to point out also that he should not be similarly lenient in battle against the Pāṇḍavas, who were also Droṇācārya's affectionate students. Arjuna, especially, was his most affectionate and brilliant student. Duryodhana also warned that such leniency in the fight would lead to defeat.

Text 4 अत्र शूरा महेष्वासा भीमार्जुनसमा युधि ।
युयुधानो विराटश्च द्रुपदश्च महारथः ॥ ४ ॥

atra śūrā maheṣv-āsā, bhīmārjuna-samā yudhi
yuyudhāno virāṭaś ca, drupadaś ca mahā-rathaḥ

atra – here; *śūrāḥ* – heroes; *mahā-iṣu-āsāḥ* – mighty bowmen; *bhīma-arjuna* – to Bhīma and Arjuna; *samāḥ* – equal; *yudhi* – in the fight; *yuyudhānaḥ* – Yuyudhāna; *virāṭaḥ* – Virāṭa; *ca* – also; *drupadaḥ* – Drupada; *ca* – also; *mahā-rathaḥ* – great fighter.

Here in this army are many heroic bowmen equal in fighting to Bhīma and Arjuna: great fighters like Yuyudhāna, Virāṭa and Drupada.

PURPORT: Even though Dhṛṣṭadyumna was not a very important obstacle in the face of Droṇācārya's very great power in the military art, there were many others who were causes of fear. They are mentioned by Duryodhana as great stumbling blocks on the path of victory because each and every one of them was as formidable as Bhīma and Arjuna. He knew the strength of Bhīma and Arjuna, and thus he compared the others with them.

Text 5 धृष्टकेतुश्चेकितानः काशिराजश्च वीर्यवान् ।
पुरुजित्कुन्तिभोजश्च शैब्यश्च नरपुङ्गवः ॥ ५ ॥

dhṛṣṭaketuś cekitānaḥ, kāśirājaś ca vīryavān
purujit kuntibhojaś ca, śaibyaś ca nara-puṅgavaḥ

dhṛṣṭaketuḥ – Dhṛṣṭaketu; *cekitānaḥ* – Cekitāna; *kāśirājaḥ* – Kāśirāja; *ca* – also; *vīrya-vān* – very powerful; *purujit* – Purujit; *kuntibhojaḥ* – Kuntibhoja; *ca* – and; *śaibyaḥ* – Śaibya; *ca* – and; *nara-puṅgavaḥ* – hero in human society.

There are also great heroic, powerful fighters like Dhṛṣṭaketu, Cekitāna, Kāśirāja, Purujit, Kuntibhoja and Śaibya.

Text 6 युधामन्युश्च विक्रान्त उत्तमौजाश्च वीर्यवान् ।
सौभद्रो द्रौपदेयाश्च सर्व एव महारथाः ॥ ६ ॥

yudhāmanyuś ca vikrānta, uttamaujāś ca vīryavān
saubhadro draupadeyāś ca, sarva eva mahā-rathāḥ

yudhāmanyuḥ – Yudhāmanyu; *ca* – and; *vikrāntaḥ* – mighty; *uttamaujāḥ* – Uttamaujā; *ca* – and; *vīrya-vān* – very powerful; *saubhadraḥ* –

the son of Subhadrā; *draupadeyāḥ* – the sons of Draupadī; *ca* – and; *sarve* – all; *eva* – certainly; *mahā-rathāḥ* – great chariot fighters.

There are the mighty Yudhāmanyu, the very powerful Uttamaujā, the son of Subhadrā and the sons of Draupadī. All these warriors are great chariot fighters.

Text 7 अस्माकं तु विशिष्टा ये तान्निबोध द्विजोत्तम ।
नायका मम सैन्यस्य संज्ञार्थं तान् ब्रवीमि ते ॥ ७ ॥

asmākaṁ tu viśiṣṭā ye, tān nibodha dvijottama
nāyakā mama sainyasya, saṁjñārthaṁ tān bravīmi te

asmākam – our; *tu* – but; *viśiṣṭāḥ* – especially powerful; *ye* – who; *tān* – them; *nibodha* – just take note of, be informed; *dvija-uttama* – O best of the *brāhmaṇas; nāyakāḥ* – captains; *mama* – my; *sainyasya* – of the soldiers; *saṁjñā-artham* – for information; *tān* – them; *bravīmi* – I am speaking; *te* – to you.

But for your information, O best of the brāhmaṇas, let me tell you about the captains who are especially qualified to lead my military force.

Text 8 भवान् भीष्मश्च कर्णश्च कृपश्च समितिंजयः ।
अश्वत्थामा विकर्णश्च सौमदत्तिस्तथैव च ॥ ८ ॥

bhavān bhīṣmaś ca karṇaś ca, kṛpaś ca samitiṁ-jayaḥ
aśvatthāmā vikarṇaś ca, saumadattis tathaiva ca

bhavān – your good self; *bhīṣmaḥ* – Grandfather Bhīṣma; *ca* – also; *karṇaḥ* – Karṇa; *ca* – and; *kṛpaḥ* – Kṛpa; *ca* – and; *samitim-jayaḥ* – always victorious in battle; *aśvatthāmā* – Aśvatthāmā; *vikarṇaḥ* – Vikarṇa; *ca* – as well as; *saumadattiḥ* – the son of Somadatta; *tathā* – as well as; *eva* – certainly; *ca* – also.

There are personalities like you, Bhīṣma, Karṇa, Kṛpa, Aśvatthāmā, Vikarṇa and the son of Somadatta called Bhūriśravā, who are always victorious in battle.

PURPORT: Duryodhana mentions the exceptional heroes in the battle, all of whom are ever victorious. Vikarṇa is the brother of Duryodhana, Aśvatthāmā is the son of Droṇācārya, and Saumadatti, or Bhūriśravā, is the son of the King of the Bāhlīkas. Karṇa is the half brother of Arjuna, as he was born of Kuntī before her marriage with King Pāṇḍu. Kṛpācārya's twin sister married Droṇācārya.

Text 9 अन्ये च बहवः शूरा मदर्थे त्यक्तजीविताः ।
नानाशस्त्रप्रहरणाः सर्वे युद्धविशारदाः ॥ ९ ॥

anye ca bahavaḥ śūrā, mad-arthe tyakta-jīvitāḥ
nānā-śastra-praharaṇāḥ, sarve yuddha-viśāradāḥ

anye – others; *ca* – also; *bahavaḥ* – in great numbers; *śūrāḥ* – heroes; *mat-arthe* – for my sake; *tyakta-jīvitāḥ* – prepared to risk life; *nānā* – many; *śastra* – weapons; *praharaṇāḥ* – equipped with; *sarve* – all of them; *yuddha-viśāradāḥ* – experienced in military science.

There are many other heroes who are prepared to lay down their lives for my sake. All of them are well equipped with different kinds of weapons, and all are experienced in military science.

PURPORT: As far as the others are concerned – like Jayadratha, Kṛtavarmā and Śalya – all are determined to lay down their lives for Duryodhana's sake. In other words, it is already concluded that all of them would die in the Battle of Kurukṣetra for joining the party of the sinful Duryodhana. Duryodhana was, of course, confident of his victory on account of the above-mentioned combined strength of his friends.

Text 10 अपर्याप्तं तदस्माकं बलं भीष्माभिरक्षितम् ।
पर्याप्तं त्विदमेतेषां बलं भीमाभिरक्षितम् ॥१०॥

aparyāptaṁ tad asmākaṁ, balaṁ bhīṣmābhirakṣitam
paryāptaṁ tv idam eteṣāṁ, balaṁ bhīmābhirakṣitam

aparyāptam – immeasurable; *tat* – that; *asmākam* – of ours; *balam* – strength; *bhīṣma* – by Grandfather Bhīṣma; *abhirakṣitam* – perfectly protected; *paryāptam* – limited; *tu* – but; *idam* – all this; *eteṣām* – of the Pāṇḍavas; *balam* – strength; *bhīma* – by Bhīma; *abhirakṣitam* – carefully protected.

Our strength is immeasurable, and we are perfectly protected by Grandfather Bhīṣma, whereas the strength of the Pāṇḍavas, carefully protected by Bhīma, is limited.

PURPORT: Herein an estimation of comparative strength is made by Duryodhana. He thinks that the strength of his armed forces is immeasurable, being specifically protected by the most experienced general, Grandfather Bhīṣma. On the other hand, the forces of the Pāṇḍavas are limited, being protected by a less experienced general, Bhīma, who is like a fig in the presence of Bhīṣma. Duryodhana was always envious of Bhīma because he knew perfectly well that if he should die at all, he would only be killed by Bhīma. But at the same time, he was confident of his victory on account of the presence of Bhīṣma, who was a far superior general. His conclusion that he would come out of the battle victorious was well ascertained.

Text 11 अयनेषु च सर्वेषु यथाभागमवस्थिताः ।
भीष्ममेवाभिरक्षन्तु भवन्तः सर्व एव हि ॥११॥

ayaneṣu ca sarveṣu, yathā-bhāgam avasthitāḥ
bhīṣmam evābhirakṣantu, bhavantaḥ sarva eva hi

ayaneṣu – in the strategic points; *ca* – also; *sarveṣu* – everywhere; *yathā-bhāgam* – as differently arranged; *avasthitāḥ* – situated; *bhīṣmam* – unto Grandfather Bhīṣma; *eva* – certainly; *abhirakṣantu* – should give support; *bhavantaḥ* – you; *sarve* – all respectively; *eva hi* – certainly.

All of you must now give full support to Grandfather Bhīṣma, as you stand at your respective strategic points of entrance into the phalanx of the army.

PURPORT: Duryodhana, after praising the prowess of Bhīṣma, further considered that others might think that they had been considered less important, so in his usual diplomatic way, he tried to adjust the situation in the above words. He emphasized that Bhīṣmadeva was undoubtedly the greatest hero, but he was an old man, so everyone must especially think of his protection from all sides. He might become engaged in the fight, and the enemy might take advantage of his full engagement on one side. Therefore, it was important that other heroes not leave their strategic positions and allow the enemy to break the phalanx. Duryodhana clearly felt that the victory of the Kurus depended on the presence of Bhīṣmadeva. He was confident of the full support of Bhīṣmadeva and Droṇācārya in the battle because he well knew that they did not even speak a word when Arjuna's wife Draupadī, in her helpless condition, had appealed to them for justice while she was being forced to appear naked in the presence of all the great generals in the assembly. Although he knew that the two generals had some sort of affection for the Pāṇḍavas, he hoped that these generals would now completely give it up, as they had done during the gambling performances.

Text 12 तस्य सञ्जनयन् हर्षं कुरुवृद्धः पितामहः ।
सिंहनादं विनद्योच्चैः शङ्खं दध्मौ प्रतापवान् ॥१२॥

tasya sañjanayan harṣaṁ, kuru-vṛddhaḥ pitāmahaḥ
siṁha-nādaṁ vinadyoccaiḥ, śaṅkhaṁ dadhmau pratāpavān

tasya – his; *sañjanayan* – increasing; *harṣam* – cheerfulness; *kuru-vṛddhaḥ* – the grandsire of the Kuru dynasty (Bhīṣma); *pitāmahaḥ* – the grandfather; *siṁha-nādam* – roaring sound, like that of a lion; *vinadya* – vibrating; *uccaiḥ* – very loudly; *śaṅkham* – conchshell; *dadhmau* – blew; *pratāpa-vān* – the valiant.

Then Bhīṣma, the great valiant grandsire of the Kuru dynasty, the grandfather of the fighters, blew his conchshell very loudly, making a sound like the roar of a lion, giving Duryodhana joy.

PURPORT: The grandsire of the Kuru dynasty could understand the inner meaning of the heart of his grandson Duryodhana, and out of his natural compassion for him he tried to cheer him by blowing his conchshell very loudly, befitting his position as a lion. Indirectly, by the symbolism of the conchshell, he informed his depressed grandson Duryodhana that he had no chance of victory in the battle, because the Supreme Lord Kṛṣṇa was on the other side. But still, it was his duty to conduct the fight, and no pains would be spared in that connection.

Text 13 ततः शङ्खाश्च भेर्यश्च पणवानकगोमुखाः ।
सहसैवाभ्यहन्यन्त स शब्दस्तुमुलोऽभवत् ॥१३॥

tataḥ śaṅkhāś ca bheryaś ca, paṇavānaka-gomukhāḥ
sahasaivābhyahanyanta, sa śabdas tumulo 'bhavat

tataḥ – thereafter; *śaṅkhāḥ* – conchshells; *ca* – also; *bheryaḥ* – large drums; *ca* – and; *paṇava-ānaka* – small drums and kettledrums; *go-mukhāḥ* – horns; *sahasā* – all of a sudden; *eva* – certainly; *abhyahanyanta* – were simultaneously sounded; *saḥ* – that; *śabdaḥ* – combined sound; *tumulaḥ* – tumultuous; *abhavat* – became.

After that, the conchshells, drums, bugles, trumpets and horns were all suddenly sounded, and the combined sound was tumultuous.

Text 14 ततः श्वेतैर्हयैर्युक्ते महति स्यन्दने स्थितौ ।
माधवः पाण्डवश्चैव दिव्यौ शङ्खौ प्रदध्मतुः ॥१४॥

tataḥ śvetair hayair yukte, mahati syandane sthitau
mādhavaḥ pāṇḍavaś caiva, divyau śaṅkhau pradadhmatuḥ

tataḥ – thereafter; *śvetaiḥ* – with white; *hayaiḥ* – horses; *yukte* – being yoked; *mahati* – in a great; *syandane* – chariot; *sthitau* – situated; *mādhavaḥ* – Kṛṣṇa (the husband of the goddess of fortune); *pāṇḍavaḥ* – Arjuna (the son of Pāṇḍu); *ca* – also; *eva* – certainly; *divyau* – transcendental; *śaṅkhau* – conchshells; *pradadhmatuḥ* – sounded.

On the other side, both Lord Kṛṣṇa and Arjuna, stationed on a great chariot drawn by white horses, sounded their transcendental conchshells.

PURPORT: In contrast with the conchshell blown by Bhīṣmadeva, the conchshells in the hands of Kṛṣṇa and Arjuna are described as transcendental. The sounding of the transcendental conchshells indicated that there was no hope of victory for the other side because Kṛṣṇa was on the side of the Pāṇḍavas. *Jayas tu pāṇḍu-putrāṇāṁ yeṣāṁ pakṣe janārdanaḥ.* Victory is always with persons like the sons of Pāṇḍu because Lord Kṛṣṇa is associated with them. And whenever and wherever the Lord is present, the goddess of fortune is also there because the goddess of fortune never lives alone without her husband. Therefore, victory and fortune were awaiting Arjuna, as indicated by the transcendental sound produced by the conchshell of Viṣṇu, or Lord Kṛṣṇa. Besides that, the chariot on which both the friends were seated had been donated by Agni (the fire-god) to Arjuna, and this indicated that this chariot was capable of conquering all sides, wherever it was drawn over the three worlds.

Text 15 पाञ्चजन्यं हृषीकेशो देवदत्तं धनञ्जयः ।
पौण्ड्रं दध्मौ महाशङ्खं भीमकर्मा वृकोदरः ॥१५॥

pāñcajanyaṁ hṛṣīkeśo, devadattaṁ dhanañ-jayaḥ
pauṇḍraṁ dadhmau mahā-śaṅkhaṁ, bhīma-karmā vṛkodaraḥ

pāñcajanyam – the conchshell named Pāñcajanya; *hṛṣīka-īśaḥ* – Hṛṣīkeśa (Kṛṣṇa, the Lord who directs the senses of the devotees);

devadattam – the conchshell named Devadatta; *dhanam-jayaḥ* – Dhanañjaya (Arjuna, the winner of wealth); *pauṇḍram* – the conch named Pauṇḍra; *dadhmau* – blew; *mahā-śaṅkham* – the terrific conchshell; *bhīma-karmā* – one who performs herculean tasks; *vṛka-udaraḥ* – the voracious eater (Bhīma).

Lord Kṛṣṇa blew His conchshell, called Pāñcajanya; Arjuna blew his, the Devadatta; and Bhīma, the voracious eater and performer of herculean tasks, blew his terrific conchshell, called Pauṇḍra.

PURPORT: Lord Kṛṣṇa is referred to as Hṛṣīkeśa in this verse because He is the owner of all senses. The living entities are part and parcel of Him, and therefore the senses of the living entities are also part and parcel of His senses. The impersonalists cannot account for the senses of the living entities, and therefore they are always anxious to describe all living entities as senseless, or impersonal. The Lord, situated in the hearts of all living entities, directs their senses. But He directs in terms of the surrender of the living entity, and in the case of a pure devotee He directly controls the senses. Here on the Battlefield of Kurukṣetra the Lord directly controls the transcendental senses of Arjuna, and thus His particular name of Hṛṣīkeśa. The Lord has different names according to His different activities. For example, His name is Madhusūdana because He killed the demon of the name Madhu; His name is Govinda because He gives pleasure to the cows and to the senses; His name is Vāsudeva because He appeared as the son of Vasudeva; His name is Devakī-nandana because He accepted Devakī as His mother; His name is Yaśodā-nandana because He awarded His childhood pastimes to Yaśodā at Vṛndāvana; His name is Pārtha-sārathi because He worked as charioteer of His friend Arjuna. Similarly, His name is Hṛṣīkeśa because He gave direction to Arjuna on the Battlefield of Kurukṣetra.

Arjuna is referred to as Dhanañjaya in this verse because he helped his elder brother in fetching wealth when it was required by the king to make expenditures for different sacrifices. Similarly, Bhīma is known as Vṛkodara because he could eat as voraciously as he could perform herculean tasks, such as killing the demon Hiḍimba. So the particular types of conchshell blown by the different personalities on the side of the Pāṇḍavas, beginning with the Lord's, were all very encouraging to the fighting soldiers. On the other side there were no such credits, nor the presence of Lord Kṛṣṇa, the supreme director, nor that of the goddess of fortune. So they were predestined to lose the battle – and that was the message announced by the sounds of the conchshells.

Texts 16–18

अनन्तविजयं राजा कुन्तीपुत्रो युधिष्ठिरः ।
नकुलः सहदेवश्च सुघोषमणिपुष्पकौ ॥१६॥
काश्यश्च परमेष्वासः शिखण्डी च महारथः ।
धृष्टद्युम्नो विराटश्च सात्यकिश्चापराजितः ॥१७॥
द्रुपदो द्रौपदेयाश्च सर्वशः पृथिवीपते ।
सौभद्रश्च महाबाहुः शङ्खान्दध्मुः पृथक्पृथक् ॥१८॥

anantavijayaṁ rājā, kuntī-putro yudhiṣṭhiraḥ
nakulaḥ sahadevaś ca, sughoṣa-maṇipuṣpakau

kāśyaś ca parameṣv-āsaḥ, śikhaṇḍī ca mahā-rathaḥ
dhṛṣṭadyumno virāṭaś ca, sātyakiś cāparājitaḥ

drupado draupadeyāś ca, sarvaśaḥ pṛthivī-pate
saubhadraś ca mahā-bāhuḥ, śaṅkhān dadhmuḥ pṛthak pṛthak

ananta-vijayam – the conch named Ananta-vijaya; *rājā* – the king; *kuntī-putraḥ* – the son of Kuntī; *yudhiṣṭhiraḥ* – Yudhiṣṭhira; *nakulaḥ* – Nakula; *sahadevaḥ* – Sahadeva; *ca* – and; *sughoṣa-maṇipuṣpakau* – the conches named Sughoṣa and Maṇipuṣpaka; *kāśyaḥ* – the King of Kāśī (Vārāṇasī); *ca* – and; *parama-iṣu-āsaḥ* – the great archer; *śikhaṇḍī* – Śikhaṇḍī; *ca* – also; *mahā-rathaḥ* – one who can fight alone against thousands; *dhṛṣṭa-dyumnaḥ* – Dhṛṣṭadyumna (the son of King Drupada); *virāṭaḥ* – Virāṭa (the prince who gave shelter to the Pāṇḍavas while they were in disguise); *ca* – also; *sātyakiḥ* – Sātyaki (the same as Yuyudhāna, the charioteer of Lord Kṛṣṇa); *ca* – and; *aparājitaḥ* – who had never been vanquished; *drupadaḥ* – Drupada, the King of Pāñcāla; *draupadeyāḥ* – the sons of Draupadī; *ca* – also; *sarvaśaḥ* – all; *pṛthivī-pate* – O King; *saubhadraḥ* – Abhimanyu, the son of Subhadrā; *ca* – also; *mahā-bāhuḥ* – mighty-armed; *śaṅkhān* – conchshells; *dadhmuḥ* – blew; *pṛthak pṛthak* – each separately.

King Yudhiṣṭhira, the son of Kuntī, blew his conchshell, the Ananta-vijaya, and Nakula and Sahadeva blew the Sughoṣa and Maṇipuṣpaka. That great archer the King of Kāśī, the great fighter Śikhaṇḍī, Dhṛṣṭa-dyumna, Virāṭa, the unconquerable Sātyaki, Drupada, the sons of Draupadī, and others, O King, such as the mighty-armed son of Subhadrā, all blew their respective conchshells.

PURPORT: Sañjaya informed King Dhṛtarāṣṭra very tactfully that his unwise policy of deceiving the sons of Pāṇḍu and endeavoring to enthrone his own sons on the seat of the kingdom was not very laudable. The signs already clearly indicated that the whole Kuru dynasty would be killed in that great battle. Beginning with the grandsire, Bhīṣma, down to the grandsons like Abhimanyu and others – including kings from many states of the world – all were present there, and all were doomed. The whole catastrophe was due to King Dhṛtarāṣṭra, because he encouraged the policy followed by his sons.

Text 19 स घोषो धार्तराष्ट्राणां हृदयानि व्यदारयत् ।
नभश्च पृथिवीं चैव तुमुलोऽभ्यनुनादयन् ॥१९॥

sa ghoṣo dhārtarāṣṭrāṇāṁ, hṛdayāni vyadārayat
nabhaś ca pṛthivīṁ caiva, tumulo 'bhyanunādayan

saḥ – that; *ghoṣaḥ* – vibration; *dhārtarāṣṭrāṇām* – of the sons of Dhṛtarāṣṭra; *hṛdayāni* – hearts; *vyadārayat* – shattered; *nabhaḥ* – the sky; *ca* – also; *pṛthivīm* – the surface of the earth; *ca* – also; *eva* – certainly; *tumulaḥ* – uproarious; *abhyanunādayan* – resounding.

The blowing of these different conchshells became uproarious. Vibrating both in the sky and on the earth, it shattered the hearts of the sons of Dhṛtarāṣṭra.

PURPORT: When Bhīṣma and the others on the side of Duryodhana blew their respective conchshells, there was no heart-breaking on the part of the Pāṇḍavas. Such occurrences are not mentioned, but in this particular verse it is mentioned that the hearts of the sons of Dhṛtarāṣṭra were shattered by the sounds vibrated by the Pāṇḍavas' party. This is due to the Pāṇḍavas and their confidence in Lord Kṛṣṇa. One who takes shelter of the Supreme Lord has nothing to fear, even in the midst of the greatest calamity.

Text 20 अथ व्यवस्थितान्दृष्ट्वा धार्तराष्ट्रान् कपिध्वजः ।
प्रवृत्ते शस्त्रसम्पाते धनुरुद्यम्य पाण्डवः ।
हृषीकेशं तदा वाक्यमिदमाह महीपते ॥२०॥

atha vyavasthitān dṛṣṭvā, dhārtarāṣṭrān kapi-dhvajaḥ
pravṛtte śastra-sampāte, dhanur udyamya pāṇḍavaḥ
hṛṣīkeśaṁ tadā vākyam, idam āha mahī-pate

atha – thereupon; *vyavasthitān* – situated; *dṛṣṭvā* – looking upon; *dhārtarāṣṭrān* – the sons of Dhṛtarāṣṭra; *kapi-dhvajaḥ* – he whose flag was marked with Hanumān; *pravṛtte* – while about to engage; *śastra-sampāte* – in releasing his arrows; *dhanuḥ* – bow; *udyamya* – taking up; *pāṇḍavaḥ* – the son of Pāṇḍu (Arjuna); *hṛṣīkeśam* – unto Lord Kṛṣṇa; *tadā* – at that time; *vākyam* – words; *idam* – these; *āha* – said; *mahī-pate* – O King.

At that time Arjuna, the son of Pāṇḍu, seated in the chariot bearing the flag marked with Hanumān, took up his bow and prepared to shoot his arrows. O King, after looking at the sons of Dhṛtarāṣṭra drawn in military array, Arjuna then spoke to Lord Kṛṣṇa these words.

PURPORT: The battle was just about to begin. It is understood from the above statement that the sons of Dhṛtarāṣṭra were more or less disheartened by the unexpected arrangement of military force by the Pāṇḍavas, who were guided by the direct instructions of Lord Kṛṣṇa on the battlefield. The emblem of Hanumān on the flag of Arjuna is another sign of victory because Hanumān cooperated with Lord Rāma in the battle between Rāma and Rāvaṇa, and Lord Rāma emerged victorious. Now both Rāma and Hanumān were present on the chariot of Arjuna to help him. Lord Kṛṣṇa is Rāma Himself, and wherever Lord Rāma is, His eternal servitor Hanumān and His eternal consort Sītā, the goddess of fortune, are present. Therefore, Arjuna had no cause to fear any enemies whatsoever. And above all, the Lord of the senses, Lord Kṛṣṇa, was personally present to give him direction. Thus, all good counsel was available to Arjuna in the matter of executing the battle. In such auspicious conditions, arranged by the Lord for His eternal devotee, lay the signs of assured victory.

Texts 21–22

अर्जुन उवाच
सेनयोरुभयोर्मध्ये रथं स्थापय मेऽच्युत ।
यावदेतान्निरीक्षेऽहं योद्धुकामानवस्थितान् ॥२१॥
कैर्मया सह योद्धव्यमस्मिन् रणसमुद्यमे ॥२२॥

arjuna uvāca
senayor ubhayor madhye, rathaṁ sthāpaya me 'cyuta
yāvad etān nirīkṣe 'haṁ, yoddhu-kāmān avasthitān

kair mayā saha yoddhavyam, asmin raṇa-samudyame

arjunaḥ uvāca – Arjuna said; *senayoḥ* – of the armies; *ubhayoḥ* – both; *madhye* – between; *ratham* – the chariot; *sthāpaya* – please keep; *me* –

my; *acyuta* – O infallible one; *yāvat* – as long as; *etān* – all these; *nirīkṣe* – may look upon; *aham* – I; *yoddhu-kāmān* – desiring to fight; *avasthitān* – arrayed on the battlefield; *kaiḥ* – with whom; *mayā* – by me; *saha* – together; *yoddhavyam* – have to fight; *asmin* – in this; *raṇa* – strife; *samudyame* – in the attempt.

Arjuna said: O infallible one, please draw my chariot between the two armies so that I may see those present here, who desire to fight, and with whom I must contend in this great trial of arms.

PURPORT: Although Lord Kṛṣṇa is the Supreme Personality of Godhead, out of His causeless mercy He was engaged in the service of His friend. He never fails in His affection for His devotees, and thus He is addressed herein as infallible. As charioteer, He had to carry out the orders of Arjuna, and since He did not hesitate to do so, He is addressed as infallible. Although He had accepted the position of a charioteer for His devotee, His supreme position was not challenged. In all circumstances, He is the Supreme Personality of Godhead, Hṛṣīkeśa, the Lord of the total senses. The relationship between the Lord and His servitor is very sweet and transcendental. The servitor is always ready to render service to the Lord, and, similarly, the Lord is always seeking an opportunity to render some service to the devotee. He takes greater pleasure in His pure devotee's assuming the advantageous position of ordering Him than He does in being the giver of orders. Since He is master, everyone is under His orders, and no one is above Him to order Him. But when He finds that a pure devotee is ordering Him, He obtains transcendental pleasure, although He is the infallible master in all circumstances.

As a pure devotee of the Lord, Arjuna had no desire to fight with his cousins and brothers, but he was forced to come onto the battlefield by the obstinacy of Duryodhana, who was never agreeable to any peaceful negotiation. Therefore, he was very anxious to see who the leading persons present on the battlefield were. Although there was no question of a peacemaking endeavor on the battlefield, he wanted to see them again, and to see how much they were bent upon demanding an unwanted war.

Text 23 योत्स्यमानानवेक्षेऽहं य एतेऽत्र समागताः ।
धार्तराष्ट्रस्य दुर्बुद्धेर्युद्धे प्रियचिकीर्षवः ॥२३॥

yotsyamānān avekṣe 'haṁ, ya ete 'tra samāgatāḥ
dhārtarāṣṭrasya durbuddher, yuddhe priya-cikīrṣavaḥ

yotsyamānān – those who will be fighting; *avekṣe* – let me see; *aham* – I; *ye* – who; *ete* – those; *atra* – here; *samāgatāḥ* – assembled; *dhārtarāṣṭrasya* – for the son of Dhṛtarāṣṭra; *durbuddheḥ* – evil-minded; *yuddhe* – in the fight; *priya* – well; *cikīrṣavaḥ* – wishing.

Let me see those who have come here to fight, wishing to please the evil-minded son of Dhṛtarāṣṭra.

PURPORT: It was an open secret that Duryodhana wanted to usurp the kingdom of the Pāṇḍavas by evil plans, in collaboration with his father, Dhṛtarāṣṭra. Therefore, all persons who had joined the side of Duryodhana must have been birds of the same feather. Arjuna wanted to see them on the battlefield before the fight was begun, just to learn who they were, but he had no intention of proposing peace negotiations with them. It was also a fact that he wanted to see them to make an estimate of the strength which he had to face, although he was quite confident of victory because Kṛṣṇa was sitting by his side.

Text 24 सञ्जय उवाच
एवमुक्तो हृषीकेशो गुडाकेशेन भारत ।
सेनयोरुभयोर्मध्ये स्थापयित्वा रथोत्तमम् ॥२४॥

sañjaya uvāca
evam ukto hṛṣīkeśo, guḍākeśena bhārata
senayor ubhayor madhye, sthāpayitvā rathottamam

sañjayaḥ uvāca – Sañjaya said; *evam* – thus; *uktaḥ* – addressed; *hṛṣīkeśaḥ* – Lord Kṛṣṇa; *guḍākeśena* – by Arjuna; *bhārata* – O descendant of Bharata; *senayoḥ* – of the armies; *ubhayoḥ* – both; *madhye* – in the midst; *sthāpayitvā* – placing; *ratha-uttamam* – the finest chariot.

Sañjaya said: O descendant of Bharata, having thus been addressed by Arjuna, Lord Kṛṣṇa drew up the fine chariot in the midst of the armies of both parties.

PURPORT: In this verse Arjuna is referred to as Guḍākeśa. *Guḍākā* means sleep, and one who conquers sleep is called *guḍākeśa.* Sleep also means ignorance. So Arjuna conquered both sleep and ignorance because of his friendship with Kṛṣṇa. As a great devotee of Kṛṣṇa, he could not forget Kṛṣṇa even for a moment, because that is the nature of a devotee. Either in waking or in sleep, a devotee of the Lord can never be free from thinking of Kṛṣṇa's name, form, qualities and pastimes. Thus a devotee of Kṛṣṇa can conquer both sleep and ignorance simply by thinking of Kṛṣṇa constantly. This is called Kṛṣṇa consciousness, or *samādhi.* As Hṛṣīkeśa, or the director of the senses and mind of every living entity, Kṛṣṇa could understand Arjuna's purpose in placing the chariot in the midst of the armies. Thus He did so, and spoke as follows.

Text 25 भीष्मद्रोणप्रमुखतः सर्वेषां च महीक्षिताम् ।
उवाच पार्थ पश्यैतान् समवेतान् कुरूनिति ॥२५॥

bhīṣma-droṇa-pramukhataḥ, sarveṣāṁ ca mahī-kṣitām
uvāca pārtha paśyaitān, samavetān kurūn iti

bhīṣma – Grandfather Bhīṣma; *droṇa* – the teacher Droṇa; *pramukhataḥ* – in front of; *sarveṣām* – all; *ca* – also; *mahī-kṣitām* – chiefs of the world; *uvāca* – said; *pārtha* – O son of Pṛthā; *paśya* – just behold; *etān* – all of them; *samavetān* – assembled; *kurūn* – the members of the Kuru dynasty; *iti* – thus.

In the presence of Bhīṣma, Droṇa and all the other chieftains of the world, the Lord said, "Just behold, Pārtha, all the Kurus assembled here."

PURPORT: As the Supersoul of all living entities, Lord Kṛṣṇa could understand what was going on in the mind of Arjuna. The use of the word Hṛṣīkeśa in this connection indicates that He knew everything. And the word Pārtha, meaning "the son of Pṛthā, or Kuntī," is also similarly significant in reference to Arjuna. As a friend, He wanted to inform Arjuna that because Arjuna was the son of Pṛthā, the sister of His own father Vasudeva, He had agreed to be the charioteer of Arjuna. Now what did Kṛṣṇa mean when He told Arjuna to "behold the Kurus"? Did Arjuna want to stop there and not fight? Kṛṣṇa never expected such things from the son of His aunt Pṛthā. The mind of Arjuna was thus predicted by the Lord in friendly joking.

Text 26 तत्रापश्यत्स्थितान् पार्थः पितॄनथ पितामहान् ।
आचार्यान्मातुलान् भ्रातॄन् पुत्रान् पौत्रान् सखींस्तथा ।
श्वशुरान् सुहृदश्चैव सेनयोरुभयोरपि ॥२६॥

tatrāpaśyat sthitān pārthaḥ, pitṝn atha pitāmahān
ācāryān mātulān bhrātṝn, putrān pautrān sakhīṁs tathā
śvaśurān suhṛdaś caiva, senayor ubhayor api

tatra – there; *apaśyat* – he could see; *sthitān* – standing; *pārthaḥ* – Arjuna; *pitṝn* – fathers; *atha* – also; *pitāmahān* – grandfathers; *ācāryān* – teachers; *mātulān* – maternal uncles; *bhrātṝn* – brothers; *putrān* – sons; *pautrān* – grandsons; *sakhīn* – friends; *tathā* – too; *śvaśurān* – fathers-in-law; *suhṛdaḥ* – well-wishers; *ca* – also; *eva* – certainly; *senayoḥ* – of the armies; *ubhayoḥ* – of both parties; *api* – including.

There Arjuna could see, within the midst of the armies of both parties, his fathers, grandfathers, teachers, maternal uncles, brothers, sons, grandsons, friends, and also his fathers-in-law and well-wishers.

PURPORT: On the battlefield Arjuna could see all kinds of relatives. He could see persons like Bhūriśravā, who were his father's contemporaries, grandfathers Bhīṣma and Somadatta, teachers like Droṇācārya and Kṛpācārya, maternal uncles like Śalya and Śakuni, brothers like Duryodhana, sons like Lakṣmaṇa, friends like Aśvatthāmā, well-wishers like Kṛtavarmā, etc. He could see also the armies which contained many of his friends.

Text 27 तान् समीक्ष्य स कौन्तेयः सर्वान् बन्धूनवस्थितान् ।
कृपया परयाविष्टो विषीदन्निदमब्रवीत् ॥२७॥

tān samīkṣya sa kaunteyaḥ, sarvān bandhūn avasthitān
kṛpayā parayāviṣṭo, viṣīdann idam abravīt

tān – all of them; *samīkṣya* – after seeing; *saḥ* – he; *kaunteyaḥ* – the son of Kuntī; *sarvān* – all kinds of; *bandhūn* – relatives; *avasthitān* – situated; *kṛpayā* – by compassion; *parayā* – of a high grade; *āviṣṭaḥ* – overwhelmed; *viṣīdan* – while lamenting; *idam* – thus; *abravīt* – spoke.

When the son of Kuntī, Arjuna, saw all these different grades of friends and relatives, he became overwhelmed with compassion and spoke thus.

Text 28 अर्जुन उवाच
दृष्ट्वेमं स्वजनं कृष्ण युयुत्सुं समुपस्थितम् ।
सीदन्ति मम गात्राणि मुखं च परिशुष्यति ॥२८॥

arjuna uvāca
dṛṣṭvemaṁ sva-janaṁ kṛṣṇa, yuyutsuṁ samupasthitam
sīdanti mama gātrāṇi, mukhaṁ ca pariśuṣyati

arjunaḥ uvāca – Arjuna said; *dṛṣṭvā* – after seeing; *imam* – all these; *sva-janam* – kinsmen; *kṛṣṇa* – O Kṛṣṇa; *yuyutsum* – all in a fighting spirit; *samupasthitam* – present; *sīdanti* – are quivering; *mama* – my; *gātrāṇi* – limbs of the body; *mukham* – mouth; *ca* – also; *pariśuṣyati* – is drying up.

Arjuna said: My dear Kṛṣṇa, seeing my friends and relatives present before me in such a fighting spirit, I feel the limbs of my body quivering and my mouth drying up.

PURPORT: Any man who has genuine devotion to the Lord has all the good qualities which are found in godly persons or in the demigods, whereas the nondevotee, however advanced he may be in material qualifications by education and culture, lacks in godly qualities. As such, Arjuna, just after seeing his kinsmen, friends and relatives on the battlefield, was at once overwhelmed by compassion for them who had so decided to fight amongst themselves. As far as his soldiers were concerned, he was sympathetic from the beginning, but he felt compassion even for the soldiers of the opposite party, foreseeing their imminent death. And while he was so thinking, the limbs of his body began to quiver, and his mouth became dry. He was more or less astonished to see their fighting spirit. Practically the whole community, all blood relatives of Arjuna, had come to fight with him. This overwhelmed a kind devotee like Arjuna. Although it is not mentioned here, still one can easily imagine that not only were Arjuna's bodily limbs quivering and his mouth drying up, but he was also crying out of compassion. Such symptoms in Arjuna were not due to weakness but to his softheartedness, a characteristic of a pure devotee of the Lord. It is said therefore:

yasyāsti bhaktir bhagavaty akiñcanā, sarvair guṇais tatra samāsate surāḥ
harāv abhaktasya kuto mahad-guṇā, mano-rathenāsati dhāvato bahiḥ

"One who has unflinching devotion for the Personality of Godhead has all the good qualities of the demigods. But one who is not a devotee of the Lord has only material qualifications that are of little value. This is because he is hovering on the mental plane and is certain to be attracted by the glaring material energy." (*Bhāgavatam* 5.18.12)

Text 29 वेपथुश्च शरीरे मे रोमहर्षश्च जायते ।
गाण्डीवं स्रंसते हस्तात्त्वक्चैव परिदह्यते ॥२९॥

vepathuś ca śarīre me, roma-harṣaś ca jāyate
gāṇḍīvaṁ sraṁsate hastāt, tvak caiva paridahyate

vepathuḥ – trembling of the body; *ca* – also; *śarīre* – on the body; *me* – my; *roma-harṣaḥ* – standing of hair on end; *ca* – also; *jāyate* – is taking place; *gāṇḍīvam* – the bow of Arjuna; *sraṁsate* – is slipping; *hastāt* – from the hand; *tvak* – skin; *ca* – also; *eva* – certainly; *paridahyate* – is burning.

My whole body is trembling, my hair is standing on end, my bow Gāṇḍīva is slipping from my hand, and my skin is burning.

PURPORT: There are two kinds of trembling of the body, and two kinds of standings of the hair on end. Such phenomena occur either in great spiritual ecstasy or out of great fear under material conditions. There is no fear in transcendental realization. Arjuna's symptoms in this situation are out of material fear – namely, loss of life. This is evident from other symptoms also; he became so impatient that his famous bow Gāṇḍīva was slipping from his hands, and, because his heart was burning within him, he was feeling a burning sensation of the skin. All these are due to a material conception of life.

Text 30 न च शक्नोम्यवस्थातुं भ्रमतीव च मे मनः ।
निमित्तानि च पश्यामि विपरीतानि केशव ॥३०॥

na ca śaknomy avasthātuṁ, bhramatīva ca me manaḥ
nimittāni ca paśyāmi, viparītāni keśava

na – nor; *ca* – also; *śaknomi* – am I able; *avasthātum* – to stay; *bhramati* – forgetting; *iva* – as; *ca* – and; *me* – my; *manaḥ* – mind; *nimittāni* – causes; *ca* – also; *paśyāmi* – I see; *viparītāni* – just the opposite; *keśava* – O killer of the demon Keśī (Kṛṣṇa).

I am now unable to stand here any longer. I am forgetting myself, and my mind is reeling. I see only causes of misfortune, O Kṛṣṇa, killer of the Keśī demon.

PURPORT: Due to his impatience, Arjuna was unable to stay on the battlefield, and he was forgetting himself on account of this weakness of his mind. Excessive attachment for material things puts a man in such a bewildering condition of existence. *Bhayaṁ dvitīyābhiniveśataḥ syāt* (*Bhāgavatam* 11.2.37): such fearfulness and loss of mental equilibrium take place in persons who are too affected by material conditions. Arjuna envisioned only painful reverses in the battlefield – he would not be happy even by gaining victory over the foe. The words *nimittāni viparītāni* are significant. When a man sees only frustration in his expectations, he thinks, "Why am I here?" Everyone is interested in himself and his own welfare. No one is interested in the Supreme Self. Arjuna is showing ignorance of his real self-interest by Kṛṣṇa's will. One's real self-interest lies in Viṣṇu, or Kṛṣṇa. The conditioned soul forgets this, and therefore suffers material pains. Arjuna thought that his victory in the battle would only be a cause of lamentation for him.

Text 31 न च श्रेयोऽनुपश्यामि हत्वा स्वजनमाहवे ।
न काङ्क्षे विजयं कृष्ण न च राज्यं सुखानि च ॥३१॥

na ca śreyo 'nupaśyāmi, hatvā sva-janam āhave
na kāṅkṣe vijayaṁ kṛṣṇa, na ca rājyaṁ sukhāni ca

na – nor; *ca* – also; *śreyaḥ* – good; *anupaśyāmi* – do I foresee; *hatvā* – by killing; *sva-janam* – own kinsmen; *āhave* – in the fight; *na* – nor; *kāṅkṣe* – do I desire; *vijayam* – victory; *kṛṣṇa* – O Kṛṣṇa; *na* – nor; *ca* – also; *rājyam* – kingdom; *sukhāni* – happiness thereof; *ca* – also.

I do not see how any good can come from killing my own kinsmen in this battle, nor can I, my dear Kṛṣṇa, desire any subsequent victory, kingdom or happiness.

PURPORT: Without knowing that one's self-interest is in Viṣṇu (or Kṛṣṇa), conditioned souls are attracted by bodily relationships, hoping to be happy in such situations. In such a blind conception of life, they forget even the causes of material happiness. Arjuna appears to have even forgotten the moral codes for a *kṣatriya.* It is said that two kinds of men, namely the *kṣatriya* who dies directly in front of the battlefield under Kṛṣṇa's personal orders and the person in the renounced order of life who is absolutely devoted to spiritual culture, are eligible to enter into the sun globe, which is so powerful and dazzling. Arjuna is reluctant even to kill his enemies, let alone his relatives. He thinks that by killing his kinsmen there would be no happiness in his life, and therefore he is not willing to fight, just as a person who does not feel hunger is not inclined to cook. He has now decided to go into the forest and live a secluded life in frustration. But as a *kṣatriya,* he requires a kingdom for his subsistence, because the *kṣatriyas* cannot engage themselves in any other occupation. But Arjuna has no kingdom. Arjuna's sole opportunity for gaining a kingdom lies in fighting with his cousins and brothers and reclaiming the kingdom inherited from his father, which he does not like to do. Therefore he considers himself fit to go to the forest to live a secluded life of frustration.

Texts 32–35

किं नो राज्येन गोविन्द किं भोगैर्जीवितेन वा ।
येषामर्थे काङ्क्षितं नो राज्यं भोगाः सुखानि च ॥३२॥
त इमेऽवस्थिता युद्धे प्राणांस्त्यक्त्वा धनानि च ।
आचार्याः पितरः पुत्रास्तथैव च पितामहाः ॥३३॥
मातुलाः श्वशुराः पौत्राः श्यालाः सम्बन्धिनस्तथा ।
एतान्न हन्तुमिच्छामि घ्नतोऽपि मधुसूदन ॥३४॥
अपि त्रैलोक्यराज्यस्य हेतोः किं नु महीकृते ।
निहत्य धार्तराष्ट्रान्नः का प्रीतिः स्याज्जनार्दन ॥३५॥

kiṁ no rājyena govinda, kiṁ bhogair jīvitena vā
yeṣām arthe kāṅkṣitaṁ no, rājyaṁ bhogāḥ sukhāni ca

ta ime 'vasthitā yuddhe, prāṇāṁs tyaktvā dhanāni ca
ācāryāḥ pitaraḥ putrās, tathaiva ca pitāmahāḥ

mātulāḥ śvaśurāḥ pautrāḥ, śyālāḥ sambandhinas tathā
etān na hantum icchāmi, ghnato 'pi madhusūdana

api trailokya-rājyasya, hetoḥ kiṁ nu mahī-kṛte
nihatya dhārtarāṣṭrān naḥ, kā prītiḥ syāj janārdana

kim – what use; *naḥ* – to us; *rājyena* – is the kingdom; *govinda* – O Kṛṣṇa; *kim* – what; *bhogaiḥ* – enjoyment; *jīvitena* – living; *vā* – either; *yeṣām* – of whom; *arthe* – for the sake; *kāṅkṣitam* – is desired; *naḥ* – by us; *rājyam* – kingdom; *bhogāḥ* – material enjoyment; *sukhāni* – all happiness; *ca* – also; *te* – all of them; *ime* – these; *avasthitāḥ* – situated; *yuddhe* – on this battlefield; *prāṇān* – lives; *tyaktvā* – giving up; *dhanāni* – riches; *ca* – also; *ācāryāḥ* – teachers; *pitaraḥ* – fathers; *putrāḥ* – sons; *tathā* – as well as; *eva* – certainly; *ca* – also; *pitāmahāḥ* – grandfathers; *mātulāḥ* – maternal uncles; *śvaśurāḥ* – fathers-in-law; *pautrāḥ* – grandsons; *śyālāḥ* – brothers-in-law; *sambandhinaḥ* – relatives; *tathā* – as well as; *etān* – all these; *na* – never; *hantum* – to kill; *icchāmi* –

do I wish; *ghnataḥ* – being killed; *api* – even; *madhusūdana* – O killer of the demon Madhu (Kṛṣṇa); *api* – even if; *trai-lokya* – of the three worlds; *rājyasya* – for the kingdom; *hetoḥ* – in exchange; *kim nu* – what to speak of; *mahī-kṛte* – for the sake of the earth; *nihatya* – by killing; *dhārtarāṣṭrān* – the sons of Dhṛtarāṣṭra; *naḥ* – our; *kā* – what; *prītiḥ* – pleasure; *syāt* – will there be; *janārdana* – O maintainer of all living entities.

O Govinda, of what avail to us are a kingdom, happiness or even life itself when all those for whom we may desire them are now arrayed on this battlefield? O Madhusūdana, when teachers, fathers, sons, grandfathers, maternal uncles, fathers-in-law, grandsons, brothers-in-law and other relatives are ready to give up their lives and properties and are standing before me, why should I wish to kill them, even though they might otherwise kill me? O maintainer of all living entities, I am not prepared to fight with them even in exchange for the three worlds, let alone this earth. What pleasure will we derive from killing the sons of Dhṛtarāṣṭra?

PURPORT: Arjuna has addressed Lord Kṛṣṇa as Govinda because Kṛṣṇa is the object of all pleasures for cows and the senses. By using this significant word, Arjuna indicates that Kṛṣṇa should understand what will satisfy Arjuna's senses. But Govinda is not meant for satisfying our senses. If we try to satisfy the senses of Govinda, however, then automatically our own senses are satisfied. Materially, everyone wants to satisfy his senses, and he wants God to be the order supplier for such satisfaction. The Lord will satisfy the senses of the living entities as much as they deserve, but not to the extent that they may covet. But when one takes the opposite way – namely, when one tries to satisfy the senses of Govinda without desiring to satisfy one's own senses – then by the grace of Govinda all desires of the living entity are satisfied. Arjuna's deep affection for community and family members is exhibited here partly due to his natural compassion for them. He is therefore not prepared to fight. Everyone wants to show his opulence to friends and relatives, but Arjuna fears that all his relatives and friends will be killed on the battlefield and he will be unable to share his opulence after victory. This is a typical calculation of material life. The transcendental life, however, is different. Since a devotee wants to satisfy the desires of the Lord, he can, Lord willing, accept all kinds of opulence for the service of the Lord, and if the Lord is not willing, he should not accept a farthing. Arjuna did not want to kill his relatives, and if there were any need to kill them, he desired that Kṛṣṇa kill them personally. At this point he did not know that Kṛṣṇa had already killed them before their coming into the battlefield and that he was only to become an instrument for Kṛṣṇa. This fact is disclosed in following chapters. As a natural devotee of the Lord, Arjuna did not like to retaliate against his miscreant cousins and brothers, but it was the Lord's plan that they should all be killed. The devotee of the Lord does not retaliate against the wrongdoer, but the Lord does not tolerate any mischief done to the devotee by the miscreants. The Lord can excuse a person on His own account, but He excuses no one who has done harm to His devotees. Therefore the Lord was determined to kill the miscreants, although Arjuna wanted to excuse them.

Text 36 पापमेवाश्रयेदस्मान् हत्वैतानाततायिनः ।
तस्मान्नार्हा वयं हन्तुं धार्तराष्ट्रान् सबान्धवान् ।
स्वजनं हि कथं हत्वा सुखिनः स्याम माधव ॥३६॥

pāpam evāśrayed asmān, hatvaitān ātatāyinaḥ
tasmān nārhā vayaṁ hantuṁ, dhārtarāṣṭrān sa-bāndhavān
sva-janaṁ hi kathaṁ hatvā, sukhinaḥ syāma mādhava

pāpam – vices; *eva* – certainly; *āśrayet* – must come upon; *asmān* – us; *hatvā* – by killing; *etān* – all these; *ātatāyinaḥ* – aggressors; *tasmāt* – therefore; *na* – never; *arhāḥ* – deserving; *vayam* – we; *hantum* – to kill; *dhārtarāṣṭrān* – the sons of Dhṛtarāṣṭra; *sa-bāndhavān* – along with friends; *sva-janam* – kinsmen; *hi* – certainly; *katham* – how; *hatvā* – by killing; *sukhinaḥ* – happy; *syāma* – will we become; *mādhava* – O Kṛṣṇa, husband of the goddess of fortune.

Sin will overcome us if we slay such aggressors. Therefore it is not proper for us to kill the sons of Dhṛtarāṣṭra and our friends. What should we gain, O Kṛṣṇa, husband of the goddess of fortune, and how could we be happy by killing our own kinsmen?

PURPORT: According to Vedic injunctions there are six kinds of aggressors: (1) a poison giver, (2) one who sets fire to the house, (3) one who attacks with deadly weapons, (4) one who plunders riches, (5) one who occupies another's land, and (6) one who kidnaps a wife. Such aggressors are at once to be killed, and no sin is incurred by killing such aggressors. Such killing of aggressors is quite befitting any ordinary man, but Arjuna was not an ordinary person. He was saintly by character, and therefore he wanted to deal with them in saintliness. This kind of saintliness, however, is not for a *kṣatriya.* Although a responsible man in the administration of a state is required to be saintly, he should not be cowardly. For example, Lord Rāma was so saintly that people even now are anxious to live in the kingdom of Lord Rāma (*rāma-rājya*), but Lord Rāma never showed any cowardice. Rāvaṇa was an aggressor against Rāma because Rāvaṇa kidnapped Rāma's wife, Sītā, but Lord Rāma gave him sufficient lessons, unparalleled in the history of the world. In Arjuna's case, however, one should consider the special type of aggressors, namely his own grandfather, own teacher, friends, sons, grandsons, etc. Because of them, Arjuna thought that he should not take the severe steps necessary against ordinary aggressors. Besides that, saintly persons are advised to forgive. Such injunctions for saintly persons are more important than any political emergency. Arjuna considered that rather than kill his own kinsmen for political reasons, it would be better to forgive them on grounds of religion and saintly behavior. He did not, therefore, consider such killing profitable simply for the matter of temporary bodily happiness. After all, kingdoms and the pleasures derived therefrom are not permanent, so why should he risk his life and eternal salvation by killing his own kinsmen? Arjuna's addressing of Kṛṣṇa as "Mādhava," or the husband of the goddess of fortune, is also significant in this connection. He wanted to point out to Kṛṣṇa that, as the husband of the goddess of fortune, He should not induce Arjuna to take up a matter which would ultimately bring about misfortune. Kṛṣṇa, however, never brings misfortune to anyone, to say nothing of His devotees.

Texts 37–38

यद्यप्येते न पश्यन्ति लोभोपहतचेतसः ।
कुलक्षयकृतं दोषं मित्रद्रोहे च पातकम् ॥३७॥
कथं न ज्ञेयमस्माभिः पापादस्मान्निवर्तितुम् ।
कुलक्षयकृतं दोषं प्रपश्यद्भिर्जनार्दन ॥३८॥

yady apy ete na paśyanti, lobhopahata-cetasaḥ
kula-kṣaya-kṛtaṁ doṣaṁ, mitra-drohe ca pātakam

kathaṁ na jñeyam asmābhiḥ, pāpād asmān nivartitum
kula-kṣaya-kṛtaṁ doṣaṁ, prapaśyadbhir janārdana

yadi – if; *api* – even; *ete* – they; *na* – do not; *paśyanti* – see; *lobha* – by greed; *upahata* – overpowered; *cetasaḥ* – their hearts; *kula-kṣaya* – in killing the family; *kṛtam* – done; *doṣam* – fault; *mitra-drohe* – in quarreling with friends; *ca* – also; *pātakam* – sinful reactions; *katham* – why;

na – should not; *jñeyam* – be known; *asmābhiḥ* – by us; *pāpāt* – from sins; *asmāt* – these; *nivartitum* – to cease; *kula-kṣaya* – in the destruction of a dynasty; *kṛtam* – done; *doṣam* – crime; *prapaśyadbhiḥ* – by those who can see; *janārdana* – O Kṛṣṇa.

O Janārdana, although these men, their hearts overtaken by greed, see no fault in killing one's family or quarreling with friends, why should we, who can see the crime in destroying a family, engage in these acts of sin?

PURPORT: A *kṣatriya* is not supposed to refuse to battle or gamble when he is so invited by some rival party. Under such an obligation, Arjuna could not refuse to fight, because he had been challenged by the party of Duryodhana. In this connection, Arjuna considered that the other party might be blind to the effects of such a challenge. Arjuna, however, could see the evil consequences and could not accept the challenge. Obligation is actually binding when the effect is good, but when the effect is otherwise, then no one can be bound. Considering all these pros and cons, Arjuna decided not to fight.

Text 39 कुलक्षये प्रणश्यन्ति कुलधर्माः सनातनाः ।
धर्मे नष्टे कुलं कृत्स्नमधर्मोऽभिभवत्युत ॥३९॥

kula-kṣaye praṇaśyanti, kula-dharmāḥ sanātanāḥ
dharme naṣṭe kulaṁ kṛtsnam, adharmo 'bhibhavaty uta

kula-kṣaye – in destroying the family; *praṇaśyanti* – become vanquished; *kula-dharmāḥ* – the family traditions; *sanātanāḥ* – eternal; *dharme* – religion; *naṣṭe* – being destroyed; *kulam* – family; *kṛtsnam* – whole; *adharmaḥ* – irreligion; *abhibhavati* – transforms; *uta* – it is said.

With the destruction of the dynasty, the eternal family tradition is vanquished, and thus the rest of the family becomes involved in irreligion.

PURPORT: In the system of the *varṇāśrama* institution there are many principles of religious traditions to help members of the family grow properly and attain spiritual values. The elder members are responsible for such purifying processes in the family, beginning from birth to death. But on the death of the elder members, such family traditions of purification may stop, and the remaining younger family members may develop irreligious habits and thereby lose their chance for spiritual salvation. Therefore, for no purpose should the elder members of the family be slain.

Text 40 अधर्माभिभवात्कृष्ण प्रदुष्यन्ति कुलस्त्रियः ।
स्त्रीषु दुष्टासु वार्ष्णेय जायते वर्णसङ्करः ॥४०॥

adharmābhibhavāt kṛṣṇa, praduṣyanti kula-striyaḥ
strīṣu duṣṭāsu vārṣṇeya, jāyate varṇa-saṅkaraḥ

adharma – irreligion; *abhibhavāt* – having become predominant; *kṛṣṇa* – O Kṛṣṇa; *praduṣyanti* – become polluted; *kula-striyaḥ* – family ladies; *strīṣu* – by the womanhood; *duṣṭāsu* – being so polluted; *vārṣṇeya* – O descendant of Vṛṣṇi; *jāyate* – comes into being; *varṇa-saṅkaraḥ* – unwanted progeny.

When irreligion is prominent in the family, O Kṛṣṇa, the women of the family become polluted, and from the degradation of womanhood, O descendant of Vṛṣṇi, comes unwanted progeny.

PURPORT: Good population in human society is the basic principle for peace, prosperity and spiritual progress in life. The *varṇāśrama* religion's principles were so designed that the good population would prevail in society for the general spiritual progress of state and community. Such population depends on the chastity and faithfulness of its womanhood. As children are very prone to be misled, women are similarly very prone to degradation. Therefore, both children and women require protection by the elder members of the family. By being engaged in various religious practices, women will not be misled into adultery. According to Cāṇakya Paṇḍita, women are generally not very intelligent and therefore not trustworthy. So the different family traditions of religious activities should always engage them, and thus their chastity and devotion will give birth to a good population eligible for participating in the *varṇāśrama* system. On the failure of such *varṇāśrama-dharma,* naturally the women become free to act and mix with men, and thus adultery is indulged in at the risk of unwanted population. Irresponsible men also provoke adultery in society, and thus unwanted children flood the human race at the risk of war and pestilence.

Text 41 सङ्करो नरकायैव कुलघ्नानां कुलस्य च ।
पतन्ति पितरो ह्येषां लुप्तपिण्डोदकक्रियाः ॥४१॥

saṅkaro narakāyaiva, kula-ghnānāṁ kulasya ca
patanti pitaro hy eṣāṁ, lupta-piṇḍodaka-kriyāḥ

saṅkaraḥ – such unwanted children; *narakāya* – make for hellish life; *eva* – certainly; *kula-ghnānām* – for those who are killers of the family; *kulasya* – for the family; *ca* – also; *patanti* – fall down; *pitaraḥ* – forefathers; *hi* – certainly; *eṣām* – of them; *lupta* – stopped; *piṇḍa* – of offerings of food; *udaka* – and water; *kriyāḥ* – performances.

An increase of unwanted population certainly causes hellish life both for the family and for those who destroy the family tradition. The ancestors of such corrupt families fall down, because the performances for offering them food and water are entirely stopped.

PURPORT: According to the rules and regulations of fruitive activities, there is a need to offer periodical food and water to the forefathers of the family. This offering is performed by worship of Viṣṇu, because eating the remnants of food offered to Viṣṇu can deliver one from all kinds of sinful reactions. Sometimes the forefathers may be suffering from various types of sinful reactions, and sometimes some of them cannot even acquire a gross material body and are forced to remain in subtle bodies as ghosts. Thus, when remnants of *prasādam* food are offered to forefathers by descendants, the forefathers are released from ghostly or other kinds of miserable life. Such help rendered to forefathers is a family tradition, and those who are not in devotional life are required to perform such rituals. One who is engaged in the devotional life is not required to perform such actions. Simply by performing devotional service, one can deliver hundreds and thousands of forefathers from all kinds of misery. It is stated in the *Bhāgavatam* (11.5.41):

devarṣi-bhūtāpta-nṛṇāṁ pitṝṇāṁ, na kiṅkaro nāyam ṛṇī ca rājan
sarvātmanā yaḥ śaraṇaṁ śaraṇyaṁ, gato mukundaṁ parihṛtya kartam

"Anyone who has taken shelter of the lotus feet of Mukunda, the giver of liberation, giving up all kinds of obligation, and has taken to the path in all seriousness, owes neither duties nor obligations to the demigods, sages, general living entities, family members, humankind or forefathers." Such obligations are automatically fulfilled by performance of devotional service to the Supreme Personality of Godhead.

Text 42 दोषैरेतैः कुलघ्नानां वर्णसङ्करकारकैः ।
उत्साद्यन्ते जातिधर्माः कुलधर्माश्च शाश्वताः ॥४२॥

doṣair etaiḥ kula-ghnānāṁ, varṇa-saṅkara-kārakaiḥ
utsādyante jāti-dharmāḥ, kula-dharmāś ca śāśvatāḥ

doṣaiḥ – by such faults; *etaiḥ* – all these; *kula-ghnānām* – of the destroyers of the family; *varṇa-saṅkara* – of unwanted children; *kārakaiḥ* – which are causes; *utsādyante* – are devastated; *jāti-dharmāḥ* – community projects; *kula-dharmāḥ* – family traditions; *ca* – also; *śāśvatāḥ* – eternal.

By the evil deeds of those who destroy the family tradition and thus give rise to unwanted children, all kinds of community projects and family welfare activities are devastated.

PURPORT: Community projects for the four orders of human society, combined with family welfare activities, as they are set forth by the institution of *sanātana-dharma,* or *varṇāśrama-dharma,* are designed to enable the human being to attain his ultimate salvation. Therefore, the breaking of the *sanātana-dharma* tradition by irresponsible leaders of society brings about chaos in that society, and consequently people forget the aim of life – Viṣṇu. Such leaders are called blind, and persons who follow such leaders are sure to be led into chaos.

Text 43 उत्सन्नकुलधर्माणां मनुष्याणां जनार्दन ।
नरके नियतं वासो भवतीत्यनुशुश्रुम ॥४३॥

utsanna-kula-dharmāṇāṁ, manuṣyāṇāṁ janārdana
narake niyataṁ vāso, bhavatīty anuśuśruma

utsanna – spoiled; *kula-dharmāṇām* – of those who have the family traditions; *manuṣyāṇām* – of such men; *janārdana* – O Kṛṣṇa; *narake* – in hell; *niyatam* – always; *vāsaḥ* – residence; *bhavati* – it so becomes; *iti* – thus; *anuśuśruma* – I have heard by disciplic succession.

O Kṛṣṇa, maintainer of the people, I have heard by disciplic succession that those whose family traditions are destroyed dwell always in hell.

PURPORT: Arjuna bases his argument not on his own personal experience, but on what he has heard from the authorities. That is the way of receiving real knowledge. One cannot reach the real point of factual knowledge without being helped by the right person who is already established in that knowledge. There is a system in the *varṇāśrama* institution by which before death one has to undergo the process of atonement for his sinful activities. One who is always engaged in sinful activities must utilize the process of atonement, called *prāyaścitta*. Without doing so, one surely will be transferred to hellish planets to undergo miserable lives as the result of sinful activities.

Text 44 अहो बत महत्पापं कर्तुं व्यवसिता वयम् ।
यद्राज्यसुखलोभेन हन्तुं स्वजनमुद्यताः ॥४४॥

aho bata mahat pāpaṁ, kartuṁ vyavasitā vayam
yad rājya-sukha-lobhena, hantuṁ sva-janam udyatāḥ

aho – alas; *bata* – how strange it is; *mahat* – great; *pāpam* – sins; *kartum* – to perform; *vyavasitāḥ* – have decided; *vayam* – we; *yat* – because; *rājya-sukha-lobhena* – driven by greed for royal happiness; *hantum* – to kill; *sva-janam* – kinsmen; *udyatāḥ* – trying.

Alas, how strange it is that we are preparing to commit greatly sinful acts. Driven by the desire to enjoy royal happiness, we are intent on killing our own kinsmen.

PURPORT: Driven by selfish motives, one may be inclined to such sinful acts as the killing of one's own brother, father or mother. There are many such instances in the history of the world. But Arjuna, being a saintly devotee of the Lord, is always conscious of moral principles and therefore takes care to avoid such activities.

Text 45 यदि मामप्रतीकारमशस्त्रं शस्त्रपाणयः ।
धार्तराष्ट्रा रणे हन्युस्तन्मे क्षेमतरं भवेत् ॥४५॥

yadi mām apratīkāram, aśastraṁ śastra-pāṇayaḥ
dhārtarāṣṭrā raṇe hanyus, tan me kṣema-taraṁ bhavet

yadi – even if; *mām* – me; *apratīkāram* – without being resistant; *aśastram* – without being fully equipped; *śastra-pāṇayaḥ* – those with weapons in hand; *dhārtarāṣṭrāḥ* – the sons of Dhṛtarāṣṭra; *raṇe* – on the battlefield; *hanyuḥ* – may kill; *tat* – that; *me* – for me; *kṣema-taram* – better; *bhavet* – would be.

Better for me if the sons of Dhṛtarāṣṭra, weapons in hand, were to kill me unarmed and unresisting on the battlefield.

PURPORT: It is the custom – according to *kṣatriya* fighting principles – that an unarmed and unwilling foe should not be attacked. Arjuna, however, decided that even if attacked by the enemy in such an awkward position, he would not fight. He did not consider how much the other party was bent upon fighting. All these symptoms are due to soft-heartedness resulting from his being a great devotee of the Lord.

Text 46 सञ्जय उवाच
एवमुक्त्वार्जुनः सङ्ख्ये रथोपस्थ उपाविशत् ।
विसृज्य सशरं चापं शोकसंविग्नमानसः ॥४६॥

sañjaya uvāca
evam uktvārjunaḥ saṅkhye, rathopastha upāviśat
visṛjya sa-śaraṁ cāpaṁ, śoka-saṁvigna-mānasaḥ

sañjayaḥ uvāca – Sañjaya said; *evam* – thus; *uktvā* – saying; *arjunaḥ* – Arjuna; *saṅkhye* – in the battlefield; *ratha* – of the chariot; *upasthe* – on the seat; *upāviśat* – sat down again; *visṛjya* – putting aside; *sa-śaram* – along with arrows; *cāpam* – the bow; *śoka* – by lamentation; *saṁvigna* – distressed; *mānasaḥ* – within the mind.

Sañjaya said: Arjuna, having thus spoken on the battlefield, cast aside his bow and arrows and sat down on the chariot, his mind overwhelmed with grief.

PURPORT: While observing the situation of his enemy, Arjuna stood up on the chariot, but he was so afflicted with lamentation that he sat down again, setting aside his bow and arrows. Such a kind and soft-hearted person, in the devotional service of the Lord, is fit to receive self-knowledge.

Thus end the Bhaktivedanta Purports to the First Chapter of the Śrīmad Bhagavad-gītā *in the matter of Observing the Armies on the Battlefield of Kurukṣetra.*

CHAPTER TWO

Contents of the Gītā Summarized

Text 1 सञ्जय उवाच
तं तथा कृपयाविष्टमश्रुपूर्णाकुलेक्षणम् ।
विषीदन्तमिदं वाक्यमुवाच मधुसूदनः ॥ १ ॥

sañjaya uvāca
taṁ tathā kṛpayāviṣṭam, aśru-pūrṇākulekṣaṇam
viṣīdantam idaṁ vākyam, uvāca madhusūdanaḥ

sañjayaḥ uvāca – Sañjaya said; *tam* – unto Arjuna; *tathā* – thus; *kṛpayā* – by compassion; *āviṣṭam* – overwhelmed; *aśru-pūrṇa-ākula* – full of tears; *īkṣaṇam* – eyes; *viṣīdantam* – lamenting; *idam* – these; *vākyam* – words; *uvāca* – said; *madhu-sūdanaḥ* – the killer of Madhu.

Sañjaya said: Seeing Arjuna full of compassion, his mind depressed, his eyes full of tears, Madhusūdana, Kṛṣṇa, spoke the following words.

PURPORT: Material compassion, lamentation and tears are all signs of ignorance of the real self. Compassion for the eternal soul is self-realization. The word "Madhusūdana" is significant in this verse. Lord Kṛṣṇa killed the demon Madhu, and now Arjuna wanted Kṛṣṇa to kill the demon of misunderstanding that had overtaken him in the discharge of his duty. No one knows where compassion should be applied.

Compassion for the dress of a drowning man is senseless. A man fallen in the ocean of nescience cannot be saved simply by rescuing his outward dress – the gross material body. One who does not know this and laments for the outward dress is called a *śūdra,* or one who laments unnecessarily. Arjuna was a *kṣatriya,* and this conduct was not expected from him. Lord Kṛṣṇa, however, can dissipate the lamentation of the ignorant man, and for this purpose the *Bhagavad-gītā* was sung by Him. This chapter instructs us in self-realization by an analytical study of the material body and the spirit soul, as explained by the supreme authority, Lord Śrī Kṛṣṇa. This realization is possible when one works without attachment to fruitive results and is situated in the fixed conception of the real self.

Text 2 श्रीभगवानुवाच
कुतस्त्वा कश्मलमिदं विषमे समुपस्थितम् ।
अनार्यजुष्टमस्वर्ग्यमकीर्तिकरमर्जुन ॥ २ ॥

śrī-bhagavān uvāca
kutas tvā kaśmalam idaṁ, viṣame samupasthitam
anārya-juṣṭam asvargyam, akīrti-karam arjuna

śrī-bhagavān uvāca – the Supreme Personality of Godhead said; *kutaḥ* – wherefrom; *tvā* – unto you; *kaśmalam* – dirtiness; *idam* – this lamentation; *viṣame* – in this hour of crisis; *samupasthitam* – arrived; *anārya* – persons who do not know the value of life; *juṣṭam* – practiced by; *asvargyam* – which does not lead to higher planets; *akīrti* – infamy; *karam* – the cause of; *arjuna* – O Arjuna.

The Supreme Personality of Godhead said: My dear Arjuna, how have these impurities come upon you? They are not at all befitting a man who knows the value of life. They lead not to higher planets but to infamy.

PURPORT: Kṛṣṇa and the Supreme Personality of Godhead are identical. Therefore Lord Kṛṣṇa is referred to as Bhagavān throughout the *Gītā.* Bhagavān is the ultimate in the Absolute Truth. The Absolute Truth is realized in three phases of understanding, namely Brahman, or the impersonal all-pervasive spirit; Paramātmā, or the localized aspect of the Supreme within the heart of all living entities; and Bhagavān, or the Supreme Personality of Godhead, Lord Kṛṣṇa. In the *Śrīmad-Bhāgavatam* (1.2.11) this conception of the Absolute Truth is explained thus:

vadanti tat tattva-vidas, tattvaṁ yaj jñānam advayam
brahmeti paramātmeti, bhagavān iti śabdyate

"The Absolute Truth is realized in three phases of understanding by the knower of the Absolute Truth, and all of them are identical. Such phases of the Absolute Truth are expressed as Brahman, Paramātmā and Bhagavān."

These three divine aspects can be explained by the example of the sun, which also has three different aspects, namely the sunshine, the sun's surface and the sun planet itself. One who studies the sunshine only is the preliminary student. One who understands the sun's surface is further advanced. And one who can enter into the sun planet is the highest. Ordinary students who are satisfied by simply understanding the sunshine – its universal pervasiveness and the glaring effulgence of its impersonal nature – may be compared to those who can realize only the Brahman feature of the Absolute Truth. The student who has advanced still further can know the sun disc, which is compared to knowledge of the Paramātmā feature of the Absolute Truth. And the student who can enter into the heart of the sun planet is compared to those who realize the personal features of the Supreme Absolute Truth. Therefore, the *bhaktas,* or the transcendentalists who have realized the Bhagavān feature of the Absolute Truth, are the topmost transcendentalists, although all students who are engaged in the study of the Absolute Truth are engaged in the same subject matter. The sunshine, the sun disc and the inner affairs of the sun planet cannot be separated from one another, and yet the students of the three different phases are not in the same category.

The Sanskrit word *bhagavān* is explained by the great authority Parāśara Muni, the father of Vyāsadeva. The Supreme Personality who possesses all riches, all strength, all fame, all beauty, all knowledge and all renunciation is called Bhagavān. There are many persons who are very rich, very powerful, very beautiful, very famous, very learned and very much detached, but no one can claim that he possesses all riches, all strength, etc., entirely. Only Kṛṣṇa can claim this because He is the Supreme Personality of Godhead. No living entity, including Brahmā, Lord Śiva or Nārāyaṇa, can possess opulences as fully as Kṛṣṇa. Therefore it is concluded in the *Brahma-saṁhitā* by Lord Brahmā himself that Lord Kṛṣṇa is the Supreme Personality of Godhead. No one is equal to or above Him. He is the primeval Lord, or Bhagavān, known as Govinda, and He is the supreme cause of all causes:

īśvaraḥ paramaḥ kṛṣṇaḥ, sac-cid-ānanda-vigrahaḥ
anādir ādir govindaḥ, sarva-kāraṇa-kāraṇam

"There are many personalities possessing the qualities of Bhagavān, but Kṛṣṇa is the supreme because none can excel Him. He is the Supreme Person, and His body is eternal, full of knowledge and bliss. He is the primeval Lord Govinda and the cause of all causes." (*Brahma-saṁhitā* 5.1)

In the *Bhāgavatam* also there is a list of many incarnations of the Supreme Personality of Godhead, but Kṛṣṇa is described as the original Personality of Godhead, from whom many, many incarnations and Personalities of Godhead expand:

ete cāṁśa-kalāḥ puṁsaḥ, kṛṣṇas tu bhagavān svayam
indrāri-vyākulaṁ lokaṁ, mṛḍayanti yuge yuge

"All the lists of the incarnations of Godhead submitted herewith are either plenary expansions or parts of the plenary expansions of the Supreme Godhead, but Kṛṣṇa is the Supreme Personality of Godhead Himself." (*Bhāgavatam* 1.3.28)

Therefore, Kṛṣṇa is the original Supreme Personality of Godhead, the Absolute Truth, the source of both the Supersoul and the impersonal Brahman.

In the presence of the Supreme Personality of Godhead, Arjuna's lamentation for his kinsmen is certainly unbecoming, and therefore Kṛṣṇa expressed His surprise with the word *kutaḥ,* "wherefrom." Such impurities were never expected from a person belonging to the civilized class of men known as Āryans. The word *āryan* is applicable to persons who know the value of life and have a civilization based on spiritual realization. Persons who are led by the material conception of life do not know that the aim of life is realization of the Absolute Truth, Viṣṇu, or Bhagavān, and they are captivated by the external features of the material world, and therefore they do not know what liberation is. Persons who have no knowledge of liberation from material bondage are called non-Āryans. Although Arjuna was a *kṣatriya,* he was deviating from his prescribed duties by declining to fight. This act of cowardice is described as befitting the non-Āryans. Such deviation from duty does not help one in the progress of spiritual life, nor does it even give one the opportunity to become famous in this world. Lord Kṛṣṇa did not approve of the so-called compassion of Arjuna for his kinsmen.

Text 3 क्लैब्यं मा स्म गमः पार्थ नैतत्त्वय्युपपद्यते ।
क्षुद्रं हृदयदौर्बल्यं त्यक्त्वोत्तिष्ठ परन्तप ॥ ३ ॥

klaibyaṁ mā sma gamaḥ pārtha, naitat tvayy upapadyate
kṣudraṁ hṛdaya-daurbalyaṁ, tyaktvottiṣṭha paran-tapa

klaibyam – impotence; *mā sma* – do not; *gamaḥ* – take to; *pārtha* – O son of Pṛthā; *na* – never; *etat* – this; *tvayi* – unto you; *upapadyate* – is befitting; *kṣudram* – petty; *hṛdaya* – of the heart; *daurbalyam* – weakness; *tyaktvā* – giving up; *uttiṣṭha* – get up; *param-tapa* – O chastiser of the enemies.

O son of Pṛthā, do not yield to this degrading impotence. It does not become you. Give up such petty weakness of heart and arise, O chastiser of the enemy.

PURPORT: Arjuna was addressed as the son of Pṛthā, who happened to be the sister of Kṛṣṇa's father Vasudeva. Therefore Arjuna had a blood relationship with Kṛṣṇa. If the son of a *kṣatriya* declines to fight, he is a *kṣatriya* in name only, and if the son of a *brāhmaṇa* acts impiously, he is a *brāhmaṇa* in name only. Such *kṣatriyas* and *brāhmaṇas* are unworthy sons of their fathers; therefore, Kṛṣṇa did not want Arjuna to become an unworthy son of a *kṣatriya*. Arjuna was the most intimate friend of Kṛṣṇa, and Kṛṣṇa was directly guiding him on the chariot; but in spite of all these credits, if Arjuna abandoned the battle he would be committing an infamous act. Therefore Kṛṣṇa said that such an attitude in Arjuna did not fit his personality. Arjuna might argue that he would give up the battle on the grounds of his magnanimous attitude for the most respectable Bhīṣma and his relatives, but Kṛṣṇa considered that sort of magnanimity mere weakness of heart. Such false magnanimity was not approved by any authority. Therefore, such magnanimity or so-called nonviolence should be given up by persons like Arjuna under the direct guidance of Kṛṣṇa.

Text 4 अर्जुन उवाच
कथं भीष्ममहं सङ्ख्ये द्रोणं च मधुसूदन ।
इषुभिः प्रतियोत्स्यामि पूजार्हावरिसूदन ॥ ४ ॥

arjuna uvāca
kathaṁ bhīṣmam ahaṁ saṅkhye, droṇaṁ ca madhusūdana
iṣubhiḥ pratiyotsyāmi, pūjārhāv ari-sūdana

arjunaḥ uvāca – Arjuna said; *katham* – how; *bhīṣmam* – Bhīṣma; *aham* – I; *saṅkhye* – in the fight; *droṇam* – Droṇa; *ca* – also; *madhu-sūdana* – O killer of Madhu; *iṣubhiḥ* – with arrows; *pratiyotsyāmi* – shall counterattack; *pūjā-arhau* – those who are worshipable; *ari-sūdana* – O killer of the enemies.

Arjuna said: O killer of enemies, O killer of Madhu, how can I counterattack with arrows in battle men like Bhīṣma and Droṇa, who are worthy of my worship?

PURPORT: Respectable superiors like Bhīṣma the grandfather and Droṇācārya the teacher are always worshipable. Even if they attack, they should not be counterattacked. It is general etiquette that superiors are not to be offered even a verbal fight. Even if they are sometimes harsh in behavior, they should not be harshly treated. Then, how is it possible for Arjuna to counterattack them? Would Kṛṣṇa ever attack His own grandfather, Ugrasena, or His teacher, Sāndīpani Muni? These were some of the arguments offered by Arjuna to Kṛṣṇa.

Text 5 गुरूनहत्वा हि महानुभावान् श्रेयो भोक्तुं भैक्ष्यमपीह लोके ।
हत्वार्थकामांस्तु गुरूनिहैव भुञ्जीय भोगान् रुधिरप्रदिग्धान् ॥ ५ ॥

gurūn ahatvā hi mahānubhāvān
śreyo bhoktuṁ bhaikṣyam apīha loke
hatvārtha-kāmāṁs tu gurūn ihaiva
bhuñjīya bhogān rudhira-pradigdhān

gurūn – the superiors; *ahatvā* – not killing; *hi* – certainly; *mahā-anubhāvān* – great souls; *śreyaḥ* – it is better; *bhoktum* – to enjoy life; *bhaikṣyam* – by begging; *api* – even; *iha* – in this life; *loke* – in this world; *hatvā* – killing; *artha* – gain; *kāmān* – desiring; *tu* – but; *gurūn* – superiors; *iha* – in this world; *eva* – certainly; *bhuñjīya* – one has to enjoy; *bhogān* – enjoyable things; *rudhira* – blood; *pradigdhān* – tainted with.

It would be better to live in this world by begging than to live at the cost of the lives of great souls who are my teachers. Even though desiring

worldly gain, they are superiors. If they are killed, everything we enjoy will be tainted with blood.

PURPORT: According to scriptural codes, a teacher who engages in an abominable action and has lost his sense of discrimination is fit to be abandoned. Bhīṣma and Droṇa were obliged to take the side of Duryodhana because of his financial assistance, although they should not have accepted such a position simply on financial considerations. Under the circumstances, they have lost the respectability of teachers. But Arjuna thinks that nevertheless they remain his superiors, and therefore to enjoy material profits after killing them would mean to enjoy spoils tainted with blood.

Text 6 न चैतद्विद्मः कतरन्नो गरीयो यद्वा जयेम यदि वा नो जयेयुः ।
यानेव हत्वा न जिजीविषामस्तेऽवस्थिताः प्रमुखे धार्तराष्ट्राः ॥ ६ ॥

na caitad vidmaḥ kataran no garīyo
yad vā jayema yadi vā no jayeyuḥ
yān eva hatvā na jijīviṣāmas
te 'vasthitāḥ pramukhe dhārtarāṣṭrāḥ

na – nor; *ca* – also; *etat* – this; *vidmaḥ* – do we know; *katarat* – which; *naḥ* – for us; *garīyaḥ* – better; *yat vā* – whether; *jayema* – we may conquer; *yadi* – if; *vā* – or; *naḥ* – us; *jayeyuḥ* – they conquer; *yān* – those who; *eva* – certainly; *hatvā* – by killing; *na* – never; *jijīviṣāmaḥ* – we would want to live; *te* – all of them; *avasthitāḥ* – are situated; *pramukhe* – in the front; *dhārtarāṣṭrāḥ* – the sons of Dhṛtarāṣṭra.

Nor do we know which is better – conquering them or being conquered by them. If we killed the sons of Dhṛtarāṣṭra, we should not care to live. Yet they are now standing before us on the battlefield.

PURPORT: Arjuna did not know whether he should fight and risk unnecessary violence, although fighting is the duty of the *kṣatriyas,* or whether he should refrain and live by begging. If he did not conquer the enemy, begging would be his only means of subsistence. Nor was there certainty of victory, because either side might emerge victorious. Even if victory awaited them (and their cause was justified), still, if the sons of Dhṛtarāṣṭra died in battle, it would be very difficult to live in their absence. Under the circumstances, that would be another kind of defeat for them.

All these considerations by Arjuna definitely proved that not only was he a great devotee of the Lord but he was also highly enlightened and had complete control over his mind and senses. His desire to live by begging, although he was born in the royal household, is another sign of detachment. He was truly virtuous, as these qualities, combined with his faith in the words of instruction of Śrī Kṛṣṇa (his spiritual master), indicate. It is concluded that Arjuna was quite fit for liberation. Unless the senses are controlled, there is no chance of elevation to the platform of knowledge, and without knowledge and devotion there is no chance of liberation. Arjuna was competent in all these attributes, over and above his enormous attributes in his material relationships.

Text 7 कार्पण्यदोषोपहतस्वभावः पृच्छामि त्वां धर्मसम्मूढचेताः ।
यच्छ्रेयः स्यान्निश्चितं ब्रूहि तन्मे शिष्यस्तेऽहं शाधि मां त्वां प्रपन्नम् ॥ ७ ॥

kārpaṇya-doṣopahata-svabhāvaḥ
pṛcchāmi tvāṁ dharma-sammūḍha-cetāḥ
yac chreyaḥ syān niścitaṁ brūhi tan me
śiṣyas te 'haṁ śādhi māṁ tvāṁ prapannam

kārpaṇya – of miserliness; *doṣa* – by the weakness; *upahata* – being afflicted; *svabhāvaḥ* – characteristics; *pṛcchāmi* – I am asking; *tvām* – unto You; *dharma* – religion; *sammūḍha* – bewildered; *cetāḥ* – in heart; *yat* – what; *śreyaḥ* – all-good; *syāt* – may be; *niścitam* – confidently; *brūhi* – tell; *tat* – that; *me* – unto me; *śiṣyaḥ* – disciple; *te* – Your; *aham* – I am; *śādhi* – just instruct; *mām* – me; *tvām* – unto You; *prapannam* – surrendered.

Now I am confused about my duty and have lost all composure because of miserly weakness. In this condition I am asking You to tell me for certain what is best for me. Now I am Your disciple, and a soul surrendered unto You. Please instruct me.

PURPORT: By nature's own way the complete system of material activities is a source of perplexity for everyone. In every step there is perplexity, and therefore it behooves one to approach a bona fide spiritual master who can give one proper guidance for executing the purpose of life. All Vedic literatures advise us to approach a bona fide spiritual master to get free from the perplexities of life, which happen without our desire. They are like a forest fire that somehow blazes without being set by anyone.

Similarly, the world situation is such that perplexities of life automatically appear, without our wanting such confusion. No one wants fire, and yet it takes place, and we become perplexed. The Vedic wisdom therefore advises that in order to solve the perplexities of life and to understand the science of the solution, one must approach a spiritual master who is in the disciplic succession. A person with a bona fide spiritual master is supposed to know everything. One should not, therefore, remain in material perplexities but should approach a spiritual master. This is the purport of this verse.

Who is the man in material perplexities? It is he who does not understand the problems of life. In the *Bṛhad-āraṇyaka Upaniṣad* (3.8.10) the perplexed man is described as follows: *yo vā etad akṣaraṁ gārgy aviditvāsmāl lokāt praiti sa kṛpaṇaḥ.* "He is a miserly man who does not solve the problems of life as a human and who thus quits this world like the cats and dogs, without understanding the science of self-realization." This human form of life is a most valuable asset for the living entity, who can utilize it for solving the problems of life; therefore, one who does not utilize this opportunity properly is a miser. On the other hand, there is the *brāhmaṇa,* or he who is intelligent enough to utilize this body to solve all the problems of life. *Ya etad akṣaraṁ gārgi viditvāsmāl lokāt praiti sa brāhmaṇaḥ.*

The *kṛpaṇas,* or miserly persons, waste their time in being overly affectionate for family, society, country, etc., in the material conception of life. One is often attached to family life, namely to wife, children and other members, on the basis of "skin disease." The *kṛpaṇa* thinks that he is able to protect his family members from death; or the *kṛpaṇa* thinks that his family or society can save him from the verge of death. Such family attachment can be found even in the lower animals, who take care of children also. Being intelligent, Arjuna could understand that his affection for family members and his wish to protect them from death were the causes of his perplexities. Although he could understand that his duty to fight was awaiting him, still, on account of miserly weakness, he could not discharge the duties. He is therefore asking Lord Kṛṣṇa, the supreme spiritual master, to make a definite solution. He offers himself to Kṛṣṇa as a disciple. He wants to stop friendly talks. Talks between the master and the disciple are serious, and now Arjuna wants to talk very seriously before the recognized spiritual master. Kṛṣṇa is therefore the original spiritual master of the science of *Bhagavad-gītā,* and Arjuna is the first disciple for understanding the *Gītā.* How Arjuna understands the *Bhagavad-gītā* is stated in the *Gītā* itself. And yet foolish mundane scholars explain that one need not submit to Kṛṣṇa as a person, but to "the unborn within Kṛṣṇa." There is no difference between Kṛṣṇa's within and without. And one who has no sense of this understanding is the greatest fool in trying to understand *Bhagavad-gītā.*

Text 8 न हि प्रपश्यामि ममापनुद्याद् यच्छोकमुच्छोषणमिन्द्रियाणाम् ।
अवाप्य भूमावसपत्नमृद्धं राज्यं सुराणामपि चाधिपत्यम् ॥ ८ ॥

na hi prapaśyāmi mamāpanudyād
yac chokam ucchoṣaṇam indriyāṇām
avāpya bhūmāv asapatnam ṛddhaṁ
rājyaṁ surāṇām api cādhipatyam

na – do not; *hi* – certainly; *prapaśyāmi* – I see; *mama* – my; *apanudyāt* – can drive away; *yat* – that which; *śokam* – lamentation; *ucchoṣaṇam* – drying up; *indriyāṇām* – of the senses; *avāpya* – achieving; *bhūmau* – on the earth; *asapatnam* – without rival; *ṛddham* – prosperous; *rājyam* – kingdom; *surāṇām* – of the demigods; *api* – even; *ca* – also; *ādhipatyam* – supremacy.

I can find no means to drive away this grief which is drying up my senses. I will not be able to dispel it even if I win a prosperous, unrivaled kingdom on earth with sovereignty like the demigods in heaven.

PURPORT: Although Arjuna was putting forward so many arguments based on knowledge of the principles of religion and moral codes, it appears that he was unable to solve his real problem without the help of the spiritual master, Lord Śrī Kṛṣṇa. He could understand that his so-called knowledge was useless in driving away his problems, which were drying up his whole existence; and it was impossible for him to solve such perplexities without the help of a spiritual master like Lord Kṛṣṇa. Academic knowledge, scholarship, high position, etc., are all useless in solving the problems of life; help can be given only by a spiritual master like Kṛṣṇa. Therefore, the conclusion is that a spiritual master who is one hundred percent Kṛṣṇa conscious is the bona fide spiritual master, for he can solve the problems of life. Lord Caitanya said that one who is a master in the science of Kṛṣṇa consciousness, regardless of his social position, is the real spiritual master.

kibā vipra, kibā nyāsī, śūdra kene naya
yei kṛṣṇa-tattva-vettā, sei 'guru' haya

"It does not matter whether a person is a *vipra* [learned scholar in Vedic wisdom], or is born in a lower family, or is in the renounced order of life – if he is a master in the science of Kṛṣṇa, he is the perfect and bona fide spiritual master." (*Caitanya-caritāmṛta, Madhya* 8.128) So without being a master in the science of Kṛṣṇa consciousness, no one is a bona fide spiritual master. It is also said in the Vedic literature:

ṣaṭ-karma-nipuṇo vipro, mantra-tantra-viśāradaḥ
avaiṣṇavo gurur na syād, vaiṣṇavaḥ śva-paco guruḥ

"A scholarly *brāhmaṇa,* expert in all subjects of Vedic knowledge, is unfit to become a spiritual master without being a Vaiṣṇava, or expert in the science of Kṛṣṇa consciousness. But a person born in a family of a lower caste can become a spiritual master if he is a Vaiṣṇava, or Kṛṣṇa conscious." (*Padma Purāṇa*)

The problems of material existence – birth, old age, disease and death – cannot be counteracted by accumulation of wealth and economic development. In many parts of the world there are states which are replete with all facilities of life, which are full of wealth and economically developed, yet the problems of material existence are still present. They are seeking peace in different ways, but they can achieve real happiness only if they consult Kṛṣṇa, or the *Bhagavad-gītā* and *Śrīmad-Bhāgavatam* – which constitute the science of Kṛṣṇa – through the bona fide representative of Kṛṣṇa, the man in Kṛṣṇa consciousness.

If economic development and material comforts could drive away one's lamentations for family, social, national or international inebrieties, then Arjuna would not have said that even an unrivaled kingdom on earth or supremacy like that of the demigods in the heavenly planets would be unable to drive away his lamentations. He sought, therefore, refuge in Kṛṣṇa consciousness, and that is the right path for peace and harmony. Economic development or supremacy over the world can be finished at any moment by the cataclysms of material nature. Even elevation into a higher planetary situation, as men are now seeking on the moon planet, can also be finished at one stroke. The *Bhagavad-gītā* confirms this: *kṣīṇe puṇye martya-lokaṁ viśanti.* "When the results of pious activities are finished, one falls down again from the peak of happiness to the lowest status of life." Many politicians of the world have fallen down in that way. Such downfalls only constitute more causes for lamentation.

Therefore, if we want to curb lamentation for good, then we have to take shelter of Kṛṣṇa, as Arjuna is seeking to do. So Arjuna asked Kṛṣṇa to solve his problem definitely, and that is the way of Kṛṣṇa consciousness.

Text 9 सञ्जय उवाच
एवमुक्त्वा हृषीकेशं गुडाकेशः परन्तपः ।
न योत्स्य इति गोविन्दमुक्त्वा तूष्णीं बभूव ह ॥ ९ ॥

sañjaya uvāca
evam uktvā hṛṣīkeśaṁ, guḍākeśaḥ paran-tapaḥ
na yotsya iti govindam, uktvā tūṣṇīṁ babhūva ha

sañjayaḥ uvāca – Sañjaya said; *evam* – thus; *uktvā* – speaking; *hṛṣīkeśam* – unto Kṛṣṇa, the master of the senses; *guḍākeśaḥ* – Arjuna, the master of curbing ignorance; *param-tapaḥ* – the chastiser of the enemies; *na yotsye* – I shall not fight; *iti* – thus; *govindam* – unto Kṛṣṇa, the giver of pleasure to the senses; *uktvā* – saying; *tūṣṇīm* – silent; *babhūva* – became; *ha* – certainly.

Sañjaya said: Having spoken thus, Arjuna, chastiser of enemies, told Kṛṣṇa, "Govinda, I shall not fight," and fell silent.

PURPORT: Dhṛtarāṣṭra must have been very glad to understand that Arjuna was not going to fight and was instead leaving the battlefield for the begging profession. But Sañjaya disappointed him again in relating that Arjuna was competent to kill his enemies (*paran-tapaḥ*). Although Arjuna was, for the time being, overwhelmed with false grief due to family affection, he surrendered unto Kṛṣṇa, the supreme spiritual master, as a disciple. This indicated that he would soon be free from the false lamentation resulting from family affection and would be enlightened with perfect knowledge of self-realization, or Kṛṣṇa consciousness, and would then surely fight. Thus Dhṛtarāṣṭra's joy would be frustrated, since Arjuna would be enlightened by Kṛṣṇa and would fight to the end.

Text 10 तमुवाच हृषीकेशः प्रहसन्निव भारत ।
सेनयोरुभयोर्मध्ये विषीदन्तमिदं वचः ॥१०॥

tam uvāca hṛṣīkeśaḥ, prahasann iva bhārata
senayor ubhayor madhye, viṣīdantam idaṁ vacaḥ

tam – unto him; *uvāca* – said; *hṛṣīkeśaḥ* – the master of the senses, Kṛṣṇa; *prahasan* – smiling; *iva* – like that; *bhārata* – O Dhṛtarāṣṭra, descendant of Bharata; *senayoḥ* – of the armies; *ubhayoḥ* – of both parties; *madhye* – between; *viṣīdantam* – unto the lamenting one; *idam* – the following; *vacaḥ* – words.

O descendant of Bharata, at that time Kṛṣṇa, smiling, in the midst of both the armies, spoke the following words to the grief-stricken Arjuna.

PURPORT: The talk was going on between intimate friends, namely the Hṛṣīkeśa and the Guḍākeśa. As friends, both of them were on the same level, but one of them voluntarily became a student of the other. Kṛṣṇa was smiling because a friend had chosen to become a disciple. As Lord of all, He is always in the superior position as the master of everyone, and yet the Lord agrees to be a friend, a son or a lover for a devotee who wants Him in such a role. But when He was accepted as the master, He at once assumed the role and talked with the disciple like the master – with gravity, as it is required. It appears that the talk between the master and the disciple was openly exchanged in the presence of both armies so that all were benefited. So the talks of *Bhagavad-gītā* are not for any particular person, society, or community, but they are for all, and friends or enemies are equally entitled to hear them.

Text 11 श्रीभगवानुवाच
अशोच्यानन्वशोचस्त्वं प्रज्ञावादांश्च भाषसे ।
गतासूनगतासूंश्च नानुशोचन्ति पण्डिताः ॥११॥

śrī-bhagavān uvāca
aśocyān anvaśocas tvaṁ, prajñā-vādāṁś ca bhāṣase
gatāsūn agatāsūṁś ca, nānuśocanti paṇḍitāḥ

śrī-bhagavān uvāca – the Supreme Personality of Godhead said; *aśocyān* – not worthy of lamentation; *anvaśocaḥ* – you are lamenting; *tvam* – you; *prajñā-vādān* – learned talks; *ca* – also; *bhāṣase* – speaking; *gata* – lost; *asūn* – life; *agata* – not passed; *asūn* – life; *ca* – also; *na* – never; *anuśocanti* – lament; *paṇḍitāḥ* – the learned.

The Supreme Personality of Godhead said: While speaking learned words, you are mourning for what is not worthy of grief. Those who are wise lament neither for the living nor for the dead.

PURPORT: The Lord at once took the position of the teacher and chastised the student, calling him, indirectly, a fool. The Lord said, "You are talking like a learned man, but you do not know that one who is learned – one who knows what is body and what is soul – does not lament for any stage of the body, neither in the living nor in the dead condition."

As explained in later chapters, it will be clear that knowledge means to know matter and spirit and the controller of both. Arjuna argued that religious principles should be given more importance than politics or sociology, but he did not know that knowledge of matter, soul and the Supreme is even more important than religious formularies. And because he was lacking in that knowledge, he should not have posed himself as a very learned man. As he did not happen to be a very learned man, he was consequently lamenting for something which was unworthy of lamentation. The body is born and is destined to be vanquished today or tomorrow; therefore the body is not as important as the soul. One who knows this is actually learned, and for him there is no cause for lamentation, regardless of the condition of the material body.

Text 12 न त्वेवाहं जातु नासं न त्वं नेमे जनाधिपाः ।
न चैव न भविष्यामः सर्वे वयमतः परम् ॥१२॥

na tv evāhaṁ jātu nāsaṁ, na tvaṁ neme janādhipāḥ
na caiva na bhaviṣyāmaḥ, sarve vayam ataḥ param

na – never; *tu* – but; *eva* – certainly; *aham* – I; *jātu* – at any time; *na* – did not; *āsam* – exist; *na* – not; *tvam* – you; *na* – not; *ime* – all these; *jana-adhipāḥ* – kings; *na* – never; *ca* – also; *eva* – certainly; *na* – not; *bhaviṣyāmaḥ* – shall exist; *sarve vayam* – all of us; *ataḥ param* – hereafter.

Never was there a time when I did not exist, nor you, nor all these kings; nor in the future shall any of us cease to be.

PURPORT: In the *Vedas* – in the *Kaṭha Upaniṣad* as well as in the *Śvetāśvatara Upaniṣad* – it is said that the Supreme Personality of Godhead is the maintainer of innumerable living entities, in terms of their different situations according to individual work and reaction of work. That Supreme Personality of Godhead is also, by His plenary portions, alive in the heart of every living entity. Only saintly persons who can see, within and without, the same Supreme Lord can actually attain to perfect and eternal peace.

nityo nityānāṁ cetanaś cetanānām, eko bahūnāṁ yo vidadhāti kāmān
tam ātma-sthaṁ ye 'nupaśyanti dhīrās, teṣāṁ śāntiḥ śāśvatī netareṣām
(*Kaṭha Upaniṣad* 2.2.13)

The same Vedic truth given to Arjuna is given to all persons in the world who pose themselves as very learned but factually have but a poor fund of knowledge. The Lord says clearly that He Himself, Arjuna and all the kings who are assembled on the battlefield are eternally individual beings and that the Lord is eternally the maintainer of the individual living entities both in their conditioned and in their liberated situations. The Supreme Personality of Godhead is the supreme individual person, and Arjuna, the Lord's eternal associate, and all the kings assembled there are individual eternal persons. It is not that they did not exist as individuals in the past, and it is not that they will not remain eternal persons. Their individuality existed in the past, and their individuality will continue in the future without interruption. Therefore, there is no cause for lamentation for anyone.

The Māyāvādī theory that after liberation the individual soul, separated by the covering of *māyā,* or illusion, will merge into the impersonal Brahman and lose its individual existence is not supported herein by Lord Kṛṣṇa, the supreme authority. Nor is the theory that we only think of individuality in the conditioned state supported herein. Kṛṣṇa clearly says herein that in the future also the individuality of the Lord and others, as it is confirmed in the *Upaniṣads,* will continue eternally. This statement of Kṛṣṇa's is authoritative because Kṛṣṇa cannot be subject to illusion. If individuality were not a fact, then Kṛṣṇa would not have stressed it so much – even for the future. The Māyāvādī may argue that the individuality spoken of by Kṛṣṇa is not spiritual, but material. Even accepting the argument that the individuality is material, then how can one distinguish Kṛṣṇa's individuality? Kṛṣṇa affirms His individuality in the past and confirms His individuality in the future also. He has confirmed His individuality in many ways, and impersonal Brahman has been declared to be subordinate to Him. Kṛṣṇa has maintained spiritual individuality all along; if He is accepted as an ordinary conditioned soul in individual consciousness, then His *Bhagavad-gītā* has no value as authoritative scripture. A common man with all the four defects of human frailty is unable to teach that which is worth hearing. The *Gītā* is above such literature. No mundane book compares with the *Bhagavad-gītā.* When one accepts Kṛṣṇa as an ordinary man, the *Gītā* loses all importance. The Māyāvādī argues that the plurality mentioned in this verse is conventional and that it refers to the body. But previous to this verse such a bodily conception is already condemned. After condemning the bodily conception of the living entities, how was it possible for Kṛṣṇa to place a conventional proposition on the body again? Therefore, individuality is maintained on spiritual grounds and is thus confirmed by great *ācāryas* like Śrī Rāmānuja and others. It is clearly mentioned in many places in the *Gītā* that this spiritual individuality is understood by those who are devotees of the Lord. Those who are envious of Kṛṣṇa as the Supreme Personality of Godhead have no bona fide access to the great literature. The nondevotee's approach to the teachings of the *Gītā* is something like that of a bee licking on a bottle of honey. One cannot have a taste of honey unless one opens the bottle. Similarly, the mysticism of the *Bhagavad-gītā* can be understood only by devotees, and no one else can taste it, as it is stated in the Fourth Chapter of the book. Nor can the *Gītā* be touched by persons who envy the very existence of the Lord. Therefore, the Māyāvādī explanation of the *Gītā* is a most misleading presentation of the whole truth. Lord Caitanya has forbidden us to read commentations made by the Māyāvādīs and warns that one who takes to such an understanding of the Māyāvādī philosophy loses all power to understand the real mystery of the *Gītā*. If individuality refers to the empirical universe, then there is no need of teaching by the Lord. The plurality of the individual soul and the Lord is an eternal fact, and it is confirmed by the *Vedas* as above mentioned.

Text 13 देहिनोऽस्मिन् यथा देहे कौमारं यौवनं जरा ।
तथा देहान्तरप्राप्तिर्धीरस्तत्र न मुह्यति ॥१३॥

dehino 'smin yathā dehe, kaumāraṁ yauvanaṁ jarā
tathā dehāntara-prāptir, dhīras tatra na muhyati

dehinaḥ – of the embodied; *asmin* – in this; *yathā* – as; *dehe* – in the body; *kaumāram* – boyhood; *yauvanam* – youth; *jarā* – old age; *tathā* – similarly; *deha-antara* – of transference of the body; *prāptiḥ* – achievement; *dhīraḥ* – the sober; *tatra* – thereupon; *na* – never; *muhyati* – is deluded.

As the embodied soul continuously passes, in this body, from boyhood to youth to old age, the soul similarly passes into another body at death. A sober person is not bewildered by such a change.

PURPORT: Since every living entity is an individual soul, each is changing his body every moment, manifesting sometimes as a child, sometimes as a youth and sometimes as an old man. Yet the same spirit soul is there and does not undergo any change. This individual soul finally changes the body at death and transmigrates to another body; and since it is sure to have another body in the next birth – either material or spiritual – there was no cause for lamentation by Arjuna on account of death, neither for Bhīṣma nor for Droṇa, for whom he was so much concerned. Rather, he should rejoice for their changing bodies from old to new ones, thereby rejuvenating their energy. Such changes of body account for varieties of enjoyment or suffering, according to one's work in life. So Bhīṣma and Droṇa, being noble souls, were surely going to have spiritual bodies in the next life, or at least life in heavenly bodies for superior enjoyment of material existence. So, in either case, there was no cause of lamentation.

Any man who has perfect knowledge of the constitution of the individual soul, the Supersoul, and nature – both material and spiritual – is called a *dhīra,* or a most sober man. Such a man is never deluded by the change of bodies.

The Māyāvādī theory of oneness of the spirit soul cannot be entertained, on the ground that the spirit soul cannot be cut into pieces as a fragmental portion. Such cutting into different individual souls would make the Supreme cleavable or changeable, against the principle of the Supreme Soul's being unchangeable. As confirmed in the *Gītā,* the fragmental portions of the Supreme exist eternally (*sanātana*) and are called *kṣara;* that is, they have a tendency to fall down into material nature. These fragmental portions are eternally so, and even after liberation the individual soul remains the same – fragmental. But once liberated, he lives an eternal life in bliss and knowledge with the Personality of Godhead. The theory of reflection can be applied to the Supersoul, who is present in each and every individual body and is known as the Paramātmā. He is different from the individual living entity. When the sky is reflected in water, the reflections represent both the sun and the moon and the stars also. The stars can be compared to the living entities and the sun or the moon to the Supreme Lord. The individual fragmental spirit soul is represented by Arjuna, and the Supreme Soul is the Personality of Godhead Śrī Kṛṣṇa. They are not on the same level, as it will be apparent in the beginning of the Fourth Chapter. If Arjuna is on the same level with Kṛṣṇa, and Kṛṣṇa is not superior to Arjuna, then their relationship of instructor and instructed becomes meaningless. If both of them are deluded by the illusory energy (*māyā*), then there is no need of one being the instructor and the other the instructed. Such instruction would be useless because, in the clutches of *māyā,* no one can be an authoritative instructor. Under the circumstances, it is admitted that Lord Kṛṣṇa is the Supreme Lord, superior in position to the living entity, Arjuna, who is a forgetful soul deluded by *māyā.*

Text 14 मात्रास्पर्शास्तु कौन्तेय शीतोष्णसुखदुःखदाः ।
आगमापायिनोऽनित्यास्तांस्तितिक्षस्व भारत ॥१४॥

mātrā-sparśās tu kaunteya, śītoṣṇa-sukha-duḥkha-dāḥ
āgamāpāyino 'nityās, tāṁs titikṣasva bhārata

mātrā-sparśāḥ – sensory perception; *tu* – only; *kaunteya* – O son of Kuntī; *śīta* – winter; *uṣṇa* – summer; *sukha* – happiness; *duḥkha* – and pain; *dāḥ* – giving; *āgama* – appearing; *apāyinaḥ* – disappearing; *anityāḥ* – nonpermanent; *tān* – all of them; *titikṣasva* – just try to tolerate; *bhārata* – O descendant of the Bharata dynasty.

O son of Kuntī, the nonpermanent appearance of happiness and distress, and their disappearance in due course, are like the appearance and disappearance of winter and summer seasons. They arise from sense perception, O scion of Bharata, and one must learn to tolerate them without being disturbed.

PURPORT: In the proper discharge of duty, one has to learn to tolerate nonpermanent appearances and disappearances of happiness and distress. According to Vedic injunction, one has to take his bath early in the morning even during the month of Māgha (January-February). It is very cold at that time, but in spite of that a man who abides by the religious principles does not hesitate to take his bath. Similarly, a woman does not hesitate to cook in the kitchen in the months of May and June, the hottest part of the summer season. One has to execute his duty in spite of climatic inconveniences. Similarly, to fight is the religious principle of the *kṣatriyas,* and although one has to fight with some friend or relative, one should not deviate from his prescribed duty. One has to follow the prescribed rules and regulations of religious principles in order to rise up to the platform of knowledge, because by knowledge and devotion only can one liberate himself from the clutches of *māyā* (illusion).

The two different names of address given to Arjuna are also significant. To address him as Kaunteya signifies his great blood relations from his mother's side; and to address him as Bhārata signifies his greatness from his father's side. From both sides he is supposed to have a great heritage. A great heritage brings responsibility in the matter of proper discharge of duties; therefore, he cannot avoid fighting.

Text 15 यं हि न व्यथयन्त्येते पुरुषं पुरुषर्षभ ।
समदुःखसुखं धीरं सोऽमृतत्वाय कल्पते ॥१५॥

yaṁ hi na vyathayanty ete, puruṣaṁ puruṣarṣabha
sama-duḥkha-sukhaṁ dhīraṁ, so 'mṛtatvāya kalpate

yam – one to whom; *hi* – certainly; *na* – never; *vyathayanti* – are distressing; *ete* – all these; *puruṣam* – to a person; *puruṣa-ṛṣabha* – O best among men; *sama* – unaltered; *duḥkha* – in distress; *sukham* – and happiness; *dhīram* – patient; *saḥ* – he; *amṛtatvāya* – for liberation; *kalpate* – is considered eligible.

O best among men [Arjuna], the person who is not disturbed by happiness and distress and is steady in both is certainly eligible for liberation.

PURPORT: Anyone who is steady in his determination for the advanced stage of spiritual realization and can equally tolerate the onslaughts of distress and happiness is certainly a person eligible for liberation. In the *varṇāśrama* institution, the fourth stage of life, namely the renounced order (*sannyāsa*), is a painstaking situation. But one who is serious about making his life perfect surely adopts the *sannyāsa* order of life in spite of all difficulties. The difficulties usually arise from having to sever family relationships, to give up the connection of wife and children. But if anyone is able to tolerate such difficulties, surely his path to spiritual realization is complete. Similarly, in Arjuna's discharge of duties as a *kṣatriya*, he is advised to persevere, even if it is difficult to fight with his family members or similarly beloved persons. Lord Caitanya took *sannyāsa* at the age of twenty-four, and His dependents, young wife as well as old mother, had no one else to look after them. Yet for a higher cause He took *sannyāsa* and was steady in the discharge of higher duties. That is the way of achieving liberation from material bondage.

Text 16 नासतो विद्यते भावो नाभावो विद्यते सतः ।
उभयोरपि दृष्टोऽन्तस्त्वनयोस्तत्त्वदर्शिभिः ॥१६॥

nāsato vidyate bhāvo, nābhāvo vidyate sataḥ
ubhayor api dṛṣṭo 'ntas, tv anayos tattva-darśibhiḥ

na – never; *asataḥ* – of the nonexistent; *vidyate* – there is; *bhāvaḥ* – endurance; *na* – never; *abhāvaḥ* – changing quality; *vidyate* – there is; *sataḥ* – of the eternal; *ubhayoḥ* – of the two; *api* – verily; *dṛṣṭaḥ* – observed; *antaḥ* – conclusion; *tu* – indeed; *anayoḥ* – of them; *tattva* – of the truth; *darśibhiḥ* – by the seers.

Those who are seers of the truth have concluded that of the nonexistent [the material body] there is no endurance and of the eternal [the soul] there is no change. This they have concluded by studying the nature of both.

PURPORT: There is no endurance of the changing body. That the body is changing every moment by the actions and reactions of the different cells is admitted by modern medical science; and thus growth and old age are taking place in the body. But the spirit soul exists permanently, remaining the same despite all changes of the body and the mind. That is the difference between matter and spirit. By nature, the body is ever changing, and the soul is eternal. This conclusion is established by all classes of seers of the truth, both impersonalist and personalist. In the *Viṣṇu Purāṇa* (2.12.38) it is stated that Viṣṇu and His abodes all have self-illuminated spiritual existence (*jyotīṁṣi viṣṇur bhuvanāni viṣṇuḥ*). The words *existent* and *nonexistent* refer only to spirit and matter. That is the version of all seers of truth.

This is the beginning of the instruction by the Lord to the living entities who are bewildered by the influence of ignorance. Removal of ignorance involves the reestablishment of the eternal relationship between the worshiper and the worshipable and the consequent understanding of the difference between the part-and-parcel living entities and the Supreme Personality of Godhead. One can understand the nature of the Supreme by thorough study of oneself, the difference between oneself and the Supreme being understood as the relationship between the part and the whole. In the *Vedānta-sūtras,* as well as in the *Śrīmad-Bhāgavatam,* the Supreme has been accepted as the origin of all emanations. Such emanations are experienced by superior and inferior natural sequences. The living entities belong to the superior nature, as it will be revealed in the Seventh Chapter. Although there is no difference between the energy and the energetic, the energetic is accepted as the Supreme, and the energy or nature is accepted as the subordinate. The living entities, therefore, are always subordinate to the Supreme Lord, as in the case of the master and the servant, or the teacher and the taught. Such clear knowledge is impossible to understand under the spell of ignorance, and to drive away such ignorance the Lord teaches the *Bhagavad-gītā* for the enlightenment of all living entities for all time.

Text 17 अविनाशि तु तद्विद्धि येन सर्वमिदं ततम् ।
विनाशमव्ययस्यास्य न कश्चित्कर्तुमर्हति ॥१७॥

avināśi tu tad viddhi, yena sarvam idaṁ tatam
vināśam avyayasyāsya, na kaścit kartum arhati

avināśi – imperishable; *tu* – but; *tat* – that; *viddhi* – know it; *yena* – by whom; *sarvam* – all of the body; *idam* – this; *tatam* – pervaded; *vināśam* – destruction; *avyayasya* – of the imperishable; *asya* – of it; *na kaścit* – no one; *kartum* – to do; *arhati* – is able.

That which pervades the entire body you should know to be indestructible. No one is able to destroy that imperishable soul.

PURPORT: This verse more clearly explains the real nature of the soul, which is spread all over the body. Anyone can understand what is spread all over the body: it is consciousness. Everyone is conscious of the pains and pleasures of the body in part or as a whole. This spreading of consciousness is limited within one's own body. The pains and pleasures of one body are unknown to another. Therefore, each and every body is the embodiment of an individual soul, and the symptom of the soul's presence is perceived as individual consciousness. This soul is described as one ten-thousandth part of the upper portion of the hair point in size. The *Śvetāśvatara Upaniṣad* (5.9) confirms this:

bālāgra-śata-bhāgasya, śatadhā kalpitasya ca
bhāgo jīvaḥ sa vijñeyaḥ, sa cānantyāya kalpate

"When the upper point of a hair is divided into one hundred parts and again each of such parts is further divided into one hundred parts, each such part is the measurement of the dimension of the spirit soul." Similarly the same version is stated:

keśāgra-śata-bhāgasya, śatāṁśaḥ sādṛśātmakaḥ
jīvaḥ sūkṣma-svarūpo 'yaṁ, saṅkhyātīto hi cit-kaṇaḥ

"There are innumerable particles of spiritual atoms, which are measured as one ten-thousandth of the upper portion of the hair."

Therefore, the individual particle of spirit soul is a spiritual atom smaller than the material atoms, and such atoms are innumerable. This very small spiritual spark is the basic principle of the material body, and the influence of such a spiritual spark is spread all over the body as the influence of the active principle of some medicine spreads throughout the body. This current of the spirit soul is felt all over the body as consciousness, and that is the proof of the presence of the soul. Any layman can understand that the material body minus consciousness is a dead body, and this consciousness cannot be revived in the body by any means of material administration. Therefore, consciousness is not due to any amount of material combination, but to the spirit soul. In the *Muṇḍaka Upaniṣad* (3.1.9) the measurement of the atomic spirit soul is further explained:

eṣo 'ṇur ātmā cetasā veditavyo
yasmin prāṇaḥ pañcadhā saṁviveśa
prāṇaiś cittaṁ sarvam otaṁ prajānāṁ
yasmin viśuddhe vibhavaty eṣa ātmā

"The soul is atomic in size and can be perceived by perfect intelligence. This atomic soul is floating in the five kinds of air (*prāṇa, apāna, vyāna, samāna* and *udāna*), is situated within the heart, and spreads its influence all over the body of the embodied living entities. When the soul is purified from the contamination of the five kinds of material air, its spiritual influence is exhibited."

The *haṭha-yoga* system is meant for controlling the five kinds of air encircling the pure soul by different kinds of sitting postures – not for any material profit, but for liberation of the minute soul from the entanglement of the material atmosphere.

So the constitution of the atomic soul is admitted in all Vedic literatures, and it is also actually felt in the practical experience of any sane man. Only the insane man can think of this atomic soul as all-pervading *viṣṇu-tattva.*

The influence of the atomic soul can be spread all over a particular body. According to the *Muṇḍaka Upaniṣad,* this atomic soul is situated in the heart of every living entity, and because the measurement of the atomic soul is beyond the power of appreciation of the material scientists, some of them assert foolishly that there is no soul. The individual atomic soul is definitely there in the heart along with the Supersoul, and thus all the energies of bodily movement are emanating from this part of the body. The corpuscles which carry the oxygen from the lungs gather energy from the soul. When the soul passes away from this position, the activity of the blood, generating fusion, ceases. Medical science accepts the importance of the red corpuscles, but it cannot ascertain that the source of the energy is the soul. Medical science, however, does admit that the heart is the seat of all energies of the body.

Such atomic particles of the spirit whole are compared to the sunshine molecules. In the sunshine there are innumerable radiant molecules. Similarly, the fragmental parts of the Supreme Lord are atomic sparks of the rays of the Supreme Lord, called by the name *prabhā,* or superior energy. So whether one follows Vedic knowledge or modern science, one cannot deny the existence of the spirit soul in the body, and the science of the soul is explicitly described in the *Bhagavad-gītā* by the Personality of Godhead Himself.

Text 18 अन्तवन्त इमे देहा नित्यस्योक्ताः शरीरिणः ।
अनाशिनोऽप्रमेयस्य तस्माद्युध्यस्व भारत ॥१८॥

antavanta ime dehā, nityasyoktāḥ śarīriṇaḥ
anāśino 'prameyasya, tasmād yudhyasva bhārata

anta-vantaḥ – perishable; *ime* – all these; *dehāḥ* – material bodies; *nityasya* – eternal in existence; *uktāḥ* – are said; *śarīriṇaḥ* – of the embodied soul; *anāśinaḥ* – never to be destroyed; *aprameyasya* – immeasurable; *tasmāt* – therefore; *yudhyasva* – fight; *bhārata* – O descendant of Bharata.

The material body of the indestructible, immeasurable and eternal living entity is sure to come to an end; therefore, fight, O descendant of Bharata.

PURPORT: The material body is perishable by nature. It may perish immediately, or it may do so after a hundred years. It is a question of time only. There is no chance of maintaining it indefinitely. But the spirit soul is so minute that it cannot even be seen by an enemy, to say nothing of being killed. As mentioned in the previous verse, it is so small that no one can have any idea how to measure its dimension. So from both viewpoints there is no cause of lamentation, because the living entity as he is cannot be killed nor can the material body be saved for any length of time or permanently protected. The minute particle of the whole spirit acquires this material body according to his work, and therefore observance of religious principles should be utilized. In the *Vedānta-sūtras* the living entity is qualified as light because he is part and parcel of the supreme light. As sunlight maintains the entire universe, so the light of the soul maintains this material body. As soon as the spirit soul is out of this material body, the body begins to decompose; therefore it is the spirit soul which maintains this body. The body itself is unimportant. Arjuna was advised to fight and not sacrifice the cause of religion for material, bodily considerations.

Text 19 य एनं वेत्ति हन्तारं यश्चैनं मन्यते हतम् ।
उभौ तौ न विजानीतो नायं हन्ति न हन्यते ॥१९॥

ya enaṁ vetti hantāraṁ, yaś cainaṁ manyate hatam
ubhau tau na vijānīto, nāyaṁ hanti na hanyate

yaḥ – anyone who; *enam* – this; *vetti* – knows; *hantāram* – the killer; *yaḥ* – anyone who; *ca* – also; *enam* – this; *manyate* – thinks; *hatam* – killed; *ubhau* – both; *tau* – they; *na* – never; *vijānītaḥ* – are in knowledge; *na* – never; *ayam* – this; *hanti* – kills; *na* – nor; *hanyate* – is killed.

Neither he who thinks the living entity the slayer nor he who thinks it slain is in knowledge, for the self slays not nor is slain.

PURPORT: When an embodied living entity is hurt by fatal weapons, it is to be known that the living entity within the body is not killed. The spirit soul is so small that it is impossible to kill him by any material weapon, as will be evident from subsequent verses. Nor is the living entity killable, because of his spiritual constitution. What is killed, or is supposed to be killed, is the body only. This, however, does not at all encourage killing of the body. The Vedic injunction is *mā hiṁsyāt sarvā bhūtāni:* never commit violence to anyone. Nor does understanding that the living entity is not killed encourage animal slaughter. Killing the body of anyone without authority is abominable and is punishable by the law of the state as well as by the law of the Lord. Arjuna, however, is being engaged in killing for the principle of religion, and not whimsically.

Text 20 न जायते म्रियते वा कदाचिन् नायं भूत्वा भविता वा न भूयः ।
अजो नित्यः शाश्वतोऽयं पुराणो न हन्यते हन्यमाने शरीरे ॥२०॥

na jāyate mriyate vā kadācin
nāyaṁ bhūtvā bhavitā vā na bhūyaḥ
ajo nityaḥ śāśvato 'yaṁ purāṇo
na hanyate hanyamāne śarīre

na – never; *jāyate* – takes birth; *mriyate* – dies; *vā* – either; *kadācit* – at any time (past, present or future); *na* – never; *ayam* – this; *bhūtvā* –

having come into being; *bhavitā* – will come to be; *vā* – or; *na* – not; *bhūyaḥ* – or is again coming to be; *ajaḥ* – unborn; *nityaḥ* – eternal; *śāśvataḥ* – permanent; *ayam* – this; *purāṇaḥ* – the oldest; *na* – never; *hanyate* – is killed; *hanyamāne* – being killed; *śarīre* – the body.

For the soul there is neither birth nor death at any time. He has not come into being, does not come into being, and will not come into being. He is unborn, eternal, ever-existing and primeval. He is not slain when the body is slain.

PURPORT: Qualitatively, the small atomic fragmental part of the Supreme Spirit is one with the Supreme. He undergoes no changes like the body. Sometimes the soul is called the steady, or *kūṭa-stha.* The body is subject to six kinds of transformations. It takes its birth from the womb of the mother's body, remains for some time, grows, produces some effects, gradually dwindles, and at last vanishes into oblivion. The soul, however, does not go through such changes. The soul is not born, but, because he takes on a material body, the body takes its birth. The soul does not take birth there, and the soul does not die. Anything which has birth also has death. And because the soul has no birth, he therefore has no past, present or future. He is eternal, ever-existing and primeval – that is, there is no trace in history of his coming into being. Under the impression of the body, we seek the history of birth, etc., of the soul. The soul does not at any time become old, as the body does. The so-called old man, therefore, feels himself to be in the same spirit as in his childhood or youth. The changes of the body do not affect the soul. The soul does not deteriorate like a tree, nor anything material. The soul has no by-product either. The by-products of the body, namely children, are also different individual souls; and, owing to the body, they appear as children of a particular man. The body develops because of the soul's presence, but the soul has neither offshoots nor change. Therefore, the soul is free from the six changes of the body.

In the *Kaṭha Upaniṣad* (1.2.18) we also find a similar passage, which reads:

na jāyate mriyate vā vipaścin, nāyaṁ kutaścin na babhūva kaścit
ajo nityaḥ śāśvato 'yaṁ purāṇo, na hanyate hanyamāne śarīre

The meaning and purport of this verse is the same as in the *Bhagavad-gītā,* but here in this verse there is one special word, *vipaścit,* which means learned or with knowledge.

The soul is full of knowledge, or full always with consciousness. Therefore, consciousness is the symptom of the soul. Even if one does not find the soul within the heart, where he is situated, one can still understand the presence of the soul simply by the presence of consciousness. Sometimes we do not find the sun in the sky owing to clouds, or for some other reason, but the light of the sun is always there, and we are convinced that it is therefore daytime. As soon as there is a little light in the sky early in the morning, we can understand that the sun is in the sky. Similarly, since there is some consciousness in all bodies – whether man or animal – we can understand the presence of the soul. This consciousness of the soul is, however, different from the consciousness of the Supreme because the supreme consciousness is all-knowledge – past, present and future. The consciousness of the individual soul is prone to be forgetful. When he is forgetful of his real nature, he obtains education and enlightenment from the superior lessons of Kṛṣṇa. But Kṛṣṇa is not like the forgetful soul. If so, Kṛṣṇa's teachings of *Bhagavad-gītā* would be useless.

There are two kinds of souls – namely the minute particle soul (*aṇu-ātmā*) and the Supersoul (*vibhu-ātmā*). This is also confirmed in the *Kaṭha Upaniṣad* (1.2.20) in this way:

aṇor aṇīyān mahato mahīyān, ātmāsya jantor nihito guhāyām
tam akratuḥ paśyati vīta-śoko, dhātuḥ prasādān mahimānam ātmanaḥ

"Both the Supersoul [Paramātmā] and the atomic soul [*jīvātmā*] are situated on the same tree of the body within the same heart of the living being, and only one who has become free from all material desires as well as lamentations can, by the grace of the Supreme, understand the glories of the soul." Kṛṣṇa is the fountainhead of the Supersoul also, as it will be disclosed in the following chapters, and Arjuna is the atomic soul, forgetful of his real nature; therefore he requires to be enlightened by Kṛṣṇa, or by His bona fide representative (the spiritual master).

Text 21 वेदाविनाशिनं नित्यं य एनमजमव्ययम् ।
कथं स पुरुषः पार्थ कं घातयति हन्ति कम् ॥२१॥

vedāvināśinaṁ nityaṁ, ya enam ajam avyayam
kathaṁ sa puruṣaḥ pārtha, kaṁ ghātayati hanti kam

veda – knows; *avināśinam* – indestructible; *nityam* – always existing; *yaḥ* – one who; *enam* – this (soul); *ajam* – unborn; *avyayam* – immutable;

katham – how; *saḥ* – that; *puruṣaḥ* – person; *pārtha* – O Pārtha (Arjuna); *kam* – whom; *ghātayati* – causes to hurt; *hanti* – kills; *kam* – whom.

O Pārtha, how can a person who knows that the soul is indestructible, eternal, unborn and immutable kill anyone or cause anyone to kill?

PURPORT: Everything has its proper utility, and a man who is situated in complete knowledge knows how and where to apply a thing for its proper utility. Similarly, violence also has its utility, and how to apply violence rests with the person in knowledge. Although the justice of the peace awards capital punishment to a person condemned for murder, the justice of the peace cannot be blamed, because he orders violence to another person according to the codes of justice. In *Manu-saṁhitā,* the lawbook for mankind, it is supported that a murderer should be condemned to death so that in his next life he will not have to suffer for the great sin he has committed. Therefore, the king's punishment of hanging a murderer is actually beneficial. Similarly, when Kṛṣṇa orders fighting, it must be concluded that violence is for supreme justice, and thus Arjuna should follow the instruction, knowing well that such violence, committed in the act of fighting for Kṛṣṇa, is not violence at all because, at any rate, the man, or rather the soul, cannot be killed; so for the administration of justice, so-called violence is permitted. A surgical operation is not meant to kill the patient, but to cure him. Therefore the fighting to be executed by Arjuna at the instruction of Kṛṣṇa is with full knowledge, so there is no possibility of sinful reaction.

Text 22 वासांसि जीर्णानि यथा विहाय नवानि गृह्णाति नरोऽपराणि ।
तथा शरीराणि विहाय जीर्णान्यन्यानि संयाति नवानि देही ॥२२॥

vāsāṁsi jīrṇāni yathā vihāya, navāni gṛhṇāti naro 'parāṇi
tathā śarīrāṇi vihāya jīrṇāny, anyāni saṁyāti navāni dehī

vāsāṁsi – garments; *jīrṇāni* – old and worn out; *yathā* – just as; *vihāya* – giving up; *navāni* – new garments; *gṛhṇāti* – does accept; *naraḥ* – a man; *aparāṇi* – others; *tathā* – in the same way; *śarīrāṇi* – bodies; *vihāya* – giving up; *jīrṇāni* – old and useless; *anyāni* – different; *saṁyāti* – verily accepts; *navāni* – new sets; *dehī* – the embodied.

As a person puts on new garments, giving up old ones, the soul similarly accepts new material bodies, giving up the old and useless ones.

PURPORT: Change of body by the atomic individual soul is an accepted fact. Even the modern scientists who do not believe in the existence of the soul, but at the same time cannot explain the source of energy from the heart, have to accept continuous changes of body which appear from childhood to boyhood and from boyhood to youth and again from youth to old age. From old age, the change is transferred to another body. This has already been explained in a previous verse (2.13).

Transference of the atomic individual soul to another body is made possible by the grace of the Supersoul. The Supersoul fulfills the desire of the atomic soul as one friend fulfills the desire of another. The *Vedas,* like the *Muṇḍaka Upaniṣad,* as well as the *Śvetāśvatara Upaniṣad,* compare the soul and the Supersoul to two friendly birds sitting on the same tree. One of the birds (the individual atomic soul) is eating the fruit of the tree, and the other bird (Kṛṣṇa) is simply watching His friend. Of these two birds – although they are the same in quality – one is captivated by the fruits of the material tree, while the other is simply witnessing the activities of His friend. Kṛṣṇa is the witnessing bird, and Arjuna is the eating bird. Although they are friends, one is still the master and the other is the servant. Forgetfulness of this relationship by the atomic soul is the cause of one's changing his position from one tree to another, or from one body to another. The *jīva* soul is struggling very hard on the tree of the material body, but as soon as he agrees to accept the other bird as the supreme spiritual master – as Arjuna agreed to do by voluntary surrender unto Kṛṣṇa for instruction – the subordinate bird immediately becomes free from all lamentations. Both the *Muṇḍaka Upaniṣad* (3.1.2) and *Śvetāśvatara Upaniṣad* (4.7) confirm this:

samāne vṛkṣe puruṣo nimagno, 'nīśayā śocati muhyamānaḥ
juṣṭaṁ yadā paśyaty anyam īśam, asya mahimānam iti vīta-śokaḥ

"Although the two birds are in the same tree, the eating bird is fully engrossed with anxiety and moroseness as the enjoyer of the fruits of the tree. But if in some way or other he turns his face to his friend the Lord and knows His glories – at once the suffering bird becomes free from all anxieties." Arjuna has now turned his face towards his eternal friend, Kṛṣṇa, and is understanding the *Bhagavad-gītā* from Him. And thus, hearing from Kṛṣṇa, he can understand the supreme glories of the Lord and be free from lamentation.

Arjuna is advised herewith by the Lord not to lament for the bodily change of his old grandfather and his teacher. He should rather be happy to kill their bodies in the righteous fight so that they may be cleansed at once of all reactions from various bodily activities. One who lays down his life on the sacrificial altar, or in the proper battlefield, is at once cleansed of bodily reactions and promoted to a higher status of life. So there was no cause for Arjuna's lamentation.

Text 23 नैनं छिन्दन्ति शस्त्राणि नैनं दहति पावकः ।
न चैनं क्लेदयन्त्यापो न शोषयति मारुतः ॥२३॥

nainaṁ chindanti śastrāṇi, nainaṁ dahati pāvakaḥ
na cainaṁ kledayanty āpo, na śoṣayati mārutaḥ

na – never; *enam* – this soul; *chindanti* – can cut to pieces; *śastrāṇi* – weapons; *na* – never; *enam* – this soul; *dahati* – burns; *pāvakaḥ* – fire; *na* – never; *ca* – also; *enam* – this soul; *kledayanti* – moistens; *āpaḥ* – water; *na* – never; *śoṣayati* – dries; *mārutaḥ* – wind.

The soul can never be cut to pieces by any weapon, nor burned by fire, nor moistened by water, nor withered by the wind.

PURPORT: All kinds of weapons – swords, flame weapons, rain weapons, tornado weapons, etc. – are unable to kill the spirit soul. It appears that there were many kinds of weapons made of earth, water, air, ether, etc., in addition to the modern weapons of fire. Even the nuclear weapons of the modern age are classified as fire weapons, but formerly there were other weapons made of all different types of material elements. Fire weapons were counteracted by water weapons, which are now unknown to modern science. Nor do modern scientists have knowledge of tornado weapons. Nonetheless, the soul can never be cut into pieces, nor annihilated by any number of weapons, regardless of scientific devices.

The Māyāvādī cannot explain how the individual soul came into existence simply by ignorance and consequently became covered by the illusory energy. Nor was it ever possible to cut the individual souls from the original Supreme Soul; rather, the individual souls are eternally separated parts of the Supreme Soul. Because they are atomic individual souls eternally (*sanātana*), they are prone to be covered by the illusory energy, and thus they become separated from the association of the Supreme Lord, just as the sparks of a fire, although one in quality with the fire, are prone to be extinguished when out of the fire. In the *Varāha Purāṇa,* the living entities are described as separated parts and parcels of the Supreme. They are eternally so, according to the *Bhagavad-gītā* also. So, even after being liberated from illusion, the living entity remains a separate identity, as is evident from the teachings of the Lord to Arjuna. Arjuna became liberated by the knowledge received from Kṛṣṇa, but he never became one with Kṛṣṇa.

Text 24 अच्छेद्योऽयमदाह्योऽयमक्लेद्योऽशोष्य एव च ।
नित्यः सर्वगतः स्थाणुरचलोऽयं सनातनः ॥२४॥

acchedyo 'yam adāhyo 'yam, akledyo 'śoṣya eva ca
nityaḥ sarva-gataḥ sthāṇur, acalo 'yaṁ sanātanaḥ

acchedyaḥ – unbreakable; *ayam* – this soul; *adāhyaḥ* – unable to be burned; *ayam* – this soul; *akledyaḥ* – insoluble; *aśoṣyaḥ* – not able to be dried; *eva* – certainly; *ca* – and; *nityaḥ* – everlasting; *sarva-gataḥ* – all-pervading; *sthāṇuḥ* – unchangeable; *acalaḥ* – immovable; *ayam* – this soul; *sanātanaḥ* – eternally the same.

This individual soul is unbreakable and insoluble, and can be neither burned nor dried. He is everlasting, present everywhere, unchangeable, immovable and eternally the same.

PURPORT: All these qualifications of the atomic soul definitely prove that the individual soul is eternally the atomic particle of the spirit whole, and he remains the same atom eternally, without change. The theory of monism is very difficult to apply in this case, because the individual soul is never expected to become one homogeneously. After liberation from material contamination, the atomic soul may prefer to remain as a spiritual spark in the effulgent rays of the Supreme Personality of Godhead, but the intelligent souls enter into the spiritual planets to associate with the Personality of Godhead.

The word *sarva-gata* ("all-pervading") is significant because there is no doubt that living entities are all over God's creation. They live on the land, in the water, in the air, within the earth and even within fire. The belief that they are sterilized in fire is not acceptable, because it is clearly stated here that the soul cannot be burned by fire. Therefore, there is no doubt that there are living entities also in the sun planet with suitable bodies to live there. If the sun globe is uninhabited, then the word *sarva-gata* – "living everywhere" – becomes meaningless.

Text 25 अव्यक्तोऽयमचिन्त्योऽयमविकार्योऽयमुच्यते ।
तस्मादेवं विदित्वैनं नानुशोचितुमर्हसि ॥२५॥

avyakto 'yam acintyo 'yam, avikāryo 'yam ucyate
tasmād evaṁ viditvainaṁ, nānuśocitum arhasi

avyaktaḥ – invisible; *ayam* – this soul; *acintyaḥ* – inconceivable; *ayam* – this soul; *avikāryaḥ* – unchangeable; *ayam* – this soul; *ucyate* – is said; *tasmāt* – therefore; *evam* – like this; *viditvā* – knowing it well; *enam* – this soul; *na* – do not; *anuśocitum* – to lament; *arhasi* – you deserve.

It is said that the soul is invisible, inconceivable and immutable. Knowing this, you should not grieve for the body.

PURPORT: As described previously, the magnitude of the soul is so small for our material calculation that he cannot be seen even by the most powerful microscope; therefore, he is invisible. As far as the soul's existence is concerned, no one can establish his existence experimentally beyond the proof of *śruti,* or Vedic wisdom. We have to accept this truth, because there is no other source of understanding the existence of the soul, although it is a fact by perception. There are many things we have to accept solely on grounds of superior authority. No one can deny the existence of his father, based upon the authority of his mother. There is no source of understanding the identity of the father except by the authority of the mother. Similarly, there is no source of understanding the soul except by studying the *Vedas.* In other words, the soul is inconceivable by human experimental knowledge. The soul is consciousness and conscious – that also is the statement of the *Vedas,* and we have to accept that. Unlike the bodily changes, there is no change in the soul. As eternally unchangeable, the soul remains atomic in comparison to the infinite Supreme Soul. The Supreme Soul is infinite, and the atomic soul is infinitesimal. Therefore, the infinitesimal soul, being unchangeable, can never become equal to the infinite soul, or the Supreme Personality of Godhead. This concept is repeated in the *Vedas* in different ways just to confirm the stability of the conception of the soul. Repetition of something is necessary in order that we understand the matter thoroughly, without error.

Text 26 अथ चैनं नित्यजातं नित्यं वा मन्यसे मृतम् ।
तथापि त्वं महाबाहो नैनं शोचितुमर्हसि ॥२६॥

atha cainaṁ nitya-jātaṁ, nityaṁ vā manyase mṛtam
tathāpi tvaṁ mahā-bāho, nainaṁ śocitum arhasi

atha – if, however; *ca* – also; *enam* – this soul; *nitya-jātam* – always born; *nityam* – forever; *vā* – either; *manyase* – you so think; *mṛtam* – dead; *tathā api* – still; *tvam* – you; *mahā-bāho* – O mighty-armed one; *na* – never; *enam* – about the soul; *śocitum* – to lament; *arhasi* – deserve.

If, however, you think that the soul [or the symptoms of life] will always be born and die forever, you still have no reason to lament, O mighty-armed.

PURPORT: There is always a class of philosophers, almost akin to the Buddhists, who do not believe in the separate existence of the soul beyond the body. When Lord Kṛṣṇa spoke the *Bhagavad-gītā,* it appears that such philosophers existed, and they were known as the Lokāyatikas and Vaibhāṣikas. Such philosophers maintain that life symptoms take place at a certain mature condition of material combination. The modern material scientist and materialist philosophers also think similarly. According to them, the body is a combination of physical elements, and at a certain stage the life symptoms develop by interaction of the physical and chemical elements. The science of anthropology is based on this philosophy. Currently, many pseudo religions – now becoming fashionable in America – are also adhering to this philosophy, as are the nihilistic nondevotional Buddhist sects.

Even if Arjuna did not believe in the existence of the soul – as in the Vaibhāṣika philosophy – there would still have been no cause for lamentation. No one laments the loss of a certain bulk of chemicals and stops discharging his prescribed duty. On the other hand, in modern science and scientific warfare, so many tons of chemicals are wasted for achieving victory over the enemy. According to the Vaibhāṣika philosophy, the so-called soul or *ātmā* vanishes along with the deterioration of the body. So, in any case, whether Arjuna accepted the Vedic conclusion that there is an atomic soul or he did not believe in the existence of the soul, he had no reason to lament. According to this theory, since there are so many living entities generating out of matter every moment, and so many of them are being vanquished every moment, there is no need to grieve for such incidents. If there were no rebirth for the soul, Arjuna had no reason to be afraid of being affected by sinful reactions due to his killing his grandfather and teacher. But at the same time, Kṛṣṇa sarcastically addressed Arjuna as *mahā-bāhu,* mighty-armed, because He, at least, did not accept the theory of the Vaibhāṣikas, which leaves aside the Vedic wisdom. As a *kṣatriya,* Arjuna belonged to the Vedic culture, and it behooved him to continue to follow its principles.

Text 27 जातस्य हि ध्रुवो मृत्युर्ध्रुवं जन्म मृतस्य च ।
तस्मादपरिहार्येऽर्थे न त्वं शोचितुमर्हसि ॥२७॥

jātasya hi dhruvo mṛtyur, dhruvaṁ janma mṛtasya ca
tasmād aparihārye 'rthe, na tvaṁ śocitum arhasi

jātasya – of one who has taken his birth; *hi* – certainly; *dhruvaḥ* – a fact; *mṛtyuḥ* – death; *dhruvam* – it is also a fact; *janma* – birth; *mṛtasya* – of the dead; *ca* – also; *tasmāt* – therefore; *aparihārye* – of that which is unavoidable; *arthe* – in the matter; *na* – do not; *tvam* – you; *śocitum* – to lament; *arhasi* – deserve.

One who has taken his birth is sure to die, and after death one is sure to take birth again. Therefore, in the unavoidable discharge of your duty, you should not lament.

PURPORT: One has to take birth according to one's activities of life. And after finishing one term of activities, one has to die to take birth for the next. In this way one is going through one cycle of birth and death after another without liberation. This cycle of birth and death does not, however, support unnecessary murder, slaughter and war. But at the same time, violence and war are inevitable factors in human society for keeping law and order.

The Battle of Kurukṣetra, being the will of the Supreme, was an inevitable event, and to fight for the right cause is the duty of a *kṣatriya.* Why should he be afraid of or aggrieved at the death of his relatives since he was discharging his proper duty? He did not deserve to break the law, thereby becoming subjected to the reactions of sinful acts, of which he was so afraid. By avoiding the discharge of his proper duty, he would not be able to stop the death of his relatives, and he would be degraded due to his selection of the wrong path of action.

Text 28 अव्यक्तादीनि भूतानि व्यक्तमध्यानि भारत ।
अव्यक्तनिधनान्येव तत्र का परिदेवना ॥२८॥

avyaktādīni bhūtāni, vyakta-madhyāni bhārata
avyakta-nidhanāny eva, tatra kā paridevanā

avyakta-ādīni – in the beginning unmanifested; *bhūtāni* – all that are created; *vyakta* – manifested; *madhyāni* – in the middle; *bhārata* – O descendant of Bharata; *avyakta* – nonmanifested; *nidhanāni* – when vanquished; *eva* – it is all like that; *tatra* – therefore; *kā* – what; *paridevanā* – lamentation.

All created beings are unmanifest in their beginning, manifest in their interim state, and unmanifest again when annihilated. So what need is there for lamentation?

PURPORT: Accepting that there are two classes of philosophers, one believing in the existence of the soul and the other not believing in the existence of the soul, there is no cause for lamentation in either case. Nonbelievers in the existence of the soul are called atheists by followers of Vedic wisdom. Yet even if, for argument's sake, we accept this atheistic theory, there is still no cause for lamentation. Apart from the separate existence of the soul, the material elements remain unmanifested before creation. From this subtle state of nonmanifestation comes manifestation, just as from ether, air is generated; from air, fire is generated; from fire, water is generated; and from water, earth becomes manifested. From the earth, many varieties of manifestations take place. Take, for example, a big skyscraper manifested from the earth. When it is dismantled, the manifestation becomes again unmanifested and remains as atoms in the ultimate stage. The law of conservation of energy remains, but in course of time things are manifested and unmanifested – that is the difference. Then what cause is there for lamentation either in the stage of manifestation or in unmanifestation? Somehow or other, even in the unmanifested stage, things are not lost. Both at the beginning and at the end, all elements remain unmanifested, and only in the middle are they manifested, and this does not make any real material difference.

And if we accept the Vedic conclusion as stated in the *Bhagavad-gītā* that these material bodies are perishable in due course of time (*antavanta ime dehāḥ*) but that the soul is eternal (*nityasyoktāḥ śarīriṇaḥ*), then we must remember always that the body is like a dress; therefore why lament the changing of a dress? The material body has no factual existence in relation to the eternal soul. It is something like a dream. In a dream we may think of flying in the sky, or sitting on a chariot as a king, but when we wake up we can see that we are neither in the sky nor seated on the chariot. The Vedic wisdom encourages self-realization on the basis of the nonexistence of the material body. Therefore, in either case, whether one believes in the existence of the soul or one does not believe in the existence of the soul, there is no cause for lamentation for loss of the body.

Text 29 आश्चर्यवत्पश्यति कश्चिदेनमाश्चर्यवद्वदति तथैव चान्यः ।
आश्चर्यवच्चैनमन्यः शृणोति श्रुत्वाप्येनं वेद न चैव कश्चित् ॥२९॥

āścarya-vat paśyati kaścid enam
āścarya-vad vadati tathaiva cānyaḥ
āścarya-vac cainam anyaḥ śṛṇoti
śrutvāpy enaṁ veda na caiva kaścit

āścarya-vat – as amazing; *paśyati* – sees; *kaścit* – someone; *enam* – this soul; *āścarya-vat* – as amazing; *vadati* – speaks of; *tathā* – thus; *eva* – certainly; *ca* – also; *anyaḥ* – another; *āścarya-vat* – similarly amazing; *ca* – also; *enam* – this soul; *anyaḥ* – another; *śṛṇoti* – hears of; *śrutvā* – having heard; *api* – even; *enam* – this soul; *veda* – knows; *na* – never; *ca* – and; *eva* – certainly; *kaścit* – someone.

Some look on the soul as amazing, some describe him as amazing, and some hear of him as amazing, while others, even after hearing about him, cannot understand him at all.

PURPORT: Since *Gītopaniṣad* is largely based on the principles of the *Upaniṣads,* it is not surprising to also find this passage in the *Kaṭha Upaniṣad* (1.2.7):

śravaṇayāpi bahubhir yo na labhyaḥ, śṛṇvanto 'pi bahavo yaṁ na vidyuḥ
āścaryo vaktā kuśalo 'sya labdhā, āścaryo 'sya jñātā kuśalānuśiṣṭaḥ

The fact that the atomic soul is within the body of a gigantic animal, in the body of a gigantic banyan tree, and also in the microbic germs, millions and billions of which occupy only an inch of space, is certainly very amazing. Men with a poor fund of knowledge and men who are not austere cannot understand the wonders of the individual atomic spark of spirit, even though it is explained by the greatest authority of knowledge, who imparted lessons even to Brahmā, the first living being in the universe. Owing to a gross material conception of things, most men in this age cannot imagine how such a small particle can become both so great and so small. So men look at the soul proper as wonderful either by constitution or by description. Illusioned by the material energy, people are so engrossed in subject matters for sense gratification that they have very little time to understand the question of self-understanding, even though it is a fact that without this self-understanding all activities result in ultimate defeat in the struggle for existence. Perhaps they have no idea that one must think of the soul, and thus make a solution to the material miseries.

Some people who are inclined to hear about the soul may be attending lectures, in good association, but sometimes, owing to ignorance, they are misguided by acceptance of the Supersoul and the atomic soul as one without distinction of magnitude. It is very difficult to find a man who perfectly understands the position of the Supersoul, the atomic soul, their respective functions and relationships and all other major and minor details. And it is still more difficult to find a man who has actually derived full benefit from knowledge of the soul, and who is able to describe the position of the soul in different aspects. But if, somehow or other, one is able to understand the subject matter of the soul, then one's life is successful.

The easiest process for understanding the subject matter of self, however, is to accept the statements of the *Bhagavad-gītā* spoken by the greatest authority, Lord Kṛṣṇa, without being deviated by other theories. But it also requires a great deal of penance and sacrifice, either in this life or in the previous ones, before one is able to accept Kṛṣṇa as the Supreme Personality of Godhead. Kṛṣṇa can, however, be known as such by the causeless mercy of the pure devotee and by no other way.

Text 30 देही नित्यमवध्योऽयं देहे सर्वस्य भारत ।
तस्मात्सर्वाणि भूतानि न त्वं शोचितुमर्हसि ॥३०॥

dehī nityam avadhyo 'yaṁ, dehe sarvasya bhārata
tasmāt sarvāṇi bhūtāni, na tvaṁ śocitum arhasi

dehī – the owner of the material body; *nityam* – eternally; *avadhyaḥ* – cannot be killed; *ayam* – this soul; *dehe* – in the body; *sarvasya* – of everyone; *bhārata* – O descendant of Bharata; *tasmāt* – therefore; *sarvāṇi* – all; *bhūtāni* – living entities (that are born); *na* – never; *tvam* – you; *śocitum* – to lament; *arhasi* – deserve.

O descendant of Bharata, he who dwells in the body can never be slain. Therefore you need not grieve for any living being.

PURPORT: The Lord now concludes the chapter of instruction on the immutable spirit soul. In describing the immortal soul in various ways, Lord Kṛṣṇa establishes that the soul is immortal and the body is temporary. Therefore Arjuna as a *kṣatriya* should not abandon his duty out of fear that his grandfather and teacher – Bhīṣma and Droṇa – will die in the battle. On the authority of Śrī Kṛṣṇa, one has to believe that there is a soul different from the material body, not that there is no such thing as soul, or that living symptoms develop at a certain stage of material maturity resulting from the interaction of chemicals. Though the soul is immortal, violence is not encouraged, but at the time of war it is not discouraged when there is actual need for it. That need must be justified in terms of the sanction of the Lord, and not capriciously.

Text 31 स्वधर्ममपि चावेक्ष्य न विकम्पितुमर्हसि ।
धर्म्याद्धि युद्धाच्छ्रेयोऽन्यत्क्षत्रियस्य न विद्यते ॥३१॥

sva-dharmam api cāvekṣya, na vikampitum arhasi
dharmyād dhi yuddhāc chreyo 'nyat, kṣatriyasya na vidyate

sva-dharmam – one's own religious principles; *api* – also; *ca* – indeed; *avekṣya* – considering; *na* – never; *vikampitum* – to hesitate; *arhasi* – you deserve; *dharmyāt* – for religious principles; *hi* – indeed; *yuddhāt* – than fighting; *śreyaḥ* – better engagement; *anyat* – any other; *kṣatriyasya* – of the *kṣatriya; na* – does not; *vidyate* – exist.

Considering your specific duty as a kṣatriya, you should know that there is no better engagement for you than fighting on religious principles; and so there is no need for hesitation.

PURPORT: Out of the four orders of social administration, the second order, for the matter of good administration, is called *kṣatriya. Kṣat* means hurt. One who gives protection from harm is called *kṣatriya* (*trāyate* – to give protection). The *kṣatriyas* are trained for killing in the forest. A *kṣatriya* would go into the forest and challenge a tiger face to face and fight with the tiger with his sword. When the tiger was killed, it would be offered the royal order of cremation. This system has been followed even up to the present day by the *kṣatriya* kings of Jaipur state. The *kṣatriyas* are specially trained for challenging and killing because religious violence is sometimes a necessary factor. Therefore, *kṣatriyas* are never meant for accepting directly the order of *sannyāsa,* or renunciation. Nonviolence in politics may be a diplomacy, but it is never a factor or principle. In the religious law books it is stated:

āhaveṣu mitho 'nyonyaṁ, jighāṁsanto mahī-kṣitaḥ
yuddhamānāḥ paraṁ śaktyā, svargaṁ yānty aparāṅ-mukhāḥ

yajñeṣu paśavo brahman, hanyante satataṁ dvijaiḥ
saṁskṛtāḥ kila mantraiś ca, te 'pi svargam avāpnuvan

"In the battlefield, a king or *kṣatriya,* while fighting another king envious of him, is eligible for achieving the heavenly planets after death, as the *brāhmaṇas* also attain the heavenly planets by sacrificing animals in the sacrificial fire." Therefore, killing on the battlefield on religious principles and killing animals in the sacrificial fire are not at all considered to be acts of violence, because everyone is benefited by the religious principles involved. The animal sacrificed gets a human life immediately without undergoing the gradual evolutionary process from one form to another, and the *kṣatriyas* killed on the battlefield also attain the heavenly planets, as do the *brāhmaṇas* who attain them by offering sacrifice.

There are two kinds of *sva-dharmas,* specific duties. As long as one is not liberated, one has to perform the duties of his particular body in accordance with religious principles in order to achieve liberation. When one is liberated, one's *sva-dharma* – specific duty – becomes spiritual and is not in the material bodily concept. In the bodily conception of life there are specific duties for the *brāhmaṇas* and *kṣatriyas* respectively, and these duties are unavoidable. Such *sva-dharma* is ordained by the Lord, and this will be clarified in the Fourth Chapter. On the bodily plane *sva-dharma* is called *varṇāśrama-dharma,* or man's steppingstone for spiritual understanding. Human civilization begins from the stage of *varṇāśrama-dharma,* or specific duties in terms of the specific modes of nature of the body obtained. Discharging one's specific duty in any field of action in accordance with the orders of higher authorities serves to elevate one to a higher status of life.

Text 32 यदृच्छया चोपपन्नं स्वर्गद्वारमपावृतम् ।
सुखिनः क्षत्रियाः पार्थ लभन्ते युद्धमीदृशम् ॥३२॥

yadṛcchayā copapannaṁ, svarga-dvāram apāvṛtam
sukhinaḥ kṣatriyāḥ pārtha, labhante yuddham īdṛśam

yadṛcchayā – by its own accord; *ca* – also; *upapannam* – arrived at; *svarga* – of the heavenly planets; *dvāram* – door; *apāvṛtam* – wide open; *sukhinaḥ* – very happy; *kṣatriyāḥ* – the members of the royal order; *pārtha* – O son of Pṛthā; *labhante* – do achieve; *yuddham* – war; *īdṛśam* – like this.

O Pārtha, happy are the kṣatriyas to whom such fighting opportunities come unsought, opening for them the doors of the heavenly planets.

PURPORT: As supreme teacher of the world, Lord Kṛṣṇa condemns the attitude of Arjuna, who said, "I do not find any good in this fighting. It will cause perpetual habitation in hell." Such statements by Arjuna were due to ignorance only. He wanted to become nonviolent in the discharge of his specific duty. For a *kṣatriya* to be on the battlefield and to become nonviolent is the philosophy of fools. In the *Parāśara-smṛti,* or religious codes made by Parāśara, the great sage and father of Vyāsadeva, it is stated:

kṣatriyo hi prajā rakṣan, śastra-pāṇiḥ pradaṇḍayan
nirjitya para-sainyādi, kṣitiṁ dharmeṇa pālayet

"The *kṣatriya's* duty is to protect the citizens from all kinds of difficulties, and for that reason he has to apply violence in suitable cases for law and order. Therefore he has to conquer the soldiers of inimical kings, and thus, with religious principles, he should rule over the world."

Considering all aspects, Arjuna had no reason to refrain from fighting. If he should conquer his enemies, he would enjoy the kingdom; and if he should die in the battle, he would be elevated to the heavenly planets, whose doors were wide open to him. Fighting would be for his benefit in either case.

Text 33 अथ चेत्त्वमिमं धर्म्यं सङ्ग्रामं न करिष्यसि ।
ततः स्वधर्मं कीर्तिं च हित्वा पापमवाप्स्यसि ॥३३॥

atha cet tvam imaṁ dharmyaṁ, saṅgrāmaṁ na kariṣyasi
tataḥ sva-dharmaṁ kīrtiṁ ca, hitvā pāpam avāpsyasi

atha – therefore; *cet* – if; *tvam* – you; *imam* – this; *dharmyam* – as a religious duty; *saṅgrāmam* – fighting; *na* – do not; *kariṣyasi* – perform; *tataḥ* – then; *sva-dharmam* – your religious duty; *kīrtim* – reputation; *ca* – also; *hitvā* – losing; *pāpam* – sinful reaction; *avāpsyasi* – will gain.

If, however, you do not perform your religious duty of fighting, then you will certainly incur sins for neglecting your duties and thus lose your reputation as a fighter.

PURPORT: Arjuna was a famous fighter, and he attained fame by fighting many great demigods, including even Lord Śiva. After fighting and defeating Lord Śiva in the dress of a hunter, Arjuna pleased the lord and received as a reward a weapon called *pāśupata-astra.* Everyone knew that he was a great warrior. Even Droṇācārya gave him benedictions and awarded him the special weapon by which he could kill even his teacher. So he was credited with so many military certificates from many authorities, including his adoptive father Indra, the heavenly king. But if he abandoned the battle, not only would he neglect his specific duty as a *kṣatriya,* but he would lose all his fame and good name and thus prepare his royal road to hell. In other words, he would go to hell not by fighting but by withdrawing from battle.

Text 34 अकीर्तिं चापि भूतानि कथयिष्यन्ति तेऽव्ययाम् ।
सम्भावितस्य चाकीर्तिर्मरणादतिरिच्यते ॥३४॥

akīrtiṁ cāpi bhūtāni, kathayiṣyanti te 'vyayām
sambhāvitasya cākīrtir, maraṇād atiricyate

akīrtim – infamy; *ca* – also; *api* – over and above; *bhūtāni* – all people; *kathayiṣyanti* – will speak; *te* – of you; *avyayām* – forever; *sambhāvitasya* – for a respectable man; *ca* – also; *akīrtiḥ* – ill fame; *maraṇāt* – than death; *atiricyate* – becomes more.

People will always speak of your infamy, and for a respectable person, dishonor is worse than death.

PURPORT: Both as friend and philosopher to Arjuna, Lord Kṛṣṇa now gives His final judgment regarding Arjuna's refusal to fight. The Lord says, "Arjuna, if you leave the battlefield before the battle even begins, people will call you a coward. And if you think that people may call you bad names but that you will save your life by fleeing the battlefield, then My advice is that you'd do better to die in the battle. For a respectable man like you, ill fame is worse than death. So, you should not flee for fear of your life; better to die in the battle. That will save you from the ill fame of misusing My friendship and from losing your prestige in society."

So, the final judgment of the Lord was for Arjuna to die in the battle and not withdraw.

Text 35 भयाद्रणादुपरतं मंस्यन्ते त्वां महारथाः ।
येषां च त्वं बहुमतो भूत्वा यास्यसि लाघवम् ॥३५॥

bhayād raṇād uparataṁ, maṁsyante tvāṁ mahā-rathāḥ
yeṣāṁ ca tvaṁ bahu-mato, bhūtvā yāsyasi lāghavam

bhayāt – out of fear; *raṇāt* – from the battlefield; *uparatam* – ceased; *maṁsyante* – they will consider; *tvām* – you; *mahā-rathāḥ* – the great generals; *yeṣām* – for whom; *ca* – also; *tvam* – you; *bahu-mataḥ* – in great estimation; *bhūtvā* – having been; *yāsyasi* – you will go; *lāghavam* – decreased in value.

The great generals who have highly esteemed your name and fame will think that you have left the battlefield out of fear only, and thus they will consider you insignificant.

PURPORT: Lord Kṛṣṇa continued to give His verdict to Arjuna: "Do not think that the great generals like Duryodhana, Karṇa, and other contemporaries will think that you have left the battlefield out of compassion for your brothers and grandfather. They will think that you have left out of fear for your life. And thus their high estimation of your personality will go to hell."

Text 36 अवाच्यवादांश्च बहून् वदिष्यन्ति तवाहिताः ।
निन्दन्तस्तव सामर्थ्यं ततो दुःखतरं नु किम् ॥३६॥

avācya-vādāṁś ca bahūn, vadiṣyanti tavāhitāḥ
nindantas tava sāmarthyaṁ, tato duḥkha-taraṁ nu kim

avācya – unkind; *vādān* – fabricated words; *ca* – also; *bahūn* – many; *vadiṣyanti* – will say; *tava* – your; *ahitāḥ* – enemies; *nindantaḥ* – while vilifying; *tava* – your; *sāmarthyam* – ability; *tataḥ* – than that; *duḥkha-taram* – more painful; *nu* – of course; *kim* – what is there.

Your enemies will describe you in many unkind words and scorn your ability. What could be more painful for you?

PURPORT: Lord Kṛṣṇa was astonished in the beginning at Arjuna's uncalled-for plea for compassion, and He described his compassion as befitting the non-Āryans. Now in so many words, He has proved His statements against Arjuna's so-called compassion.

Text 37 हतो वा प्राप्स्यसि स्वर्गं जित्वा वा भोक्ष्यसे महीम् ।
तस्मादुत्तिष्ठ कौन्तेय युद्धाय कृतनिश्चयः ॥३७॥

hato vā prāpsyasi svargaṁ, jitvā vā bhokṣyase mahīm
tasmād uttiṣṭha kaunteya, yuddhāya kṛta-niścayaḥ

hataḥ – being killed; *vā* – either; *prāpsyasi* – you gain; *svargam* – the heavenly kingdom; *jitvā* – by conquering; *vā* – or; *bhokṣyase* – you enjoy; *mahīm* – the world; *tasmāt* – therefore; *uttiṣṭha* – get up; *kaunteya* – O son of Kuntī; *yuddhāya* – to fight; *kṛta* – determined; *niścayaḥ* – in certainty.

O son of Kuntī, either you will be killed on the battlefield and attain the heavenly planets, or you will conquer and enjoy the earthly kingdom. Therefore, get up with determination and fight.

PURPORT: Even though there was no certainty of victory for Arjuna's side, he still had to fight; for, even being killed there, he could be elevated into the heavenly planets.

Text 38 सुखदुःखे समे कृत्वा लाभालाभौ जयाजयौ ।
ततो युद्धाय युज्यस्व नैवं पापमवाप्स्यसि ॥३८॥

sukha-duḥkhe same kṛtvā, lābhālābhau jayājayau
tato yuddhāya yujyasva, naivaṁ pāpam avāpsyasi

sukha – happiness; *duḥkhe* – and distress; *same* – in equanimity; *kṛtvā* – doing so; *lābha-alābhau* – both profit and loss; *jaya-ajayau* – both victory and defeat; *tataḥ* – thereafter; *yuddhāya* – for the sake of fighting; *yujyasva* – engage (fight); *na* – never; *evam* – in this way; *pāpam* – sinful reaction; *avāpsyasi* – you will gain.

Do thou fight for the sake of fighting, without considering happiness or distress, loss or gain, victory or defeat – and by so doing you shall never incur sin.

PURPORT: Lord Kṛṣṇa now directly says that Arjuna should fight for the sake of fighting because He desires the battle. There is no consideration of happiness or distress, profit or loss, victory or defeat in the activities of Kṛṣṇa consciousness. That everything should be performed for the sake of Kṛṣṇa is transcendental consciousness; so there is no reaction to material activities. He who acts for his own sense gratification, either in goodness or in passion, is subject to the reaction, good or bad. But he who has completely surrendered himself in the activities of Kṛṣṇa consciousness is no longer obliged to anyone, nor is he a debtor to anyone, as one is in the ordinary course of activities. It is said:

devarṣi-bhūtāpta-nṛṇāṁ pitṝṇāṁ, na kiṅkaro nāyam ṛṇī ca rājan
sarvātmanā yaḥ śaraṇaṁ śaraṇyaṁ, gato mukundaṁ parihṛtya kartam

"Anyone who has completely surrendered unto Kṛṣṇa, Mukunda, giving up all other duties, is no longer a debtor, nor is he obliged to anyone – not the demigods, nor the sages, nor the people in general, nor kinsmen, nor humanity, nor forefathers." (*Bhāgavatam* 11.5.41) That is the indirect hint given by Kṛṣṇa to Arjuna in this verse, and the matter will be more clearly explained in the following verses.

Text 39 एषा तेऽभिहिता साङ्ख्ये बुद्धिर्योगे त्विमां शृणु ।
बुद्ध्या युक्तो यया पार्थ कर्मबन्धं प्रहास्यसि ॥३९॥

eṣā te 'bhihitā sāṅkhye, buddhir yoge tv imāṁ śṛṇu
buddhyā yukto yayā pārtha, karma-bandhaṁ prahāsyasi

eṣā – all this; *te* – unto you; *abhihitā* – described; *sāṅkhye* – in analytical study; *buddhiḥ* – intelligence; *yoge* – in work without fruitive result; *tu* – but; *imām* – this; *śṛṇu* – just hear; *buddhyā* – by intelligence; *yuktaḥ* – dovetailed; *yayā* – by which; *pārtha* – O son of Pṛthā; *karma-bandham* – bondage of reaction; *prahāsyasi* – you can be released from.

Thus far I have described this knowledge to you through analytical study. Now listen as I explain it in terms of working without fruitive results. O son of Pṛthā, when you act in such knowledge you can free yourself from the bondage of works.

PURPORT: According to the *Nirukti,* or the Vedic dictionary, *saṅkhyā* means that which describes things in detail, and *sāṅkhya* refers to that philosophy which describes the real nature of the soul. And *yoga* involves controlling the senses. Arjuna's proposal not to fight was based on sense gratification. Forgetting his prime duty, he wanted to cease fighting, because he thought that by not killing his relatives and kinsmen he would be happier than by enjoying the kingdom after conquering his cousins and brothers, the sons of Dhṛtarāṣṭra. In both ways, the basic principles were for sense gratification. Happiness derived from conquering them and happiness derived by seeing kinsmen alive are both on the basis of personal sense gratification, even at a sacrifice of wisdom and duty. Kṛṣṇa, therefore, wanted to explain to Arjuna that by killing the body of his grandfather he would not be killing the soul proper, and He explained that all individual persons, including the Lord Himself, are eternal individuals; they were individuals in the past, they are individuals in the present, and they will continue to remain individuals in the future, because all of us are individual souls eternally. We simply change our bodily dress in different manners, but actually we keep our individuality even after liberation from the bondage of material dress. An analytical study of the soul and the body has been very graphically explained by Lord Kṛṣṇa. And this descriptive knowledge of the soul and the body from different angles of vision has been described here as Sāṅkhya, in terms of the *Nirukti* dictionary. This Sāṅkhya has nothing to do with the Sāṅkhya philosophy of the atheist Kapila. Long before the imposter Kapila's Sāṅkhya, the Sāṅkhya philosophy was expounded in the *Śrīmad-Bhāgavatam* by the true Lord Kapila, the incarnation of Lord Kṛṣṇa, who explained it to His mother, Devahūti. It is clearly explained by Him that the *puruṣa,* or the Supreme Lord, is active and that He creates by looking over the *prakṛti.* This is accepted in the *Vedas* and in the *Gītā.* The description in the *Vedas* indicates that the Lord glanced over the *prakṛti,* or nature, and impregnated it with atomic individual souls. All these individuals are working in the material world for sense gratification, and under the spell of material energy they are thinking of being enjoyers. This mentality is dragged to the last point of liberation when the living entity wants to become one with the Lord. This is the last snare of *māyā,* or sense gratificatory illusion, and it is only after many, many births of such sense gratificatory activities that a great soul surrenders unto Vāsudeva, Lord Kṛṣṇa, thereby fulfilling the search after the ultimate truth.

Arjuna has already accepted Kṛṣṇa as his spiritual master by surrendering himself unto Him: *śiṣyas te 'haṁ śādhi māṁ tvāṁ prapannam.* Consequently, Kṛṣṇa will now tell him about the working process in *buddhi-yoga,* or *karma-yoga,* or in other words, the practice of devotional service only for the sense gratification of the Lord. This *buddhi-yoga* is clearly explained in Chapter Ten, verse ten, as being direct communion with the Lord, who is sitting as Paramātmā in everyone's heart. But such communion does not take place without devotional service. One who is therefore situated in devotional or transcendental loving service to the Lord, or, in other words, in Kṛṣṇa consciousness, attains to this stage of *buddhi-yoga* by the special grace of the Lord. The Lord says, therefore, that only to those who are always engaged in devotional service out of transcendental love does He award the pure knowledge of devotion in love. In that way the devotee can reach Him easily in the ever-blissful kingdom of God.

Thus the *buddhi-yoga* mentioned in this verse is the devotional service of the Lord, and the word Sāṅkhya mentioned herein has nothing to do with the atheistic *sāṅkhya-yoga* enunciated by the imposter Kapila. One should not, therefore, misunderstand that the *sāṅkhya-yoga* mentioned herein has any connection with the atheistic Sāṅkhya. Nor did that philosophy have any influence during that time; nor would Lord Kṛṣṇa care to mention such godless philosophical speculations. Real Sāṅkhya philosophy is described by Lord Kapila in the *Śrīmad-Bhāgavatam,* but even that Sāṅkhya has nothing to do with the current topics. Here, Sāṅkhya means analytical description of the body and the soul. Lord Kṛṣṇa made an analytical description of the soul just to bring Arjuna to the point of *buddhi-yoga,* or *bhakti-yoga.* Therefore, Lord Kṛṣṇa's Sāṅkhya and Lord Kapila's Sāṅkhya, as described in the *Bhāgavatam,* are one and the same. They are all *bhakti-yoga.* Lord Kṛṣṇa said, therefore, that only the less intelligent class of men make a distinction between *sāṅkhya-yoga* and *bhakti-yoga* (*sāṅkhya-yogau pṛthag bālāḥ pravadanti na paṇḍitāḥ*).

Of course, atheistic *sāṅkhya-yoga* has nothing to do with *bhakti-yoga,* yet the unintelligent claim that the atheistic *sāṅkhya-yoga* is referred to in the *Bhagavad-gītā.*

One should therefore understand that *buddhi-yoga* means to work in Kṛṣṇa consciousness, in the full bliss and knowledge of devotional service. One who works for the satisfaction of the Lord only, however difficult such work may be, is working under the principles of *buddhi-yoga* and finds himself always in transcendental bliss. By such transcendental engagement, one achieves all transcendental understanding automatically, by the grace of the Lord, and thus his liberation is complete in itself, without his making extraneous endeavors to acquire knowledge. There is much difference between work in Kṛṣṇa consciousness and work for fruitive results, especially in the matter of sense gratification for achieving results in terms of family or material happiness. *Buddhi-yoga* is therefore the transcendental quality of the work that we perform.

Text 40 नेहाभिक्रमनाशोऽस्ति प्रत्यवायो न विद्यते ।
स्वल्पमप्यस्य धर्मस्य त्रायते महतो भयात् ॥४०॥

nehābhikrama-nāśo 'sti, pratyavāyo na vidyate
sv-alpam apy asya dharmasya, trāyate mahato bhayāt

na – there is not; *iha* – in this *yoga; abhikrama* – in endeavoring; *nāśaḥ* – loss; *asti* – there is; *pratyavāyaḥ* – diminution; *na* – never; *vidyate* – there is; *su-alpam* – a little; *api* – although; *asya* – of this; *dharmasya* – occupation; *trāyate* – releases; *mahataḥ* – from very great; *bhayāt* – danger.

In this endeavor there is no loss or diminution, and a little advancement on this path can protect one from the most dangerous type of fear.

PURPORT: Activity in Kṛṣṇa consciousness, or acting for the benefit of Kṛṣṇa without expectation of sense gratification, is the highest transcendental quality of work. Even a small beginning of such activity finds no impediment, nor can that small beginning be lost at any stage. Any work begun on the material plane has to be completed, otherwise the whole attempt becomes a failure. But any work begun in Kṛṣṇa consciousness has a permanent effect, even though not finished. The performer of such work is therefore not at a loss even if his work in Kṛṣṇa consciousness is incomplete. One percent done in Kṛṣṇa consciousness bears permanent results, so that the next beginning is from the point of two percent, whereas in material activity without a hundred percent success there is no profit. Ajāmila performed his duty in some percentage of Kṛṣṇa consciousness, but the result he enjoyed at the end was a hundred percent, by the grace of the Lord. There is a nice verse in this connection in *Śrīmad-Bhāgavatam* (1.5.17):

tyaktvā sva-dharmaṁ caraṇāmbujaṁ harer
bhajann apakvo 'tha patet tato yadi
yatra kva vābhadram abhūd amuṣya kiṁ
ko vārtha āpto 'bhajatāṁ sva-dharmataḥ

"If someone gives up his occupational duties and works in Kṛṣṇa consciousness and then falls down on account of not completing his work, what loss is there on his part? And what can one gain if one performs his material activities perfectly?" Or, as the Christians say, "What profiteth a man if he gain the whole world yet suffer the loss of his eternal soul?"

Material activities and their results end with the body. But work in Kṛṣṇa consciousness carries a person again to Kṛṣṇa consciousness, even after the loss of the body. At least one is sure to have a chance in the next life of being born again as a human being, either in the family of a great cultured *brāhmaṇa* or in a rich aristocratic family that will give one a further chance for elevation. That is the unique quality of work done in Kṛṣṇa consciousness.

Text 41 व्यवसायात्मिका बुद्धिरेकेह कुरुनन्दन ।
बहुशाखा ह्यनन्ताश्च बुद्धयोऽव्यवसायिनाम् ॥४१॥

vyavasāyātmikā buddhir, ekeha kuru-nandana
bahu-śākhā hy anantāś ca, buddhayo 'vyavasāyinām

vyavasāya-ātmikā – resolute in Kṛṣṇa consciousness; *buddhiḥ* – intelligence; *ekā* – only one; *iha* – in this world; *kuru-nandana* – O beloved child of the Kurus; *bahu-śākhāḥ* – having various branches; *hi* – indeed; *anantāḥ* – unlimited; *ca* – also; *buddhayaḥ* – intelligence; *avyavasāyinām* – of those who are not in Kṛṣṇa consciousness.

Those who are on this path are resolute in purpose, and their aim is one. O beloved child of the Kurus, the intelligence of those who are irresolute is many-branched.

PURPORT: A strong faith that by Kṛṣṇa consciousness one will be elevated to the highest perfection of life is called *vyavasāyātmikā* intelligence. The *Caitanya-caritāmṛta* (*Madhya* 22.62) states:

'śraddhā'-śabde – viśvāsa kahe sudṛḍha niścaya
kṛṣṇe bhakti kaile sarva-karma kṛta haya

Faith means unflinching trust in something sublime. When one is engaged in the duties of Kṛṣṇa consciousness, he need not act in relationship to the material world with obligations to family traditions, humanity, or nationality. Fruitive activities are the engagements of one's reactions from past good or bad deeds. When one is awake in Kṛṣṇa consciousness, he need no longer endeavor for good results in his activities. When one is situated in Kṛṣṇa consciousness, all activities are on the absolute plane, for they are no longer subject to dualities like good and bad. The highest perfection of Kṛṣṇa consciousness is renunciation of the material conception of life. This state is automatically achieved by progressive Kṛṣṇa consciousness.

The resolute purpose of a person in Kṛṣṇa consciousness is based on knowledge. *Vāsudevaḥ sarvam iti sa mahātmā su-durlabhaḥ:* a person in Kṛṣṇa consciousness is the rare good soul who knows perfectly that Vāsudeva, or Kṛṣṇa, is the root of all manifested causes. As by watering the root of a tree one automatically distributes water to the leaves and branches, so by acting in Kṛṣṇa consciousness one can render the highest service to everyone – namely self, family, society, country, humanity, etc. If Kṛṣṇa is satisfied by one's actions, then everyone will be satisfied.

Service in Kṛṣṇa consciousness is, however, best practiced under the able guidance of a spiritual master who is a bona fide representative of Kṛṣṇa, who knows the nature of the student and who can guide him to act in Kṛṣṇa consciousness. As such, to be well versed in Kṛṣṇa consciousness one has to act firmly and obey the representative of Kṛṣṇa, and one should accept the instruction of the bona fide spiritual master as one's mission in life. Śrīla Viśvanātha Cakravartī Ṭhākura instructs us, in his famous prayers for the spiritual master, as follows:

yasya prasādād bhagavat-prasādo
yasyāprasādān na gatiḥ kuto 'pi
dhyāyan stuvaṁs tasya yaśas tri-sandhyaṁ
vande guroḥ śrī-caraṇāravindam

"By satisfaction of the spiritual master, the Supreme Personality of Godhead becomes satisfied. And by not satisfying the spiritual master, there is no chance of being promoted to the plane of Kṛṣṇa consciousness. I should, therefore, meditate and pray for his mercy three times a day, and offer my respectful obeisances unto him, my spiritual master."

The whole process, however, depends on perfect knowledge of the soul beyond the conception of the body – not theoretically but practically, when there is no longer a chance for sense gratification manifested in fruitive activities. One who is not firmly fixed in mind is diverted by various types of fruitive acts.

Texts 42–43

यामिमां पुष्पितां वाचं प्रवदन्त्यविपश्चितः ।
वेदवादरताः पार्थ नान्यदस्तीति वादिनः ॥४२॥
कामात्मानः स्वर्गपरा जन्मकर्मफलप्रदाम् ।
क्रियाविशेषबहुलां भोगैश्वर्यगतिं प्रति ॥४३॥

yām imāṁ puṣpitāṁ vācaṁ, pravadanty avipaścitaḥ
veda-vāda-ratāḥ pārtha, nānyad astīti vādinaḥ

kāmātmānaḥ svarga-parā, janma-karma-phala-pradām
kriyā-viśeṣa-bahulāṁ, bhogaiśvarya-gatiṁ prati

yām imām – all these; *puṣpitām* – flowery; *vācam* – words; *pravadanti* – say; *avipaścitaḥ* – men with a poor fund of knowledge; *veda-vāda-ratāḥ* – supposed followers of the *Vedas; pārtha* – O son of Pṛthā; *na* – never; *anyat* – anything else; *asti* – there is; *iti* – thus; *vādinaḥ* – the advocates;

kāma-ātmānaḥ – desirous of sense gratification; *svarga-parāḥ* – aiming to achieve heavenly planets; *janma-karma-phala-pradām* – resulting in good birth and other fruitive reactions; *kriyā-viśeṣa* – pompous ceremonies; *bahulām* – various; *bhoga* – in sense enjoyment; *aiśvarya* – and opulence; *gatim* – progress; *prati* – towards.

Men of small knowledge are very much attached to the flowery words of the Vedas, which recommend various fruitive activities for elevation to heavenly planets, resultant good birth, power, and so forth. Being desirous of sense gratification and opulent life, they say that there is nothing more than this.

PURPORT: People in general are not very intelligent, and due to their ignorance they are most attached to the fruitive activities recommended in the *karma-kāṇda* portions of the *Vedas.* They do not want anything more than sense gratificatory proposals for enjoying life in heaven, where wine and women are available and material opulence is very common. In the *Vedas* many sacrifices are recommended for elevation to the heavenly planets, especially the Jyotiṣṭoma sacrifices. In fact, it is stated that anyone desiring elevation to heavenly planets must perform these sacrifices, and men with a poor fund of knowledge think that this is the whole purpose of Vedic wisdom. It is very difficult for such inexperienced persons to be situated in the determined action of Kṛṣṇa consciousness. As fools are attached to the flowers of poisonous trees without knowing the results of such attractions, unenlightened men are similarly attracted by such heavenly opulence and the sense enjoyment thereof.

In the *karma-kāṇḍa* section of the *Vedas* it is said, *apāma somam amṛtā abhūma* and *akṣayyaṁ ha vai cāturmāsya-yājinaḥ sukṛtaṁ bhavati.* In other words, those who perform the four-month penances become eligible to drink the *soma-rasa* beverages to become immortal and happy forever. Even on this earth some are very eager to have *soma-rasa* to become strong and fit to enjoy sense gratifications. Such persons have no faith in liberation from material bondage, and they are very much attached to the pompous ceremonies of Vedic sacrifices. They are generally sensual, and they do not want anything other than the heavenly pleasures of life. It is understood that there are gardens called Nandana-kānana in which there is good opportunity for association with angelic, beautiful women and having a profuse supply of *soma-rasa* wine. Such bodily happiness is certainly sensual; therefore there are those who are purely attached to such material, temporary happiness, as lords of the material world.

Text 44 भोगैश्वर्यप्रसक्तानां तयापहृतचेतसाम् ।
व्यवसायात्मिका बुद्धिः समाधौ न विधीयते ॥४४॥

bhogaiśvarya-prasaktānāṁ, tayāpahṛta-cetasām
vyavasāyātmikā buddhiḥ, samādhau na vidhīyate

bhoga – to material enjoyment; *aiśvarya* – and opulence; *prasaktānām* – for those who are attached; *tayā* – by such things; *apahṛta-cetasām* – bewildered in mind; *vyavasāya-ātmikā* – fixed in determination; *buddhiḥ* – devotional service to the Lord; *samādhau* – in the controlled mind; *na* – never; *vidhīyate* – does take place.

In the minds of those who are too attached to sense enjoyment and material opulence, and who are bewildered by such things, the resolute determination for devotional service to the Supreme Lord does not take place.

PURPORT: *Samādhi* means "fixed mind." The Vedic dictionary, the *Nirukti,* says, *samyag ādhīyate 'sminn ātma-tattva-yāthātmyam:* "When the mind is fixed for understanding the self, it is said to be in *samādhi.*" *Samādhi* is never possible for persons interested in material sense enjoyments and bewildered by such temporary things. They are more or less condemned by the process of material energy.

Text 45 त्रैगुण्यविषया वेदा निस्त्रैगुण्यो भवार्जुन ।
निर्द्वन्द्वो नित्यसत्त्वस्थो निर्योगक्षेम आत्मवान् ॥४५॥

trai-guṇya-viṣayā vedā, nistrai-guṇyo bhavārjuna
nirdvandvo nitya-sattva-stho, niryoga-kṣema ātmavān

trai-guṇya – pertaining to the three modes of material nature; *viṣayāḥ* – on the subject matter; *vedāḥ* – Vedic literatures; *nistrai-guṇyaḥ* – transcendental to the three modes of material nature; *bhava* – be; *arjuna* – O Arjuna; *nirdvandvaḥ* – without duality; *nitya-sattva-sthaḥ* – in a pure state of spiritual existence; *niryoga-kṣemaḥ* – free from ideas of gain and protection; *ātma-vān* – established in the self.

The Vedas deal mainly with the subject of the three modes of material nature. O Arjuna, become transcendental to these three modes. Be free from all dualities and from all anxieties for gain and safety, and be established in the self.

PURPORT: All material activities involve actions and reactions in the three modes of material nature. They are meant for fruitive results, which cause bondage in the material world. The *Vedas* deal mostly with fruitive activities to gradually elevate the general public from the field of sense gratification to a position on the transcendental plane. Arjuna, as a student and friend of Lord Kṛṣṇa, is advised to raise himself to the transcendental position of *Vedānta* philosophy where, in the beginning, there is *brahma-jijñāsā,* or questions on the supreme transcendence. All the living entities who are in the material world are struggling very hard for existence. For them the Lord, after creation of the material world, gave the Vedic wisdom advising how to live and get rid of the material entanglement. When the activities for sense gratification, namely the *karma-kāṇḍa* chapter, are finished, then the chance for spiritual realization is offered in the form of the *Upaniṣads,* which are part of different *Vedas,* as the *Bhagavad-gītā* is a part of the fifth *Veda,* namely the *Mahābhārata.* The *Upaniṣads* mark the beginning of transcendental life.

As long as the material body exists, there are actions and reactions in the material modes. One has to learn tolerance in the face of dualities such as happiness and distress, or cold and warmth, and by tolerating such dualities become free from anxieties regarding gain and loss. This transcendental position is achieved in full Kṛṣṇa consciousness when one is fully dependent on the good will of Kṛṣṇa.

Text 46 यावानर्थ उदपाने सर्वतः सम्प्लुतोदके ।
तावान् सर्वेषु वेदेषु ब्राह्मणस्य विजानतः ॥४६॥

yāvān artha uda-pāne, sarvataḥ samplutodake
tāvān sarveṣu vedeṣu, brāhmaṇasya vijānataḥ

yāvān – all that; *arthah* – is meant; *uda-pāne* – in a well of water; *sarvataḥ* – in all respects; *sampluta-udake* – in a great reservoir of water; *tāvān* – similarly; *sarveṣu* – in all; *vedeṣu* – Vedic literatures; *brāhmaṇasya* – of the man who knows the Supreme Brahman; *vijānataḥ* – who is in complete knowledge.

All purposes served by a small well can at once be served by a great reservoir of water. Similarly, all the purposes of the Vedas can be served to one who knows the purpose behind them.

PURPORT: The rituals and sacrifices mentioned in the *karma-kāṇḍa* division of the Vedic literature are meant to encourage gradual development of self-realization. And the purpose of self-realization is clearly stated in the Fifteenth Chapter of the *Bhagavad-gītā* (15.15): the purpose of studying the *Vedas* is to know Lord Kṛṣṇa, the primeval cause of everything. So, self-realization means understanding Kṛṣṇa and one's eternal relationship with Him. The relationship of the living entities with Kṛṣṇa is also mentioned in the Fifteenth Chapter of *Bhagavad-gītā* (15.7). The living entities are parts and parcels of Kṛṣṇa; therefore, revival of Kṛṣṇa consciousness by the individual living entity is the highest perfectional stage of Vedic knowledge. This is confirmed in the *Śrīmad-Bhāgavatam* (3.33.7) as follows:

aho bata śva-paco 'to garīyān, yaj-jihvāgre vartate nāma tubhyam
tepus tapas te juhuvuḥ sasnur āryā, brahmānūcur nāma gṛṇanti ye te

"O my Lord, a person who is chanting Your holy name, although born of a low family like that of a *caṇḍāla* [dog-eater], is situated on the highest platform of self-realization. Such a person must have performed all kinds of penances and sacrifices according to Vedic rituals and studied the Vedic literatures many, many times after taking his bath in all the holy places of pilgrimage. Such a person is considered to be the best of the Āryan family."

So one must be intelligent enough to understand the purpose of the *Vedas,* without being attached to the rituals only, and must not desire to be elevated to the heavenly kingdoms for a better quality of sense gratification. It is not possible for the common man in this age to follow all the rules and regulations of the Vedic rituals, nor is it possible to study all of the *Vedānta* and the *Upaniṣads* thoroughly. It requires much time, energy, knowledge and resources to execute the purposes of the *Vedas.* This is hardly possible in this age. The best purpose of Vedic culture is served, however, by chanting the holy name of the Lord, as recommended by Lord Caitanya, the deliverer of all fallen souls. When Lord Caitanya was asked by a great Vedic scholar, Prakāśānanda Sarasvatī, why He, the Lord, was chanting the holy name of the Lord like a sentimentalist instead of studying *Vedānta* philosophy, the Lord replied that His spiritual master had found Him to be a great fool and thus asked Him to chant the holy name of Lord Kṛṣṇa. He did so, and became ecstatic like a madman. In this Age of Kali, most of the population is foolish and not adequately educated to understand *Vedānta* philosophy; the best purpose of *Vedānta* philosophy is served by inoffensively chanting the holy name of the Lord. *Vedānta* is the last word in Vedic wisdom, and the author and knower of the *Vedānta* philosophy is Lord Kṛṣṇa; and the highest Vedāntist is the great soul who takes pleasure in chanting the holy name of the Lord. That is the ultimate purpose of all Vedic mysticism.

Text 47 कर्मण्येवाधिकारस्ते मा फलेषु कदाचन ।
मा कर्मफलहेतुर्भूर्मा ते सङ्गोऽस्त्वकर्मणि ॥४७॥

karmaṇy evādhikāras te, mā phaleṣu kadācana
mā karma-phala-hetur bhūr, mā te saṅgo 'stv akarmaṇi

karmaṇi – in prescribed duties; *eva* – certainly; *adhikāraḥ* – right; *te* – of you; *mā* – never; *phaleṣu* – in the fruits; *kadācana* – at any time; *mā* – never; *karma-phala* – in the result of the work; *hetuḥ* – cause; *bhūḥ* – become; *mā* – never; *te* – of you; *saṅgaḥ* – attachment; *astu* – there should be; *akarmaṇi* – in not doing prescribed duties.

You have a right to perform your prescribed duty, but you are not entitled to the fruits of action. Never consider yourself the cause of the results of your activities, and never be attached to not doing your duty.

PURPORT: There are three considerations here: prescribed duties, capricious work, and inaction. Prescribed duties are activities enjoined in terms of one's acquired modes of material nature. Capricious work means actions without the sanction of authority, and inaction means not performing one's prescribed duties. The Lord advised that Arjuna not be inactive, but that he perform his prescribed duty without being attached to the result. One who is attached to the result of his work is also the cause of the action. Thus he is the enjoyer or sufferer of the result of such actions.

As far as prescribed duties are concerned, they can be fitted into three subdivisions, namely routine work, emergency work and desired activities. Routine work performed as an obligation in terms of the scriptural injunctions, without desire for results, is action in the mode of goodness. Work with results becomes the cause of bondage; therefore such work is not auspicious. Everyone has his proprietary right in regard to prescribed duties, but should act without attachment to the result; such disinterested obligatory duties doubtlessly lead one to the path of liberation.

Arjuna was therefore advised by the Lord to fight as a matter of duty without attachment to the result. His nonparticipation in the battle is another side of attachment. Such attachment never leads one to the path of salvation. Any attachment, positive or negative, is cause for bondage. Inaction is sinful. Therefore, fighting as a matter of duty was the only auspicious path of salvation for Arjuna.

Text 48 योगस्थः कुरु कर्माणि सङ्गं त्यक्त्वा धनञ्जय ।
सिद्ध्यसिद्ध्योः समो भूत्वा समत्वं योग उच्यते ॥४८॥

yoga-sthaḥ kuru karmāṇi, saṅgaṁ tyaktvā dhanañ-jaya
siddhy-asiddhyoḥ samo bhūtvā, samatvaṁ yoga ucyate

yoga-sthaḥ – equipoised; *kuru* – perform; *karmāṇi* – your duties; *saṅgam* – attachment; *tyaktvā* – giving up; *dhanam-jaya* – O Arjuna; *siddhi-asiddhyoḥ* – in success and failure; *samaḥ* – equipoised; *bhūtvā* – becoming; *samatvam* – equanimity; *yogaḥ* – *yoga; ucyate* – is called.

Perform your duty equipoised, O Arjuna, abandoning all attachment to success or failure. Such equanimity is called yoga.

PURPORT: Kṛṣṇa tells Arjuna that he should act in *yoga.* And what is that *yoga*? *Yoga* means to concentrate the mind upon the Supreme by controlling the ever-disturbing senses. And who is the Supreme? The Supreme is the Lord. And because He Himself is telling Arjuna to fight, Arjuna has nothing to do with the results of the fight. Gain or victory are Kṛṣṇa's concern; Arjuna is simply advised to act according to the dictation of Kṛṣṇa. The following of Kṛṣṇa's dictation is real *yoga,* and this is practiced in the process called Kṛṣṇa consciousness. By Kṛṣṇa consciousness only can one give up the sense of proprietorship. One has to become the servant of Kṛṣṇa, or the servant of the servant of Kṛṣṇa. That is the right way to discharge duty in Kṛṣṇa consciousness, which alone can help one to act in *yoga.*

Arjuna is a *kṣatriya,* and as such he is participating in the *varṇāśrama-dharma* institution. It is said in the *Viṣṇu Purāṇa* that in the *varṇāśrama-dharma,* the whole aim is to satisfy Viṣṇu. No one should satisfy himself, as is the rule in the material world, but one should satisfy Kṛṣṇa. So unless one satisfies Kṛṣṇa, one cannot correctly observe the principles of *varṇāśrama-dharma.* Indirectly, Arjuna was advised to act as Kṛṣṇa told him.

Text 49 दूरेण ह्यवरं कर्म बुद्धियोगाद्धनञ्जय ।
बुद्धौ शरणमन्विच्छ कृपणाः फलहेतवः ॥४९॥

dūreṇa hy avaraṁ karma, buddhi-yogād dhanañ-jaya
buddhau śaraṇam anviccha, kṛpaṇāḥ phala-hetavaḥ

dūreṇa – discard it at a long distance; *hi* – certainly; *avaram* – abominable; *karma* – activity; *buddhi-yogāt* – on the strength of Kṛṣṇa consciousness; *dhanam-jaya* – O conqueror of wealth; *buddhau* – in such consciousness; *śaraṇam* – full surrender; *anviccha* – try for; *kṛpaṇāḥ* – misers; *phala-hetavaḥ* – those desiring fruitive results.

O Dhanañjaya, keep all abominable activities far distant by devotional service, and in that consciousness surrender unto the Lord. Those who want to enjoy the fruits of their work are misers.

PURPORT: One who has actually come to understand one's constitutional position as an eternal servitor of the Lord gives up all engagements save working in Kṛṣṇa consciousness. As already explained, *buddhi-yoga* means transcendental loving service to the Lord. Such devotional service is the right course of action for the living entity. Only misers desire to enjoy the fruit of their own work just to be further entangled in material bondage. Except for work in Kṛṣṇa consciousness, all activities are abominable because they continually bind the worker to the cycle of birth and death. One should therefore never desire to be the cause of work. Everything should be done in Kṛṣṇa consciousness, for the satisfaction of Kṛṣṇa. Misers do not know how to utilize the assets of riches which they acquire by good fortune or by hard labor. One should spend all energies working in Kṛṣṇa consciousness, and that will make one's life successful. Like misers, unfortunate persons do not employ their human energy in the service of the Lord.

Text 50 बुद्धियुक्तो जहातीह उभे सुकृतदुष्कृते ।
तस्माद्योगाय युज्यस्व योगः कर्मसु कौशलम् ॥५०॥

buddhi-yukto jahātīha, ubhe sukṛta-duṣkṛte
tasmād yogāya yujyasva, yogaḥ karmasu kauśalam

buddhi-yuktaḥ – one who is engaged in devotional service; *jahāti* – can get rid of; *iha* – in this life; *ubhe* – both; *sukṛta-duṣkṛte* – good and bad results; *tasmāt* – therefore; *yogāya* – for the sake of devotional service; *yujyasva* – be so engaged; *yogaḥ* – Kṛṣṇa consciousness; *karmasu* – in all activities; *kauśalam* – art.

A man engaged in devotional service rids himself of both good and bad reactions even in this life. Therefore strive for yoga, which is the art of all work.

PURPORT: Since time immemorial each living entity has accumulated the various reactions of his good and bad work. As such, he is continuously ignorant of his real constitutional position. One's ignorance can be removed by the instruction of the *Bhagavad-gītā,* which teaches one to surrender unto Lord Śrī Kṛṣṇa in all respects and become liberated from the chained victimization of action and reaction, birth after birth. Arjuna is therefore advised to act in Kṛṣṇa consciousness, the purifying process of resultant action.

Text 51 कर्मजं बुद्धियुक्ता हि फलं त्यक्त्वा मनीषिणः ।
जन्मबन्धविनिर्मुक्ताः पदं गच्छन्त्यनामयम् ॥५१॥

karma-jaṁ buddhi-yuktā hi, phalaṁ tyaktvā manīṣiṇaḥ
janma-bandha-vinirmuktāḥ, padaṁ gacchanty anāmayam

karma-jam – due to fruitive activities; *buddhi-yuktāḥ* – being engaged in devotional service; *hi* – certainly; *phalam* – results; *tyaktvā* – giving up; *manīṣiṇaḥ* – great sages or devotees; *janma-bandha* – from the bondage of birth and death; *vinirmuktāḥ* – liberated; *padam* – position; *gacchanti* – they reach; *anāmayam* – without miseries.

By thus engaging in devotional service to the Lord, great sages or devotees free themselves from the results of work in the material world. In this way they become free from the cycle of birth and death and attain the state beyond all miseries [by going back to Godhead].

PURPORT: The liberated living entities belong to that place where there are no material miseries. The *Bhāgavatam* (10.14.58) says:

samāśritā ye pada-pallava-plavaṁ
mahat-padaṁ puṇya-yaśo murāreḥ
bhavāmbudhir vatsa-padaṁ paraṁ padaṁ
padaṁ padaṁ yad vipadāṁ na teṣām

"For one who has accepted the boat of the lotus feet of the Lord, who is the shelter of the cosmic manifestation and is famous as Mukunda, or the giver of *mukti,* the ocean of the material world is like the water contained in a calf's footprint. *Paraṁ padam,* or the place where there are no material miseries, or Vaikuṇṭha, is his goal, not the place where there is danger in every step of life."

Owing to ignorance, one does not know that this material world is a miserable place where there are dangers at every step. Out of ignorance only, less intelligent persons try to adjust to the situation by fruitive activities, thinking that the resultant actions will make them happy. They do not know that no kind of material body anywhere within the universe can give life without miseries. The miseries of life, namely birth, death, old age and diseases, are present everywhere within the material world. But one who understands his real constitutional position as the eternal servitor of the Lord, and thus knows the position of the Personality of Godhead, engages himself in the transcendental loving service of the Lord. Consequently he becomes qualified to enter into the Vaikuṇṭha planets, where there is neither material, miserable life nor the influence of time and death. To know one's constitutional position means to know also the sublime position of the Lord. One who wrongly thinks that the living entity's position and the Lord's position are on the same level is to be understood to be in darkness and therefore unable to engage himself in the devotional service of the Lord. He becomes a lord himself and thus paves the way for the repetition of birth and death. But one who, understanding that his position is to serve, transfers himself to the service of the Lord, at once becomes eligible for Vaikuṇṭha-loka. Service for the cause of the Lord is called *karma-yoga* or *buddhi-yoga,* or in plain words, devotional service to the Lord.

Text 52 यदा ते मोहकलिलं बुद्धिर्व्यतितरिष्यति ।
तदा गन्तासि निर्वेदं श्रोतव्यस्य श्रुतस्य च ॥५२॥

yadā te moha-kalilaṁ, buddhir vyatitariṣyati
tadā gantāsi nirvedaṁ, śrotavyasya śrutasya ca

yadā – when; *te* – your; *moha* – of illusion; *kalilam* – dense forest; *buddhiḥ* – transcendental service with intelligence; *vyatitariṣyati* – surpasses; *tadā* – at that time; *gantā asi* – you shall go; *nirvedam* – callousness; *śrotavyasya* – toward all that is to be heard; *śrutasya* – all that is already heard; *ca* – also.

When your intelligence has passed out of the dense forest of delusion, you shall become indifferent to all that has been heard and all that is to be heard.

PURPORT: There are many good examples in the lives of the great devotees of the Lord of those who became indifferent to the rituals of the *Vedas* simply by devotional service to the Lord. When a person factually understands Kṛṣṇa and his relationship with Kṛṣṇa, he naturally becomes completely indifferent to the rituals of fruitive activities, even though an experienced *brāhmaṇa.* Śrī Mādhavendra Purī, a great devotee and *ācārya* in the line of the devotees, says:

sandhyā-vandana bhadram astu bhavato bhoḥ snāna tubhyaṁ namo
bho devāḥ pitaraś ca tarpaṇa-vidhau nāhaṁ kṣamaḥ kṣamyatām
yatra kvāpi niṣadya yādava-kulottaṁsasya kaṁsa-dviṣaḥ
smāraṁ smāram aghaṁ harāmi tad alaṁ manye kim anyena me

"O my prayers three times a day, all glory to you. O bathing, I offer my obeisances unto you. O demigods! O forefathers! Please excuse me for my inability to offer you my respects. Now wherever I sit, I can remember the great descendant of the Yadu dynasty [Kṛṣṇa], the enemy of Kaṁsa, and thereby I can free myself from all sinful bondage. I think this is sufficient for me."

The Vedic rites and rituals are imperative for neophytes: comprehending all kinds of prayer three times a day, taking a bath early in the morning, offering respects to the forefathers, etc. But when one is fully in Kṛṣṇa consciousness and is engaged in His transcendental loving service, one becomes indifferent to all these regulative principles because he has already attained perfection. If one can reach the platform of understanding by service to the Supreme Lord Kṛṣṇa, he has no longer to execute different types of penances and sacrifices as recommended in revealed scriptures. And, similarly, if one has not understood that the purpose of the *Vedas* is to reach Kṛṣṇa and simply engages in the rituals, etc., then he is uselessly wasting time in such engagements. Persons in Kṛṣṇa consciousness transcend the limit of *śabda-brahma,* or the range of the *Vedas* and *Upaniṣads.*

Text 53 श्रुतिविप्रतिपन्ना ते यदा स्थास्यति निश्चला ।
समाधावचला बुद्धिस्तदा योगमवाप्स्यसि ॥५३॥

śruti-vipratipannā te, yadā sthāsyati niścalā
samādhāv acalā buddhis, tadā yogam avāpsyasi

śruti – of Vedic revelation; *vipratipannā* – without being influenced by the fruitive results; *te* – your; *yadā* – when; *sthāsyati* – remains; *niścalā* –

unmoved; *samādhau* – in transcendental consciousness, or Kṛṣṇa consciousness; *acalā* – unflinching; *buddhiḥ* – intelligence; *tadā* – at that time; *yogam* – self-realization; *avāpsyasi* – you will achieve.

When your mind is no longer disturbed by the flowery language of the Vedas, and when it remains fixed in the trance of self-realization, then you will have attained the divine consciousness.

PURPORT: To say that one is in *samādhi* is to say that one has fully realized Kṛṣṇa consciousness; that is, one in full *samādhi* has realized Brahman, Paramātmā and Bhagavān. The highest perfection of self-realization is to understand that one is eternally the servitor of Kṛṣṇa and that one's only business is to discharge one's duties in Kṛṣṇa consciousness. A Kṛṣṇa conscious person, or unflinching devotee of the Lord, should not be disturbed by the flowery language of the *Vedas* nor be engaged in fruitive activities for promotion to the heavenly kingdom. In Kṛṣṇa consciousness, one comes directly into communion with Kṛṣṇa, and thus all directions from Kṛṣṇa may be understood in that transcendental state. One is sure to achieve results by such activities and attain conclusive knowledge. One has only to carry out the orders of Kṛṣṇa or His representative, the spiritual master.

Text 54 अर्जुन उवाच
स्थितप्रज्ञस्य का भाषा समाधिस्थस्य केशव ।
स्थितधीः किं प्रभाषेत किमासीत व्रजेत किम् ॥५४॥

arjuna uvāca
sthita-prajñasya kā bhāṣā, samādhi-sthasya keśava
sthita-dhīḥ kiṁ prabhāṣeta, kim āsīta vrajeta kim

arjunaḥ uvāca – Arjuna said; *sthita-prajñasya* – of one who is situated in fixed Kṛṣṇa consciousness; *kā* – what; *bhāṣā* – language; *samādhi-sthasya* – of one situated in trance; *keśava* – O Kṛṣṇa; *sthita-dhīḥ* – one fixed in Kṛṣṇa consciousness; *kim* – what; *prabhāṣeta* – speaks; *kim* – how; *āsīta* – does remain still; *vrajeta* – walks; *kim* – how.

Arjuna said: O Kṛṣṇa, what are the symptoms of one whose consciousness is thus merged in transcendence? How does he speak, and what is his language? How does he sit, and how does he walk?

PURPORT: As there are symptoms for each and every man, in terms of his particular situation, similarly one who is Kṛṣṇa conscious has his particular nature – talking, walking, thinking, feeling, etc. As a rich man has his symptoms by which he is known as a rich man, as a diseased man has his symptoms by which he is known as diseased, or as a learned man has his symptoms, so a man in transcendental consciousness of Kṛṣṇa has specific symptoms in various dealings. One can know his specific symptoms from the *Bhagavad-gītā.* Most important is how the man in Kṛṣṇa consciousness speaks; for speech is the most important quality of any man. It is said that a fool is undiscovered as long as he does not speak, and certainly a well-dressed fool cannot be identified unless he speaks, but as soon as he speaks, he reveals himself at once. The immediate symptom of a Kṛṣṇa conscious man is that he speaks only of Kṛṣṇa and of matters relating to Him. Other symptoms then automatically follow, as stated below.

Text 55 श्रीभगवानुवाच
प्रजहाति यदा कामान् सर्वान् पार्थ मनोगतान् ।
आत्मन्येवात्मना तुष्टः स्थितप्रज्ञस्तदोच्यते ॥५५॥

śrī-bhagavān uvāca
prajahāti yadā kāmān, sarvān pārtha mano-gatān
ātmany evātmanā tuṣṭaḥ, sthita-prajñas tadocyate

śrī-bhagavān uvāca – the Supreme Personality of Godhead said; *prajahāti* – gives up; *yadā* – when; *kāmān* – desires for sense gratification; *sarvān* – of all varieties; *pārtha* – O son of Pṛthā; *manaḥ-gatān* – of mental concoction; *ātmani* – in the pure state of the soul; *eva* – certainly; *ātmanā* – by the purified mind; *tuṣṭaḥ* – satisfied; *sthita-prajñaḥ* – transcendentally situated; *tadā* – at that time; *ucyate* – is said.

The Supreme Personality of Godhead said: O Pārtha, when a man gives up all varieties of desire for sense gratification, which arise from mental concoction, and when his mind, thus purified, finds satisfaction in the self alone, then he is said to be in pure transcendental consciousness.

PURPORT: The *Bhāgavatam* affirms that any person who is fully in Kṛṣṇa consciousness, or devotional service of the Lord, has all the good qualities of the great sages, whereas a person who is not so transcendentally situated has no good qualifications, because he is sure to be taking refuge in his own mental concoctions. Consequently, it is rightly said herein that one has to give up all kinds of sense desire manufactured by mental concoction. Artificially, such sense desires cannot be stopped. But if one is engaged in Kṛṣṇa consciousness, then, automatically, sense desires subside without extraneous efforts. Therefore, one has to engage himself in Kṛṣṇa consciousness without hesitation, for this devotional service will instantly help one onto the platform of transcendental consciousness. The highly developed soul always remains satisfied in himself by realizing himself as the eternal servitor of the Supreme Lord. Such a transcendentally situated person has no sense desires resulting from petty materialism; rather, he remains always happy in his natural position of eternally serving the Supreme Lord.

Text 56 दुःखेष्वनुद्विग्नमनाः सुखेषु विगतस्पृहः ।
वीतरागभयक्रोधः स्थितधीर्मुनिरुच्यते ॥५६॥

duḥkheṣv anudvigna-manāḥ, sukheṣu vigata-spṛhaḥ
vīta-rāga-bhaya-krodhaḥ, sthita-dhīr munir ucyate

duḥkheṣu – in the threefold miseries; *anudvigna-manāḥ* – without being agitated in mind; *sukheṣu* – in happiness; *vigata-spṛhaḥ* – without being interested; *vīta* – free from; *rāga* – attachment; *bhaya* – fear; *krodhaḥ* – and anger; *sthita-dhīḥ* – whose mind is steady; *muniḥ* – a sage; *ucyate* – is called.

One who is not disturbed in mind even amidst the threefold miseries or elated when there is happiness, and who is free from attachment, fear and anger, is called a sage of steady mind.

PURPORT: The word *muni* means one who can agitate his mind in various ways for mental speculation without coming to a factual conclusion. It is said that every *muni* has a different angle of vision, and unless a *muni* differs from other *munis,* he cannot be called a *muni* in the strict sense of the term. *Nāsāv ṛṣir yasya mataṁ na bhinnam* (*Mahābhārata, Vana-parva* 313.117). But a *sthita-dhīr muni,* as mentioned herein by the Lord, is different from an ordinary *muni.* The *sthita-dhīr muni* is always in Kṛṣṇa consciousness, for he has exhausted all his business of creative speculation. He is called *praśānta-niḥśeṣa-mano-rathāntara* (*Stotra-ratna* 43), or one who has surpassed the stage of mental speculations and has come to the conclusion that Lord Śrī Kṛṣṇa, or Vāsudeva, is everything (*vāsudevaḥ sarvam iti sa mahātmā su-durlabhaḥ*). He is called a *muni* fixed in mind. Such a fully Kṛṣṇa conscious person is not at all disturbed by the onslaughts of the threefold miseries, for he accepts all miseries as the mercy of the Lord, thinking himself only worthy of more trouble due to his past misdeeds; and he sees that his miseries, by the grace of the Lord, are minimized to the lowest. Similarly, when he is happy he gives credit to the Lord, thinking himself unworthy of the happiness; he realizes that it is due only to the Lord's grace that he is in such a comfortable condition and able to render better service to the Lord. And, for the service of the Lord, he is always daring and active and is not influenced by attachment or aversion. Attachment means accepting things for one's own sense gratification, and detachment is the absence of such sensual attachment. But one fixed in Kṛṣṇa consciousness has neither attachment nor detachment because his life is dedicated in the service of the Lord. Consequently he is not at all angry even when his attempts are unsuccessful. Success or no success, a Kṛṣṇa conscious person is always steady in his determination.

Text 57 यः सर्वत्रानभिस्नेहस्तत्तत्प्राप्य शुभाशुभम् ।
नाभिनन्दति न द्वेष्टि तस्य प्रज्ञा प्रतिष्ठिता ॥५७॥

yaḥ sarvatrānabhisnehas, tat tat prāpya śubhāśubham
nābhinandati na dveṣṭi, tasya prajñā pratiṣṭhitā

yaḥ – one who; *sarvatra* – everywhere; *anabhisnehaḥ* – without affection; *tat* – that; *tat* – that; *prāpya* – achieving; *śubha* – good; *aśubham* – evil; *na* – never; *abhinandati* – praises; *na* – never; *dveṣṭi* – envies; *tasya* – his; *prajñā* – perfect knowledge; *pratiṣṭhitā* – fixed.

In the material world, one who is unaffected by whatever good or evil he may obtain, neither praising it nor despising it, is firmly fixed in perfect knowledge.

PURPORT: There is always some upheaval in the material world which may be good or evil. One who is not agitated by such material upheavals, who is unaffected by good and evil, is to be understood to be fixed in Kṛṣṇa consciousness. As long as one is in the material world there is always the possibility of good and evil because this world is full of duality. But one who is fixed in Kṛṣṇa consciousness is not affected by good and evil, because he is simply concerned with Kṛṣṇa, who is all-good absolute. Such consciousness in Kṛṣṇa situates one in a perfect transcendental position called, technically, *samādhi.*

Text 58 यदा संहरते चायं कूर्मोऽङ्गानीव सर्वशः ।
इन्द्रियाणीन्द्रियार्थेभ्यस्तस्य प्रज्ञा प्रतिष्ठिता ॥५८॥

yadā saṁharate cāyaṁ, kūrmo 'ṅgānīva sarvaśaḥ
indriyāṇīndriyārthebhyas, tasya prajñā pratiṣṭhitā

yadā – when; *saṁharate* – winds up; *ca* – also; *ayam* – he; *kūrmaḥ* – tortoise; *aṅgāni* – limbs; *iva* – like; *sarvaśaḥ* – altogether; *indriyāṇi* – senses; *indriya-arthebhyaḥ* – from the sense objects; *tasya* – his; *prajñā* – consciousness; *pratiṣṭhitā* – fixed.

One who is able to withdraw his senses from sense objects, as the tortoise draws its limbs within the shell, is firmly fixed in perfect consciousness.

PURPORT: The test of a *yogī,* devotee, or self-realized soul is that he is able to control the senses according to his plan. Most people, however, are servants of the senses and are thus directed by the dictation of the senses. That is the answer to the question as to how the *yogī* is situated. The senses are compared to venomous serpents. They want to act very loosely and without restriction. The *yogī,* or the devotee, must be very strong to control the serpents – like a snake charmer. He never allows them to act independently. There are many injunctions in the revealed scriptures; some of them are do-not's, and some of them are do's. Unless one is able to follow the do's and the do-not's, restricting oneself from sense enjoyment, it is not possible to be firmly fixed in Kṛṣṇa consciousness. The best example, set herein, is the tortoise. The tortoise can at any moment wind up its senses and exhibit them again at any time for particular purposes. Similarly, the senses of the Kṛṣṇa conscious persons are used only for some particular purpose in the service of the Lord and are withdrawn otherwise. Arjuna is being taught here to use his senses for the service of the Lord, instead of for his own satisfaction. Keeping the senses always in the service of the Lord is the example set by the analogy of the tortoise, who keeps the senses within.

Text 59 विषया विनिवर्तन्ते निराहारस्य देहिनः ।
रसवर्जं रसोऽप्यस्य परं दृष्ट्वा निवर्तते ॥५९॥

viṣayā vinivartante, nirāhārasya dehinaḥ
rasa-varjaṁ raso 'py asya, paraṁ dṛṣṭvā nivartate

viṣayāḥ – objects for sense enjoyment; *vinivartante* – are practiced to be refrained from; *nirāhārasya* – by negative restrictions; *dehinaḥ* – for the embodied; *rasa-varjam* – giving up the taste; *rasaḥ* – sense of enjoyment; *api* – although there is; *asya* – his; *param* – far superior things; *dṛṣṭvā* – by experiencing; *nivartate* – he ceases from.

Though the embodied soul may be restricted from sense enjoyment, the taste for sense objects remains. But, ceasing such engagements by experiencing a higher taste, he is fixed in consciousness.

PURPORT: Unless one is transcendentally situated, it is not possible to cease from sense enjoyment. The process of restriction from sense enjoyment by rules and regulations is something like restricting a diseased person from certain types of eatables. The patient, however, neither likes such restrictions nor loses his taste for eatables. Similarly, sense restriction by some spiritual process like *aṣṭāṅga-yoga,* in the matter of *yama, niyama, āsana, prāṇāyāma, pratyāhāra, dhāraṇā, dhyāna,* etc., is recommended for less intelligent persons who have no better knowledge. But one who has tasted the beauty of the Supreme Lord Kṛṣṇa, in the course of his advancement in Kṛṣṇa consciousness, no longer has a taste for dead, material things. Therefore, restrictions are there for the less intelligent neophytes in the spiritual advancement of life, but such restrictions are only good until one actually has a taste for Kṛṣṇa consciousness. When one is actually Kṛṣṇa conscious, he automatically loses his taste for pale things.

Text 60 यततो ह्यपि कौन्तेय पुरुषस्य विपश्चितः ।
इन्द्रियाणि प्रमाथीनि हरन्ति प्रसभं मनः ॥६०॥

yatato hy api kaunteya, puruṣasya vipaścitaḥ
indriyāṇi pramāthīni, haranti prasabhaṁ manaḥ

yatataḥ – while endeavoring; *hi* – certainly; *api* – in spite of; *kaunteya* – O son of Kuntī; *puruṣasya* – of a man; *vipaścitaḥ* – full of discriminating knowledge; *indriyāṇi* – the senses; *pramāthīni* – agitating; *haranti* – throw; *prasabham* – by force; *manaḥ* – the mind.

The senses are so strong and impetuous, O Arjuna, that they forcibly carry away the mind even of a man of discrimination who is endeavoring to control them.

PURPORT: There are many learned sages, philosophers and transcendentalists who try to conquer the senses, but in spite of their endeavors, even the greatest of them sometimes fall victim to material sense enjoyment due to the agitated mind. Even Viśvāmitra, a great sage and perfect *yogī,* was misled by Menakā into sex enjoyment, although the *yogī* was endeavoring for sense control with severe types of penance and *yoga* practice. And, of course, there are so many similar instances in the history of the world. Therefore, it is very difficult to control the mind and senses without being fully Kṛṣṇa conscious. Without engaging the mind in Kṛṣṇa, one cannot cease such material engagements. A practical example is given by Śrī Yāmunācārya, a great saint and devotee, who says:

yad-avadhi mama cetaḥ kṛṣṇa-pādāravinde
nava-nava-rasa-dhāmany udyataṁ rantum āsīt
tad-avadhi bata nārī-saṅgame smaryamāne
bhavati mukha-vikāraḥ suṣṭhu niṣṭhīvanaṁ ca

"Since my mind has been engaged in the service of the lotus feet of Lord Kṛṣṇa, and I have been enjoying an ever new transcendental humor, whenever I think of sex life with a woman, my face at once turns from it, and I spit at the thought."

Kṛṣṇa consciousness is such a transcendentally nice thing that automatically material enjoyment becomes distasteful. It is as if a hungry man had satisfied his hunger by a sufficient quantity of nutritious eatables. Mahārāja Ambarīṣa also conquered a great *yogī,* Durvāsā Muni, simply because his mind was engaged in Kṛṣṇa consciousness (*sa vai manaḥ kṛṣṇa-padāravindayor vacāṁsi vaikuṇṭha-guṇānuvarṇane*).

Text 61 **तानि सर्वाणि संयम्य युक्त आसीत मत्परः ।**
वशे हि यस्येन्द्रियाणि तस्य प्रज्ञा प्रतिष्ठिता ॥६१॥

tāni sarvāṇi saṁyamya, yukta āsīta mat-paraḥ
vaśe hi yasyendriyāṇi, tasya prajñā pratiṣṭhitā

tāni – those senses; *sarvāṇi* – all; *saṁyamya* – keeping under control; *yuktaḥ* – engaged; *āsīta* – should be situated; *mat-paraḥ* – in relationship with Me; *vaśe* – in full subjugation; *hi* – certainly; *yasya* – one whose; *indriyāṇi* – senses; *tasya* – his; *prajñā* – consciousness; *pratiṣṭhitā* – fixed.

One who restrains his senses, keeping them under full control, and fixes his consciousness upon Me, is known as a man of steady intelligence.

PURPORT: That the highest conception of *yoga* perfection is Kṛṣṇa consciousness is clearly explained in this verse. And unless one is Kṛṣṇa conscious it is not at all possible to control the senses. As cited above, the great sage Durvāsā Muni picked a quarrel with Mahārāja Ambarīṣa, and Durvāsā Muni unnecessarily became angry out of pride and therefore could not check his senses. On the other hand, the king, although not as powerful a *yogī* as the sage, but a devotee of the Lord, silently tolerated all the sage's injustices and thereby emerged victorious. The king was able to control his senses because of the following qualifications, as mentioned in the *Śrīmad-Bhāgavatam* (9.4.18–20):

sa vai manaḥ kṛṣṇa-padāravindayor
vacāṁsi vaikuṇṭha-guṇānuvarṇane
karau harer mandira-mārjanādiṣu
śrutiṁ cakārācyuta-sat-kathodaye

mukunda-liṅgālaya-darśane dṛśau
tad-bhṛtya-gātra-sparśe 'ṅga-saṅgamam
ghrāṇaṁ ca tat-pāda-saroja-saurabhe
śrīmat-tulasyā rasanāṁ tad-arpite

pādau hareḥ kṣetra-padānusarpaṇe
śiro hṛṣīkeśa-padābhivandane
kāmaṁ ca dāsye na tu kāma-kāmyayā
yathottama-śloka-janāśrayā ratiḥ

"King Ambarīṣa fixed his mind on the lotus feet of Lord Kṛṣṇa, engaged his words in describing the abode of the Lord, his hands in cleansing the temple of the Lord, his ears in hearing the pastimes of the Lord, his eyes in seeing the form of the Lord, his body in touching the body of the devotee, his nostrils in smelling the flavor of the flowers offered to the lotus feet of the Lord, his tongue in tasting the *tulasī* leaves offered to Him, his legs in traveling to the holy place where His temple is situated, his head in offering obeisances unto the Lord, and his desires in fulfilling the desires of the Lord... and all these qualifications made him fit to become a *mat-para* devotee of the Lord."

The word *mat-para* is most significant in this connection. How one can become *mat-para* is described in the life of Mahārāja Ambarīṣa. Śrīla Baladeva Vidyābhūṣaṇa, a great scholar and *ācārya* in the line of the *mat-para,* remarks, *mad-bhakti-prabhāvena sarvendriya-vijaya-pūrvikā svātma-dṛṣṭiḥ su-labheti bhāvaḥ.* "The senses can be completely controlled only by the strength of devotional service to Kṛṣṇa." Also, the example of fire is sometimes given: "As a blazing fire burns everything within a room, Lord Viṣṇu, situated in the heart of the *yogī,* burns up all kinds of impurities." The *Yoga-sūtra* also prescribes meditation on

Viṣṇu, and not meditation on the void. The so-called *yogīs* who meditate on something other than the Viṣṇu form simply waste their time in a vain search after some phantasmagoria. We have to be Kṛṣṇa conscious – devoted to the Personality of Godhead. This is the aim of the real *yoga.*

Text 62 ध्यायतो विषयान् पुंसः सङ्गस्तेषूपजायते ।
सङ्गात्सञ्जायते कामः कामात्क्रोधोऽभिजायते ॥६२॥

dhyāyato viṣayān puṁsaḥ, saṅgas teṣūpajāyate
saṅgāt sañjāyate kāmaḥ, kāmāt krodho 'bhijāyate

dhyāyataḥ – while contemplating; *viṣayān* – sense objects; *puṁsaḥ* – of a person; *saṅgaḥ* – attachment; *teṣu* – in the sense objects; *upajāyate* – develops; *saṅgāt* – from attachment; *sañjāyate* – develops; *kāmaḥ* – desire; *kāmāt* – from desire; *krodhaḥ* – anger; *abhijāyate* – becomes manifest.

While contemplating the objects of the senses, a person develops attachment for them, and from such attachment lust develops, and from lust anger arises.

PURPORT: One who is not Kṛṣṇa conscious is subjected to material desires while contemplating the objects of the senses. The senses require real engagements, and if they are not engaged in the transcendental loving service of the Lord, they will certainly seek engagement in the service of materialism. In the material world everyone, including Lord Śiva and Lord Brahmā – to say nothing of other demigods in the heavenly planets – is subjected to the influence of sense objects, and the only method to get out of this puzzle of material existence is to become Kṛṣṇa conscious. Lord Śiva was deep in meditation, but when Pārvatī agitated him for sense pleasure, he agreed to the proposal, and as a result Kārtikeya was born. When Haridāsa Ṭhākura was a young devotee of the Lord, he was similarly allured by the incarnation of Māyā-devī, but Haridāsa easily passed the test because of his unalloyed devotion to Lord Kṛṣṇa. As illustrated in the above-mentioned verse of Śrī Yāmunācārya, a sincere devotee of the Lord shuns all material sense enjoyment due to his higher taste for spiritual enjoyment in the association of the Lord. That is the secret of success. One who is not, therefore, in Kṛṣṇa consciousness, however powerful he may be in controlling the senses by artificial repression, is sure ultimately to fail, for the slightest thought of sense pleasure will agitate him to gratify his desires.

Text 63 क्रोधाद्भवति सम्मोहः सम्मोहात्स्मृतिविभ्रमः ।
स्मृतिभ्रंशाद् बुद्धिनाशो बुद्धिनाशात्प्रणश्यति ॥६३॥

krodhād bhavati sammohaḥ, sammohāt smṛti-vibhramaḥ
smṛti-bhraṁśād buddhi-nāśo, buddhi-nāśāt praṇaśyati

krodhāt – from anger; *bhavati* – takes place; *sammohaḥ* – perfect illusion; *sammohāt* – from illusion; *smṛti* – of memory; *vibhramaḥ* – bewilderment; *smṛti-bhraṁśāt* – after bewilderment of memory; *buddhi-nāśaḥ* – loss of intelligence; *buddhi-nāśāt* – and from loss of intelligence; *praṇaśyati* – one falls down.

From anger, complete delusion arises, and from delusion bewilderment of memory. When memory is bewildered, intelligence is lost, and when intelligence is lost one falls down again into the material pool.

PURPORT: Śrīla Rūpa Gosvāmī has given us this direction:

prāpañcikatayā buddhyā, hari-sambandhi-vastunaḥ
mumukṣubhiḥ parityāgo, vairāgyaṁ phalgu kathyate
(*Bhakti-rasāmṛta-sindhu* 1.2.258)

By development of Kṛṣṇa consciousness one can know that everything has its use in the service of the Lord. Those who are without knowledge of Kṛṣṇa consciousness artificially try to avoid material objects, and as a result, although they desire liberation from material bondage, they do not attain to the perfect stage of renunciation. Their so-called renunciation is called *phalgu,* or less important. On the other hand, a person in Kṛṣṇa consciousness knows how to use everything in the service of the Lord; therefore he does not become a victim of material consciousness. For example, for an impersonalist, the Lord, or the Absolute, being impersonal, cannot eat. Whereas an impersonalist tries to avoid good eatables, a devotee knows that Kṛṣṇa is the supreme enjoyer and that He eats all that is offered to Him in devotion. So, after offering good eatables to the Lord, the devotee takes the remnants, called *prasādam.* Thus everything becomes spiritualized, and there is no danger of a downfall. The devotee takes *prasādam* in Kṛṣṇa consciousness, whereas the nondevotee rejects it as material. The impersonalist, therefore, cannot enjoy life, due to his artificial renunciation; and for this reason, a slight agitation of the mind pulls him down again into the pool of material existence. It is said that such a soul, even though rising up to the point of liberation, falls down again due to his not having support in devotional service.

Text 64 रागद्वेषविमुक्तैस्तु विषयानिन्द्रियैश्चरन् ।
आत्मवश्यैर्विधेयात्मा प्रसादमधिगच्छति ॥६४॥

rāga-dveṣa-vimuktais tu, viṣayān indriyaiś caran
ātma-vaśyair vidheyātmā, prasādam adhigacchati

rāga – attachment; *dveṣa* – and detachment; *vimuktaiḥ* – by one who has become free from; *tu* – but; *viṣayān* – sense objects; *indriyaiḥ* – by the senses; *caran* – acting upon; *ātma-vaśyaiḥ* – under one's control; *vidheya-ātmā* – one who follows regulated freedom; *prasādam* – the mercy of the Lord; *adhigacchati* – attains.

But a person free from all attachment and aversion and able to control his senses through regulative principles of freedom can obtain the complete mercy of the Lord.

PURPORT: It is already explained that one may externally control the senses by some artificial process, but unless the senses are engaged in the transcendental service of the Lord, there is every chance of a fall. Although the person in full Kṛṣṇa consciousness may apparently be on the sensual plane, because of his being Kṛṣṇa conscious he has no attachment to sensual activities. The Kṛṣṇa conscious person is concerned only with the satisfaction of Kṛṣṇa, and nothing else. Therefore he is transcendental to all attachment and detachment. If Kṛṣṇa wants, the devotee can do anything which is ordinarily undesirable; and if Kṛṣṇa does not want, he shall not do that which he would have ordinarily done for his own satisfaction. Therefore to act or not to act is within his control because he acts only under the direction of Kṛṣṇa. This consciousness is the causeless mercy of the Lord, which the devotee can achieve in spite of his being attached to the sensual platform.

Text 65 प्रसादे सर्वदुःखानां हानिरस्योपजायते ।
प्रसन्नचेतसो ह्याशु बुद्धिः पर्यवतिष्ठते ॥६५॥

prasāde sarva-duḥkhānāṁ, hānir asyopajāyate
prasanna-cetaso hy āśu, buddhiḥ paryavatiṣṭhate

prasāde – on achievement of the causeless mercy of the Lord; *sarva* – of all; *duḥkhānām* – material miseries; *hāniḥ* – destruction; *asya* – his; *upajāyate* – takes place; *prasanna-cetasaḥ* – of the happy-minded; *hi* – certainly; *āśu* – very soon; *buddhiḥ* – intelligence; *pari* – sufficiently; *avatiṣṭhate* – becomes established.

For one thus satisfied [in Kṛṣṇa consciousness], the threefold miseries of material existence exist no longer; in such satisfied consciousness, one's intelligence is soon well established.

Text 66 नास्ति बुद्धिरयुक्तस्य न चायुक्तस्य भावना ।
न चाभावयतः शान्तिरशान्तस्य कुतः सुखम् ॥६६॥

nāsti buddhir ayuktasya, na cāyuktasya bhāvanā
na cābhāvayataḥ śāntir, aśāntasya kutaḥ sukham

na asti – there cannot be; *buddhiḥ* – transcendental intelligence; *ayuktasya* – of one who is not connected (with Kṛṣṇa consciousness); *na* – not; *ca* – and; *ayuktasya* – of one devoid of Kṛṣṇa consciousness; *bhāvanā* – fixed mind (in happiness); *na* – not; *ca* – and; *abhāvayataḥ* – of one who is not fixed; *śāntiḥ* – peace; *aśāntasya* – of the unpeaceful; *kutaḥ* – where is; *sukham* – happiness.

One who is not connected with the Supreme [in Kṛṣṇa consciousness] can have neither transcendental intelligence nor a steady mind, without which there is no possibility of peace. And how can there be any happiness without peace?

PURPORT: Unless one is in Kṛṣṇa consciousness, there is no possibility of peace. So it is confirmed in the Fifth Chapter (5.29) that when one understands that Kṛṣṇa is the only enjoyer of all the good results of sacrifice and penance, that He is the proprietor of all universal manifestations, and that He is the real friend of all living entities, then only can one have real peace. Therefore, if one is not in Kṛṣṇa consciousness, there cannot be a final goal for the mind. Disturbance is due to want of an ultimate goal, and when one is certain that Kṛṣṇa is the enjoyer, proprietor and friend of everyone and everything, then one can, with a steady mind, bring about peace. Therefore, one who is engaged without a relationship with Kṛṣṇa is certainly always in distress and is without peace, however much he may make a show of peace and spiritual advancement in life. Kṛṣṇa consciousness is a self-manifested peaceful condition which can be achieved only in relationship with Kṛṣṇa.

Text 67 इन्द्रियाणां हि चरतां यन्मनोऽनुविधीयते ।
तदस्य हरति प्रज्ञां वायुर्नावमिवाम्भसि ॥६७॥

indriyāṇāṁ hi caratāṁ, yan mano 'nuvidhīyate
tad asya harati prajñāṁ, vāyur nāvam ivāmbhasi

indriyāṇām – of the senses; *hi* – certainly; *caratām* – while roaming; *yat* – with which; *manaḥ* – the mind; *anuvidhīyate* – becomes constantly engaged; *tat* – that; *asya* – his; *harati* – takes away; *prajñām* – intelligence; *vāyuḥ* – wind; *nāvam* – a boat; *iva* – like; *ambhasi* – on the water.

As a strong wind sweeps away a boat on the water, even one of the roaming senses on which the mind focuses can carry away a man's intelligence.

PURPORT: Unless all of the senses are engaged in the service of the Lord, even one of them engaged in sense gratification can deviate the devotee from the path of transcendental advancement. As mentioned in the life of Mahārāja Ambarīṣa, all of the senses must be engaged in Kṛṣṇa consciousness, for that is the correct technique for controlling the mind.

Text 68 तस्माद्यस्य महाबाहो निगृहीतानि सर्वशः ।
इन्द्रियाणीन्द्रियार्थेभ्यस्तस्य प्रज्ञा प्रतिष्ठिता ॥६८॥

tasmād yasya mahā-bāho, nigṛhītāni sarvaśaḥ
indriyāṇīndriyārthebhyas, tasya prajñā pratiṣṭhitā

tasmāt – therefore; *yasya* – whose; *mahā-bāho* – O mighty-armed one; *nigṛhītāni* – so curbed down; *sarvaśaḥ* – all around; *indriyāṇi* – the senses; *indriya-arthebhyaḥ* – from sense objects; *tasya* – his; *prajñā* – intelligence; *pratiṣṭhitā* – fixed.

Therefore, O mighty-armed, one whose senses are restrained from their objects is certainly of steady intelligence.

PURPORT: One can curb the forces of sense gratification only by means of Kṛṣṇa consciousness, or engaging all the senses in the transcendental loving service of the Lord. As enemies are curbed by superior force, the senses can similarly be curbed, not by any human endeavor, but only by keeping them engaged in the service of the Lord. One who has understood this – that only by Kṛṣṇa consciousness is one really established in intelligence and that one should practice this art under the guidance of a bona fide spiritual master – is called a *sādhaka,* or a suitable candidate for liberation.

Text 69 या निशा सर्वभूतानां तस्यां जागर्ति संयमी ।
यस्यां जाग्रति भूतानि सा निशा पश्यतो मुनेः ॥६९॥

yā niśā sarva-bhūtānāṁ, tasyāṁ jāgarti saṁyamī
yasyāṁ jāgrati bhūtāni, sā niśā paśyato muneḥ

yā – what; *niśā* – is night; *sarva* – all; *bhūtānām* – of living entities; *tasyām* – in that; *jāgarti* – is wakeful; *saṁyamī* – the self-controlled; *yasyām* – in which; *jāgrati* – are awake; *bhūtāni* – all beings; *sā* – that is; *niśā* – night; *paśyataḥ* – for the introspective; *muneḥ* – sage.

What is night for all beings is the time of awakening for the self-controlled; and the time of awakening for all beings is night for the introspective sage.

PURPORT: There are two classes of intelligent men. One is intelligent in material activities for sense gratification, and the other is introspective and awake to the cultivation of self-realization. Activities of the introspective sage, or thoughtful man, are night for persons materially absorbed. Materialistic persons remain asleep in such a night due to their ignorance of self-realization. The introspective sage remains alert in the "night" of the materialistic men. The sage feels transcendental pleasure in the gradual advancement of spiritual culture, whereas the man in materialistic activities, being asleep to self-realization, dreams of varieties of sense pleasure, feeling sometimes happy and sometimes distressed in his sleeping condition. The introspective man is always indifferent to materialistic happiness and distress. He goes on with his self-realization activities undisturbed by material reactions.

Text 70 आपूर्यमाणमचलप्रतिष्ठं समुद्रमापः प्रविशन्ति यद्वत् ।
तद्वत्कामा यं प्रविशन्ति सर्वे स शान्तिमाप्नोति न कामकामी ॥७०॥

āpūryamāṇam acala-pratiṣṭhaṁ
samudram āpaḥ praviśanti yadvat
tadvat kāmā yaṁ praviśanti sarve
sa śāntim āpnoti na kāma-kāmī

āpūryamāṇam – always being filled; *acala-pratiṣṭham* – steadily situated; *samudram* – the ocean; *āpaḥ* – waters; *praviśanti* – enter; *yadvat* – as; *tadvat* – so; *kāmāḥ* – desires; *yam* – unto whom; *praviśanti* – enter;

sarve – all; *saḥ* – that person; *śāntim* – peace; *āpnoti* – achieves; *na* – not; *kāma-kāmī* – one who desires to fulfill desires.

A person who is not disturbed by the incessant flow of desires – that enter like rivers into the ocean, which is ever being filled but is always still – can alone achieve peace, and not the man who strives to satisfy such desires.

PURPORT: Although the vast ocean is always filled with water, it is always, especially during the rainy season, being filled with much more water. But the ocean remains the same – steady; it is not agitated, nor does it cross beyond the limit of its brink. That is also true of a person fixed in Kṛṣṇa consciousness. As long as one has the material body, the demands of the body for sense gratification will continue. The devotee, however, is not disturbed by such desires, because of his fullness. A Kṛṣṇa conscious man is not in need of anything, because the Lord fulfills all his material necessities. Therefore he is like the ocean – always full in himself. Desires may come to him like the waters of the rivers that flow into the ocean, but he is steady in his activities, and he is not even slightly disturbed by desires for sense gratification. That is the proof of a Kṛṣṇa conscious man – one who has lost all inclinations for material sense gratification, although the desires are present. Because he remains satisfied in the transcendental loving service of the Lord, he can remain steady, like the ocean, and therefore enjoy full peace. Others, however, who want to fulfill desires even up to the limit of liberation, what to speak of material success, never attain peace. The fruitive workers, the salvationists, and also the *yogīs* who are after mystic powers are all unhappy because of unfulfilled desires. But the person in Kṛṣṇa consciousness is happy in the service of the Lord, and he has no desires to be fulfilled. In fact, he does not even desire liberation from the so-called material bondage. The devotees of Kṛṣṇa have no material desires, and therefore they are in perfect peace.

Text 71 विहाय कामान् यः सर्वान् पुमांश्चरति निःस्पृहः ।
निर्ममो निरहङ्कारः स शान्तिमधिगच्छति ॥७१॥

vihāya kāmān yaḥ sarvān, pumāṁś carati niḥspṛhaḥ
nirmamo nirahaṅkāraḥ, sa śāntim adhigacchati

vihāya – giving up; *kāmān* – material desires for sense gratification; *yaḥ* – who; *sarvān* – all; *pumān* – a person; *carati* – lives; *niḥspṛhaḥ* – desireless;

nirmamaḥ – without a sense of proprietorship; *nirahaṅkāraḥ* – without false ego; *saḥ* – he; *śāntim* – perfect peace; *adhigacchati* – attains.

A person who has given up all desires for sense gratification, who lives free from desires, who has given up all sense of proprietorship and is devoid of false ego – he alone can attain real peace.

PURPORT: To become desireless means not to desire anything for sense gratification. In other words, desire for becoming Kṛṣṇa conscious is actually desirelessness. To understand one's actual position as the eternal servitor of Kṛṣṇa, without falsely claiming this material body to be oneself and without falsely claiming proprietorship over anything in the world, is the perfect stage of Kṛṣṇa consciousness. One who is situated in this perfect stage knows that because Kṛṣṇa is the proprietor of everything, everything must be used for the satisfaction of Kṛṣṇa. Arjuna did not want to fight for his own sense satisfaction, but when he became fully Kṛṣṇa conscious he fought because Kṛṣṇa wanted him to fight. For himself there was no desire to fight, but for Kṛṣṇa the same Arjuna fought to his best ability. Real desirelessness is desire for the satisfaction of Kṛṣṇa, not an artificial attempt to abolish desires. The living entity cannot be desireless or senseless, but he does have to change the quality of the desires. A materially desireless person certainly knows that everything belongs to Kṛṣṇa (*īśāvāsyam idaṁ sarvam*), and therefore he does not falsely claim proprietorship over anything. This transcendental knowledge is based on self-realization – namely, knowing perfectly well that every living entity is an eternal part and parcel of Kṛṣṇa in spiritual identity, and that the eternal position of the living entity is therefore never on the level of Kṛṣṇa or greater than Him. This understanding of Kṛṣṇa consciousness is the basic principle of real peace.

Text 72 एषा ब्राह्मी स्थितिः पार्थ नैनां प्राप्य विमुह्यति ।
स्थित्वास्यामन्तकालेऽपि ब्रह्मनिर्वाणमृच्छति ॥७२॥

eṣā brāhmī sthitiḥ pārtha, naināṁ prāpya vimuhyati
sthitvāsyām anta-kāle 'pi, brahma-nirvāṇam ṛcchati

eṣā – this; *brāhmī* – spiritual; *sthitiḥ* – situation; *pārtha* – O son of Pṛthā; *na* – never; *enām* – this; *prāpya* – achieving; *vimuhyati* – one is bewildered; *sthitvā* – being situated; *asyām* – in this; *anta-kāle* – at the end of life; *api* – also; *brahma-nirvāṇam* – the spiritual kingdom of God; *ṛcchati* – one attains.

That is the way of the spiritual and godly life, after attaining which a man is not bewildered. If one is thus situated even at the hour of death, one can enter into the kingdom of God.

PURPORT: One can attain Kṛṣṇa consciousness or divine life at once, within a second – or one may not attain such a state of life even after millions of births. It is only a matter of understanding and accepting the fact. Khaṭvāṅga Mahārāja attained this state of life just a few minutes before his death, by surrendering unto Kṛṣṇa. *Nirvāṇa* means ending the process of materialistic life. According to Buddhist philosophy, there is only void after the completion of this material life, but *Bhagavad-gītā* teaches differently. Actual life begins after the completion of this material life. For the gross materialist it is sufficient to know that one has to end this materialistic way of life, but for persons who are spiritually advanced, there is another life after this materialistic life. Before ending this life, if one fortunately becomes Kṛṣṇa conscious, he at once attains the stage of *brahma-nirvāṇa.* There is no difference between the kingdom of God and the devotional service of the Lord. Since both of them are on the absolute plane, to be engaged in the transcendental loving service of the Lord is to have attained the spiritual kingdom. In the material world there are activities of sense gratification, whereas in the spiritual world there are activities of Kṛṣṇa consciousness. Attainment of Kṛṣṇa consciousness even during this life is immediate attainment of Brahman, and one who is situated in Kṛṣṇa consciousness has certainly already entered into the kingdom of God.

Brahman is just the opposite of matter. Therefore *brāhmī sthiti* means "not on the platform of material activities." Devotional service of the Lord is accepted in the *Bhagavad-gītā* as the liberated stage (*sa guṇān samatītyaitān brahma-bhūyāya kalpate*). Therefore, *brāhmī sthiti* is liberation from material bondage.

Śrīla Bhaktivinoda Ṭhākura has summarized this Second Chapter of the *Bhagavad-gītā* as being the contents for the whole text. In the *Bhagavad-gītā,* the subject matters are *karma-yoga, jñāna-yoga,* and *bhakti-yoga*. In the Second Chapter *karma-yoga* and *jñāna-yoga* have been clearly discussed, and a glimpse of *bhakti-yoga* has also been given, as the contents for the complete text.

Thus end the Bhaktivedanta Purports to the Second Chapter of the Śrīmad Bhagavad-gītā *in the matter of its Contents.*

CHAPTER THREE

Karma-yoga

Text 1 अर्जुन उवाच
ज्यायसी चेत्कर्मणस्ते मता बुद्धिर्जनार्दन ।
तत्किं कर्मणि घोरे मां नियोजयसि केशव ॥ १ ॥

arjuna uvāca
jyāyasī cet karmaṇas te, matā buddhir janārdana
tat kiṁ karmaṇi ghore māṁ, niyojayasi keśava

arjunaḥ uvāca – Arjuna said; *jyāyasī* – better; *cet* – if; *karmaṇaḥ* – than fruitive action; *te* – by You; *matā* – is considered; *buddhiḥ* – intelligence; *janārdana* – O Kṛṣṇa; *tat* – therefore; *kim* – why; *karmaṇi* – in action; *ghore* – ghastly; *mām* – me; *niyojayasi* – You are engaging; *keśava* – O Kṛṣṇa.

Arjuna said: O Janārdana, O Keśava, why do You want to engage me in this ghastly warfare, if You think that intelligence is better than fruitive work?

PURPORT: The Supreme Personality of Godhead Śrī Kṛṣṇa has very elaborately described the constitution of the soul in the previous chapter, with a view to delivering His intimate friend Arjuna from the ocean of material grief. And the path of realization has been recommended: *buddhi-yoga,* or Kṛṣṇa consciousness. Sometimes Kṛṣṇa consciousness is misunderstood to be inertia, and one with such a misunderstanding often withdraws to a secluded place to become fully Kṛṣṇa conscious by chanting the holy name of Lord Kṛṣṇa. But without being trained in the philosophy of Kṛṣṇa consciousness, it is not advisable to chant the holy name of Kṛṣṇa in a secluded place, where one may acquire only cheap adoration from the innocent public. Arjuna also thought of Kṛṣṇa consciousness or *buddhi-yoga,* or intelligence in spiritual advancement of knowledge, as something like retirement from active life and the practice of penance and austerity at a secluded place. In other words, he wanted to skillfully avoid the fighting by using Kṛṣṇa consciousness as an excuse. But as a sincere student, he placed the matter before his master and questioned Kṛṣṇa as to his best course of action. In answer, Lord Kṛṣṇa elaborately explained *karma-yoga,* or work in Kṛṣṇa consciousness, in this Third Chapter.

Text 2 व्यामिश्रेणेव वाक्येन बुद्धिं मोहयसीव मे ।
तदेकं वद निश्चित्य येन श्रेयोऽहमाप्नुयाम् ॥ २ ॥

vyāmiśreṇeva vākyena, buddhiṁ mohayasīva me
tad ekaṁ vada niścitya, yena śreyo 'ham āpnuyām

vyāmiśreṇa – by equivocal; *iva* – certainly; *vākyena* – words; *buddhim* – intelligence; *mohayasi* – You are bewildering; *iva* – certainly; *me* – my; *tat* – therefore; *ekam* – only one; *vada* – please tell; *niścitya* – ascertaining; *yena* – by which; *śreyaḥ* – real benefit; *aham* – I; *āpnuyām* – may have.

My intelligence is bewildered by Your equivocal instructions. Therefore, please tell me decisively which will be most beneficial for me.

PURPORT: In the previous chapter, as a prelude to the *Bhagavad-gītā,* many different paths were explained, such as *sāṅkhya-yoga, buddhi-yoga,* control of the senses by intelligence, work without fruitive desire, and the position of the neophyte. This was all presented unsystematically. A more organized outline of the path would be necessary for action and understanding. Arjuna, therefore, wanted to clear up these apparently confusing matters so that any common man could accept them without misinterpretation. Although Kṛṣṇa had no intention of confusing Arjuna by any jugglery of words, Arjuna could not follow the process of Kṛṣṇa consciousness – either by inertia or by active service. In other words, by his questions he is clearing the path of Kṛṣṇa consciousness for all students who seriously want to understand the mystery of the *Bhagavad-gītā.*

Text 3 श्रीभगवानुवाच
लोकेऽस्मिन्द्विविधा निष्ठा पुरा प्रोक्ता मयानघ ।
ज्ञानयोगेन साङ्ख्यानां कर्मयोगेन योगिनाम् ॥ ३ ॥

śrī-bhagavān uvāca
loke 'smin dvi-vidhā niṣṭhā, purā proktā mayānagha
jñāna-yogena sāṅkhyānāṁ, karma-yogena yoginām

śrī-bhagavān uvāca – the Supreme Personality of Godhead said; *loke* – in the world; *asmin* – this; *dvi-vidhā* – two kinds of; *niṣṭhā* – faith; *purā* – formerly; *proktā* – were said; *mayā* – by Me; *anagha* – O sinless one; *jñāna-yogena* – by the linking process of knowledge; *sāṅkhyānām* – of the empiric philosophers; *karma-yogena* – by the linking process of devotion; *yoginām* – of the devotees.

The Supreme Personality of Godhead said: O sinless Arjuna, I have already explained that there are two classes of men who try to realize the self. Some are inclined to understand it by empirical, philosophical speculation, and others by devotional service.

PURPORT: In the Second Chapter, verse 39, the Lord explained two kinds of procedures – namely *sāṅkhya-yoga* and *karma-yoga,* or *buddhi-yoga.* In this verse, the Lord explains the same more clearly. *Sāṅkhya-yoga,* or the analytical study of the nature of spirit and matter, is the subject matter for persons who are inclined to speculate and understand things by experimental knowledge and philosophy. The other class of men work in Kṛṣṇa consciousness, as it is explained in the 61st verse of the Second Chapter. The Lord has explained, also in the 39th verse, that by working by the principles of *buddhi-yoga,* or Kṛṣṇa consciousness, one can be relieved from the bonds of action; and, furthermore, there is no flaw in the process. The same principle is more clearly explained in the 61st verse – that this *buddhi-yoga* is to depend entirely on the Supreme (or more specifically, on Kṛṣṇa), and in this way all the senses can be brought under control very easily. Therefore, both the *yogas* are interdependent, as religion and philosophy. Religion without philosophy is sentiment, or sometimes fanaticism, while philosophy without religion is mental speculation. The ultimate goal is Kṛṣṇa, because the philosophers who are also sincerely searching after the Absolute Truth come in the end to Kṛṣṇa consciousness. This is also stated in the *Bhagavad-gītā*. The whole process is to understand the real position of the self in relation to the Superself. The indirect process is philosophical speculation, by which, gradually, one may come to the point of Kṛṣṇa consciousness; and the other process is directly connecting everything with Kṛṣṇa in Kṛṣṇa consciousness. Of these two, the path of Kṛṣṇa consciousness is better because it does not depend on purifying the senses by a philosophical process. Kṛṣṇa consciousness is itself the purifying process, and by the direct method of devotional service it is simultaneously easy and sublime.

Text 4 न कर्मणामनारम्भान्नैष्कर्म्यं पुरुषोऽश्नुते ।
न च सन्न्यसनादेव सिद्धिं समधिगच्छति ॥ ४ ॥

na karmaṇām anārambhān, naiṣkarmyaṁ puruṣo 'śnute
na ca sannyasanād eva, siddhiṁ samadhigacchati

na – not; *karmaṇām* – of prescribed duties; *anārambhāt* – by nonperformance; *naiṣkarmyam* – freedom from reaction; *puruṣaḥ* – a man; *aśnute* – achieves; *na* – nor; *ca* – also; *sannyasanāt* – by renunciation; *eva* – simply; *siddhim* – success; *samadhigacchati* – attains.

Not by merely abstaining from work can one achieve freedom from reaction, nor by renunciation alone can one attain perfection.

PURPORT: The renounced order of life can be accepted when one has been purified by the discharge of the prescribed form of duties which are laid down just to purify the hearts of materialistic men. Without purification, one cannot attain success by abruptly adopting the fourth order of life (*sannyāsa*). According to the empirical philosophers, simply by adopting *sannyāsa,* or retiring from fruitive activities, one at once becomes as good as Nārāyaṇa. But Lord Kṛṣṇa does not approve this principle. Without purification of heart, *sannyāsa* is simply a disturbance to the social order. On the other hand, if someone takes to the transcendental service of the Lord, even without discharging his prescribed duties, whatever he may be able to advance in the cause is accepted by the Lord (*buddhi-yoga*). *Sv-alpam apy asya dharmasya trāyate mahato bhayāt.* Even a slight performance of such a principle enables one to overcome great difficulties.

Text 5 न हि कश्चित्क्षणमपि जातु तिष्ठत्यकर्मकृत् ।
कार्यते ह्यवशः कर्म सर्वः प्रकृतिजैर्गुणैः ॥ ५ ॥

na hi kaścit kṣaṇam api, jātu tiṣṭhaty akarma-kṛt
kāryate hy avaśaḥ karma, sarvaḥ prakṛti-jair guṇaiḥ

na – nor; *hi* – certainly; *kaścit* – anyone; *kṣaṇam* – a moment; *api* – also; *jātu* – at any time; *tiṣṭhati* – remains; *akarma-kṛt* – without doing something; *kāryate* – is forced to do; *hi* – certainly; *avaśaḥ* – helplessly; *karma* – work; *sarvaḥ* – all; *prakṛti-jaiḥ* – born of the modes of material nature; *guṇaiḥ* – by the qualities.

Everyone is forced to act helplessly according to the qualities he has acquired from the modes of material nature; therefore no one can refrain from doing something, not even for a moment.

PURPORT: It is not a question of embodied life, but it is the nature of the soul to be always active. Without the presence of the spirit soul, the material body cannot move. The body is only a dead vehicle to be worked by the spirit soul, which is always active and cannot stop even for a moment. As such, the spirit soul has to be engaged in the good work of Kṛṣṇa consciousness, otherwise it will be engaged in occupations dictated by the illusory energy. In contact with material energy, the spirit soul acquires material modes, and to purify the soul from such affinities it is necessary to engage in the prescribed duties enjoined in the *śāstras.* But if the soul is engaged in his natural function of Kṛṣṇa consciousness, whatever he is able to do is good for him. The *Śrīmad-Bhāgavatam* (1.5.17) affirms this:

tyaktvā sva-dharmaṁ caraṇāmbujaṁ harer
bhajann apakvo 'tha patet tato yadi
yatra kva vābhadram abhūd amuṣya kiṁ
ko vārtha āpto 'bhajatāṁ sva-dharmataḥ

"If someone takes to Kṛṣṇa consciousness, even though he may not follow the prescribed duties in the *śāstras* or execute the devotional service properly, and even though he may fall down from the standard, there is no loss or evil for him. But if he carries out all the injunctions for purification in the *śāstras,* what does it avail him if he is not Kṛṣṇa conscious?" So the purificatory process is necessary for reaching this point of Kṛṣṇa consciousness. Therefore, *sannyāsa,* or any purificatory process, is to help reach the ultimate goal of becoming Kṛṣṇa conscious, without which everything is considered a failure.

Text 6 कर्मेन्द्रियाणि संयम्य य आस्ते मनसा स्मरन् ।
इन्द्रियार्थान् विमूढात्मा मिथ्याचारः स उच्यते ॥ ६ ॥

karmendriyāṇi saṁyamya, ya āste manasā smaran
indriyārthān vimūḍhātmā, mithyācāraḥ sa ucyate

karma-indriyāṇi – the five working sense organs; *saṁyamya* – controlling; *yaḥ* – anyone who; *āste* – remains; *manasā* – by the mind; *smaran* – thinking of; *indriya-arthān* – sense objects; *vimūḍha* – foolish; *ātmā* – soul; *mithyā-ācāraḥ* – pretender; *saḥ* – he; *ucyate* – is called.

One who restrains the senses of action but whose mind dwells on sense objects certainly deludes himself and is called a pretender.

PURPORT: There are many pretenders who refuse to work in Kṛṣṇa consciousness but make a show of meditation, while actually dwelling within the mind upon sense enjoyment. Such pretenders may also speak on dry philosophy in order to bluff sophisticated followers, but according to this verse these are the greatest cheaters. For sense enjoyment one can act in any capacity of the social order, but if one follows the rules and regulations of his particular status, he can make gradual progress in purifying his existence. But he who makes a show of being a *yogī* while actually searching for the objects of sense gratification must be called the greatest cheater, even though he sometimes speaks of philosophy. His knowledge has no value, because the effects of such a sinful man's knowledge are taken away by the illusory energy of the Lord. Such a pretender's mind is always impure, and therefore his show of yogic meditation has no value whatsoever.

Text 7 यस्त्विन्द्रियाणि मनसा नियम्यारभतेऽर्जुन ।
कर्मेन्द्रियैः कर्मयोगमसक्तः स विशिष्यते ॥ ७ ॥

yas tv indriyāṇi manasā, niyamyārabhate 'rjuna
karmendriyaiḥ karma-yogam, asaktaḥ sa viśiṣyate

yaḥ – one who; *tu* – but; *indriyāṇi* – the senses; *manasā* – by the mind; *niyamya* – regulating; *ārabhate* – begins; *arjuna* – O Arjuna; *karma-indriyaiḥ* – by the active sense organs; *karma-yogam* – devotion; *asaktaḥ* – without attachment; *saḥ* – he; *viśiṣyate* – is by far the better.

On the other hand, if a sincere person tries to control the active senses by the mind and begins karma-yoga [in Kṛṣṇa consciousness] without attachment, he is by far superior.

PURPORT: Instead of becoming a pseudo transcendentalist for the sake of wanton living and sense enjoyment, it is far better to remain in one's own business and execute the purpose of life, which is to get free from material bondage and enter into the kingdom of God. The prime *svārtha-gati,* or goal of self-interest, is to reach Viṣṇu. The whole institution of *varṇa* and *āśrama* is designed to help us reach this goal of life. A householder can also reach this destination by regulated service in Kṛṣṇa consciousness. For self-realization, one can live a controlled life, as prescribed in the *śāstras,* and continue carrying out his business without attachment, and in that way make progress. A sincere person who follows this method is far better situated than the false pretender who adopts show-bottle spiritualism to cheat the innocent public. A sincere sweeper in the street is far better than the charlatan meditator who meditates only for the sake of making a living.

Text 8 नियतं कुरु कर्म त्वं कर्म ज्यायो ह्यकर्मणः ।
शरीरयात्रापि च ते न प्रसिध्येदकर्मणः ॥ ८ ॥

niyataṁ kuru karma tvaṁ, karma jyāyo hy akarmaṇaḥ
śarīra-yātrāpi ca te, na prasidhyed akarmaṇaḥ

niyatam – prescribed; *kuru* – do; *karma* – duties; *tvam* – you; *karma* – work; *jyāyaḥ* – better; *hi* – certainly; *akarmaṇaḥ* – than no work; *śarīra* – bodily; *yātrā* – maintenance; *api* – even; *ca* – also; *te* – your; *na* – never; *prasidhyet* – is effected; *akarmaṇaḥ* – without work.

Perform your prescribed duty, for doing so is better than not working. One cannot even maintain one's physical body without work.

PURPORT: There are many pseudo meditators who misrepresent themselves as belonging to high parentage, and great professional men who falsely pose that they have sacrificed everything for the sake of advancement in spiritual life. Lord Kṛṣṇa did not want Arjuna to become a pretender. Rather, the Lord desired that Arjuna perform his prescribed duties as set forth for *kṣatriyas.* Arjuna was a householder and a military general, and therefore it was better for him to remain as such and perform his religious duties as prescribed for the householder *kṣatriya.*

Such activities gradually cleanse the heart of a mundane man and free him from material contamination. So-called renunciation for the purpose of maintenance is never approved by the Lord, nor by any religious scripture. After all, one has to maintain one's body and soul together by some work. Work should not be given up capriciously, without purification of materialistic propensities. Anyone who is in the material world is certainly possessed of the impure propensity for lording it over material nature, or, in other words, for sense gratification. Such polluted propensities have to be cleared. Without doing so, through prescribed duties, one should never attempt to become a so-called transcendentalist, renouncing work and living at the cost of others.

Text 9 यज्ञार्थात्कर्मणोऽन्यत्र लोकोऽयं कर्मबन्धनः ।
तदर्थं कर्म कौन्तेय मुक्तसङ्गः समाचर ॥ ९ ॥

yajñārthāt karmaṇo 'nyatra, loko 'yaṁ karma-bandhanaḥ
tad-arthaṁ karma kaunteya, mukta-saṅgaḥ samācara

yajña-arthāt – done only for the sake of Yajña, or Viṣṇu; *karmaṇaḥ* – than work; *anyatra* – otherwise; *lokaḥ* – world; *ayam* – this; *karma-bandhanaḥ* – bondage by work; *tat* – of Him; *artham* – for the sake; *karma* – work; *kaunteya* – O son of Kuntī; *mukta-saṅgaḥ* – liberated from association; *samācara* – do perfectly.

Work done as a sacrifice for Viṣṇu has to be performed; otherwise work causes bondage in this material world. Therefore, O son of Kuntī, perform your prescribed duties for His satisfaction, and in that way you will always remain free from bondage.

PURPORT: Since one has to work even for the simple maintenance of the body, the prescribed duties for a particular social position and quality are so made that that purpose can be fulfilled. *Yajña* means Lord Viṣṇu, or sacrificial performances. All sacrificial performances also are meant for the satisfaction of Lord Viṣṇu. The *Vedas* enjoin: *yajño vai viṣṇuḥ.* In other words, the same purpose is served whether one performs prescribed *yajñas* or directly serves Lord Viṣṇu. Kṛṣṇa consciousness is therefore performance of *yajña* as it is prescribed in this verse. The *varṇāśrama* institution also aims at satisfying Lord Viṣṇu. *Varṇāśram-ācāravatā puruṣeṇa paraḥ pumān/ viṣṇur ārādhyate* (*Viṣṇu Purāṇa* 3.8.8).

Therefore one has to work for the satisfaction of Viṣṇu. Any other work done in this material world will be a cause of bondage, for both good and evil work have their reactions, and any reaction binds the performer. Therefore, one has to work in Kṛṣṇa consciousness to satisfy Kṛṣṇa (or Viṣṇu); and while performing such activities one is in a liberated stage. This is the great art of doing work, and in the beginning this process requires very expert guidance. One should therefore act very diligently, under the expert guidance of a devotee of Lord Kṛṣṇa, or under the direct instruction of Lord Kṛṣṇa Himself (under whom Arjuna had the opportunity to work). Nothing should be performed for sense gratification, but everything should be done for the satisfaction of Kṛṣṇa. This practice will not only save one from the reaction of work, but also gradually elevate one to transcendental loving service of the Lord, which alone can raise one to the kingdom of God.

Text 10 सहयज्ञाः प्रजाः सृष्ट्वा पुरोवाच प्रजापतिः ।
अनेन प्रसविष्यध्वमेष वोऽस्त्विष्टकामधुक् ॥१०॥

saha-yajñāḥ prajāḥ sṛṣṭvā, purovāca prajāpatiḥ
anena prasaviṣyadhvam, eṣa vo 'stv iṣṭa-kāma-dhuk

saha – along with; *yajñāḥ* – sacrifices; *prajāḥ* – generations; *sṛṣṭvā* – creating; *purā* – anciently; *uvāca* – said; *prajā-patiḥ* – the Lord of creatures; *anena* – by this; *prasaviṣyadhvam* – be more and more prosperous; *eṣaḥ* – this; *vaḥ* – your; *astu* – let it be; *iṣṭa* – of all desirable things; *kāma-dhuk* – bestower.

In the beginning of creation, the Lord of all creatures sent forth generations of men and demigods, along with sacrifices for Viṣṇu, and blessed them by saying, "Be thou happy by this yajña [sacrifice] because its performance will bestow upon you everything desirable for living happily and achieving liberation."

PURPORT: The material creation by the Lord of creatures (Viṣṇu) is a chance offered to the conditioned souls to come back home – back to Godhead. All living entities within the material creation are conditioned by material nature because of their forgetfulness of their relationship to Viṣṇu, or Kṛṣṇa, the Supreme Personality of Godhead. The Vedic principles are to help us understand this eternal relation, as it is stated in the *Bhagavad-gītā: vedaiś ca sarvair aham eva vedyaḥ.* The Lord says that the purpose of the *Vedas* is to understand Him. In the Vedic hymns it is said: *patiṁ viśvasyātmeśvaram.* Therefore, the Lord of the living entities is the Supreme Personality of Godhead, Viṣṇu. In the *Śrīmad-Bhāgavatam* also

(2.4.20) Śrīla Śukadeva Gosvāmī describes the Lord as *pati* in so many ways:

śriyaḥ patir yajña-patiḥ prajā-patir
dhiyāṁ patir loka-patir dharā-patiḥ
patir gatiś cāndhaka-vṛṣṇi-sātvatāṁ
prasīdatāṁ me bhagavān satāṁ patiḥ

The *prajā-pati* is Lord Viṣṇu, and He is the Lord of all living creatures, all worlds, and all beauties, and the protector of everyone. The Lord created this material world to enable the conditioned souls to learn how to perform *yajñas* (sacrifices) for the satisfaction of Viṣṇu, so that while in the material world they can live very comfortably without anxiety and after finishing the present material body they can enter into the kingdom of God. That is the whole program for the conditioned soul. By performance of *yajña,* the conditioned souls gradually become Kṛṣṇa conscious and become godly in all respects. In the Age of Kali, the *saṅkīrtana-yajña* (the chanting of the names of God) is recommended by the Vedic scriptures, and this transcendental system was introduced by Lord Caitanya for the deliverance of all men in this age. *Saṅkīrtana-yajña* and Kṛṣṇa consciousness go well together. Lord Kṛṣṇa in His devotional form (as Lord Caitanya) is mentioned in the *Śrīmad-Bhāgavatam* (11.5.32) as follows, with special reference to the *saṅkīrtana-yajña:*

kṛṣṇa-varṇaṁ tviṣākṛṣṇaṁ, sāṅgopāṅgāstra-pārṣadam
yajñaiḥ saṅkīrtana-prāyair, yajanti hi su-medhasaḥ

"In this Age of Kali, people who are endowed with sufficient intelligence will worship the Lord, who is accompanied by His associates, by performance of *saṅkīrtana-yajña.*" Other *yajñas* prescribed in the Vedic literatures are not easy to perform in this Age of Kali, but the *saṅkīrtana-yajña* is easy and sublime for all purposes, as recommended in *Bhagavad-gītā* also (9.14).

Text 11 देवान् भावयतानेन ते देवा भावयन्तु वः ।
परस्परं भावयन्तः श्रेयः परमवाप्स्यथ ॥११॥

devān bhāvayatānena, te devā bhāvayantu vaḥ
parasparaṁ bhāvayantaḥ, śreyaḥ param avāpsyatha

devān – demigods; *bhāvayatā* – having pleased; *anena* – by this sacrifice; *te* – those; *devāḥ* – demigods; *bhāvayantu* – will please; *vaḥ* – you;

parasparam – mutually; *bhāvayantaḥ* – pleasing one another; *śreyaḥ* – benediction; *param* – the supreme; *avāpsyatha* – you will achieve.

The demigods, being pleased by sacrifices, will also please you, and thus, by cooperation between men and demigods, prosperity will reign for all.

PURPORT: The demigods are empowered administrators of material affairs. The supply of air, light, water and all other benedictions for maintaining the body and soul of every living entity is entrusted to the demigods, who are innumerable assistants in different parts of the body of the Supreme Personality of Godhead. Their pleasures and displeasures are dependent on the performance of *yajñas* by the human being. Some of the *yajñas* are meant to satisfy particular demigods; but even in so doing, Lord Viṣṇu is worshiped in all *yajñas* as the chief beneficiary. It is stated also in the *Bhagavad-gītā* that Kṛṣṇa Himself is the beneficiary of all kinds of *yajñas: bhoktāraṁ yajña-tapasām.* Therefore, ultimate satisfaction of the *yajña-pati* is the chief purpose of all *yajñas.* When these *yajñas* are perfectly performed, naturally the demigods in charge of the different departments of supply are pleased, and there is no scarcity in the supply of natural products.

Performance of *yajñas* has many side benefits, ultimately leading to liberation from material bondage. By performance of *yajñas,* all activities become purified, as it is stated in the *Vedas: āhāra-śuddhau sattva-śuddhiḥ sattva-śuddhau dhruvā smṛtiḥ smṛti-lambhe sarva-granthīnāṁ vipramokṣaḥ.* By performance of *yajña* one's eatables become sanctified, and by eating sanctified foodstuffs one's very existence becomes purified; by the purification of existence finer tissues in the memory become sanctified, and when memory is sanctified one can think of the path of liberation, and all these combined together lead to Kṛṣṇa consciousness, the great necessity of present-day society.

Text 12 इष्टान् भोगान् हि वो देवा दास्यन्ते यज्ञभाविताः ।
तैर्दत्तानप्रदायैभ्यो यो भुङ्क्ते स्तेन एव सः ॥१२॥

iṣṭān bhogān hi vo devā, dāsyante yajña-bhāvitāḥ
tair dattān apradāyaibhyo, yo bhuṅkte stena eva saḥ

iṣṭān – desired; *bhogān* – necessities of life; *hi* – certainly; *vaḥ* – unto you; *devāḥ* – the demigods; *dāsyante* – will award; *yajña-bhāvitāḥ* – being satisfied by the performance of sacrifices; *taiḥ* – by them; *dattān* – things given; *apradāya* – without offering; *ebhyaḥ* – to these demigods; *yaḥ* – he who; *bhuṅkte* – enjoys; *stenaḥ* – thief; *eva* – certainly; *saḥ* – he.

In charge of the various necessities of life, the demigods, being satisfied by the performance of yajña [sacrifice], will supply all necessities to you. But he who enjoys such gifts without offering them to the demigods in return is certainly a thief.

PURPORT: The demigods are authorized supplying agents on behalf of the Supreme Personality of Godhead, Viṣṇu. Therefore, they must be satisfied by the performance of prescribed *yajñas.* In the *Vedas,* there are different kinds of *yajñas* prescribed for different kinds of demigods, but all are ultimately offered to the Supreme Personality of Godhead. For one who cannot understand what the Personality of Godhead is, sacrifice to the demigods is recommended. According to the different material qualities of the persons concerned, different types of *yajñas* are recommended in the *Vedas.* Worship of different demigods is also on the same basis – namely, according to different qualities. For example, the meat-eaters are recommended to worship the goddess Kālī, the ghastly form of material nature, and before the goddess the sacrifice of animals is recommended. But for those who are in the mode of goodness, the transcendental worship of Viṣṇu is recommended. But ultimately all *yajñas* are meant for gradual promotion to the transcendental position. For ordinary men, at least five *yajñas,* known as *pañca-mahā-yajña,* are necessary.

One should know, however, that all the necessities of life that the human society requires are supplied by the demigod agents of the Lord. No one can manufacture anything. Take, for example, all the eatables of human society. These eatables include grains, fruits, vegetables, milk, sugar, etc., for the persons in the mode of goodness, and also eatables for the nonvegetarians, like meats, none of which can be manufactured by men. Then again, take for example heat, light, water, air, etc., which are also necessities of life – none of them can be manufactured by the human society. Without the Supreme Lord, there can be no profuse sunlight, moonlight, rainfall, breeze, etc., without which no one can live. Obviously, our life is dependent on supplies from the Lord. Even for our manufacturing enterprises, we require so many raw materials like metal, sulphur, mercury, manganese, and so many essentials – all of which are supplied by the agents of the Lord, with the purpose that we should make proper use of them to keep ourselves fit and healthy for the purpose of self-realization, leading to the ultimate goal of life, namely, liberation from the material struggle for existence. This aim of life is attained by performance of *yajñas.* If we forget the purpose of human life and simply take supplies from the agents of the Lord for sense gratification and become more and more entangled in material existence, which is not the purpose of creation, certainly we become thieves, and therefore we are punished by the laws of material nature. A society of thieves can never be happy, because they have no aim in life. The gross materialist thieves have no ultimate goal of life. They are simply directed to sense gratification; nor do they have knowledge of how to perform *yajñas.* Lord Caitanya, however, inaugurated the easiest performance of *yajña,* namely the *saṅkīrtana-yajña,* which can be performed by anyone in the world who accepts the principles of Kṛṣṇa consciousness.

Text 13 यज्ञशिष्टाशिनः सन्तो मुच्यन्ते सर्वकिल्बिषैः ।
भुञ्जते ते त्वघं पापा ये पचन्त्यात्मकारणात् ॥१३॥

yajña-śiṣṭāśinaḥ santo, mucyante sarva-kilbiṣaiḥ
bhuñjate te tv aghaṁ pāpā, ye pacanty ātma-kāraṇāt

yajña-śiṣṭa – of food taken after performance of *yajña; aśinaḥ* – eaters; *santaḥ* – the devotees; *mucyante* – get relief; *sarva* – all kinds of; *kilbiṣaiḥ* – from sins; *bhuñjate* – enjoy; *te* – they; *tu* – but; *agham* – grievous sins; *pāpāḥ* – sinners; *ye* – who; *pacanti* – prepare food; *ātma-kāraṇāt* – for sense enjoyment.

The devotees of the Lord are released from all kinds of sins because they eat food which is offered first for sacrifice. Others, who prepare food for personal sense enjoyment, verily eat only sin.

PURPORT: The devotees of the Supreme Lord, or the persons who are in Kṛṣṇa consciousness, are called *santas,* and they are always in love with the Lord as it is described in the *Brahma-saṁhitā* (5.38): *premāñjana-cchurita-bhakti-vilocanena santaḥ sadaiva hṛdayeṣu vilokayanti.* The *santas,* being always in a compact of love with the Supreme Personality of Godhead, Govinda (the giver of all pleasures), or Mukunda (the giver of liberation), or Kṛṣṇa (the all-attractive person), cannot accept anything without first offering it to the Supreme Person. Therefore, such devotees always perform *yajñas* in different modes of devotional service, such as *śravaṇam, kīrtanam, smaraṇam, arcanam,* etc., and these performances of *yajñas* keep them always aloof from all kinds of contamination of sinful association in the material world. Others, who prepare food for self or sense gratification, are not only thieves but also the eaters of all kinds of sins. How can a person be happy if he is both a thief and sinful? It is not possible. Therefore, in order for people to become happy in all respects, they must be taught to perform the easy process of *saṅkīrtana-yajña,* in full Kṛṣṇa consciousness. Otherwise, there can be no peace or happiness in the world.

Text 14 अन्नाद्भवन्ति भूतानि पर्जन्यादन्नसम्भवः ।
यज्ञाद्भवति पर्जन्यो यज्ञः कर्मसमुद्भवः ॥१४॥

annād bhavanti bhūtāni, parjanyād anna-sambhavaḥ
yajñād bhavati parjanyo, yajñaḥ karma-samudbhavaḥ

annāt – from grains; *bhavanti* – grow; *bhūtāni* – the material bodies; *parjanyāt* – from rains; *anna* – of food grains; *sambhavaḥ* – production; *yajñāt* – from the performance of sacrifice; *bhavati* – becomes possible; *parjanyaḥ* – rain; *yajñaḥ* – performance of *yajña; karma* – prescribed duties; *samudbhavaḥ* – born of.

All living bodies subsist on food grains, which are produced from rains. Rains are produced by performance of yajña [sacrifice], and yajña is born of prescribed duties.

PURPORT: Śrīla Baladeva Vidyābhūṣaṇa, a great commentator on the *Bhagavad-gītā,* writes as follows: *ye indrādy-aṅgatayāvasthitaṁ yajñaṁ sarveśvaraṁ viṣṇum abhyarcya tac-cheṣam aśnanti tena tad deha-yātrāṁ sampādayanti, te santaḥ sarveśvarasya yajña-puruṣasya bhaktāḥ sarva-kilbiṣair anādi-kāla-vivṛddhair ātmānubhava-pratibandhakair nikhilaiḥ pāpair vimucyante.* The Supreme Lord, who is known as the *yajña-puruṣa,* or the personal beneficiary of all sacrifices, is the master of all the demigods, who serve Him as the different limbs of the body serve the whole. Demigods like Indra, Candra and Varuṇa are appointed officers who manage material affairs, and the *Vedas* direct sacrifices to satisfy these demigods so that they may be pleased to supply air, light and water sufficiently to produce food grains. When Lord Kṛṣṇa is worshiped, the demigods, who are different limbs of the Lord, are also automatically worshiped; therefore there is no separate need to worship the demigods. For this reason, the devotees of the Lord, who are in Kṛṣṇa consciousness, offer food to Kṛṣṇa and then eat – a process which nourishes the body spiritually. By such action not only are past sinful reactions in the body vanquished, but the body becomes immunized to all contamination of material nature. When there is an epidemic disease, an antiseptic vaccine protects a person from the attack of such an epidemic. Similarly, food offered to Lord Viṣṇu and then taken by us makes us sufficiently resistant to material affection, and one who is accustomed to this practice is called a devotee of the Lord. Therefore, a person in Kṛṣṇa consciousness, who eats only food offered to Kṛṣṇa, can counteract all reactions of past material infections, which are impediments to the progress of self-realization. On the other hand, one who does not do so continues to increase the volume of sinful action, and this prepares the next body to resemble hogs and dogs, to suffer the resultant reactions of all sins. The material world is full of contaminations, and one who is immunized by accepting *prasādam* of the Lord (food offered to Viṣṇu) is saved from the attack, whereas one who does not do so becomes subjected to contamination.

Food grains or vegetables are factually eatables. The human being eats different kinds of food grains, vegetables, fruits, etc., and the animals eat the refuse of the food grains and vegetables, grass, plants, etc. Human beings who are accustomed to eating meat and flesh must also depend on the production of vegetation in order to eat the animals. Therefore, ultimately, we have to depend on the production of the field and not on the production of big factories. The field production is due to sufficient rain from the sky, and such rains are controlled by demigods like Indra, sun, moon, etc., and they are all servants of the Lord. The Lord can be satisfied by sacrifices; therefore, one who cannot perform them will find himself in scarcity – that is the law of nature. *Yajña,* specifically the *saṅkīrtana-yajña* prescribed for this age, must therefore be performed to save us at least from scarcity of food supply.

Text 15 कर्म ब्रह्मोद्भवं विद्धि ब्रह्माक्षरसमुद्भवम् ।
तस्मात्सर्वगतं ब्रह्म नित्यं यज्ञे प्रतिष्ठितम् ॥१५॥

karma brahmodbhavaṁ viddhi, brahmākṣara-samudbhavam
tasmāt sarva-gataṁ brahma, nityaṁ yajñe pratiṣṭhitam

karma – work; *brahma* – from the *Vedas; udbhavam* – produced; *viddhi* – you should know; *brahma* – the *Vedas; akṣara* – from the Supreme Brahman (Personality of Godhead); *samudbhavam* – directly manifested; *tasmāt* – therefore; *sarva-gatam* – all-pervading; *brahma* – transcendence; *nityam* – eternally; *yajñe* – in sacrifice; *pratiṣṭhitam* – situated.

Regulated activities are prescribed in the Vedas, and the Vedas are directly manifested from the Supreme Personality of Godhead. Consequently the all-pervading Transcendence is eternally situated in acts of sacrifice.

PURPORT: *Yajñārtha-karma,* or the necessity of work for the satisfaction of Kṛṣṇa only, is more expressly stated in this verse. If we have to work for the satisfaction of the *yajña-puruṣa,* Viṣṇu, then we must find out the direction of work in Brahman, or the transcendental *Vedas*. The *Vedas* are therefore codes of working directions. Anything performed without the direction of the *Vedas* is called *vikarma,* or unauthorized or sinful work. Therefore, one should always take direction from the *Vedas* to be saved from the reaction of work. As one has to work in ordinary life by the direction of the state, one similarly has to work under direction of the supreme state of the Lord. Such directions in the *Vedas* are directly manifested from the breathing of the Supreme Personality of Godhead. It is said, *asya mahato bhūtasya niśvasitam etad yad ṛg-vedo yajur-vedaḥ sāma-vedo 'tharvāṅgirasaḥ.* "The four *Vedas* – namely the *Ṛg Veda, Yajur Veda, Sāma Veda* and *Atharva Veda* – are all emanations from the breathing of the great Personality of Godhead." (*Bṛhad-āraṇyaka Upaniṣad* 4.5.11) The Lord, being omnipotent, can speak by breathing air, for as it is confirmed in the *Brahma-saṁhitā,* the Lord has the omnipotence to perform through each of His senses the actions of all other senses. In other words, the Lord can speak through His breathing, and He can impregnate by His eyes. In fact, it is said that He glanced over material nature and thus fathered all living entities. After creating or impregnating the conditioned souls into the womb of material nature, He gave His directions in the Vedic wisdom as to how such conditioned souls can return home, back to Godhead. We should always remember that the conditioned souls in material nature are all eager for material enjoyment. But the Vedic directions are so made that one can satisfy one's perverted desires, then return to Godhead, having finished his so-called enjoyment. It is a chance for the conditioned souls to attain liberation; therefore the conditioned souls must try to follow the process of *yajña* by becoming Kṛṣṇa conscious. Even those who have not followed the Vedic injunctions may adopt the principles of Kṛṣṇa consciousness, and that will take the place of performance of Vedic *yajñas,* or *karmas.*

Text 16 एवं प्रवर्तितं चक्रं नानुवर्तयतीह यः ।
अघायुरिन्द्रियारामो मोघं पार्थ स जीवति ॥१६॥

evaṁ pravartitaṁ cakraṁ, nānuvartayatīha yaḥ
aghāyur indriyārāmo, moghaṁ pārtha sa jīvati

evam – thus; *pravartitam* – established by the *Vedas; cakram* – cycle; *na* – does not; *anuvartayati* – adopt; *iha* – in this life; *yaḥ* – one who; *agha-āyuḥ* – whose life is full of sins; *indriya-ārāmaḥ* – satisfied in sense gratification; *mogham* – uselessly; *pārtha* – O son of Pṛthā (Arjuna); *saḥ* – he; *jīvati* – lives.

My dear Arjuna, one who does not follow in human life the cycle of sacrifice thus established by the Vedas certainly leads a life full of sin. Living only for the satisfaction of the senses, such a person lives in vain.

PURPORT: The mammonist philosophy of "work very hard and enjoy sense gratification" is condemned herein by the Lord. Therefore, for those who want to enjoy this material world, the above-mentioned cycle of performing *yajñas* is absolutely necessary. One who does not follow such regulations is living a very risky life, being condemned more and more. By nature's law, this human form of life is specifically meant for self-realization, in either of the three ways – namely *karma-yoga, jñāna-yoga* or *bhakti-yoga.* There is no necessity of rigidly following the performances of the prescribed *yajñas* for the transcendentalists who are above vice and virtue; but those who are engaged in sense gratification require purification by the above-mentioned cycle of *yajña* performances. There are different kinds of activities. Those who are not Kṛṣṇa conscious are certainly engaged in sensory consciousness; therefore they need to execute pious work. The *yajña* system is planned in such a way that sensory conscious persons may satisfy their desires without becoming entangled in the reaction of sense-gratificatory work. The prosperity of the world depends not on our own efforts but on the background arrangement of the Supreme Lord, directly carried out by the demigods. Therefore, the *yajñas* are directly aimed at the particular demigods mentioned in the *Vedas.* Indirectly, it is the practice of Kṛṣṇa consciousness, because when one masters the performance of *yajñas* one is sure to become Kṛṣṇa conscious. But if by performing *yajñas* one does not become Kṛṣṇa conscious, such principles are counted as only moral codes. One should not, therefore, limit his progress only to the point of moral codes, but should transcend them, to attain Kṛṣṇa consciousness.

Text 17 यस्त्वात्मरतिरेव स्यादात्मतृप्तश्च मानवः ।
आत्मन्येव च सन्तुष्टस्तस्य कार्यं न विद्यते ॥१७॥

yas tv ātma-ratir eva syād, ātma-tṛptaś ca mānavaḥ
ātmany eva ca santuṣṭas, tasya kāryaṁ na vidyate

yaḥ – one who; *tu* – but; *ātma-ratiḥ* – taking pleasure in the Self; *eva* – certainly; *syāt* – remains; *ātma-tṛptaḥ* – self-illuminated; *ca* – and; *mānavaḥ* – a man; *ātmani* – in himself; *eva* – only; *ca* – and; *santuṣṭaḥ* – perfectly satiated; *tasya* – his; *kāryam* – duty; *na* – does not; *vidyate* – exist.

But for one who takes pleasure in the Self, whose human life is one of self-realization, and who is satisfied in the Self only, fully satiated – for him there is no duty.

PURPORT: A person who is *fully* Kṛṣṇa conscious, and is fully satisfied by his acts in Kṛṣṇa consciousness, no longer has any duty to perform. Due to his being Kṛṣṇa conscious, all impiety within is instantly cleansed, an effect of many, many thousands of *yajña* performances. By such clearing of consciousness, one becomes fully confident of his eternal position in relationship with the Supreme. His duty thus becomes self-illuminated by the grace of the Lord, and therefore he no longer has any obligations to the Vedic injunctions. Such a Kṛṣṇa conscious person is no longer interested in material activities and no longer takes pleasure in material arrangements like wine, women and similar infatuations.

Text 18 नैव तस्य कृतेनार्थो नाकृतेनेह कश्चन ।
न चास्य सर्वभूतेषु कश्चिदर्थव्यपाश्रयः ॥१८॥

naiva tasya kṛtenārtho, nākṛteneha kaścana
na cāsya sarva-bhūteṣu, kaścid artha-vyapāśrayaḥ

na – never; *eva* – certainly; *tasya* – his; *kṛtena* – by discharge of duty; *arthaḥ* – purpose; *na* – nor; *akṛtena* – without discharge of duty; *iha* – in this world; *kaścana* – whatever; *na* – never; *ca* – and; *asya* – of him; *sarva-bhūteṣu* – among all living beings; *kaścit* – any; *artha* – purpose; *vyapāśrayaḥ* – taking shelter of.

A self-realized man has no purpose to fulfill in the discharge of his prescribed duties, nor has he any reason not to perform such work. Nor has he any need to depend on any other living being.

PURPORT: A self-realized man is no longer obliged to perform any prescribed duty, save and except activities in Kṛṣṇa consciousness. Kṛṣṇa consciousness is not inactivity either, as will be explained in the following verses. A Kṛṣṇa conscious man does not take shelter of any person – man or demigod. Whatever he does in Kṛṣṇa consciousness is sufficient in the discharge of his obligation.

Text 19 तस्मादसक्तः सततं कार्यं कर्म समाचर ।
असक्तो ह्याचरन् कर्म परमाप्नोति पूरुषः ॥१९॥

tasmād asaktaḥ satataṁ, kāryaṁ karma samācara
asakto hy ācaran karma, param āpnoti pūruṣaḥ

tasmāt – therefore; *asaktaḥ* – without attachment; *satatam* – constantly; *kāryam* – as duty; *karma* – work; *samācara* – perform; *asaktaḥ* – unattached; *hi* – certainly; *ācaran* – performing; *karma* – work; *param* – the Supreme; *āpnoti* – achieves; *pūruṣaḥ* – a man.

Therefore, without being attached to the fruits of activities, one should act as a matter of duty, for by working without attachment one attains the Supreme.

PURPORT: The Supreme is the Personality of Godhead for the devotees, and liberation for the impersonalist. A person, therefore, acting for Kṛṣṇa, or in Kṛṣṇa consciousness, under proper guidance and without attachment to the result of the work, is certainly making progress toward the supreme goal of life. Arjuna is told that he should fight in the Battle of Kurukṣetra for the interest of Kṛṣṇa because Kṛṣṇa wanted him to fight. To be a good man or a nonviolent man is a personal attachment, but to act on behalf of the Supreme is to act without attachment for the result. That is perfect action of the highest degree, recommended by the Supreme Personality of Godhead, Śrī Kṛṣṇa.

Vedic rituals, like prescribed sacrifices, are performed for purification of impious activities that were performed in the field of sense gratification. But action in Kṛṣṇa consciousness is transcendental to the reactions of good or evil work. A Kṛṣṇa conscious person has no attachment for the result but acts on behalf of Kṛṣṇa alone. He engages in all kinds of activities, but is completely nonattached.

Text 20 कर्मणैव हि संसिद्धिमास्थिता जनकादयः ।
लोकसङ्ग्रहमेवापि सम्पश्यन् कर्तुमर्हसि ॥२०॥

karmaṇaiva hi saṁsiddhim, āsthitā janakādayaḥ
loka-saṅgraham evāpi, sampaśyan kartum arhasi

karmaṇā – by work; *eva* – even; *hi* – certainly; *saṁsiddhim* – in perfection; *āsthitāḥ* – situated; *janaka-ādayaḥ* – Janaka and other kings; *loka-saṅgraham* – the people in general; *eva api* – also; *sampaśyan* – considering; *kartum* – to act; *arhasi* – you deserve.

Kings such as Janaka attained perfection solely by performance of prescribed duties. Therefore, just for the sake of educating the people in general, you should perform your work.

PURPORT: Kings like Janaka were all self-realized souls; consequently they had no obligation to perform the prescribed duties in the *Vedas.* Nonetheless they performed all prescribed activities just to set examples for the people in general. Janaka was the father of Sītā and father-in-law of Lord Śrī Rāma. Being a great devotee of the Lord, he was transcendentally situated, but because he was the king of Mithilā (a subdivision of Bihar province in India), he had to teach his subjects how to perform prescribed duties. Lord Kṛṣṇa and Arjuna, the Lord's eternal friend, had no need to fight in the Battle of Kurukṣetra, but they fought to teach people in general that violence is also necessary in a situation where good arguments fail. Before the Battle of Kurukṣetra, every effort was made to avoid the war, even by the Supreme Personality of Godhead, but the other party was determined to fight. So for such a right cause, there is a necessity for fighting. Although one who is situated in Kṛṣṇa consciousness may not have any interest in the world, he still works to teach the public how to live and how to act. Experienced persons in Kṛṣṇa consciousness can act in such a way that others will follow, and this is explained in the following verse.

Text 21 यद्यदाचरति श्रेष्ठस्तत्तदेवेतरो जनः ।
स यत्प्रमाणं कुरुते लोकस्तदनुवर्तते ॥२१॥

yad yad ācarati śreṣṭhas, tat tad evetaro janaḥ
sa yat pramāṇaṁ kurute, lokas tad anuvartate

yat yat – whatever; *ācarati* – he does; *śreṣṭhaḥ* – a respectable leader; *tat* – that; *tat* – and that alone; *eva* – certainly; *itaraḥ* – common; *janaḥ* – person; *saḥ* – he; *yat* – whichever; *pramāṇam* – example; *kurute* – does perform; *lokaḥ* – all the world; *tat* – that; *anuvartate* – follows in the footsteps.

Whatever action a great man performs, common men follow. And whatever standards he sets by exemplary acts, all the world pursues.

PURPORT: People in general always require a leader who can teach the public by practical behavior. A leader cannot teach the public to stop smoking if he himself smokes. Lord Caitanya said that a teacher should behave properly before he begins teaching. One who teaches in that way is called *ācārya,* or the ideal teacher. Therefore, a teacher must follow the principles of *śāstra* (scripture) to teach the common man. The teacher cannot manufacture rules against the principles of revealed scriptures. The revealed scriptures, like *Manu-saṁhitā* and similar others, are considered the standard books to be followed by human society. Thus the leader's teaching should be based on the principles of such standard *śāstras.* One who desires to improve himself must follow the standard rules as they are practiced by the great teachers. The *Śrīmad-Bhāgavatam* also affirms that one should follow in the footsteps of great devotees, and that is the way of progress on the path of spiritual realization. The king or the executive head of a state, the father and the schoolteacher are all considered to be natural leaders of the innocent people in general. All such natural leaders have a great responsibility to their dependents; therefore they must be conversant with standard books of moral and spiritual codes.

Text 22 न मे पार्थास्ति कर्तव्यं त्रिषु लोकेषु किञ्चन ।
नानवाप्तमवाप्तव्यं वर्त एव च कर्मणि ॥२२॥

na me pārthāsti kartavyaṁ, triṣu lokeṣu kiñcana
nānavāptam avāptavyaṁ, varta eva ca karmaṇi

na – not; *me* – Mine; *pārtha* – O son of Pṛthā; *asti* – there is; *kartavyam* – prescribed duty; *triṣu* – in the three; *lokesu* – planetary systems; *kiñcana* – any; *na* – nothing; *anavāptam* – wanted; *avāptavyam* – to be gained; *varte* – I am engaged; *eva* – certainly; *ca* – also; *karmaṇi* – in prescribed duty.

O son of Pṛthā, there is no work prescribed for Me within all the three planetary systems. Nor am I in want of anything, nor have I a need to obtain anything – and yet I am engaged in prescribed duties.

PURPORT: The Supreme Personality of Godhead is described in the Vedic literatures as follows:

tam īśvarāṇāṁ paramaṁ maheśvaraṁ
taṁ devatānāṁ paramaṁ ca daivatam

patiṁ patīnāṁ paramaṁ parastād
vidāma devaṁ bhuvaneśam īḍyam

na tasya kāryaṁ karaṇaṁ ca vidyate
na tat-samaś cābhyadhikaś ca dṛśyate
parāsya śaktir vividhaiva śrūyate
svābhāvikī jñāna-bala-kriyā ca

"The Supreme Lord is the controller of all other controllers, and He is the greatest of all the diverse planetary leaders. Everyone is under His control. All entities are delegated with particular power only by the Supreme Lord; they are not supreme themselves. He is also worshipable by all demigods and is the supreme director of all directors. Therefore, He is transcendental to all kinds of material leaders and controllers and is worshipable by all. There is no one greater than Him, and He is the supreme cause of all causes.

"He does not possess a bodily form like that of an ordinary living entity. There is no difference between His body and His soul. He is absolute. All His senses are transcendental. Any one of His senses can perform the action of any other sense. Therefore, no one is greater than Him or equal to Him. His potencies are multifarious, and thus His deeds are automatically performed as a natural sequence." (*Śvetāśvatara Upaniṣad* 6.7–8)

Since everything is in full opulence in the Personality of Godhead and is existing in full truth, there is no duty for the Supreme Personality of Godhead to perform. One who must receive the results of work has some designated duty, but one who has nothing to achieve within the three planetary systems certainly has no duty. And yet Lord Kṛṣṇa is engaged on the Battlefield of Kurukṣetra as the leader of the *kṣatriyas* because the *kṣatriyas* are duty-bound to give protection to the distressed. Although He is above all the regulations of the revealed scriptures, He does not do anything that violates the revealed scriptures.

Text 23 यदि ह्यहं न वर्तेयं जातु कर्मण्यतन्द्रितः ।
मम वर्त्मानुवर्तन्ते मनुष्याः पार्थ सर्वशः ॥२३॥

yadi hy ahaṁ na varteyaṁ, jātu karmaṇy atandritaḥ
mama vartmānuvartante, manuṣyāḥ pārtha sarvaśaḥ

yadi – if; *hi* – certainly; *aham* – I; *na* – do not; *varteyam* – thus engage; *jātu* – ever; *karmaṇi* – in the performance of prescribed duties;

atandritaḥ – with great care; *mama* – My; *vartma* – path; *anuvartante* – would follow; *manuṣyāḥ* – all men; *pārtha* – O son of Pṛthā; *sarvaśaḥ* – in all respects.

For if I ever failed to engage in carefully performing prescribed duties, O Pārtha, certainly all men would follow My path.

PURPORT: In order to keep the balance of social tranquillity for progress in spiritual life, there are traditional family usages meant for every civilized man. Although such rules and regulations are for the conditioned souls and not Lord Kṛṣṇa, because He descended to establish the principles of religion He followed the prescribed rules. Otherwise, common men would follow in His footsteps, because He is the greatest authority. From the *Śrīmad-Bhāgavatam* it is understood that Lord Kṛṣṇa was performing all the religious duties at home and out of home, as required of a householder.

Text 24 उत्सीदेयुरिमे लोका न कुर्यां कर्म चेदहम् ।
सङ्करस्य च कर्ता स्यामुपहन्यामिमाः प्रजाः ॥२४॥

utsīdeyur ime lokā, na kuryāṁ karma ced aham
saṅkarasya ca kartā syām, upahanyām imāḥ prajāḥ

utsīdeyuḥ – would be put into ruin; *ime* – all these; *lokāḥ* – worlds; *na* – not; *kuryām* – I perform; *karma* – prescribed duties; *cet* – if; *aham* – I; *saṅkarasya* – of unwanted population; *ca* – and; *kartā* – creator; *syām* – would be; *upahanyām* – would destroy; *imāḥ* – all these; *prajāḥ* – living entities.

If I did not perform prescribed duties, all these worlds would be put to ruination. I would be the cause of creating unwanted population, and I would thereby destroy the peace of all living beings.

PURPORT: *Varṇa-saṅkara* is unwanted population which disturbs the peace of the general society. In order to check this social disturbance, there are prescribed rules and regulations by which the population can automatically become peaceful and organized for spiritual progress in life. When Lord Kṛṣṇa descends, naturally He deals with such rules and regulations in order to maintain the prestige and necessity of such important performances. The Lord is the father of all living entities, and if the living entities are misguided, indirectly the responsibility goes to the

Lord. Therefore, whenever there is general disregard of regulative principles, the Lord Himself descends and corrects the society. We should, however, note carefully that although we have to follow in the footsteps of the Lord, we still have to remember that we cannot imitate Him. Following and imitating are not on the same level. We cannot imitate the Lord by lifting Govardhana Hill, as the Lord did in His childhood. It is impossible for any human being. We have to follow His instructions, but we may not imitate Him at any time. The *Śrīmad-Bhāgavatam* (10.33.30–31) affirms:

naitat samācarej jātu, manasāpi hy anīśvaraḥ
vinaśyaty ācaran mauḍhyād, yathārudro 'bdhi-jaṁ viṣam

īśvarāṇāṁ vacaḥ satyaṁ, tathaivācaritaṁ kvacit
teṣāṁ yat sva-vaco-yuktaṁ, buddhimāṁs tat samācaret

"One should simply follow the instructions of the Lord and His empowered servants. Their instructions are all good for us, and any intelligent person will perform them as instructed. However, one should guard against trying to imitate their actions. One should not try to drink the ocean of poison in imitation of Lord Śiva."

We should always consider the position of the *īśvaras,* or those who can actually control the movements of the sun and moon, as superior. Without such power, one cannot imitate the *īśvaras,* who are superpowerful. Lord Śiva drank poison to the extent of swallowing an ocean, but if any common man tries to drink even a fragment of such poison, he will be killed. There are many pseudo devotees of Lord Śiva who want to indulge in smoking *gañjā* (marijuana) and similar intoxicating drugs, forgetting that by so imitating the acts of Lord Śiva they are calling death very near. Similarly, there are some pseudo devotees of Lord Kṛṣṇa who prefer to imitate the Lord in His *rāsa-līlā,* or dance of love, forgetting their inability to lift Govardhana Hill. It is best, therefore, that one not try to imitate the powerful, but simply follow their instructions; nor should one try to occupy their posts without qualification. There are so many "incarnations" of God without the power of the Supreme Godhead.

Text 25 सक्ताः कर्मण्यविद्वांसो यथा कुर्वन्ति भारत ।
कुर्याद्विद्वांस्तथासक्तश्चिकीर्षुर्लोकसङ्ग्रहम् ॥२५॥

saktāḥ karmaṇy avidvāṁso, yathā kurvanti bhārata
kuryād vidvāṁs tathāsaktaś, cikīrṣur loka-saṅgraham

saktāḥ – being attached; *karmaṇi* – in prescribed duties; *avidvāṁsaḥ* – the ignorant; *yathā* – as much as; *kurvanti* – they do; *bhārata* – O descendant of Bharata; *kuryāt* – must do; *vidvān* – the learned; *tathā* – thus; *asaktaḥ* – without attachment; *cikīrṣuḥ* – desiring to lead; *loka-saṅgraham* – the people in general.

As the ignorant perform their duties with attachment to results, the learned may similarly act, but without attachment, for the sake of leading people on the right path.

PURPORT: A person in Kṛṣṇa consciousness and a person not in Kṛṣṇa consciousness are differentiated by different desires. A Kṛṣṇa conscious person does not do anything which is not conducive to development of Kṛṣṇa consciousness. He may even act exactly like the ignorant person, who is too much attached to material activities, but one is engaged in such activities for the satisfaction of his sense gratification, whereas the other is engaged for the satisfaction of Kṛṣṇa. Therefore, the Kṛṣṇa conscious person is required to show the people how to act and how to engage the results of action for the purpose of Kṛṣṇa consciousness.

Text 26 न बुद्धिभेदं जनयेदज्ञानां कर्मसङ्गिनाम् ।
जोषयेत्सर्वकर्माणि विद्वान् युक्तः समाचरन् ॥२६॥

na buddhi-bhedaṁ janayed, ajñānāṁ karma-saṅginām
joṣayet sarva-karmāṇi, vidvān yuktaḥ samācaran

na – not; *buddhi-bhedam* – disruption of intelligence; *janayet* – he should cause; *ajñānām* – of the foolish; *karma-saṅginām* – who are attached to fruitive work; *joṣayet* – he should dovetail; *sarva* – all; *karmāṇi* – work; *vidvān* – a learned person; *yuktaḥ* – engaged; *samācaran* – practicing.

So as not to disrupt the minds of ignorant men attached to the fruitive results of prescribed duties, a learned person should not induce them to stop work. Rather, by working in the spirit of devotion, he should engage them in all sorts of activities [for the gradual development of Kṛṣṇa consciousness].

PURPORT: *Vedaiś ca sarvair aham eva vedyaḥ.* That is the end of all Vedic rituals. All rituals, all performances of sacrifices, and everything that is put into the *Vedas,* including all direction for material activities, are meant for understanding Kṛṣṇa, who is the ultimate goal of life. But because the conditioned souls do not know anything beyond sense gratification, they study the *Vedas* to that end. But through fruitive activities and sense gratification regulated by the Vedic rituals one is gradually elevated to Kṛṣṇa consciousness. Therefore a realized soul in Kṛṣṇa consciousness should not disturb others in their activities or understanding, but he should act by showing how the results of all work can be dedicated to the service of Kṛṣṇa. The learned Kṛṣṇa conscious person may act in such a way that the ignorant person working for sense gratification may learn how to act and how to behave. Although the ignorant man is not to be disturbed in his activities, a slightly developed Kṛṣṇa conscious person may directly be engaged in the service of the Lord without waiting for other Vedic formulas. For this fortunate man there is no need to follow the Vedic rituals, because by direct Kṛṣṇa consciousness one can have all the results one would otherwise derive from following one's prescribed duties.

Text 27 प्रकृतेः क्रियमाणानि गुणैः कर्माणि सर्वशः ।
अहङ्कारविमूढात्मा कर्ताहमिति मन्यते ॥२७॥

prakṛteḥ kriyamāṇāni, guṇaiḥ karmāṇi sarvaśaḥ
ahaṅkāra-vimūḍhātmā, kartāham iti manyate

prakṛteḥ – of material nature; *kriyamāṇāni* – being done; *guṇaiḥ* – by the modes; *karmāṇi* – activities; *sarvaśaḥ* – all kinds of; *ahaṅkāra-vimūḍha* – bewildered by false ego; *ātmā* – the spirit soul; *kartā* – doer; *aham* – I; *iti* – thus; *manyate* – he thinks.

The spirit soul bewildered by the influence of false ego thinks himself the doer of activities that are in actuality carried out by the three modes of material nature.

PURPORT: Two persons, one in Kṛṣṇa consciousness and the other in material consciousness, working on the same level, may appear to be working on the same platform, but there is a wide gulf of difference in their respective positions. The person in material consciousness is convinced by false ego that he is the doer of everything. He does not know that the mechanism of the body is produced by material nature, which works under the supervision of the Supreme Lord. The materialistic person has no knowledge that ultimately he is under the control of Kṛṣṇa. The person in false ego takes all credit for doing everything independently, and that is the symptom of his nescience. He does not know that this gross and subtle body is the creation of material nature, under the order of the Supreme Personality of Godhead, and as such his bodily and mental activities should be engaged in the service of Kṛṣṇa, in Kṛṣṇa consciousness. The ignorant man forgets that the Supreme Personality of Godhead is known as Hṛṣīkeśa, or the master of the senses of the material body, for due to his long misuse of the senses in sense gratification, he is factually bewildered by the false ego, which makes him forget his eternal relationship with Kṛṣṇa.

Text 28 **तत्त्ववित्तु महाबाहो गुणकर्मविभागयोः ।**
गुणा गुणेषु वर्तन्त इति मत्वा न सज्जते ॥२८॥

tattva-vit tu mahā-bāho, guṇa-karma-vibhāgayoḥ
guṇā guṇeṣu vartanta, iti matvā na sajjate

tattva-vit – the knower of the Absolute Truth; *tu* – but; *mahā-bāho* – O mighty-armed one; *guṇa-karma* – of works under material influence; *vibhāgayoḥ* – differences; *guṇāḥ* – senses; *guṇeṣu* – in sense gratification; *vartante* – are being engaged; *iti* – thus; *matvā* – thinking; *na* – never; *sajjate* – becomes attached.

One who is in knowledge of the Absolute Truth, O mighty-armed, does not engage himself in the senses and sense gratification, knowing well the differences between work in devotion and work for fruitive results.

PURPORT: The knower of the Absolute Truth is convinced of his awkward position in material association. He knows that he is part and parcel of the Supreme Personality of Godhead, Kṛṣṇa, and that his position should not be in the material creation. He knows his real identity as part and parcel of the Supreme, who is eternal bliss and knowledge, and he realizes that somehow or other he is entrapped in the material conception of life. In his pure state of existence he is meant to dovetail his activities in devotional service to the Supreme Personality of Godhead, Kṛṣṇa. He therefore engages himself in the activities of Kṛṣṇa consciousness and becomes naturally unattached to the activities of the material senses, which are all circumstantial and temporary. He knows that his material condition of life is under the supreme control of the Lord; consequently he is not disturbed by all kinds of material reactions, which he considers to be the mercy of the Lord. According to *Śrīmad-Bhāgavatam,* one who knows the Absolute Truth in three different features – namely Brahman, Paramātmā, and the Supreme Personality of Godhead – is called *tattva-*

vit, for he knows also his own factual position in relationship with the Supreme.

Text 29 प्रकृतेर्गुणसम्मूढाः सज्जन्ते गुणकर्मसु ।
तानकृत्स्नविदो मन्दान् कृत्स्नविन्न विचालयेत् ॥२९॥

prakṛter guṇa-sammūḍhāḥ, sajjante guṇa-karmasu
tān akṛtsna-vido mandān, kṛtsna-vin na vicālayet

prakṛteḥ – of material nature; *guṇa* – by the modes; *sammūḍhāḥ* – befooled by material identification; *sajjante* – they become engaged; *guṇa-karmasu* – in material activities; *tān* – those; *akṛtsna-vidaḥ* – persons with a poor fund of knowledge; *mandān* – lazy to understand self-realization; *kṛtsna-vit* – one who is in factual knowledge; *na* – not; *vicālayet* – should try to agitate.

Bewildered by the modes of material nature, the ignorant fully engage themselves in material activities and become attached. But the wise should not unsettle them, although these duties are inferior due to the performers' lack of knowledge.

PURPORT: Persons who are unknowledgeable falsely identify with gross material consciousness and are full of material designations. This body is a gift of the material nature, and one who is too much attached to the bodily consciousness is called *manda,* or a lazy person without understanding of spirit soul. Ignorant men think of the body as the self; they accept bodily connections with others as kinsmanship, the land in which the body is obtained is their object of worship, and they consider the formalities of religious rituals to be ends in themselves. Social work, nationalism and altruism are some of the activities for such materially designated persons. Under the spell of such designations, they are always busy in the material field; for them spiritual realization is a myth, and so they are not interested. Those who are enlightened in spiritual life, however, should not try to agitate such materially engrossed persons. Better to prosecute one's own spiritual activities silently. Such bewildered persons may be engaged in such primary moral principles of life as nonviolence and similar materially benevolent work.

Men who are ignorant cannot appreciate activities in Kṛṣṇa consciousness, and therefore Lord Kṛṣṇa advises us not to disturb them and simply waste valuable time. But the devotees of the Lord are more kind than the Lord because they understand the purpose of the Lord.

Consequently they undertake all kinds of risks, even to the point of approaching ignorant men to try to engage them in the acts of Kṛṣṇa consciousness, which are absolutely necessary for the human being.

Text 30 मयि सर्वाणि कर्माणि सन्न्यस्याध्यात्मचेतसा ।
निराशीर्निर्ममो भूत्वा युध्यस्व विगतज्वरः ॥३०॥

mayi sarvāṇi karmāṇi, sannyasyādhyātma-cetasā
nirāśīr nirmamo bhūtvā, yudhyasva vigata-jvaraḥ

mayi – unto Me; *sarvāṇi* – all sorts of; *karmāṇi* – activities; *sannyasya* – giving up completely; *adhyātma* – with full knowledge of the self; *cetasā* – by consciousness; *nirāśīḥ* – without desire for profit; *nirmamaḥ* – without ownership; *bhūtvā* – so being; *yudhyasva* – fight; *vigata-jvaraḥ* – without being lethargic.

Therefore, O Arjuna, surrendering all your works unto Me, with full knowledge of Me, without desires for profit, with no claims to proprietorship, and free from lethargy, fight.

PURPORT: This verse clearly indicates the purpose of the *Bhagavad-gītā.* The Lord instructs that one has to become fully Kṛṣṇa conscious to discharge duties, as if in military discipline. Such an injunction may make things a little difficult; nevertheless duties must be carried out, with dependence on Kṛṣṇa, because that is the constitutional position of the living entity. The living entity cannot be happy independent of the cooperation of the Supreme Lord, because the eternal constitutional position of the living entity is to become subordinate to the desires of the Lord. Arjuna was therefore ordered by Śrī Kṛṣṇa to fight as if the Lord were his military commander. One has to sacrifice everything for the good will of the Supreme Lord, and at the same time discharge prescribed duties without claiming proprietorship. Arjuna did not have to consider the order of the Lord; he had only to execute His order. The Supreme Lord is the soul of all souls; therefore, one who depends solely and wholly on the Supreme Soul without personal consideration, or in other words, one who is fully Kṛṣṇa conscious, is called *adhyātma-cetās.* *Nirāśīḥ* means that one has to act on the order of the master but should not expect fruitive results. The cashier may count millions of dollars for his employer, but he does not claim a cent for himself. Similarly, one has to realize that nothing in the world belongs to any individual person, but that everything belongs to the Supreme Lord. That is the real purport of *mayi,* or "unto Me." And when one acts in such Kṛṣṇa consciousness, certainly he does not claim proprietorship over anything. This consciousness is called *nirmama,* or "nothing is mine." And if there is any reluctance to execute such a stern order, which is without consideration of so-called kinsmen in the bodily relationship, that reluctance should be thrown off; in this way one may become *vigata-jvara,* or without feverish mentality or lethargy. Everyone, according to his quality and position, has a particular type of work to discharge, and all such duties may be discharged in Kṛṣṇa consciousness, as described above. That will lead one to the path of liberation.

Text 31 ये मे मतमिदं नित्यमनुतिष्ठन्ति मानवाः ।
श्रद्धावन्तोऽनसूयन्तो मुच्यन्ते तेऽपि कर्मभिः ॥३१॥

ye me matam idaṁ nityam, anutiṣṭhanti mānavāḥ
śraddhāvanto 'nasūyanto, mucyante te 'pi karmabhiḥ

ye – those who; *me* – My; *matam* – injunctions; *idam* – these; *nityam* – as an eternal function; *anutiṣṭhanti* – execute regularly; *mānavāḥ* – human beings; *śraddhā-vantaḥ* – with faith and devotion; *anasūyantaḥ* – without envy; *mucyante* – become free; *te* – all of them; *api* – even; *karmabhiḥ* – from the bondage of the law of fruitive actions.

Those persons who execute their duties according to My injunctions and who follow this teaching faithfully, without envy, become free from the bondage of fruitive actions.

PURPORT: The injunction of the Supreme Personality of Godhead, Kṛṣṇa, is the essence of all Vedic wisdom and therefore is eternally true without exception. As the *Vedas* are eternal, so this truth of Kṛṣṇa consciousness is also eternal. One should have firm faith in this injunction, without envying the Lord. There are many philosophers who write comments on the *Bhagavad-gītā* but have no faith in Kṛṣṇa. They will never be liberated from the bondage of fruitive action. But an ordinary man with firm faith in the eternal injunctions of the Lord, even though unable to execute such orders, becomes liberated from the bondage of the law of *karma.* In the beginning of Kṛṣṇa consciousness, one may not fully discharge the injunctions of the Lord, but because one is not resentful of this principle and works sincerely without consideration of defeat and hopelessness, he will surely be promoted to the stage of pure Kṛṣṇa consciousness.

Text 32 ये त्वेतदभ्यसूयन्तो नानुतिष्ठन्ति मे मतम् ।
सर्वज्ञानविमूढांस्तान् विद्धि नष्टानचेतसः ॥३२॥

ye tv etad abhyasūyanto, nānutiṣṭhanti me matam
sarva-jñāna-vimūḍhāṁs tān, viddhi naṣṭān acetasaḥ

ye – those; *tu* – however; *etat* – this; *abhyasūyantaḥ* – out of envy; *na* – do not; *anutiṣṭhanti* – regularly perform; *me* – My; *matam* – injunction; *sarva-jñāna* – in all sorts of knowledge; *vimūḍhān* – perfectly befooled; *tān* – they are; *viddhi* – know it well; *naṣṭān* – all ruined; *acetasaḥ* – without Kṛṣṇa consciousness.

But those who, out of envy, disregard these teachings and do not follow them regularly are to be considered bereft of all knowledge, befooled, and ruined in their endeavors for perfection.

PURPORT: The flaw of not being Kṛṣṇa conscious is clearly stated herein. As there is punishment for disobedience to the order of the supreme executive head, so there is certainly punishment for disobedience to the order of the Supreme Personality of Godhead. A disobedient person, however great he may be, is ignorant of his own self, and of the Supreme Brahman, Paramātmā and the Personality of Godhead, due to a vacant heart. Therefore there is no hope of perfection of life for him.

Text 33 सदृशं चेष्टते स्वस्याः प्रकृतेर्ज्ञानवानपि ।
प्रकृतिं यान्ति भूतानि निग्रहः किं करिष्यति ॥३३॥

sadṛśaṁ ceṣṭate svasyāḥ, prakṛter jñānavān api
prakṛtiṁ yānti bhūtāni, nigrahaḥ kiṁ kariṣyati

sadṛśam – accordingly; *ceṣṭate* – tries; *svasyāḥ* – by his own; *prakṛteḥ* – modes of nature; *jñāna-vān* – learned; *api* – although; *prakṛtim* – nature; *yānti* – undergo; *bhūtāni* – all living entities; *nigrahaḥ* – repression; *kim* – what; *kariṣyati* – can do.

Even a man of knowledge acts according to his own nature, for everyone follows the nature he has acquired from the three modes. What can repression accomplish?

PURPORT: Unless one is situated on the transcendental platform of Kṛṣṇa consciousness, he cannot get free from the influence of the modes of material nature, as it is confirmed by the Lord in the Seventh Chapter (7.14). Therefore, even for the most highly educated person on the mundane plane, it is impossible to get out of the entanglement of *māyā* simply by theoretical knowledge, or by separating the soul from the body. There are many so-called spiritualists who outwardly pose as advanced in the science but inwardly or privately are completely under particular modes of nature which they are unable to surpass. Academically, one may be very learned, but because of his long association with material nature, he is in bondage. Kṛṣṇa consciousness helps one to get out of the material entanglement, even though one may be engaged in his prescribed duties in terms of material existence. Therefore, without being fully in Kṛṣṇa consciousness, one should not give up his occupational duties. No one should suddenly give up his prescribed duties and become a so-called *yogī* or transcendentalist artificially. It is better to be situated in one's position and to try to attain Kṛṣṇa consciousness under superior training. Thus one may be freed from the clutches of Kṛṣṇa's *māyā*.

Text 34 इन्द्रियस्येन्द्रियस्यार्थे रागद्वेषौ व्यवस्थितौ ।
तयोर्न वशमागच्छेत्तौ ह्यस्य परिपन्थिनौ ॥३४॥

indriyasyendriyasyārthe, rāga-dveṣau vyavasthitau
tayor na vaśam āgacchet, tau hy asya paripanthinau

indriyasya – of the senses; *indriyasya arthe* – in the sense objects; *rāga* – attachment; *dveṣau* – also detachment; *vyavasthitau* – put under regulations; *tayoḥ* – of them; *na* – never; *vaśam* – control; *āgacchet* – one should come; *tau* – those; *hi* – certainly; *asya* – his; *paripanthinau* – stumbling blocks.

There are principles to regulate attachment and aversion pertaining to the senses and their objects. One should not come under the control of such attachment and aversion, because they are stumbling blocks on the path of self-realization.

PURPORT: Those who are in Kṛṣṇa consciousness are naturally reluctant to engage in material sense gratification. But those who are not in such consciousness should follow the rules and regulations of the revealed scriptures. Unrestricted sense enjoyment is the cause of material encagement, but one who follows the rules and regulations of the revealed scriptures does not become entangled by the sense objects. For example, sex enjoyment is a necessity for the conditioned soul, and sex enjoyment is allowed under the license of marriage ties. According to scriptural injunctions, one is forbidden to engage in sex relationships with any women other than one's wife. All other women are to be considered as one's mother. But in spite of such injunctions, a man is still inclined to have sex relationships with other women. These propensities are to be curbed; otherwise they will be stumbling blocks on the path of self-realization. As long as the material body is there, the necessities of the material body are allowed, but under rules and regulations. And yet, we should not rely upon the control of such allowances. One has to follow those rules and regulations, unattached to them, because practice of sense gratification under regulations may also lead one to go astray – as much as there is always the chance of an accident, even on the royal roads. Although they may be very carefully maintained, no one can guarantee that there will be no danger even on the safest road. The sense enjoyment spirit has been current a very long, long time, owing to material association. Therefore, in spite of regulated sense enjoyment, there is every chance of falling down; therefore any attachment for regulated sense enjoyment must also be avoided by all means. But attachment to Kṛṣṇa consciousness, or acting always in the loving service of Kṛṣṇa, detaches one from all kinds of sensory activities. Therefore, no one should try to be detached from Kṛṣṇa consciousness at any stage of life. The whole purpose of detachment from all kinds of sense attachment is ultimately to become situated on the platform of Kṛṣṇa consciousness.

Text 35 श्रेयान् स्वधर्मो विगुणः परधर्मात्स्वनुष्ठितात् ।
स्वधर्मे निधनं श्रेयः परधर्मो भयावहः ॥३५॥

śreyān sva-dharmo viguṇaḥ, para-dharmāt sv-anuṣṭhitāt
sva-dharme nidhanaṁ śreyaḥ, para-dharmo bhayāvahaḥ

śreyān – far better; *sva-dharmaḥ* – one's prescribed duties; *viguṇaḥ* – even faulty; *para-dharmāt* – than duties mentioned for others; *su-anuṣṭhitāt* – perfectly done; *sva-dharme* – in one's prescribed duties; *nidhanam* – destruction; *śreyaḥ* – better; *para-dharmaḥ* – duties prescribed for others; *bhaya-āvahaḥ* – dangerous.

It is far better to discharge one's prescribed duties, even though faultily, than another's duties perfectly. Destruction in the course of performing one's own duty is better than engaging in another's duties, for to follow another's path is dangerous.

PURPORT: One should therefore discharge his prescribed duties in full Kṛṣṇa consciousness rather than those prescribed for others. Materially, prescribed duties are duties enjoined according to one's psychophysical condition, under the spell of the modes of material nature. Spiritual duties are as ordered by the spiritual master for the transcendental service of Kṛṣṇa. But whether material or spiritual, one should stick to his prescribed duties even up to death, rather than imitate another's prescribed duties. Duties on the spiritual platform and duties on the material platform may be different, but the principle of following the authorized direction is always good for the performer. When one is under the spell of the modes of material nature, one should follow the prescribed rules for his particular situation and should not imitate others. For example, a *brāhmaṇa,* who is in the mode of goodness, is nonviolent, whereas a *kṣatriya,* who is in the mode of passion, is allowed to be violent. As such, for a *kṣatriya* it is better to be vanquished following the rules of violence than to imitate a *brāhmaṇa* who follows the principles of nonviolence. Everyone has to cleanse his heart by a gradual process, not abruptly. However, when one transcends the modes of material nature and is fully situated in Kṛṣṇa consciousness, he can perform anything and everything under the direction of a bona fide spiritual master. In that complete stage of Kṛṣṇa consciousness, the *kṣatriya* may act as a *brāhmaṇa,* or a *brāhmaṇa* may act as a *kṣatriya.* In the transcendental stage, the distinctions of the material world do not apply. For example, Viśvāmitra was originally a *kṣatriya,* but later on he acted as a *brāhmaṇa,* whereas Paraśurāma was a *brāhmaṇa* but later on he acted as a *kṣatriya.* Being transcendentally situated, they could do so; but as long as one is on the material platform, he must perform his duties according to the modes of material nature. At the same time, he must have a full sense of Kṛṣṇa consciousness.

Text 36 अर्जुन उवाच
अथ केन प्रयुक्तोऽयं पापं चरति पूरुषः ।
अनिच्छन्नपि वार्ष्णेय बलादिव नियोजितः ॥३६॥

arjuna uvāca
atha kena prayukto 'yaṁ, pāpaṁ carati pūruṣaḥ
anicchann api vārṣṇeya, balād iva niyojitaḥ

arjunaḥ uvāca – Arjuna said; *atha* – then; *kena* – by what; *prayuktaḥ* – impelled; *ayam* – one; *pāpam* – sins; *carati* – does; *pūruṣaḥ* – a man;

anicchan – without desiring; *api* – although; *vārṣṇeya* – O descendant of Vṛṣṇi; *balāt* – by force; *iva* – as if; *niyojitaḥ* – engaged.

Arjuna said: O descendant of Vṛṣṇi, by what is one impelled to sinful acts, even unwillingly, as if engaged by force?

PURPORT: A living entity, as part and parcel of the Supreme, is originally spiritual, pure, and free from all material contaminations. Therefore, by nature he is not subject to the sins of the material world. But when he is in contact with the material nature, he acts in many sinful ways without hesitation, and sometimes even against his will. As such, Arjuna's question to Kṛṣṇa is very sanguine, as to the perverted nature of the living entities. Although the living entity sometimes does not want to act in sin, he is still forced to act. Sinful actions are not, however, impelled by the Supersoul within, but are due to another cause, as the Lord explains in the next verse.

Text 37 श्रीभगवानुवाच
काम एष क्रोध एष रजोगुणसमुद्भवः ।
महाशनो महापाप्मा विद्ध्येनमिह वैरिणम् ॥३७॥

śrī-bhagavān uvāca
kāma eṣa krodha eṣa, rajo-guṇa-samudbhavaḥ
mahāśano mahā-pāpmā, viddhy enam iha vairiṇam

śrī-bhagavān uvāca – the Personality of Godhead said; *kāmaḥ* – lust; *eṣaḥ* – this; *krodhaḥ* – wrath; *eṣaḥ* – this; *rajaḥ-guṇa* – the mode of passion; *samudbhavaḥ* – born of; *mahā-aśanaḥ* – all-devouring; *mahā-pāpmā* – greatly sinful; *viddhi* – know; *enam* – this; *iha* – in the material world; *vairiṇam* – greatest enemy.

The Supreme Personality of Godhead said: It is lust only, Arjuna, which is born of contact with the material mode of passion and later transformed into wrath, and which is the all-devouring sinful enemy of this world.

PURPORT: When a living entity comes in contact with the material creation, his eternal love for Kṛṣṇa is transformed into lust, in association with the mode of passion. Or, in other words, the sense of love of God becomes transformed into lust, as milk in contact with sour tamarind is transformed into yogurt. Then again, when lust is unsatisfied, it turns into wrath; wrath is transformed into illusion, and illusion continues the material existence. Therefore, lust is the greatest enemy of the living entity, and it is lust only which induces the pure living entity to remain entangled in the material world. Wrath is the manifestation of the mode of ignorance; these modes exhibit themselves as wrath and other corollaries. If, therefore, the mode of passion, instead of being degraded into the mode of ignorance, is elevated to the mode of goodness by the prescribed method of living and acting, then one can be saved from the degradation of wrath by spiritual attachment.

The Supreme Personality of Godhead expanded Himself into many for His ever-increasing spiritual bliss, and the living entities are parts and parcels of this spiritual bliss. They also have partial independence, but by misuse of their independence, when the service attitude is transformed into the propensity for sense enjoyment, they come under the sway of lust. This material creation is created by the Lord to give facility to the conditioned souls to fulfill these lustful propensities, and when completely baffled by prolonged lustful activities, the living entities begin to inquire about their real position.

This inquiry is the beginning of the *Vedānta-sūtras,* wherein it is said, *athāto brahma-jijñāsā:* one should inquire into the Supreme. And the Supreme is defined in *Śrīmad-Bhāgavatam* as *janmādy asya yato 'nvayād itarataś ca,* or, "The origin of everything is the Supreme Brahman." Therefore the origin of lust is also in the Supreme. If, therefore, lust is transformed into love for the Supreme, or transformed into Kṛṣṇa consciousness – or, in other words, desiring everything for Kṛṣṇa – then both lust and wrath can be spiritualized. Hanumān, the great servitor of Lord Rāma, exhibited his wrath by burning the golden city of Rāvaṇa, but by doing so he became the greatest devotee of the Lord. Here also, in *Bhagavad-gītā,* the Lord induces Arjuna to engage his wrath upon his enemies for the satisfaction of the Lord. Therefore, lust and wrath, when they are employed in Kṛṣṇa consciousness, become our friends instead of our enemies.

Text 38 धूमेनाव्रियते वह्निर्यथादर्शो मलेन च ।
यथोल्बेनावृतो गर्भस्तथा तेनेदमावृतम् ॥३८॥

dhūmenāvriyate vahnir, yathādarśo malena ca
yatholbenāvṛto garbhas, tathā tenedam āvṛtam

dhūmena – by smoke; *āvriyate* – is covered; *vahniḥ* – fire; *yathā* – just as; *ādarśaḥ* – mirror; *malena* – by dust; *ca* – also; *yathā* – just as; *ulbena* –

by the womb; *āvṛtaḥ* – is covered; *garbhaḥ* – embryo; *tathā* – so; *tena* – by that lust; *idam* – this; *āvṛtam* – is covered.

As fire is covered by smoke, as a mirror is covered by dust, or as the embryo is covered by the womb, the living entity is similarly covered by different degrees of this lust.

PURPORT: There are three degrees of covering of the living entity by which his pure consciousness is obscured. This covering is but lust under different manifestations like smoke in the fire, dust on the mirror, and the womb about the embryo. When lust is compared to smoke, it is understood that the fire of the living spark can be a little perceived. In other words, when the living entity exhibits his Kṛṣṇa consciousness slightly, he may be likened to the fire covered by smoke. Although fire is necessary where there is smoke, there is no overt manifestation of fire in the early stage. This stage is like the beginning of Kṛṣṇa consciousness. The dust on the mirror refers to a cleansing process of the mirror of the mind by so many spiritual methods. The best process is to chant the holy names of the Lord. The embryo covered by the womb is an analogy illustrating a helpless position, for the child in the womb is so helpless that he cannot even move. This stage of living condition can be compared to that of the trees. The trees are also living entities, but they have been put in such a condition of life by such a great exhibition of lust that they are almost void of all consciousness. The covered mirror is compared to the birds and beasts, and the smoke-covered fire is compared to the human being. In the form of a human being, the living entity may revive a little Kṛṣṇa consciousness, and, if he makes further development, the fire of spiritual life can be kindled in the human form of life. By careful handling of the smoke in the fire, fire can be made to blaze. Therefore the human form of life is a chance for the living entity to escape the entanglement of material existence. In the human form of life, one can conquer the enemy, lust, by cultivation of Kṛṣṇa consciousness under able guidance.

Text 39 आवृतं ज्ञानमेतेन ज्ञानिनो नित्यवैरिणा ।
कामरूपेण कौन्तेय दुष्पूरेणानलेन च ॥३९॥

āvṛtaṁ jñānam etena, jñānino nitya-vairiṇā
kāma-rūpeṇa kaunteya, duṣpūreṇānalena ca

āvṛtam – covered; *jñānam* – pure consciousness; *etena* – by this; *jñāninaḥ* – of the knower; *nitya-vairiṇā* – by the eternal enemy; *kāma-rūpeṇa* –

in the form of lust; *kaunteya* – O son of Kuntī; *duṣpūreṇa* – never to be satisfied; *analena* – by the fire; *ca* – also.

Thus the wise living entity's pure consciousness becomes covered by his eternal enemy in the form of lust, which is never satisfied and which burns like fire.

PURPORT: It is said in the *Manu-smṛti* that lust cannot be satisfied by any amount of sense enjoyment, just as fire is never extinguished by a constant supply of fuel. In the material world, the center of all activities is sex, and thus this material world is called *maithunya-āgāra,* or the shackles of sex life. In the ordinary prison house, criminals are kept within bars; similarly, the criminals who are disobedient to the laws of the Lord are shackled by sex life. Advancement of material civilization on the basis of sense gratification means increasing the duration of the material existence of a living entity. Therefore, this lust is the symbol of ignorance by which the living entity is kept within the material world. While one enjoys sense gratification, it may be that there is some feeling of happiness, but actually that so-called feeling of happiness is the ultimate enemy of the sense enjoyer.

Text 40 इन्द्रियाणि मनो बुद्धिरस्याधिष्ठानमुच्यते ।
एतैर्विमोहयत्येष ज्ञानमावृत्य देहिनम् ॥४०॥

indriyāṇi mano buddhir, asyādhiṣṭhānam ucyate
etair vimohayaty eṣa, jñānam āvṛtya dehinam

indriyāṇi – the senses; *manaḥ* – the mind; *buddhiḥ* – the intelligence; *asya* – of this lust; *adhiṣṭhānam* – sitting place; *ucyate* – is called; *etaiḥ* – by all these; *vimohayati* – bewilders; *eṣaḥ* – this lust; *jñānam* – knowledge; *āvṛtya* – covering; *dehinam* – of the embodied.

The senses, the mind and the intelligence are the sitting places of this lust. Through them lust covers the real knowledge of the living entity and bewilders him.

PURPORT: The enemy has captured different strategic positions in the body of the conditioned soul, and therefore Lord Kṛṣṇa is giving hints of those places, so that one who wants to conquer the enemy may know where he can be found. Mind is the center of all the activities of the senses, and thus when we hear about sense objects the mind generally becomes a reservoir of all ideas of sense gratification; and, as a result, the mind and the senses become the repositories of lust. Next, the intelligence department becomes the capital of such lustful propensities. Intelligence is the immediate next-door neighbor of the spirit soul. Lusty intelligence influences the spirit soul to acquire the false ego and identify itself with matter, and thus with the mind and senses. The spirit soul becomes addicted to enjoying the material senses and mistakes this as true happiness. This false identification of the spirit soul is very nicely explained in the *Śrīmad-Bhāgavatam* (10.84.13):

yasyātma-buddhiḥ kuṇape tri-dhātuke
sva-dhīḥ kalatrādiṣu bhauma ijya-dhīḥ
yat-tīrtha-buddhiḥ salile na karhicij
janeṣv abhijñeṣu sa eva go-kharaḥ

"A human being who identifies this body made of three elements with his self, who considers the by-products of the body to be his kinsmen, who considers the land of birth worshipable, and who goes to the place of pilgrimage simply to take a bath rather than meet men of transcendental knowledge there, is to be considered like an ass or a cow."

Text 41 तस्मात्त्वमिन्द्रियाण्यादौ नियम्य भरतर्षभ ।
पाप्मानं प्रजहि ह्येनं ज्ञानविज्ञाननाशनम् ॥४१॥

tasmāt tvam indriyāṇy ādau, niyamya bharatarṣabha
pāpmānaṁ prajahi hy enaṁ, jñāna-vijñāna-nāśanam

tasmāt – therefore; *tvam* – you; *indriyāṇi* – senses; *ādau* – in the beginning; *niyamya* – by regulating; *bharata-ṛṣabha* – O chief amongst the descendants of Bharata; *pāpmānam* – the great symbol of sin; *prajahi* – curb; *hi* – certainly; *enam* – this; *jñāna* – of knowledge; *vijñāna* – and scientific knowledge of the pure soul; *nāśanam* – the destroyer.

Therefore, O Arjuna, best of the Bhāratas, in the very beginning curb this great symbol of sin [lust] by regulating the senses, and slay this destroyer of knowledge and self-realization.

PURPORT: The Lord advised Arjuna to regulate the senses from the very beginning so that he could curb the greatest sinful enemy, lust, which destroys the urge for self-realization and specific knowledge of the self. *Jñāna* refers to knowledge of self as distinguished from non-self, or in other words, knowledge that the spirit soul is not the body. *Vijñāna* refers to specific knowledge of the spirit soul's constitutional position and his relationship to the Supreme Soul. It is explained thus in the *Śrīmad-Bhāgavatam* (2.9.31):

jñānaṁ parama-guhyaṁ me, yad vijñāna-samanvitam
sa-rahasyaṁ tad-aṅgaṁ ca, gṛhāṇa gaditaṁ mayā

"The knowledge of the self and Supreme Self is very confidential and mysterious, but such knowledge and specific realization can be understood if explained with their various aspects by the Lord Himself." *Bhagavad-gītā* gives us that general and specific knowledge of the self. The living entities are parts and parcels of the Lord, and therefore they are simply meant to serve the Lord. This consciousness is called Kṛṣṇa consciousness. So, from the very beginning of life one has to learn this Kṛṣṇa consciousness, and thereby one may become fully Kṛṣṇa conscious and act accordingly.

Lust is only the perverted reflection of the love of God which is natural for every living entity. But if one is educated in Kṛṣṇa consciousness from the very beginning, that natural love of God cannot deteriorate into lust. When love of God deteriorates into lust, it is very difficult to return to the normal condition. Nonetheless, Kṛṣṇa consciousness is so powerful that even a late beginner can become a lover of God by following the regulative principles of devotional service. So, from any stage of life, or from the time of understanding its urgency, one can begin regulating the senses in Kṛṣṇa consciousness, devotional service of the Lord, and turn the lust into love of Godhead – the highest perfectional stage of human life.

Text 42 इन्द्रियाणि पराण्याहुरिन्द्रियेभ्यः परं मनः ।
मनसस्तु परा बुद्धिर्यो बुद्धेः परतस्तु सः ॥४२॥

indriyāṇi parāṇy āhur, indriyebhyaḥ paraṁ manaḥ
manasas tu parā buddhir, yo buddheḥ paratas tu saḥ

indriyāṇi – senses; *parāṇi* – superior; *āhuḥ* – are said; *indriyebhyaḥ* – more than the senses; *param* – superior; *manaḥ* – the mind; *manasaḥ* – more than the mind; *tu* – also; *parā* – superior; *buddhiḥ* – intelligence; *yaḥ* – who; *buddheḥ* – more than the intelligence; *parataḥ* – superior; *tu* – but; *saḥ* – he.

The working senses are superior to dull matter; mind is higher than the senses; intelligence is still higher than the mind; and he [the soul] is even higher than the intelligence.

PURPORT: The senses are different outlets for the activities of lust. Lust is reserved within the body, but it is given vent through the senses. Therefore, the senses are superior to the body as a whole. These outlets are not in use when there is superior consciousness, or Kṛṣṇa consciousness. In Kṛṣṇa consciousness the soul makes direct connection with the Supreme Personality of Godhead; therefore the hierarchy of bodily functions, as described here, ultimately ends in the Supreme Soul. Bodily action means the functions of the senses, and stopping the senses means stopping all bodily actions. But since the mind is active, then even though the body may be silent and at rest, the mind will act – as it does during dreaming. But above the mind is the determination of the intelligence, and above the intelligence is the soul proper. If, therefore, the soul is directly engaged with the Supreme, naturally all other subordinates, namely, the intelligence, mind and senses, will be automatically engaged. In the *Kaṭha Upaniṣad* there is a similar passage, in which it is said that the objects of sense gratification are superior to the senses, and mind is superior to the sense objects. If, therefore, the mind is directly engaged in the service of the Lord constantly, then there is no chance that the senses will become engaged in other ways. This mental attitude has already been explained. *Paraṁ dṛṣṭvā nivartate.* If the mind is engaged in the transcendental service of the Lord, there is no chance of its being engaged in the lower propensities. In the *Kaṭha Upaniṣad* the soul has been described as *mahān,* the great. Therefore the soul is above all – namely, the sense objects, the senses, the mind and the intelligence. Therefore, directly understanding the constitutional position of the soul is the solution of the whole problem.

With intelligence one has to seek out the constitutional position of the soul and then engage the mind always in Kṛṣṇa consciousness. That solves the whole problem. A neophyte spiritualist is generally advised to keep aloof from the objects of the senses. But aside from that, one has to strengthen the mind by use of intelligence. If by intelligence one engages one's mind in Kṛṣṇa consciousness, by complete surrender unto the Supreme Personality of Godhead, then, automatically, the mind becomes stronger, and even though the senses are very strong, like serpents, they will be no more effective than serpents with broken fangs. But even though the soul is the master of intelligence and mind, and the senses also, still, unless it is strengthened by association with Kṛṣṇa in Kṛṣṇa consciousness, there is every chance of falling down due to the agitated mind.

Text 43 एवं बुद्धेः परं बुद्ध्वा संस्तभ्यात्मानमात्मना ।
जहि शत्रुं महाबाहो कामरूपं दुरासदम् ॥४३॥

evaṁ buddheḥ paraṁ buddhvā, saṁstabhyātmānam ātmanā
jahi śatruṁ mahā-bāho, kāma-rūpaṁ durāsadam

evam – thus; *buddheḥ* – to intelligence; *param* – superior; *buddhvā* – knowing; *saṁstabhya* – by steadying; *ātmānam* – the mind; *ātmanā* – by deliberate intelligence; *jahi* – conquer; *śatrum* – the enemy; *mahā-bāho* – O mighty-armed one; *kāma-rūpam* – in the form of lust; *durāsadam* – formidable.

Thus knowing oneself to be transcendental to the material senses, mind and intelligence, O mighty-armed Arjuna, one should steady the mind by deliberate spiritual intelligence [Kṛṣṇa consciousness] and thus – by spiritual strength – conquer this insatiable enemy known as lust.

PURPORT: This Third Chapter of the *Bhagavad-gītā* is conclusively directive to Kṛṣṇa consciousness by knowing oneself as the eternal servitor of the Supreme Personality of Godhead, without considering impersonal voidness the ultimate end. In the material existence of life, one is certainly influenced by propensities for lust and desire for dominating the resources of material nature. Desire for overlording and for sense gratification is the greatest enemy of the conditioned soul; but by the strength of Kṛṣṇa consciousness, one can control the material senses, the mind and the intelligence. One may not give up work and prescribed duties all of a sudden; but by gradually developing Kṛṣṇa consciousness, one can be situated in a transcendental position without being influenced by the material senses and the mind – by steady intelligence directed toward one's pure identity. This is the sum total of this chapter. In the immature stage of material existence, philosophical speculations and artificial attempts to control the senses by the so-called practice of yogic postures can never help a man toward spiritual life. He must be trained in Kṛṣṇa consciousness by higher intelligence.

Thus end the Bhaktivedanta Purports to the Third Chapter of the Śrīmad Bhagavad-gītā *in the matter of* Karma-yoga, *or the Discharge of One's Prescribed Duty in Kṛṣṇa Consciousness.*

CHAPTER FOUR

Transcendental Knowledge

Text 1 श्रीभगवानुवाच
इमं विवस्वते योगं प्रोक्तवानहमव्ययम् ।
विवस्वान्मनवे प्राह मनुरिक्ष्वाकवेऽब्रवीत् ॥ १ ॥

śrī-bhagavān uvāca
imaṁ vivasvate yogaṁ, proktavān aham avyayam
vivasvān manave prāha, manur ikṣvākave 'bravīt

śrī-bhagavān uvāca – the Supreme Personality of Godhead said; *imam* – this; *vivasvate* – unto the sun-god; *yogam* – the science of one's relationship to the Supreme; *proktavān* – instructed; *aham* – I; *avyayam* – imperishable; *vivasvān* – Vivasvān (the sun-god's name); *manave* – unto the father of mankind (of the name Vaivasvata); *prāha* – told; *manuḥ* – the father of mankind; *ikṣvākave* – unto King Ikṣvāku; *abravīt* – said.

The Personality of Godhead, Lord Śrī Kṛṣṇa, said: I instructed this imperishable science of yoga to the sun-god, Vivasvān, and Vivasvān instructed it to Manu, the father of mankind, and Manu in turn instructed it to Ikṣvāku.

PURPORT: Herein we find the history of the *Bhagavad-gītā* traced from a remote time when it was delivered to the royal order of all planets, beginning from the sun planet. The kings of all planets are especially meant for the protection of the inhabitants, and therefore the royal order should understand the science of *Bhagavad-gītā* in order to be able to rule the citizens and protect them from material bondage to lust. Human life is meant for cultivation of spiritual knowledge, in eternal relationship with the Supreme Personality of Godhead, and the executive heads of all states and all planets are obliged to impart this lesson to the citizens by education, culture and devotion. In other words, the executive heads of all states are intended to spread the science of Kṛṣṇa consciousness so that the people may take advantage of this great science and pursue a successful path, utilizing the opportunity of the human form of life.

In this millennium, the sun-god is known as Vivasvān, the king of the sun, which is the origin of all planets within the solar system. In the *Brahma-saṁhitā* (5.52) it is stated:

yac-cakṣur eṣa savitā sakala-grahāṇāṁ
rājā samasta-sura-mūrtir aśeṣa-tejāḥ
yasyājñayā bhramati sambhṛta-kāla-cakro
govindam ādi-puruṣaṁ tam ahaṁ bhajāmi

"Let me worship," Lord Brahmā said, "the Supreme Personality of Godhead, Govinda [Kṛṣṇa], who is the original person and under whose order the sun, which is the king of all planets, is assuming immense power and heat. The sun represents the eye of the Lord and traverses its orbit in obedience to His order."

The sun is the king of the planets, and the sun-god (at present of the name Vivasvān) rules the sun planet, which is controlling all other planets by supplying heat and light. He is rotating under the order of Kṛṣṇa, and Lord Kṛṣṇa originally made Vivasvān His first disciple to understand the science of *Bhagavad-gītā*. The *Gītā* is not, therefore, a speculative treatise for the insignificant mundane scholar but is a standard book of knowledge coming down from time immemorial.

In the *Mahābhārata* (*Śānti-parva* 348.51–52) we can trace out the history of the *Gītā* as follows:

tretā-yugādau ca tato, vivasvān manave dadau
manuś ca loka-bhṛty-arthaṁ, sutāyekṣvākave dadau
ikṣvākuṇā ca kathito, vyāpya lokān avasthitaḥ

"In the beginning of the millennium known as Tretā-yuga this science of the relationship with the Supreme was delivered by Vivasvān to Manu.

Manu, being the father of mankind, gave it to his son Mahārāja Ikṣvāku, the king of this earth planet and forefather of the Raghu dynasty, in which Lord Rāmacandra appeared. Therefore, *Bhagavad-gītā* existed in human society from the time of Mahārāja Ikṣvāku."

At the present moment we have just passed through five thousand years of the Kali-yuga, which lasts 432,000 years. Before this there was Dvāpara-yuga (800,000 years), and before that there was Tretā-yuga (1,200,000 years). Thus, some 2,005,000 years ago, Manu spoke the *Bhagavad-gītā* to his disciple and son Mahārāja Ikṣvāku, the king of this planet earth. The age of the current Manu is calculated to last some 305,300,000 years, of which 120,400,000 have passed. Accepting that before the birth of Manu the *Gītā* was spoken by the Lord to His disciple the sun-god Vivasvān, a rough estimate is that the *Gītā* was spoken at least 120,400,000 years ago; and in human society it has been extant for two million years. It was respoken by the Lord again to Arjuna about five thousand years ago. That is the rough estimate of the history of the *Gītā,* according to the *Gītā* itself and according to the version of the speaker, Lord Śrī Kṛṣṇa. It was spoken to the sun-god Vivasvān because he is also a *kṣatriya* and is the father of all *kṣatriyas* who are descendants of the sun-god, or the *sūrya-vaṁśa kṣatriyas.* Because *Bhagavad-gītā* is as good as the *Vedas,* being spoken by the Supreme Personality of Godhead, this knowledge is *apauruṣeya,* superhuman. Since the Vedic instructions are accepted as they are, without human interpretation, the *Gītā* must therefore be accepted without mundane interpretation. The mundane wranglers may speculate on the *Gītā* in their own ways, but that is not *Bhagavad-gītā* as it is. Therefore, *Bhagavad-gītā* has to be accepted as it is, from the disciplic succession, and it is described herein that the Lord spoke to the sun-god, the sun-god spoke to his son Manu, and Manu spoke to his son Ikṣvāku.

Text 2 एवं परम्पराप्राप्तमिमं राजर्षयो विदुः ।
स कालेनेह महता योगो नष्टः परन्तप ॥ २ ॥

evaṁ paramparā-prāptam, imaṁ rājarṣayo viduḥ
sa kāleneha mahatā, yogo naṣṭaḥ paran-tapa

evam – thus; *paramparā* – by disciplic succession; *prāptam* – received; *imam* – this science; *rāja-ṛṣayaḥ* – the saintly kings; *viduḥ* – understood; *saḥ* – that knowledge; *kālena* – in the course of time; *iha* – in this world; *mahatā* – great; *yogaḥ* – the science of one's relationship with the Supreme; *naṣṭaḥ* – scattered; *param-tapa* – O Arjuna, subduer of the enemies.

This supreme science was thus received through the chain of disciplic succession, and the saintly kings understood it in that way. But in course of time the succession was broken, and therefore the science as it is appears to be lost.

PURPORT: It is clearly stated that the *Gītā* was especially meant for the saintly kings because they were to execute its purpose in ruling over the citizens. Certainly *Bhagavad-gītā* was never meant for the demonic persons, who would dissipate its value for no one's benefit and would devise all types of interpretations according to personal whims. As soon as the original purpose was scattered by the motives of the unscrupulous commentators, there arose the need to reestablish the disciplic succession. Five thousand years ago it was detected by the Lord Himself that the disciplic succession was broken, and therefore He declared that the purpose of the *Gītā* appeared to be lost. In the same way, at the present moment also there are so many editions of the *Gītā* (especially in English), but almost all of them are not according to authorized disciplic succession. There are innumerable interpretations rendered by different mundane scholars, but almost all of them do not accept the Supreme Personality of Godhead, Kṛṣṇa, although they make a good business on the words of Śrī Kṛṣṇa. This spirit is demonic, because demons do not believe in God but simply enjoy the property of the Supreme. Since there is a great need of an edition of the *Gītā* in English, as it is received by the *paramparā* (disciplic succession) system, an attempt is made herewith to fulfill this great want. *Bhagavad-gītā* – accepted as it is – is a great boon to humanity; but if it is accepted as a treatise of philosophical speculations, it is simply a waste of time.

Text 3 स एवायं मया तेऽद्य योगः प्रोक्तः पुरातनः ।
भक्तोऽसि मे सखा चेति रहस्यं ह्येतदुत्तमम् ॥ ३ ॥

sa evāyaṁ mayā te 'dya, yogaḥ proktaḥ purātanaḥ
bhakto 'si me sakhā ceti, rahasyaṁ hy etad uttamam

saḥ – the same; *eva* – certainly; *ayam* – this; *mayā* – by Me; *te* – unto you; *adya* – today; *yogaḥ* – the science of *yoga; proktaḥ* – spoken; *purātanaḥ* – very old; *bhaktaḥ* – devotee; *asi* – you are; *me* – My; *sakhā* – friend;

ca – also; *iti* – therefore; *rahasyam* – mystery; *hi* – certainly; *etat* – this; *uttamam* – transcendental.

That very ancient science of the relationship with the Supreme is today told by Me to you because you are My devotee as well as My friend and can therefore understand the transcendental mystery of this science.

PURPORT: There are two classes of men, namely the devotee and the demon. The Lord selected Arjuna as the recipient of this great science owing to his being a devotee of the Lord, but for the demon it is not possible to understand this great mysterious science. There are a number of editions of this great book of knowledge. Some of them have commentaries by the devotees, and some of them have commentaries by the demons. Commentation by the devotees is real, whereas that of the demons is useless. Arjuna accepts Śrī Kṛṣṇa as the Supreme Personality of Godhead, and any commentary on the *Gītā* following in the footsteps of Arjuna is real devotional service to the cause of this great science. The demonic, however, do not accept Lord Kṛṣṇa as He is. Instead they concoct something about Kṛṣṇa and mislead general readers from the path of Kṛṣṇa's instructions. Here is a warning about such misleading paths. One should try to follow the disciplic succession from Arjuna, and thus be benefited by this great science of *Śrīmad Bhagavad-gītā.*

Text 4 अर्जुन उवाच
अपरं भवतो जन्म परं जन्म विवस्वतः ।
कथमेतद्विजानीयां त्वमादौ प्रोक्तवानिति ॥ ४ ॥

arjuna uvāca
aparaṁ bhavato janma, paraṁ janma vivasvataḥ
katham etad vijānīyāṁ, tvam ādau proktavān iti

arjunaḥ uvāca – Arjuna said; *aparam* – junior; *bhavataḥ* – Your; *janma* – birth; *param* – superior; *janma* – birth; *vivasvataḥ* – of the sun-god; *katham* – how; *etat* – this; *vijānīyām* – shall I understand; *tvam* – You; *ādau* – in the beginning; *proktavān* – instructed; *iti* – thus.

Arjuna said: The sun-god Vivasvān is senior by birth to You. How am I to understand that in the beginning You instructed this science to him?

PURPORT: Arjuna is an accepted devotee of the Lord, so how could he not believe Kṛṣṇa's words? The fact is that Arjuna is not inquiring for himself but for those who do not believe in the Supreme Personality of Godhead or for the demons who do not like the idea that Kṛṣṇa should be accepted as the Supreme Personality of Godhead; for them only Arjuna inquires on this point, as if he were himself not aware of the Personality of Godhead, or Kṛṣṇa. As it will be evident from the Tenth Chapter, Arjuna knew perfectly well that Kṛṣṇa is the Supreme Personality of Godhead, the fountainhead of everything and the last word in transcendence. Of course, Kṛṣṇa also appeared as the son of Devakī on this earth. How Kṛṣṇa remained the same Supreme Personality of Godhead, the eternal original person, is very difficult for an ordinary man to understand. Therefore, to clarify this point, Arjuna put this question before Kṛṣṇa so that He Himself could speak authoritatively. That Kṛṣṇa is the supreme authority is accepted by the whole world, not only at present but from time immemorial, and the demons alone reject Him. Anyway, since Kṛṣṇa is the authority accepted by all, Arjuna put this question before Him in order that Kṛṣṇa would describe Himself without being depicted by the demons, who always try to distort Him in a way understandable to the demons and their followers. It is necessary that everyone, for his own interest, know the science of Kṛṣṇa. Therefore, when Kṛṣṇa Himself speaks about Himself, it is auspicious for all the worlds. To the demons, such explanations by Kṛṣṇa Himself may appear to be strange because the demons always study Kṛṣṇa from their own standpoint, but those who are devotees heartily welcome the statements of Kṛṣṇa when they are spoken by Kṛṣṇa Himself. The devotees will always worship such authoritative statements of Kṛṣṇa because they are always eager to know more and more about Him. The atheists, who consider Kṛṣṇa an ordinary man, may in this way come to know that Kṛṣṇa is superhuman, that He is *sac-cid-ānanda-vigraha* – the eternal form of bliss and knowledge – that He is transcendental, and that He is above the domination of the modes of material nature and above the influence of time and space. A devotee of Kṛṣṇa, like Arjuna, is undoubtedly above any misunderstanding of the transcendental position of Kṛṣṇa. Arjuna's putting this question before the Lord is simply an attempt by the devotee to defy the atheistic attitude of persons who consider Kṛṣṇa to be an ordinary human being, subject to the modes of material nature.

Text 5 श्रीभगवानुवाच
बहूनि मे व्यतीतानि जन्मानि तव चार्जुन ।
तान्यहं वेद सर्वाणि न त्वं वेत्थ परन्तप ॥५॥

śrī-bhagavān uvāca
bahūni me vyatītāni, janmāni tava cārjuna
tāny ahaṁ veda sarvāṇi, na tvaṁ vettha paran-tapa

śrī-bhagavān uvāca – the Personality of Godhead said; *bahūni* – many; *me* – of Mine; *vyatītāni* – have passed; *janmāni* – births; *tava* – of yours; *ca* – and also; *arjuna* – O Arjuna; *tāni* – those; *aham* – I; *veda* – do know; *sarvāṇi* – all; *na* – not; *tvam* – you; *vettha* – know; *param-tapa* – O subduer of the enemy.

The Personality of Godhead said: Many, many births both you and I have passed. I can remember all of them, but you cannot, O subduer of the enemy!

PURPORT: In the *Brahma-saṁhitā* (5.33) we have information of many, many incarnations of the Lord. It is stated there:

advaitam acyutam anādim ananta-rūpam
ādyaṁ purāṇa-puruṣaṁ nava-yauvanaṁ ca
vedeṣu durlabham adurlabham ātma-bhaktau
govindam ādi-puruṣaṁ tam ahaṁ bhajāmi

"I worship the Supreme Personality of Godhead, Govinda [Kṛṣṇa], who is the original person – absolute, infallible, without beginning. Although expanded into unlimited forms, He is still the same original, the oldest, and the person always appearing as a fresh youth. Such eternal, blissful, all-knowing forms of the Lord are usually not understood by even the best Vedic scholars, but they are always manifest to pure, unalloyed devotees."

It is also stated in *Brahma-saṁhitā* (5.39):

rāmādi-mūrtiṣu kalā-niyamena tiṣṭhan
nānāvatāram akarod bhuvaneṣu kintu
kṛṣṇaḥ svayaṁ samabhavat paramaḥ pumān yo
govindam ādi-puruṣaṁ tam ahaṁ bhajāmi

"I worship the Supreme Personality of Godhead, Govinda [Kṛṣṇa], who is always situated in various incarnations such as Rāma, Nṛsiṁha and many subincarnations as well, but who is the original Personality of Godhead known as Kṛṣṇa, and who incarnates personally also."

In the *Vedas* also it is said that the Lord, although one without a second, manifests Himself in innumerable forms. He is like the *vaidūrya* stone, which changes color yet still remains one. All those multiforms are understood by the pure, unalloyed devotees, but not by a simple study of the *Vedas* (*vedeṣu durlabham adurlabham ātma-bhaktau*). Devotees like Arjuna are constant companions of the Lord, and whenever the Lord incarnates, the associate devotees also incarnate in order to serve the Lord in different capacities. Arjuna is one of these devotees, and in this verse it is understood that some millions of years ago when Lord Kṛṣṇa spoke the *Bhagavad-gītā* to the sun-god Vivasvān, Arjuna, in a different capacity, was also present. But the difference between the Lord and Arjuna is that the Lord remembered the incident whereas Arjuna could not remember. That is the difference between the part-and-parcel living entity and the Supreme Lord. Although Arjuna is addressed herein as the mighty hero who could subdue the enemies, he is unable to recall what had happened in his various past births. Therefore, a living entity, however great he may be in the material estimation, can never equal the Supreme Lord. Anyone who is a constant companion of the Lord is certainly a liberated person, but he cannot be equal to the Lord. The Lord is described in the *Brahma-saṁhitā* as infallible (*acyuta*), which means that He never forgets Himself, even though He is in material contact. Therefore, the Lord and the living entity can never be equal in all respects, even if the living entity is as liberated as Arjuna. Although Arjuna is a devotee of the Lord, he sometimes forgets the nature of the Lord, but by the divine grace a devotee can at once understand the infallible condition of the Lord, whereas a nondevotee or a demon cannot understand this transcendental nature. Consequently these descriptions in the *Gītā* cannot be understood by demonic brains. Kṛṣṇa remembered acts which were performed by Him millions of years before, but Arjuna could not, despite the fact that both Kṛṣṇa and Arjuna are eternal in nature. We may also note herein that a living entity forgets everything due to his change of body, but the Lord remembers because He does not change His *sac-cid-ānanda* body. He is *advaita,* which means there is no distinction between His body and Himself. Everything in relation to Him is spirit – whereas the conditioned soul is different from his material body. And because the Lord's body and self are identical, His position is always different from that of the ordinary living entity, even when He descends to the material platform. The demons cannot adjust themselves to this transcendental nature of the Lord, which the Lord Himself explains in the following verse.

Text 6 अजोऽपि सन्नव्ययात्मा भूतानामीश्वरोऽपि सन् ।
प्रकृतिं स्वामधिष्ठाय सम्भवाम्यात्ममायया ॥ ६ ॥

ajo 'pi sann avyayātmā, bhūtānām īśvaro 'pi san
prakṛtiṁ svām adhiṣṭhāya, sambhavāmy ātma-māyayā

ajaḥ – unborn; *api* – although; *san* – being so; *avyaya* – without deterioration; *ātmā* – body; *bhūtānām* – of all those who are born; *īśvaraḥ* – the Supreme Lord; *api* – although; *san* – being so; *prakṛtim* – in the transcendental form; *svām* – of Myself; *adhiṣṭhāya* – being so situated; *sambhavāmi* – I do incarnate; *ātma-māyayā* – by My internal energy.

Although I am unborn and My transcendental body never deteriorates, and although I am the Lord of all living entities,by My internal energy I still appear in every millennium in My original transcendental form.

PURPORT: The Lord has spoken about the peculiarity of His birth: although He may appear like an ordinary person, He remembers everything of His many, many past "births," whereas a common man cannot remember what he has done even a few hours before. If someone is asked what he did exactly at the same time one day earlier, it would be very difficult for a common man to answer immediately. He would surely have to dredge his memory to recall what he was doing exactly at the same time one day before. And yet, men often dare claim to be God, or Kṛṣṇa. One should not be misled by such meaningless claims. Then again, the Lord explains His *prakṛti,* or His form. *Prakṛti* means "nature," as well as *svarūpa,* or "one's own form." The Lord says that He appears in His own body. He does not change His body, as the common living entity changes from one body to another. The conditioned soul may have one kind of body in the present birth, but he has a different body in the next birth. In the material world, the living entity has no fixed body but transmigrates from one body to another. The Lord, however, does not do so. Whenever He appears, He does so in the same original body, by His internal potency. In other words, Kṛṣṇa appears in this material world in His original eternal form, with two hands, holding a flute. He appears exactly in His eternal body, uncontaminated by this material world. Although He appears in the same transcendental body and is Lord of the universe, it still appears that He takes His birth like an ordinary living entity. And although His body does not deteriorate like a material body, it still appears that Lord Kṛṣṇa grows from childhood to boyhood and from boyhood to youth. But astonishingly enough He never ages beyond youth. At the time of the Battle of Kurukṣetra, He had many grandchildren at home; or, in other words, He had sufficiently aged by material calculations. Still He looked just like a young man twenty or twenty-five years old. We never see a picture of Kṛṣṇa in old age because He never grows old like us, although He is the oldest person in the whole creation – past, present, and future. Neither His body nor His intelligence ever deteriorates or changes. Therefore, it is clear that in spite of His being in the material world, He is the same unborn, eternal form of bliss and knowledge, changeless in His transcendental body and intelligence. Factually, His appearance and disappearance are like the sun's rising, moving before us, and then disappearing from our eyesight. When the sun is out of sight, we think that the sun has set, and when the sun is before our eyes, we think that the sun is on the horizon. Actually, the sun is always in its fixed position, but owing to our defective, insufficient senses, we calculate the appearance and disappearance of the sun in the sky. And because Lord Kṛṣṇa's appearance and disappearance are completely different from that of any ordinary, common living entity, it is evident that He is eternal, blissful knowledge by His internal potency – and He is never contaminated by material nature. The *Vedas* also confirm that the Supreme Personality of Godhead is unborn yet He still appears to take His birth in multimanifestations. The Vedic supplementary literatures also confirm that even though the Lord appears to be taking His birth, He is still without change of body. In the *Bhāgavatam,* He appears before His mother as Nārāyaṇa, with four hands and the decorations of the six kinds of full opulences. His appearance in His original eternal form is His causeless mercy, bestowed upon the living entities so that they can concentrate on the Supreme Lord as He is, and not on mental concoctions or imaginations, which the impersonalist wrongly thinks the Lord's forms to be. The word *māyā,* or *ātma-māyā,* refers to the Lord's causeless mercy, according to the *Viśva-kośa* dictionary. The Lord is conscious of all of His previous appearances and disappearances, but a common living entity forgets everything about his past body as soon as he gets another body. He is the Lord of all living entities because He performs wonderful and superhuman activities while He is on this earth. Therefore, the Lord is always the same Absolute Truth and is without differentiation between His form and self, or between His quality and body. A question may now be raised as to why the Lord appears and disappears in this world. This is explained in the next verse.

Text 7 यदा यदा हि धर्मस्य ग्लानिर्भवति भारत ।
अभ्युत्थानमधर्मस्य तदात्मानं सृजाम्यहम् ॥ ७ ॥

yadā yadā hi dharmasya, glānir bhavati bhārata
abhyutthānam adharmasya, tadātmānaṁ sṛjāmy aham

yadā yadā – whenever and wherever; *hi* – certainly; *dharmasya* – of religion; *glāniḥ* – discrepancies; *bhavati* – become manifested; *bhārata* – O descendant of Bharata; *abhyutthānam* – predominance; *adharmasya* – of irreligion; *tadā* – at that time; *ātmānam* – self; *sṛjāmi* – manifest; *aham* – I.

Whenever and wherever there is a decline in religious practice, O descendant of Bharata, and a predominant rise of irreligion – at that time I descend Myself.

PURPORT: The word *sṛjāmi* is significant herein. *Sṛjāmi* cannot be used in the sense of creation, because, according to the previous verse, there is no creation of the Lord's form or body, since all of the forms are eternally existent. Therefore, *sṛjāmi* means that the Lord manifests Himself as He is. Although the Lord appears on schedule, namely at the end of the Dvāpara-yuga of the twenty-eighth millennium of the seventh Manu in one day of Brahmā, He has no obligation to adhere to such rules and regulations, because He is completely free to act in many ways at His will. He therefore appears by His own will whenever there is a predominance of irreligiosity and a disappearance of true religion. Principles of religion are laid down in the *Vedas,* and any discrepancy in the matter of properly executing the rules of the *Vedas* makes one irreligious. In the *Bhāgavatam* it is stated that such principles are the laws of the Lord. Only the Lord can manufacture a system of religion. The *Vedas* are also accepted as originally spoken by the Lord Himself to Brahmā, from within his heart. Therefore, the principles of *dharma,* or religion, are the direct orders of the Supreme Personality of Godhead (*dharmaṁ tu sākṣād bhagavat-praṇītam*). These principles are clearly indicated throughout the *Bhagavad-gītā.* The purpose of the *Vedas* is to establish such principles under the order of the Supreme Lord, and the Lord directly orders, at the end of the *Gītā,* that the highest principle of religion is to surrender unto Him only, and nothing more. The Vedic principles push one towards complete surrender unto Him; and whenever such principles are disturbed by the demoniac, the Lord appears. From the *Bhāgavatam* we understand that Lord Buddha is the incarnation of Kṛṣṇa who appeared when materialism was rampant and materialists were using the pretext of the authority of the *Vedas.* Although there are certain restrictive rules and regulations regarding animal sacrifice for particular purposes in the

Vedas, people of demonic tendency still took to animal sacrifice without reference to the Vedic principles. Lord Buddha appeared in order to stop this nonsense and to establish the Vedic principles of nonviolence. Therefore each and every *avatāra,* or incarnation of the Lord, has a particular mission, and they are all described in the revealed scriptures. No one should be accepted as an *avatāra* unless he is referred to by scriptures. It is not a fact that the Lord appears only on Indian soil. He can manifest Himself anywhere and everywhere, and whenever He desires to appear. In each and every incarnation, He speaks as much about religion as can be understood by the particular people under their particular circumstances. But the mission is the same – to lead people to God consciousness and obedience to the principles of religion. Sometimes He descends personally, and sometimes He sends His bona fide representative in the form of His son, or servant, or Himself in some disguised form.

The principles of the *Bhagavad-gītā* were spoken to Arjuna, and, for that matter, to other highly elevated persons, because he was highly advanced compared to ordinary persons in other parts of the world. Two plus two equals four is a mathematical principle that is true in the beginner's arithmetic class and in the advanced class as well. Still, there are higher and lower mathematics. In all incarnations of the Lord, therefore, the same principles are taught, but they appear to be higher and lower in varied circumstances. The higher principles of religion begin with the acceptance of the four orders and the four statuses of social life, as will be explained later. The whole purpose of the mission of incarnations is to arouse Kṛṣṇa consciousness everywhere. Such consciousness is manifest and nonmanifest only under different circumstances.

Text 8 परित्राणाय साधूनां विनाशाय च दुष्कृताम् ।
धर्मसंस्थापनार्थाय सम्भवामि युगे युगे ॥ ८ ॥

paritrāṇāya sādhūnāṁ, vināśāya ca duṣkṛtām
dharma-saṁsthāpanārthāya, sambhavāmi yuge yuge

paritrāṇāya – for the deliverance; *sādhūnām* – of the devotees; *vināśāya* – for the annihilation; *ca* – and; *duṣkṛtām* – of the miscreants; *dharma* – principles of religion; *saṁsthāpana-arthāya* – to reestablish; *sambhavāmi* – I do appear; *yuge* – millennium; *yuge* – after millennium.

To deliver the pious and to annihilate the miscreants, as well as to reestablish the principles of religion, I Myself appear, millennium after millennium.

PURPORT: According to *Bhagavad-gītā,* a *sādhu* (holy man) is a man in Kṛṣṇa consciousness. A person may appear to be irreligious, but if he has the qualifications of Kṛṣṇa consciousness wholly and fully, he is to be understood to be a *sādhu.* And *duṣkṛtām* applies to those who do not care for Kṛṣṇa consciousness. Such miscreants, or *duṣkṛtām,* are described as foolish and the lowest of mankind, even though they may be decorated with mundane education, whereas a person who is one hundred percent engaged in Kṛṣṇa consciousness is accepted as a *sādhu,* even though such a person may be neither learned nor well cultured. As far as the atheistic are concerned, it is not necessary for the Supreme Lord to appear as He is to destroy them, as He did with the demons Rāvaṇa and Kaṁsa. The Lord has many agents who are quite competent to vanquish demons. But the Lord especially descends to appease His unalloyed devotees, who are always harassed by the demoniac. The demon harasses the devotee, even though the latter may happen to be his kin. Although Prahlāda Mahārāja was the son of Hiraṇyakaśipu, he was nonetheless persecuted by his father; although Devakī, the mother of Kṛṣṇa, was the sister of Kaṁsa, she and her husband Vasudeva were persecuted only because Kṛṣṇa was to be born of them. So Lord Kṛṣṇa appeared primarily to deliver Devakī, rather than kill Kaṁsa, but both were performed simultaneously. Therefore it is said here that to deliver the devotee and vanquish the demon miscreants, the Lord appears in different incarnations.

In the *Caitanya-caritāmṛta* of Kṛṣṇadāsa Kavirāja, the following verses (*Madhya* 20.263–264) summarize these principles of incarnation:

sṛṣṭi-hetu yei mūrti prapañce avatare
sei īśvara-mūrti 'avatāra' nāma dhare

māyātīta paravyome sabāra avasthāna
viśve avatari' dhare 'avatāra' nāma

"The *avatāra,* or incarnation of Godhead, descends from the kingdom of God for material manifestation. And the particular form of the Personality of Godhead who so descends is called an incarnation, or *avatāra.* Such incarnations are situated in the spiritual world, the kingdom of God. When they descend to the material creation, they assume the name *avatāra.*"

There are various kinds of *avatāras,* such as *puruṣāvatāras, guṇāvatāras, līlāvatāras, śakty-āveśa avatāras, manvantara-avatāras* and *yugāvatāras* – all appearing on schedule all over the universe. But Lord Kṛṣṇa is the primeval Lord, the fountainhead of all *avatāras.* Lord Śrī Kṛṣṇa descends for the specific purpose of mitigating the anxieties of the pure devotees, who are very anxious to see Him in His original Vṛndāvana pastimes. Therefore, the prime purpose of the Kṛṣṇa *avatāra* is to satisfy His unalloyed devotees.

The Lord says that He incarnates Himself in every millennium. This indicates that He incarnates also in the Age of Kali. As stated in the *Śrīmad-Bhāgavatam,* the incarnation in the Age of Kali is Lord Caitanya Mahāprabhu, who spread the worship of Kṛṣṇa by the *saṅkīrtana* movement (congregational chanting of the holy names) and spread Kṛṣṇa consciousness throughout India. He predicted that this culture of *saṅkīrtana* would be broadcast all over the world, from town to town and village to village. Lord Caitanya as the incarnation of Kṛṣṇa, the Personality of Godhead, is described secretly but not directly in the confidential parts of the revealed scriptures, such as the *Upaniṣads, Mahābhārata* and *Bhāgavatam.* The devotees of Lord Kṛṣṇa are very much attracted by the *saṅkīrtana* movement of Lord Caitanya. This *avatāra* of the Lord does not kill the miscreants, but delivers them by His causeless mercy.

Text 9 जन्म कर्म च मे दिव्यमेवं यो वेत्ति तत्त्वतः ।
त्यक्त्वा देहं पुनर्जन्म नैति मामेति सोऽर्जुन ॥ ९ ॥

janma karma ca me divyam, evaṁ yo vetti tattvataḥ
tyaktvā dehaṁ punar janma, naiti mām eti so 'rjuna

janma – birth; *karma* – work; *ca* – also; *me* – of Mine; *divyam* – transcendental; *evam* – like this; *yaḥ* – anyone who; *vetti* – knows; *tattvataḥ* – in reality; *tyaktvā* – leaving aside; *deham* – this body; *punaḥ* – again; *janma* – birth; *na* – never; *eti* – does attain; *mām* – unto Me; *eti* – does attain; *saḥ* – he; *arjuna* – O Arjuna.

One who knows the transcendental nature of My appearance and activities does not, upon leaving the body, take his birth again in this material world, but attains My eternal abode, O Arjuna.

PURPORT: The Lord's descent from His transcendental abode is already explained in the sixth verse. One who can understand the truth of the appearance of the Personality of Godhead is already liberated from material bondage, and therefore he returns to the kingdom of God immediately after quitting this present material body. Such liberation of the living entity from material bondage is not at all easy. The impersonalists and the *yogīs* attain liberation only after much trouble and many, many births. Even then, the liberation they achieve – merging into the impersonal *brahma-jyotir* of the Lord – is only partial, and there is the risk of returning to this material world. But the devotee, simply by understanding the transcendental nature of the body and activities of the Lord, attains the abode of the Lord after ending this body and does not run the risk of returning to this material world. In the *Brahma-saṁhitā* (5.33) it is stated that the Lord has many, many forms and incarnations: *advaitam acyutam anādim ananta-rūpam.* Although there are many transcendental forms of the Lord, they are still one and the same Supreme Personality of Godhead. One has to understand this fact with conviction, although it is incomprehensible to mundane scholars and empiric philosophers. As stated in the *Vedas* (*Puruṣa-bodhinī Upaniṣad*):

eko devo nitya-līlānurakto, bhakta-vyāpī hṛdy antar-ātmā

"The one Supreme Personality of Godhead is eternally engaged in many, many transcendental forms in relationships with His unalloyed devotees." This Vedic version is confirmed in this verse of the *Gītā* personally by the Lord. He who accepts this truth on the strength of the authority of the *Vedas* and of the Supreme Personality of Godhead and who does not waste time in philosophical speculations attains the highest perfectional stage of liberation. Simply by accepting this truth on faith, one can, without a doubt, attain liberation. The Vedic version *tat tvam asi* is actually applied in this case. Anyone who understands Lord Kṛṣṇa to be the Supreme, or who says unto the Lord "You are the same Supreme Brahman, the Personality of Godhead," is certainly liberated instantly, and consequently his entrance into the transcendental association of the Lord is guaranteed. In other words, such a faithful devotee of the Lord attains perfection, and this is confirmed by the following Vedic assertion:

tam eva viditvāti mṛtyum eti, nānyaḥ panthā vidyate 'yanāya

"One can attain the perfect stage of liberation from birth and death simply by knowing the Lord, the Supreme Personality of Godhead, and there is no other way to achieve this perfection." (*Śvetāśvatara Upaniṣad* 3.8) That there is no alternative means that anyone who does not understand Lord Kṛṣṇa as the Supreme Personality of Godhead is surely in the mode of ignorance and consequently he will not attain salvation simply, so to speak, by licking the outer surface of the bottle of honey, or by interpreting the *Bhagavad-gītā* according to mundane scholarship. Such empiric philosophers may assume very important roles in the material world, but they are not necessarily eligible for liberation. Such puffed-up mundane scholars have to wait for the causeless mercy of the devotee of the Lord. One should therefore cultivate Kṛṣṇa consciousness with faith and knowledge, and in this way attain perfection.

Text 10 वीतरागभयक्रोधा मन्मया मामुपाश्रिताः ।
बहवो ज्ञानतपसा पूता मद्भावमागताः ॥१०॥

vīta-rāga-bhaya-krodhā, man-mayā mām upāśritāḥ
bahavo jñāna-tapasā, pūtā mad-bhāvam āgatāḥ

vīta – freed from; *rāga* – attachment; *bhaya* – fear; *krodhāḥ* – and anger; *mat-mayāḥ* – fully in Me; *mām* – in Me; *upāśritāḥ* – being fully situated; *bahavaḥ* – many; *jñāna* – of knowledge; *tapasā* – by the penance; *pūtāḥ* – being purified; *mat-bhāvam* – transcendental love for Me; *āgatāḥ* – attained.

Being freed from attachment, fear and anger, being fully absorbed in Me and taking refuge in Me, many, many persons in the past became purified by knowledge of Me – and thus they all attained transcendental love for Me.

PURPORT: As described above, it is very difficult for a person who is too materially affected to understand the personal nature of the Supreme Absolute Truth. Generally, people who are attached to the bodily conception of life are so absorbed in materialism that it is almost impossible for them to understand how the Supreme can be a person. Such materialists cannot even imagine that there is a transcendental body which is imperishable, full of knowledge and eternally blissful. In the materialistic concept, the body is perishable, full of ignorance and completely miserable. Therefore, people in general keep this same bodily idea in mind when they are informed of the personal form of the Lord. For such materialistic men, the form of the gigantic material manifestation is supreme. Consequently they consider the Supreme to be impersonal. And because they are too materially absorbed, the conception of retaining the personality after liberation from matter frightens them. When they are informed that spiritual life is also individual and personal, they become afraid of becoming persons again, and so they naturally prefer a kind of merging into the impersonal void. Generally, they compare the living entities to the bubbles of the ocean, which merge into the ocean. That is the highest perfection of spiritual existence attainable without individual personality. This is a kind of fearful stage of life, devoid of perfect knowledge of spiritual existence. Furthermore there are many persons who cannot understand spiritual existence at all. Being embarrassed by so many theories and by contradictions of various types of philosophical speculation, they become disgusted or angry and foolishly conclude that there is no supreme cause and that everything is ultimately void. Such people are in a diseased condition of life. Some people are too materially attached and therefore do not give attention to spiritual life, some of them want to merge into the supreme spiritual cause, and some of them disbelieve in everything, being angry at all sorts of spiritual speculation out of hopelessness. This last class of men take to the shelter of some kind of intoxication, and their affective hallucinations are sometimes accepted as spiritual vision. One has to get rid of all three stages of material consciousness: attachment to material life, fear of a spiritual personal identity, and the conception of void that arises from frustration in life. To get free from these three stages of the material concept of life, one has to take complete shelter of the Lord, guided by the bona fide spiritual master, and follow the disciplines and regulative principles of devotional life. The last stage of the devotional life is called *bhāva,* or transcendental love of Godhead.

According to *Bhakti-rasāmṛta-sindhu* (1.4.15–16), the science of devotional service:

ādau śraddhā tataḥ sādhu-, saṅgo 'tha bhajana-kriyā
tato 'nartha-nivṛttiḥ syāt, tato niṣṭhā rucis tataḥ

athāsaktis tato bhāvas, tataḥ premābhyudañcati
sādhakānām ayaṁ premṇaḥ, prādurbhāve bhavet kramaḥ

"In the beginning one must have a preliminary desire for self-realization. This will bring one to the stage of trying to associate with persons who are spiritually elevated. In the next stage one becomes initiated by an elevated spiritual master, and under his instruction the neophyte devotee begins the process of devotional service. By execution of devotional service under the guidance of the spiritual master, one becomes free from all material attachment, attains steadiness in self-realization, and acquires a taste for hearing about the Absolute Personality of Godhead, Śrī Kṛṣṇa. This taste leads one further forward to attachment for Kṛṣṇa consciousness, which is matured in *bhāva,* or the preliminary stage of transcendental love of God. Real love for God is called *prema,* the highest perfectional stage of life." In the *prema* stage there is constant engagement in the transcendental loving service of the Lord. So, by the slow process of devotional service, under the guidance of the bona fide spiritual master, one can attain the highest stage, being freed from all material attachment, from the fearfulness of one's individual spiritual personality, and from the frustrations that result in void philosophy. Then one can ultimately attain to the abode of the Supreme Lord.

Text 11 ये यथा मां प्रपद्यन्ते तांस्तथैव भजाम्यहम् ।
मम वर्त्मानुवर्तन्ते मनुष्याः पार्थ सर्वशः ॥११॥

ye yathā māṁ prapadyante, tāṁs tathaiva bhajāmy aham
mama vartmānuvartante, manuṣyāḥ pārtha sarvaśaḥ

ye – all who; *yathā* – as; *mām* – unto Me; *prapadyante* – surrender; *tān* – them; *tathā* – so; *eva* – certainly; *bhajāmi* – reward; *aham* – I; *mama* – My; *vartma* – path; *anuvartante* – follow; *manuṣyāḥ* – all men; *pārtha* – O son of Pṛthā; *sarvaśaḥ* – in all respects.

As all surrender unto Me, I reward them accordingly. Everyone follows My path in all respects, O son of Pṛthā.

PURPORT: Everyone is searching for Kṛṣṇa in the different aspects of His manifestations. Kṛṣṇa, the Supreme Personality of Godhead, is partially realized in His impersonal *brahma-jyotir* effulgence and as the all-pervading Supersoul dwelling within everything, including the particles of atoms. But Kṛṣṇa is fully realized only by His pure devotees. Consequently, Kṛṣṇa is the object of everyone's realization, and thus anyone and everyone is satisfied according to one's desire to have Him. In the transcendental world also, Kṛṣṇa reciprocates with His pure devotees in the transcendental attitude, just as the devotee wants Him. One devotee may want Kṛṣṇa as supreme master, another as his personal friend, another as his son, and still another as his lover. Kṛṣṇa rewards all the devotees equally, according to their different intensities of love for Him. In the material world, the same reciprocations of feelings are there, and they are equally exchanged by the Lord with the different types of worshipers. The pure devotees both here and in the transcendental abode associate with Him in person and are able to render personal service to the Lord and thus derive transcendental bliss in His loving service. As for those who are impersonalists and who want to commit spiritual suicide by annihilating the individual existence of the living entity, Kṛṣṇa helps also by absorbing them into His effulgence. Such impersonalists do not agree to accept the eternal, blissful Personality of Godhead; consequently they cannot relish the bliss of transcendental personal service to the Lord, having extinguished their individuality. Some of them, who are not firmly situated even in the impersonal existence, return to this material field to exhibit their dormant desires for activities. They are not admitted into the spiritual planets, but they are again given a chance to act on the material planets. For those who are fruitive workers, the Lord awards the desired results of their prescribed duties, as the *yajñeśvara;* and those who are *yogīs* seeking mystic powers are awarded such powers. In other words, everyone is dependent for success upon His mercy alone, and all kinds of spiritual processes are but different degrees of success on the same path. Unless, therefore, one comes to the highest perfection of Kṛṣṇa consciousness, all attempts remain imperfect, as is stated in the *Śrīmad-Bhāgavatam* (2.3.10):

akāmaḥ sarva-kāmo vā, mokṣa-kāma udāra-dhīḥ
tīvreṇa bhakti-yogena, yajeta puruṣaṁ param

"Whether one is without desire [the condition of the devotees], or is desirous of all fruitive results, or is after liberation, one should with all efforts try to worship the Supreme Personality of Godhead for complete perfection, culminating in Kṛṣṇa consciousness."

Text 12 काङ्क्षन्तः कर्मणां सिद्धिं यजन्त इह देवताः ।
क्षिप्रं हि मानुषे लोके सिद्धिर्भवति कर्मजा ॥१२॥

kāṅkṣantaḥ karmaṇāṁ siddhiṁ, yajanta iha devatāḥ
kṣipraṁ hi mānuṣe loke, siddhir bhavati karma-jā

kāṅkṣantaḥ – desiring; *karmaṇām* – of fruitive activities; *siddhim* – perfection; *yajante* – they worship by sacrifices; *iha* – in the material world; *devatāḥ* – the demigods; *kṣipram* – very quickly; *hi* – certainly; *mānuṣe* – in human society; *loke* – within this world; *siddhiḥ* – success; *bhavati* – comes; *karma-jā* – from fruitive work.

Men in this world desire success in fruitive activities, and therefore they worship the demigods. Quickly, of course, men get results from fruitive work in this world.

PURPORT: There is a great misconception about the gods or demigods of this material world, and men of less intelligence, although passing as great scholars, take these demigods to be various forms of the Supreme Lord. Actually, the demigods are not different forms of God, but they are God's different parts and parcels. God is one, and the parts and parcels are many. The *Vedas* say, *nityo nityānām:* God is one. *Īśvaraḥ paramaḥ kṛṣṇaḥ.* The Supreme God is one – Kṛṣṇa – and the demigods are delegated with powers to manage this material world. These demigods are all living entities (*nityānām*) with different grades of material power. They cannot be equal to the Supreme God – Nārāyaṇa, Viṣṇu, or Kṛṣṇa. Anyone who thinks that God and the demigods are on the same level is called an atheist, or *pāṣaṇḍī.* Even the great demigods like Brahmā and Śiva cannot be compared to the Supreme Lord. In fact, the Lord is worshiped by demigods such as Brahmā and Śiva (*śiva-viriñci-nutam*). Yet curiously enough there are many human leaders who are worshiped by foolish men under the misunderstanding of anthropomorphism or zoomorphism. *Iha devatāḥ* denotes a powerful man or demigod of this material world. But Nārāyaṇa, Viṣṇu, or Kṛṣṇa, the Supreme Personality of Godhead, does not belong to this world. He is above, or transcendental to, material creation. Even Śrīpāda Śaṅkarācārya, the leader of the impersonalists, maintains that Nārāyaṇa, or Kṛṣṇa, is beyond this material creation. However, foolish people (*hṛta-jñāna*) worship the demigods because they want immediate results. They get the results, but do not know that results so obtained are temporary and are meant for less intelligent persons. The intelligent person is in Kṛṣṇa consciousness, and he has no need to worship the paltry demigods for some immediate, temporary benefit. The demigods of this material world, as well as their worshipers, will vanish with the annihilation of this material world. The boons of the demigods are material and temporary. Both the material worlds and their inhabitants, including the demigods and their worshipers, are bubbles in the cosmic ocean. In this world, however, human society is mad after temporary things such as the material opulence of possessing land, family and enjoyable paraphernalia. To achieve such temporary things, people worship the demigods or powerful men in human society. If a man gets some ministership in the government by worshiping a political leader, he considers that he has achieved a great boon. All of them are therefore kowtowing to the so-called leaders or "big guns" in order to achieve temporary boons, and they indeed achieve such things. Such foolish men are not interested in Kṛṣṇa consciousness for the permanent solution to the hardships of material existence. They are all after sense enjoyment, and to get a little facility for sense enjoyment they are attracted to worshiping empowered living entities known as demigods. This verse indicates that people are rarely interested in Kṛṣṇa consciousness. They are mostly interested in material enjoyment, and therefore they worship some powerful living entity.

Text 13 चातुर्वर्ण्यं मया सृष्टं गुणकर्मविभागशः ।
तस्य कर्तारमपि मां विद्ध्यकर्तारमव्ययम् ॥१३॥

cātur-varṇyaṁ mayā sṛṣṭaṁ, guṇa-karma-vibhāgaśaḥ
tasya kartāram api māṁ, viddhy akartāram avyayam

cātuḥ-varṇyam – the four divisions of human society; *mayā* – by Me; *sṛṣṭam* – created; *guṇa* – of quality; *karma* – and work; *vibhāgaśaḥ* – in terms of division; *tasya* – of that; *kartāram* – the father; *api* – although; *mām* – Me; *viddhi* – you may know; *akartāram* – as the nondoer; *avyayam* – unchangeable.

According to the three modes of material nature and the work associated with them, the four divisions of human society are created by Me. And although I am the creator of this system, you should know that I am yet the nondoer, being unchangeable.

PURPORT: The Lord is the creator of everything. Everything is born of Him, everything is sustained by Him, and everything, after annihilation, rests in Him. He is therefore the creator of the four divisions of the social order, beginning with the intelligent class of men, technically called *brāhmaṇas* due to their being situated in the mode of goodness. Next is the administrative class, technically called the *kṣatriyas* due to their being situated in the mode of passion. The mercantile men, called the *vaiśyas,* are situated in the mixed modes of passion and ignorance, and the *śūdras,* or laborer class, are situated in the ignorant mode of material nature. In spite of His creating the four divisions of human society, Lord Kṛṣṇa does not belong to any of these divisions, because He is not one of the conditioned souls, a section of whom form human society. Human society is similar to any other animal society, but to elevate men from the animal status, the above-mentioned divisions are created by the Lord for the systematic development of Kṛṣṇa consciousness. The tendency of a particular man toward work is determined by the modes of material nature which he has acquired. Such symptoms of life, according to the different modes of material nature, are described in the Eighteenth Chapter of this book. A person in Kṛṣṇa consciousness, however, is above even the *brāhmaṇas.* Although *brāhmaṇas* by quality are supposed to know about

Brahman, the Supreme Absolute Truth, most of them approach only the impersonal Brahman manifestation of Lord Kṛṣṇa. But a man who transcends the limited knowledge of a *brāhmaṇa* and reaches the knowledge of the Supreme Personality of Godhead, Lord Śrī Kṛṣṇa, becomes a person in Kṛṣṇa consciousness – or, in other words, a Vaiṣṇava. Kṛṣṇa consciousness includes knowledge of all different plenary expansions of Kṛṣṇa, namely Rāma, Nṛsiṁha, Varāha, etc. And as Kṛṣṇa is transcendental to this system of the four divisions of human society, a person in Kṛṣṇa consciousness is also transcendental to all divisions of human society, whether we consider the divisions of community, nation or species.

Text 14 न मां कर्माणि लिम्पन्ति न मे कर्मफले स्पृहा ।
इति मां योऽभिजानाति कर्मभिर्न स बध्यते ॥१४॥

na māṁ karmāṇi limpanti, na me karma-phale spṛhā
iti māṁ yo 'bhijānāti, karmabhir na sa badhyate

na – never; *mām* – Me; *karmāṇi* – all kinds of work; *limpanti* – do affect; *na* – nor; *me* – My; *karma-phale* – in fruitive action; *spṛhā* – aspiration; *iti* – thus; *mām* – Me; *yaḥ* – one who; *abhijānāti* – does know; *karmabhiḥ* – by the reaction of such work; *na* – never; *saḥ* – he; *badhyate* – becomes entangled.

There is no work that affects Me; nor do I aspire for the fruits of action. One who understands this truth about Me also does not become entangled in the fruitive reactions of work.

PURPORT: As there are constitutional laws in the material world stating that the king can do no wrong, or that the king is not subject to the state laws, similarly the Lord, although He is the creator of this material world, is not affected by the activities of the material world. He creates and remains aloof from the creation, whereas the living entities are entangled in the fruitive results of material activities because of their propensity for lording it over material resources. The proprietor of an establishment is not responsible for the right and wrong activities of the workers, but the workers are themselves responsible. The living entities are engaged in their respective activities of sense gratification, and these activities are not ordained by the Lord. For advancement of sense gratification, the living entities are engaged in the work of this world, and they aspire to heavenly happiness after death. The Lord, being full in Himself, has no attraction for so-called heavenly happiness. The heavenly demigods are only His engaged servants. The proprietor never desires the low-grade happiness such as the workers may desire. He is aloof from the material actions and reactions. For example, the rains are not responsible for different types of vegetation that appear on the earth, although without such rains there is no possibility of vegetative growth. Vedic *smṛti* confirms this fact as follows:

nimitta-mātram evāsau, sṛjyānāṁ sarga-karmaṇi
pradhāna-kāraṇī-bhūtā, yato vai sṛjya-śaktayaḥ

"In the material creations, the Lord is only the supreme cause. The immediate cause is material nature, by which the cosmic manifestation is made visible." The created beings are of many varieties, such as the demigods, human beings and lower animals, and all of them are subject to the reactions of their past good or bad activities. The Lord only gives them the proper facilities for such activities and the regulations of the modes of nature, but He is never responsible for their past and present activities. In the *Vedānta-sūtra* (2.1.34) it is confirmed, *vaiṣamya-nairghṛṇye na sāpekṣatvāt:* the Lord is never partial to any living entity. The living entity is responsible for his own acts. The Lord only gives him facilities, through the agency of material nature, the external energy. Anyone who is fully conversant with all the intricacies of this law of *karma,* or fruitive activities, does not become affected by the results of his activities. In other words, the person who understands this transcendental nature of the Lord is an experienced man in Kṛṣṇa consciousness, and thus he is never subjected to the laws of *karma.* One who does not know the transcendental nature of the Lord and who thinks that the activities of the Lord are aimed at fruitive results, as are the activities of the ordinary living entities, certainly becomes entangled himself in fruitive reactions. But one who knows the Supreme Truth is a liberated soul fixed in Kṛṣṇa consciousness.

Text 15 एवं ज्ञात्वा कृतं कर्म पूर्वैरपि मुमुक्षुभिः ।
कुरु कर्मैव तस्मात्त्वं पूर्वैः पूर्वतरं कृतम् ॥१५॥

evaṁ jñātvā kṛtaṁ karma, pūrvair api mumukṣubhiḥ
kuru karmaiva tasmāt tvaṁ, pūrvaiḥ pūrva-taraṁ kṛtam

evam – thus; *jñātvā* – knowing well; *kṛtam* – was performed; *karma* – work; *pūrvaiḥ* – by past authorities; *api* – indeed; *mumukṣubhiḥ* – who attained liberation; *kuru* – just perform; *karma* – prescribed duty; *eva* – certainly; *tasmāt* – therefore; *tvam* – you; *pūrvaiḥ* – by the predecessors; *pūrva-taram* – in ancient times; *kṛtam* – as performed.

All the liberated souls in ancient times acted with this understanding of My transcendental nature. Therefore you should perform your duty, following in their footsteps.

PURPORT: There are two classes of men. Some of them are full of polluted material things within their hearts, and some of them are materially free. Kṛṣṇa consciousness is equally beneficial for both of these persons. Those who are full of dirty things can take to the line of Kṛṣṇa consciousness for a gradual cleansing process, following the regulative principles of devotional service. Those who are already cleansed of the impurities may continue to act in the same Kṛṣṇa consciousness so that others may follow their exemplary activities and thereby be benefited. Foolish persons or neophytes in Kṛṣṇa consciousness often want to retire from activities without having knowledge of Kṛṣṇa consciousness. Arjuna's desire to retire from activities on the battlefield was not approved by the Lord. One need only know how to act. To retire from the activities of Kṛṣṇa consciousness and to sit aloof making a show of Kṛṣṇa consciousness is less important than actually engaging in the field of activities for the sake of Kṛṣṇa. Arjuna is here advised to act in Kṛṣṇa consciousness, following in the footsteps of the Lord's previous disciples, such as the sun-god Vivasvān, as mentioned hereinbefore. The Supreme Lord knows all His past activities, as well as those of persons who acted in Kṛṣṇa consciousness in the past. Therefore He recommends the acts of the sun-god, who learned this art from the Lord some millions of years before. All such students of Lord Kṛṣṇa are mentioned here as past liberated persons, engaged in the discharge of duties allotted by Kṛṣṇa.

Text 16 किं कर्म किमकर्मेति कवयोऽप्यत्र मोहिताः ।
तत्ते कर्म प्रवक्ष्यामि यज्ज्ञात्वा मोक्ष्यसेऽशुभात् ॥१६॥

kiṁ karma kim akarmeti, kavayo 'py atra mohitāḥ
tat te karma pravakṣyāmi, yaj jñātvā mokṣyase 'śubhāt

kim – what is; *karma* – action; *kim* – what is; *akarma* – inaction; *iti* – thus; *kavayaḥ* – the intelligent; *api* – also; *atra* – in this matter; *mohitāḥ* – are bewildered; *tat* – that; *te* – unto you; *karma* – work;

pravakṣyāmi – I shall explain; *yat* – which; *jñātvā* – knowing; *mokṣyase* – you will be liberated; *aśubhāt* – from ill fortune.

Even the intelligent are bewildered in determining what is action and what is inaction. Now I shall explain to you what action is, knowing which you shall be liberated from all misfortune.

PURPORT: Action in Kṛṣṇa consciousness has to be executed in accord with the examples of previous bona fide devotees. This is recommended in the fifteenth verse. Why such action should not be independent will be explained in the text to follow.

To act in Kṛṣṇa consciousness, one has to follow the leadership of authorized persons who are in a line of disciplic succession as explained in the beginning of this chapter. The system of Kṛṣṇa consciousness was first narrated to the sun-god, the sun-god explained it to his son Manu, Manu explained it to his son Ikṣvāku, and the system is current on this earth from that very remote time. Therefore, one has to follow in the footsteps of previous authorities in the line of disciplic succession. Otherwise even the most intelligent men will be bewildered regarding the standard actions of Kṛṣṇa consciousness. For this reason, the Lord decided to instruct Arjuna in Kṛṣṇa consciousness directly. Because of the direct instruction of the Lord to Arjuna, anyone who follows in the footsteps of Arjuna is certainly not bewildered.

It is said that one cannot ascertain the ways of religion simply by imperfect experimental knowledge. Actually, the principles of religion can only be laid down by the Lord Himself. *Dharmaṁ tu sākṣād bhagavat-praṇītam* (*Bhāgavatam* 6.3.19). No one can manufacture a religious principle by imperfect speculation. One must follow in the footsteps of great authorities like Brahmā, Śiva, Nārada, Manu, the Kumāras, Kapila, Prahlāda, Bhīṣma, Śukadeva Gosvāmī, Yamarāja, Janaka, and Bali Mahārāja. By mental speculation one cannot ascertain what is religion or self-realization. Therefore, out of causeless mercy to His devotees, the Lord explains directly to Arjuna what action is and what inaction is. Only action performed in Kṛṣṇa consciousness can deliver a person from the entanglement of material existence.

Text 17 कर्मणो ह्यपि बोद्धव्यं बोद्धव्यं च विकर्मणः ।
अकर्मणश्च बोद्धव्यं गहना कर्मणो गतिः ॥१७॥

karmaṇo hy api boddhavyaṁ, boddhavyaṁ ca vikarmaṇaḥ
akarmaṇaś ca boddhavyaṁ, gahanā karmaṇo gatiḥ

karmaṇaḥ – of work; *hi* – certainly; *api* – also; *boddhavyam* – should be understood; *boddhavyam* – should be understood; *ca* – also; *vikarmaṇaḥ* – of forbidden work; *akarmaṇaḥ* – of inaction; *ca* – also; *boddhavyam* – should be understood; *gahanā* – very difficult; *karmaṇaḥ* – of work; *gatiḥ* – entrance.

The intricacies of action are very hard to understand. Therefore one should know properly what action is, what forbidden action is, and what inaction is.

PURPORT: If one is serious about liberation from material bondage, one has to understand the distinctions between action, inaction and unauthorized actions. One has to apply oneself to such an analysis of action, reaction and perverted actions because it is a very difficult subject matter. To understand Kṛṣṇa consciousness and action according to its modes, one has to learn one's relationship with the Supreme; i.e., one who has learned perfectly knows that every living entity is an eternal servitor of the Lord and that consequently one has to act in Kṛṣṇa consciousness. The entire *Bhagavad-gītā* is directed toward this conclusion. Any other conclusions, against this consciousness and its attendant actions, are *vikarmas,* or prohibited actions. To understand all this one has to associate with authorities in Kṛṣṇa consciousness and learn the secret from them; this is as good as learning from the Lord directly. Otherwise, even the most intelligent persons will be bewildered.

Text 18 कर्मण्यकर्म यः पश्येदकर्मणि च कर्म यः ।
स बुद्धिमान्मनुष्येषु स युक्तः कृत्स्नकर्मकृत् ॥१८॥

karmaṇy akarma yaḥ paśyed, akarmaṇi ca karma yaḥ
sa buddhimān manuṣyeṣu, sa yuktaḥ kṛtsna-karma-kṛt

karmaṇi – in action; *akarma* – inaction; *yaḥ* – one who; *paśyet* – observes; *akarmaṇi* – in inaction; *ca* – also; *karma* – fruitive action; *yaḥ* – one who; *saḥ* – he; *buddhi-mān* – is intelligent; *manuṣyeṣu* – in human society; *saḥ* – he; *yuktaḥ* – is in the transcendental position; *kṛtsna-karma-kṛt* – although engaged in all activities.

One who sees inaction in action, and action in inaction, is intelligent among men, and he is in the transcendental position, although engaged in all sorts of activities.

PURPORT: A person acting in Kṛṣṇa consciousness is naturally free from the bonds of *karma.* His activities are all performed for Krsna; therefore he does not enjoy or suffer any of the effects of work. Consequently he is intelligent in human society, even though he is engaged in all sorts of activities for Kṛṣṇa. *Akarma* means without reaction to work. The impersonalist ceases fruitive activities out of fear, so that the resultant action may not be a stumbling block on the path of self-realization, but the personalist knows rightly his position as the eternal servitor of the Supreme Personality of Godhead. Therefore he engages himself in the activities of Kṛṣṇa consciousness. Because everything is done for Kṛṣṇa, he enjoys only transcendental happiness in the discharge of this service. Those who are engaged in this process are known to be without desire for personal sense gratification. The sense of eternal servitorship to Kṛṣṇa makes one immune to all sorts of reactionary elements of work.

Text 19 यस्य सर्वे समारम्भाः कामसङ्कल्पवर्जिताः ।
ज्ञानाग्निदग्धकर्माणं तमाहुः पण्डितं बुधाः ॥१९॥

yasya sarve samārambhāḥ, kāma-saṅkalpa-varjitāḥ
jñānāgni-dagdha-karmāṇaṁ, tam āhuḥ paṇḍitaṁ budhāḥ

yasya – one whose; *sarve* – all sorts of; *samārambhāḥ* – attempts; *kāma* – based on desire for sense gratification; *saṅkalpa* – determination; *varjitāḥ* – are devoid of; *jñāna* – of perfect knowledge; *agni* – by the fire; *dagdha* – burned; *karmāṇam* – whose work; *tam* – him; *āhuḥ* – declare; *paṇḍitam* – learned; *budhāḥ* – those who know.

One is understood to be in full knowledge whose every endeavor is devoid of desire for sense gratification. He is said by sages to be a worker for whom the reactions of work have been burned up by the fire of perfect knowledge.

PURPORT: Only a person in full knowledge can understand the activities of a person in Kṛṣṇa consciousness. Because the person in Kṛṣṇa consciousness is devoid of all kinds of sense-gratificatory propensities, it is to be understood that he has burned up the reactions of his work by perfect knowledge of his constitutional position as the eternal servitor of the Supreme Personality of Godhead. He is actually learned who has attained to such perfection of knowledge. Development of this knowledge of eternal servitorship to the Lord is compared to fire. Such a fire, once kindled, can burn up all kinds of reactions to work.

Text 20 त्यक्त्वा कर्मफलासङ्गं नित्यतृप्तो निराश्रयः ।
कर्मण्यभिप्रवृत्तोऽपि नैव किञ्चित्करोति सः ॥२०॥

tyaktvā karma-phalāsaṅgaṁ, nitya-tṛpto nirāśrayaḥ
karmaṇy abhipravṛtto 'pi, naiva kiñcit karoti saḥ

tyaktvā – having given up; *karma-phala-āsaṅgam* – attachment for fruitive results; *nitya* – always; *tṛptaḥ* – being satisfied; *nirāśrayaḥ* – without any shelter; *karmaṇi* – in activity; *abhipravṛttaḥ* – being fully engaged; *api* – in spite of; *na* – does not; *eva* – certainly; *kiñcit* – anything; *karoti* – do; *saḥ* – he.

Abandoning all attachment to the results of his activities, ever satisfied and independent, he performs no fruitive action, although engaged in all kinds of undertakings.

PURPORT: This freedom from the bondage of actions is possible only in Kṛṣṇa consciousness, when one is doing everything for Kṛṣṇa. A Kṛṣṇa conscious person acts out of pure love for the Supreme Personality of Godhead, and therefore he has no attraction for the results of the action. He is not even attached to his personal maintenance, for everything is left to Kṛṣṇa. Nor is he anxious to secure things, nor to protect things already in his possession. He does his duty to the best of his ability and leaves everything to Kṛṣṇa. Such an unattached person is always free from the resultant reactions of good and bad; it is as though he were not doing anything. This is the sign of *akarma,* or actions without fruitive reactions. Any other action, therefore, devoid of Kṛṣṇa consciousness, is binding upon the worker, and that is the real aspect of *vikarma,* as explained hereinbefore.

Text 21 निराशीर्यतचित्तात्मा त्यक्तसर्वपरिग्रहः ।
शारीरं केवलं कर्म कुर्वन्नाप्नोति किल्बिषम् ॥२१॥

nirāśīr yata-cittātmā, tyakta-sarva-parigrahaḥ
śārīraṁ kevalaṁ karma, kurvan nāpnoti kilbiṣam

nirāśīḥ – without desire for the result; *yata* – controlled; *citta-ātmā* – mind and intelligence; *tyakta* – giving up; *sarva* – all; *parigrahaḥ* – sense of proprietorship over possessions; *śārīram* – in keeping body and soul together; *kevalam* – only; *karma* – work; *kurvan* – doing; *na* – never; *āpnoti* – does acquire; *kilbiṣam* – sinful reactions.

Such a man of understanding acts with mind and intelligence perfectly controlled, gives up all sense of proprietorship over his possessions, and acts only for the bare necessities of life. Thus working, he is not affected by sinful reactions.

PURPORT: A Kṛṣṇa conscious person does not expect good or bad results in his activities. His mind and intelligence are fully controlled. He knows that because he is part and parcel of the Supreme, the part played by him, as a part and parcel of the whole, is not his own activity but is only being done through him by the Supreme. When the hand moves, it does not move out of its own accord, but by the endeavor of the whole body. A Kṛṣṇa conscious person is always dovetailed with the supreme desire, for he has no desire for personal sense gratification. He moves exactly like a part of a machine. As a machine part requires oiling and cleaning for maintenance, so a Kṛṣṇa conscious man maintains himself by his work just to remain fit for action in the transcendental loving service of the Lord. He is therefore immune to all the reactions of his endeavors. Like an animal, he has no proprietorship even over his own body. A cruel proprietor of an animal sometimes kills the animal in his possession, yet the animal does not protest. Nor does it have any real independence. A Kṛṣṇa conscious person, fully engaged in self-realization, has very little time to falsely possess any material object. For maintaining body and soul, he does not require unfair means of accumulating money. He does not, therefore, become contaminated by such material sins. He is free from all reactions to his actions.

Text 22 यदृच्छालाभसन्तुष्टो द्वन्द्वातीतो विमत्सरः ।
समः सिद्धावसिद्धौ च कृत्वापि न निबध्यते ॥२२॥

yadṛcchā-lābha-santuṣṭo, dvandvātīto vimatsaraḥ
samaḥ siddhāv asiddhau ca, kṛtvāpi na nibadhyate

yadṛcchā – out of its own accord; *lābha* – with gain; *santuṣṭaḥ* – satisfied; *dvandva* – duality; *atītaḥ* – surpassed; *vimatsaraḥ* – free from envy; *samaḥ* – steady; *siddhau* – in success; *asiddhau* – failure; *ca* – also; *kṛtvā* – doing; *api* – although; *na* – never; *nibadhyate* – becomes affected.

He who is satisfied with gain which comes of its own accord, who is free from duality and does not envy, who is steady in both success and failure, is never entangled, although performing actions.

PURPORT: A Kṛṣṇa conscious person does not make much endeavor even to maintain his body. He is satisfied with gains which are obtained of their own accord. He neither begs nor borrows, but he labors honestly as far as is in his power, and is satisfied with whatever is obtained by his own honest labor. He is therefore independent in his livelihood. He does not allow anyone's service to hamper his own service in Kṛṣṇa consciousness. However, for the service of the Lord he can participate in any kind of action without being disturbed by the duality of the material world. The duality of the material world is felt in terms of heat and cold, or misery and happiness. A Kṛṣṇa conscious person is above duality because he does not hesitate to act in any way for the satisfaction of Kṛṣṇa. Therefore he is steady both in success and in failure. These signs are visible when one is fully in transcendental knowledge.

Text 23 गतसङ्गस्य मुक्तस्य ज्ञानावस्थितचेतसः ।
यज्ञायाचरतः कर्म समग्रं प्रविलीयते ॥२३॥

gata-saṅgasya muktasya, jñānāvasthita-cetasaḥ
yajñāyācarataḥ karma, samagraṁ pravilīyate

gata-saṅgasya – of one unattached to the modes of material nature; *muktasya* – of the liberated; *jñāna-avasthita* – situated in transcendence; *cetasaḥ* – whose wisdom; *yajñāya* – for the sake of Yajña (Kṛṣṇa); *ācarataḥ* – acting; *karma* – work; *samagram* – in total; *pravilīyate* – merges entirely.

The work of a man who is unattached to the modes of material nature and who is fully situated in transcendental knowledge merges entirely into transcendence.

PURPORT: Becoming fully Kṛṣṇa conscious, one is freed from all dualities and thus is free from the contaminations of the material modes. He can become liberated because he knows his constitutional position in relationship with Kṛṣṇa, and thus his mind cannot be drawn from Kṛṣṇa consciousness. Consequently, whatever he does, he does for Kṛṣṇa, who is the primeval Viṣṇu. Therefore, all his works are technically sacrifices because sacrifice aims at satisfying the Supreme Person, Kṛṣṇa (or Viṣṇu. The resultant reactions to all such work certainly merge into transcendence, and one does not suffer material effects.

Text 24 **ब्रह्मार्पणं ब्रह्म हविर्ब्रह्माग्नौ ब्रह्मणा हुतम् ।**
ब्रह्मैव तेन गन्तव्यं ब्रह्मकर्मसमाधिना ॥२४॥

brahmārpaṇaṁ brahma havir, brahmāgnau brahmaṇā hutam
brahmaiva tena gantavyaṁ, brahma-karma-samādhinā

brahma – spiritual in nature; *arpaṇam* – contribution; *brahma* – the Supreme; *haviḥ* – butter; *brahma* – spiritual; *agnau* – in the fire of consummation; *brahmaṇā* – by the spirit soul; *hutam* – offered; *brahma* – spiritual kingdom; *eva* – certainly; *tena* – by him; *gantavyam* – to be reached; *brahma* – spiritual; *karma* – in activities; *samādhinā* – by complete absorption.

A person who is fully absorbed in Kṛṣṇa consciousness is sure to attain the spiritual kingdom because of his full contribution to spiritual activities, in which the consummation is absolute and that which is offered is of the same spiritual nature.

PURPORT: How activities in Kṛṣṇa consciousness can lead one ultimately to the spiritual goal is described here. There are various activities in Kṛṣṇa consciousness, and all of them will be described in the following verses. But, for the present, just the principle of Kṛṣṇa consciousness is described. A conditioned soul, entangled in material contamination, is sure to act in the material atmosphere, and yet he has to get out of such an environment. The process by which the conditioned soul can get out of the material atmosphere is Kṛṣṇa consciousness. For example, a patient who is suffering from a disorder of the bowels due to overindulgence in milk products is cured by another milk product, namely curds. The materially absorbed conditioned soul can be cured by Kṛṣṇa consciousness as set forth here in the *Gītā.* This process is generally known as *yajña,* or activities (sacrifices) simply meant for the satisfaction of Viṣṇu, or Kṛṣṇa. The more the activities of the material world are performed in Kṛṣṇa consciousness, or for Viṣṇu only, the more the atmosphere becomes spiritualized by complete absorption. The word *brahma* (Brahman) means "spiritual." The Lord is spiritual, and the rays of His transcendental body are called *brahma-jyotir,* His spiritual effulgence. Everything that exists is situated in that *brahma-jyotir,* but when the *jyotir* is covered by illusion (*māyā*) or sense gratification, it is called material. This material veil can be removed at once by Kṛṣṇa consciousness; thus the offering for the sake of Kṛṣṇa consciousness, the consuming agent of such an offering or contribution, the process of consumption, the contributor, and the result are – all combined together – Brahman, or the Absolute Truth. The Absolute Truth covered by *māyā* is called matter. Matter dovetailed for the cause of the Absolute Truth regains its spiritual quality. Kṛṣṇa consciousness is the process of converting the illusory consciousness into Brahman, or the Supreme. When the mind is fully absorbed in Kṛṣṇa consciousness, it is said to be in *samādhi,* or trance. Anything done in such transcendental consciousness is called *yajña,* or sacrifice for the Absolute. In that condition of spiritual consciousness, the contributor, the contribution, the consumption, the performer or leader of the performance, and the result or ultimate gain – everything – becomes one in the Absolute, the Supreme Brahman. That is the method of Kṛṣṇa consciousness.

Text 25 दैवमेवापरे यज्ञं योगिनः पर्युपासते ।
ब्रह्माग्नावपरे यज्ञं यज्ञेनैवोपजुह्वति ॥२५॥

daivam evāpare yajñaṁ, yoginaḥ paryupāsate
brahmāgnāv apare yajñaṁ, yajñenaivopajuhvati

daivam – in worshiping the demigods; *eva* – like this; *apare* – some others; *yajñam* – sacrifices; *yoginaḥ* – mystics; *paryupāsate* – worship perfectly; *brahma* – of the Absolute Truth; *agnau* – in the fire; *apare* – others; *yajñam* – sacrifice; *yajñena* – by sacrifice; *eva* – thus; *upajuhvati* – offer.

Some yogīs perfectly worship the demigods by offering different sacrifices to them, and some offer sacrifices in the fire of the Supreme Brahman.

PURPORT: As described above, a person engaged in discharging duties in Kṛṣṇa consciousness is also called a perfect *yogī* or a first-class mystic. But there are others also, who perform similar sacrifices in the worship of demigods, and still others who sacrifice to the Supreme Brahman, or the impersonal feature of the Supreme Lord. So there are different kinds of sacrifices in terms of different categories. Such different categories of sacrifice by different types of performers only superficially demark varieties of sacrifice. Factually sacrifice means to satisfy the Supreme Lord, Viṣṇu, who is also known as Yajña. All the different varieties of sacrifice can be placed within two primary divisions: namely, sacrifice of worldly possessions and sacrifice in pursuit of transcendental knowledge. Those who are in Kṛṣṇa consciousness sacrifice all material possessions for the satisfaction of the Supreme Lord, while others, who want some temporary material happiness, sacrifice their material possessions to satisfy demigods such as Indra, the sun-god, etc. And others, who are impersonalists, sacrifice their identity by merging into the existence of impersonal Brahman. The demigods are powerful living entities appointed by the Supreme Lord for the maintenance and supervision of all material functions like the heating, watering and lighting of the universe. Those who are interested in material benefits worship the demigods by various sacrifices according to the Vedic rituals. They are called *bahv-īśvara-vādī,* or believers in many gods. But others, who worship the impersonal feature of the Absolute Truth and regard the forms of the demigods as temporary, sacrifice their individual selves in the supreme fire and thus end their individual existences by merging into the existence of the Supreme. Such impersonalists sacrifice their time in philosophical speculation to understand the transcendental nature of the Supreme. In other words, the fruitive workers sacrifice their material possessions for material enjoyment, whereas the impersonalist sacrifices his material designations with a view to merging into the existence of the Supreme. For the impersonalist, the fire altar of sacrifice is the Supreme Brahman, and the offering is the self being consumed by the fire of Brahman. The Kṛṣṇa conscious person, like Arjuna, however, sacrifices everything for the satisfaction of Kṛṣṇa, and thus all his material possessions as well as his own self – everything – is sacrificed for Kṛṣṇa. Thus, he is the first-class *yogī;* but he does not lose his individual existence.

Text 26 श्रोत्रादीनीन्द्रियाण्यन्ये संयमाग्निषु जुह्वति ।
शब्दादीन् विषयानन्य इन्द्रियाग्निषु जुह्वति ॥२६॥

śrotrādīnīndriyāṇy anye, saṁyamāgniṣu juhvati
śabdādīn viṣayān anya, indriyāgniṣu juhvati

śrotra-ādīni – such as the hearing process; *indriyāṇi* – senses; *anye* – others; *saṁyama* – of restraint; *agniṣu* – in the fires; *juhvati* – offer; *śabda-ādīn* – sound vibration, etc.; *viṣayān* – objects of sense gratification; *anye* – others; *indriya* – of the sense organs; *agniṣu* – in the fires; *juhvati* – they sacrifice.

Some [the unadulterated brahmacārīs] sacrifice the hearing process and the senses in the fire of mental control, and others [the regulated householders] sacrifice the objects of the senses in the fire of the senses.

PURPORT: The members of the four divisions of human life, namely the *brahmacārī,* the *gṛhastha,* the *vānaprastha* and the *sannyāsī,* are all meant to become perfect *yogīs* or transcendentalists. Since human life is not meant for our enjoying sense gratification like the animals, the four orders of human life are so arranged that one may become perfect in spiritual life. The *brahmacārīs,* or students under the care of a bona fide spiritual master, control the mind by abstaining from sense gratification. A *brahmacārī* hears only words concerning Kṛṣṇa consciousness; hearing is the basic principle for understanding, and therefore the pure *brahmacārī* engages fully in *harer nāmānukīrtanam* – chanting and hearing the glories of the Lord. He restrains himself from the vibrations of material sounds, and his hearing is engaged in the transcendental sound vibration of Hare Kṛṣṇa, Hare Kṛṣṇa. Similarly, the householders, who have some license for sense gratification, perform such acts with great restraint. Sex life, intoxication and meat-eating are general tendencies of human society, but a regulated householder does not indulge in unrestricted sex life and other sense gratification. Marriage on the principles of religious life is therefore current in all civilized human society because that is the way for restricted sex life. This restricted, unattached sex life is also a kind of *yajña* because the restricted householder sacrifices his general tendency toward sense gratification for higher, transcendental life.

Text 27 सर्वाणीन्द्रियकर्माणि प्राणकर्माणि चापरे ।
आत्मसंयमयोगाग्नौ जुह्वति ज्ञानदीपिते ॥२७॥

sarvāṇīndriya-karmāṇi, prāṇa-karmāṇi cāpare
ātma-saṁyama-yogāgnau, juhvati jñāna-dīpite

sarvāṇi – of all; *indriya* – the senses; *karmāṇi* – functions; *prāṇa-karmāṇi* – functions of the life breath; *ca* – also; *apare* – others; *ātma-saṁyama* – of controlling the mind; *yoga* – the linking process; *agnau* – in the fire of; *juhvati* – offer; *jñāna-dīpite* – because of the urge for self-realization.

Others, who are interested in achieving self-realization through control of the mind and senses, offer the functions of all the senses, and of the life breath, as oblations into the fire of the controlled mind.

PURPORT: The *yoga* system conceived by Patañjali is referred to herein. In the *Yoga-sūtra* of Patañjali, the soul is called *pratyag-ātmā* and *parāg-ātmā.* As long as the soul is attached to sense enjoyment it is called *parāg-*

ātmā, but as soon as the same soul becomes detached from such sense enjoyment it is called *pratyag-ātmā.* The soul is subjected to the functions of ten kinds of air at work within the body, and this is perceived through the breathing system. The Patañjali system of *yoga* instructs one on how to control the functions of the body's air in a technical manner so that ultimately all the functions of the air within become favorable for purifying the soul of material attachment. According to this *yoga* system, *pratyag-ātmā* is the ultimate goal. This *pratyag-ātmā* is withdrawn from activities in matter. The senses interact with the sense objects, like the ear for hearing, eyes for seeing, nose for smelling, tongue for tasting, and hand for touching, and all of them are thus engaged in activities outside the self. They are called the functions of the *prāṇa-vāyu.* The *apāna-vāyu* goes downwards, *vyāna-vāyu* acts to shrink and expand, *samāna-vāyu* adjusts equilibrium, *udāna-vāyu* goes upwards – and when one is enlightened, one engages all these in searching for self-realization.

Text 28 द्रव्ययज्ञास्तपोयज्ञा योगयज्ञास्तथापरे ।
स्वाध्यायज्ञानयज्ञाश्च यतयः संशितव्रताः ॥२८॥

dravya-yajñās tapo-yajñā, yoga-yajñās tathāpare
svādhyāya-jñāna-yajñāś ca, yatayaḥ saṁśita-vratāḥ

dravya-yajñāḥ – sacrificing one's possessions; *tapaḥ-yajñāḥ* – sacrifice in austerities; *yoga-yajñāḥ* – sacrifice in eightfold mysticism; *tathā* – thus; *apare* – others; *svādhyāya* – sacrifice in the study of the *Vedas; jñāna-yajñāḥ* – sacrifice in advancement of transcendental knowledge; *ca* – also; *yatayaḥ* – enlightened persons; *saṁśita-vratāḥ* – taken to strict vows.

Having accepted strict vows, some become enlightened by sacrificing their possessions, and others by performing severe austerities, by practicing the yoga of eightfold mysticism, or by studying the Vedas to advance in transcendental knowledge.

PURPORT: These sacrifices may be fitted into various divisions. There are persons who are sacrificing their possessions in the form of various kinds of charities. In India, the rich mercantile community or princely orders open various kinds of charitable institutions like *dharma-śālā, anna-kṣetra, atithi-śālā, anāthālaya* and *vidyā-pīṭha.* In other countries, too, there are many hospitals, old age homes and similar charitable foundations meant for distributing food, education and medical treatment free to the poor. All these charitable activities are called *dravyamaya-*

yajña. There are others who, for higher elevation in life or for promotion to higher planets within the universe, voluntarily accept many kinds of austerities such as *candrāyaṇa* and *cāturmāsya.* These processes entail severe vows for conducting life under certain rigid rules. For example, under the *cāturmāsya* vow the candidate does not shave for four months during the year (July to October), he does not eat certain foods, does not eat twice in a day or does not leave home. Such sacrifice of the comforts of life is called *tapomaya-yajña.* There are still others who engage themselves in different kinds of mystic *yogas* like the Patañjali system (for merging into the existence of the Absolute), or *haṭha-yoga* or *aṣṭāṅga-yoga* (for particular perfections). And some travel to all the sanctified places of pilgrimage. All these practices are called *yoga-yajña,* sacrifice for a certain type of perfection in the material world. There are others who engage themselves in the studies of different Vedic literatures, specifically the *Upaniṣads* and *Vedānta-sūtras,* or the Sāṅkhya philosophy. All of these are called *svādhyāya-yajña,* or engagement in the sacrifice of studies. All these *yogīs* are faithfully engaged in different types of sacrifice and are seeking a higher status of life. Kṛṣṇa consciousness, however, is different from these because it is the direct service of the Supreme Lord. Kṛṣṇa consciousness cannot be attained by any one of the above-mentioned types of sacrifice but can be attained only by the mercy of the Lord and His bona fide devotees. Therefore, Kṛṣṇa consciousness is transcendental.

Text 29 अपाने जुह्वति प्राणं प्राणेऽपानं तथापरे ।
प्राणापानगती रुद्ध्वा प्राणायामपरायणाः ।
अपरे नियताहाराः प्राणान् प्राणेषु जुह्वति ॥२९॥

apāne juhvati prāṇaṁ, prāṇe 'pānaṁ tathāpare
prāṇāpāna-gatī ruddhvā, prāṇāyāma-parāyaṇāḥ
apare niyatāhārāḥ, prāṇān prāṇeṣu juhvati

apāne – in the air which acts downward; *juhvati* – offer; *prāṇam* – the air which acts outward; *prāṇe* – in the air going outward; *apānam* – the air going downward; *tathā* – as also; *apare* – others; *prāṇa* – of the air going outward; *apāna* – and the air going downward; *gatī* – the movement; *ruddhvā* – checking; *prāṇa-āyāma* – trance induced by stopping all breathing; *parāyaṇāḥ* – so inclined; *apare* – others; *niyata* – having controlled; *āhārāḥ* – eating; *prāṇān* – the outgoing air; *prāṇeṣu* – in the outgoing air; *juhvati* – sacrifice.

Still others, who are inclined to the process of breath restraint to remain in trance, practice by offering the movement of the outgoing breath into the incoming, and the incoming breath into the outgoing, and thus at last remain in trance, stopping all breathing. Others, curtailing the eating process, offer the outgoing breath into itself as a sacrifice.

PURPORT: This system of *yoga* for controlling the breathing process is called *prāṇāyāma,* and in the beginning it is practiced in the *haṭha-yoga* system through different sitting postures. All of these processes are recommended for controlling the senses and for advancement in spiritual realization. This practice involves controlling the airs within the body so as to reverse the directions of their passage. The *apāna* air goes downward, and the *prāṇa* air goes up. The *prāṇāyāma-yogī* practices breathing the opposite way until the currents are neutralized into *pūraka,* equilibrium. Offering the exhaled breath into the inhaled breath is called *recaka.* When both air currents are completely stopped, one is said to be in *kumbhaka-yoga.* By practice of *kumbhaka-yoga,* one can increase the duration of life for perfection in spiritual realization. The intelligent *yogī* is interested in attaining perfection in one life, without waiting for the next. For by practicing *kumbhaka-yoga,* the *yogīs* increase the duration of life by many, many years. A Kṛṣṇa conscious person, however, being always situated in the transcendental loving service of the Lord, automatically becomes the controller of the senses. His senses, being always engaged in the service of Kṛṣṇa, have no chance of becoming otherwise engaged. So at the end of life, he is naturally transferred to the transcendental plane of Lord Kṛṣṇa; consequently he makes no attempt to increase his longevity. He is at once raised to the platform of liberation, as stated in *Bhagavad-gītā* (14.26):

māṁ ca yo 'vyabhicāreṇa, bhakti-yogena sevate
sa guṇān samatītyaitān, brahma-bhūyāya kalpate

"One who engages in unalloyed devotional service to the Lord transcends the modes of material nature and is immediately elevated to the spiritual platform." A Kṛṣṇa conscious person begins from the transcendental stage, and he is constantly in that consciousness. Therefore, there is no falling down, and ultimately he enters into the abode of the Lord without delay. The practice of reduced eating is automatically done when one eats only *kṛṣṇa-prasādam,* or food which is offered first to the Lord. Reducing the eating process is very helpful in the matter of sense control. And without sense control there is no possibility of getting out of the material entanglement.

Text 30 सर्वेऽप्येते यज्ञविदो यज्ञक्षपितकल्मषाः ।
यज्ञशिष्टामृतभुजो यान्ति ब्रह्म सनातनम् ॥३०॥

sarve 'py ete yajña-vido, yajña-kṣapita-kalmaṣāḥ
yajña-śiṣṭāmṛta-bhujo, yānti brahma sanātanam

sarve – all; *api* – although apparently different; *ete* – these; *yajña-vidaḥ* – conversant with the purpose of performing sacrifices; *yajña-kṣapita* – being cleansed as the result of such performances; *kalmaṣāḥ* – of sinful reactions; *yajña-śiṣṭa* – of the result of such performances of *yajña; amṛta-bhujaḥ* – those who have tasted such nectar; *yānti* – do approach; *brahma* – the supreme; *sanātanam* – eternal atmosphere.

All these performers who know the meaning of sacrifice become cleansed of sinful reactions, and, having tasted the nectar of the results of sacrifices, they advance toward the supreme eternal atmosphere.

PURPORT: From the foregoing explanation of different types of sacrifice (namely sacrifice of one's possessions, study of the *Vedas* or philosophical doctrines, and performance of the *yoga* system), it is found that the common aim of all is to control the senses. Sense gratification is the root cause of material existence; therefore, unless and until one is situated on a platform apart from sense gratification, there is no chance of being elevated to the eternal platform of full knowledge, full bliss and full life. This platform is in the eternal atmosphere, or Brahman atmosphere. All the above-mentioned sacrifices help one to become cleansed of the sinful reactions of material existence. By this advancement in life, not only does one become happy and opulent in this life, but also, at the end, he enters into the eternal kingdom of God, either merging into the impersonal Brahman or associating with the Supreme Personality of Godhead, Kṛṣṇa.

Text 31 नायं लोकोऽस्त्ययज्ञस्य कुतोऽन्यः कुरुसत्तम ॥३१॥

nāyaṁ loko 'sty ayajñasya, kuto 'nyaḥ kuru-sattama

na – never; *ayam* – this; *lokaḥ* – planet; *asti* – there is; *ayajñasya* – for one who performs no sacrifice; *kutaḥ* – where is; *anyaḥ* – the other; *kuru-sat-tama* – O best amongst the Kurus.

O best of the Kuru dynasty, without sacrifice one can never live happily on this planet or in this life: what then of the next?

PURPORT: Whatever form of material existence one is in, one is invariably ignorant of his real situation. In other words, existence in the material world is due to the multiple reactions to our sinful lives. Ignorance is the cause of sinful life, and sinful life is the cause of one's dragging on in material existence. The human form of life is the only loophole by which one may get out of this entanglement. The *Vedas,* therefore, give us a chance for escape by pointing out the paths of religion, economic comfort, regulated sense gratification and, at last, the means to get out of the miserable condition entirely. The path of religion, or the different kinds of sacrifice recommended above, automatically solves our economic problems. By performance of *yajña* we can have enough food, enough milk, etc. – even if there is a so-called increase of population. When the body is fully supplied, naturally the next stage is to satisfy the senses. The *Vedas* prescribe, therefore, sacred marriage for regulated sense gratification. Thereby one is gradually elevated to the platform of release from material bondage, and the highest perfection of liberated life is to associate with the Supreme Lord. Perfection is achieved by performance of *yajña* (sacrifice), as described above. Now, if a person is not inclined to perform *yajña* according to the *Vedas,* how can he expect a happy life even in this body, and what to speak of another body on another planet? There are different grades of material comforts in different heavenly planets, and in all cases there is immense happiness for persons engaged in different kinds of *yajña.* But the highest kind of happiness that a man can achieve is to be promoted to the spiritual planets by practice of Kṛṣṇa consciousness. A life of Kṛṣṇa consciousness is therefore the solution to all the problems of material existence.

Text 32 एवं बहुविधा यज्ञा वितता ब्रह्मणो मुखे ।
कर्मजान् विद्धि तान् सर्वानेवं ज्ञात्वा विमोक्ष्यसे ॥३२॥

evaṁ bahu-vidhā yajñā, vitatā brahmaṇo mukhe
karma-jān viddhi tān sarvān, evaṁ jñātvā vimokṣyase

evam – thus; *bahu-vidhāḥ* – various kinds of; *yajñāḥ* – sacrifices; *vitatāḥ* – are spread; *brahmaṇaḥ* – of the *Vedas; mukhe* – through the mouth; *karma-jān* – born of work; *viddhi* – you should know; *tān* – them; *sarvān* – all; *evam* – thus; *jñātvā* – knowing; *vimokṣyase* – you will be liberated.

All these different types of sacrifice are approved by the Vedas, and all of them are born of different types of work. Knowing them as such, you will become liberated.

PURPORT: Different types of sacrifice, as discussed above, are mentioned in the *Vedas* to suit the different types of worker. Because men are so deeply absorbed in the bodily concept, these sacrifices are so arranged that one can work either with the body, with the mind, or with the intelligence. But all of them are recommended for ultimately bringing about liberation from the body. This is confirmed by the Lord herewith from His own mouth.

Text 33 श्रेयान्द्रव्यमयाद्यज्ञाज्ज्ञानयज्ञः परन्तप ।
सर्वं कर्माखिलं पार्थ ज्ञाने परिसमाप्यते ॥३३॥

śreyān dravya-mayād yajñāj, jñāna-yajñaḥ paran-tapa
sarvaṁ karmākhilaṁ pārtha, jñāne parisamāpyate

śreyān – greater; *dravya-mayāt* – of material possessions; *yajñāt* – than the sacrifice; *jñāna-yajñaḥ* – sacrifice in knowledge; *param-tapa* – O chastiser of the enemy; *sarvam* – all; *karma* – activities; *akhilam* – in totality; *pārtha* – O son of Pṛthā; *jñāne* – in knowledge; *parisamāpyate* – end.

O chastiser of the enemy, the sacrifice performed in knowledge is better than the mere sacrifice of material possessions. After all, O son of Pṛthā, all sacrifices of work culminate in transcendental knowledge.

PURPORT: The purpose of all sacrifices is to arrive at the status of complete knowledge, then to gain release from material miseries, and, ultimately, to engage in loving transcendental service to the Supreme Lord (Kṛṣṇa consciousness). Nonetheless, there is a mystery about all these different activities of sacrifice, and one should know this mystery. Sacrifices sometimes take different forms according to the particular faith of the performer. When one's faith reaches the stage of transcendental knowledge, the performer of sacrifices should be considered more advanced than those who simply sacrifice material possessions without such knowledge, for without attainment of knowledge, sacrifices remain on the material platform and bestow no spiritual benefit. Real knowledge culminates in Kṛṣṇa consciousness, the highest stage of transcendental knowledge. Without the elevation of knowledge, sacrifices are simply material activities. When, however, they are elevated to the level of transcendental knowledge, all such activities enter onto the spiritual platform. Depending on differences in consciousness, sacrificial activities are sometimes called *karma-kāṇḍa* (fruitive activities) and sometimes *jñāna-kāṇḍa* (knowledge in the pursuit of truth). It is better when the end is knowledge.

Text 34 तद्विद्धि प्रणिपातेन परिप्रश्नेन सेवया ।
उपदेक्ष्यन्ति ते ज्ञानं ज्ञानिनस्तत्त्वदर्शिनः ॥३४॥

tad viddhi praṇipātena, paripraśnena sevayā
upadekṣyanti te jñānaṁ, jñāninas tattva-darśinaḥ

tat – that knowledge of different sacrifices; *viddhi* – try to understand; *praṇipātena* – by approaching a spiritual master; *paripraśnena* – by submissive inquiries; *sevayā* – by the rendering of service; *upadekṣyanti* – they will initiate; *te* – you; *jñānam* – into knowledge; *jñāninaḥ* – the self-realized; *tattva* – of the truth; *darśinaḥ* – seers.

Just try to learn the truth by approaching a spiritual master. Inquire from him submissively and render service unto him. The self-realized souls can impart knowledge unto you because they have seen the truth.

PURPORT: The path of spiritual realization is undoubtedly difficult. The Lord therefore advises us to approach a bona fide spiritual master in the line of disciplic succession from the Lord Himself. No one can be a bona fide spiritual master without following this principle of disciplic succession. The Lord is the original spiritual master, and a person in the disciplic succession can convey the message of the Lord as it is to his disciple. No one can be spiritually realized by manufacturing his own process, as is the fashion of the foolish pretenders. The *Bhāgavatam* (6.3.19) says, *dharmaṁ tu sākṣād bhagavat-praṇītam:* the path of religion is directly enunciated by the Lord. Therefore, mental speculation or dry arguments cannot help lead one to the right path. Nor by independent study of books of knowledge can one progress in spiritual life. One has to approach a bona fide spiritual master to receive the knowledge. Such a spiritual master should be accepted in full surrender, and one should serve the spiritual master like a menial servant, without false prestige. Satisfaction of the self-realized spiritual master is the secret of advancement in spiritual life. Inquiries and submission constitute the proper combination for spiritual understanding. Unless there is submission and service, inquiries from the learned spiritual master will not be effective. One must be able to pass the test of the spiritual master, and when he sees the genuine desire of the disciple, he automatically blesses the disciple with genuine spiritual understanding. In this verse, both blind following and absurd inquiries are condemned. Not only should one hear submissively from the spiritual master, but one must also get a clear understanding from him, in submission and service and inquiries. A bona fide spiritual master is by nature very kind toward the disciple. Therefore when the student is submissive and is always ready to render service, the reciprocation of knowledge and inquiries becomes perfect.

Text 35 यज्ज्ञात्वा न पुनर्मोहमेवं यास्यसि पाण्डव ।
येन भूतान्यशेषाणि द्रक्ष्यस्यात्मन्यथो मयि ॥३५॥

yaj jñātvā na punar moham, evaṁ yāsyasi pāṇḍava
yena bhūtāny aśeṣāṇi, drakṣyasy ātmany atho mayi

yat – which; *jñātvā* – knowing; *na* – never; *punaḥ* – again; *moham* – to illusion; *evam* – like this; *yāsyasi* – you shall go; *pāṇḍava* – O son of Pāṇḍu; *yena* – by which; *bhūtāni* – living entities; *aśeṣāṇi* – all; *drakṣyasi* – you will see; *ātmani* – in the Supreme Soul; *atha u* – or in other words; *mayi* – in Me.

Having obtained real knowledge from a self-realized soul, you will never fall again into such illusion, for by this knowledge you will see that all living beings are but part of the Supreme, or, in other words, that they are Mine.

PURPORT: The result of receiving knowledge from a self-realized soul, or one who knows things as they are, is learning that all living beings are parts and parcels of the Supreme Personality of Godhead, Lord Śrī Kṛṣṇa. The sense of an existence separate from Kṛṣṇa is called *māyā* (*mā* – not, *yā* – this). Some think that we have nothing to do with Kṛṣṇa, that Kṛṣṇa is only a great historical personality and that the Absolute is the impersonal Brahman. Factually, as it is stated in the *Bhagavad-gītā,* this impersonal Brahman is the personal effulgence of Kṛṣṇa. Kṛṣṇa, as the Supreme Personality of Godhead, is the cause of everything. In the *Brahma-saṁhitā* it is clearly stated that Kṛṣṇa is the Supreme Personality of Godhead, the cause of all causes. Even the millions of incarnations are only His different expansions. Similarly, the living entities are also expansions of Kṛṣṇa. The Māyāvādī philosophers wrongly think that

Kṛṣṇa loses His own separate existence in His many expansions. This thought is material in nature. We have experience in the material world that a thing, when fragmentally distributed, loses its own original identity. But the Māyāvādī philosophers fail to understand that *absolute* means that one plus one is equal to one, and that one minus one is also equal to one. This is the case in the absolute world.

For want of sufficient knowledge in the absolute science, we are now covered with illusion, and therefore we think that we are separate from Kṛṣṇa. Although we are separated parts of Kṛṣṇa, we are nevertheless not different from Him. The bodily difference of the living entities is *māyā,* or not actual fact. We are all meant to satisfy Kṛṣṇa. By *māyā* alone Arjuna thought that the temporary bodily relationship with his kinsmen was more important than his eternal spiritual relationship with Kṛṣṇa. The whole teaching of the *Gītā* is targeted toward this end: that a living being, as Kṛṣṇa's eternal servitor, cannot be separated from Kṛṣṇa, and his sense of being an identity apart from Kṛṣṇa is called *māyā.* The living entities, as separate parts and parcels of the Supreme, have a purpose to fulfill. Having forgotten that purpose since time immemorial, they are situated in different bodies, as men, animals, demigods, etc. Such bodily differences arise from forgetfulness of the transcendental service of the Lord. But when one is engaged in transcendental service through Kṛṣṇa consciousness, one becomes at once liberated from this illusion. One can acquire such pure knowledge only from the bona fide spiritual master and thereby avoid the delusion that the living entity is equal to Kṛṣṇa. Perfect knowledge is that the Supreme Soul, Kṛṣṇa, is the supreme shelter for all living entities, and giving up such shelter, the living entities are deluded by the material energy, imagining themselves to have a separate identity. Thus, under different standards of material identity, they become forgetful of Kṛṣṇa. When, however, such deluded living entities become situated in Kṛṣṇa consciousness, it is to be understood that they are on the path of liberation, as confirmed in the *Bhāgavatam* (2.10.6): *muktir hitvānyathā-rūpaṁ svarūpena vyavasthitiḥ.* Liberation means to be situated in one's constitutional position as an eternal servitor of Kṛṣṇa (Kṛṣṇa consciousness).

Text 36 अपि चेदसि पापेभ्यः सर्वेभ्यः पापकृत्तमः ।
सर्वं ज्ञानप्लवेनैव वृजिनं सन्तरिष्यसि ॥३६॥

api ced asi pāpebhyaḥ, sarvebhyaḥ pāpa-kṛt-tamaḥ
sarvaṁ jñāna-plavenaiva, vṛjinaṁ santariṣyasi

api – even; *cet* – if; *asi* – you are; *pāpebhyaḥ* – of sinners; *sarvebhyaḥ* – of all; *pāpa-kṛt-tamaḥ* – the greatest sinner; *sarvam* – all such sinful reactions; *jñāna-plavena* – by the boat of transcendental knowledge; *eva* – certainly; *vṛjinam* – the ocean of miseries; *santariṣyasi* – you will cross completely.

Even if you are considered to be the most sinful of all sinners, when you are situated in the boat of transcendental knowledge you will be able to cross over the ocean of miseries.

PURPORT: Proper understanding of one's constitutional position in relationship to Kṛṣṇa is so nice that it can at once lift one from the struggle for existence which goes on in the ocean of nescience. This material world is sometimes regarded as an ocean of nescience and sometimes as a blazing forest. In the ocean, however expert a swimmer one may be, the struggle for existence is very severe. If someone comes forward and lifts the struggling swimmer from the ocean, he is the greatest savior. Perfect knowledge, received from the Supreme Personality of Godhead, is the path of liberation. The boat of Kṛṣṇa consciousness is very simple, but at the same time the most sublime.

Text 37 यथैधांसि समिद्धोऽग्निर्भस्मसात्कुरुतेऽर्जुन ।
ज्ञानाग्निः सर्वकर्माणि भस्मसात्कुरुते तथा ॥३७॥

yathaidhāṁsi samiddho 'gnir, bhasma-sāt kurute 'rjuna
jñānāgniḥ sarva-karmāṇi, bhasma-sāt kurute tathā

yathā – just as; *edhāṁsi* – firewood; *samiddhaḥ* – blazing; *agniḥ* – fire; *bhasma-sāt* – ashes; *kurute* – turns; *arjuna* – O Arjuna; *jñāna-agniḥ* – the fire of knowledge; *sarva-karmāṇi* – all reactions to material activities; *bhasma-sāt* – to ashes; *kurute* – it turns; *tathā* – similarly.

As a blazing fire turns firewood to ashes, O Arjuna, so does the fire of knowledge burn to ashes all reactions to material activities.

PURPORT: Perfect knowledge of self and Superself and of their relationship is compared herein to fire. This fire not only burns up all reactions to impious activities, but also all reactions to pious activities, turning them to ashes. There are many stages of reaction: reaction in the making, reaction fructifying, reaction already achieved, and reaction *a priori.* But knowledge of the constitutional position of the living entity burns everything to ashes. When one is in complete knowledge, all reactions, both *a priori* and *a posteriori,* are consumed. In the *Vedas* (*Bṛhad-āraṇyaka Upaniṣad* 4.4.22) it is stated, *ubhe uhaivaiṣa ete taraty amṛtaḥ sādhv-asādhūnī:* "One overcomes both the pious and impious reactions of work."

Text 38 न हि ज्ञानेन सदृशं पवित्रमिह विद्यते ।
तत्स्वयं योगसंसिद्धः कालेनात्मनि विन्दति ॥३८॥

na hi jñānena sadṛśaṁ, pavitram iha vidyate
tat svayaṁ yoga-saṁsiddhaḥ, kālenātmani vindati

na – nothing; *hi* – certainly; *jñānena* – with knowledge; *sadṛśam* – in comparison; *pavitram* – sanctified; *iha* – in this world; *vidyate* – exists; *tat* – that; *svayam* – himself; *yoga* – in devotion; *saṁsiddhaḥ* – he who is mature; *kālena* – in course of time; *ātmani* – in himself; *vindati* – enjoys.

In this world, there is nothing so sublime and pure as transcendental knowledge. Such knowledge is the mature fruit of all mysticism. And one who has become accomplished in the practice of devotional service enjoys this knowledge within himself in due course of time.

PURPORT: When we speak of transcendental knowledge, we do so in terms of spiritual understanding. As such, there is nothing so sublime and pure as transcendental knowledge. Ignorance is the cause of our bondage, and knowledge is the cause of our liberation. This knowledge is the mature fruit of devotional service, and when one is situated in transcendental knowledge, he need not search for peace elsewhere, for he enjoys peace within himself. In other words, this knowledge and peace culminate in Kṛṣṇa consciousness. That is the last word in the *Bhagavad-gītā.*

Text 39 श्रद्धावाँल्लभते ज्ञानं तत्परः संयतेन्द्रियः ।
ज्ञानं लब्ध्वा परां शान्तिमचिरेणाधिगच्छति ॥३९॥

śraddhāvāl̐ labhate jñānaṁ, tat-paraḥ saṁyatendriyaḥ
jñānaṁ labdhvā parāṁ śāntim, acireṇādhigacchati

śraddhā-vān – a faithful man; *labhate* – achieves; *jñānam* – knowledge; *tat-paraḥ* – very much attached to it; *saṁyata* – controlled; *indriyaḥ* – senses; *jñānam* – knowledge; *labdhvā* – having achieved; *parām* – transcendental; *śāntim* – peace; *acireṇa* – very soon; *adhigacchati* – attains.

A faithful man who is dedicated to transcendental knowledge and who subdues his senses is eligible to achieve such knowledge, and having achieved it he quickly attains the supreme spiritual peace.

PURPORT: Such knowledge in Kṛṣṇa consciousness can be achieved by a faithful person who believes firmly in Kṛṣṇa. One is called a faithful man who thinks that simply by acting in Kṛṣṇa consciousness he can attain the highest perfection. This faith is attained by the discharge of devotional service, and by chanting Hare Kṛṣṇa, Hare Kṛṣṇa, Kṛṣṇa Kṛṣṇa, Hare Hare/ Hare Rāma, Hare Rāma, Rāma Rāma, Hare Hare, which cleanses one's heart of all material dirt. Over and above this, one should control the senses. A person who is faithful to Kṛṣṇa and who controls the senses can easily attain perfection in the knowledge of Kṛṣṇa consciousness without delay.

Text 40 अज्ञश्चाश्रद्दधानश्च संशयात्मा विनश्यति ।
नायं लोकोऽस्ति न परो न सुखं संशयात्मनः ॥४०॥

ajñaś cāśraddadhānaś ca, saṁśayātmā vinaśyati
nāyaṁ loko 'sti na paro, na sukhaṁ saṁśayātmanaḥ

ajñaḥ – a fool who has no knowledge in standard scriptures; *ca* – and; *aśraddadhānaḥ* – without faith in revealed scriptures; *ca* – also; *saṁśaya* – of doubts; *ātmā* – a person; *vinaśyati* – falls back; *na* – never; *ayam* – in this; *lokaḥ* – world; *asti* – there is; *na* – nor; *paraḥ* – in the next life; *na* – not; *sukham* – happiness; *saṁśaya* – doubtful; *ātmanaḥ* – of the person.

But ignorant and faithless persons who doubt the revealed scriptures do not attain God consciousness; they fall down. For the doubting soul there is happiness neither in this world nor in the next.

PURPORT: Out of many standard and authoritative revealed scriptures, the *Bhagavad-gītā* is the best. Persons who are almost like animals have no faith in, or knowledge of, the standard revealed scriptures; and some, even though they have knowledge of, or can cite passages from, the revealed scriptures, have actually no faith in these words. And even though others may have faith in scriptures like *Bhagavad-gītā,* they do not believe in or worship the Personality of Godhead, Śrī Kṛṣṇa. Such persons cannot have any standing in Kṛṣṇa consciousness. They fall down. Out of all the above-mentioned persons, those who have no faith and are always doubtful make no progress at all. Men without faith in God and His revealed word find no good in this world, nor in the next. For them there is no happiness whatsoever. One should therefore follow the principles of revealed scriptures with faith and thereby be raised to the platform of knowledge. Only this knowledge will help one become promoted to the transcendental platform of spiritual understanding. In other words, doubtful persons have no status whatsoever in spiritual emancipation. One should therefore follow in the footsteps of great *ācāryas* who are in the disciplic succession and thereby attain success.

Text 41 योगसन्न्यस्तकर्माणं ज्ञानसञ्छिन्नसंशयम् ।
आत्मवन्तं न कर्माणि निबध्नन्ति धनञ्जय ॥४१॥

yoga-sannyasta-karmāṇaṁ, jñāna-sañchinna-saṁśayam
ātmavantaṁ na karmāṇi, nibadhnanti dhanañ-jaya

yoga – by devotional service in *karma-yoga; sannyasta* – one who has renounced; *karmāṇam* – the fruits of actions; *jñāna* – by knowledge; *sañchinna* – cut; *saṁśayam* – doubts; *ātma-vantam* – situated in the self; *na* – never; *karmāṇi* – works; *nibadhnanti* – do bind; *dhanam-jaya* – O conqueror of riches.

One who acts in devotional service, renouncing the fruits of his actions, and whose doubts have been destroyed by transcendental knowledge, is situated factually in the self. Thus he is not bound by the reactions of work, O conqueror of riches.

PURPORT: One who follows the instruction of the *Bhagavad-gītā,* as it is imparted by the Lord, the Personality of Godhead Himself, becomes free from all doubts by the grace of transcendental knowledge. He, as a part and parcel of the Lord, in full Kṛṣṇa consciousness, is already established in self-knowledge. As such, he is undoubtedly above bondage to action.

Text 42 तस्मादज्ञानसम्भूतं हृत्स्थं ज्ञानासिनात्मनः ।
छित्त्वैनं संशयं योगमातिष्ठोत्तिष्ठ भारत ॥४२॥

tasmād ajñāna-sambhūtaṁ, hṛt-sthaṁ jñānāsinātmanaḥ
chittvainaṁ saṁśayaṁ yogam, ātiṣṭhottiṣṭha bhārata

tasmāt – therefore; *ajñāna-sambhūtam* – born of ignorance; *hṛt-stham* – situated in the heart; *jñāna* – of knowledge; *asinā* – by the weapon;

ātmanaḥ – of the self; *chittvā* – cutting off; *enam* – this; *saṁśayam* – doubt; *yogam* – in *yoga; ātiṣṭha* – be situated; *uttiṣṭha* – stand up to fight; *bhārata* – O descendant of Bharata.

Therefore the doubts which have arisen in your heart out of ignorance should be slashed by the weapon of knowledge. Armed with yoga, O Bhārata, stand and fight.

PURPORT: The *yoga* system instructed in this chapter is called *sanātana-yoga,* or eternal activities performed by the living entity. This *yoga* has two divisions of sacrificial actions: one is called sacrifice of one's material possessions, and the other is called knowledge of self, which is pure spiritual activity. If sacrifice of one's material possessions is not dovetailed for spiritual realization, then such sacrifice becomes material. But one who performs such sacrifices with a spiritual objective, or in devotional service, makes a perfect sacrifice. When we come to spiritual activities, we find that these are also divided into two: namely, understanding of one's own self (or one's constitutional position), and the truth regarding the Supreme Personality of Godhead. One who follows the path of *Bhagavad-gītā* as it is can very easily understand these two important divisions of spiritual knowledge. For him there is no difficulty in obtaining perfect knowledge of the self as part and parcel of the Lord. And such understanding is beneficial, for such a person can easily understand the transcendental activities of the Lord. In the beginning of this chapter, the transcendental activities of the Lord were discussed by the Supreme Lord Himself. One who does not understand the instructions of the *Gītā* is faithless, and is to be considered to be misusing the fragmental independence awarded to him by the Lord. In spite of such instructions, one who does not understand the real nature of the Lord as the eternal, blissful, all-knowing Personality of Godhead is certainly fool number one. Ignorance can be removed by gradual acceptance of the principles of Kṛṣṇa consciousness. Kṛṣṇa consciousness is awakened by different types of sacrifices to the demigods, sacrifice to Brahman, sacrifice in celibacy, in household life, in controlling the senses, in practicing mystic yoga, in penance, in forgoing material possessions, in studying the *Vedas,* and in partaking of the social institution called *varṇāśrama-dharma*. All of these are known as sacrifice, and all of them are based on regulated action. But within all these activities, the important factor is self-realization. One who seeks that objective is the real student of *Bhagavad-gītā,* but one who doubts the authority of Kṛṣṇa falls back. One is therefore advised to study *Bhagavad-gītā,* or any other scripture, under a bona fide spiritual master, with service and surrender. A bona fide spiritual master is in the disciplic succession from time eternal, and he does not deviate at all from the instructions of the Supreme Lord as they were imparted millions of years ago to the sun-god, from whom the instructions of *Bhagavad-gītā* have come down to the earthly kingdom. One should, therefore, follow the path of *Bhagavad-gītā* as it is expressed in the *Gītā* itself and beware of self-interested people after personal aggrandizement who deviate others from the actual path. The Lord is definitely the supreme person, and His activities are transcendental. One who understands this is a liberated person from the very beginning of his study of *Bhagavad-gītā*.

Thus end the Bhaktivedanta Purports to the Fourth Chapter of the Śrīmad Bhagavad-gītā *in the matter of Transcendental Knowledge.*

CHAPTER FIVE

Karma-yoga – Action in Kṛṣṇa Consciousness

Text 1 अर्जुन उवाच
सन्न्यासं कर्मणां कृष्ण पुनर्योगं च शंससि ।
यच्छ्रेय एतयोरेकं तन्मे ब्रूहि सुनिश्चितम् ॥ १ ॥

arjuna uvāca
sannyāsaṁ karmaṇāṁ kṛṣṇa, punar yogaṁ ca śaṁsasi
yac chreya etayor ekaṁ, tan me brūhi su-niścitam

arjunaḥ uvāca – Arjuna said; *sannyāsam* – renunciation; *karmaṇām* – of all activities; *kṛṣṇa* – O Kṛṣṇa; *punaḥ* – again; *yogam* – devotional service; *ca* – also; *śaṁsasi* – You are praising; *yat* – which; *śreyaḥ* – is more beneficial; *etayoḥ* – of these two; *ekam* – one; *tat* – that; *me* – unto me; *brūhi* – please tell; *su-niścitam* – definitely.

Arjuna said: O Kṛṣṇa, first of all You ask me to renounce work, and then again You recommend work with devotion. Now will You kindly tell me definitely which of the two is more beneficial?

PURPORT: In this Fifth Chapter of the *Bhagavad-gītā,* the Lord says that work in devotional service is better than dry mental speculation. Devotional service is easier than the latter because, being transcendental in nature, it frees one from reaction. In the Second Chapter, preliminary knowledge of the soul and its entanglement in the material body were explained. How to get out of this material encagement by *buddhi-yoga,* or devotional service, was also explained therein. In the Third Chapter, it was explained that a person who is situated on the platform of knowledge no longer has any duties to perform. And in the Fourth Chapter the Lord told Arjuna that all kinds of sacrificial work culminate in knowledge. However, at the end of the Fourth Chapter, the Lord advised Arjuna to wake up and fight, being situated in perfect knowledge. Therefore, by simultaneously stressing the importance of both work in devotion and inaction in knowledge, Kṛṣṇa has perplexed Arjuna and confused his determination. Arjuna understands that renunciation in knowledge involves cessation of all kinds of work performed as sense activities. But if one performs work in devotional service, then how is work stopped? In other words, he thinks that *sannyāsa,* or renunciation in knowledge, should be altogether free from all kinds of activity, because work and renunciation appear to him to be incompatible. He appears not to have understood that work in full knowledge is nonreactive and is therefore the same as inaction. He inquires, therefore, whether he should cease work altogether or work with full knowledge.

Text 2 श्रीभगवानुवाच
सन्न्यासः कर्मयोगश्च निःश्रेयसकरावुभौ ।
तयोस्तु कर्मसन्न्यासात्कर्मयोगो विशिष्यते ॥ २ ॥

śrī-bhagavān uvāca
sannyāsaḥ karma-yogaś ca, niḥśreyasa-karāv ubhau
tayos tu karma-sannyāsāt, karma-yogo viśiṣyate

śrī-bhagavān uvāca – the Personality of Godhead said; *sannyāsaḥ* – renunciation of work; *karma-yogaḥ* – work in devotion; *ca* – also; *niḥśreyasa-karau* – leading to the path of liberation; *ubhau* – both; *tayoḥ* – of the two; *tu* – but; *karma-sannyāsāt* – in comparison to the renunciation of fruitive work; *karma-yogaḥ* – work in devotion; *viśiṣyate* – is better.

The Personality of Godhead replied: The renunciation of work and work in devotion are both good for liberation. But, of the two, work in devotional service is better than renunciation of work.

PURPORT: Fruitive activities (seeking sense gratification) are cause for material bondage. As long as one is engaged in activities aimed at improving the standard of bodily comfort, one is sure to transmigrate to different types of bodies, thereby continuing material bondage perpetually. *Śrīmad-Bhāgavatam* (5.5.4–6) confirms this as follows:

nūnaṁ pramattaḥ kurute vikarma, yad indriya-prītaya āpṛṇoti
na sādhu manye yata ātmano 'yam, asann api kleśa-da āsa dehaḥ

parābhavas tāvad abodha-jāto, yāvan na jijñāsata ātma-tattvam
yāvat kriyās tāvad idaṁ mano vai, karmātmakaṁ yena śarīra-bandhaḥ

evaṁ manaḥ karma-vaśaṁ prayuṅkte, avidyayātmany upadhīyamāne
prītir na yāvan mayi vāsudeve, na mucyate deha-yogena tāvat

"People are mad after sense gratification, and they do not know that this present body, which is full of miseries, is a result of one's fruitive activities in the past. Although this body is temporary, it is always giving one trouble in many ways. Therefore, to act for sense gratification is not good. One is considered to be a failure in life as long as he makes no inquiry about his real identity. As long as he does not know his real identity, he has to work for fruitive results for sense gratification, and as long as one is engrossed in the consciousness of sense gratification one has to transmigrate from one body to another. Although the mind may be engrossed in fruitive activities and influenced by ignorance, one must develop a love for devotional service to Vāsudeva. Only then can one have the opportunity to get out of the bondage of material existence."

Therefore, *jñāna* (or knowledge that one is not this material body but spirit soul) is not sufficient for liberation. One has to *act* in the status of spirit soul, otherwise there is no escape from material bondage. Action in Kṛṣṇa consciousness is not, however, action on the fruitive platform. Activities performed in full knowledge strengthen one's advancement in real knowledge. Without Kṛṣṇa consciousness, mere renunciation of fruitive activities does not actually purify the heart of a conditioned soul. As long as the heart is not purified, one has to work on the fruitive platform. But action in Kṛṣṇa consciousness automatically helps one escape the result of fruitive action so that one need not descend to the material platform. Therefore action in Kṛṣṇa consciousness is always superior to renunciation, which always entails a risk of falling. Renunciation without Kṛṣṇa consciousness is incomplete, as is confirmed by Śrīla Rūpa Gosvāmī in his *Bhakti-rasāmṛta-sindhu* (1.2.258):

prāpañcikatayā buddhyā, hari-sambandhi-vastunaḥ
mumukṣubhiḥ parityāgo, vairāgyaṁ phalgu kathyate

"When persons eager to achieve liberation renounce things related to the Supreme Personality of Godhead, thinking them to be material, their renunciation is called incomplete." Renunciation is complete when it is in the knowledge that everything in existence belongs to the Lord and that no one should claim proprietorship over anything. One should understand that, factually, nothing belongs to anyone. Then where is the question of renunciation? One who knows that everything is Kṛṣṇa's property is always situated in renunciation. Since everything belongs to Kṛṣṇa, everything should be employed in the service of Kṛṣṇa. This perfect form of action in Kṛṣṇa consciousness is far better than any amount of artificial renunciation by a *sannyāsī* of the Māyāvādī school.

Text 3 ज्ञेयः स नित्यसन्न्यासी यो न द्वेष्टि न काङ्क्षति ।
निर्द्वन्द्वो हि महाबाहो सुखं बन्धात्प्रमुच्यते ॥ ३ ॥

jñeyaḥ sa nitya-sannyāsī, yo na dveṣṭi na kāṅkṣati
nirdvandvo hi mahā-bāho, sukhaṁ bandhāt pramucyate

jñeyaḥ – should be known; *saḥ* – he; *nitya* – always; *sannyāsī* – renouncer; *yaḥ* – who; *na* – never; *dveṣṭi* – abhors; *na* – nor; *kāṅkṣati* – desires; *nirdvandvaḥ* – free from all dualities; *hi* – certainly; *mahā-bāho* – O mighty-armed one; *sukham* – happily; *bandhāt* – from bondage; *pramucyate* – is completely liberated.

One who neither hates nor desires the fruits of his activities is known to be always renounced. Such a person, free from all dualities, easily overcomes material bondage and is completely liberated, O mighty-armed Arjuna.

PURPORT: One who is fully in Kṛṣṇa consciousness is always a renouncer because he feels neither hatred nor desire for the results of his actions. Such a renouncer, dedicated to the transcendental loving service of the Lord, is fully qualified in knowledge because he knows his constitutional position in his relationship with Kṛṣṇa. He knows fully well that Kṛṣṇa is the whole and that he is part and parcel of Kṛṣṇa. Such knowledge is perfect because it is qualitatively and quantitatively correct. The concept of oneness with Kṛṣṇa is incorrect because the part cannot be equal to the whole. Knowledge that one is one in quality yet different in quantity is correct transcendental knowledge leading one to become full in himself, having nothing to aspire to or lament over. There is no duality in his mind because whatever he does, he does for Kṛṣṇa. Being thus freed from the platform of dualities, he is liberated – even in this material world.

Text 4 साङ्ख्ययोगौ पृथग्बालाः प्रवदन्ति न पण्डिताः ।
एकमप्यास्थितः सम्यगुभयोर्विन्दते फलम् ॥ ४ ॥

sāṅkhya-yogau pṛthag bālāḥ, pravadanti na paṇḍitāḥ
ekam apy āsthitaḥ samyag, ubhayor vindate phalam

sāṅkhya – analytical study of the material world; *yogau* – work in devotional service; *pṛthak* – different; *bālāḥ* – the less intelligent; *pravadanti* – say; *na* – never; *paṇḍitāḥ* – the learned; *ekam* – in one; *api* – even; *āsthitaḥ* – being situated; *samyak* – complete; *ubhayoḥ* – of both; *vindate* – enjoys; *phalam* – the result.

Only the ignorant speak of devotional service [karma-yoga] as being different from the analytical study of the material world [Sāṅkhya]. Those who are actually learned say that he who applies himself well to one of these paths achieves the results of both.

PURPORT: The aim of the analytical study of the material world is to find the soul of existence. The soul of the material world is Viṣṇu, or the Supersoul. Devotional service to the Lord entails service to the Supersoul. One process is to find the root of the tree, and the other is to water the root. The real student of Sāṅkhya philosophy finds the root of the material world, Viṣṇu, and then, in perfect knowledge, engages himself in the service of the Lord. Therefore, in essence, there is no difference between the two because the aim of both is Viṣṇu. Those who do not know the ultimate end say that the purposes of Sāṅkhya and *karma-yoga* are not the same, but one who is learned knows the unifying aim in these different processes.

Text 5 यत्साङ्ख्यैः प्राप्यते स्थानं तद्योगैरपि गम्यते ।
एकं साङ्ख्यं च योगं च यः पश्यति स पश्यति ॥ ५ ॥

yat sāṅkhyaiḥ prāpyate sthānaṁ, tad yogair api gamyate
ekaṁ sāṅkhyaṁ ca yogaṁ ca, yaḥ paśyati sa paśyati

yat – what; *sāṅkhyaiḥ* – by means of Sāṅkhya philosophy; *prāpyate* – is achieved; *sthānam* – place; *tat* – that; *yogaiḥ* – by devotional service;

api – also; *gamyate* – one can attain; *ekam* – one; *sāṅkhyam* – analytical study; *ca* – and; *yogam* – action in devotion; *ca* – and; *yaḥ* – one who; *paśyati* – sees; *saḥ* – he; *paśyati* – actually sees.

One who knows that the position reached by means of analytical study can also be attained by devotional service, and who therefore sees analytical study and devotional service to be on the same level, sees things as they are.

PURPORT: The real purpose of philosophical research is to find the ultimate goal of life. Since the ultimate goal of life is self-realization, there is no difference between the conclusions reached by the two processes. By Sāṅkhya philosophical research one comes to the conclusion that a living entity is not a part and parcel of the material world but of the supreme spirit whole. Consequently, the spirit soul has nothing to do with the material world; his actions must be in some relation with the Supreme. When he acts in Kṛṣṇa consciousness, he is actually in his constitutional position. In the first process, Sāṅkhya, one has to become detached from matter, and in the devotional *yoga* process one has to attach himself to the work of Kṛṣṇa consciousness. Factually, both processes are the same, although superficially one process appears to involve detachment and the other process appears to involve attachment. Detachment from matter and attachment to Kṛṣṇa are one and the same. One who can see this sees things as they are.

Text 6 सन्न्यासस्तु महाबाहो दुःखमाप्तुमयोगतः ।
योगयुक्तो मुनिर्ब्रह्म न चिरेणाधिगच्छति ॥ ६ ॥

sannyāsas tu mahā-bāho, duḥkham āptum ayogataḥ
yoga-yukto munir brahma, na cireṇādhigacchati

sannyāsaḥ – the renounced order of life; *tu* – but; *mahā-bāho* – O mighty-armed one; *duḥkham* – distress; *āptum* – afflicts one with; *ayogataḥ* – without devotional service; *yoga-yuktaḥ* – one engaged in devotional service; *muniḥ* – a thinker; *brahma* – the Supreme; *na cireṇa* – without delay; *adhigacchati* – attains.

Merely renouncing all activities yet not engaging in the devotional service of the Lord cannot make one happy. But a thoughtful person engaged in devotional service can achieve the Supreme without delay.

PURPORT: There are two classes of *sannyāsīs,* or persons in the renounced order of life. The Māyāvādī *sannyāsīs* are engaged in the study of Sāṅkhya philosophy, whereas the Vaiṣṇava *sannyāsīs* are engaged in the study of *Bhāgavatam* philosophy, which affords the proper commentary on the *Vedānta-sūtras.* The Māyāvādī *sannyāsīs* also study the *Vedānta-sūtras,* but use their own commentary, called *Śārīraka-bhāṣya,* written by Śaṅkarācārya. The students of the *Bhāgavata* school are engaged in the devotional service of the Lord, according to *pāñcarātrikī* regulations, and therefore the Vaiṣṇava *sannyāsīs* have multiple engagements in the transcendental service of the Lord. The Vaiṣṇava *sannyāsīs* have nothing to do with material activities, and yet they perform various activities in their devotional service to the Lord. But the Māyāvādī *sannyāsīs,* engaged in the studies of Sāṅkhya and Vedānta and speculation, cannot relish the transcendental service of the Lord. Because their studies become very tedious, they sometimes become tired of Brahman speculation, and thus they take shelter of the *Bhāgavatam* without proper understanding. Consequently their study of the *Śrīmad-Bhāgavatam* becomes troublesome. Dry speculations and impersonal interpretations by artificial means are all useless for the Māyāvādī *sannyāsīs.* The Vaiṣṇava *sannyāsīs,* who are engaged in devotional service, are happy in the discharge of their transcendental duties, and they have the guarantee of ultimate entrance into the kingdom of God. The Māyāvādī *sannyāsīs* sometimes fall down from the path of self-realization and again enter into material activities of a philanthropic and altruistic nature, which are nothing but material engagements. Therefore, the conclusion is that those who are engaged in Kṛṣṇa conscious activities are better situated than the *sannyāsīs* engaged in simple speculation about what is Brahman and what is not Brahman, although they too come to Kṛṣṇa consciousness, after many births.

Text 7 योगयुक्तो विशुद्धात्मा विजितात्मा जितेन्द्रियः ।
सर्वभूतात्मभूतात्मा कुर्वन्नपि न लिप्यते ॥ ७ ॥

yoga-yukto viśuddhātmā, vijitātmā jitendriyaḥ
sarva-bhūtātma-bhūtātmā, kurvann api na lipyate

yoga-yuktaḥ – engaged in devotional service; *viśuddha-ātmā* – a purified soul; *vijita-ātmā* – self-controlled; *jita-indriyaḥ* – having conquered the senses; *sarva-bhūta* – to all living entities; *ātma-bhūta-ātmā* –

compassionate; *kurvan api* – although engaged in work; *na* – never; *lipyate* – is entangled.

One who works in devotion, who is a pure soul, and who controls his mind and senses is dear to everyone, and everyone is dear to him. Though always working, such a man is never entangled.

PURPORT: One who is on the path of liberation by Kṛṣṇa consciousness is very dear to every living being, and every living being is dear to him. This is due to his Kṛṣṇa consciousness. Such a person cannot think of any living being as separate from Kṛṣṇa, just as the leaves and branches of a tree are not separate from the tree. He knows very well that by pouring water on the root of the tree, the water will be distributed to all the leaves and branches, or by supplying food to the stomach, the energy is automatically distributed throughout the body. Because one who works in Kṛṣṇa consciousness is servant to all, he is very dear to everyone. And because everyone is satisfied by his work, he is pure in consciousness. Because he is pure in consciousness, his mind is completely controlled. And because his mind is controlled, his senses are also controlled. Because his mind is always fixed on Kṛṣṇa, there is no chance of his being deviated from Kṛṣṇa. Nor is there a chance that he will engage his senses in matters other than the service of the Lord. He does not like to hear anything except topics relating to Kṛṣṇa; he does not like to eat anything which is not offered to Kṛṣṇa; and he does not wish to go anywhere if Kṛṣṇa is not involved. Therefore, his senses are controlled. A man of controlled senses cannot be offensive to anyone. One may ask, "Why then was Arjuna offensive (in battle) to others? Wasn't he in Kṛṣṇa consciousness?" Arjuna was only superficially offensive because (as has already been explained in the Second Chapter) all the assembled persons on the battlefield would continue to live individually, as the soul cannot be slain. So, spiritually, no one was killed on the Battlefield of Kurukṣetra. Only their dresses were changed by the order of Kṛṣṇa, who was personally present. Therefore Arjuna, while fighting on the Battlefield of Kurukṣetra, was not really fighting at all; he was simply carrying out the orders of Kṛṣṇa in full Kṛṣṇa consciousness. Such a person is never entangled in the reactions of work.

Texts नैव किञ्चित्करोमीति युक्तो मन्येत तत्त्ववित् ।
8–9 पश्यञ्शृण्वन् स्पृशञ्जिघ्रन्नश्नन् गच्छन् स्वपन् श्वसन् ॥ ८ ॥

प्रलपन् विसृजन् गृह्णन्नुन्मिषन्निमिषन्नपि ।
इन्द्रियाणीन्द्रियार्थेषु वर्तन्त इति धारयन् ॥ ९ ॥

naiva kiñcit karomīti, yukto manyeta tattva-vit
paśyañ śṛṇvan spṛśañ jighrann, aśnan gacchan svapañ śvasan

pralapan visṛjan gṛhṇann, unmiṣan nimiṣann api
indriyāṇīndriyārtheṣu, vartanta iti dhārayan

na – never; *eva* – certainly; *kiñcit* – anything; *karomi* – I do; *iti* – thus; *yuktaḥ* – engaged in the divine consciousness; *manyeta* – thinks; *tattva-vit* – one who knows the truth; *paśyan* – seeing; *śṛṇvan* – hearing; *spṛśan* – touching; *jighran* – smelling; *aśnan* – eating; *gacchan* – going; *svapan* – dreaming; *śvasan* – breathing; *pralapan* – talking; *visṛjan* – giving up; *gṛhṇan* – accepting; *unmiṣan* – opening; *nimiṣan* – closing; *api* – in spite of; *indriyāṇi* – the senses; *indriya-artheṣu* – in sense gratification; *vartante* – let them be so engaged; *iti* – thus; *dhārayan* – considering.

A person in the divine consciousness, although engaged in seeing, hearing, touching, smelling, eating, moving about, sleeping and breathing, always knows within himself that he actually does nothing at all. Because while speaking, evacuating, receiving, or opening or closing his eyes, he always knows that only the material senses are engaged with their objects and that he is aloof from them.

PURPORT: A person in Kṛṣṇa consciousness is pure in his existence, and consequently he has nothing to do with any work which depends upon five immediate and remote causes: the doer, the work, the situation, the endeavor and fortune. This is because he is engaged in the loving transcendental service of Kṛṣṇa. Although he appears to be acting with his body and senses, he is always conscious of his actual position, which is spiritual engagement. In material consciousness, the senses are engaged in sense gratification, but in Kṛṣṇa consciousness the senses are engaged in the satisfaction of Kṛṣṇa's senses. Therefore, the Kṛṣṇa conscious person is always free, even though he appears to be engaged in affairs of the senses. Activities such as seeing and hearing are actions of the senses meant for receiving knowledge, whereas moving, speaking, evacuating, etc., are actions of the senses meant for work. A Kṛṣṇa conscious person is never affected by the actions of the senses. He cannot perform any act except in the service of the Lord because he knows that he is the eternal servitor of the Lord.

Text 10 ब्रह्मण्याधाय कर्माणि सङ्गं त्यक्त्वा करोति यः ।
लिप्यते न स पापेन पद्मपत्रमिवाम्भसा ॥१०॥

brahmaṇy ādhāya karmāṇi, saṅgaṁ tyaktvā karoti yaḥ
lipyate na sa pāpena, padma-patram ivāmbhasā

brahmaṇi – unto the Supreme Personality of Godhead; *ādhāya* – resigning; *karmāṇi* – all works; *saṅgam* – attachment; *tyaktvā* – giving up; *karoti* – performs; *yaḥ* – who; *lipyate* – is affected; *na* – never; *saḥ* – he; *pāpena* – by sin; *padma-patram* – a lotus leaf; *iva* – like; *ambhasā* – by the water.

One who performs his duty without attachment, surrendering the results unto the Supreme Lord, is unaffected by sinful action, as the lotus leaf is untouched by water.

PURPORT: Here *brahmaṇi* means in Kṛṣṇa consciousness. The material world is a sum total manifestation of the three modes of material nature, technically called the *pradhāna*. The Vedic hymns *sarvaṁ hy etad brahma* (*Māṇḍūkya Upaniṣad* 2), *tasmād etad brahma nāma-rūpam annaṁ ca jāyate* (*Muṇḍaka Upaniṣad* 1.1.9), and, in the *Bhagavad-gītā* (14.3), *mama yonir mahad brahma* indicate that everything in the material world is a manifestation of Brahman; and although the effects are differently manifested, they are nondifferent from the cause. In the *Īśopaniṣad* it is said that everything is related to the Supreme Brahman, or Kṛṣṇa, and thus everything belongs to Him only. One who knows perfectly well that everything belongs to Kṛṣṇa, that He is the proprietor of everything and that, therefore, everything is engaged in the service of the Lord, naturally has nothing to do with the results of his activities, whether virtuous or sinful. Even one's material body, being a gift of the Lord for carrying out a particular type of action, can be engaged in Kṛṣṇa consciousness. It is then beyond contamination by sinful reactions, exactly as the lotus leaf, though remaining in the water, is not wet. The Lord also says in the *Gītā* (3.30), *mayi sarvāṇi karmāṇi sannyasya:* "Resign all works unto Me [Kṛṣṇa]." The conclusion is that a person without Kṛṣṇa consciousness acts according to the concept of the material body and senses, but a person in Kṛṣṇa consciousness acts according to the knowledge that the body is the property of Kṛṣṇa and should therefore be engaged in the service of Kṛṣṇa.

Text 11 कायेन मनसा बुद्ध्या केवलैरिन्द्रियैरपि ।
योगिनः कर्म कुर्वन्ति सङ्गं त्यक्त्वात्मशुद्धये ॥११॥

kāyena manasā buddhyā, kevalair indriyair api
yoginaḥ karma kurvanti, saṅgaṁ tyaktvātma-śuddhaye

kāyena – with the body; *manasā* – with the mind; *buddhyā* – with the intelligence; *kevalaiḥ* – purified; *indriyaiḥ* – with the senses; *api* – even; *yoginaḥ* – Kṛṣṇa conscious persons; *karma* – actions; *kurvanti* – they perform; *saṅgam* – attachment; *tyaktvā* – giving up; *ātma* – of the self; *śuddhaye* – for the purpose of purification.

The yogīs, abandoning attachment, act with body, mind, intelligence and even with the senses, only for the purpose of purification.

PURPORT: When one acts in Kṛṣṇa consciousness for the satisfaction of the senses of Kṛṣṇa, any action, whether of the body, mind, intelligence or even the senses, is purified of material contamination. There are no material reactions resulting from the activities of a Kṛṣṇa conscious person. Therefore purified activities, which are generally called *sad-ācāra,* can be easily performed by acting in Kṛṣṇa consciousness. Śrī Rūpa Gosvāmī in his *Bhakti-rasāmṛta-sindhu* (1.2.187) describes this as follows:

īhā yasya harer dāsye, karmaṇā manasā girā
nikhilāsv apy avasthāsu, jīvan-muktaḥ sa ucyate

"A person acting in Kṛṣṇa consciousness (or, in other words, in the service of Kṛṣṇa) with his body, mind, intelligence and words is a liberated person even within the material world, although he may be engaged in many so-called material activities." He has no false ego, for he does not believe that he is this material body, or that he possesses the body. He knows that he is not this body and that this body does not belong to him. He himself belongs to Kṛṣṇa, and the body too belongs to Kṛṣṇa. When he applies everything produced of the body, mind, intelligence, words, life, wealth, etc. – whatever he may have within his possession – to Kṛṣṇa's service, he is at once dovetailed with Kṛṣṇa. He is one with Kṛṣṇa and is devoid of the false ego that leads one to believe that he is the body, etc. This is the perfect stage of Kṛṣṇa consciousness.

Text 12 युक्तः कर्मफलं त्यक्त्वा शान्तिमाप्नोति नैष्ठिकीम् ।
अयुक्तः कामकारेण फले सक्तो निबध्यते ॥१२॥

yuktaḥ karma-phalaṁ tyaktvā, śāntim āpnoti naiṣṭhikīm
ayuktaḥ kāma-kāreṇa, phale sakto nibadhyate

yuktaḥ – one who is engaged in devotional service; *karma-phalam* – the results of all activities; *tyaktvā* – giving up; *śāntim* – perfect peace; *āpnoti* – achieves; *naiṣṭhikīm* – unflinching; *ayuktaḥ* – one who is not in Kṛṣṇa consciousness; *kāma-kāreṇa* – for enjoying the result of work; *phale* – in the result; *saktaḥ* – attached; *nibadhyate* – becomes entangled.

The steadily devoted soul attains unadulterated peace because he offers the result of all activities to Me; whereas a person who is not in union with the Divine, who is greedy for the fruits of his labor, becomes entangled.

PURPORT: The difference between a person in Kṛṣṇa consciousness and a person in bodily consciousness is that the former is attached to Kṛṣṇa whereas the latter is attached to the results of his activities. The person who is attached to Kṛṣṇa and works for Him only is certainly a liberated person, and he has no anxiety over the results of his work. In the *Bhāgavatam,* the cause of anxiety over the result of an activity is explained as being one's functioning in the conception of duality, that is, without knowledge of the Absolute Truth. Kṛṣṇa is the Supreme Absolute Truth, the Personality of Godhead. In Kṛṣṇa consciousness, there is no duality. All that exists is a product of Kṛṣṇa's energy, and Kṛṣṇa is all good. Therefore, activities in Kṛṣṇa consciousness are on the absolute plane; they are transcendental and have no material effect. One is therefore filled with peace in Kṛṣṇa consciousness. But one who is entangled in profit calculation for sense gratification cannot have that peace. This is the secret of Kṛṣṇa consciousness – realization that there is no existence besides Kṛṣṇa is the platform of peace and fearlessness.

Text 13 सर्वकर्माणि मनसा सन्न्यस्यास्ते सुखं वशी ।
नवद्वारे पुरे देही नैव कुर्वन्न कारयन् ॥१३॥

sarva-karmāṇi manasā, sannyasyāste sukhaṁ vaśī
nava-dvāre pure dehī, naiva kurvan na kārayan

sarva – all; *karmāṇi* – activities; *manasā* – by the mind; *sannyasya* – giving up; *āste* – remains; *sukham* – in happiness; *vaśī* – one who is controlled; *nava-dvāre* – in the place where there are nine gates; *pure* – in the city; *dehī* – the embodied soul; *na* – never; *eva* – certainly; *kurvan* – doing anything; *na* – not; *kārayan* – causing to be done.

When the embodied living being controls his nature and mentally renounces all actions, he resides happily in the city of nine gates [the material body], neither working nor causing work to be done.

PURPORT: The embodied soul lives in the city of nine gates. The activities of the body, or the figurative city of the body, are conducted automatically by its particular modes of nature. The soul, although subjecting himself to the conditions of the body, can be beyond those conditions, if he so desires. Owing only to forgetfulness of his superior nature, he identifies with the material body, and therefore suffers. By Kṛṣṇa consciousness, he can revive his real position and thus come out of his embodiment. Therefore, when one takes to Kṛṣṇa consciousness, one at once becomes completely aloof from bodily activities. In such a controlled life, in which his deliberations are changed, he lives happily within the city of nine gates. The nine gates are mentioned as follows:

nava-dvāre pure dehī, haṁso lelāyate bahiḥ
vaśī sarvasya lokasya, sthāvarasya carasya ca

"The Supreme Personality of Godhead, who is living within the body of a living entity, is the controller of all living entities all over the universe. The body consists of nine gates [two eyes, two nostrils, two ears, one mouth, the anus and the genitals]. The living entity in his conditioned stage identifies himself with the body, but when he identifies himself with the Lord within himself, he becomes just as free as the Lord, even while in the body." (*Śvetāśvatara Upaniṣad* 3.18)

Therefore, a Kṛṣṇa conscious person is free from both the outer and inner activities of the material body.

Text 14 न कर्तृत्वं न कर्माणि लोकस्य सृजति प्रभुः ।
न कर्मफलसंयोगं स्वभावस्तु प्रवर्तते ॥१४॥

na kartṛtvaṁ na karmāṇi, lokasya sṛjati prabhuḥ
na karma-phala-saṁyogaṁ, svabhāvas tu pravartate

na – never; *kartṛtvam* – proprietorship; *na* – nor; *karmāṇi* – activities; *lokasya* – of the people; *sṛjati* – creates; *prabhuḥ* – the master of the city of the body; *na* – nor; *karma-phala* – with the results of activities;

saṁyogam – connection; *svabhāvaḥ* – the modes of material nature; *tu* – but; *pravartate* – act.

The embodied spirit, master of the city of his body, does not create activities, nor does he induce people to act, nor does he create the fruits of action. All this is enacted by the modes of material nature.

PURPORT: The living entity, as will be explained in the Seventh Chapter, is one of the energies or natures of the Supreme Lord but is distinct from matter, which is another nature – called inferior – of the Lord. Somehow the superior nature, the living entity, has been in contact with material nature since time immemorial. The temporary body or material dwelling place which he obtains is the cause of varieties of activities and their resultant reactions. Living in such a conditional atmosphere, one suffers the results of the activities of the body by identifying himself (in ignorance) with the body. It is ignorance acquired from time immemorial that is the cause of bodily suffering and distress. As soon as the living entity becomes aloof from the activities of the body, he becomes free from the reactions as well. As long as he is in the city of the body, he appears to be the master of it, but actually he is neither its proprietor nor controller of its actions and reactions. He is simply in the midst of the material ocean, struggling for existence. The waves of the ocean are tossing him, and he has no control over them. His best solution is to get out of the water by transcendental Kṛṣṇa consciousness. That alone will save him from all turmoil.

Text 15 नादत्ते कस्यचित्पापं न चैव सुकृतं विभुः ।
अज्ञानेनावृतं ज्ञानं तेन मुह्यन्ति जन्तवः ॥१५॥

nādatte kasyacit pāpaṁ, na caiva sukṛtaṁ vibhuḥ
ajñānenāvṛtaṁ jñānaṁ, tena muhyanti jantavaḥ

na – never; *ādatte* – accepts; *kasyacit* – anyone's; *pāpam* – sin; *na* – nor; *ca* – also; *eva* – certainly; *su-kṛtam* – pious activities; *vibhuḥ* – the Supreme Lord; *ajñānena* – by ignorance; *āvṛtam* – covered; *jñānam* – knowledge; *tena* – by that; *muhyanti* – are bewildered; *jantavaḥ* – the living entities.

Nor does the Supreme Lord assume anyone's sinful or pious activities. Embodied beings, however, are bewildered because of the ignorance which covers their real knowledge.

PURPORT: The Sanskrit word *vibhu* means the Supreme Lord who is full of unlimited knowledge, riches, strength, fame, beauty and renunciation. He is always satisfied in Himself, undisturbed by sinful or pious activities. He does not create a particular situation for any living entity, but the living entity, bewildered by ignorance, desires to be put into certain conditions of life, and thereby his chain of action and reaction begins. A living entity is, by superior nature, full of knowledge. Nevertheless, he is prone to be influenced by ignorance due to his limited power. The Lord is omnipotent, but the living entity is not. The Lord is *vibhu,* or omniscient, but the living entity is *aṇu,* or atomic. Because he is a living soul, he has the capacity to desire by his free will. Such desire is fulfilled only by the omnipotent Lord. And so, when the living entity is bewildered in his desires, the Lord allows him to fulfill those desires, but the Lord is never responsible for the actions and reactions of the particular situation which may be desired. Being in a bewildered condition, therefore, the embodied soul identifies himself with the circumstantial material body and becomes subjected to the temporary misery and happiness of life. The Lord is the constant companion of the living entity as Paramātmā, or the Supersoul, and therefore He can understand the desires of the individual soul, as one can smell the flavor of a flower by being near it. Desire is a subtle form of conditioning for the living entity. The Lord fulfills his desire as he deserves: Man proposes and God disposes. The individual is not, therefore, omnipotent in fulfilling his desires. The Lord, however, can fulfill all desires, and the Lord, being neutral to everyone, does not interfere with the desires of the minute independent living entities. However, when one desires Kṛṣṇa, the Lord takes special care and encourages one to desire in such a way that one can attain to Him and be eternally happy. The Vedic hymns therefore declare, *eṣa u hy eva sādhu karma kārayati taṁ yam ebhyo lokebhya unninīṣate. eṣa u evāsādhu karma kārayati yam adho ninīṣate:* "The Lord engages the living entity in pious activities so that he may be elevated. The Lord engages him in impious activities so that he may go to hell." (*Kauṣītakī Upaniṣad* 3.8) Similarly, the *Mahābhārata* (*Vana-parva* 31.27) states:

ajño jantur anīśo 'yam, ātmanaḥ sukha-duḥkhayoḥ
īśvara-prerito gacchet, svargaṁ vāśv abhram eva ca

"The living entity is completely dependent in his distress and happiness. By the will of the Supreme he can go to heaven or hell, as a cloud is driven by the air."

Therefore the embodied soul, by his immemorial desire to avoid Kṛṣṇa consciousness, causes his own bewilderment. Consequently, although he is constitutionally eternal, blissful and cognizant, due to the littleness of his existence he forgets his constitutional position of service to the Lord and is thus entrapped by nescience. And, under the spell of ignorance, the living entity claims that the Lord is responsible for his conditional existence. The *Vedānta-sūtras* (2.1.34) also confirm this. *Vaiṣamya-nairghṛṇye na sāpekṣatvāt tathā hi darśayati:* "The Lord neither hates nor likes anyone, though He appears to."

Text 16 ज्ञानेन तु तदज्ञानं येषां नाशितमात्मनः ।
तेषामादित्यवज्ज्ञानं प्रकाशयति तत्परम् ॥१६॥

jñānena tu tad ajñānaṁ, yeṣāṁ nāśitam ātmanaḥ
teṣām āditya-vaj jñānaṁ, prakāśayati tat param

jñānena – by knowledge; *tu* – but; *tat* – that; *ajñānam* – nescience; *yeṣām* – whose; *nāśitam* – is destroyed; *ātmanaḥ* – of the living entity; *teṣām* – their; *āditya-vat* – like the rising sun; *jñānam* – knowledge; *prakāśayati* – discloses; *tat param* – Kṛṣṇa consciousness.

When, however, one is enlightened with the knowledge by which nescience is destroyed, then his knowledge reveals everything, as the sun lights up everything in the daytime.

PURPORT: Those who have forgotten Kṛṣṇa must certainly be bewildered, but those who are in Kṛṣṇa consciousness are not bewildered at all. It is stated in the *Bhagavad-gītā, sarvaṁ jñāna-plavena, jñānāgniḥ sarva-karmāṇi* and *na hi jñānena sadṛśam.* Knowledge is always highly esteemed. And what is that knowledge? Perfect knowledge is achieved when one surrenders unto Kṛṣṇa, as is said in the Seventh Chapter, 19th verse: *bahūnāṁ janmanām ante jñānavān māṁ prapadyate.* After passing through many, many births, when one perfect in knowledge surrenders unto Kṛṣṇa, or when one attains Kṛṣṇa consciousness, then everything is revealed to him, as everything is revealed by the sun in the daytime. The living entity is bewildered in so many ways. For instance, when he unceremoniously thinks himself God, he actually falls into the last snare of nescience. If a living entity is God, then how can he become bewildered by nescience? Does God become bewildered by nescience? If so, then nescience, or Satan, is greater than God. Real knowledge can be obtained from a person who is in perfect Kṛṣṇa consciousness. Therefore, one has to seek out such a bona fide spiritual master and, under him, learn what Kṛṣṇa consciousness is, for Kṛṣṇa consciousness will certainly drive away all nescience, as the sun drives away darkness. Even though a person may be in full knowledge that he is not this body but is transcendental to the body, he still may not be able to discriminate between the soul and the Supersoul. However, he can know everything well if he cares to take shelter of the perfect, bona fide Kṛṣṇa conscious spiritual master. One can know God and one's relationship with God only when one actually meets a representative of God. A representative of God never claims that he is God, although he is paid all the respect ordinarily paid to God because he has knowledge of God. One has to learn the distinction between God and the living entity. Lord Śrī Kṛṣṇa therefore stated in the Second Chapter (2.12) that every living being is individual and that the Lord also is individual. They were all individuals in the past, they are individuals at present, and they will continue to be individuals in the future, even after liberation. At night we see everything as one in the darkness, but in the daytime, when the sun is up, we see everything in its real identity. Identity with individuality in spiritual life is real knowledge.

Text 17 तद्बुद्धयस्तदात्मानस्तन्निष्ठास्तत्परायणाः ।
गच्छन्त्यपुनरावृत्तिं ज्ञाननिर्धूतकल्मषाः ॥१७॥

tad-buddhayas tad-ātmānas, tan-niṣṭhās tat-parāyaṇāḥ
gacchanty apunar-āvṛttiṁ, jñāna-nirdhūta-kalmaṣāḥ

tat-buddhayaḥ – those whose intelligence is always in the Supreme; *tat-ātmānaḥ* – those whose minds are always in the Supreme; *tat-niṣṭhāḥ* – those whose faith is only meant for the Supreme; *tat-parāyaṇāḥ* – who have completely taken shelter of Him; *gacchanti* – go; *apunaḥ-āvṛttim* – to liberation; *jñāna* – by knowledge; *nirdhūta* – cleansed; *kalmaṣāḥ* – misgivings.

When one's intelligence, mind, faith and refuge are all fixed in the Supreme, then one becomes fully cleansed of misgivings through complete knowledge and thus proceeds straight on the path of liberation.

PURPORT: The Supreme Transcendental Truth is Lord Kṛṣṇa. The whole *Bhagavad-gītā* centers around the declaration that Kṛṣṇa is the Supreme Personality of Godhead. That is the version of all Vedic literature. *Para-tattva* means the Supreme Reality, who is understood by the knowers of the Supreme as Brahman, Paramātmā and Bhagavān. Bhagavān, or the Supreme Personality of Godhead, is the last word in the Absolute. There is nothing more than that. The Lord says, *mattaḥ parataraṁ nānyat kiñcid asti dhanañ-jaya.* Impersonal Brahman is also supported by Kṛṣṇa: *brahmaṇo hi pratiṣṭhāham.* Therefore in all ways Kṛṣṇa is the Supreme Reality. One whose mind, intelligence, faith and refuge are always in Kṛṣṇa, or, in other words, one who is fully in Kṛṣṇa consciousness, is undoubtedly washed clean of all misgivings and is in perfect knowledge in everything concerning transcendence. A Kṛṣṇa conscious person can thoroughly understand that there is duality (simultaneous identity and individuality) in Kṛṣṇa, and, equipped with such transcendental knowledge, one can make steady progress on the path of liberation.

Text 18 विद्याविनयसम्पन्ने ब्राह्मणे गवि हस्तिनि ।
शुनि चैव श्वपाके च पण्डिताः समदर्शिनः ॥१८॥

vidyā-vinaya-sampanne, brāhmaṇe gavi hastini
śuni caiva śva-pāke ca, paṇḍitāḥ sama-darśinaḥ

vidyā – with education; *vinaya* – and gentleness; *sampanne* – fully equipped; *brāhmaṇe* – in the *brāhmaṇa; gavi* – in the cow; *hastini* – in the elephant; *śuni* – in the dog; *ca* – and; *eva* – certainly; *śva-pāke* – in the dog-eater (the outcaste); *ca* – respectively; *paṇḍitāḥ* – those who are wise; *sama-darśinaḥ* – who see with equal vision.

The humble sages, by virtue of true knowledge, see with equal vision a learned and gentle brāhmaṇa, a cow, an elephant, a dog and a dog-eater [outcaste].

PURPORT: A Kṛṣṇa conscious person does not make any distinction between species or castes. The *brāhmaṇa* and the outcaste may be different from the social point of view, or a dog, a cow, and an elephant may be different from the point of view of species, but these differences of body are meaningless from the viewpoint of a learned transcendentalist. This is due to their relationship to the Supreme, for the Supreme Lord, by His plenary portion as Paramātmā, is present in everyone's heart. Such an understanding of the Supreme is real knowledge. As far as the bodies are concerned in different castes or different species of life, the Lord is equally kind to everyone because He treats every living being as a friend yet maintains Himself as Paramātmā regardless of the circumstances of the living entities. The Lord as Paramātmā is present both in the outcaste and in the *brāhmaṇa,* although the body of a *brāhmaṇa* and that of an outcaste are not the same. The bodies are material productions of different modes of material nature, but the soul and the Supersoul within the body are of the same spiritual quality. The similarity in the quality of the soul and the Supersoul, however, does not make them equal in quantity, for the individual soul is present only in that particular body whereas the Paramātmā is present in each and every body. A Kṛṣṇa conscious person has full knowledge of this, and therefore he is truly learned and has equal vision. The similar characteristics of the soul and Supersoul are that they are both conscious, eternal and blissful. But the difference is that the individual soul is conscious within the limited jurisdiction of the body whereas the Supersoul is conscious of all bodies. The Supersoul is present in all bodies without distinction.

Text 19 **इहैव तैर्जितः सर्गो येषां साम्ये स्थितं मनः ।**
निर्दोषं हि समं ब्रह्म तस्माद् ब्रह्मणि ते स्थिताः ॥१९॥

ihaiva tair jitaḥ sargo, yeṣāṁ sāmye sthitaṁ manaḥ
nirdoṣaṁ hi samaṁ brahma, tasmād brahmaṇi te sthitāḥ

iha – in this life; *eva* – certainly; *taiḥ* – by them; *jitaḥ* – conquered; *sargaḥ* – birth and death; *yeṣām* – whose; *sāmye* – in equanimity; *sthitam* – situated; *manaḥ* – mind; *nirdoṣam* – flawless; *hi* – certainly; *samam* – in equanimity; *brahma* – like the Supreme; *tasmāt* – therefore; *brahmaṇi* – in the Supreme; *te* – they; *sthitāḥ* – are situated.

Those whose minds are established in sameness and equanimity have already conquered the conditions of birth and death. They are flawless like Brahman, and thus they are already situated in Brahman.

PURPORT: Equanimity of mind, as mentioned above, is the sign of self-realization. Those who have actually attained to such a stage should be considered to have conquered material conditions, specifically birth and death. As long as one identifies with this body, he is considered a conditioned soul, but as soon as he is elevated to the stage of equanimity through realization of self, he is liberated from conditional life. In other words, he is no longer subject to take birth in the material world but can enter into the spiritual sky after his death. The Lord is flawless because He is without attraction or hatred. Similarly, when a living entity is without attraction or hatred, he also becomes flawless and eligible to enter into the spiritual sky. Such persons are to be considered already liberated, and their symptoms are described below.

Text 20 न प्रहृष्येत्प्रियं प्राप्य नोद्विजेत्प्राप्य चाप्रियम् ।
स्थिरबुद्धिरसम्मूढो ब्रह्मविद् ब्रह्मणि स्थितः ॥२०॥

na prahṛṣyet priyaṁ prāpya, nodvijet prāpya cāpriyam
sthira-buddhir asammūḍho, brahma-vid brahmaṇi sthitaḥ

na – never; *prahṛṣyet* – rejoices; *priyam* – the pleasant; *prāpya* – achieving; *na* – does not; *udvijet* – become agitated; *prāpya* – obtaining; *ca* – also; *apriyam* – the unpleasant; *sthira-buddhiḥ* – self-intelligent; *asammūḍhaḥ* – unbewildered; *brahma-vit* – one who knows the Supreme perfectly; *brahmaṇi* – in the transcendence; *sthitaḥ* – situated.

A person who neither rejoices upon achieving something pleasant nor laments upon obtaining something unpleasant, who is self-intelligent, who is unbewildered, and who knows the science of God, is already situated in transcendence.

PURPORT: The symptoms of the self-realized person are given herein. The first symptom is that he is not illusioned by the false identification of the body with his true self. He knows perfectly well that he is not this body, but is the fragmental portion of the Supreme Personality of Godhead. He is therefore not joyful in achieving something, nor does he lament in losing anything which is related to his body. This steadiness of mind is called *sthira-buddhi,* or self-intelligence. He is therefore never bewildered by mistaking the gross body for the soul, nor does he accept the body as permanent and disregard the existence of the soul. This knowledge elevates him to the station of knowing the complete science of the Absolute Truth, namely Brahman, Paramātmā and Bhagavān. He thus knows his constitutional position perfectly well, without falsely trying to become one with the Supreme in all respects. This is called Brahman realization, or self-realization. Such steady consciousness is called Kṛṣṇa consciousness.

Text 21 बाह्यस्पर्शेष्वसक्तात्मा विन्दत्यात्मनि यत्सुखम् ।
स ब्रह्मयोगयुक्तात्मा सुखमक्षयमश्नुते ॥२१॥

bāhya-sparśeṣv asaktātmā, vindaty ātmani yat sukham
sa brahma-yoga-yuktātmā, sukham akṣayam aśnute

bāhya-sparśeṣu – in external sense pleasure; *asakta-ātmā* – one who is not attached; *vindati* – enjoys; *ātmani* – in the self; *yat* – that which; *sukham* – happiness; *saḥ* – he; *brahma-yoga* – by concentration in Brahman; *yukta-ātmā* – self-connected; *sukham* – happiness; *akṣayam* – unlimited; *aśnute* – enjoys.

Such a liberated person is not attracted to material sense pleasure but is always in trance, enjoying the pleasure within. In this way the self-realized person enjoys unlimited happiness, for he concentrates on the Supreme.

PURPORT: Śrī Yāmunācārya, a great devotee in Kṛṣṇa consciousness, said:

yad-avadhi mama cetaḥ kṛṣṇa-pādāravinde
nava-nava-rasa-dhāmany udyataṁ rantum āsīt
tad-avadhi bata nārī-saṅgame smaryamāne
bhavati mukha-vikāraḥ suṣṭhu niṣṭhīvanaṁ ca

"Since I have been engaged in the transcendental loving service of Kṛṣṇa, realizing ever-new pleasure in Him, whenever I think of sex pleasure I spit at the thought, and my lips curl with distaste." A person in *brahma-yoga,* or Kṛṣṇa consciousness, is so absorbed in the loving service of the Lord that he loses his taste for material sense pleasure altogether. The highest pleasure in terms of matter is sex pleasure. The whole world is moving under its spell, and a materialist cannot work at all without this motivation. But a person engaged in Kṛṣṇa consciousness can work with greater vigor without sex pleasure, which he avoids. That is the test in spiritual realization. Spiritual realization and sex pleasure go ill together. A Kṛṣṇa conscious person is not attracted to any kind of sense pleasure, due to his being a liberated soul.

Text 22 ये हि संस्पर्शजा भोगा दुःखयोनय एव ते ।
आद्यन्तवन्तः कौन्तेय न तेषु रमते बुधः ॥२२॥

ye hi saṁsparśa-jā bhogā, duḥkha-yonaya eva te
ādy-antavantaḥ kaunteya, na teṣu ramate budhaḥ

ye – those; *hi* – certainly; *saṁsparśa-jāḥ* – by contact with the material senses; *bhogāḥ* – enjoyments; *duḥkha* – distress; *yonayaḥ* – sources of; *eva* – certainly; *te* – they are; *ādi* – beginning; *anta* – end; *vantaḥ* –

subject to; *kaunteya* – O son of Kuntī; *na* – never; *teṣu* – in those; *ramate* – takes delight; *budhaḥ* – the intelligent person.

An intelligent person does not take part in the sources of misery, which are due to contact with the material senses. O son of Kuntī, such pleasures have a beginning and an end, and so the wise man does not delight in them.

PURPORT: Material sense pleasures are due to the contact of the material senses, which are all temporary because the body itself is temporary. A liberated soul is not interested in anything which is temporary. Knowing well the joys of transcendental pleasures, how can a liberated soul agree to enjoy false pleasure? In the *Padma Purāṇa* it is said:

ramante yogino 'nante, satyānande cid-ātmani
iti rāma-padenāsau, paraṁ brahmābhidhīyate

"The mystics derive unlimited transcendental pleasures from the Absolute Truth, and therefore the Supreme Absolute Truth, the Personality of Godhead, is also known as Rāma."

In the *Śrīmad-Bhāgavatam* also (5.5.1) it is said:

nāyaṁ deho deha-bhājāṁ nṛ-loke
kaṣṭān kāmān arhate viḍ-bhujāṁ ye
tapo divyaṁ putrakā yena sattvaṁ
śuddhyed yasmād brahma-saukhyaṁ tv anantam

"My dear sons, there is no reason to labor very hard for sense pleasure while in this human form of life; such pleasures are available to the stool-eaters [hogs]. Rather, you should undergo penances in this life by which your existence will be purified, and as a result you will be able to enjoy unlimited transcendental bliss."

Therefore, those who are true *yogīs* or learned transcendentalists are not attracted by sense pleasures, which are the causes of continuous material existence. The more one is addicted to material pleasures, the more he is entrapped by material miseries.

Text 23 शक्नोतीहैव यः सोढुं प्राक्शरीरविमोक्षणात् ।
कामक्रोधोद्भवं वेगं स युक्तः स सुखी नरः ॥२३॥

śaknotīhaiva yaḥ soḍhuṁ, prāk śarīra-vimokṣaṇāt
kāma-krodhodbhavaṁ vegaṁ, sa yuktaḥ sa sukhī naraḥ

śaknoti – is able; *iha eva* – in the present body; *yaḥ* – one who; *soḍhum* – to tolerate; *prāk* – before; *śarīra* – the body; *vimokṣaṇāt* – giving up; *kāma* – desire; *krodha* – and anger; *udbhavam* – generated from; *vegam* – urges; *saḥ* – he; *yuktaḥ* – in trance; *saḥ* – he; *sukhī* – happy; *naraḥ* – human being.

Before giving up this present body, if one is able to tolerate the urges of the material senses and check the force of desire and anger, he is well situated and is happy in this world.

PURPORT: If one wants to make steady progress on the path of self-realization, he must try to control the forces of the material senses. There are the forces of talk, forces of anger, forces of mind, forces of the stomach, forces of the genitals, and forces of the tongue. One who is able to control the forces of all these different senses, and the mind, is called *gosvāmī,* or *svāmī.* Such *gosvāmīs* live strictly controlled lives, and forgo altogether the forces of the senses. Material desires, when unsatiated, generate anger, and thus the mind, eyes and chest become agitated. Therefore, one must practice to control them before one gives up this material body. One who can do this is understood to be self-realized and is thus happy in the state of self-realization. It is the duty of the transcendentalist to try strenuously to control desire and anger.

Text 24 योऽन्तःसुखोऽन्तरारामस्तथान्तर्ज्योतिरेव यः ।
स योगी ब्रह्मनिर्वाणं ब्रह्मभूतोऽधिगच्छति ॥२४॥

yo 'ntaḥ-sukho 'ntar-ārāmas, tathāntar-jyotir eva yaḥ
sa yogī brahma-nirvāṇaṁ, brahma-bhūto 'dhigacchati

yaḥ – one who; *antaḥ-sukhaḥ* – happy from within; *antaḥ-ārāmaḥ* – actively enjoying within; *tathā* – as well as; *antaḥ-jyotiḥ* – aiming within; *eva* – certainly; *yaḥ* – anyone; *saḥ* – he; *yogī* – a mystic; *brahma-nirvāṇam* – liberation in the Supreme; *brahma-bhūtaḥ* – being self-realized; *adhigacchati* – attains.

One whose happiness is within, who is active and rejoices within, and whose aim is inward is actually the perfect mystic. He is liberated in the Supreme, and ultimately he attains the Supreme.

PURPORT: Unless one is able to relish happiness from within, how can one retire from the external engagements meant for deriving superficial happiness? A liberated person enjoys happiness by factual experience. He can, therefore, sit silently at any place and enjoy the activities of life from within. Such a liberated person no longer desires external material happiness. This state is called *brahma-bhūta,* attaining which one is assured of going back to Godhead, back to home.

Text 25 लभन्ते ब्रह्मनिर्वाणमृषयः क्षीणकल्मषाः ।
छिन्नद्वैधा यतात्मानः सर्वभूतहिते रताः ॥२५॥

labhante brahma-nirvāṇam, ṛṣayaḥ kṣīṇa-kalmaṣāḥ
chinna-dvaidhā yatātmānaḥ, sarva-bhūta-hite ratāḥ

labhante – achieve; *brahma-nirvāṇam* – liberation in the Supreme; *ṛṣayaḥ* – those who are active within; *kṣīṇa-kalmaṣāḥ* – who are devoid of all sins; *chinna* – having torn off; *dvaidhāḥ* – duality; *yata-ātmānaḥ* – engaged in self-realization; *sarva-bhūta* – for all living entities; *hite* – in welfare work; *ratāḥ* – engaged.

Those who are beyond the dualities that arise from doubts, whose minds are engaged within, who are always busy working for the welfare of all living beings, and who are free from all sins achieve liberation in the Supreme.

PURPORT: Only a person who is fully in Kṛṣṇa consciousness can be said to be engaged in welfare work for all living entities. When a person is actually in the knowledge that Kṛṣṇa is the fountainhead of everything, then when he acts in that spirit he acts for everyone. The sufferings of humanity are due to forgetfulness of Kṛṣṇa as the supreme enjoyer, the supreme proprietor, and the supreme friend. Therefore, to act to revive this consciousness within the entire human society is the highest welfare work. One cannot be engaged in such first-class welfare work without being liberated in the Supreme. A Kṛṣṇa conscious person has no doubt about the supremacy of Kṛṣṇa. He has no doubt because he is completely freed from all sins. This is the state of divine love.

A person engaged only in ministering to the physical welfare of human society cannot factually help anyone. Temporary relief of the external body and the mind is not satisfactory. The real cause of one's difficulties in the hard struggle for life may be found in one's forgetfulness of his relationship with the Supreme Lord. When a man is fully conscious of his relationship with Kṛṣṇa, he is actually a liberated soul, although he may be in the material tabernacle.

Text 26 **कामक्रोधविमुक्तानां यतीनां यतचेतसाम् ।**
अभितो ब्रह्मनिर्वाणं वर्तते विदितात्मनाम् ॥२६॥

kāma-krodha-vimuktānāṁ, yatīnāṁ yata-cetasām
abhito brahma-nirvāṇaṁ, vartate viditātmanām

kāma – from desires; *krodha* – and anger; *vimuktānām* – of those who are liberated; *yatīnām* – of the saintly persons; *yata-cetasām* – who have full control over the mind; *abhitaḥ* – assured in the near future; *brahma-nirvāṇam* – liberation in the Supreme; *vartate* – is there; *vidita-ātmanām* – of those who are self-realized.

Those who are free from anger and all material desires, who are self-realized, self-disciplined and constantly endeavoring for perfection, are assured of liberation in the Supreme in the very near future.

PURPORT: Of the saintly persons who are constantly engaged in striving toward salvation, one who is in Kṛṣṇa consciousness is the best of all. The *Bhāgavatam* (4.22.39) confirms this fact as follows:

yat-pāda-paṅkaja-palāśa-vilāsa-bhaktyā
karmāśayaṁ grathitam udgrathayanti santaḥ
tadvan na rikta-matayo yatayo 'pi ruddha-
sroto-gaṇās tam araṇaṁ bhaja vāsudevam

"Just try to worship, in devotional service, Vāsudeva, the Supreme Personality of Godhead. Even great sages are not able to control the forces of the senses as effectively as those who are engaged in transcendental bliss by serving the lotus feet of the Lord, uprooting the deep-grown desire for fruitive activities."

In the conditioned soul the desire to enjoy the fruitive results of work is so deep-rooted that it is very difficult even for the great sages to control such desires, despite great endeavors. A devotee of the Lord, constantly engaged in devotional service in Kṛṣṇa consciousness, perfect in self-realization, very quickly attains liberation in the Supreme. Owing to his complete knowledge in self-realization, he always remains in trance. To cite an analogous example of this:

darśana-dhyāna-saṁsparśair, matsya-kūrma-vihaṅgamāḥ
svāny apatyāni puṣṇanti, tathāham api padma-ja

"By vision, by meditation and by touch only do the fish, the tortoise and the birds maintain their offspring. Similarly do I also, O Padmaja!"

The fish brings up its offspring simply by looking at them. The tortoise brings up its offspring simply by meditation. The eggs of the tortoise are laid on land, and the tortoise meditates on the eggs while in the water. Similarly, the devotee in Kṛṣṇa consciousness, although far away from the Lord's abode, can elevate himself to that abode simply by thinking of Him constantly – by engagement in Kṛṣṇa consciousness. He does not feel the pangs of material miseries; this state of life is called *brahma-nirvāṇa,* or the absence of material miseries due to being constantly immersed in the Supreme.

Texts 27–28

स्पर्शान् कृत्वा बहिर्बाह्यांश्चक्षुश्चैवान्तरे भ्रुवोः ।
प्राणापानौ समौ कृत्वा नासाभ्यन्तरचारिणौ ॥२७॥
यतेन्द्रियमनोबुद्धिर्मुनिर्मोक्षपरायणः ।
विगतेच्छाभयक्रोधो यः सदा मुक्त एव सः ॥२८॥

sparśān kṛtvā bahir bāhyāṁś, cakṣuś caivāntare bhruvoḥ
prāṇāpānau samau kṛtvā, nāsābhyantara-cāriṇau

yatendriya-mano-buddhir, munir mokṣa-parāyaṇaḥ
vigatecchā-bhaya-krodho, yaḥ sadā mukta eva saḥ

sparśān – sense objects, such as sound; *kṛtvā* – keeping; *bahiḥ* – external; *bāhyān* – unnecessary; *cakṣuḥ* – eyes; *ca* – also; *eva* – certainly; *antare* – between; *bhruvoḥ* – the eyebrows; *prāṇa-apānau* – up-and down-moving air; *samau* – in suspension; *kṛtvā* – keeping; *nāsa-abhyantara* – within the nostrils; *cāriṇau* – blowing; *yata* – controlled; *indriya* – senses; *manaḥ* – mind; *buddhiḥ* – intelligence; *muniḥ* – the transcendentalist; *mokṣa* – for liberation; *parāyaṇaḥ* – being so destined; *vigata* – having discarded; *icchā* – wishes; *bhaya* – fear; *krodhaḥ* – anger; *yaḥ* – one who; *sadā* – always; *muktaḥ* – liberated; *eva* – certainly; *saḥ* – he is.

Shutting out all external sense objects, keeping the eyes and vision concentrated between the two eyebrows, suspending the inward and outward breaths within the nostrils, and thus controlling the mind, senses and intelligence, the transcendentalist aiming at liberation becomes free from desire, fear and anger. One who is always in this state is certainly liberated.

PURPORT: Being engaged in Kṛṣṇa consciousness, one can immediately understand one's spiritual identity, and then one can understand the

Supreme Lord by means of devotional service. When one is well situated in devotional service, one comes to the transcendental position, qualified to feel the presence of the Lord in the sphere of one's activity. This particular position is called liberation in the Supreme.

After explaining the above principles of liberation in the Supreme, the Lord gives instruction to Arjuna as to how one can come to that position by the practice of the mysticism or *yoga* known as *aṣṭāṅga-yoga,* which is divisible into an eightfold procedure called *yama, niyama, āsana, prāṇāyāma, pratyāhāra, dhāraṇā, dhyāna* and *samādhi.* In the Sixth Chapter the subject of *yoga* is explicitly detailed, and at the end of the Fifth it is only preliminarily explained. One has to drive out the sense objects such as sound, touch, form, taste and smell by the *pratyāhāra* process in *yoga,* and then keep the vision of the eyes between the two eyebrows and concentrate on the tip of the nose with half-closed lids. There is no benefit in closing the eyes altogether, because then there is every chance of falling asleep. Nor is there benefit in opening the eyes completely, because then there is the hazard of being attracted by sense objects. The breathing movement is restrained within the nostrils by neutralizing the up-moving and down-moving air within the body. By practice of such *yoga* one is able to gain control over the senses, refrain from outward sense objects, and thus prepare oneself for liberation in the Supreme.

This *yoga* process helps one become free from all kinds of fear and anger and thus feel the presence of the Supersoul in the transcendental situation. In other words, Kṛṣṇa consciousness is the easiest process of executing *yoga* principles. This will be thoroughly explained in the next chapter. A Kṛṣṇa conscious person, however, being always engaged in devotional service, does not risk losing his senses to some other engagement. This is a better way of controlling the senses than by *aṣṭāṅga-yoga.*

Text 29

भोक्तारं यज्ञतपसां सर्वलोकमहेश्वरम् ।
सुहृदं सर्वभूतानां ज्ञात्वा मां शान्तिमृच्छति ॥२९॥

bhoktāraṁ yajña-tapasāṁ, sarva-loka-maheśvaram
suhṛdaṁ sarva-bhūtānāṁ, jñātvā māṁ śāntim ṛcchati

bhoktāram – the beneficiary; *yajña* – of sacrifices; *tapasām* – and penances and austerities; *sarva-loka* – of all planets and the demigods thereof; *mahā-īśvaram* – the Supreme Lord; *su-hṛdam* – the benefactor; *sarva* – of all; *bhūtānām* – the living entities; *jñātvā* – thus knowing;

mām – Me (Lord Kṛṣṇa); *śāntim* – relief from material pangs; *ṛcchati* – one achieves.

A person in full consciousness of Me, knowing Me to be the ultimate beneficiary of all sacrifices and austerities, the Supreme Lord of all planets and demigods, and the benefactor and well-wisher of all living entities, attains peace from the pangs of material miseries.

PURPORT: The conditioned souls within the clutches of the illusory energy are all anxious to attain peace in the material world. But they do not know the formula for peace, which is explained in this part of the *Bhagavad-gītā.* The greatest peace formula is simply this: Lord Kṛṣṇa is the beneficiary in all human activities. Men should offer everything to the transcendental service of the Lord because He is the proprietor of all planets and the demigods thereon. No one is greater than He. He is greater than the greatest of the demigods, Lord Śiva and Lord Brahmā. In the *Vedas* (*Śvetāśvatara Upaniṣad* 6.7) the Supreme Lord is described as *tam īśvarāṇāṁ paramaṁ maheśvaram.* Under the spell of illusion, living entities are trying to be lords of all they survey, but actually they are dominated by the material energy of the Lord. The Lord is the master of material nature, and the conditioned souls are under the stringent rules of material nature. Unless one understands these bare facts, it is not possible to achieve peace in the world either individually or collectively. This is the sense of Kṛṣṇa consciousness: Lord Kṛṣṇa is the supreme predominator, and all living entities, including the great demigods, are His subordinates. One can attain perfect peace only in complete Kṛṣṇa consciousness.

This Fifth Chapter is a practical explanation of Kṛṣṇa consciousness, generally known as *karma-yoga.* The question of mental speculation as to how *karma-yoga* can give liberation is answered herewith. To work in Kṛṣṇa consciousness is to work with the complete knowledge of the Lord as the predominator. Such work is not different from transcendental knowledge. Direct Kṛṣṇa consciousness is *bhakti-yoga,* and *jñāna-yoga* is a path leading to *bhakti-yoga.* Kṛṣṇa consciousness means to work in full knowledge of one's relationship with the Supreme Absolute, and the perfection of this consciousness is full knowledge of Kṛṣṇa, or the Supreme Personality of Godhead. A pure soul is the eternal servant of God as His fragmental part and parcel. He comes into contact with *māyā* (illusion) due to the desire to lord it over *māyā,* and that is the cause of his many sufferings. As long as he is in contact with matter, he has to execute work in terms of material necessities. Kṛṣṇa consciousness, however, brings one into spiritual life even while one is within the jurisdiction of matter, for it is an arousing of spiritual existence by practice in the material world. The more one is advanced, the more he is freed from the clutches of matter. The Lord is not partial toward anyone. Everything depends on one's practical performance of duties in Kṛṣṇa consciousness, which in every respect helps one control the senses and conquer the influence of desire and anger. And one who stands fast in Kṛṣṇa consciousness, controlling the abovementioned passions, remains factually in the transcendental stage, or *brahma-nirvāṇa.* The eightfold *yoga* mysticism is automatically practiced in Kṛṣṇa consciousness because the ultimate purpose is served. There is a gradual process of elevation in the practice of *yama, niyama, āsana, prāṇāyāma, pratyāhāra, dhāraṇā, dhyāna* and *samādhi.* But these only preface perfection by devotional service, which alone can award peace to the human being. It is the highest perfection of life.

Thus end the Bhaktivedanta Purports to the Fifth Chapter of the Śrīmad Bhagavad-gītā *in the matter of* Karma-yoga, *or Action in Kṛṣṇa Consciousness.*

CHAPTER SIX

Dhyāna-yoga

Text 1 श्रीभगवानुवाच
अनाश्रितः कर्मफलं कार्यं कर्म करोति यः ।
स सन्न्यासी च योगी च न निरग्निर्न चाक्रियः ॥१॥

śrī-bhagavān uvāca
anāśritaḥ karma-phalaṁ, kāryaṁ karma karoti yaḥ
sa sannyāsī ca yogī ca, na niragnir na cākriyaḥ

śrī-bhagavān uvāca – the Lord said; *anāśritaḥ* – without taking shelter; *karma-phalam* – of the result of work; *kāryam* – obligatory; *karma* – work; *karoti* – performs; *yaḥ* – one who; *saḥ* – he; *sannyāsī* – in the renounced order; *ca* – also; *yogī* – mystic; *ca* – also; *na* – not; *niḥ* – without; *agniḥ* – fire; *na* – nor; *ca* – also; *akriyaḥ* – without duty.

The Supreme Personality of Godhead said: One who is unattached to the fruits of his work and who works as he is obligated is in the renounced order of life, and he is the true mystic, not he who lights no fire and performs no duty.

PURPORT: In this chapter the Lord explains that the process of the eightfold *yoga* system is a means to control the mind and the senses. However, this is very difficult for people in general to perform, especially in the Age of Kali. Although the eightfold *yoga* system is recommended in this chapter, the Lord emphasizes that the process of *karma-yoga,* or acting in Kṛṣṇa consciousness, is better. Everyone acts in this world to maintain his family and their paraphernalia, but no one is working without some self-interest, some personal gratification, be it concentrated or extended. The criterion of perfection is to act in Kṛṣṇa consciousness, and not with a view to enjoying the fruits of work. To act in Kṛṣṇa consciousness is the duty of every living entity because all are constitutionally parts and parcels of the Supreme. The parts of the body work for the satisfaction of the whole body. The limbs of the body do not act for self-satisfaction but for the satisfaction of the complete whole. Similarly, the living entity who acts for satisfaction of the supreme whole and not for personal satisfaction is the perfect *sannyāsī,* the perfect *yogī.*

The *sannyāsīs* sometimes artificially think that they have become liberated from all material duties, and therefore they cease to perform *agnihotra yajñas* (fire sacrifices), but actually they are self-interested because their goal is to become one with the impersonal Brahman. Such a desire is greater than any material desire, but it is not without self-interest. Similarly, the mystic *yogī* who practices the *yoga* system with half-open eyes, ceasing all material activities, desires some satisfaction for his personal self. But a person acting in Kṛṣṇa consciousness works for the satisfaction of the whole, without self-interest. A Kṛṣṇa conscious person has no desire for self-satisfaction. His criterion of success is the satisfaction of Kṛṣṇa, and thus he is the perfect *sannyāsī,* or perfect *yogī.* Lord Caitanya, the highest perfectional symbol of renunciation, prays in this way:

na dhanaṁ na janaṁ na sundarīṁ, kavitāṁ vā jagad-īśa kāmaye
mama janmani janmanīśvare, bhavatād bhaktir ahaitukī tvayi

"O Almighty Lord, I have no desire to accumulate wealth, nor to enjoy beautiful women. Nor do I want any number of followers. What I want only is the causeless mercy of Your devotional service in my life, birth after birth."

Text 2 यं सन्न्यासमिति प्राहुर्योगं तं विद्धि पाण्डव ।
न ह्यसन्न्यस्तसङ्कल्पो योगी भवति कश्चन ॥ २ ॥

yaṁ sannyāsam iti prāhur, yogaṁ taṁ viddhi pāṇḍava
na hy asannyasta-saṅkalpo, yogī bhavati kaścana

yam – what; *sannyāsam* – renunciation; *iti* – thus; *prāhuḥ* – they say; *yogam* – linking with the Supreme; *tam* – that; *viddhi* – you must know; *pāṇḍava* – O son of Pāṇḍu; *na* – never; *hi* – certainly; *asannyasta* – without giving up; *saṅkalpaḥ* – desire for self-satisfaction; *yogī* – a mystic transcendentalist; *bhavati* – becomes; *kaścana* – anyone.

What is called renunciation you should know to be the same as yoga, or linking oneself with the Supreme, O son of Pāṇḍu, for one can never become a yogī unless he renounces the desire for sense gratification.

PURPORT: Real *sannyāsa-yoga* or *bhakti* means that one should know his constitutional position as the living entity, and act accordingly. The living entity has no separate independent identity. He is the marginal energy of the Supreme. When he is entrapped by material energy, he is conditioned, and when he is Kṛṣṇa conscious, or aware of the spiritual energy, then he is in his real and natural state of life. Therefore, when one is in complete knowledge, one ceases all material sense gratification, or renounces all kinds of sense gratificatory activities. This is practiced by the *yogīs* who restrain the senses from material attachment. But a person in Kṛṣṇa consciousness has no opportunity to engage his senses in anything which is not for the purpose of Kṛṣṇa. Therefore, a Kṛṣṇa conscious person is simultaneously a *sannyāsī* and a *yogī.* The purpose of knowledge and of restraining the senses, as prescribed in the *jñāna* and *yoga* processes, is automatically served in Kṛṣṇa consciousness. If one is unable to give up the activities of his selfish nature, then *jñāna* and *yoga* are of no avail. The real aim is for a living entity to give up all selfish satisfaction and to be prepared to satisfy the Supreme. A Kṛṣṇa conscious person has no desire for any kind of self-enjoyment. He is always engaged for the enjoyment of the Supreme. One who has no information of the Supreme must therefore be engaged in self-satisfaction, because no one can stand on the platform of inactivity. All purposes are perfectly served by the practice of Kṛṣṇa consciousness.

Text 3 आरुरुक्षोर्मुनेर्योगं कर्म कारणमुच्यते ।
योगारूढस्य तस्यैव शमः कारणमुच्यते ॥ ३ ॥

ārurukṣor muner yogaṁ, karma kāraṇam ucyate
yogārūḍhasya tasyaiva, śamaḥ kāraṇam ucyate

ārurukṣoḥ – who has just begun *yoga; muneḥ* – of the sage; *yogam* – the eightfold *yoga* system; *karma* – work; *kāraṇam* – the means; *ucyate* – is said to be; *yoga* – eightfold *yoga; ārūḍhasya* – of one who has attained; *tasya* – his; *eva* – certainly; *śamaḥ* – cessation of all material activities; *kāraṇam* – the means; *ucyate* – is said to be.

For one who is a neophyte in the eightfold yoga system, work is said to be the means; and for one who is already elevated in yoga, cessation of all material activities is said to be the means.

PURPORT: The process of linking oneself with the Supreme is called *yoga.* It may be compared to a ladder for attaining the topmost spiritual realization. This ladder begins from the lowest material condition of the living entity and rises up to perfect self-realization in pure spiritual life. According to various elevations, different parts of the ladder are known by different names. But all in all, the complete ladder is called *yoga* and may be divided into three parts, namely *jñāna-yoga, dhyāna-yoga* and *bhakti-yoga.* The beginning of the ladder is called the *yogārurukṣu* stage, and the highest rung is called *yogārūḍha.*

Concerning the eightfold *yoga* system, attempts in the beginning to enter into meditation through regulative principles of life and practice of different sitting postures (which are more or less bodily exercises) are considered fruitive material activities. All such activities lead to achieving perfect mental equilibrium to control the senses. When one is accomplished in the practice of meditation, he ceases all disturbing mental activities.

A Kṛṣṇa conscious person, however, is situated from the beginning on the platform of meditation because he always thinks of Kṛṣṇa. And, being constantly engaged in the service of Kṛṣṇa, he is considered to have ceased all material activities.

Text 4 यदा हि नेन्द्रियार्थेषु न कर्मस्वनुषज्जते ।
सर्वसङ्कल्पसन्न्यासी योगारूढस्तदोच्यते ॥ ४ ॥

yadā hi nendriyārtheṣu, na karmasv anuṣajjate
sarva-saṅkalpa-sannyāsī, yogārūḍhas tadocyate

yadā – when; *hi* – certainly; *na* – not; *indriya-artheṣu* – in sense gratification; *na* – never; *karmasu* – in fruitive activities; *anuṣajjate* – one necessarily engages; *sarva-saṅkalpa* – of all material desires; *sannyāsī* – renouncer; *yoga-ārūḍhaḥ* – elevated in *yoga; tadā* – at that time; *ucyate* – is said to be.

A person is said to be elevated in yoga when, having renounced all material desires, he neither acts for sense gratification nor engages in fruitive activities.

PURPORT: When a person is fully engaged in the transcendental loving service of the Lord, he is pleased in himself, and thus he is no longer engaged in sense gratification or in fruitive activities. Otherwise, one must be engaged in sense gratification, since one cannot live without engagement. Without Kṛṣṇa consciousness, one must be always seeking self-centered or extended selfish activities. But a Kṛṣṇa conscious person can do everything for the satisfaction of Kṛṣṇa and thereby be perfectly detached from sense gratification. One who has no such realization must mechanically try to escape material desires before being elevated to the top rung of the *yoga* ladder.

Text 5 उद्धरेदात्मनात्मानं नात्मानमवसादयेत् ।
आत्मैव ह्यात्मनो बन्धुरात्मैव रिपुरात्मनः ॥ ५ ॥

uddhared ātmanātmānaṁ, nātmānam avasādayet
ātmaiva hy ātmano bandhur, ātmaiva ripur ātmanaḥ

uddharet – one must deliver; *ātmanā* – by the mind; *ātmānam* – the conditioned soul; *na* – never; *ātmānam* – the conditioned soul; *avasādayet* – put into degradation; *ātmā* – mind; *eva* – certainly; *hi* – indeed; *ātmanaḥ* – of the conditioned soul; *bandhuḥ* – friend; *ātmā* – mind; *eva* – certainly; *ripuḥ* – enemy; *ātmanaḥ* – of the conditioned soul.

One must deliver himself with the help of his mind, and not degrade himself. The mind is the friend of the conditioned soul, and his enemy as well.

PURPORT: The word *ātmā* denotes body, mind and soul – depending upon different circumstances. In the *yoga* system, the mind and the conditioned soul are especially important. Since the mind is the central point of *yoga* practice, *ātmā* refers here to the mind. The purpose of the *yoga* system is to control the mind and to draw it away from attachment to sense objects. It is stressed herein that the mind must be so trained that it can deliver the conditioned soul from the mire of nescience. In material existence one is subjected to the influence of the mind and the senses. In fact, the pure soul is entangled in the material world because the mind is involved with the false ego, which desires to lord it over material nature. Therefore, the mind should be trained so that it will not be attracted by the glitter of material nature, and in this way the conditioned soul may be saved. One should not degrade oneself by attraction to sense objects. The more one is attracted by sense objects, the more one becomes entangled in material existence. The best way to disentangle oneself is to always engage the mind in Kṛṣṇa consciousness. The word *hi* is used for emphasizing this point, i.e., that one *must* do this. It is also said:

mana eva manuṣyāṇāṁ, kāraṇaṁ bandha-mokṣayoḥ
bandhāya viṣayāsaṅgo, muktyai nirviṣayaṁ manaḥ

"For man, mind is the cause of bondage and mind is the cause of liberation. Mind absorbed in sense objects is the cause of bondage, and mind detached from the sense objects is the cause of liberation." (*Amṛta-bindu Upaniṣad* 2) Therefore, the mind which is always engaged in Kṛṣṇa consciousness is the cause of supreme liberation.

Text 6 बन्धुरात्मात्मनस्तस्य येनात्मैवात्मना जितः ।
अनात्मनस्तु शत्रुत्वे वर्तेतात्मैव शत्रुवत् ॥६॥

bandhur ātmātmanas tasya, yenātmaivātmanā jitaḥ
anātmanas tu śatrutve, vartetātmaiva śatru-vat

bandhuḥ – friend; *ātmā* – the mind; *ātmanaḥ* – of the living entity; *tasya* – of him; *yena* – by whom; *ātmā* – the mind; *eva* – certainly; *ātmanā* – by the living entity; *jitaḥ* – conquered; *anātmanaḥ* – of one who has failed to control the mind; *tu* – but; *śatrutve* – because of enmity; *varteta* – remains; *ātmā eva* – the very mind; *śatru-vat* – as an enemy.

For him who has conquered the mind, the mind is the best of friends; but for one who has failed to do so, his mind will remain the greatest enemy.

PURPORT: The purpose of practicing eightfold *yoga* is to control the mind in order to make it a friend in discharging the human mission. Unless the mind is controlled, the practice of *yoga* (for show) is simply a waste of time. One who cannot control his mind lives always with the greatest enemy, and thus his life and its mission are spoiled. The constitutional position of the living entity is to carry out the order of the superior. As long as one's mind remains an unconquered enemy, one has to serve the dictations of lust, anger, avarice, illusion, etc. But when the mind is conquered, one voluntarily agrees to abide by the dictation of the Personality of Godhead, who is situated within the heart of everyone as

Paramātmā. Real *yoga* practice entails meeting the Paramātmā within the heart and then following His dictation. For one who takes to Kṛṣṇa consciousness directly, perfect surrender to the dictation of the Lord follows automatically.

Text 7 जितात्मनः प्रशान्तस्य परमात्मा समाहितः ।
शीतोष्णसुखदुःखेषु तथा मानापमानयोः ॥ ७ ॥

jitātmanaḥ praśāntasya, paramātmā samāhitaḥ
śītoṣṇa-sukha-duḥkheṣu, tathā mānāpamānayoḥ

jita-ātmanaḥ – of one who has conquered his mind; *praśāntasya* – who has attained tranquillity by such control over the mind; *parama-ātmā* – the Supersoul; *samāhitaḥ* – approached completely; *śīta* – in cold; *uṣṇa* – heat; *sukha* – happiness; *duḥkheṣu* – and distress; *tathā* – also; *māna* – in honor; *apamānayoḥ* – and dishonor.

For one who has conquered the mind, the Supersoul is already reached, for he has attained tranquillity. To such a man happiness and distress, heat and cold, honor and dishonor are all the same.

PURPORT: Actually, every living entity is intended to abide by the dictation of the Supreme Personality of Godhead, who is seated in everyone's heart as Paramātmā. When the mind is misled by the external, illusory energy, one becomes entangled in material activities. Therefore, as soon as one's mind is controlled through one of the *yoga* systems, one should be considered to have already reached the destination. One has to abide by superior dictation. When one's mind is fixed on the superior nature, he has no alternative but to follow the dictation of the Supreme. The mind must admit some superior dictation and follow it. The effect of controlling the mind is that one automatically follows the dictation of the Paramātmā, or Supersoul. Because this transcendental position is at once achieved by one who is in Kṛṣṇa consciousness, the devotee of the Lord is unaffected by the dualities of material existence, namely distress and happiness, cold and heat, etc. This state is practical *samādhi,* or absorption in the Supreme.

Text 8 ज्ञानविज्ञानतृप्तात्मा कूटस्थो विजितेन्द्रियः ।
युक्त इत्युच्यते योगी समलोष्ट्राश्मकाञ्चनः ॥ ८ ॥

jñāna-vijñāna-tṛptātmā, kūṭa-stho vijitendriyaḥ
yukta ity ucyate yogī, sama-loṣṭrāśma-kāñcanaḥ

jñāna – by acquired knowledge; *vijñāna* – and realized knowledge; *tṛpta* – satisfied; *ātmā* – a living entity; *kūṭa-sthaḥ* – spiritually situated; *vijita-indriyaḥ* – sensually controlled; *yuktaḥ* – competent for self-realization; *iti* – thus; *ucyate* – is said; *yogī* – a mystic; *sama* – equipoised; *loṣtra* – pebbles; *aśma* – stone; *kāñcanaḥ* – gold.

A person is said to be established in self-realization and is called a yogī [or mystic] when he is fully satisfied by virtue of acquired knowledge and realization. Such a person is situated in transcendence and is self-controlled. He sees everything – whether it be pebbles, stones or gold – as the same.

PURPORT: Book knowledge without realization of the Supreme Truth is useless. This is stated as follows:

ataḥ śrī-kṛṣṇa-nāmādi, na bhaved grāhyam indriyaiḥ
sevonmukhe hi jihvādau, svayam eva sphuraty adaḥ

"No one can understand the transcendental nature of the name, form, quality and pastimes of Śrī Kṛṣṇa through his materially contaminated senses. Only when one becomes spiritually saturated by transcendental service to the Lord are the transcendental name, form, quality and pastimes of the Lord revealed to him." (*Bhakti-rasāmṛta-sindhu* 1.2.234)

This *Bhagavad-gītā* is the science of Kṛṣṇa consciousness. No one can become Kṛṣṇa conscious simply by mundane scholarship. One must be fortunate enough to associate with a person who is in pure consciousness. A Kṛṣṇa conscious person has realized knowledge, by the grace of Kṛṣṇa, because he is satisfied with pure devotional service. By realized knowledge, one becomes perfect. By transcendental knowledge one can remain steady in his convictions, but by mere academic knowledge one can be easily deluded and confused by apparent contradictions. It is the realized soul who is actually self-controlled, because he is surrendered to Kṛṣṇa. He is transcendental because he has nothing to do with mundane scholarship. For him mundane scholarship and mental speculation, which may be as good as gold to others, are of no greater value than pebbles or stones.

Text 9 सुहृन्मित्रार्युदासीनमध्यस्थद्वेष्यबन्धुषु ।
साधुष्वपि च पापेषु समबुद्धिर्विशिष्यते ॥ ९ ॥

suhṛn-mitrāry-udāsīna-, madhyastha-dveṣya-bandhuṣu
sādhuṣv api ca pāpeṣu, sama-buddhir viśiṣyate

su-hṛt – to well-wishers by nature; *mitra* – benefactors with affection; *ari* – enemies; *udāsīna* – neutrals between belligerents; *madhya-stha* – mediators between belligerents; *dveṣya* – the envious; *bandhuṣu* – and the relatives or well-wishers; *sādhuṣu* – unto the pious; *api* – as well as; *ca* – and; *pāpeṣu* – unto the sinners; *sama-buddhiḥ* – having equal intelligence; *viśiṣyate* – is far advanced.

A person is considered still further advanced when he regards honest well-wishers, affectionate benefactors, the neutral, mediators, the envious, friends and enemies, the pious and the sinners all with an equal mind.

Text 10 योगी युञ्जीत सततमात्मानं रहसि स्थितः ।
एकाकी यतचित्तात्मा निराशीरपरिग्रहः ॥१०॥

yogī yuñjīta satatam, ātmānaṁ rahasi sthitaḥ
ekākī yata-cittātmā, nirāśīr aparigrahaḥ

yogī – a transcendentalist; *yuñjīta* – must concentrate in Kṛṣṇa consciousness; *satatam* – constantly; *ātmānam* – himself (by body, mind and self); *rahasi* – in a secluded place; *sthitaḥ* – being situated; *ekākī* – alone; *yata-citta-ātmā* – always careful in mind; *nirāśīḥ* – without being attracted by anything else; *aparigrahaḥ* – free from the feeling of possessiveness.

A transcendentalist should always engage his body, mind and self in relationship with the Supreme; he should live alone in a secluded place and should always carefully control his mind. He should be free from desires and feelings of possessiveness.

PURPORT: Kṛṣṇa is realized in different degrees as Brahman, Paramātmā and the Supreme Personality of Godhead. Kṛṣṇa consciousness means, concisely, to be always engaged in the transcendental loving service of the Lord. But those who are attached to the impersonal Brahman or the localized Supersoul are also partially Kṛṣṇa conscious, because the impersonal Brahman is the spiritual ray of Kṛṣṇa and the Supersoul is the all-pervading partial expansion of Kṛṣṇa. Thus the impersonalist and the meditator are also indirectly Kṛṣṇa conscious. A directly Kṛṣṇa conscious person is the topmost transcendentalist because such a devotee knows what is meant by Brahman and Paramātmā. His knowledge of the Absolute Truth is perfect, whereas the impersonalist and the meditative *yogī* are imperfectly Kṛṣṇa conscious.

Nevertheless, all of these are instructed herewith to be constantly engaged in their particular pursuits so that they may come to the highest perfection sooner or later. The first business of a transcendentalist is to keep the mind always on Kṛṣṇa. One should always think of Kṛṣṇa and not forget Him even for a moment. Concentration of the mind on the Supreme is called *samādhi,* or trance. In order to concentrate the mind, one should always remain in seclusion and avoid disturbance by external objects. He should be very careful to accept favorable and reject unfavorable conditions that affect his realization. And, in perfect determination, he should not hanker after unnecessary material things that entangle him by feelings of possessiveness.

All these perfections and precautions are perfectly executed when one is directly in Kṛṣṇa consciousness, because direct Kṛṣṇa consciousness means self-abnegation, wherein there is very little chance for material possessiveness. Śrīla Rūpa Gosvāmī characterizes Kṛṣṇa consciousness in this way:

anāsaktasya viṣayān, yathārham upayuñjataḥ
nirbandhaḥ kṛṣṇa-sambandhe, yuktaṁ vairāgyam ucyate

prāpañcikatayā buddhyā, hari-sambandhi-vastunaḥ
mumukṣubhiḥ parityāgo, vairāgyaṁ phalgu kathyate

"When one is not attached to anything, but at the same time accepts everything in relation to Kṛṣṇa, one is rightly situated above possessiveness. On the other hand, one who rejects everything without knowledge of its relationship to Kṛṣṇa is not as complete in his renunciation." (*Bhakti-rasāmṛta-sindhu* 1.2.255–256)

A Kṛṣṇa conscious person well knows that everything belongs to Kṛṣṇa, and thus he is always free from feelings of personal possession. As such, he has no hankering for anything on his own personal account. He knows how to accept things in favor of Kṛṣṇa consciousness and how to reject things unfavorable to Kṛṣṇa consciousness. He is always aloof from material things because he is always transcendental, and he is always alone, having nothing to do with persons not in Kṛṣṇa consciousness. Therefore a person in Kṛṣṇa consciousness is the perfect *yogī.*

Texts 11–12

शुचौ देशे प्रतिष्ठाप्य स्थिरमासनमात्मनः ।
नात्युच्छ्रितं नातिनीचं चैलाजिनकुशोत्तरम् ॥११॥
तत्रैकाग्रं मनः कृत्वा यतचित्तेन्द्रियक्रियः ।
उपविश्यासने युञ्ज्याद्योगमात्मविशुद्धये ॥१२॥

śucau deśe pratiṣṭhāpya, sthiram āsanam ātmanaḥ
nāty-ucchritaṁ nāti-nīcaṁ, cailājina-kuśottaram

tatraikāgraṁ manaḥ kṛtvā, yata-cittendriya-kriyaḥ
upaviśyāsane yuñjyād, yogam ātma-viśuddhaye

śucau – in a sanctified; *deśe* – land; *pratiṣṭhāpya* – placing; *sthiram* – firm; *āsanam* – seat; *ātmanaḥ* – his own; *na* – not; *ati* – too; *ucchritam* – high; *na* – nor; *ati* – too; *nīcam* – low; *caila-ajina* – of soft cloth and deerskin; *kuśa* – and *kuśa* grass; *uttaram* – covering; *tatra* – thereupon; *eka-agram* – with one attention; *manaḥ* – mind; *kṛtvā* – making; *yata-citta* – controlling the mind; *indriya* – senses; *kriyaḥ* – and activities; *upaviśya* – sitting; *āsane* – on the seat; *yuñjyāt* – should execute; *yogam* – *yoga* practice; *ātma* – the heart; *viśuddhaye* – for clarifying.

To practice yoga, one should go to a secluded place and should lay kuśa grass on the ground and then cover it with a deerskin and a soft cloth. The seat should be neither too high nor too low and should be situated in a sacred place. The yogī should then sit on it very firmly and practice yoga to purify the heart by controlling his mind, senses and activities and fixing the mind on one point.

PURPORT: "Sacred place" refers to places of pilgrimage. In India the *yogīs* – the transcendentalists or the devotees – all leave home and reside in sacred places such as Prayāga, Mathurā, Vṛndāvana, Hṛṣīkeśa and Hardwar and in solitude practice *yoga* where the sacred rivers like the Yamunā and the Ganges flow. But often this is not possible, especially for Westerners. The so-called *yoga* societies in big cities may be successful in earning material benefit, but they are not at all suitable for the actual practice of *yoga.* One who is not self-controlled and whose mind is not undisturbed cannot practice meditation. Therefore, in the *Bṛhan-nāradīya Purāṇa* it is said that in Kali-yuga (the present *yuga,* or age), when people in general are short-lived, slow in spiritual realization and always disturbed by various anxieties, the best means of spiritual realization is chanting the holy name of the Lord.

harer nāma harer nāma, harer nāmaiva kevalam
kalau nāsty eva nāsty eva, nāsty eva gatir anyathā

"In this age of quarrel and hypocrisy the only means of deliverance is chanting the holy name of the Lord. There is no other way. There is no other way. There is no other way."

Texts 13–14

समं कायशिरोग्रीवं धारयन्नचलं स्थिरः ।
सम्प्रेक्ष्य नासिकाग्रं स्वं दिशश्चानवलोकयन् ॥१३॥
प्रशान्तात्मा विगतभीर्ब्रह्मचारिव्रते स्थितः ।
मनः संयम्य मच्चित्तो युक्त आसीत मत्परः ॥१४॥

samaṁ kāya-śiro-grīvaṁ, dhārayann acalaṁ sthiraḥ
samprekṣya nāsikāgraṁ svaṁ, diśaś cānavalokayan

praśāntātmā vigata-bhīr, brahmacāri-vrate sthitaḥ
manaḥ saṁyamya mac-citto, yukta āsīta mat-paraḥ

samam – straight; *kāya* – body; *śiraḥ* – head; *grīvam* – and neck; *dhārayan* – holding; *acalam* – unmoving; *sthiraḥ* – still; *samprekṣya* – looking; *nāsikā* – of the nose; *agram* – at the tip; *svam* – own; *diśaḥ* – on all sides; *ca* – also; *anavalokayan* – not looking; *praśānta* – unagitated; *ātmā* – mind; *vigata-bhīḥ* – devoid of fear; *brahmacāri-vrate* – in the vow of celibacy; *sthitaḥ* – situated; *manaḥ* – mind; *saṁyamya* – completely subduing; *mat* – upon Me (Kṛṣṇa); *cittaḥ* – concentrating the mind; *yuktaḥ* – the actual *yogī; āsīta* – should sit; *mat* – Me; *paraḥ* – the ultimate goal.

One should hold one's body, neck and head erect in a straight line and stare steadily at the tip of the nose. Thus, with an unagitated, subdued mind, devoid of fear, completely free from sex life, one should meditate upon Me within the heart and make Me the ultimate goal of life.

PURPORT: The goal of life is to know Kṛṣṇa, who is situated within the heart of every living being as Paramātmā, the four-handed Viṣṇu form. The *yoga* process is practiced in order to discover and see this localized form of Viṣṇu, and not for any other purpose. The localized *viṣṇu-mūrti* is the plenary representation of Kṛṣṇa dwelling within one's heart. One who has no program to realize this *viṣṇu-mūrti* is uselessly engaged in mock *yoga* practice and is certainly wasting his time. Kṛṣṇa is the ultimate goal of life, and the *viṣṇu-mūrti* situated in one's heart is the object of *yoga* practice. To realize this *viṣṇu-mūrti* within the heart, one has to observe complete abstinence from sex life; therefore one has to leave home and live alone in a secluded place, remaining seated as mentioned above. One cannot enjoy sex life daily at home or elsewhere and attend a so-called *yoga* class and thus become a *yogī.* One has to practice controlling the mind and avoiding all kinds of sense gratification, of which sex life is the chief. In the rules of celibacy written by the great sage Yājñavalkya it is said:

karmaṇā manasā vācā, sarvāvasthāsu sarvadā
sarvatra maithuna-tyāgo, brahmacaryaṁ pracakṣate

"The vow of *brahmacarya* is meant to help one completely abstain from sex indulgence in work, words and mind – at all times, under all circumstances, and in all places." No one can perform correct *yoga* practice through sex indulgence. *Brahmacarya* is taught, therefore, from childhood, when one has no knowledge of sex life. Children at the age of five are sent to the *guru-kula,* or the place of the spiritual master, and the master trains the young boys in the strict discipline of becoming *brahmacārīs.* Without such practice, no one can make advancement in any *yoga,* whether it be *dhyāna, jñāna* or *bhakti.* One who, however, follows the rules and regulations of married life, having a sexual relationship only with his wife (and that also under regulation), is also called a *brahmacārī.* Such a restrained householder *brahmacārī* may be accepted in the *bhakti* school, but the *jñāna* and *dhyāna* schools do not even admit householder *brahmacārīs.* They require complete abstinence without compromise. In the *bhakti* school, a householder *brahmacārī* is allowed controlled sex life because the cult of *bhakti-yoga* is so powerful that one automatically loses sexual attraction, being engaged in the superior service of the Lord. In the *Bhagavad-gītā* (2.59) it is said:

viṣayā vinivartante, nirāhārasya dehinaḥ
rasa-varjaṁ raso 'py asya, paraṁ dṛṣṭvā nivartate

Whereas others are forced to restrain themselves from sense gratification, a devotee of the Lord automatically refrains because of superior taste. Other than the devotee, no one has any information of that superior taste.

Vigata-bhīḥ. One cannot be fearless unless one is fully in Kṛṣṇa consciousness. A conditioned soul is fearful due to his perverted memory, his forgetfulness of his eternal relationship with Kṛṣṇa. The *Bhāgavatam*

(11.2.37) says, *bhayaṁ dvitīyābhiniveśataḥ syād īśād apetasya viparyayo 'smṛtiḥ.* Kṛṣṇa consciousness is the only basis for fearlessness. Therefore, perfect practice is possible for a person who is Kṛṣṇa conscious. And since the ultimate goal of *yoga* practice is to see the Lord within, a Kṛṣṇa conscious person is already the best of all *yogīs.* The principles of the *yoga* system mentioned herein are different from those of the popular so-called *yoga* societies.

Text 15 युञ्जन्नेवं सदात्मानं योगी नियतमानसः ।
शान्तिं निर्वाणपरमां मत्संस्थामधिगच्छति ॥१५॥

yuñjann evaṁ sadātmānaṁ, yogī niyata-mānasaḥ
śāntiṁ nirvāṇa-paramāṁ, mat-saṁsthām adhigacchati

yuñjan – practicing; *evam* – as mentioned above; *sadā* – constantly; *ātmānam* – body, mind and soul; *yogī* – the mystic transcendentalist; *niyata-mānasaḥ* – with a regulated mind; *śāntim* – peace; *nirvāṇa-paramām* – cessation of material existence; *mat-saṁsthām* – the spiritual sky (the kingdom of God); *adhigacchati* – does attain.

Thus practicing constant control of the body, mind and activities, the mystic transcendentalist, his mind regulated, attains to the kingdom of God [or the abode of Kṛṣṇa] by cessation of material existence.

PURPORT: The ultimate goal in practicing *yoga* is now clearly explained. *Yoga* practice is not meant for attaining any kind of material facility; it is to enable the cessation of all material existence. One who seeks an improvement in health or aspires after material perfection is no *yogī* according to *Bhagavad-gītā.* Nor does cessation of material existence entail one's entering into "the void," which is only a myth. There is no void anywhere within the creation of the Lord. Rather, the cessation of material existence enables one to enter into the spiritual sky, the abode of the Lord. The abode of the Lord is also clearly described in the *Bhagavad-gītā* as that place where there is no need of sun, moon or electricity. All the planets in the spiritual kingdom are self-illuminated like the sun in the material sky. The kingdom of God is everywhere, but the spiritual sky and the planets thereof are called *paraṁ dhāma,* or superior abodes.

A consummate *yogī,* who is perfect in understanding Lord Kṛṣṇa, as is clearly stated herein by the Lord Himself (*mat-cittaḥ, mat-paraḥ, mat-sthānam*), can attain real peace and can ultimately reach His supreme abode, Kṛṣṇaloka, known as Goloka Vṛndāvana. In the *Brahma-saṁhitā* (5.37) it is clearly stated, *goloka eva nivasaty akhilātma-bhūtaḥ:* the Lord, although residing always in His abode called Goloka, is the all-pervading Brahman and the localized Paramātmā as well by dint of His superior spiritual energies. No one can reach the spiritual sky (Vaikuṇṭha) or enter into the Lord's eternal abode (Goloka Vṛndāvana) without the proper understanding of Kṛṣṇa and His plenary expansion Viṣṇu. Therefore a person working in Kṛṣṇa consciousness is the perfect *yogī,* because his mind is always absorbed in Kṛṣṇa's activities (*sa vai manaḥ kṛṣṇa-padāravindayoḥ*). In the *Vedas* also (*Śvetāśvatara Upaniṣad* 3.8) we learn, *tam eva viditvāti mṛtyum eti:* "One can overcome the path of birth and death only by understanding the Supreme Personality of Godhead, Kṛṣṇa." In other words, perfection of the *yoga* system is the attainment of freedom from material existence and not some magical jugglery or gymnastic feats to befool innocent people.

Text 16 **नात्यश्नतस्तु योगोऽस्ति न चैकान्तमनश्नतः ।**
न चातिस्वप्नशीलस्य जाग्रतो नैव चार्जुन ॥१६॥

nāty-aśnatas tu yogo 'sti, na caikāntam anaśnataḥ
na cāti-svapna-śīlasya, jāgrato naiva cārjuna

na – never; *ati* – too much; *aśnataḥ* – of one who eats; *tu* – but; *yogaḥ* – linking with the Supreme; *asti* – there is; *na* – nor; *ca* – also; *ekāntam* – overly; *anaśnataḥ* – abstaining from eating; *na* – nor; *ca* – also; *ati* – too much; *svapna-śīlasya* – of one who sleeps; *jāgrataḥ* – or one who keeps night watch too much; *na* – not; *eva* – ever; *ca* – and; *arjuna* – O Arjuna.

There is no possibility of one's becoming a yogī, O Arjuna, if one eats too much or eats too little, sleeps too much or does not sleep enough.

PURPORT: Regulation of diet and sleep is recommended herein for the *yogīs.* Too much eating means eating more than is required to keep the body and soul together. There is no need for men to eat animals, because there is an ample supply of grains, vegetables, fruits and milk. Such simple foodstuff is considered to be in the mode of goodness according to the *Bhagavad-gītā.* Animal food is for those in the mode of ignorance. Therefore, those who indulge in animal food, drinking, smoking and eating food which is not first offered to Kṛṣṇa will suffer sinful reactions because of eating only polluted things. *Bhuñjate te tv aghaṁ pāpā ye pacanty ātma-kāraṇāt.* Anyone who eats for sense pleasure, or cooks for himself, not offering his food to Kṛṣṇa, eats only sin. One who eats sin and eats more than is allotted to him cannot execute perfect *yoga.* It is best that one eat only the remnants of foodstuff offered to Kṛṣṇa. A person in Kṛṣṇa consciousness does not eat anything which is not first offered to Kṛṣṇa. Therefore, only the Kṛṣṇa conscious person can attain perfection in *yoga* practice. Nor can one who artificially abstains from eating, manufacturing his own personal process of fasting, practice *yoga.* The Kṛṣṇa conscious person observes fasting as it is recommended in the scriptures. He does not fast or eat more than is required, and he is thus competent to perform *yoga* practice. One who eats more than required will dream very much while sleeping, and he must consequently sleep more than is required. One should not sleep more than six hours daily. One who sleeps more than six hours out of twenty-four is certainly influenced by the mode of ignorance. A person in the mode of ignorance is lazy and prone to sleep a great deal. Such a person cannot perform *yoga.*

Text 17 युक्ताहारविहारस्य युक्तचेष्टस्य कर्मसु ।
युक्तस्वप्नावबोधस्य योगो भवति दुःखहा ॥१७॥

yuktāhāra-vihārasya, yukta-ceṣṭasya karmasu
yukta-svapnāvabodhasya, yogo bhavati duḥkha-hā

yukta – regulated; *āhāra* – eating; *vihārasya* – recreation; *yukta* – regulated; *ceṣṭasya* – of one who works for maintenance; *karmasu* – in discharging duties; *yukta* – regulated; *svapna-avabodhasya* – sleep and wakefulness; *yogaḥ* – practice of *yoga; bhavati* – becomes; *duḥkha-hā* – diminishing pains.

He who is regulated in his habits of eating, sleeping, recreation and work can mitigate all material pains by practicing the yoga system.

PURPORT: Extravagance in the matter of eating, sleeping, defending and mating – which are demands of the body – can block advancement in the practice of *yoga.* As far as eating is concerned, it can be regulated only when one is practiced to take and accept *prasādam,* sanctified food. Lord Kṛṣṇa is offered, according to the *Bhagavad-gītā* (9.26), vegetables, flowers, fruits, grains, milk, etc. In this way, a person in Kṛṣṇa consciousness becomes automatically trained not to accept food not meant for human consumption, or not in the category of goodness. As far as sleeping is concerned, a Kṛṣṇa conscious person is always alert in the discharge of his duties in Kṛṣṇa consciousness, and therefore any unnecessary time spent sleeping is considered a great loss. *Avyartha-kālatvam:* a Kṛṣṇa conscious person cannot bear to pass a minute of his life without being engaged in the service of the Lord. Therefore, his sleeping is kept to a minimum. His ideal in this respect is Śrīla Rūpa Gosvāmī, who was always engaged in the service of Kṛṣṇa and who could not sleep more than two hours a day, and sometimes not even that. Ṭhākura Haridāsa would not even accept *prasādam* nor even sleep for a moment without finishing his daily routine of chanting with his beads three hundred thousand names. As far as work is concerned, a Kṛṣṇa conscious person does not do anything which is not connected with Kṛṣṇa's interest, and thus his work is always regulated and is untainted by sense gratification. Since there is no question of sense gratification, there is no material leisure for a person in Kṛṣṇa consciousness. And because he is regulated in all his work, speech, sleep, wakefulness and all other bodily activities, there is no material misery for him.

Text 18 यदा विनियतं चित्तमात्मन्येवावतिष्ठते ।
निस्पृहः सर्वकामेभ्यो युक्त इत्युच्यते तदा ॥१८॥

yadā viniyataṁ cittam, ātmany evāvatiṣṭhate
nispṛhaḥ sarva-kāmebhyo, yukta ity ucyate tadā

yadā – when; *viniyatam* – particularly disciplined; *cittam* – the mind and its activities; *ātmani* – in the transcendence; *eva* – certainly; *avatiṣṭhate* – becomes situated; *nispṛhaḥ* – devoid of desire; *sarva* – for all kinds of; *kāmebhyaḥ* – material sense gratification; *yuktaḥ* – well situated in *yoga; iti* – thus; *ucyate* – is said to be; *tadā* – at that time.

When the yogī, by practice of yoga, disciplines his mental activities and becomes situated in transcendence – devoid of all material desires – he is said to be well established in yoga.

PURPORT: The activities of the *yogī* are distinguished from those of an ordinary person by his characteristic cessation from all kinds of material desires – of which sex is the chief. A perfect *yogī* is so well disciplined in the activities of the mind that he can no longer be disturbed by any kind of material desire. This perfectional stage can automatically be attained by persons in Kṛṣṇa consciousness, as stated in the *Śrīmad-Bhāgavatam* (9.4.18–20):

sa vai manaḥ kṛṣṇa-padāravindayor
vacāṁsi vaikuṇṭha-guṇānuvarṇane
karau harer mandira-mārjanādiṣu
śrutiṁ cakārācyuta-sat-kathodaye

mukunda-liṅgālaya-darśane dṛśau
tad-bhṛtya-gātra-sparśe 'ṅga-saṅgamam
ghrāṇaṁ ca tat-pāda-saroja-saurabhe
śrīmat-tulasyā rasanāṁ tad-arpite

pādau hareḥ kṣetra-padānusarpaṇe
śiro hṛṣīkeśa-padābhivandane
kāmaṁ ca dāsye na tu kāma-kāmyayā
yathottama-śloka-janāśrayā ratiḥ

"King Ambarīṣa first of all engaged his mind on the lotus feet of Lord Kṛṣṇa; then, one after another, he engaged his words in describing the transcendental qualities of the Lord, his hands in mopping the temple of the Lord, his ears in hearing of the activities of the Lord, his eyes in seeing the transcendental forms of the Lord, his body in touching the bodies of the devotees, his sense of smell in smelling the scents of the lotus flowers offered to the Lord, his tongue in tasting the *tulasī* leaf offered at the lotus feet of the Lord, his legs in going to places of pilgrimage and the temple of the Lord, his head in offering obeisances unto the Lord, and his desires in executing the mission of the Lord. All these transcendental activities are quite befitting a pure devotee."

This transcendental stage may be inexpressible subjectively by the followers of the impersonalist path, but it becomes very easy and practical for a person in Kṛṣṇa consciousness, as is apparent in the above description of the engagements of Mahārāja Ambarīṣa. Unless the mind is fixed on the lotus feet of the Lord by constant remembrance, such transcendental engagements are not practical. In the devotional service of the Lord, therefore, these prescribed activities are called *arcana,* or engaging all the senses in the service of the Lord. The senses and the mind require engagements. Simple abnegation is not practical. Therefore, for people in general – especially those who are not in the renounced order of life – transcendental engagement of the senses and the mind as described above is the perfect process for transcendental achievement, which is called *yukta* in the *Bhagavad-gītā.*

Text 19 यथा दीपो निवातस्थो नेङ्गते सोपमा स्मृता ।
योगिनो यतचित्तस्य युञ्जतो योगमात्मनः ॥१९॥

yathā dīpo nivāta-stho, neṅgate sopamā smṛtā
yogino yata-cittasya, yuñjato yogam ātmanaḥ

yathā – as; *dīpaḥ* – a lamp; *nivāta-sthaḥ* – in a place without wind; *na* – does not; *iṅgate* – waver; *sā* – this; *upamā* – comparison; *smṛtā* – is considered; *yoginaḥ* – of the *yogī; yata-cittasya* – whose mind is controlled; *yuñjataḥ* – constantly engaged; *yogam* – in meditation; *ātmanaḥ* – on transcendence.

As a lamp in a windless place does not waver, so the transcendentalist, whose mind is controlled, remains always steady in his meditation on the transcendent Self.

PURPORT: A truly Kṛṣṇa conscious person, always absorbed in transcendence, in constant undisturbed meditation on his worshipable Lord, is as steady as a lamp in a windless place.

Texts 20–23 यत्रोपरमते चित्तं निरुद्धं योगसेवया ।
यत्र चैवात्मनात्मानं पश्यन्नात्मनि तुष्यति ॥२०॥
सुखमात्यन्तिकं यत्तद् बुद्धिग्राह्यमतीन्द्रियम् ।
वेत्ति यत्र न चैवायं स्थितश्चलति तत्त्वतः ॥२१॥
यं लब्ध्वा चापरं लाभं मन्यते नाधिकं ततः ।
यस्मिन् स्थितो न दुःखेन गुरुणापि विचाल्यते ॥२२॥
तं विद्याद् दुःखसंयोगवियोगं योगसंज्ञितम् ॥२३॥

yatroparamate cittaṁ, niruddhaṁ yoga-sevayā
yatra caivātmanātmānaṁ, paśyann ātmani tuṣyati
sukham ātyantikaṁ yat tad, buddhi-grāhyam atīndriyam
vetti yatra na caivāyaṁ, sthitaś calati tattvataḥ

yaṁ labdhvā cāparaṁ lābhaṁ, manyate nādhikaṁ tataḥ
yasmin sthito na duḥkhena, guruṇāpi vicālyate
taṁ vidyād duḥkha-saṁyoga-, viyogaṁ yoga-saṁjñitam

yatra – in that state of affairs where; *uparamate* – cease (because one feels transcendental happiness); *cittam* – mental activities; *niruddham* – being restrained from matter; *yoga-sevayā* – by performance of *yoga; yatra* – in which; *ca* – also; *eva* – certainly; *ātmanā* – by the pure mind;

ātmānam – the Self; *paśyan* – realizing the position of; *ātmani* – in the Self; *tuṣyati* – one becomes satisfied; *sukham* – happiness; *ātyantikam* – supreme; *yat* – which; *tat* – that; *buddhi* – by intelligence; *grāhyam* – accessible; *atīndriyam* – transcendental; *vetti* – one knows; *yatra* – wherein; *na* – never; *ca* – also; *eva* – certainly; *ayam* – he; *sthitaḥ* – situated; *calati* – moves; *tattvataḥ* – from the truth; *yam* – that which; *labdhvā* – by attainment; *ca* – also; *aparam* – any other; *lābham* – gain; *manyate* – considers; *na* – never; *adhikam* – more; *tataḥ* – than that; *yasmin* – in which; *sthitaḥ* – being situated; *na* – never; *duḥkhena* – by miseries; *guruṇā api* – even though very difficult; *vicālyate* – becomes shaken; *tam* – that; *vidyāt* – you must know; *duḥkha-saṁyoga* – of the miseries of material contact; *viyogam* – extermination; *yoga-saṁjñitam* – called trance in *yoga.*

In the stage of perfection called trance, or samādhi, one's mind is completely restrained from material mental activities by practice of yoga. This perfection is characterized by one's ability to see the Self by the pure mind and to relish and rejoice in the Self. In that joyous state, one is situated in boundless transcendental happiness, realized through transcendental senses. Established thus, one never departs from the truth, and upon gaining this he thinks there is no greater gain. Being situated in such a position, one is never shaken, even in the midst of greatest difficulty. This indeed is actual freedom from all miseries arising from material contact.

PURPORT: By practice of *yoga* one becomes gradually detached from material concepts. This is the primary characteristic of the *yoga* principle. And after this, one becomes situated in trance, or *samādhi,* which means that the *yogī* realizes the Supersoul through transcendental mind and intelligence, without any of the misgivings of identifying the self with the Superself. *Yoga* practice is more or less based on the principles of the Patañjali system. Some unauthorized commentators try to identify the individual soul with the Supersoul, and the monists think this to be liberation, but they do not understand the real purpose of the Patañjali system of *yoga.* There is an acceptance of transcendental pleasure in the Patañjali system, but the monists do not accept this transcendental pleasure, out of fear of jeopardizing the theory of oneness. The duality of knowledge and knower is not accepted by the nondualist, but in this verse transcendental pleasure – realized through transcendental senses – is accepted. And this is corroborated by Patañjali Muni, the famous exponent of the *yoga* system. The great sage declares in his *Yoga-sūtras*

(4.33): *puruṣārtha-śūnyānāṁ guṇānāṁ pratiprasavaḥ kaivalyaṁ svarūpa-pratiṣṭhā vā citi-śaktir iti.*

This *citi-śakti,* or internal potency, is transcendental. *Puruṣārtha* means material religiosity, economic development, sense gratification and, at the end, the attempt to become one with the Supreme. This "oneness with the Supreme" is called *kaivalyam* by the monist. But according to Patañjali, this *kaivalyam* is an internal, or transcendental, potency by which the living entity becomes aware of his constitutional position. In the words of Lord Caitanya, this state of affairs is called *ceto-darpaṇa-mārjanam,* or clearance of the impure mirror of the mind. This "clearance" is actually liberation, or *bhava-mahā-dāvāgni-nirvāpaṇam.* The theory of *nirvāṇa* – also preliminary – corresponds with this principle. In the *Bhāgavatam* (2.10.6) this is called *svarūpeṇa vyavasthitiḥ.* The *Bhagavad-gītā* also confirms this situation in this verse.

After *nirvāṇa,* or material cessation, there is the manifestation of spiritual activities, or devotional service to the Lord, known as Kṛṣṇa consciousness. In the words of the *Bhāgavatam, svarūpeṇa vyavasthitiḥ:* this is the "real life of the living entity." *Māyā,* or illusion, is the condition of spiritual life contaminated by material infection. Liberation from this material infection does not mean destruction of the original eternal position of the living entity. Patañjali also accepts this by his words *kaivalyaṁ svarūpa-pratiṣṭhā vā citi-śaktir iti.* This *citi-śakti,* or transcendental pleasure, is real life. This is confirmed in the *Vedānta-sūtra* (1.1.12) as *ānanda-mayo 'bhyāsāt.* This natural transcendental pleasure is the ultimate goal of *yoga* and is easily achieved by execution of devotional service, or *bhakti-yoga. Bhakti-yoga* will be vividly described in the Seventh Chapter of *Bhagavad-gītā.*

In the *yoga* system, as described in this chapter, there are two kinds of *samādhi,* called *samprajñāta-samādhi* and *asamprajñāta-samādhi.* When one becomes situated in the transcendental position by various philosophical researches, he is said to have achieved *samprajñāta-samādhi.* In the *asamprajñāta-samādhi* there is no longer any connection with mundane pleasure, for one is then transcendental to all sorts of happiness derived from the senses. When the *yogī* is once situated in that transcendental position, he is never shaken from it. Unless the *yogī* is able to reach this position, he is unsuccessful. Today's so-called *yoga* practice, which involves various sense pleasures, is contradictory. A *yogī* indulging in sex and intoxication is a mockery. Even those *yogīs* who are attracted by the *siddhis* (perfections) in the process of *yoga* are not perfectly situated. If *yogīs* are attracted by the by-products of *yoga,* then they cannot attain the stage of perfection, as is stated in this verse. Persons, therefore, indulging in the make-show practice of gymnastic feats or *siddhis* should know that the aim of *yoga* is lost in that way.

The best practice of *yoga* in this age is Kṛṣṇa consciousness, which is not baffling. A Kṛṣṇa conscious person is so happy in his occupation that he does not aspire after any other happiness. There are many impediments, especially in this age of hypocrisy, to practicing *haṭha-yoga, dhyāna-yoga* and *jñāna-yoga,* but there is no such problem in executing *karma-yoga* or *bhakti-yoga.*

As long as the material body exists, one has to meet the demands of the body, namely eating, sleeping, defending and mating. But a person who is in pure *bhakti-yoga,* or in Kṛṣṇa consciousness, does not arouse the senses while meeting the demands of the body. Rather, he accepts the bare necessities of life, making the best use of a bad bargain, and enjoys transcendental happiness in Kṛṣṇa consciousness. He is callous toward incidental occurrences – such as accidents, disease, scarcity and even the death of a most dear relative – but he is always alert to execute his duties in Kṛṣṇa consciousness, or *bhakti-yoga.* Accidents never deviate him from his duty. As stated in the *Bhagavad-gītā* (2.14), *āgamāpāyino 'nityās tāṁs titikṣasva bhārata.* He endures all such incidental occurrences because he knows that they come and go and do not affect his duties. In this way he achieves the highest perfection in *yoga* practice.

Text 24 स निश्चयेन योक्तव्यो योगोऽनिर्विण्णचेतसा ।
सङ्कल्पप्रभवान् कामांस्त्यक्त्वा सर्वानशेषतः ।
मनसैवेन्द्रियग्रामं विनियम्य समन्ततः ॥२४॥

sa niścayena yoktavyo, yogo 'nirviṇṇa-cetasā
saṅkalpa-prabhavān kāmāṁs, tyaktvā sarvān aśeṣataḥ
manasaivendriya-grāmaṁ, viniyamya samantataḥ

saḥ – that; *niścayena* – with firm determination; *yoktavyaḥ* – must be practiced; *yogaḥ* – *yoga* system; *anirviṇṇa-cetasā* – without deviation; *saṅkalpa* – mental speculations; *prabhavān* – born of; *kāmān* – material desires; *tyaktvā* – giving up; *sarvān* – all; *aśeṣataḥ* – completely; *manasā* – by the mind; *eva* – certainly; *indriya-grāmam* – the full set of senses; *viniyamya* – regulating; *samantataḥ* – from all sides.

One should engage oneself in the practice of yoga with determination and faith and not be deviated from the path. One should abandon, with-

out exception, all material desires born of mental speculation and thus control all the senses on all sides by the mind.

PURPORT: The *yoga* practitioner should be determined and should patiently prosecute the practice without deviation. One should be sure of success at the end and pursue this course with great perseverance, not becoming discouraged if there is any delay in the attainment of success. Success is sure for the rigid practitioner. Regarding *bhakti-yoga,* Rūpa Gosvāmī says:

utsāhān niścayād dhairyāt, tat-tat-karma-pravartanāt
saṅga-tyāgāt sato vṛtteḥ, ṣaḍbhir bhaktiḥ prasidhyati

"One can execute the process of *bhakti-yoga* successfully with full-hearted enthusiasm, perseverance, and determination, by following the prescribed duties in the association of devotees and by engaging completely in activities of goodness." (*Upadeśāmṛta* 3)

As for determination, one should follow the example of the sparrow who lost her eggs in the waves of the ocean. A sparrow laid her eggs on the shore of the ocean, but the big ocean carried away the eggs on its waves. The sparrow became very upset and asked the ocean to return her eggs. The ocean did not even consider her appeal. So the sparrow decided to dry up the ocean. She began to pick out the water in her small beak, and everyone laughed at her for her impossible determination. The news of her activity spread, and at last Garuḍa, the gigantic bird carrier of Lord Viṣṇu, heard it. He became compassionate toward his small sister bird, and so he came to see the sparrow. Garuḍa was very pleased by the determination of the small sparrow, and he promised to help. Thus Garuḍa at once asked the ocean to return her eggs lest he himself take up the work of the sparrow. The ocean was frightened at this, and returned the eggs. Thus the sparrow became happy by the grace of Garuḍa.

Similarly, the practice of *yoga,* especially *bhakti-yoga* in Kṛṣṇa consciousness, may appear to be a very difficult job. But if anyone follows the principles with great determination, the Lord will surely help, for God helps those who help themselves.

Text 25 शनैः शनैरुपरमेद् बुद्ध्या धृतिगृहीतया ।
आत्मसंस्थं मनः कृत्वा न किञ्चिदपि चिन्तयेत् ॥२५॥

śanaiḥ śanair uparamed, buddhyā dhṛti-gṛhītayā
ātma-saṁsthaṁ manaḥ kṛtvā, na kiñcid api cintayet

śanaiḥ – gradually; *śanaiḥ* – step by step; *uparamet* – one should hold back; *buddhyā* – by intelligence; *dhṛti-gṛhītayā* – carried by conviction; *ātma-saṁstham* – placed in transcendence; *manaḥ* – mind; *kṛtvā* – making; *na* – not; *kiñcit* – anything else; *api* – even; *cintayet* – should think of.

Gradually, step by step, one should become situated in trance by means of intelligence sustained by full conviction, and thus the mind should be fixed on the Self alone and should think of nothing else.

PURPORT: By proper conviction and intelligence one should gradually cease sense activities. This is called *pratyāhāra.* The mind, being controlled by conviction, meditation, and cessation from the senses, should be situated in trance, or *samādhi.* At that time there is no longer any danger of becoming engaged in the material conception of life. In other words, although one is involved with matter as long as the material body exists, one should not think about sense gratification. One should think of no pleasure aside from the pleasure of the Supreme Self. This state is easily attained by directly practicing Kṛṣṇa consciousness.

Text 26 यतो यतो निश्चलति मनश्चञ्चलमस्थिरम् ।
ततस्ततो नियम्यैतदात्मन्येव वशं नयेत् ॥२६॥

yato yato niścalati, manaś cañcalam asthiram
tatas tato niyamyaitad, ātmany eva vaśaṁ nayet

yataḥ yataḥ – wherever; *niścalati* – becomes verily agitated; *manaḥ* – the mind; *cañcalam* – flickering; *asthiram* – unsteady; *tataḥ tataḥ* – from there; *niyamya* – regulating; *etat* – this; *ātmani* – in the Self; *eva* – certainly; *vaśam* – control; *nayet* – must bring under.

From wherever the mind wanders due to its flickering and unsteady nature, one must certainly withdraw it and bring it back under the control of the Self.

PURPORT: The nature of the mind is flickering and unsteady. But a self-realized *yogī* has to control the mind; the mind should not control him. One who controls the mind (and therefore the senses as well) is called *gosvāmī,* or *svāmī,* and one who is controlled by the mind is called *go-dāsa,* or the servant of the senses. A *gosvāmī* knows the standard of sense happiness. In transcendental sense happiness, the senses are engaged in the service of Hṛṣīkeśa, or the supreme owner of the senses – Kṛṣṇa. Serving Kṛṣṇa with purified senses is called Kṛṣṇa consciousness.

That is the way of bringing the senses under full control. What is more, that is the highest perfection of *yoga* practice.

Text 27 प्रशान्तमनसं ह्येनं योगिनं सुखमुत्तमम् ।
उपैति शान्तरजसं ब्रह्मभूतमकल्मषम् ॥२७॥

praśānta-manasaṁ hy enaṁ, yoginaṁ sukham uttamam
upaiti śānta-rajasaṁ, brahma-bhūtam akalmaṣam

praśānta – peaceful, fixed on the lotus feet of Kṛṣṇa; *manasam* – whose mind; *hi* – certainly; *enam* – this; *yoginam* – *yogī; sukham* – happiness; *uttamam* – the highest; *upaiti* – attains; *śānta-rajasam* – his passion pacified; *brahma-bhūtam* – liberation by identification with the Absolute; *akalmaṣam* – freed from all past sinful reactions.

The yogī whose mind is fixed on Me verily attains the highest perfection of transcendental happiness. He is beyond the mode of passion, he realizes his qualitative identity with the Supreme, and thus he is freed from all reactions to past deeds.

PURPORT: *Brahma-bhūta* is the state of being free from material contamination and situated in the transcendental service of the Lord. *Mad-bhaktiṁ labhate parām* (*Bhagavad-gītā* 18.54). One cannot remain in the quality of Brahman, the Absolute, until one's mind is fixed on the lotus feet of the Lord. *Sa vai manaḥ kṛṣṇa-padāravindayoḥ.* To be always engaged in the transcendental loving service of the Lord, or to remain in Kṛṣṇa consciousness, is to be factually liberated from the mode of passion and all material contamination.

Text 28 युञ्जन्नेवं सदात्मानं योगी विगतकल्मषः ।
सुखेन ब्रह्मसंस्पर्शमत्यन्तं सुखमश्नुते ॥२८॥

yuñjann evaṁ sadātmānaṁ, yogī vigata-kalmaṣaḥ
sukhena brahma-saṁsparśam, atyantaṁ sukham aśnute

yuñjan – engaging in *yoga* practice; *evam* – thus; *sadā* – always; *ātmānam* – the self; *yogī* – one who is in touch with the Supreme Self; *vigata* – freed from; *kalmaṣaḥ* – all material contamination; *sukhena* – in transcendental happiness; *brahma-saṁsparśam* – being in constant touch with the Supreme; *atyantam* – the highest; *sukham* – happiness; *aśnute* – attains.

Thus the self-controlled yogī, constantly engaged in yoga practice, becomes free from all material contamination and achieves the highest stage of perfect happiness in transcendental loving service to the Lord.

PURPORT: Self-realization means knowing one's constitutional position in relationship to the Supreme. The individual soul is part and parcel of the Supreme, and his position is to render transcendental service to the Lord. This transcendental contact with the Supreme is called *brahma-saṁsparśa.*

Text 29 सर्वभूतस्थमात्मानं सर्वभूतानि चात्मनि ।
ईक्षते योगयुक्तात्मा सर्वत्र समदर्शनः ॥२९॥

sarva-bhūta-stham ātmānaṁ, sarva-bhūtāni cātmani
īkṣate yoga-yuktātmā, sarvatra sama-darśanaḥ

sarva-bhūta-stham – situated in all beings; *ātmānam* – the Supersoul; *sarva* – all; *bhūtāni* – entities; *ca* – also; *ātmani* – in the Self; *īkṣate* – does see; *yoga-yukta-ātmā* – one who is dovetailed in Kṛṣṇa consciousness; *sarvatra* – everywhere; *sama-darśanaḥ* – seeing equally.

A true yogī observes Me in all beings and also sees every being in Me. Indeed, the self-realized person sees Me, the same Supreme Lord, everywhere.

PURPORT: A Kṛṣṇa conscious *yogī* is the perfect seer because he sees Kṛṣṇa, the Supreme, situated in everyone's heart as Supersoul (Paramātmā). *Īśvaraḥ sarva-bhūtānāṁ hṛd-deśe 'rjuna tiṣṭhati.* The Lord in His Paramātmā feature is situated within both the heart of the dog and that of a *brāhmaṇa*. The perfect *yogī* knows that the Lord is eternally transcendental and is not materially affected by His presence in either a dog or a *brāhmaṇa*. That is the supreme neutrality of the Lord. The individual soul is also situated in the individual heart, but he is not present in all hearts. That is the distinction between the individual soul and the Supersoul. One who is not factually in the practice of *yoga* cannot see so clearly. A Kṛṣṇa conscious person can see Kṛṣṇa in the heart of both the believer and the nonbeliever. In the *smṛti* this is confirmed as follows: *ātatatvāc ca mātṛtvāc ca ātmā hi paramo hariḥ.* The Lord, being the source of all beings, is like the mother and the maintainer. As the mother is neutral to all different kinds of children, the supreme father (or mother) is also. Consequently the Supersoul is always in every living being.

Outwardly, also, every living being is situated in the energy of the Lord. As will be explained in the Seventh Chapter, the Lord has, primarily, two energies – the spiritual (or superior) and the material (or inferior). The living entity, although part of the superior energy, is conditioned by the inferior energy; the living entity is always in the Lord's energy. Every living entity is situated in Him in one way or another.

The *yogī* sees equally because he sees that all living entities, although in different situations according to the results of fruitive work, in all circumstances remain the servants of God. While in the material energy, the living entity serves the material senses; and while in the spiritual energy, he serves the Supreme Lord directly. In either case the living entity is the servant of God. This vision of equality is perfect in a person in Kṛṣṇa consciousness.

Text 30 यो मां पश्यति सर्वत्र सर्वं च मयि पश्यति ।
तस्याहं न प्रणश्यामि स च मे न प्रणश्यति ॥३०॥

yo māṁ paśyati sarvatra, sarvaṁ ca mayi paśyati
tasyāhaṁ na praṇaśyāmi, sa ca me na praṇaśyati

yaḥ – whoever; *mām* – Me; *paśyati* – sees; *sarvatra* – everywhere; *sarvam* – everything; *ca* – and; *mayi* – in Me; *paśyati* – sees; *tasya* – for him; *aham* – I; *na* – not; *praṇaśyāmi* – am lost; *saḥ* – he; *ca* – also; *me* – to Me; *na* – nor; *praṇaśyati* – is lost.

For one who sees Me everywhere and sees everything in Me, I am never lost, nor is he ever lost to Me.

PURPORT: A person in Kṛṣṇa consciousness certainly sees Lord Kṛṣṇa everywhere, and he sees everything in Kṛṣṇa. Such a person may appear to see all separate manifestations of the material nature, but in each and every instance he is conscious of Kṛṣṇa, knowing that everything is a manifestation of Kṛṣṇa's energy. Nothing can exist without Kṛṣṇa, and Kṛṣṇa is the Lord of everything – this is the basic principle of Kṛṣṇa consciousness. Kṛṣṇa consciousness is the development of love of Kṛṣṇa – a position transcendental even to material liberation. At this stage of Kṛṣṇa consciousness, beyond self-realization, the devotee becomes one with Kṛṣṇa in the sense that Kṛṣṇa becomes everything for the devotee and the devotee becomes full in loving Kṛṣṇa. An intimate relationship between the Lord and the devotee then exists. In that stage, the living entity can never be annihilated, nor is the Personality of Godhead ever out of the sight of the devotee. To merge in Kṛṣṇa is spiritual annihilation. A devotee takes no such risk. It is stated in the *Brahma-saṁhitā* (5.38):

premāñjana-cchurita-bhakti-vilocanena
santaḥ sadaiva hṛdayeṣu vilokayanti
yaṁ śyāmasundaram acintya-guṇa-svarūpaṁ
govindam ādi-puruṣaṁ tam ahaṁ bhajāmi

"I worship the primeval Lord, Govinda, who is always seen by the devotee whose eyes are anointed with the pulp of love. He is seen in His eternal form of Śyāmasundara, situated within the heart of the devotee."

At this stage, Lord Kṛṣṇa never disappears from the sight of the devotee, nor does the devotee ever lose sight of the Lord. In the case of a *yogī* who sees the Lord as Paramātmā within the heart, the same applies. Such a *yogī* turns into a pure devotee and cannot bear to live for a moment without seeing the Lord within himself.

Text 31 सर्वभूतस्थितं यो मां भजत्येकत्वमास्थितः ।
सर्वथा वर्तमानोऽपि स योगी मयि वर्तते ॥३१॥

sarva-bhūta-sthitaṁ yo māṁ, bhajaty ekatvam āsthitaḥ
sarvathā vartamāno 'pi, sa yogī mayi vartate

sarva-bhūta-sthitam – situated in everyone's heart; *yaḥ* – he who; *mām* – Me; *bhajati* – serves in devotional service; *ekatvam* – in oneness; *āsthitaḥ* – situated; *sarvathā* – in all respects; *vartamānaḥ* – being situated; *api* – in spite of; *saḥ* – he; *yogī* – the transcendentalist; *mayi* – in Me; *vartate* – remains.

Such a yogī, who engages in the worshipful service of the Supersoul, knowing that I and the Supersoul are one, remains always in Me in all circumstances.

PURPORT: A *yogī* who is practicing meditation on the Supersoul sees within himself the plenary portion of Kṛṣṇa as Viṣṇu – with four hands, holding conchshell, wheel, club and lotus flower. The *yogī* should know that Viṣṇu is not different from Kṛṣṇa. Kṛṣṇa in this form of Supersoul is situated in everyone's heart. Furthermore, there is no difference between the innumerable Supersouls present in the innumerable hearts of living entities. Nor is there a difference between a Kṛṣṇa conscious person always engaged in the transcendental loving service of Kṛṣṇa and a perfect *yogī* engaged in meditation on the Supersoul. The *yogī* in Kṛṣṇa consciousness – even though he may be engaged in various activities while in material existence – remains always situated in Kṛṣṇa. This is confirmed in the *Bhakti-rasāmṛta-sindhu* (1.2.187) of Śrīla Rūpa Gosvāmī: *nikhilāsv apy avasthāsu jīvan-muktaḥ sa ucyate.* A devotee of the Lord, always acting in Kṛṣṇa consciousness, is automatically liberated. In the *Nārada Pañcarātra* this is confirmed in this way:

dik-kālādy-anavacchinne, kṛṣṇe ceto vidhāya ca
tan-mayo bhavati kṣipraṁ, jīvo brahmaṇi yojayet

"By concentrating one's attention on the transcendental form of Kṛṣṇa, who is all-pervading and beyond time and space, one becomes absorbed in thinking of Kṛṣṇa and then attains the happy state of transcendental association with Him."

Kṛṣṇa consciousness is the highest stage of trance in yoga practice. This very understanding that Kṛṣṇa is present as Paramātmā in everyone's heart makes the *yogī* faultless. The *Vedas* (*Gopāla-tāpanī Upaniṣad* 1.21) confirm this inconceivable potency of the Lord as follows: *eko 'pi san bahudhā yo 'vabhāti.* "Although the Lord is one, He is present in innumerable hearts as many." Similarly, in the *smṛti-śāstra* it is said:

eka eva paro viṣṇuḥ, sarva-vyāpī na saṁśayaḥ
aiśvaryād rūpam ekaṁ ca, sūrya-vat bahudheyate

"Viṣṇu is one, and yet He is certainly all-pervading. By His inconceivable potency, in spite of His one form, He is present everywhere, as the sun appears in many places at once."

Text 32 आत्मौपम्येन सर्वत्र समं पश्यति योऽर्जुन ।
सुखं वा यदि वा दुःखं स योगी परमो मतः ॥३२॥

ātmaupamyena sarvatra, samaṁ paśyati yo 'rjuna
sukhaṁ vā yadi vā duḥkhaṁ, sa yogī paramo mataḥ

ātma – with his self; *aupamyena* – by comparison; *sarvatra* – everywhere; *samam* – equally; *paśyati* – sees; *yaḥ* – he who; *arjuna* – O Arjuna; *sukham* – happiness; *vā* – or; *yadi* – if; *vā* – or; *duḥkham* – distress; *saḥ* – such; *yogī* – a transcendentalist; *paramaḥ* – perfect; *mataḥ* – is considered.

He is a perfect yogī who, by comparison to his own self, sees the true equality of all beings, in both their happiness and their distress, O Arjuna!

PURPORT: One who is Kṛṣṇa conscious is a perfect *yogī;* he is aware of everyone's happiness and distress by dint of his own personal experience. The cause of the distress of a living entity is forgetfulness of his relationship with God. And the cause of happiness is knowing Kṛṣṇa to be the supreme enjoyer of all the activities of the human being, the proprietor of all lands and planets, and the sincerest friend of all living entities. The perfect *yogī* knows that the living being who is conditioned by the modes of material nature is subjected to the threefold material miseries due to forgetfulness of his relationship with Kṛṣṇa. And because one in Kṛṣṇa consciousness is happy, he tries to distribute the knowledge of Kṛṣṇa everywhere. Since the perfect *yogī* tries to broadcast the importance of becoming Kṛṣṇa conscious, he is the best philanthropist in the world, and he is the dearest servitor of the Lord. *Na ca tasmān manuṣyeṣu kaścin me priya-kṛttamaḥ* (*Bhagavad-gītā* 18.69). In other words, a devotee of the Lord always looks to the welfare of all living entities, and in this way he is factually the friend of everyone. He is the best *yogī* because he does not desire perfection in *yoga* for his personal benefit, but tries for others also. He does not envy his fellow living entities. Here is a contrast between a pure devotee of the Lord and a *yogī* interested only in his personal elevation. The *yogī* who has withdrawn to a secluded place in order to meditate perfectly may not be as perfect as a devotee who is trying his best to turn every man toward Kṛṣṇa consciousness.

Text 33 अर्जुन उवाच
योऽयं योगस्त्वया प्रोक्तः साम्येन मधुसूदन ।
एतस्याहं न पश्यामि चञ्चलत्वात्स्थितिं स्थिराम् ॥३३॥

arjuna uvāca
yo 'yaṁ yogas tvayā proktaḥ, sāmyena madhusūdana
etasyāhaṁ na paśyāmi, cañcalatvāt sthitiṁ sthirām

arjunaḥ uvāca – Arjuna said; *yaḥ ayam* – this system; *yogaḥ* – mysticism; *tvayā* – by You; *proktaḥ* – described; *sāmyena* – generally; *madhusūdana* – O killer of the demon Madhu; *etasya* – of this; *aham* – I; *na* – do not; *paśyāmi* – see; *cañcalatvāt* – due to being restless; *sthitim* – situation; *sthirām* – stable.

Arjuna said: O Madhusūdana, the system of yoga which You have summarized appears impractical and unendurable to me, for the mind is restless and unsteady.

PURPORT: The system of mysticism described by Lord Kṛṣṇa to Arjuna beginning with the words *śucau deśe* and ending with *yogī paramaḥ* is here being rejected by Arjuna out of a feeling of inability. It is not possible for an ordinary man to leave home and go to a secluded place in the mountains or jungles to practice *yoga* in this Age of Kali. The present age is characterized by a bitter struggle for a life of short duration. People are not serious about self-realization even by simple, practical means, and what to speak of this difficult *yoga* system, which regulates the mode of living, the manner of sitting, selection of place, and detachment of the mind from material engagements. As a practical man, Arjuna thought it was impossible to follow this system of *yoga,* even though he was favorably endowed in many ways. He belonged to the royal family and was highly elevated in terms of numerous qualities; he was a great warrior, he had great longevity, and, above all, he was the most intimate friend of Lord Kṛṣṇa, the Supreme Personality of Godhead. Five thousand years ago, Arjuna had much better facilities than we do now, yet he refused to accept this system of *yoga.* In fact, we do not find any record in history of his practicing it at any time. Therefore this system must be considered generally impossible in this Age of Kali. Of course it may be possible for some very few, rare men, but for the people in general it is an impossible proposal. If this were so five thousand years ago, then what of the present day? Those who are imitating this *yoga* system in different so-called schools and societies, although complacent, are certainly wasting their time. They are completely in ignorance of the desired goal.

Text 34 चञ्चलं हि मनः कृष्ण प्रमाथि बलवद् दृढम् ।
तस्याहं निग्रहं मन्ये वायोरिव सुदुष्करम् ॥३४॥

cañcalaṁ hi manaḥ kṛṣṇa, pramāthi balavad dṛḍham
tasyāhaṁ nigrahaṁ manye, vāyor iva su-duṣkaram

cañcalam – flickering; *hi* – certainly; *manaḥ* – mind; *kṛṣṇa* – O Kṛṣṇa; *pramāthi* – agitating; *bala-vat* – strong; *dṛḍham* – obstinate; *tasya* – its; *aham* – I; *nigraham* – subduing; *manye* – think; *vāyoḥ* – of the wind; *iva* – like; *su-duṣkaram* – difficult.

The mind is restless, turbulent, obstinate and very strong, O Kṛṣṇa, and to subdue it, I think, is more difficult than controlling the wind.

PURPORT: The mind is so strong and obstinate that it sometimes overcomes the intelligence, although the mind is supposed to be subservient to the intelligence. For a man in the practical world who has to fight so many opposing elements, it is certainly very difficult to control the mind. Artificially, one may establish a mental equilibrium toward both friend and enemy, but ultimately no worldly man can do so, for this is more difficult than controlling the raging wind. In the Vedic literature (*Kaṭha Upaniṣad* 1.3.3–4) it is said:

ātmānaṁ rathinaṁ viddhi, śarīraṁ ratham eva ca
buddhiṁ tu sārathiṁ viddhi, manaḥ pragraham eva ca

indriyāṇi hayān āhur, viṣayāṁs teṣu gocarān
ātmendriya-mano-yuktaṁ, bhoktety āhur manīṣiṇaḥ

"The individual is the passenger in the car of the material body, and intelligence is the driver. Mind is the driving instrument, and the senses are the horses. The self is thus the enjoyer or sufferer in the association of the mind and senses. So it is understood by great thinkers." Intelligence is supposed to direct the mind, but the mind is so strong and obstinate that it often overcomes even one's own intelligence, as an acute infection may surpass the efficacy of medicine. Such a strong mind is supposed to be controlled by the practice of *yoga*, but such practice is never practical for a worldly person like Arjuna. And what can we say of modern man? The simile used here is appropriate: one cannot capture the blowing wind. And it is even more difficult to capture the turbulent mind. The easiest way to control the mind, as suggested by Lord Caitanya, is chanting "Hare Kṛṣṇa," the great *mantra* for deliverance, in all humility. The method prescribed is *sa vai manaḥ kṛṣṇa-padāravindayoḥ:* one must engage one's mind fully in Kṛṣṇa. Only then will there remain no other engagements to agitate the mind.

Text 35 श्रीभगवानुवाच
असंशयं महाबाहो मनो दुर्निग्रहं चलम् ।
अभ्यासेन तु कौन्तेय वैराग्येण च गृह्यते ॥३५॥

śrī-bhagavān uvāca
asaṁśayaṁ mahā-bāho, mano durnigrahaṁ calam
abhyāsena tu kaunteya, vairāgyeṇa ca gṛhyate

śrī-bhagavān uvāca – the Personality of Godhead said; *asaṁśayam* – undoubtedly; *mahā-bāho* – O mighty-armed one; *manaḥ* – the mind; *durnigraham* – difficult to curb; *calam* – flickering; *abhyāsena* – by practice; *tu* – but; *kaunteya* – O son of Kuntī; *vairāgyeṇa* – by detachment; *ca* – also; *gṛhyate* – can be so controlled.

Lord Śrī Kṛṣṇa said: O mighty-armed son of Kuntī, it is undoubtedly very difficult to curb the restless mind, but it is possible by suitable practice and by detachment.

PURPORT: The difficulty of controlling the obstinate mind, as expressed by Arjuna, is accepted by the Personality of Godhead. But at the same time He suggests that by practice and detachment it is possible. What is that practice? In the present age no one can observe the strict rules and regulations of placing oneself in a sacred place, focusing the mind on the Supersoul, restraining the senses and mind, observing celibacy, remaining alone, etc. By the practice of Kṛṣṇa consciousness, however, one engages in nine types of devotional service to the Lord. The first and foremost of such devotional engagements is hearing about Kṛṣṇa. This is a very powerful transcendental method for purging the mind of all misgivings. The more one hears about Kṛṣṇa, the more one becomes enlightened and detached from everything that draws the mind away from Kṛṣṇa. By detaching the mind from activities not devoted to the Lord, one can very easily learn *vairāgya. Vairāgya* means detachment from matter and engagement of the mind in spirit. Impersonal spiritual detachment is more difficult than attaching the mind to the activities of Kṛṣṇa. This is practical because by hearing about Kṛṣṇa one becomes automatically attached to the Supreme Spirit. This attachment is called *pareśānubhava,* spiritual satisfaction. It is just like the feeling of satisfaction a hungry man has for every morsel of food he eats. The more one eats while hungry, the more one feels satisfaction and strength. Similarly, by discharge of devotional service one feels transcendental satisfaction as the mind becomes detached from material objectives. It is something like curing a disease by expert treatment and appropriate diet. Hearing of the transcendental activities of Lord Kṛṣṇa is therefore expert treatment for the mad mind, and eating the foodstuff offered to Kṛṣṇa is the appropriate diet for the suffering patient. This treatment is the process of Kṛṣṇa consciousness.

Text 36 असंयतात्मना योगो दुष्प्राप इति मे मतिः ।
वश्यात्मना तु यतता शक्योऽवाप्तुमुपायतः ॥३६॥

asaṁyatātmanā yogo, duṣprāpa iti me matiḥ
vaśyātmanā tu yatatā, śakyo 'vāptum upāyataḥ

asaṁyata – unbridled; *ātmanā* – by the mind; *yogaḥ* – self-realization; *duṣprāpaḥ* – difficult to obtain; *iti* – thus; *me* – My; *matiḥ* – opinion; *vaśya* – controlled; *ātmanā* – by the mind; *tu* – but; *yatatā* – while endeavoring; *śakyaḥ* – practical; *avāptum* – to achieve; *upāyataḥ* – by appropriate means.

For one whose mind is unbridled, self-realization is difficult work. But he whose mind is controlled and who strives by appropriate means is assured of success. That is My opinion.

PURPORT: The Supreme Personality of Godhead declares that one who does not accept the proper treatment to detach the mind from material engagement can hardly achieve success in self-realization. Trying to practice *yoga* while engaging the mind in material enjoyment is like trying to ignite a fire while pouring water on it. *Yoga* practice without mental control is a waste of time. Such a show of *yoga* may be materially lucrative, but it is useless as far as spiritual realization is concerned. Therefore, one must control the mind by engaging it constantly in the transcendental loving service of the Lord. Unless one is engaged in Kṛṣṇa consciousness, he cannot steadily control the mind. A Kṛṣṇa conscious person easily achieves the result of *yoga* practice without separate endeavor, but a *yoga* practitioner cannot achieve success without becoming Kṛṣṇa conscious.

Text 37 अर्जुन उवाच
अयतिः श्रद्धयोपेतो योगाच्चलितमानसः ।
अप्राप्य योगसंसिद्धिं कां गतिं कृष्ण गच्छति ॥३७॥

arjuna uvāca
ayatiḥ śraddhayopeto, yogāc calita-mānasaḥ
aprāpya yoga-saṁsiddhiṁ, kāṁ gatiṁ kṛṣṇa gacchati

arjunaḥ uvāca – Arjuna said; *ayatiḥ* – the unsuccessful transcendentalist; *śraddhayā* – with faith; *upetaḥ* – engaged; *yogāt* – from the mystic link; *calita* – deviated; *mānasaḥ* – who has such a mind; *aprāpya* – failing to attain; *yoga-saṁsiddhim* – the highest perfection in mysticism; *kām* – which; *gatim* – destination; *kṛṣṇa* – O Kṛṣṇa; *gacchati* – achieves.

Arjuna said: O Kṛṣṇa, what is the destination of the unsuccessful transcendentalist, who in the beginning takes to the process of self-realization with faith but who later desists due to worldly-mindedness and thus does not attain perfection in mysticism?

PURPORT: The path of self-realization or mysticism is described in the *Bhagavad-gītā*. The basic principle of self-realization is knowledge that the living entity is not this material body but that he is different from it and that his happiness is in eternal life, bliss and knowledge. These are transcendental, beyond both body and mind. Self-realization is sought by the path of knowledge, by the practice of the eightfold system or by *bhakti-yoga*. In each of these processes one has to realize the constitutional position of the living entity, his relationship with God, and the activities whereby he can reestablish the lost link and achieve the highest perfectional stage of Kṛṣṇa consciousness. Following any of the abovementioned three methods, one is sure to reach the supreme goal sooner or later. This was asserted by the Lord in the Second Chapter: even a little endeavor on the transcendental path offers a great hope for deliverance. Out of these three methods, the path of *bhakti-yoga* is especially suitable for this age because it is the most direct method of God realization. To be doubly assured, Arjuna is asking Lord Kṛṣṇa to confirm His former statement. One may sincerely accept the path of self-realization, but the process of cultivation of knowledge and the practice of the eightfold *yoga* system are generally very difficult for this age. Therefore, despite constant endeavor one may fail, for many reasons. First of all, one may not be sufficiently serious about following the process. To pursue the transcendental path is more or less to declare war on the illusory energy. Consequently, whenever a person tries to escape the clutches of the illusory energy, she tries to defeat the practitioner by various allurements. A conditioned soul is already allured by the modes of material energy, and there is every chance of being allured again, even while performing transcendental disciplines. This is called *yogāc calita-mānasaḥ:* deviation from the transcendental path. Arjuna is inquisitive to know the results of deviation from the path of self-realization.

Text 38 कच्चिन्नोभयविभ्रष्टश्छिन्नाभ्रमिव नश्यति ।
अप्रतिष्ठो महाबाहो विमूढो ब्रह्मणः पथि ॥३८॥

kaccin nobhaya-vibhraṣṭaś, chinnābhram iva naśyati
apratiṣṭho mahā-bāho, vimūḍho brahmaṇaḥ pathi

kaccit – whether; *na* – not; *ubhaya* – both; *vibhraṣṭaḥ* – deviated from; *chinna* – torn; *abhram* – cloud; *iva* – like; *naśyati* – perishes; *apratiṣṭhaḥ* – without any position; *mahā-bāho* – O mighty-armed Kṛṣṇa; *vimūḍhaḥ* – bewildered; *brahmaṇaḥ* – of transcendence; *pathi* – on the path.

O mighty-armed Kṛṣṇa, does not such a man, who is bewildered from the path of transcendence, fall away from both spiritual and material success and perish like a riven cloud, with no position in any sphere?

PURPORT: There are two ways to progress. Those who are materialists have no interest in transcendence; therefore they are more interested in material advancement by economic development, or in promotion to the higher planets by appropriate work. When one takes to the path of transcendence, one has to cease all material activities and sacrifice all forms of so-called material happiness. If the aspiring transcendentalist fails, then he apparently loses both ways; in other words, he can enjoy neither material happiness nor spiritual success. He has no position; he is like a riven cloud. A cloud in the sky sometimes deviates from a small cloud and joins a big one. But if it cannot join a big one, then it is blown away by the wind and becomes a nonentity in the vast sky. The *brahmaṇaḥ pathi* is the path of transcendental realization through knowing oneself to be spiritual in essence, part and parcel of the Supreme Lord, who is manifested as Brahman, Paramātmā and Bhagavān. Lord Śrī Kṛṣṇa is the fullest manifestation of the Supreme Absolute Truth, and therefore one who is surrendered to the Supreme Person is a successful transcendentalist. To reach this goal of life through Brahman and Paramātmā realization takes many, many births (*bahūnāṁ janmanām ante*). Therefore the supermost path of transcendental realization is *bhakti-yoga,* or Kṛṣṇa consciousness, the direct method.

Text 39 एतन्मे संशयं कृष्ण छेत्तुमर्हस्यशेषतः ।
त्वदन्यः संशयस्यास्य छेत्ता न ह्युपपद्यते ॥३९॥

etan me saṁśayaṁ kṛṣṇa, chettum arhasy aśeṣataḥ
tvad-anyaḥ saṁśayasyāsya, chettā na hy upapadyate

etat – this is; *me* – my; *saṁśayam* – doubt; *kṛṣṇa* – O Kṛṣṇa; *chettum* – to dispel; *arhasi* – You are requested; *aśeṣataḥ* – completely; *tvat* – than You; *anyaḥ* – other; *saṁśayasya* – of the doubt; *asya* – this; *chettā* – remover; *na* – never; *hi* – certainly; *upapadyate* – is to be found.

This is my doubt, O Kṛṣṇa, and I ask You to dispel it completely. But for You, no one is to be found who can destroy this doubt.

PURPORT: Kṛṣṇa is the perfect knower of past, present and future. In the beginning of the *Bhagavad-gītā,* the Lord said that all living entities existed individually in the past, they exist now in the present, and they continue to retain individual identity in the future, even after liberation from the material entanglement. So He has already cleared up the question of the future of the individual living entity. Now, Arjuna wants to know of the future of the unsuccessful transcendentalist. No one is equal to or above Kṛṣṇa, and certainly the so-called great sages and philosophers who are at the mercy of material nature cannot equal Him. Therefore the verdict of Kṛṣṇa is the final and complete answer to all doubts, because He knows past, present and future perfectly – but no one knows Him. Kṛṣṇa and Kṛṣṇa conscious devotees alone can know what is what.

Text 40 श्रीभगवानुवाच
पार्थ नैवेह नामुत्र विनाशस्तस्य विद्यते ।
न हि कल्याणकृत्कश्चिद् दुर्गतिं तात गच्छति ॥४०॥

śrī-bhagavān uvāca
pārtha naiveha nāmutra, vināśas tasya vidyate
na hi kalyāṇa-kṛt kaścid, durgatiṁ tāta gacchati

śrī-bhagavān uvāca – the Supreme Personality of Godhead said; *pārtha* – O son of Pṛthā; *na eva* – never is it so; *iha* – in this material world; *na* – never; *amutra* – in the next life; *vināśaḥ* – destruction; *tasya* – his; *vidyate* – exists; *na* – never; *hi* – certainly; *kalyāṇa-kṛt* – one who is engaged in auspicious activities; *kaścit* – anyone; *durgatim* – to degradation; *tāta* – My friend; *gacchati* – goes.

The Supreme Personality of Godhead said: Son of Pṛthā, a transcendentalist engaged in auspicious activities does not meet with destruction either in this world or in the spiritual world; one who does good, My friend, is never overcome by evil.

PURPORT: In the *Śrīmad-Bhāgavatam* (1.5.17) Śrī Nārada Muni instructs Vyāsadeva as follows:

tyaktvā sva-dharmaṁ caraṇāmbujaṁ harer
bhajann apakvo 'tha patet tato yadi
yatra kva vābhadram abhūd amuṣya kiṁ
ko vārtha āpto 'bhajatāṁ sva-dharmataḥ

"If someone gives up all material prospects and takes complete shelter of the Supreme Personality of Godhead, there is no loss or degradation in any way. On the other hand a nondevotee may fully engage in his occupational duties and yet not gain anything." For material prospects there are many activities, both scriptural and customary. A transcendentalist is supposed to give up all material activities for the sake of spiritual advancement in life, Kṛṣṇa consciousness. One may argue that by Kṛṣṇa consciousness one may attain the highest perfection if it is completed, but if one does not attain such a perfectional stage, then he loses both materially and spiritually. It is enjoined in the scriptures that one has to suffer the reaction for not executing prescribed duties; therefore one who fails to discharge transcendental activities properly becomes subjected to these reactions. The *Bhāgavatam* assures the unsuccessful transcendentalist that there need be no worries. Even though he may be subjected to the reaction for not perfectly executing prescribed duties, he is still not a loser, because auspicious Kṛṣṇa consciousness is never forgotten, and one so engaged will continue to be so even if he is lowborn in the next life. On the other hand, one who simply follows strictly the prescribed duties need not necessarily attain auspicious results if he is lacking in Kṛṣṇa consciousness.

The purport may be understood as follows. Humanity may be divided into two sections, namely, the regulated and the nonregulated. Those who are engaged simply in bestial sense gratifications without knowledge of their next life or spiritual salvation belong to the nonregulated section. And those who follow the principles of prescribed duties in the scriptures are classified amongst the regulated section. The nonregulated section, both civilized and noncivilized, educated and noneducated, strong and weak, are full of animal propensities. Their activities are never auspicious, because while enjoying the animal propensities of eating, sleeping, defending and mating, they perpetually remain in material existence, which is always miserable. On the other hand, those who are regulated by scriptural injunctions, and who thus rise gradually to Kṛṣṇa consciousness, certainly progress in life.

Those who are following the path of auspiciousness can be divided into three sections, namely (1) the followers of scriptural rules and regulations who are enjoying material prosperity, (2) those who are trying to find ultimate liberation from material existence, and (3) those who are devotees in Kṛṣṇa consciousness. Those who are following the rules and regulations of the scriptures for material happiness may be further divided into two classes: those who are fruitive workers and those who desire no fruit for sense gratification. Those who are after fruitive results for sense gratification may be elevated to a higher standard of life – even to the higher planets – but still, because they are not free from material existence, they are not following the truly auspicious path. The only auspicious activities are those which lead one to liberation. Any activity which is not aimed at ultimate self-realization or liberation from the material bodily concept of life is not at all auspicious. Activity in Kṛṣṇa consciousness is the only auspicious activity, and anyone who voluntarily accepts all bodily discomforts for the sake of making progress on the path of Kṛṣṇa consciousness can be called a perfect transcendentalist under severe austerity. And because the eightfold *yoga* system is directed toward the ultimate realization of Kṛṣṇa consciousness, such practice is also auspicious, and no one who is trying his best in this matter need fear degradation.

Text 41 प्राप्य पुण्यकृतां लोकानुषित्वा शाश्वतीः समाः ।
शुचीनां श्रीमतां गेहे योगभ्रष्टोऽभिजायते ॥४१॥

prāpya puṇya-kṛtāṁ lokān, uṣitvā śāśvatīḥ samāḥ
śucīnāṁ śrīmatāṁ gehe, yoga-bhraṣṭo 'bhijāyate

prāpya – after achieving; *puṇya-kṛtām* – of those who performed pious activities; *lokān* – planets; *uṣitvā* – after dwelling; *śāśvatīḥ* – many; *samāḥ* – years; *śucīnām* – of the pious; *śrī-matām* – of the prosperous; *gehe* – in the house; *yoga-bhraṣṭaḥ* – one who has fallen from the path of self-realization; *abhijāyate* – takes his birth.

The unsuccessful yogī, after many, many years of enjoyment on the planets of the pious living entities, is born into a family of righteous people, or into a family of rich aristocracy.

PURPORT: The unsuccessful *yogīs* are divided into two classes: one is fallen after very little progress, and one is fallen after long practice of *yoga.* The *yogī* who falls after a short period of practice goes to the higher planets, where pious living entities are allowed to enter. After prolonged life there, one is sent back again to this planet, to take birth in the family of a righteous *brāhmaṇa* Vaiṣṇava or of aristocratic merchants.

The real purpose of *yoga* practice is to achieve the highest perfection of Kṛṣṇa consciousness, as explained in the last verse of this chapter. But those who do not persevere to such an extent and who fail because of material allurements are allowed, by the grace of the Lord, to make full utilization of their material propensities. And after that, they are given opportunities to live prosperous lives in righteous or aristocratic families.

Those who are born in such families may take advantage of the facilities and try to elevate themselves to full Kṛṣṇa consciousness.

Text 42 अथ वा योगिनामेव कुले भवति धीमताम् ।
एतद्धि दुर्लभतरं लोके जन्म यदीदृशम् ॥४२॥

atha vā yoginām eva, kule bhavati dhīmatām
etad dhi durlabha-taraṁ, loke janma yad īdṛśam

atha vā – or; *yoginām* – of learned transcendentalists; *eva* – certainly; *kule* – in the family; *bhavati* – takes birth; *dhī-matām* – of those who are endowed with great wisdom; *etat* – this; *hi* – certainly; *durlabha-taram* – very rare; *loke* – in this world; *janma* – birth; *yat* – that which; *īdṛśam* – like this.

Or [if unsuccessful after long practice of yoga] he takes his birth in a family of transcendentalists who are surely great in wisdom. Certainly, such a birth is rare in this world.

PURPORT: Birth in a family of *yogīs* or transcendentalists – those with great wisdom – is praised herein because the child born in such a family receives a spiritual impetus from the very beginning of his life. It is especially the case in the *ācārya* or *gosvāmī* families. Such families are very learned and devoted by tradition and training, and thus they become spiritual masters. In India there are many such *ācārya* families, but they have now degenerated due to insufficient education and training. By the grace of the Lord, there are still families that foster transcendentalists generation after generation. It is certainly very fortunate to take birth in such families. Fortunately, both our spiritual master, Oṁ Viṣṇupāda Śrī Śrīmad Bhaktisiddhānta Sarasvatī Gosvāmī Mahārāja, and our humble self had the opportunity to take birth in such families, by the grace of the Lord, and both of us were trained in the devotional service of the Lord from the very beginning of our lives. Later on we met by the order of the transcendental system.

Text 43 तत्र तं बुद्धिसंयोगं लभते पौर्वदेहिकम् ।
यतते च ततो भूयः संसिद्धौ कुरुनन्दन ॥४३॥

tatra taṁ buddhi-saṁyogaṁ, labhate paurva-dehikam
yatate ca tato bhūyaḥ, saṁsiddhau kuru-nandana

tatra – thereupon; *tam* – that; *buddhi-saṁyogam* – revival of consciousness; *labhate* – gains; *paurva-dehikam* – from the previous body; *yatate* – he endeavors; *ca* – also; *tataḥ* – thereafter; *bhūyaḥ* – again; *saṁsiddhau* – for perfection; *kuru-nandana* – O son of Kuru.

On taking such a birth, he revives the divine consciousness of his previous life, and he again tries to make further progress in order to achieve complete success, O son of Kuru.

PURPORT: King Bharata, who took his third birth in the family of a good *brāhmaṇa,* is an example of good birth for the revival of previous transcendental consciousness. King Bharata was the emperor of the world, and since his time this planet has been known among the demigods as Bhārata-varṣa. Formerly it was known as Ilāvṛta-varṣa. The emperor, at an early age, retired for spiritual perfection but failed to achieve success. In his next life he took birth in the family of a good *brāhmaṇa* and was known as Jaḍa Bharata because he always remained secluded and did not talk to anyone. And later on he was discovered as the greatest transcendentalist by King Rahūgaṇa. From his life it is understood that transcendental endeavors, or the practice of *yoga,* never go in vain. By the grace of the Lord the transcendentalist gets repeated opportunities for complete perfection in Kṛṣṇa consciousness.

Text 44 पूर्वाभ्यासेन तेनैव ह्रियते ह्यवशोऽपि सः ।
जिज्ञासुरपि योगस्य शब्दब्रह्मातिवर्तते ॥४४॥

pūrvābhyāsena tenaiva, hriyate hy avaśo 'pi saḥ
jijñāsur api yogasya, śabda-brahmātivartate

pūrva – previous; *abhyāsena* – by practice; *tena* – by that; *eva* – certainly; *hriyate* – is attracted; *hi* – surely; *avaśaḥ* – automatically; *api* – also; *saḥ* – he; *jijñāsuḥ* – inquisitive; *api* – even; *yogasya* – about *yoga; śabda-brahma* – ritualistic principles of scriptures; *ativartate* – transcends.

By virtue of the divine consciousness of his previous life, he automatically becomes attracted to the yogic principles – even without seeking them. Such an inquisitive transcendentalist stands always above the ritualistic principles of the scriptures.

PURPORT: Advanced *yogīs* are not very much attracted to the rituals of the scriptures, but they automatically become attracted to the *yoga* principles, which can elevate them to complete Kṛṣṇa consciousness, the highest *yoga* perfection. In the *Śrīmad-Bhāgavatam* (3.33.7), such disregard of Vedic rituals by the advanced transcendentalists is explained as follows:

aho bata śva-paco 'to garīyān, yaj-jihvāgre vartate nāma tubhyam
tepus tapas te juhuvuḥ sasnur āryā, brahmānūcur nāma gṛṇanti ye te

"O my Lord! Persons who chant the holy names of Your Lordship are far, far advanced in spiritual life, even if born in families of dog-eaters. Such chanters have undoubtedly performed all kinds of austerities and sacrifices, bathed in all sacred places, and finished all scriptural studies."

The famous example of this was presented by Lord Caitanya, who accepted Ṭhākura Haridāsa as one of His most important disciples. Although Ṭhākura Haridāsa happened to take his birth in a Muslim family, he was elevated to the post of *nāmācārya* by Lord Caitanya due to his rigidly attended principle of chanting three hundred thousand holy names of the Lord daily: Hare Kṛṣṇa, Hare Kṛṣṇa, Kṛṣṇa Kṛṣṇa, Hare Hare/ Hare Rāma, Hare Rāma, Rāma Rāma, Hare Hare. And because he chanted the holy name of the Lord constantly, it is understood that in his previous life he must have passed through all the ritualistic methods of the *Vedas,* known as *śabda-brahma.* Unless, therefore, one is purified, one cannot take to the principles of Kṛṣṇa consciousness or become engaged in chanting the holy name of the Lord, Hare Kṛṣṇa.

Text 45 प्रयत्नाद्यतमानस्तु योगी संशुद्धकिल्बिषः ।
अनेकजन्मसंसिद्धस्ततो याति परां गतिम् ॥४५॥

prayatnād yatamānas tu, yogī saṁśuddha-kilbiṣaḥ
aneka-janma-saṁsiddhas, tato yāti parāṁ gatim

prayatnāt – by rigid practice; *yatamānaḥ* – endeavoring; *tu* – and; *yogī* – such a transcendentalist; *saṁśuddha* – washed off; *kilbiṣaḥ* – all of whose sins; *aneka* – after many, many; *janma* – births; *saṁsiddhaḥ* – having achieved perfection; *tataḥ* – thereafter; *yāti* – attains; *parām* – the highest; *gatim* – destination.

And when the yogī engages himself with sincere endeavor in making further progress, being washed of all contaminations, then ultimately, achieving perfection after many, many births of practice, he attains the supreme goal.

PURPORT: A person born in a particularly righteous, aristocratic or sacred family becomes conscious of his favorable condition for executing *yoga* practice. With determination, therefore, he begins his unfinished task, and thus he completely cleanses himself of all material contaminations. When he is finally free from all contaminations, he attains the supreme perfection – Kṛṣṇa consciousness. Kṛṣṇa consciousness is the perfect stage of being freed of all contaminations. This is confirmed in the *Bhagavad-gītā* (7.28):

yeṣāṁ tv anta-gataṁ pāpaṁ, janānāṁ puṇya-karmaṇām
te dvandva-moha-nirmuktā, bhajante māṁ dṛḍha-vratāḥ

"After many, many births of executing pious activities, when one is completely freed from all contaminations, and from all illusory dualities, one becomes engaged in the transcendental loving service of the Lord."

Text 46 तपस्विभ्योऽधिको योगी ज्ञानिभ्योऽपि मतोऽधिकः ।
कर्मिभ्यश्चाधिको योगी तस्माद्योगी भवार्जुन ॥४६॥

tapasvibhyo 'dhiko yogī, jñānibhyo 'pi mato 'dhikaḥ
karmibhyaś cādhiko yogī, tasmād yogī bhavārjuna

tapasvibhyaḥ – than the ascetics; *adhikaḥ* – greater; *yogī* – the *yogī; jñānibhyaḥ* – than the wise; *api* – also; *mataḥ* – considered; *adhikaḥ* – greater; *karmibhyaḥ* – than the fruitive workers; *ca* – also; *adhikaḥ* – greater; *yogī* – the *yogī; tasmāt* – therefore; *yogī* – a transcendentalist; *bhava* – just become; *arjuna* – O Arjuna.

A yogī is greater than the ascetic, greater than the empiricist and greater than the fruitive worker. Therefore, O Arjuna, in all circumstances, be a yogī.

PURPORT: When we speak of *yoga* we refer to linking our consciousness with the Supreme Absolute Truth. Such a process is named differently by various practitioners in terms of the particular method adopted. When the linking process is predominantly in fruitive activities it is called *karma-yoga,* when it is predominantly empirical it is called *jñāna-yoga,* and when it is predominantly in a devotional relationship with the Supreme Lord it is called *bhakti-yoga. Bhakti-yoga,* or Kṛṣṇa consciousness, is the ultimate perfection of all *yogas,* as will be explained in the next verse. The Lord has confirmed herein the superiority of *yoga,* but He has not mentioned that it is better than *bhakti-yoga. Bhakti-yoga* is full spiritual knowledge, and therefore nothing can excel it. Asceticism without self-knowledge is imperfect. Empiric knowledge without surrender to the Supreme Lord is also imperfect. And fruitive work without Kṛṣṇa consciousness is a waste of time. Therefore, the most highly praised form of *yoga* performance mentioned here is *bhakti-yoga,* and this is still more clearly explained in the next verse.

Text 47 योगिनामपि सर्वेषां मद्गतेनान्तरात्मना ।
श्रद्धावान् भजते यो मां स मे युक्ततमो मतः ॥४७॥

yoginām api sarveṣāṁ, mad-gatenāntar-ātmanā
śraddhāvān bhajate yo māṁ, sa me yukta-tamo mataḥ

yoginām – of *yogīs; api* – also; *sarveṣām* – all types of; *mat-gatena* – abiding in Me, always thinking of Me; *antaḥ-ātmanā* – within himself; *śraddhā-vān* – in full faith; *bhajate* – renders transcendental loving service; *yaḥ* – one who; *mām* – to Me (the Supreme Lord); *saḥ* – he; *me* – by Me; *yukta-tamaḥ* – the greatest *yogī; mataḥ* – is considered.

And of all yogīs, the one with great faith who always abides in Me, thinks of Me within himself, and renders transcendental loving service to Me – he is the most intimately united with Me in yoga and is the highest of all. That is My opinion.

PURPORT: The word *bhajate* is significant here. *Bhajate* has its root in the verb *bhaj,* which is used when there is need of service. The English word "worship" cannot be used in the same sense as *bhaj.* Worship means to adore, or to show respect and honor to the worthy one. But service with love and faith is especially meant for the Supreme Personality of Godhead. One can avoid worshiping a respectable man or a demigod and may be called discourteous, but one cannot avoid serving the Supreme Lord without being thoroughly condemned. Every living entity is part and parcel of the Supreme Personality of Godhead, and thus every living entity is intended to serve the Supreme Lord by his own constitution. Failing to do this, he falls down. The *Bhāgavatam* (11.5.3) confirms this as follows:

ya eṣāṁ puruṣaṁ sākṣād, ātma-prabhavam īśvaram
na bhajanty avajānanti, sthānād bhraṣṭāḥ patanty adhaḥ

"Anyone who does not render service and neglects his duty unto the primeval Lord, who is the source of all living entities, will certainly fall down from his constitutional position."

In this verse also the word *bhajanti* is used. Therefore, *bhajanti* is applicable to the Supreme Lord only, whereas the word "worship" can be applied to demigods or to any other common living entity. The word *avajānanti,* used in this verse of *Śrīmad-Bhāgavatam,* is also found in the *Bhagavad-gītā. Avajānanti māṁ mūḍhāḥ:* "Only the fools and rascals deride the Supreme Personality of Godhead, Lord Kṛṣṇa." Such fools take it upon themselves to write commentaries on the *Bhagavad-gītā* without an attitude of service to the Lord. Consequently they cannot properly distinguish between the word *bhajanti* and the word "worship."

The culmination of all kinds of *yoga* practices lies in *bhakti yoga.* All other *yogas* are but means to come to the point of *bhakti* in *bhakti-yoga. Yoga* actually means *bhakti-yoga;* all other *yogas* are progressions toward the destination of *bhakti-yoga.* From the beginning of *karma-yoga* to the end of *bhakti-yoga* is a long way to self-realization. *Karma-yoga,* without fruitive results, is the beginning of this path. When *karma-yoga* increases in knowledge and renunciation, the stage is called *jñāna-yoga.* When *jñāna-yoga* increases in meditation on the Supersoul by different physical processes, and the mind is on Him, it is called *aṣṭāṅga-yoga.* And when one surpasses the *aṣṭāṅga-yoga* and comes to the point of the Supreme Personality of Godhead Kṛṣṇa, it is called *bhakti-yoga,* the culmination. Factually, *bhakti-yoga* is the ultimate goal, but to analyze *bhakti-yoga* minutely one has to understand these other *yogas.* The *yogī* who is progressive is therefore on the true path of eternal good fortune. One who sticks to a particular point and does not make further progress is called by that particular name: *karma-yogī, jñāna-yogī* or *dhyāna-yogī, rāja-yogī, haṭha-yogī,* etc. If one is fortunate enough to come to the point of *bhakti-yoga,* it is to be understood that he has surpassed all other *yogas.* Therefore, to become Kṛṣṇa conscious is the highest stage of *yoga,* just as, when we speak of Himālayan, we refer to the world's highest mountains, of which the highest peak, Mount Everest, is considered to be the culmination.

It is by great fortune that one comes to Kṛṣṇa consciousness on the path of *bhakti-yoga* to become well situated according to the Vedic direction. The ideal *yogī* concentrates his attention on Kṛṣṇa, who is called Śyāmasundara, who is as beautifully colored as a cloud, whose lotuslike face is as effulgent as the sun, whose dress is brilliant with jewels, and whose body is flower-garlanded. Illuminating all sides is His gorgeous luster, which is called the *brahma-jyotir.* He incarnates in different forms such as Rāma, Nṛsiṁha, Varāha and Kṛṣṇa, the Supreme Personality of Godhead, and He descends like a human being, as the son of mother Yaśodā, and He is known as Kṛṣṇa, Govinda and Vāsudeva. He is the perfect child, husband, friend and master, and He is full with all opulences and transcendental qualities. If one remains fully conscious of these features of the Lord, he is called the highest *yogī.*

This stage of highest perfection in *yoga* can be attained only by *bhakti-yoga,* as is confirmed in all Vedic literature:

yasya deve parā bhaktir, yathā deve tathā gurau
tasyaite kathitā hy arthāḥ, prakāśante mahātmanaḥ

"Only unto those great souls who have implicit faith in both the Lord and the spiritual master are all the imports of Vedic knowledge automatically revealed." (*Śvetāśvatara Upaniṣad* 6.23)

Bhaktir asya bhajanaṁ tad ihāmutropādhi-nairāsyenāmuṣmin manaḥ-kalpanam, etad eva naiṣkarmyam. "*Bhakti* means devotional service to the Lord which is free from desire for material profit, either in this life or in the next. Devoid of such inclinations, one should fully absorb the mind in the Supreme. That is the purpose of *naiṣkarmya.*" (*Gopāla-tāpanī Upaniṣad* 1.15)

These are some of the means for performance of *bhakti,* or Kṛṣṇa consciousness, the highest perfectional stage of the *yoga* system.

Thus end the Bhaktivedanta Purports to the Sixth Chapter of the Śrīmad Bhagavad-gītā *in the matter of* Dhyāna-yoga.

CHAPTER SEVEN

Knowledge of the Absolute

Text 1 श्रीभगवानुवाच
मय्यासक्तमनाः पार्थ योगं युञ्जन्मदाश्रयः ।
असंशयं समग्रं मां यथा ज्ञास्यसि तच्छृणु ॥ १ ॥

śrī-bhagavān uvāca
mayy āsakta-manāḥ pārtha, yogaṁ yuñjan mad-āśrayaḥ
asaṁśayaṁ samagraṁ māṁ, yathā jñāsyasi tac chṛṇu

śrī-bhagavān uvāca – the Supreme Lord said; *mayi* – to Me; *āsakta-manāḥ* – mind attached; *pārtha* – O son of Pṛthā; *yogam* – self-realization; *yuñjan* – practicing; *mat-āśrayaḥ* – in consciousness of Me (Kṛṣṇa consciousness); *asaṁśayam* – without doubt; *samagram* – completely; *mām* – Me; *yathā* – how; *jñāsyasi* – you can know; *tat* – that; *śṛṇu* – try to hear.

The Supreme Personality of Godhead said: Now hear, O son of Pṛthā, how by practicing yoga in full consciousness of Me, with mind attached to Me, you can know Me in full, free from doubt.

PURPORT: In this Seventh Chapter of *Bhagavad-gītā*, the nature of Kṛṣṇa consciousness is fully described. Kṛṣṇa is full in all opulences, and how He manifests such opulences is described herein. Also, four kinds of fortunate people who become attached to Kṛṣṇa and four kinds of unfortunate people who never take to Kṛṣṇa are described in this chapter.

In the first six chapters of *Bhagavad-gītā,* the living entity has been described as nonmaterial spirit soul capable of elevating himself to self-realization by different types of *yogas.* At the end of the Sixth Chapter, it has been clearly stated that the steady concentration of the mind upon Kṛṣṇa, or in other words Kṛṣṇa consciousness, is the highest form of all *yoga.* By concentrating one's mind upon Kṛṣṇa, one is able to know the Absolute Truth completely, but not otherwise. Impersonal *brahma-jyotir* or localized Paramātmā realization is not perfect knowledge of the Absolute Truth, because it is partial. Full and scientific knowledge is Kṛṣṇa, and everything is revealed to the person in Kṛṣṇa consciousness. In complete Kṛṣṇa consciousness one knows that Kṛṣṇa is ultimate knowledge beyond any doubts. Different types of *yoga* are only stepping-stones on the path of Kṛṣṇa consciousness. One who takes directly to Kṛṣṇa consciousness automatically knows about *brahma-jyotir* and Paramātmā in full. By practice of Kṛṣṇa consciousness *yoga,* one can know everything in full – namely the Absolute Truth, the living entities, the material nature, and their manifestations with paraphernalia.

One should therefore begin *yoga* practice as directed in the last verse of the Sixth Chapter. Concentration of the mind upon Kṛṣṇa the Supreme is made possible by prescribed devotional service in nine different forms, of which *śravaṇam* is the first and most important. The Lord therefore says to Arjuna, *tac chṛṇu,* or "Hear from Me." No one can be a greater authority than Kṛṣṇa, and therefore by hearing from Him one receives the greatest opportunity to become a perfectly Kṛṣṇa conscious person. One has therefore to learn from Kṛṣṇa directly or from a pure devotee of Kṛṣṇa – and not from a nondevotee upstart, puffed up with academic education.

In the *Śrīmad-Bhāgavatam* this process of understanding Kṛṣṇa, the Supreme Personality of Godhead, the Absolute Truth, is described in the Second Chapter of the First Canto as follows:

śṛṇvatāṁ sva-kathāḥ kṛṣṇaḥ, puṇya-śravaṇa-kīrtanaḥ
hṛdy antaḥ-stho hy abhadrāṇi, vidhunoti suhṛt satām

naṣṭa-prāyeṣv abhadreṣu, nityaṁ bhāgavata-sevayā
bhagavaty uttama-śloke, bhaktir bhavati naiṣṭhikī

tadā rajas-tamo-bhāvāḥ, kāma-lobhādayaś ca ye
ceta etair anāviddhaṁ, sthitaṁ sattve prasīdati

evaṁ prasanna-manaso, bhagavad-bhakti-yogataḥ
bhagavat-tattva-vijñānaṁ, mukta-saṅgasya jāyate

bhidyate hṛdaya-granthiś, chidyante sarva-saṁśayāḥ
kṣīyante cāsya karmāṇi, dṛṣṭa evātmanīśvare

"To hear about Kṛṣṇa from Vedic literatures, or to hear from Him directly through the *Bhagavad-gītā,* is itself righteous activity. And for one who hears about Kṛṣṇa, Lord Kṛṣṇa, who is dwelling in everyone's heart, acts as a best-wishing friend and purifies the devotee who constantly engages in hearing of Him. In this way, a devotee naturally develops his dormant transcendental knowledge. As he hears more about Kṛṣṇa from the *Bhāgavatam* and from the devotees, he becomes fixed in the devotional service of the Lord. By development of devotional service one becomes freed from the modes of passion and ignorance, and thus material lusts and avarice are diminished. When these impurities are wiped away, the candidate remains steady in his position of pure goodness, becomes enlivened by devotional service and understands the science of God perfectly. Thus *bhakti-yoga* severs the hard knot of material affection and enables one to come at once to the stage of *asaṁśayaṁ samagram,* understanding of the Supreme Absolute Truth Personality of Godhead." (*Bhāgavatam* 1.2.17–21)

Therefore only by hearing from Kṛṣṇa or from His devotee in Kṛṣṇa consciousness can one understand the science of Kṛṣṇa.

Text 2 ज्ञानं तेऽहं सविज्ञानमिदं वक्ष्याम्यशेषतः ।
यज्ज्ञात्वा नेह भूयोऽन्यज्ज्ञातव्यमवशिष्यते ॥ २ ॥

jñānaṁ te 'haṁ sa-vijñānam, idaṁ vakṣyāmy aśeṣataḥ
yaj jñātvā neha bhūyo 'nyaj, jñātavyam avaśiṣyate

jñānam – phenomenal knowledge; *te* – unto you; *aham* – I; *sa* – with; *vijñānam* – numinous knowledge; *idam* – this; *vakṣyāmi* – shall explain; *aśeṣataḥ* – in full; *yat* – which; *jñātvā* – knowing; *na* – not; *iha* – in this world; *bhūyaḥ* – further; *anyat* – anything more; *jñātavyam* – knowable; *avaśiṣyate* – remains.

I shall now declare unto you in full this knowledge, both phenomenal and numinous. This being known, nothing further shall remain for you to know.

PURPORT: Complete knowledge includes knowledge of the phenomenal world, the spirit behind it, and the source of both of them. This is transcendental knowledge. The Lord wants to explain the above-mentioned system of knowledge because Arjuna is Kṛṣṇa's confidential devotee and friend. In the beginning of the Fourth Chapter this explanation was given by the Lord, and it is again confirmed here: complete knowledge can be achieved only by the devotee of the Lord in disciplic succession directly from the Lord. Therefore one should be intelligent enough to know the source of all knowledge, who is the cause of all causes and the only object for meditation in all types of *yoga* practice. When the cause of all causes becomes known, then everything knowable becomes known, and nothing remains unknown. The *Vedas* (*Muṇḍaka Upaniṣad* 1.1.3) say, *kasminn u bhagavo vijñāte sarvam idaṁ vijñātaṁ bhavatīti.*

Text 3 मनुष्याणां सहस्रेषु कश्चिद्यतति सिद्धये ।
यततामपि सिद्धानां कश्चिन्मां वेत्ति तत्त्वतः ॥३॥

manuṣyāṇāṁ sahasreṣu, kaścid yatati siddhaye
yatatām api siddhānāṁ, kaścin māṁ vetti tattvataḥ

manuṣyāṇām – of men; *sahasreṣu* – out of many thousands; *kaścit* – someone; *yatati* – endeavors; *siddhaye* – for perfection; *yatatām* – of those so endeavoring; *api* – indeed; *siddhānām* – of those who have achieved perfection; *kaścit* – someone; *mām* – Me; *vetti* – does know; *tattvataḥ* – in fact.

Out of many thousands among men, one may endeavor for perfection, and of those who have achieved perfection, hardly one knows Me in truth.

PURPORT: There are various grades of men, and out of many thousands, one may be sufficiently interested in transcendental realization to try to know what is the self, what is the body, and what is the Absolute Truth. Generally mankind is simply engaged in the animal propensities, namely eating, sleeping, defending and mating, and hardly anyone is interested in transcendental knowledge. The first six chapters of the *Gītā* are meant for those who are interested in transcendental knowledge, in understanding the self, the Superself and the process of realization by *jñāna-yoga, dhyāna-yoga* and discrimination of the self from matter. However, Kṛṣṇa can be known only by persons who are in Kṛṣṇa consciousness. Other transcendentalists may achieve impersonal Brahman realization, for this is easier than understanding Kṛṣṇa. Kṛṣṇa is the Supreme Person, but at the same time He is beyond the knowledge of Brahman and Paramātmā. The *yogīs* and *jñānīs* are confused in their attempts to understand Kṛṣṇa. Although the greatest of the impersonalists, Śrīpāda Śaṅkarācārya, has admitted in his *Gītā* commentary that Kṛṣṇa is the Supreme Personality of Godhead, his followers do not accept Kṛṣṇa as such, for it is very difficult to know Kṛṣṇa, even though one has transcendental realization of impersonal Brahman.

Kṛṣṇa is the Supreme Personality of Godhead, the cause of all causes, the primeval Lord Govinda. *Īśvaraḥ paramaḥ kṛṣṇaḥ sac-cid-ānanda-vigrahaḥ/ anādir ādir govindaḥ sarva-kāraṇa-kāraṇam.* It is very difficult for the nondevotees to know Him. Although nondevotees declare that the path of *bhakti,* or devotional service, is very easy, they cannot practice it. If the path of *bhakti* is so easy, as the nondevotee class of men proclaim, then why do they take up the difficult path? Actually the path of *bhakti* is not easy. The so-called path of *bhakti* practiced by unauthorized persons without knowledge of *bhakti* may be easy, but when it is practiced factually according to the rules and regulations, the speculative scholars and philosophers fall away from the path. Śrīla Rūpa Gosvāmī writes in his *Bhakti-rasāmṛta-sindhu* (1.2.101):

śruti-smṛti-purāṇādi-, pañcarātra-vidhiṁ vinā
aikāntikī harer bhaktir, utpātāyaiva kalpate

"Devotional service of the Lord that ignores the authorized Vedic literatures like the *Upaniṣads, Purāṇas* and *Nārada Pañcarātra* is simply an unnecessary disturbance in society."

It is not possible for the Brahman-realized impersonalist or the Paramātmā-realized *yogī* to understand Kṛṣṇa the Supreme Personality of Godhead as the son of mother Yaśodā or the charioteer of Arjuna. Even the great demigods are sometimes confused about Kṛṣṇa (*muhyanti yat sūrayaḥ*). *Māṁ tu veda na kaścana:* "No one knows Me as I am," the Lord says. And if one does know Him, then *sa mahātmā su-durlabhaḥ:* "Such a great soul is very rare." Therefore unless one practices devotional service to the Lord, one cannot know Kṛṣṇa as He is (*tattvataḥ*), even though one is a great scholar or philosopher. Only the pure devotees can know something of the inconceivable transcendental qualities in Kṛṣṇa – His being the cause of all causes, His omnipotence and opulence, and His wealth, fame, strength, beauty, knowledge and renunciation – because Kṛṣṇa is benevolently inclined to His devotees. He is the last word in Brahman realization, and the devotees alone can realize Him as He is. Therefore it is said:

ataḥ śrī-kṛṣṇa-nāmādi, na bhaved grāhyam indriyaiḥ
sevonmukhe hi jihvādau, svayam eva sphuraty adaḥ

"No one can understand Kṛṣṇa as He is by the blunt material senses. But He reveals Himself to the devotees, being pleased with them for their transcendental loving service unto Him." (*Bhakti-rasāmṛta-sindhu* 1.2.234)

Text 4 भूमिरापोऽनलो वायुः खं मनो बुद्धिरेव च ।
अहङ्कार इतीयं मे भिन्ना प्रकृतिरष्टधा ॥ ४ ॥

bhūmir āpo 'nalo vāyuḥ, khaṁ mano buddhir eva ca
ahaṅkāra itīyaṁ me, bhinnā prakṛtir aṣṭadhā

bhūmiḥ – earth; *āpaḥ* – water; *analaḥ* – fire; *vāyuḥ* – air; *kham* – ether; *manaḥ* – mind; *buddhiḥ* – intelligence; *eva* – certainly; *ca* – and; *ahaṅkāraḥ* – false ego; *iti* – thus; *iyam* – all these; *me* – My; *bhinnā* – separated; *prakṛtiḥ* – energies; *aṣṭadhā* – eightfold.

Earth, water, fire, air, ether, mind, intelligence and false ego – all together these eight constitute My separated material energies.

PURPORT: The science of God analyzes the constitutional position of God and His diverse energies. Material nature is called *prakṛti,* or the energy of the Lord in His different *puruṣa* incarnations (expansions) as described in the *Nārada Pañcarātra,* one of the *Sātvata-tantras:*

viṣṇos tu trīṇi rūpāṇi, puruṣākhyāny atho viduḥ
ekaṁ tu mahataḥ sraṣṭṛ, dvitīyaṁ tv aṇḍa-saṁsthitam
tṛtīyaṁ sarva-bhūta-sthaṁ, tāni jñātvā vimucyate

"For material creation, Lord Kṛṣṇa's plenary expansion assumes three Viṣṇus. The first one, Mahā-viṣṇu, creates the total material energy, known as the *mahat-tattva.* The second, Garbhodaka-śāyī Viṣṇu, enters into all the universes to create diversities in each of them. The third, Kṣīrodaka-śāyī Viṣṇu, is diffused as the all-pervading Supersoul in all the universes and is known as Paramātmā. He is present even within the atoms. Anyone who knows these three Viṣṇus can be liberated from material entanglement."

This material world is a temporary manifestation of one of the energies of the Lord. All the activities of the material world are directed by these three Viṣṇu expansions of Lord Kṛṣṇa. These *puruṣas* are called incarnations. Generally one who does not know the science of God (Kṛṣṇa) assumes that this material world is for the enjoyment of the living entities and that the living entities are the *puruṣas* – the causes, controllers and enjoyers of the material energy. According to *Bhagavad-gītā* this atheistic conclusion is false. In the verse under discussion it is stated that Kṛṣṇa is the original cause of the material manifestation. *Śrīmad-Bhāgavatam* also confirms this. The ingredients of the material manifestation are separated energies of the Lord. Even the *brahma-jyotir,* which is the ultimate goal of the impersonalists, is a spiritual energy manifested in the spiritual sky. There are no spiritual diversities in the *brahma-jyotir* as there are in the Vaikuṇṭha-lokas, and the impersonalist accepts this *brahma-jyotir* as the ultimate eternal goal. The Paramātmā manifestation is also a temporary all-pervasive aspect of the Kṣīrodaka-śāyī Viṣṇu. The Paramātmā manifestation is not eternal in the spiritual world. Therefore the factual Absolute Truth is the Supreme Personality of Godhead Kṛṣṇa. He is the complete energetic person, and He possesses different separated and internal energies.

In the material energy, the principal manifestations are eight, as above mentioned. Out of these, the first five manifestations, namely earth, water, fire, air and sky, are called the five gigantic creations or the gross creations, within which the five sense objects are included. They are the manifestations of physical sound, touch, form, taste and smell. Material science comprises these ten items and nothing more. But the other three items, namely mind, intelligence and false ego, are neglected by the materialists. Philosophers who deal with mental activities are also not perfect in knowledge because they do not know the ultimate source, Kṛṣṇa. The false ego – "I am," and "It is mine," which constitute the basic principle of material existence – includes ten sense organs for material activities. Intelligence refers to the total material creation, called the *mahat-tattva.* Therefore from the eight separated energies of the Lord are manifest the twenty-four elements of the material world, which are the subject matter of Sāṅkhya atheistic philosophy; they are originally offshoots from Kṛṣṇa's energies and are separated from Him, but atheistic Sāṅkhya philosophers with a poor fund of knowledge do not know Kṛṣṇa as the cause of all causes. The subject matter for discussion in the Sāṅkhya philosophy is only the manifestation of the external energy of Kṛṣṇa, as it is described in the *Bhagavad-gītā.*

Text 5 अपरेयमितस्त्वन्यां प्रकृतिं विद्धि मे पराम् ।
जीवभूतां महाबाहो ययेदं धार्यते जगत् ॥ ५ ॥

apareyam itas tv anyāṁ, prakṛtiṁ viddhi me parām
jīva-bhūtāṁ mahā-bāho, yayedaṁ dhāryate jagat

aparā – inferior; *iyam* – this; *itaḥ* – besides this; *tu* – but; *anyām* – another; *prakṛtim* – energy; *viddhi* – just try to understand; *me* – My; *parām* – superior; *jīva-bhūtām* – comprising the living entities; *mahā-bāho* – O mighty-armed one; *yayā* – by whom; *idam* – this; *dhāryate* – is utilized or exploited; *jagat* – the material world.

Besides these, O mighty-armed Arjuna, there is another, superior energy of Mine, which comprises the living entities who are exploiting the resources of this material, inferior nature.

PURPORT: Here it is clearly mentioned that living entities belong to the superior nature (or energy) of the Supreme Lord. The inferior energy is matter manifested in different elements, namely earth, water, fire, air, ether, mind, intelligence and false ego. Both forms of material nature, namely gross (earth, etc.) and subtle (mind, etc.), are products of the inferior energy. The living entities, who are exploiting these inferior energies for different purposes, are the superior energy of the Supreme Lord, and it is due to this energy that the entire material world functions. The cosmic manifestation has no power to act unless it is moved by the superior energy, the living entity. Energies are always controlled by the energetic, and therefore the living entities are always controlled by the Lord – they have no independent existence. They are never equally powerful, as unintelligent men think. The distinction between the living entities and the Lord is described in *Śrīmad-Bhāgavatam* (10.87.30) as follows:

aparimitā dhruvās tanu-bhṛto yadi sarva-gatās
tarhi na śāsyateti niyamo dhruva netarathā
ajani ca yan-mayaṁ tad avimucya niyantṛ bhavet
samam anujānatāṁ yad amataṁ mata-duṣṭatayā

"O Supreme Eternal! If the embodied living entities were eternal and all-pervading like You, then they would not be under Your control. But if the living entities are accepted as minute energies of Your Lordship, then they are at once subject to Your supreme control. Therefore real liberation entails surrender by the living entities to Your control, and that surrender will make them happy. In that constitutional position only can they be controllers. Therefore, men with limited knowledge who advocate the monistic theory that God and the living entities are equal in all respects are actually guided by a faulty and polluted opinion."

The Supreme Lord, Kṛṣṇa, is the only controller, and all living entities are controlled by Him. These living entities are His superior energy because the quality of their existence is one and the same with the Supreme, but they are never equal to the Lord in quantity of power. While exploiting the gross and subtle inferior energy (matter), the superior energy (the living entity) forgets his real spiritual mind and intelligence. This forgetfulness is due to the influence of matter upon the living entity. But when the living entity becomes free from the influence of the illusory material energy, he attains the stage called *mukti,* or liberation. The false ego, under the influence of material illusion, thinks, "I am matter, and material acquisitions are mine." His actual position is realized when he is liberated from all material ideas, including the conception of his becoming one in all respects with God. Therefore one may conclude that the *Gītā* confirms the living entity to be only one of the multi-energies of Kṛṣṇa; and when this energy is freed from material contamination, it becomes fully Kṛṣṇa conscious, or liberated.

Text 6 एतद्योनीनि भूतानि सर्वाणीत्युपधारय ।
अहं कृत्स्नस्य जगतः प्रभवः प्रलयस्तथा ॥ ६ ॥

etad-yonīni bhūtāni, sarvāṇīty upadhāraya
ahaṁ kṛtsnasya jagataḥ, prabhavaḥ pralayas tathā

etat – these two natures; *yonīni* – whose source of birth; *bhūtāni* – everything created; *sarvāṇi* – all; *iti* – thus; *upadhāraya* – know; *aham* – I; *kṛtsnasya* – all-inclusive; *jagataḥ* – of the world; *prabhavaḥ* – the source of manifestation; *pralayaḥ* – annihilation; *tathā* – as well as.

All created beings have their source in these two natures. Of all that is material and all that is spiritual in this world, know for certain that I am both the origin and the dissolution.

PURPORT: Everything that exists is a product of matter and spirit. Spirit is the basic field of creation, and matter is created by spirit. Spirit is not created at a certain stage of material development. Rather, this material world is manifested only on the basis of spiritual energy. This material body is developed because spirit is present within matter; a child grows gradually to boyhood and then to manhood because that superior energy, spirit soul, is present. Similarly, the entire cosmic manifestation of the gigantic universe is developed because of the presence of the Supersoul, Viṣṇu. Therefore spirit and matter, which combine to manifest this gigantic universal form, are originally two energies of the Lord, and consequently the Lord is the original cause of everything. A fragmental part and parcel of the Lord, namely the living entity, may be the cause of a big skyscraper, a big factory, or even a big city, but he cannot be the cause of a big universe. The cause of the big universe is the big soul, or the Supersoul. And Kṛṣṇa, the Supreme, is the cause of both the big and small souls. Therefore He is the original cause of all causes. This is confirmed in the *Kaṭha Upaniṣad* (2.2.13). *Nityo nityānāṁ cetanaś cetanānām.*

Text 7 मत्तः परतरं नान्यत्किञ्चिदस्ति धनञ्जय ।
मयि सर्वमिदं प्रोतं सूत्रे मणिगणा इव ॥ ७ ॥

mattaḥ parataraṁ nānyat, kiñcid asti dhanañ-jaya
mayi sarvam idaṁ protaṁ, sūtre maṇi-gaṇā iva

mattaḥ – beyond Me; *para-taram* – superior; *na* – not; *anyat kiñcit* – anything else; *asti* – there is; *dhanam-jaya* – O conqueror of wealth; *mayi* – in Me; *sarvam* – all that be; *idam* – which we see; *protam* – is strung; *sūtre* – on a thread; *maṇi-gaṇāḥ* – pearls; *iva* – like.

O conqueror of wealth, there is no truth superior to Me. Everything rests upon Me, as pearls are strung on a thread.

PURPORT: There is a common controversy over whether the Supreme Absolute Truth is personal or impersonal. As far as *Bhagavad-gītā* is concerned, the Absolute Truth is the Personality of Godhead, Śrī Kṛṣṇa, and this is confirmed in every step. In this verse, in particular, it is stressed that the Absolute Truth is a person. That the Personality of Godhead is the Supreme Absolute Truth is also the affirmation of the *Brahma-saṁhitā: īśvaraḥ paramaḥ kṛṣṇaḥ sac-cid-ānanda-vigrahaḥ;* that is, the Supreme Absolute Truth Personality of Godhead is Lord Kṛṣṇa, who is the primeval Lord, the reservoir of all pleasure, Govinda, and the eternal form of complete bliss and knowledge. These authorities leave no doubt that the Absolute Truth is the Supreme Person, the cause of all causes. The impersonalist, however, argues on the strength of the Vedic version given in the *Śvetāśvatara Upaniṣad* (3.10): *tato yad uttara-taraṁ tad arūpam anāmayam/ ya etad vidur amṛtās te bhavanti athetare duḥkham evāpiyanti.* "In the material world Brahmā, the primeval living entity within the universe, is understood to be the supreme amongst the demigods, human beings and lower animals. But beyond Brahmā there is the Transcendence, who has no material form and is free from all material contaminations. Anyone who can know Him also becomes transcendental, but those who do not know Him suffer the miseries of the material world."

The impersonalist puts more stress on the word *arūpam*. But this *arūpam* is not impersonal. It indicates the transcendental form of eternity, bliss and knowledge as described in the *Brahma-saṁhitā* quoted above. Other verses in the *Śvetāśvatara Upaniṣad* (3.8–9) substantiate this as follows:

vedāham etaṁ puruṣaṁ mahāntam, āditya-varṇaṁ tamasaḥ parastāt
tam eva viditvāti mṛtyum eti, nānyaḥ panthā vidyate 'yanāya

yasmāt paraṁ nāparam asti kiñcid, yasmān nāṇīyo no jyāyo 'sti kiñcit
vṛkṣa iva stabdho divi tiṣṭhaty ekas, tenedaṁ pūrṇaṁ puruṣeṇa sarvam

"I know that Supreme Personality of Godhead who is transcendental to all material conceptions of darkness. Only he who knows Him can transcend the bonds of birth and death. There is no way for liberation other than this knowledge of that Supreme Person.

"There is no truth superior to that Supreme Person, because He is the supermost. He is smaller than the smallest, and He is greater than the greatest. He is situated as a silent tree, and He illumines the transcendental sky, and as a tree spreads its roots, He spreads His extensive energies."

From these verses one concludes that the Supreme Absolute Truth is the Supreme Personality of Godhead, who is all-pervading by His multi-energies, both material and spiritual.

Text 8 रसोऽहमप्सु कौन्तेय प्रभास्मि शशिसूर्ययोः ।
प्रणवः सर्ववेदेषु शब्दः खे पौरुषं नृषु ॥ ८ ॥

raso 'ham apsu kaunteya, prabhāsmi śaśi-sūryayoḥ
praṇavaḥ sarva-vedeṣu, śabdaḥ khe pauruṣaṁ nṛṣu

rasaḥ – taste; *aham* – I; *apsu* – in water; *kaunteya* – O son of Kuntī; *prabhā* – the light; *asmi* – I am; *śaśi-sūryayoḥ* – of the moon and the sun; *praṇavaḥ* – the three letters *a-u-m; sarva* – in all; *vedeṣu* – the *Vedas; śabdaḥ* – sound vibration; *khe* – in the ether; *pauruṣam* – ability; *nṛṣu* – in men.

O son of Kuntī, I am the taste of water, the light of the sun and the moon, the syllable oṁ in the Vedic mantras; I am the sound in ether and ability in man.

PURPORT: This verse explains how the Lord is all-pervasive by His diverse material and spiritual energies. The Supreme Lord can be preliminarily perceived by His different energies, and in this way He is realized impersonally. As the demigod in the sun is a person and is perceived by his all-pervading energy, the sunshine, so the Lord, although in His eternal abode, is perceived by His all-pervading diffusive energies. The taste of water is the active principle of water. No one likes to drink sea water, because the pure taste of water is mixed with salt. Attraction for water depends on the purity of the taste, and this pure taste is one of the energies of the Lord. The impersonalist perceives the presence of the Lord in water by its taste, and the personalist also glorifies the Lord for His kindly supplying tasty water to quench man's thirst. That is the way of perceiving the Supreme. Practically speaking, there is no conflict between personalism and impersonalism. One who knows God knows that the impersonal conception and personal conception are simultaneously present in everything and that there is no contradiction. Therefore Lord Caitanya established His sublime doctrine: *acintya -bheda* and *abheda-tattva* – simultaneous oneness and difference.

The light of the sun and the moon is also originally emanating from the *brahma-jyotir,* which is the impersonal effulgence of the Lord. And *praṇava,* or the *oṁ-kāra* transcendental sound in the beginning of every Vedic hymn, addresses the Supreme Lord. Because the impersonalists are very much afraid of addressing the Supreme Lord Kṛṣṇa by His innumerable names, they prefer to vibrate the transcendental sound *oṁ-kāra.* But they do not realize that *oṁ-kāra* is the sound representation of Kṛṣṇa. The jurisdiction of Kṛṣṇa consciousness extends everywhere, and one who knows Kṛṣṇa consciousness is blessed. Those who do not know Kṛṣṇa are in illusion, and so knowledge of Kṛṣṇa is liberation, and ignorance of Him is bondage.

Text 9 पुण्यो गन्धः पृथिव्यां च तेजश्चास्मि विभावसौ ।
जीवनं सर्वभूतेषु तपश्चास्मि तपस्विषु ॥ ९ ॥

puṇyo gandhaḥ pṛthivyāṁ ca, tejaś cāsmi vibhāvasau
jīvanaṁ sarva-bhūteṣu, tapaś cāsmi tapasviṣu

puṇyaḥ – original; *gandhaḥ* – fragrance; *pṛthivyām* – in the earth; *ca* – also; *tejaḥ* – heat; *ca* – also; *asmi* – I am; *vibhāvasau* – in the fire; *jīvanam* – life; *sarva* – in all; *bhūteṣu* – living entities; *tapaḥ* – penance; *ca* – also; *asmi* – I am; *tapasviṣu* – in those who practice penance.

I am the original fragrance of the earth, and I am the heat in fire. I am the life of all that lives, and I am the penances of all ascetics.

PURPORT: *Puṇya* means that which is not decomposed; *puṇya* is original. Everything in the material world has a certain flavor or fragrance, as the flavor and fragrance in a flower, or in the earth, in water, in fire, in air, etc. The uncontaminated flavor, the original flavor, which permeates everything, is Kṛṣṇa. Similarly, everything has a particular original taste, and this taste can be changed by the mixture of chemicals. So everything original has some smell, some fragrance, and some taste. *Vibhāvasu* means fire. Without fire we cannot run factories, we cannot cook, etc., and that fire is Kṛṣṇa. The heat in the fire is Kṛṣṇa. According to Vedic medicine, indigestion is due to a low temperature in the belly. So even for digestion fire is needed. In Kṛṣṇa consciousness we become aware that earth, water, fire, air and every active principle, all chemicals and all material elements are due to Kṛṣṇa. The duration of man's life is also due to Kṛṣṇa. Therefore by the grace of Kṛṣṇa, man can prolong his life or diminish it. So Kṛṣṇa consciousness is active in every sphere.

Text 10 बीजं मां सर्वभूतानां विद्धि पार्थ सनातनम् ।
बुद्धिर्बुद्धिमतामस्मि तेजस्तेजस्विनामहम् ॥१०॥

bījaṁ māṁ sarva-bhūtānāṁ, viddhi pārtha sanātanam
buddhir buddhimatām asmi, tejas tejasvinām aham

bījam – the seed; *mām* – Me; *sarva-bhūtānām* – of all living entities; *viddhi* – try to understand; *pārtha* – O son of Pṛthā; *sanātanam* – original, eternal; *buddhiḥ* – intelligence; *buddhi-matām* – of the intelligent; *asmi* – I am; *tejaḥ* – prowess; *tejasvinām* – of the powerful; *aham* – I am.

O son of Pṛthā, know that I am the original seed of all existences, the intelligence of the intelligent, and the prowess of all powerful men.

PURPORT: *Bījam* means seed; Kṛṣṇa is the seed of everything. There are various living entities, moving and inert. Birds, beasts, men and many other living creatures are moving living entities; trees and plants, however, are inert – they cannot move, but only stand. Every entity is contained within the scope of 8,400,000 species of life; some of them are moving and some of them are inert. In all cases, however, the seed of their life is Kṛṣṇa. As stated in Vedic literature (*Taittirīya Upaniṣad* 3.1), *yato vā imāni bhūtāni jāyante:* Brahman, or the Supreme Absolute Truth, is that from which everything is emanating. Kṛṣṇa is Para-brahman, the Supreme Spirit. Brahman is impersonal and Para-brahman is personal. Impersonal Brahman is situated in the personal aspect – that is stated in *Bhagavad-gītā* (14.27): *brahmaṇo hi pratiṣṭhāham.* Therefore, originally, Kṛṣṇa is the source of everything. He is the root. As the root of a tree maintains the whole tree, Kṛṣṇa, being the original root of all things, maintains everything in this material manifestation. This is also confirmed in the Vedic literature (*Kaṭha Upaniṣad* 2.2.13):

nityo nityānāṁ cetanaś cetanānām, eko bahūnāṁ yo vidadhāti kāmān

He is the prime eternal among all eternals. He is the supreme living entity of all living entities, and He alone is maintaining all life. One cannot do anything without intelligence, and Kṛṣṇa also says that He is the root of all intelligence. Unless a person is intelligent he cannot understand the Supreme Personality of Godhead, Kṛṣṇa.

Text 11 बलं बलवतां चाहं कामरागविवर्जितम् ।
धर्माविरुद्धो भूतेषु कामोऽस्मि भरतर्षभ ॥११॥

balaṁ balavatāṁ cāhaṁ, kāma-rāga-vivarjitam
dharmāviruddho bhūteṣu, kāmo 'smi bharatarṣabha

balam – strength; *bala-vatām* – of the strong; *ca* – and; *aham* – I am; *kāma* – passion; *rāga* – and attachment; *vivarjitam* – devoid of; *dharma-aviruddhaḥ* – not against religious principles; *bhūteṣu* – in all beings; *kāmaḥ* – sex life; *asmi* – I am; *bharata-ṛṣabha* – O lord of the Bhāratas.

I am the strength of the strong, devoid of passion and desire. I am sex life which is not contrary to religious principles, O lord of the Bhāratas [Arjuna].

PURPORT: The strong man's strength should be applied to protect the weak, not for personal aggression. Similarly, sex life, according to religious principles (*dharma*), should be for the propagation of children, not otherwise. The responsibility of parents is then to make their offspring Kṛṣṇa conscious.

Text 12 ये चैव सात्त्विका भावा राजसास्तामसाश्च ये ।
मत्त एवेति तान् विद्धि न त्वहं तेषु ते मयि ॥१२॥

ye caiva sāttvikā bhāvā, rājasās tāmasāś ca ye
matta eveti tān viddhi, na tv ahaṁ teṣu te mayi

ye – all which; *ca* – and; *eva* – certainly; *sāttvikāḥ* – in goodness; *bhāvāḥ* – states of being; *rājasāḥ* – in the mode of passion; *tāmasāḥ* – in the mode of ignorance; *ca* – also; *ye* – all which; *mattaḥ* – from Me; *eva* – certainly; *iti* – thus; *tān* – those; *viddhi* – try to know; *na* – not; *tu* – but; *aham* – I; *teṣu* – in them; *te* – they; *mayi* – in Me.

Know that all states of being – be they of goodness, passion or ignorance – are manifested by My energy. I am, in one sense, everything, but I am independent. I am not under the modes of material nature, for they, on the contrary, are within Me.

PURPORT: All material activities in the world are being conducted under the three modes of material nature. Although these material modes of nature are emanations from the Supreme Lord, Kṛṣṇa, He is not subject to them. For instance, under the state laws one may be punished, but the king, the lawmaker, is not subject to that law. Similarly, all the modes of material nature – goodness, passion and ignorance – are emanations from the Supreme Lord, Kṛṣṇa, but Kṛṣṇa is not subject to material nature. Therefore He is *nirguṇa,* which means that these *guṇas,* or modes, although issuing from Him, do not affect Him. That is one of the special characteristics of Bhagavān, or the Supreme Personality of Godhead.

Text 13 त्रिभिर्गुणमयैर्भावैरेभिः सर्वमिदं जगत् ।
मोहितं नाभिजानाति मामेभ्यः परमव्ययम् ॥१३॥

tribhir guṇa-mayair bhāvair, ebhiḥ sarvam idaṁ jagat
mohitaṁ nābhijānāti, mām ebhyaḥ param avyayam

tribhiḥ – three; *guṇa-mayaiḥ* – consisting of the *guṇas; bhāvaiḥ* – by the states of being; *ebhiḥ* – all these; *sarvam* – whole; *idam* – this; *jagat* – universe; *mohitam* – deluded; *na abhijānāti* – does not know; *mām* – Me; *ebhyaḥ* – above these; *param* – the Supreme; *avyayam* – inexhaustible.

Deluded by the three modes [goodness, passion and ignorance], the whole world does not know Me, who am above the modes and inexhaustible.

PURPORT: The whole world is enchanted by the three modes of material nature. Those who are bewildered by these three modes cannot understand that transcendental to this material nature is the Supreme Lord, Kṛṣṇa.

Every living entity under the influence of material nature has a particular type of body and a particular type of psychological and biological activities accordingly. There are four classes of men functioning in the three material modes of nature. Those who are purely in the mode of goodness are called *brāhmaṇas.* Those who are purely in the mode of passion are called *kṣatriyas.* Those who are in the modes of both passion and ignorance are called *vaiśyas.* Those who are completely in ignorance are called *śūdras.* And those who are less than that are animals or animal life. However, these designations are not permanent. I may be either a *brāhmaṇa, kṣatriya, vaiśya* or whatever – in any case, this life is temporary. But although life is temporary and we do not know what we are going to be in the next life, by the spell of this illusory energy we consider ourselves in terms of this bodily conception of life, and we thus think that we are American, Indian, Russian, or *brāhmaṇa,* Hindu, Muslim, etc. And if we become entangled with the modes of material nature, then we forget the Supreme Personality of Godhead, who is behind all these modes. So Lord Kṛṣṇa says that living entities deluded by these three modes of nature do not understand that behind the material background is the Supreme Personality of Godhead.

There are many different kinds of living entities – human beings, demigods, animals, etc. – and each and every one of them is under the influence of material nature, and all of them have forgotten the transcendent Personality of Godhead. Those who are in the modes of passion and ignorance, and even those who are in the mode of goodness, cannot go beyond the impersonal Brahman conception of the Absolute Truth. They are bewildered before the Supreme Lord in His personal feature, which possesses all beauty, opulence, knowledge, strength, fame and renunciation. When even those who are in goodness cannot understand, what hope is there for those in passion and ignorance? Kṛṣṇa consciousness is transcendental to all these three modes of material nature, and those who are truly established in Kṛṣṇa consciousness are actually liberated.

Text 14 दैवी ह्येषा गुणमयी मम माया दुरत्यया ।
मामेव ये प्रपद्यन्ते मायामेतां तरन्ति ते ॥१४॥

daivī hy eṣā guṇa-mayī, mama māyā duratyayā
mām eva ye prapadyante, māyām etāṁ taranti te

daivī – transcendental; *hi* – certainly; *eṣā* – this; *guṇa-mayī* – consisting of the three modes of material nature; *mama* – My; *māyā* – energy;

duratyayā – very difficult to overcome; *mām* – unto Me; *eva* – certainly; *ye* – those who; *prapadyante* – surrender; *māyām etām* – this illusory energy; *taranti* – overcome; *te* – they.

This divine energy of Mine, consisting of the three modes of material nature, is difficult to overcome. But those who have surrendered unto Me can easily cross beyond it.

PURPORT: The Supreme Personality of Godhead has innumerable energies, and all these energies are divine. Although the living entities are part of His energies and are therefore divine, due to contact with material energy their original superior power is covered. Being thus covered by material energy, one cannot possibly overcome its influence. As previously stated, both the material and spiritual natures, being emanations from the Supreme Personality of Godhead, are eternal. The living entities belong to the eternal superior nature of the Lord, but due to contamination by the inferior nature, matter, their illusion is also eternal. The conditioned soul is therefore called *nitya-baddha,* or eternally conditioned. No one can trace out the history of his becoming conditioned at a certain date in material history. Consequently, his release from the clutches of material nature is very difficult, even though that material nature is an inferior energy, because material energy is ultimately conducted by the supreme will, which the living entity cannot overcome. Inferior, material nature is defined herein as divine nature due to its divine connection and movement by the divine will. Being conducted by divine will, material nature, although inferior, acts so wonderfully in the construction and destruction of the cosmic manifestation. The *Vedas* confirm this as follows: *māyāṁ tu prakṛtiṁ vidyān māyinaṁ tu maheś-varam.* "Although *māyā* [illusion] is false or temporary, the background of *māyā* is the supreme magician, the Personality of Godhead, who is Maheśvara, the supreme controller." (*Śvetāśvatara Upaniṣad* 4.10)

Another meaning of *guṇa* is rope; it is to be understood that the conditioned soul is tightly tied by the ropes of illusion. A man bound by the hands and feet cannot free himself – he must be helped by a person who is unbound. Because the bound cannot help the bound, the rescuer must be liberated. Therefore, only Lord Kṛṣṇa, or His bona fide representative the spiritual master, can release the conditioned soul. Without such superior help, one cannot be freed from the bondage of material nature. Devotional service, or Kṛṣṇa consciousness, can help one gain such release. Kṛṣṇa, being the Lord of the illusory energy, can order this insurmountable energy to release the conditioned soul. He orders this release out of His causeless mercy on the surrendered soul and out of His paternal affection for the living entity, who is originally a beloved son of the Lord. Therefore surrender unto the lotus feet of the Lord is the only means to get free from the clutches of the stringent material nature.

The words *mām eva* are also significant. *Mām* means unto Kṛṣṇa (Viṣṇu) only, and not Brahmā or Śiva. Although Brahmā and Śiva are greatly elevated and are almost on the level of Viṣṇu, it is not possible for such incarnations of *rajo-guṇa* (passion) and *tamo-guṇa* (ignorance) to release the conditioned soul from the clutches of *māyā.* In other words, both Brahmā and Śiva are also under the influence of *māyā.* Only Viṣṇu is the master of *māyā;* therefore He alone can give release to the conditioned soul. The *Vedas* (*Śvetāśvatara Upaniṣad* 3.8) confirm this in the phrase *tam eva viditvā,* or "Freedom is possible only by understanding Kṛṣṇa." Even Lord Śiva affirms that liberation can be achieved only by the mercy of Viṣṇu. Lord Śiva says, *mukti-pradātā sarveṣāṁ viṣṇur eva na saṁśayaḥ:* "There is no doubt that Viṣṇu is the deliverer of liberation for everyone."

Text 15 न मां दुष्कृतिनो मूढाः प्रपद्यन्ते नराधमाः ।
माययापहृतज्ञाना आसुरं भावमाश्रिताः ॥१५॥

na māṁ duṣkṛtino mūḍhāḥ, prapadyante narādhamāḥ
māyayāpahṛta-jñānā, āsuraṁ bhāvam āśritāḥ

na – not; *mām* – unto Me; *duṣkṛtinaḥ* – miscreants; *mūḍhāḥ* – foolish; *prapadyante* – surrender; *nara-adhamāḥ* – lowest among mankind; *māyayā* – by the illusory energy; *apahṛta* – stolen; *jñānāḥ* – whose knowledge; *āsuram* – demonic; *bhāvam* – nature; *āśritāḥ* – accepting.

Those miscreants who are grossly foolish, who are lowest among mankind, whose knowledge is stolen by illusion, and who partake of the atheistic nature of demons do not surrender unto Me.

PURPORT: It is said in *Bhagavad-gītā* that simply by surrendering oneself unto the lotus feet of the Supreme Personality Kṛṣṇa one can surmount the stringent laws of material nature. At this point a question arises: How is it that educated philosophers, scientists, businessmen, administrators and all the leaders of ordinary men do not surrender to the lotus feet of Śrī Kṛṣṇa, the all-powerful Personality of Godhead? *Mukti,* or liberation from the laws of material nature, is sought by the leaders of mankind in different ways and with great plans and perseverance for a great many years and births. But if that liberation is possible by simply surrendering unto the lotus feet of the Supreme Personality of Godhead, then why don't these intelligent and hard-working leaders adopt this simple method?

The *Gītā* answers this question very frankly. Those really learned leaders of society like Brahmā, Śiva, Kapila, the Kumāras, Manu, Vyāsa, Devala, Asita, Janaka, Prahlāda, Bali, and later on Madhvācārya, Rāmānujācārya, Śrī Caitanya and many others – who are faithful philosophers, politicians, educators, scientists, etc. – surrender to the lotus feet of the Supreme Person, the all-powerful authority. Those who are not actually philosophers, scientists, educators, administrators, etc., but who pose themselves as such for material gain, do not accept the plan or path of the Supreme Lord. They have no idea of God; they simply manufacture their own worldly plans and consequently complicate the problems of material existence in their vain attempts to solve them. Because material energy (nature) is so powerful, it can resist the unauthorized plans of the atheists and baffle the knowledge of "planning commissions."

The atheistic planmakers are described herein by the word *duṣkṛtinaḥ,* or "miscreants." *Kṛtī* means one who has performed meritorious work. The atheist planmaker is sometimes very intelligent and meritorious also, because any gigantic plan, good or bad, must take intelligence to execute. But because the atheist's brain is improperly utilized in opposing the plan of the Supreme Lord, the atheistic planmaker is called *duṣkṛtī,* which indicates that his intelligence and efforts are misdirected.

In the *Gītā* it is clearly mentioned that material energy works fully under the direction of the Supreme Lord. It has no independent authority. It works as the shadow moves, in accordance with the movements of the object. But still material energy is very powerful, and the atheist, due to his godless temperament, cannot know how it works; nor can he know the plan of the Supreme Lord. Under illusion and the modes of passion and ignorance, all his plans are baffled, as in the case of Hiraṇyakaśipu and Rāvaṇa, whose plans were smashed to dust although they were both materially learned as scientists, philosophers, administrators and educators. These *duṣkṛtinas,* or miscreants, are of four different patterns, as outlined below.

(1) The *mūḍhas* are those who are grossly foolish, like hardworking beasts of burden. They want to enjoy the fruits of their labor by themselves, and so do not want to part with them for the Supreme. The typical example of the beast of burden is the ass. This humble beast is made to work very hard by his master. The ass does not really know for whom he

works so hard day and night. He remains satisfied by filling his stomach with a bundle of grass, sleeping for a while under fear of being beaten by his master, and satisfying his sex appetite at the risk of being repeatedly kicked by the opposite party. The ass sings poetry and philosophy sometimes, but this braying sound only disturbs others. This is the position of the foolish fruitive worker who does not know for whom he should work. He does not know that *karma* (action) is meant for *yajña* (sacrifice).

Most often, those who work very hard day and night to clear the burden of self-created duties say that they have no time to hear of the immortality of the living being. To such *mūḍhas,* material gains, which are destructible, are life's all in all – despite the fact that the *mūḍhas* enjoy only a very small fraction of the fruit of labor. Sometimes they spend sleepless days and nights for fruitive gain, and although they may have ulcers or indigestion, they are satisfied with practically no food; they are simply absorbed in working hard day and night for the benefit of illusory masters. Ignorant of their real master, the foolish workers waste their valuable time serving mammon. Unfortunately, they never surrender to the supreme master of all masters, nor do they take time to hear of Him from the proper sources. The swine who eat the night soil do not care to accept sweetmeats made of sugar and ghee. Similarly, the foolish worker will untiringly continue to hear of the sense-enjoyable tidings of the flickering mundane world, but will have very little time to hear about the eternal living force that moves the material world.

(2) Another class of *duṣkṛtī,* or miscreant, is called the *narādhama,* or the lowest of mankind. *Nara* means human being, and *adhama* means the lowest. Out of the 8,400,000 different species of living beings, there are 400,000 human species. Out of these there are numerous lower forms of human life that are mostly uncivilized. The civilized human beings are those who have regulative principles of social, political and religious life. Those who are socially and politically developed but who have no religious principles must be considered *narādhamas.* Nor is religion without God religion, because the purpose of following religious principles is to know the Supreme Truth and man's relation with Him. In the *Gītā* the Personality of Godhead clearly states that there is no authority above Him and that He is the Supreme Truth. The civilized form of human life is meant for man's *reviving the lost consciousness* of his eternal relation with the Supreme Truth, the Personality of Godhead Śrī Kṛṣṇa, who is all-powerful. Whoever loses this chance is classified as a *narādhama.* We get information from revealed scriptures that when the baby is in the mother's womb (an extremely uncomfortable situation) he prays to God

for deliverance and promises to worship Him alone as soon as he gets out. To pray to God when he is in difficulty is a natural instinct in every living being because he is eternally related with God. But after his deliverance, the child forgets the difficulties of birth and forgets his deliverer also, being influenced by *māyā,* the illusory energy.

It is the duty of the guardians of children to revive the divine consciousness dormant in them. The ten processes of reformatory ceremonies, as enjoined in the *Manu-smṛti,* which is the guide to religious principles, are meant for reviving God consciousness in the system of *varṇāśrama.* However, no process is strictly followed now in any part of the world, and therefore 99.9 percent of the population is *narādhama.*

When the whole population becomes *narādhama,* naturally all their so-called education is made null and void by the all-powerful energy of physical nature. According to the standard of the *Gītā,* a learned man is he who sees on equal terms the learned *brāhmaṇa,* the dog, the cow, the elephant and the dog-eater. That is the vision of a true devotee. Śrī Nityānanda Prabhu, who is the incarnation of Godhead as divine master, delivered the typical *narādhamas,* the brothers Jagāi and Mādhāi, and showed how the mercy of a real devotee is bestowed upon the lowest of mankind. So the *narādhama* who is condemned by the Personality of Godhead can again revive his spiritual consciousness only by the mercy of a devotee.

Śrī Caitanya Mahāprabhu, in propagating the *bhāgavata-dharma,* or activities of the devotees, has recommended that people submissively hear the message of the Personality of Godhead. The essence of this message is *Bhagavad-gītā.* The lowest amongst human beings can be delivered by this submissive hearing process only, but unfortunately they even refuse to give an aural reception to these messages, and what to speak of surrendering to the will of the Supreme Lord? *Narādhamas,* or the lowest of mankind, willfully neglect the prime duty of the human being.

(3) The next class of *duṣkṛtī* is called *māyayāpahṛta-jñānāḥ,* or those persons whose erudite knowledge has been nullified by the influence of illusory material energy. They are mostly very learned fellows – great philosophers, poets, literati, scientists, etc. – but the illusory energy misguides them, and therefore they disobey the Supreme Lord.

There are a great number of *māyayāpahṛta-jñānāḥ* at the present moment, even amongst the scholars of the *Bhagavad-gītā.* In the *Gītā,* in plain and simple language, it is stated that Śrī Kṛṣṇa is the Supreme Personality of Godhead. There is none equal to or greater than Him. He is mentioned as the father of Brahmā, the original father of all human beings. In fact, Śrī Kṛṣṇa is said to be not only the father of Brahmā but also the father of all species of life. He is the root of the impersonal Brahman and Paramātmā; the Supersoul in every entity is His plenary portion. He is the fountainhead of everything, and everyone is advised to surrender unto His lotus feet. Despite all these clear statements, the *māyayāpahṛta-jñānāḥ* deride the personality of the Supreme Lord and consider Him merely another human being. They do not know that the blessed form of human life is designed after the eternal and transcendental feature of the Supreme Lord.

All the unauthorized interpretations of the *Gītā* by the class of *māyayāpahṛta-jñānāḥ,* outside the purview of the *paramparā* system, are so many stumbling blocks on the path of spiritual understanding. The deluded interpreters do not surrender unto the lotus feet of Śrī Kṛṣṇa, nor do they teach others to follow this principle.

(4) The last class of *duṣkṛtī* is called *āsuraṁ bhāvam āśritāḥ,* or those of demonic principles. This class is openly atheistic. Some of them argue that the Supreme Lord can never descend upon this material world, but they are unable to give any tangible reasons as to why not. There are others who make Him subordinate to the impersonal feature, although the opposite is declared in the *Gītā.* Envious of the Supreme Personality of Godhead, the atheist will present a number of illicit incarnations manufactured in the factory of his brain. Such persons, whose very principle of life is to decry the Personality of Godhead, cannot surrender unto the lotus feet of Śrī Kṛṣṇa.

Śrī Yāmunācārya Ālabandaru of South India said, "O my Lord! You are unknowable to persons involved with atheistic principles, despite Your uncommon qualities, features and activities, despite Your personality's being confirmed by all the revealed scriptures in the quality of goodness, and despite Your being acknowledged by the famous authorities renowned for their depth of knowledge in the transcendental science and situated in the godly qualities."

Therefore, (1) grossly foolish persons, (2) the lowest of mankind, (3) the deluded speculators, and (4) the professed atheists, as above mentioned, never surrender unto the lotus feet of the Personality of Godhead in spite of all scriptural and authoritative advice.

Text 16 चतुर्विधा भजन्ते मां जनाः सुकृतिनोऽर्जुन ।
आर्तो जिज्ञासुरर्थार्थी ज्ञानी च भरतर्षभ ॥१६॥

catur-vidhā bhajante māṁ, janāḥ su-kṛtino 'rjuna
ārto jijñāsur arthārthī, jñānī ca bharatarṣabha

catuḥ-vidhāḥ – four kinds of; *bhajante* – render services; *mām* – unto Me; *janāḥ* – persons; *su-kṛtinaḥ* – those who are pious; *arjuna* – O Arjuna; *ārtaḥ* – the distressed; *jijñāsuḥ* – the inquisitive; *artha-arthī* – one who desires material gain; *jñānī* – one who knows things as they are; *ca* – also; *bharata-ṛṣabha* – O great one amongst the descendants of Bharata.

O best among the Bhāratas, four kinds of pious men begin to render devotional service unto Me – the distressed, the desirer of wealth, the inquisitive, and he who is searching for knowledge of the Absolute.

PURPORT: Unlike the miscreants, these are adherents of the regulative principles of the scriptures, and they are called *sukṛtinaḥ,* or those who obey the rules and regulations of scriptures, the moral and social laws, and are, more or less, devoted to the Supreme Lord. Out of these there are four classes of men – those who are sometimes distressed, those who are in need of money, those who are sometimes inquisitive, and those who are sometimes searching after knowledge of the Absolute Truth. These persons come to the Supreme Lord for devotional service under different conditions. These are not pure devotees, because they have some aspiration to fulfill in exchange for devotional service. Pure devotional service is without aspiration and without desire for material profit. The *Bhakti-rasāmṛta-sindhu* (1.1.11) defines pure devotion thus:

anyābhilāṣitā-śūnyaṁ, jñāna-karmādy-anāvṛtam
ānukūlyena kṛṣṇānu-, śīlanaṁ bhaktir uttamā

"One should render transcendental loving service to the Supreme Lord Kṛṣṇa favorably and without desire for material profit or gain through fruitive activities or philosophical speculation. That is called pure devotional service."

When these four kinds of persons come to the Supreme Lord for devotional service and are completely purified by the association of a pure devotee, they also become pure devotees. As far as the miscreants are concerned, for them devotional service is very difficult because their lives are selfish, irregular and without spiritual goals. But even some of them, by chance, when they come in contact with a pure devotee, also become pure devotees.

Those who are always busy with fruitive activities come to the Lord in material distress and at that time associate with pure devotees and become, in their distress, devotees of the Lord. Those who are simply frustrated also come sometimes to associate with the pure devotees and become inquisitive to know about God. Similarly, when the dry philosophers are frustrated in every field of knowledge, they sometimes want to learn of God, and they come to the Supreme Lord to render devotional service and thus transcend knowledge of the impersonal Brahman and the localized Paramātmā and come to the personal conception of Godhead by the grace of the Supreme Lord or His pure devotee. On the whole, when the distressed, the inquisitive, the seekers of knowledge, and those who are in need of money are free from all material desires, and when they fully understand that material remuneration has nothing to do with spiritual improvement, they become pure devotees. As long as such a purified stage is not attained, devotees in transcendental service to the Lord are tainted with fruitive activities, the search for mundane knowledge, etc. So one has to transcend all this before one can come to the stage of pure devotional service.

Text 17 तेषां ज्ञानी नित्ययुक्त एकभक्तिर्विशिष्यते ।
प्रियो हि ज्ञानिनोऽत्यर्थमहं स च मम प्रियः ॥१७॥

teṣāṁ jñānī nitya-yukta, eka-bhaktir viśiṣyate
priyo hi jñānino 'tyartham, ahaṁ sa ca mama priyaḥ

teṣām – out of them; *jñānī* – one in full knowledge; *nitya-yuktaḥ* – always engaged; *eka* – only; *bhaktiḥ* – in devotional service; *viśiṣyate* – is special; *priyaḥ* – very dear; *hi* – certainly; *jñāninaḥ* – to the person in knowledge; *atyartham* – highly; *aham* – I am; *saḥ* – he; *ca* – also; *mama* – to Me; *priyaḥ* – dear.

Of these, the one who is in full knowledge and who is always engaged in pure devotional service is the best. For I am very dear to him, and he is dear to Me.

PURPORT: Free from all contaminations of material desires, the distressed, the inquisitive, the penniless and the seeker after supreme knowledge can all become pure devotees. But out of them, he who is in knowledge of the Absolute Truth and free from all material desires becomes a really pure devotee of the Lord. And of the four orders, the devotee who is in full knowledge and is at the same time engaged in devotional service is, the Lord says, the best. By searching after knowledge one realizes that his self is different from his material body, and when further advanced he comes to the knowledge of impersonal Brahman and Paramātmā. When one is fully purified, he realizes that his constitutional position is to be the eternal servant of God. So by association with pure devotees the inquisitive, the distressed, the seeker after material amelioration and the man in knowledge all become themselves pure. But in the preparatory stage, the man who is in full knowledge of the Supreme Lord and is at the same time executing devotional service is very dear to the Lord. He who is situated in pure knowledge of the transcendence of the Supreme Personality of God is so protected in devotional service that material contamination cannot touch him.

Text 18 उदाराः सर्व एवैते ज्ञानी त्वात्मैव मे मतम् ।
आस्थितः स हि युक्तात्मा मामेवानुत्तमां गतिम् ॥१८॥

udārāḥ sarva evaite, jñānī tv ātmaiva me matam
āsthitaḥ sa hi yuktātmā, mām evānuttamāṁ gatim

udārāḥ – magnanimous; *sarve* – all; *eva* – certainly; *ete* – these; *jñānī* – one who is in knowledge; *tu* – but; *ātmā eva* – just like Myself; *me* – My; *matam* – opinion; *āsthitaḥ* – situated; *saḥ* – he; *hi* – certainly; *yukta-ātmā* – engaged in devotional service; *mām* – in Me; *eva* – certainly; *anuttamām* – the highest; *gatim* – destination.

All these devotees are undoubtedly magnanimous souls, but he who is situated in knowledge of Me I consider to be just like My own self. Being engaged in My transcendental service, he is sure to attain Me, the highest and most perfect goal.

PURPORT: It is not that devotees who are less complete in knowledge are not dear to the Lord. The Lord says that all are magnanimous because anyone who comes to the Lord for any purpose is called a *mahātmā,* or great soul. The devotees who want some benefit out of devotional service are accepted by the Lord because there is an exchange of affection. Out of affection they ask the Lord for some material benefit, and when they get it they become so satisfied that they also advance in devotional service. But the devotee in full knowledge is considered to be very dear to the Lord because his only purpose is to serve the Supreme Lord with love and devotion. Such a devotee cannot live a second without contacting or serving the Supreme Lord. Similarly, the Supreme Lord is very fond of His devotee and cannot be separated from him.

In the *Śrīmad-Bhāgavatam* (9.4.68), the Lord says:

sādhavo hṛdayaṁ mahyaṁ, sādhūnāṁ hṛdayaṁ tv aham
mad-anyat te na jānanti, nāhaṁ tebhyo manāg api

"The devotees are always in My heart, and I am always in the hearts of the devotees. The devotee does not know anything beyond Me, and I also cannot forget the devotee. There is a very intimate relationship between Me and the pure devotees. Pure devotees in full knowledge are never out of spiritual touch, and therefore they are very much dear to Me."

Text 19 बहूनां जन्मनामन्ते ज्ञानवान्मां प्रपद्यते ।
वासुदेवः सर्वमिति स महात्मा सुदुर्लभः ॥१९॥

bahūnāṁ janmanām ante, jñānavān māṁ prapadyate
vāsudevaḥ sarvam iti, sa mahātmā su-durlabhaḥ

bahūnām – many; *janmanām* – repeated births and deaths; *ante* – after; *jñāna-vān* – one who is in full knowledge; *mām* – unto Me; *prapadyate* – surrenders; *vāsudevaḥ* – the Personality of Godhead, Kṛṣṇa; *sarvam* – everything; *iti* – thus; *saḥ* – that; *mahā-ātmā* – great soul; *su-durlabhaḥ* – very rare to see.

After many births and deaths, he who is actually in knowledge surrenders unto Me, knowing Me to be the cause of all causes and all that is. Such a great soul is very rare.

PURPORT: The living entity, while executing devotional service or transcendental rituals after many, many births, may actually become situated in transcendental pure knowledge that the Supreme Personality of Godhead is the ultimate goal of spiritual realization. In the beginning of spiritual realization, while one is trying to give up one's attachment to materialism, there is some leaning towards impersonalism, but when one is further advanced he can understand that there are activities in the spiritual life and that these activities constitute devotional service. Realizing this, he becomes attached to the Supreme Personality of Godhead and surrenders to Him. At such a time one can understand that Lord Śrī Kṛṣṇa's mercy is everything, that He is the cause of all causes, and that this material manifestation is not independent from Him. He realizes the material world to be a perverted reflection of spiritual variegatedness and realizes that in everything there is a relationship with the Supreme Lord Kṛṣṇa. Thus he thinks of everything in relation to Vāsudeva, or Śrī Kṛṣṇa. Such a universal vision of Vāsudeva precipitates one's full surrender to the Supreme Lord Śrī Kṛṣṇa as the highest goal. Such surrendered great souls are very rare.

This verse is very nicely explained in the Third Chapter (verses 14 and 15) of the *Śvetāśvatara Upaniṣad:*

sahasra-śīrṣā puruṣaḥ, sahasrākṣaḥ sahasra-pāt
sa bhūmiṁ viśvato vṛtvā-, tyātiṣṭhad daśāṅgulam

puruṣa evedaṁ sarvaṁ, yad bhūtaṁ yac ca bhavyam
utāmṛtatvasyeśāno, yad annenātirohati

"Lord Viṣṇu has thousands of heads, thousands of eyes and thousands of feet. Entirely encompassing the whole universe, He still extends beyond it by ten fingers' breadth. He is in fact this entire universe. He is all that was and all that will be. He is the Lord of immortality and of all that is nourished by food." In the *Chāndogya Upaniṣad* (5.1.15) it is said, *na vai vāco na cakṣūṁṣi na śrotrāṇi na manāṁsīty ācakṣate prāṇa iti evācakṣate prāṇo hy evaitāni sarvāṇi bhavanti:* "In the body of a living being neither the power to speak, nor the power to see, nor the power to hear, nor the power to think is the prime factor; it is life air, which is the center of all activities." Similarly Lord Vāsudeva, or the Personality of Godhead, Lord Śrī Kṛṣṇa, is the prime entity in everything. And because Vāsudeva is all-pervading and everything is Vāsudeva, the devotee surrenders in full knowledge (cf. *Bhagavad-gītā* 7.17 and 11.40).

Text 20 कामैस्तैस्तैर्हृतज्ञानाः प्रपद्यन्तेऽन्यदेवताः ।
तं तं नियममास्थाय प्रकृत्या नियताः स्वया ॥२०॥

kāmais tais tair hṛta-jñānāḥ, prapadyante 'nya-devatāḥ
taṁ taṁ niyamam āsthāya, prakṛtyā niyatāḥ svayā

kāmaiḥ – by desires; *taiḥ taiḥ* – various; *hṛta* – deprived of; *jñānāḥ* – knowledge; *prapadyante* – surrender; *anya* – to other; *devatāḥ* – demigods; *tam tam* – corresponding; *niyamam* – regulations; *āsthāya* – following; *prakṛtyā* – by nature; *niyatāḥ* – controlled; *svayā* – by their own.

Those whose intelligence has been stolen by material desires surrender unto demigods and follow the particular rules and regulations of worship according to their own natures.

PURPORT: Those who are freed from all material contaminations surrender unto the Supreme Lord and engage in His devotional service. As long as the material contamination is not completely washed off, they are by nature nondevotees. But even those who have material desires and who resort to the Supreme Lord are not so much attracted by external nature; because of approaching the right goal, they soon become free from all material lust. In the *Śrīmad-Bhāgavatam* it is recommended that whether one is a pure devotee and is free from all material desires, or is full of material desires, or desires liberation from material contamination, he should in all cases surrender to Vāsudeva and worship Him. As stated in the *Bhāgavatam* (2.3.10):

akāmaḥ sarva-kāmo vā, mokṣa-kāma udāra-dhīḥ
tīvreṇa bhakti-yogena, yajeta puruṣaṁ param

Less intelligent people who have lost their spiritual sense take shelter of demigods for immediate fulfillment of material desires. Generally, such people do not go to the Supreme Personality of Godhead, because they are in the lower modes of nature (ignorance and passion) and therefore worship various demigods. Following the rules and regulations of worship, they are satisfied. The worshipers of demigods are motivated by small desires and do not know how to reach the supreme goal, but a devotee of the Supreme Lord is not misguided. Because in Vedic literature there are recommendations for worshiping different gods for different purposes (e.g., a diseased man is recommended to worship the sun), those who are not devotees of the Lord think that for certain purposes demigods are better than the Supreme Lord. But a pure devotee knows that the Supreme Lord Kṛṣṇa is the master of all. In the *Caitanya-caritāmṛta* (*Ādi* 5.142) it is said, *ekale īśvara kṛṣṇa, āra saba bhṛtya:* only the Supreme Personality of Godhead, Kṛṣṇa, is master, and all others are servants. Therefore a pure devotee never goes to demigods for satisfaction of his material needs. He depends on the Supreme Lord. And the pure devotee is satisfied with whatever He gives.

Text 21 यो यो यां यां तनुं भक्तः श्रद्धयार्चितुमिच्छति ।
तस्य तस्याचलां श्रद्धां तामेव विदधाम्यहम् ॥२१॥

yo yo yāṁ yāṁ tanuṁ bhaktaḥ, śraddhayārcitum icchati
tasya tasyācalāṁ śraddhāṁ, tām eva vidadhāmy aham

yaḥ yaḥ – whoever; *yām yām* – whichever; *tanum* – form of a demigod; *bhaktaḥ* – devotee; *śraddhayā* – with faith; *arcitum* – to worship; *icchati* – desires; *tasya tasya* – to him; *acalām* – steady; *śraddhām* – faith; *tām* – that; *eva* – surely; *vidadhāmi* – give; *aham* – I.

I am in everyone's heart as the Supersoul. As soon as one desires to worship some demigod, I make his faith steady so that he can devote himself to that particular deity.

PURPORT: God has given independence to everyone; therefore, if a person desires to have material enjoyment and wants very sincerely to have such facilities from the material demigods, the Supreme Lord, as Supersoul in everyone's heart, understands and gives facilities to such persons. As the supreme father of all living entities, He does not interfere with their independence, but gives all facilities so that they can fulfill their material desires. Some may ask why the all-powerful God gives facilities to the living entities for enjoying this material world and so lets them fall into the trap of the illusory energy. The answer is that if the Supreme Lord as Supersoul does not give such facilities, then there is no meaning to independence. Therefore He gives everyone full independence – whatever one likes – but His ultimate instruction we find in the *Bhagavad-gītā:* one should give up all other engagements and fully surrender unto Him. That will make man happy.

Both the living entity and the demigods are subordinate to the will of the Supreme Personality of Godhead; therefore the living entity cannot worship the demigod by his own desire, nor can the demigod bestow any benediction without the supreme will. As it is said, not a blade of grass moves without the will of the Supreme Personality of Godhead. Generally, persons who are distressed in the material world go to the demigods, as they are advised in the Vedic literature. A person wanting some particular thing may worship such and such a demigod. For example, a diseased person is recommended to worship the sun-god; a person wanting education may worship the goddess of learning, Sarasvatī; and a person wanting a beautiful wife may worship the goddess Umā, the wife of Lord Śiva. In this way there are recommendations in the *śāstras* (Vedic scriptures) for different modes of worship of different demigods. And because a particular living entity wants to enjoy a particular material facility, the Lord inspires him with a strong desire to achieve that benediction from that particular demigod, and so he successfully receives the benediction. The particular mode of the devotional attitude of the living entity toward a particular type of demigod is also arranged by the Supreme Lord. The demigods cannot infuse the living entities with such an affinity, but because He is the Supreme Lord, or the Supersoul who is present in the hearts of all living entities, Kṛṣṇa gives impetus to man to worship certain demigods. The demigods are actually different parts of the universal body of the Supreme Lord; therefore they have no independence. In the Vedic literature it is stated: "The Supreme Personality of Godhead as Supersoul is also present within the heart of the demigod; therefore He arranges through the demigod to fulfill the desire of the living entity. But both the demigod and the living entity are dependent on the supreme will. They are not independent."

Text 22 स तया श्रद्धया युक्तस्तस्याराधनमीहते ।
लभते च ततः कामान्मयैव विहितान् हि तान् ॥२२॥

sa tayā śraddhayā yuktas, tasyārādhanam īhate
labhate ca tataḥ kāmān, mayaiva vihitān hi tān

saḥ – he; *tayā* – with that; *śraddhayā* – inspiration; *yuktaḥ* – endowed; *tasya* – of that demigod; *ārādhanam* – for the worship; *īhate* – he aspires; *labhate* – obtains; *ca* – and; *tataḥ* – from that; *kāmān* – his desires; *mayā* – by Me; *eva* – alone; *vihitān* – arranged; *hi* – certainly; *tān* – those.

Endowed with such a faith, he endeavors to worship a particular demigod and obtains his desires. But in actuality these benefits are bestowed by Me alone.

PURPORT: The demigods cannot award benedictions to their devotees without the permission of the Supreme Lord. The living entity may forget that everything is the property of the Supreme Lord, but the demigods do not forget. So the worship of demigods and achievement of desired results are due not to the demigods but to the Supreme Personality of Godhead, by arrangement. The less intelligent living entity does not know this, and therefore he foolishly goes to the demigods for some benefit. But the pure devotee, when in need of something, prays only to the Supreme Lord. Asking for material benefit, however, is not a sign of a pure devotee. A living entity goes to the demigods usually because he is mad to fulfill his lust. This happens when something undue is desired by the living entity and the Lord Himself does not fulfill the desire. In the *Caitanya-caritāmṛta* it is said that one who worships the Supreme Lord and at the same time desires material enjoyment is contradictory in his desires. Devotional service to the Supreme Lord and the worship of a demigod cannot be on the same platform, because worship of a demigod is material and devotional service to the Supreme Lord is completely spiritual.

For the living entity who desires to return to Godhead, material desires are impediments. A pure devotee of the Lord is therefore not awarded the material benefits desired by less intelligent living entities, who therefore prefer to worship demigods of the material world rather than engage in the devotional service of the Supreme Lord.

Text 23 अन्तवत्तु फलं तेषां तद्भवत्यल्पमेधसाम् ।
देवान्देवयजो यान्ति मद्भक्ता यान्ति मामपि ॥२३॥

antavat tu phalaṁ teṣāṁ, tad bhavaty alpa-medhasām
devān deva-yajo yānti, mad-bhaktā yānti mām api

anta-vat – perishable; *tu* – but; *phalam* – fruit; *teṣām* – their; *tat* – that; *bhavati* – becomes; *alpa-medhasām* – of those of small intelligence; *devān* – to the demigods; *deva-yajaḥ* – the worshipers of the demigods; *yānti* – go; *mat* – My; *bhaktāḥ* – devotees; *yānti* – go; *mām* – to Me; *api* – also.

Men of small intelligence worship the demigods, and their fruits are limited and temporary. Those who worship the demigods go to the planets of the demigods, but My devotees ultimately reach My supreme planet.

PURPORT: Some commentators on the *Bhagavad-gītā* say that one who worships a demigod can reach the Supreme Lord, but here it is clearly stated that the worshipers of demigods go to the different planetary systems where various demigods are situated, just as a worshiper of the sun achieves the sun or a worshiper of the demigod of the moon achieves the moon. Similarly, if anyone wants to worship a demigod like Indra, he can attain that particular god's planet. It is not that everyone, regardless of whatever demigod is worshiped, will reach the Supreme Personality of Godhead. That is denied here, for it is clearly stated that the worshipers of demigods go to different planets in the material world but the devotee of the Supreme Lord goes directly to the supreme planet of the Personality of Godhead.

Here the point may be raised that if the demigods are different parts of the body of the Supreme Lord, then the same end should be achieved by worshiping them. However, worshipers of the demigods are less intelligent because they don't know to what part of the body food must be supplied. Some of them are so foolish that they claim that there are many parts and many ways to supply food. This isn't very sanguine. Can anyone supply food to the body through the ears or eyes? They do not know that these demigods are different parts of the universal body of the Supreme Lord, and in their ignorance they believe that each and every demigod is a separate God and a competitor of the Supreme Lord.

Not only are the demigods parts of the Supreme Lord, but ordinary living entities are also. In the *Śrīmad-Bhāgavatam* it is stated that the *brāhmaṇas* are the head of the Supreme Lord, the *kṣatriyas* are His arms, the *vaiśyas* are His waist, the *śūdras* are His legs, and all serve different functions. Regardless of the situation, if one knows that both the demigods and he himself are part and parcel of the Supreme Lord, his knowledge is perfect. But if he does not understand this, he achieves different planets where the demigods reside. This is not the same destination the devotee reaches.

The results achieved by the demigods' benedictions are perishable because within this material world the planets, the demigods and their worshipers are all perishable. Therefore it is clearly stated in this verse that all results achieved by worshiping demigods are perishable, and therefore such worship is performed by the less intelligent living entity. Because the pure devotee engaged in Kṛṣṇa consciousness in devotional service of the Supreme Lord achieves eternal blissful existence that is full of knowledge, his achievements and those of the common worshiper of the demigods are different. The Supreme Lord is unlimited; His favor is unlimited; His mercy is unlimited. Therefore the mercy of the Supreme Lord upon His pure devotees is unlimited.

Text 24 अव्यक्तं व्यक्तिमापन्नं मन्यन्ते मामबुद्धयः ।
परं भावमजानन्तो ममाव्ययमनुत्तमम् ॥२४॥

avyaktaṁ vyaktim āpannaṁ, manyante mām abuddhayaḥ
paraṁ bhāvam ajānanto, mamāvyayam anuttamam

avyaktam – nonmanifested; *vyaktim* – personality; *āpannam* – achieved; *manyante* – think; *mām* – Me; *abuddhayaḥ* – less intelligent persons; *param* – supreme; *bhāvam* – existence; *ajānantaḥ* – without knowing; *mama* – My; *avyayam* – imperishable; *anuttamam* – the finest.

Unintelligent men, who do not know Me perfectly, think that I, the Supreme Personality of Godhead, Kṛṣṇa, was impersonal before and have now assumed this personality. Due to their small knowledge, they do not know My higher nature, which is imperishable and supreme.

PURPORT: Those who are worshipers of demigods have been described as less intelligent persons, and here the impersonalists are similarly described. Lord Kṛṣṇa in His personal form is here speaking before Arjuna, and still, due to ignorance, impersonalists argue that the Supreme Lord ultimately has no form. Yāmunācārya, a great devotee of the Lord in the disciplic succession of Rāmānujācārya, has written a very appropriate verse in this connection. He says,

tvāṁ śīla-rūpa-caritaiḥ parama-prakṛṣṭaiḥ
sattvena sāttvikatayā prabalaiś ca śāstraiḥ
prakhyāta-daiva-paramārtha-vidāṁ mataiś ca
naivāsura-prakṛtayaḥ prabhavanti boddhum

"My dear Lord, devotees like Vyāsadeva and Nārada know You to be the Personality of Godhead. By understanding different Vedic literatures, one can come to know Your characteristics, Your form and Your activities, and one can thus understand that You are the Supreme Personality of Godhead. But those who are in the modes of passion and ignorance, the demons, the nondevotees, cannot understand You. They are unable to understand You. However expert such nondevotees may be in discussing *Vedānta* and the *Upaniṣads* and other Vedic literatures, it is not possible for them to understand the Personality of Godhead." (*Stotra-ratna* 12)

In the *Brahma-saṁhitā* it is stated that the Personality of Godhead cannot be understood simply by study of the *Vedānta* literature. Only by the mercy of the Supreme Lord can the Personality of the Supreme be known. Therefore in this verse it is clearly stated that not only are the worshipers of the demigods less intelligent, but those nondevotees who are engaged in *Vedānta* and speculation on Vedic literature without any tinge of true Kṛṣṇa consciousness are also less intelligent, and for them it is not possible to understand God's personal nature. Persons who are under the impression that the Absolute Truth is impersonal are described as *abuddhayaḥ,* which means those who do not know the ultimate feature of the Absolute Truth. In the *Śrīmad-Bhāgavatam* it is stated that supreme realization begins from the impersonal Brahman and then rises to the localized Supersoul – but the ultimate word in the Absolute Truth is the Personality of Godhead. Modern impersonalists are still less intelligent, for they do not even follow their great predecessor Śaṅkarācārya, who has specifically stated that Kṛṣṇa is the Supreme Personality of Godhead. Impersonalists, therefore, not knowing the Supreme Truth, think Kṛṣṇa to be only the son of Devakī and Vasudeva, or a prince, or a powerful living entity. This is also condemned in the *Bhagavad-gītā* (9.11). *Avajānanti māṁ mūḍhā mānuṣīṁ tanum āśritam:* "Only the fools regard Me as an ordinary person."

The fact is that no one can understand Kṛṣṇa without rendering devotional service and without developing Kṛṣṇa consciousness. The *Bhāgavatam* (10.14.29) confirms this:

athāpi te deva padāmbuja-dvaya-, prasāda-leśānugṛhīta eva hi
jānāti tattvaṁ bhagavan-mahimno, na cānya eko 'pi ciraṁ vicinvan

"My Lord, if one is favored by even a slight trace of the mercy of Your lotus feet, he can understand the greatness of Your personality. But those who speculate to understand the Supreme Personality of Godhead are unable to know You, even though they continue to study the *Vedas* for many years." One cannot understand the Supreme Personality of Godhead, Kṛṣṇa, or His form, quality or name simply by mental speculation or by discussing Vedic literature. One must understand Him by devotional service. When one is fully engaged in Kṛṣṇa consciousness, beginning by chanting the *mahā-mantra* – Hare Kṛṣṇa, Hare Kṛṣṇa, Kṛṣṇa Kṛṣṇa, Hare Hare/ Hare Rāma, Hare Rāma, Rāma Rāma, Hare Hare – then only can one understand the Supreme Personality of Godhead. Nondevotee impersonalists think that Kṛṣṇa has a body made of this material nature and that all His activities, His form and everything are *māyā*. These impersonalists are known as Māyāvādīs. They do not know the ultimate truth.

The twentieth verse clearly states, *kāmais tais tair hṛta-jñānāḥ prapadyante 'nya-devatāḥ.* "Those who are blinded by lusty desires surrender unto the different demigods." It is accepted that besides the Supreme Personality of Godhead, there are demigods who have their different planets, and the Lord also has a planet. As stated in the twenty-third verse, *devān deva-yajo yānti mad-bhaktā yānti mām api:* the worshipers of the demigods go to the different planets of the demigods, and those who are devotees of Lord Kṛṣṇa go to the Kṛṣṇaloka planet. Although this is clearly stated, the foolish impersonalists still maintain that the Lord is formless and that these forms are impositions. From the study of the *Gītā* does it appear that the demigods and their abodes are impersonal? Clearly, neither the demigods nor Kṛṣṇa, the Supreme Personality of Godhead, are impersonal. They are all persons; Lord Kṛṣṇa is the Supreme Personality of Godhead, and He has His own planet, and the demigods have theirs.

Therefore the monistic contention that ultimate truth is formless and that form is imposed does not hold true. It is clearly stated here that it is not imposed. From the *Bhagavad-gītā* we can clearly understand that the forms of the demigods and the form of the Supreme Lord are simultaneously existing and that Lord Kṛṣṇa is *sac-cid-ānanda,* eternal blissful knowledge. The Vedic literature confirms that the Supreme Absolute Truth is knowledge and blissful pleasure, *vijñānam ānandaṁ brahma* (*Bṛhad-āraṇyaka Upaniṣad* 3.9.28), and that He is the reservoir of unlimited auspicious qualities, *ananta-kalyāṇa-guṇātmako 'sau* (*Viṣṇu Purāṇa* 6.5.84). And in the *Gītā* the Lord says that although He is *aja* (unborn), He still appears. These are the facts that we should understand from the *Bhagavad-gītā.* We cannot understand how the Supreme Personality of Godhead can be impersonal; the imposition theory of the impersonalist monist is false as far as the statements of the *Gītā* are concerned. It is clear herein that the Supreme Absolute Truth, Lord Kṛṣṇa, has both form and personality.

Text 25 नाहं प्रकाशः सर्वस्य योगमायासमावृतः ।
मूढोऽयं नाभिजानाति लोको मामजमव्ययम् ॥२५॥

nāhaṁ prakāśaḥ sarvasya, yoga-māyā-samāvṛtaḥ
mūḍho 'yaṁ nābhijānāti, loko mām ajam avyayam

na – nor; *aham* – I; *prakāśaḥ* – manifest; *sarvasya* – to everyone; *yoga-māyā* – by internal potency; *samāvṛtaḥ* – covered; *mūḍhaḥ* – foolish; *ayam* – these; *na* – not; *abhijānāti* – can understand; *lokaḥ* – persons; *mām* – Me; *ajam* – unborn; *avyayam* – inexhaustible.

I am never manifest to the foolish and unintelligent. For them I am covered by My internal potency, and therefore they do not know that I am unborn and infallible.

PURPORT: It may be argued that since Kṛṣṇa was visible to everyone when He was present on this earth, how can it be said that He is not manifest to everyone? But actually He was not manifest to everyone. When Kṛṣṇa was present there were only a few people who could understand Him to be the Supreme Personality of Godhead. In the assembly of Kurus, when Śiśupāla spoke against Kṛṣṇa's being elected president of the assembly, Bhīṣma supported Him and proclaimed Him to be the Supreme God. Similarly, the Pāṇḍavas and a few others knew that He was the Supreme, but not everyone. He was not revealed to the nondevotees and the common man. Therefore in the *Bhagavad-gītā* Kṛṣṇa says that but for His pure devotees, all men consider Him to be like themselves. He was manifest only to His devotees as the reservoir of all pleasure. But to others, to unintelligent nondevotees, He was covered by His internal potency.

In the prayers of Kuntī in the *Śrīmad-Bhāgavatam* (1.8.19) it is said that the Lord is covered by the curtain of *yoga-māyā* and thus ordinary people cannot understand Him. This *yoga-māyā* curtain is also confirmed in the *Īśopaniṣad* (Mantra 15), in which the devotee prays:

hiraṇmayena pātreṇa, satyasyāpihitaṁ mukham
tat tvaṁ pūṣann apāvṛṇu, satya-dharmāya dṛṣṭaye

"O my Lord, You are the maintainer of the entire universe, and devotional service to You is the highest religious principle. Therefore, I pray that You will also maintain me. Your transcendental form is covered by the *yoga-māyā.* The *brahma-jyotir* is the covering of the internal potency. May You kindly remove this glowing effulgence that impedes my seeing Your *sac-cid-ānanda-vigraha,* Your eternal form of bliss and knowledge." The Supreme Personality of Godhead in His transcendental form of bliss and knowledge is covered by the internal potency of the *brahma-jyotir,* and the less intelligent impersonalists cannot see the Supreme on this account.

Also in the *Śrīmad-Bhāgavatam* (10.14.7) there is this prayer by Brahmā: "O Supreme Personality of Godhead, O Supersoul, O master of all mystery, who can calculate Your potency and pastimes in this world? You are always expanding Your internal potency, and therefore no one can understand You. Learned scientists and learned scholars can examine the atomic constitution of the material world or even the planets, but still they are unable to calculate Your energy and potency, although You are present before them." The Supreme Personality of Godhead, Lord Kṛṣṇa, is not only unborn but also *avyaya,* inexhaustible. His eternal form is bliss and knowledge, and His energies are all inexhaustible.

Text 26 वेदाहं समतीतानि वर्तमानानि चार्जुन ।
भविष्याणि च भूतानि मां तु वेद न कश्चन ॥२६॥

vedāhaṁ samatītāni, vartamānāni cārjuna
bhaviṣyāṇi ca bhūtāni, māṁ tu veda na kaścana

veda – know; *aham* – I; *samatītāni* – completely past; *vartamānāni* – present; *ca* – and; *arjuna* – O Arjuna; *bhaviṣyāṇi* – future; *ca* – also;

bhūtāni – all living entities; *mām* – Me; *tu* – but; *veda* – knows; *na* – not; *kaścana* – anyone.

O Arjuna, as the Supreme Personality of Godhead, I know everything that has happened in the past, all that is happening in the present, and all things that are yet to come. I also know all living entities; but Me no one knows.

PURPORT: Here the question of personality and impersonality is clearly stated. If Kṛṣṇa, the form of the Supreme Personality of Godhead, were *māyā,* material, as the impersonalists consider Him to be, then like the living entity He would change His body and forget everything about His past life. Anyone with a material body cannot remember his past life, nor can he foretell his future life, nor can he predict the outcome of his present life; therefore he cannot know what is happening in past, present and future. Unless one is liberated from material contamination, he cannot know past, present and future.

Unlike the ordinary human being, Lord Kṛṣṇa clearly says that He completely knows what happened in the past, what is happening in the present, and what will happen in the future. In the Fourth Chapter we have seen that Lord Kṛṣṇa remembers instructing Vivasvān, the sun-god, millions of years ago. Kṛṣṇa knows every living entity because He is situated in every living being's heart as the Supersoul. But despite His presence in every living entity as Supersoul and His presence as the Supreme Personality of Godhead, the less intelligent, even if able to realize the impersonal Brahman, cannot realize Śrī Kṛṣṇa as the Supreme Person. Certainly the transcendental body of Śrī Kṛṣṇa is not perishable. He is just like the sun, and *māyā* is like a cloud. In the material world we can see that there is the sun and that there are clouds and different stars and planets. The clouds may cover all these in the sky temporarily, but this covering is only apparent to our limited vision. The sun, moon and stars are not actually covered. Similarly, *māyā* cannot cover the Supreme Lord. By His internal potency He is not manifest to the less intelligent class of men. As it is stated in the third verse of this chapter, out of millions and millions of men, some try to become perfect in this human form of life, and out of thousands and thousands of such perfected men, hardly one can understand what Lord Krṣṇa is. Even if one is perfected by realization of impersonal Brahman or localized Paramātmā, he cannot possibly understand the Supreme Personality of Godhead, Śrī Kṛṣṇa, without being in Kṛṣṇa consciousness.

Text 27 इच्छाद्वेषसमुत्थेन द्वन्द्वमोहेन भारत ।
सर्वभूतानि सम्मोहं सर्गे यान्ति परन्तप ॥२७॥

icchā-dveṣa-samutthena, dvandva-mohena bhārata
sarva-bhūtāni sammohaṁ, sarge yānti paran-tapa

icchā – desire; *dveṣa* – and hate; *samutthena* – arisen from; *dvandva* – of duality; *mohena* – by the illusion; *bhārata* – O scion of Bharata; *sarva* – all; *bhūtāni* – living entities; *sammoham* – into delusion; *sarge* – while taking birth; *yānti* – go; *param-tapa* – O conqueror of enemies.

O scion of Bharata, O conqueror of the foe, all living entities are born into delusion, bewildered by dualities arisen from desire and hate.

PURPORT: The real constitutional position of the living entity is that of subordination to the Supreme Lord, who is pure knowledge. When one is deluded into separation from this pure knowledge, he becomes controlled by the illusory energy and cannot understand the Supreme Personality of Godhead. The illusory energy is manifested in the duality of desire and hate. Due to desire and hate, the ignorant person wants to become one with the Supreme Lord and envies Kṛṣṇa as the Supreme Personality of Godhead. Pure devotees, who are not deluded or contaminated by desire and hate, can understand that Lord Śrī Kṛṣṇa appears by His internal potencies, but those who are deluded by duality and nescience think that the Supreme Personality of Godhead is created by material energies. This is their misfortune. Such deluded persons, symptomatically,dwell in dualities of dishonor and honor, misery and happiness, woman and man, good and bad, pleasure and pain, etc., thinking, "This is my wife; this is my house; I am the master of this house; I am the husband of this wife." These are the dualities of delusion. Those who are so deluded by dualities are completely foolish and therefore cannot understand the Supreme Personality of Godhead.

Text 28 येषां त्वन्तगतं पापं जनानां पुण्यकर्मणाम् ।
ते द्वन्द्वमोहनिर्मुक्ता भजन्ते मां दृढव्रताः ॥२८॥

yeṣāṁ tv anta-gataṁ pāpaṁ, janānāṁ puṇya-karmaṇām
te dvandva-moha-nirmuktā, bhajante māṁ dṛḍha-vratāḥ

yeṣām – whose; *tu* – but; *anta-gatam* – completely eradicated; *pāpam* – sin; *janānām* – of the persons; *puṇya* – pious; *karmaṇām* – whose previous activities; *te* – they; *dvandva* – of duality; *moha* – delusion; *nirmuktāḥ* – free from; *bhajante* – engage in devotional service; *mām* – to Me; *dṛḍha-vratāḥ* – with determination.

Persons who have acted piously in previous lives and in this life and whose sinful actions are completely eradicated are freed from the dualities of delusion, and they engage themselves in My service with determination.

PURPORT: Those eligible for elevation to the transcendental position are mentioned in this verse. For those who are sinful, atheistic, foolish and deceitful, it is very difficult to transcend the duality of desire and hate. Only those who have passed their lives in practicing the regulative principles of religion, who have acted piously, and who have conquered sinful reactions can accept devotional service and gradually rise to the pure knowledge of the Supreme Personality of Godhead. Then, gradually, they can meditate in trance on the Supreme Personality of Godhead. That is the process of being situated on the spiritual platform. This elevation is possible in Kṛṣṇa consciousness in the association of pure devotees, for in the association of great devotees one can be delivered from delusion.

It is stated in the *Śrīmad-Bhāgavatam* (5.5.2) that if one actually wants to be liberated he must render service to the devotees (*mahat-sevāṁ dvāram āhur vimukteḥ*); but one who associates with materialistic people is on the path leading to the darkest region of existence (*tamo-dvāraṁ yoṣitāṁ saṅgi-saṅgam*). All the devotees of the Lord traverse this earth just to recover the conditioned souls from their delusion. The impersonalists do not know that forgetting their constitutional position as subordinate to the Supreme Lord is the greatest violation of God's law. Unless one is reinstated in his own constitutional position, it is not possible to understand the Supreme Personality or to be fully engaged in His transcendental loving service with determination.

Text 29 जरामरणमोक्षाय मामाश्रित्य यतन्ति ये ।
ते ब्रह्म तद्विदुः कृत्स्नमध्यात्मं कर्म चाखिलम् ॥२९॥

jarā-maraṇa-mokṣāya, mām āśritya yatanti ye
te brahma tad viduḥ kṛtsnam, adhyātmaṁ karma cākhilam

jarā – from old age; *maraṇa* – and death; *mokṣāya* – for the purpose of liberation; *mām* – Me; *āśritya* – taking shelter of; *yatanti* – endeavor;

ye – all those who; *te* – such persons; *brahma* – Brahman; *tat* – actually that; *viduḥ* – they know; *kṛtsnam* – everything; *adhyātmam* – transcendental; *karma* – activities; *ca* – also; *akhilam* – entirely.

Intelligent persons who are endeavoring for liberation from old age and death take refuge in Me in devotional service. They are actually Brahman because they entirely know everything about transcendental activities.

PURPORT: Birth, death, old age and diseases affect this material body, but not the spiritual body. There is no birth, death, old age and disease for the spiritual body, so one who attains a spiritual body, becomes one of the associates of the Supreme Personality of Godhead and engages in eternal devotional service is really liberated. *Ahaṁ brahmāsmi:* I am spirit. It is said that one should understand that he is Brahman, spirit soul. This Brahman conception of life is also in devotional service, as described in this verse. The pure devotees are transcendentally situated on the Brahman platform, and they know everything about transcendental activities.

Four kinds of impure devotees who engage themselves in the transcendental service of the Lord achieve their respective goals, and by the grace of the Supreme Lord, when they are fully Kṛṣṇa conscious, they actually enjoy spiritual association with the Supreme Lord. But those who are worshipers of demigods never reach the Supreme Lord in His supreme planet. Even the less intelligent Brahman-realized persons cannot reach the supreme planet of Kṛṣṇa known as Goloka Vṛndāvana. Only persons who perform activities in Kṛṣṇa consciousness (*mām āśritya*) are actually entitled to be called Brahman, because they are actually endeavoring to reach the Kṛṣṇa planet. Such persons have no misgivings about Kṛṣṇa, and thus they are factually Brahman.

Those who are engaged in worshiping the form or *arcā* of the Lord, or who are engaged in meditation on the Lord simply for liberation from material bondage, also know, by the grace of the Lord, the purports of Brahman, *adhibhūta,* etc., as explained by the Lord in the next chapter.

Text 30 साधिभूताधिदैवं मां साधियज्ञं च ये विदुः ।
प्रयाणकालेऽपि च मां ते विदुर्युक्तचेतसः ॥३०॥

sādhibhūtādhidaivaṁ māṁ, sādhiyajñaṁ ca ye viduḥ
prayāṇa-kāle 'pi ca māṁ, te vidur yukta-cetasaḥ

sa-adhibhūta – and the governing principle of the material manifestation; *adhidaivam* – governing all the demigods; *mām* – Me; *sa-adhiyajñam* – and governing all sacrifices; *ca* – also; *ye* – those who; *viduḥ* – know; *prayāṇa* – of death; *kāle* – at the time; *api* – even; *ca* – and; *mām* – Me; *te* – they; *viduḥ* – know; *yukta-cetasaḥ* – their minds engaged in Me.

Those in full consciousness of Me, who know Me, the Supreme Lord, to be the governing principle of the material manifestation, of the demigods, and of all methods of sacrifice, can understand and know Me, the Supreme Personality of Godhead, even at the time of death.

PURPORT: Persons acting in Kṛṣṇa consciousness are never deviated from the path of entirely understanding the Supreme Personality of Godhead. In the transcendental association of Kṛṣṇa consciousness, one can understand how the Supreme Lord is the governing principle of the material manifestation and even of the demigods. Gradually, by such transcendental association, one becomes convinced of the Supreme Personality of Godhead, and at the time of death such a Kṛṣṇa conscious person can never forget Kṛṣṇa. Naturally he is thus promoted to the planet of the Supreme Lord, Goloka Vṛndāvana.

This Seventh Chapter particularly explains how one can become a fully Kṛṣṇa conscious person. The beginning of Kṛṣṇa consciousness is association of persons who are Kṛṣṇa conscious. Such association is spiritual and puts one directly in touch with the Supreme Lord, and, by His grace, one can understand Kṛṣṇa to be the Supreme Personality of Godhead. At the same time one can really understand the constitutional position of the living entity and how the living entity forgets Kṛṣṇa and becomes entangled in material activities. By gradual development of Kṛṣṇa consciousness in good association, the living entity can understand that due to forgetfulness of Kṛṣṇa he has become conditioned by the laws of material nature. He can also understand that this human form of life is an opportunity to regain Kṛṣṇa consciousness and that it should be fully utilized to attain the causeless mercy of the Supreme Lord.

Many subjects have been discussed in this chapter: the man in distress, the inquisitive man, the man in want of material necessities, knowledge of Brahman, knowledge of Paramātmā, liberation from birth, death and diseases, and worship of the Supreme Lord. However, he who is actually elevated in Kṛṣṇa consciousness does not care for the different processes. He simply directly engages himself in activities of Kṛṣṇa consciousness and thereby factually attains his constitutional position as an eternal servitor of Lord Kṛṣṇa. In such a situation he takes pleasure in hearing and glorifying the Supreme Lord in pure devotional service. He is convinced that by his doing so, all his objectives will be fulfilled. This determined faith is called *dṛḍha-vrata,* and it is the beginning of *bhakti-yoga,* or transcendental loving service. That is the verdict of all scriptures. This Seventh Chapter of the *Bhagavad-gītā* is the substance of that conviction.

Thus end the Bhaktivedanta Purports to the Seventh Chapter of the Śrīmad Bhagavad-gītā *in the matter of Knowledge of the Absolute.*

CHAPTER EIGHT

Attaining the Supreme

Text 1 अर्जुन उवाच
किं तद् ब्रह्म किमध्यात्मं किं कर्म पुरुषोत्तम ।
अधिभूतं च किं प्रोक्तमधिदैवं किमुच्यते ॥ १ ॥

arjuna uvāca
kiṁ tad brahma kim adhyātmaṁ, kiṁ karma puruṣottama
adhibhūtaṁ ca kiṁ proktam, adhidaivaṁ kim ucyate

arjunaḥ uvāca – Arjuna said; *kim* – what; *tat* – that; *brahma* – Brahman; *kim* – what; *adhyātmam* – the self; *kim* – what; *karma* – fruitive activities; *puruṣa-uttama* – O Supreme Person; *adhibhūtam* – the material manifestation; *ca* – and; *kim* – what; *proktam* – is called; *adhidaivam* – the demigods; *kim* – what; *ucyate* – is called.

Arjuna inquired: O my Lord, O Supreme Person, what is Brahman? What is the self? What are fruitive activities? What is this material manifestation? And what are the demigods? Please explain this to me.

PURPORT: In this chapter Lord Kṛṣṇa answers different questions from Arjuna, beginning with "What is Brahman?" The Lord also explains *karma* (fruitive activities), devotional service and *yoga* principles, and devotional service in its pure form. The *Śrīmad-Bhāgavatam* explains that the Supreme Absolute Truth is known as Brahman, Paramātmā and Bhagavān. In addition, the living entity, the individual soul, is also called Brahman. Arjuna also inquires about *ātmā,* which refers to body, soul and mind. According to the Vedic dictionary, *ātmā* refers to the mind, soul, body and senses also.

Arjuna has addressed the Supreme Lord as Puruṣottama, Supreme Person, which means that he was putting these questions not simply to a friend but to the Supreme Person, knowing Him to be the supreme authority able to give definitive answers.

Text 2 अधियज्ञः कथं कोऽत्र देहेऽस्मिन्मधुसूदन ।
प्रयाणकाले च कथं ज्ञेयोऽसि नियतात्मभिः ॥ २ ॥

adhiyajñaḥ kathaṁ ko 'tra, dehe 'smin madhusūdana
prayāṇa-kāle ca kathaṁ, jñeyo 'si niyatātmabhiḥ

adhiyajñaḥ – the Lord of sacrifice; *katham* – how; *kaḥ* – who; *atra* – here; *dehe* – in the body; *asmin* – this; *madhusūdana* – O Madhusūdana; *prayāṇa-kāle* – at the time of death; *ca* – and; *katham* – how; *jñeyaḥ asi* – You can be known; *niyata-ātmabhiḥ* – by the self-controlled.

Who is the Lord of sacrifice, and how does He live in the body, O Madhusūdana? And how can those engaged in devotional service know You at the time of death?

PURPORT: "Lord of sacrifice" may refer to either Indra or Viṣṇu. Viṣṇu is the chief of the primal demigods, including Brahmā and Śiva, and Indra is the chief of the administrative demigods. Both Indra and Viṣṇu are worshiped by *yajña* performances. But here Arjuna asks who is actually the Lord of *yajña* (sacrifice) and how the Lord is residing within the body of the living entity.

Arjuna addresses the Lord as Madhusūdana because Kṛṣṇa once killed a demon named Madhu. Actually these questions, which are of the nature of doubts, should not have arisen in the mind of Arjuna, because Arjuna is a Kṛṣṇa conscious devotee. Therefore these doubts are like demons. Since Kṛṣṇa is so expert in killing demons, Arjuna here addresses Him as Madhusūdana so that Kṛṣṇa might kill the demonic doubts that arise in Arjuna's mind.

Now the word *prayāṇa-kāle* in this verse is very significant because whatever we do in life will be tested at the time of death. Arjuna is very anxious to know of those who are constantly engaged in Kṛṣṇa consciousness. What should be their position at that final moment? At the time of death all the bodily functions are disrupted, and the mind is not in a proper condition. Thus disturbed by the bodily situation, one may not be able to remember the Supreme Lord. Mahārāja Kulaśekhara, a great devotee, prays, "My dear Lord, just now I am quite healthy, and it is better that I die immediately so that the swan of my mind can seek entrance at the stem of Your lotus feet." The metaphor is used because the swan, a bird of the water, takes pleasure in digging into the lotus flowers; its sporting proclivity is to enter the lotus flower. Mahārāja Kulaśekhara says to the Lord, "Now my mind is undisturbed, and I am quite healthy. If I die immediately, thinking of Your lotus feet, then I am sure that my performance of Your devotional service will become perfect. But if I have to wait for my natural death, then I do not know what will happen, because at that time the bodily functions will be disrupted, my throat will be choked up, and I do not know whether I shall be able to chant Your name. Better let me die immediately." Arjuna questions how a person can fix his mind on Kṛṣṇa's lotus feet at such a time.

Text 3 श्रीभगवानुवाच
अक्षरं ब्रह्म परमं स्वभावोऽध्यात्ममुच्यते ।
भूतभावोद्भवकरो विसर्गः कर्मसंज्ञितः ॥ ३ ॥

śrī-bhagavān uvāca
akṣaraṁ brahma paramaṁ, svabhāvo 'dhyātmam ucyate
bhūta-bhāvodbhava-karo, visargaḥ karma-saṁjñitaḥ

śrī-bhagavān uvāca – the Supreme Personality of Godhead said; *akṣaram* – indestructible; *brahma* – Brahman; *paramam* – transcendental; *svabhāvaḥ* – eternal nature; *adhyātmam* – the self; *ucyate* – is called; *bhūta-bhāva-udbhava-karaḥ* – producing the material bodies of the living entities; *visargaḥ* – creation; *karma* – fruitive activities; *saṁjñitaḥ* – is called.

The Supreme Personality of Godhead said: The indestructible, transcendental living entity is called Brahman, and his eternal nature is called adhyātma, the self. Action pertaining to the development of the material bodies of the living entities is called karma, or fruitive activities.

PURPORT: Brahman is indestructible and eternally existing, and its constitution is not changed at any time. But beyond Brahman there is Para-brahman. Brahman refers to the living entity, and Para-brahman refers to the Supreme Personality of Godhead. The constitutional position of the living entity is different from the position he takes in the material world. In material consciousness his nature is to try to be the lord of matter, but in spiritual consciousness, Kṛṣṇa consciousness, his position is to serve the Supreme. When the living entity is in material consciousness, he has to take on various bodies in the material world. That is called *karma,* or varied creation by the force of material consciousness.

In Vedic literature the living entity is called *jīvātmā* and Brahman, but he is never called Para-brahman. The living entity (*jīvātmā*) takes different positions – sometimes he merges into the dark material nature and identifies himself with matter, and sometimes he identifies himself with the superior, spiritual nature. Therefore he is called the Supreme Lord's marginal energy. According to his identification with material or spiritual nature, he receives a material or spiritual body. In material nature he may take a body from any of the 8,400,000 species of life, but in spiritual nature he has only one body. In material nature he is manifested sometimes as a man, demigod, animal, beast, bird, etc., according to his *karma.* To attain material heavenly planets and enjoy their facilities, he sometimes performs sacrifices (*yajña*), but when his merit is exhausted he returns to earth again in the form of a man. This process is called *karma.*

The *Chāndogya Upaniṣad* describes the Vedic sacrificial process. On the sacrificial altar, five kinds of offerings are made into five kinds of fire. The five kinds of fire are conceived of as the heavenly planets, clouds, the earth, man and woman, and the five kinds of sacrificial offerings are faith, the enjoyer on the moon, rain, grains and semen.

In the process of sacrifice, the living entity makes specific sacrifices to attain specific heavenly planets and consequently reaches them. When the merit of sacrifice is exhausted, the living entity descends to earth in the form of rain, then takes on the form of grains, and the grains are eaten by man and transformed into semen, which impregnates a woman, and thus the living entity once again attains the human form to perform sacrifice and so repeat the same cycle. In this way, the living entity perpetually comes and goes on the material path. The Kṛṣṇa conscious person, however, avoids such sacrifices. He takes directly to Kṛṣṇa consciousness and thereby prepares himself to return to Godhead.

Impersonalist commentators on the *Bhagavad-gītā* unreasonably assume that Brahman takes the form of *jīva* in the material world, and to substantiate this they refer to Chapter Fifteen, verse 7, of the *Gītā.* But in this verse the Lord also speaks of the living entity as "an eternal fragment of Myself." The fragment of God, the living entity, may fall down into the material world, but the Supreme Lord (Acyuta) never falls down. Therefore this assumption that the Supreme Brahman assumes the form of *jīva* is not acceptable. It is important to remember that in Vedic literature Brahman (the living entity) is distinguished from Para-brahman (the Supreme Lord).

Text 4 अधिभूतं क्षरो भावः पुरुषश्चाधिदैवतम् ।
अधियज्ञोऽहमेवात्र देहे देहभृतां वर ॥ ४ ॥

adhibhūtaṁ kṣaro bhāvaḥ, puruṣaś cādhidaivatam
adhiyajño 'ham evātra, dehe deha-bhṛtāṁ vara

adhibhūtam – the physical manifestation; *kṣaraḥ* – constantly changing; *bhāvaḥ* – nature; *puruṣaḥ* – the universal form, including all the demigods, like the sun and moon; *ca* – and; *adhidaivatam* – called *adhidaiva; adhiyajñaḥ* – the Supersoul; *aham* – I (Kṛṣṇa); *eva* – certainly; *atra* – in this; *dehe* – body; *deha-bhṛtām* – of the embodied; *vara* – O best.

O best of the embodied beings, the physical nature, which is constantly changing, is called adhibhūta [the material manifestation]. The universal form of the Lord, which includes all the demigods, like those of the sun and moon, is called adhidaiva. And I, the Supreme Lord, represented as the Supersoul in the heart of every embodied being, am called adhiyajña [the Lord of sacrifice].

PURPORT: The physical nature is constantly changing. Material bodies generally pass through six stages: they are born, they grow, they remain for some duration, they produce some by-products, they dwindle, and then they vanish. This physical nature is called *adhibhūta.* It is created at a certain point and will be annihilated at a certain point. The conception of the universal form of the Supreme Lord, which includes all the demigods and their different planets, is called *adhidaivata.* And present in the body along with the individual soul is the Supersoul, a plenary representation of Lord Kṛṣṇa. The Supersoul is called the Paramātmā or *adhiyajña* and is situated in the heart. The word *eva* is particularly important in the context of this verse because by this word the Lord stresses that the Paramātmā is not different from Him. The Supersoul, the Supreme Personality of Godhead, seated beside the individual soul, is the witness of the individual soul's activities and is the source of the soul's various types of consciousness. The Supersoul gives the individual soul an opportunity to act freely and witnesses his activities. The functions of all these different manifestations of the Supreme Lord automatically become clarified for the pure Kṛṣṇa conscious devotee engaged in transcendental service to the Lord. The gigantic universal form of the Lord called *adhidaivata* is contemplated by the neophyte who cannot approach the Supreme Lord in His manifestation as Supersoul. The neophyte is advised to contemplate the universal form, or *virāt-puruṣa,* whose legs are considered the lower planets, whose eyes are considered the sun and moon, and whose head is considered the upper planetary system.

Text 5 अन्तकाले च मामेव स्मरन्मुक्त्वा कलेवरम् ।
यः प्रयाति स मद्भावं याति नास्त्यत्र संशयः ॥ ५ ॥

anta-kāle ca mām eva, smaran muktvā kalevaram
yaḥ prayāti sa mad-bhāvaṁ, yāti nāsty atra saṁśayaḥ

anta-kāle – at the end of life; *ca* – also; *mām* – Me; *eva* – certainly; *smaran* – remembering; *muktvā* – quitting; *kalevaram* – the body; *yaḥ* – he who; *prayāti* – goes; *saḥ* – he; *mat-bhāvam* – My nature; *yāti* – achieves; *na* – not; *asti* – there is; *atra* – here; *saṁśayaḥ* – doubt.

And whoever, at the end of his life, quits his body remembering Me alone at once attains My nature. Of this there is no doubt.

PURPORT: In this verse the importance of Kṛṣṇa consciousness is stressed. Anyone who quits his body in Kṛṣṇa consciousness is at once transferred to the transcendental nature of the Supreme Lord. The Supreme Lord is the purest of the pure. Therefore anyone who is constantly Kṛṣṇa conscious is also the purest of the pure. The word *smaran* ("remembering") is important. Remembrance of Kṛṣṇa is not possible for the impure soul who has not practiced Kṛṣṇa consciousness in devotional service. Therefore one should practice Kṛṣṇa consciousness from the very beginning of life. If one wants to achieve success at the end of his life, the process of remembering Kṛṣṇa is essential. Therefore one should constantly, incessantly chant the *mahā-mantra* – Hare Kṛṣṇa, Hare Kṛṣṇa, Kṛṣṇa Kṛṣṇa, Hare Hare/ Hare Rāma, Hare Rāma, Rāma Rāma, Hare Hare. Lord Caitanya has advised that one be as tolerant as a tree (*taror api sahiṣṇunā*). There may be so many impediments for a person who is chanting Hare Kṛṣṇa. Nonetheless, tolerating all these impediments, one should continue to chant Hare Kṛṣṇa, Hare Kṛṣṇa, Kṛṣṇa Kṛṣṇa,

Hare Hare/ Hare Rāma, Hare Rāma, Rāma Rāma, Hare Hare, so that at the end of one's life one can have the full benefit of Kṛṣṇa consciousness.

Text 6 यं यं वापि स्मरन् भावं त्यजत्यन्ते कलेवरम् ।
तं तमेवैति कौन्तेय सदा तद्भावभावितः ॥ ६ ॥

yaṁ yaṁ vāpi smaran bhāvaṁ, tyajaty ante kalevaram
taṁ tam evaiti kaunteya, sadā tad-bhāva-bhāvitaḥ

yam yam – whatever; *vā api* – at all; *smaran* – remembering; *bhāvam* – nature; *tyajati* – gives up; *ante* – at the end; *kalevaram* – this body; *tam tam* – similar; *eva* – certainly; *eti* – gets; *kaunteya* – O son of Kuntī; *sadā* – always; *tat* – that; *bhāva* – state of being; *bhāvitaḥ* – remembering.

Whatever state of being one remembers when he quits his body, O son of Kuntī, that state he will attain without fail.

PURPORT: The process of changing one's nature at the critical moment of death is here explained. A person who at the end of his life quits his body thinking of Kṛṣṇa attains the transcendental nature of the Supreme Lord, but it is not true that a person who thinks of something other than Kṛṣṇa attains the same transcendental state. This is a point we should note very carefully. How can one die in the proper state of mind? Mahārāja Bharata, although a great personality, thought of a deer at the end of his life, and so in his next life he was transferred into the body of a deer. Although as a deer he remembered his past activities, he had to accept that animal body. Of course, one's thoughts during the course of one's life accumulate to influence one's thoughts at the moment of death, so this life creates one's next life. If in one's present life one lives in the mode of goodness and always thinks of Kṛṣṇa, it is possible for one to remember Kṛṣṇa at the end of one's life. That will help one be transferred to the transcendental nature of Kṛṣṇa. If one is transcendentally absorbed in Kṛṣṇa's service, then his next body will be transcendental (spiritual), not material. Therefore the chanting of Hare Kṛṣṇa, Hare Kṛṣṇa, Kṛṣṇa Kṛṣṇa, Hare Hare/ Hare Rāma, Hare Rāma, Rāma Rāma, Hare Hare is the best process for successfully changing one's state of being at the end of one's life.

Text 7 तस्मात्सर्वेषु कालेषु मामनुस्मर युध्य च ।
मय्यर्पितमनोबुद्धिर्मामेवैष्यस्यसंशयः ॥ ७ ॥

tasmāt sarveṣu kāleṣu, mām anusmara yudhya ca
mayy arpita-mano-buddhir, mām evaiṣyasy asaṁśayaḥ

tasmāt – therefore; *sarveṣu* – at all; *kāleṣu* – times; *mām* – Me; *anusmara* – go on remembering; *yudhya* – fight; *ca* – also; *mayi* – unto Me; *arpita* – surrendering; *manaḥ* – mind; *buddhiḥ* – intellect; *mām* – unto Me; *eva* – surely; *eṣyasi* – you will attain; *asaṁśayaḥ* – beyond a doubt.

Therefore, Arjuna, you should always think of Me in the form of Kṛṣṇa and at the same time carry out your prescribed duty of fighting. With your activities dedicated to Me and your mind and intelligence fixed on Me, you will attain Me without doubt.

PURPORT: This instruction to Arjuna is very important for all men engaged in material activities. The Lord does not say that one should give up his prescribed duties or engagements. One can continue them and at the same time think of Kṛṣṇa by chanting Hare Kṛṣṇa. This will free one from material contamination and engage the mind and intelligence in Kṛṣṇa. By chanting Kṛṣṇa's names, one will be transferred to the supreme planet, Kṛṣṇaloka, without a doubt.

Text 8 अभ्यासयोगयुक्तेन चेतसा नान्यगामिना ।
परमं पुरुषं दिव्यं याति पार्थानुचिन्तयन् ॥ ८ ॥

abhyāsa-yoga-yuktena, cetasā nānya-gāminā
paramaṁ puruṣaṁ divyaṁ, yāti pārthānucintayan

abhyāsa-yoga – in the practice of meditation; *yuktena* – being engaged in meditation; *cetasā* – by the mind and intelligence; *na anya-gāminā* – without their being deviated; *paramam* – the Supreme; *puruṣam* – Personality of Godhead; *divyam* – transcendental; *yāti* – one achieves; *pārtha* – O son of Pṛthā; *anucintayan* – constantly thinking of.

He who meditates on Me as the Supreme Personality of Godhead, his mind constantly engaged in remembering Me, undeviated from the path, he, O Pārtha, is sure to reach Me.

PURPORT: In this verse Lord Kṛṣṇa stresses the importance of remembering Him. One's memory of Kṛṣṇa is revived by chanting the *mahā-mantra,* Hare Kṛṣṇa. By this practice of chanting and hearing the sound vibration of the Supreme Lord, one's ear, tongue and mind are engaged.

This mystic meditation is very easy to practice, and it helps one attain the Supreme Lord. *Puruṣam* means enjoyer. Although living entities belong to the marginal energy of the Supreme Lord, they are in material contamination. They think themselves enjoyers, but they are not the supreme enjoyer. Here it is clearly stated that the supreme enjoyer is the Supreme Personality of Godhead in His different manifestations and plenary expansions as Nārāyaṇa, Vāsudeva, etc.

The devotee can constantly think of the object of worship, the Supreme Lord, in any of His features – Nārāyaṇa, Kṛṣṇa, Rāma, etc. – by chanting Hare Kṛṣṇa. This practice will purify him, and at the end of his life, due to his constant chanting, he will be transferred to the kingdom of God. *Yoga* practice is meditation on the Supersoul within; similarly, by chanting Hare Kṛṣṇa one fixes his mind always on the Supreme Lord. The mind is fickle, and therefore it is necessary to engage the mind by force to think of Kṛṣṇa. One example often given is that of the caterpillar that thinks of becoming a butterfly and so is transformed into a butterfly in the same life. Similarly, if we constantly think of Kṛṣṇa, it is certain that at the end of our lives we shall have the same bodily constitution as Kṛṣṇa.

Text 9 कविं पुराणमनुशासितारमणोरणीयांसमनुस्मरेद्यः ।
सर्वस्य धातारमचिन्त्यरूपमादित्यवर्णं तमसः परस्तात् ॥ ९ ॥

kaviṁ purāṇam anuśāsitāram
aṇor aṇīyāṁsam anusmared yaḥ
sarvasya dhātāram acintya-rūpam
āditya-varṇaṁ tamasaḥ parastāt

kavim – the one who knows everything; *purāṇam* – the oldest; *anuśāsitāram* – the controller; *aṇoḥ* – than the atom; *aṇīyāṁsam* – smaller; *anusmaret* – always thinks of; *yaḥ* – one who; *sarvasya* – of everything; *dhātāram* – the maintainer; *acintya* – inconceivable; *rūpam* – whose form; *āditya-varṇam* – luminous like the sun; *tamasaḥ* – to darkness; *parastāt* – transcendental.

One should meditate upon the Supreme Person as the one who knows everything, as He who is the oldest, who is the controller, who is smaller than the smallest, who is the maintainer of everything, who is beyond all material conception, who is inconceivable, and who is always a person. He is luminous like the sun, and He is transcendental, beyond this material nature.

PURPORT: The process of thinking of the Supreme is mentioned in this verse. The foremost point is that He is not impersonal or void. One cannot meditate on something impersonal or void. That is very difficult. The process of thinking of Kṛṣṇa, however, is very easy and is factually stated herein. First of all, the Lord is *puruṣa,* a person – we think of the person Rāma and the person Kṛṣṇa. And whether one thinks of Rāma or of Kṛṣṇa, what He is like is described in this verse of *Bhagavad-gītā.* The Lord is *kavi;* that is, He knows past, present and future and therefore knows everything. He is the oldest personality because He is the origin of everything; everything is born out of Him. He is also the supreme controller of the universe, and He is the maintainer and instructor of humanity. He is smaller than the smallest. The living entity is one ten-thousandth part of the tip of a hair, but the Lord is so inconceivably small that He enters into the heart of this particle. Therefore He is called smaller than the smallest. As the Supreme, He can enter into the atom and into the heart of the smallest and control him as the Supersoul. Although so small, He is still all-pervading and is maintaining everything. By Him all these planetary systems are sustained. We often wonder how these big planets are floating in the air. It is stated here that the Supreme Lord, by His inconceivable energy, is sustaining all these big planets and systems of galaxies. The word *acintya* ("inconceivable") is very significant in this connection. God's energy is beyond our conception, beyond our thinking jurisdiction, and is therefore called inconceivable (*acintya*). Who can argue this point? He pervades this material world and yet is beyond it. We cannot comprehend even this material world, which is insignificant compared to the spiritual world – so how can we comprehend what is beyond? *Acintya* means that which is beyond this material world, that which our argument, logic and philosophical speculation cannot touch, that which is inconceivable. Therefore intelligent persons, avoiding useless argument and speculation, should accept what is stated in scriptures like the *Vedas, Bhagavad-gītā* and *Śrīmad-Bhāgavatam* and follow the principles they set down. This will lead one to understanding.

Text 10 प्रयाणकाले मनसाचलेन भक्त्या युक्तो योगबलेन चैव ।
भ्रुवोर्मध्ये प्राणमावेश्य सम्यक् स तं परं पुरुषमुपैति दिव्यम् ॥१०॥

prayāṇa-kāle manasācalena
bhaktyā yukto yoga-balena caiva
bhruvor madhye prāṇam āveśya samyak
sa taṁ paraṁ puruṣam upaiti divyam

prayāṇa-kāle – at the time of death; *manasā* – by the mind; *acalena* – without its being deviated; *bhaktyā* – in full devotion; *yuktaḥ* – engaged; *yoga-balena* – by the power of mystic *yoga; ca* – also; *eva* – certainly; *bhruvoḥ* – the two eyebrows; *madhye* – between; *prāṇam* – the life air; *āveśya* – establishing; *samyak* – completely; *saḥ* – he; *tam* – that; *param* – transcendental; *puruṣam* – Personality of Godhead; *upaiti* – achieves; *divyam* – in the spiritual kingdom.

One who, at the time of death, fixes his life air between the eyebrows and, by the strength of yoga, with an undeviating mind, engages himself in remembering the Supreme Lord in full devotion, will certainly attain to the Supreme Personality of Godhead.

PURPORT: In this verse it is clearly stated that at the time of death the mind must be fixed in devotion to the Supreme Personality of Godhead. For those practiced in *yoga,* it is recommended that they raise the life force between the eyebrows (to the *ājñā-cakra*). The practice of *ṣaṭ-cakra-yoga,* involving meditation on the six *cakras,* is suggested here. A pure devotee does not practice such *yoga,* but because he is always engaged in Kṛṣṇa consciousness, at death he can remember the Supreme Personality of Godhead by His grace. This is explained in verse fourteen.

The particular use of the word *yoga-balena* is significant in this verse because without practice of *yoga* – whether *ṣaṭ-cakra-yoga* or *bhakti-yoga* – one cannot come to this transcendental state of being at the time of death. One cannot suddenly remember the Supreme Lord at death; one must have practiced some *yoga* system, especially the system of *bhakti-yoga.* Since one's mind at death is very disturbed, one should practice transcendence through *yoga* during one's life.

Text 11 यदक्षरं वेदविदो वदन्ति विशन्ति यद्यतयो वीतरागाः ।
यदिच्छन्तो ब्रह्मचर्यं चरन्ति तत्ते पदं सङ्ग्रहेण प्रवक्ष्ये ॥११॥

yad akṣaraṁ veda-vido vadanti
viśanti yad yatayo vīta-rāgāḥ
yad icchanto brahma-caryaṁ caranti
tat te padaṁ saṅgraheṇa pravakṣye

yat – that which; *akṣaram* – syllable *oṁ; veda-vidaḥ* – persons conversant with the *Vedas; vadanti* – say; *viśanti* – enter; *yat* – in which; *yatayaḥ* – great sages; *vīta-rāgāḥ* – in the renounced order of life; *yat* – that which; *icchantaḥ* – desiring; *brahma-caryam* – celibacy; *caranti* –

practice; *tat* – that; *te* – unto you; *padam* – situation; *saṅgraheṇa* – in summary; *pravakṣye* – I shall explain.

Persons who are learned in the Vedas, who utter oṁ-kāra, and who are great sages in the renounced order enter into Brahman. Desiring such perfection, one practices celibacy. I shall now briefly explain to you this process by which one may attain salvation.

PURPORT: Lord Śrī Kṛṣṇa has recommended to Arjuna the practice of *ṣaṭ-cakra-yoga,* in which one places the air of life between the eyebrows. Taking it for granted that Arjuna might not know how to practice *ṣaṭ-cakra-yoga,* the Lord explains the process in the following verses. The Lord says that Brahman, although one without a second, has various manifestations and features. Especially for the impersonalists, the *akṣara,* or *oṁ-kāra* – the syllable *oṁ* – is identical with Brahman. Kṛṣṇa here explains the impersonal Brahman, into which the renounced order of sages enter.

In the Vedic system of knowledge, students, from the very beginning, are taught to vibrate *oṁ* and learn of the ultimate impersonal Brahman by living with the spiritual master in complete celibacy. In this way they realize two of Brahman's features. This practice is very essential for the student's advancement in spiritual life, but at the moment such *brahmacārī* (unmarried celibate) life is not at all possible. The social construction of the world has changed so much that there is no possibility of one's practicing celibacy from the beginning of student life. Throughout the world there are many institutions for different departments of knowledge, but there is no recognized institution where students can be educated in the *brahmacārī* principles. Unless one practices celibacy, advancement in spiritual life is very difficult. Therefore Lord Caitanya has announced, according to the scriptural injunctions for this Age of Kali, that in this age no process of realizing the Supreme is possible except the chanting of the holy names of Lord Kṛṣṇa: Hare Kṛṣṇa, Hare Kṛṣṇa, Kṛṣṇa Kṛṣṇa, Hare Hare/ Hare Rāma, Hare Rāma, Rāma Rāma, Hare Hare.

Text 12 सर्वद्वाराणि संयम्य मनो हृदि निरुध्य च ।
मूर्ध्न्याधायात्मनः प्राणमास्थितो योगधारणाम् ॥१२॥

sarva-dvārāṇi saṁyamya, mano hṛdi nirudhya ca
mūrdhny ādhāyātmanaḥ prāṇam, āsthito yoga-dhāraṇām

sarva-dvārāṇi – all the doors of the body; *saṁyamya* – controlling; *manaḥ* – the mind; *hṛdi* – in the heart; *nirudhya* – confining; *ca* – also; *mūrdhni* – on the head; *ādhāya* – fixing; *ātmanaḥ* – of the soul; *prāṇam* – the life air; *āsthitaḥ* – situated in; *yoga-dhāraṇām* – the yogic situation.

The yogic situation is that of detachment from all sensual engagements. Closing all the doors of the senses and fixing the mind on the heart and the life air at the top of the head, one establishes himself in yoga.

PURPORT: To practice *yoga* as suggested here, one first has to close the doors of all sense enjoyment. This practice is called *pratyāhāra,* or withdrawing the senses from the sense objects. The sense organs for acquiring knowledge – the eyes, ears, nose, tongue and touch – should be fully controlled and should not be allowed to engage in self-gratification. In this way the mind focuses on the Supersoul in the heart, and the life force is raised to the top of the head. In the Sixth Chapter this process is described in detail. But as mentioned before, this practice is not practical in this age. The best process is Kṛṣṇa consciousness. If one is always able to fix his mind on Kṛṣṇa in devotional service, it is very easy for him to remain in an undisturbed transcendental trance, or in *samādhi.*

Text 13 ॐ इत्येकाक्षरं ब्रह्म व्याहरन्मामनुस्मरन् ।
यः प्रयाति त्यजन्देहं स याति परमां गतिम् ॥१३॥

oṁ ity ekākṣaraṁ brahma, vyāharan mām anusmaran
yaḥ prayāti tyajan dehaṁ, sa yāti paramāṁ gatim

oṁ – the combination of letters *oṁ* (*oṁ-kāra*); *iti* – thus; *eka-akṣaram* – the one syllable; *brahma* – absolute; *vyāharan* – vibrating; *mām* – Me (Kṛṣṇa); *anusmaran* – remembering; *yaḥ* – anyone who; *prayāti* – leaves; *tyajan* – quitting; *deham* – this body; *saḥ* – he; *yāti* – achieves; *paramām* – the supreme; *gatim* – destination.

After being situated in this yoga practice and vibrating the sacred syllable oṁ, the supreme combination of letters, if one thinks of the Supreme Personality of Godhead and quits his body, he will certainly reach the spiritual planets.

PURPORT: It is clearly stated here that *oṁ,* Brahman and Lord Kṛṣṇa are not different. The impersonal sound of Kṛṣṇa is *oṁ,* but the sound Hare

Kṛṣṇa contains *oṁ.* The chanting of the Hare Kṛṣṇa *mantra* is clearly recommended for this age. So if one quits his body at the end of life chanting Hare Kṛṣṇa, Hare Kṛṣṇa, Kṛṣṇa Kṛṣṇa, Hare Hare/ Hare Rāma, Hare Rāma, Rāma Rāma, Hare Hare, he certainly reaches one of the spiritual planets, according to the mode of his practice. The devotees of Kṛṣṇa enter the Kṛṣṇa planet, Goloka Vṛndāvana. For the personalists there are also innumerable other planets, known as Vaikuṇṭha planets, in the spiritual sky, whereas the impersonalists remain in the *brahma-jyotir.*

Text 14 अनन्यचेताः सततं यो मां स्मरति नित्यशः ।
तस्याहं सुलभः पार्थ नित्ययुक्तस्य योगिनः ॥१४॥

ananya-cetāḥ satataṁ, yo māṁ smarati nityaśaḥ
tasyāhaṁ su-labhaḥ pārtha, nitya-yuktasya yoginaḥ

ananya-cetāḥ – without deviation of the mind; *satatam* – always; *yaḥ* – anyone who; *mām* – Me (Kṛṣṇa); *smarati* – remembers; *nityaśaḥ* – regularly; *tasya* – to him; *aham* – I am; *su-labhaḥ* – very easy to achieve; *pārtha* – O son of Pṛthā; *nitya* – regularly; *yuktasya* – engaged; *yoginaḥ* – for the devotee.

For one who always remembers Me without deviation, I am easy to obtain, O son of Pṛthā, because of his constant engagement in devotional service.

PURPORT: This verse especially describes the final destination attained by the unalloyed devotees who serve the Supreme Personality of Godhead in *bhakti-yoga.* Previous verses have mentioned four different kinds of devotees – the distressed, the inquisitive, those who seek material gain, and the speculative philosophers. Different processes of liberation have also been described: *karma-yoga, jñāna-yoga* and *haṭha-yoga.* The principles of these *yoga* systems have some *bhakti* added, but this verse particularly mentions pure *bhakti-yoga,* without any mixture of *jñāna, karma* or *haṭha.* As indicated by the word *ananya-cetāḥ,* in pure *bhakti-yoga* the devotee desires nothing but Kṛṣṇa. A pure devotee does not desire promotion to heavenly planets, nor does he seek oneness with the *brahma-jyotir* or salvation or liberation from material entanglement. A pure devotee does not desire anything. In the *Caitanya-caritāmṛta* the pure devotee is called *niṣkāma,* which means he has no desire for self-interest. Perfect peace belongs to him alone, not to them who strive for personal gain. Whereas a *jñāna-yogī, karma-yogī* or *haṭha-yogī* has his own selfish interests, a perfect devotee has no desire other than to please the Supreme Personality of Godhead. Therefore the Lord says that for anyone who is unflinchingly devoted to Him, He is easy to attain.

A pure devotee always engages in devotional service to Kṛṣṇa in one of His various personal features. Kṛṣṇa has various plenary expansions and incarnations, such as Rāma and Nṛsiṁha, and a devotee can choose to fix his mind in loving service to any of these transcendental forms of the Supreme Lord. Such a devotee meets with none of the problems that plague the practitioners of other *yogas. Bhakti-yoga* is very simple and pure and easy to perform. One can begin simply by chanting Hare Kṛṣṇa. The Lord is merciful to all, but as we have already explained, He is especially inclined toward those who always serve Him without deviation. The Lord helps such devotees in various ways. As stated in the *Vedas* (*Kaṭha Upaniṣad* 1.2.23), *yam evaiṣa vṛṇute tena labhyas/ tasyaiṣa ātmā vivṛṇute tanuṁ svām:* one who is fully surrendered and engaged in the devotional service of the Supreme Lord can understand the Supreme Lord as He is. And as stated in *Bhagavad-gītā* (10.10), *dadāmi buddhi-yogaṁ tam:* the Lord gives such a devotee sufficient intelligence so that ultimately the devotee can attain Him in His spiritual kingdom.

The special qualification of the pure devotee is that he is always thinking of Kṛṣṇa without deviation and without considering the time or place. There should be no impediments. He should be able to carry out his service anywhere and at any time. Some say that the devotee should remain in holy places like Vṛndāvana or some holy town where the Lord lived, but a pure devotee can live anywhere and create the atmosphere of Vṛndāvana by his devotional service. It was Śrī Advaita who told Lord Caitanya, "Wherever You are, O Lord – *there* is Vṛndāvana."

As indicated by the words *satatam* and *nityaśaḥ,* which mean "always," "regularly," or "every day," a pure devotee constantly remembers Kṛṣṇa and meditates upon Him. These are qualifications of the pure devotee for whom the Lord is most easily attainable. *Bhakti-yoga* is the system that the *Gītā* recommends above all others. Generally, the *bhakti-yogīs* are engaged in five different ways: (1) *śānta-bhakta,* engaged in devotional service in neutrality; (2) *dāsya-bhakta,* engaged in devotional service as servant; (3) *sakhya-bhakta,* engaged as friend; (4) *vātsalya-bhakta,* engaged as parent; and (5) *mādhurya-bhakta,* engaged as conjugal lover of the Supreme Lord. In any of these ways, the pure devotee is always constantly engaged in the transcendental loving service of the Supreme Lord and cannot forget the Supreme Lord, and so for him the

Lord is easily attained. A pure devotee cannot forget the Supreme Lord for a moment, and similarly the Supreme Lord cannot forget His pure devotee for a moment. This is the great blessing of the Kṛṣṇa conscious process of chanting the *mahā-mantra* – Hare Kṛṣṇa, Hare Kṛṣṇa, Kṛṣṇa Kṛṣṇa, Hare Hare/ Hare Rāma, Hare Rāma, Rāma Rāma, Hare Hare.

Text 15 मामुपेत्य पुनर्जन्म दुःखालयमशाश्वतम् ।
नाप्नुवन्ति महात्मानः संसिद्धिं परमां गताः ॥१५॥

mām upetya punar janma, duḥkhālayam aśāśvatam
nāpnuvanti mahātmānaḥ, saṁsiddhiṁ paramāṁ gatāḥ

mām – Me; *upetya* – achieving; *punaḥ* – again; *janma* – birth; *duḥkha-ālayam* – place of miseries; *aśāśvatam* – temporary; *na* – never; *āpnuvanti* – attain; *mahā-ātmānaḥ* – the great souls; *saṁsiddhim* – perfection; *paramām* – ultimate; *gatāḥ* – having achieved.

After attaining Me, the great souls, who are yogīs in devotion, never return to this temporary world, which is full of miseries, because they have attained the highest perfection.

PURPORT: Since this temporary material world is full of the miseries of birth, old age, disease and death, naturally he who achieves the highest perfection and attains the supreme planet, Kṛṣṇaloka, Goloka Vṛndāvana, does not wish to return. The supreme planet is described in Vedic literature as *avyakta* and *akṣara* and *paramā gati;* in other words, that planet is beyond our material vision, and it is inexplicable, but it is the highest goal, the destination for the *mahātmās* (great souls). The *mahātmās* receive transcendental messages from the realized devotees and thus gradually develop devotional service in Kṛṣṇa consciousness and become so absorbed in transcendental service that they no longer desire elevation to any of the material planets, nor do they even want to be transferred to any spiritual planet. They only want Kṛṣṇa and Kṛṣṇa's association, and nothing else. That is the highest perfection of life. This verse specifically mentions the personalist devotees of the Supreme Lord, Kṛṣṇa. These devotees in Kṛṣṇa consciousness achieve the highest perfection of life. In other words, they are the supreme souls.

Text 16 आब्रह्मभुवनाल्लोकाः पुनरावर्तिनोऽर्जुन ।
मामुपेत्य तु कौन्तेय पुनर्जन्म न विद्यते ॥१६॥

ā-brahma-bhuvanāl lokāḥ, punar āvartino 'rjuna
mām upetya tu kaunteya, punar janma na vidyate

ā-brahma-bhuvanāt – up to the Brahmaloka planet; *lokāḥ* – the planetary systems; *punaḥ* – again; *āvartinaḥ* – returning; *arjuna* – O Arjuna; *mām* – unto Me; *upetya* – arriving; *tu* – but; *kaunteya* – O son of Kuntī; *punaḥ janma* – rebirth; *na* – never; *vidyate* – takes place.

From the highest planet in the material world down to the lowest, all are places of misery wherein repeated birth and death take place. But one who attains to My abode, O son of Kuntī, never takes birth again.

PURPORT: All kinds of *yogīs* – *karma, jñāna, haṭha,* etc. – eventually have to attain devotional perfection in *bhakti-yoga,* or Kṛṣṇa consciousness, before they can go to Kṛṣṇa's transcendental abode and never return. Those who attain the highest material planets, the planets of the demigods, are again subjected to repeated birth and death. As persons on earth are elevated to higher planets, people on higher planets such as Brahmaloka, Candraloka and Indraloka fall down to earth. The practice of sacrifice called *pañcāgni-vidyā,* recommended in the *Chāndogya Upaniṣad,* enables one to achieve Brahmaloka, but if, on Brahmaloka, one does not cultivate Kṛṣṇa consciousness, then he must return to earth. Those who progress in Kṛṣṇa consciousness on the higher planets are gradually elevated to higher and higher planets and at the time of universal devastation are transferred to the eternal spiritual kingdom. Baladeva Vidyābhūṣaṇa, in his commentary on *Bhagavad-gītā,* quotes this verse:

brahmaṇā saha te sarve, samprāpte pratisañcare
parasyānte kṛtātmānaḥ, praviśanti paraṁ padam

"When there is devastation of this material universe, Brahmā and his devotees, who are constantly engaged in Kṛṣṇa consciousness, are all transferred to the spiritual universe and to specific spiritual planets according to their desires."

Text 17 सहस्रयुगपर्यन्तमहर्यद् ब्रह्मणो विदुः ।
रात्रिं युगसहस्रान्तां तेऽहोरात्रविदो जनाः ॥१७॥

sahasra-yuga-paryantam, ahar yad brahmaṇo viduḥ
rātriṁ yuga-sahasrāntāṁ, te 'ho-rātra-vido janāḥ

sahasra – one thousand; *yuga* – millenniums; *paryantam* – including; *ahaḥ* – day; *yat* – that which; *brahmaṇaḥ* – of Brahmā; *viduḥ* – they know; *rātrim* – night; *yuga* – millenniums; *sahasra-antām* – similarly, ending after one thousand; *te* – they; *ahaḥ-rātra* – day and night; *vidaḥ* – who understand; *janāḥ* – people.

By human calculation, a thousand ages taken together form the duration of Brahmā's one day. And such also is the duration of his night.

PURPORT: The duration of the material universe is limited. It is manifested in cycles of *kalpas.* A *kalpa* is a day of Brahmā, and one day of Brahmā consists of a thousand cycles of four *yugas,* or ages: Satya, Tretā, Dvāpara and Kali. The cycle of Satya is characterized by virtue, wisdom and religion, there being practically no ignorance and vice, and the *yuga* lasts 1,728,000 years. In the Tretā-yuga vice is introduced, and this *yuga* lasts 1,296,000 years. In the Dvāpara-yuga there is an even greater decline in virtue and religion, vice increasing, and this *yuga* lasts 864,000 years. And finally in Kali-yuga (the *yuga* we have now been experiencing over the past 5,000 years) there is an abundance of strife, ignorance, irreligion and vice, true virtue being practically nonexistent, and this *yuga* lasts 432,000 years. In Kali-yuga vice increases to such a point that at the termination of the *yuga* the Supreme Lord Himself appears as the Kalki *avatāra,* vanquishes the demons, saves His devotees, and commences another Satya-yuga. Then the process is set rolling again. These four *yugas,* rotating a thousand times, comprise one day of Brahmā, and the same number comprise one night. Brahmā lives one hundred of such "years" and then dies. These "hundred years" by earth calculations total to 311 trillion and 40 billion earth years. By these calculations the life of Brahmā seems fantastic and interminable, but from the viewpoint of eternity it is as brief as a lightning flash. In the Causal Ocean there are innumerable Brahmās rising and disappearing like bubbles in the Atlantic. Brahmā and his creation are all part of the material universe, and therefore they are in constant flux.

In the material universe not even Brahmā is free from the process of birth, old age, disease and death. Brahmā, however, is directly engaged in the service of the Supreme Lord in the management of this universe – therefore he at once attains liberation. Elevated *sannyāsīs* are promoted to Brahmā's particular planet, Brahmaloka, which is the highest planet in the material universe and which survives all the heavenly planets in the upper strata of the planetary system, but in due course Brahmā and all the inhabitants of Brahmaloka are subject to death, according to the law of material nature.

Text 18 अव्यक्ताद्व्यक्तयः सर्वाः प्रभवन्त्यहरागमे ।
रात्र्यागमे प्रलीयन्ते तत्रैवाव्यक्तसंज्ञके ॥१८॥

avyaktād vyaktayaḥ sarvāḥ, prabhavanty ahar-āgame
rātry-āgame pralīyante, tatraivāvyakta-saṁjñake

avyaktāt – from the unmanifest; *vyaktayaḥ* – living entities; *sarvāḥ* – all; *prabhavanti* – become manifest; *ahaḥ-āgame* – at the beginning of the day; *rātri-āgame* – at the fall of night; *pralīyante* – are annihilated; *tatra* – into that; *eva* – certainly; *avyakta* – the unmanifest; *saṁjñake* – which is called.

At the beginning of Brahmā's day, all living entities become manifest from the unmanifest state, and thereafter, when the night falls, they are merged into the unmanifest again.

Text 19 भूतग्रामः स एवायं भूत्वा भूत्वा प्रलीयते ।
रात्र्यागमेऽवशः पार्थ प्रभवत्यहरागमे ॥१९॥

bhūta-grāmaḥ sa evāyaṁ, bhūtvā bhūtvā pralīyate
rātry-āgame 'vaśaḥ pārtha, prabhavaty ahar-āgame

bhūta-grāmaḥ – the aggregate of all living entities; *saḥ* – these; *eva* – certainly; *ayam* – this; *bhūtvā bhūtvā* – repeatedly taking birth; *pralīyate* – is annihilated; *rātri* – of night; *āgame* – on the arrival; *avaśaḥ* – automatically; *pārtha* – O son of Pṛthā; *prabhavati* – is manifest; *ahaḥ* – of daytime; *āgame* – on the arrival.

Again and again, when Brahmā's day arrives, all living entities come into being, and with the arrival of Brahmā's night they are helplessly annihilated.

PURPORT: The less intelligent, who try to remain within this material world, may be elevated to higher planets and then again must come down to this planet earth. During the daytime of Brahmā they can exhibit their activities on higher and lower planets within this material world, but at the coming of Brahmā's night they are all annihilated. In the day they receive various bodies for material activities, and at night they no longer have bodies but remain compact in the body of Viṣṇu. Then again they are manifest at the arrival of Brahmā's day. *Bhūtvā bhūtvā pralīyate:* during the day they become manifest, and at night they are annihilated again.

Ultimately, when Brahmā's life is finished, they are all annihilated and remain unmanifest for millions and millions of years. And when Brahmā is born again in another millennium they are again manifest. In this way they are captivated by the spell of the material world. But those intelligent persons who take to Kṛṣṇa consciousness use the human life fully in the devotional service of the Lord, chanting Hare Kṛṣṇa, Hare Kṛṣṇa, Kṛṣṇa Kṛṣṇa, Hare Hare/ Hare Rāma, Hare Rāma, Rāma Rāma, Hare Hare. Thus they transfer themselves, even in this life, to the spiritual planet of Kṛṣṇa and become eternally blissful there, not being subject to such rebirths.

Text 20 परस्तस्मात्तु भावोऽन्योऽव्यक्तोऽव्यक्तात्सनातनः ।
यः स सर्वेषु भूतेषु नश्यत्सु न विनश्यति ॥२०॥

paras tasmāt tu bhāvo 'nyo, 'vyakto 'vyaktāt sanātanaḥ
yaḥ sa sarveṣu bhūteṣu, naśyatsu na vinaśyati

paraḥ – transcendental; *tasmāt* – to that; *tu* – but; *bhāvaḥ* – nature; *anyaḥ* – another; *avyaktaḥ* – unmanifest; *avyaktāt* – to the unmanifest; *sanātanaḥ* – eternal; *yaḥ saḥ* – that which; *sarveṣu* – all; *bhūteṣu* – manifestation; *naśyatsu* – being annihilated; *na* – never; *vinaśyati* – is annihilated.

Yet there is another unmanifest nature, which is eternal and is transcendental to this manifested and unmanifested matter. It is supreme and is never annihilated. When all in this world is annihilated, that part remains as it is.

PURPORT: Kṛṣṇa's superior, spiritual energy is transcendental and eternal. It is beyond all the changes of material nature, which is manifest and annihilated during the days and nights of Brahmā. Kṛṣṇa's superior energy is completely opposite in quality to material nature. Superior and inferior nature are explained in the Seventh Chapter.

Text 21 अव्यक्तोऽक्षर इत्युक्तस्तमाहुः परमां गतिम् ।
यं प्राप्य न निवर्तन्ते तद्धाम परमं मम ॥२१॥

avyakto 'kṣara ity uktas, tam āhuḥ paramāṁ gatim
yaṁ prāpya na nivartante, tad dhāma paramaṁ mama

avyaktaḥ – unmanifested; *akṣaraḥ* – infallible; *iti* – thus; *uktaḥ* – is said; *tam* – that; *āhuḥ* – is known; *paramām* – the ultimate; *gatim* – destination; *yam* – which; *prāpya* – gaining; *na* – never; *nivartante* – come back; *tat* – that; *dhāma* – abode; *paramam* – supreme; *mama* – My.

That which the Vedāntists describe as unmanifest and infallible, that which is known as the supreme destination, that place from which, having attained it, one never returns – that is My supreme abode.

PURPORT: The supreme abode of the Personality of Godhead, Kṛṣṇa, is described in the *Brahma-saṁhitā* as *cintāmaṇi-dhāma,* a place where all desires are fulfilled. The supreme abode of Lord Kṛṣṇa, known as Goloka Vṛndāvana, is full of palaces made of touchstone. There are also trees, called "desire trees," that supply any type of eatable upon demand, and there are cows, known as *surabhi* cows, which supply a limitless supply of milk. In this abode, the Lord is served by hundreds of thousands of goddesses of fortune (Lakṣmīs), and He is called Govinda, the primal Lord and the cause of all causes. The Lord is accustomed to blow His flute (*veṇuṁ kvaṇantam*). His transcendental form is the most attractive in all the worlds – His eyes are like lotus petals, and the color of His body is like the color of clouds. He is so attractive that His beauty excels that of thousands of Cupids. He wears saffron cloth, a garland around His neck and a peacock feather in His hair. In the *Bhagavad-gītā* Lord Kṛṣṇa gives only a small hint of His personal abode, Goloka Vṛndāvana, which is the supermost planet in the spiritual kingdom. A vivid description is given in the *Brahma-saṁhitā.* Vedic literatures (*Kaṭha Upaniṣad* 1.3.11) state that there is nothing superior to the abode of the Supreme Godhead, and that that abode is the ultimate destination (*puruṣān na paraṁ kiñcit sā kāṣṭhā paramā gatiḥ*). When one attains to it, he never returns to the material world. Kṛṣṇa's supreme abode and Kṛṣṇa Himself are nondifferent, being of the same quality. On this earth, Vṛndāvana, ninety miles southeast of Delhi, is a replica of that supreme Goloka Vṛndāvana located in the spiritual sky. When Kṛṣṇa descended on this earth, He sported on that particular tract of land known as Vṛndāvana, comprising about 168 square miles in the district of Mathurā, India.

Text 22 पुरुषः स परः पार्थ भक्त्या लभ्यस्त्वनन्यया ।
यस्यान्तःस्थानि भूतानि येन सर्वमिदं ततम् ॥२२॥

puruṣaḥ sa paraḥ pārtha, bhaktyā labhyas tv ananyayā
yasyāntaḥ-sthāni bhūtāni, yena sarvam idaṁ tatam

puruṣaḥ – the Supreme Personality; *saḥ* – He; *paraḥ* – the Supreme, than whom no one is greater; *pārtha* – O son of Pṛthā; *bhaktyā* – by devotional service; *labhyaḥ* – can be achieved; *tu* – but; *ananyayā* – unalloyed, undeviating; *yasya* – whom; *antaḥ-sthāni* – within; *bhūtāni* – all of this material manifestation; *yena* – by whom; *sarvam* – all; *idam* – whatever we can see; *tatam* – is pervaded.

The Supreme Personality of Godhead, who is greater than all, is attainable by unalloyed devotion. Although He is present in His abode, He is all-pervading, and everything is situated within Him.

PURPORT: It is here clearly stated that the supreme destination, from which there is no return, is the abode of Kṛṣṇa, the Supreme Person. The *Brahma-saṁhitā* describes this supreme abode as *ānanda-cinmaya-rasa,* a place where everything is full of spiritual bliss. All the variegatedness manifest there is of the quality of spiritual bliss – nothing there is material. That variegatedness is expanded as the spiritual expansion of the Supreme Godhead Himself, for the manifestation there is totally of the spiritual energy, as explained in Chapter Seven. As far as this material world is concerned, although the Lord is always in His supreme abode, He is nonetheless all-pervading by His material energy. So by His spiritual and material energies He is present everywhere – both in the material and in the spiritual universes. *Yasyāntaḥ-sthāni* means that everything is sustained within Him, within either His spiritual or material energy. The Lord is all-pervading by these two energies.

To enter Kṛṣṇa's supreme abode or the innumerable Vaikuṇṭha planets is possible only by *bhakti,* devotional service, as clearly indicated here by the word *bhaktyā.* No other process can help one attain that supreme abode. The *Vedas* (*Gopāla-tāpanī Upaniṣad* 1.21) also describe the supreme abode and the Supreme Personality of Godhead. *Eko vaśī sarvagaḥ kṛṣṇaḥ.* In that abode there is only one Supreme Personality of Godhead, whose name is Kṛṣṇa. He is the supreme merciful Deity, and although situated there as one He has expanded Himself into millions and millions of plenary expansions. The *Vedas* compare the Lord to a tree standing still yet bearing many varieties of fruits, flowers and changing leaves. The plenary expansions of the Lord who preside over the Vaikuṇṭha planets are four-armed, and they are known by a variety of names – Puruṣottama, Trivikrama, Keśava, Mādhava, Aniruddha, Hṛṣīkeśa, Saṅkarṣaṇa, Pradyumna, Śrīdhara, Vāsudeva, Dāmodara, Janārdana, Nārāyaṇa, Vāmana, Padmanābha, etc.

The *Brahma-saṁhitā* (5.37) also confirms that although the Lord is always in the supreme abode, Goloka Vṛndāvana, He is all-pervading, so that everything is going on nicely (*goloka eva nivasaty akhilātma-bhūtah*). As stated in the *Vedas* (*Śvetāśvatara Upaniṣad* 6.8), *parāsya śaktir vividhaiva śrūyate/ svābhāvikī jñāna-bala-kriyā ca:* His energies are so expansive that they systematically conduct everything in the cosmic manifestation without a flaw, although the Supreme Lord is far, far away.

Text 23 यत्र काले त्वनावृत्तिमावृत्तिं चैव योगिनः ।
प्रयाता यान्ति तं कालं वक्ष्यामि भरतर्षभ ॥२३॥

yatra kāle tv anāvṛttim, āvṛttiṁ caiva yoginaḥ
prayātā yānti taṁ kālaṁ, vakṣyāmi bharatarṣabha

yatra – at which; *kāle* – time; *tu* – and; *anāvṛttim* – no return; *āvṛttim* – return; *ca* – also; *eva* – certainly; *yoginah* – different kinds of mystics; *prayātāḥ* – having departed; *yānti* – attain; *tam* – that; *kālam* – time; *vakṣyāmi* – I shall describe; *bharata-ṛṣabha* – O best of the Bhāratas.

O best of the Bhāratas, I shall now explain to you the different times at which, passing away from this world, the yogī does or does not come back.

PURPORT: The unalloyed devotees of the Supreme Lord, who are totally surrendered souls, do not care when they leave their bodies or by what method. They leave everything in Kṛṣṇa's hands and so easily and happily return to Godhead. But those who are not unalloyed devotees and who depend instead on such methods of spiritual realization as *karma-yoga, jñāna-yoga* and *haṭha-yoga* must leave the body at a suitable time in order to be sure of whether or not they will return to the world of birth and death.

If the *yogī* is perfect he can select the time and situation for leaving this material world. But if he is not so expert his success depends on his accidentally passing away at a certain suitable time. The suitable times at which one passes away and does not come back are explained by the Lord in the next verse. According to Ācārya Baladeva Vidyābhūṣaṇa, the Sanskrit word *kāla* used herein refers to the presiding deity of time.

Text 24 अग्निर्ज्योतिरहः शुक्लः षण्मासा उत्तरायणम् ।
तत्र प्रयाता गच्छन्ति ब्रह्म ब्रह्मविदो जनाः ॥२४॥

agnir jyotir ahaḥ śuklaḥ, ṣaṇ-māsā uttarāyaṇam
tatra prayātā gacchanti, brahma brahma-vido janāḥ

agniḥ – fire; *jyotiḥ* – light; *ahaḥ* – day; *śuklaḥ* – the white fortnight; *ṣaṭ-māsāḥ* – the six months; *uttara-ayanam* – when the sun passes on the northern side; *tatra* – there; *prayātāḥ* – those who pass away; *gacchanti* – go; *brahma* – to the Absolute; *brahma-vidaḥ* – who know the Absolute; *janāḥ* – persons.

Those who know the Supreme Brahman attain that Supreme by passing away from the world during the influence of the fiery god, in the light, at an auspicious moment of the day, during the fortnight of the waxing moon, or during the six months when the sun travels in the north.

PURPORT: When fire, light, day and the fortnight of the moon are mentioned, it is to be understood that over all of them there are various presiding deities who make arrangements for the passage of the soul. At the time of death, the mind carries one on the path to a new life. If one leaves the body at the time designated above, either accidentally or by arrangement, it is possible for him to attain the impersonal *brahma-jyotir.* Mystics who are advanced in *yoga* practice can arrange the time and place to leave the body. Others have no control – if by accident they leave at an auspicious moment, then they will not return to the cycle of birth and death, but otherwise there is every possibility that they will have to return. However, for the pure devotee in Kṛṣṇa consciousness, there is no fear of returning, whether he leaves the body at an auspicious or inauspicious moment, by accident or arrangement.

Text 25 धूमो रात्रिस्तथा कृष्णः षण्मासा दक्षिणायनम् ।
तत्र चान्द्रमसं ज्योतिर्योगी प्राप्य निवर्तते ॥२५॥

dhūmo rātris tathā kṛṣṇaḥ, ṣaṇ-māsā dakṣiṇāyanam
tatra cāndramasaṁ jyotir, yogī prāpya nivartate

dhūmaḥ – smoke; *rātriḥ* – night; *tathā* – also; *kṛṣṇaḥ* – the fortnight of the dark moon; *ṣaṭ-māsāḥ* – the six months; *dakṣiṇa-ayanam* – when the sun passes on the southern side; *tatra* – there; *cāndramasam* – the moon planet; *jyotiḥ* – the light; *yogī* – the mystic; *prāpya* – achieving; *nivartate* – comes back.

The mystic who passes away from this world during the smoke, the night, the fortnight of the waning moon, or the six months when the sun passes to the south reaches the moon planet but again comes back.

PURPORT: In the Third Canto of *Śrīmad-Bhāgavatam* Kapila Muni mentions that those who are expert in fruitive activities and sacrificial methods on earth attain to the moon at death. These elevated souls live on the moon for about 10,000 years (by demigod calculations) and enjoy life by drinking *soma-rasa.* They eventually return to earth. This means that on the moon there are higher classes of living beings, though they may not be perceived by the gross senses.

Text 26 शुक्लकृष्णे गती ह्येते जगतः शाश्वते मते ।
एकया यात्यनावृत्तिमन्ययावर्तते पुनः ॥२६॥

śukla-kṛṣṇe gatī hy ete, jagataḥ śāśvate mate
ekayā yāty anāvṛttim, anyayāvartate punaḥ

śukla – light; *kṛṣṇe* – and darkness; *gatī* – ways of passing; *hi* – certainly; *ete* – these two; *jagataḥ* – of the material world; *śāśvate* – of the *Vedas; mate* – in the opinion; *ekayā* – by one; *yāti* – goes; *anāvṛttim* – to no return; *anyayā* – by the other; *āvartate* – comes back; *punaḥ* – again.

According to Vedic opinion, there are two ways of passing from this world – one in light and one in darkness. When one passes in light, he does not come back; but when one passes in darkness, he returns.

PURPORT: The same description of departure and return is quoted by Ācārya Baladeva Vidyābhūṣaṇa from the *Chāndogya Upaniṣad* (5.10.3–5). Those who are fruitive laborers and philosophical speculators from time immemorial are constantly going and coming. Actually they do not attain ultimate salvation, for they do not surrender to Kṛṣṇa.

Text 27 नैते सृती पार्थ जानन् योगी मुह्यति कश्चन ।
तस्मात्सर्वेषु कालेषु योगयुक्तो भवार्जुन ॥२७॥

naite sṛtī pārtha jānan, yogī muhyati kaścana
tasmāt sarveṣu kāleṣu, yoga-yukto bhavārjuna

na – never; *ete* – these two; *sṛtī* – different paths; *pārtha* – O son of Pṛthā; *jānan* – even if he knows; *yogī* – the devotee of the Lord; *muhyati* – is bewildered; *kaścana* – any; *tasmāt* – therefore; *sarveṣu kāleṣu* – always;

yoga-yuktaḥ – engaged in Kṛṣṇa consciousness; *bhava* – just become; *arjuna* – O Arjuna.

Although the devotees know these two paths, O Arjuna, they are never bewildered. Therefore be always fixed in devotion.

PURPORT: Kṛṣṇa is here advising Arjuna that he should not be disturbed by the different paths the soul can take when leaving the material world. A devotee of the Supreme Lord should not worry whether he will depart by arrangement or by accident. The devotee should be firmly established in Kṛṣṇa consciousness and chant Hare Kṛṣṇa. He should know that concern over either of these two paths is troublesome. The best way to be absorbed in Kṛṣṇa consciousness is to be always dovetailed in His service, and this will make one's path to the spiritual kingdom safe, certain and direct. The word *yoga-yukta* is especially significant in this verse. One who is firm in *yoga* is constantly engaged in Kṛṣṇa consciousness in all his activities. Śrī Rūpa Gosvāmī advises, *anāsaktasya viṣayān yathārham upayuñjataḥ:* one should be unattached in material affairs and do everything in Kṛṣṇa consciousness. By this system, which is called *yukta-vairāgya,* one attains perfection. Therefore the devotee is not disturbed by these descriptions, because he knows that his passage to the supreme abode is guaranteed by devotional service.

Text 28 वेदेषु यज्ञेषु तपःसु चैव दानेषु यत्पुण्यफलं प्रदिष्टम् ।
अत्येति तत्सर्वमिदं विदित्वा योगी परं स्थानमुपैति चाद्यम् ॥२८॥

vedeṣu yajñeṣu tapaḥsu caiva
dāneṣu yat puṇya-phalaṁ pradiṣṭam
atyeti tat sarvam idaṁ viditvā
yogī paraṁ sthānam upaiti cādyam

vedeṣu – in the study of the *Vedas; yajñeṣu* – in the performances of *yajña,* sacrifice; *tapaḥsu* – in undergoing different types of austerities; *ca* – also; *eva* – certainly; *dāneṣu* – in giving charities; *yat* – that which; *puṇya-phalam* – result of pious work; *pradiṣṭam* – indicated; *atyeti* – surpasses; *tat sarvam* – all those; *idam* – this; *viditvā* – knowing; *yogī* – the devotee; *param* – supreme; *sthānam* – abode; *upaiti* – achieves; *ca* – also; *ādyam* – original.

A person who accepts the path of devotional service is not bereft of the results derived from studying the Vedas, performing sacrifices, under-

going austerities, giving charity or pursuing philosophical and fruitive activities. Simply by performing devotional service, he attains all these, and at the end he reaches the supreme eternal abode.

PURPORT: This verse is the summation of the Seventh and Eighth chapters, which particularly deal with Kṛṣṇa consciousness and devotional service. One has to study the *Vedas* under the guidance of the spiritual master and undergo many austerities and penances while living under his care. A *brahmacārī* has to live in the home of the spiritual master just like a servant, and he must beg alms from door to door and bring them to the spiritual master. He takes food only under the master's order, and if the master neglects to call the student for food that day, the student fasts. These are some of the Vedic principles for observing *brahmacarya.*

After the student studies the *Vedas* under the master for some time – at least from age five to twenty – he becomes a man of perfect character. Study of the *Vedas* is not meant for the recreation of armchair speculators, but for the formation of character. After this training, the *brahmacārī* is allowed to enter into household life and marry. When he is a householder, he has to perform many sacrifices so that he may achieve further enlightenment. He must also give charity according to the country, time and candidate, discriminating among charity in goodness, in passion and in ignorance, as described in *Bhagavad-gītā.* Then after retiring from household life, upon accepting the order of *vānaprastha,* he undergoes severe penances – living in forests, dressing with tree bark, not shaving, etc. By carrying out the orders of *brahmacarya,* householder life, *vānaprastha* and finally *sannyāsa,* one becomes elevated to the perfectional stage of life. Some are then elevated to the heavenly kingdoms, and when they become even more advanced they are liberated in the spiritual sky, either in the impersonal *brahma-jyotir* or in the Vaikuṇṭha planets or Kṛṣṇaloka. This is the path outlined by Vedic literatures.

The beauty of Kṛṣṇa consciousness, however, is that by one stroke, by engaging in devotional service, one can surpass all the rituals of the different orders of life.

The words *idaṁ viditvā* indicate that one should understand the instructions given by Śrī Kṛṣṇa in this chapter and the Seventh Chapter of *Bhagavad-gītā.* One should try to understand these chapters not by scholarship or mental speculation but by hearing them in association with devotees. Chapters Seven through Twelve are the essence of the *Bhagavad-gītā.* The first six and the last six chapters are like coverings for the middle six chapters, which are especially protected by the Lord. If one is fortunate enough to understand *Bhagavad-gītā* – especially these middle six chapters – in the association of devotees, then his life at once becomes glorified beyond all penances, sacrifices, charities, speculations, etc., for one can achieve all the results of these activities simply by Kṛṣṇa consciousness.

One who has a little faith in *Bhagavad-gītā* should learn *Bhagavad-gītā* from a devotee, because in the beginning of the Fourth Chapter it is stated clearly that *Bhagavad-gītā* can be understood only by devotees; no one else can perfectly understand the purpose of *Bhagavad-gītā.* One should therefore learn *Bhagavad-gītā* from a devotee of Kṛṣṇa, not from mental speculators. This is a sign of faith. When one searches for a devotee and fortunately gets a devotee's association one actually begins to study and understand *Bhagavad-gītā.* By advancement in the association of the devotee one is placed in devotional service, and this service dispels all one's misgivings about Kṛṣṇa, or God, and Kṛṣṇa's activities, form, pastimes, name and other features. After these misgivings have been perfectly cleared away, one becomes fixed in one's study. Then one relishes the study of *Bhagavad-gītā* and attains the state of feeling always Kṛṣṇa conscious. In the advanced stage, one falls completely in love with Kṛṣṇa. This highest perfectional stage of life enables the devotee to be transferred to Kṛṣṇa's abode in the spiritual sky, Goloka Vṛndāvana, where the devotee becomes eternally happy.

Thus end the Bhaktivedanta Purports to the Eighth Chapter of the Śrīmad Bhagavad-gītā *in the matter of Attaining the Supreme.*

CHAPTER NINE

The Most Confidential Knowledge

Text 1 श्रीभगवानुवाच
इदं तु ते गुह्यतमं प्रवक्ष्याम्यनसूयवे ।
ज्ञानं विज्ञानसहितं यज्ज्ञात्वा मोक्ष्यसेऽशुभात् ॥ १ ॥

śrī-bhagavān uvāca
idaṁ tu te guhya-tamaṁ, pravakṣyāmy anasūyave
jñānaṁ vijñāna-sahitaṁ, yaj jñātvā mokṣyase 'śubhāt

śrī-bhagavān uvāca – the Supreme Personality of Godhead said; *idam* – this; *tu* – but; *te* – unto you; *guhya-tamam* – the most confidential; *pravakṣyāmi* – I am speaking; *anasūyave* – to the nonenvious; *jñānam* – knowledge; *vijñāna* – realized knowledge; *sahitam* – with; *yat* – which; *jñātvā* – knowing; *mokṣyase* – you will be released; *aśubhāt* – from this miserable material existence.

The Supreme Personality of Godhead said: My dear Arjuna, because you are never envious of Me, I shall impart to you this most confidential knowledge and realization, knowing which you shall be relieved of the miseries of material existence.

PURPORT: As a devotee hears more and more about the Supreme Lord, he becomes enlightened. This hearing process is recommended in the *Śrīmad-Bhāgavatam:* "The messages of the Supreme Personality of

Godhead are full of potencies, and these potencies can be realized if topics regarding the Supreme Godhead are discussed amongst devotees." This cannot be achieved by the association of mental speculators or academic scholars, for it is realized knowledge.

The devotees are constantly engaged in the Supreme Lord's service. The Lord understands the mentality and sincerity of a particular living entity who is engaged in Kṛṣṇa consciousness and gives him the intelligence to understand the science of Kṛṣṇa in the association of devotees. Discussion of Kṛṣṇa is very potent, and if a fortunate person has such association and tries to assimilate the knowledge, then he will surely make advancement toward spiritual realization. Lord Kṛṣṇa, in order to encourage Arjuna to higher and higher elevation in His potent service, describes in this Ninth Chapter matters more confidential than any He has already disclosed.

The very beginning of *Bhagavad-gītā,* the First Chapter, is more or less an introduction to the rest of the book; and in the Second and Third chapters, the spiritual knowledge described is called confidential. Topics discussed in the Seventh and Eighth chapters are specifically related to devotional service, and because they bring enlightenment in Kṛṣṇa consciousness, they are called more confidential. But the matters which are described in the Ninth Chapter deal with unalloyed, pure devotion. Therefore this is called the most confidential. One who is situated in the most confidential knowledge of Kṛṣṇa is naturally transcendental; he therefore has no material pangs, although he is in the material world. In the *Bhakti-rasāmṛta-sindhu* it is said that although one who has a sincere desire to render loving service to the Supreme Lord is situated in the conditional state of material existence, he is to be considered liberated. Similarly, we shall find in the *Bhagavad-gītā,* Tenth Chapter, that anyone who is engaged in that way is a liberated person.

Now this first verse has specific significance. The words *idaṁ jñānam* ("this knowledge") refer to pure devotional service, which consists of nine different activities: hearing, chanting, remembering, serving, worshiping, praying, obeying, maintaining friendship and surrendering everything. By the practice of these nine elements of devotional service one is elevated to spiritual consciousness, Kṛṣṇa consciousness. When one's heart is thus cleared of material contamination, one can understand this science of Kṛṣṇa. Simply to understand that a living entity is not material is not sufficient. That may be the beginning of spiritual realization, but one should recognize the difference between activities of the body and the spiritual activities of one who understands that he is not the body.

In the Seventh Chapter we have already discussed the opulent potency of the Supreme Personality of Godhead, His different energies, the inferior and superior natures, and all this material manifestation. Now in Chapter Nine the glories of the Lord will be delineated.

The Sanskrit word *anasūyave* in this verse is also very significant. Generally the commentators, even if they are highly scholarly, are all envious of Kṛṣṇa, the Supreme Personality of Godhead. Even the most erudite scholars write on *Bhagavad-gītā* very inaccurately. Because they are envious of Kṛṣṇa, their commentaries are useless. The commentaries given by devotees of the Lord are bona fide. No one can explain *Bhagavad-gītā* or give perfect knowledge of Kṛṣṇa if he is envious. One who criticizes the character of Kṛṣṇa without knowing Him is a fool. So such commentaries should be very carefully avoided. For one who understands that Kṛṣṇa is the Supreme Personality of Godhead, the pure and transcendental Personality, these chapters will be very beneficial.

Text 2 राजविद्या राजगुह्यं पवित्रमिदमुत्तमम् ।
प्रत्यक्षावगमं धर्म्यं सुसुखं कर्तुमव्ययम् ॥ २ ॥

rāja-vidyā rāja-guhyaṁ
pavitram idam uttamam
pratyakṣāvagamaṁ dharmyaṁ
su-sukhaṁ kartum avyayam

rāja-vidyā – the king of education; *rāja-guhyam* – the king of confidential knowledge; *pavitram* – the purest; *idam* – this; *uttamam* – transcendental; *pratyakṣa* – by direct experience; *avagamam* – understood; *dharmyam* – the principle of religion; *su-sukham* – very happy; *kartum* – to execute; *avyayam* – everlasting.

This knowledge is the king of education, the most secret of all secrets. It is the purest knowledge, and because it gives direct perception of the self by realization, it is the perfection of religion. It is everlasting, and it is joyfully performed.

PURPORT: This chapter of *Bhagavad-gītā* is called the king of education because it is the essence of all doctrines and philosophies explained before. Among the principal philosophers in India are Gautama, Kaṇāda, Kapila, Yājñavalkya, Śāṇḍilya and Vaiśvānara. And finally there is Vyāsadeva, the author of the *Vedānta-sūtra.* So there is no dearth of knowledge in the field of philosophy or transcendental knowledge. Now the Lord says that this Ninth Chapter is the king of all such knowledge, the essence of all knowledge that can be derived from the study of the *Vedas* and different kinds of philosophy. It is the most confidential because confidential or transcendental knowledge involves understanding the difference between the soul and the body. And the king of all confidential knowledge culminates in devotional service.

Generally, people are not educated in this confidential knowledge; they are educated in external knowledge. As far as ordinary education is concerned, people are involved with so many departments: politics, sociology, physics, chemistry, mathematics, astronomy, engineering, etc. There are so many departments of knowledge all over the world and many huge universities, but there is, unfortunately, no university or educational institution where the science of the spirit soul is instructed. Yet the soul is the most important part of the body; without the presence of the soul, the body has no value. Still people are placing great stress on the bodily necessities of life, not caring for the vital soul.

The *Bhagavad-gītā,* especially from the Second Chapter on, stresses the importance of the soul. In the very beginning, the Lord says that this body is perishable and that the soul is not perishable (*antavanta ime dehā nityasyoktāḥ śarīriṇaḥ*). That is a confidential part of knowledge: simply knowing that the spirit soul is different from this body and that its nature is immutable, indestructible and eternal. But that gives no positive information about the soul. Sometimes people are under the impression that the soul is different from the body and that when the body is finished, or one is liberated from the body, the soul remains in a void and becomes impersonal. But actually that is not the fact. How can the soul, which is so active within this body, be inactive after being liberated from the body? It is always active. If it is eternal, then it is eternally active, and its activities in the spiritual kingdom are the most confidential part of spiritual knowledge. These activities of the spirit soul are therefore indicated here as constituting the king of all knowledge, the most confidential part of all knowledge.

This knowledge is the purest form of all activities, as explained in Vedic literature. In the *Padma Purāṇa,* man's sinful activities have been analyzed and are shown to be the results of sin after sin. Those who are engaged in fruitive activities are entangled in different stages and forms of sinful reactions. For instance, when the seed of a particular tree is sown, the tree does not appear immediately to grow; it takes some time. It is first a small, sprouting plant, then it assumes the form of a tree, then it flowers and bears fruit, and, when it is complete, the flowers and fruits are enjoyed by persons who have sown the seed of the tree. Similarly, a man performs a sinful act, and like a seed it takes time to fructify. There are different stages. The sinful action may have already stopped within the individual, but the results or the fruit of that sinful action are still to be enjoyed. There are sins which are still in the form of a seed, and there are others which are already fructified and are giving us fruit, which we are enjoying as distress and pain.

As explained in the twenty-eighth verse of the Seventh Chapter, a person who has completely ended the reactions of all sinful activities and who is fully engaged in pious activities, being freed from the duality of this material world, becomes engaged in devotional service to the Supreme Personality of Godhead, Kṛṣṇa. In other words, those who are actually engaged in the devotional service of the Supreme Lord are already freed from all reactions. This statement is confirmed in the *Padma Purāṇa:*

aprārabdha-phalaṁ pāpaṁ, kūṭaṁ bījaṁ phalonmukham
krameṇaiva pralīyeta, viṣṇu-bhakti-ratātmanām

For those who are engaged in the devotional service of the Supreme Personality of Godhead, all sinful reactions, whether fructified, in the stock, or in the form of a seed, gradually vanish. Therefore the purifying potency of devotional service is very strong, and it is called *pavitram uttamam,* the purest. *Uttama* means transcendental. *Tamas* means this material world or darkness, and *uttama* means that which is transcendental to material activities. Devotional activities are never to be considered material, although sometimes it appears that devotees are engaged just like ordinary men. One who can see and is familiar with devotional service will know that they are not material activities. They are all spiritual and devotional, uncontaminated by the material modes of nature.

It is said that the execution of devotional service is so perfect that one can perceive the results directly. This direct result is actually perceived, and we have practical experience that any person who is chanting the holy names of Kṛṣṇa (Hare Kṛṣṇa, Hare Kṛṣṇa, Kṛṣṇa Kṛṣṇa, Hare Hare/ Hare Rāma, Hare Rāma, Rāma Rāma, Hare Hare) in course of chanting without offenses feels some transcendental pleasure and very quickly becomes purified of all material contamination. This is actually seen. Furthermore, if one engages not only in hearing but in trying to broadcast the message of devotional activities as well, or if he engages himself in helping the missionary activities of Kṛṣṇa consciousness, he gradually feels spiritual progress. This advancement in spiritual life does not depend on any kind of previous education or qualification. The method itself is so pure that by simply engaging in it one becomes pure.

In the *Vedānta-sūtra* (3.2.26) this is also described in the following words: *prakāśaś ca karmaṇy abhyāsāt.* "Devotional service is so potent that simply by engaging in the activities of devotional service one becomes enlightened without a doubt." A practical example of this can be seen in the previous life of Nārada, who in that life happened to be the son of a maidservant. He had no education, nor was he born into a high family. But when his mother was engaged in serving great devotees, Nārada also became engaged, and sometimes, in the absence of his mother, he would serve the great devotees himself. Nārada personally says,

ucchiṣṭa-lepān anumodito dvijaiḥ
sakṛt sma bhuñje tad-apāsta-kilbiṣaḥ
evaṁ pravṛttasya viśuddha-cetasas
tad-dharma evātma-ruciḥ prajāyate

In this verse from *Śrīmad-Bhāgavatam* (1.5.25) Nārada describes his previous life to his disciple Vyāsadeva. He says that while engaged as a boy servant for those purified devotees during the four months of their stay, he was intimately associating with them. Sometimes those sages left remnants of food on their dishes, and the boy, who would wash their dishes, wanted to taste the remnants. So he asked the great devotees for their permission, and when they gave it Nārada ate those remnants and consequently became freed from all sinful reactions. As he went on eating, he gradually became as pure-hearted as the sages. The great devotees relished the taste of unceasing devotional service to the Lord by hearing and chanting, and Nārada gradually developed the same taste. Nārada says further,

tatrānv-ahaṁ kṛṣṇa-kathāḥ pragāyatām
anugraheṇāśṛṇavaṁ mano-harāḥ
tāḥ śraddhayā me 'nu-padaṁ viśṛṇvataḥ
priyaśravasy aṅga mamābhavad ruciḥ

By associating with the sages, Nārada got the taste for hearing and chanting the glories of the Lord, and he developed a great desire for devotional service. Therefore, as described in the *Vedānta-sūtra, prakāśaś ca karmaṇy abhyāsāt:* if one is engaged simply in the acts of devotional service, everything is revealed to him automatically, and he can understand. This is called *pratyakṣa,* directly perceived.

The word *dharmyam* means "the path of religion." Nārada was actually a son of a maidservant. He had no opportunity to go to school. He was simply assisting his mother, and fortunately his mother rendered some service to the devotees. The child Nārada also got the opportunity and simply by association achieved the highest goal of all religion. The highest goal of all religion is devotional service, as stated in *Śrīmad-Bhāgavatam* (*sa vai puṁsāṁ paro dharmo yato bhaktir adhokṣaje*). Religious people generally do not know that the highest perfection of religion is the attainment of devotional service. As we have already discussed in regard to the last verse of Chapter Eight (*vedeṣu yajñeṣu tapaḥsu caiva*), generally Vedic knowledge is required for self-realization. But here, although Nārada never went to the school of the spiritual master and was not educated in the Vedic principles, he acquired the highest results of Vedic study. This process is so potent that even without performing the religious process regularly, one can be raised to the highest perfection. How is this possible? This is also confirmed in Vedic literature: *ācāryavān puruṣo veda.* One who is in association with great *ācāryas,* even if he is not educated or has never studied the *Vedas,* can become familiar with all the knowledge necessary for realization.

The process of devotional service is a very happy one (*su-sukham*). Why? Devotional service consists of *śravaṇaṁ kīrtanaṁ viṣṇoḥ,* so one can simply hear the chanting of the glories of the Lord or can attend philosophical lectures on transcendental knowledge given by authorized *ācāryas.* Simply by sitting, one can learn; then one can eat the remnants of the food offered to God, nice palatable dishes. In every state devotional service is joyful. One can execute devotional service even in the most poverty-stricken condition. The Lord says, *patraṁ puṣpaṁ phalaṁ toyam:* He is ready to accept from the devotee any kind of offering, never mind what. Even a leaf, a flower, a bit of fruit, or a little water, which are all available in every part of the world, can be offered by *any* person, regardless of social position, and will be accepted if offered with love. There are many instances in history. Simply by tasting the *tulasī* leaves offered to the lotus feet of the Lord, great sages like Sanat-kumāra became great devotees. Therefore the devotional process is very nice, and it can be executed in a happy mood. God accepts only the love with which things are offered to Him.

It is said here that this devotional service is eternally existing. It is not as the Māyāvādī philosophers claim. Although they sometimes take to so-called devotional service, their idea is that as long as they are not liberated they will continue their devotional service, but at the end, when they become liberated, they will "become one with God." Such temporary time-serving devotional service is not accepted as pure devotional service. Actual devotional service continues even after liberation. When the devotee goes to the spiritual planet in the kingdom of God, he is also engaged there in serving the Supreme Lord. He does not try to become one with the Supreme Lord.

As will be seen in *Bhagavad-gītā,* actual devotional service begins after liberation. After one is liberated, when one is situated in the Brahman position (*brahma-bhūta*), one's devotional service begins (*samaḥ sarveṣu bhūteṣu mad-bhaktiṁ labhate parām*). No one can understand the Supreme Personality of Godhead by executing *karma-yoga, jñāna-yoga, aṣṭāṅga-yoga* or any other *yoga* independently. By these yogic methods one may make a little progress toward *bhakti-yoga,* but without coming to the stage of devotional service one cannot understand what is the Personality of Godhead. In the *Śrīmad-Bhāgavatam* it is also confirmed that when one becomes purified by executing the process of devotional service, especially by hearing *Śrīmad-Bhāgavatam* or *Bhagavad-gītā* from realized souls, then he can understand the science of Kṛṣṇa, or the science of God. *Evaṁ prasanna-manaso bhagavad-bhakti-yogataḥ.* When one's heart is cleared of all nonsense, then one can understand what God is. Thus the process of devotional service, of Kṛṣṇa consciousness, is the king of all education and the king of all confidential knowledge. It is the purest form of religion, and it can be executed joyfully without difficulty. Therefore one should adopt it.

Text 3 अश्रद्दधानाः पुरुषा धर्मस्यास्य परन्तप ।
अप्राप्य मां निवर्तन्ते मृत्युसंसारवर्त्मनि ॥ ३ ॥

aśraddadhānāḥ puruṣā, dharmasyāsya paran-tapa
aprāpya māṁ nivartante, mṛtyu-saṁsāra-vartmani

aśraddadhānāḥ – those who are faithless; *puruṣāḥ* – such persons; *dharmasya* – toward the process of religion; *asya* – this; *param-tapa* – O killer of the enemies; *aprāpya* – without obtaining; *mām* – Me; *nivartante* – come back; *mṛtyu* – of death; *saṁsāra* – in material existence; *vartmani* – on the path.

Those who are not faithful in this devotional service cannot attain Me, O conqueror of enemies. Therefore they return to the path of birth and death in this material world.

PURPORT: The faithless cannot accomplish this process of devotional service; that is the purport of this verse. Faith is created by association with devotees. Unfortunate people, even after hearing all the evidence of Vedic literature from great personalities, still have no faith in God. They are hesitant and cannot stay fixed in the devotional service of the Lord. Thus faith is a most important factor for progress in Kṛṣṇa consciousness. In the *Caitanya-caritāmṛta* it is said that faith is the complete conviction that simply by serving the Supreme Lord, Śrī Kṛṣṇa, one can achieve all perfection. That is called real faith. As stated in the *Śrīmad-Bhāgavatam* (4.31.14),

yathā taror mūla-niṣecanena, tṛpyanti tat-skandha-bhujopaśākhāḥ
prāṇopahārāc ca yathendriyāṇāṁ, tathaiva sarvārhaṇam acyutejyā

"By giving water to the root of a tree one satisfies its branches, twigs and leaves, and by supplying food to the stomach one satisfies all the senses of the body. Similarly, by engaging in the transcendental service of the Supreme Lord one automatically satisfies all the demigods and all other living entities." Therefore, after reading *Bhagavad-gītā* one should promptly come to the conclusion of *Bhagavad-gītā:* one should give up all other engagements and adopt the service of the Supreme Lord, Kṛṣṇa, the Personality of Godhead. If one is convinced of this philosophy of life, that is faith.

Now, the development of that faith is the process of Kṛṣṇa consciousness. There are three divisions of Kṛṣṇa conscious men. In the third class are those who have no faith. Even if they are officially engaged in devotional service, they cannot achieve the highest perfectional stage. Most probably they will slip, after some time. They may become engaged, but because they haven't complete conviction and faith, it is very difficult for them to continue in Kṛṣṇa consciousness. We have practical experience in discharging our missionary activity that some people come and apply themselves to Kṛṣṇa consciousness with some hidden motive, and as soon as they are economically a little well situated they give up this process and take to their old ways again. It is only by faith that one can advance in Kṛṣṇa consciousness. As far as the development of faith is concerned, one who is well versed in the literatures of devotional service and has attained the stage of firm faith is called a first-class person in Kṛṣṇa consciousness. And in the second class are those who are not very advanced in understanding the devotional scriptures but who automatically have firm faith that *kṛṣṇa-bhakti,* or service to Kṛṣṇa, is the best course and so in good faith have taken it up. Thus they are superior to the third class, who have neither perfect knowledge of the scriptures nor good faith but by association and simplicity are trying to follow. The third-class person in Kṛṣṇa consciousness may fall down, but when one is in the second class he does not fall down, and for the first-class person in Kṛṣṇa consciousness there is no chance of falling down. One in the first class will surely make progress and achieve the result at the end. As far as the third-class person in Kṛṣṇa consciousness is concerned, although he has faith in the conviction that devotional service to Kṛṣṇa is very good, he has not yet gained adequate knowledge of Kṛṣṇa through the scriptures like *Śrīmad-Bhāgavatam* and *Bhagavad-gītā.* Sometimes these third-class persons in Kṛṣṇa consciousness have some tendency toward *karma-yoga* and *jñāna-yoga,* and sometimes they are disturbed, but as soon as the infection of *karma-yoga* or *jñāna-yoga* is vanquished, they become second-class or first-class persons in Kṛṣṇa consciousness. Faith in Kṛṣṇa is also divided into three stages and described in *Śrīmad-Bhāgavatam.* First-class attachment, second-class attachment and third-class attachment are also explained in *Śrīmad-Bhāgavatam* in the Eleventh Canto. Those who have no faith even after hearing about Kṛṣṇa and the excellence of devotional service, who think that it is simply eulogy, find the path very difficult, even if they are supposedly engaged in devotional service. For them there is very little hope of gaining perfection. Thus faith is very important in the discharge of devotional service.

Text 4 मया ततमिदं सर्वं जगदव्यक्तमूर्तिना ।
मत्स्थानि सर्वभूतानि न चाहं तेष्ववस्थितः ॥ ४ ॥

mayā tatam idaṁ sarvaṁ, jagad avyakta-mūrtinā
mat-sthāni sarva-bhūtāni, na cāhaṁ teṣv avasthitaḥ

mayā – by Me; *tatam* – pervaded; *idam* – this; *sarvam* – all; *jagat* – cosmic manifestation; *avyakta-mūrtinā* – by the unmanifested form; *mat-sthāni* – in Me; *sarva-bhūtāni* – all living entities; *na* – not; *ca* – also; *aham* – I; *teṣu* – in them; *avasthitaḥ* – situated.

By Me, in My unmanifested form, this entire universe is pervaded. All beings are in Me, but I am not in them.

His Divine Grace
A. C. Bhaktivedanta Swami Prabhupāda
Founder-*Ācārya* of the International Society for Krishna Consciousness

Śrīla Bhaktisiddhānta Sarasvatī Ṭhākura, the spiritual master of His Divine Grace A.C. Bhaktivedanta Swami Prabhupāda.

Śrīla Gaurakiśora dāsa Bābājī Mahārāja, the spiritual master of Śrīla Bhaktisiddhānta Sarasvatī.

Śrīla Ṭhākura Bhaktivinoda, the pioneer of the program to bless the entire world with Kṛṣṇa consciousness.

Śrī Rūpa Gosvāmī and Śrī Sanātana Gosvāmī, two of the most intimate associates of Śrī Caitanya Mahāprabhu.

Śrī Pañca-tattva

Lord Śrī Kṛṣṇa Caitanya, the ideal preacher of *Śrīmad Bhagavad-gītā,* surrounded by His principal associates.

Dhṛtarāṣṭra inquires from Sañjaya about the events of the battle. (p. 31)

Kṛṣṇa and Arjuna sounded their transcendental conchshells. (p. 40)

When Arjuna saw many of his friends and relatives in the opposing army, he became overwhelmed with compassion. (p. 48)

The Supreme Lord said, "Those who are wise lament neither for the living nor for the dead." (p. 75)

As the embodied soul continuously passes, in this body, from boyhood to youth to old age, the soul similarly passes into another body at death. (p. 78)

Lord Kṛṣṇa first instructed the imperishable science of *bhakti-yoga* to the sun-god, Vivasvān. Vivasvān instructed it to Manu, the father of mankind, and Manu in turn instructed it to Ikṣvāku. (p. 181)

The humble sages, by virtue of true knowledge, see with equal vision a learned and gentle *brāhmaṇa,* a cow, an elephant, a dog and a dog-eater [outcaste]. (p. 248)

The perfection of *yoga* is to meditate on the Supreme Personality of Godhead within one's heart and make Him the ultimate goal of life. (p. 272)

A *yogī* who is not a devotee of Lord Kṛṣṇa must perform severe austerities to be able to choose a suitable moment to leave his body. (p. 373)

As he gazed upon the universal form of the Lord, Arjuna prayed with joined palms. (p. 474)

At the time of death, the consciousness created by the living being carries it to its next body. (p. 609)

If the living being has made its consciousness like an animal's,
it is sure to get an animal's body. (p. 610)

The Supreme Personality of Godhead, Śrī Kṛṣṇa, displayed His four-armed form to Arjuna, and at last He showed him His two-armed form. (p. 502)

PURPORT: The Supreme Personality of Godhead is not perceivable through the gross material senses. It is said,

ataḥ śrī-kṛṣṇa-nāmādi, na bhaved grāhyam indriyaiḥ
sevonmukhe hi jihvādau, svayam eva sphuraty adaḥ
(*Bhakti-rasāmṛta-sindhu* 1.2.234)

Lord Śrī Kṛṣṇa's name, fame, pastimes, etc., cannot be understood by material senses. Only to one who is engaged in pure devotional service under proper guidance is He revealed. In the *Brahma-saṁhitā* (5.38) it is stated, *premāñjana-cchurita-bhakti-vilocanena santaḥ sadaiva hṛdayeṣu vilokayanti:* one can see the Supreme Personality of Godhead, Govinda, always within himself and outside himself if one has developed the transcendental loving attitude towards Him. Thus for people in general He is not visible. Here it is said that although He is all-pervading, everywhere present, He is not conceivable by the material senses. This is indicated here by the word *avyakta-mūrtinā.* But actually, although we cannot see Him, everything is resting in Him. As we have discussed in the Seventh Chapter, the entire material cosmic manifestation is only a combination of His two different energies – the superior, spiritual energy and the inferior, material energy. Just as the sunshine is spread all over the universe, the energy of the Lord is spread all over the creation, and everything is resting in that energy.

Yet one should not conclude that because He is spread all over He has lost His personal existence. To refute such an argument the Lord says, "I am everywhere, and everything is in Me, but still I am aloof." For example, a king heads a government which is but the manifestation of the king's energy; the different governmental departments are nothing but the energies of the king, and each department is resting on the king's power. But still one cannot expect the king to be present in every department personally. That is a crude example. Similarly, all the manifestations that we see and everything that exists, both in this material world and in the spiritual world, are resting on the energy of the Supreme Personality of Godhead. The creation takes place by the diffusion of His different energies, and, as stated in the *Bhagavad-gītā, viṣṭabhyāham idaṁ kṛtsnam:* He is everywhere present by His personal representation, the diffusion of His different energies.

Text 5 न च मत्स्थानि भूतानि पश्य मे योगमैश्वरम् ।
भूतभृन्न च भूतस्थो ममात्मा भूतभावनः ॥ ५ ॥

na ca mat-sthāni bhūtāni, paśya me yogam aiśvaram
bhūta-bhṛn na ca bhūta-stho, mamātmā bhūta-bhāvanaḥ

na – never; *ca* – also; *mat-sthāni* – situated in Me; *bhūtāni* – all creation; *paśya* – just see; *me* – My; *yogam aiśvaram* – inconceivable mystic power; *bhūta-bhṛt* – the maintainer of all living entities; *na* – never; *ca* – also; *bhūta-sthaḥ* – in the cosmic manifestation; *mama* – My; *ātmā* – Self; *bhūta-bhāvanaḥ* – the source of all manifestations.

And yet everything that is created does not rest in Me. Behold My mystic opulence! Although I am the maintainer of all living entities and although I am everywhere, I am not a part of this cosmic manifestation, for My Self is the very source of creation.

PURPORT: The Lord says that everything is resting on Him (*mat-sthāni sarva-bhūtāni*). This should not be misunderstood. The Lord is not directly concerned with the maintenance and sustenance of this material manifestation. Sometimes we see a picture of Atlas holding the globe on his shoulders; he seems to be very tired, holding this great earthly planet. Such an image should not be entertained in connection with Kṛṣṇa's upholding this created universe. He says that although everything is resting on Him, He is aloof. The planetary systems are floating in space, and this space is the energy of the Supreme Lord. But He is different from space. He is differently situated. Therefore the Lord says, "Although they are situated on My inconceivable energy, as the Supreme Personality of Godhead I am aloof from them." This is the inconceivable opulence of the Lord.

In the *Nirukti* Vedic dictionary it is said, *yujyate 'nena durghaṭeṣu kāryeṣu:* "The Supreme Lord is performing inconceivably wonderful pastimes, displaying His energy." His person is full of different potent energies, and His determination is itself actual fact. In this way the Personality of Godhead is to be understood. We may think of doing something, but there are so many impediments, and sometimes it is not possible to do as we like. But when Kṛṣṇa wants to do something, simply by His willing, everything is performed so perfectly that one cannot imagine how it is being done. The Lord explains this fact: although He is the maintainer and sustainer of the entire material manifestation, He does not touch this material manifestation. Simply by His supreme will, everything is created, everything is sustained, everything is maintained, and everything is annihilated. There is no difference between His mind and Himself (as there is a difference between ourselves and our present material mind) because He is absolute spirit. Simultaneously the Lord is present in everything; yet the common man cannot understand how He is also present personally. He is different from this material manifestation, yet everything is resting on Him. This is explained here as *yogam aiśvaram,* the mystic power of the Supreme Personality of Godhead.

Text 6 यथाकाशस्थितो नित्यं वायुः सर्वत्रगो महान् ।
तथा सर्वाणि भूतानि मत्स्थानीत्युपधारय ॥ ६ ॥

yathākāśa-sthito nityaṁ, vāyuḥ sarvatra-go mahān
tathā sarvāṇi bhūtāni, mat-sthānīty upadhāraya

yathā – just as; *ākāśa-sthitaḥ* – situated in the sky; *nityam* – always; *vāyuḥ* – the wind; *sarvatra-gaḥ* – blowing everywhere; *mahān* – great; *tathā* – similarly; *sarvāṇi bhūtāni* – all created beings; *mat-sthāni* – situated in Me; *iti* – thus; *upadhāraya* – try to understand.

Understand that as the mighty wind, blowing everywhere, rests always in the sky, all created beings rest in Me.

PURPORT: For the ordinary person it is almost inconceivable how the huge material creation is resting in Him. But the Lord is giving an example which may help us to understand. The sky may be the biggest manifestation we can conceive. And in that sky the wind or air is the biggest manifestation in the cosmic world. The movement of the air influences the movements of everything. But although the wind is great, it is still situated within the sky; the wind is not beyond the sky. Similarly, all the wonderful cosmic manifestations are existing by the supreme will of God, and all of them are subordinate to that supreme will. As we generally say, not a blade of grass moves without the will of the Supreme Personality of Godhead. Thus everything is moving under His will: by His will everything is being created, everything is being maintained, and everything is being annihilated. Still He is aloof from everything, as the sky is always aloof from the activities of the wind.

In the *Upaniṣads* it is stated, *yad-bhīṣā vātaḥ pavate:* "It is out of the fear of the Supreme Lord that the wind is blowing." (*Taittirīya Upaniṣad* 2.8.1) In the *Bṛhad-āraṇyaka Upaniṣad* (3.8.9) it is stated, *etasya vā akṣarasya praśāsane gārgi sūrya-candramasau vidhṛtau tiṣṭhata etasya vā akṣarasya praśāsane gārgi dyāv-āpṛthivyau vidhṛtau tiṣṭhataḥ.* "By the supreme order, under the superintendence of the Supreme Personality of

Godhead, the moon, the sun, and the other great planets are moving." In the *Brahma-saṁhitā* (5.52) also it is stated,

yac-cakṣur eṣa savitā sakala-grahāṇāṁ
rājā samasta-sura-mūrtir aśeṣa-tejāḥ
yasyājñayā bhramati sambhṛta-kāla-cakro
govindam ādi-puruṣaṁ tam ahaṁ bhajāmi

This is a description of the movement of the sun. It is said that the sun is considered to be one of the eyes of the Supreme Lord and that it has immense potency to diffuse heat and light. Still it is moving in its prescribed orbit by the order and the supreme will of Govinda. So, from the Vedic literature we can find evidence that this material manifestation, which appears to us to be very wonderful and great, is under the complete control of the Supreme Personality of Godhead. This will be further explained in the later verses of this chapter.

Text 7 सर्वभूतानि कौन्तेय प्रकृतिं यान्ति मामिकाम् ।
कल्पक्षये पुनस्तानि कल्पादौ विसृजाम्यहम् ॥ ७ ॥

sarva-bhūtāni kaunteya, prakṛtiṁ yānti māmikām
kalpa-kṣaye punas tāni, kalpādau visṛjāmy aham

sarva-bhūtāni – all created entities; *kaunteya* – O son of Kuntī; *prakṛtim* – nature; *yānti* – enter; *māmikām* – My; *kalpa-kṣaye* – at the end of the millennium; *punaḥ* – again; *tāni* – all those; *kalpa-ādau* – in the beginning of the millennium; *visṛjāmi* – create; *aham* – I.

O son of Kuntī, at the end of the millennium all material manifestations enter into My nature, and at the beginning of another millennium, by My potency, I create them again.

PURPORT: The creation, maintenance and annihilation of this material cosmic manifestation are completely dependent on the supreme will of the Personality of Godhead. "At the end of the millennium" means at the death of Brahmā. Brahmā lives for one hundred years, and his one day is calculated at 4,300,000,000 of our earthly years. His night is of the same duration. His month consists of thirty such days and nights, and his year of twelve months. After one hundred such years, when Brahmā dies, the devastation or annihilation takes place; this means that the energy manifested by the Supreme Lord is again wound up in Himself. Then again, when there is a need to manifest the cosmic world, it is done by His will. *Bahu syām:* "Although I am one, I shall become many." This is the Vedic aphorism (*Chāndogya Upaniṣad* 6.2.3). He expands Himself in this material energy, and the whole cosmic manifestation again takes place.

Text 8 प्रकृतिं स्वामवष्टभ्य विसृजामि पुनः पुनः ।
भूतग्राममिमं कृत्स्नमवशं प्रकृतेर्वशात् ॥ ८ ॥

prakṛtiṁ svām avaṣṭabhya, visṛjāmi punaḥ punaḥ
bhūta-grāmam imaṁ kṛtsnam, avaśaṁ prakṛter vaśāt

prakṛtim – the material nature; *svām* – of My personal Self; *avaṣṭabhya* – entering into; *visṛjāmi* – I create; *punaḥ punaḥ* – again and again; *bhūta-grāmam* – all the cosmic manifestations; *imam* – these; *kṛtsnam* – in total; *avaśam* – automatically; *prakṛteḥ* – of the force of nature; *vaśāt* – under obligation.

The whole cosmic order is under Me. Under My will it is automatically manifested again and again, and under My will it is annihilated at the end.

PURPORT: This material world is the manifestation of the inferior energy of the Supreme Personality of Godhead. This has already been explained several times. At the creation, the material energy is let loose as the *mahat-tattva,* into which the Lord as His first *puruṣa* incarnation, Mahā-viṣṇu, enters. He lies within the Causal Ocean and breathes out innumerable universes, and into each universe the Lord again enters as Garbhodaka-śāyī Viṣṇu. Each universe is in that way created. He still further manifests Himself as Kṣīrodaka-śāyī Viṣṇu, and that Viṣṇu enters into everything – even into the minute atom. This fact is explained here. He enters into everything.

Now, as far as the living entities are concerned, they are impregnated into this material nature, and as a result of their past deeds they take different positions. Thus the activities of this material world begin. The activities of the different species of living beings are begun from the very moment of the creation. It is not that all is evolved. The different species of life are created immediately along with the universe. Men, animals, beasts, birds – everything is simultaneously created, because whatever desires the living entities had at the last annihilation are again manifested. It is clearly indicated here by the word *avaśam* that the living entities have nothing to do with this process. The state of being in their past life in the past creation is simply manifested again, and all this is done simply by His will. This is the inconceivable potency of the Supreme Personality of God. And after creating different species of life, He has no connection with them. The creation takes place to accommodate the inclinations of the various living entities, and so the Lord does not become involved with it.

Text 9 न च मां तानि कर्माणि निबध्नन्ति धनञ्जय ।
उदासीनवदासीनमसक्तं तेषु कर्मसु ॥ ९ ॥

na ca māṁ tāni karmāṇi, nibadhnanti dhanañ-jaya
udāsīna-vad āsīnam, asaktaṁ teṣu karmasu

na – never; *ca* – also; *mām* – Me; *tāni* – all those; *karmāṇi* – activities; *nibadhnanti* – bind; *dhanam-jaya* – O conqueror of riches; *udāsīna-vat* – as neutral; *āsīnam* – situated; *asaktam* – without attraction; *teṣu* – for those; *karmasu* – activities.

O Dhanañjaya, all this work cannot bind Me. I am ever detached from all these material activities, seated as though neutral.

PURPORT: One should not think, in this connection, that the Supreme Personality of Godhead has no engagement. In His spiritual world He is always engaged. In the *Brahma-saṁhitā* (5.6) it is stated, *ātmārāmasya tasyāsti prakṛtyā na samāgamaḥ:* "He is always involved in His eternal, blissful, spiritual activities, but He has nothing to do with these material activities." Material activities are being carried on by His different potencies. The Lord is always neutral in the material activities of the created world. This neutrality is mentioned here with the word *udāsīna-vat.* Although He has control over every minute detail of material activities, He is sitting as if neutral. The example can be given of a high-court judge sitting on his bench. By his order so many things are happening – someone is being hanged, someone is being put into jail, someone is awarded a huge amount of wealth – but still he is neutral. He has nothing to do with all that gain and loss. Similarly, the Lord is always neutral, although He has His hand in every sphere of activity. In the *Vedānta-sūtra* (2.1.34) it is stated, *vaiṣamya-nairghṛṇye na:* He is not situated in the dualities of this material world. He is transcendental to these dualities. Nor is He attached to the creation and annihilation of this material world. The living entities take their different forms in the various species of life according to their past deeds, and the Lord doesn't interfere with them.

Text 10 मयाध्यक्षेण प्रकृतिः सूयते सचराचरम् ।
हेतुनानेन कौन्तेय जगद्विपरिवर्तते ॥१०॥

mayādhyakṣeṇa prakṛtiḥ, sūyate sa-carācaram
hetunānena kaunteya, jagad viparivartate

mayā – by Me; *adhyakṣeṇa* – by superintendence; *prakṛtiḥ* – material nature; *sūyate* – manifests; *sa* – both; *cara-acaram* – the moving and the nonmoving; *hetunā* – for the reason; *anena* – this; *kaunteya* – O son of Kuntī; *jagat* – the cosmic manifestation; *viparivartate* – is working.

This material nature, which is one of My energies, is working under My direction, O son of Kuntī, producing all moving and nonmoving beings. Under its rule this manifestation is created and annihilated again and again.

PURPORT: It is clearly stated here that the Supreme Lord, although aloof from all the activities of the material world, remains the supreme director. The Supreme Lord is the supreme will and the background of this material manifestation, but the management is being conducted by material nature. Kṛṣṇa also states in *Bhagavad-gītā* that of all the living entities in different forms and species, "I am the father." The father gives seeds to the womb of the mother for the child, and similarly the Supreme Lord by His mere glance injects all the living entities into the womb of material nature, and they come out in their different forms and species, according to their last desires and activities. All these living entities, although born under the glance of the Supreme Lord, take their different bodies according to their past deeds and desires. So the Lord is not directly attached to this material creation. He simply glances over material nature; material nature is thus activated, and everything is created immediately. Because He glances over material nature, there is undoubtedly activity on the part of the Supreme Lord, but He has nothing to do with the manifestation of the material world directly. This example is given in the *smṛti:* when there is a fragrant flower before someone, the fragrance is touched by the smelling power of the person, yet the smelling and the flower are detached from one another. There is a similar connection between the material world and the Supreme Personality of Godhead; actually He has nothing to do with this material world, but He creates by His glance and ordains. In summary, material nature, without the superintendence of the Supreme Personality of Godhead, cannot do anything. Yet the Supreme Personality is detached from all material activities.

Text 11 अवजानन्ति मां मूढा मानुषीं तनुमाश्रितम् ।
परं भावमजानन्तो मम भूतमहेश्वरम् ॥११॥

avajānanti māṁ mūḍhā, mānuṣīṁ tanum āśritam
paraṁ bhāvam ajānanto, mama bhūta-maheśvaram

avajānanti – deride; *mām* – Me; *mūḍhāḥ* – foolish men; *mānuṣīm* – in a human form; *tanum* – a body; *āśritam* – assuming; *param* – transcendental; *bhāvam* – nature; *ajānantaḥ* – not knowing; *mama* – My; *bhūta* – of everything that be; *mahā-īśvaram* – the supreme proprietor.

Fools deride Me when I descend in the human form. They do not know My transcendental nature as the Supreme Lord of all that be.

PURPORT: From the other explanations of the previous verses in this chapter, it is clear that the Supreme Personality of Godhead, although appearing like a human being, is not a common man. The Personality of Godhead, who conducts the creation, maintenance and annihilation of the complete cosmic manifestation, cannot be a human being. Yet there are many foolish men who consider Kṛṣṇa to be merely a powerful man and nothing more. Actually, He is the original Supreme Personality, as is confirmed in the *Brahma-saṁhitā* (*īśvaraḥ paramaḥ kṛṣṇaḥ*); He is the Supreme Lord.

There are many *īśvaras,* controllers, and one appears greater than another. In the ordinary management of affairs in the material world, we find some official or director, and above him there is a secretary, and above him a minister, and above him a president. Each of them is a controller, but one is controlled by another. In the *Brahma-saṁhitā* it is said that Kṛṣṇa is the supreme controller; there are many controllers undoubtedly, both in the material and spiritual world, but Kṛṣṇa is the supreme controller (*īśvaraḥ paramaḥ kṛṣṇaḥ*), and His body is *sac-cid-ānanda,* nonmaterial.

Material bodies cannot perform the wonderful acts described in previous verses. His body is eternal, blissful and full of knowledge. Although He is not a common man, the foolish deride Him and consider Him to be a man. His body is called here *mānuṣīm* because He is acting just like a man, a friend of Arjuna's, a politician involved in the Battle of Kurukṣetra. In so many ways He is acting just like an ordinary man, but actually His body is *sac-cid-ānanda-vigraha* – eternal bliss and knowledge absolute. This is confirmed in the Vedic language also. *Sac-cid-ānanda-rūpāya kṛṣṇāya:* "I offer my obeisances unto the Supreme Personality of Godhead, Kṛṣṇa, who is the eternal blissful form of knowledge." (*Gopāla-tāpanī Upaniṣad* 1.1) There are other descriptions in the Vedic language also. *Tam ekaṁ govindam:* "You are Govinda, the pleasure of the senses and the cows." *Sac-cid-ānanda-vigraham:* "And Your form is transcendental, full of knowledge, bliss and eternality." (*Gopāla-tāpanī Upaniṣad* 1.38)

Despite the transcendental qualities of Lord Kṛṣṇa's body, its full bliss and knowledge, there are many so-called scholars and commentators of *Bhagavad-gītā* who deride Kṛṣṇa as an ordinary man. The scholar may be born an extraordinary man due to his previous good work, but this conception of Śrī Kṛṣṇa is due to a poor fund of knowledge. Therefore he is called *mūḍha,* for only foolish persons consider Kṛṣṇa to be an ordinary human being. The foolish consider Kṛṣṇa an ordinary human being because they do not know the confidential activities of the Supreme Lord and His different energies. They do not know that Kṛṣṇa's body is a symbol of complete knowledge and bliss, that He is the proprietor of everything that be and that He can award liberation to anyone. Because they do not know that Kṛṣṇa has so many transcendental qualifications, they deride Him.

Nor do they know that the appearance of the Supreme Personality of Godhead in this material world is a manifestation of His internal energy. He is the master of the material energy. As has been explained in several places (*mama māyā duratyayā*), He claims that the material energy, although very powerful, is under His control, and whoever surrenders unto Him can get out of the control of this material energy. If a soul surrendered to Kṛṣṇa can get out of the influence of material energy, then how can the Supreme Lord, who conducts the creation, maintenance and annihilation of the whole cosmic nature, have a material body like us? So this conception of Kṛṣṇa is complete foolishness. Foolish persons, however, cannot conceive that the Personality of Godhead, Kṛṣṇa, appearing just like an ordinary man, can be the controller of all the atoms and of the gigantic manifestation of the universal form. The biggest and the minutest are beyond their conception, so they cannot imagine that a form like that of a human being can simultaneously control the infinite and the minute. Actually, although He is controlling the infinite and the finite, He is apart from all this manifestation. It is clearly stated concerning His *yogam aiśvaram,* His inconceivable transcendental energy, that He can control the infinite and the finite simultaneously and that He can remain aloof from them. Although the foolish cannot imagine how Kṛṣṇa, who appears just like a human being, can control the infinite and the finite, those who are pure devotees accept this, for they know that Kṛṣṇa is the Supreme Personality of Godhead. Therefore they completely surrender unto Him and engage in Kṛṣṇa consciousness, devotional service of the Lord.

There are many controversies between the impersonalists and the personalists about the Lord's appearance as a human being. But if we consult *Bhagavad-gītā* and *Śrīmad-Bhāgavatam,* the authoritative texts for understanding the science of Kṛṣṇa, then we can understand that Kṛṣṇa is the Supreme Personality of Godhead. He is not an ordinary man, although He appeared on this earth as an ordinary human. In the *Śrīmad-Bhāgavatam,* First Canto, First Chapter, when the sages headed by Śaunaka inquired about the activities of Kṛṣṇa, they said:

kṛtavān kila karmāṇi, saha rāmeṇa keśavaḥ
ati-martyāni bhagavān, gūḍhaḥ kapaṭa-mānuṣaḥ

"Lord Śrī Kṛṣṇa, the Supreme Personality of Godhead, along with Balarāma, played like a human being, and so masked He performed many superhuman acts." (*Bhāgavatam* 1.1.20) The Lord's appearance as a man bewilders the foolish. No human being could perform the wonderful acts that Kṛṣṇa performed while He was present on this earth. When Kṛṣṇa appeared before His father and mother, Vasudeva and Devakī, He appeared with four hands, but after the prayers of the parents He transformed Himself into an ordinary child. As stated in the *Bhāgavatam* (10.3.46), *babhūva prākṛtaḥ śiśuḥ:* He became just like an ordinary child, an ordinary human being. Now, here again it is indicated that the Lord's appearance as an ordinary human being is one of the features of His transcendental body. In the Eleventh Chapter of *Bhagavad-gītā* also it is stated that Arjuna prayed to see Kṛṣṇa's form of four hands (*tenaiva rūpeṇa catur-bhujena*). After revealing this form, Kṛṣṇa, when petitioned by Arjuna, again assumed His original humanlike form (*mānuṣaṁ rūpam*). These different features of the Supreme Lord are certainly not those of an ordinary human being.

Some of those who deride Kṛṣṇa and who are infected with the Māyāvādī philosophy quote the following verse from the *Śrīmad-Bhāgavatam*

(3.29.21) to prove that Kṛṣṇa is just an ordinary man. *Ahaṁ sarveṣu bhūteṣu bhūtātmāvasthitaḥ sadā:* "The Supreme is present in every living entity." We should better take note of this particular verse from the Vaiṣṇava *ācāryas* like Jīva Gosvāmī and Viśvanātha Cakravartī Ṭhākura instead of following the interpretation of unauthorized persons who deride Kṛṣṇa. Jīva Gosvāmī, commenting on this verse, says that Kṛṣṇa, in His plenary expansion as Paramātmā, is situated in the moving and the nonmoving entities as the Supersoul, so any neophyte devotee who simply gives his attention to the *arcā-mūrti,* the form of the Supreme Lord in the temple, and does not respect other living entities is uselessly worshiping the form of the Lord in the temple. There are three kinds of devotees of the Lord, and the neophyte is in the lowest stage. The neophyte devotee gives more attention to the Deity in the temple than to other devotees, so Viśvanātha Cakravartī Ṭhākura warns that this sort of mentality should be corrected. A devotee should see that because Kṛṣṇa is present in everyone's heart as Paramātmā, every body is the embodiment or the temple of the Supreme Lord; so as one offers respect to the temple of the Lord, he should similarly properly respect each and every body in which the Paramātmā dwells. Everyone should therefore be given proper respect and should not be neglected.

There are also many impersonalists who deride temple worship. They say that since God is everywhere, why should one restrict himself to temple worship? But if God is everywhere, is He not in the temple or in the Deity? Although the personalist and the impersonalist will fight with one another perpetually, a perfect devotee in Kṛṣṇa consciousness knows that although Kṛṣṇa is the Supreme Personality, He is all-pervading, as confirmed in the *Brahma-saṁhitā.* Although His personal abode is Goloka Vṛndāvana and He is always staying there, by His different manifestations of energy and by His plenary expansion He is present everywhere in all parts of the material and spiritual creation.

Text 12 मोघाशा मोघकर्माणो मोघज्ञाना विचेतसः ।
राक्षसीमासुरीं चैव प्रकृतिं मोहिनीं श्रिताः ॥१२॥

moghāśā mogha-karmāṇo, mogha-jñānā vicetasaḥ
rākṣasīm āsurīṁ caiva, prakṛtiṁ mohinīṁ śritāḥ

mogha-āśāḥ – baffled in their hopes; *mogha-karmāṇaḥ* – baffled in fruitive activities; *mogha-jñānāḥ* – baffled in knowledge; *vicetasaḥ* – bewildered; *rākṣasīm* – demonic; *āsurīm* – atheistic; *ca* – and; *eva* –

certainly; *prakṛtim* – nature; *mohinīm* – bewildering; *śritāḥ* – taking shelter of.

Those who are thus bewildered are attracted by demonic and atheistic views. In that deluded condition, their hopes for liberation, their fruitive activities, and their culture of knowledge are all defeated.

PURPORT: There are many devotees who assume themselves to be in Kṛṣṇa consciousness and devotional service but at heart do not accept the Supreme Personality of Godhead, Kṛṣṇa, as the Absolute Truth. For them, the fruit of devotional service – going back to Godhead – will never be tasted. Similarly, those who are engaged in fruitive pious activities and who are ultimately hoping to be liberated from this material entanglement will never be successful either, because they deride the Supreme Personality of Godhead, Kṛṣṇa. In other words, persons who mock Kṛṣṇa are to be understood to be demonic or atheistic. As described in the Seventh Chapter of *Bhagavad-gītā,* such demonic miscreants never surrender to Kṛṣṇa. Therefore their mental speculations to arrive at the Absolute Truth bring them to the false conclusion that the ordinary living entity and Kṛṣṇa are one and the same. With such a false conviction, they think that the body of any human being is now simply covered by material nature and that as soon as one is liberated from this material body there is no difference between God and himself. This attempt to become one with Kṛṣṇa will be baffled because of delusion. Such atheistic and demoniac cultivation of spiritual knowledge is always futile. That is the indication of this verse. For such persons, cultivation of the knowledge in the Vedic literature, like the *Vedānta-sūtra* and the *Upaniṣads,* is always baffled.

It is a great offense, therefore, to consider Kṛṣṇa, the Supreme Personality of Godhead, to be an ordinary man. Those who do so are certainly deluded because they cannot understand the eternal form of Kṛṣṇa. The *Bṛhad-viṣṇu-smṛti* clearly states:

yo vetti bhautikaṁ dehaṁ, kṛṣṇasya paramātmanaḥ
sa sarvasmād bahiṣ-kāryaḥ, śrauta-smārta-vidhānataḥ
mukhaṁ tasyāvalokyāpi, sa-celaṁ snānam ācaret

"One who considers the body of Kṛṣṇa to be material should be driven out from all rituals and activities of the *śruti* and the *smṛti.* And if one by chance sees his face, one should at once take bath in the Ganges to rid himself of infection." People jeer at Kṛṣṇa because they are envious of the Supreme Personality of Godhead. Their destiny is certainly to take birth after birth in the species of atheistic and demoniac life. Perpetually, their real knowledge will remain under delusion, and gradually they will regress to the darkest region of creation.

Text 13 महात्मानस्तु मां पार्थ दैवीं प्रकृतिमाश्रिताः ।
भजन्त्यनन्यमनसो ज्ञात्वा भूतादिमव्ययम् ॥१३॥

mahātmānas tu māṁ pārtha, daivīṁ prakṛtim āśritāḥ
bhajanty ananya-manaso, jñātvā bhūtādim avyayam

mahā-ātmānaḥ – the great souls; *tu* – but; *mām* – unto Me; *pārtha* – O son of Pṛthā; *daivīm* – divine; *prakṛtim* – nature; *āśritāḥ* – having taken shelter of; *bhajanti* – render service; *ananya-manasaḥ* – without deviation of the mind; *jñātvā* – knowing; *bhūta* – of creation; *ādim* – the origin; *avyayam* – inexhaustible.

O son of Pṛthā, those who are not deluded, the great souls, are under the protection of the divine nature. They are fully engaged in devotional service because they know Me as the Supreme Personality of Godhead, original and inexhaustible.

PURPORT: In this verse the description of the *mahātmā* is clearly given. The first sign of the *mahātmā* is that he is already situated in the divine nature. He is not under the control of material nature. And how is this effected? That is explained in the Seventh Chapter: one who surrenders unto the Supreme Personality of Godhead, Śrī Kṛṣṇa, at once becomes freed from the control of material nature. That is the qualification. One can become free from the control of material nature as soon as he surrenders his soul to the Supreme Personality of Godhead. That is the preliminary formula. Being marginal potency, as soon as the living entity is freed from the control of material nature, he is put under the guidance of the spiritual nature. The guidance of the spiritual nature is called *daivī prakṛti,* divine nature. So when one is promoted in that way – by surrendering to the Supreme Personality of Godhead – one attains to the stage of great soul, *mahātmā.*

The *mahātmā* does not divert his attention to anything outside Kṛṣṇa, because he knows perfectly well that Kṛṣṇa is the original Supreme Person, the cause of all causes. There is no doubt about it. Such a *mahātmā,* or great soul, develops through association with other *mahātmās,* pure devotees. Pure devotees are not even attracted by Kṛṣṇa's other features, such as the four-armed Mahā-viṣṇu. They are simply attracted by the two-armed form of Kṛṣṇa. They are not attracted to other features of Kṛṣṇa, nor are they concerned with any form of a demigod or of a human being. They meditate only upon Kṛṣṇa in Kṛṣṇa consciousness. They are always engaged in the unswerving service of the Lord in Kṛṣṇa consciousness.

Text 14 सततं कीर्तयन्तो मां यतन्तश्च दृढव्रताः ।
नमस्यन्तश्च मां भक्त्या नित्ययुक्ता उपासते ॥१४॥

satataṁ kīrtayanto māṁ, yatantaś ca dṛḍha-vratāḥ
namasyantaś ca māṁ bhaktyā, nitya-yuktā upāsate

satatam – always; *kīrtayantaḥ* – chanting; *mām* – about Me; *yatantaḥ* – fully endeavoring; *ca* – also; *dṛḍha-vratāḥ* – with determination; *namasyantaḥ* – offering obeisances; *ca* – and; *mām* – Me; *bhaktyā* – in devotion; *nitya-yuktāḥ* – perpetually engaged; *upāsate* – worship.

Always chanting My glories, endeavoring with great determination, bowing down before Me, these great souls perpetually worship Me with devotion.

PURPORT: The *mahātmā* cannot be manufactured by rubber-stamping an ordinary man. His symptoms are described here: a *mahātmā* is always engaged in chanting the glories of the Supreme Lord Kṛṣṇa, the Personality of Godhead. He has no other business. He is always engaged in the glorification of the Lord. In other words, he is not an impersonalist. When the question of glorification is there, one has to glorify the Supreme Lord, praising His holy name, His eternal form, His transcendental qualities and His uncommon pastimes. One has to glorify all these things; therefore a *mahātmā* is attached to the Supreme Personality of Godhead.

One who is attached to the impersonal feature of the Supreme Lord, the *brahma-jyotir,* is not described as *mahātmā* in the *Bhagavad-gītā.* He is described in a different way in the next verse. The *mahātmā* is always engaged in different activities of devotional service, as described in the *Śrīmad-Bhāgavatam,* hearing and chanting about Viṣṇu, not a demigod or human being. That is devotion: *śravaṇaṁ kīrtanaṁ viṣṇoḥ* and *smaraṇam,* remembering Him. Such a *mahātmā* has firm determination to achieve at the ultimate end the association of the Supreme Lord in any one of the five transcendental *rasas.* To achieve that success, he engages all activities – mental, bodily and vocal, everything – in the service of the Supreme Lord, Śrī Kṛṣṇa. That is called full Kṛṣṇa consciousness.

In devotional service there are certain activities which are called determined, such as fasting on certain days, like the eleventh day of the moon, Ekādaśī, and on the appearance day of the Lord. All these rules and regulations are offered by the great *ācāryas* for those who are actually interested in getting admission into the association of the Supreme Personality of Godhead in the transcendental world. The *mahātmās,* great souls, strictly observe all these rules and regulations, and therefore they are sure to achieve the desired result.

As described in the second verse of this chapter, not only is this devotional service easy, but it can be performed in a happy mood. One does not need to undergo any severe penance and austerity. He can live this life in devotional service, guided by an expert spiritual master, and in any position, either as a householder or a *sannyāsī* or a *brahmacārī;* in any position and anywhere in the world, he can perform this devotional service to the Supreme Personality of Godhead and thus become actually *mahātmā,* a great soul.

Text 15 ज्ञानयज्ञेन चाप्यन्ये यजन्तो मामुपासते ।
एकत्वेन पृथक्त्वेन बहुधा विश्वतोमुखम् ॥१५॥

jñāna-yajñena cāpy anye, yajanto mām upāsate
ekatvena pṛthaktvena, bahudhā viśvato-mukham

jñāna-yajñena – by cultivation of knowledge; *ca* – also; *api* – certainly; *anye* – others; *yajantaḥ* – sacrificing; *mām* – Me; *upāsate* – worship; *ekatvena* – in oneness; *pṛthaktvena* – in duality; *bahudhā* – in diversity; *viśvataḥ-mukham* – and in the universal form.

Others, who engage in sacrifice by the cultivation of knowledge, worship the Supreme Lord as the one without a second, as diverse in many, and in the universal form.

PURPORT: This verse is the summary of the previous verses. The Lord tells Arjuna that those who are purely in Kṛṣṇa consciousness and do not know anything other than Kṛṣṇa are called *mahātmā;* yet there are other persons who are not exactly in the position of *mahātmā* but who worship Kṛṣṇa also, in different ways. Some of them have already been described as the distressed, the financially destitute, the inquisitive, and those who are engaged in the cultivation of knowledge. But there are others who are still lower, and these are divided into three: (1) he who worships himself as one with the Supreme Lord, (2) he who concocts some form of the Supreme Lord and worships that, and (3) he who accepts the universal form, the *viśva-rūpa* of the Supreme Personality of Godhead, and worships that. Out of the above three, the lowest, those who worship themselves as the Supreme Lord, thinking themselves to be monists, are most predominant. Such people think themselves to be the Supreme Lord, and in this mentality they worship themselves. This is also a type of God worship, for they can understand that they are not the material body but are actually spiritual soul; at least, such a sense is prominent. Generally the impersonalists worship the Supreme Lord in this way. The second class includes the worshipers of the demigods, those who by imagination consider any form to be the form of the Supreme Lord. And the third class includes those who cannot conceive of anything beyond the manifestation of this material universe. They consider the universe to be the supreme organism or entity and worship that. The universe is also a form of the Lord.

Text 16 अहं क्रतुरहं यज्ञः स्वधाहमहमौषधम् ।
मन्त्रोऽहमहमेवाज्यमहमग्निरहं हुतम् ॥१६॥

ahaṁ kratur ahaṁ yajñaḥ, svadhāham aham auṣadham
mantro 'ham aham evājyam, aham agnir ahaṁ hutam

aham – I; *kratuḥ* – Vedic ritual; *aham* – I; *yajñaḥ* – *smṛti* sacrifice; *svadhā* – oblation; *aham* – I; *aham* – I; *auṣadham* – healing herb; *mantraḥ* – transcendental chant; *aham* – I; *aham* – I; *eva* – certainly; *ājyam* – melted butter; *aham* – I; *agniḥ* – fire; *aham* – I; *hutam* – offering.

But it is I who am the ritual, I the sacrifice, the offering to the ancestors, the healing herb, the transcendental chant. I am the butter and the fire and the offering.

PURPORT: The Vedic sacrifice known as Jyotiṣṭoma is also Kṛṣṇa, and He is also the *mahā-yajña* mentioned in the *smṛti.* The oblations offered to the Pitṛloka or the sacrifice performed to please the Pitṛloka, considered as a kind of drug in the form of clarified butter, is also Kṛṣṇa. The *mantras* chanted in this connection are also Kṛṣṇa. And many other commodities made with milk products for offering in the sacrifices are also Kṛṣṇa. The fire is also Kṛṣṇa because fire is one of the five material elements and is therefore claimed as the separated energy of Kṛṣṇa. In other words, the Vedic sacrifices recommended in the *karma-kāṇḍa* division of the *Vedas* are in total also Kṛṣṇa. Or, in other words, those who are engaged in rendering devotional service unto Kṛṣṇa are to be understood to have performed all the sacrifices recommended in the *Vedas.*

Text 17 पिताहमस्य जगतो माता धाता पितामहः ।
वेद्यं पवित्रमोंकार ऋक्साम यजुरेव च ॥१७॥

pitāham asya jagato, mātā dhātā pitāmahaḥ
vedyaṁ pavitram oṁkāra, ṛk sāma yajur eva ca

pitā – father; *aham* – I; *asya* – of this; *jagataḥ* – universe; *mātā* – mother; *dhātā* – supporter; *pitāmahaḥ* – grandfather; *vedyam* – what is to be known; *pavitram* – that which purifies; *om-kāraḥ* – the syllable *oṁ; ṛk* – the *Ṛg Veda; sāma* – the *Sāma Veda; yajuḥ* – the *Yajur Veda; eva* – certainly; *ca* – and.

I am the father of this universe, the mother, the support and the grandsire. I am the object of knowledge, the purifier and the syllable oṁ. I am also the Ṛg, the Sāma and the Yajur Vedas.

PURPORT: The entire cosmic manifestations, moving and nonmoving, are manifested by different activities of Kṛṣṇa's energy. In the material existence we create different relationships with different living entities who are nothing but Kṛṣṇa's marginal energy; under the creation of *prakṛti* some of them appear as our father, mother, grandfather, creator, etc., but actually they are parts and parcels of Kṛṣṇa. As such, these living entities who appear to be our father, mother, etc., are nothing but Kṛṣṇa. In this verse the word *dhātā* means "creator." Not only are our father and mother parts and parcels of Kṛṣṇa, but the creator, grandmother and grandfather, etc., are also Kṛṣṇa. Actually any living entity, being part and parcel of Kṛṣṇa, is Kṛṣṇa. All the *Vedas,* therefore, aim only toward Kṛṣṇa. Whatever we want to know through the *Vedas* is but a progressive step toward understanding Kṛṣṇa. That subject matter which helps us purify our constitutional position is especially Kṛṣṇa. Similarly, the living entity who is inquisitive to understand all Vedic principles is also part and parcel of Kṛṣṇa and as such is also Kṛṣṇa. In all the Vedic *mantras* the word *oṁ,* called *praṇava,* is a transcendental sound vibration and is also Kṛṣṇa. And because in all the hymns of the four *Vedas* – *Sāma, Yajur, Ṛg* and *Atharva* – the *praṇava,* or *oṁ-kāra,* is very prominent, it is understood to be Kṛṣṇa.

Text 18 गतिर्भर्ता प्रभुः साक्षी निवासः शरणं सुहृत् ।
प्रभवः प्रलयः स्थानं निधानं बीजमव्ययम् ॥१८॥

gatir bhartā prabhuḥ sākṣī, nivāsaḥ śaraṇaṁ suhṛt
prabhavaḥ pralayaḥ sthānaṁ, nidhānaṁ bījam avyayam

gatiḥ – goal; *bhartā* – sustainer; *prabhuḥ* – Lord; *sākṣī* – witness; *nivāsaḥ* – abode; *śaraṇam* – refuge; *su-hṛt* – most intimate friend; *prabhavaḥ* – creation; *pralayaḥ* – dissolution; *sthānam* – ground; *nidhānam* – resting place; *bījam* – seed; *avyayam* – imperishable.

I am the goal, the sustainer, the master, the witness, the abode, the refuge, and the most dear friend. I am the creation and the annihilation, the basis of everything, the resting place and the eternal seed.

PURPORT: *Gati* means the destination where we want to go. But the ultimate goal is Kṛṣṇa, although people do not know it. One who does not know Kṛṣṇa is misled, and his so-called progressive march is either partial or hallucinatory. There are many who make as their destination different demigods, and by rigid performance of the strict respective methods they reach different planets known as Candraloka, Sūryaloka, Indraloka, Maharloka, etc. But all such *lokas,* or planets, being creations of Kṛṣṇa, are simultaneously Kṛṣṇa and not Kṛṣṇa. Such planets, being manifestations of Kṛṣṇa's energy, are also Kṛṣṇa, but actually they serve only as a step forward for realization of Kṛṣṇa. To approach the different energies of Kṛṣṇa is to approach Kṛṣṇa indirectly. One should directly approach Kṛṣṇa, for that will save time and energy. For example, if there is a possibility of going to the top of a building by the help of an elevator, why should one go by the staircase, step by step? Everything is resting on Kṛṣṇa's energy; therefore without Kṛṣṇa's shelter nothing can exist. Kṛṣṇa is the supreme ruler because everything belongs to Him and everything exists on His energy. Kṛṣṇa, being situated in everyone's heart, is the supreme witness. The residences, countries or planets on which we live are also Kṛṣṇa. Kṛṣṇa is the ultimate goal of shelter, and therefore one should take shelter of Kṛṣṇa either for protection or for annihilation of his distress. And whenever we have to take protection, we should know that our protection must be a living force. Kṛṣṇa is the supreme living entity. And since Kṛṣṇa is the source of our generation, or the supreme father, no one can be a better friend than Kṛṣṇa, nor can anyone be a better well-wisher. Kṛṣṇa is the original source of creation and the ultimate rest after annihilation. Kṛṣṇa is therefore the eternal cause of all causes.

Text 19 तपाम्यहमहं वर्षं निगृह्णाम्युत्सृजामि च ।
अमृतं चैव मृत्युश्च सदसच्चाहमर्जुन ॥१९॥

tapāmy aham ahaṁ varṣaṁ, nigṛhṇāmy utsṛjāmi ca
amṛtaṁ caiva mṛtyuś ca, sad asac cāham arjuna

tapāmi – give heat; *aham* – I; *aham* – I; *varṣam* – rain; *nigṛhṇāmi* – withhold; *utsṛjāmi* – send forth; *ca* – and; *amṛtam* – immortality; *ca* – and; *eva* – certainly; *mṛtyuḥ* – death; *ca* – and; *sat* – spirit; *asat* – matter; *ca* – and; *aham* – I; *arjuna* – O Arjuna.

O Arjuna, I give heat, and I withhold and send forth the rain. I am immortality, and I am also death personified. Both spirit and matter are in Me.

PURPORT: Kṛṣṇa, by His different energies, diffuses heat and light through the agency of electricity and the sun. During the summer season it is Kṛṣṇa who checks rain from falling from the sky, and then during the rainy season He gives unceasing torrents of rain. The energy which sustains us by prolonging the duration of our life is Kṛṣṇa, and Kṛṣṇa meets us at the end as death. By analyzing all these different energies of Kṛṣṇa, one can ascertain that for Kṛṣṇa there is no distinction between matter and spirit, or, in other words, He is both matter and spirit. In the advanced stage of Kṛṣṇa consciousness, one therefore makes no such distinctions. He sees only Kṛṣṇa in everything.

Since Kṛṣṇa is both matter and spirit, the gigantic universal form comprising all material manifestations is also Kṛṣṇa, and His pastimes in Vṛndāvana as two-handed Śyāmasundara, playing on a flute, are those of the Supreme Personality of Godhead.

Text 20 त्रैविद्या मां सोमपाः पूतपापा यज्ञैरिष्ट्वा स्वर्गतिं प्रार्थयन्ते ।
ते पुण्यमासाद्य सुरेन्द्रलोकमश्नन्ति दिव्यान्दिवि देवभोगान् ॥२०॥

trai-vidyā māṁ soma-pāḥ pūta-pāpā
yajñair iṣṭvā svar-gatiṁ prārthayante
te puṇyam āsādya surendra-lokam
aśnanti divyān divi deva-bhogān

trai-vidyāḥ – the knowers of the three *Vedas; mām* – Me; *soma-pāḥ* – drinkers of *soma* juice; *pūta* – purified; *pāpāḥ* – of sins; *yajñaiḥ* – with sacrifices; *iṣṭvā* – worshiping; *svaḥ-gatim* – passage to heaven; *prārthayante* – pray for; *te* – they; *puṇyam* – pious; *āsādya* – attaining; *sura-indra* – of Indra; *lokam* – the world; *aśnanti* – enjoy; *divyān* – celestial; *divi* – in heaven; *deva-bhogān* – the pleasures of the gods.

Those who study the Vedas and drink the soma juice, seeking the heavenly planets, worship Me indirectly. Purified of sinful reactions, they take birth on the pious, heavenly planet of Indra, where they enjoy godly delights.

PURPORT: The word *trai-vidyāḥ* refers to the three *Vedas – Sāma, Yajur* and *Ṛg.* A *brāhmaṇa* who has studied these three *Vedas* is called a *tri-vedī.* Anyone who is very much attached to knowledge derived from these three *Vedas* is respected in society. Unfortunately, there are many great scholars of the *Vedas* who do not know the ultimate purport of studying them. Therefore Kṛṣṇa herein declares Himself to be the ultimate goal for the *tri-vedīs.* Actual *tri-vedīs* take shelter under the lotus feet of Kṛṣṇa and engage in pure devotional service to satisfy the Lord. Devotional service begins with the chanting of the Hare Kṛṣṇa *mantra* and side by side trying to understand Kṛṣṇa in truth. Unfortunately those who are simply official students of the *Vedas* become more interested in offering sacrifices to the different demigods like Indra and Candra. By such endeavor, the worshipers of different demigods are certainly purified of the contamination of the lower qualities of nature and are thereby elevated to the higher planetary systems or heavenly planets known as Maharloka, Janaloka, Tapoloka, etc. Once situated on those higher planetary systems, one can satisfy his senses hundreds of thousands of times better than on this planet.

Text 21 ते तं भुक्त्वा स्वर्गलोकं विशालं क्षीणे पुण्ये मर्त्यलोकं विशन्ति ।
एवं त्रयीधर्ममनुप्रपन्ना गतागतं कामकामा लभन्ते ॥२१॥

te taṁ bhuktvā svarga-lokaṁ viśālaṁ
kṣīṇe puṇye martya-lokaṁ viśanti
evaṁ trayī-dharmam anuprapannā
gatāgataṁ kāma-kāmā labhante

te – they; *tam* – that; *bhuktvā* – having enjoyed; *svarga-lokam* – heaven; *viśālam* – vast; *kṣīṇe* – being exhausted; *puṇye* – the results of their pious activities; *martya-lokam* – to the mortal earth; *viśanti* – fall down; *evam* – thus; *trayī* – of the three *Vedas; dharmam* – doctrines; *anuprapannāḥ* – following; *gata-āgatam* – death and birth; *kāma-kāmāḥ* – desiring sense enjoyments; *labhante* – attain.

When they have thus enjoyed vast heavenly sense pleasure and the results of their pious activities are exhausted, they return to this mortal planet again. Thus those who seek sense enjoyment by adhering to the principles of the three Vedas achieve only repeated birth and death.

PURPORT: One who is promoted to the higher planetary systems enjoys a longer duration of life and better facilities for sense enjoyment, yet one is not allowed to stay there forever. One is again sent back to this earth upon finishing the resultant fruits of pious activities. He who has not attained perfection of knowledge, as indicated in the *Vedānta-sūtra* (*janmādy asya yataḥ*), or, in other words, he who fails to understand Kṛṣṇa, the cause of all causes, becomes baffled about achieving the ultimate goal of life and is thus subjected to the routine of being promoted to the higher planets and then again coming down, as if situated on a ferris wheel which sometimes goes up and sometimes comes down. The purport is that instead of being elevated to the spiritual world, from which there is no longer any possibility of coming down, one simply revolves in the cycle of birth and death on higher and lower planetary systems. One should better take to the spiritual world to enjoy an eternal life full of bliss and knowledge and never return to this miserable material existence.

Text 22 अनन्याश्चिन्तयन्तो मां ये जनाः पर्युपासते ।
तेषां नित्याभियुक्तानां योगक्षेमं वहाम्यहम् ॥२२॥

ananyāś cintayanto māṁ, ye janāḥ paryupāsate
teṣāṁ nityābhiyuktānāṁ, yoga-kṣemaṁ vahāmy aham

ananyāḥ – having no other object; *cintayantaḥ* – concentrating; *mām* – on Me; *ye* – those who; *janāḥ* – persons; *paryupāsate* – properly worship; *teṣām* – of them; *nitya* – always; *abhiyuktānām* – fixed in devotion; *yoga* – requirements; *kṣemam* – protection; *vahāmi* – carry; *aham* – I.

But those who always worship Me with exclusive devotion, meditating on My transcendental form – to them I carry what they lack, and I preserve what they have.

PURPORT: One who is unable to live for a moment without Kṛṣṇa consciousness cannot but think of Kṛṣṇa twenty-four hours a day, being engaged in devotional service by hearing, chanting, remembering, offering prayers, worshiping, serving the lotus feet of the Lord, rendering other services, cultivating friendship and surrendering fully to the Lord. Such activities are all auspicious and full of spiritual potencies, which make the devotee perfect in self-realization, so that his only desire is to achieve the association of the Supreme Personality of Godhead. Such a devotee undoubtedly approaches the Lord without difficulty. This is called *yoga.* By the mercy of the Lord, such a devotee never comes back to this material condition of life. *Kṣema* refers to the merciful protection of the Lord. The Lord helps the devotee to achieve Kṛṣṇa consciousness by *yoga,* and when he becomes fully Kṛṣṇa conscious the Lord protects him from falling down to a miserable conditioned life.

Text 23 येऽप्यन्यदेवताभक्ता यजन्ते श्रद्धयान्विताः ।
तेऽपि मामेव कौन्तेय यजन्त्यविधिपूर्वकम् ॥२३॥

ye 'py anya-devatā-bhaktā, yajante śraddhayānvitāḥ
te 'pi mām eva kaunteya, yajanty avidhi-pūrvakam

ye – those who; *api* – also; *anya* – of other; *devatā* – gods; *bhaktāḥ* – devotees; *yajante* – worship; *śraddhayā anvitāḥ* – with faith; *te* – they; *api* – also; *mām* – Me; *eva* – only; *kaunteya* – O son of Kuntī; *yajanti* – they worship; *avidhi-pūrvakam* – in a wrong way.

Those who are devotees of other gods and who worship them with faith actually worship only Me, O son of Kuntī, but they do so in a wrong way.

PURPORT: "Persons who are engaged in the worship of demigods are not very intelligent, although such worship is offered to Me indirectly," Kṛṣṇa says. For example, when a man pours water on the leaves and branches of a tree without pouring water on the root, he does so without sufficient knowledge or without observing regulative principles. Similarly, the process of rendering service to different parts of the body is to supply food to the stomach. The demigods are, so to speak, different officers and directors in the government of the Supreme Lord. One has to follow the laws made by the government, not by the officers or directors. Similarly, everyone is to offer his worship to the Supreme Lord only. That will automatically satisfy the different officers and directors of the Lord. The officers and directors are engaged as representatives of the government, and to offer some bribe to the officers and directors is illegal. This is stated here as *avidhi-pūrvakam.* In other words, Kṛṣṇa does not approve the unnecessary worship of the demigods.

Text 24 अहं हि सर्वयज्ञानां भोक्ता च प्रभुरेव च ।
न तु मामभिजानन्ति तत्त्वेनातश्च्यवन्ति ते ॥२४॥

ahaṁ hi sarva-yajñānāṁ, bhoktā ca prabhur eva ca
na tu mām abhijānanti, tattvenātaś cyavanti te

aham – I; *hi* – surely; *sarva* – of all; *yajñānām* – sacrifices; *bhoktā* – the enjoyer; *ca* – and; *prabhuḥ* – the Lord; *eva* – also; *ca* – and; *na* – not; *tu* – but; *mām* – Me; *abhijānanti* – they know; *tattvena* – in reality; *ataḥ* – therefore; *cyavanti* – fall down; *te* – they.

I am the only enjoyer and master of all sacrifices. Therefore, those who do not recognize My true transcendental nature fall down.

PURPORT: Here it is clearly stated that there are many types of *yajña* performances recommended in the Vedic literatures, but actually all of them are meant for satisfying the Supreme Lord. *Yajña* means Viṣṇu. In the Third Chapter of *Bhagavad-gītā* it is clearly stated that one should only work for satisfying Yajña, or Viṣṇu. The perfectional form of human civilization, known as *varṇāśrama-dharma,* is specifically meant for satisfying Viṣṇu. Therefore, Kṛṣṇa says in this verse, "I am the enjoyer of all sacrifices because I am the supreme master." Less intelligent persons, however, without knowing this fact, worship demigods for temporary benefit. Therefore they fall down to material existence and do not achieve the desired goal of life. If, however, anyone has any material desire to be fulfilled, he had better pray for it to the Supreme Lord (although that is not pure devotion), and he will thus achieve the desired result.

Text 25 यान्ति देवव्रता देवान् पितॄन् यान्ति पितृव्रताः ।
भूतानि यान्ति भूतेज्या यान्ति मद्याजिनोऽपि माम् ॥२५॥

yānti deva-vratā devān, pitṝn yānti pitṛ-vratāḥ
bhūtāni yānti bhūtejyā, yānti mad-yājino 'pi mām

yānti – go; *deva-vratāḥ* – worshipers of demigods; *devān* – to the demigods; *pitṝn* – to the ancestors; *yānti* – go; *pitṛ-vratāḥ* – worshipers of ancestors; *bhūtāni* – to the ghosts and spirits; *yānti* – go; *bhūta-ijyāḥ* – worshipers of ghosts and spirits; *yānti* – go; *mat* – My; *yājinaḥ* – devotees; *api* – but; *mām* – unto Me.

Those who worship the demigods will take birth among the demigods; those who worship the ancestors go to the ancestors; those who worship ghosts and spirits will take birth among such beings; and those who worship Me will live with Me.

PURPORT: If one has any desire to go to the moon, the sun or any other planet, one can attain the desired destination by following specific Vedic principles recommended for that purpose, such as the process technically known as Darśa-paurṇamāsa. These are vividly described in the fruitive activities portion of the *Vedas,* which recommends a specific worship of demigods situated on different heavenly planets. Similarly, one can attain the Pitā planets by performing a specific *yajña.* Similarly, one can go to many ghostly planets and become a Yakṣa, Rakṣa or Piśāca. Piśāca worship is called "black arts" or "black magic." There are many men who practice this black art, and they think that it is spiritualism, but such activities are completely materialistic. Similarly, a pure devotee, who worships the Supreme Personality of Godhead only, achieves the planets of Vaikuṇṭha and Kṛṣṇaloka without a doubt. It is very easy to understand through this important verse that if by simply worshiping the demigods one can achieve the heavenly planets, or by worshiping the Pitās achieve the Pitā planets, or by practicing the black arts achieve the ghostly planets, why can the pure devotee not achieve the planet of Kṛṣṇa or Viṣṇu? Unfortunately many people have no information of these sublime planets where Kṛṣṇa and Viṣṇu live, and because they do not know of them they fall down. Even the impersonalists fall down from the *brahmajyotir.* The Kṛṣṇa consciousness movement is therefore distributing sublime information to the entire human society to the effect that by simply chanting the Hare Kṛṣṇa *mantra* one can become perfect in this life and go back home, back to Godhead.

Text 26 पत्रं पुष्पं फलं तोयं यो मे भक्त्या प्रयच्छति ।
तदहं भक्त्युपहृतमश्नामि प्रयतात्मनः ॥२६॥

patraṁ puṣpaṁ phalaṁ toyaṁ, yo me bhaktyā prayacchati
tad ahaṁ bhakty-upahṛtam, aśnāmi prayatātmanaḥ

patram – a leaf; *puṣpam* – a flower; *phalam* – a fruit; *toyam* – water; *yaḥ* – whoever; *me* – unto Me; *bhaktyā* – with devotion; *prayacchati* – offers; *tat* – that; *aham* – I; *bhakti-upahṛtam* – offered in devotion; *aśnāmi* – accept; *prayata-ātmanaḥ* – from one in pure consciousness.

If one offers Me with love and devotion a leaf, a flower, a fruit or water, I will accept it.

PURPORT: For the intelligent person, it is essential to be in Kṛṣṇa consciousness, engaged in the transcendental loving service of the Lord, in order to achieve a permanent, blissful abode for eternal happiness. The process of achieving such a marvelous result is very easy and can be attempted even by the poorest of the poor, without any kind of qualification. The only qualification required in this connection is to be a pure devotee of the Lord. It does not matter what one is or where one is situated. The process is so easy that even a leaf or a little water or fruit can be offered to the Supreme Lord in genuine love and the Lord will be pleased to accept it. No one, therefore, can be barred from Kṛṣṇa consciousness, because it is so easy and universal. Who is such a fool that he does not want to be Kṛṣṇa conscious by this simple method and thus attain the highest perfectional life of eternity, bliss and knowledge? Kṛṣṇa wants only loving service and nothing more. Kṛṣṇa accepts even a little flower from His pure devotee. He does not want any kind of offering from a nondevotee. He is not in need of anything from anyone, because He is self-sufficient, and yet He accepts the offering of His devotee in an exchange of love and affection. To develop Kṛṣṇa consciousness is the highest perfection of life. *Bhakti* is mentioned twice in this verse in order to declare more emphatically that *bhakti,* or devotional service, is the only means to approach Kṛṣṇa. No other condition, such as becoming a *brāhmaṇa,* a learned scholar, a very rich man or a great philosopher, can induce Kṛṣṇa to accept some offering. Without the basic principle of *bhakti,* nothing can induce the Lord to agree to accept anything from anyone. *Bhakti* is never causal. The process is eternal. It is direct action in service to the absolute whole.

Here Lord Kṛṣṇa, having established that He is the only enjoyer, the primeval Lord and the real object of all sacrificial offerings, reveals what types of sacrifices He desires to be offered. If one wishes to engage in devotional service to the Supreme in order to be purified and to reach the goal of life – the transcendental loving service of God – then one should find out what the Lord desires of him. One who loves Kṛṣṇa will give Him whatever He wants, and he avoids offering anything which is undesirable or unasked. Thus meat, fish and eggs should not be offered to Kṛṣṇa. If He desired such things as offerings, He would have said so. Instead He clearly requests that a leaf, fruit, flowers and water be given to Him, and He says of this offering, "I will accept it." Therefore, we should understand that He will not accept meat, fish and eggs. Vegetables, grains, fruits, milk and water are the proper foods for human beings and are prescribed by Lord Kṛṣṇa Himself. Whatever else we eat cannot be offered to Him, since He will not accept it. Thus we cannot be acting on the level of loving devotion if we offer such foods.

In the Third Chapter, verse thirteen, Śrī Kṛṣṇa explains that only the remains of sacrifice are purified and fit for consumption by those who are seeking advancement in life and release from the clutches of the material entanglement. Those who do not make an offering of their food, He says in the same verse, are eating only sin. In other words, their every mouthful is simply deepening their involvement in the complexities of material nature. But preparing nice, simple vegetable dishes, offering them before the picture or Deity of Lord Kṛṣṇa and bowing down and praying for Him to accept such a humble offering enable one to advance steadily in life, to purify the body, and to create fine brain tissues which will lead to clear thinking. Above all, the offering should be made with an attitude of love. Kṛṣṇa has no need of food, since He already possesses everything that be, yet He will accept the offering of one who desires to please Him in that way. The important element, in preparation, in serving and in offering, is to act with love for Kṛṣṇa.

The impersonalist philosophers, who wish to maintain that the Absolute Truth is without senses, cannot comprehend this verse of *Bhagavad-gītā*. To them, it is either a metaphor or proof of the mundane character of Kṛṣṇa, the speaker of the *Bhagavad-gītā*. But, in actuality, Kṛṣṇa, the Supreme Godhead, has senses, and it is stated that His senses are interchangeable; in other words, one sense can perform the function of any other. This is what it means to say that Kṛṣṇa is absolute. Lacking senses, He could hardly be considered full in all opulences. In the Seventh Chapter, Kṛṣṇa has explained that He impregnates the living entities into material nature. This is done by His looking upon material nature. And so in this instance, Kṛṣṇa's hearing the devotee's words of love in offering foodstuffs is *wholly* identical with His eating and actually tasting. This point should be emphasized: because of His absolute position, His hearing is wholly identical with His eating and tasting. Only the devotee, who accepts Kṛṣṇa as He describes Himself, without interpretation, can understand that the Supreme Absolute Truth can eat food and enjoy it.

Text 27 यत्करोषि यदश्नासि यज्जुहोषि ददासि यत् ।
यत्तपस्यसि कौन्तेय तत्कुरुष्व मदर्पणम् ॥२७॥

yat karoṣi yad aśnāsi, yaj juhoṣi dadāsi yat
yat tapasyasi kaunteya, tat kuruṣva mad-arpaṇam

yat – whatever; *karoṣi* – you do; *yat* – whatever; *aśnāsi* – you eat; *yat* – whatever; *juhoṣi* – you offer; *dadāsi* – you give away; *yat* – whatever; *yat* – whatever; *tapasyasi* – austerities you perform; *kaunteya* – O son of Kuntī; *tat* – that; *kuruṣva* – do; *mat* – unto Me; *arpaṇam* – as an offering.

Whatever you do, whatever you eat, whatever you offer or give away, and whatever austerities you perform – do that, O son of Kuntī, as an offering to Me.

PURPORT: Thus, it is the duty of everyone to mold his life in such a way that he will not forget Kṛṣṇa in any circumstance. Everyone has to work for maintenance of his body and soul together, and Kṛṣṇa recommends herein that one should work for Him. Everyone has to eat something to live; therefore he should accept the remnants of foodstuffs offered to Kṛṣṇa. Any civilized man has to perform some religious ritualistic ceremonies; therefore Kṛṣṇa recommends, "Do it for Me," and this is called *arcana.* Everyone has a tendency to give something in charity; Kṛṣṇa says, "Give it to Me," and this means that all surplus money accumulated should be utilized in furthering the Kṛṣṇa consciousness movement. Nowadays people are very much inclined to the meditational process, which is not practical in this age, but if anyone practices meditating on Kṛṣṇa twenty-four hours a day by chanting the Hare Kṛṣṇa *mantra* round his beads, he is surely the greatest meditator and the greatest *yogī,* as substantiated by the Sixth Chapter of *Bhagavad-gītā.*

Text 28 शुभाशुभफलैरेवं मोक्ष्यसे कर्मबन्धनैः ।
सन्न्यासयोगयुक्तात्मा विमुक्तो मामुपैष्यसि ॥२८॥

śubhāśubha-phalair evaṁ, mokṣyase karma-bandhanaiḥ
sannyāsa-yoga-yuktātmā, vimukto mām upaiṣyasi

śubha – from auspicious; *aśubha* – and inauspicious; *phalaiḥ* – results; *evam* – thus; *mokṣyase* – you will become free; *karma* – of work; *bandhanaiḥ* – from the bondage; *sannyāsa* – of renunciation; *yoga* – the *yoga; yukta-ātmā* – having the mind firmly set on; *vimuktaḥ* – liberated; *mām* – to Me; *upaiṣyasi* – you will attain.

In this way you will be freed from bondage to work and its auspicious and inauspicious results. With your mind fixed on Me in this principle of renunciation, you will be liberated and come to Me.

PURPORT: One who acts in Kṛṣṇa consciousness under superior direction is called *yukta.* The technical term is *yukta-vairāgya.* This is further explained by Rūpa Gosvāmī as follows:

anāsaktasya viṣayān, yathārham upayuñjataḥ
nirbandhaḥ kṛṣṇa-sambandhe, yuktaṁ vairāgyam ucyate
(*Bhakti-rasāmṛta-sindhu,* 1.2.255)

Rūpa Gosvāmī says that as long as we are in this material world we have to act; we cannot cease acting. Therefore if actions are performed and the fruits are given to Kṛṣṇa, then that is called *yukta-vairāgya.* Actually situated in renunciation, such activities clear the mirror of the mind, and as the actor gradually makes progress in spiritual realization he becomes completely surrendered to the Supreme Personality of Godhead. Therefore at the end he becomes liberated, and this liberation is also specified. By this liberation he does not become one with the *brahma-jyotir,* but rather enters into the planet of the Supreme Lord. It is clearly mentioned here: *mām upaiṣyasi,* "he comes to Me," back home, back to Godhead. There are five different stages of liberation, and here it is specified that the devotee who has always lived his lifetime here under the direction of the Supreme Lord, as stated, has evolved to the point where he can, after quitting this body, go back to Godhead and engage directly in the association of the Supreme Lord.

Anyone who has no interest but to dedicate his life to the service of the Lord is actually a *sannyāsī.* Such a person always thinks of himself as an eternal servant, dependent on the supreme will of the Lord. As such, whatever he does, he does it for the benefit of the Lord. Whatever action he performs, he performs it as service to the Lord. He does not give serious attention to the fruitive activities or prescribed duties mentioned in the *Vedas.* For ordinary persons it is obligatory to execute the prescribed duties mentioned in the *Vedas,* but although a pure devotee who is completely engaged in the service of the Lord may sometimes appear to go against the prescribed Vedic duties, actually it is not so.

It is said, therefore, by Vaiṣṇava authorities that even the most intelligent person cannot understand the plans and activities of a pure devotee. The exact words are *tāṅra vakya, kriyā, mudrā vijñeha nā bujhaya* (*Caitanya-caritāmṛta, Madhya* 23.39). A person who is thus always engaged in the service of the Lord or is always thinking and planning how to serve the Lord is to be considered completely liberated at present, and in the future his going back home, back to Godhead, is guaranteed. He is above all materialistic criticism, just as Kṛṣṇa is above all criticism.

Text 29 समोऽहं सर्वभूतेषु न मे द्वेष्योऽस्ति न प्रियः ।
ये भजन्ति तु मां भक्त्या मयि ते तेषु चाप्यहम् ॥२९॥

samo 'haṁ sarva-bhūteṣu, na me dveṣyo 'sti na priyaḥ
ye bhajanti tu māṁ bhaktyā, mayi te teṣu cāpy aham

samaḥ – equally disposed; *aham* – I; *sarva-bhūteṣu* – to all living entities; *na* – no one; *me* – to Me; *dveṣyaḥ* – hateful; *asti* – is; *na* – nor; *priyaḥ* – dear; *ye* – those who; *bhajanti* – render transcendental service; *tu* – but; *mām* – unto Me; *bhaktyā* – in devotion; *mayi* – are in Me; *te* – such persons; *teṣu* – in them; *ca* – also; *api* – certainly; *aham* – I.

I envy no one, nor am I partial to anyone. I am equal to all. But whoever renders service unto Me in devotion is a friend, is in Me, and I am also a friend to him.

PURPORT: One may question here that if Kṛṣna is equal to everyone and no one is His special friend, then why does He take a special interest in the devotees who are always engaged in His transcendental service? But this is not discrimination; it is natural. Any man in this material world may be very charitably disposed, yet he has a special interest in his own children. The Lord claims that every living entity – in whatever form – is His son, and so He provides everyone with a generous supply of the necessities of life. He is just like a cloud which pours rain all over, regardless of whether it falls on rock or land or water. But for His devotees, He gives specific attention. Such devotees are mentioned here: they are always in Kṛṣṇa consciousness, and therefore they are always transcendentally situated in Kṛṣṇa. The very phrase "Kṛṣṇa consciousness" suggests that those who are in such consciousness are living transcendentalists, situated in Him. The Lord says here distinctly, *mayi te:* "They are in Me." Naturally, as a result, the Lord is also in them. This is reciprocal. This also explains the words *ye yathā māṁ prapadyante tāṁs tathaiva bhajāmy aham:* "Whoever surrenders unto Me, proportionately I take care of him." This transcendental reciprocation exists because both the

Lord and the devotee are conscious. When a diamond is set in a golden ring, it looks very nice. The gold is glorified, and at the same time the diamond is glorified. The Lord and the living entity eternally glitter, and when a living entity becomes inclined to the service of the Supreme Lord he looks like gold. The Lord is a diamond, and so this combination is very nice. Living entities in a pure state are called devotees. The Supreme Lord becomes the devotee of His devotees. If a reciprocal relationship is not present between the devotee and the Lord, then there is no personalist philosophy. In the impersonal philosophy there is no reciprocation between the Supreme and the living entity, but in the personalist philosophy there is.

The example is often given that the Lord is like a desire tree, and whatever one wants from this desire tree, the Lord supplies. But here the explanation is more complete. The Lord is here stated to be partial to the devotees. This is the manifestation of the Lord's special mercy to the devotees. The Lord's reciprocation should not be considered to be under the law of *karma*. It belongs to the transcendental situation in which the Lord and His devotees function. Devotional service to the Lord is not an activity of this material world; it is part of the spiritual world, where eternity, bliss and knowledge predominate.

Text 30 अपि चेत्सुदुराचारो भजते मामनन्यभाक् ।
साधुरेव स मन्तव्यः सम्यग्व्यवसितो हि सः ॥३०॥

api cet su-durācāro, bhajate mām ananya-bhāk
sādhur eva sa mantavyaḥ, samyag vyavasito hi saḥ

api – even; *cet* – if; *su-durācāraḥ* – one committing the most abominable actions; *bhajate* – is engaged in devotional service; *mām* – unto Me; *ananya-bhāk* – without deviation; *sādhuḥ* – a saint; *eva* – certainly; *saḥ* – he; *mantavyaḥ* – is to be considered; *samyak* – completely; *vyavasitaḥ* – situated in determination; *hi* – certainly; *saḥ* – he.

Even if one commits the most abominable action, if he is engaged in devotional service he is to be considered saintly because he is properly situated in his determination.

PURPORT: The word *su-durācāraḥ* used in this verse is very significant, and we should understand it properly. When a living entity is conditioned, he has two kinds of activities: one is conditional, and the other is constitutional. As for protecting the body or abiding by the rules of society and state, certainly there are different activities, even for the devotees, in connection with the conditional life, and such activities are called conditional. Besides these, the living entity who is fully conscious of his spiritual nature and is engaged in Kṛṣṇa consciousness, or the devotional service of the Lord, has activities which are called transcendental. Such activities are performed in his constitutional position, and they are technically called devotional service. Now, in the conditioned state, sometimes devotional service and the conditional service in relation to the body will parallel one another. But then again, sometimes these activities become opposed to one another. As far as possible, a devotee is very cautious so that he does not do anything that could disrupt his wholesome condition. He knows that perfection in his activities depends on his progressive realization of Kṛṣṇa consciousness. Sometimes, however, it may be seen that a person in Kṛṣṇa consciousness commits some act which may be taken as most abominable socially or politically. But such a temporary falldown does not disqualify him. In the *Śrīmad-Bhāgavatam* it is stated that if a person falls down but is wholeheartedly engaged in the transcendental service of the Supreme Lord, the Lord, being situated within his heart, purifies him and excuses him from that abomination. The material contamination is so strong that even a *yogī* fully engaged in the service of the Lord sometimes becomes ensnared; but Kṛṣṇa consciousness is so strong that such an occasional falldown is at once rectified. Therefore the process of devotional service is always a success. No one should deride a devotee for some accidental falldown from the ideal path, for, as explained in the next verse, such occasional falldowns will be stopped in due course, as soon as a devotee is completely situated in Kṛṣṇa consciousness.

Therefore a person who is situated in Kṛṣṇa consciousness and is engaged with determination in the process of chanting Hare Kṛṣṇa, Hare Kṛṣṇa, Kṛṣṇa Kṛṣṇa, Hare Hare/ Hare Rāma, Hare Rāma, Rāma Rāma, Hare Hare should be considered to be in the transcendental position, even if by chance or accident he is found to have fallen. The words *sādhur eva,* "he is saintly," are very emphatic. They are a warning to the nondevotees that because of an accidental falldown a devotee should not be derided; he should still be considered saintly even if he has accidentally fallen down. And the word *mantavyaḥ* is still more emphatic. If one does not follow this rule, and derides a devotee for his accidental falldown, then one is disobeying the order of the Supreme Lord. The only qualification of a devotee is to be unflinchingly and exclusively engaged in devotional service.

In the *Nṛsiṁha Purāṇa* the following statement is given:

bhagavati ca harāv ananya-cetā, bhṛśa-malino 'pi virājate manuṣyaḥ
na hi śaśa-kaluṣa-cchabiḥ kadācit, timira-parābhavatām upaiti candraḥ

The meaning is that even if one fully engaged in the devotional service of the Lord is sometimes found engaged in abominable activities, these activities should be considered to be like the spots that resemble the mark of a rabbit on the moon. Such spots do not become an impediment to the diffusion of moonlight. Similarly, the accidental falldown of a devotee from the path of saintly character does not make him abominable.

On the other hand, one should not misunderstand that a devotee in transcendental devotional service can act in all kinds of abominable ways; this verse only refers to an accident due to the strong power of material connections. Devotional service is more or less a declaration of war against the illusory energy. As long as one is not strong enough to fight the illusory energy, there may be accidental falldowns. But when one is strong enough, he is no longer subjected to such falldowns, as previously explained. No one should take advantage of this verse and commit nonsense and think that he is still a devotee. If he does not improve in his character by devotional service, then it is to be understood that he is not a high devotee.

Text 31 क्षिप्रं भवति धर्मात्मा शश्वच्छान्तिं निगच्छति ।
कौन्तेय प्रतिजानीहि न मे भक्तः प्रणश्यति ॥३१॥

kṣipraṁ bhavati dharmātmā, śaśvac-chāntiṁ nigacchati
kaunteya pratijānīhi, na me bhaktaḥ praṇaśyati

kṣipram – very soon; *bhavati* – becomes; *dharma-ātmā* – righteous; *śaśvat-śāntim* – lasting peace; *nigacchati* – attains; *kaunteya* – O son of Kuntī; *pratijānīhi* – declare; *na* – never; *me* – My; *bhaktaḥ* – devotee; *praṇaśyati* – perishes.

He quickly becomes righteous and attains lasting peace. O son of Kuntī, declare it boldly that My devotee never perishes.

PURPORT: This should not be misunderstood. In the Seventh Chapter the Lord says that one who is engaged in mischievous activities cannot become a devotee of the Lord. One who is not a devotee of the Lord has no good qualifications whatsoever. The question remains, then, How can a person engaged in abominable activities – either by accident or by intention – be a pure devotee? This question may justly be raised. The miscreants, as stated in the Seventh Chapter, who never come to the devotional service of the Lord, have no good qualifications, as is stated in the *Śrīmad-Bhāgavatam.* Generally, a devotee who is engaged in the nine kinds of devotional activities is engaged in the process of cleansing all material contamination from the heart. He puts the Supreme Personality of Godhead within his heart, and all sinful contaminations are naturally washed away. Continuous thinking of the Supreme Lord makes him pure by nature. According to the *Vedas,* there is a certain regulation that if one falls down from his exalted position he has to undergo certain ritualistic processes to purify himself. But here there is no such condition, because the purifying process is already there in the heart of the devotee, due to his remembering the Supreme Personality of Godhead constantly. Therefore, the chanting of Hare Kṛṣṇa, Hare Kṛṣṇa, Kṛṣṇa Kṛṣṇa, Hare Hare/ Hare Rāma, Hare Rāma, Rāma Rāma, Hare Hare should be continued without stoppage. This will protect a devotee from all accidental falldowns. He will thus remain perpetually free from all material contaminations.

Text 32 मां हि पार्थ व्यपाश्रित्य येऽपि स्युः पापयोनयः ।
स्त्रियो वैश्यास्तथा शूद्रास्तेऽपि यान्ति परां गतिम् ॥३२॥

māṁ hi pārtha vyapāśritya, ye 'pi syuḥ pāpa-yonayaḥ
striyo vaiśyās tathā śūdrās, te 'pi yānti parāṁ gatim

mām – of Me; *hi* – certainly; *pārtha* – O son of Pṛthā; *vyapāśritya* – particularly taking shelter; *ye* – those who; *api* – also; *syuḥ* – are; *pāpa-yonayaḥ* – born of a lower family; *striyaḥ* – women; *vaiśyāḥ* – mercantile people; *tathā* – also; *śūdrāḥ* – lower-class men; *te api* – even they; *yānti* – go; *parām* – to the supreme; *gatim* – destination.

O son of Pṛthā, those who take shelter in Me, though they be of lower birth – women, vaiśyas [merchants] and śūdras [workers] – can attain the supreme destination.

PURPORT: It is clearly declared here by the Supreme Lord that in devotional service there is no distinction between the lower and higher classes of people. In the material conception of life there are such divisions, but for a person engaged in transcendental devotional service to the Lord there are not. Everyone is eligible for the supreme destination. In the

Śrīmad-Bhāgavatam (2.4.18) it is stated that even the lowest, who are called *caṇḍālas* (dog-eaters), can be purified by association with a pure devotee. Therefore devotional service and the guidance of a pure devotee are so strong that there is no discrimination between the lower and higher classes of men; anyone can take to it. The most simple man taking shelter of the pure devotee can be purified by proper guidance. According to the different modes of material nature, men are classified in the mode of goodness (*brāhmaṇas*), the mode of passion (*kṣatriyas,* or administrators), the mixed modes of passion and ignorance (*vaiśyas,* or merchants), and the mode of ignorance (*śūdras,* or workers). Those lower than them are called *caṇḍālas,* and they are born in sinful families. Generally, the association of those born in sinful families is not accepted by the higher classes. But the process of devotional service is so strong that the pure devotee of the Supreme Lord can enable people of all the lower classes to attain the highest perfection of life. This is possible only when one takes shelter of Kṛṣṇa. As indicated here by the word *vyapāśritya,* one has to take shelter completely of Kṛṣṇa. Then one can become much greater than great *jñānīs* and *yogīs.*

Text 33 किं पुनर्ब्राह्मणाः पुण्या भक्ता राजर्षयस्तथा ।
अनित्यमसुखं लोकमिमं प्राप्य भजस्व माम् ॥३३॥

kiṁ punar brāhmaṇāḥ puṇyā, bhaktā rājarṣayas tathā
anityam asukhaṁ lokam, imaṁ prāpya bhajasva mām

kim – how much; *punaḥ* – again; *brāhmaṇāḥ* – *brāhmaṇas; puṇyāḥ* – righteous; *bhaktāḥ* – devotees; *rāja-ṛṣayaḥ* – saintly kings; *tathā* – also; *anityam* – temporary; *asukham* – full of miseries; *lokam* – planet; *imam* – this; *prāpya* – gaining; *bhajasva* – be engaged in loving service; *mām* – unto Me.

How much more this is so of the righteous brāhmaṇas, the devotees and the saintly kings. Therefore, having come to this temporary, miserable world, engage in loving service unto Me.

PURPORT: In this material world there are classifications of people, but, after all, this world is not a happy place for anyone. It is clearly stated here, *anityam asukhaṁ lokam:* this world is temporary and full of miseries, not habitable for any sane gentleman. This world is declared by the Supreme Personality of Godhead to be temporary and full of miseries. Some philosophers, especially Māyāvādī philosophers, say that this world is false, but we can understand from *Bhagavad-gītā* that the world is not false; it is temporary. There is a difference between temporary and false. This world is temporary, but there is another world, which is eternal. This world is miserable, but the other world is eternal and blissful.

Arjuna was born in a saintly royal family. To him also the Lord says, "Take to My devotional service and come quickly back to Godhead, back home." No one should remain in this temporary world, full as it is with miseries. Everyone should attach himself to the bosom of the Supreme Personality of Godhead so that he can be eternally happy. The devotional service of the Supreme Lord is the only process by which all problems of all classes of men can be solved. Everyone should therefore take to Kṛṣṇa consciousness and make his life perfect.

Text 34 मन्मना भव मद्भक्तो मद्याजी मां नमस्कुरु ।
मामेवैष्यसि युक्त्वैवमात्मानं मत्परायणः ॥३४॥

man-manā bhava mad-bhakto, mad-yājī māṁ namaskuru
mām evaiṣyasi yuktvaivam, ātmānaṁ mat-parāyaṇaḥ

mat-manāḥ – always thinking of Me; *bhava* – become; *mat* – My; *bhaktaḥ* – devotee; *mat* – My; *yājī* – worshiper; *mām* – unto Me; *namaskuru* – offer obeisances; *mām* – unto Me; *eva* – completely; *eṣyasi* – you will come; *yuktvā* – being absorbed; *evam* – thus; *ātmānam* – your soul; *mat-parāyaṇaḥ* – devoted to Me.

Engage your mind always in thinking of Me, become My devotee, offer obeisances to Me and worship Me. Being completely absorbed in Me, surely you will come to Me.

PURPORT: In this verse it is clearly indicated that Kṛṣṇa consciousness is the only means of being delivered from the clutches of this contaminated material world. Sometimes unscrupulous commentators distort the meaning of what is clearly stated here: that all devotional service should be offered to the Supreme Personality of Godhead, Kṛṣṇa. Unfortunately, unscrupulous commentators divert the mind of the reader to that which is not at all feasible. Such commentators do not know that there is no difference between Kṛṣṇa's mind and Kṛṣṇa. Kṛṣṇa is not an ordinary human being; He is Absolute Truth. His body, His mind and He Himself are one and absolute. It is stated in the *Kūrma Purāṇa,* as it is quoted by Bhaktisiddhānta Sarasvatī Gosvāmī in his *Anubhāṣya* comments on *Caitanya-caritāmṛta* (Fifth Chapter, *Ādi-līlā,* verses 41–48), *deha-dehi-vibhedo 'yaṁ neśvare vidyate kvacit.* This means that there is no difference in Kṛṣṇa, the Supreme Lord, between Himself and His body. But because the commentators do not know this science of Kṛṣṇa, they hide Kṛṣṇa and divide His personality from His mind or from His body. Although this is sheer ignorance of the science of Kṛṣṇa, some men make profit out of misleading people.

There are some who are demonic; they also think of Kṛṣṇa, but enviously, just like King Kaṁsa, Kṛṣṇa's uncle. He was also thinking of Kṛṣṇa always, but he thought of Kṛṣṇa as his enemy. He was always in anxiety, wondering when Kṛṣṇa would come to kill him. That kind of thinking will not help us. One should be thinking of Kṛṣṇa in devotional love. That is *bhakti.* One should cultivate the knowledge of Kṛṣṇa continuously. What is that favorable cultivation? It is to learn from a bona fide teacher. Kṛṣṇa is the Supreme Personality of Godhead, and we have several times explained that His body is not material, but is eternal, blissful knowledge. This kind of talk about Kṛṣṇa will help one become a devotee. Understanding Kṛṣṇa otherwise, from the wrong source, will prove fruitless.

One should therefore engage his mind in the eternal form, the primal form of Kṛṣṇa; with conviction in his heart that Kṛṣṇa is the Supreme, he should engage himself in worship. There are hundreds of thousands of temples in India for the worship of Kṛṣṇa, and devotional service is practiced there. When such practice is made, one has to offer obeisances to Kṛṣṇa. One should lower his head before the Deity and engage his mind, his body, his activities – everything. That will make one fully absorbed in Kṛṣṇa without deviation. This will help one transfer to Kṛṣṇaloka. One should not be deviated by unscrupulous commentators. One must engage in the nine different processes of devotional service, beginning with hearing and chanting about Kṛṣṇa. Pure devotional service is the highest achievement of human society.

The Seventh and Eighth chapters of *Bhagavad-gītā* have explained pure devotional service to the Lord that is free from speculative knowledge, mystic *yoga* and fruitive activities. Those who are not purely sanctified may be attracted by different features of the Lord like the impersonal *brahma-jyotir* and localized Paramātmā, but a pure devotee directly takes to the service of the Supreme Lord.

There is a beautiful poem about Kṛṣṇa in which it is clearly stated that any person who is engaged in the worship of demigods is most unintelligent and cannot achieve at any time the supreme award of Kṛṣṇa. The devotee, in the beginning, may sometimes fall from the standard, but still he should be considered superior to all other philosophers and *yogīs.* One who always engages in Kṛṣṇa consciousness should be understood to be a perfectly saintly person. His accidental nondevotional activities will diminish, and he will soon be situated without any doubt in complete perfection. The pure devotee has no actual chance to fall down, because the Supreme Godhead personally takes care of His pure devotees. Therefore, the intelligent person should take directly to the process of Kṛṣṇa consciousness and happily live in this material world. He will eventually receive the supreme award of Kṛṣṇa.

Thus end the Bhaktivedanta Purports to the Ninth Chapter of the Śrīmad Bhagavad-gītā *in the matter of the Most Confidential Knowledge.*

CHAPTER TEN

The Opulence of the Absolute

Text 1 श्रीभगवानुवाच
भूय एव महाबाहो शृणु मे परमं वचः ।
यत्तेऽहं प्रीयमाणाय वक्ष्यामि हितकाम्यया ॥ १ ॥

śrī-bhagavān uvāca
bhūya eva mahā-bāho, śṛṇu me paramaṁ vacaḥ
yat te 'haṁ prīyamāṇāya, vakṣyāmi hita-kāmyayā

śrī-bhagavān uvāca – the Supreme Personality of Godhead said; *bhūyaḥ* – again; *eva* – certainly; *mahā-bāho* – O mighty-armed; *śṛṇu* – just hear; *me* – My; *paramam* – supreme; *vacaḥ* – instruction; *yat* – that which; *te* – to you; *aham* – I; *prīyamāṇāya* – thinking you dear to Me; *vakṣyāmi* – say; *hita-kāmyayā* – for your benefit.

The Supreme Personality of Godhead said: Listen again, O mighty-armed Arjuna. Because you are My dear friend, for your benefit I shall speak to you further, giving knowledge that is better than what I have already explained.

PURPORT: The word *bhagavān* is explained thus by Parāśara Muni: one who is full in six opulences, who has full strength, full fame, wealth, knowledge, beauty and renunciation, is Bhagavān, or the Supreme Personality of Godhead. While Kṛṣṇa was present on this earth,

He displayed all six opulences. Therefore great sages like Parāśara Muni have all accepted Kṛṣṇa as the Supreme Personality of Godhead. Now Kṛṣṇa is instructing Arjuna in more confidential knowledge of His opulences and His work. Previously, beginning with the Seventh Chapter, the Lord has already explained His different energies and how they are acting. Now in this chapter He explains His specific opulences to Arjuna. In the previous chapter He has clearly explained His different energies to establish devotion in firm conviction. Again in this chapter He tells Arjuna about His manifestations and various opulences.

The more one hears about the Supreme God, the more one becomes fixed in devotional service. One should always hear about the Lord in the association of devotees; that will enhance one's devotional service. Discourses in the society of devotees can take place only among those who are really anxious to be in Kṛṣṇa consciousness. Others cannot take part in such discourses. The Lord clearly tells Arjuna that because Arjuna is very dear to Him, for his benefit such discourses are taking place.

Text 2 न मे विदुः सुरगणाः प्रभवं न महर्षयः ।
अहमादिर्हि देवानां महर्षीणां च सर्वशः ॥ २ ॥

na me viduḥ sura-gaṇāḥ
prabhavaṁ na maharṣayaḥ
aham ādir hi devānāṁ
maharṣīṇāṁ ca sarvaśaḥ

na – never; *me* – My; *viduḥ* – know; *sura-gaṇāḥ* – the demigods; *prabhavam* – origin, opulences; *na* – never; *mahā-ṛṣayaḥ* – great sages; *aham* – I am; *ādiḥ* – the origin; *hi* – certainly; *devānām* – of the demigods; *mahā-ṛṣīṇām* – of the great sages; *ca* – also; *sarvaśaḥ* – in all respects.

Neither the hosts of demigods nor the great sages know My origin or opulences, for, in every respect, I am the source of the demigods and sages.

PURPORT: As stated in the *Brahma-saṁhitā,* Lord Kṛṣṇa is the Supreme Lord. No one is greater than Him; He is the cause of all causes. Here it is also stated by the Lord personally that He is the cause of all the demigods and sages. Even the demigods and great sages cannot understand Kṛṣṇa; they can understand neither His name nor His personality, so what is the position of the so-called scholars of this tiny planet? No one can understand why this Supreme God comes to earth as an ordinary human being and executes such wonderful, uncommon activities. One should know, then, that scholarship is not the qualification necessary to understand Kṛṣṇa. Even the demigods and the great sages have tried to understand Kṛṣṇa by their mental speculation, and they have failed to do so. In the *Śrīmad-Bhāgavatam* also it is clearly said that even the great demigods are not able to understand the Supreme Personality of Godhead. They can speculate to the limits of their imperfect senses and can reach the opposite conclusion of impersonalism, of something not manifested by the three qualities of material nature, or they can imagine something by mental speculation, but it is not possible to understand Kṛṣṇa by such foolish speculation.

Here the Lord indirectly says that if anyone wants to know the Absolute Truth, "Here I am present as the Supreme Personality of Godhead. I am the Supreme." One should know this. Although one cannot understand the inconceivable Lord who is personally present, He nonetheless exists. We can actually understand Kṛṣṇa, who is eternal, full of bliss and knowledge, simply by studying His words in *Bhagavad-gītā* and *Śrīmad-Bhāgavatam.* The conception of God as some ruling power or as the impersonal Brahman can be reached by persons who are in the inferior energy of the Lord, but the Personality of Godhead cannot be conceived unless one is in the transcendental position.

Because most men cannot understand Kṛṣṇa in His actual situation, out of His causeless mercy He descends to show favor to such speculators. Yet despite the Supreme Lord's uncommon activities, these speculators, due to contamination in the material energy, still think that the impersonal Brahman is the Supreme. Only the devotees who are fully surrendered unto the Supreme Lord can understand, by the grace of the Supreme Personality, that He is Kṛṣṇa. The devotees of the Lord do not bother about the impersonal Brahman conception of God; their faith and devotion bring them to surrender immediately unto the Supreme Lord, and out of the causeless mercy of Kṛṣṇa they can understand Kṛṣṇa. No one else can understand Him. So even great sages agree: What is *ātmā,* what is the Supreme? It is He whom we have to worship.

Text 3 यो मामजमनादिं च वेत्ति लोकमहेश्वरम् ।
असम्मूढः स मर्त्येषु सर्वपापैः प्रमुच्यते ॥ ३ ॥

yo mām ajam anādiṁ ca, vetti loka-maheśvaram
asammūḍhaḥ sa martyeṣu, sarva-pāpaiḥ pramucyate

yaḥ – anyone who; *mām* – Me; *ajam* – unborn; *anādim* – without beginning; *ca* – also; *vetti* – knows; *loka* – of the planets; *mahā-īśvaram* – the supreme master; *asammūḍhaḥ* – undeluded; *saḥ* – he; *martyeṣu* – among those subject to death; *sarva-pāpaiḥ* – from all sinful reactions; *pramucyate* – is delivered.

He who knows Me as the unborn, as the beginningless, as the Supreme Lord of all the worlds – he only, undeluded among men, is freed from all sins.

PURPORT: As stated in the Seventh Chapter (7.3), *manuṣyāṇāṁ sahasreṣu kaścid yatati siddhaye:* those who are trying to elevate themselves to the platform of spiritual realization are not ordinary men; they are superior to millions and millions of ordinary men who have no knowledge of spiritual realization. But out of those actually trying to understand their spiritual situation, one who can come to the understanding that Kṛṣṇa is the Supreme Personality of Godhead, the proprietor of everything, the unborn, is the most successful spiritually realized person. In that stage only, when one has fully understood Kṛṣṇa's supreme position, can one be free completely from all sinful reactions.

Here the Lord is described by the word *aja,* meaning "unborn," but He is distinct from the living entities who are described in the Second Chapter as *aja.* The Lord is different from the living entities who are taking birth and dying due to material attachment. The conditioned souls are changing their bodies, but His body is not changeable. Even when He comes to this material world, He comes as the same unborn; therefore in the Fourth Chapter it is said that the Lord, by His internal potency, is not under the inferior, material energy, but is always in the superior energy.

In this verse the words *vetti loka-maheśvaram* indicate that one should know that Lord Kṛṣṇa is the supreme proprietor of the planetary systems of the universe. He was existing before the creation, and He is different from His creation. All the demigods were created within this material world, but as far as Kṛṣṇa is concerned, it is said that He is not created; therefore Kṛṣṇa is different even from the great demigods like Brahmā and Śiva. And because He is the creator of Brahmā, Śiva and all the other demigods, He is the Supreme Person of all planets.

Śrī Kṛṣṇa is therefore different from everything that is created, and anyone who knows Him as such immediately becomes liberated from all sinful reactions. One must be liberated from all sinful activities to be in the knowledge of the Supreme Lord. Only by devotional service can He be known and not by any other means, as stated in *Bhagavad-gītā.*

One should not try to understand Kṛṣṇa as a human being. As stated previously, only a foolish person thinks Him to be a human being. This is again expressed here in a different way. A man who is not foolish, who is intelligent enough to understand the constitutional position of the Godhead, is always free from all sinful reactions.

If Kṛṣṇa is known as the son of Devakī, then how can He be unborn? That is also explained in *Śrīmad-Bhāgavatam:* When He appeared before Devakī and Vasudeva, He was not born as an ordinary child; He appeared in His original form, and then He transformed Himself into an ordinary child.

Anything done under the direction of Kṛṣṇa is transcendental. It cannot be contaminated by material reactions, which may be auspicious or inauspicious. The conception that there are things auspicious and inauspicious in the material world is more or less a mental concoction because there is nothing auspicious in the material world. Everything is inauspicious because the very material nature is inauspicious. We simply imagine it to be auspicious. Real auspiciousness depends on activities in Kṛṣṇa consciousness in full devotion and service. Therefore if we at all want our activities to be auspicious, then we should work under the directions of the Supreme Lord. Such directions are given in authoritative scriptures such as *Śrīmad-Bhāgavatam* and *Bhagavad-gītā,* or from a bona fide spiritual master. Because the spiritual master is the representative of the Supreme Lord, his direction is directly the direction of the Supreme Lord. The spiritual master, saintly persons and scriptures direct in the same way. There is no contradiction in these three sources. All actions done under such direction are free from the reactions of pious or impious activities of this material world. The transcendental attitude of the devotee in the performance of activities is actually that of renunciation, and this is called *sannyāsa.* As stated in the first verse of the Sixth Chapter of *Bhagavad-gītā,* one who acts as a matter of duty because he has been ordered to do so by the Supreme Lord, and who does not seek shelter in the fruits of his activities (*anāśritaḥ karma-phalam*), is a true renouncer. Anyone acting under the direction of the Supreme Lord is actually a *sannyāsī* and a *yogī,* and not the man who has simply taken the dress of the *sannyāsī,* or a pseudo *yogī.*

Texts 4–5

बुद्धिर्ज्ञानमसम्मोहः क्षमा सत्यं दमः शमः ।
सुखं दुःखं भवोऽभावो भयं चाभयमेव च ॥ ४ ॥

अहिंसा समता तुष्टिस्तपो दानं यशोऽयशः ।
भवन्ति भावा भूतानां मत्त एव पृथग्विधाः ॥ ५ ॥

buddhir jñānam asammohaḥ, kṣamā satyaṁ damaḥ śamaḥ
sukhaṁ duḥkhaṁ bhavo 'bhāvo, bhayaṁ cābhayam eva ca

ahiṁsā samatā tuṣṭis, tapo dānaṁ yaśo 'yaśaḥ
bhavanti bhāvā bhūtānāṁ, matta eva pṛthag-vidhāḥ

buddhiḥ – intelligence; *jñānam* – knowledge; *asammohaḥ* – freedom from doubt; *kṣamā* – forgiveness; *satyam* – truthfulness; *damaḥ* – control of the senses; *śamaḥ* – control of the mind; *sukham* – happiness; *duḥkham* – distress; *bhavaḥ* – birth; *abhāvaḥ* – death; *bhayam* – fear; *ca* – also; *abhayam* – fearlessness; *eva* – also; *ca* – and; *ahiṁsā* – nonviolence; *samatā* – equilibrium; *tuṣṭiḥ* – satisfaction; *tapaḥ* – penance; *dānam* – charity; *yaśaḥ* – fame; *ayaśaḥ* – infamy; *bhavanti* – come about; *bhāvāḥ* – natures; *bhūtānām* – of living entities; *mattaḥ* – from Me; *eva* – certainly; *pṛthak-vidhāḥ* – variously arranged.

Intelligence, knowledge, freedom from doubt and delusion, forgiveness, truthfulness, control of the senses, control of the mind, happiness and distress, birth, death, fear, fearlessness, nonviolence, equanimity, satisfaction, austerity, charity, fame and infamy – all these various qualities of living beings are created by Me alone.

PURPORT: The different qualities of living entities, be they good or bad, are all created by Kṛṣṇa, and they are described here.

Intelligence refers to the power to analyze things in their proper perspective, and knowledge refers to understanding what is spirit and what is matter. Ordinary knowledge obtained by a university education pertains only to matter, and it is not accepted here as knowledge. Knowledge means knowing the distinction between spirit and matter. In modern education there is no knowledge about spirit; they are simply taking care of the material elements and bodily needs. Therefore academic knowledge is not complete.

Asammoha, freedom from doubt and delusion, can be achieved when one is not hesitant and when he understands the transcendental philosophy. Slowly but surely he becomes free from bewilderment. Nothing should be accepted blindly; everything should be accepted with care and with caution. *Kṣamā,* tolerance and forgiveness, should be practiced; one should be tolerant and excuse the minor offenses of others. *Satyam,* truthfulness, means that facts should be presented as they are, for the benefit of others. Facts should not be misrepresented. According to social conventions, it is said that one can speak the truth only when it is palatable to others. But that is not truthfulness. The truth should be spoken in a straightforward way, so that others will understand actually what the facts are. If a man is a thief and if people are warned that he is a thief, that is truth. Although sometimes the truth is unpalatable, one should not refrain from speaking it. Truthfulness demands that the facts be presented as they are for the benefit of others. That is the definition of truth.

Control of the senses means that the senses should not be used for unnecessary personal enjoyment. There is no prohibition against meeting the proper needs of the senses, but unnecessary sense enjoyment is detrimental for spiritual advancement. Therefore the senses should be restrained from unnecessary use. Similarly, one should restrain the mind from unnecessary thoughts; that is called *śama.* One should not spend one's time pondering over earning money. That is a misuse of the thinking power. The mind should be used to understand the prime necessity of human beings, and that should be presented authoritatively. The power of thought should be developed in association with persons who are authorities in the scriptures, saintly persons and spiritual masters and those whose thinking is highly developed. *Sukham,* pleasure or happiness, should always be in that which is favorable for the cultivation of the spiritual knowledge of Kṛṣṇa consciousness. And similarly, that which is painful or which causes distress is that which is unfavorable for the cultivation of Kṛṣṇa consciousness. Anything favorable for the development of Kṛṣṇa consciousness should be accepted, and anything unfavorable should be rejected.

Bhava, birth, should be understood to refer to the body. As far as the soul is concerned, there is neither birth nor death; that we have discussed in the beginning of *Bhagavad-gītā.* Birth and death apply to one's embodiment in the material world. Fear is due to worrying about the future. A person in Kṛṣṇa consciousness has no fear because by his activities he is sure to go back to the spiritual sky, back home, back to Godhead. Therefore his future is very bright. Others, however, do not know what their future holds; they have no knowledge of what the next life holds. So they are therefore in constant anxiety. If we want to get free from anxiety, then the best course is to understand Kṛṣṇa and be situated always in Kṛṣṇa consciousness. In that way we will be free from all fear. In the *Śrīmad-Bhāgavatam* (11.2.37) it is stated, *bhayaṁ dvitīyābhiniveśataḥ syāt:* fear is caused by our absorption in the illusory energy. But those who are free from the illusory energy, those who are confident that they are not the material body, that they are spiritual parts of the Supreme Personality of Godhead, and who are therefore engaged in the transcendental service of the Supreme Godhead, have nothing to fear. Their future is very bright. This fear is a condition of persons who are not in Kṛṣṇa consciousness. *Abhayam,* fearlessness, is possible only for one in Kṛṣṇa consciousness.

Ahiṁsā, nonviolence, means that one should not do anything which will put others into misery or confusion. Material activities that are promised by so many politicians, sociologists, philanthropists, etc., do not produce very good results because the politicians and philanthropists have no transcendental vision; they do not know what is actually beneficial for human society. *Ahiṁsā* means that people should be trained in such a way that the full utilization of the human body can be achieved. The human body is meant for spiritual realization, so any movement or any commissions which do not further that end commit violence on the human body. That which furthers the future spiritual happiness of the people in general is called nonviolence.

Samatā, equanimity, refers to freedom from attachment and aversion. To be very much attached or to be very much detached is not the best. This material world should be accepted without attachment or aversion. That which is favorable for prosecuting Kṛṣṇa consciousness should be accepted; that which is unfavorable should be rejected. That is called *samatā,* equanimity. A person in Kṛṣṇa consciousness has nothing to reject and nothing to accept save in terms of its usefulness in the prosecution of Kṛṣṇa consciousness.

Tuṣṭi, satisfaction, means that one should not be eager to gather more and more material goods by unnecessary activity. One should be satisfied with whatever is obtained by the grace of the Supreme Lord; that is called satisfaction. *Tapas* means austerity or penance. There are many rules and regulations in the *Vedas* which apply here, like rising early in the morning and taking a bath. Sometimes it is very troublesome to rise early in the morning, but whatever voluntary trouble one may suffer in this way is called penance. Similarly, there are prescriptions for fasting on certain days of the month. One may not be inclined to practice such fasting, but because of his determination to make advancement in the science of Kṛṣṇa consciousness, he should accept such bodily troubles when they are recommended. However, one should not fast unnecessarily or against Vedic injunctions. One should not fast for some political purpose; that is described in *Bhagavad-gītā* as fasting in ignorance, and anything done in ignorance or passion does not lead to spiritual advancement. Everything done in the mode of goodness does advance one, however, and fasting done in terms of the Vedic injunctions enriches one in spiritual knowledge.

As far as charity is concerned, one should give fifty percent of his earnings to some good cause. And what is a good cause? It is that which is conducted in terms of Kṛṣṇa consciousness. That is not only a good cause, but the best cause. Because Kṛṣṇa is good, His cause is also good. Thus charity should be given to a person who is engaged in Kṛṣṇa consciousness. According to the Vedic literature, it is enjoined that charity should be given to the *brāhmaṇas.* This practice is still followed, although not very nicely in terms of the Vedic injunction. But still the injunction is that charity should be given to the *brāhmaṇas.* Why? Because they are engaged in higher cultivation of spiritual knowledge. A *brāhmaṇa* is supposed to devote his whole life to understanding Brahman. *Brahma jānātīti brāhmaṇaḥ:* one who knows Brahman is called a *brāhmaṇa.* Thus charity is offered to the *brāhmaṇas* because they are always engaged in higher spiritual service and have no time to earn their livelihood. In the Vedic literature, charity is also to be awarded to one in the renounced order of life, the *sannyāsī.* The *sannyāsīs* beg from door to door, not for money but for missionary purposes. The system is that they go from door to door to awaken the householders from the slumber of ignorance. Because the householders are engaged in family affairs and have forgotten their actual purpose in life – awakening their Kṛṣṇa consciousness – it is the business of the *sannyāsīs* to go as beggars to the householders and encourage them to be Kṛṣṇa conscious. As it is said in the *Vedas,* one should awake and achieve what is due him in this human form of life. This knowledge and method is distributed by the *sannyāsīs;* hence charity is to be given to the renouncer of life, to the *brāhmaṇas,* and similar good causes, not to any whimsical cause.

Yaśas, fame, should be according to Lord Caitanya, who said that a man is famous when he is known as a great devotee. That is real fame. If one has become a great man in Kṛṣṇa consciousness and it is known, then he is truly famous. One who does not have such fame is infamous.

All these qualities are manifest throughout the universe in human society and in the society of the demigods. There are many forms of humanity on other planets, and these qualities are there. Now, for one who wants to advance in Kṛṣṇa consciousness, Kṛṣṇa creates all these qualities, but the person develops them himself from within. One who engages in the devotional service of the Supreme Lord develops all the good qualities, as arranged by the Supreme Lord.

Of whatever we find, good or bad, the origin is Kṛṣṇa. Nothing can manifest itself in this material world which is not in Kṛṣṇa. That is knowledge; although we know that things are differently situated, we should realize that everything flows from Kṛṣṇa.

Text 6 महर्षयः सप्त पूर्वे चत्वारो मनवस्तथा ।
मद्भावा मानसा जाता येषां लोक इमाः प्रजाः ॥ ६ ॥

maharṣayaḥ sapta pūrve, catvāro manavas tathā
mad-bhāvā mānasā jātā, yeṣāṁ loka imāḥ prajāḥ

mahā-ṛṣayaḥ – the great sages; *sapta* – seven; *pūrve* – before; *catvāraḥ* – four; *manavaḥ* – Manus; *tathā* – also; *mat-bhāvāḥ* – born of Me; *mānasāḥ* – from the mind; *jātāḥ* – born; *yeṣām* – of them; *loke* – in the world; *imāḥ* – all this; *prajāḥ* – population.

The seven great sages and before them the four other great sages and the Manus [progenitors of mankind] come from Me, born from My mind, and all the living beings populating the various planets descend from them.

PURPORT: The Lord is giving a genealogical synopsis of the universal population. Brahmā is the original creature born out of the energy of the Supreme Lord, who is known as Hiraṇyagarbha. And from Brahmā all the seven great sages, and before them four other great sages, named Sanaka, Sananda, Sanātana and Sanat-kumāra, and the fourteen Manus, are manifested. All these twenty-five great sages are known as the patriarchs of the living entities all over the universe. There are innumerable universes and innumerable planets within each universe, and each planet is full of population of different varieties. All of them are born of these twenty-five patriarchs. Brahmā underwent penance for one thousand years of the demigods before he realized by the grace of Kṛṣṇa how to create. Then from Brahmā came Sanaka, Sananda, Sanātana and Sanat-kumāra, then Rudra, and then the seven sages, and in this way all the *brāhmaṇas* and *kṣatriyas* are born out of the energy of the Supreme Personality of Godhead. Brahmā is known as Pitāmaha, the grandfather, and Kṛṣṇa is known as Prapitāmaha, the father of the grandfather. That is stated in the Eleventh Chapter of the *Bhagavad-gītā* (11.39).

Text 7 एतां विभूतिं योगं च मम यो वेत्ति तत्त्वतः ।
सोऽविकल्पेन योगेन युज्यते नात्र संशयः ॥ ७ ॥

etāṁ vibhutiṁ yogaṁ ca, mama yo vetti tattvataḥ
so 'vikalpena yogena, yujyate nātra saṁśayaḥ

etām – all this; *vibhūtim* – opulence; *yogam* – mystic power; *ca* – also; *mama* – of Mine; *yaḥ* – anyone who; *vetti* – knows; *tattvataḥ* – factually; *saḥ* – he; *avikalpena* – without division; *yogena* – in devotional service; *yujyate* – is engaged; *na* – never; *atra* – here; *saṁśayaḥ* – doubt.

One who is factually convinced of this opulence and mystic power of Mine engages in unalloyed devotional service; of this there is no doubt.

PURPORT: The highest summit of spiritual perfection is knowledge of the Supreme Personality of Godhead. Unless one is firmly convinced of the different opulences of the Supreme Lord, he cannot engage in devotional service. Generally people know that God is great, but they do not know in detail how God is great. Here are the details. If one knows factually how God is great, then naturally he becomes a surrendered soul and engages himself in the devotional service of the Lord. When one factually knows the opulences of the Supreme, there is no alternative but to surrender to Him. This factual knowledge can be known from the descriptions in *Śrīmad-Bhāgavatam* and *Bhagavad-gītā* and similar literatures.

In the administration of this universe there are many demigods distributed throughout the planetary system, and the chief of them are Brahmā, Lord Śiva and the four great Kumāras and the other patriarchs. There are many forefathers of the population of the universe, and all of them are born of the Supreme Lord, Kṛṣṇa. The Supreme Personality of Godhead, Kṛṣṇa, is the original forefather of all forefathers.

These are some of the opulences of the Supreme Lord. When one is firmly convinced of them, he accepts Kṛṣṇa with great faith and without any doubt, and he engages in devotional service. All this particular knowledge is required in order to increase one's interest in the loving devotional service of the Lord. One should not neglect to understand fully how great Kṛṣṇa is, for by knowing the greatness of Kṛṣṇa one will be able to be fixed in sincere devotional service.

Text 8 अहं सर्वस्य प्रभवो मत्तः सर्वं प्रवर्तते ।
इति मत्वा भजन्ते मां बुधा भावसमन्विताः ॥ ८ ॥

ahaṁ sarvasya prabhavo, mattaḥ sarvaṁ pravartate
iti matvā bhajante māṁ, budhā bhāva-samanvitāḥ

aham – I; *sarvasya* – of all; *prabhavaḥ* – the source of generation; *mattaḥ* – from Me; *sarvam* – everything; *pravartate* – emanates; *iti* – thus; *matvā* – knowing; *bhajante* – become devoted; *mām* – unto Me; *budhāḥ* – the learned; *bhāva-samanvitāḥ* – with great attention.

I am the source of all spiritual and material worlds. Everything emanates from Me. The wise who perfectly know this engage in My devotional service and worship Me with all their hearts.

PURPORT: A learned scholar who has studied the *Vedas* perfectly and has information from authorities like Lord Caitanya and who knows how to apply these teachings can understand that Kṛṣṇa is the origin of everything in both the material and spiritual worlds, and because he knows this perfectly he becomes firmly fixed in the devotional service of the Supreme Lord. He can never be deviated by any amount of nonsensical commentaries or by fools. All Vedic literature agrees that Kṛṣṇa is the source of Brahmā, Śiva and all other demigods. In the *Atharva Veda* (*Gopāla-tāpanī Upaniṣad* 1.24) it is said, *yo brahmāṇaṁ vidadhāti pūrvaṁ yo vai vedāṁś ca gāpayati sma kṛṣṇaḥ:* "It was Kṛṣṇa who in the beginning instructed Brahmā in Vedic knowledge and who disseminated Vedic knowledge in the past." Then again the *Nārāyaṇa Upaniṣad* (1) says, *atha puruṣo ha vai nārāyaṇo 'kāmayata prajāḥ sṛjeyeti:* "Then the Supreme Personality Nārāyaṇa desired to create living entities." The *Upaniṣad* continues, *nārāyaṇād brahmā jāyate, nārāyaṇād prajāpatiḥ prajāyate, nārāyaṇād indro jāyate, nārāyaṇād aṣṭau vasavo jāyante, nārāyaṇād ekādaśa rudrā jāyante, nārāyaṇād dvādaśādityāḥ:* "From Nārāyaṇa, Brahmā is born, and from Nārāyaṇa the patriarchs are also born. From Nārāyaṇa, Indra is born, from Nārāyaṇa the eight Vasus are born, from Nārāyaṇa the eleven Rudras are born, from Nārāyaṇa the twelve Ādityas are born." This Nārāyaṇa is an expansion of Kṛṣṇa.

It is said in the same *Vedas, brahmaṇyo devakī-putraḥ:* "The son of Devakī, Kṛṣṇa, is the Supreme Personality." (*Nārāyaṇa Upaniṣad* 4) Then it is said, *eko vai nārāyaṇa āsīn na brahmā neśāno nāpo nāgnisomau neme dyāv-āpṛthivī na nakṣatrāṇi na sūryaḥ:* "In the beginning of the creation there was only the Supreme Personality Nārāyaṇa. There was no Brahmā, no Śiva, no water, no fire, no moon, no heaven and earth, no stars in the sky, no sun." (*Mahā Upaniṣad* 1.2) In the *Mahā Upaniṣad* it is also said that Lord Śiva was born from the forehead of the Supreme Lord. Thus the *Vedas* say that it is the Supreme Lord, the creator of Brahmā and Śiva, who is to be worshiped.

In the *Mokṣa-dharma* section of the *Mahābhārata,* Kṛṣṇa also says,

prajāpatiṁ ca rudraṁ cāpy, aham eva sṛjāmi vai
tau hi māṁ na vijānīto, mama māyā-vimohitau

"The patriarchs, Śiva and others are created by Me, though they do not know that they are created by Me because they are deluded by My illusory energy." In the *Varāha Purāṇa* it is also said,

nārāyaṇaḥ paro devas, tasmāj jātaś caturmukhaḥ
tasmād rudro 'bhavad devaḥ, sa ca sarva-jñatāṁ gataḥ

"Nārāyaṇa is the Supreme Personality of Godhead, and from Him Brahmā was born, from whom Śiva was born."

Lord Kṛṣṇa is the source of all generations, and He is called the most efficient cause of everything. He says, "Because everything is born of Me, I am the original source of all. Everything is under Me; no one is above Me." There is no supreme controller other than Kṛṣṇa. One who understands Kṛṣṇa in such a way from a bona fide spiritual master, with references from Vedic literature, engages all his energy in Kṛṣṇa consciousness and becomes a truly learned man. In comparison to him, all others, who do not know Kṛṣṇa properly, are but fools. Only a fool would consider Kṛṣṇa to be an ordinary man. A Kṛṣṇa conscious person should not be bewildered by fools; he should avoid all unauthorized commentaries and interpretations on *Bhagavad-gītā* and proceed in Kṛṣṇa consciousness with determination and firmness.

Text 9 मच्चित्ता मद्गतप्राणा बोधयन्तः परस्परम् ।
कथयन्तश्च मां नित्यं तुष्यन्ति च रमन्ति च ॥ ९ ॥

mac-cittā mad-gata-prāṇā, bodhayantaḥ parasparam
kathayantaś ca māṁ nityaṁ, tuṣyanti ca ramanti ca

mat-cittāḥ – their minds fully engaged in Me; *mat-gata-prāṇāḥ* – their lives devoted to Me; *bodhayantaḥ* – preaching; *parasparam* – among themselves; *kathayantaḥ* – talking; *ca* – also; *mām* – about Me; *nityam* – perpetually; *tuṣyanti* – become pleased; *ca* – also; *ramanti* – enjoy transcendental bliss; *ca* – also.

The thoughts of My pure devotees dwell in Me, their lives are fully devoted to My service, and they derive great satisfaction and bliss from always enlightening one another and conversing about Me.

PURPORT: Pure devotees, whose characteristics are mentioned here, engage themselves fully in the transcendental loving service of the Lord. Their minds cannot be diverted from the lotus feet of Kṛṣṇa. Their talks are solely on the transcendental subjects. The symptoms of the pure devotees are described in this verse specifically. Devotees of the Supreme Lord are twenty-four hours daily engaged in glorifying the qualities and pastimes of the Supreme Lord. Their hearts and souls are constantly submerged in Kṛṣṇa, and they take pleasure in discussing Him with other devotees.

In the preliminary stage of devotional service they relish the transcendental pleasure from the service itself, and in the mature stage they are actually situated in love of God. Once situated in that transcendental position, they can relish the highest perfection which is exhibited by the Lord in His abode. Lord Caitanya likens transcendental devotional service to the sowing of a seed in the heart of the living entity. There are innumerable living entities traveling throughout the different planets of the universe, and out of them there are a few who are fortunate enough to meet a pure devotee and get the chance to understand devotional service. This devotional service is just like a seed, and if it is sown in the heart of a living entity, and if he goes on hearing and chanting Hare Kṛṣṇa, Hare Kṛṣṇa, Kṛṣṇa Kṛṣṇa, Hare Hare/ Hare Rāma, Hare Rāma, Rāma Rāma, Hare Hare, that seed fructifies, just as the seed of a tree fructifies with regular watering. The spiritual plant of devotional service gradually grows and grows until it penetrates the covering of the material universe and enters into the *brahma-jyotir* effulgence in the spiritual sky. In the spiritual sky also that plant grows more and more until it reaches the highest planet, which is called Goloka Vṛndāvana, the supreme planet of Kṛṣṇa. Ultimately, the plant takes shelter under the lotus feet of Kṛṣṇa and rests there. Gradually, as a plant grows fruits and flowers, that plant of devotional service also produces fruits, and the watering process in the form of chanting and hearing goes on. This plant of devotional service is fully described in the *Caitanya-caritāmṛta* (*Madhya-līlā,* Chapter Nineteen). It is explained there that when the complete plant takes shelter under the lotus feet of the Supreme Lord, one becomes fully absorbed in love of God; then he cannot live even for a moment without being in contact with the Supreme Lord, just as a fish cannot live without water. In such a state, the devotee actually attains the transcendental qualities in contact with the Supreme Lord.

The *Śrīmad-Bhāgavatam* is also full of such narrations about the relationship between the Supreme Lord and His devotees; therefore the *Śrīmad-Bhāgavatam* is very dear to the devotees, as stated in the *Bhāgavatam* itself (12.13.18). *Śrīmad-bhāgavataṁ purāṇam amalaṁ yad vaiṣṇavānāṁ priyam.* In this narration there is nothing about material activities, economic development, sense gratification or liberation. *Śrīmad-Bhāgavatam* is the only narration in which the transcendental nature of the Supreme Lord and His devotees is fully described. Thus the realized souls in Kṛṣṇa consciousness take continual pleasure in hearing such transcendental literatures, just as a young boy and girl take pleasure in association.

Text 10 तेषां सततयुक्तानां भजतां प्रीतिपूर्वकम् ।
ददामि बुद्धियोगं तं येन मामुपयान्ति ते ॥१०॥

teṣāṁ satata-yuktānāṁ, bhajatāṁ prīti-pūrvakam
dadāmi buddhi-yogaṁ taṁ, yena mām upayānti te

teṣām – unto them; *satata-yuktānām* – always engaged; *bhajatām* – in rendering devotional service; *prīti-pūrvakam* – in loving ecstasy; *dadāmi* – I give; *buddhi-yogam* – real intelligence; *tam* – that; *yena* – by which; *mām* – unto Me; *upayānti* – come; *te* – they.

To those who are constantly devoted to serving Me with love, I give the understanding by which they can come to Me.

PURPORT: In this verse the word *buddhi-yogam* is very significant. We may remember that in the Second Chapter the Lord, instructing Arjuna, said that He had spoken to him of many things and that He would instruct him in the way of *buddhi-yoga.* Now *buddhi-yoga* is explained. *Buddhi-yoga* itself is action in Kṛṣṇa consciousness; that is the highest intelligence. *Buddhi* means intelligence, and *yoga* means mystic activities or mystic elevation. When one tries to go back home, back to Godhead, and takes fully to Kṛṣṇa consciousness in devotional service, his action is called *buddhi-yoga.* In other words, *buddhi-yoga* is the process by which one gets out of the entanglement of this material world. The ultimate goal of progress is Kṛṣṇa. People do not know this; therefore the association of devotees and a bona fide spiritual master are important. One should know that the goal is Kṛṣṇa, and when the goal is assigned, then the path is slowly but progressively traversed, and the ultimate goal is achieved.

When a person knows the goal of life but is addicted to the fruits of activities, he is acting in *karma-yoga.* When he knows that the goal is Kṛṣṇa but he takes pleasure in mental speculations to understand Kṛṣṇa, he is acting in *jñāna-yoga.* And when he knows the goal and seeks Kṛṣṇa completely in Kṛṣṇa consciousness and devotional service, he is acting in *bhakti-yoga,* or *buddhi-yoga,* which is the complete *yoga.* This complete *yoga* is the highest perfectional stage of life.

A person may have a bona fide spiritual master and may be attached to a spiritual organization, but if he is still not intelligent enough to make progress, then Kṛṣṇa from within gives him instructions so that he may ultimately come to Him without difficulty. The qualification is that a person always engage himself in Kṛṣṇa consciousness and with love and devotion render all kinds of services. He should perform some sort of work for Kṛṣṇa, and that work should be with love. If a devotee is not intelligent enough to make progress on the path of self-realization but is sincere and devoted to the activities of devotional service, the Lord gives him a chance to make progress and ultimately attain to Him.

Text 11 तेषामेवानुकम्पार्थमहमज्ञानजं तमः ।
नाशयाम्यात्मभावस्थो ज्ञानदीपेन भास्वता ॥११॥

teṣām evānukampārtham, aham ajñāna-jaṁ tamaḥ
nāśayāmy ātma-bhāva-stho, jñāna-dīpena bhāsvatā

teṣām – for them; *eva* – certainly; *anukampā-artham* – to show special mercy; *aham* – I; *ajñāna-jam* – due to ignorance; *tamaḥ* – darkness; *nāśayāmi* – dispel; *ātma-bhāva* – within their hearts; *sthaḥ* – situated; *jñāna* – of knowledge; *dīpena* – with the lamp; *bhāsvatā* – glowing.

To show them special mercy, I, dwelling in their hearts, destroy with the shining lamp of knowledge the darkness born of ignorance.

PURPORT: When Lord Caitanya was in Benares promulgating the chanting of Hare Kṛṣṇa, Hare Kṛṣṇa, Kṛṣṇa Kṛṣṇa, Hare Hare/ Hare Rāma, Hare Rāma, Rāma Rāma, Hare Hare, thousands of people were following Him. Prakāśānanda Sarasvatī, a very influential and learned scholar in Benares at that time, derided Lord Caitanya for being a sentimentalist. Sometimes Māyāvādī philosophers criticize the devotees because they think that most of the devotees are in the darkness of ignorance and are philosophically naive sentimentalists. Actually that is not the fact. There are very, very learned scholars who have put forward the philosophy of devotion. But even if a devotee does not take advantage of their literatures or of his spiritual master, if he is sincere in his devotional service he is helped by Kṛṣṇa Himself within his heart. So the sincere devotee engaged in Kṛṣṇa consciousness cannot be without knowledge. The only qualification is that one carry out devotional service in full Kṛṣṇa consciousness.

The Māyāvādī philosophers think that without discriminating one cannot have pure knowledge. For them this answer is given by the Supreme Lord: those who are engaged in pure devotional service, even though they be without sufficient education and even without sufficient knowledge of the Vedic principles, are still helped by the Supreme God, as stated in this verse.

The Lord tells Arjuna that basically there is no possibility of understanding the Supreme Truth, the Absolute Truth, the Supreme Personality of Godhead, simply by speculating, for the Supreme Truth is so great that it is not possible to understand Him or to achieve Him simply by making a mental effort. Man can go on speculating for several millions of years, and if he is not devoted, if he is not a lover of the Supreme Truth, he will never understand Kṛṣṇa, or the Supreme Truth. Only by devotional service is the Supreme Truth, Kṛṣṇa, pleased, and by His inconceivable energy He can reveal Himself to the heart of the pure devotee. The pure devotee always has Kṛṣṇa within his heart; and with the presence of Kṛṣṇa, who is just like the sun, the darkness of ignorance is at once dissipated. This is the special mercy rendered to the pure devotee by Kṛṣṇa.

Due to the contamination of material association, through many, many millions of births, one's heart is always covered with the dust of materialism, but when one engages in devotional service and constantly chants Hare Kṛṣṇa, the dust quickly clears, and one is elevated to the platform of pure knowledge. The ultimate goal, Viṣṇu, can be attained only by this chant and by devotional service, and not by mental speculation or argument. The pure devotee does not have to worry about the material necessities of life; he need not be anxious, because when he removes the darkness from his heart, everything is provided automatically by the Supreme Lord, who is pleased by the loving devotional service of the devotee. This is the essence of the teachings of *Bhagavad-gītā*. By studying *Bhagavad-gītā,* one can become a soul completely surrendered to the Supreme Lord and engage himself in pure devotional service. As the Lord takes charge, one becomes completely free from all kinds of materialistic endeavors.

Texts 12–13

अर्जुन उवाच
परं ब्रह्म परं धाम पवित्रं परमं भवान् ।
पुरुषं शाश्वतं दिव्यमादिदेवमजं विभुम् ॥१२॥
आहुस्त्वामृषयः सर्वे देवर्षिर्नारदस्तथा ।
असितो देवलो व्यासः स्वयं चैव ब्रवीषि मे ॥१३॥

arjuna uvāca
paraṁ brahma paraṁ dhāma, pavitraṁ paramaṁ bhavān
puruṣaṁ śāśvataṁ divyam, ādi-devam ajaṁ vibhum

āhus tvām ṛṣayaḥ sarve, devarṣir nāradas tathā
asito devalo vyāsaḥ, svayaṁ caiva bravīṣi me

arjunaḥ uvāca – Arjuna said; *param* – supreme; *brahma* – truth; *param* – supreme; *dhāma* – sustenance; *pavitram* – pure; *paramam* – supreme; *bhavān* – You; *puruṣam* – personality; *śāśvatam* – eternal; *divyam* – transcendental; *ādi-devam* – the original Lord; *ajam* – unborn; *vibhum* – greatest; *āhuḥ* – say; *tvām* – of You; *ṛṣayaḥ* – sages; *sarve* – all; *deva-ṛṣiḥ* – the sage among the demigods; *nāradaḥ* – Nārada; *tathā* – also; *asitaḥ* – Asita; *devalaḥ* – Devala; *vyāsaḥ* – Vyāsa; *svayam* – personally; *ca* – also; *eva* – certainly; *bravīṣi* – You are explaining; *me* – unto me.

Arjuna said: You are the Supreme Personality of Godhead, the ultimate abode, the purest, the Absolute Truth. You are the eternal, transcendental, original person, the unborn, the greatest. All the great sages such as Nārada, Asita, Devala and Vyāsa confirm this truth about You, and now You Yourself are declaring it to me.

PURPORT: In these two verses the Supreme Lord gives a chance to the Māyāvādī philosopher, for here it is clear that the Supreme is different from the individual soul. Arjuna, after hearing the essential four verses of *Bhagavad-gītā* in this chapter, became completely free from all doubts and accepted Kṛṣṇa as the Supreme Personality of Godhead. He at once boldly declares, "You are *paraṁ brahma,* the Supreme Personality of Godhead." And previously Kṛṣṇa stated that He is the originator of everything and everyone. Every demigod and every human being is dependent on Him. Men and demigods, out of ignorance, think that they are absolute and independent of the Supreme Personality of Godhead. That ignorance is removed perfectly by the discharge of devotional service. This has already been explained in the previous verse by the Lord. Now, by His grace, Arjuna is accepting Him as the Supreme Truth, in concordance with the Vedic injunction. It is not that because Kṛṣṇa is Arjuna's intimate friend Arjuna is flattering Him by calling Him the Supreme Personality of Godhead, the Absolute Truth. Whatever Arjuna says in these two verses is confirmed by Vedic truth. Vedic injunctions affirm that only one who takes to devotional service to the Supreme Lord can understand Him, whereas others cannot. Each and every word of this verse spoken by Arjuna is confirmed by Vedic injunction.

In the *Kena Upaniṣad* it is stated that the Supreme Brahman is the rest for everything, and Kṛṣṇa has already explained that everything is resting on Him. The *Muṇḍaka Upaniṣad* confirms that the Supreme Lord, in whom everything is resting, can be realized only by those who engage constantly in thinking of Him. This constant thinking of Kṛṣṇa is *smaraṇam,* one of the methods of devotional service. It is only by devotional service to Kṛṣṇa that one can understand his position and get rid of this material body.

In the *Vedas* the Supreme Lord is accepted as the purest of the pure. One who understands that Kṛṣṇa is the purest of the pure can become purified from all sinful activities. One cannot be disinfected from sinful activities unless he surrenders unto the Supreme Lord. Arjuna's acceptance of Kṛṣṇa as the supreme pure complies with the injunctions of Vedic literature. This is also confirmed by great personalities, of whom Nārada is the chief.

Kṛṣṇa is the Supreme Personality of Godhead, and one should always meditate upon Him and enjoy one's transcendental relationship with Him. He is the supreme existence. He is free from bodily needs, birth and death. Not only does Arjuna confirm this, but all the Vedic literatures, the *Purāṇas* and histories. In all Vedic literatures Kṛṣṇa is thus described, and the Supreme Lord Himself also says in the Fourth Chapter, "Although I am unborn, I appear on this earth to establish religious principles." He is the supreme origin; He has no cause, for He is the cause of all causes, and everything is emanating from Him. This perfect knowledge can be had by the grace of the Supreme Lord.

Here Arjuna expresses himself through the grace of Kṛṣṇa. If we want to understand *Bhagavad-gītā,* we should accept the statements in these two verses. This is called the *paramparā* system, acceptance of the disciplic succession. Unless one is in the disciplic succession, he cannot understand *Bhagavad-gītā.* It is not possible by so-called academic education. Unfortunately those proud of their academic education, despite so much evidence in Vedic literatures, stick to their obstinate conviction that Kṛṣṇa is an ordinary person.

Text 14 सर्वमेतदृतं मन्ये यन्मां वदसि केशव ।
न हि ते भगवन् व्यक्तिं विदुर्देवा न दानवाः ॥१४॥

sarvam etad ṛtaṁ manye, yan māṁ vadasi keśava
na hi te bhagavan vyaktiṁ, vidur devā na dānavāḥ

sarvam – all; *etat* – this; *ṛtam* – truth; *manye* – I accept; *yat* – which; *mām* – unto me; *vadasi* – You tell; *keśava* – O Kṛṣṇa; *na* – never; *hi* – certainly; *te* – Your; *bhagavan* – O Personality of Godhead; *vyaktim* – revelation; *viduḥ* – can know; *devāḥ* – the demigods; *na* – nor; *dānavāḥ* – the demons.

O Kṛṣṇa, I totally accept as truth all that You have told me. Neither the demigods nor the demons, O Lord, can understand Your personality.

PURPORT: Arjuna herein confirms that persons of faithless and demonic nature cannot understand Kṛṣṇa. He is not known even by the demigods, so what to speak of the so-called scholars of this modern world? By the grace of the Supreme Lord, Arjuna has understood that the Supreme Truth is Kṛṣṇa and that He is the perfect one. One should therefore follow the path of Arjuna. He received the authority of *Bhagavad-gītā.* As described in the Fourth Chapter, the *paramparā* system of disciplic succession for the understanding of *Bhagavad-gītā* was lost, and therefore Kṛṣṇa reestablished that disciplic succession with Arjuna because He considered Arjuna His intimate friend and a great devotee. Therefore, as stated in our Introduction to *Gītopaniṣad, Bhagavad-gītā* should be understood in the *paramparā* system. When the *paramparā* system was lost, Arjuna was selected to rejuvenate it. The acceptance by Arjuna of all that Kṛṣṇa says should be emulated; then we can understand the essence of *Bhagavad-gītā,* and then only can we understand that Kṛṣṇa is the Supreme Personality of Godhead.

Text 15 स्वयमेवात्मनात्मानं वेत्थ त्वं पुरुषोत्तम ।
भूतभावन भूतेश देवदेव जगत्पते ॥१५॥

svayam evātmanātmānaṁ, vettha tvaṁ puruṣottama
bhūta-bhāvana bhūteśa, deva-deva jagat-pate

svayam – personally; *eva* – certainly; *ātmanā* – by Yourself; *ātmānam* – Yourself; *vettha* – know; *tvam* – You; *puruṣa-uttama* – O greatest of all persons; *bhūta-bhāvana* – O origin of everything; *bhūta-īśa* – O Lord of everything; *deva-deva* – O Lord of all demigods; *jagat-pate* – O Lord of the entire universe.

Indeed, You alone know Yourself by Your own internal potency, O Supreme Person, origin of all, Lord of all beings, God of gods, Lord of the universe!

PURPORT: The Supreme Lord, Kṛṣṇa, can be known by persons who are in a relationship with Him through the discharge of devotional service, like Arjuna and his followers. Persons of demonic or atheistic mentality cannot know Kṛṣṇa. Mental speculation that leads one away from the Supreme Lord is a serious sin, and one who does not know Kṛṣṇa should not try to comment on *Bhagavad-gītā*. *Bhagavad-gītā* is the statement of Kṛṣṇa, and since it is the science of Kṛṣṇa, it should be understood from Kṛṣṇa as Arjuna understood it. It should not be received from atheistic persons.

As stated in *Śrīmad-Bhāgavatam* (1.2.11):

vadanti tat tattva-vidas, tattvaṁ yaj jñānam advayam
brahmeti paramātmeti, bhagavān iti śabdyate

The Supreme Truth is realized in three aspects: as impersonal Brahman, localized Paramātmā and at last as the Supreme Personality of Godhead. So at the last stage of understanding the Absolute Truth, one comes to the Supreme Personality of Godhead. A common man or even a liberated man who has realized impersonal Brahman or localized Paramātmā may not understand God's personality. Such men, therefore, may endeavor to understand the Supreme Person from the verses of *Bhagavad-gītā,* which are being spoken by this person, Kṛṣṇa. Sometimes the impersonalists accept Kṛṣṇa as Bhagavān, or they accept His authority. Yet many liberated persons cannot understand Kṛṣṇa as Puruṣottama, the Supreme Person. Therefore Arjuna addresses Him as Puruṣottama. Yet one still may not understand that Kṛṣṇa is the father of all living entities. Therefore Arjuna addresses Him as Bhūta-bhāvana. And if one comes to know Him as the father of all the living entities, still one may not know Him as the supreme controller; therefore He is addressed here as Bhūteśa, the supreme controller of everyone. And even if one knows Kṛṣṇa as the supreme controller of all living entities, still one may not know that He is the origin of all the demigods; therefore He is addressed herein as Deva-deva, the worshipful God of all demigods. And even if one knows Him as the worshipful God of all demigods, one may not know that He is the supreme proprietor of everything; therefore He is addressed as Jagat-pati. Thus the truth about Kṛṣṇa is established in this verse by the realization of Arjuna, and we should follow in the footsteps of Arjuna to understand Kṛṣṇa as He is.

Text 16 वक्तुमर्हस्यशेषेण दिव्या ह्यात्मविभूतयः ।
याभिर्विभूतिभिर्लोकानिमांस्त्वं व्याप्य तिष्ठसि ॥१६॥

vaktum arhasy aśeṣeṇa, divyā hy ātma-vibhūtayaḥ
yābhir vibhūtibhir lokān, imāṁs tvaṁ vyāpya tiṣṭhasi

vaktum – to say; *arhasi* – You deserve; *aśeṣeṇa* – in detail; *divyāḥ* – divine; *hi* – certainly; *ātma* – Your own; *vibhūtayaḥ* – opulences; *yābhiḥ* – by which; *vibhūtibhiḥ* – opulences; *lokān* – all the planets; *imān* – these; *tvam* – You; *vyāpya* – pervading; *tiṣṭhasi* – remain.

Please tell me in detail of Your divine opulences by which You pervade all these worlds.

PURPORT: In this verse it appears that Arjuna is already satisfied with his understanding of the Supreme Personality of Godhead, Kṛṣṇa. By Kṛṣṇa's grace, Arjuna has personal experience, intelligence and knowledge and whatever else a person may have, and through all these agencies he has understood Kṛṣṇa to be the Supreme Personality of Godhead. For him there is no doubt, yet he is asking Kṛṣṇa to explain His all-pervading nature. People in general and the impersonalists in particular concern themselves mainly with the all-pervading nature of the Supreme. So Arjuna is asking Kṛṣṇa how He exists in His all-pervading aspect through His different energies. One should know that this is being asked by Arjuna on behalf of the common people.

Text 17 कथं विद्यामहं योगिंस्त्वां सदा परिचिन्तयन् ।
केषु केषु च भावेषु चिन्त्योऽसि भगवन्मया ॥१७॥

kathaṁ vidyām ahaṁ yogiṁs, tvāṁ sadā paricintayan
keṣu keṣu ca bhāveṣu, cintyo 'si bhagavan mayā

katham – how; *vidyām aham* – shall I know; *yogin* – O supreme mystic; *tvām* – You; *sadā* – always; *paricintayan* – thinking of; *keṣu* – in which; *keṣu* – in which; *ca* – also; *bhāveṣu* – natures; *cintyaḥ asi* – You are to be remembered; *bhagavan* – O Supreme; *mayā* – by me.

O Kṛṣṇa, O supreme mystic, how shall I constantly think of You, and how shall I know You? In what various forms are You to be remembered, O Supreme Personality of Godhead?

PURPORT: As it is stated in the previous chapter, the Supreme Personality of Godhead is covered by His *yoga-māyā.* Only surrendered souls and devotees can see Him. Now Arjuna is convinced that His friend, Kṛṣṇa, is the Supreme Godhead, but he wants to know the general process by which the all-pervading Lord can be understood by the common man. Common men, including the demons and atheists, cannot know Kṛṣṇa, because He is guarded by His *yoga-māyā* energy. Again, these questions are asked by Arjuna for their benefit. The superior devotee is concerned not only for his own understanding but for the understanding of all mankind. So Arjuna, out of his mercy, because he is a Vaiṣṇava, a devotee, is opening for the common man the understanding of the all-pervasiveness of the Supreme Lord. He addresses Kṛṣṇa specifically as *yogin* because Śrī Kṛṣṇa is the master of the *yoga-māyā* energy, by which He is covered and uncovered to the common man. The common man who has no love for Kṛṣṇa cannot always think of Kṛṣṇa; therefore he has to think materially. Arjuna is considering the mode of thinking of the materialistic persons of this world. The words *keṣu keṣu ca bhāveṣu* refer to material nature (the word *bhāva* means "physical things"). Because materialists cannot understand Kṛṣṇa spiritually, they are advised to concentrate the mind on physical things and try to see how Kṛṣṇa is manifested by physical representations.

Text 18 विस्तरेणात्मनो योगं विभूतिं च जनार्दन ।
भूयः कथय तृप्तिर्हि शृण्वतो नास्ति मेऽमृतम् ॥१८॥

vistareṇātmano yogaṁ, vibhūtiṁ ca janārdana
bhūyaḥ kathaya tṛptir hi, śṛṇvato nāsti me 'mṛtam

vistareṇa – in detail; *ātmanaḥ* – Your; *yogam* – mystic power; *vibhūtim* – opulences; *ca* – also; *jana-ardana* – O killer of the atheists; *bhūyaḥ* – again; *kathaya* – describe; *tṛptiḥ* – satisfaction; *hi* – certainly; *śṛṇvataḥ* – hearing; *na asti* – there is not; *me* – my; *amṛtam* – nectar.

O Janārdana, again please describe in detail the mystic power of Your opulences. I am never satiated in hearing about You, for the more I hear the more I want to taste the nectar of Your words.

PURPORT: A similar statement was made to Sūta Gosvāmī by the *ṛṣis* of Naimiṣāraṇya, headed by Śaunaka. That statement is:

vayaṁ tu na vitṛpyāma, uttama-śloka-vikrame
yac chṛṇvatāṁ rasa-jñānāṁ, svādu svādu pade pade

"One can never be satiated even though one continuously hears the transcendental pastimes of Kṛṣṇa, who is glorified by excellent prayers. Those who have entered into a transcendental relationship with Kṛṣṇa relish at every step the descriptions of the pastimes of the Lord." (*Śrīmad-Bhāgavatam* 1.1.19) Thus Arjuna is interested in hearing about Kṛṣṇa, and specifically how He remains as the all-pervading Supreme Lord.

Now as far as *amṛtam,* nectar, is concerned, any narration or statement concerning Kṛṣṇa is just like nectar. And this nectar can be perceived by practical experience. Modern stories, fiction and histories are different from the transcendental pastimes of the Lord in that one will tire of hearing mundane stories but one never tires of hearing about Kṛṣṇa. It is for this reason only that the history of the whole universe is replete with references to the pastimes of the incarnations of Godhead. The *Purāṇas* are histories of bygone ages that relate the pastimes of the various incarnations of the Lord. In this way the reading matter remains forever fresh, despite repeated readings.

Text 19 श्रीभगवानुवाच
हन्त ते कथयिष्यामि दिव्या ह्यात्मविभूतयः ।
प्राधान्यतः कुरुश्रेष्ठ नास्त्यन्तो विस्तरस्य मे ॥१९॥

śrī-bhagavān uvāca
hanta te kathayiṣyāmi, divyā hy ātma-vibhūtayaḥ
prādhānyataḥ kuru-śreṣṭha, nāsty anto vistarasya me

śrī-bhagavān uvāca – the Supreme Personality of Godhead said; *hanta* – yes; *te* – unto you; *kathayiṣyāmi* – I shall speak; *divyāḥ* – divine; *hi* – certainly; *ātma-vibhūtayaḥ* – personal opulences; *prādhānyataḥ* – which are principal; *kuru-śreṣṭha* – O best of the Kurus; *na asti* – there is not; *antaḥ* – limit; *vistarasya* – to the extent; *me* – My.

The Supreme Personality of Godhead said: Yes, I will tell you of My splendorous manifestations, but only of those which are prominent, O Arjuna, for My opulence is limitless.

PURPORT: It is not possible to comprehend the greatness of Kṛṣṇa and His opulences. The senses of the individual soul are limited and do not permit him to understand the totality of Kṛṣṇa's affairs. Still the devotees try to understand Kṛṣṇa, but not on the principle that they will be able to understand Kṛṣṇa fully at any specific time or in any state of life. Rather, the very topics of Kṛṣṇa are so relishable that they appear to the devotees as nectar. Thus the devotees enjoy them. In discussing Kṛṣṇa's opulences and His diverse energies, the pure devotees take transcendental pleasure. Therefore they want to hear and discuss them. Kṛṣṇa knows that living entities do not understand the extent of His opulences; He therefore agrees to state only the principal manifestations of His different energies. The word *prādhānyataḥ* ("principal") is very important because we can understand only a few of the principal details of the Supreme Lord, for His features are unlimited. It is not possible to understand them all. And *vibhūti,* as used in this verse, refers to the opulences by which He controls the whole manifestation. In the *Amara-kośa* dictionary it is stated that *vibhūti* indicates an exceptional opulence.

The impersonalist or pantheist cannot understand the exceptional opulences of the Supreme Lord nor the manifestations of His divine energies. Both in the material world and in the spiritual world His energies are distributed in every variety of manifestation. Now Kṛṣṇa is describing what can be directly perceived by the common man; thus part of His variegated energy is described in this way.

Text 20 अहमात्मा गुडाकेश सर्वभूताशयस्थितः ।
अहमादिश्च मध्यं च भूतानामन्त एव च ॥२०॥

aham ātmā guḍākeśa, sarva-bhūtāśaya-sthitaḥ
aham ādiś ca madhyaṁ ca, bhūtānām anta eva ca

aham – I; *ātmā* – the soul; *guḍākeśa* – O Arjuna; *sarva-bhūta* – of all living entities; *āśaya-sthitaḥ* – situated within the heart; *aham* – I am; *ādiḥ* – the origin; *ca* – also; *madhyam* – middle; *ca* – also; *bhūtānām* – of all living entities; *antaḥ* – end; *eva* – certainly; *ca* – and.

I am the Supersoul, O Arjuna, seated in the hearts of all living entities. I am the beginning, the middle and the end of all beings.

PURPORT: In this verse Arjuna is addressed as Guḍākeśa, which means "one who has conquered the darkness of sleep." For those who are sleeping in the darkness of ignorance, it is not possible to understand how the Supreme Personality of Godhead manifests Himself in various ways in the material and spiritual worlds. Thus this address by Kṛṣṇa to Arjuna is significant. Because Arjuna is above such darkness, the Personality of Godhead agrees to describe His various opulences.

Kṛṣṇa first informs Arjuna that He is the soul of the entire cosmic manifestation by dint of His primary expansion. Before the material creation, the Supreme Lord, by His plenary expansion, accepts the *puruṣa* incarnation, and from Him everything begins. Therefore He is *ātmā,* the soul of the *mahat-tattva,* the universal elements. The total material energy is not the cause of the creation; actually the Mahā-viṣṇu enters into the *mahat-tattva,* the total material energy. He is the soul. When Mahā-viṣṇu enters into the manifested universes, He again manifests Himself as the Supersoul in each and every entity. We have experience that the personal body of the living entity exists due to the presence of the spiritual spark. Without the existence of the spiritual spark, the body cannot develop. Similarly, the material manifestation cannot develop unless the Supreme Soul, Kṛṣṇa, enters. As stated in the *Subāla Upaniṣad, prakṛty-ādi-sarva-bhūtāntar-yāmī sarva-śeṣī ca nārāyaṇaḥ:* "The Supreme Personality of Godhead is existing as the Supersoul in all manifested universes."

The three *puruṣa-avatāras* are described in *Śrīmad-Bhāgavatam.* They are also described in the *Nārada Pañcarātra,* one of the *Sātvata-tantras. Viṣṇos tu trīṇi rūpāṇi puruṣākhyāny atho viduḥ:* the Supreme Personality of Godhead manifests three features – as Kāraṇodaka-śāyī Viṣṇu, Garbhodaka-śāyī Viṣṇu and Kṣīrodaka-śāyī Viṣṇu – in this material manifestation. The Mahā-viṣṇu, or Kāraṇodaka-śāyī Viṣṇu, is described in the *Brahma-saṁhitā* (5.47). *Yaḥ kāraṇārṇava-jale bhajati sma yoga-nidrām:* the Supreme Lord, Kṛṣṇa, the cause of all causes, lies down in the cosmic ocean as Mahā-viṣṇu. Therefore the Supreme Personality of Godhead is the beginning of this universe, the maintainer of the universal manifestations, and the end of all energy.

Text 21 आदित्यानामहं विष्णुर्ज्योतिषां रविरंशुमान् ।
मरीचिर्मरुतामस्मि नक्षत्राणामहं शशी ॥२१॥

ādityānām ahaṁ viṣṇur, jyotiṣāṁ ravir aṁśumān
marīcir marutām asmi, nakṣatrāṇām ahaṁ śaśī

ādityānām – of the Ādityas; *aham* – I am; *viṣṇuḥ* – the Supreme Lord; *jyotiṣām* – of all luminaries; *raviḥ* – the sun; *aṁśu-mān* – radiant; *marī-*

ciḥ – Marīci; *marutām* – of the Maruts; *asmi* – I am; *nakṣatrāṇām* – of the stars; *aham* – I am; *śaśī* – the moon.

Of the Ādityas I am Viṣṇu, of lights I am the radiant sun, of the Maruts I am Marīci, and among the stars I am the moon.

PURPORT: There are twelve Ādityas, of which Kṛṣṇa is the principal. Among all the luminaries shining in the sky, the sun is the chief, and in the *Brahma-saṁhitā* the sun is accepted as the glowing eye of the Supreme Lord. There are fifty varieties of wind blowing in space, and of these winds the controlling deity, Marīci, represents Kṛṣṇa.

Among the stars, the moon is the most prominent at night, and thus the moon represents Kṛṣṇa. It appears from this verse that the moon is one of the stars; therefore the stars that twinkle in the sky also reflect the light of the sun. The theory that there are many suns within the universe is not accepted by Vedic literature. The sun is one, and as by the reflection of the sun the moon illuminates, so also do the stars. Since *Bhagavad-gītā* indicates herein that the moon is one of the stars, the twinkling stars are not suns but are similar to the moon.

Text 22 वेदानां सामवेदोऽस्मि देवानामस्मि वासवः ।
इन्द्रियाणां मनश्चास्मि भूतानामस्मि चेतना ॥२२॥

vedānāṁ sāma-vedo 'smi, devānām asmi vāsavaḥ
indriyāṇāṁ manaś cāsmi, bhūtānām asmi cetanā

vedānām – of all the *Vedas; sāma-vedaḥ* – the *Sāma Veda; asmi* – I am; *devānām* – of all the demigods; *asmi* – I am; *vāsavaḥ* – the heavenly king; *indriyāṇām* – of all the senses; *manaḥ* – the mind; *ca* – also; *asmi* – I am; *bhūtānām* – of all living entities; *asmi* – I am; *cetanā* – the living force.

Of the Vedas I am the Sāma Veda; of the demigods I am Indra, the king of heaven; of the senses I am the mind; and in living beings I am the living force [consciousness].

PURPORT: The difference between matter and spirit is that matter has no consciousness like the living entity; therefore this consciousness is supreme and eternal. Consciousness cannot be produced by a combination of matter.

Text 23 रुद्राणां शङ्करश्चास्मि वित्तेशो यक्षरक्षसाम् ।
वसूनां पावकश्चास्मि मेरुः शिखरिणामहम् ॥२३॥

rudrāṇāṁ śaṅkaraś cāsmi, vitteśo yakṣa-rakṣasām
vasūnāṁ pāvakaś cāsmi, meruḥ śikhariṇām aham

rudrāṇām – of all the Rudras; *śaṅkaraḥ* – Lord Śiva; *ca* – also; *asmi* – I am; *vitta-īśaḥ* – the lord of the treasury of the demigods; *yakṣa-rakṣasām* – of the Yakṣas and Rākṣasas; *vasūnām* – of the Vasus; *pāvakaḥ* – fire; *ca* – also; *asmi* – I am; *meruḥ* – Meru; *śikhariṇām* – of all mountains; *aham* – I am.

Of all the Rudras I am Lord Śiva, of the Yakṣas and Rākṣasas I am the Lord of wealth [Kuvera], of the Vasus I am fire [Agni], and of mountains I am Meru.

PURPORT: There are eleven Rudras, of whom Śaṅkara, Lord Śiva, is predominant. He is the incarnation of the Supreme Lord in charge of the mode of ignorance in the universe. The leader of the Yakṣas and Rākṣasas is Kuvera, the master treasurer of the demigods, and he is a representation of the Supreme Lord. Meru is a mountain famed for its rich natural resources.

Text 24 पुरोधसां च मुख्यं मां विद्धि पार्थ बृहस्पतिम् ।
सेनानीनामहं स्कन्दः सरसामस्मि सागरः ॥२४॥

purodhasāṁ ca mukhyaṁ māṁ, viddhi pārtha bṛhaspatim
senānīnām ahaṁ skandaḥ, sarasām asmi sāgaraḥ

purodhasām – of all priests; *ca* – also; *mukhyam* – the chief; *mām* – Me; *viddhi* – understand; *pārtha* – O son of Pṛthā; *bṛhaspatim* – Bṛhaspati; *senānīnām* – of all commanders; *aham* – I am; *skandaḥ* – Kārttikeya; *sarasām* – of all reservoirs of water; *asmi* – I am; *sāgaraḥ* – the ocean.

Of priests, O Arjuna, know Me to be the chief, Bṛhaspati. Of generals I am Kārttikeya, and of bodies of water I am the ocean.

PURPORT: Indra is the chief demigod of the heavenly planets and is known as the king of the heavens. The planet on which he reigns is called Indraloka. Bṛhaspati is Indra's priest, and since Indra is the chief of all kings, Bṛhaspati is the chief of all priests. And as Indra is the chief of all kings, similarly Skanda, or Kārttikeya, the son of Pārvatī and Lord Śiva, is the chief of all military commanders. And of all bodies of water, the ocean is the greatest. These representations of Kṛṣṇa only give hints of His greatness.

Text 25 महर्षीणां भृगुरहं गिरामस्म्येकमक्षरम् ।
यज्ञानां जपयज्ञोऽस्मि स्थावराणां हिमालयः ॥२५॥

maharṣīṇāṁ bhṛgur ahaṁ, girām asmy ekam akṣaram
yajñānāṁ japa-yajño 'smi, sthāvarāṇāṁ himālayaḥ

mahā-ṛṣīṇām – among the great sages; *bhṛguḥ* – Bhṛgu; *aham* – I am; *girām* – of vibrations; *asmi* – I am; *ekam akṣaram* – *praṇava; yajñānām* – of sacrifices; *japa-yajñaḥ* – chanting; *asmi* – I am; *sthāvarāṇām* – of immovable things; *himālayaḥ* – the Himālayan mountains.

Of the great sages I am Bhṛgu; of vibrations I am the transcendental oṁ. Of sacrifices I am the chanting of the holy names [japa], and of immovable things I am the Himālayas.

PURPORT: Brahmā, the first living creature within the universe, created several sons for the propagation of various kinds of species. Among these sons, Bhṛgu is the most powerful sage. Of all the transcendental vibrations, *oṁ* (*oṁkāra*) represents Kṛṣṇa. Of all sacrifices, the chanting of Hare Kṛṣṇa, Hare Kṛṣṇa, Kṛṣṇa Kṛṣṇa, Hare Hare/ Hare Rāma, Hare Rāma, Rāma Rāma, Hare Hare is the purest representation of Kṛṣṇa. Sometimes animal sacrifices are recommended, but in the sacrifice of Hare Kṛṣṇa, Hare Kṛṣṇa, there is no question of violence. It is the simplest and the purest. Whatever is sublime in the worlds is a representation of Kṛṣṇa. Therefore the Himālayas, the greatest mountains in the world, also represent Him. The mountain named Meru was mentioned in a previous verse, but Meru is sometimes movable, whereas the Himālayas are never movable. Thus the Himālayas are greater than Meru.

Text 26 अश्वत्थः सर्ववृक्षाणां देवर्षीणां च नारदः ।
गन्धर्वाणां चित्ररथः सिद्धानां कपिलो मुनिः ॥२६॥

aśvatthaḥ sarva-vṛkṣāṇāṁ, devarṣīṇāṁ ca nāradaḥ
gandharvāṇāṁ citrarathaḥ, siddhānāṁ kapilo muniḥ

aśvatthaḥ – the banyan tree; *sarva-vṛkṣāṇām* – of all trees; *deva-ṛṣīṇām* – of all the sages amongst the demigods; *ca* – and; *nāradaḥ* – Nārada; *gandharvāṇām* – of the citizens of the Gandharva planet; *citrarathaḥ* – Citraratha; *siddhānām* – of all those who are perfected; *kapilaḥ muniḥ* – Kapila Muni.

Of all trees I am the banyan tree, and of the sages among the demigods I am Nārada. Of the Gandharvas I am Citraratha, and among perfected beings I am the sage Kapila.

PURPORT: The banyan tree (*aśvattha*) is one of the highest and most beautiful trees, and people in India often worship it as one of their daily morning rituals. Amongst the demigods they also worship Nārada, who is considered the greatest devotee in the universe. Thus he is the representation of Kṛṣṇa as a devotee. The Gandharva planet is filled with entities who sing beautifully, and among them the best singer is Citraratha. Amongst the perfect living entities, Kapila, the son of Devahūti, is a representative of Kṛṣṇa. He is considered an incarnation of Kṛṣṇa, and His philosophy is mentioned in the *Śrīmad-Bhāgavatam.* Later on another Kapila became famous, but his philosophy was atheistic. Thus there is a gulf of difference between them.

Text 27 उच्चैःश्रवसमश्वानां विद्धि माममृतोद्भवम् ।
ऐरावतं गजेन्द्राणां नराणां च नराधिपम् ॥२७॥

uccaiḥśravasam aśvānāṁ, viddhi māṁ amṛtodbhavam
airāvataṁ gajendrāṇāṁ, narāṇāṁ ca narādhipam

uccaiḥśravasam – Uccaiḥśravā; *aśvānām* – among horses; *viddhi* – know; *mām* – Me; *amṛta-udbhavam* – produced from the churning of the ocean; *airāvatam* – Airāvata; *gaja-indrāṇām* – of lordly elephants; *narāṇām* – among human beings; *ca* – and; *nara-adhipam* – the king.

Of horses know Me to be Uccaiḥśravā, produced during the churning of the ocean for nectar. Of lordly elephants I am Airāvata, and among men I am the monarch.

PURPORT: The devotee demigods and the demons (*asuras*) once took part in churning the sea. From this churning, nectar and poison were produced, and Lord Śiva drank the poison. From the nectar were produced many entities, of which there was a horse named Uccaiḥśravā. Another animal produced from the nectar was an elephant named Airāvata. Because these two animals were produced from nectar, they have special significance, and they are representatives of Kṛṣṇa.

Amongst the human beings, the king is the representative of Kṛṣṇa because Kṛṣṇa is the maintainer of the universe, and the kings, who are appointed on account of their godly qualifications, are maintainers of their kingdoms. Kings like Mahārāja Yudhiṣṭhira, Mahārāja Parīkṣit and Lord Rāma were all highly righteous kings who always thought of the citizens' welfare. In Vedic literature, the king is considered to be the representative of God. In this age, however, with the corruption of the principles of religion, monarchy decayed and is now finally abolished. It is to be understood that in the past, however, people were more happy under righteous kings.

Text 28 आयुधानामहं वज्रं धेनूनामस्मि कामधुक् ।
प्रजनश्चास्मि कन्दर्पः सर्पाणामस्मि वासुकिः ॥२८॥

āyudhānām ahaṁ vajraṁ, dhenūnām asmi kāma-dhuk
prajanaś cāsmi kandarpaḥ, sarpāṇām asmi vāsukiḥ

āyudhānām – of all weapons; *aham* – I am; *vajram* – the thunderbolt; *dhenūnām* – of cows; *asmi* – I am; *kāma-dhuk* – the *surabhi* cow; *prajanaḥ* – the cause for begetting children; *ca* – and; *asmi* – I am; *kandarpaḥ* – Cupid; *sarpāṇām* – of serpents; *asmi* – I am; *vāsukiḥ* – Vāsuki.

Of weapons I am the thunderbolt; among cows I am the surabhi. Of causes for procreation I am Kandarpa, the god of love, and of serpents I am Vāsuki.

PURPORT: The thunderbolt, indeed a mighty weapon, represents Kṛṣṇa's power. In Kṛṣṇaloka in the spiritual sky there are cows which can be milked at any time, and they give as much milk as one likes. Of course such cows do not exist in this material world, but there is mention of them in Kṛṣṇaloka. The Lord keeps many such cows, which are called *surabhi*. It is stated that the Lord is engaged in herding the *surabhi* cows. Kandarpa is the sex desire for presenting good sons; therefore Kandarpa is the representative of Kṛṣṇa. Sometimes sex is engaged in only for sense gratification; such sex does not represent Kṛṣṇa. But sex for the generation of good children is called Kandarpa and represents Kṛṣṇa.

Text 29 अनन्तश्चास्मि नागानां वरुणो यादसामहम् ।
पितॄणामर्यमा चास्मि यमः संयमतामहम् ॥२९॥

anantaś cāsmi nāgānāṁ, varuṇo yādasām aham
pitṝṇām aryamā cāsmi, yamaḥ saṁyamatām aham

anantaḥ – Ananta; *ca* – also; *asmi* – I am; *nāgānām* – of the many-hooded serpents; *varuṇaḥ* – the demigod controlling the water; *yādasām* – of all aquatics; *aham* – I am; *pitṝṇām* – of the ancestors; *aryamā* – Aryamā; *ca* – also; *asmi* – I am; *yamaḥ* – the controller of death; *saṁyamatām* – of all regulators; *aham* – I am.

Of the many-hooded Nāgas I am Ananta, and among the aquatics I am the demigod Varuṇa. Of departed ancestors I am Aryamā, and among the dispensers of law I am Yama, the lord of death.

PURPORT: Among the many-hooded Nāga serpents, Ananta is the greatest, as is the demigod Varuṇa among the aquatics. They both represent Kṛṣṇa. There is also a planet of Pitās, ancestors, presided over by Aryamā, who represents Kṛṣṇa. There are many living entities who give punishment to the miscreants, and among them Yama is the chief. Yama is situated in a planet near this earthly planet. After death those who are very sinful are taken there, and Yama arranges different kinds of punishments for them.

Text 30 प्रह्लादश्चास्मि दैत्यानां कालः कलयतामहम् ।
मृगाणां च मृगेन्द्रोऽहं वैनतेयश्च पक्षिणाम् ॥३०॥

prahlādaś cāsmi daityānāṁ, kālaḥ kalayatām aham
mṛgāṇāṁ ca mṛgendro 'haṁ, vainateyaś ca pakṣiṇām

prahlādaḥ – Prahlāda; *ca* – also; *asmi* – I am; *daityānām* – of the demons; *kālaḥ* – time; *kalayatām* – of subduers; *aham* – I am; *mṛgāṇām* – of animals; *ca* – and; *mṛga-indraḥ* – the lion; *aham* – I am; *vainateyaḥ* – Garuḍa; *ca* – also; *pakṣiṇām* – of birds.

Among the Daitya demons I am the devoted Prahlāda, among subduers I am time, among beasts I am the lion, and among birds I am Garuḍa.

PURPORT: Diti and Aditi are two sisters. The sons of Aditi are called Ādityas, and the sons of Diti are called Daityas. All the Ādityas are devotees of the Lord, and all the Daityas are atheistic. Although Prahlāda was born in the family of the Daityas, he was a great devotee from his childhood. Because of his devotional service and godly nature, he is considered to be a representative of Kṛṣṇa.

There are many subduing principles, but time wears down all things in the material universe and so represents Kṛṣṇa. Of the many animals, the lion is the most powerful and ferocious, and of the million varieties of birds, Garuḍa, the bearer of Lord Viṣṇu, is the greatest.

Text 31 पवनः पवतामस्मि रामः शस्त्रभृतामहम् ।
झषाणां मकरश्चास्मि स्रोतसामस्मि जाह्नवी ॥३१॥

pavanaḥ pavatām asmi, rāmaḥ śastra-bhṛtām aham
jhaṣāṇāṁ makaraś cāsmi, srotasām asmi jāhnavī

pavanaḥ – the wind; *pavatām* – of all that purifies; *asmi* – I am; *rāmaḥ* – Rāma; *śastra-bhṛtām* – of the carriers of weapons; *aham* – I am; *jhaṣāṇām* – of all fish; *makaraḥ* – the shark; *ca* – also; *asmi* – I am; *srotasām* – of flowing rivers; *asmi* – I am; *jāhnavī* – the river Ganges.

Of purifiers I am the wind, of the wielders of weapons I am Rāma, of fishes I am the shark, and of flowing rivers I am the Ganges.

PURPORT: Of all the aquatics the shark is one of the biggest and is certainly the most dangerous to man. Thus the shark represents Kṛṣṇa.

Text 32 सर्गाणामादिरन्तश्च मध्यं चैवाहमर्जुन ।
अध्यात्मविद्या विद्यानां वादः प्रवदतामहम् ॥३२॥

sargāṇām ādir antaś ca, madhyaṁ caivāham arjuna
adhyātma-vidyā vidyānāṁ, vādaḥ pravadatām aham

sargāṇām – of all creations; *ādiḥ* – the beginning; *antaḥ* – end; *ca* – and; *madhyam* – middle; *ca* – also; *eva* – certainly; *aham* – I am; *arjuna* – O Arjuna; *adhyātma-vidyā* – spiritual knowledge; *vidyānām* – of all education; *vādaḥ* – the natural conclusion; *pravadatām* – of arguments; *aham* – I am.

Of all creations I am the beginning and the end and also the middle, O Arjuna. Of all sciences I am the spiritual science of the self, and among logicians I am the conclusive truth.

PURPORT: Among the created manifestations, the first is the creation of the total material elements. As explained before, the cosmic manifestation is created and conducted by Mahā-viṣṇu, Garbhodaka-śāyī Viṣṇu and Kṣīrodaka-śāyī Viṣṇu, and then again it is annihilated by Lord Śiva. Brahmā is a secondary creator. All these agents of creation, maintenance and annihilation are incarnations of the material qualities of the Supreme Lord. Therefore He is the beginning, the middle and the end of all creation.

For advanced education there are various kinds of books of knowledge, such as the four *Vedas,* their six supplements, the *Vedānta-sūtra,* books of logic, books of religiosity and the *Purāṇas.* So all together there are fourteen divisions of books of education. Of these, the book which presents *adhyātma-vidyā,* spiritual knowledge – in particular, the *Vedānta-sūtra* – represents Kṛṣṇa.

Among logicians there are different kinds of argument. Supporting one's argument with evidence that also supports the opposing side is called *jalpa.* Merely trying to defeat one's opponent is called *vitaṇḍā.* But the actual conclusion is called *vāda.* This conclusive truth is a representation of Kṛṣṇa.

Text 33 अक्षराणामकारोऽस्मि द्वन्द्वः सामासिकस्य च ।
अहमेवाक्षयः कालो धाताहं विश्वतोमुखः ॥३३॥

akṣarāṇām a-kāro 'smi, dvandvaḥ sāmāsikasya ca
aham evākṣayaḥ kālo, dhātāhaṁ viśvato-mukhaḥ

akṣarāṇām – of letters; *a-kāraḥ* – the first letter; *asmi* – I am; *dvandvaḥ* – the dual; *sāmāsikasya* – of compounds; *ca* – and; *aham* – I am; *eva* – certainly; *akṣayaḥ* – eternal; *kālaḥ* – time; *dhātā* – the creator; *aham* – I am; *viśvataḥ-mukhaḥ* – Brahmā.

Of letters I am the letter A, and among compound words I am the dual compound. I am also inexhaustible time, and of creators I am Brahmā.

PURPORT: *A-kāra,* the first letter of the Sanskrit alphabet, is the beginning of the Vedic literature. Without *a-kāra,* nothing can be sounded; therefore it is the beginning of sound. In Sanskrit there are also many compound words, of which the dual word, like *rāma-kṛṣṇa,* is called *dvandva.* In this compound, the words *rāma* and *kṛṣṇa* have the same form, and therefore the compound is called dual.

Among all kinds of killers, time is the ultimate because time kills everything. Time is the representative of Kṛṣṇa because in due course of time there will be a great fire and everything will be annihilated.

Among the living entities who are creators, Brahmā, who has four heads, is the chief. Therefore he is a representative of the Supreme Lord, Kṛṣṇa.

Text 34 मृत्युः सर्वहरश्चाहमुद्भवश्च भविष्यताम् ।
कीर्तिः श्रीर्वाक्च नारीणां स्मृतिर्मेधा धृतिः क्षमा ॥३४॥

mṛtyuḥ sarva-haraś cāham, udbhavaś ca bhaviṣyatām
kīrtiḥ śrīr vāk ca nārīṇāṁ, smṛtir medhā dhṛtiḥ kṣamā

mṛtyuḥ – death; *sarva-haraḥ* – all-devouring; *ca* – also; *aham* – I am; *udbhavaḥ* – generation; *ca* – also; *bhaviṣyatām* – of future manifestations; *kīrtiḥ* – fame; *śrīḥ* – opulence or beauty; *vāk* – fine speech; *ca* – also; *nārīṇām* – of women; *smṛtiḥ* – memory; *medhā* – intelligence; *dhṛtiḥ* – firmness; *kṣamā* – patience.

I am all-devouring death, and I am the generating principle of all that is yet to be. Among women I am fame, fortune, fine speech, memory, intelligence, steadfastness and patience.

PURPORT: As soon as a man is born, he dies at every moment. Thus death is devouring every living entity at every moment, but the last stroke is called death itself. That death is Kṛṣṇa. As for future development, all living entities undergo six basic changes. They are born, they grow, they remain for some time, they reproduce, they dwindle, and finally they vanish. Of these changes, the first is deliverance from the womb, and that is Kṛṣṇa. The first generation is the beginning of all future activities.

The seven opulences listed – fame, fortune, fine speech, memory, intelligence, steadfastness and patience – are considered feminine. If a person possesses all of them or some of them he becomes glorious. If a man is famous as a righteous man, that makes him glorious. Sanskrit is a perfect language and is therefore very glorious. If after studying one can remember a subject matter, he is gifted with a good memory, or *smṛti*. And the ability not only to read many books on different subject matters but to understand them and apply them when necessary is intelligence (*medhā*), another opulence. The ability to overcome unsteadiness is called firmness or steadfastness (*dhṛti*). And when one is fully qualified yet is humble and gentle, and when one is able to keep his balance both in sorrow and in the ecstasy of joy, he has the opulence called patience (*kṣamā*).

Text 35 बृहत्साम तथा साम्नां गायत्री छन्दसामहम् ।
मासानां मार्गशीर्षोऽहमृतूनां कुसुमाकरः ॥३५॥

bṛhat-sāma tathā sāmnāṁ, gāyatrī chandasām aham
māsānāṁ mārga-śīrṣo 'ham, ṛtūnāṁ kusumākaraḥ

bṛhat-sāma – the *Bṛhat-sāma; tathā* – also; *sāmnām* – of the *Sāma Veda* songs; *gāyatrī* – the Gāyatrī hymns; *chandasām* – of all poetry; *aham* – I am; *māsānām* – of months; *mārga-śīrṣaḥ* – the month of November-December; *aham* – I am; *ṛtūnām* – of all seasons; *kusuma-ākaraḥ* – spring.

Of the hymns in the Sāma Veda I am the Bṛhat-sāma, and of poetry I am the Gāyatrī. Of months I am Mārgaśīrṣa [November-December], and of seasons I am flower-bearing spring.

PURPORT: It has already been explained by the Lord that amongst all the *Vedas,* He is the *Sāma Veda.* The *Sāma Veda* is rich with beautiful songs played by the various demigods. One of these songs is the *Bṛhat-sāma,* which has an exquisite melody and is sung at midnight.

In Sanskrit, there are definite rules that regulate poetry; rhyme and meter are not written whimsically, as in much modern poetry. Amongst the regulated poetry, the Gāyatrī *mantra,* which is chanted by the duly qualified *brāhmaṇas,* is the most prominent. The Gāyatrī *mantra* is mentioned in the *Śrīmad-Bhāgavatam.* Because the Gāyatrī *mantra* is especially meant for God realization, it represents the Supreme Lord. This *mantra* is meant for spiritually advanced people, and when one attains success in chanting it, he can enter into the transcendental position of the Lord. One must first acquire the qualities of the perfectly situated person, the qualities of goodness according to the laws of material nature, in order to chant the Gāyatrī *mantra.* The Gāyatrī *mantra* is very important in Vedic civilization and is considered to be the sound incarnation of Brahman. Brahmā is its initiator, and it is passed down from him in disciplic succession.

The month of November-December is considered the best of all months because in India grains are collected from the fields at this time and the people become very happy. Of course spring is a season universally liked because it is neither too hot nor too cold and the flowers and trees blossom and flourish. In spring there are also many ceremonies commemorating Kṛṣṇa's pastimes; therefore this is considered to be the most joyful of all seasons, and it is the representative of the Supreme Lord, Kṛṣṇa.

Text 36 द्यूतं छलयतामस्मि तेजस्तेजस्विनामहम् ।
जयोऽस्मि व्यवसायोऽस्मि सत्त्वं सत्त्ववतामहम् ॥३६॥

dyūtaṁ chalayatām asmi, tejas tejasvinām aham
jayo 'smi vyavasāyo 'smi, sattvaṁ sattvavatām aham

dyūtam – gambling; *chalayatām* – of all cheats; *asmi* – I am; *tejaḥ* – the splendor; *tejasvinām* – of everything splendid; *aham* – I am; *jayaḥ* – victory; *asmi* – I am; *vyavasāyaḥ* – enterprise or adventure; *asmi* – I am; *sattvam* – the strength; *sattva-vatām* – of the strong; *aham* – I am.

I am also the gambling of cheats, and of the splendid I am the splendor. I am victory, I am adventure, and I am the strength of the strong.

PURPORT: There are many kinds of cheaters all over the universe. Of all cheating processes, gambling stands supreme and therefore represents Kṛṣṇa. As the Supreme, Kṛṣṇa can be more deceitful than any mere man. The unfortunate commentator who wants to cheat Kṛṣṇa is cheated by Kṛṣṇa, and the commentator cannot understand Kṛṣṇa after any length of time. If Kṛṣṇa chooses to deceive a person, no one can surpass Him in His deceit. His greatness is not simply one-sided – it is all-sided.

Among the victorious, He is victory. He is the splendor of the splendid. Among the enterprising and industrious, He is the most enterprising, the most industrious. Among adventurers He is the most adventurous, and among the strong He is the strongest. When Kṛṣṇa was present on earth, no one could surpass Him in strength. Even in His childhood He lifted Govardhana Hill. No one can surpass Him in cheating, no one can surpass Him in splendor, no one can surpass Him in victory, no one can surpass Him in enterprise, and no one can surpass Him in strength.

Text 37 वृष्णीनां वासुदेवोऽस्मि पाण्डवानां धनञ्जयः ।
मुनीनामप्यहं व्यासः कवीनामुशना कविः ॥३७॥

vṛṣṇīnāṁ vāsudevo 'smi, pāṇḍavānāṁ dhanañ-jayaḥ
munīnām apy ahaṁ vyāsaḥ, kavīnām uśanā kaviḥ

vṛṣṇīnām – of the descendants of Vṛṣṇi; *vāsudevaḥ* – Kṛṣṇa in Dvārakā; *asmi* – I am; *pāṇḍavānām* – of the Pāṇḍavas; *dhanam-jayaḥ* – Arjuna; *munīnām* – of the sages; *api* – also; *aham* – I am; *vyāsaḥ* – Vyāsa, the compiler of all Vedic literature; *kavīnām* – of all great thinkers; *uśanā* – Uśanā; *kaviḥ* – the thinker.

Of the descendants of Vṛṣṇi I am Vāsudeva, and of the Pāṇḍavas I am Arjuna. Of the sages I am Vyāsa, and among great thinkers I am Uśanā.

PURPORT: Kṛṣṇa is the original Supreme Personality of Godhead, and Baladeva is Kṛṣṇa's immediate expansion. Both Lord Kṛṣṇa and Baladeva appeared as sons of Vasudeva, so both of Them may be called Vāsudeva. From another point of view, because Kṛṣṇa never leaves Vṛndāvana, all the forms of Kṛṣṇa that appear elsewhere are His expansions. Vāsudeva is Kṛṣṇa's immediate expansion, so Vāsudeva is not different from Kṛṣṇa. It is to be understood that the Vāsudeva referred to in this verse of *Bhagavad-gītā* is Baladeva, or Balarāma, because He is the original source of all incarnations and thus He is the sole source of Vāsudeva. The immediate expansions of the Lord are called *svāṁśa* (personal expansions), and there are also expansions called *vibhinnāṁśa* (separated expansions).

Amongst the sons of Pāṇḍu, Arjuna is famous as Dhanañjaya. He is the best of men and therefore represents Kṛṣṇa. Among the *munis,* or learned men conversant in Vedic knowledge, Vyāsa is the greatest because he explained Vedic knowledge in many different ways for the understanding of the common mass of people in this Age of Kali. And Vyāsa is also known as an incarnation of Kṛṣṇa; therefore Vyāsa also represents Kṛṣṇa. *Kavis* are those who are capable of thinking thoroughly on any subject matter. Among the *kavis,* Uśanā, Śukrācārya, was the spiritual master of the demons; he was an extremely intelligent and far-seeing politician. Thus Śukrācārya is another representative of the opulence of Kṛṣṇa.

Text 38 दण्डो दमयतामस्मि नीतिरस्मि जिगीषताम् ।
मौनं चैवास्मि गुह्यानां ज्ञानं ज्ञानवतामहम् ॥३८॥

daṇḍo damayatām asmi, nītir asmi jigīṣatam
maunaṁ caivāsmi guhyānāṁ, jñānaṁ jñānavatām aham

daṇḍaḥ – punishment; *damayatām* – of all means of suppression; *asmi* – I am; *nītiḥ* – morality; *asmi* – I am; *jigīṣatām* – of those who seek victory; *maunam* – silence; *ca* – and; *eva* – also; *asmi* – I am; *guhyānām* – of secrets; *jñānam* – knowledge; *jñāna-vatām* – of the wise; *aham* – I am.

Among all means of suppressing lawlessness I am punishment, and of those who seek victory I am morality. Of secret things I am silence, and of the wise I am the wisdom.

PURPORT: There are many suppressing agents, of which the most important are those that cut down miscreants. When miscreants are punished, the agency of chastisement represents Kṛṣṇa. Among those who are trying to be victorious in some field of activity, the most victorious element is morality. Among the confidential activities of hearing, thinking and meditating, silence is most important because by silence one can make progress very quickly. The wise man is he who can discriminate between matter and spirit, between God's superior and inferior natures. Such knowledge is Kṛṣṇa Himself.

Text 39 यच्चापि सर्वभूतानां बीजं तदहमर्जुन ।
न तदस्ति विना यत्स्यान्मया भूतं चराचरम् ॥३९॥

yac cāpi sarva-bhūtānāṁ, bījaṁ tad aham arjuna
na tad asti vinā yat syān, mayā bhūtaṁ carācaram

yat – whatever; *ca* – also; *api* – may be; *sarva-bhūtānām* – of all creations; *bījam* – seed; *tat* – that; *aham* – I am; *arjuna* – O Arjuna; *na* – not; *tat* – that; *asti* – there is; *vinā* – without; *yat* – which; *syāt* – exists; *mayā* – Me; *bhūtam* – created being; *cara-acaram* – moving and nonmoving.

Furthermore, O Arjuna, I am the generating seed of all existences. There is no being – moving or nonmoving – that can exist without Me.

PURPORT: Everything has a cause, and that cause or seed of manifestation is Kṛṣṇa. Without Kṛṣṇa's energy, nothing can exist; therefore He is called omnipotent. Without His potency, neither the movable nor the immovable can exist. Whatever existence is not founded on the energy of Kṛṣṇa is called *māyā,* "that which is not."

Text 40 नान्तोऽस्ति मम दिव्यानां विभूतीनां परन्तप ।
एष तूद्देशतः प्रोक्तो विभूतेर्विस्तरो मया ॥४०॥

nānto 'sti mama divyānāṁ, vibhūtīnāṁ paran-tapa
eṣa tūddeśataḥ prokto, vibhūter vistaro mayā

na – nor; *antaḥ* – a limit; *asti* – there is; *mama* – My; *divyānām* – of the divine; *vibhūtīnām* – opulences; *param-tapa* – O conqueror of the enemies; *eṣaḥ* – all this; *tu* – but; *uddeśataḥ* – as examples; *proktaḥ* – spoken; *vibhūteḥ* – of opulences; *vistaraḥ* – the expanse; *mayā* – by Me.

O mighty conqueror of enemies, there is no end to My divine manifestations. What I have spoken to you is but a mere indication of My infinite opulences.

PURPORT: As stated in the Vedic literature, although the opulences and energies of the Supreme are understood in various ways, there is no limit to such opulences; therefore not all the opulences and energies can be explained. Simply a few examples are being described to Arjuna to pacify his inquisitiveness.

Text 41 यद्यद्विभूतिमत्सत्त्वं श्रीमदूर्जितमेव वा ।
तत्तदेवावगच्छ त्वं मम तेजोंऽशसम्भवम् ॥४१॥

yad yad vibhūtimat sattvaṁ, śrīmad ūrjitam eva vā
tat tad evāvagaccha tvaṁ, mama tejo-'ṁśa-sambhavam

yat yat – whatever; *vibhūti* – opulences; *mat* – having; *sattvam* – existence; *śrī-mat* – beautiful; *ūrjitam* – glorious; *eva* – certainly; *vā* – or; *tat tat* – all those; *eva* – certainly; *avagaccha* – must know; *tvam* – you; *mama* – My; *tejaḥ* – of the splendor; *aṁśa* – a part; *sambhavam* – born of.

Know that all opulent, beautiful and glorious creations spring from but a spark of My splendor.

PURPORT: Any glorious or beautiful existence should be understood to be but a fragmental manifestation of Kṛṣṇa's opulence, whether it be in the spiritual or material world. Anything extraordinarily opulent should be considered to represent Kṛṣṇa's opulence.

Text 42 अथ वा बहुनैतेन किं ज्ञातेन तवार्जुन ।
विष्टभ्याहमिदं कृत्स्नमेकांशेन स्थितो जगत् ॥४२॥

atha vā bahunaitena, kiṁ jñātena tavārjuna
viṣṭabhyāham idaṁ kṛtsnam, ekāṁśena sthito jagat

atha vā – or; *bahunā* – many; *etena* – by this kind; *kim* – what; *jñātena* – by knowing; *tava* – your; *arjuna* – O Arjuna; *viṣṭabhya* – pervading; *aham* – I; *idam* – this; *kṛtsnam* – entire; *eka* – by one; *aṁśena* – part; *sthitaḥ* – am situated; *jagat* – universe.

But what need is there, Arjuna, for all this detailed knowledge? With a single fragment of Myself I pervade and support this entire universe.

PURPORT: The Supreme Lord is represented throughout the entire material universes by His entering into all things as the Supersoul. The Lord here tells Arjuna that there is no point in understanding how things exist in their separate opulence and grandeur. He should know that all things are existing due to Kṛṣṇa's entering them as Supersoul. From Brahmā, the most gigantic entity, on down to the smallest ant, all are existing because the Lord has entered each and all and is sustaining them.

There is a Mission that regularly propounds that worship of any demigod will lead one to the Supreme Personality of Godhead, or the supreme goal. But worship of demigods is thoroughly discouraged herein because even the greatest demigods like Brahmā and Śiva represent only part of the opulence of the Supreme Lord. He is the origin of everyone born, and no one is greater than Him. He is *asamaurdhva,* which means that no one is superior to Him and that no one is equal to Him. In the *Padma Purāṇa* it is said that one who considers the Supreme Lord Kṛṣṇa in the same category with demigods – be they even Brahmā or Śiva – becomes at once an atheist. If, however, one thoroughly studies the different descriptions of the opulences and expansions of Kṛṣṇa's energy, then one can understand without any doubt the position of Lord Śrī Kṛṣṇa and can fix his mind in the worship of Kṛṣṇa without deviation. The Lord is all-pervading by the expansion of His partial representation, the Supersoul, who enters into everything that is. Pure devotees, therefore, concentrate their minds in Kṛṣṇa consciousness in full devotional service; therefore they are always situated in the transcendental position. Devotional service and worship of Kṛṣṇa are very clearly indicated in this chapter in verses eight through eleven. That is the way of pure devotional service. How one can attain the highest devotional perfection of association with the Supreme Personality of Godhead has been thoroughly explained in this chapter. Śrīla Baladeva Vidyābhūṣaṇa, a great *ācārya* in disciplic succession from Kṛṣṇa, concludes his commentary on this chapter by saying,

yac-chakti-leśāt sūryādyā, bhavanty aty-ugra-tejasaḥ
yad-aṁśena dhṛtaṁ viśvaṁ, sa kṛṣṇo daśame 'rcyate

From Lord Kṛṣṇa's potent energy even the powerful sun gets its power, and by Kṛṣṇa's partial expansion the whole world is maintained. Therefore Lord Śrī Kṛṣṇa is worshipable.

Thus end the Bhaktivedanta Purports to the Tenth Chapter of the Śrīmad Bhagavad-gītā *in the matter of the Opulence of the Absolute.*

CHAPTER ELEVEN

The Universal Form

Text 1 अर्जुन उवाच
मदनुग्रहाय परमं गुह्यमध्यात्मसंज्ञितम् ।
यत्त्वयोक्तं वचस्तेन मोहोऽयं विगतो मम ॥ १ ॥

arjuna uvāca
mad-anugrahāya paramaṁ, guhyam adhyātma-saṁjñitam
yat tvayoktaṁ vacas tena, moho 'yaṁ vigato mama

arjunaḥ uvāca – Arjuna said; *mat-anugrahāya* – just to show me favor; *paramam* – supreme; *guhyam* – confidential subject; *adhyātma* – spiritual; *saṁjñitam* – in the matter of; *yat* – what; *tvayā* – by You; *uktam* – said; *vacaḥ* – words; *tena* – by that; *mohaḥ* – illusion; *ayam* – this; *vigataḥ* – is removed; *mama* – my.

Arjuna said: By my hearing the instructions You have kindly given me about these most confidential spiritual subjects, my illusion has now been dispelled.

PURPORT: This chapter reveals Kṛṣṇa as the cause of all causes. He is even the cause of the Mahā-viṣṇu, from whom the material universes emanate. Kṛṣṇa is not an incarnation; He is the source of all incarnations. That has been completely explained in the last chapter.

Now, as far as Arjuna is concerned, he says that his illusion is over. This means that Arjuna no longer thinks of Kṛṣṇa as a mere human being, as a friend of his, but as the source of everything. Arjuna is very enlightened and is glad that he has such a great friend as Kṛṣṇa, but now he is thinking that although he may accept Kṛṣṇa as the source of everything, others may not. So in order to establish Kṛṣṇa's divinity for all, he is requesting Kṛṣṇa in this chapter to show His universal form. Actually when one sees the universal form of Kṛṣṇa one becomes frightened, like Arjuna, but Kṛṣṇa is so kind that after showing it He converts Himself again into His original form. Arjuna agrees to what Kṛṣṇa has several times said: Kṛṣṇa is speaking to him just for his benefit. So Arjuna acknowledges that all this is happening to him by Kṛṣṇa's grace. He is now convinced that Kṛṣṇa is the cause of all causes and is present in everyone's heart as the Supersoul.

Text 2 भवाप्ययौ हि भूतानां श्रुतौ विस्तरशो मया ।
त्वत्तः कमलपत्राक्ष माहात्म्यमपि चाव्ययम् ॥ २ ॥

bhavāpyayau hi bhūtānāṁ, śrutau vistaraśo mayā
tvattaḥ kamala-patrākṣa, māhātmyam api cāvyayam

bhava – appearance; *apyayau* – disappearance; *hi* – certainly; *bhūtānām* – of all living entities; *śrutau* – have been heard; *vistaraśaḥ* – in detail; *mayā* – by me; *tvattaḥ* – from You; *kamala-patra-akṣa* – O lotus-eyed one; *māhātmyam* – glories; *api* – also; *ca* – and; *avyayam* – inexhaustible.

O lotus-eyed one, I have heard from You in detail about the appearance and disappearance of every living entity and have realized Your inexhaustible glories.

PURPORT: Arjuna addresses Lord Kṛṣṇa as "lotus-eyed" (Kṛṣṇa's eyes appear just like the petals of a lotus flower) out of his joy, for Kṛṣṇa has assured him, in a previous chapter, *ahaṁ kṛtsnasya jagataḥ prabhavaḥ pralayas tathā:* "I am the source of the appearance and disappearance of this entire material manifestation." Arjuna has heard of this from the Lord in detail. Arjuna further knows that in spite of His being the source of all appearances and disappearances, He is aloof from them. As the Lord has said in the Ninth Chapter, He is all-pervading, yet He is not personally present everywhere. That is the inconceivable opulence of Kṛṣṇa which Arjuna admits that he has thoroughly understood.

Text 3 एवमेतद्यथात्थ त्वमात्मानं परमेश्वर ।
द्रष्टुमिच्छामि ते रूपमैश्वरं पुरुषोत्तम ॥ ३ ॥

evam etad yathāttha tvam, ātmānaṁ parameśvara
draṣṭum icchāmi te rūpam, aiśvaraṁ puruṣottama

evam – thus; *etat* – this; *yathā* – as it is; *āttha* – have spoken; *tvam* – You; *ātmānam* – Yourself; *parama-īśvara* – O Supreme Lord; *draṣṭum* – to see; *icchāmi* – I wish; *te* – Your; *rūpam* – form; *aiśvaram* – divine; *puruṣa-uttama* – O best of personalities.

O greatest of all personalities, O supreme form, though I see You here before me in Your actual position, as You have described Yourself, I wish to see how You have entered into this cosmic manifestation. I want to see that form of Yours.

PURPORT: The Lord said that because He entered into the material universe by His personal representation, the cosmic manifestation has been made possible and is going on. Now as far as Arjuna is concerned, he is inspired by the statements of Kṛṣṇa, but in order to convince others in the future who may think that Kṛṣṇa is an ordinary person, Arjuna desires to see Him actually in His universal form, to see how He is acting from within the universe, although He is apart from it. Arjuna's addressing the Lord as *puruṣottama* is also significant. Since the Lord is the Supreme Personality of Godhead, He is present within Arjuna himself; therefore He knows the desire of Arjuna, and He can understand that Arjuna has no special desire to see Him in His universal form, for Arjuna is completely satisfied to see Him in His personal form of Kṛṣṇa. But the Lord can understand also that Arjuna wants to see the universal form to convince others. Arjuna did not have any personal desire for confirmation. Kṛṣṇa also understands that Arjuna wants to see the universal form to set a criterion, for in the future there would be so many imposters who would pose themselves as incarnations of God. The people, therefore, should be careful; one who claims to be Kṛṣṇa should be prepared to show his universal form to confirm his claim to the people.

Text 4 मन्यसे यदि तच्छक्यं मया द्रष्टुमिति प्रभो ।
योगेश्वर ततो मे त्वं दर्शयात्मानमव्ययम् ॥ ४ ॥

manyase yadi tac chakyaṁ, mayā draṣṭum iti prabho
yogeśvara tato me tvaṁ, darśayātmānam avyayam

manyase – You think; *yadi* – if; *tat* – that; *śakyam* – is able; *mayā* – by me; *draṣṭum* – to be seen; *iti* – thus; *prabho* – O Lord; *yoga-īśvara* –

O Lord of all mystic power; *tataḥ* – then; *me* – unto me; *tvam* – You; *darśaya* – show; *ātmānam* – Your Self; *avyayam* – eternal.

If You think that I am able to behold Your cosmic form, O my Lord, O master of all mystic power, then kindly show me that unlimited universal Self.

PURPORT: It is said that one can neither see, hear, understand nor perceive the Supreme Lord, Kṛṣṇa, by the material senses. But if one is engaged in loving transcendental service to the Lord from the beginning, then one can see the Lord by revelation. Every living entity is only a spiritual spark; therefore it is not possible to see or to understand the Supreme Lord. Arjuna, as a devotee, does not depend on his speculative strength; rather, he admits his limitations as a living entity and acknowledges Kṛṣṇa's inestimable position. Arjuna could understand that for a living entity it is not possible to understand the unlimited infinite. If the infinite reveals Himself, then it is possible to understand the nature of the infinite by the grace of the infinite. The word *yogeśvara* is also very significant here because the Lord has inconceivable power. If He likes, He can reveal Himself by His grace, although He is unlimited. Therefore Arjuna pleads for the inconceivable grace of Kṛṣṇa. He does not give Kṛṣṇa orders. Kṛṣṇa is not obliged to reveal Himself unless one surrenders fully in Kṛṣṇa consciousness and engages in devotional service. Thus it is not possible for persons who depend on the strength of their mental speculations to see Kṛṣṇa.

Text 5 श्रीभगवानुवाच
पश्य मे पार्थ रूपाणि शतशोऽथ सहस्रशः ।
नानाविधानि दिव्यानि नानावर्णाकृतीनि च ॥ ५ ॥

śrī-bhagavān uvāca
paśya me pārtha rūpāṇi, śataśo 'tha sahasraśaḥ
nānā-vidhāni divyāni, nānā-varṇākṛtīni ca

śrī-bhagavān uvāca – the Supreme Personality of Godhead said; *paśya* – just see; *me* – My; *pārtha* – O son of Pṛthā; *rūpāṇi* – forms; *śataśaḥ* – hundreds; *atha* – also; *sahasraśaḥ* – thousands; *nānā-vidhāni* – variegated; *divyāni* – divine; *nānā* – variegated; *varṇa* – colors; *ākṛtīni* – forms; *ca* – also.

The Supreme Personality of Godhead said: My dear Arjuna, O son of Pṛthā, see now My opulences, hundreds of thousands of varied divine and multicolored forms.

PURPORT: Arjuna wanted to see Kṛṣṇa in His universal form, which, although a transcendental form, is just manifested for the cosmic manifestation and is therefore subject to the temporary time of this material nature. As the material nature is manifested and not manifested, similarly this universal form of Kṛṣṇa is manifested and nonmanifested. It is not eternally situated in the spiritual sky like Kṛṣṇa's other forms. As far as a devotee is concerned, he is not eager to see the universal form, but because Arjuna wanted to see Kṛṣṇa in this way, Kṛṣṇa reveals this form. This universal form is not possible to be seen by any ordinary man. Kṛṣṇa must give one the power to see it.

Text 6 पश्यादित्यान् वसून् रुद्रानश्विनौ मरुतस्तथा ।
बहून्यदृष्टपूर्वाणि पश्याश्चर्याणि भारत ॥ ६ ॥

paśyādityān vasūn rudrān, aśvinau marutas tathā
bahūny adṛṣṭa-pūrvāṇi, paśyāścaryāṇi bhārata

paśya – see; *ādityān* – the twelve sons of Aditi; *vasūn* – the eight Vasus; *rudrān* – the eleven forms of Rudra; *aśvinau* – the two Aśvinīs; *marutaḥ* – the forty-nine Maruts (demigods of the wind); *tathā* – also; *bahūni* – many; *adṛṣṭa* – that you have not seen; *pūrvāṇi* – before; *paśya* – see; *āścaryāṇi* – all the wonders; *bhārata* – O best of the Bhāratas.

O best of the Bhāratas, see here the different manifestations of Ādityas, Vasus, Rudras, Aśvini-kumāras and all the other demigods. Behold the many wonderful things which no one has ever seen or heard of before.

PURPORT: Even though Arjuna was a personal friend of Kṛṣṇa and the most advanced of learned men, it was still not possible for him to know everything about Kṛṣṇa. Here it is stated that humans have neither heard nor known of all these forms and manifestations. Now Kṛṣṇa reveals these wonderful forms.

Text 7 इहैकस्थं जगत्कृत्स्नं पश्याद्य सचराचरम् ।
मम देहे गुडाकेश यच्चान्यद्द्रष्टुमिच्छसि ॥ ७ ॥

ihaika-sthaṁ jagat kṛtsnaṁ, paśyādya sa-carācaram
mama dehe guḍākeśa, yac cānyad draṣṭum icchasi

iha – in this; *eka-stham* – in one place; *jagat* – the universe; *kṛtsnam* – completely; *paśya* – see; *adya* – immediately; *sa* – with; *cara* – the moving; *acaram* – and not moving; *mama* – My; *dehe* – in this body; *guḍākeśa* – O Arjuna; *yat* – that which; *ca* – also; *anyat* – other; *draṣṭum* – to see; *icchasi* – you wish.

O Arjuna, whatever you wish to see, behold at once in this body of Mine! This universal form can show you whatever you now desire to see and whatever you may want to see in the future. Everything – moving and nonmoving – is here completely, in one place.

PURPORT: No one can see the entire universe while sitting in one place. Even the most advanced scientist cannot see what is going on in other parts of the universe. But a devotee like Arjuna can see everything that exists in any part of the universe. Kṛṣṇa gives him the power to see anything he wants to see, past, present and future. Thus by the mercy of Kṛṣṇa, Arjuna is able to see everything.

Text 8 न तु मां शक्यसे द्रष्टुमनेनैव स्वचक्षुषा ।
दिव्यं ददामि ते चक्षुः पश्य मे योगमैश्वरम् ॥ ८ ॥

na tu māṁ śakyase draṣṭum, anenaiva sva-cakṣuṣā
divyaṁ dadāmi te cakṣuḥ, paśya me yogam aiśvaram

na – never; *tu* – but; *mām* – Me; *śakyase* – are able; *draṣṭum* – to see; *anena* – with these; *eva* – certainly; *sva-cakṣuṣā* – your own eyes; *divyam* – divine; *dadāmi* – I give; *te* – to you; *cakṣuḥ* – eyes; *paśya* – see; *me* – My; *yogam aiśvaram* – inconceivable mystic power.

But you cannot see Me with your present eyes. Therefore I give you divine eyes. Behold My mystic opulence!

PURPORT: A pure devotee does not like to see Kṛṣṇa in any form except His form with two hands; a devotee must see His universal form by His grace, not with the mind but with spiritual eyes. To see the universal form of Kṛṣṇa, Arjuna is told not to change his mind but his vision. The universal form of Kṛṣṇa is not very important; that will be clear in subsequent verses. Yet because Arjuna wanted to see it, the Lord gives him the particular vision required to see that universal form.

Devotees who are correctly situated in a transcendental relationship with Kṛṣṇa are attracted by loving features, not by a godless display of opulences. The playmates of Kṛṣṇa, the friends of Kṛṣṇa and the parents of Kṛṣṇa never want Kṛṣṇa to show His opulences. They are so immersed in pure love that they do not even know that Kṛṣṇa is the Supreme Personality of Godhead. In their loving exchange they forget that Kṛṣṇa is the Supreme Lord. In the *Śrīmad-Bhāgavatam* it is stated that the boys who play with Kṛṣṇa are all highly pious souls and after many, many births they are able to play with Kṛṣṇa. Such boys do not know that Kṛṣṇa is the Supreme Personality of Godhead. They take Him as a personal friend. Therefore Śukadeva Gosvāmī recites this verse:

itthaṁ satāṁ brahma-sukhānubhūtyā, dāsyaṁ gatānāṁ para-daivatena
māyāśritānāṁ nara-dārakeṇa, sākaṁ vijahruḥ kṛta-puṇya-puñjāḥ

"Here is the Supreme Person, who is considered the impersonal Brahman by great sages, the Supreme Personality of Godhead by devotees, and a product of material nature by ordinary men. Now these boys, who have performed many, many pious activities in their past lives, are playing with that Supreme Personality of Godhead." (*Śrīmad-Bhāgavatam* 10.12.11)

The fact is that the devotee is not concerned with seeing the *viśva-rūpa,* the universal form, but Arjuna wanted to see it to substantiate Kṛṣṇa's statements so that in the future people could understand that Kṛṣṇa not only theoretically or philosophically presented Himself as the Supreme but actually presented Himself as such to Arjuna. Arjuna must confirm this because Arjuna is the beginning of the *paramparā* system. Those who are actually interested in understanding the Supreme Personality of Godhead, Kṛṣṇa, and who follow in the footsteps of Arjuna should understand that Kṛṣṇa not only theoretically presented Himself as the Supreme, but actually revealed Himself as the Supreme.

The Lord gave Arjuna the necessary power to see His universal form because He knew that Arjuna did not particularly want to see it, as we have already explained.

Text 9 सञ्जय उवाच

एवमुक्त्वा ततो राजन्महायोगेश्वरो हरिः ।
दर्शयामास पार्थाय परमं रूपमैश्वरम् ॥ ९ ॥

sañjaya uvāca
evam uktvā tato rājan, mahā-yogeśvaro hariḥ
darśayām āsa pārthāya, paramaṁ rūpam aiśvaram

sañjayaḥ uvāca – Sañjaya said; *evam* – thus; *uktvā* – saying; *tataḥ* – thereafter; *rājan* – O King; *mahā-yoga-īśvaraḥ* – the most powerful mystic; *hariḥ* – the Supreme Personality of Godhead, Kṛṣṇa; *darśayām āsa* – showed; *pārthāya* – unto Arjuna; *paramam* – the divine; *rūpam aiśvaram* – universal form.

Sañjaya said: O King, having spoken thus, the Supreme Lord of all mystic power, the Personality of Godhead, displayed His universal form to Arjuna.

Texts 10–11

अनेकवक्त्रनयनमनेकाद्भुतदर्शनम् ।
अनेकदिव्याभरणं दिव्यानेकोद्यतायुधम् ॥१०॥
दिव्यमाल्याम्बरधरं दिव्यगन्धानुलेपनम् ।
सर्वाश्चर्यमयं देवमनन्तं विश्वतोमुखम् ॥११॥

aneka-vaktra-nayanam, anekādbhuta-darśanam
aneka-divyābharaṇaṁ, divyānekodyatāyudham

divya-mālyāmbara-dharaṁ, divya-gandhānulepanam
sarvāścarya-mayaṁ devam, anantaṁ viśvato-mukham

aneka – various; *vaktra* – mouths; *nayanam* – eyes; *aneka* – various; *adbhuta* – wonderful; *darśanam* – sights; *aneka* – many; *divya* – divine; *ābharaṇam* – ornaments; *divya* – divine; *aneka* – various; *udyata* – uplifted; *āyudham* – weapons; *divya* – divine; *mālya* – garlands; *ambara* – dresses; *dharam* – wearing; *divya* – divine; *gandha* – fragrances; *anulepanam* – smeared with; *sarva* – all; *āścarya-mayam* – wonderful; *devam* – shining; *anantam* – unlimited; *viśvataḥ-mukham* – all-pervading.

Arjuna saw in that universal form unlimited mouths, unlimited eyes, unlimited wonderful visions. The form was decorated with many celestial ornaments and bore many divine upraised weapons. He wore celestial garlands and garments, and many divine scents were smeared over His body. All was wondrous, brilliant, unlimited, all-expanding.

PURPORT: In these two verses the repeated use of the word *many* indicates that there was no limit to the number of hands, mouths, legs and other manifestations Arjuna was seeing. These manifestations were distributed throughout the universe, but by the grace of the Lord, Arjuna could see them while sitting in one place. That was due to the inconceivable potency of Kṛṣṇa.

Text 12 दिवि सूर्यसहस्रस्य भवेद्युगपदुत्थिता ।
यदि भाः सदृशी सा स्याद्भासस्तस्य महात्मनः ॥१२॥

divi sūrya-sahasrasya, bhaved yugapad utthitā
yadi bhāḥ sadṛśī sā syād, bhāsas tasya mahātmanaḥ

divi – in the sky; *sūrya* – of suns; *sahasrasya* – of many thousands; *bhavet* – there were; *yugapat* – simultaneously; *utthitā* – present; *yadi* – if; *bhāḥ* – light; *sadṛśī* – like that; *sā* – that; *syāt* – might be; *bhāsaḥ* – effulgence; *tasya* – of Him; *mahā-ātmanaḥ* – the great Lord.

If hundreds of thousands of suns were to rise at once into the sky, their radiance might resemble the effulgence of the Supreme Person in that universal form.

PURPORT: What Arjuna saw was indescribable, yet Sañjaya is trying to give a mental picture of that great revelation to Dhṛtarāṣṭra. Neither Sañjaya nor Dhṛtarāṣṭra was present, but Sañjaya, by the grace of Vyāsa, could see whatever happened. Thus he now compares the situation, as far as it can be understood, to an imaginable phenomenon (i.e., thousands of suns).

Text 13 तत्रैकस्थं जगत्कृत्स्नं प्रविभक्तमनेकधा ।
अपश्यद्देवदेवस्य शरीरे पाण्डवस्तदा ॥१३॥

tatraika-sthaṁ jagat kṛtsnaṁ, pravibhaktam anekadhā
apaśyad deva-devasya, śarīre pāṇḍavas tadā

tatra – there; *eka-stham* – in one place; *jagat* – the universe; *kṛtsnam* – complete; *pravibhaktam* – divided; *anekadhā* – into many; *apaśyat* – could see; *deva-devasya* – of the Supreme Personality of Godhead; *śarīre* – in the universal form; *pāṇḍavaḥ* – Arjuna; *tadā* – at that time.

At that time Arjuna could see in the universal form of the Lord the unlimited expansions of the universe situated in one place although divided into many, many thousands.

PURPORT: The word *tatra* ("there") is very significant. It indicates that both Arjuna and Kṛṣṇa were sitting on the chariot when Arjuna saw the universal form. Others on the battlefield could not see this form, because Kṛṣṇa gave the vision only to Arjuna. Arjuna could see in the body of

Kṛṣṇa many thousands of planets. As we learn from Vedic scriptures, there are many universes and many planets. Some of them are made of earth, some are made of gold, some are made of jewels, some are very great, some are not so great, etc. Sitting on his chariot, Arjuna could see all these. But no one could understand what was going on between Arjuna and Kṛṣṇa.

Text 14 ततः स विस्मयाविष्टो हृष्टरोमा धनञ्जयः ।
प्रणम्य शिरसा देवं कृताञ्जलिरभाषत ॥१४॥

tataḥ sa vismayāviṣṭo, hṛṣṭa-romā dhanañ-jayaḥ
praṇamya śirasā devaṁ, kṛtāñjalir abhāṣata

tataḥ – thereafter; *saḥ* – he; *vismaya-āviṣṭaḥ* – being overwhelmed with wonder; *hṛṣṭa-romā* – with his bodily hairs standing on end due to his great ecstasy; *dhanam-jaya* – Arjuna; *praṇamya* – offering obeisances; *śirasā* – with the head; *devam* – to the Supreme Personality of Godhead; *kṛta-añjaliḥ* – with folded hands; *abhāṣata* – began to speak.

Then, bewildered and astonished, his hair standing on end, Arjuna bowed his head to offer obeisances and with folded hands began to pray to the Supreme Lord.

PURPORT: Once the divine vision is revealed, the relationship between Kṛṣṇa and Arjuna changes immediately. Before, Kṛṣṇa and Arjuna had a relationship based on friendship, but here, after the revelation, Arjuna is offering obeisances with great respect, and with folded hands he is praying to Kṛṣṇa. He is praising the universal form. Thus Arjuna's relationship becomes one of wonder rather than friendship. Great devotees see Kṛṣṇa as the reservoir of all relationships. In the scriptures there are twelve basic kinds of relationships mentioned, and all of them are present in Kṛṣṇa. It is said that He is the ocean of all the relationships exchanged between two living entities, between the gods, or between the Supreme Lord and His devotees.

Here Arjuna was inspired by the relationship of wonder, and in that wonder, although he was by nature very sober, calm and quiet, he became ecstatic, his hair stood up, and he began to offer his obeisances unto the Supreme Lord with folded hands. He was not, of course, afraid. He was affected by the wonders of the Supreme Lord. The immediate context is wonder; his natural loving friendship was overwhelmed by wonder, and thus he reacted in this way.

Text 15 अर्जुन उवाच
पश्यामि देवांस्तव देव देहे सर्वांस्तथा भूतविशेषसङ्घान् ।
ब्रह्माणमीशं कमलासनस्थमृषींश्च सर्वानुरगांश्च दिव्यान् ॥१५॥

arjuna uvāca
paśyāmi devāṁs tava deva dehe
sarvāṁs tathā bhūta-viśeṣa-saṅghān
brahmāṇam īśaṁ kamalāsana-stham
ṛṣīṁś ca sarvān uragāṁś ca divyān

arjunaḥ uvāca – Arjuna said; *paśyāmi* – I see; *devān* – all the demigods; *tava* – Your; *deva* – O Lord; *dehe* – in the body; *sarvān* – all; *tathā* – also; *bhūta* – living entities; *viśeṣa-saṅghān* – specifically assembled; *brahmāṇam* – Lord Brahmā; *īśam* – Lord Śiva; *kamala-āsana-stham* – sitting on the lotus flower; *ṛṣīn* – great sages; *ca* – also; *sarvān* – all; *uragān* – serpents; *ca* – also; *divyān* – divine.

Arjuna said: My dear Lord Kṛṣṇa, I see assembled in Your body all the demigods and various other living entities. I see Brahmā sitting on the lotus flower, as well as Lord Śiva and all the sages and divine serpents.

PURPORT: Arjuna sees everything in the universe; therefore he sees Brahmā, who is the first creature in the universe, and the celestial serpent upon which the Garbhodaka-śāyī Viṣṇu lies in the lower regions of the universe. This snake bed is called Vāsuki. There are also other snakes known as Vāsuki. Arjuna can see from the Garbhodaka-śāyī Viṣṇu up to the topmost part of the universe on the lotus-flower planet where Brahmā, the first creature of the universe, resides. That means that from the beginning to the end, everything could be seen by Arjuna, who was sitting in one place on his chariot. This was possible by the grace of the Supreme Lord, Kṛṣṇa.

Text 16 अनेकबाहूदरवक्त्रनेत्रं पश्यामि त्वां सर्वतोऽनन्तरूपम् ।
नान्तं न मध्यं न पुनस्तवादिं पश्यामि विश्वेश्वर विश्वरूप ॥१६॥

aneka-bāhūdara-vaktra-netraṁ
paśyāmi tvāṁ sarvato 'nanta-rūpam
nāntaṁ na madhyaṁ na punas tavādiṁ
paśyāmi viśveśvara viśva-rūpa

aneka – many; *bāhu* – arms; *udara* – bellies; *vaktra* – mouths; *netram* – eyes; *paśyāmi* – I see; *tvām* – You; *sarvataḥ* – on all sides; *ananta-rūpam* – unlimited form; *na antam* – no end; *na madhyam* – no middle; *na punaḥ* – nor again; *tava* – Your; *ādim* – beginning; *paśyāmi* – I see; *viśva-īśvara* – O Lord of the universe; *viśva-rūpa* – in the form of the universe.

O Lord of the universe, O universal form, I see in Your body many, many arms, bellies, mouths and eyes, expanded everywhere, without limit. I see in You no end, no middle and no beginning.

PURPORT: Kṛṣṇa is the Supreme Personality of Godhead and is unlimited; thus through Him everything could be seen.

Text 17 किरीटिनं गदिनं चक्रिणं च तेजोराशिं सर्वतो दीप्तिमन्तम् ।
पश्यामि त्वां दुर्निरीक्ष्यं समन्ताद् दीप्तानलार्कद्युतिमप्रमेयम् ॥१७॥

kirīṭinaṁ gadinaṁ cakriṇaṁ ca
tejo-rāśiṁ sarvato dīptimantam
paśyāmi tvāṁ durnirīkṣyaṁ samantād
dīptānalārka-dyutim aprameyam

kirīṭinam – with helmets; *gadinam* – with maces; *cakriṇam* – with discs; *ca* – and; *tejaḥ-rāśim* – effulgence; *sarvataḥ* – on all sides; *dīpti-mantam* – glowing; *paśyāmi* – I see; *tvām* – You; *durnirīkṣyam* – difficult to see; *samantāt* – everywhere; *dīpta-anala* – blazing fire; *arka* – of the sun; *dyutim* – the sunshine; *aprameyam* – immeasurable.

Your form is difficult to see because of its glaring effulgence, spreading on all sides, like blazing fire or the immeasurable radiance of the sun. Yet I see this glowing form everywhere, adorned with various crowns, clubs and discs.

Text 18 त्वमक्षरं परमं वेदितव्यं त्वमस्य विश्वस्य परं निधानम् ।
त्वमव्ययः शाश्वतधर्मगोप्ता सनातनस्त्वं पुरुषो मतो मे ॥१८॥

tvam akṣaraṁ paramaṁ veditavyaṁ
tvam asya viśvasya paraṁ nidhānam
tvam avyayaḥ śāśvata-dharma-goptā
sanātanas tvaṁ puruṣo mato me

tvam – You; *akṣaram* – the infallible; *paramam* – supreme; *veditavyam* – to be understood; *tvam* – You; *asya* – of this; *viśvasya* – universe; *param* – supreme; *nidhānam* – basis; *tvam* – You; *avyayaḥ* – inexhaustible; *śāśvata-dharma-goptā* – maintainer of the eternal religion; *sanātanaḥ* – eternal; *tvam* – You; *puruṣaḥ* – the Supreme Personality; *mataḥ me* – this is my opinion.

You are the supreme primal objective. You are the ultimate resting place of all this universe. You are inexhaustible, and You are the oldest. You are the maintainer of the eternal religion, the Personality of Godhead. This is my opinion.

Text 19 अनादिमध्यान्तमनन्तवीर्यमनन्तबाहुं शशिसूर्यनेत्रम् ।
पश्यामि त्वां दीप्तहुताशवक्त्रं स्वतेजसा विश्वमिदं तपन्तम् ॥१९॥

anādi-madhyāntam ananta-vīryam
ananta-bāhuṁ śaśi-sūrya-netram
paśyāmi tvāṁ dīpta-hutāśa-vaktraṁ
sva-tejasā viśvam idaṁ tapantam

anādi – without beginning; *madhya* – middle; *antam* – or end; *ananta* – unlimited; *vīryam* – glories; *ananta* – unlimited; *bāhum* – arms; *śaśi* – the moon; *sūrya* – and sun; *netram* – eyes; *paśyāmi* – I see; *tvām* – You; *dīpta* – blazing; *hutāśa-vaktram* – fire coming out of Your mouth; *sva-tejasā* – by Your radiance; *viśvam* – universe; *idam* – this; *tapantam* – heating.

You are without origin, middle or end. Your glory is unlimited. You have numberless arms, and the sun and moon are Your eyes. I see You with blazing fire coming forth from Your mouth, burning this entire universe by Your own radiance.

PURPORT: There is no limit to the extent of the six opulences of the Supreme Personality of Godhead. Here and in many other places there is repetition, but according to the scriptures, repetition of the glories of Kṛṣṇa is not a literary weakness. It is said that at a time of bewilderment or wonder or of great ecstasy, statements are repeated over and over. That is not a flaw.

Text 20 द्यावापृथिव्योरिदमन्तरं हि व्याप्तं त्वयैकेन दिशश्च सर्वाः ।
दृष्ट्वाद्भुतं रूपमुग्रं तवेदं लोकत्रयं प्रव्यथितं महात्मन् ॥२०॥

dyāv ā-pṛthivyor idam antaraṁ hi
vyāptaṁ tvayaikena diśaś ca sarvāḥ
dṛṣṭvādbhutaṁ rūpam ugraṁ tavedaṁ
loka-trayaṁ pravyathitaṁ mahātman

dyau – from outer space; *ā-pṛthivyoḥ* – to the earth; *idam* – this; *antaram* – between; *hi* – certainly; *vyāptam* – pervaded; *tvayā* – by You; *ekena* – alone; *diśaḥ* – directions; *ca* – and; *sarvāḥ* – all; *dṛṣṭvā* – by seeing; *adbhutam* – wonderful; *rūpam* – form; *ugram* – terrible; *tava* – Your; *idam* – this; *loka* – the planetary systems; *trayam* – three; *pravyathitam* – perturbed; *mahā-ātman* – O great one.

Although You are one, You spread throughout the sky and the planets and all space between. O great one, seeing this wondrous and terrible form, all the planetary systems are perturbed.

PURPORT: *Dyāv ā-pṛthivyoḥ* ("the space between heaven and earth") and *loka-trayam* ("the three worlds") are significant words in this verse because it appears that not only did Arjuna see this universal form of the Lord, but others in other planetary systems saw it also. Arjuna's seeing of the universal form was not a dream. All whom the Lord endowed with divine vision saw that universal form on the battlefield.

Text 21 अमी हि त्वां सुरसङ्घा विशन्ति केचिद्भीताः प्राञ्जलयो गृणन्ति ।
स्वस्तीत्युक्त्वा महर्षिसिद्धसङ्घाः स्तुवन्ति त्वां स्तुतिभिः पुष्कलाभिः ॥२१॥

amī hi tvāṁ sura-saṅghā viśanti
kecid bhītāḥ prāñjalayo gṛṇanti
svastīty uktvā maharṣi-siddha-saṅghāḥ
stuvanti tvāṁ stutibhiḥ puṣkalābhiḥ

amī – all those; *hi* – certainly; *tvām* – You; *sura-saṅghāḥ* – groups of demigods; *viśanti* – are entering; *kecit* – some of them; *bhītāḥ* – out of fear; *prāñjalayaḥ* – with folded hands; *gṛṇanti* – are offering prayers; *svasti* – all peace; *iti* – thus; *uktvā* – speaking; *mahā-ṛṣi* – great sages; *siddha-saṅghāḥ* – perfect beings; *stuvanti* – are singing hymns; *tvām* – unto You; *stutibhiḥ* – with prayers; *puṣkalābhiḥ* – Vedic hymns.

All the hosts of demigods are surrendering before You and entering into You. Some of them, very much afraid, are offering prayers with folded hands. Hosts of great sages and perfected beings, crying "All peace!" are praying to You by singing the Vedic hymns.

PURPORT: The demigods in all the planetary systems feared the terrific manifestation of the universal form and its glaring effulgence and so prayed for protection.

Text 22 रुद्रादित्या वसवो ये च साध्या विश्वेऽश्विनौ मरुतश्चोष्मपाश्च ।
गन्धर्वयक्षासुरसिद्धसङ्घा वीक्षन्ते त्वां विस्मिताश्चैव सर्वे ॥२२॥

rudrādityā vasavo ye ca sādhyā
viśve 'śvinau marutaś coṣmapāś ca
gandharva-yakṣāsura-siddha-saṅghā
vīkṣante tvāṁ vismitāś caiva sarve

rudra – manifestations of Lord Śiva; *ādityāḥ* – the Ādityas; *vasavaḥ* – the Vasus; *ye* – all those; *ca* – and; *sādhyāḥ* – the Sādhyas; *viśve* – the Viśvedevas; *aśvinau* – the Aśvinī-kumāras; *marutaḥ* – the Maruts; *ca* – and; *uṣma-pāḥ* – the forefathers; *ca* – and; *gandharva* – of the Gandharvas; *yakṣa* – the Yakṣas; *asura* – the demons; *siddha* – and the perfected demigods; *saṅghāḥ* – the assemblies; *vīkṣante* – are beholding; *tvām* – You; *vismitāḥ* – in wonder; *ca* – also; *eva* – certainly; *sarve* – all.

All the various manifestations of Lord Śiva, the Ādityas, the Vasus, the Sādhyas, the Viśvedevas, the two Aśvīs, the Maruts, the forefathers, the Gandharvas, the Yakṣas, the Asuras and the perfected demigods are beholding You in wonder.

Text 23 रूपं महत्ते बहुवक्त्रनेत्रं महाबाहो बहुबाहूरुपादम् ।
बहूदरं बहुदंष्ट्राकरालं दृष्ट्वा लोकाः प्रव्यथितास्तथाहम् ॥२३॥

rūpaṁ mahat te bahu-vaktra-netraṁ
mahā-bāho bahu-bāhūru-pādam
bahūdaraṁ bahu-daṁṣṭrā-karālaṁ
dṛṣṭvā lokāḥ pravyathitās tathāham

rūpam – the form; *mahat* – very great; *te* – of You; *bahu* – many; *vaktra* – faces; *netram* – and eyes; *mahā-bāho* – O mighty-armed one; *bahu* – many; *bāhu* – arms; *ūru* – thighs; *pādam* – and legs; *bahu-udaram* – many bellies; *bahu-daṁṣṭrā* – many teeth; *karālam* – horrible; *dṛṣṭvā* – seeing; *lokāḥ* – all the planets; *pravyathitāḥ* – perturbed; *tathā* – similarly; *aham* – I.

O mighty-armed one, all the planets with their demigods are disturbed at seeing Your great form, with its many faces, eyes, arms, thighs, legs,

and bellies and Your many terrible teeth; and as they are disturbed, so am I.

Text 24 नभःस्पृशं दीप्तमनेकवर्णं व्यात्ताननं दीप्तविशालनेत्रम् ।
दृष्ट्वा हि त्वां प्रव्यथितान्तरात्मा धृतिं न विन्दामि शमं च विष्णो ॥२४॥

nabhaḥ-spṛśaṁ dīptam aneka-varṇaṁ
vyāttānanaṁ dīpta-viśāla-netram
dṛṣṭvā hi tvāṁ pravyathitāntar-ātmā
dhṛtiṁ na vindāmi śamaṁ ca viṣṇo

nabhaḥ-spṛśam – touching the sky; *dīptam* – glowing; *aneka* – many; *varṇam* – colors; *vyātta* – open; *ānanam* – mouths; *dīpta* – glowing; *viśāla* – very great; *netram* – eyes; *dṛṣṭvā* – seeing; *hi* – certainly; *tvām* – You; *pravyathita* – perturbed; *antaḥ* – within; *ātmā* – soul; *dhṛtim* – steadiness; *na* – not; *vindāmi* – I have; *śamam* – mental tranquillity; *ca* – also; *viṣṇo* – O Lord Viṣṇu.

O all-pervading Viṣṇu, seeing You with Your many radiant colors touching the sky, Your gaping mouths, and Your great glowing eyes, my mind is perturbed by fear. I can no longer maintain my steadiness or equilibrium of mind.

Text 25 दंष्ट्राकरालानि च ते मुखानि दृष्ट्वैव कालानलसन्निभानि ।
दिशो न जाने न लभे च शर्म प्रसीद देवेश जगन्निवास ॥२५॥

daṁṣṭrā-karālāni ca te mukhāni
dṛṣṭvaiva kālānala-sannibhāni
diśo na jāne na labhe ca śarma
prasīda deveśa jagan-nivāsa

daṁṣṭrā – teeth; *karālāni* – terrible; *ca* – also; *te* – Your; *mukhāni* – faces; *dṛṣṭvā* – seeing; *eva* – thus; *kāla-anala* – the fire of death; *sannibhāni* – as if; *diśaḥ* – the directions; *na* – not; *jāne* – I know; *na* – not; *labhe* – I obtain; *ca* – and; *śarma* – grace; *prasīda* – be pleased; *deva-īśa* – O Lord of all lords; *jagat-nivāsa* – O refuge of the worlds.

O Lord of lords, O refuge of the worlds, please be gracious to me. I cannot keep my balance seeing thus Your blazing deathlike faces and awful teeth. In all directions I am bewildered.

Texts 26–27

अमी च त्वां धृतराष्ट्रस्य पुत्राः सर्वे सहैवावनिपालसङ्घैः ।
भीष्मो द्रोणः सूतपुत्रस्तथासौ सहास्मदीयैरपि योधमुख्यैः ॥२६॥
वक्त्राणि ते त्वरमाणा विशन्ति दंष्ट्राकरालानि भयानकानि ।
केचिद्विलग्ना दशनान्तरेषु सन्दृश्यन्ते चूर्णितैरुत्तमाङ्गैः ॥२७॥

amī ca tvāṁ dhṛtarāṣṭrasya putrāḥ
sarve sahaivāvani-pāla-saṅghaiḥ
bhīṣmo droṇaḥ sūta-putras tathāsau
sahāsmadīyair api yodha-mukhyaiḥ

vaktrāṇi te tvaramāṇā viśanti
daṁṣṭrā-karālāni bhayānakāni
kecid vilagnā daśanāntareṣu
sandṛśyante cūrṇitair uttamāṅgaiḥ

amī – these; *ca* – also; *tvām* – You; *dhṛtarāṣṭrasya* – of Dhṛtarāṣṭra; *putrāḥ* – the sons; *sarve* – all; *saha* – with; *eva* – indeed; *avani-pāla* – of warrior kings; *saṅghaiḥ* – the groups; *bhīṣmaḥ* – Bhīṣmadeva; *droṇaḥ* – Droṇācārya; *sūta-putraḥ* – Karṇa; *tathā* – also; *asau* – that; *saha* – with; *asmadīyaiḥ* – our; *api* – also; *yodha-mukhyaiḥ* – chiefs among the warriors; *vaktrāṇi* – mouths; *te* – Your; *tvaramāṇāḥ* – rushing; *viśanti* – are entering; *daṁṣṭrā* – teeth; *karālāni* – terrible; *bhayānakāni* – very fearful; *kecit* – some of them; *vilagnāḥ* – becoming attached; *daśana-antareṣu* – between the teeth; *sandṛśyante* – are seen; *cūrṇitaiḥ* – with smashed; *uttama-aṅgaiḥ* – heads.

All the sons of Dhṛtarāṣṭra, along with their allied kings, and Bhīṣma, Droṇa, Karṇa – and our chief soldiers also – are rushing into Your fearful mouths. And some I see trapped with heads smashed between Your teeth.

PURPORT: In a previous verse the Lord promised to show Arjuna things he would be very interested in seeing. Now Arjuna sees that the leaders of the opposite party (Bhīṣma, Droṇa, Karṇa and all the sons of Dhṛtarāṣṭra) and their soldiers and Arjuna's own soldiers are all being annihilated. This is an indication that after the death of nearly all the persons assembled at Kurukṣetra, Arjuna will emerge victorious. It is also mentioned here that Bhīṣma, who is supposed to be unconquerable, will also be smashed. So also Karṇa. Not only will the great warriors of the other party like Bhīṣma be smashed, but some of the great warriors of Arjuna's side also.

Text 28 यथा नदीनां बहवोऽम्बुवेगाः समुद्रमेवाभिमुखा द्रवन्ति ।
तथा तवामी नरलोकवीरा विशन्ति वक्त्राण्यभिविज्वलन्ति ॥२८॥

yathā nadīnāṁ bahavo 'mbu-vegāḥ
samudram evābhimukhā dravanti
tathā tavāmī nara-loka-vīrā
viśanti vaktrāṇy abhivijvalanti

yathā – as; *nadīnām* – of the rivers; *bahavaḥ* – the many; *ambu-vegāḥ* – waves of the waters; *samudram* – the ocean; *eva* – certainly; *abhimukhāḥ* – towards; *dravanti* – glide; *tathā* – similarly; *tava* – Your; *amī* – all these; *nara-loka-vīrāḥ* – kings of human society; *viśanti* – are entering; *vaktrāṇi* – the mouths; *abhivijvalanti* – and are blazing.

As the many waves of the rivers flow into the ocean, so do all these great warriors enter blazing into Your mouths.

Text 29 यथा प्रदीप्तं ज्वलनं पतङ्गा विशन्ति नाशाय समृद्धवेगाः ।
तथैव नाशाय विशन्ति लोकास्तवापि वक्त्राणि समृद्धवेगाः ॥२९॥

yathā pradīptaṁ jvalanaṁ pataṅgā
viśanti nāśāya samṛddha-vegāḥ
tathaiva nāśāya viśanti lokās
tavāpi vaktrāṇi samṛddha-vegāḥ

yathā – as; *pradīptam* – blazing; *jvalanam* – a fire; *pataṅgāḥ* – moths; *viśanti* – enter; *nāśāya* – for destruction; *samṛddha* – with full; *vegāḥ* – speed; *tathā eva* – similarly; *nāśāya* – for destruction; *viśanti* – are entering; *lokāḥ* – all people; *tava* – Your; *api* – also; *vaktrāṇi* – mouths; *samṛddha-vegāḥ* – with full speed.

I see all people rushing full speed into Your mouths, as moths dash to destruction in a blazing fire.

Text 30 लेलिह्यसे ग्रसमानः समन्ताल्लोकान् समग्रान् वदनैर्ज्वलद्भिः ।
तेजोभिरापूर्य जगत्समग्रं भासस्तवोग्राः प्रतपन्ति विष्णो ॥३०॥

lelihyase grasamānaḥ samantāl
lokān samagrān vadanair jvaladbhiḥ
tejobhir āpūrya jagat samagraṁ
bhāsas tavogrāḥ pratapanti viṣṇo

lelihyase – You are licking; *grasamānaḥ* – devouring; *samantāt* – from all directions; *lokān* – people; *samagrān* – all; *vadanaiḥ* – by the mouths; *jvaladbhiḥ* – blazing; *tejobhiḥ* – by effulgence; *āpūrya* – covering; *jagat* – the universe; *samagram* – all; *bhāsaḥ* – rays; *tava* – Your; *ugrāḥ* – terrible; *pratapanti* – are scorching; *viṣṇo* – O all-pervading Lord.

O Viṣṇu, I see You devouring all people from all sides with Your flaming mouths. Covering all the universe with Your effulgence, You are manifest with terrible, scorching rays.

Text 31 आख्याहि मे को भवानुग्ररूपो नमोऽस्तु ते देववर प्रसीद ।
विज्ञातुमिच्छामि भवन्तमाद्यं न हि प्रजानामि तव प्रवृत्तिम् ॥३१॥

ākhyāhi me ko bhavān ugra-rūpo
namo 'stu te deva-vara prasīda
vijñātum icchāmi bhavantam ādyaṁ
na hi prajānāmi tava pravṛttim

ākhyāhi – please explain; *me* – unto me; *kaḥ* – who; *bhavān* – You; *ugra-rūpaḥ* – fierce form; *namaḥ astu* – obeisances; *te* – unto You; *deva-vara* – O great one amongst the demigods; *prasīda* – be gracious; *vijñātum* – to know; *icchāmi* – I wish; *bhavantam* – You; *ādyam* – the original; *na* – not; *hi* – certainly; *prajānāmi* – do I know; *tava* – Your; *pravṛttim* – mission.

O Lord of lords, so fierce of form, please tell me who You are. I offer my obeisances unto You; please be gracious to me. You are the primal Lord. I want to know about You, for I do not know what Your mission is.

Text 32 श्रीभगवानुवाच
कालोऽस्मि लोकक्षयकृत्प्रवृद्धो लोकान् समाहर्तुमिह प्रवृत्तः ।
ऋतेऽपि त्वां न भविष्यन्ति सर्वे येऽवस्थिताः प्रत्यनीकेषु योधाः ॥३२॥

śrī-bhagavān uvāca
kālo 'smi loka-kṣaya-kṛt pravṛddho
lokān samāhartum iha pravṛttaḥ
ṛte 'pi tvāṁ na bhaviṣyanti sarve
ye 'vasthitāḥ praty-anīkeṣu yodhāḥ

śrī-bhagavān uvāca – the Personality of Godhead said; *kālaḥ* – time; *asmi* – I am; *loka* – of the worlds; *kṣaya-kṛt* – the destroyer; *pravṛddhaḥ* –

great; *lokān* – all people; *samāhartum* – in destroying; *iha* – in this world; *pravṛttaḥ* – engaged; *ṛte* – without, except for; *api* – even; *tvām* – you; *na* – never; *bhaviṣyanti* – will be; *sarve* – all; *ye* – who; *avasthitāḥ* – situated; *prati-anīkeṣu* – on the opposite sides; *yodhāḥ* – the soldiers.

The Supreme Personality of Godhead said: Time I am, the great destroyer of the worlds, and I have come here to destroy all people. With the exception of you [the Pāṇḍavas], all the soldiers here on both sides will be slain.

PURPORT: Although Arjuna knew that Kṛṣṇa was his friend and the Supreme Personality of Godhead, he was puzzled by the various forms exhibited by Kṛṣṇa. Therefore he asked further about the actual mission of this devastating force. It is written in the *Vedas* that the Supreme Truth destroys everything, even the *brāhmaṇas.* As stated in the *Kaṭha Upaniṣad* (1.2.25),

yasya brahma ca kṣatraṁ ca, ubhe bhavata odanaḥ
mṛtyur yasyopasecanaṁ, ka itthā veda yatra saḥ

Eventually all the *brāhmaṇas, kṣatriyas* and everyone else are devoured like a meal by the Supreme. This form of the Supreme Lord is the all-devouring giant, and here Kṛṣṇa presents Himself in that form of all-devouring time. Except for a few Pāṇḍavas, everyone who was present on that battlefield would be devoured by Him. Arjuna was not in favor of the fight, and he thought it was better not to fight; then there would be no frustration. In reply, the Lord is saying that even if he did not fight, every one of them would be destroyed, for that was His plan. If Arjuna stopped fighting, they would die in another way. Death could not be checked, even if he did not fight. In fact, they were already dead. Time is destruction, and all manifestations are to be vanquished by the desire of the Supreme Lord. That is the law of nature.

Text 33 तस्मात्त्वमुत्तिष्ठ यशो लभस्व जित्वा शत्रून् भुङ्क्ष्व राज्यं समृद्धम् ।
मयैवैते निहताः पूर्वमेव निमित्तमात्रं भव सव्यसाचिन् ॥३३॥

tasmāt tvam uttiṣṭha yaśo labhasva
jitvā śatrūn bhuṅkṣva rājyaṁ samṛddham
mayaivaite nihatāḥ pūrvam eva
nimitta-mātraṁ bhava savya-sācin

tasmāt – therefore; *tvam* – you; *uttiṣṭha* – get up; *yaśaḥ* – fame; *labhasva* – gain; *jitvā* – conquering; *śatrūn* – enemies; *bhuṅkṣva* – enjoy; *rājyam* – kingdom; *samṛddham* – flourishing; *mayā* – by Me; *eva* – certainly; *ete* – all these; *nihatāḥ* – killed; *pūrvam eva* – by previous arrangement; *nimitta-mātram* – just the cause; *bhava* – become; *savya-sācin* – O Savyasācī.

Therefore get up. Prepare to fight and win glory. Conquer your enemies and enjoy a flourishing kingdom. They are already put to death by My arrangement, and you, O Savyasācī, can be but an instrument in the fight.

PURPORT: *Savya-sācin* refers to one who can shoot arrows very expertly in the field; thus Arjuna is addressed as an expert warrior capable of delivering arrows to kill his enemies. "Just become an instrument": *nimitta-mātram.* This word is also very significant. The whole world is moving according to the plan of the Supreme Personality of Godhead. Foolish persons who do not have sufficient knowledge think that nature is moving without a plan and all manifestations are but accidental formations. There are many so-called scientists who suggest that perhaps it was like this, or maybe like that, but there is no question of "perhaps" and "maybe." There is a specific plan being carried out in this material world. What is this plan? This cosmic manifestation is a chance for the conditioned souls to go back to Godhead, back to home. As long as they have the domineering mentality which makes them try to lord it over material nature, they are conditioned. But anyone who can understand the plan of the Supreme Lord and cultivate Kṛṣṇa consciousness is most intelligent. The creation and destruction of the cosmic manifestation are under the superior guidance of God. Thus the Battle of Kurukṣetra was fought according to the plan of God. Arjuna was refusing to fight, but he was told that he should fight in accordance with the desire of the Supreme Lord. Then he would be happy. If one is in full Kṛṣṇa consciousness and his life is devoted to the Lord's transcendental service, he is perfect.

Text 34 द्रोणं च भीष्मं च जयद्रथं च कर्णं तथान्यानपि योधवीरान् ।
मया हतांस्त्वं जहि मा व्यथिष्ठा युध्यस्व जेतासि रणे सपत्नान् ॥३४॥

droṇaṁ ca bhīṣmaṁ ca jayadrathaṁ ca
karṇaṁ tathānyān api yodha-vīrān
mayā hatāṁs tvaṁ jahi mā vyathiṣṭhā
yudhyasva jetāsi raṇe sapatnān

droṇam ca – also Droṇa; *bhīṣmam ca* – also Bhīṣma; *jayadratham ca* – also Jayadratha; *karṇam* – Karṇa; *tathā* – also; *anyān* – others; *api* – certainly; *yodha-vīrān* – great warriors; *mayā* – by Me; *hatān* – already killed; *tvam* – you; *jahi* – destroy; *mā* – do not; *vyathiṣṭhāḥ* – be disturbed; *yudhyasva* – just fight; *jetā asi* – you will conquer; *raṇe* – in the fight; *sapatnān* – enemies.

Droṇa, Bhīṣma, Jayadratha, Karṇa and the other great warriors have already been destroyed by Me. Therefore, kill them and do not be disturbed. Simply fight, and you will vanquish your enemies in battle.

PURPORT: Every plan is made by the Supreme Personality of Godhead, but He is so kind and merciful to His devotees that He wants to give the credit to His devotees who carry out His plan according to His desire. Life should therefore move in such a way that everyone acts in Kṛṣṇa consciousness and understands the Supreme Personality of Godhead through the medium of a spiritual master. The plans of the Supreme Personality of Godhead are understood by His mercy, and the plans of the devotees are as good as His plans. One should follow such plans and be victorious in the struggle for existence.

Text 35 सञ्जय उवाच

एतच्छ्रुत्वा वचनं केशवस्य कृताञ्जलिर्वेपमानः किरीती ।
नमस्कृत्वा भूय एवाह कृष्णं सगद्गदं भीतभीतः प्रणम्य ॥३५॥

sañjaya uvāca
etac chrutvā vacanaṁ keśavasya
kṛtāñjalir vepamānaḥ kirīṭī
namaskṛtvā bhūya evāha kṛṣṇaṁ
sa-gadgadaṁ bhīta-bhītaḥ praṇamya

sañjayaḥ uvāca – Sañjaya said; *etat* – thus; *śrutvā* – hearing; *vacanam* – the speech; *keśavasya* – of Kṛṣṇa; *kṛta-añjaliḥ* – with folded hands; *vepamānaḥ* – trembling; *kirīṭī* – Arjuna; *namaskṛtvā* – offering obeisances; *bhūyaḥ* – again; *eva* – also; *āha* – said; *kṛṣṇam* – unto Kṛṣṇa; *sa-gadgadam* – with a faltering voice; *bhīta-bhītaḥ* – fearful; *praṇamya* – offering obeisances.

Sañjaya said to Dhṛtarāṣṭra: O King, after hearing these words from the Supreme Personality of Godhead, the trembling Arjuna offered obei-

sances with folded hands again and again. He fearfully spoke to Lord Kṛṣṇa in a faltering voice, as follows.

PURPORT: As we have already explained, because of the situation created by the universal form of the Supreme Personality of Godhead, Arjuna became bewildered in wonder; thus he began to offer his respectful obeisances to Kṛṣṇa again and again, and with faltering voice he began to pray, not as a friend, but as a devotee in wonder.

Text 36 अर्जुन उवाच
स्थाने हृषीकेश तव प्रकीर्त्या जगत्प्रहृष्यत्यनुरज्यते च ।
रक्षांसि भीतानि दिशो द्रवन्ति सर्वे नमस्यन्ति च सिद्धसङ्घाः ॥३६॥

arjuna uvāca
sthāne hṛṣīkeśa tava prakīrtyā
jagat prahṛṣyaty anurajyate ca
rakṣāṁsi bhītāni diśo dravanti
sarve namasyanti ca siddha-saṅghāḥ

arjunaḥ uvāca – Arjuna said; *sthāne* – rightly; *hṛṣīka-īśa* – O master of all senses; *tava* – Your; *prakīrtyā* – by the glories; *jagat* – the entire world; *prahṛṣyati* – is rejoicing; *anurajyate* – is becoming attached; *ca* – and; *rakṣāṁsi* – the demons; *bhītāni* – out of fear; *diśaḥ* – in all directions; *dravanti* – are fleeing; *sarve* – all; *namasyanti* – are offering respects; *ca* – also; *siddha-saṅghāḥ* – the perfect human beings.

Arjuna said: O master of the senses, the world becomes joyful upon hearing Your name, and thus everyone becomes attached to You. Although the perfected beings offer You their respectful homage, the demons are afraid, and they flee here and there. All this is rightly done.

PURPORT: Arjuna, after hearing from Kṛṣṇa about the outcome of the Battle of Kurukṣetra, became enlightened, and as a great devotee and friend of the Supreme Personality of Godhead he said that everything done by Kṛṣṇa is quite fit. Arjuna confirmed that Kṛṣṇa is the maintainer and the object of worship for the devotees and the destroyer of the undesirables. His actions are equally good for all. Arjuna understood herein that when the Battle of Kurukṣetra was being concluded, in outer space there were present many demigods, *siddhas,* and the intelligentsia of the higher planets, and they were observing the fight because Kṛṣṇa was present there. When Arjuna saw the universal form of the Lord, the demigods took pleasure in it, but others, who were demons and atheists, could not stand it when the Lord was praised. Out of their natural fear of the devastating form of the Supreme Personality of Godhead, they fled. Kṛṣṇa's treatment of the devotees and the atheists is praised by Arjuna. In all cases a devotee glorifies the Lord because he knows that whatever He does is good for all.

Text 37 कस्माच्च ते न नमेरन्महात्मन् गरीयसे ब्रह्मणोऽप्यादिकर्त्रे ।
अनन्त देवेश जगन्निवास त्वमक्षरं सदसत्तत्परं यत् ॥३७॥

kasmāc ca te na nameran mahātman
garīyase brahmaṇo 'py ādi-kartre
ananta deveśa jagan-nivāsa
tvam akṣaraṁ sad-asat tat paraṁ yat

kasmāt – why; *ca* – also; *te* – unto You; *na* – not; *nameran* – they should offer proper obeisances; *mahā-ātman* – O great one; *garīyase* – who are better; *brahmaṇaḥ* – than Brahmā; *api* – although; *ādi-kartre* – to the supreme creator; *ananta* – O unlimited; *deva-īśa* – O God of the gods; *jagat-nivāsa* – O refuge of the universe; *tvam* – You are; *akṣaram* – imperishable; *sat-asat* – to cause and effect; *tat param* – transcendental; *yat* – because.

O great one, greater even than Brahmā, You are the original creator. Why then should they not offer their respectful obeisances unto You? O limitless one, God of gods, refuge of the universe! You are the invincible source, the cause of all causes, transcendental to this material manifestation.

PURPORT: By this offering of obeisances, Arjuna indicates that Kṛṣṇa is worshipable by everyone. He is all-pervading, and He is the Soul of every soul. Arjuna is addressing Kṛṣṇa as *mahātmā,* which means that He is most magnanimous and unlimited. *Ananta* indicates that there is nothing which is not covered by the influence and energy of the Supreme Lord, and *deveśa* means that He is the controller of all demigods and is above them all. He is the shelter of the whole universe. Arjuna also thought that it was fitting that all the perfect living entities and powerful demigods offer their respectful obeisances unto Him, because no one is greater than Him. Arjuna especially mentions that Kṛṣṇa is greater than

Brahmā because Brahmā is created by Him. Brahmā is born out of the lotus stem grown from the navel abdomen of Garbhodaka-śāyī Viṣṇu, who is Kṛṣṇa's plenary expansion; therefore Brahmā and Lord Śiva, who is born of Brahmā, and all other demigods must offer their respectful obeisances. It is stated in *Śrīmad-Bhāgavatam* that the Lord is respected by Lord Śiva and Brahmā and similar other demigods. The word *akṣaram* is very significant because this material creation is subject to destruction but the Lord is above this material creation. He is the cause of all causes, and being so, He is superior to all the conditioned souls within this material nature as well as the material cosmic manifestation itself. He is therefore the all-great Supreme.

Text 38 त्वमादिदेवः पुरुषः पुराणस्त्वमस्य विश्वस्य परं निधानम् ।
वेत्तासि वेद्यं च परं च धाम त्वया ततं विश्वमनन्तरूप ॥३८॥

tvam ādi-devaḥ puruṣaḥ purāṇas
tvam asya viśvasya paraṁ nidhānam
vettāsi vedyaṁ ca paraṁ ca dhāma
tvayā tataṁ viśvam ananta-rūpa

tvam – You; *ādi-devaḥ* – the original Supreme God; *puruṣaḥ* – personality; *purāṇaḥ* – old; *tvam* – You; *asya* – of this; *viśvasya* – universe; *param* – transcendental; *nidhānam* – refuge; *vettā* – the knower; *asi* – You are; *vedyam* – the knowable; *ca* – and; *param* – transcendental; *ca* – and; *dhāma* – refuge; *tvayā* – by You; *tatam* – pervaded; *viśvam* – the universe; *ananta-rūpa* – O unlimited form.

You are the original Personality of Godhead, the oldest, the ultimate sanctuary of this manifested cosmic world. You are the knower of everything, and You are all that is knowable. You are the supreme refuge, above the material modes. O limitless form! This whole cosmic manifestation is pervaded by You!

PURPORT: Everything is resting on the Supreme Personality of Godhead; therefore He is the ultimate rest. *Nidhānam* means that everything, even the Brahman effulgence, rests on the Supreme Personality of Godhead, Kṛṣṇa. He is the knower of everything that is happening in this world, and if knowledge has any end, He is the end of all knowledge; therefore He is the known and the knowable. He is the object of knowledge because He is all-pervading. Because He is the cause in the spiritual world, He is transcendental. He is also the chief personality in the transcendental world.

Text 39 **वायुर्यमोऽग्निर्वरुणः शशाङ्कः प्रजापतिस्त्वं प्रपितामहश्च ।**
नमो नमस्तेऽस्तु सहस्रकृत्वः पुनश्च भूयोऽपि नमो नमस्ते ॥३९॥

vāyur yamo 'gnir varuṇaḥ śaśāṅkaḥ
prajāpatis tvaṁ prapitāmahaś ca
namo namas te 'stu sahasra-kṛtvaḥ
punaś ca bhūyo 'pi namo namas te

vāyuḥ – air; *yamaḥ* – the controller; *agniḥ* – fire; *varuṇaḥ* – water; *śaśa-aṅkaḥ* – the moon; *prajāpatiḥ* – Brahmā; *tvam* – You; *prapitāmahaḥ* – the great-grandfather; *ca* – also; *namaḥ* – my respects; *namaḥ* – again my respects; *te* – unto You; *astu* – let there be; *sahasra-kṛtvaḥ* – a thousand times; *punaḥ ca* – and again; *bhūyaḥ* – again; *api* – also; *namaḥ* – offering my respects; *namaḥ te* – offering my respects unto You.

You are air, and You are the supreme controller! You are fire, You are water, and You are the moon! You are Brahmā, the first living creature, and You are the great-grandfather. I therefore offer my respectful obeisances unto You a thousand times, and again and yet again!

PURPORT: The Lord is addressed here as air because the air is the most important representation of all the demigods, being all-pervasive. Arjuna also addresses Kṛṣṇa as the great-grandfather because He is the father of Brahmā, the first living creature in the universe.

Text 40 **नमः पुरस्तादथ पृष्ठतस्ते नमोऽस्तु ते सर्वत एव सर्व ।**
अनन्तवीर्यामितविक्रमस्त्वं सर्वं समाप्नोषि ततोऽसि सर्वः ॥४०॥

namaḥ purastād atha pṛṣṭhatas te
namo 'stu te sarvata eva sarva
ananta-vīryāmita-vikramas tvaṁ
sarvaṁ samāpnoṣi tato 'si sarvaḥ

namaḥ – offering obeisances; *purastāt* – from the front; *atha* – also; *pṛṣṭhataḥ* – from behind; *te* – unto You; *namaḥ astu* – I offer my respects; *te* – unto You; *sarvataḥ* – from all sides; *eva* – indeed; *sarva* – because You are everything; *ananta-vīrya* – unlimited potency; *amita-vikramaḥ* – and unlimited force; *tvam* – You; *sarvam* – everything; *samāpnoṣi* – You cover; *tataḥ* – therefore; *asi* – You are; *sarvaḥ* – everything.

Obeisances to You from the front, from behind and from all sides! O unbounded power, You are the master of limitless might! You are all-pervading, and thus You are everything!

PURPORT: Out of loving ecstasy for Kṛṣṇa, his friend, Arjuna is offering his respects from all sides. He is accepting that He is the master of all potencies and all prowess and far superior to all the great warriors assembled on the battlefield. It is said in the *Viṣṇu Purāṇa* (1.9.69):

yo 'yaṁ tavāgato deva, samīpaṁ devatā-gaṇaḥ
sa tvam eva jagat-sraṣṭā, yataḥ sarva-gato bhavān

"Whoever comes before You, even if he be a demigod, is created by You, O Supreme Personality of Godhead."

Texts 41–42 सखेति मत्वा प्रसभं यदुक्तं हे कृष्ण हे यादव हे सखेति ।
अजानता महिमानं तवेदं मया प्रमादात्प्रणयेन वापि ॥४१॥
यच्चावहासार्थमसत्कृतोऽसि विहारशय्यासनभोजनेषु ।
एकोऽथ वाप्यच्युत तत्समक्षं तत्क्षामये त्वामहमप्रमेयम् ॥४२॥

sakheti matvā prasabhaṁ yad uktaṁ
he kṛṣṇa he yādava he sakheti
ajānatā mahimānaṁ tavedaṁ
mayā pramādāt praṇayena vāpi

yac cāvahāsārtham asat-kṛto 'si
vihāra-śayyāsana-bhojaneṣu
eko 'tha vāpy acyuta tat-samakṣaṁ
tat kṣāmaye tvām aham aprameyam

sakhā – friend; *iti* – thus; *matvā* – thinking; *prasabham* – presumptuously; *yat* – whatever; *uktam* – said; *he kṛṣṇa* – O Kṛṣṇa; *he yādava* – O Yādava; *he sakhe* – O my dear friend; *iti* – thus; *ajānatā* – without knowing; *mahimānam* – glories; *tava* – Your; *idam* – this; *mayā* – by me; *pramādāt* – out of foolishness; *praṇayena* – out of love; *vā api* – either; *yat* – whatever; *ca* – also; *avahāsa-artham* – for joking; *asat-kṛtaḥ* – dishonored; *asi* – You have been; *vihāra* – in relaxation; *śayyā* – in lying down; *āsana* – in sitting; *bhojaneṣu* – or while eating together; *ekaḥ* – alone; *atha vā* – or; *api* – also; *acyuta* – O infallible one; *tat-samakṣam* – among companions; *tat* – all those; *kṣāmaye* – ask forgiveness; *tvām* – from You; *aham* – I; *aprameyam* – immeasurable.

Thinking of You as my friend, I have rashly addressed You "O Kṛṣṇa," "O Yādava," "O my friend," not knowing Your glories. Please forgive whatever I may have done in madness or in love. I have dishonored You many times, jesting as we relaxed, lay on the same bed, or sat or ate together, sometimes alone and sometimes in front of many friends. O infallible one, please excuse me for all those offenses.

PURPORT: Although Kṛṣṇa is manifested before Arjuna in His universal form, Arjuna remembers his friendly relationship with Kṛṣṇa and is therefore asking pardon and requesting Kṛṣṇa to excuse him for the many informal gestures which arise out of friendship. He is admitting that formerly he did not know that Kṛṣṇa could assume such a universal form, although Kṛṣṇa explained it as his intimate friend. Arjuna did not know how many times he may have dishonored Kṛṣṇa by addressing Him "O my friend," "O Kṛṣṇa," "O Yādava," etc., without acknowledging His opulence. But Kṛṣṇa is so kind and merciful that in spite of such opulence He played with Arjuna as a friend. Such is the transcendental loving reciprocation between the devotee and the Lord. The relationship between the living entity and Kṛṣṇa is fixed eternally; it cannot be forgotten, as we can see from the behavior of Arjuna. Although Arjuna has seen the opulence in the universal form, he cannot forget his friendly relationship with Kṛṣṇa.

Text 43 पितासि लोकस्य चराचरस्य त्वमस्य पूज्यश्च गुरुर्गरीयान् ।
न त्वत्समोऽस्त्यभ्यधिकः कुतोऽन्यो लोकत्रयेऽप्यप्रतिमप्रभाव ॥४३॥

pitāsi lokasya carācarasya
tvam asya pūjyaś ca gurur garīyān
na tvat-samo 'sty abhyadhikaḥ kuto 'nyo
loka-traye 'py apratima-prabhāva

pitā – the father; *asi* – You are; *lokasya* – of all the world; *cara* – moving; *acarasya* – and nonmoving; *tvam* – You are; *asya* – of this; *pūjyaḥ* – worshipable; *ca* – also; *guruḥ* – master; *garīyān* – glorious; *na* – never; *tvat-samaḥ* – equal to You; *asti* – there is; *abhyadhikaḥ* – greater; *kutaḥ* – how is it possible; *anyaḥ* – other; *loka-traye* – in the three planetary systems; *api* – also; *apratima-prabhāva* – O immeasurable power.

You are the father of this complete cosmic manifestation, of the moving and the nonmoving. You are its worshipable chief, the supreme spiritual master. No one is greater than You, nor can anyone be one

with You. How then could there be anyone greater than You within the three worlds, O Lord of immeasurable power?

PURPORT: The Supreme Personality of Godhead, Kṛṣṇa, is worshipable as a father is worshipable for his son. He is the spiritual master because He originally gave the Vedic instructions to Brahmā and presently He is also instructing *Bhagavad-gītā* to Arjuna; therefore He is the original spiritual master, and any bona fide spiritual master at the present moment must be a descendant in the line of disciplic succession stemming from Kṛṣṇa. Without being a representative of Kṛṣṇa, one cannot become a teacher or spiritual master of transcendental subject matter.

The Lord is being paid obeisances in all respects. He is of immeasurable greatness. No one can be greater than the Supreme Personality of Godhead, Kṛṣṇa, because no one is equal to or higher than Kṛṣṇa within any manifestation, spiritual or material. Everyone is below Him. No one can excel Him. This is stated in the *Śvetāśvatara Upaniṣad* (6.8):

na tasya kāryaṁ karaṇaṁ ca vidyate
na tat-samaś cābhyadhikaś ca dṛśyate

The Supreme Lord, Kṛṣṇa, has senses and a body like the ordinary man, but for Him there is no difference between His senses, His body, His mind and Himself. Foolish persons who do not perfectly know Him say that Kṛṣṇa is different from His soul, mind, heart and everything else. Kṛṣṇa is absolute; therefore His activities and potencies are supreme. It is also stated that although He does not have senses like ours, He can perform all sensory activities; therefore His senses are neither imperfect nor limited. No one can be greater than Him, no one can be equal to Him, and everyone is lower than Him.

The knowledge, strength and activities of the Supreme Personality are all transcendental. As stated in *Bhagavad-gītā* (4.9):

janma karma ca me divyam, evaṁ yo vetti tattvataḥ
tyaktvā dehaṁ punar janma, naiti mām eti so 'rjuna

Whoever knows Kṛṣṇa's transcendental body, activities and perfection, after quitting his body, returns to Him and doesn't come back again to this miserable world. Therefore one should know that Kṛṣṇa's activities are different from others. The best policy is to follow the principles of Kṛṣṇa; that will make one perfect. It is also stated that there is no one who is master of Kṛṣṇa; everyone is His servant. The *Caitanya-caritāmṛta* (*Ādi* 5.142) confirms, *ekale īśvara kṛṣṇa, āra saba bhṛtya:* only Kṛṣṇa is

God, and everyone else is His servant. Everyone is complying with His order. There is no one who can deny His order. Everyone is acting according to His direction, being under His superintendence. As stated in the *Brahma-saṁhitā,* He is the cause of all causes.

Text 44 तस्मात्प्रणम्य प्रणिधाय कायं प्रसादये त्वामहमीशमीड्यम् ।
पितेव पुत्रस्य सखेव सख्युः प्रियः प्रियायार्हसि देव सोढुम् ॥४४॥

tasmāt praṇamya praṇidhāya kāyaṁ
prasādaye tvām aham īśam īḍyam
piteva putrasya sakheva sakhyuḥ
priyaḥ priyāyārhasi deva soḍhum

tasmāt – therefore; *praṇamya* – offering obeisances; *praṇidhāya* – laying down; *kāyam* – the body; *prasādaye* – to beg mercy; *tvām* – unto You; *aham* – I; *īśam* – unto the Supreme Lord; *īḍyam* – worshipable; *pitā iva* – like a father; *putrasya* – with a son; *sakhā iva* – like a friend; *sakhyuḥ* – with a friend; *priyaḥ* – a lover; *priyāyāḥ* – with the dearmost; *arhasi* – You should; *deva* – my Lord; *soḍhum* – tolerate.

You are the Supreme Lord, to be worshiped by every living being. Thus I fall down to offer You my respectful obeisances and ask Your mercy. As a father tolerates the impudence of his son, a friend the impertinence of a friend, or a husband the familiarity of his wife, please tolerate the wrongs I may have done You.

PURPORT: Kṛṣṇa's devotees relate to Kṛṣṇa in various relationships; one might treat Kṛṣṇa as a son, or one might treat Kṛṣṇa as a husband, as a friend, or as a master. Kṛṣṇa and Arjuna are related in friendship. As the father tolerates, or the husband or a master tolerates, so Kṛṣṇa tolerates.

Text 45 अदृष्टपूर्वं हृषितोऽस्मि दृष्ट्वा भयेन च प्रव्यथितं मनो मे ।
तदेव मे दर्शय देव रूपं प्रसीद देवेश जगन्निवास ॥४५॥

adṛṣṭa-pūrvaṁ hṛṣito 'smi dṛṣṭvā
bhayena ca pravyathitaṁ mano me
tad eva me darśaya deva rūpaṁ
prasīda deveśa jagan-nivāsa

adṛṣṭa-pūrvam – never seen before; *hṛṣitaḥ* – gladdened; *asmi* – I am; *dṛṣṭvā* – by seeing; *bhayena* – out of fear; *ca* – also; *pravyathitam* – perturbed; *manaḥ* – mind; *me* – my; *tat* – that; *eva* – certainly; *me* – unto me; *darśaya* – show; *deva* – O Lord; *rūpam* – the form; *prasīda* – just be gracious; *deva-īśa* – O Lord of lords; *jagat-nivāsa* – O refuge of the universe.

After seeing this universal form, which I have never seen before, I am gladdened, but at the same time my mind is disturbed with fear. Therefore please bestow Your grace upon me and reveal again Your form as the Personality of Godhead, O Lord of lords, O abode of the universe.

PURPORT: Arjuna is always in confidence with Kṛṣṇa because he is a very dear friend, and as a dear friend is gladdened by his friend's opulence, Arjuna is very joyful to see that his friend Kṛṣṇa is the Supreme Personality of Godhead and can show such a wonderful universal form. But at the same time, after seeing that universal form, he is afraid that he has committed so many offenses to Kṛṣṇa out of his unalloyed friendship. Thus his mind is disturbed out of fear, although he had no reason to fear. Arjuna therefore is asking Kṛṣṇa to show His Nārāyaṇa form, because He can assume any form. This universal form is material and temporary, as the material world is temporary. But in the Vaikuṇṭha planets He has His transcendental form with four hands as Nārāyaṇa. There are innumerable planets in the spiritual sky, and in each of them Kṛṣṇa is present by His plenary manifestations of different names. Thus Arjuna desired to see one of the forms manifest in the Vaikuṇṭha planets. Of course in each Vaikuṇṭha planet the form of Nārāyaṇa is four-handed, but the four hands hold different arrangements of symbols – the conchshell, mace, lotus and disc. According to the different hands these four things are held in, the Nārāyaṇas are variously named. All of these forms are one with Kṛṣṇa; therefore Arjuna requests to see His four-handed feature.

Text 46 किरीटिनं गदिनं चक्रहस्तमिच्छामि त्वां द्रष्टुमहं तथैव ।
तेनैव रूपेण चतुर्भुजेन सहस्रबाहो भव विश्वमूर्ते ॥४६॥

kirīṭinaṁ gadinaṁ cakra-hastam
icchāmi tvāṁ draṣṭum ahaṁ tathaiva
tenaiva rūpeṇa catur-bhujena
sahasra-bāho bhava viśva-mūrte

kirīṭinam – with helmet; *gadinam* – with club; *cakra-hastam* – disc in hand; *icchāmi* – I wish; *tvām* – You; *draṣṭum* – to see; *aham* – I; *tathā eva* – in that position; *tena eva* – in that; *rūpeṇa* – form; *catuḥ-bhujena* –

four-handed; *sahasra-bāho* – O thousand-handed one; *bhava* – just become; *viśva-mūrte* – O universal form.

O universal form, O thousand-armed Lord, I wish to see You in Your four-armed form, with helmeted head and with club, wheel, conch and lotus flower in Your hands. I long to see You in that form.

PURPORT: In the *Brahma-saṁhitā* (5.39) it is stated, *rāmādi-mūrtiṣu kalā-niyamena tiṣṭhan:* the Lord is eternally situated in hundreds and thousands of forms, and the main forms are those like Rāma, Nṛsiṁha, Nārāyaṇa, etc. There are innumerable forms. But Arjuna knew that Kṛṣṇa is the original Personality of Godhead assuming His temporary universal form. He is now asking to see the form of Nārāyaṇa, a spiritual form. This verse establishes without any doubt the statement of the *Śrīmad-Bhāgavatam* that Kṛṣṇa is the original Personality of Godhead and all other features originate from Him. He is not different from His plenary expansions, and He is God in any of His innumerable forms. In all of these forms He is fresh like a young man. That is the constant feature of the Supreme Personality of Godhead. One who knows Kṛṣṇa becomes free at once from all contamination of the material world.

Text 47 श्रीभगवानुवाच
मया प्रसन्नेन तवार्जुनेदं रूपं परं दर्शितमात्मयोगात् ।
तेजोमयं विश्वमनन्तमाद्यं यन्मे त्वदन्येन न दृष्टपूर्वम् ॥४७॥

śrī-bhagavān uvāca
mayā prasannena tavārjunedaṁ
rūpaṁ paraṁ darśitam ātma-yogāt
tejo-mayaṁ viśvam anantam ādyaṁ
yan me tvad anyena na dṛṣṭa-pūrvam

śrī-bhagavān uvāca – the Supreme Personality of Godhead said; *mayā* – by Me; *prasannena* – happily; *tava* – unto you; *arjuna* – O Arjuna; *idam* – this; *rūpam* – form; *param* – transcendental; *darśitam* – shown; *ātma-yogāt* – by My internal potency; *tejaḥ-mayam* – full of effulgence; *viśvam* – the entire universe; *anantam* – unlimited; *ādyam* – original; *yat* – that which; *me* – My; *tvat anyena* – besides you; *na dṛṣṭa-pūrvam* – no one has previously seen.

The Supreme Personality of Godhead said: My dear Arjuna, happily have I shown you, by My internal potency, this supreme universal form

within the material world. No one before you has ever seen this primal form, unlimited and full of glaring effulgence.

PURPORT: Arjuna wanted to see the universal form of the Supreme Lord, so Lord Kṛṣṇa, out of His mercy upon His devotee Arjuna, showed His universal form, full of effulgence and opulence. This form was glaring like the sun, and its many faces were rapidly changing. Kṛṣṇa showed this form just to satisfy the desire of His friend Arjuna. This form was manifested by Kṛṣṇa through His internal potency, which is inconceivable by human speculation. No one had seen this universal form of the Lord before Arjuna, but because the form was shown to Arjuna, other devotees in the heavenly planets and in other planets in outer space could also see it. They had not seen it before, but because of Arjuna they were also able to see it. In other words, all the disciplic devotees of the Lord could see the universal form which was shown to Arjuna by the mercy of Kṛṣṇa. Someone has commented that this form was shown to Duryodhana also when Kṛṣṇa went to Duryodhana to negotiate for peace. Unfortunately, Duryodhana did not accept the peace offer, but at that time Kṛṣṇa manifested some of His universal forms. But those forms are different from this one shown to Arjuna. It is clearly said that no one had ever seen this form before.

Text 48 न वेदयज्ञाध्ययनैर्न दानैर्न च क्रियाभिर्न तपोभिरुग्रैः ।
एवंरूपः शक्य अहं नृलोके द्रष्टुं त्वदन्येन कुरुप्रवीर ॥४८॥

na veda-yajñādhyayanair na dānair
na ca kriyābhir na tapobhir ugraiḥ
evaṁ-rūpaḥ śakya ahaṁ nṛ-loke
draṣṭuṁ tvad anyena kuru-pravīra

na – never; *veda-yajña* – by sacrifice; *adhyayanaiḥ* – or Vedic study; *na* – never; *dānaiḥ* – by charity; *na* – never; *ca* – also; *kriyābhiḥ* – by pious activities; *na* – never; *tapobhiḥ* – by serious penances; *ugraiḥ* – severe; *evam-rūpaḥ* – in this form; *śakyaḥ* – can; *aham* – I; *nṛ-loke* – in this material world; *draṣṭum* – be seen; *tvat* – than you; *anyena* – by another; *kuru-pravīra* – O best among the Kuru warriors.

O best of the Kuru warriors, no one before you has ever seen this universal form of Mine, for neither by studying the Vedas, nor by performing sacrifices, nor by charity, nor by pious activities, nor by severe penances can I be seen in this form in the material world.

PURPORT: The divine vision in this connection should be clearly understood. Who can have divine vision? Divine means godly. Unless one attains the status of divinity as a demigod, he cannot have divine vision. And what is a demigod? It is stated in the Vedic scriptures that those who are devotees of Lord Viṣṇu are demigods (*viṣṇu-bhaktaḥ smṛto daivāḥ*). Those who are atheistic, i.e., who do not believe in Viṣṇu, or who recognize only the impersonal part of Kṛṣṇa as the Supreme, cannot have the divine vision. It is not possible to decry Kṛṣṇa and at the same time have the divine vision. One cannot have the divine vision without becoming divine. In other words, those who have divine vision can also see like Arjuna.

The *Bhagavad-gītā* gives the description of the universal form. Although this description was unknown to everyone before Arjuna, now one can have some idea of the *viśva-rūpa* after this incident. Those who are actually divine can see the universal form of the Lord. But one cannot be divine without being a pure devotee of Kṛṣṇa. The devotees, however, who are actually in the divine nature and who have divine vision, are not very much interested in seeing the universal form of the Lord. As described in the previous verse, Arjuna desired to see the four-handed form of Lord Kṛṣṇa as Viṣṇu, and he was actually afraid of the universal form.

In this verse there are some significant words, just like *veda-yajñādhyayanaiḥ,* which refers to studying Vedic literature and the subject matter of sacrificial regulations. *Veda* refers to all kinds of Vedic literature, such as the four *Vedas* (*Ṛg, Yajur, Sāma* and *Atharva*) and the eighteen *Purāṇas,* the *Upaniṣads* and the *Vedānta-sūtra.* One can study these at home or anywhere else. Similarly, there are *sūtras – Kalpa-sūtras* and *Mīmāṁsā-sūtras* – for studying the method of sacrifice. *Dānaiḥ* refers to charity which is offered to a suitable party, such as those who are engaged in the transcendental loving service of the Lord – the *brāhmaṇas* and the Vaiṣṇavas. Similarly, "pious activities" refers to the *agni-hotra* and the prescribed duties of the different castes. And the voluntary acceptance of some bodily pains is called *tapasya.* So one can perform all these – can accept bodily penances, give charity, study the *Vedas,* etc. – but unless he is a devotee like Arjuna, it is not possible to see that universal form. Those who are impersonalists are also imagining that they are seeing the universal form of the Lord, but from *Bhagavad-gītā* we understand that the impersonalists are not devotees. Therefore they are unable to see the universal form of the Lord.

There are many persons who create incarnations. They falsely claim an ordinary human to be an incarnation, but this is all foolishness. We should follow the principles of *Bhagavad-gītā,* otherwise there is no possibility of attaining perfect spiritual knowledge. Although *Bhagavad-gītā* is considered the preliminary study of the science of God, still it is so perfect that it enables one to distinguish what is what. The followers of a pseudo incarnation may say that they have also seen the transcendental incarnation of God, the universal form, but that is unacceptable because it is clearly stated here that unless one becomes a devotee of Kṛṣṇa one cannot see the universal form of God. So one first of all has to become a pure devotee of Kṛṣṇa; then he can claim that he can show the universal form of what he has seen. A devotee of Kṛṣṇa cannot accept false incarnations or followers of false incarnations.

Text 49 मा ते व्यथा मा च विमूढभावो दृष्ट्वा रूपं घोरमीदृङ् ममेदम् ।
व्यपेतभीः प्रीतमनाः पुनस्त्वं तदेव मे रूपमिदं प्रपश्य ॥४९॥

mā te vyathā mā ca vimūḍha-bhāvo
dṛṣṭvā rūpaṁ ghoram īdṛṅ mamedam
vyapeta-bhīḥ prīta-manāḥ punas tvaṁ
tad eva me rūpam idaṁ prapaśya

mā – let it not be; *te* – unto you; *vyathā* – trouble; *mā* – let it not be; *ca* – also; *vimūḍha-bhāvaḥ* – bewilderment; *dṛṣṭvā* – by seeing; *rūpam* – form; *ghoram* – horrible; *īdṛk* – as it is; *mama* – My; *idam* – this; *vyapeta-bhīḥ* – free from all fear; *prīta-manāḥ* – pleased in mind; *punaḥ* – again; *tvam* – you; *tat* – that; *eva* – thus; *me* – My; *rūpam* – form; *idam* – this; *prapaśya* – just see.

You have been perturbed and bewildered by seeing this horrible feature of Mine. Now let it be finished. My devotee, be free again from all disturbances. With a peaceful mind you can now see the form you desire.

PURPORT: In the beginning of *Bhagavad-gītā* Arjuna was worried about killing Bhīṣma and Droṇa, his worshipful grandfather and master. But Kṛṣṇa said that he need not be afraid of killing his grandfather. When the sons of Dhṛtarāṣṭra tried to disrobe Draupadī in the assembly of the Kurus, Bhīṣma and Droṇa were silent, and for such negligence of duty they should be killed. Kṛṣṇa showed His universal form to Arjuna just to show him that these people were already killed for their unlawful action. That scene was shown to Arjuna because devotees are always peaceful and they cannot perform such horrible actions. The purpose of the revelation of the universal form was shown; now Arjuna wanted to see the four-armed form, and Kṛṣṇa showed him. A devotee is not much interested in the universal form, for it does not enable one to reciprocate loving feelings. Either a devotee wants to offer his respectful worshipful feelings, or he wants to see the two-handed Kṛṣṇa form so that he can reciprocate in loving service with the Supreme Personality of Godhead.

Text 50 सञ्जय उवाच
इत्यर्जुनं वासुदेवस्तथोक्त्वा स्वकं रूपं दर्शयामास भूयः ।
आश्वासयामास च भीतमेनं भूत्वा पुनः सौम्यवपुर्महात्मा ॥५०॥

sañjaya uvāca
ity arjunaṁ vāsudevas tathoktvā
svakaṁ rūpaṁ darśayām āsa bhūyaḥ
āśvāsayām āsa ca bhītam enaṁ
bhūtvā punaḥ saumya-vapur mahātmā

sañjayaḥ uvāca – Sañjaya said; *iti* – thus; *arjunam* – unto Arjuna; *vāsudevaḥ* – Kṛṣṇa; *tathā* – in that way; *uktvā* – speaking; *svakam* – His own; *rūpam* – form; *darśayām āsa* – showed; *bhūyaḥ* – again; *āśvāsayām āsa* – encouraged; *ca* – also; *bhītam* – fearful; *enam* – him; *bhūtvā* – becoming; *punaḥ* – again; *saumya-vapuḥ* – the beautiful form; *mahā-ātmā* – the great one.

Sañjaya said to Dhṛtarāṣṭra: The Supreme Personality of Godhead, Kṛṣṇa, having spoken thus to Arjuna, displayed His real four-armed form and at last showed His two-armed form, thus encouraging the fearful Arjuna.

PURPORT: When Kṛṣṇa appeared as the son of Vasudeva and Devakī, He first of all appeared as four-armed Nārāyaṇa, but when He was requested by His parents, He transformed Himself into an ordinary child in appearance. Similarly, Kṛṣṇa knew that Arjuna was not interested in seeing a four-handed form, but since Arjuna asked to see this four-handed form, Kṛṣṇa also showed him this form again and then showed Himself in His two-handed form. The word *saumya-vapuḥ* is very significant. *Saumya-vapuḥ* is a very beautiful form; it is known as the most beautiful form. When He was present, everyone was attracted simply by Kṛṣṇa's form, and because Kṛṣṇa is the director of the universe, He just banished the fear of Arjuna, His devotee, and showed him again His beautiful form of Kṛṣṇa. In the *Brahma-saṁhitā* (5.38) it is stated, *prem-*

āñjana-cchurita-bhakti-vilocanena: only a person whose eyes are smeared with the ointment of love can see the beautiful form of Śrī Kṛṣṇa.

Text 51 अर्जुन उवाच
दृष्ट्वेदं मानुषं रूपं तव सौम्यं जनार्दन ।
इदानीमस्मि संवृत्तः सचेताः प्रकृतिं गतः ॥५१॥

arjuna uvāca
dṛṣṭvedaṁ mānuṣaṁ rūpaṁ, tava saumyaṁ janārdana
idānīm asmi saṁvṛttaḥ, sa-cetāḥ prakṛtiṁ gataḥ

arjunaḥ uvāca – Arjuna said; *dṛṣṭvā* – seeing; *idam* – this; *mānuṣam* – human; *rūpam* – form; *tava* – Your; *saumyam* – very beautiful; *janārdana* – O chastiser of the enemies; *idānīm* – now; *asmi* – I am; *saṁvṛttaḥ* – settled; *sa-cetāḥ* – in my consciousness; *prakṛtim* – to my own nature; *gataḥ* – returned.

When Arjuna thus saw Kṛṣṇa in His original form, he said: O Janārdana, seeing this humanlike form, so very beautiful, I am now composed in mind, and I am restored to my original nature.

PURPORT: Here the words *mānuṣaṁ rūpam* clearly indicate the Supreme Personality of Godhead to be originally two-handed. Those who deride Kṛṣṇa as if He were an ordinary person are shown here to be ignorant of His divine nature. If Kṛṣṇa is like an ordinary human being, then how is it possible for Him to show the universal form and again to show the four-handed Nārāyaṇa form? So it is very clearly stated in *Bhagavad-gītā* that one who thinks that Kṛṣṇa is an ordinary person and who misguides the reader by claiming that it is the impersonal Brahman within Kṛṣṇa speaking is doing the greatest injustice. Kṛṣṇa has actually shown His universal form and His four-handed Viṣṇu form. So how can He be an ordinary human being? A pure devotee is not confused by misguiding commentaries on *Bhagavad-gītā* because he knows what is what. The original verses of *Bhagavad-gītā* are as clear as the sun; they do not require lamplight from foolish commentators.

Text 52 श्रीभगवानुवाच
सुदुर्दर्शमिदं रूपं दृष्टवानसि यन्मम ।
देवा अप्यस्य रूपस्य नित्यं दर्शनकाङ्क्षिणः ॥५२॥

śrī-bhagavān uvāca
su-durdarśam idaṁ rūpaṁ, dṛṣṭavān asi yan mama
devā apy asya rūpasya, nityaṁ darśana-kāṅkṣiṇaḥ

śrī-bhagavān uvāca – the Supreme Personality of Godhead said; *su-durdarśam* – very difficult to see; *idam* – this; *rūpam* – form; *dṛṣṭavān asi* – as you have seen; *yat* – which; *mama* – of Mine; *devāḥ* – the demigods; *api* – also; *asya* – this; *rūpasya* – form; *nityam* – eternally; *darśana-kāṅkṣiṇaḥ* – aspiring to see.

The Supreme Personality of Godhead said: My dear Arjuna, this form of Mine you are now seeing is very difficult to behold. Even the demigods are ever seeking the opportunity to see this form, which is so dear.

PURPORT: In the forty-eighth verse of this chapter Lord Kṛṣṇa concluded revealing His universal form and informed Arjuna that this form is not possible to be seen by so many pious activities, sacrifices, etc. Now here the word *su-durdarśam* is used, indicating that Kṛṣṇa's two-handed form is still more confidential. One may be able to see the universal form of Kṛṣṇa by adding a little tinge of devotional service to various activities like penances, Vedic study and philosophical speculation. It may be possible, but without a tinge of *bhakti* one cannot see; that has already been explained. Still, beyond that universal form, the form of Kṛṣṇa with two hands is still more difficult to see, even for demigods like Brahmā and Lord Śiva. They desire to see Him, and we have evidence in the *Śrīmad-Bhāgavatam* that when He was supposed to be in the womb of His mother, Devakī, all the demigods from heaven came to see the marvel of Kṛṣṇa, and they offered nice prayers to the Lord, although He was not at that time visible to them. They waited to see Him. A foolish person may deride Him, thinking Him an ordinary person, and may offer respect not to Him but to the impersonal "something" within Him, but these are all nonsensical postures. Kṛṣṇa in His two-armed form is actually desired to be seen by demigods like Brahmā and Śiva.

In *Bhagavad-gītā* (9.11) it is also confirmed, *avajānanti māṁ mūḍhā mānuṣīṁ tanum āśritam:* He is not visible to the foolish persons who deride Him. Kṛṣṇa's body, as confirmed by *Brahma-saṁhitā* and confirmed by Kṛṣṇa Himself in *Bhagavad-gītā,* is completely spiritual and full of bliss and eternality. His body is never like a material body. But for some who make a study of Kṛṣṇa by reading *Bhagavad-gītā* or similar Vedic scriptures, Kṛṣṇa is a problem. For one using a material process,

Kṛṣṇa is considered to be a great historical personality and very learned philosopher, but He is an ordinary man, and even though He was so powerful He had to accept a material body. Ultimately they think that the Absolute Truth is impersonal; therefore they think that from His impersonal feature He assumed a personal feature attached to material nature. This is a materialistic calculation of the Supreme Lord. Another calculation is speculative. Those who are in search of knowledge also speculate on Kṛṣṇa and consider Him to be less important than the universal form of the Supreme. Thus some think that the universal form of Kṛṣṇa which was manifested to Arjuna is more important than His personal form. According to them, the personal form of the Supreme is something imaginary. They believe that in the ultimate issue, the Absolute Truth is not a person. But the transcendental process is described in *Bhagavad-gītā,* Chapter Four: to hear about Kṛṣṇa from authorities. That is the actual Vedic process, and those who are actually in the Vedic line hear about Kṛṣṇa from authority, and by repeated hearing about Him, Kṛṣṇa becomes dear. As we have several times discussed, Kṛṣṇa is covered by His *yoga-māyā* potency. He is not to be seen or revealed to anyone and everyone. Only by one to whom He reveals Himself can He be seen. This is confirmed in the Vedic literature; for one who is a surrendered soul, the Absolute Truth can actually be understood. The transcendentalist, by continuous Kṛṣṇa consciousness and by devotional service to Kṛṣṇa, can have his spiritual eyes opened and can see Kṛṣṇa by revelation. Such a revelation is not possible even for the demigods; therefore it is difficult even for the demigods to understand Kṛṣṇa, and the advanced demigods are always in hope of seeing Kṛṣṇa in His two-handed form. The conclusion is that although to see the universal form of Kṛṣṇa is very, very difficult and not possible for anyone and everyone, it is still more difficult to understand His personal form as Śyāmasundara.

Text 53

नाहं वेदैर्न तपसा न दानेन न चेज्यया ।
शक्य एवंविधो द्रष्टुं दृष्टवानसि मां यथा ॥५३॥

nāhaṁ vedair na tapasā, na dānena na cejyayā
śakya evaṁ-vidho draṣṭuṁ, dṛṣṭavān asi māṁ yathā

na – never; *aham* – I; *vedaiḥ* – by study of the *Vedas; na* – never; *tapasā* – by serious penances; *na* – never; *dānena* – by charity; *na* – never; *ca* – also; *ijyayā* – by worship; *śakyaḥ* – it is possible; *evam-vidhaḥ* – like this; *draṣṭum* – to see; *dṛṣṭavān* – seeing; *asi* – you are; *mām* – Me; *yathā* – as.

The form you are seeing with your transcendental eyes cannot be understood simply by studying the Vedas, nor by undergoing serious penances, nor by charity, nor by worship. It is not by these means that one can see Me as I am.

PURPORT: Kṛṣṇa first appeared before His parents Devakī and Vasudeva in a four-handed form, and then He transformed Himself into the two-handed form. This mystery is very difficult to understand for those who are atheists or who are devoid of devotional service. For scholars who have simply studied Vedic literature by way of grammatical knowledge or mere academic qualifications, Kṛṣṇa is not possible to understand. Nor is He to be understood by persons who officially go to the temple to offer worship. They make their visit, but they cannot understand Kṛṣṇa as He is. Kṛṣṇa can be understood only through the path of devotional service, as explained by Kṛṣṇa Himself in the next verse.

Text 54 भक्त्या त्वनन्यया शक्य अहमेवंविधोऽर्जुन ।
ज्ञातुं द्रष्टुं च तत्त्वेन प्रवेष्टुं च परन्तप ॥५४॥

bhaktyā tv ananyayā śakya, aham evaṁ-vidho 'rjuna
jñātuṁ draṣṭuṁ ca tattvena, praveṣṭuṁ ca paran-tapa

bhaktyā – by devotional service; *tu* – but; *ananyayā* – without being mixed with fruitive activities or speculative knowledge; *śakyaḥ* – possible; *aham* – I; *evam-vidhaḥ* – like this; *arjuna* – O Arjuna; *jñātum* – to know; *draṣṭum* – to see; *ca* – and; *tattvena* – in fact; *praveṣṭum* – to enter into; *ca* – also; *param-tapa* – O subduer of the enemy.

My dear Arjuna, only by undivided devotional service can I be understood as I am, standing before you, and can thus be seen directly. Only in this way can you enter into the mysteries of My understanding.

PURPORT: Kṛṣṇa can be understood only by the process of undivided devotional service. He explicitly explains this in this verse so that unauthorized commentators, who try to understand *Bhagavad-gītā* by the speculative process, will know that they are simply wasting their time. No one can understand Kṛṣṇa or how He came from parents in a four-handed form and at once changed Himself into a two-handed form. These things are very difficult to understand by study of the *Vedas* or by philosophical speculation. Therefore it is clearly stated here that no one can see Him or enter into understanding of these matters. Those who, however, are very experienced students of Vedic literature can learn about Him from the Vedic literature in so many ways. There are so many rules and regulations, and if one at all wants to understand Kṛṣṇa, he must follow the regulative principles described in the authoritative literature. One can perform penance in accordance with those principles. For example, to undergo serious penances one may observe fasting on Janmāṣṭamī, the day on which Kṛṣṇa appeared, and on the two days of Ekādaśī (the eleventh day after the new moon and the eleventh day after the full moon). As far as charity is concerned, it is plain that charity should be given to the devotees of Kṛṣṇa who are engaged in His devotional service to spread the Kṛṣṇa philosophy, or Kṛṣṇa consciousness, throughout the world. Kṛṣṇa consciousness is a benediction to humanity. Lord Caitanya was appreciated by Rūpa Gosvāmī as the most munificent man of charity because love of Kṛṣṇa, which is very difficult to achieve, was distributed freely by Him. So if one gives some amount of his money to persons involved in distributing Kṛṣṇa consciousness, that charity, given to spread Kṛṣṇa consciousness, is the greatest charity in the world. And if one worships as prescribed in the temple (in the temples in India there is always some statue, usually of Viṣṇu or Kṛṣṇa), that is a chance to progress by offering worship and respect to the Supreme Personality of Godhead. For the beginners in devotional service to the Lord, temple worship is essential, and this is confirmed in the Vedic literature (*Śvetāśvatara Upaniṣad* 6.23):

yasya deve parā bhaktir, yathā deve tathā gurau
tasyaite kathitā hy arthāḥ, prakāśante mahātmanaḥ

One who has unflinching devotion for the Supreme Lord and is directed by the spiritual master, in whom he has similar unflinching faith, can see the Supreme Personality of Godhead by revelation. One cannot understand Kṛṣṇa by mental speculation. For one who does not take personal training under the guidance of a bona fide spiritual master, it is impossible to even begin to understand Kṛṣṇa. The word *tu* is specifically used here to indicate that no other process can be used, can be recommended, or can be successful in understanding Kṛṣṇa.

The personal forms of Kṛṣṇa, the two-handed form and the four-handed, are described as *su-durdarśam*, very difficult to see. They are completely different from the temporary universal form shown to Arjuna. The four-handed form of Nārāyaṇa and the two-handed form of Kṛṣṇa are eternal and transcendental, whereas the universal form exhibited to Arjuna is temporary. The words *tvad anyena na dṛṣṭa-pūrvam* (text 47) state that before Arjuna, no one had seen that universal form. Also, they suggest that amongst the devotees there was no necessity of showing it. That form was exhibited by Kṛṣṇa at the request of Arjuna so that in the future, when one represents himself as an incarnation of God, people can ask to see his universal form.

The word *na,* used repeatedly in the previous verse, indicates that one should not be very much proud of such credentials as an academic education in Vedic literature. One must take to the devotional service of Kṛṣṇa. Only then can one attempt to write commentaries on *Bhagavad-gītā.*

Kṛṣṇa changes from the universal form to the four-handed form of Nārāyaṇa and then to His own natural form of two hands. This indicates that the four-handed forms and other forms mentioned in Vedic literature are all emanations of the original two-handed Kṛṣṇa. He is the origin of all emanations. Kṛṣṇa is distinct even from these forms, what to speak of the impersonal conception. As far as the four-handed forms of Kṛṣṇa are concerned, it is stated clearly that even the most identical four-handed form of Kṛṣṇa (which is known as Mahā-viṣṇu, who is lying on the cosmic ocean and from whose breathing so many innumerable universes are passing out and entering) is also an expansion of the Supreme Lord. As stated in the *Brahma-saṁhitā* (5.48),

yasyaika-niśvasita-kālam athāvalambya
jīvanti loma-vila-jā jagad-aṇḍa-nāthāḥ
viṣṇur mahān sa iha yasya kalā-viśeṣo
govindam ādi-puruṣaṁ tam ahaṁ bhajāmi

"The Mahā-viṣṇu, into whom all the innumerable universes enter and from whom they come forth again simply by His breathing process, is a plenary expansion of Kṛṣṇa. Therefore I worship Govinda, Kṛṣṇa, the cause of all causes." Therefore one should conclusively worship the personal form of Kṛṣṇa as the Supreme Personality of Godhead who has eternal bliss and knowledge. He is the source of all forms of Viṣṇu, He is the source of all forms of incarnation, and He is the original Supreme Personality, as confirmed in *Bhagavad-gītā.*

In the Vedic literature (*Gopāla-tāpanī Upaniṣad* 1.1) the following statement appears:

sac-cid-ānanda-rūpāya, kṛṣṇāyākliṣṭa-kāriṇe
namo vedānta-vedyāya, gurave buddhi-sākṣiṇe

"I offer my respectful obeisances unto Kṛṣṇa, who has a transcendental form of bliss, eternity and knowledge. I offer my respect to Him, because understanding Him means understanding the *Vedas* and He is therefore the supreme spiritual master." Then it is said, *kṛṣṇo vai paramaṁ daivatam:* "Kṛṣṇa is the Supreme Personality of Godhead." (*Gopāla-tāpanī Upaniṣad* 1.3) *Eko vaśī sarva-gaḥ kṛṣṇa īḍyaḥ:* "That one Kṛṣṇa is the Supreme Personality of Godhead, and He is worshipable." *Eko 'pi san bahudhā yo 'vabhāti:* "Kṛṣṇa is one, but He is manifested in unlimited forms and expanded incarnations." (*Gopāla-tāpanī Upaniṣad* 1.21)

The *Brahma-saṁhitā* (5.1) says,

īśvaraḥ paramaḥ kṛṣṇaḥ, sac-cid-ānanda-vigrahaḥ
anādir ādir govindaḥ, sarva-kāraṇa-kāraṇam

"The Supreme Personality of Godhead is Kṛṣṇa, who has a body of eternity, knowledge and bliss. He has no beginning, for He is the beginning of everything. He is the cause of all causes."

Elsewhere it is said, *yatrāvatīrṇaṁ kṛṣṇākhyaṁ paraṁ brahma narākṛti:* "The Supreme Absolute Truth is a person, His name is Kṛṣṇa, and He sometimes descends on this earth." Similarly, in the *Śrīmad-Bhāgavatam* we find a description of all kinds of incarnations of the Supreme Personality of Godhead, and in this list the name of Kṛṣṇa also appears. But then it is said that this Kṛṣṇa is not an incarnation of God but is the original Supreme Personality of Godhead Himself (*ete cāṁśa-kalāḥ puṁsaḥ kṛṣṇas tu bhagavān svayam*).

Similarly, in *Bhagavad-gītā* the Lord says, *mattaḥ parataraṁ nānyat:* "There is nothing superior to My form as the Personality of Godhead Kṛṣṇa." He also says elsewhere in *Bhagavad-gītā, aham ādir hi devānām:* "I am the origin of all the demigods." And after understanding *Bhagavad-gītā* from Kṛṣṇa, Arjuna also confirms this in the following words: *paraṁ brahma paraṁ dhāma pavitraṁ paramaṁ bhavān,* "I now fully understand that You are the Supreme Personality of Godhead, the Absolute Truth, and that You are the refuge of everything." Therefore the universal form which Kṛṣṇa showed to Arjuna is not the original form of God. The original is the Kṛṣṇa form. The universal form, with its thousands and thousands of heads and hands, is manifest just to draw the attention of those who have no love for God. It is not God's original form.

The universal form is not attractive for pure devotees, who are in love with the Lord in different transcendental relationships. The Supreme Godhead exchanges transcendental love in His original form of Kṛṣṇa. Therefore to Arjuna, who was so intimately related with Kṛṣṇa in friendship, this form of the universal manifestation was not pleasing; rather, it was fearful. Arjuna, who was a constant companion of Kṛṣṇa's, must have had transcendental eyes; he was not an ordinary man. Therefore he was not captivated by the universal form. This form may seem wonderful to persons who are involved in elevating themselves by fruitive activities, but to persons who are engaged in devotional service the two-handed form of Kṛṣṇa is the most dear.

Text 55 मत्कर्मकृन्मत्परमो मद्भक्तः सङ्गवर्जितः ।
निर्वैरः सर्वभूतेषु यः स मामेति पाण्डव ॥५५॥

mat-karma-kṛn mat-paramo, mad-bhaktaḥ saṅga-varjitaḥ
nirvairaḥ sarva-bhūteṣu, yaḥ sa mām eti pāṇḍava

mat-karma-kṛt – engaged in doing My work; *mat-paramaḥ* – considering Me the Supreme; *mat-bhaktaḥ* – engaged in My devotional service; *saṅga-varjitaḥ* – freed from the contamination of fruitive activities and mental speculation; *nirvairaḥ* – without an enemy; *sarva-bhūteṣu* – among all living entities; *yaḥ* – one who; *saḥ* – he; *mām* – unto Me; *eti* – comes; *pāṇḍava* – O son of Pāṇḍu.

My dear Arjuna, he who engages in My pure devotional service, free from the contaminations of fruitive activities and mental speculation, he who works for Me, who makes Me the supreme goal of his life, and who is friendly to every living being – he certainly comes to Me.

PURPORT: Anyone who wants to approach the supreme of all the Personalities of Godhead, on the Kṛṣṇaloka planet in the spiritual sky, and be intimately connected with the Supreme Personality, Kṛṣṇa, must take this formula, as stated by the Supreme Himself. Therefore, this verse is considered to be the essence of *Bhagavad-gītā.* The *Bhagavad-gītā* is a book directed to the conditioned souls, who are engaged in the material world with the purpose of lording it over nature and who do not know of the real, spiritual life. The *Bhagavad-gītā* is meant to show how one can understand his spiritual existence and his eternal relationship with the supreme spiritual personality and to teach one how to go back home, back to Godhead. Now here is the verse which clearly explains the process by which one can attain success in his spiritual activity: devotional service.

As far as work is concerned, one should transfer his energy entirely to Kṛṣṇa conscious activities. As stated in the *Bhakti-rasāmṛta-sindhu* (1.2.255),

anāsaktasya viṣayān, yathārham upayuñjataḥ
nirbandhaḥ kṛṣṇa-sambandhe, yuktaṁ vairāgyam ucyate

No work should be done by any man except in relationship to Kṛṣṇa. This is called *kṛṣṇa-karma.* One may be engaged in various activities, but one should not be attached to the result of his work; the result should be done only for Him. For example, one may be engaged in business, but to transform that activity into Kṛṣṇa consciousness, one has to do business for Kṛṣṇa. If Kṛṣṇa is the proprietor of the business, then Kṛṣṇa should enjoy the profit of the business. If a businessman is in possession of thousands and thousands of dollars, and if he has to offer all this to Kṛṣṇa, he can do it. This is work for Kṛṣṇa. Instead of constructing a big building for his sense gratification, he can construct a nice temple for Kṛṣṇa, and he can install the Deity of Kṛṣṇa and arrange for the Deity's service, as is outlined in the authorized books of devotional service. This is all *kṛṣṇa-karma.* One should not be attached to the result of his work, but the result should be offered to Kṛṣṇa, and one should accept as *prasādam* the remnants of offerings to Kṛṣṇa. If one constructs a very big building for Kṛṣṇa and installs the Deity of Kṛṣṇa, one is not prohibited from living there, but it is understood that the proprietor of the building is Kṛṣṇa. That is called Kṛṣṇa consciousness. If, however, one is not able to construct a temple for Kṛṣṇa, one can engage himself in cleansing the temple of Kṛṣṇa; that is also *kṛṣṇa-karma.* One can cultivate a garden. Anyone who has land – in India, at least, any poor man has a certain amount of land – can utilize that for Kṛṣṇa by growing flowers to offer Him. One can sow *tulasī* plants, because *tulasī* leaves are very important and Kṛṣṇa has recommended this in *Bhagavad-gītā. Patraṁ puṣpaṁ phalaṁ toyam.* Kṛṣṇa desires that one offer Him either a leaf, or a flower, or fruit, or a little water – and by such an offering He is satisfied. This leaf especially refers to the *tulasī.* So one can sow *tulasī* and pour water on the plant. Thus, even the poorest man can engage in the service of Kṛṣṇa. These are some of the examples of how one can engage in working for Kṛṣṇa.

The word *mat-paramaḥ* refers to one who considers the association of Kṛṣṇa in His supreme abode to be the highest perfection of life. Such a person does not wish to be elevated to the higher planets such as the moon or sun or heavenly planets, or even the highest planet of this universe, Brahmaloka. He has no attraction for that. He is only attracted to being transferred to the spiritual sky. And even in the spiritual sky he is not satisfied with merging into the glowing *brahma-jyotir* effulgence, for he wants to enter the highest spiritual planet, namely Kṛṣṇaloka, Goloka Vṛndāvana. He has full knowledge of that planet, and therefore he is not interested in any other. As indicated by the word *mad-bhaktaḥ,* he fully engages in devotional service, specifically in the nine processes of devotional engagement: hearing, chanting, remembering, worshiping, serving the lotus feet of the Lord, offering prayers, carrying out the orders of the Lord, making friends with Him, and surrendering everything to Him. One can engage in all nine devotional processes, or eight, or seven, or at least in one, and that will surely make one perfect.

The term *saṅga-varjitaḥ* is very significant. One should disassociate himself from persons who are against Kṛṣṇa. Not only are the atheistic persons against Kṛṣṇa, but so also are those who are attracted to fruitive activities and mental speculation. Therefore the pure form of devotional service is described in *Bhakti-rasāmṛta-sindhu* (1.1.11) as follows:

anyābhilāṣitā-śūnyaṁ, jñāna-karmādy-anāvṛtam
ānukūlyena kṛṣṇānu-, śīlanaṁ bhaktir uttamā

In this verse Śrīla Rūpa Gosvāmī clearly states that if anyone wants to execute unalloyed devotional service, he must be freed from all kinds of material contamination. He must be freed from the association of persons who are addicted to fruitive activities and mental speculation. When, freed from such unwanted association and from the contamination of material desires, one favorably cultivates knowledge of Kṛṣṇa, that is called pure devotional service. *Ānukūlyasya saṅkalpaḥ prātikūlyasya varjanam* (*Hari-bhakti-vilāsa* 11.676). One should think of Kṛṣṇa and act for Kṛṣṇa favorably, not unfavorably. Kaṁsa was an enemy of Kṛṣṇa's. From the very beginning of Kṛṣṇa's birth, Kaṁsa planned in so many ways to kill Him, and because he was always unsuccessful, he was always thinking of Kṛṣṇa. Thus while working, while eating and while sleeping, he was always Kṛṣṇa conscious in every respect, but that Kṛṣṇa consciousness was not favorable, and therefore in spite of his always thinking of Kṛṣṇa twenty-four hours a day, he was considered a demon, and Kṛṣṇa at last killed him. Of course anyone who is killed by Kṛṣṇa attains salvation immediately, but that is not the aim of the pure devotee. The pure devotee does not even want salvation. He does not want to be transferred even to the highest planet, Goloka Vṛndāvana. His only objective is to serve Kṛṣṇa wherever he may be.

A devotee of Kṛṣṇa is friendly to everyone. Therefore it is said here that he has no enemy (*nirvairaḥ*). How is this? A devotee situated in Kṛṣṇa consciousness knows that only devotional service to Kṛṣṇa can relieve a person from all the problems of life. He has personal experience of this, and therefore he wants to introduce this system, Kṛṣṇa consciousness, into human society. There are many examples in history of devotees of the Lord who risked their lives for the spreading of God consciousness. The favorite example is Lord Jesus Christ. He was crucified by the nondevotees, but he sacrificed his life for spreading God consciousness. Of course, it would be superficial to understand that he was killed. Similarly, in India also there are many examples, such as Ṭhākura Haridāsa and Prahlāda Mahārāja. Why such risk? Because they wanted to spread Kṛṣṇa consciousness, and it is difficult. A Kṛṣṇa conscious person knows that if a man is suffering it is due to his forgetfulness of his eternal relationship with Kṛṣṇa. Therefore, the highest benefit one can render to human society is relieving one's neighbor from all material problems. In such a way, a pure devotee is engaged in the service of the Lord. Now, we can imagine how merciful Kṛṣṇa is to those engaged in His service, risking everything for Him. Therefore it is certain that such persons must reach the supreme planet after leaving the body.

In summary, the universal form of Kṛṣṇa, which is a temporary manifestation, and the form of time which devours everything, and even the form of Viṣṇu, four-handed, have all been exhibited by Kṛṣṇa. Thus Kṛṣṇa is the origin of all these manifestations. It is not that Kṛṣṇa is a manifestation of the original *viśva-rūpa,* or Viṣṇu. Kṛṣṇa is the origin of all forms. There are hundreds and thousands of Viṣṇus, but for a devotee no form of Kṛṣṇa is important but the original form, two-handed Śyāmasundara. In the *Brahma-saṁhitā* it is stated that those who are attached to the Śyāmasundara form of Kṛṣṇa in love and devotion can see Him always within the heart and cannot see anything else. One should understand, therefore, that the purport of this Eleventh Chapter is that the form of Kṛṣṇa is essential and supreme.

Thus end the Bhaktivedanta Purports to the Eleventh Chapter of the Śrīmad Bhagavad-gītā *in the matter of the Universal Form.*

CHAPTER TWELVE

Devotional Service

Text 1 अर्जुन उवाच
एवं सततयुक्ता ये भक्तास्त्वां पर्युपासते ।
ये चाप्यक्षरमव्यक्तं तेषां के योगवित्तमाः ॥ १ ॥

arjuna uvāca
evaṁ satata-yuktā ye, bhaktās tvāṁ paryupāsate
ye cāpy akṣaram avyaktaṁ, teṣāṁ ke yoga-vittamāḥ

arjunaḥ uvāca – Arjuna said; *evam* – thus; *satata* – always; *yuktāḥ* – engaged; *ye* – those who; *bhaktāḥ* – devotees; *tvām* – You; *paryupāsate* – properly worship; *ye* – those who; *ca* – also; *api* – again; *akṣaram* – beyond the senses; *avyaktam* – the unmanifested; *teṣām* – of them; *ke* – who; *yoga-vit-tamāḥ* – the most perfect in knowledge of *yoga*.

Arjuna inquired: Which are considered to be more perfect, those who are always properly engaged in Your devotional service or those who worship the impersonal Brahman, the unmanifested?

PURPORT: Kṛṣṇa has now explained about the personal, the impersonal and the universal and has described all kinds of devotees and *yogīs*. Generally, the transcendentalists can be divided into two classes. One is the impersonalist, and the other is the personalist. The personalist devotee engages himself with all energy in the service of the Supreme Lord. The impersonalist also engages himself, not directly in the service of Kṛṣṇa but in meditation on the impersonal Brahman, the unmanifested.

We find in this chapter that of the different processes for realization of the Absolute Truth, *bhakti-yoga,* devotional service, is the highest. If one at all desires to have the association of the Supreme Personality of Godhead, then he must take to devotional service.

Those who worship the Supreme Lord directly by devotional service are called personalists. Those who engage themselves in meditation on the impersonal Brahman are called impersonalists. Arjuna is here questioning which position is better. There are different ways to realize the Absolute Truth, but Kṛṣṇa indicates in this chapter that *bhakti-yoga,* or devotional service to Him, is the highest of all. It is the most direct, and it is the easiest means for association with the Godhead.

In the Second Chapter of *Bhagavad-gītā,* the Supreme Lord explained that a living entity is not the material body; he is a spiritual spark. And the Absolute Truth is the spiritual whole. In the Seventh Chapter He spoke of the living entity as being part and parcel of the supreme whole and recommended that he transfer his attention fully to the whole. Then again in the Eighth Chapter it was said that anyone who thinks of Kṛṣṇa at the time of quitting his body is at once transferred to the spiritual sky, to the abode of Kṛṣṇa. And at the end of the Sixth Chapter the Lord clearly said that of all *yogīs,* one who always thinks of Kṛṣṇa within himself is considered the most perfect. So in practically every chapter the conclusion has been that one should be attached to the personal form of Kṛṣṇa, for that is the highest spiritual realization.

Nevertheless, there are those who are not attached to the personal form of Kṛṣṇa. They are so firmly detached that even in the preparation of commentaries to *Bhagavad-gītā* they want to distract other people from Kṛṣṇa and transfer all devotion to the impersonal *brahma-jyotir.* They prefer to meditate on the impersonal form of the Absolute Truth, which is beyond the reach of the senses and is not manifest.

And so, factually, there are two classes of transcendentalists. Now Arjuna is trying to settle the question of which process is easier and which of the classes is most perfect. In other words, he is clarifying his own position because he is attached to the personal form of Kṛṣṇa. He is not attached to the impersonal Brahman. He wants to know whether his position is secure. The impersonal manifestation, either in this material world or in the spiritual world of the Supreme Lord, is a problem for meditation. Actually, one cannot perfectly conceive of the impersonal feature of the Absolute Truth. Therefore Arjuna wants to say, "What is the use of such a waste of time?" Arjuna experienced in the Eleventh Chapter that to be attached to the personal form of Kṛṣṇa is best because he could thus understand all other forms at the same time and there was no disturbance to his love for Kṛṣṇa. This important question asked of Kṛṣṇa by Arjuna will clarify the distinction between the impersonal and personal conceptions of the Absolute Truth.

Text 2 श्रीभगवानुवाच
मय्यावेश्य मनो ये मां नित्ययुक्ता उपासते ।
श्रद्धया परयोपेतास्ते मे युक्ततमा मताः ॥ २ ॥

śrī-bhagavān uvāca
mayy āveśya mano ye māṁ, nitya-yuktā upāsate
śraddhayā parayopetās, te me yukta-tamā matāḥ

śrī-bhagavān uvāca – the Supreme Personality of Godhead said; *mayi* – upon Me; *āveśya* – fixing; *manah* – the mind; *ye* – those who; *mām* – Me; *nitya* – always; *yuktāḥ* – engaged; *upāsate* – worship; *śraddhayā* – with faith; *parayā* – transcendental; *upetāḥ* – endowed; *te* – they; *me* – by Me; *yukta-tamāḥ* – most perfect in *yoga; matāḥ* – are considered.

The Supreme Personality of Godhead said: Those who fix their minds on My personal form and are always engaged in worshiping Me with great and transcendental faith are considered by Me to be most perfect.

PURPORT: In answer to Arjuna's question, Kṛṣṇa clearly says that he who concentrates upon His personal form and who worships Him with faith and devotion is to be considered most perfect in *yoga.* For one in such Kṛṣṇa consciousness there are no material activities, because everything is done for Kṛṣṇa. A pure devotee is constantly engaged. Sometimes he chants, sometimes he hears or reads books about Kṛṣṇa, or sometimes he cooks *prasādam* or goes to the marketplace to purchase something for Kṛṣṇa, or sometimes he washes the temple or the dishes – whatever he does, he does not let a single moment pass without devoting his activities to Kṛṣṇa. Such action is in full *samādhi.*

Texts 3–4 ये त्वक्षरमनिर्देश्यमव्यक्तं पर्युपासते ।
सर्वत्रगमचिन्त्यं च कूटस्थमचलं ध्रुवम् ॥ ३ ॥
सन्नियम्येन्द्रियग्रामं सर्वत्र समबुद्धयः ।
ते प्राप्नुवन्ति मामेव सर्वभूतहिते रताः ॥ ४ ॥

ye tv akṣaram anirdeśyam, avyaktaṁ paryupāsate
sarvatra-gam acintyaṁ ca, kūṭa-stham acalaṁ dhruvam

sanniyamyendriya-grāmaṁ, sarvatra sama-buddhayaḥ
te prāpnuvanti mām eva, sarva-bhūta-hite ratāḥ

ye – those who; *tu* – but; *akṣaram* – that which is beyond the perception of the senses; *anirdeśyam* – indefinite; *avyaktam* – unmanifested; *paryupāsate* – completely engage in worshiping; *sarvatra-gam* – all-pervading; *acintyam* – inconceivable; *ca* – also; *kūṭa-stham* – unchanging; *acalam* – immovable; *dhruvam* – fixed; *sanniyamya* – controlling; *indriya-grāmam* – all the senses; *sarvatra* – everywhere; *sama-buddhayaḥ* – equally disposed; *te* – they; *prāpnuvanti* – achieve; *mām* – Me; *eva* – certainly; *sarva-bhūta-hite* – for the welfare of all living entities; *ratāḥ* – engaged.

But those who fully worship the unmanifested, that which lies beyond the perception of the senses, the all-pervading, inconceivable, unchanging, fixed and immovable – the impersonal conception of the Absolute Truth – by controlling the various senses and being equally disposed to everyone, such persons, engaged in the welfare of all, at last achieve Me.

PURPORT: Those who do not directly worship the Supreme Godhead, Kṛṣṇa, but who attempt to achieve the same goal by an indirect process, also ultimately achieve the same goal, Śrī Kṛṣṇa. "After many births the man of wisdom seeks refuge in Me, knowing that Vāsudeva is all." When a person comes to full knowledge after many births, he surrenders unto Lord Kṛṣṇa. If one approaches the Godhead by the method mentioned in this verse, he has to control the senses, render service to everyone and engage in the welfare of all beings. It is inferred that one has to approach Lord Kṛṣṇa, otherwise there is no perfect realization. Often there is much penance involved before one fully surrenders unto Him.

In order to perceive the Supersoul within the individual soul, one has to cease the sensual activities of seeing, hearing, tasting, working, etc. Then one comes to understand that the Supreme Soul is present everywhere. Realizing this, one envies no living entity – he sees no difference between man and animal because he sees soul only, not the outer covering. But for the common man, this method of impersonal realization is very difficult.

Text 5 क्लेशोऽधिकतरस्तेषामव्यक्तासक्तचेतसाम् ।
अव्यक्ता हि गतिर्दुःखं देहवद्भिरवाप्यते ॥ ५ ॥

kleśo 'dhika-taras teṣām, avyaktāsakta-cetasām
avyaktā hi gatir duḥkhaṁ, dehavadbhir avāpyate

kleśaḥ – trouble; *adhika-taraḥ* – very much; *teṣām* – of them; *avyakta* – to the unmanifested; *āsakta* – attached; *cetasām* – of those whose minds; *avyaktā* – toward the unmanifested; *hi* – certainly; *gatiḥ* – progress; *duḥkham* – with trouble; *deha-vadbhiḥ* – by the embodied; *avāpyate* – is achieved.

For those whose minds are attached to the unmanifested, impersonal feature of the Supreme, advancement is very troublesome. To make progress in that discipline is always difficult for those who are embodied.

PURPORT: The group of transcendentalists who follow the path of the inconceivable, unmanifested, impersonal feature of the Supreme Lord are called *jñāna-yogīs,* and persons who are in full Kṛṣṇa consciousness, engaged in devotional service to the Lord, are called *bhakti-yogīs.* Now, here the difference between *jñāna-yoga* and *bhakti-yoga* is definitely expressed. The process of *jñāna-yoga,* although ultimately bringing one to the same goal, is very troublesome, whereas the path of *bhakti-yoga,* the process of being in direct service to the Supreme Personality of Godhead, is easier and is natural for the embodied soul. The individual soul is embodied since time immemorial. It is very difficult for him to simply theoretically understand that he is not the body. Therefore, the *bhakti-yogī* accepts the Deity of Kṛṣṇa as worshipable because there is some bodily conception fixed in the mind, which can thus be applied. Of course, worship of the Supreme Personality of Godhead in His form within the temple is not idol worship. There is evidence in the Vedic literature that worship may be *saguṇa* or *nirguṇa* – of the Supreme possessing or not possessing attributes. Worship of the Deity in the temple is *saguṇa* worship, for the Lord is represented by material qualities. But the form of the Lord, though represented by material qualities such as stone, wood or oil paint, is not actually material. That is the absolute nature of the Supreme Lord.

A crude example may be given here. We may find some mailboxes on the street, and if we post our letters in those boxes, they will naturally go to their destination without difficulty. But any old box, or an imitation which we may find somewhere but which is not authorized by the post office, will not do the work. Similarly, God has an authorized representation in the Deity form, which is called *arcā-vigraha.* This *arcā-vigraha* is an incarnation of the Supreme Lord. God will accept service through that form. The Lord is omnipotent, all-powerful; therefore, by His incarnation as *arcā-vigraha* He can accept the services of the devotee, just to make it convenient for the man in conditioned life.

So for a devotee there is no difficulty in approaching the Supreme immediately and directly, but for those who are following the impersonal way to spiritual realization the path is difficult. They have to understand the unmanifested representation of the Supreme through such Vedic literatures as the *Upaniṣads,* and they have to learn the language, understand the nonperceptual feelings, and realize all these processes. This is not very easy for a common man. A person in Kṛṣṇa consciousness, engaged in devotional service, simply by the guidance of the bona fide spiritual master, simply by offering regulative obeisances unto the Deity, simply by hearing the glories of the Lord, and simply by eating the remnants of foodstuffs offered to the Lord, realizes the Supreme Personality of Godhead very easily. There is no doubt that the impersonalists are unnecessarily taking a troublesome path with the risk of not realizing the Absolute Truth at the ultimate end. But the personalist, without any risk, trouble or difficulty, approaches the Supreme Personality directly. A similar passage appears in *Śrīmad-Bhāgavatam.* It is stated there that if one ultimately has to surrender unto the Supreme Personality of Godhead (this surrendering process is called *bhakti*), but instead takes the trouble to understand what is Brahman and what is not Brahman and spends his whole life in that way, the result is simply troublesome. Therefore it is advised here that one should not take up this troublesome path of self-realization, because there is uncertainty in the ultimate result.

A living entity is eternally an individual soul, and if he wants to merge into the spiritual whole, he may accomplish the realization of the eternal and knowledgeable aspects of his original nature, but the blissful portion is not realized. By the grace of some devotee, such a transcendentalist, highly learned in the process of *jñāna-yoga,* may come to the point of *bhakti-yoga,* or devotional service. At that time, long practice in impersonalism also becomes a source of trouble, because he cannot give up the idea. Therefore an embodied soul is always in difficulty with the unmanifest, both at the time of practice and at the time of realization. Every living soul is partially independent, and one should know for certain that this unmanifested realization is against the nature of his spiritual blissful self. One should not take up this process. For every individual living entity the process of Kṛṣṇa consciousness, which entails full engagement in devotional service, is the best way. If one wants to ignore this devotional service, there is the danger of turning to atheism. Thus the process of centering attention on the unmanifested, the inconceivable, which is beyond the approach of the senses, as already expressed in this verse, should never be encouraged at any time, especially in this age. It is not advised by Lord Kṛṣṇa.

Texts 6–7

ये तु सर्वाणि कर्माणि मयि सन्न्यस्य मत्पराः ।
अनन्येनैव योगेन मां ध्यायन्त उपासते ॥ ६ ॥
तेषामहं समुद्धर्ता मृत्युसंसारसागरात् ।
भवामि न चिरात्पार्थ मय्यावेशितचेतसाम् ॥ ७ ॥

ye tu sarvāṇi karmāṇi, mayi sannyasya mat-parāḥ
ananyenaiva yogena, māṁ dhyāyanta upāsate

teṣām ahaṁ samuddhartā, mṛtyu-saṁsāra-sāgarāt
bhavāmi na cirāt pārtha, mayy āveśita-cetasām

ye – those who; *tu* – but; *sarvāṇi* – all; *karmāṇi* – activities; *mayi* – unto Me; *sannyasya* – giving up; *mat-parāḥ* – being attached to Me; *ananyena* – without division; *eva* – certainly; *yogena* – by practice of such *bhakti-yoga; mām* – upon Me; *dhyāyantaḥ* – meditating; *upāsate* – worship; *teṣām* – of them; *aham* – I; *samuddhartā* – the deliverer; *mṛtyu* – of death; *saṁsāra* – in material existence; *sāgarāt* – from the ocean; *bhavāmi* – I become; *na* – not; *cirāt* – after a long time; *pārtha* – O son of Pṛthā; *mayi* – upon Me; *āveśita* – fixed; *cetasām* – of those whose minds.

But those who worship Me, giving up all their activities unto Me and being devoted to Me without deviation, engaged in devotional service and always meditating upon Me, having fixed their minds upon Me, O son of Pṛthā – for them I am the swift deliverer from the ocean of birth and death.

PURPORT: It is explicitly stated here that the devotees are very fortunate to be delivered very soon from material existence by the Lord. In pure devotional service one comes to the realization that God is great and that the individual soul is subordinate to Him. His duty is to render service to the Lord – and if he does not, then he will render service to *māyā.*

As stated before, the Supreme Lord can be appreciated only by devotional service. Therefore, one should be fully devoted. One should fix his mind fully on Kṛṣṇa in order to achieve Him. One should work only for Kṛṣṇa. It does not matter in what kind of work one engages, but that work should be done only for Kṛṣṇa. That is the standard of devotional service. The devotee does not desire any achievement other than pleasing the Supreme Personality of Godhead. His life's mission is to please Kṛṣṇa, and he can sacrifice everything for Kṛṣṇa's satisfaction, just as Arjuna did in the Battle of Kurukṣetra. The process is very simple: one can devote himself in his occupation and engage at the same time in chanting Hare Kṛṣṇa, Hare Kṛṣṇa, Kṛṣṇa Kṛṣṇa, Hare Hare/ Hare Rāma, Hare Rāma, Rāma Rāma, Hare Hare. Such transcendental chanting attracts the devotee to the Personality of Godhead.

The Supreme Lord herein promises that without delay He will deliver a pure devotee thus engaged from the ocean of material existence. Those who are advanced in *yoga* practice can willfully transfer the soul to whatever planet they like by the *yoga* process, and others take the opportunity in various ways, but as far as the devotee is concerned, it is clearly stated here that the Lord Himself takes him. The devotee does not need to wait to become very experienced in order to transfer himself to the spiritual sky.

In the *Varāha Purāṇa* this verse appears:

nayāmi paramaṁ sthānam, arcir-ādi-gatiṁ vinā
garuḍa-skandham āropya, yatheccham anivāritaḥ

The purport of this verse is that a devotee does not need to practice *aṣṭāṅga-yoga* in order to transfer his soul to the spiritual planets. The responsibility is taken by the Supreme Lord Himself. He clearly states here that He Himself becomes the deliverer. A child is completely cared for by his parents, and thus his position is secure. Similarly, a devotee does not need to endeavor to transfer himself by *yoga* practice to other planets. Rather, the Supreme Lord, by His great mercy, comes at once, riding on His bird carrier Garuḍa, and at once delivers the devotee from material existence. Although a man who has fallen in the ocean may struggle very hard and may be very expert in swimming, he cannot save himself. But if someone comes and picks him up from the water, then he is easily rescued. Similarly, the Lord picks up the devotee from this material existence. One simply has to practice the easy process of Kṛṣṇa consciousness and fully engage himself in devotional service. Any intelligent man should always prefer the process of devotional service to all other paths. In the *Nārāyaṇīya* this is confirmed as follows:

yā vai sādhana-sampattiḥ, puruṣārtha-catuṣṭaye
tayā vinā tad āpnoti, naro nārāyaṇāśrayaḥ

The purport of this verse is that one should not engage in the different processes of fruitive activity or cultivate knowledge by the mental speculative process. One who is devoted to the Supreme Personality can attain all the benefits derived from other yogic processes, speculation, rituals, sacrifices, charities, etc. That is the specific benediction of devotional service.

Simply by chanting the holy name of Kṛṣṇa – Hare Kṛṣṇa, Hare Kṛṣṇa, Kṛṣṇa Kṛṣṇa, Hare Hare/ Hare Rāma, Hare Rāma, Rāma Rāma, Hare Hare – a devotee of the Lord can approach the supreme destination easily and happily, but this destination cannot be approached by any other process of religion.

The conclusion of *Bhagavad-gītā* is stated in the Eighteenth Chapter:

sarva-dharmān parityajya, māṁ ekaṁ śaraṇaṁ vraja
ahaṁ tvāṁ sarva-pāpebhyo, mokṣayiṣyāmi mā śucaḥ

One should give up all other processes of self-realization and simply execute devotional service in Kṛṣṇa consciousness. That will enable one to reach the highest perfection of life. There is no need for one to consider the sinful actions of his past life, because the Supreme Lord fully takes charge of him. Therefore one should not futilely try to deliver himself in spiritual realization. Let everyone take shelter of the supreme omnipotent Godhead, Kṛṣṇa. That is the highest perfection of life.

Text 8 मय्येव मन आधत्स्व मयि बुद्धिं निवेशय ।
निवसिष्यसि मय्येव अत ऊर्ध्वं न संशयः ॥ ८ ॥

mayy eva mana ādhatsva, mayi buddhiṁ niveśaya
nivasiṣyasi mayy eva, ata ūrdhvaṁ na saṁśayaḥ

mayi – upon Me; *eva* – certainly; *manaḥ* – mind; *ādhatsva* – fix; *mayi* – upon Me; *buddhim* – intelligence; *niveśaya* – apply; *nivasiṣyasi* – you will live; *mayi* – in Me; *eva* – certainly; *ataḥ ūrdhvam* – thereafter; *na* – never; *saṁśayaḥ* – doubt.

Just fix your mind upon Me, the Supreme Personality of Godhead, and engage all your intelligence in Me. Thus you will live in Me always, without a doubt.

PURPORT: One who is engaged in Lord Kṛṣṇa's devotional service lives in a direct relationship with the Supreme Lord, so there is no doubt that his position is transcendental from the very beginning. A devotee does not live on the material plane – he lives in Kṛṣṇa. The holy name of the Lord and the Lord are nondifferent; therefore when a devotee chants Hare Kṛṣṇa, Kṛṣṇa and His internal potency are dancing on the tongue of the devotee. When he offers Kṛṣṇa food, Kṛṣṇa directly accepts these eatables, and the devotee becomes Kṛṣṇa-ized by eating the remnants. One who does not engage in such service cannot understand how this is so, although this is a process recommended in the *Bhagavad-gītā* and in other Vedic literatures.

Text 9 अथ चित्तं समाधातुं न शक्नोषि मयि स्थिरम् ।
अभ्यासयोगेन ततो मामिच्छाप्तुं धनञ्जय ॥ ९ ॥

atha cittaṁ samādhātuṁ, na śaknoṣi mayi sthiram
abhyāsa-yogena tato, mām icchāptuṁ dhanañ-jaya

atha – if, therefore; *cittam* – mind; *samādhātum* – to fix; *na* – not; *śaknoṣi* – you are able; *mayi* – upon Me; *sthiram* – steadily; *abhyāsa-yogena* – by the practice of devotional service; *tataḥ* – then; *mām* – Me; *icchā* – desire; *āptum* – to get; *dhanam-jaya* – O winner of wealth, Arjuna.

My dear Arjuna, O winner of wealth, if you cannot fix your mind upon Me without deviation, then follow the regulative principles of bhakti-yoga. In this way develop a desire to attain Me.

PURPORT: In this verse, two different processes of *bhakti-yoga* are indicated. The first applies to one who has actually developed an attachment for Kṛṣṇa, the Supreme Personality of Godhead, by transcendental love. And the other is for one who has not developed an attachment for the Supreme Person by transcendental love. For this second class there are different prescribed rules and regulations one can follow to be ultimately elevated to the stage of attachment to Kṛṣṇa.

Bhakti-yoga is the purification of the senses. At the present moment in material existence the senses are always impure, being engaged in sense gratification. But by the practice of *bhakti-yoga* these senses can become purified, and in the purified state they come directly in contact with the Supreme Lord. In this material existence, I may be engaged in some service to some master, but I don't really lovingly serve my master. I simply serve to get some money. And the master also is not in love; he takes service from me and pays me. So there is no question of love. But for spiritual life, one must be elevated to the pure stage of love. That stage of love can be achieved by practice of devotional service, performed with the present senses.

This love of God is now in a dormant state in everyone's heart. And, there, love of God is manifested in different ways, but it is contaminated by material association. Now the heart has to be purified of the material association, and that dormant, natural love for Kṛṣṇa has to be revived. That is the whole process.

To practice the regulative principles of *bhakti-yoga* one should, under the guidance of an expert spiritual master, follow certain principles: one should rise early in the morning, take bath, enter the temple and offer prayers and chant Hare Kṛṣṇa, then collect flowers to offer to the Deity, cook foodstuffs to offer to the Deity, take *prasādam,* and so on. There are various rules and regulations which one should follow. And one should constantly hear *Bhagavad-gītā* and *Śrīmad-Bhāgavatam* from pure devotees. This practice can help anyone rise to the level of love of God, and then he is sure of his progress into the spiritual kingdom of God. This practice of *bhakti-yoga,* under the rules and regulations, with the direction of a spiritual master, will surely bring one to the stage of love of God.

Text 10 अभ्यासेऽप्यसमर्थोऽसि मत्कर्मपरमो भव ।
मदर्थमपि कर्माणि कुर्वन् सिद्धिमवाप्स्यसि ॥१०॥

abhyāse 'py asamartho 'si, mat-karma-paramo bhava
mad-artham api karmāṇi, kurvan siddhim avāpsyasi

abhyāse – in practice; *api* – even if; *asamarthaḥ* – unable; *asi* – you are; *mat-karma* – My work; *paramaḥ* – dedicated to; *bhava* – become; *mat-artham* – for My sake; *api* – even; *karmāṇi* – work; *kurvan* – performing; *siddhim* – perfection; *avāpsyasi* – you will achieve.

If you cannot practice the regulations of bhakti-yoga, then just try to work for Me, because by working for Me you will come to the perfect stage.

PURPORT: One who is not able even to practice the regulative principles of *bhakti-yoga,* under the guidance of a spiritual master, can still be drawn to this perfectional stage by working for the Supreme Lord. How to do this work has already been explained in the fifty-fifth verse of the Eleventh Chapter. One should be sympathetic to the propagation of

Kṛṣṇa consciousness. There are many devotees who are engaged in the propagation of Kṛṣṇa consciousness, and they require help. So, even if one cannot directly practice the regulative principles of *bhakti-yoga,* he can try to help such work. Every endeavor requires land, capital, organization and labor. Just as in business one requires a place to stay, some capital to use, some labor and some organization to expand, so the same is required in the service of Kṛṣṇa. The only difference is that in materialism one works for sense gratification. The same work, however, can be performed for the satisfaction of Kṛṣṇa, and that is spiritual activity. If one has sufficient money, he can help in building an office or temple for propagating Kṛṣṇa consciousness. Or he can help with publications. There are various fields of activity, and one should be interested in such activities. If one cannot sacrifice the results of his activities, the same person can still sacrifice some percentage to propagate Kṛṣṇa consciousness. This voluntary service to the cause of Kṛṣṇa consciousness will help one to rise to a higher state of love for God, whereupon one becomes perfect.

Text 11 अथैतदप्यशक्तोऽसि कर्तुं मद्योगमाश्रितः ।
सर्वकर्मफलत्यागं ततः कुरु यतात्मवान् ॥११॥

athaitad apy aśakto 'si, kartuṁ mad-yogam āśritaḥ
sarva-karma-phala-tyāgaṁ, tataḥ kuru yatātmavān

atha – even though; *etat* – this; *api* – also; *aśaktaḥ* – unable; *asi* – you are; *kartum* – to perform; *mat* – unto Me; *yogam* – in devotional service; *āśritaḥ* – taking refuge; *sarva-karma* – of all activities; *phala* – of the results; *tyāgam* – renunciation; *tataḥ* – then; *kuru* – do; *yata-ātma-vān* – self-situated.

If, however, you are unable to work in this consciousness of Me, then try to act giving up all results of your work and try to be self-situated.

PURPORT: It may be that one is unable even to sympathize with the activities of Kṛṣṇa consciousness because of social, familial or religious considerations or because of some other impediments. If one attaches himself directly to the activities of Kṛṣṇa consciousness, there may be objections from family members, or so many other difficulties. For one who has such a problem, it is advised that he sacrifice the accumulated result of his activities to some good cause. Such procedures are described in the Vedic rules. There are many descriptions of sacrifices and special functions for the full-moon day, and there is special work in which the result of one's previous action may be applied. Thus one may gradually become elevated to the state of knowledge. It is also found that when one who is not even interested in the activities of Kṛṣṇa consciousness gives charity to some hospital or some other social institution, he gives up the hard-earned results of his activities. That is also recommended here because by the practice of giving up the fruits of one's activities one is sure to purify his mind gradually, and in that purified stage of mind one becomes able to understand Kṛṣṇa consciousness. Of course, Kṛṣṇa consciousness is not dependent on any other experience, because Kṛṣṇa consciousness itself can purify one's mind, but if there are impediments to accepting Kṛṣṇa consciousness, one may try to give up the results of his actions. In that respect, social service, community service, national service, sacrifice for one's country, etc., may be accepted so that some day one may come to the stage of pure devotional service to the Supreme Lord. In *Bhagavad-gītā* (18.46) we find it is stated, *yataḥ pravṛttir bhūtānām:* if one decides to sacrifice for the supreme cause, even if he does not know that the supreme cause is Kṛṣṇa, he will come gradually to understand that Kṛṣṇa is the supreme cause by the sacrificial method.

Text 12 श्रेयो हि ज्ञानमभ्यासाज्ज्ञानाद्ध्यानं विशिष्यते ।
ध्यानात्कर्मफलत्यागस्त्यागाच्छान्तिरनन्तरम् ॥१२॥

śreyo hi jñānam abhyāsāj, jñānād dhyānaṁ viśiṣyate
dhyānāt karma-phala-tyāgas, tyāgāc chāntir anantaram

śreyaḥ – better; *hi* – certainly; *jñānam* – knowledge; *abhyāsāt* – than practice; *jñānāt* – than knowledge; *dhyānam* – meditation; *viśiṣyate* – is considered better; *dhyānāt* – than meditation; *karma-phala-tyāgaḥ* – renunciation of the results of fruitive action; *tyāgāt* – by such renunciation; *śāntiḥ* – peace; *anantaram* – thereafter.

If you cannot take to this practice, then engage yourself in the cultivation of knowledge. Better than knowledge, however, is meditation, and better than meditation is renunciation of the fruits of action, for by such renunciation one can attain peace of mind.

PURPORT: As mentioned in the previous verses, there are two kinds of devotional service: the way of regulative principles and the way of full attachment in love to the Supreme Personality of Godhead. For those who are actually not able to follow the principles of Kṛṣṇa consciousness it is better to cultivate knowledge, because by knowledge one can be able to understand his real position. Gradually knowledge will develop to the point of meditation. By meditation one can be able to understand the Supreme Personality of Godhead by a gradual process. There are processes which make one understand that one himself is the Supreme, and that sort of meditation is preferred if one is unable to engage in devotional service. If one is not able to meditate in such a way, then there are prescribed duties, as enjoined in the Vedic literature, for the *brāhmaṇas, kṣatriyas, vaiśyas* and *śūdras,* which we shall find in the last chapter of *Bhagavad-gītā.* But in all cases, one should give up the result or fruits of labor; this means to employ the result of *karma* for some good cause.

In summary, to reach the Supreme Personality of Godhead, the highest goal, there are two processes: one process is by gradual development, and the other process is direct. Devotional service in Kṛṣṇa consciousness is the direct method, and the other method involves renouncing the fruits of one's activities. Then one can come to the stage of knowledge, then to the stage of meditation, then to the stage of understanding the Supersoul, and then to the stage of the Supreme Personality of Godhead. One may take either the step-by-step process or the direct path. The direct process is not possible for everyone; therefore the indirect process is also good. It is, however, to be understood that the indirect process is not recommended for Arjuna, because he is already at the stage of loving devotional service to the Supreme Lord. It is for others, who are not at this stage; for them the gradual process of renunciation, knowledge, meditation and realization of the Supersoul and Brahman should be followed. But as far as *Bhagavad-gītā* is concerned, it is the direct method that is stressed. Everyone is advised to take to the direct method and surrender unto the Supreme Personality of Godhead, Kṛṣṇa.

Texts 13–14

अद्वेष्टा सर्वभूतानां मैत्रः करुण एव च ।
निर्ममो निरहङ्कारः समदुःखसुखः क्षमी ॥१३॥
सन्तुष्टः सततं योगी यतात्मा दृढनिश्चयः ।
मय्यर्पितमनोबुद्धिर्यो मद्भक्तः स मे प्रियः ॥१४॥

adveṣṭā sarva-bhūtānāṁ, maitraḥ karuṇa eva ca
nirmamo nirahaṅkāraḥ, sama-duḥkha-sukhaḥ kṣamī
santuṣṭaḥ satataṁ yogī, yatātmā dṛḍha-niścayaḥ
mayy arpita-mano-buddhir, yo mad-bhaktaḥ sa me priyaḥ

adveṣṭā – nonenvious; *sarva-bhūtānām* – toward all living entities; *maitraḥ* – friendly; *karuṇaḥ* – kindly; *eva* – certainly; *ca* – also; *nirmamaḥ* – with no sense of proprietorship; *nirahaṅkāraḥ* – without false ego; *sama* – equal; *duḥkha* – in distress; *sukhaḥ* – and happiness; *kṣamī* – forgiving; *santuṣṭaḥ* – satisfied; *satatam* – always; *yogī* – one engaged in devotion; *yata-ātmā* – self-controlled; *dṛḍha-niścayaḥ* – with determination; *mayi* – upon Me; *arpita* – engaged; *manaḥ* – mind; *buddhiḥ* – and intelligence; *yaḥ* – one who; *mat-bhaktaḥ* – My devotee; *saḥ* – he; *me* – to Me; *priyaḥ* – dear.

One who is not envious but is a kind friend to all living entities, who does not think himself a proprietor and is free from false ego, who is equal in both happiness and distress, who is tolerant, always satisfied, self-controlled, and engaged in devotional service with determination, his mind and intelligence fixed on Me – such a devotee of Mine is very dear to Me.

PURPORT: Coming again to the point of pure devotional service, the Lord is describing the transcendental qualifications of a pure devotee in these two verses. A pure devotee is never disturbed in any circumstances. Nor is he envious of anyone. Nor does a devotee become his enemy's enemy; he thinks, "This person is acting as my enemy due to my own past misdeeds. So it is better to suffer than to protest." In the *Śrīmad-Bhāgavatam* (10.14.8) it is stated: *tat te 'nukampāṁ su-samīkṣamāṇo bhuñjāna evātma-kṛtaṁ vipākam.* Whenever a devotee is in distress or has fallen into difficulty, he thinks that it is the Lord's mercy upon him. He thinks, "Thanks to my past misdeeds I should suffer far, far greater than I am suffering now. So it is by the mercy of the Supreme Lord that I am not getting all the punishment I am due. I am just getting a little, by the mercy of the Supreme Personality of Godhead." Therefore he is always calm, quiet and patient, despite many distressful conditions. A devotee is also always kind to everyone, even to his enemy. *Nirmama* means that a devotee does not attach much importance to the pains and trouble pertaining to the body because he knows perfectly well that he is not the material body. He does not identify with the body; therefore he is freed from the conception of false ego and is equipoised in happiness and distress. He is tolerant, and he is satisfied with whatever comes by the grace of the Supreme Lord. He does not endeavor much to achieve something with great difficulty; therefore he is always joyful. He is a completely perfect mystic because he is fixed in the instructions received from the spiritual master, and because his senses are controlled he is determined. He is not swayed by false arguments, because no one can lead him from the fixed determination of devotional service. He is fully conscious that Kṛṣṇa is the eternal Lord, so no one can disturb him. All these qualifications enable him to fix his mind and intelligence entirely on the Supreme Lord. Such a standard of devotional service is undoubtedly very rare, but a devotee becomes situated in that stage by following the regulative principles of devotional service. Furthermore, the Lord says that such a devotee is very dear to Him, for the Lord is always pleased with all his activities in full Kṛṣṇa consciousness.

Text 15 यस्मान्नोद्विजते लोको लोकान्नोद्विजते च यः ।
हर्षामर्षभयोद्वेगैर्मुक्तो यः स च मे प्रियः ॥१५॥

yasmān nodvijate loko, lokān nodvijate ca yaḥ
harṣāmarṣa-bhayodvegair, mukto yaḥ sa ca me priyaḥ

yasmāt – from whom; *na* – never; *udvijate* – are agitated; *lokaḥ* – people; *lokāt* – from people; *na* – never; *udvijate* – is disturbed; *ca* – also; *yaḥ* – anyone who; *harṣa* – from happiness; *amarṣa* – distress; *bhaya* – fear; *udvegaiḥ* – and anxiety; *muktaḥ* – freed; *yaḥ* – who; *saḥ* – anyone; *ca* – also; *me* – to Me; *priyaḥ* – very dear.

He by whom no one is put into difficulty and who is not disturbed by anyone, who is equipoised in happiness and distress, fear and anxiety, is very dear to Me.

PURPORT: A few of a devotee's qualifications are further being described. No one is put into difficulty, anxiety, fearfulness or dissatisfaction by such a devotee. Since a devotee is kind to everyone, he does not act in such a way as to put others into anxiety. At the same time, if others try to put a devotee into anxiety, he is not disturbed. It is by the grace of the Lord that he is so practiced that he is not disturbed by any outward disturbance. Actually because a devotee is always engrossed in Kṛṣṇa consciousness and engaged in devotional service, such material circumstances cannot move him. Generally a materialistic person becomes very happy when there is something for his sense gratification and his body, but when he sees that others have something for their sense gratification and he hasn't, he is sorry and envious. When he is expecting some retaliation from an enemy, he is in a state of fear, and when he cannot successfully execute something he becomes dejected. A devotee who is always transcendental to all these disturbances is very dear to Kṛṣṇa.

Text 16 अनपेक्षः शुचिर्दक्ष उदासीनो गतव्यथः ।
सर्वारम्भपरित्यागी यो मद्भक्तः स मे प्रियः ॥१६॥

anapekṣaḥ śucir dakṣa, udāsīno gata-vyathaḥ
sarvārambha-parityāgī, yo mad-bhaktaḥ sa me priyaḥ

anapekṣaḥ – neutral; *śuciḥ* – pure; *dakṣaḥ* – expert; *udāsīnaḥ* – free from care; *gata-vyathaḥ* – freed from all distress; *sarva-ārambha* – of all endeavors; *parityāgī* – renouncer; *yaḥ* – anyone who; *mat-bhaktaḥ* – My devotee; *saḥ* – he; *me* – to Me; *priyaḥ* – very dear.

My devotee who is not dependent on the ordinary course of activities, who is pure, expert, without cares, free from all pains, and not striving for some result, is very dear to Me.

PURPORT: Money may be offered to a devotee, but he should not struggle to acquire it. If automatically, by the grace of the Supreme, money comes to him, he is not agitated. Naturally a devotee takes a bath at least twice in a day and rises early in the morning for devotional service. Thus he is naturally clean both inwardly and outwardly. A devotee is always expert because he fully knows the essence of all activities of life and he is convinced of the authoritative scriptures. A devotee never takes the part of a particular party; therefore he is carefree. He is never pained, because he is free from all designations; he knows that his body is a designation, so if there are some bodily pains, he is free. The pure devotee does not endeavor for anything which is against the principles of devotional service. For example, constructing a big building requires great energy, and a devotee does not take to such business if it does not benefit him by advancing his devotional service. He may construct a temple for the Lord, and for that he may take all kinds of anxiety, but he does not construct a big house for his personal relations.

Text 17 यो न हृष्यति न द्वेष्टि न शोचति न काङ्क्षति ।
शुभाशुभपरित्यागी भक्तिमान् यः स मे प्रियः ॥१७॥

yo na hṛṣyati na dveṣṭi, na śocati na kāṅkṣati
śubhāśubha-parityāgī, bhaktimān yaḥ sa me priyaḥ

yaḥ – one who; *na* – never; *hṛṣyati* – takes pleasure; *na* – never; *dveṣṭi* – grieves; *na* – never; *śocati* – laments; *na* – never; *kāṅkṣati* – desires; *śubha* – of the auspicious; *aśubha* – and the inauspicious; *parityāgī* –

renouncer; *bhakti-mān* – devotee; *yaḥ* – one who; *saḥ* – he is; *me* – to Me; *priyaḥ* – dear.

One who neither rejoices nor grieves, who neither laments nor desires, and who renounces both auspicious and inauspicious things – such a devotee is very dear to Me.

PURPORT: A pure devotee is neither happy nor distressed over material gain and loss, nor is he very much anxious to get a son or disciple, nor is he distressed by not getting them. If he loses anything which is very dear to him, he does not lament. Similarly, if he does not get what he desires, he is not distressed. He is transcendental in the face of all kinds of auspicious, inauspicious and sinful activities. He is prepared to accept all kinds of risks for the satisfaction of the Supreme Lord. Nothing is an impediment in the discharge of his devotional service. Such a devotee is very dear to Kṛṣṇa.

Texts 18–19

समः शत्रौ च मित्रे च तथा मानापमानयोः ।
शीतोष्णसुखदुःखेषु समः सङ्गविवर्जितः ॥१८॥
तुल्यनिन्दास्तुतिर्मौनी सन्तुष्टो येन केनचित् ।
अनिकेतः स्थिरमतिर्भक्तिमान्मे प्रियो नरः ॥१९॥

samaḥ śatrau ca mitre ca, tathā mānāpamānayoḥ
śītoṣṇa-sukha-duḥkheṣu, samaḥ saṅga-vivarjitaḥ

tulya-nindā-stutir maunī, santuṣṭo yena kenacit
aniketaḥ sthira-matir, bhaktimān me priyo naraḥ

samaḥ – equal; *śatrau* – to an enemy; *ca* – also; *mitre* – to a friend; *ca* – also; *tathā* – so; *māna* – in honor; *apamānayoḥ* – and dishonor; *śīta* – in cold; *uṣṇa* – heat; *sukha* – happiness; *duḥkheṣu* – and distress; *samaḥ* – equipoised; *saṅga-vivarjitaḥ* – free from all association; *tulya* – equal; *nindā* – in defamation; *stutiḥ* – and repute; *maunī* – silent; *santuṣṭaḥ* – satisfied; *yena kenacit* – with anything; *aniketaḥ* – having no residence; *sthira* – fixed; *matiḥ* – determination; *bhakti-mān* – engaged in devotion; *me* – to Me; *priyaḥ* – dear; *naraḥ* – a man.

One who is equal to friends and enemies, who is equipoised in honor and dishonor, heat and cold, happiness and distress, fame and infamy, who is always free from contaminating association, always silent and satisfied with anything, who doesn't care for any residence, who is fixed

in knowledge and who is engaged in devotional service – such a person is very dear to Me.

PURPORT: A devotee is always free from all bad association. Sometimes one is praised and sometimes one is defamed; that is the nature of human society. But a devotee is always transcendental to artificial fame and infamy, distress or happiness. He is very patient. He does not speak of anything but the topics about Kṛṣṇa; therefore he is called silent. Silent does not mean that one should not speak; silent means that one should not speak nonsense. One should speak only of essentials, and the most essential speech for the devotee is to speak for the sake of the Supreme Lord. A devotee is happy in all conditions; sometimes he may get very palatable foodstuffs, sometimes not, but he is satisfied. Nor does he care for any residential facility. He may sometimes live underneath a tree, and he may sometimes live in a very palatial building; he is attracted to neither. He is called fixed because he is fixed in his determination and knowledge. We may find some repetition in the descriptions of the qualifications of a devotee, but this is just to emphasize the fact that a devotee must acquire all these qualifications. Without good qualifications, one cannot be a pure devotee. *Harāv abhaktasya kuto mahad-guṇāḥ:* one who is not a devotee has no good qualification. One who wants to be recognized as a devotee should develop the good qualifications. Of course he does not extraneously endeavor to acquire these qualifications, but engagement in Kṛṣṇa consciousness and devotional service automatically helps him develop them.

Text 20 ये तु धर्मामृतमिदं यथोक्तं पर्युपासते ।
श्रद्दधाना मत्परमा भक्तास्तेऽतीव मे प्रियाः ॥२०॥

ye tu dharmāmṛtam idaṁ, yathoktaṁ paryupāsate
śraddadhānā mat-paramā, bhaktās te 'tīva me priyāḥ

ye – those who; *tu* – but; *dharma* – of religion; *amṛtam* – nectar; *idam* – this; *yathā* – as; *uktam* – said; *paryupāsate* – completely engage; *śraddadhānāḥ* – with faith; *mat-paramāḥ* – taking Me, the Supreme Lord, as everything; *bhaktāḥ* – devotees; *te* – they; *atīva* – very, very; *me* – to Me; *priyāḥ* – dear.

Those who follow this imperishable path of devotional service and who completely engage themselves with faith, making Me the supreme goal, are very, very dear to Me.

PURPORT: In this chapter, from verse 2 through the end – from *mayy āveśya mano ye mām* ("fixing the mind on Me") through *ye tu dharmāmṛtam idam* ("this religion of eternal engagement") – the Supreme Lord has explained the processes of transcendental service for approaching Him. Such processes are very dear to the Lord, and He accepts a person engaged in them. The question of who is better – one who is engaged in the path of impersonal Brahman or one who is engaged in the personal service of the Supreme Personality of Godhead – was raised by Arjuna, and the Lord replied to him so explicitly that there is no doubt that devotional service to the Personality of Godhead is the best of all processes of spiritual realization. In other words, in this chapter it is decided that through good association one develops attachment for pure devotional service and thereby accepts a bona fide spiritual master and from him begins to hear and chant and observe the regulative principles of devotional service with faith, attachment and devotion and thus becomes engaged in the transcendental service of the Lord. This path is recommended in this chapter; therefore there is no doubt that devotional service is the only absolute path for self-realization, for the attainment of the Supreme Personality of Godhead. The impersonal conception of the Supreme Absolute Truth, as described in this chapter, is recommended only up to the time one surrenders himself for self-realization. In other words, as long as one does not have the chance to associate with a pure devotee, the impersonal conception may be beneficial. In the impersonal conception of the Absolute Truth one works without fruitive result, meditates and cultivates knowledge to understand spirit and matter. This is necessary as long as one is not in the association of a pure devotee. Fortunately, if one develops directly a desire to engage in Kṛṣṇa consciousness in pure devotional service, he does not need to undergo step-by-step improvements in spiritual realization. Devotional service, as described in the middle six chapters of *Bhagavad-gītā,* is more congenial. One need not bother about materials to keep body and soul together, because by the grace of the Lord everything is carried out automatically.

Thus end the Bhaktivedanta Purports to the Twelfth Chapter of the Śrīmad Bhagavad-gītā *in the matter of Devotional Service.*

CHAPTER THIRTEEN

Nature, the Enjoyer and Consciousness

Texts 1–2 अर्जुन उवाच
प्रकृतिं पुरुषं चैव क्षेत्रं क्षेत्रज्ञमेव च ।
एतद्वेदितुमिच्छामि ज्ञानं ज्ञेयं च केशव ॥ १ ॥

श्रीभगवानुवाच
इदं शरीरं कौन्तेय क्षेत्रमित्यभिधीयते ।
एतद्यो वेत्ति तं प्राहुः क्षेत्रज्ञ इति तद्विदः ॥ २ ॥

arjuna uvāca
prakṛtiṁ puruṣaṁ caiva, kṣetraṁ kṣetra-jñam eva ca
etad veditum icchāmi, jñānaṁ jñeyaṁ ca keśava

śrī-bhagavān uvāca
idaṁ śarīraṁ kaunteya, kṣetram ity abhidhīyate
etad yo vetti taṁ prāhuḥ, kṣetra-jña iti tad-vidaḥ

arjunaḥ uvāca – Arjuna said; *prakṛtim* – nature; *puruṣam* – the enjoyer; *ca* – also; *eva* – certainly; *kṣetram* – the field; *kṣetra-jñam* – the knower of the field; *eva* – certainly; *ca* – also; *etat* – all this; *veditum* – to understand; *icchāmi* – I wish; *jñānam* – knowledge; *jñeyam* – the object of knowledge; *ca* – also; *keśava* – O Kṛṣṇa; *śrī-bhagavān uvāca* – the Personality of Godhead said; *idam* – this; *śarīram* – body; *kaunteya* – O son of Kuntī; *kṣetram* – the field; *iti* – thus; *abhidhīyate* – is called; *etat* – this; *yaḥ* – one who; *vetti* – knows; *tam* – he; *prāhuḥ* – is called; *kṣetra-jñaḥ* – the knower of the field; *iti* – thus; *tat-vidaḥ* – by those who know this.

Arjuna said: O my dear Kṛṣṇa, I wish to know about prakṛti [nature], puruṣa [the enjoyer], and the field and the knower of the field, and of knowledge and the object of knowledge.

The Supreme Personality of Godhead said: This body, O son of Kuntī, is called the field, and one who knows this body is called the knower of the field.

PURPORT: Arjuna was inquisitive about *prakṛti* (nature), *puruṣa* (the enjoyer), *kṣetra* (the field), *kṣetra-jña* (its knower), and knowledge and the object of knowledge. When he inquired about all these, Kṛṣṇa said that this body is called the field and that one who knows this body is called the knower of the field. This body is the field of activity for the conditioned soul. The conditioned soul is entrapped in material existence, and he attempts to lord it over material nature. And so, according to his capacity to dominate material nature, he gets a field of activity. That field of activity is the body. And what is the body? The body is made of senses. The conditioned soul wants to enjoy sense gratification, and, according to his capacity to enjoy sense gratification, he is offered a body, or field of activity. Therefore the body is called *kṣetra,* or the field of activity for the conditioned soul. Now, the person, who should not identify himself with the body, is called *kṣetra-jña,* the knower of the field. It is not very difficult to understand the difference between the field and its knower, the body and the knower of the body. Any person can consider that from childhood to old age he undergoes so many changes of body and yet is still one person, remaining. Thus there is a difference between the knower of the field of activities and the actual field of activities. A living conditioned soul can thus understand that he is different from the body. It is described in the beginning – *dehino 'smin* – that the living entity is within the body and that the body is changing from childhood to boyhood and from boyhood to youth and from youth to old age, and the person who owns the body knows that the body is changing. The owner is distinctly *kṣetra-jña.* Sometimes we think, "I am happy," "I am a man," "I am a woman," "I am a dog," "I am a cat." These are the bodily designations of the knower. But the knower is different from the body. Although we may use many articles – our clothes, etc. – we know that we are different from the things used. Similarly, we also understand by a little contemplation that we are different from the body. I or you or anyone else who owns the body is called *kṣetra-jña,* the knower of the field of activities, and the body is called *kṣetra,* the field of activities itself.

In the first six chapters of *Bhagavad-gītā* the knower of the body (the living entity) and the position by which he can understand the Supreme Lord are described. In the middle six chapters of the *Bhagavad-gītā* the Supreme Personality of Godhead and the relationship between the individual soul and the Supersoul in regard to devotional service are described. The superior position of the Supreme Personality of Godhead and the subordinate position of the individual soul are definitely defined in these chapters. The living entities are subordinate under all circumstances, but in their forgetfulness they are suffering. When enlightened by pious activities, they approach the Supreme Lord in different capacities – as the distressed, those in want of money, the inquisitive, and those in search of knowledge. That is also described. Now, starting with the Thirteenth Chapter, how the living entity comes into contact with material nature and how he is delivered by the Supreme Lord through the different methods of fruitive activities, cultivation of knowledge, and the discharge of devotional service are explained. Although the living entity is completely different from the material body, he somehow becomes related. This also is explained.

Text 3 क्षेत्रज्ञं चापि मां विद्धि सर्वक्षेत्रेषु भारत ।
क्षेत्रक्षेत्रज्ञयोर्ज्ञानं यत्तज्ज्ञानं मतं मम ॥ ३ ॥

kṣetra-jñaṁ cāpi māṁ viddhi, sarva-kṣetreṣu bhārata
kṣetra-kṣetrajñayor jñānaṁ, yat taj jñānaṁ mataṁ mama

kṣetra-jñam – the knower of the field; *ca* – also; *api* – certainly; *mām* – Me; *viddhi* – know; *sarva* – all; *kṣetreṣu* – in bodily fields; *bhārata* – O son of Bharata; *kṣetra* – the field of activities (the body); *kṣetra-jñayoḥ* – and the knower of the field; *jñānam* – knowledge of; *yat* – that which; *tat* – that; *jñānam* – knowledge; *matam* – opinion; *mama* – My.

O scion of Bharata, you should understand that I am also the knower in all bodies, and to understand this body and its knower is called knowledge. That is My opinion.

PURPORT: While discussing the subject of the body and the knower of the body, the soul and the Supersoul, we shall find three different topics of study: the Lord, the living entity, and matter. In every field of activities, in every body, there are two souls: the individual soul and the Supersoul. Because the Supersoul is the plenary expansion of the Supreme Personality of Godhead, Kṛṣṇa, Kṛṣṇa says, "I am also the knower, but I am not the individual knower of the body. I am the superknower. I am present in every body as the Paramātmā, or Supersoul."

One who studies the subject matter of the field of activity and the knower of the field very minutely, in terms of this *Bhagavad-gītā,* can attain to knowledge.

The Lord says, "I am the knower of the field of activities in every individual body." The individual may be the knower of his own body, but he is not in knowledge of other bodies. The Supreme Personality of Godhead, who is present as the Supersoul in all bodies, knows everything about all bodies. He knows all the different bodies of all the various species of life. A citizen may know everything about his patch of land, but the king knows not only his palace but all the properties possessed by the individual citizens. Similarly, one may be the proprietor of the body individually, but the Supreme Lord is the proprietor of all bodies. The king is the original proprietor of the kingdom, and the citizen is the secondary proprietor. Similarly, the Supreme Lord is the supreme proprietor of all bodies.

The body consists of the senses. The Supreme Lord is Hṛṣīkeśa, which means "the controller of the senses." He is the original controller of the senses, just as the king is the original controller of all the activities of the state; the citizens are secondary controllers. The Lord says, "I am also the knower." This means that He is the superknower; the individual soul knows only his particular body. In the Vedic literature, it is stated as follows:

kṣetrāṇi hi śarīrāṇi, bījaṁ cāpi śubhāśubhe
tāni vetti sa yogātmā, tataḥ kṣetra-jña ucyate

This body is called the *kṣetra,* and within it dwells the owner of the body and the Supreme Lord, who knows both the body and the owner of the body. Therefore He is called the knower of all fields. The distinction between the field of activities, the knower of activities, and the supreme knower of activities is described as follows. Perfect knowledge of the constitution of the body, the constitution of the individual soul, and the constitution of the Supersoul is known in terms of Vedic literature as *jñāna.* That is the opinion of Kṛṣṇa. To understand both the soul and the Supersoul as one yet distinct is knowledge. One who does not understand the field of activity and the knower of activity is not in perfect knowledge. One has to understand the position of *prakṛti* (nature), *puruṣa* (the enjoyer of nature) and *īśvara* (the knower who dominates or controls nature and the individual soul). One should not confuse the three in their different capacities. One should not confuse the painter, the painting and the easel. This material world, which is the field of activities, is nature, and the enjoyer of nature is the living entity, and above them both is the supreme controller, the Personality of Godhead. It is stated in the Vedic language (in the *Śvetāśvatara Upaniṣad* 1.12), *bhoktā bhogyaṁ preritāraṁ ca matvā/ sarvaṁ proktaṁ tri-vidhaṁ brahmam etat.* There are three Brahman conceptions: *prakṛti* is Brahman as the field of activities, and the *jīva* (individual soul) is also Brahman and is trying to control material nature, and the controller of both of them is also Brahman, but He is the factual controller.

In this chapter it will also be explained that out of the two knowers, one is fallible and the other is infallible. One is superior and the other is subordinate. One who understands the two knowers of the field to be one and the same contradicts the Supreme Personality of Godhead, who states here very clearly, "I am also the knower of the field of activity." One who misunderstands a rope to be a serpent is not in knowledge. There are different kinds of bodies, and there are different owners of the bodies. Because each individual soul has his individual capacity for lording it over material nature, there are different bodies. But the Supreme also is present in them as the controller. The word *ca* is significant, for it indicates the total number of bodies. That is the opinion of Śrīla Baladeva Vidyābhūṣaṇa. Kṛṣṇa is the Supersoul present in each and every body apart from the individual soul. And Kṛṣṇa explicitly says here that real knowledge is to know that the Supersoul is the controller of both the field of activities and the finite enjoyer.

Text 4 तत्क्षेत्रं यच्च यादृक्च यद्विकारि यतश्च यत् ।
स च यो यत्प्रभावश्च तत्समासेन मे शृणु ॥ ४ ॥

tat kṣetraṁ yac ca yādṛk ca, yad-vikāri yataś ca yat
sa ca yo yat-prabhāvaś ca, tat samāsena me śṛṇu

tat – that; *kṣetram* – field of activities; *yat* – what; *ca* – also; *yādṛk* – as it is; *ca* – also; *yat* – having what; *vikāri* – changes; *yataḥ* – from which; *ca* – also; *yat* – what; *saḥ* – he; *ca* – also; *yaḥ* – who; *yat* – having what;

prabhāvaḥ – influence; *ca* – also; *tat* – that; *samāsena* – in summary; *me* – from Me; *śṛṇu* – understand.

Now please hear My brief description of this field of activity and how it is constituted, what its changes are, whence it is produced, who that knower of the field of activities is, and what his influences are.

PURPORT: The Lord is describing the field of activities and the knower of the field of activities in their constitutional positions. One has to know how this body is constituted, the materials of which this body is made, under whose control this body is working, how the changes are taking place, wherefrom the changes are coming, what the causes are, what the reasons are, what the ultimate goal of the individual soul is, and what the actual form of the individual soul is. One should also know the distinction between the individual living soul and the Supersoul, their different influences, their potentials, etc. One just has to understand this *Bhagavad-gītā* directly from the description given by the Supreme Personality of Godhead, and all this will be clarified. But one should be careful not to consider the Supreme Personality of Godhead in every body to be one with the individual soul, the *jīva.* This is something like equating the potent and the impotent.

Text 5 ऋषिभिर्बहुधा गीतं छन्दोभिर्विविधैः पृथक् ।
ब्रह्मसूत्रपदैश्चैव हेतुमद्भिर्विनिश्चितैः ॥ ५ ॥

ṛṣibhir bahudhā gītaṁ, chandobhir vividhaiḥ pṛthak
brahma-sūtra-padaiś caiva, hetumadbhir viniścitaiḥ

ṛṣibhiḥ – by the wise sages; *bahudhā* – in many ways; *gītam* – described; *chandobhiḥ* – by Vedic hymns; *vividhaiḥ* – various; *pṛthak* – variously; *brahma-sūtra* – of the *Vedānta; padaiḥ* – by the aphorisms; *ca* – also; *eva* – certainly; *hetu-madbhiḥ* – with cause and effect; *viniścitaiḥ* – certain.

That knowledge of the field of activities and of the knower of activities is described by various sages in various Vedic writings. It is especially presented in Vedānta-sūtra with all reasoning as to cause and effect.

PURPORT: The Supreme Personality of Godhead, Kṛṣṇa, is the highest authority in explaining this knowledge. Still, as a matter of course, learned scholars and standard authorities always give evidence from previous authorities. Kṛṣṇa is explaining this most controversial point regarding the duality and nonduality of the soul and the Supersoul by referring to a scripture, the *Vedānta,* which is accepted as authority. First He says, "This is according to different sages." As far as the sages are concerned, besides Himself, Vyāsadeva (the author of the *Vedānta-sūtra*) is a great sage, and in the *Vedānta-sūtra* duality is perfectly explained. And Vyāsadeva's father, Parāśara, is also a great sage, and he writes in his books of religiosity, *ahaṁ tvaṁ ca tathānye . . .* "we – you, I and the various other living entities – are all transcendental, although in material bodies. Now we are fallen into the ways of the three modes of material nature according to our different *karma.* As such, some are on higher levels, and some are in the lower nature. The higher and lower natures exist due to ignorance and are being manifested in an infinite number of living entities. But the Supersoul, which is infallible, is uncontaminated by the three qualities of nature and is transcendental." Similarly, in the original *Vedas,* a distinction between the soul, the Supersoul and the body is made, especially in the *Kaṭha Upaniṣad.* There are many great sages who have explained this, and Parāśara is considered principal among them.

The word *chandobhiḥ* refers to the various Vedic literatures. The *Taittirīya Upaniṣad,* for example, which is a branch of the *Yajur Veda,* describes nature, the living entity and the Supreme Personality of Godhead.

As stated before, *kṣetra* is the field of activities, and there are two kinds of *kṣetra-jña:* the individual living entity and the supreme living entity. As stated in the *Taittirīya Upaniṣad* (2.5), *brahma pucchaṁ pratiṣṭhā.* There is a manifestation of the Supreme Lord's energy known as *anna-maya,* dependence upon food for existence. This is a materialistic realization of the Supreme. Then, in *prāṇa-maya,* after realizing the Supreme Absolute Truth in food, one can realize the Absolute Truth in the living symptoms or life forms. In *jñāna-maya,* realization extends beyond the living symptoms to the point of thinking, feeling and willing. Then there is Brahman realization, called *vijñāna-maya,* in which the living entity's mind and life symptoms are distinguished from the living entity himself. The next and supreme stage is *ānanda-maya,* realization of the all-blissful nature. Thus there are five stages of Brahman realization, which are called *brahma puccham.* Out of these, the first three – *anna-maya, prāṇa-maya* and *jñāna-maya* – involve the fields of activities of the living entities. Transcendental to all these fields of activities is the Supreme Lord, who is called *ānanda-maya.* The *Vedānta-sūtra* also describes the Supreme by saying, *ānanda-mayo 'bhyāsāt:* the Supreme Personality of Godhead is by nature full of joy. To enjoy His transcendental bliss, He expands into *vijñāna-maya, prāṇa-maya, jñāna-maya* and *anna-maya.* In the field of activities the living entity is considered to be the enjoyer, and different from him is the *ānanda-maya.* That means that if the living entity decides to enjoy in dovetailing himself with the *ānanda-maya,* then he becomes perfect. This is the real picture of the Supreme Lord as the supreme knower of the field, the living entity as the subordinate knower, and the nature of the field of activities. One has to search for this truth in the *Vedānta-sūtra,* or *Brahma-sūtra.*

It is mentioned here that the codes of the *Brahma-sūtra* are very nicely arranged according to cause and effect. Some of the *sūtras,* or aphorisms, are *na viyad aśruteḥ* (2.3.2), *nātmā śruteḥ* (2.3.18), and *parāt tu tac-chruteḥ* (2.3.40). The first aphorism indicates the field of activities, the second indicates the living entity, and the third indicates the Supreme Lord, the *summum bonum* among all the manifestations of various entities.

Texts 6–7

महाभूतान्यहङ्कारो बुद्धिरव्यक्तमेव च ।
इन्द्रियाणि दशैकं च पञ्च चेन्द्रियगोचराः ॥ ६ ॥
इच्छा द्वेषः सुखं दुःखं सङ्घातश्चेतना धृतिः ।
एतत्क्षेत्रं समासेन सविकारमुदाहृतम् ॥ ७ ॥

mahā-bhūtāny ahaṅkāro, buddhir avyaktam eva ca
indriyāṇi daśaikaṁ ca, pañca cendriya-gocarāḥ

icchā dveṣaḥ sukhaṁ duḥkhaṁ, saṅghātaś cetanā dhṛtiḥ
etat kṣetraṁ samāsena, sa-vikāram udāhṛtam

mahā-bhūtāni – the great elements; *ahaṅkāraḥ* – false ego; *buddhiḥ* – intelligence; *avyaktam* – the unmanifested; *eva* – certainly; *ca* – also; *indriyāṇi* – the senses; *daśa-ekam* – eleven; *ca* – also; *pañca* – five; *ca* – also; *indriya-go-carāḥ* – the objects of the senses; *icchā* – desire; *dveṣaḥ* – hatred; *sukham* – happiness; *duḥkham* – distress; *saṅghātaḥ* – the aggregate; *cetanā* – living symptoms; *dhṛtiḥ* – conviction; *etat* – all this; *kṣetram* – the field of activities; *samāsena* – in summary; *sa-vikāram* – with interactions; *udāhṛtam* – exemplified.

The five great elements, false ego, intelligence, the unmanifested, the ten senses and the mind, the five sense objects, desire, hatred, happi-

ness, distress, the aggregate, the life symptoms, and convictions – all these are considered, in summary, to be the field of activities and its interactions.

PURPORT: From all the authoritative statements of the great sages, the Vedic hymns and the aphorisms of the *Vedānta-sūtra,* the components of this world can be understood as follows. First there are earth, water, fire, air and ether. These are the five great elements (*mahā-bhūta*). Then there are false ego, intelligence and the unmanifested stage of the three modes of nature. Then there are five senses for acquiring knowledge: the eyes, ears, nose, tongue and skin. Then five working senses: voice, legs, hands, anus and genitals. Then, above the senses, there is the mind, which is within and which can be called the sense within. Therefore, including the mind, there are eleven senses altogether. Then there are the five objects of the senses: smell, taste, form, touch and sound. Now the aggregate of these twenty-four elements is called the field of activity. If one makes an analytical study of these twenty-four subjects, then he can very well understand the field of activity. Then there are desire, hatred, happiness and distress, which are interactions, representations of the five great elements in the gross body. The living symptoms, represented by consciousness, and convictions are the manifestation of the subtle body – mind, ego and intelligence. These subtle elements are included within the field of activities.

The five great elements are a gross representation of the false ego, which in turn represents the primal stage of false ego technically called the materialistic conception, or *tāmasa-buddhi,* intelligence in ignorance. This, further, represents the unmanifested stage of the three modes of material nature. The unmanifested modes of material nature are called *pradhāna.*

One who desires to know the twenty-four elements in detail along with their interactions should study the philosophy in more detail. In *Bhagavad-gītā,* a summary only is given.

The body is the representation of all these factors, and there are changes of the body, which are six in number: the body is born, it grows, it stays, it produces by-products, then it begins to decay, and at the last stage it vanishes. Therefore the field is a nonpermanent material thing. However, the *kṣetra-jña,* the knower of the field, its proprietor, is different.

Texts 8–12

अमानित्वमदम्भित्वमहिंसा क्षान्तिरार्जवम् ।
आचार्योपासनं शौचं स्थैर्यमात्मविनिग्रहः ॥ ८ ॥

इन्द्रियार्थेषु वैराग्यमनहङ्कार एव च ।
जन्ममृत्युजराव्याधिदुःखदोषानुदर्शनम् ॥ ९ ॥
असक्तिरनभिष्वङ्गः पुत्रदारगृहादिषु ।
नित्यं च समचित्तत्वमिष्टानिष्टोपपत्तिषु ॥१०॥
मयि चानन्ययोगेन भक्तिरव्यभिचारिणी ।
विविक्तदेशसेवित्वमरतिर्जनसंसदि ॥११॥
अध्यात्मज्ञाननित्यत्वं तत्त्वज्ञानार्थदर्शनम् ।
एतज्ज्ञानमिति प्रोक्तमज्ञानं यदतोऽन्यथा ॥१२॥

amānitvam adambhitvam, ahiṁsā kṣāntir ārjavam
ācāryopāsanaṁ śaucaṁ, sthairyam ātma-vinigrahaḥ

indriyārtheṣu vairāgyam, anahaṅkāra eva ca
janma-mṛtyu-jarā-vyādhi-, duḥkha-doṣānudarśanam

asaktir anabhiṣvaṅgaḥ, putra-dāra-gṛhādiṣu
nityaṁ ca sama-cittatvam, iṣṭāniṣṭopapattiṣu

mayi cānanya-yogena, bhaktir avyabhicāriṇī
vivikta-deśa-sevitvam, aratir jana-saṁsadi

adhyātma-jñāna-nityatvaṁ, tattva-jñānārtha-darśanam
etaj jñānam iti proktam, ajñānaṁ yad ato 'nyathā

amānitvam – humility; *adambhitvam* – pridelessness; *ahiṁsā* – nonviolence; *kṣāntiḥ* – tolerance; *ārjavam* – simplicity; *ācārya-upāsanam* – approaching a bona fide spiritual master; *śaucam* – cleanliness; *sthairyam* – steadfastness; *ātma-vinigrahaḥ* – self-control; *indriya-artheṣu* – in the matter of the senses; *vairāgyam* – renunciation; *anahaṅkāraḥ* – being without false egoism; *eva* – certainly; *ca* – also; *janma* – of birth; *mṛtyu* – death; *jarā* – old age; *vyādhi* – and disease; *duḥkha* – of the distress; *doṣa* – the fault; *anudarśanam* – observing; *asaktiḥ* – being without attachment; *anabhiṣvaṅgaḥ* – being without association; *putra* – for son; *dāra* – wife; *gṛha-ādiṣu* – home, etc.; *nityam* – constant; *ca* – also; *sama-cittatvam* – equilibrium; *iṣṭa* – the desirable; *aniṣṭa* – and undesirable; *upapattiṣu* – having obtained; *mayi* – unto Me; *ca* – also; *ananya-yogena* – by unalloyed devotional service; *bhaktiḥ* – devotion; *avyabhicāriṇī* – without any break; *vivikta* – to solitary; *deśa* – places; *sevitvam* – aspiring; *aratiḥ* – being without attachment; *jana-saṁsadi* – to people in general; *adhyātma* – pertaining to the self; *jñāna* – in knowledge; *nityatvam* –

constancy; *tattva-jñāna* – of knowledge of the truth; *artha* – for the object; *darśanam* – philosophy; *etat* – all this; *jñānam* – knowledge; *iti* – thus; *proktam* – declared; *ajñānam* – ignorance; *yat* – that which; *ataḥ* – from this; *anyathā* – other.

Humility; pridelessness; nonviolence; tolerance; simplicity; approaching a bona fide spiritual master; cleanliness; steadiness; self-control; renunciation of the objects of sense gratification; absence of false ego; the perception of the evil of birth, death, old age and disease; detachment; freedom from entanglement with children, wife, home and the rest; even-mindedness amid pleasant and unpleasant events; constant and unalloyed devotion to Me; aspiring to live in a solitary place; detachment from the general mass of people; accepting the importance of self-realization; and philosophical search for the Absolute Truth – all these I declare to be knowledge, and besides this whatever there may be is ignorance.

PURPORT: This process of knowledge is sometimes misunderstood by less intelligent men as being the interaction of the field of activity. But actually this is the real process of knowledge. If one accepts this process, then the possibility of approaching the Absolute Truth exists. This is not the interaction of the twenty-four elements, as described before. This is actually the means to get out of the entanglement of those elements. The embodied soul is entrapped by the body, which is a casing made of the twenty-four elements, and the process of knowledge as described here is the means to get out of it. Of all the descriptions of the process of knowledge, the most important point is described in the first line of the eleventh verse. *Mayi cānanya-yogena bhaktir avyabhicāriṇī:* the process of knowledge terminates in unalloyed devotional service to the Lord. So if one does not approach, or is not able to approach, the transcendental service of the Lord, then the other nineteen items are of no particular value. But if one takes to devotional service in full Kṛṣṇa consciousness, the other nineteen items automatically develop within him. As stated in *Śrīmad-Bhāgavatam* (5.18.12), *yasyāsti bhaktir bhagavaty akiñcanā sarvair guṇais tatra samāsate surāḥ.* All the good qualities of knowledge develop in one who has attained the stage of devotional service. The principle of accepting a spiritual master, as mentioned in the eighth verse, is essential. Even for one who takes to devotional service, it is most important. Transcendental life begins when one accepts a bona fide spiritual master. The Supreme Personality of Godhead, Śrī Kṛṣṇa, clearly states here that this process of knowledge is the actual path. Anything speculated beyond this is nonsense.

As for the knowledge outlined here, the items may be analyzed as follows. Humility means that one should not be anxious to have the satisfaction of being honored by others. The material conception of life makes us very eager to receive honor from others, but from the point of view of a man in perfect knowledge – who knows that he is not this body – anything, honor or dishonor, pertaining to this body is useless. One should not be hankering after this material deception. People are very anxious to be famous for their religion, and consequently sometimes it is found that without understanding the principles of religion one enters into some group which is not actually following religious principles and then wants to advertise himself as a religious mentor. As for actual advancement in spiritual science, one should have a test to see how far he is progressing. He can judge by these items.

Nonviolence is generally taken to mean not killing or destroying the body, but actually nonviolence means not to put others into distress. People in general are trapped by ignorance in the material concept of life, and they perpetually suffer material pains. So unless one elevates people to spiritual knowledge, one is practicing violence. One should try his best to distribute real knowledge to the people, so that they may become enlightened and leave this material entanglement. That is nonviolence.

Tolerance means that one should be practiced to bear insult and dishonor from others. If one is engaged in the advancement of spiritual knowledge, there will be so many insults and much dishonor from others. This is expected because material nature is so constituted. Even a boy like Prahlāda, who, only five years old, was engaged in the cultivation of spiritual knowledge, was endangered when his father became antagonistic to his devotion. The father tried to kill him in so many ways, but Prahlāda tolerated him. So there may be many impediments to making advancement in spiritual knowledge, but we should be tolerant and continue our progress with determination.

Simplicity means that without diplomacy one should be so straightforward that he can disclose the real truth even to an enemy. As for acceptance of the spiritual master, that is essential, because without the instruction of a bona fide spiritual master one cannot progress in the spiritual science. One should approach the spiritual master with all humility and offer him all services so that he will be pleased to bestow his blessings upon the disciple. Because a bona fide spiritual master is a representative of Kṛṣṇa, if he bestows any blessings upon his disciple, that will make the disciple immediately advanced without the disciple's following the regulative principles. Or, the regulative principles will be easier for one who has served the spiritual master without reservation.

Cleanliness is essential for making advancement in spiritual life. There are two kinds of cleanliness: external and internal. External cleanliness means taking a bath, but for internal cleanliness one has to think of Kṛṣṇa always and chant Hare Kṛṣṇa, Hare Kṛṣṇa, Kṛṣṇa Kṛṣṇa, Hare Hare/ Hare Rāma, Hare Rāma, Rāma Rāma, Hare Hare. This process cleans the accumulated dust of past *karma* from the mind.

Steadiness means that one should be very determined to make progress in spiritual life. Without such determination, one cannot make tangible progress. And self-control means that one should not accept anything which is detrimental to the path of spiritual progress. One should become accustomed to this and reject anything which is against the path of spiritual progress. This is real renunciation. The senses are so strong that they are always anxious to have sense gratification. One should not cater to these demands, which are not necessary. The senses should only be gratified to keep the body fit so that one can discharge his duty in advancing in spiritual life. The most important and uncontrollable sense is the tongue. If one can control the tongue, then there is every possibility of controlling the other senses. The function of the tongue is to taste and to vibrate. Therefore, by systematic regulation, the tongue should always be engaged in tasting the remnants of foodstuffs offered to Kṛṣṇa and chanting Hare Kṛṣṇa. As far as the eyes are concerned, they should not be allowed to see anything but the beautiful form of Kṛṣṇa. That will control the eyes. Similarly, the ears should be engaged in hearing about Kṛṣṇa and the nose in smelling the flowers offered to Kṛṣṇa. This is the process of devotional service, and it is understood here that *Bhagavad-gītā* is simply expounding the science of devotional service. Devotional service is the main and sole objective. Unintelligent commentators on the *Bhagavad-gītā* try to divert the mind of the reader to other subjects, but there is no other subject in *Bhagavad-gītā* than devotional service.

False ego means accepting this body as oneself. When one understands that he is not his body and is spirit soul, he comes to his real ego. Ego is there. False ego is condemned, but not real ego. In the Vedic literature (*Bṛhad-āraṇyaka Upaniṣad* 1.4.10) it is said, *ahaṁ brahmāsmi:* I am Brahman, I am spirit. This "I am," the sense of self, also exists in the liberated stage of self-realization. This sense of "I am" is ego, but when the sense of "I am" is applied to this false body it is false ego. When the sense of self is applied to reality, that is real ego. There are some philosophers who say we should give up our ego, but we cannot give up our ego, because ego means identity. We ought, of course, to give up the false identification with the body.

One should try to understand the distress of accepting birth, death, old age and disease. There are descriptions in various Vedic literatures of birth. In the *Śrīmad-Bhāgavatam* the world of the unborn, the child's stay in the womb of the mother, its suffering, etc., are all very graphically described. It should be thoroughly understood that birth is distressful. Because we forget how much distress we have suffered within the womb of the mother, we do not make any solution to the repetition of birth and death. Similarly at the time of death there are all kinds of sufferings, and they are also mentioned in the authoritative scriptures. These should be discussed. And as far as disease and old age are concerned, everyone gets practical experience. No one wants to be diseased, and no one wants to become old, but there is no avoiding these. Unless we have a pessimistic view of this material life, considering the distresses of birth, death, old age and disease, there is no impetus for our making advancement in spiritual life.

As for detachment from children, wife and home, it is not meant that one should have no feeling for these. They are natural objects of affection. But when they are not favorable to spiritual progress, then one should not be attached to them. The best process for making the home pleasant is Kṛṣṇa consciousness. If one is in full Kṛṣṇa consciousness, he can make his home very happy, because this process of Kṛṣṇa consciousness is very easy. One need only chant Hare Kṛṣṇa, Hare Kṛṣṇa, Kṛṣṇa Kṛṣṇa, Hare Hare/ Hare Rāma, Hare Rāma, Rāma Rāma, Hare Hare, accept the remnants of foodstuffs offered to Kṛṣṇa, have some discussion on books like *Bhagavad-gītā* and *Śrīmad-Bhāgavatam,* and engage oneself in Deity worship. These four things will make one happy. One should train the members of his family in this way. The family members can sit down morning and evening and chant together Hare Kṛṣṇa, Hare Kṛṣṇa, Kṛṣṇa Kṛṣṇa, Hare Hare/ Hare Rāma, Hare Rāma, Rāma Rāma, Hare Hare. If one can mold his family life in this way to develop Kṛṣṇa consciousness, following these four principles, then there is no need to change from family life to renounced life. But if it is not congenial, not favorable for spiritual advancement, then family life should be abandoned. One must sacrifice everything to realize or serve Kṛṣṇa, just as Arjuna did. Arjuna did not want to kill his family members, but when he understood that these family members were impediments to his Kṛṣṇa realization, he accepted the instruction of Kṛṣṇa and fought and killed them. In all cases, one should be detached from the happiness and distress of family life, because in this world one can never be fully happy or fully miserable.

Happiness and distress are concomitant factors of material life. One should learn to tolerate, as advised in *Bhagavad-gītā.* One can never restrict the coming and going of happiness and distress, so one should be detached from the materialistic way of life and be automatically equipoised in both cases. Generally, when we get something desirable we are very happy, and when we get something undesirable we are distressed. But if we are actually in the spiritual position these things will not agitate us. To reach that stage, we have to practice unbreakable devotional service. Devotional service to Kṛṣṇa without deviation means engaging oneself in the nine processes of devotional service – chanting, hearing, worshiping, offering respect, etc. – as described in the last verse of the Ninth Chapter. That process should be followed.

Naturally, when one is adapted to the spiritual way of life, he will not want to mix with materialistic men. That would go against his grain. One may test himself by seeing how far he is inclined to live in a solitary place, without unwanted association. Naturally a devotee has no taste for unnecessary sporting or cinema-going or enjoying some social function, because he understands that these are simply a waste of time. There are many research scholars and philosophers who study sex life or some other subject, but according to *Bhagavad-gītā* such research work and philosophical speculation have no value. That is more or less nonsensical. According to *Bhagavad-gītā,* one should make research, by philosophical discretion, into the nature of the soul. One should make research to understand the self. That is recommended here.

As far as self-realization is concerned, it is clearly stated here that *bhakti-yoga* is especially practical. As soon as there is a question of devotion, one must consider the relationship between the Supersoul and the individual soul. The individual soul and the Supersoul cannot be one, at least not in the *bhakti* conception, the devotional conception of life. This service of the individual soul to the Supreme Soul is eternal, *nityam,* as it is clearly stated. So *bhakti,* or devotional service, is eternal. One should be established in that philosophical conviction.

In the *Śrīmad-Bhāgavatam* (1.2.11) this is explained. *Vadanti tat tattvavidas tattvaṁ yaj jñānam advayam.* "Those who are actually knowers of the Absolute Truth know that the Self is realized in three different phases, as Brahman, Paramātmā and Bhagavān." Bhagavān is the last word in the realization of the Absolute Truth; therefore one should reach up to that platform of understanding the Supreme Personality of Godhead and thus engage in the devotional service of the Lord. That is the perfection of knowledge.

Beginning from practicing humility up to the point of realization of the Supreme Truth, the Absolute Personality of Godhead, this process is just like a staircase beginning from the ground floor and going up to the top floor. Now on this staircase there are so many people who have reached the first floor, the second or the third floor, etc., but unless one reaches the top floor, which is the understanding of Kṛṣṇa, he is at a lower stage of knowledge. If anyone wants to compete with God and at the same time make advancement in spiritual knowledge, he will be frustrated. It is clearly stated that without humility, understanding is not truly possible. To think oneself God is most puffed up. Although the living entity is always being kicked by the stringent laws of material nature, he still thinks, "I am God" because of ignorance. The beginning of knowledge, therefore, is *amānitva,* humility. One should be humble and know that he is subordinate to the Supreme Lord. Due to rebellion against the Supreme Lord, one becomes subordinate to material nature. One must know and be convinced of this truth.

Text 13 ज्ञेयं यत्तत्प्रवक्ष्यामि यज्ज्ञात्वामृतमश्नुते ।
अनादि मत्परं ब्रह्म न सत्तन्नासदुच्यते ॥१३॥

jñeyaṁ yat tat pravakṣyāmi, yaj jñātvāmṛtam aśnute
anādi mat-paraṁ brahma, na sat tan nāsad ucyate

jñeyam – the knowable; *yat* – which; *tat* – that; *pravakṣyāmi* – I shall now explain; *yat* – which; *jñātvā* – knowing; *amṛtam* – nectar; *aśnute* – one tastes; *anādi* – beginningless; *mat-param* – subordinate to Me; *brahma* – spirit; *na* – neither; *sat* – cause; *tat* – that; *na* – nor; *asat* – effect; *ucyate* – is said to be.

I shall now explain the knowable, knowing which you will taste the eternal. Brahman, the spirit, beginningless and subordinate to Me, lies beyond the cause and effect of this material world.

PURPORT: The Lord has explained the field of activities and the knower of the field. He has also explained the process of knowing the knower of the field of activities. Now He begins to explain the knowable, first the soul and then the Supersoul. By knowledge of the knower, both the soul and the Supersoul, one can relish the nectar of life. As explained in the Second Chapter, the living entity is eternal. This is also confirmed here. There is no specific date at which the *jīva* was born. Nor can anyone trace out the history of the *jīvātmā's* manifestation from the Supreme Lord. Therefore it is beginningless. The Vedic literature confirms this: *na jāyate mriyate vā vipaścit* (*Kaṭha Upaniṣad* 1.2.18). The knower of the body is never born and never dies, and he is full of knowledge.

The Supreme Lord as the Supersoul is also stated in the Vedic literature (*Śvetāśvatara Upaniṣad* 6.16) to be *pradhāna-kṣetrajña-patir guṇeśaḥ,* the chief knower of the body and the master of the three modes of material nature. In the *smṛti* it is said, *dāsa-bhūto harer eva nānyasyaiva kadācana.* The living entities are eternally in the service of the Supreme Lord. This is also confirmed by Lord Caitanya in His teachings. Therefore the description of Brahman mentioned in this verse is in relation to the individual soul, and when the word Brahman is applied to the living entity, it is to be understood that he is *vijñāna-brahma* as opposed to *ānanda-brahma. Ānanda-brahma* is the Supreme Brahman Personality of Godhead.

Text 14 सर्वतः पाणिपादं तत्सर्वतोऽक्षिशिरोमुखम् ।
सर्वतः श्रुतिमल्लोके सर्वमावृत्य तिष्ठति ॥१४॥

sarvataḥ pāṇi-pādaṁ tat, sarvato 'kṣi-śiro-mukham
sarvataḥ śrutimal loke, sarvam āvṛtya tiṣṭhati

sarvataḥ – everywhere; *pāṇi* – hands; *pādam* – legs; *tat* – that; *sarvataḥ* – everywhere; *akṣi* – eyes; *śiraḥ* – heads; *mukham* – faces; *sarvataḥ* – everywhere; *śruti-mat* – having ears; *loke* – in the world; *sarvam* – everything; *āvṛtya* – covering; *tiṣṭhati* – exists.

Everywhere are His hands and legs, His eyes, heads and faces, and He has ears everywhere. In this way the Supersoul exists, pervading everything.

PURPORT: As the sun exists diffusing its unlimited rays, so does the Supersoul, or Supreme Personality of Godhead. He exists in His all-pervading form, and in Him exist all the individual living entities, beginning from the first great teacher, Brahmā, down to the small ants. There are unlimited heads, legs, hands and eyes, and unlimited living entities. All are existing in and on the Supersoul. Therefore the Supersoul is all-pervading. The individual soul, however, cannot say that he has his hands, legs and eyes everywhere. That is not possible. If he thinks that under ignorance he is not conscious that his hands and legs are diffused all over but when he attains to proper knowledge he will come to that stage, his thinking is contradictory. This means that the individual soul, having become conditioned by material nature, is not supreme. The Supreme is different from the individual soul. The Supreme Lord can extend His hand without limit; the individual soul cannot. In *Bhagavad-gītā* the Lord says that if anyone offers Him a flower, or a fruit, or a little water, He accepts it. If the Lord is a far distance away, how can He accept things? This is the omnipotence of the Lord: even though He is situated in His own abode, far, far away from earth, He can extend His hand to accept what anyone offers. That is His potency. In the *Brahma-saṁhitā* (5.37) it is stated, *goloka eva nivasaty akhilātma-bhūtaḥ:* although He is always engaged in pastimes in His transcendental planet, He is all-pervading. The individual soul cannot claim that he is all-pervading. Therefore this verse describes the Supreme Soul, the Personality of Godhead, not the individual soul.

Text 15 सर्वेन्द्रियगुणाभासं सर्वेन्द्रियविवर्जितम् ।
असक्तं सर्वभृच्चैव निर्गुणं गुणभोक्तृ च ॥१५॥

sarvendriya-guṇābhāsaṁ, sarvendriya-vivarjitam
asaktaṁ sarva-bhṛc caiva, nirguṇaṁ guṇa-bhoktṛ ca

sarva – of all; *indriya* – senses; *guṇa* – of the qualities; *ābhāsam* – the original source; *sarva* – all; *indriya* – senses; *vivarjitam* – being without; *asaktam* – without attachment; *sarva-bhṛt* – the maintainer of everyone; *ca* – also; *eva* – certainly; *nirguṇam* – without material qualities; *guṇa-bhoktṛ* – master of the *guṇas; ca* – also.

The Supersoul is the original source of all senses, yet He is without senses. He is unattached, although He is the maintainer of all living beings. He transcends the modes of nature, and at the same time He is the master of all the modes of material nature.

PURPORT: The Supreme Lord, although the source of all the senses of the living entities, doesn't have material senses like they have. Actually, the individual souls have spiritual senses, but in conditioned life they are covered with the material elements, and therefore the sense activities are exhibited through matter. The Supreme Lord's senses are not so covered. His senses are transcendental and are therefore called *nirguṇa. Guṇa* means the material modes, but His senses are without material covering. It should be understood that His senses are not exactly like ours. Although He is the source of all our sensory activities, He has His transcendental senses, which are uncontaminated. This is very nicely explained in the *Śvetāśvatara Upaniṣad* (3.19) in the verse *apāṇi-pādo javano grahītā.* The Supreme Personality of Godhead has no hands which are materially contaminated, but He has His hands and accepts whatever sacrifice is offered to Him. That is the distinction between the conditioned soul and the Supersoul. He has no material eyes, but He has eyes – otherwise how could He see? He sees everything – past, present and future. He lives within the heart of the living being, and He knows what we have done in the past, what we are doing now, and what is awaiting us in the future. This is also confirmed in *Bhagavad-gītā:* He knows everything, but no one knows Him. It is said that the Supreme Lord has no legs like us, but He can travel throughout space because He has spiritual legs. In other words, the Lord is not impersonal; He has His eyes, legs, hands and everything else, and because we are part and parcel of the Supreme Lord we also have these things. But His hands, legs, eyes and senses are not contaminated by material nature.

Bhagavad-gītā also confirms that when the Lord appears He appears as He is by His internal potency. He is not contaminated by the material energy, because He is the Lord of material energy. In the Vedic literature we find that His whole embodiment is spiritual. He has His eternal form, called *sac-cid-ānanda-vigraha.* He is full of all opulence. He is the proprietor of all wealth and the owner of all energy. He is the most intelligent and is full of knowledge. These are some of the symptoms of the Supreme Personality of Godhead. He is the maintainer of all living entities and the witness of all activity. As far as we can understand from Vedic literature, the Supreme Lord is always transcendental. Although we do not see His head, face, hands or legs, He has them, and when we are elevated to the transcendental situation we can see the Lord's form. Due to materially contaminated senses, we cannot see His form. Therefore the impersonalists, who are still materially affected, cannot understand the Personality of Godhead.

Text 16 बहिरन्तश्च भूतानामचरं चरमेव च ।
सूक्ष्मत्वात्तदविज्ञेयं दूरस्थं चान्तिके च तत् ॥१६॥

bahir antaś ca bhūtānām, acaraṁ caram eva ca
sūkṣmatvāt tad avijñeyaṁ, dūra-sthaṁ cāntike ca tat

bahiḥ – outside; *antaḥ* – inside; *ca* – also; *bhūtānām* – of all living entities; *acaram* – not moving; *caram* – moving; *eva* – also; *ca* – and; *sūkṣmatvāt* – on account of being subtle; *tat* – that; *avijñeyam* – unknowable; *dūra-stham* – far away; *ca* – also; *antike* – near; *ca* – and; *tat* – that.

The Supreme Truth exists outside and inside of all living beings, the moving and the nonmoving. Because He is subtle, He is beyond the power of the material senses to see or to know. Although far, far away, He is also near to all.

PURPORT: In Vedic literature we understand that Nārāyaṇa, the Supreme Person, is residing both outside and inside of every living entity. He is present in both the spiritual and material worlds. Although He is far, far away, still He is near to us. These are the statements of Vedic literature. *Āsīno dūraṁ vrajati śayāno yāti sarvataḥ* (*Kaṭha Upaniṣad* 1.2.21). And because He is always engaged in transcendental bliss, we cannot understand how He is enjoying His full opulence. We cannot see or understand with these material senses. Therefore in the Vedic language it is said that to understand Him our material mind and senses cannot act. But one who has purified his mind and senses by practicing Kṛṣṇa consciousness in devotional service can see Him constantly. It is confirmed in *Brahma-saṁhitā* that the devotee who has developed love for the Supreme God can see Him always, without cessation. And it is confirmed in *Bhagavad-gītā* (11.54) that He can be seen and understood only by devotional service. *Bhaktyā tv ananyayā śakyaḥ.*

Text 17 अविभक्तं च भूतेषु विभक्तमिव च स्थितम् ।
भूतभर्तृ च तज्ज्ञेयं ग्रसिष्णु प्रभविष्णु च ॥१७॥

avibhaktaṁ ca bhūteṣu, vibhaktam iva ca sthitam
bhūta-bhartṛ ca taj jñeyaṁ, grasiṣṇu prabhaviṣṇu ca

avibhaktam – without division; *ca* – also; *bhūteṣu* – in all living beings; *vibhaktam* – divided; *iva* – as if; *ca* – also; *sthitam* – situated; *bhūta-bhartṛ* – the maintainer of all living entities; *ca* – also; *tat* – that; *jñeyam* – to be understood; *grasiṣṇu* – devouring; *prabhaviṣṇu* – developing; *ca* – also.

Although the Supersoul appears to be divided among all beings, He is never divided. He is situated as one. Although He is the maintainer

of every living entity, it is to be understood that He devours and develops all.

PURPORT: The Lord is situated in everyone's heart as the Supersoul. Does this mean that He has become divided? No. Actually, He is one. The example is given of the sun: The sun, at the meridian, is situated in its place. But if one goes for five thousand miles in all directions and asks, "Where is the sun?" everyone will say that it is shining on his head. In the Vedic literature this example is given to show that although He is undivided, He is situated as if divided. Also it is said in Vedic literature that one Viṣṇu is present everywhere by His omnipotence, just as the sun appears in many places to many persons. And the Supreme Lord, although the maintainer of every living entity, devours everything at the time of annihilation. This was confirmed in the Eleventh Chapter when the Lord said that He had come to devour all the warriors assembled at Kurukṣetra. He also mentioned that in the form of time He devours also. He is the annihilator, the killer of all. When there is creation, He develops all from their original state, and at the time of annihilation He devours them. The Vedic hymns confirm the fact that He is the origin of all living entities and the rest of all. After creation, everything rests in His omnipotence, and after annihilation everything again returns to rest in Him. These are the confirmations of Vedic hymns. *Yato vā imāni bhūtāni jāyante yena jātāni jīvanti yat prayanty abhisaṁ viśanti tad brahma tad vijijñāsasva* (*Taittirīya Upaniṣad* 3.1).

Text 18 ज्योतिषामपि तज्ज्योतिस्तमसः परमुच्यते ।
ज्ञानं ज्ञेयं ज्ञानगम्यं हृदि सर्वस्य विष्ठितम् ॥१८॥

jyotiṣām api taj jyotis, tamasaḥ param ucyate
jñānaṁ jñeyaṁ jñāna-gamyaṁ, hṛdi sarvasya viṣṭhitam

jyotiṣām – in all luminous objects; *api* – also; *tat* – that; *jyotiḥ* – the source of light; *tamasaḥ* – the darkness; *param* – beyond; *ucyate* – is said; *jñānam* – knowledge; *jñeyam* – to be known; *jñāna-gamyam* – to be approached by knowledge; *hṛdi* – in the heart; *sarvasya* – of everyone; *viṣṭhitam* – situated.

He is the source of light in all luminous objects. He is beyond the darkness of matter and is unmanifested. He is knowledge, He is the object of knowledge, and He is the goal of knowledge. He is situated in everyone's heart.

PURPORT: The Supersoul, the Supreme Personality of Godhead, is the source of light in all luminous objects like the sun, moon and stars. In the Vedic literature we find that in the spiritual kingdom there is no need of sun or moon, because the effulgence of the Supreme Lord is there. In the material world that *brahma-jyotir,* the Lord's spiritual effulgence, is covered by the *mahat-tattva,* the material elements; therefore in this material world we require the assistance of sun, moon, electricity, etc., for light. But in the spiritual world there is no need of such things. It is clearly stated in the Vedic literature that because of His luminous effulgence, everything is illuminated. It is clear, therefore, that His situation is not in the material world. He is situated in the spiritual world, which is far, far away in the spiritual sky. That is also confirmed in the Vedic literature. *Āditya-varṇaṁ tamasaḥ parastāt* (*Śvetāśvatara Upaniṣad* 3.8). He is just like the sun, eternally luminous, but He is far, far beyond the darkness of this material world.

His knowledge is transcendental. The Vedic literature confirms that Brahman is concentrated transcendental knowledge. To one who is anxious to be transferred to that spiritual world, knowledge is given by the Supreme Lord, who is situated in everyone's heart. One Vedic *mantra* (*Śvetāśvatara Upaniṣad* 6.18) says, *taṁ ha devam ātma-buddhi-prakāśaṁ mumukṣur vai śaraṇam ahaṁ prapadye.* One must surrender unto the Supreme Personality of Godhead if he at all wants liberation. As far as the goal of ultimate knowledge is concerned, it is also confirmed in Vedic literature: *tam eva viditvāti mṛtyum eti.* "Only by knowing Him can one surpass the boundary of birth and death." (*Śvetāśvatara Upaniṣad* 3.8)

He is situated in everyone's heart as the supreme controller. The Supreme has legs and hands distributed everywhere, and this cannot be said of the individual soul. Therefore that there are two knowers of the field of activity – the individual soul and the Supersoul – must be admitted. One's hands and legs are distributed locally, but Kṛṣṇa's hands and legs are distributed everywhere. This is confirmed in the *Śvetāśvatara Upaniṣad* (3.17): *sarvasya prabhum īśānaṁ sarvasya śaraṇaṁ bṛhat.* That Supreme Personality of Godhead, Supersoul, is the *prabhu,* or master, of all living entities; therefore He is the ultimate shelter of all living entities. So there is no denying the fact that the Supreme Supersoul and the individual soul are always different.

Text 19 इति क्षेत्रं तथा ज्ञानं ज्ञेयं चोक्तं समासतः ।
मद्भक्त एतद्विज्ञाय मद्भावायोपपद्यते ॥१९॥

iti kṣetraṁ tathā jñānaṁ, jñeyaṁ coktaṁ samāsataḥ
mad-bhakta etad vijñāya, mad-bhāvāyopapadyate

iti – thus; *kṣetram* – the field of activities (the body); *tathā* – also; *jñānam* – knowledge; *jñeyam* – the knowable; *ca* – also; *uktam* – described; *samāsataḥ* – in summary; *mat-bhaktaḥ* – My devotee; *etat* – all this; *vijñāya* – after understanding; *mat-bhāvāya* – to My nature; *upapadyate* – attains.

Thus the field of activities [the body], knowledge and the knowable have been summarily described by Me. Only My devotees can understand this thoroughly and thus attain to My nature.

PURPORT: The Lord has described in summary the body, knowledge and the knowable. This knowledge is of three things: the knower, the knowable and the process of knowing. Combined, these are called *vijñāna,* or the science of knowledge. Perfect knowledge can be understood by the unalloyed devotees of the Lord directly. Others are unable to understand. The monists say that at the ultimate stage these three items become one, but the devotees do not accept this. Knowledge and development of knowledge mean understanding oneself in Kṛṣṇa consciousness. We are being led by material consciousness, but as soon as we transfer all consciousness to Kṛṣṇa's activities and realize that Kṛṣṇa is everything, then we attain real knowledge. In other words, knowledge is nothing but the preliminary stage of understanding devotional service perfectly. In the Fifteenth Chapter this will be very clearly explained.

Now, to summarize, one may understand that verses 6 and 7, beginning from *mahā-bhūtāni* and continuing through *cetanā dhṛtiḥ,* analyze the material elements and certain manifestations of the symptoms of life. These combine to form the body, or the field of activities. And verses 8 through 12, from *amānitvam* through *tattva-jñānārtha-darśanam,* describe the process of knowledge for understanding both types of knower of the field of activities, namely the soul and the Supersoul. Then verses 13 through 18, beginning from *anādi mat-param* and continuing through *hṛdi sarvasya viṣṭhitam,* describe the soul and the Supreme Lord, or the Supersoul.

Thus three items have been described: the field of activity (the body), the process of understanding, and both the soul and the Supersoul. It is especially described here that only the unalloyed devotees of the Lord can understand these three items clearly. So for these devotees *Bhagavad-gītā* is fully useful; it is they who can attain the supreme goal, the nature of the Supreme Lord, Kṛṣṇa. In other words, only devotees, and not others, can understand *Bhagavad-gītā* and derive the desired result.

Text 20 प्रकृतिं पुरुषं चैव विद्ध्यनादी उभावपि ।
विकारांश्च गुणांश्चैव विद्धि प्रकृतिसम्भवान् ॥२०॥

prakṛtiṁ puruṣaṁ caiva, viddhy anādī ubhāv api
vikārāṁś ca guṇāṁś caiva, viddhi prakṛti-sambhavān

prakṛtim – material nature; *puruṣam* – the living entities; *ca* – also; *eva* – certainly; *viddhi* – you must know; *anādī* – without beginning; *ubhau* – both; *api* – also; *vikārān* – transformations; *ca* – also; *guṇān* – the three modes of nature; *ca* – also; *eva* – certainly; *viddhi* – know; *prakṛti* – material nature; *sambhavān* – produced of.

Material nature and the living entities should be understood to be beginningless. Their transformations and the modes of matter are products of material nature.

PURPORT: By the knowledge given in this chapter, one can understand the body (the field of activities) and the knowers of the body (both the individual soul and the Supersoul). The body is the field of activity and is composed of material nature. The individual soul that is embodied and enjoying the activities of the body is the *puruṣa,* or the living entity. He is one knower, and the other is the Supersoul. Of course, it is to be understood that both the Supersoul and the individual entity are different manifestations of the Supreme Personality of Godhead. The living entity is in the category of His energy, and the Supersoul is in the category of His personal expansion.

Both material nature and the living entity are eternal. That is to say that they existed before the creation. The material manifestation is from the energy of the Supreme Lord, and so also are the living entities, but the living entities are of the superior energy. Both the living entities and material nature existed before this cosmos was manifested. Material nature was absorbed in the Supreme Personality of Godhead, Mahā-viṣṇu, and when it was required, it was manifested by the agency of the *mahat-tattva.* Similarly, the living entities are also in Him, and because they are conditioned, they are averse to serving the Supreme Lord. Thus they are not allowed to enter into the spiritual sky. But with the coming forth of material nature these living entities are again given a chance to act in the material world and prepare themselves to enter into the spiritual world. That is the mystery of this material creation. Actually the living entity is originally the spiritual part and parcel of the Supreme Lord, but due to his rebellious nature, he is conditioned within material nature. It really does not matter how these living entities or superior entities of the Supreme Lord have come in contact with material nature. The Supreme Personality of Godhead knows, however, how and why this actually took place. In the scriptures the Lord says that those attracted by this material nature are undergoing a hard struggle for existence. But we should know it with certainty from the descriptions of these few verses that all transformations and influences of material nature by the three modes are also productions of material nature. All transformations and variety in respect to living entities are due to the body. As far as spirit is concerned, living entities are all the same.

Text 21 कार्यकारणकर्तृत्वे हेतुः प्रकृतिरुच्यते ।
पुरुषः सुखदुःखानां भोक्तृत्वे हेतुरुच्यते ॥२१॥

kārya-kāraṇa-kartṛtve, hetuḥ prakṛtir ucyate
puruṣaḥ sukha-duḥkhānāṁ, bhoktṛtve hetur ucyate

kārya – of effect; *kāraṇa* – and cause; *kartṛtve* – in the matter of creation; *hetuḥ* – the instrument; *prakṛtiḥ* – material nature; *ucyate* – is said to be; *puruṣaḥ* – the living entity; *sukha* – of happiness; *duḥkhānām* – and distress; *bhoktṛtve* – in enjoyment; *hetuḥ* – the instrument; *ucyate* – is said to be.

Nature is said to be the cause of all material causes and effects, whereas the living entity is the cause of the various sufferings and enjoyments in this world.

PURPORT: The different manifestations of body and senses among the living entities are due to material nature. There are 8,400,000 different species of life, and these varieties are creations of the material nature. They arise from the different sensual pleasures of the living entity, who thus desires to live in this body or that. When he is put into different bodies, he enjoys different kinds of happiness and distress. His material happiness and distress are due to his body, and not to himself as he is. In his original state there is no doubt of enjoyment; therefore that is his real state. Because of the desire to lord it over material nature, he is in the material world. In the spiritual world there is no such thing. The spiritual world is pure, but in the material world everyone is struggling hard to acquire different kinds of pleasures for the body. It might be more clear to state that this body is the effect of the senses. The senses are instruments for gratifying desire. Now, the sum total – body and instrument senses – are offered by material nature, and as will be clear in the next verse, the living entity is blessed or damned with circumstances according to his past desire and activity. According to one's desires and activities, material nature places one in various residential quarters. The being himself is the cause of his attaining such residential quarters and his attendant enjoyment or suffering. Once placed in some particular kind of body, he comes under the control of nature because the body, being matter, acts according to the laws of nature. At that time, the living entity has no power to change that law. Suppose an entity is put into the body of a dog. As soon as he is put into the body of a dog, he must act like a dog. He cannot act otherwise. And if the living entity is put into the body of a hog, then he is forced to eat stool and act like a hog. Similarly, if the living entity is put into the body of a demigod, he must act according to his body. This is the law of nature. But in all circumstances, the Supersoul is with the individual soul. That is explained in the *Vedas* (*Muṇḍaka Upaniṣad* 3.1.1) as follows: *dvā suparṇā sayujā sakhāyaḥ.* The Supreme Lord is so kind upon the living entity that He always accompanies the individual soul and in all circumstances is present as the Supersoul, or Paramātmā.

Text 22 पुरुषः प्रकृतिस्थो हि भुङ्क्ते प्रकृतिजान् गुणान् ।
कारणं गुणसङ्गोऽस्य सदसद्योनिजन्मसु ॥२२॥

puruṣaḥ prakṛti-stho hi, bhuṅkte prakṛti-jān guṇān
kāraṇaṁ guṇa-saṅgo 'sya, sad-asad-yoni-janmasu

puruṣaḥ – the living entity; *prakṛti-sthaḥ* – being situated in the material energy; *hi* – certainly; *bhuṅkte* – enjoys; *prakṛti-jān* – produced by the material nature; *guṇān* – the modes of nature; *kāraṇam* – the cause; *guṇa-saṅgaḥ* – the association with the modes of nature; *asya* – of the living entity; *sat-asat* – in good and bad; *yoni* – species of life; *janmasu* – in births.

The living entity in material nature thus follows the ways of life, enjoying the three modes of nature. This is due to his association with that

material nature. Thus he meets with good and evil among various species.

PURPORT: This verse is very important for an understanding of how the living entities transmigrate from one body to another. It is explained in the Second Chapter that the living entity is transmigrating from one body to another just as one changes dress. This change of dress is due to his attachment to material existence. As long as he is captivated by this false manifestation, he has to continue transmigrating from one body to another. Due to his desire to lord it over material nature, he is put into such undesirable circumstances. Under the influence of material desire, the entity is born sometimes as a demigod, sometimes as a man, sometimes as a beast, as a bird, as a worm, as an aquatic, as a saintly man, as a bug. This is going on. And in all cases the living entity thinks himself to be the master of his circumstances, yet he is under the influence of material nature.

How he is put into such different bodies is explained here. It is due to association with the different modes of nature. One has to rise, therefore, above the three material modes and become situated in the transcendental position. That is called Kṛṣṇa consciousness. Unless one is situated in Kṛṣṇa consciousness, his material consciousness will oblige him to transfer from one body to another because he has material desires since time immemorial. But he has to change that conception. That change can be effected only by hearing from authoritative sources. The best example is here: Arjuna is hearing the science of God from Kṛṣṇa. The living entity, if he submits to this hearing process, will lose his long-cherished desire to dominate material nature, and gradually and proportionately, as he reduces his long desire to dominate, he comes to enjoy spiritual happiness. In a Vedic *mantra* it is said that as he becomes learned in association with the Supreme Personality of Godhead, he proportionately relishes his eternal blissful life.

Text 23 उपद्रष्टानुमन्ता च भर्ता भोक्ता महेश्वरः ।
परमात्मेति चाप्युक्तो देहेऽस्मिन् पुरुषः परः ॥२३॥

upadraṣṭānumantā ca, bhartā bhoktā maheśvaraḥ
paramātmeti cāpy ukto, dehe 'smin puruṣaḥ paraḥ

upadraṣṭā – overseer; *anumantā* – permitter; *ca* – also; *bhartā* – master; *bhoktā* – supreme enjoyer; *mahā-īśvaraḥ* – the Supreme Lord; *parama-*

ātmā – the Supersoul; *iti* – also; *ca* – and; *api* – indeed; *uktaḥ* – is said; *dehe* – in the body; *asmin* – this; *puruṣaḥ* – enjoyer; *paraḥ* – transcendental.

Yet in this body there is another, a transcendental enjoyer, who is the Lord, the supreme proprietor, who exists as the overseer and permitter, and who is known as the Supersoul.

PURPORT: It is stated here that the Supersoul, who is always with the individual soul, is the representation of the Supreme Lord. He is not an ordinary living entity. Because the monist philosophers take the knower of the body to be one, they think that there is no difference between the Supersoul and the individual soul. To clarify this, the Lord says that He is represented as the Paramātmā in every body. He is different from the individual soul; He is *para,* transcendental. The individual soul enjoys the activities of a particular field, but the Supersoul is present not as finite enjoyer nor as one taking part in bodily activities, but as the witness, overseer, permitter and supreme enjoyer. His name is Paramātmā, not *ātmā,* and He is transcendental. It is distinctly clear that the *ātmā* and Paramātmā are different. The Supersoul, the Paramātmā, has legs and hands everywhere, but the individual soul does not. And because the Paramātmā is the Supreme Lord, He is present within to sanction the individual soul's desiring material enjoyment. Without the sanction of the Supreme Soul, the individual soul cannot do anything. The individual is *bhukta,* or the sustained, and the Lord is *bhoktā,* or the maintainer. There are innumerable living entities, and He is staying in them as a friend.

The fact is that every individual living entity is eternally part and parcel of the Supreme Lord, and both of them are very intimately related as friends. But the living entity has the tendency to reject the sanction of the Supreme Lord and act independently in an attempt to dominate nature, and because he has this tendency he is called the marginal energy of the Supreme Lord. The living entity can be situated either in the material energy or in the spiritual energy. As long as he is conditioned by the material energy, the Supreme Lord, as his friend, the Supersoul, stays with him just to get him to return to the spiritual energy. The Lord is always eager to take him back to the spiritual energy, but due to his minute independence the individual entity is continually rejecting the association of spiritual light. This misuse of independence is the cause of his material strife in the conditioned nature. The Lord, therefore, is always giving instruction from within and from without. From without He gives instructions as stated in *Bhagavad-gītā,* and from within He tries to convince the living entity that his activities in the material field are not conducive to real happiness. "Just give it up and turn your faith toward Me. Then you will be happy," He says. Thus the intelligent person who places his faith in the Paramātmā or the Supreme Personality of Godhead begins to advance toward a blissful eternal life of knowledge.

Text 24 य एवं वेत्ति पुरुषं प्रकृतिं च गुणैः सह ।
सर्वथा वर्तमानोऽपि न स भूयोऽभिजायते ॥२४॥

ya evaṁ vetti puruṣaṁ, prakṛtiṁ ca guṇaiḥ saha
sarvathā vartamāno 'pi, na sa bhūyo 'bhijāyate

yaḥ – anyone who; *evam* – thus; *vetti* – understands; *puruṣam* – the living entity; *prakṛtim* – material nature; *ca* – and; *guṇaiḥ* – the modes of material nature; *saha* – with; *sarvathā* – in all ways; *vartamānaḥ* – being situated; *api* – in spite of; *na* – never; *saḥ* – he; *bhūyaḥ* – again; *abhijāyate* – takes his birth.

One who understands this philosophy concerning material nature, the living entity and the interaction of the modes of nature is sure to attain liberation. He will not take birth here again, regardless of his present position.

PURPORT: Clear understanding of material nature, the Supersoul, the individual soul and their interrelation makes one eligible to become liberated and turn to the spiritual atmosphere without being forced to return to this material nature. This is the result of knowledge. The purpose of knowledge is to understand distinctly that the living entity has by chance fallen into this material existence. By his personal endeavor in association with authorities, saintly persons and a spiritual master, he has to understand his position and then revert to spiritual consciousness or Kṛṣṇa consciousness by understanding *Bhagavad-gītā* as it is explained by the Personality of Godhead. Then it is certain that he will never come again into this material existence; he will be transferred into the spiritual world for a blissful eternal life of knowledge.

Text 25 ध्यानेनात्मनि पश्यन्ति केचिदात्मानमात्मना ।
अन्ये साङ्ख्येन योगेन कर्मयोगेन चापरे ॥२५॥

dhyānenātmani paśyanti, kecid ātmānam ātmanā
anye sāṅkhyena yogena, karma-yogena cāpare

dhyānena – by meditation; *ātmani* – within the self; *paśyanti* – see; *kecit* – some; *ātmānam* – the Supersoul; *ātmanā* – by the mind; *anye* – others; *sāṅkhyena* – of philosophical discussion; *yogena* – by the *yoga* system; *karma-yogena* – by activities without fruitive desire; *ca* – also; *apare* – others.

Some perceive the Supersoul within themselves through meditation, others through the cultivation of knowledge, and still others through working without fruitive desires.

PURPORT: The Lord informs Arjuna that the conditioned souls can be divided into two classes as far as man's search for self-realization is concerned. Those who are atheists, agnostics and skeptics are beyond the sense of spiritual understanding. But there are others, who are faithful in their understanding of spiritual life, and they are called introspective devotees, philosophers, and workers who have renounced fruitive results. Those who always try to establish the doctrine of monism are also counted among the atheists and agnostics. In other words, only the devotees of the Supreme Personality of Godhead are best situated in spiritual understanding, because they understand that beyond this material nature are the spiritual world and the Supreme Personality of Godhead, who is expanded as the Paramātmā, the Supersoul in everyone, the all-pervading Godhead. Of course there are those who try to understand the Supreme Absolute Truth by cultivation of knowledge, and they can be counted in the class of the faithful. The Sāṅkhya philosophers analyze this material world into twenty-four elements, and they place the individual soul as the twenty-fifth item. When they are able to understand the nature of the individual soul to be transcendental to the material elements, they are able to understand also that above the individual soul there is the Supreme Personality of Godhead. He is the twenty-sixth element. Thus gradually they also come to the standard of devotional service in Kṛṣṇa consciousness. Those who work without fruitive results are also perfect in their attitude. They are given a chance to advance to the platform of devotional service in Kṛṣṇa consciousness. Here it is stated that there are some people who are pure in consciousness and who try to find out the Supersoul by meditation, and when they discover the Supersoul within themselves, they become transcendentally situated. Similarly, there are others who also try to understand the Supreme Soul by cultivation of knowledge, and there are others who cultivate the *haṭha-yoga* system and who try to satisfy the Supreme Personality of Godhead by childish activities.

Text 26 अन्ये त्वेवमजानन्तः श्रुत्वान्येभ्य उपासते ।
तेऽपि चातितरन्त्येव मृत्युं श्रुतिपरायणाः ॥२६॥

anye tv evam ajānantaḥ, śrutvānyebhya upāsate
te 'pi cātitaranty eva, mṛtyuṁ śruti-parāyaṇāḥ

anye – others; *tu* – but; *evam* – thus; *ajānantaḥ* – without spiritual knowledge; *śrutvā* – by hearing; *anyebhyaḥ* – from others; *upāsate* – begin to worship; *te* – they; *api* – also; *ca* – and; *atitaranti* – transcend; *eva* – certainly; *mṛtyum* – the path of death; *śruti-parāyaṇāḥ* – inclined to the process of hearing.

Again there are those who, although not conversant in spiritual knowledge, begin to worship the Supreme Person upon hearing about Him from others. Because of their tendency to hear from authorities, they also transcend the path of birth and death.

PURPORT: This verse is particularly applicable to modern society because in modern society there is practically no education in spiritual matters. Some of the people may appear to be atheistic or agnostic or philosophical, but actually there is no knowledge of philosophy. As for the common man, if he is a good soul, then there is a chance for advancement by hearing. This hearing process is very important. Lord Caitanya, who preached Kṛṣṇa consciousness in the modern world, gave great stress to hearing because if the common man simply hears from authoritative sources he can progress, especially, according to Lord Caitanya, if he hears the transcendental vibration Hare Kṛṣṇa, Hare Kṛṣṇa, Kṛṣṇa Kṛṣṇa, Hare Hare/ Hare Rāma, Hare Rāma, Rāma Rāma, Hare Hare. It is stated, therefore, that all men should take advantage of hearing from realized souls and gradually become able to understand everything. The worship of the Supreme Lord will then undoubtedly take place. Lord Caitanya has said that in this age no one needs to change his position, but one should give up the endeavor to understand the Absolute Truth by speculative reasoning. One should learn to become the servant of those who are in knowledge of the Supreme Lord. If one is fortunate enough to take shelter of a pure devotee, hear from him about self-realization and follow in his footsteps, one will be gradually elevated to the position of a pure devotee. In this verse particularly, the process of hearing is strongly recommended, and this is very appropriate. Although the common man is often not as capable as so-called philosophers, faithful hearing from an authoritative person will help one transcend this material existence and go back to Godhead, back to home.

Text 27 यावत्सञ्जायते किञ्चित्सत्त्वं स्थावरजङ्गमम् ।
क्षेत्रक्षेत्रज्ञसंयोगात्तद्विद्धि भरतर्षभ ॥२७॥

yāvat sañjāyate kiñcit, sattvaṁ sthāvara-jaṅgamam
kṣetra-kṣetrajña-saṁyogāt, tad viddhi bharatarṣabha

yāvat – whatever; *sañjāyate* – comes into being; *kiñcit* – anything; *sattvam* – existence; *sthāvara* – not moving; *jaṅgamam* – moving; *kṣetra* – of the body; *kṣetra-jña* – and the knower of the body; *saṁyogāt* – by the union between; *tat viddhi* – you must know it; *bharata-ṛṣabha* – O chief of the Bhāratas.

O chief of the Bhāratas, know that whatever you see in existence, both the moving and the nonmoving, is only a combination of the field of activities and the knower of the field.

PURPORT: Both material nature and the living entity, which were existing before the creation of the cosmos, are explained in this verse. Whatever is created is but a combination of the living entity and material nature. There are many manifestations like trees, mountains and hills which are not moving, and there are many existences which are moving, and all of them are but combinations of material nature and the superior nature, the living entity. Without the touch of the superior nature, the living entity, nothing can grow. The relationship between material nature and spiritual nature is eternally going on, and this combination is effected by the Supreme Lord; therefore He is the controller of both the superior and inferior natures. The material nature is created by Him, and the superior nature is placed in this material nature, and thus all these activities and manifestations take place.

Text 28 समं सर्वेषु भूतेषु तिष्ठन्तं परमेश्वरम् ।
विनश्यत्स्वविनश्यन्तं यः पश्यति स पश्यति ॥२८॥

samaṁ sarveṣu bhūteṣu, tiṣṭhan-taṁ parameśvaram
vinaśyatsv avinaśyantaṁ, yaḥ paśyati sa paśyati

samam – equally; *sarveṣu* – in all; *bhūteṣu* – living entities; *tiṣṭhan-tam* – residing; *parama-īśvaram* – the Supersoul; *vinaśyatsu* – in the destructible; *avinaśyantam* – not destroyed; *yaḥ* – anyone who; *paśyati* – sees; *saḥ* – he; *paśyati* – actually sees.

One who sees the Supersoul accompanying the individual soul in all bodies, and who understands that neither the soul nor the Supersoul within the destructible body is ever destroyed, actually sees.

PURPORT: Anyone who by good association can see three things combined together – the body, the proprietor of the body, or individual soul, and the friend of the individual soul – is actually in knowledge. Unless one has the association of a real knower of spiritual subjects, one cannot see these three things. Those who do not have such association are ignorant; they simply see the body, and they think that when the body is destroyed everything is finished. But actually it is not so. After the destruction of the body, both the soul and the Supersoul exist, and they go on eternally in many various moving and nonmoving forms. The Sanskrit word *parameśvara* is sometimes translated as "the individual soul" because the soul is the master of the body and after the destruction of the body he transfers to another form. In that way he is master. But there are others who interpret this *parameśvara* to be the Supersoul. In either case, both the Supersoul and the individual soul continue. They are not destroyed. One who can see in this way can actually see what is happening.

Text 29 समं पश्यन् हि सर्वत्र समवस्थितमीश्वरम् ।
न हिनस्त्यात्मनात्मानं ततो याति परां गतिम् ॥२९॥

samaṁ paśyan hi sarvatra, samavasthitam īśvaram
na hinasty ātmanātmānaṁ, tato yāti parāṁ gatim

samam – equally; *paśyan* – seeing; *hi* – certainly; *sarvatra* – everywhere; *samavasthitam* – equally situated; *īśvaram* – the Supersoul; *na* – does not; *hinasti* – degrade; *ātmanā* – by the mind; *ātmānam* – the soul; *tataḥ* – then; *yāti* – reaches; *parām* – the transcendental; *gatim* – destination.

One who sees the Supersoul equally present everywhere, in every living being, does not degrade himself by his mind. Thus he approaches the transcendental destination.

PURPORT: The living entity, by accepting his material existence, has become situated differently than in his spiritual existence. But if one understands that the Supreme is situated in His Paramātmā manifestation everywhere, that is, if one can see the presence of the Supreme Personality of Godhead in every living thing, he does not degrade himself by a destructive mentality, and he therefore gradually advances to the spiritual world. The mind is generally addicted to sense gratifying processes; but when the mind turns to the Supersoul, one becomes advanced in spiritual understanding.

Text 30 प्रकृत्यैव च कर्माणि क्रियमाणानि सर्वशः ।
यः पश्यति तथात्मानमकर्तारं स पश्यति ॥३०॥

prakṛtyaiva ca karmāṇi, kriyamāṇāni sarvaśaḥ
yaḥ paśyati tathātmānam, akartāraṁ sa paśyati

prakṛtyā – by material nature; *eva* – certainly; *ca* – also; *karmāṇi* – activities; *kriyamāṇāni* – being performed; *sarvaśaḥ* – in all respects; *yaḥ* – anyone who; *paśyati* – sees; *tathā* – also; *ātmānam* – himself; *akartāram* – the nondoer; *saḥ* – he; *paśyati* – sees perfectly.

One who can see that all activities are performed by the body, which is created of material nature, and sees that the self does nothing, actually sees.

PURPORT: This body is made by material nature under the direction of the Supersoul, and whatever activities are going on in respect to one's body are not his doing. Whatever one is supposed to do, either for happiness or for distress, one is forced to do because of the bodily constitution. The self, however, is outside all these bodily activities. This body is given according to one's past desires. To fulfill desires, one is given the body, with which he acts accordingly. Practically speaking, the body is a machine, designed by the Supreme Lord, to fulfill desires. Because of desires, one is put into difficult circumstances to suffer or to enjoy. This transcendental vision of the living entity, when developed, makes one separate from bodily activities. One who has such a vision is an actual seer.

Text 31 यदा भूतपृथग्भावमेकस्थमनुपश्यति ।
तत एव च विस्तारं ब्रह्म सम्पद्यते तदा ॥३१॥

yadā bhūta-pṛthag-bhāvam, eka-stham anupaśyati
tata eva ca vistāraṁ, brahma sampadyate tadā

yadā – when; *bhūta* – of living entities; *pṛthak-bhāvam* – separated identities; *eka-stham* – situated in one; *anupaśyati* – one tries to see through authority; *tataḥ eva* – thereafter; *ca* – also; *vistāram* – the expansion; *brahma* – the Absolute; *sampadyate* – he attains; *tadā* – at that time.

When a sensible man ceases to see different identities due to different material bodies and he sees how beings are expanded everywhere, he attains to the Brahman conception.

PURPORT: When one can see that the various bodies of living entities arise due to the different desires of the individual soul and do not actually belong to the soul itself, one actually sees. In the material conception of life, we find someone a demigod, someone a human being, a dog, a cat, etc. This is material vision, not actual vision. This material differentiation is due to a material conception of life. After the destruction of the material body, the spirit soul is one. The spirit soul, due to contact with material nature, gets different types of bodies. When one can see this, he attains spiritual vision; thus being freed from differentiations like man, animal, big, low, etc., one becomes purified in his consciousness and able to develop Kṛṣṇa consciousness in his spiritual identity. How he then sees things will be explained in the next verse.

Text 32 अनादित्वान्निर्गुणत्वात्परमात्मायमव्ययः ।
शरीरस्थोऽपि कौन्तेय न करोति न लिप्यते ॥३२॥

anāditvān nirguṇatvāt, paramātmāyam avyayaḥ
śarīra-stho 'pi kaunteya, na karoti na lipyate

anāditvāt – due to eternity; *nirguṇatvāt* – due to being transcendental; *parama* – beyond material nature; *ātmā* – spirit; *ayam* – this; *avyayaḥ* – inexhaustible; *śarīra-sthaḥ* – dwelling in the body; *api* – though; *kaunteya* – O son of Kuntī; *na karoti* – never does anything; *na lipyate* – nor is he entangled.

Those with the vision of eternity can see that the imperishable soul is transcendental, eternal, and beyond the modes of nature. Despite contact with the material body, O Arjuna, the soul neither does anything nor is entangled.

PURPORT: A living entity appears to be born because of the birth of the material body, but actually the living entity is eternal; he is not born, and in spite of his being situated in a material body, he is transcendental and eternal. Thus he cannot be destroyed. By nature he is full of bliss. He does not engage himself in any material activities; therefore the activities performed due to his contact with material bodies do not entangle him.

Text 33 यथा सर्वगतं सौक्ष्म्यादाकाशं नोपलिप्यते ।
सर्वत्रावस्थितो देहे तथात्मा नोपलिप्यते ॥३३॥

yathā sarva-gataṁ saukṣmyād, ākāśaṁ nopalipyate
sarvatrāvasthito dehe, tathātmā nopalipyate

yathā – as; *sarva-gatam* – all-pervading; *saukṣmyāt* – due to being subtle; *ākāśam* – the sky; *na* – never; *upalipyate* – mixes; *sarvatra* – everywhere; *avasthitaḥ* – situated; *dehe* – in the body; *tathā* – so; *ātmā* – the self; *na* – never; *upalipyate* – mixes.

The sky, due to its subtle nature, does not mix with anything, although it is all-pervading. Similarly, the soul situated in Brahman vision does not mix with the body, though situated in that body.

PURPORT: The air enters into water, mud, stool and whatever else is there; still it does not mix with anything. Similarly, the living entity, even though situated in varieties of bodies, is aloof from them due to his subtle nature. Therefore it is impossible to see with the material eyes how the living entity is in contact with this body and how he is out of it after the destruction of the body. No one in science can ascertain this.

Text 34 यथा प्रकाशयत्येकः कृत्स्नं लोकमिमं रविः ।
क्षेत्रं क्षेत्री तथा कृत्स्नं प्रकाशयति भारत ॥३४॥

yathā prakāśayaty ekaḥ, kṛtsnaṁ lokam imaṁ raviḥ
kṣetraṁ kṣetrī tathā kṛtsnaṁ, prakāśayati bhārata

yathā – as; *prakāśayati* – illuminates; *ekaḥ* – one; *kṛtsnam* – the whole; *lokam* – universe; *imam* – this; *raviḥ* – sun; *kṣetram* – this body; *kṣetrī* – the soul; *tathā* – similarly; *kṛtsnam* – all; *prakāśayati* – illuminates; *bhārata* – O son of Bharata.

O son of Bharata, as the sun alone illuminates all this universe, so does the living entity, one within the body, illuminate the entire body by consciousness.

PURPORT: There are various theories regarding consciousness. Here in *Bhagavad-gītā* the example of the sun and the sunshine is given. As the sun is situated in one place but is illuminating the whole universe, so a small particle of spirit soul, although situated in the heart of this body, is illuminating the whole body by consciousness. Thus consciousness is the proof of the presence of the soul, as sunshine or light is the proof of the presence of the sun. When the soul is present in the body, there is consciousness all over the body, and as soon as the soul has passed from the body there is no more consciousness. This can be easily understood by any intelligent man. Therefore consciousness is not a product of the combinations of matter. It is the symptom of the living entity. The consciousness of the living entity, although qualitatively one with the supreme consciousness, is not supreme, because the consciousness of one particular body does not share that of another body. But the Supersoul, which is situated in all bodies as the friend of the individual soul, is conscious of all bodies. That is the difference between supreme consciousness and individual consciousness.

Text 35 क्षेत्रक्षेत्रज्ञयोरेवमन्तरं ज्ञानचक्षुषा ।
भूतप्रकृतिमोक्षं च ये विदुर्यान्ति ते परम् ॥३५॥

kṣetra-kṣetrajñayor evam, antaraṁ jñāna-cakṣuṣā
bhūta-prakṛti-mokṣaṁ ca, ye vidur yānti te param

kṣetra – of the body; *kṣetra-jñayoḥ* – of the proprietor of the body; *evam* – thus; *antaram* – the difference; *jñāna-cakṣuṣā* – by the vision of knowledge; *bhūta* – of the living entity; *prakṛti* – from material nature; *mokṣam* – the liberation; *ca* – also; *ye* – those who; *viduḥ* – know; *yānti* – approach; *te* – they; *param* – the Supreme.

Those who see with eyes of knowledge the difference between the body and the knower of the body, and can also understand the process of liberation from bondage in material nature, attain to the supreme goal.

PURPORT: The purport of this Thirteenth Chapter is that one should know the distinction between the body, the owner of the body, and the Supersoul. One should recognize the process of liberation, as described in verses eight through twelve. Then one can go on to the supreme destination.

A faithful person should at first have some good association to hear of God and thus gradually become enlightened. If one accepts a spiritual master, one can learn to distinguish between matter and spirit, and that becomes the steppingstone for further spiritual realization. A spiritual master, by various instructions, teaches his students to get free from the material concept of life. For instance, in *Bhagavad-gītā* we find Kṛṣṇa instructing Arjuna to free him from materialistic considerations.

One can understand that this body is matter; it can be analyzed with its twenty-four elements. The body is the gross manifestation. And the subtle manifestation is the mind and psychological effects. And the symptoms of life are the interaction of these features. But over and above this, there is the soul, and there is also the Supersoul. The soul and the Supersoul are two. This material world is working by the conjunction of the soul and the twenty-four material elements. One who can see the constitution of the whole material manifestation as this combination of the soul and material elements and can also see the situation of the Supreme Soul becomes eligible for transfer to the spiritual world. These things are meant for contemplation and for realization, and one should have a complete understanding of this chapter with the help of the spiritual master.

Thus end the Bhaktivedanta Purports to the Thirteenth Chapter of the Śrīmad Bhagavad-gītā *in the matter of Nature, the Enjoyer and Consciousness.*

CHAPTER FOURTEEN

The Three Modes of Material Nature

Text 1 श्रीभगवानुवाच
परं भूयः प्रवक्ष्यामि ज्ञानानां ज्ञानमुत्तमम् ।
यज्ज्ञात्वा मुनयः सर्वे परां सिद्धिमितो गताः ॥१॥

śrī-bhagavān uvāca
paraṁ bhūyaḥ pravakṣyāmi, jñānānāṁ jñānam uttamam
yaj jñātvā munayaḥ sarve, parāṁ siddhim ito gatāḥ

śrī-bhagavān uvāca – the Supreme Personality of Godhead said; *param* – transcendental; *bhūyaḥ* – again; *pravakṣyāmi* – I shall speak; *jñānā-nām* – of all knowledge; *jñānam* – knowledge; *uttamam* – the supreme; *yat* – which; *jñātvā* – knowing; *munayaḥ* – the sages; *sarve* – all; *parām* – transcendental; *siddhim* – perfection; *itaḥ* – from this world; *gatāḥ* – attained.

The Supreme Personality of Godhead said: Again I shall declare to you this supreme wisdom, the best of all knowledge, knowing which all the sages have attained the supreme perfection.

PURPORT: From the Seventh Chapter to the end of the Twelfth Chapter, Śrī Kṛṣṇa in detail reveals the Absolute Truth, the Supreme Personality of Godhead. Now, the Lord Himself is further enlightening

Arjuna. If one understands this chapter through the process of philosophical speculation, he will come to an understanding of devotional service. In the Thirteenth Chapter, it was clearly explained that by humbly developing knowledge one may possibly be freed from material entanglement. It has also been explained that it is due to association with the modes of nature that the living entity is entangled in this material world. Now, in this chapter, the Supreme Personality explains what those modes of nature are, how they act, how they bind and how they give liberation. The knowledge explained in this chapter is proclaimed by the Supreme Lord to be superior to the knowledge given so far in other chapters. By understanding this knowledge, various great sages attained perfection and transferred to the spiritual world. The Lord now explains the same knowledge in a better way. This knowledge is far, far superior to all other processes of knowledge thus far explained, and knowing this many attained perfection. Thus it is expected that one who understands this Fourteenth Chapter will attain perfection.

Text 2 इदं ज्ञानमुपाश्रित्य मम साधर्म्यमागताः ।
सर्गेऽपि नोपजायन्ते प्रलये न व्यथन्ति च ॥ २ ॥

idaṁ jñānam upāśritya, mama sādharmyam āgatāḥ
sarge 'pi nopajāyante, pralaye na vyathanti ca

idam – this; *jñānam* – knowledge; *upāśritya* – taking shelter of; *mama* – My; *sādharmyam* – same nature; *āgatāḥ* – having attained; *sarge api* – even in the creation; *na* – never; *upajāyante* – are born; *pralaye* – in the annihilation; *na* – nor; *vyathanti* – are disturbed; *ca* – also.

By becoming fixed in this knowledge, one can attain to the transcendental nature like My own. Thus established, one is not born at the time of creation or disturbed at the time of dissolution.

PURPORT: After acquiring perfect transcendental knowledge, one acquires qualitative equality with the Supreme Personality of Godhead, becoming free from the repetition of birth and death. One does not, however, lose his identity as an individual soul. It is understood from Vedic literature that the liberated souls who have reached the transcendental planets of the spiritual sky always look to the lotus feet of the Supreme Lord, being engaged in His transcendental loving service. So, even after liberation, the devotees do not lose their individual identities.

Generally, in the material world, whatever knowledge we get is contaminated by the three modes of material nature. Knowledge which is not contaminated by the three modes of nature is called transcendental knowledge. As soon as one is situated in that transcendental knowledge, he is on the same platform as the Supreme Person. Those who have no knowledge of the spiritual sky hold that after being freed from the material activities of the material form, this spiritual identity becomes formless, without any variegatedness. However, just as there is material variegatedness in this world, in the spiritual world there is also variegatedness. Those in ignorance of this think that spiritual existence is opposed to material variety. But actually, in the spiritual sky, one attains a spiritual form. There are spiritual activities, and the spiritual situation is called devotional life. That atmosphere is said to be uncontaminated, and there one is equal in quality with the Supreme Lord. To obtain such knowledge, one must develop all the spiritual qualities. One who thus develops the spiritual qualities is not affected either by the creation or by the destruction of the material world.

Text 3 मम योनिर्महद् ब्रह्म तस्मिन् गर्भं दधाम्यहम् ।
सम्भवः सर्वभूतानां ततो भवति भारत ॥ ३ ॥

mama yonir mahad brahma, tasmin garbhaṁ dadhāmy aham
sambhavaḥ sarva-bhūtānāṁ, tato bhavati bhārata

mama – My; *yoniḥ* – source of birth; *mahat* – the total material existence; *brahma* – supreme; *tasmin* – in that; *garbham* – pregnancy; *dadhāmi* – create; *aham* – I; *sambhavaḥ* – the possibility; *sarva-bhūtānām* – of all living entities; *tataḥ* – thereafter; *bhavati* – becomes; *bhārata* – O son of Bharata.

The total material substance, called Brahman, is the source of birth, and it is that Brahman that I impregnate, making possible the births of all living beings, O son of Bharata.

PURPORT: This is an explanation of the world: everything that takes place is due to the combination of *kṣetra* and *kṣetra-jña,* the body and the spirit soul. This combination of material nature and the living entity is made possible by the Supreme God Himself. The *mahat-tattva* is the total cause of the total cosmic manifestation; and that total substance of the material cause, in which there are three modes of nature, is sometimes called Brahman. The Supreme Personality impregnates that total substance, and thus innumerable universes become possible. This total material substance, the *mahat-tattva,* is described as Brahman in the Vedic literature (*Muṇḍaka Upaniṣad* 1.1.19): *tasmād etad brahma nāma-rūpam annaṁ ca jāyate.* The Supreme Person impregnates that Brahman with the seeds of the living entities. The twenty-four elements, beginning from earth, water, fire and air, are all material energy, and they constitute what is called *mahad brahma,* or the great Brahman, the material nature. As explained in the Seventh Chapter, beyond this there is another, superior nature – the living entity. Into material nature the superior nature is mixed by the will of the Supreme Personality of Godhead, and thereafter all living entities are born of this material nature.

The scorpion lays its eggs in piles of rice, and sometimes it is said that the scorpion is born out of rice. But the rice is not the cause of the scorpion. Actually, the eggs were laid by the mother. Similarly, material nature is not the cause of the birth of the living entities. The seed is given by the Supreme Personality of Godhead, and they only seem to come out as products of material nature. Thus every living entity, according to his past activities, has a different body, created by this material nature, so that the entity can enjoy or suffer according to his past deeds. The Lord is the cause of all the manifestations of living entities in this material world.

Text 4 सर्वयोनिषु कौन्तेय मूर्तयः सम्भवन्ति याः ।
तासां ब्रह्म महद्योनिरहं बीजप्रदः पिता ॥ ४ ॥

sarva-yoniṣu kaunteya, mūrtayaḥ sambhavanti yāḥ
tāsāṁ brahma mahad yonir, ahaṁ bīja-pradaḥ pitā

sarva-yoniṣu – in all species of life; *kaunteya* – O son of Kuntī; *mūrtayaḥ* – forms; *sambhavanti* – they appear; *yāḥ* – which; *tāsām* – of all of them; *brahma* – the supreme; *mahat yoniḥ* – source of birth in the material substance; *aham* – I; *bīja-pradaḥ* – the seed-giving; *pitā* – father.

It should be understood that all species of life, O son of Kuntī, are made possible by birth in this material nature, and that I am the seed-giving father.

PURPORT: In this verse it is clearly explained that the Supreme Personality of Godhead, Kṛṣṇa, is the original father of all living entities. The living entities are combinations of the material nature and the spiritual nature. Such living entities are seen not only on this planet but on every planet, even on the highest, where Brahmā is situated. Everywhere there are living entities; within the earth there are living entities, even within water and within fire. All these appearances are due to the mother, material nature, and Kṛṣṇa's seed-giving process. The purport is that the material world is impregnated with living entities, who come out in various forms at the time of creation according to their past deeds.

Text 5 सत्त्वं रजस्तम इति गुणाः प्रकृतिसम्भवाः ।
निबध्नन्ति महाबाहो देहे देहिनमव्ययम् ॥ ५ ॥

sattvaṁ rajas tama iti, guṇāḥ prakṛti-sambhavāḥ
nibadhnanti mahā-bāho, dehe dehinam avyayam

sattvam – the mode of goodness; *rajaḥ* – the mode of passion; *tamaḥ* – the mode of ignorance; *iti* – thus; *guṇāḥ* – the qualities; *prakṛti* – material nature; *sambhavāḥ* – produced of; *nibadhnanti* – do condition; *mahā-bāho* – O mighty-armed one; *dehe* – in this body; *dehinam* – the living entity; *avyayam* – eternal.

Material nature consists of three modes – goodness, passion and ignorance. When the eternal living entity comes in contact with nature, O mighty-armed Arjuna, he becomes conditioned by these modes.

PURPORT: The living entity, because he is transcendental, has nothing to do with this material nature. Still, because he has become conditioned by the material world, he is acting under the spell of the three modes of material nature. Because living entities have different kinds of bodies, in terms of the different aspects of nature, they are induced to act according to that nature. This is the cause of the varieties of happiness and distress.

Text 6 तत्र सत्त्वं निर्मलत्वात्प्रकाशकमनामयम् ।
सुखसङ्गेन बध्नाति ज्ञानसङ्गेन चानघ ॥ ६ ॥

tatra sattvaṁ nirmalatvāt, prakāśakam anāmayam
sukha-saṅgena badhnāti, jñāna-saṅgena cānagha

tatra – there; *sattvam* – the mode of goodness; *nirmalatvāt* – being purest in the material world; *prakāśakam* – illuminating; *anāmayam* –

without any sinful reaction; *sukha* – with happiness; *saṅgena* – by association; *badhnāti* – conditions; *jñāna* – with knowledge; *saṅgena* – by association; *ca* – also; *anagha* – O sinless one.

O sinless one, the mode of goodness, being purer than the others, is illuminating, and it frees one from all sinful reactions. Those situated in that mode become conditioned by a sense of happiness and knowledge.

PURPORT: The living entities conditioned by material nature are of various types. One is happy, another is very active, and another is helpless. All these types of psychological manifestations are causes of the entities' conditioned status in nature. How they are differently conditioned is explained in this section of *Bhagavad-gītā.* The mode of goodness is first considered. The effect of developing the mode of goodness in the material world is that one becomes wiser than those otherwise conditioned. A man in the mode of goodness is not so much affected by material miseries, and he has a sense of advancement in material knowledge. The representative type is the *brāhmaṇa,* who is supposed to be situated in the mode of goodness. This sense of happiness is due to understanding that, in the mode of goodness, one is more or less free from sinful reactions. Actually, in the Vedic literature it is said that the mode of goodness means greater knowledge and a greater sense of happiness.

The difficulty here is that when a living entity is situated in the mode of goodness he becomes conditioned to feel that he is advanced in knowledge and is better than others. In this way he becomes conditioned. The best examples are the scientist and the philosopher. Each is very proud of his knowledge, and because they generally improve their living conditions, they feel a sort of material happiness. This sense of advanced happiness in conditioned life makes them bound by the mode of goodness of material nature. As such, they are attracted toward working in the mode of goodness, and, as long as they have an attraction for working in that way, they have to take some type of body in the modes of nature. Thus there is no likelihood of liberation, or of being transferred to the spiritual world. Repeatedly one may become a philosopher, a scientist or a poet, and repeatedly become entangled in the same disadvantages of birth and death. But, due to the illusion of the material energy, one thinks that that sort of life is pleasant.

Text 7 रजो रागात्मकं विद्धि तृष्णासङ्गसमुद्भवम् ।
तन्निबध्नाति कौन्तेय कर्मसङ्गेन देहिनम् ॥ ७ ॥

rajo rāgātmakaṁ viddhi, tṛṣṇā-saṅga-samudbhavam
tan nibadhnāti kaunteya, karma-saṅgena dehinam

rajaḥ – the mode of passion; *rāga-ātmakam* – born of desire or lust; *viddhi* – know; *tṛṣṇā* – with hankering; *saṅga* – association; *samud-bhavam* – produced of; *tat* – that; *nibadhnāti* – binds; *kaunteya* – O son of Kuntī; *karma-saṅgena* – by association with fruitive activity; *dehinam* – the embodied.

The mode of passion is born of unlimited desires and longings, O son of Kuntī, and because of this the embodied living entity is bound to material fruitive actions.

PURPORT: The mode of passion is characterized by the attraction between man and woman. Woman has attraction for man, and man has attraction for woman. This is called the mode of passion. And when the mode of passion is increased, one develops the hankering for material enjoyment. He wants to enjoy sense gratification. For sense gratification, a man in the mode of passion wants some honor in society, or in the nation, and he wants to have a happy family, with nice children, wife and house. These are the products of the mode of passion. As long as one is hankering after these things, he has to work very hard. Therefore it is clearly stated here that he becomes associated with the fruits of his activities and thus becomes bound by such activities. In order to please his wife, children and society and to keep up his prestige, one has to work. Therefore, the whole material world is more or less in the mode of passion. Modern civilization is considered to be advanced in the standard of the mode of passion. Formerly, the advanced condition was considered to be in the mode of goodness. If there is no liberation for those in the mode of goodness, what to speak of those who are entangled in the mode of passion?

Text 8 तमस्त्वज्ञानजं विद्धि मोहनं सर्वदेहिनाम् ।
प्रमादालस्यनिद्राभिस्तन्निबध्नाति भारत ॥ ८ ॥

tamas tv ajñāna-jaṁ viddhi, mohanaṁ sarva-dehinām
pramādālasya-nidrābhis, tan nibadhnāti bhārata

tamaḥ – the mode of ignorance; *tu* – but; *ajñāna-jam* – produced of ignorance; *viddhi* – know; *mohanam* – the delusion; *sarva-dehinām* – of all embodied beings; *pramāda* – with madness; *ālasya* – indolence;

nidrābhiḥ – and sleep; *tat* – that; *nibadhnāti* – binds; *bhārata* – O son of Bharata.

O son of Bharata, know that the mode of darkness, born of ignorance, is the delusion of all embodied living entities. The results of this mode are madness, indolence and sleep, which bind the conditioned soul.

PURPORT: In this verse the specific application of the word *tu* is very significant. This means that the mode of ignorance is a very peculiar qualification of the embodied soul. The mode of ignorance is just the opposite of the mode of goodness. In the mode of goodness, by development of knowledge, one can understand what is what, but the mode of ignorance is just the opposite. Everyone under the spell of the mode of ignorance becomes mad, and a madman cannot understand what is what. Instead of making advancement, one becomes degraded. The definition of the mode of ignorance is stated in the Vedic literature. *Vastu-yāthātmya-jñānāvarakaṁ viparyaya-jñāna-janakaṁ tamaḥ:* under the spell of ignorance, one cannot understand a thing as it is. For example, everyone can see that his grandfather has died and therefore he will also die; man is mortal. The children that he conceives will also die. So death is sure. Still, people are madly accumulating money and working very hard all day and night, not caring for the eternal spirit. This is madness. In their madness, they are very reluctant to make advancement in spiritual understanding. Such people are very lazy. When they are invited to associate for spiritual understanding, they are not much interested. They are not even active like the man who is controlled by the mode of passion. Thus another symptom of one embedded in the mode of ignorance is that he sleeps more than is required. Six hours of sleep is sufficient, but a man in the mode of ignorance sleeps at least ten or twelve hours a day. Such a man appears to be always dejected and is addicted to intoxicants and sleeping. These are the symptoms of a person conditioned by the mode of ignorance.

Text 9 सत्त्वं सुखे सञ्जयति रजः कर्मणि भारत ।
ज्ञानमावृत्य तु तमः प्रमादे सञ्जयत्युत ॥ ९ ॥

sattvaṁ sukhe sañjayati, rajaḥ karmaṇi bhārata
jñānam āvṛtya tu tamaḥ, pramāde sañjayaty uta

sattvam – the mode of goodness; *sukhe* – in happiness; *sañjayati* – binds; *rajaḥ* – the mode of passion; *karmaṇi* – in fruitive activity; *bhārata* – O son of Bharata; *jñānam* – knowledge; *āvṛtya* – covering; *tu* – but; *tamaḥ* – the mode of ignorance; *pramāde* – in madness; *sañjayati* – binds; *uta* – it is said.

O son of Bharata, the mode of goodness conditions one to happiness; passion conditions one to fruitive action; and ignorance, covering one's knowledge, binds one to madness.

PURPORT: A person in the mode of goodness is satisfied by his work or intellectual pursuit, just as a philosopher, scientist or educator may be engaged in a particular field of knowledge and may be satisfied in that way. A man in the mode of passion may be engaged in fruitive activity; he owns as much as he can and spends for good causes. Sometimes he tries to open hospitals, give to charity institutions, etc. These are signs of one in the mode of passion. And the mode of ignorance covers knowledge. In the mode of ignorance, whatever one does is good neither for him nor for anyone.

Text 10 रजस्तमश्चाभिभूय सत्त्वं भवति भारत ।
रजः सत्त्वं तमश्चैव तमः सत्त्वं रजस्तथा ॥१०॥

rajas tamaś cābhibhūya, sattvaṁ bhavati bhārata
rajaḥ sattvaṁ tamaś caiva, tamaḥ sattvaṁ rajas tathā

rajaḥ – the mode of passion; *tamah* – the mode of ignorance; *ca* – also; *abhibhūya* – surpassing; *sattvam* – the mode of goodness; *bhavati* – becomes prominent; *bhārata* – O son of Bharata; *rajaḥ* – the mode of passion; *sattvam* – the mode of goodness; *tamaḥ* – the mode of ignorance; *ca* – also; *eva* – like that; *tamaḥ* – the mode of ignorance; *sattvam* – the mode of goodness; *rajaḥ* – the mode of passion; *tathā* – thus.

Sometimes the mode of goodness becomes prominent, defeating the modes of passion and ignorance, O son of Bharata. Sometimes the mode of passion defeats goodness and ignorance, and at other times ignorance defeats goodness and passion. In this way there is always competition for supremacy.

PURPORT: When the mode of passion is prominent, the modes of goodness and ignorance are defeated. When the mode of goodness is prominent, passion and ignorance are defeated. And when the mode of ignorance is prominent, passion and goodness are defeated. This competition is always going on. Therefore, one who is actually intent on advancing in Kṛṣṇa consciousness has to transcend these three modes. The prominence of some certain mode of nature is manifested in one's dealings, in his activities, in eating, etc. All this will be explained in later chapters. But if one wants, he can develop, by practice, the mode of goodness and thus defeat the modes of ignorance and passion. One can similarly develop the mode of passion and defeat goodness and ignorance. Or one can develop the mode of ignorance and defeat goodness and passion. Although there are these three modes of material nature, if one is determined he can be blessed by the mode of goodness, and by transcending the mode of goodness he can be situated in pure goodness, which is called the *vasudeva* state, a state in which one can understand the science of God. By the manifestation of particular activities, it can be understood in what mode of nature one is situated.

Text 11 सर्वद्वारेषु देहेऽस्मिन् प्रकाश उपजायते ।
ज्ञानं यदा तदा विद्याद्विवृद्धं सत्त्वमित्युत ॥११॥

sarva-dvāreṣu dehe 'smin, prakāśa upajāyate
jñānaṁ yadā tadā vidyād, vivṛddhaṁ sattvam ity uta

sarva-dvāreṣu – in all the gates; *dehe asmin* – in this body; *prakāśaḥ* – the quality of illumination; *upajāyate* – develops; *jñānam* – knowledge; *yadā* – when; *tadā* – at that time; *vidyāt* – know; *vivṛddham* – increased; *sattvam* – the mode of goodness; *iti uta* – thus it is said.

The manifestation of the mode of goodness can be experienced when all the gates of the body are illuminated by knowledge.

PURPORT: There are nine gates in the body: two eyes, two ears, two nostrils, the mouth, the genitals and the anus. When every gate is illuminated by the symptoms of goodness, it should be understood that one has developed the mode of goodness. In the mode of goodness, one can see things in the right position, one can hear things in the right position, and one can taste things in the right position. One becomes cleansed inside and outside. In every gate there is development of the symptoms of happiness, and that is the position of goodness.

Text 12 लोभः प्रवृत्तिरारम्भः कर्मणामशमः स्पृहा ।
रजस्येतानि जायन्ते विवृद्धे भरतर्षभ ॥१२॥

lobhaḥ pravṛttir ārambhaḥ, karmaṇām aśamaḥ spṛhā
rajasy etāni jāyante, vivṛddhe bharatarṣabha

lobhaḥ – greed; *pravṛttiḥ* – activity; *ārambhaḥ* – endeavor; *karmaṇām* – in activities; *aśamaḥ* – uncontrollable; *spṛhā* – desire; *rajasi* – of the mode of passion; *etāni* – all these; *jāyante* – develop; *vivṛddhe* – when there is an excess; *bharata-ṛṣabha* – O chief of the descendants of Bharata.

O chief of the Bhāratas, when there is an increase in the mode of passion the symptoms of great attachment, fruitive activity, intense endeavor, and uncontrollable desire and hankering develop.

PURPORT: One in the mode of passion is never satisfied with the position he has already acquired; he hankers to increase his position. If he wants to construct a residential house, he tries his best to have a palatial house, as if he would be able to reside in that house eternally. And he develops a great hankering for sense gratification. There is no end to sense gratification. He always wants to remain with his family and in his house and to continue the process of sense gratification. There is no cessation of this. All these symptoms should be understood as characteristic of the mode of passion.

Text 13 अप्रकाशोऽप्रवृत्तिश्च प्रमादो मोह एव च ।
तमस्येतानि जायन्ते विवृद्धे कुरुनन्दन ॥१३॥

aprakāśo 'pravṛttiś ca, pramādo moha eva ca
tamasy etāni jāyante, vivṛddhe kuru-nandana

aprakāśaḥ – darkness; *apravṛttiḥ* – inactivity; *ca* – and; *pramādaḥ* – madness; *mohaḥ* – illusion; *eva* – certainly; *ca* – also; *tamasi* – the mode of ignorance; *etāni* – these; *jāyante* – are manifested; *vivṛddhe* – when developed; *kuru-nandana* – O son of Kuru.

When there is an increase in the mode of ignorance, O son of Kuru, darkness, inertia, madness and illusion are manifested.

PURPORT: When there is no illumination, knowledge is absent. One in the mode of ignorance does not work by a regulative principle; he wants to act whimsically, for no purpose. Even though he has the capacity to work, he makes no endeavor. This is called illusion. Although consciousness is going on, life is inactive. These are the symptoms of one in the mode of ignorance.

Text 14 यदा सत्त्वे प्रवृद्धे तु प्रलयं याति देहभृत् ।
तदोत्तमविदां लोकानमलान् प्रतिपद्यते ॥१४॥

yadā sattve pravṛddhe tu, pralayaṁ yāti deha-bhṛt
tadottama-vidāṁ lokān, amalān pratipadyate

yadā – when; *sattve* – the mode of goodness; *pravṛddhe* – developed; *tu* – but; *pralayam* – dissolution; *yāti* – goes; *deha-bhṛt* – the embodied; *tadā* – at that time; *uttama-vidām* – of the great sages; *lokān* – the planets; *amalān* – pure; *pratipadyate* – attains.

When one dies in the mode of goodness, he attains to the pure higher planets of the great sages.

PURPORT: One in goodness attains higher planetary systems, like Brahmaloka or Janaloka, and there enjoys godly happiness. The word *amalān* is significant; it means "free from the modes of passion and ignorance." There are impurities in the material world, but the mode of goodness is the purest form of existence in the material world. There are different kinds of planets for different kinds of living entities. Those who die in the mode of goodness are elevated to the planets where great sages and great devotees live.

Text 15 रजसि प्रलयं गत्वा कर्मसङ्गिषु जायते ।
तथा प्रलीनस्तमसि मूढयोनिषु जायते ॥१५॥

rajasi pralayaṁ gatvā, karma-saṅgiṣu jāyate
tathā pralīnas tamasi, mūḍha-yoniṣu jāyate

rajasi – in passion; *pralayam* – dissolution; *gatvā* – attaining; *karma-saṅgiṣu* – in the association of those engaged in fruitive activities; *jāyate* – takes birth; *tathā* – similarly; *pralīnaḥ* – being dissolved; *tamasi* – in ignorance; *mūḍha-yoniṣu* – in animal species; *jāyate* – takes birth.

When one dies in the mode of passion, he takes birth among those engaged in fruitive activities; and when one dies in the mode of ignorance, he takes birth in the animal kingdom.

PURPORT: Some people have the impression that when the soul reaches the platform of human life it never goes down again. This is incorrect. According to this verse, if one develops the mode of ignorance, after his death he is degraded to an animal form of life. From there one has to again elevate himself, by an evolutionary process, to come again to the human form of life. Therefore, those who are actually serious about human life should take to the mode of goodness and in good association transcend the modes and become situated in Kṛṣṇa consciousness. This is the aim of human life. Otherwise, there is no guarantee that the human being will again attain to the human status.

Text 16 कर्मणः सुकृतस्याहुः सात्त्विकं निर्मलं फलम् ।
रजसस्तु फलं दुःखमज्ञानं तमसः फलम् ॥१६॥

karmaṇaḥ sukṛtasyāhuḥ, sāttvikaṁ nirmalaṁ phalam
rajasas tu phalaṁ duḥkham, ajñānaṁ tamasaḥ phalam

karmaṇaḥ – of work; *su-kṛtasya* – pious; *āhuḥ* – is said; *sāttvikam* – in the mode of goodness; *nirmalam* – purified; *phalam* – the result; *rajasaḥ* – of the mode of passion; *tu* – but; *phalam* – the result; *duḥkham* – misery; *ajñānam* – nonsense; *tamasaḥ* – of the mode of ignorance; *phalam* – the result.

The result of pious action is pure and is said to be in the mode of goodness. But action done in the mode of passion results in misery, and action performed in the mode of ignorance results in foolishness.

PURPORT: The result of pious activities in the mode of goodness is pure. Therefore the sages, who are free from all illusion, are situated in happiness. But activities in the mode of passion are simply miserable. Any activity for material happiness is bound to be defeated. If, for example, one wants to have a skyscraper, so much human misery has to be undergone before a big skyscraper can be built. The financier has to take much trouble to earn a mass of wealth, and those who are slaving to construct the building have to render physical toil. The miseries are there. Thus *Bhagavad-gītā* says that in any activity performed under the spell of the mode of passion, there is definitely great misery. There may be a little so-called mental happiness – "I have this house or this money" – but this is not actual happiness.

As far as the mode of ignorance is concerned, the performer is without knowledge, and therefore all his activities result in present misery, and afterwards he will go on toward animal life. Animal life is always miserable, although, under the spell of the illusory energy, *māyā,* the animals do not understand this. Slaughtering poor animals is also due to the mode of ignorance. The animal killers do not know that in the future the animal will have a body suitable to kill them. That is the law of nature. In human society, if one kills a man he has to be hanged. That is the law of the state. Because of ignorance, people do not perceive that there is a complete state controlled by the Supreme Lord. Every living creature is a son of the Supreme Lord, and He does not tolerate even an ant's being killed. One has to pay for it. So indulgence in animal killing for the taste of the tongue is the grossest kind of ignorance. A human being has no need to kill animals, because God has supplied so many nice things. If one indulges in meat-eating anyway, it is to be understood that he is acting in ignorance and is making his future very dark. Of all kinds of animal killing, the killing of cows is most vicious because the cow gives us all kinds of pleasure by supplying milk. Cow slaughter is an act of the grossest type of ignorance. In the Vedic literature (*Ṛg Veda* 9.46.4) the words *gobhiḥ prīṇita-matsaram* indicate that one who, being fully satisfied by milk, is desirous of killing the cow is in the grossest ignorance. There is also a prayer in the Vedic literature that states:

namo brahmaṇya-devāya, go-brāhmaṇa-hitāya ca
jagad-dhitāya kṛṣṇāya, govindāya namo namaḥ

"My Lord, You are the well-wisher of the cows and the *brāhmaṇas,* and You are the well-wisher of the entire human society and world." (*Viṣṇu Purāṇa* 1.19.65) The purport is that special mention is given in that prayer for the protection of the cows and the *brāhmaṇas. Brāhmaṇas* are the symbol of spiritual education, and cows are the symbol of the most valuable food; these two living creatures, the *brāhmaṇas* and the cows, must be given all protection – that is real advancement of civilization. In modern human society, spiritual knowledge is neglected, and cow killing is encouraged. It is to be understood, then, that human society is advancing in the wrong direction and is clearing the path to its own condemnation. A civilization which guides the citizens to become animals in their next lives is certainly not a human civilization. The present human civilization is, of course, grossly misled by the modes of passion and ignorance. It is a very dangerous age, and all nations should take care to provide the easiest process, Kṛṣṇa consciousness, to save humanity from the greatest danger.

Text 17 सत्त्वात्सञ्जायते ज्ञानं रजसो लोभ एव च ।
प्रमादमोहौ तमसो भवतोऽज्ञानमेव च ॥१७॥

sattvāt sañjāyate jñānaṁ, rajaso lobha eva ca
pramāda-mohau tamaso, bhavato 'jñānam eva ca

sattvāt – from the mode of goodness; *sañjāyate* – develops; *jñānam* – knowledge; *rajasaḥ* – from the mode of passion; *lobhaḥ* – greed; *eva* – certainly; *ca* – also; *pramāda* – madness; *mohau* – and illusion; *tamasaḥ* – from the mode of ignorance; *bhavataḥ* – develop; *ajñānam* – nonsense; *eva* – certainly; *ca* – also.

From the mode of goodness, real knowledge develops; from the mode of passion, greed develops; and from the mode of ignorance develop foolishness, madness and illusion.

PURPORT: Since the present civilization is not very congenial to the living entities, Kṛṣṇa consciousness is recommended. Through Kṛṣṇa consciousness, society will develop the mode of goodness. When the mode of goodness is developed, people will see things as they are. In the mode of ignorance, people are just like animals and cannot see things clearly. In the mode of ignorance, for example, they do not see that by killing one animal they are taking the chance of being killed by the same animal in the next life. Because people have no education in actual knowledge, they become irresponsible. To stop this irresponsibility, education for developing the mode of goodness of the people in general must be there. When they are actually educated in the mode of goodness, they will become sober, in full knowledge of things as they are. Then people will be happy and prosperous. Even if the majority of the people aren't happy and prosperous, if a certain percentage of the population develops Kṛṣṇa consciousness and becomes situated in the mode of goodness, then there is the possibility for peace and prosperity all over the world. Otherwise, if the world is devoted to the modes of passion and ignorance, there can be no peace or prosperity. In the mode of passion, people become greedy, and their hankering for sense enjoyment has no limit. One can see that even if one has enough money and adequate arrangements for sense gratification, there is neither happiness nor peace of mind. That is not possible, because one is situated in the mode of passion. If one wants happiness at all, his money will not help him; he has to elevate himself to the mode of goodness by practicing Kṛṣṇa consciousness. When one is engaged in the mode of passion, not only is he mentally unhappy, but his profession and occupation are also very troublesome. He has to devise so many plans and schemes to acquire enough money to maintain his status quo. This is all miserable. In the mode of ignorance, people become mad.

Being distressed by their circumstances, they take shelter of intoxication, and thus they sink further into ignorance. Their future in life is very dark.

Text 18 ऊर्ध्वं गच्छन्ति सत्त्वस्था मध्ये तिष्ठन्ति राजसाः ।
जघन्यगुणवृत्तिस्था अधो गच्छन्ति तामसाः ॥१८॥

ūrdhvaṁ gacchanti sattva-sthā, madhye tiṣṭhanti rājasāḥ
jaghanya-guṇa-vṛtti-sthā, adho gacchanti tāmasāḥ

ūrdhvam – upwards; *gacchanti* – go; *sattva-sthāḥ* – those situated in the mode of goodness; *madhye* – in the middle; *tiṣṭhanti* – dwell; *rājasāḥ* – those situated in the mode of passion; *jaghanya* – of abominable; *guṇa* – quality; *vṛtti-sthāḥ* – whose occupation; *adhaḥ* – down; *gacchanti* – go; *tāmasāḥ* – persons in the mode of ignorance.

Those situated in the mode of goodness gradually go upward to the higher planets; those in the mode of passion live on the earthly planets; and those in the abominable mode of ignorance go down to the hellish worlds.

PURPORT: In this verse the results of actions in the three modes of nature are more explicitly set forth. There is an upper planetary system, consisting of the heavenly planets, where everyone is highly elevated. According to the degree of development of the mode of goodness, the living entity can be transferred to various planets in this system. The highest planet is Satyaloka, or Brahmaloka, where the prime person of this universe, Lord Brahmā, resides. We have seen already that we can hardly calculate the wondrous condition of life in Brahmaloka, but the highest condition of life, the mode of goodness, can bring us to this.

The mode of passion is mixed. It is in the middle, between the modes of goodness and ignorance. A person is not always pure, but even if he should be purely in the mode of passion, he will simply remain on this earth as a king or a rich man. But because there are mixtures, one can also go down. People on this earth, in the mode of passion or ignorance, cannot forcibly approach the higher planets by machine. In the mode of passion, there is also the chance of becoming mad in the next life.

The lowest quality, the mode of ignorance, is described here as abominable. The result of developing ignorance is very, very risky. It is the lowest quality in material nature. Beneath the human level there are eight million species of life – birds, beasts, reptiles, trees, etc. – and according to the development of the mode of ignorance, people are brought down to these abominable conditions. The word *tāmasāḥ* is very significant here. *Tāmasāḥ* indicates those who stay continuously in the mode of ignorance without rising to a higher mode. Their future is very dark.

There is an opportunity for men in the modes of ignorance and passion to be elevated to the mode of goodness, and that system is called Kṛṣṇa consciousness. But one who does not take advantage of this opportunity will certainly continue in the lower modes.

Text 19 नान्यं गुणेभ्यः कर्तारं यदा द्रष्टानुपश्यति ।
गुणेभ्यश्च परं वेत्ति मद्भावं सोऽधिगच्छति ॥१९॥

nānyaṁ guṇebhyaḥ kartāraṁ, yadā draṣṭānupaśyati
guṇebhyaś ca paraṁ vetti, mad-bhāvaṁ so 'dhigacchati

na – no; *anyam* – other; *guṇebhyaḥ* – than the qualities; *kartāram* – performer; *yadā* – when; *draṣṭā* – a seer; *anupaśyati* – sees properly; *guṇebhyaḥ* – to the modes of nature; *ca* – and; *param* – transcendental; *vetti* – knows; *mat-bhāvam* – to My spiritual nature; *saḥ* – he; *adhigacchati* – is promoted.

When one properly sees that in all activities no other performer is at work than these modes of nature, and he knows the Supreme Lord, who is transcendental to all these modes, he attains My spiritual nature.

PURPORT: One can transcend all the activities of the modes of material nature simply by understanding them properly by learning from the proper souls. The real spiritual master is Kṛṣṇa, and He is imparting this spiritual knowledge to Arjuna. Similarly, it is from those who are fully in Kṛṣṇa consciousness that one has to learn this science of activities in terms of the modes of nature. Otherwise, one's life will be misdirected. By the instruction of a bona fide spiritual master, a living entity can know of his spiritual position, his material body, his senses, how he is entrapped, and how he is under the spell of the material modes of nature. He is helpless, being in the grip of these modes, but when he can see his real position, then he can attain to the transcendental platform, having the scope for spiritual life. Actually, the living entity is not the performer of different activities. He is forced to act because he is situated in a particular type of body, conducted by some particular mode of material nature. Unless one has the help of spiritual authority, he cannot understand in what position he is actually situated. With the association of a bona fide spiritual master, he can see his real position, and by such an understanding he can become fixed in full Kṛṣṇa consciousness. A man in Kṛṣṇa consciousness is not controlled by the spell of the material modes of nature. It has already been stated in the Seventh Chapter that one who has surrendered to Kṛṣṇa is relieved from the activities of material nature. For one who is able to see things as they are, the influence of material nature gradually ceases.

Text 20 गुणानेतानतीत्य त्रीन्देही देहसमुद्भवान् ।
जन्ममृत्युजरादुःखैर्विमुक्तोऽमृतमश्नुते ॥२०॥

guṇān etān atītya trīn, dehī deha-samudbhavān
janma-mṛtyu-jarā-duḥkhair, vimukto 'mṛtam aśnute

guṇān – qualities; *etān* – all these; *atītya* – transcending; *trīn* – three; *dehī* – the embodied; *deha* – the body; *samudbhavān* – produced of; *janma* – of birth; *mṛtyu* – death; *jarā* – and old age; *duḥkhaiḥ* – the distresses; *vimuktaḥ* – being freed from; *amṛtam* – nectar; *aśnute* – he enjoys.

When the embodied being is able to transcend these three modes associated with the material body, he can become free from birth, death, old age and their distresses and can enjoy nectar even in this life.

PURPORT: How one can stay in the transcendental position, even in this body, in full Kṛṣṇa consciousness, is explained in this verse. The Sanskrit word *dehī* means "embodied." Although one is within this material body, by his advancement in spiritual knowledge he can be free from the influence of the modes of nature. He can enjoy the happiness of spiritual life even in this body because, after leaving this body, he is certainly going to the spiritual sky. But even in this body he can enjoy spiritual happiness. In other words, devotional service in Kṛṣṇa consciousness is the sign of liberation from material entanglement, and this will be explained in the Eighteenth Chapter. When one is freed from the influence of the modes of material nature, he enters into devotional service.

Text 21 अर्जुन उवाच
कैर्लिङ्गैस्त्रीन् गुणानेतानतीतो भवति प्रभो ।
किमाचारः कथं चैतांस्त्रीन् गुणानतिवर्तते ॥२१॥

arjuna uvāca
kair liṅgais trīn guṇān etān, atīto bhavati prabho
kim-ācāraḥ kathaṁ caitāṁs, trīn guṇān ativartate

arjunaḥ uvāca – Arjuna said; *kaiḥ* – by which; *liṅgaiḥ* – symptoms; *trīn* – three; *guṇān* – qualities; *etān* – all these; *atītaḥ* – having transcended; *bhavati* – is; *prabho* – O my Lord; *kim* – what; *ācāraḥ* – behavior; *katham* – how; *ca* – also; *etān* – these; *trīn* – three; *guṇān* – qualities; *ativartate* – transcends.

Arjuna inquired: O my dear Lord, by which symptoms is one known who is transcendental to these three modes? What is his behavior? And how does he transcend the modes of nature?

PURPORT: In this verse, Arjuna's questions are very appropriate. He wants to know the symptoms of a person who has already transcended the material modes. He first inquires of the symptoms of such a transcendental person. How can one understand that he has already transcended the influence of the modes of material nature? The second question asks how he lives and what his activities are. Are they regulated or nonregulated? Then Arjuna inquires of the means by which he can attain the transcendental nature. That is very important. Unless one knows the direct means by which one can be situated always transcendentally, there is no possibility of showing the symptoms. So all these questions put by Arjuna are very important, and the Lord answers them.

Texts 22–25

श्रीभगवानुवाच
प्रकाशं च प्रवृत्तिं च मोहमेव च पाण्डव ।
न द्वेष्टि सम्प्रवृत्तानि न निवृत्तानि काङ्क्षति ॥२२॥
उदासीनवदासीनो गुणैर्यो न विचाल्यते ।
गुणा वर्तन्त इत्येवं योऽवतिष्ठति नेङ्गते ॥२३॥
समदुःखसुखः स्वस्थः समलोष्टाश्मकाञ्चनः ।
तुल्यप्रियाप्रियो धीरस्तुल्यनिन्दात्मसंस्तुतिः ॥२४॥
मानापमानयोस्तुल्यस्तुल्यो मित्रारिपक्षयोः ।
सर्वारम्भपरित्यागी गुणातीतः स उच्यते ॥२५॥

śrī-bhagavān uvāca
prakāśaṁ ca pravṛttiṁ ca, moham eva ca pāṇḍava
na dveṣṭi sampravṛttāni, na nivṛttāni kāṅkṣati

udāsīna-vad āsīno, guṇair yo na vicālyate
guṇā vartanta ity evaṁ, yo 'vatiṣṭhati neṅgate

sama-duḥkha-sukhaḥ sva-sthaḥ, sama-loṣṭāśma-kāñcanaḥ
tulya-priyāpriyo dhīras, tulya-nindātma-saṁstutiḥ

mānāpamānayos tulyas, tulyo mitrāri-pakṣayoḥ
sarvārambha-parityāgī, guṇātītaḥ sa ucyate

śrī-bhagavān uvāca – the Supreme Personality of Godhead said; *prakāśam* – illumination; *ca* – and; *pravṛttim* – attachment; *ca* – and; *moham* – illusion; *eva ca* – also; *pāṇḍava* – O son of Pāṇḍu; *na dveṣṭi* – does not hate; *sampravṛttāni* – although developed; *na nivṛttāni* – nor stopping development; *kāṅkṣati* – desires; *udāsīna-vat* – as if neutral; *āsīnaḥ* – situated; *guṇaiḥ* – by the qualities; *yaḥ* – one who; *na* – never; *vicālyate* – is agitated; *guṇāḥ* – the qualities; *vartante* – are acting; *iti evam* – knowing thus; *yaḥ* – one who; *avatiṣṭhati* – remains; *na* – never; *iṅgate* – flickers; *sama* – equal; *duḥkha* – in distress; *sukhaḥ* – and happiness; *sva-sthaḥ* – being situated in himself; *sama* – equally; *loṣṭa* – a lump of earth; *aśma* – stone; *kāñcanaḥ* – gold; *tulya* – equally disposed; *priya* – to the dear; *apriyaḥ* – and the undesirable; *dhīraḥ* – steady; *tulya* – equal; *nindā* – in defamation; *ātma-saṁstutiḥ* – and praise of himself; *māna* – in honor; *apamānayoḥ* – and dishonor; *tulyaḥ* – equal; *tulyaḥ* – equal; *mitra* – of friends; *ari* – and enemies; *pakṣayoḥ* – to the parties; *sarva* – of all; *ārambha* – endeavors; *parityāgī* – renouncer; *guṇa-atītaḥ* – transcendental to the material modes of nature; *saḥ* – he; *ucyate* – is said to be.

The Supreme Personality of Godhead said: O son of Pāṇḍu, he who does not hate illumination, attachment and delusion when they are present or long for them when they disappear; who is unwavering and undisturbed through all these reactions of the material qualities, remaining neutral and transcendental, knowing that the modes alone are active; who is situated in the self and regards alike happiness and distress; who looks upon a lump of earth, a stone and a piece of gold with an equal eye; who is equal toward the desirable and the undesirable; who is steady, situated equally well in praise and blame, honor and dishonor; who treats alike both friend and enemy; and who has renounced all material activities – such a person is said to have transcended the modes of nature.

PURPORT: Arjuna submitted three different questions, and the Lord answers them one after another. In these verses, Kṛṣṇa first indicates that a person transcendentally situated has no envy and does not hanker for anything. When a living entity stays in this material world embodied by the material body, it is to be understood that he is under the control of one of the three modes of material nature. When he is actually out of the body, then he is out of the clutches of the material modes of nature. But as long as he is not out of the material body, he should be neutral. He should engage himself in the devotional service of the Lord so that his identity with the material body will automatically be forgotten. When one is conscious of the material body, he acts only for sense gratification, but when one transfers the consciousness to Kṛṣṇa, sense gratification automatically stops. One does not need this material body, and he does not need to accept the dictations of the material body. The qualities of the material modes in the body will act, but as spirit soul the self is aloof from such activities. How does he become aloof? He does not desire to enjoy the body, nor does he desire to get out of it. Thus transcendentally situated, the devotee becomes automatically free. He need not try to become free from the influence of the modes of material nature.

The next question concerns the dealings of a transcendentally situated person. The materially situated person is affected by so-called honor and dishonor offered to the body, but the transcendentally situated person is not affected by such false honor and dishonor. He performs his duty in Kṛṣṇa consciousness and does not mind whether a man honors or dishonors him. He accepts things that are favorable for his duty in Kṛṣṇa consciousness, otherwise he has no necessity of anything material, either a stone or gold. He takes everyone as his dear friend who helps him in his execution of Kṛṣṇa consciousness, and he does not hate his so-called enemy. He is equally disposed and sees everything on an equal level because he knows perfectly well that he has nothing to do with material existence. Social and political issues do not affect him, because he knows the situation of temporary upheavals and disturbances. He does not attempt anything for his own sake. He can attempt anything for Kṛṣṇa, but for his personal self he does not attempt anything. By such behavior one becomes actually transcendentally situated.

Text 26 मां च योऽव्यभिचारेण भक्तियोगेन सेवते ।
स गुणान् समतीत्यैतान् ब्रह्मभूयाय कल्पते ॥२६॥

māṁ ca yo 'vyabhicāreṇa, bhakti-yogena sevate
sa guṇān samatītyaitān, brahma-bhūyāya kalpate

mām – unto Me; *ca* – also; *yaḥ* – a person who; *avyabhicāreṇa* – without fail; *bhakti-yogena* – by devotional service; *sevate* – renders service; *saḥ* – he; *guṇān* – the modes of material nature; *samatītya* – transcending; *etān* – all these; *brahma-bhūyāya* – elevated to the Brahman platform; *kalpate* – becomes.

One who engages in full devotional service, unfailing in all circumstances, at once transcends the modes of material nature and thus comes to the level of Brahman.

PURPORT: This verse is a reply to Arjuna's third question: What is the means of attaining to the transcendental position? As explained before, the material world is acting under the spell of the modes of material nature. One should not be disturbed by the activities of the modes of nature; instead of putting his consciousness into such activities, he may transfer his consciousness to Kṛṣṇa activities. Kṛṣṇa activities are known as *bhakti-yoga* – always acting for Kṛṣṇa. This includes not only Kṛṣṇa, but His different plenary expansions such as Rāma and Nārāyaṇa. He has innumerable expansions. One who is engaged in the service of any of the forms of Kṛṣṇa, or of His plenary expansions, is considered to be transcendentally situated. One should also note that all the forms of Kṛṣṇa are fully transcendental, blissful, full of knowledge and eternal. Such personalities of Godhead are omnipotent and omniscient, and they possess all transcendental qualities. So if one engages himself in the service of Kṛṣṇa or His plenary expansions with unfailing determination, although these modes of material nature are very difficult to overcome, one can overcome them easily. This has already been explained in the Seventh Chapter. One who surrenders unto Kṛṣṇa at once surmounts the influence of the modes of material nature. To be in Kṛṣṇa consciousness or in devotional service means to acquire equality with Kṛṣṇa. The Lord says that His nature is eternal, blissful and full of knowledge, and the living entities are part and parcel of the Supreme, as gold particles are part of a gold mine. Thus the living entity, in his spiritual position, is as good as gold, as good as Kṛṣṇa in quality. The difference of individuality continues, otherwise there would be no question of *bhakti-yoga. Bhakti-yoga* means that the Lord is there, the devotee is there and the activity of exchange of love between the Lord and the devotee is there. Therefore the individuality of two persons is present in the Supreme Personality of Godhead and the individual person, otherwise there would be no meaning to *bhakti-yoga*. If one is not situated in the same transcendental position with the Lord, one cannot serve the Supreme Lord. To be a personal assistant to a king, one must acquire the qualifications. Thus the qualification is to become Brahman, or freed from all material contamination. It is said in the Vedic literature, *brahmaiva san brahmāpy eti*. One can attain the Supreme Brahman by becoming Brahman. This means that one must qualitatively become one with Brahman. By attainment of Brahman, one does not lose his eternal Brahman identity as an individual soul.

Text 27 ब्रह्मणो हि प्रतिष्ठाहममृतस्याव्ययस्य च ।
शाश्वतस्य च धर्मस्य सुखस्यैकान्तिकस्य च ॥२७॥

brahmaṇo hi pratiṣṭhāham, amṛtasyāvyayasya ca
śāśvatasya ca dharmasya, sukhasyaikāntikasya ca

brahmaṇaḥ – of the impersonal *brahma-jyotir; hi* – certainly; *pratiṣṭhā* – the rest; *aham* – I am; *amṛtasya* – of the immortal; *avyayasya* – of the imperishable; *ca* – also; *śāśvatasya* – of the eternal; *ca* – and; *dharmasya* – of the constitutional position; *sukhasya* – of happiness; *aikāntikasya* – ultimate; *ca* – also.

And I am the basis of the impersonal Brahman, which is immortal, imperishable and eternal and is the constitutional position of ultimate happiness.

PURPORT: The constitution of Brahman is immortality, imperishability, eternity, and happiness. Brahman is the beginning of transcendental realization. Paramātmā, the Supersoul, is the middle, the second stage in transcendental realization, and the Supreme Personality of Godhead is the ultimate realization of the Absolute Truth. Therefore, both Paramātmā and the impersonal Brahman are within the Supreme Person. It is explained in the Seventh Chapter that material nature is the manifestation of the inferior energy of the Supreme Lord. The Lord impregnates the inferior, material nature with fragments of the superior nature, and that is the spiritual touch in the material nature. When a living entity conditioned by this material nature begins the cultivation of spiritual knowledge, he elevates himself from the position of material existence and gradually rises up to the Brahman conception of the Supreme. This attainment of the Brahman conception of life is the first stage in self-realization. At this stage the Brahman-realized person is transcendental to the material position, but he is not actually perfect in Brahman realization. If he wants, he can continue to stay in the Brahman position and then gradually rise up to Paramātmā realization and then to the realization of the Supreme Personality of Godhead. There are many examples of this in Vedic literature. The four Kumāras were situated first in the impersonal Brahman conception of truth, but then they gradually rose to the platform of devotional service. One who cannot elevate himself beyond the impersonal conception of Brahman runs the risk of falling down. In *Śrīmad-Bhāgavatam* it is stated that although a person may rise to the stage of impersonal Brahman, without going further, with no information of the Supreme Person, his intelligence is not perfectly clear. Therefore, in spite of being raised to the Brahman platform, there is the chance of falling down if one is not engaged in the devotional service of the Lord. In the Vedic language it is also said, *raso vai saḥ, rasaṁ hy evāyaṁ labdhvānandī bhavati:* "When one understands the Personality of Godhead, the reservoir of pleasure, Kṛṣṇa, he actually becomes transcendentally blissful." (*Taittirīya Upaniṣad* 2.7.1) The Supreme Lord is full in six opulences, and when a devotee approaches Him there is an exchange of these six opulences. The servant of the king enjoys on an almost equal level with the king. And so eternal happiness, imperishable happiness, and eternal life accompany devotional service. Therefore, realization of Brahman, or eternity, or imperishability, is included in devotional service. This is already possessed by a person who is engaged in devotional service.

The living entity, although Brahman by nature, has the desire to lord it over the material world, and due to this he falls down. In his constitutional position, a living entity is above the three modes of material nature, but association with material nature entangles him in the different modes of material nature – goodness, passion and ignorance. Due to the association of these three modes, his desire to dominate the material world is there. By engagement in devotional service in full Kṛṣṇa consciousness, he is immediately situated in the transcendental position, and his unlawful desire to control material nature is removed. Therefore the process of devotional service, beginning with hearing, chanting, remembering – the prescribed nine methods for realizing devotional service – should be practiced in the association of devotees. Gradually, by such association, by the influence of the spiritual master, one's material desire to dominate is removed, and one becomes firmly situated in the Lord's transcendental loving service. This method is prescribed from the twenty-second to the last verse of this chapter. Devotional service to the Lord is very simple: one should always engage in the service of the Lord, should eat the remnants of foodstuffs offered to the Deity, smell the flowers offered to the lotus feet of the Lord, see the places where the Lord had His transcendental pastimes, read of the different activities of the Lord, His reciprocation of love with His devotees, chant always the transcendental vibration Hare Kṛṣṇa, Hare Kṛṣṇa, Kṛṣṇa Kṛṣṇa, Hare Hare/ Hare Rāma, Hare Rāma, Rāma Rāma, Hare Hare, and observe the fasting days commemorating the appearances and disappearances of the Lord and His devotees. By following such a process one becomes completely detached from all material activities. One who can thus situate himself in the *brahma-jyotir* or the different varieties of the Brahman conception is equal to the Supreme Personality of Godhead in quality.

Thus end the Bhaktivedanta Purports to the Fourteenth Chapter of the Śrīmad Bhagavad-gītā *in the matter of the Three Modes of Material Nature.*

CHAPTER FIFTEEN

The Yoga of the Supreme Person

Text 1 श्रीभगवानुवाच
ऊर्ध्वमूलमधःशाखमश्वत्थं प्राहुरव्ययम् ।
छन्दांसि यस्य पर्णानि यस्तं वेद स वेदवित् ॥१॥

śrī-bhagavān uvāca
ūrdhva-mūlam adhaḥ-śākham, aśvatthaṁ prāhur avyayam
chandāṁsi yasya parṇāni, yas taṁ veda sa veda-vit

śrī-bhagavān uvāca – the Supreme Personality of Godhead said; *ūrdhva-mūlam* – with roots above; *adhaḥ* – downwards; *śākham* – branches; *aśvattham* – a banyan tree; *prāhuḥ* – is said; *avyayam* – eternal; *chandāṁsi* – the Vedic hymns; *yasya* – of which; *parṇāni* – the leaves; *yaḥ* – anyone who; *tam* – that; *veda* – knows; *saḥ* – he; *veda-vit* – the knower of the *Vedas.*

The Supreme Personality of Godhead said: It is said that there is an imperishable banyan tree that has its roots upward and its branches down and whose leaves are the Vedic hymns. One who knows this tree is the knower of the Vedas.

PURPORT: After the discussion of the importance of *bhakti-yoga,* one may question, "What about the *Vedas*?" It is explained in this chapter that the purpose of Vedic study is to understand Kṛṣṇa. Therefore one who is in Kṛṣṇa consciousness, who is engaged in devotional service, already knows the *Vedas.*

The entanglement of this material world is compared here to a banyan tree. For one who is engaged in fruitive activities, there is no end to the banyan tree. He wanders from one branch to another, to another, to another. The tree of this material world has no end, and for one who is attached to this tree, there is no possibility of liberation. The Vedic hymns, meant for elevating oneself, are called the leaves of this tree. This tree's roots grow upward because they begin from where Brahmā is located, the topmost planet of this universe. If one can understand this indestructible tree of illusion, then one can get out of it.

This process of extrication should be understood. In the previous chapters it has been explained that there are many processes by which to get out of the material entanglement. And, up to the Thirteenth Chapter, we have seen that devotional service to the Supreme Lord is the best way. Now, the basic principle of devotional service is detachment from material activities and attachment to the transcendental service of the Lord. The process of breaking attachment to the material world is discussed in the beginning of this chapter. The root of this material existence grows upward. This means that it begins from the total material substance, from the topmost planet of the universe. From there, the whole universe is expanded, with so many branches, representing the various planetary systems. The fruits represent the results of the living entities' activities, namely, religion, economic development, sense gratification and liberation.

Now, there is no ready experience in this world of a tree situated with its branches down and its roots upward, but there is such a thing. That tree can be found beside a reservoir of water. We can see that the trees on the bank reflect upon the water with their branches down and roots up. In other words, the tree of this material world is only a reflection of the real tree of the spiritual world. This reflection of the spiritual world is situated on desire, just as a tree's reflection is situated on water. Desire is the cause of things' being situated in this reflected material light. One who wants to get out of this material existence must know this tree thoroughly through analytical study. Then he can cut off his relationship with it.

This tree, being the reflection of the real tree, is an exact replica. Everything is there in the spiritual world. The impersonalists take Brahman to be the root of this material tree, and from the root, according to Sāṅkhya philosophy, come *prakṛti, puruṣa,* then the three *guṇas,* then the five gross elements (*pañca-mahā-bhūta*), then the ten senses (*daśendriya*), mind, etc. In this way they divide up the whole material world into twenty-four elements. If Brahman is the center of all manifestations, then this material world is a manifestation of the center by 180 degrees, and the other 180 degrees constitute the spiritual world. The material world is the perverted reflection, so the spiritual world must have the same variegatedness, but in reality. The *prakṛti* is the external energy of the Supreme Lord, and the *puruṣa* is the Supreme Lord Himself, and that is explained in *Bhagavad-gītā*. Since this manifestation is material, it is temporary. A reflection is temporary, for it is sometimes seen and sometimes not seen. But the origin from whence the reflection is reflected is eternal. The material reflection of the real tree has to be cut off. When it is said that a person knows the *Vedas*, it is assumed that he knows how to cut off attachment to this material world. If one knows that process, he actually knows the *Vedas*. One who is attracted by the ritualistic formulas of the *Vedas* is attracted by the beautiful green leaves of the tree. He does not exactly know the purpose of the *Vedas*. The purpose of the *Vedas*, as disclosed by the Personality of Godhead Himself, is to cut down this reflected tree and attain the real tree of the spiritual world.

Text 2 अधश्चोर्ध्वं प्रसृतास्तस्य शाखा गुणप्रवृद्धा विषयप्रवालाः ।
अधश्च मूलान्यनुसन्ततानि कर्मानुबन्धीनि मनुष्यलोके ॥ २ ॥

adhaś cordhvaṁ prasṛtās tasya śākhā
guṇa-pravṛddhā viṣaya-pravālāḥ
adhaś ca mūlāny anusantatāni
karmānubandhīni manuṣya-loke

adhaḥ – downward; *ca* – and; *ūrdhvam* – upward; *prasṛtāḥ* – extended; *tasya* – its; *śākhāḥ* – branches; *guṇa* – by the modes of material nature; *pravṛddhāḥ* – developed; *viṣaya* – sense objects; *pravālāḥ* – twigs; *adhaḥ* – downward; *ca* – and; *mūlāni* – roots; *anusantatāni* – extended; *karma* – to work; *anubandhīni* – bound; *manuṣya-loke* – in the world of human society.

The branches of this tree extend downward and upward, nourished by the three modes of material nature. The twigs are the objects of the senses. This tree also has roots going down, and these are bound to the fruitive actions of human society.

PURPORT: The description of the banyan tree is further explained here. Its branches spread in all directions. In the lower parts, there are variegated manifestations of living entities – human beings, animals, horses, cows, dogs, cats, etc. These are situated on the lower parts of the branches, whereas on the upper parts are higher forms of living entities: the demigods, Gandharvas and many other higher species of life. As a tree is nourished by water, so this tree is nourished by the three modes of material nature. Sometimes we find that a tract of land is barren for want of sufficient water, and sometimes a tract is very green; similarly, where particular modes of material nature are proportionately greater in quantity, the different species of life are manifested accordingly.

The twigs of the tree are considered to be the sense objects. By development of the different modes of nature we develop different senses, and by the senses we enjoy different varieties of sense objects. The tips of the branches are the senses – the ears, nose, eyes, etc. – which are attached to the enjoyment of different sense objects. The twigs are sound, form, touch, and so on – the sense objects. The subsidiary roots are attachments and aversions, which are by-products of different varieties of suffering and sense enjoyment. The tendencies toward piety and impiety are considered to develop from these secondary roots, which spread in all directions. The real root is from Brahmaloka, and the other roots are in the human planetary systems. After one enjoys the results of virtuous activities in the upper planetary systems, he comes down to this earth and renews his *karma,* or fruitive activities for promotion. This planet of human beings is considered the field of activities.

Texts 3–4

न रूपमस्येह तथोपलभ्यते नान्तो न चादिर्न च सम्प्रतिष्ठा ।
अश्वत्थमेनं सुविरूढमूल मसङ्गशस्त्रेण दृढेन छित्त्वा ॥ ३ ॥
ततः पदं तत्परिमार्गितव्यं यस्मिन् गता न निवर्तन्ति भूयः ।
तमेव चाद्यं पुरुषं प्रपद्ये यतः प्रवृत्तिः प्रसृता पुराणी ॥ ४ ॥

na rūpam asyeha tathopalabhyate
nānto na cādir na ca sampratiṣṭhā
aśvattham enaṁ su-virūḍha-mūlam
asaṅga-śastreṇa dṛḍhena chittvā

tataḥ padaṁ tat parimārgitavyaṁ
yasmin gatā na nivartanti bhūyaḥ
tam eva cādyaṁ puruṣaṁ prapadye
yataḥ pravṛttiḥ prasṛtā purāṇī

na – not; *rūpam* – the form; *asya* – of this tree; *iha* – in this world; *tathā* – also; *upalabhyate* – can be perceived; *na* – never; *antaḥ* – end; *na* – never; *ca* – also; *ādiḥ* – beginning; *na* – never; *ca* – also; *sampratiṣṭhā* – the foundation; *aśvattham* – banyan tree; *enam* – this; *su-virūḍha* – strongly; *mūlam* – rooted; *asaṅga-śastreṇa* – by the weapon of detachment; *dṛḍhena* – strong; *chittvā* – cutting; *tataḥ* – thereafter; *padam* – situation; *tat* – that; *parimārgitavyam* – has to be searched out; *yasmin* – where; *gatāḥ* – going; *na* – never; *nivartanti* – they come back; *bhūyaḥ* – again; *tam* – to Him; *eva* – certainly; *ca* – also; *ādyam* – original; *puruṣam* – the Personality of Godhead; *prapadye* – surrender; *yataḥ* – from whom; *pravṛttiḥ* – the beginning; *prasṛtā* – extended; *purāṇi* – very old.

The real form of this tree cannot be perceived in this world. No one can understand where it ends, where it begins, or where its foundation is. But with determination one must cut down this strongly rooted tree with the weapon of detachment. Thereafter, one must seek that place from which, having gone, one never returns, and there surrender to that Supreme Personality of Godhead from whom everything began and from whom everything has extended since time immemorial.

PURPORT: It is now clearly stated that the real form of this banyan tree cannot be understood in this material world. Since the root is upwards, the extension of the real tree is at the other end. When entangled with the material expansions of the tree, one cannot see how far the tree extends, nor can one see the beginning of this tree. Yet one has to find out the cause. "I am the son of my father, my father is the son of such-and-such a person, etc." By searching in this way, one comes to Brahmā, who is generated by the Garbhodaka-śāyī Viṣṇu. Finally, in this way, when one reaches the Supreme Personality of Godhead, that is the end of research work. One has to search out that origin of this tree, the Supreme Personality of Godhead, through the association of persons who are in knowledge of that Supreme Personality of Godhead. Then by understanding one becomes gradually detached from this false reflection of reality, and by knowledge one can cut off the connection and actually become situated in the real tree.

The word *asaṅga* is very important in this connection because the attachment for sense enjoyment and lording it over the material nature is very strong. Therefore one must learn detachment by discussion of spiritual science based on authoritative scriptures, and one must hear from persons who are actually in knowledge. As a result of such discussion in the association of devotees, one comes to the Supreme Personality of

Godhead. Then the first thing one must do is surrender to Him. The description of that place whence having gone one never returns to this false reflected tree is given here. The Supreme Personality of Godhead, Kṛṣṇa, is the original root from whom everything has emanated. To gain the favor of that Personality of Godhead, one has only to surrender, and this is a result of performing devotional service by hearing, chanting, etc. He is the cause of the extension of the material world. This has already been explained by the Lord Himself. *Ahaṁ sarvasya prabhavaḥ:* "I am the origin of everything." Therefore to get out of the entanglement of this strong banyan tree of material life, one must surrender to Kṛṣṇa. As soon as one surrenders unto Kṛṣṇa, one becomes detached automatically from this material extension.

Text 5 निर्मानमोहा जितसङ्गदोषा अध्यात्मनित्या विनिवृत्तकामाः ।
द्वन्द्वैर्विमुक्ताः सुखदुःखसंज्ञैर्गच्छन्त्यमूढाः पदमव्ययं तत् ॥ ५ ॥

nirmāna-mohā jita-saṅga-doṣā
adhyātma-nityā vinivṛtta-kāmāḥ
dvandvair vimuktāḥ sukha-duḥkha-saṁjñair
gacchanty amūḍhāḥ padam avyayaṁ tat

niḥ – without; *māna* – false prestige; *mohāḥ* – and illusion; *jita* – having conquered; *saṅga* – of association; *doṣāḥ* – the faults; *adhyātma* – in spiritual knowledge; *nityāḥ* – in eternity; *vinivṛtta* – disassociated; *kāmāḥ* – from lust; *dvandvaiḥ* – from the dualities; *vimuktāḥ* – liberated; *sukha-duḥkha* – happiness and distress; *saṁjñaiḥ* – named; *gacchanti* – attain; *amūḍhāḥ* – unbewildered; *padam* – situation; *avyayam* – eternal; *tat* – that.

Those who are free from false prestige, illusion and false association, who understand the eternal, who are done with material lust, who are freed from the dualities of happiness and distress, and who, unbewildered, know how to surrender unto the Supreme Person attain to that eternal kingdom.

PURPORT: The surrendering process is described here very nicely. The first qualification is that one should not be deluded by pride. Because the conditioned soul is puffed up, thinking himself the lord of material nature, it is very difficult for him to surrender unto the Supreme Personality of Godhead. One should know by the cultivation of real knowledge that he is not lord of material nature; the Supreme Personality of Godhead is the Lord. When one is free from delusion caused by pride, he can begin the process of surrender. For one who is always expecting some honor in this material world, it is not possible to surrender to the Supreme Person. Pride is due to illusion, for although one comes here, stays for a brief time and then goes away, he has the foolish notion that he is the lord of the world. He thus makes all things complicated, and he is always in trouble. The whole world moves under this impression. People are considering the land, this earth, to belong to human society, and they have divided the land under the false impression that they are the proprietors. One has to get out of this false notion that human society is the proprietor of this world. When one is freed from such a false notion, he becomes free from all the false associations caused by familial, social and national affections. These faulty associations bind one to this material world. After this stage, one has to develop spiritual knowledge. One has to cultivate knowledge of what is actually his own and what is actually not his own. And when one has an understanding of things as they are, he becomes free from all dual conceptions such as happiness and distress, pleasure and pain. He becomes full in knowledge; then it is possible for him to surrender to the Supreme Personality of Godhead.

Text 6 न तद्भासयते सूर्यो न शशाङ्को न पावकः ।
यद्गत्वा न निवर्तन्ते तद्धाम परमं मम ॥ ६ ॥

na tad bhāsayate sūryo, na śaśāṅko na pāvakaḥ
yad gatvā na nivartante, tad dhāma paramaṁ mama

na – not; *tat* – that; *bhāsayate* – illuminates; *sūryaḥ* – the sun; *na* – nor; *śaśāṅkaḥ* – the moon; *na* – nor; *pāvakaḥ* – fire, electricity; *yat* – where; *gatvā* – going; *na* – never; *nivartante* – they come back; *tat dhāma* – that abode; *paramam* – supreme; *mama* – My.

That supreme abode of Mine is not illumined by the sun or moon, nor by fire or electricity. Those who reach it never return to this material world.

PURPORT: The spiritual world, the abode of the Supreme Personality of Godhead, Kṛṣṇa – which is known as Kṛṣṇaloka, Goloka Vṛndāvana – is described here. In the spiritual sky there is no need of sunshine, moonshine, fire or electricity, because all the planets are self-luminous. We have only one planet in this universe, the sun, which is self-luminous, but all the planets in the spiritual sky are self-luminous. The shining effulgence of all those planets (called Vaikuṇṭhas) constitutes the shining sky known as the *brahma-jyotir.* Actually, the effulgence is emanating from the planet of Kṛṣṇa, Goloka Vṛndāvana. Part of that shining effulgence is covered by the *mahat-tattva,* the material world. Other than this, the major portion of that shining sky is full of spiritual planets, which are called Vaikuṇṭhas, chief of which is Goloka Vṛndāvana.

As long as a living entity is in this dark material world, he is in conditional life, but as soon as he reaches the spiritual sky by cutting through the false, perverted tree of this material world, he becomes liberated. Then there is no chance of his coming back here. In his conditional life, the living entity considers himself to be the lord of this material world, but in his liberated state he enters into the spiritual kingdom and becomes an associate of the Supreme Lord. There he enjoys eternal bliss, eternal life, and full knowledge.

One should be captivated by this information. He should desire to transfer himself to that eternal world and extricate himself from this false reflection of reality. For one who is too much attached to this material world, it is very difficult to cut that attachment, but if he takes to Kṛṣṇa consciousness there is a chance of gradually becoming detached. One has to associate himself with devotees, those who are in Kṛṣṇa consciousness. One should search out a society dedicated to Kṛṣṇa consciousness and learn how to discharge devotional service. In this way he can cut off his attachment to the material world. One cannot become detached from the attraction of the material world simply by dressing himself in saffron cloth. He must become attached to the devotional service of the Lord. Therefore one should take it very seriously that devotional service as described in the Twelfth Chapter is the only way to get out of this false representation of the real tree. In Chapter Fourteen the contamination of all kinds of processes by material nature is described. Only devotional service is described as purely transcendental.

The words *paramaṁ mama* are very important here. Actually every nook and corner is the property of the Supreme Lord, but the spiritual world is *paramam,* full of six opulences. The *Kaṭha Upaniṣad* (2.2.15) also confirms that in the spiritual world there is no need of sunshine, moonshine or stars (*na tatra sūryo bhāti na candra-tārakam*), for the whole spiritual sky is illuminated by the internal potency of the Supreme Lord. That supreme abode can be achieved only by surrender and by no other means.

Text 7 मममैवांशो जीवलोके जीवभूतः सनातनः ।
मनःषष्ठानीन्द्रियाणि प्रकृतिस्थानि कर्षति ॥ ७ ॥

mamaivāṁśo jīva-loke, jīva-bhūtaḥ sanātanaḥ
manaḥ-ṣaṣṭhānīndriyāṇi, prakṛti-sthāni karṣati

mama – My; *eva* – certainly; *aṁśaḥ* – fragmental particle; *jīva-loke* – in the world of conditional life; *jīva-bhūtaḥ* – the conditioned living entity; *sanātanaḥ* – eternal; *manaḥ* – with the mind; *ṣaṣṭhāni* – the six; *indriyāṇi* – senses; *prakṛti* – in material nature; *sthāni* – situated; *karṣati* – is struggling hard.

The living entities in this conditioned world are My eternal fragmental parts. Due to conditioned life, they are struggling very hard with the six senses, which include the mind.

PURPORT: In this verse the identity of the living being is clearly given. The living entity is the fragmental part and parcel of the Supreme Lord – eternally. It is not that he assumes individuality in his conditional life and in his liberated state becomes one with the Supreme Lord. He is eternally fragmented. It is clearly said, *sanātanaḥ.* According to the Vedic version, the Supreme Lord manifests and expands Himself in innumerable expansions, of which the primary expansions are called *viṣṇu-tattva* and the secondary expansions are called the living entities. In other words, the *viṣṇu-tattva* is the personal expansion, and the living entities are the separated expansions. By His personal expansion, He is manifested in various forms like Lord Rāma, Nṛsiṁha-deva, Viṣṇu-mūrti and all the predominating Deities in the Vaikuṇṭha planets. The separated expansions, the living entities, are eternally servitors. The personal expansions of the Supreme Personality of Godhead, the individual identities of the Godhead, are always present. Similarly, the separated expansions of living entities have their identities. As fragmental parts and parcels of the Supreme Lord, the living entities also have fragmental portions of His qualities, of which independence is one. Every living entity, as an individual soul, has his personal individuality and a minute form of independence. By misuse of that independence one becomes a conditioned soul, and by proper use of independence he is always liberated. In either case, he is qualitatively eternal, as the Supreme Lord is. In his liberated state he is freed from this material condition, and he is under the engagement of transcendental service unto the Lord; in his conditioned life he is dominated by the material modes of nature, and he forgets the transcendental loving service of the Lord. As a result, he has to struggle very hard to maintain his existence in the material world.

The living entities, not only human beings and the cats and dogs, but even the greater controllers of the material world – Brahmā, Lord Śiva and even Viṣṇu – are all parts and parcels of the Supreme Lord. They are all eternal, not temporary manifestations. The word *karṣati* ("struggling" or "grappling hard") is very significant. The conditioned soul is bound up, as though shackled by iron chains. He is bound up by the false ego, and the mind is the chief agent which is driving him in this material existence. When the mind is in the mode of goodness, his activities are good; when the mind is in the mode of passion, his activities are troublesome; and when the mind is in the mode of ignorance, he travels in the lower species of life. It is clear, however, in this verse, that the conditioned soul is covered by the material body, with the mind and the senses, and when he is liberated this material covering perishes, but his spiritual body manifests itself in its individual capacity. The following information is there in the *Mādhyandināyana-śruti: sa vā eṣa brahma-niṣṭha idaṁ śarīraṁ martyam atisṛjya brahmābhisampadya brahmaṇā paśyati brahmaṇā śṛṇoti brahmaṇaivedaṁ sarvam anubhavati.* It is stated here that when a living entity gives up this material embodiment and enters into the spiritual world, he revives his spiritual body, and in his spiritual body he can see the Supreme Personality of Godhead face to face. He can hear and speak to Him face to face, and he can understand the Supreme Personality as He is. From *smṛti* also it is understood, *vasanti yatra puruṣāḥ sarve vaikuṇṭha-mūrtayaḥ:* in the spiritual planets everyone lives in bodies featured like the Supreme Personality of Godhead's. As far as bodily construction is concerned, there is no difference between the part-and-parcel living entities and the expansions of *viṣṇu-mūrti.* In other words, at liberation the living entity gets a spiritual body by the grace of the Supreme Personality of Godhead.

The words *mamaivāṁśaḥ* ("fragmental parts and parcels of the Supreme Lord") are also very significant. The fragmental portion of the Supreme Lord is not like some material broken part. We have already understood in the Second Chapter that the spirit cannot be cut into pieces. This fragment is not materially conceived. It is not like matter, which can be cut into pieces and joined together again. That conception is not applicable here, because the Sanskrit word *sanātana* ("eternal") is used. The fragmental portion is eternal. It is also stated in the beginning of the Second Chapter that in each and every individual body the fragmental portion of the Supreme Lord is present (*dehino 'smin yathā dehe*).

That fragmental portion, when liberated from the bodily entanglement, revives its original spiritual body in the spiritual sky in a spiritual planet and enjoys association with the Supreme Lord. It is, however, understood here that the living entity, being the fragmental part and parcel of the Supreme Lord, is qualitatively one with the Lord, just as the parts and parcels of gold are also gold.

Text 8 शरीरं यदवाप्नोति यच्चाप्युत्क्रामतीश्वरः ।
गृहीत्वैतानि संयाति वायुर्गन्धानिवाशयात् ॥ ८ ॥

śarīraṁ yad avāpnoti, yac cāpy utkrāmatīśvaraḥ
gṛhītvaitāni saṁyāti, vāyur gandhān ivāśayāt

śarīram – the body; *yat* – as; *avāpnoti* – gets; *yat* – as; *ca api* – also; *utkrāmati* – gives up; *īśvaraḥ* – the lord of the body; *gṛhītvā* – taking; *etāni* – all these; *saṁyāti* – goes away; *vāyuḥ* – the air; *gandhān* – smells; *iva* – like; *āśayāt* – from their source.

The living entity in the material world carries his different conceptions of life from one body to another, as the air carries aromas. Thus he takes one kind of body and again quits it to take another.

PURPORT: Here the living entity is described as *īśvara,* the controller of his own body. If he likes, he can change his body to a higher grade, and if he likes he can move to a lower class. Minute independence is there. The change his body undergoes depends upon him. At the time of death, the consciousness he has created will carry him on to the next type of body. If he has made his consciousness like that of a cat or dog, he is sure to change to a cat's or dog's body. And if he has fixed his consciousness on godly qualities, he will change into the form of a demigod. And if he is in Kṛṣṇa consciousness, he will be transferred to Kṛṣṇaloka in the spiritual world and will associate with Kṛṣṇa. It is a false claim that after the annihilation of this body everything is finished. The individual soul is transmigrating from one body to another, and his present body and present activities are the background of his next body. One gets a different body according to *karma,* and he has to quit this body in due course. It is stated here that the subtle body, which carries the conception of the next body, develops another body in the next life. This process of transmigrating from one body to another and struggling while in the body is called *karṣati,* or struggle for existence.

Text 9 श्रोत्रं चक्षुः स्पर्शनं च रसनं घ्राणमेव च ।
अधिष्ठाय मनश्चायं विषयानुपसेवते ॥ ९ ॥

śrotraṁ cakṣuḥ sparśanaṁ ca, rasanaṁ ghrāṇam eva ca
adhiṣṭhāya manaś cāyaṁ, viṣayān upasevate

śrotram – ears; *cakṣuḥ* – eyes; *sparśanam* – touch; *ca* – also; *rasanam* – tongue; *ghrāṇam* – smelling power; *eva* – also; *ca* – and; *adhiṣṭhāya* – being situated in; *manaḥ* – mind; *ca* – also; *ayam* – he; *viṣayān* – sense objects; *upasevate* – enjoys.

The living entity, thus taking another gross body, obtains a certain type of ear, eye, tongue, nose and sense of touch, which are grouped about the mind. He thus enjoys a particular set of sense objects.

PURPORT: In other words, if the living entity adulterates his consciousness with the qualities of cats and dogs, in his next life he gets a cat or dog body and enjoys. Consciousness is originally pure, like water. But if we mix water with a certain color, it changes. Similarly, consciousness is pure, for the spirit soul is pure. But consciousness is changed according to the association of the material qualities. Real consciousness is Kṛṣṇa consciousness. When, therefore, one is situated in Kṛṣṇa consciousness, he is in his pure life. But if his consciousness is adulterated by some type of material mentality, in the next life he gets a corresponding body. He does not necessarily get a human body again; he can get the body of a cat, dog, hog, demigod or one of many other forms, for there are 8,400,000 species.

Text 10 उत्क्रामन्तं स्थितं वापि भुञ्जानं वा गुणान्वितम् ।
विमूढा नानुपश्यन्ति पश्यन्ति ज्ञानचक्षुषः ॥१०॥

utkrāmantaṁ sthitaṁ vāpi, bhuñjānaṁ vā guṇānvitam
vimūḍhā nānupaśyanti, paśyanti jñāna-cakṣuṣaḥ

utkrāmantam – quitting the body; *sthitam* – situated in the body; *vā api* – either; *bhuñjānam* – enjoying; *vā* – or; *guṇa-anvitam* – under the spell of the modes of material nature; *vimūḍhāḥ* – foolish persons; *na* – never; *anupaśyanti* – can see; *paśyanti* – can see; *jñāna-cakṣuṣaḥ* – those who have the eyes of knowledge.

The foolish cannot understand how a living entity can quit his body, nor can they understand what sort of body he enjoys under the spell of the

modes of nature. But one whose eyes are trained in knowledge can see all this.

PURPORT: The word *jñāna-cakṣuṣaḥ* is very significant. Without knowledge, one cannot understand how a living entity leaves his present body, nor what form of body he is going to take in the next life, nor even why he is living in a particular type of body. This requires a great amount of knowledge understood from *Bhagavad-gītā* and similar literatures heard from a bona fide spiritual master. One who is trained to perceive all these things is fortunate. Every living entity is quitting his body under certain circumstances, he is living under certain circumstances, and he is enjoying under certain circumstances under the spell of material nature. As a result, he is suffering different kinds of happiness and distress, under the illusion of sense enjoyment. Persons who are everlastingly fooled by lust and desire lose all power to understand their change of body and their stay in a particular body. They cannot comprehend it. Those who have developed spiritual knowledge, however, can see that the spirit is different from the body and is changing its body and enjoying in different ways. A person in such knowledge can understand how the conditioned living entity is suffering in this material existence. Therefore those who are highly developed in Kṛṣṇa consciousness try their best to give this knowledge to the people in general, for their conditional life is very much troublesome. They should come out of it and be Kṛṣṇa conscious and liberate themselves to transfer to the spiritual world.

Text 11 यतन्तो योगिनश्चैनं पश्यन्त्यात्मन्यवस्थितम् ।
यतन्तोऽप्यकृतात्मानो नैनं पश्यन्त्यचेतसः ॥११॥

yatanto yoginaś cainaṁ, paśyanty ātmany avasthitam
yatanto 'py akṛtātmāno, nainaṁ paśyanty acetasaḥ

yatantaḥ – endeavoring; *yoginaḥ* – transcendentalists; *ca* – also; *enam* – this; *paśyanti* – can see; *ātmani* – in the self; *avasthitam* – situated; *yatantaḥ* – endeavoring; *api* – although; *akṛta-ātmānaḥ* – those without self-realization; *na* – do not; *enam* – this; *paśyanti* – see; *acetasaḥ* – having undeveloped minds.

The endeavoring transcendentalists who are situated in self-realization can see all this clearly. But those whose minds are not developed and who are not situated in self-realization cannot see what is taking place, though they may try.

PURPORT: There are many transcendentalists on the path of spiritual self-realization, but one who is not situated in self-realization cannot see how things are changing in the body of the living entity. The word *yoginaḥ* is significant in this connection. In the present day there are many so-called *yogīs,* and there are many so-called associations of *yogīs,* but they are actually blind in the matter of self-realization. They are simply addicted to some sort of gymnastic exercise and are satisfied if the body is well built and healthy. They have no other information. They are called *yatanto 'py akṛtātmānaḥ.* Even though they are endeavoring in a so-called *yoga* system, they are not self-realized. Such people cannot understand the process of the transmigration of the soul. Only those who are actually in the *yoga* system and have realized the self, the world, and the Supreme Lord – in other words, the *bhakti-yogīs,* those engaged in pure devotional service in Kṛṣṇa consciousness – can understand how things are taking place.

Text 12 यदादित्यगतं तेजो जगद्भासयतेऽखिलम् ।
यच्चन्द्रमसि यच्चाग्नौ तत्तेजो विद्धि मामकम् ॥१२॥

yad āditya-gataṁ tejo, jagad bhāsayate 'khilam
yac candramasi yac cāgnau, tat tejo viddhi māmakam

yat – that which; *āditya-gatam* – in the sunshine; *tejaḥ* – splendor; *jagat* – the whole world; *bhāsayate* – illuminates; *akhilam* – entirely; *yat* – that which; *candramasi* – in the moon; *yat* – that which; *ca* – also; *agnau* – in fire; *tat* – that; *tejaḥ* – splendor; *viddhi* – understand; *māmakam* – from Me.

The splendor of the sun, which dissipates the darkness of this whole world, comes from Me. And the splendor of the moon and the splendor of fire are also from Me.

PURPORT: The unintelligent cannot understand how things are taking place. But one can begin to be established in knowledge by understanding what the Lord explains here. Everyone sees the sun, moon, fire and electricity. One should simply try to understand that the splendor of the sun, the splendor of the moon, and the splendor of electricity or fire are coming from the Supreme Personality of Godhead. In such a conception of life, the beginning of Kṛṣṇa consciousness, lies a great deal of advancement for the conditioned soul in this material world. The living entities are essentially the parts and parcels of the Supreme Lord, and He is giving herewith the hint how they can come back to Godhead, back to home.

From this verse we can understand that the sun is illuminating the whole solar system. There are different universes and solar systems, and there are different suns, moons and planets also, but in each universe there is only one sun. As stated in *Bhagavad-gītā* (10.21), the moon is one of the stars (*nakṣatrāṇām ahaṁ śaśī*). Sunlight is due to the spiritual effulgence in the spiritual sky of the Supreme Lord. With the rise of the sun, the activities of human beings are set up. They set fire to prepare their foodstuff, they set fire to start the factories, etc. So many things are done with the help of fire. Therefore sunrise, fire and moonlight are so pleasing to the living entities. Without their help no living entity can live. So if one can understand that the light and splendor of the sun, moon and fire are emanating from the Supreme Personality of Godhead, Kṛṣṇa, then one's Kṛṣṇa consciousness will begin. By the moonshine, all the vegetables are nourished. The moonshine is so pleasing that people can easily understand that they are living by the mercy of the Supreme Personality of Godhead, Kṛṣṇa. Without His mercy there cannot be sun, without His mercy there cannot be moon, and without His mercy there cannot be fire, and without the help of sun, moon and fire, no one can live. These are some thoughts to provoke Kṛṣṇa consciousness in the conditioned soul.

Text 13 गामाविश्य च भूतानि धारयाम्यहमोजसा ।
पुष्णामि चौषधीः सर्वाः सोमो भूत्वा रसात्मकः ॥१३॥

gām āviśya ca bhūtāni, dhārayāmy aham ojasā
puṣṇāmi cauṣadhīḥ sarvāḥ, somo bhūtvā rasātmakaḥ

gām – the planets; *āviśya* – entering; *ca* – also; *bhūtāni* – the living entities; *dhārayāmi* – sustain; *aham* – I; *ojasā* – by My energy; *puṣṇāmi* – am nourishing; *ca* – and; *auṣadhīḥ* – vegetables; *sarvāḥ* – all; *somaḥ* – the moon; *bhūtvā* – becoming; *rasa-ātmakaḥ* – supplying the juice.

I enter into each planet, and by My energy they stay in orbit. I become the moon and thereby supply the juice of life to all vegetables.

PURPORT: It is understood that all the planets are floating in the air only by the energy of the Lord. The Lord enters into every atom, every planet, and every living being. That is discussed in the *Brahma-saṁhitā.* It is said there that one plenary portion of the Supreme Personality of Godhead,

Paramātmā, enters into the planets, the universe, the living entity, and even into the atom. So due to His entrance, everything is appropriately manifested. When the spirit soul is there, a living man can float on the water, but when the living spark is out of the body and the body is dead, the body sinks. Of course when it is decomposed it floats just like straw and other things, but as soon as the man is dead, he at once sinks in the water. Similarly, all these planets are floating in space, and this is due to the entrance of the supreme energy of the Supreme Personality of Godhead. His energy is sustaining each planet, just like a handful of dust. If someone holds a handful of dust, there is no possibility of the dust's falling, but if one throws it in the air it will fall down. Similarly, these planets, which are floating in the air, are actually held in the fist of the universal form of the Supreme Lord. By His strength and energy, all moving and nonmoving things stay in their place. It is said in the Vedic hymns that because of the Supreme Personality of Godhead the sun is shining and the planets are steadily moving. Were it not for Him, all the planets would scatter, like dust in air, and perish. Similarly, it is due to the Supreme Personality of Godhead that the moon nourishes all vegetables. Due to the moon's influence, the vegetables become delicious. Without the moonshine, the vegetables can neither grow nor taste succulent. Human society is working, living comfortably and enjoying food due to the supply from the Supreme Lord. Otherwise, mankind could not survive. The word *rasātmakaḥ* is very significant. Everything becomes palatable by the agency of the Supreme Lord through the influence of the moon.

Text 14 अहं वैश्वानरो भूत्वा प्राणिनां देहमाश्रितः ।
प्राणापानसमायुक्तः पचाम्यन्नं चतुर्विधम् ॥१४॥

ahaṁ vaiśvānaro bhūtvā, prāṇināṁ deham āśritaḥ
prāṇāpāna-samāyuktaḥ, pacāmy annaṁ catur-vidham

aham – I; *vaiśvānaraḥ* – My plenary portion as the digesting fire; *bhūtvā* – becoming; *prāṇinām* – of all living entities; *deham* – in the bodies; *āśritaḥ* – situated; *prāṇa* – the outgoing air; *apāna* – the downgoing air; *samāyuktaḥ* – keeping in balance; *pacāmi* – I digest; *annam* – foodstuff; *catuḥ-vidham* – the four kinds.

I am the fire of digestion in the bodies of all living entities, and I join with the air of life, outgoing and incoming, to digest the four kinds of foodstuff.

PURPORT: According to Āyur-vedic *śāstra,* we understand that there is a fire in the stomach which digests all food sent there. When the fire is not blazing there is no hunger, and when the fire is in order we become hungry. Sometimes when the fire is not going nicely, treatment is required. In any case, this fire is representative of the Supreme Personality of Godhead. Vedic *mantras* (*Bṛhad-āraṇyaka Upaniṣad* 5.9.1) also confirm that the Supreme Lord or Brahman is situated in the form of fire within the stomach and is digesting all kinds of foodstuff (*ayam agnir vaiśvānaro yo 'yam antaḥ puruṣe yenedam annaṁ pacyate*). Therefore since He is helping the digestion of all kinds of foodstuff, the living entity is not independent in the eating process. Unless the Supreme Lord helps him in digesting, there is no possibility of eating. He thus produces and digests foodstuff, and by His grace we are enjoying life. In the *Vedānta-sūtra* (1.2.27) this is also confirmed. *Śabdādibhyo 'ntaḥ pratiṣṭhānāc ca:* the Lord is situated within sound and within the body, within the air and even within the stomach as the digestive force. There are four kinds of foodstuff – some are drunk, some are chewed, some are licked up, and some are sucked – and He is the digestive force for all of them.

Text 15 सर्वस्य चाहं हृदि सन्निविष्टो मत्तः स्मृतिर्ज्ञानमपोहनं च ।
वेदैश्च सर्वैरहमेव वेद्यो वेदान्तकृद्वेदविदेव चाहम् ॥१५॥

sarvasya cāhaṁ hṛdi sanniviṣṭo
mattaḥ smṛtir jñānam apohanaṁ ca
vedaiś ca sarvair aham eva vedyo
vedānta-kṛd veda-vid eva cāham

sarvasya – of all living beings; *ca* – and; *aham* – I; *hṛdi* – in the heart; *sanniviṣṭaḥ* – situated; *mattaḥ* – from Me; *smṛtiḥ* – remembrance; *jñānam* – knowledge; *apohanam* – forgetfulness; *ca* – and; *vedaiḥ* – by the *Vedas; ca* – also; *sarvaiḥ* – all; *aham* – I am; *eva* – certainly; *vedyaḥ* – knowable; *vedānta-kṛt* – the compiler of the *Vedānta; veda-vit* – the knower of the *Vedas; eva* – certainly; *ca* – and; *aham* – I.

I am seated in everyone's heart, and from Me come remembrance, knowledge and forgetfulness. By all the Vedas, I am to be known. Indeed, I am the compiler of Vedānta, and I am the knower of the Vedas.

PURPORT: The Supreme Lord is situated as Paramātmā in everyone's heart, and it is from Him that all activities are initiated. The living entity forgets everything of his past life, but he has to act according to the direction of the Supreme Lord, who is witness to all his work. Therefore he begins his work according to his past deeds. Required knowledge is supplied to him, and remembrance is given to him, and he forgets, also, about his past life. Thus, the Lord is not only all-pervading; He is also localized in every individual heart. He awards the different fruitive results. He is worshipable not only as the impersonal Brahman, the Supreme Personality of Godhead, and the localized Paramātmā, but as the form of the incarnation of the *Vedas* as well. The *Vedas* give the right direction to people so that they can properly mold their lives and come back to Godhead, back to home. The *Vedas* offer knowledge of the Supreme Personality of Godhead, Kṛṣṇa, and Kṛṣṇa in His incarnation as Vyāsadeva is the compiler of the *Vedānta-sūtra.* The commentation on the *Vedānta-sūtra* by Vyāsadeva in the *Śrīmad-Bhāgavatam* gives the real understanding of *Vedānta-sūtra.* The Supreme Lord is so full that for the deliverance of the conditioned soul He is the supplier and digester of foodstuff, the witness of his activity, and the giver of knowledge in the form of the *Vedas* and as the Supreme Personality of Godhead, Śrī Kṛṣṇa, the teacher of the *Bhagavad-gītā.* He is worshipable by the conditioned soul. Thus God is all-good; God is all-merciful.

Antaḥ-praviṣṭaḥ śāstā janānām. The living entity forgets as soon as he quits his present body, but he begins his work again, initiated by the Supreme Lord. Although he forgets, the Lord gives him the intelligence to renew his work where he ended his last life. So not only does a living entity enjoy or suffer in this world according to the dictation from the Supreme Lord situated locally in the heart, but he receives the opportunity to understand the *Vedas* from Him. If one is serious about understanding the Vedic knowledge, then Kṛṣṇa gives the required intelligence. Why does He present the Vedic knowledge for understanding? Because a living entity individually needs to understand Kṛṣṇa. Vedic literature confirms this: *yo 'sau sarvair vedair gīyate.* In all Vedic literature, beginning from the four *Vedas, Vedānta-sūtra* and the *Upaniṣads* and *Purāṇas,* the glories of the Supreme Lord are celebrated. By performance of Vedic rituals, discussion of the Vedic philosophy and worship of the Lord in devotional service, He is attained. Therefore the purpose of the *Vedas* is to understand Kṛṣṇa. The *Vedas* give us direction by which to understand Kṛṣṇa and the process of realizing Him. The ultimate goal is the Supreme Personality of Godhead. *Vedānta-sūtra* (1.1.4) confirms this in the following words: *tat tu samanvayāt.* One can attain perfection in three stages. By understanding Vedic literature one can understand his relationship with the Supreme Personality of Godhead, by performing the different processes one can approach Him, and at the end one can attain the supreme goal, who is no other than the Supreme Personality of Godhead. In this verse the purpose of the *Vedas,* the understanding of the *Vedas,* and the goal of the *Vedas* are clearly defined.

Text 16 द्वाविमौ पुरुषौ लोके क्षरश्चाक्षर एव च ।
क्षरः सर्वाणि भूतानि कूटस्थोऽक्षर उच्यते ॥१६॥

dvāv imau puruṣau loke, kṣaraś cākṣara eva ca
kṣaraḥ sarvāṇi bhūtāni, kūṭa-stho 'kṣara ucyate

dvau – two; *imau* – these; *puruṣau* – living entities; *loke* – in the world; *kṣaraḥ* – fallible; *ca* – and; *akṣaraḥ* – infallible; *eva* – certainly; *ca* – and; *kṣaraḥ* – fallible; *sarvāṇi* – all; *bhūtāni* – living entities; *kūṭa-sthaḥ* – in oneness; *akṣaraḥ* – infallible; *ucyate* – is said.

There are two classes of beings, the fallible and the infallible. In the material world every living entity is fallible, and in the spiritual world every living entity is called infallible.

PURPORT: As already explained, the Lord in His incarnation as Vyāsadeva compiled the *Vedānta-sūtra.* Here the Lord is giving, in summary, the contents of the *Vedānta-sūtra.* He says that the living entities, who are innumerable, can be divided into two classes – the fallible and the infallible. The living entities are eternally separated parts and parcels of the Supreme Personality of Godhead. When they are in contact with the material world they are called *jīva-bhūta,* and the Sanskrit words given here, *kṣaraḥ sarvāṇi bhūtāni,* mean that they are fallible. Those who are in oneness with the Supreme Personality of Godhead, however, are called infallible. Oneness does not mean that they have no individuality, but that there is no disunity. They are all agreeable to the purpose of the creation. Of course, in the spiritual world there is no such thing as creation, but since the Supreme Personality of Godhead, as stated in the *Vedānta-sūtra,* is the source of all emanations, that conception is explained.

According to the statement of the Supreme Personality of Godhead, Lord Kṛṣṇa, there are two classes of living entities. The *Vedas* give evidence of this, so there is no doubt about it. The living entities who are struggling in this world with the mind and five senses have their material bodies, which are changing. As long as a living entity is conditioned, his body changes due to contact with matter; matter is changing, so the living entity appears to be changing. But in the spiritual world the body is not made of matter; therefore there is no change. In the material world the living entity undergoes six changes – birth, growth, duration, reproduction, then dwindling and vanishing. These are the changes of the material body. But in the spiritual world the body does not change; there is no old age, there is no birth, there is no death. There all exists in oneness. *Kṣaraḥ sarvāṇi bhūtāni:* any living entity who has come in contact with matter, beginning from the first created being, Brahmā, down to a small ant, is changing its body; therefore they are all fallible. In the spiritual world, however, they are always liberated in oneness.

Text 17 उत्तमः पुरुषस्त्वन्यः परमात्मेत्युदाहृतः ।
यो लोकत्रयमाविश्य बिभर्त्यव्यय ईश्वरः ॥१७॥

uttamaḥ puruṣas tv anyaḥ, paramātmety udāhṛtaḥ
yo loka-trayam āviśya, bibharty avyaya īśvaraḥ

uttamaḥ – the best; *puruṣaḥ* – personality; *tu* – but; *anyaḥ* – another; *parama-ātmā* – the Supreme Self; *iti* – thus; *udāhṛtaḥ* – is said; *yaḥ* – who; *loka* – of the universe; *trayam* – the three divisions; *āviśya* – entering; *bibharti* – is maintaining; *avyayaḥ* – inexhaustible; *īśvaraḥ* – the Lord.

Besides these two, there is the greatest living personality, the Supreme Soul, the imperishable Lord Himself, who has entered the three worlds and is maintaining them.

PURPORT: The idea of this verse is very nicely expressed in the *Kaṭha Upaniṣad* (2.2.13) and *Śvetāśvatara Upaniṣad* (6.13). It is clearly stated there that above the innumerable living entities, some of whom are conditioned and some of whom are liberated, there is the Supreme Personality, who is Paramātmā. The Upaniṣadic verse runs as follows: *nityo nityānāṁ cetanaś cetanānām.* The purport is that amongst all the living entities, both conditioned and liberated, there is one supreme living personality, the Supreme Personality of Godhead, who maintains them and gives them all the facility of enjoyment according to different work. That Supreme Personality of Godhead is situated in everyone's heart as Paramātmā. A wise man who can understand Him is eligible to attain perfect peace, not others.

Text 18 यस्मात्क्षरमतीतोऽहमक्षरादपि चोत्तमः ।
अतोऽस्मि लोके वेदे च प्रथितः पुरुषोत्तमः ॥१८॥

yasmāt kṣaram atīto 'ham, akṣarād api cottamaḥ
ato 'smi loke vede ca, prathitaḥ puruṣottamaḥ

yasmāt – because; *kṣaram* – to the fallible; *atītaḥ* – transcendental; *aham* – I am; *akṣarāt* – beyond the infallible; *api* – also; *ca* – and; *uttamaḥ* – the best; *ataḥ* – therefore; *asmi* – I am; *loke* – in the world; *vede* – in the Vedic literature; *ca* – and; *prathitaḥ* – celebrated; *puruṣa-uttamaḥ* – as the Supreme Personality.

Because I am transcendental, beyond both the fallible and the infallible, and because I am the greatest, I am celebrated both in the world and in the Vedas as that Supreme Person.

PURPORT: No one can surpass the Supreme Personality of Godhead, Kṛṣṇa – neither the conditioned soul nor the liberated soul. He is therefore the greatest of personalities. Now it is clear here that the living entities and the Supreme Personality of Godhead are individuals. The difference is that the living entities, either in the conditioned state or in the liberated state, cannot surpass in quantity the inconceivable potencies of the Supreme Personality of Godhead. It is incorrect to think of the Supreme Lord and the living entities as being on the same level or equal in all respects. There is always the question of superiority and inferiority between their personalities. The word *uttama* is very significant. No one can surpass the Supreme Personality of Godhead.

The word *loke* signifies "in the *pauruṣa āgama* [the *smṛti* scriptures]." As confirmed in the *Nirukti* dictionary, *lokyate vedārtho 'nena:* "The purpose of the *Vedas* is explained by the *smṛti* scriptures."

The Supreme Lord, in His localized aspect of Paramātmā, is also described in the *Vedas* themselves. The following verse appears in the *Vedas* (*Chāndogya Upaniṣad* 8.12.3): *tāvad eṣa samprasādo 'smāc charīrāt samutthāya paraṁ jyoti-rūpaṁ sampadya svena rūpeṇābhiniṣpadyate sa uttamaḥ puruṣaḥ.* "The Supersoul coming out of the body enters the impersonal *brahma-jyotir;* then in His form He remains in His spiritual identity. That Supreme is called the Supreme Personality." This means that the Supreme Personality is exhibiting and diffusing His spiritual effulgence, which is the ultimate illumination. That Supreme Personality also has a localized aspect as Paramātmā. By incarnating Himself as the son of Satyavatī and Parāśara, He explains the Vedic knowledge as Vyāsadeva.

Text 19 यो मामेवमसम्मूढो जानाति पुरुषोत्तमम् ।
स सर्वविद्भजति मां सर्वभावेन भारत ॥१९॥

yo mām evam asammūḍho, jānāti puruṣottamam
sa sarva-vid bhajati māṁ, sarva-bhāvena bhārata

yaḥ – anyone who; *mām* – Me; *evam* – thus; *asammūḍhaḥ* – without a doubt; *jānāti* – knows; *puruṣa-uttamam* – the Supreme Personality of Godhead; *saḥ* – he; *sarva-vit* – the knower of everything; *bhajati* – renders devotional service; *mām* – unto Me; *sarva-bhāvena* – in all respects; *bhārata* – O son of Bharata.

Whoever knows Me as the Supreme Personality of Godhead, without doubting, is the knower of everything. He therefore engages himself in full devotional service to Me, O son of Bharata.

PURPORT: There are many philosophical speculations about the constitutional position of the living entities and the Supreme Absolute Truth. Now in this verse the Supreme Personality of Godhead clearly explains that anyone who knows Lord Kṛṣṇa to be the Supreme Person is actually the knower of everything. The imperfect knower goes on simply speculating about the Absolute Truth, but the perfect knower, without wasting his valuable time, engages directly in Kṛṣṇa consciousness, the devotional service of the Supreme Lord. Throughout the whole of *Bhagavad-gītā,* this fact is being stressed at every step. And still there are so many stubborn commentators on *Bhagavad-gītā* who consider the Supreme Absolute Truth and the living entities to be one and the same.

Vedic knowledge is called *śruti,* learning by aural reception. One should actually receive the Vedic message from authorities like Kṛṣṇa and His representatives. Here Kṛṣṇa distinguishes everything very nicely, and one should hear from this source. Simply to hear like the hogs is not sufficient; one must be able to understand from the authorities. It is not that one should simply speculate academically. One should submissively hear from *Bhagavad-gītā* that these living entities are always subordinate to the Supreme Personality of Godhead. Anyone who is able to understand this, according to the Supreme Personality of Godhead, Śrī Kṛṣṇa, knows the purpose of the *Vedas;* no one else knows the purpose of the *Vedas.*

The word *bhajati* is very significant. In many places the word *bhajati* is expressed in relationship with the service of the Supreme Lord. If a person is engaged in full Kṛṣṇa consciousness, in the devotional service of the Lord, it is to be understood that he has understood all the Vedic knowledge. In the Vaiṣṇava *paramparā* it is said that if one is engaged in the devotional service of Kṛṣṇa, then there is no need for any other spiritual process for understanding the Supreme Absolute Truth. He has already come to the point, because he is engaged in the devotional service of the Lord. He has ended all preliminary processes of understanding. But if anyone, after speculating for hundreds of thousands of lives, does not come to the point that Kṛṣṇa is the Supreme Personality of Godhead and that one has to surrender there, all his speculation for so many years and lives is a useless waste of time.

Text 20 इति गुह्यतमं शास्त्रमिदमुक्तं मयानघ ।
एतद् बुद्ध्वा बुद्धिमान् स्यात्कृतकृत्यश्च भारत ॥२०॥

iti guhya-tamaṁ śāstram, idam uktaṁ mayānagha
etad buddhvā buddhimān syāt, kṛta-kṛtyaś ca bhārata

iti – thus; *guhya-tamam* – the most confidential; *śāstram* – revealed scripture; *idam* – this; *uktam* – disclosed; *mayā* – by Me; *anagha* – O sinless one; *etat* – this; *buddhvā* – understanding; *buddhi-mān* – intelligent; *syāt* – one becomes; *kṛta-kṛtyaḥ* – the most perfect in his endeavors; *ca* – and; *bhārata* – O son of Bharata.

This is the most confidential part of the Vedic scriptures, O sinless one, and it is disclosed now by Me. Whoever understands this will become wise, and his endeavors will know perfection.

PURPORT: The Lord clearly explains here that this is the substance of all revealed scriptures. And one should understand this as it is given by the Supreme Personality of Godhead. Thus one will become intelligent and perfect in transcendental knowledge. In other words, by understanding this philosophy of the Supreme Personality of Godhead and engaging in His transcendental service, everyone can become freed from all contaminations of the modes of material nature. Devotional service is a process of spiritual understanding. Wherever devotional service exists, the material contamination cannot coexist. Devotional service to the Lord and the Lord Himself are one and the same because they are spiritual; devotional service takes place within the internal energy of the Supreme

Lord. The Lord is said to be the sun, and ignorance is called darkness. Where the sun is present, there is no question of darkness. Therefore, whenever devotional service is present under the proper guidance of a bona fide spiritual master, there is no question of ignorance.

Everyone must take to this consciousness of Kṛṣṇa and engage in devotional service to become intelligent and purified. Unless one comes to this position of understanding Kṛṣṇa and engages in devotional service, however intelligent he may be in the estimation of some common man, he is not perfectly intelligent.

The word *anagha,* by which Arjuna is addressed, is significant. *Anagha,* "O sinless one," means that unless one is free from all sinful reactions it is very difficult to understand Kṛṣṇa. One has to become free from all contamination, all sinful activities; then he can understand. But devotional service is so pure and potent that once one is engaged in devotional service he automatically comes to the stage of sinlessness.

While one is performing devotional service in the association of pure devotees in full Kṛṣṇa consciousness, there are certain things which require to be vanquished altogether. The most important thing one has to surmount is weakness of the heart. The first falldown is caused by the desire to lord it over material nature. Thus one gives up the transcendental loving service of the Supreme Lord. The second weakness of the heart is that as one increases the propensity to lord it over material nature, he becomes attached to matter and the possession of matter. The problems of material existence are due to these weaknesses of the heart. In this chapter the first five verses describe the process of freeing oneself from these weaknesses of heart, and the rest of the chapter, from the sixth verse through the end, discusses *puruṣottama-yoga.*

Thus end the Bhaktivedanta Purports to the Fifteenth Chapter of the Śrīmad Bhagavad-gītā *in the matter of* Puruṣottama-yoga, *the Yoga of the Supreme Person.*

CHAPTER SIXTEEN

The Divine and Demoniac Natures

Texts 1–3

श्रीभगवानुवाच
अभयं सत्त्वसंशुद्धिर्ज्ञानयोगव्यवस्थितिः ।
दानं दमश्च यज्ञश्च स्वाध्यायस्तप आर्जवम् ॥ १ ॥
अहिंसा सत्यमक्रोधस्त्यागः शान्तिरपैशुनम् ।
दया भूतेष्वलोलुप्त्वं मार्दवं ह्रीरचापलम् ॥ २ ॥
तेजः क्षमा धृतिः शौचमद्रोहो नातिमानिता ।
भवन्ति सम्पदं दैवीमभिजातस्य भारत ॥ ३ ॥

śrī-bhagavān uvāca
abhayaṁ sattva-saṁśuddhir, jñāna-yoga-vyavasthitiḥ
dānaṁ damaś ca yajñaś ca, svādhyāyas tapa ārjavam

ahiṁsā satyam akrodhas, tyāgaḥ śāntir apaiśunam
dayā bhūteṣv aloluptvaṁ, mārdavaṁ hrīr acāpalam

tejaḥ kṣamā dhṛtiḥ śaucam, adroho nāti-mānitā
bhavanti sampadaṁ daivīm, abhijātasya bhārata

śrī-bhagavān uvāca – the Supreme Personality of Godhead said; *abhayam* – fearlessness; *sattva-saṁśuddhiḥ* – purification of one's existence; *jñāna* – in knowledge; *yoga* – of linking up; *vyavasthitiḥ* – the situation; *dānam* – charity; *damaḥ* – controlling the mind; *ca* – and; *yajñaḥ* – performance of sacrifice; *ca* – and; *svādhyāyaḥ* – study of Vedic literature; *tapaḥ* – austerity; *ārjavam* – simplicity; *ahiṁsā* – nonviolence;

satyam – truthfulness; *akrodhaḥ* – freedom from anger; *tyāgaḥ* – renunciation; *śāntiḥ* – tranquillity; *apaiśunam* – aversion to fault-finding; *dayā* – mercy; *bhūteṣu* – towards all living entities; *aloluptvam* – freedom from greed; *mārdavam* – gentleness; *hrīḥ* – modesty; *acāpalam* – determination; *tejaḥ* – vigor; *kṣamā* – forgiveness; *dhṛtiḥ* – fortitude; *śaucam* – cleanliness; *adrohaḥ* – freedom from envy; *na* – not; *ati-mānitā* – expectation of honor; *bhavanti* – are; *sampadam* – the qualities; *daivīm* – the transcendental nature; *abhijātasya* – of one who is born of; *bhārata* – O son of Bharata.

The Supreme Personality of Godhead said: Fearlessness; purification of one's existence; cultivation of spiritual knowledge; charity; self-control; performance of sacrifice; study of the Vedas; austerity; simplicity; nonviolence; truthfulness; freedom from anger; renunciation; tranquillity; aversion to faultfinding; compassion for all living entities; freedom from covetousness; gentleness; modesty; steady determination; vigor; forgiveness; fortitude; cleanliness; and freedom from envy and from the passion for honor – these transcendental qualities, O son of Bharata, belong to godly men endowed with divine nature.

PURPORT: In the beginning of the Fifteenth Chapter, the banyan tree of this material world was explained. The extra roots coming out of it were compared to the activities of the living entities, some auspicious, some inauspicious. In the Ninth Chapter, also, the *devas,* or godly, and the *asuras,* the ungodly, or demons, were explained. Now, according to Vedic rites, activities in the mode of goodness are considered auspicious for progress on the path of liberation, and such activities are known as *daivī prakṛti,* transcendental by nature. Those who are situated in the transcendental nature make progress on the path of liberation. For those who are acting in the modes of passion and ignorance, on the other hand, there is no possibility of liberation. Either they will have to remain in this material world as human beings, or they will descend among the species of animals or even lower life forms. In this Sixteenth Chapter the Lord explains both the transcendental nature and its attendant qualities and the demoniac nature and its qualities. He also explains the advantages and disadvantages of these qualities.

The word *abhijātasya* in reference to one born of transcendental qualities or godly tendencies is very significant. To beget a child in a godly atmosphere is known in the Vedic scriptures as Garbhādhāna-saṁskāra. If the parents want a child in the godly qualities they should follow the ten principles recommended for the social life of the human being. In

Bhagavad-gītā we have studied also before that sex life for begetting a good child is Kṛṣṇa Himself. Sex life is not condemned, provided the process is used in Kṛṣṇa consciousness. Those who are in Kṛṣṇa consciousness at least should not beget children like cats and dogs but should beget them so that they may become Kṛṣṇa conscious after birth. That should be the advantage of children born of a father and mother absorbed in Kṛṣṇa consciousness.

The social institution known as *varṇāśrama-dharma* – the institution dividing society into four divisions of social life and four occupational divisions or castes – is not meant to divide human society according to birth. Such divisions are in terms of educational qualifications. They are to keep the society in a state of peace and prosperity. The qualities mentioned herein are explained as transcendental qualities meant for making a person progress in spiritual understanding so that he can get liberated from the material world.

In the *varṇāśrama* institution the *sannyāsī,* or the person in the renounced order of life, is considered to be the head or the spiritual master of all the social statuses and orders. A *brāhmaṇa* is considered to be the spiritual master of the three other sections of a society, namely, the *kṣatriyas,* the *vaiśyas* and the *śūdras,* but a *sannyāsī,* who is on the top of the institution, is considered to be the spiritual master of the *brāhmaṇas* also. For a *sannyāsī,* the first qualification should be fearlessness. Because a *sannyāsī* has to be alone without any support or guarantee of support, he has simply to depend on the mercy of the Supreme Personality of Godhead. If one thinks, "After I leave my connections, who will protect me?" he should not accept the renounced order of life. One must be fully convinced that Kṛṣṇa or the Supreme Personality of Godhead in His localized aspect as Paramātmā is always within, that He is seeing everything and He always knows what one intends to do. One must thus have firm conviction that Kṛṣṇa as Paramātmā will take care of a soul surrendered to Him. "I shall never be alone," one should think. "Even if I live in the darkest regions of a forest I shall be accompanied by Kṛṣṇa, and He will give me all protection." That conviction is called *abhayam,* fearlessness. This state of mind is necessary for a person in the renounced order of life.

Then he has to purify his existence. There are so many rules and regulations to be followed in the renounced order of life. Most important of all, a *sannyāsī* is strictly forbidden to have any intimate relationship with a woman. He is even forbidden to talk with a woman in a secluded place. Lord Caitanya was an ideal *sannyāsī,* and when He was at Purī His feminine devotees could not even come near to offer their respects. They were advised to bow down from a distant place. This is not a sign of hatred for women as a class, but it is a stricture imposed on the *sannyāsī* not to have close connections with women. One has to follow the rules and regulations of a particular status of life in order to purify his existence. For a *sannyāsī,* intimate relations with women and possession of wealth for sense gratification are strictly forbidden. The ideal *sannyāsī* was Lord Caitanya Himself, and we can learn from His life that He was very strict in regards to women. Although He is considered to be the most liberal incarnation of Godhead, accepting the most fallen conditioned souls, He strictly followed the rules and regulations of the *sannyāsa* order of life in connection with association with women. One of His personal associates, namely Choṭa Haridāsa, was associated with Lord Caitanya along with His other confidential personal associates, but somehow or other this Choṭa Haridāsa looked lustily on a young woman, and Lord Caitanya was so strict that He at once rejected him from the society of His personal associates. Lord Caitanya said, "For a *sannyāsī* or anyone who is aspiring to get out of the clutches of material nature and trying to elevate himself to the spiritual nature and go back home, back to Godhead, for him, looking toward material possessions and women for sense gratification – not even enjoying them, but just looking toward them with such a propensity – is so condemned that he had better commit suicide before experiencing such illicit desires." So these are the processes for purification.

The next item is *jñāna-yoga-vyavasthiti:* being engaged in the cultivation of knowledge. *Sannyāsī* life is meant for distributing knowledge to the householders and others who have forgotten their real life of spiritual advancement. A *sannyāsī* is supposed to beg from door to door for his livelihood, but this does not mean that he is a beggar. Humility is also one of the qualifications of a transcendentally situated person, and out of sheer humility the *sannyāsī* goes from door to door, not exactly for the purpose of begging, but to see the householders and awaken them to Kṛṣṇa consciousness. This is the duty of a *sannyāsī.* If he is actually advanced and so ordered by his spiritual master, he should preach Kṛṣṇa consciousness with logic and understanding, and if one is not so advanced he should not accept the renounced order of life. But even if one has accepted the renounced order of life without sufficient knowledge, he should engage himself fully in hearing from a bona fide spiritual master to cultivate knowledge. A *sannyāsī,* or one in the renounced order of life, must be situated in fearlessness, *sattva-saṁśuddhi* (purity) and *jñāna-yoga* (knowledge).

The next item is charity. Charity is meant for the householders. The householders should earn a livelihood by an honorable means and spend fifty percent of their income to propagate Kṛṣṇa consciousness all over the world. Thus a householder should give in charity to institutional societies that are engaged in that way. Charity should be given to the right receiver. There are different kinds of charity, as will be explained later on – charity in the modes of goodness, passion and ignorance. Charity in the mode of goodness is recommended by the scriptures, but charity in the modes of passion and ignorance is not recommended, because it is simply a waste of money. Charity should be given only to propagate Kṛṣṇa consciousness all over the world. That is charity in the mode of goodness.

Then as far as *dama* (self-control) is concerned, it is not only meant for other orders of religious society, but is especially meant for the householder. Although he has a wife, a householder should not use his senses for sex life unnecessarily. There are restrictions for the householders even in sex life, which should only be engaged in for the propagation of children. If he does not require children, he should not enjoy sex life with his wife. Modern society enjoys sex life with contraceptive methods or more abominable methods to avoid the responsibility of children. This is not in the transcendental quality, but is demoniac. If anyone, even if he is a householder, wants to make progress in spiritual life, he must control his sex life and should not beget a child without the purpose of serving Kṛṣṇa. If he is able to beget children who will be in Kṛṣṇa consciousness, one can produce hundreds of children, but without this capacity one should not indulge only for sense pleasure.

Sacrifice is another item to be performed by the householders, because sacrifices require a large amount of money. Those in other orders of life, namely *brahmacarya, vānaprastha* and *sannyāsa,* have no money; they live by begging. So performance of different types of sacrifice is meant for the householders. They should perform *agni-hotra* sacrifices as enjoined in the Vedic literature, but such sacrifices at the present moment are very expensive, and it is not possible for any householder to perform them. The best sacrifice recommended in this age is called *saṅkīrtana-yajña.* This *saṅkīrtana-yajña,* the chanting of Hare Kṛṣṇa, Hare Kṛṣṇa, Kṛṣṇa Kṛṣṇa, Hare Hare/ Hare Rāma, Hare Rāma, Rāma Rāma, Hare Hare, is the best and most inexpensive sacrifice; everyone can adopt it and derive benefit. So these three items, namely charity, sense control and performance of sacrifice, are meant for the householder.

Then *svādhyāya,* Vedic study, is meant for *brahmacarya,* or student life. *Brahmacārīs* should have no connection with women; they should live a life of celibacy and engage the mind in the study of Vedic literature for cultivation of spiritual knowledge. This is called *svādhyāya.*

Tapas, or austerity, is especially meant for the retired life. One should not remain a householder throughout his whole life; he must always remember that there are four divisions of life – *brahmacarya, gṛhastha, vānaprastha* and *sannyāsa.* So after *gṛhastha,* householder life, one should retire. If one lives for a hundred years, he should spend twenty-five years in student life, twenty-five in householder life, twenty-five in retired life and twenty-five in the renounced order of life. These are the regulations of the Vedic religious discipline. A man retired from household life must practice austerities of the body, mind and tongue. That is *tapasya.* The entire *varṇāśrama-dharma* society is meant for *tapasya.* Without *tapasya,* or austerity, no human being can get liberation. The theory that there is no need of austerity in life, that one can go on speculating and everything will be nice, is recommended neither in the Vedic literature nor in *Bhagavad-gītā.* Such theories are manufactured by show-bottle spiritualists who are trying to gather more followers. If there are restrictions, rules and regulations, people will not become attracted. Therefore those who want followers in the name of religion, just to have a show only, don't restrict the lives of their students, nor their own lives. But that method is not approved by the *Vedas.*

As far as the brahminical quality of simplicity is concerned, not only should a particular order of life follow this principle, but every member, be he in the *brahmacārī āśrama, gṛhastha āśrama, vānaprastha āśrama* or *sannyāsa āśrama.* One should be very simple and straightforward.

Ahiṁsā means not arresting the progressive life of any living entity. One should not think that since the spirit spark is never killed even after the killing of the body there is no harm in killing animals for sense gratification. People are now addicted to eating animals, in spite of having an ample supply of grains, fruits and milk. There is no necessity for animal killing. This injunction is for everyone. When there is no alternative, one may kill an animal, but it should be offered in sacrifice. At any rate, when there is an ample food supply for humanity, persons who are desiring to make advancement in spiritual realization should not commit violence to animals. Real *ahiṁsā* means not checking anyone's progressive life. The animals are also making progress in their evolutionary life by transmigrating from one category of animal life to another. If a particular animal is killed, then his progress is checked. If an animal is staying in a particular body for so many days or so many years and is untimely killed, then he has to come back again in that form of life to complete the remaining days in order to be promoted to another species of life. So their progress should not be checked simply to satisfy one's palate. This is called *ahiṁsā.*

Satyam. This word means that one should not distort the truth for some personal interest. In Vedic literature there are some difficult passages, but the meaning or the purpose should be learned from a bona fide spiritual master. That is the process for understanding the *Vedas. Śruti* means that one should hear from the authority. One should not construe some interpretation for his personal interest. There are so many commentaries on *Bhagavad-gītā* that misinterpret the original text. The real import of the word should be presented, and that should be learned from a bona fide spiritual master.

Akrodha means to check anger. Even if there is provocation one should be tolerant, for once one becomes angry his whole body becomes polluted. Anger is a product of the mode of passion and lust, so one who is transcendentally situated should check himself from anger. *Apaiśunam* means that one should not find fault with others or correct them unnecessarily. Of course to call a thief a thief is not faultfinding, but to call an honest person a thief is very much offensive for one who is making advancement in spiritual life. *Hrī* means that one should be very modest and must not perform some act which is abominable. *Acāpalam,* determination, means that one should not be agitated or frustrated in some attempt. There may be failure in some attempt, but one should not be sorry for that; he should make progress with patience and determination.

The word *tejas* used here is meant for the *kṣatriyas.* The *kṣatriyas* should always be very strong to be able to give protection to the weak. They should not pose themselves as nonviolent. If violence is required, they must exhibit it. But a person who is able to curb down his enemy may under certain conditions show forgiveness. He may excuse minor offenses.

Śaucam means cleanliness, not only in mind and body but in one's dealings also. It is especially meant for the mercantile people, who should not deal in the black market. *Nāti-mānitā,* not expecting honor, applies to the *śūdras,* the worker class, which are considered, according to Vedic injunctions, to be the lowest of the four classes. They should not be puffed up with unnecessary prestige or honor and should remain in their own status. It is the duty of the *śūdras* to offer respect to the higher class for the upkeep of the social order.

All these twenty-six qualifications mentioned are transcendental qualities. They should be cultivated according to the different statuses of social and occupational order. The purport is that even though material conditions are miserable, if these qualities are developed by practice, by all classes of men, then gradually it is possible to rise to the highest platform of transcendental realization.

Text 4 दम्भो दर्पोऽभिमानश्च क्रोधः पारुष्यमेव च ।
अज्ञानं चाभिजातस्य पार्थ सम्पदमासुरीम् ॥ ४ ॥

dambho darpo 'bhimānaś ca, krodhaḥ pāruṣyam eva ca
ajñānaṁ cābhijātasya, pārtha sampadam āsurīm

dambhaḥ – pride; *darpaḥ* – arrogance; *abhimānaḥ* – conceit; *ca* – and; *krodhaḥ* – anger; *pāruṣyam* – harshness; *eva* – certainly; *ca* – and; *ajñānam* – ignorance; *ca* – and; *abhijātasya* – of one who is born of; *pārtha* – O son of Pṛthā; *sampadam* – the qualities; *āsurīm* – of the demoniac nature.

Pride, arrogance, conceit, anger, harshness and ignorance – these qualities belong to those of demoniac nature, O son of Pṛthā.

PURPORT: In this verse, the royal road to hell is described. The demoniac want to make a show of religion and advancement in spiritual science, although they do not follow the principles. They are always arrogant or proud in possessing some type of education or so much wealth. They desire to be worshiped by others, and demand respectability, although they do not command respect. Over trifles they become very angry and speak harshly, not gently. They do not know what should be done and what should not be done. They do everything whimsically, according to their own desire, and they do not recognize any authority. These demoniac qualities are taken on by them from the beginning of their bodies in the wombs of their mothers, and as they grow they manifest all these inauspicious qualities.

Text 5 दैवी सम्पद्विमोक्षाय निबन्धायासुरी मता ।
मा शुचः सम्पदं दैवीमभिजातोऽसि पाण्डव ॥ ५ ॥

daivī sampad vimokṣāya, nibandhāyāsurī matā
mā śucaḥ sampadaṁ daivīm, abhijāto 'si pāṇḍava

daivī – transcendental; *sampat* – assets; *vimokṣāya* – meant for liberation; *nibandhāya* – for bondage; *āsurī* – demoniac qualities; *matā* – are considered; *mā* – do not; *śucaḥ* – worry; *sampadam* – assets; *daivīm* – transcendental; *abhijātaḥ* – born of; *asi* – you are; *pāṇḍava* – O son of Pāṇḍu.

The transcendental qualities are conducive to liberation, whereas the demoniac qualities make for bondage. Do not worry, O son of Pāṇḍu, for you are born with the divine qualities.

PURPORT: Lord Kṛṣṇa encouraged Arjuna by telling him that he was not born with demoniac qualities. His involvement in the fight was not demoniac, because he was considering the pros and cons. He was considering whether respectable persons such as Bhīṣma and Droṇa should be killed or not, so he was not acting under the influence of anger, false prestige or harshness. Therefore he was not of the quality of the demons. For a *kṣatriya,* a military man, shooting arrows at the enemy is considered transcendental, and refraining from such a duty is demoniac. Therefore there was no cause for Arjuna to lament. Anyone who performs the regulative principles of the different orders of life is transcendentally situated.

Text 6 द्वौ भूतसर्गौ लोकेऽस्मिन्दैव आसुर एव च ।
दैवो विस्तरशः प्रोक्त आसुरं पार्थ मे शृणु ॥ ६ ॥

dvau bhūta-sargau loke 'smin, daiva āsura eva ca
daivo vistaraśaḥ prokta, āsuraṁ pārtha me śṛṇu

dvau – two; *bhūta-sargau* – created living beings; *loke* – in the world; *asmin* – this; *daivaḥ* – godly; *āsuraḥ* – demoniac; *eva* – certainly; *ca* – and; *daivaḥ* – the divine; *vistaraśaḥ* – at great length; *proktaḥ* – said; *āsuram* – the demoniac; *pārtha* – O son of Pṛthā; *me* – from Me; *śṛṇu* – just hear.

O son of Pṛthā, in this world there are two kinds of created beings. One is called divine and the other demoniac. I have already explained to you at length the divine qualities. Now hear from Me of the demoniac.

PURPORT: Lord Kṛṣṇa, having assured Arjuna that he was born with the divine qualities, is now describing the demoniac way. The conditioned living entities are divided into two classes in this world. Those who are born with divine qualities follow a regulated life; that is to say they abide by the injunctions in scriptures and by the authorities. One should perform duties in the light of authoritative scripture. This mentality is called divine. One who does not follow the regulative principles as they are laid down in the scriptures and who acts according to his whims is called demoniac or asuric. There is no other criterion but obedience to the regulative principles of scriptures. It is mentioned in Vedic literature that both the demigods and the demons are born of the Prajāpati; the only difference is that one class obeys the Vedic injunctions and the other does not.

Text 7 प्रवृत्तिं च निवृत्तिं च जना न विदुरासुराः ।
न शौचं नापि चाचारो न सत्यं तेषु विद्यते ॥ ७ ॥

pravṛttiṁ ca nivṛttiṁ ca, janā na vidur āsurāḥ
na śaucaṁ nāpi cācāro, na satyaṁ teṣu vidyate

pravṛttim – acting properly; *ca* – also; *nivṛttim* – not acting improperly; *ca* – and; *janāḥ* – persons; *na* – never; *viduḥ* – know; *āsurāḥ* – of demoniac quality; *na* – never; *śaucam* – cleanliness; *na* – nor; *api* – also; *ca* – and; *ācāraḥ* – behavior; *na* – never; *satyam* – truth; *teṣu* – in them; *vidyate* – there is.

Those who are demoniac do not know what is to be done and what is not to be done. Neither cleanliness nor proper behavior nor truth is found in them.

PURPORT: In every civilized human society there is some set of scriptural rules and regulations which is followed from the beginning. Especially among the Āryans, those who adopt the Vedic civilization and who are known as the most advanced civilized peoples, those who do not follow the scriptural injunctions are supposed to be demons. Therefore it is stated here that the demons do not know the scriptural rules, nor do they have any inclination to follow them. Most of them do not know them, and even if some of them know, they have not the tendency to follow them. They have no faith, nor are they willing to act in terms of the Vedic injunctions. The demons are not clean, either externally or internally. One should always be careful to keep his body clean by bathing, brushing teeth, shaving, changing clothes, etc. As far as internal cleanliness is concerned, one should always remember the holy names of God and chant Hare Kṛṣṇa, Hare Kṛṣṇa, Kṛṣṇa Kṛṣṇa, Hare Hare/ Hare Rāma, Hare Rāma, Rāma Rāma, Hare Hare. The demons neither like nor follow all these rules for external and internal cleanliness.

As for behavior, there are many rules and regulations guiding human behavior, such as the *Manu-saṁhitā,* which is the law of the human race. Even up to today, those who are Hindu follow the *Manu-saṁhitā.* Laws of inheritance and other legalities are derived from this book. Now, in the *Manu-saṁhitā* it is clearly stated that a woman should not be given freedom. That does not mean that women are to be kept as slaves, but they are like children. Children are not given freedom, but that does not mean that they are kept as slaves. The demons have now neglected such injunctions, and they think that women should be given as much freedom as men. However, this has not improved the social condition of the world. Actually, a woman should be given protection at every stage of life. She should be given protection by the father in her younger days, by the husband in her youth, and by the grown-up sons in her old age. This is proper social behavior according to the *Manu-saṁhitā.* But modern education has artificially devised a puffed-up concept of womanly life, and therefore marriage is practically now an imagination in human society. The social condition of women is thus not very good now, although those who are married are in a better condition than those who are proclaiming their so-called freedom. The demons, therefore, do not accept any instruction which is good for society, and because they do not follow the experience of great sages and the rules and regulations laid down by the sages, the social condition of the demoniac people is very miserable.

Text 8 असत्यमप्रतिष्ठं ते जगदाहुरनीश्वरम् ।
अपरस्परसम्भूतं किमन्यत्कामहैतुकम् ॥ ८ ॥

asatyam apratiṣṭhaṁ te, jagad āhur anīśvaram
aparaspara-sambhūtaṁ, kim anyat kāma-haitukam

asatyam – unreal; *apratiṣṭham* – without foundation; *te* – they; *jagat* – the cosmic manifestation; *āhuḥ* – say; *anīśvaram* – with no controller; *aparaspara* – without cause; *sambhūtam* – arisen; *kim anyat* – there is no other cause; *kāma-haitukam* – it is due to lust only.

They say that this world is unreal, with no foundation, no God in control. They say it is produced of sex desire and has no cause other than lust.

PURPORT: The demonic conclude that the world is phantasmagoria. There is no cause and effect, no controller, no purpose: everything is unreal. They say that this cosmic manifestation arises due to chance material actions and reactions. They do not think that the world was created by God for a certain purpose. They have their own theory: that the world has come about in its own way and that there is no reason to believe that there is a God behind it. For them there is no difference between spirit and matter, and they do not accept the Supreme Spirit. Everything is matter only, and the whole cosmos is supposed to be a mass of ignorance. According to them, everything is void, and whatever manifestation exists is due to our ignorance in perception. They take it for granted that all manifestation of diversity is a display of ignorance, just as in a dream we may create so many things which actually have no existence. Then when we are awake we shall see that everything is simply a dream. But factually, although the demons say that life is a dream, they are very expert in enjoying this dream. And so, instead of acquiring knowledge, they become more and more implicated in their dreamland. They conclude that as a child is simply the result of sexual intercourse between man and woman, this world is born without any soul. For them it is only a combination of matter that has produced the living entities, and there is no question of the existence of the soul. As many living creatures come out from perspiration and from a dead body without any cause, the whole living world has come out of the material combinations of the cosmic manifestation. Therefore material nature is the cause of this manifestation, and there is no other cause. They do not believe in the words of Kṛṣṇa in *Bhagavad-gītā: mayādhyakṣeṇa prakṛtiḥ sūyate sa-carācaram.* "Under My direction the whole material world is moving." In other words, among the demons there is no perfect knowledge of the creation of the world; every one of them has some particular theory of his own. According to them, one interpretation of the scriptures is as good as another, for they do not believe in a standard understanding of the scriptural injunctions.

Text 9 एतां दृष्टिमवष्टभ्य नष्टात्मानोऽल्पबुद्धयः ।
प्रभवन्त्युग्रकर्माणः क्षयाय जगतोऽहिताः ॥ ९ ॥

etāṁ dṛṣṭim avaṣṭabhya, naṣṭātmāno 'lpa-buddhayaḥ
prabhavanty ugra-karmāṇaḥ, kṣayāya jagato 'hitāḥ

etām – this; *dṛṣṭim* – vision; *avaṣṭabhya* – accepting; *naṣṭa* – having lost; *ātmānaḥ* – themselves; *alpa-buddhayaḥ* – the less intelligent; *prabhavanti* – flourish; *ugra-karmāṇaḥ* – engaged in painful activities; *kṣayāya* – for destruction; *jagataḥ* – of the world; *ahitāḥ* – unbeneficial.

Following such conclusions, the demoniac, who are lost to themselves and who have no intelligence, engage in unbeneficial, horrible works meant to destroy the world.

PURPORT: The demoniac are engaged in activities that will lead the world to destruction. The Lord states here that they are less intelligent. The materialists, who have no concept of God, think that they are advancing. But according to *Bhagavad-gītā,* they are unintelligent and devoid of all sense. They try to enjoy this material world to the utmost limit and therefore always engage in inventing something for sense gratification. Such materialistic inventions are considered to be advancement of human civilization, but the result is that people grow more and more violent and more and more cruel, cruel to animals and cruel to other human beings. They have no idea how to behave toward one another. Animal killing is very prominent amongst demoniac people. Such people are considered the enemies of the world because ultimately they will invent or create something which will bring destruction to all. Indirectly, this verse anticipates the invention of nuclear weapons, of which the whole world is today very proud. At any moment war may take place, and these atomic weapons may create havoc. Such things are created solely for the destruction of the world, and this is indicated here. Due to godlessness, such weapons are invented in human society; they are not meant for the peace and prosperity of the world.

Text 10 काममाश्रित्य दुष्पूरं दम्भमानमदान्विताः ।
मोहाद् गृहीत्वासद्ग्राहान् प्रवर्तन्तेऽशुचिव्रताः ॥१०॥

kāmam āśritya duṣpūraṁ, dambha-māna-madānvitāḥ
mohād gṛhītvāsad-grāhān, pravartante 'śuci-vratāḥ

kāmam – lust; *āśritya* – taking shelter of; *duṣpūram* – insatiable; *dambha* – of pride; *māna* – and false prestige; *mada-anvitāḥ* – absorbed in the conceit; *mohāt* – by illusion; *gṛhītvā* – taking; *asat* – nonpermanent; *grāhān* – things; *pravartante* – they flourish; *aśuci* – to the unclean; *vratāḥ* – avowed.

Taking shelter of insatiable lust and absorbed in the conceit of pride and false prestige, the demoniac, thus illusioned, are always sworn to unclean work, attracted by the impermanent.

PURPORT: The demoniac mentality is described here. The demons have no satiation for their lust. They will go on increasing and increasing their insatiable desires for material enjoyment. Although they are always full of anxieties on account of accepting nonpermanent things, they still continue to engage in such activities out of illusion. They have no knowledge and cannot tell that they are heading the wrong way. Accepting nonpermanent things, such demoniac people create their own God, create their own hymns and chant accordingly. The result is that they become more and more attracted to two things – sex enjoyment and accumulation of material wealth. The word *aśuci-vratāḥ,* "unclean vows," is very significant in this connection. Such demoniac people are only attracted by wine, women, gambling and meat-eating; those are their *aśuci,* unclean habits. Induced by pride and false prestige, they create some principles of religion which are not approved by the Vedic injunctions. Although such demoniac people are most abominable in the world, by artificial means the world creates a false honor for them. Although they are gliding toward hell, they consider themselves very much advanced.

Texts 11–12

चिन्तामपरिमेयां च प्रलयान्तामुपाश्रिताः ।
कामोपभोगपरमा एतावदिति निश्चिताः ॥११॥
आशापाशशतैर्बद्धाः कामक्रोधपरायणाः ।
ईहन्ते कामभोगार्थमन्यायेनार्थसञ्चयान् ॥१२॥

cintām aparimeyāṁ ca, pralayāntām upāśritāḥ
kāmopabhoga-paramā, etāvad iti niścitāḥ

āśā-pāśa-śatair baddhāḥ, kāma-krodha-parāyaṇāḥ
īhante kāma-bhogārtham, anyāyenārtha-sañcayān

cintām – fears and anxieties; *aparimeyām* – immeasurable; *ca* – and; *pralaya-antām* – unto the point of death; *upāśritāḥ* – having taken shelter of; *kāma-upabhoga* – sense gratification; *paramāḥ* – the highest goal of life; *etāvat* – thus; *iti* – in this way; *niścitāḥ* – having ascertained; *āśā-pāśa* – entanglements in a network of hope; *śataiḥ* – by hundreds; *baddhāḥ* – being bound; *kāma* – of lust; *krodha* – and anger; *parāyaṇāḥ* – always situated in the mentality; *īhante* – they desire; *kāma* – lust; *bhoga* – sense enjoyment; *artham* – for the purpose of; *anyāyena* – illegally; *artha* – of wealth; *sañcayān* – accumulation.

They believe that to gratify the senses is the prime necessity of human civilization. Thus until the end of life their anxiety is immeasurable. Bound by a network of hundreds of thousands of desires and

absorbed in lust and anger, they secure money by illegal means for sense gratification.

PURPORT: The demoniac accept that the enjoyment of the senses is the ultimate goal of life, and this concept they maintain until death. They do not believe in life after death, and they do not believe that one takes on different types of bodies according to one's *karma,* or activities in this world. Their plans for life are never finished, and they go on preparing plan after plan, all of which are never finished. We have personal experience of a person of such demoniac mentality who, even at the point of death, was requesting the physician to prolong his life for four years more because his plans were not yet complete. Such foolish people do not know that a physician cannot prolong life even for a moment. When the notice is there, there is no consideration of the man's desire. The laws of nature do not allow a second beyond what one is destined to enjoy.

The demoniac person, who has no faith in God or the Supersoul within himself, performs all kinds of sinful activities simply for sense gratification. He does not know that there is a witness sitting within his heart. The Supersoul is observing the activities of the individual soul. As it is stated in the *Upaniṣads,* there are two birds sitting in one tree; one is acting and enjoying or suffering the fruits of the branches, and the other is witnessing. But one who is demoniac has no knowledge of Vedic scripture, nor has he any faith; therefore he feels free to do anything for sense enjoyment, regardless of the consequences.

Texts 13–15

इदमद्य मया लब्धमिमं प्राप्स्ये मनोरथम् ।
इदमस्तीदमपि मे भविष्यति पुनर्धनम् ॥१३॥
असौ मया हतः शत्रुर्हनिष्ये चापरानपि ।
ईश्वरोऽहमहं भोगी सिद्धोऽहं बलवान् सुखी ॥१४॥
आढ्योऽभिजनवानस्मि कोऽन्योऽस्ति सदृशो मया ।
यक्ष्ये दास्यामि मोदिष्य इत्यज्ञानविमोहिताः ॥१५॥

idam adya mayā labdham, imaṁ prāpsye manoratham
idam astīdam api me, bhaviṣyati punar dhanam

asau mayā hataḥ śatrur, haniṣye cāparān api
īśvaro 'ham ahaṁ bhogī, siddho 'haṁ balavān sukhī

āḍhyo 'bhijanavān asmi, ko 'nyo 'sti sadṛśo mayā
yakṣye dāsyāmi modiṣya, ity ajñāna-vimohitāḥ

idam – this; *adya* – today; *mayā* – by me; *labdham* – gained; *imam* – this; *prāpsye* – I shall gain; *manaḥ-ratham* – according to my desires; *idam* – this; *asti* – there is; *idam* – this; *api* – also; *me* – mine; *bhaviṣyati* – it will increase in the future; *punaḥ* – again; *dhanam* – wealth; *asau* – that; *mayā* – by me; *hataḥ* – has been killed; *śatruḥ* – enemy; *haniṣye* – I shall kill; *ca* – also; *aparān* – others; *api* – certainly; *īśvaraḥ* – the lord; *aham* – I am; *aham* – I am; *bhogī* – the enjoyer; *siddhaḥ* – perfect; *aham* – I am; *bala-vān* – powerful; *sukhī* – happy; *āḍhyaḥ* – wealthy; *abhijana-vān* – surrounded by aristocratic relatives; *asmi* – I am; *kaḥ* – who; *anyaḥ* – other; *asti* – there is; *sadṛśaḥ* – like; *mayā* – me; *yakṣye* – I shall sacrifice; *dāsyāmi* – I shall give charity; *modiṣye* – I shall rejoice; *iti* – thus; *ajñāna* – by ignorance; *vimohitāḥ* – deluded.

The demoniac person thinks: "So much wealth do I have today, and I will gain more according to my schemes. So much is mine now, and it will increase in the future, more and more. He is my enemy, and I have killed him, and my other enemies will also be killed. I am the lord of everything. I am the enjoyer. I am perfect, powerful and happy. I am the richest man, surrounded by aristocratic relatives. There is none so powerful and happy as I am. I shall perform sacrifices, I shall give some charity, and thus I shall rejoice." In this way, such persons are deluded by ignorance.

Text 16 अनेकचित्तविभ्रान्ता मोहजालसमावृताः ।
प्रसक्ताः कामभोगेषु पतन्ति नरकेऽशुचौ ॥१६॥

aneka-citta-vibhrāntā, moha-jāla-samāvṛtāḥ
prasaktāḥ kāma-bhogeṣu, patanti narake 'śucau

aneka – numerous; *citta* – by anxieties; *vibhrāntāḥ* – perplexed; *moha* – of illusions; *jāla* – by a network; *samāvṛtāḥ* – surrounded; *prasaktāḥ* – attached; *kāma-bhogeṣu* – to sense gratification; *patanti* – they glide down; *narake* – into hell; *aśucau* – unclean.

Thus perplexed by various anxieties and bound by a network of illusions, they become too strongly attached to sense enjoyment and fall down into hell.

PURPORT: The demoniac man knows no limit to his desire to acquire money. That is unlimited. He thinks only of how much assessment he has just now and schemes to engage that stock of wealth further and further.

For that reason, he does not hesitate to act in any sinful way and so deals in the black market for illegal gratification. He is enamored by the possessions he has already, such as land, family, house and bank balance, and he is always planning to improve them. He believes in his own strength, and he does not know that whatever he is gaining is due to his past good deeds. He is given an opportunity to accumulate such things, but he has no conception of past causes. He simply thinks that all his mass of wealth is due to his own endeavor. A demoniac person believes in the strength of his personal work, not in the law of *karma.* According to the law of *karma,* a man takes his birth in a high family, or becomes rich, or very well educated, or very beautiful because of good work in the past. The demoniac think that all these things are accidental and due to the strength of one's personal ability. They do not sense any arrangement behind all the varieties of people, beauty and education. Anyone who comes into competition with such a demoniac man is his enemy. There are many demoniac people, and each is enemy to the others. This enmity becomes more and more deep – between persons, then between families, then between societies, and at last between nations. Therefore there is constant strife, war and enmity all over the world.

Each demoniac person thinks that he can live at the sacrifice of all others. Generally, a demoniac person thinks of himself as the Supreme God, and a demoniac preacher tells his followers: "Why are you seeking God elsewhere? You are all yourselves God! Whatever you like, you can do. Don't believe in God. Throw away God. God is dead." These are the demoniac's preachings.

Although the demoniac person sees others equally rich and influential, or even more so, he thinks that no one is richer than he and that no one is more influential than he. As far as promotion to the higher planetary system is concerned, he does not believe in performing *yajñas,* or sacrifices. Demons think that they will manufacture their own process of *yajña* and prepare some machine by which they will be able to reach any higher planet. The best example of such a demoniac man was Rāvaṇa. He offered a program to the people by which he would prepare a staircase so that anyone could reach the heavenly planets without performing sacrifices, such as are prescribed in the *Vedas.* Similarly, in the present age such demoniac men are striving to reach the higher planetary systems by mechanical arrangements. These are examples of bewilderment. The result is that, without their knowledge, they are gliding toward hell. Here the Sanskrit word *moha-jāla* is very significant. *Jāla* means "net"; like fish caught in a net, they have no way to come out.

Text 17 आत्मसम्भाविताः स्तब्धा धनमानमदान्विताः ।
यजन्ते नामयज्ञैस्ते दम्भेनाविधिपूर्वकम् ॥१७॥

ātma-sambhāvitāḥ stabdhā, dhana-māna-madānvitāḥ
yajante nāma-yajñais te, dambhenāvidhi-pūrvakam

ātma-sambhāvitāḥ – self-complacent; *stabdhāḥ* – impudent; *dhana-māna* – of wealth and false prestige; *mada* – in the delusion; *anvitāḥ* – absorbed; *yajante* – they perform sacrifice; *nāma* – in name only; *yajñaiḥ* – with sacrifices; *te* – they; *dambhena* – out of pride; *avidhi-pūrvakam* – without following any rules and regulations.

Self-complacent and always impudent, deluded by wealth and false prestige, they sometimes proudly perform sacrifices in name only, without following any rules or regulations.

PURPORT: Thinking themselves all in all, not caring for any authority or scripture, the demoniac sometimes perform so-called religious or sacrificial rites. And since they do not believe in authority, they are very impudent. This is due to illusion caused by accumulating some wealth and false prestige. Sometimes such demons take up the role of preacher, mislead the people, and become known as religious reformers or as incarnations of God. They make a show of performing sacrifices, or they worship the demigods, or manufacture their own God. Common men advertise them as God and worship them, and by the foolish they are considered advanced in the principles of religion, or in the principles of spiritual knowledge. They take the dress of the renounced order of life and engage in all nonsense in that dress. Actually there are so many restrictions for one who has renounced this world. The demons, however, do not care for such restrictions. They think that whatever path one can create is one's own path; there is no such thing as a standard path one has to follow. The word *avidhi-pūrvakam,* meaning a disregard for the rules and regulations, is especially stressed here. These things are always due to ignorance and illusion.

Text 18 अहङ्कारं बलं दर्पं कामं क्रोधं च संश्रिताः ।
मामात्मपरदेहेषु प्रद्विषन्तोऽभ्यसूयकाः ॥१८॥

ahaṅkāraṁ balaṁ darpaṁ, kāmaṁ krodhaṁ ca saṁśritāḥ
māṁ ātma-para-deheṣu, pradviṣanto 'bhyasūyakāḥ

ahaṅkāram – false ego; *balam* – strength; *darpam* – pride; *kāmam* – lust; *krodham* – anger; *ca* – also; *saṁśritāḥ* – having taken shelter of; *mām* – Me; *ātma* – in their own; *para* – and in other; *deheṣu* – bodies; *pradviṣantaḥ* – blaspheming; *abhyasūyakāḥ* – envious.

Bewildered by false ego, strength, pride, lust and anger, the demons become envious of the Supreme Personality of Godhead, who is situated in their own bodies and in the bodies of others, and blaspheme against the real religion.

PURPORT: A demoniac person, being always against God's supremacy, does not like to believe in the scriptures. He is envious of both the scriptures and the existence of the Supreme Personality of Godhead. This is caused by his so-called prestige and his accumulation of wealth and strength. He does not know that the present life is a preparation for the next life. Not knowing this, he is actually envious of his own self, as well as of others. He commits violence on other bodies and on his own. He does not care for the supreme control of the Personality of Godhead, because he has no knowledge. Being envious of the scriptures and the Supreme Personality of Godhead, he puts forward false arguments against the existence of God and denies the scriptural authority. He thinks himself independent and powerful in every action. He thinks that since no one can equal him in strength, power or wealth, he can act in any way and no one can stop him. If he has an enemy who might check the advancement of his sensual activities, he makes plans to cut him down by his own power.

Text 19 तानहं द्विषतः क्रूरान् संसारेषु नराधमान् ।
क्षिपाम्यजस्रमशुभानासुरीष्वेव योनिषु ॥१९॥

tān ahaṁ dviṣataḥ krūrān, saṁsāreṣu narādhamān
kṣipāmy ajasram aśubhān, āsurīṣv eva yoniṣu

tān – those; *aham* – I; *dviṣataḥ* – envious; *krūrān* – mischievous; *saṁsāreṣu* – into the ocean of material existence; *nara-adhamān* – the lowest of mankind; *kṣipāmi* – I put; *ajasram* – forever; *aśubhān* – inauspicious; *āsurīṣu* – demoniac; *eva* – certainly; *yoniṣu* – into the wombs.

Those who are envious and mischievous, who are the lowest among men, I perpetually cast into the ocean of material existence, into various demoniac species of life.

PURPORT: In this verse it is clearly indicated that the placing of a particular individual soul in a particular body is the prerogative of the supreme will. The demoniac person may not agree to accept the supremacy of the Lord, and it is a fact that he may act according to his own whims, but his next birth will depend upon the decision of the Supreme Personality of Godhead and not on himself. In the *Śrīmad-Bhāgavatam,* Third Canto, it is stated that an individual soul, after his death, is put into the womb of a mother where he gets a particular type of body under the supervision of superior power. Therefore in the material existence we find so many species of life – animals, insects, men, and so on. All are arranged by the superior power. They are not accidental. As for the demoniac, it is clearly said here that they are perpetually put into the wombs of demons, and thus they continue to be envious, the lowest of mankind. Such demoniac species of men are held to be always full of lust, always violent and hateful and always unclean. The many kinds of hunters in the jungle are considered to belong to the demoniac species of life.

Text 20 आसुरीं योनिमापन्ना मूढा जन्मनि जन्मनि ।
मामप्राप्यैव कौन्तेय ततो यान्त्यधमां गतिम् ॥२०॥

āsurīṁ yonim āpannā, mūḍhā janmani janmani
mām aprāpyaiva kaunteya, tato yānty adhamāṁ gatim

āsurīm – demoniac; *yonim* – species; *āpannāḥ* – gaining; *mūḍhāḥ* – the foolish; *janmani janmani* – in birth after birth; *mām* – Me; *aprāpya* – without achieving; *eva* – certainly; *kaunteya* – O son of Kuntī; *tataḥ* – thereafter; *yānti* – go; *adhamām* – condemned; *gatim* – destination.

Attaining repeated birth amongst the species of demoniac life, O son of Kuntī, such persons can never approach Me. Gradually they sink down to the most abominable type of existence.

PURPORT: It is known that God is all-merciful, but here we find that God is never merciful to the demoniac. It is clearly stated that the demoniac people, life after life, are put into the wombs of similar demons, and, not achieving the mercy of the Supreme Lord, they go down and down, so that at last they achieve bodies like those of cats, dogs and hogs. It is clearly stated that such demons have practically no chance of receiving the mercy of God at any stage of later life. In the *Vedas* also it is stated that such persons gradually sink to become dogs and hogs. It may be then argued in this connection that God should not be advertised as all-merciful if He is not merciful to such demons. In answer to this question, in the *Vedānta-sūtra* we find that the Supreme Lord has no hatred for anyone. The placing of the *asuras,* the demons, in the lowest status of life is simply another feature of His mercy. Sometimes the *asuras* are killed by the Supreme Lord, but this killing is also good for them, for in Vedic literature we find that anyone who is killed by the Supreme Lord becomes liberated. There are instances in history of many *asuras* – Rāvaṇa, Kaṁsa, Hiraṇyakaśipu – to whom the Lord appeared in various incarnations just to kill them. Therefore God's mercy is shown to the *asuras* if they are fortunate enough to be killed by Him.

Text 21 त्रिविधं नरकस्येदं द्वारं नाशनमात्मनः ।
कामः क्रोधस्तथा लोभस्तस्मादेतत्त्रयं त्यजेत् ॥२१॥

tri-vidhaṁ narakasyedaṁ, dvāraṁ nāśanam ātmanaḥ
kāmaḥ krodhas tathā lobhas, tasmād etat trayaṁ tyajet

tri-vidham – of three kinds; *narakasya* – of hell; *idam* – this; *dvāram* – gate; *nāśanam* – destructive; *ātmanaḥ* – of the self; *kāmaḥ* – lust; *krodhaḥ* – anger; *tathā* – as well as; *lobhaḥ* – greed; *tasmāt* – therefore; *etat* – these; *trayam* – three; *tyajet* – one must give up.

There are three gates leading to this hell – lust, anger and greed. Every sane man should give these up, for they lead to the degradation of the soul.

PURPORT: The beginning of demoniac life is described herein. One tries to satisfy his lust, and when he cannot, anger and greed arise. A sane man who does not want to glide down to the species of demoniac life must try to give up these three enemies, which can kill the self to such an extent that there will be no possibility of liberation from this material entanglement.

Text 22 एतैर्विमुक्तः कौन्तेय तमोद्वारैस्त्रिभिर्नरः ।
आचरत्यात्मनः श्रेयस्ततो याति परां गतिम् ॥२२॥

etair vimuktaḥ kaunteya, tamo-dvārais tribhir naraḥ
ācaraty ātmanaḥ śreyas, tato yāti parāṁ gatim

etaiḥ – from these; *vimuktaḥ* – being liberated; *kaunteya* – O son of Kuntī; *tamaḥ-dvāraiḥ* – from the gates of ignorance; *tribhiḥ* – of three kinds; *naraḥ* – a person; *ācarati* – performs; *ātmanaḥ* – for the self; *śreyaḥ* – benediction; *tataḥ* – thereafter; *yāti* – he goes; *parām* – to the supreme; *gatim* – destination.

The man who has escaped these three gates of hell, O son of Kuntī, performs acts conducive to self-realization and thus gradually attains the supreme destination.

PURPORT: One should be very careful of these three enemies to human life: lust, anger and greed. The more a person is freed from lust, anger and greed, the more his existence becomes pure. Then he can follow the rules and regulations enjoined in the Vedic literature. By following the regulative principles of human life, one gradually raises himself to the platform of spiritual realization. If one is so fortunate, by such practice, to rise to the platform of Kṛṣṇa consciousness, then success is guaranteed for him. In the Vedic literature, the ways of action and reaction are prescribed to enable one to come to the stage of purification. The whole method is based on giving up lust, greed and anger. By cultivating knowledge of this process, one can be elevated to the highest position of self-realization; this self-realization is perfected in devotional service. In that devotional service, the liberation of the conditioned soul is guaranteed. Therefore, according to the Vedic system, there are instituted the four orders of life and the four statuses of life, called the caste system and the spiritual order system. There are different rules and regulations for different castes or divisions of society, and if a person is able to follow them, he will be automatically raised to the highest platform of spiritual realization. Then he can have liberation without a doubt.

Text 23 यः शास्त्रविधिमुत्सृज्य वर्तते कामकारतः ।
न स सिद्धिमवाप्नोति न सुखं न परां गतिम् ॥२३॥

yaḥ śāstra-vidhim utsṛjya, vartate kāma-kārataḥ
na sa siddhim avāpnoti, na sukhaṁ na parāṁ gatim

yaḥ – anyone who; *śāstra-vidhim* – the regulations of the scriptures; *utsṛjya* – giving up; *vartate* – remains; *kāma-kārataḥ* – acting whimsically in lust; *na* – never; *saḥ* – he; *siddhim* – perfection; *avāpnoti* – achieves; *na* – never; *sukham* – happiness; *na* – never; *parām* – the supreme; *gatim* – perfectional stage.

He who discards scriptural injunctions and acts according to his own whims attains neither perfection, nor happiness, nor the supreme destination.

PURPORT: As described before, the *śāstra-vidhi,* or the direction of the *śāstra,* is given to the different castes and orders of human society. Everyone is expected to follow these rules and regulations. If one does not follow them and acts whimsically according to his lust, greed and desire, then he never will be perfect in his life. In other words, a man may theoretically know all these things, but if he does not apply them in his own life, then he is to be known as the lowest of mankind. In the human form of life, a living entity is expected to be sane and to follow the regulations given for elevating his life to the highest platform, but if he does not follow them, then he degrades himself. But even if he follows the rules and regulations and moral principles and ultimately does not come to the stage of understanding the Supreme Lord, then all his knowledge becomes spoiled. And even if he accepts the existence of God, if he does not engage himself in the service of the Lord his attempts are spoiled. Therefore one should gradually raise himself to the platform of Kṛṣṇa consciousness and devotional service; it is then and there that he can attain the highest perfectional stage, not otherwise.

The word *kāma-kārataḥ* is very significant. A person who knowingly violates the rules acts in lust. He knows that this is forbidden, but still he acts. This is called acting whimsically. He knows that this should be done, but still he does not do it; therefore he is called whimsical. Such persons are destined to be condemned by the Supreme Lord. Such persons cannot have the perfection which is meant for the human life. The human life is especially meant for purifying one's existence, and one who does not follow the rules and regulations cannot purify himself, nor can he attain the real stage of happiness.

Text 24 तस्माच्छास्त्रं प्रमाणं ते कार्याकार्यव्यवस्थितौ ।
ज्ञात्वा शास्त्रविधानोक्तं कर्म कर्तुमिहार्हसि ॥२४॥

tasmāc chāstraṁ pramāṇaṁ te, kāryākārya-vyavasthitau
jñātvā śāstra-vidhānoktaṁ, karma kartum ihārhasi

tasmāt – therefore; *śāstram* – the scriptures; *pramāṇam* – evidence; *te* – your; *kārya* – duty; *akārya* – and forbidden activities; *vyavasthitau* – in determining; *jñātvā* – knowing; *śāstra* – of scripture; *vidhāna* – the regulations; *uktam* – as declared; *karma* – work; *kartum* – do; *iha* – in this world; *arhasi* – you should.

One should therefore understand what is duty and what is not duty by the regulations of the scriptures. Knowing such rules and regulations, one should act so that he may gradually be elevated.

PURPORT: As stated in the Fifteenth Chapter, all the rules and regulations of the *Vedas* are meant for knowing Kṛṣṇa. If one understands Kṛṣṇa from the *Bhagavad-gītā* and becomes situated in Kṛṣṇa consciousness, engaging himself in devotional service, he has reached the highest perfection of knowledge offered by the Vedic literature. Lord Caitanya Mahāprabhu made this process very easy: He asked people simply to chant Hare Kṛṣṇa, Hare Kṛṣṇa, Kṛṣṇa Kṛṣṇa, Hare Hare/ Hare Rāma, Hare Rāma, Rāma Rāma, Hare Hare and to engage in the devotional service of the Lord and eat the remnants of foodstuff offered to the Deity. One who is directly engaged in all these devotional activities is to be understood as having studied all Vedic literature. He has come to the conclusion perfectly. Of course, for the ordinary persons who are not in Kṛṣṇa consciousness or who are not engaged in devotional service, what is to be done and what is not to be done must be decided by the injunctions of the *Vedas*. One should act accordingly, without argument. That is called following the principles of *śāstra,* or scripture. *Śāstra* is without the four principal defects that are visible in the conditioned soul: imperfect senses, the propensity for cheating, certainty of committing mistakes, and certainty of being illusioned. These four principal defects in conditioned life disqualify one from putting forth rules and regulations. Therefore, the rules and regulations as described in the *śāstra* – being above these defects – are accepted without alteration by all great saints, *ācāryas* and great souls.

In India there are many parties of spiritual understanding, generally classified as two: the impersonalist and the personalist. Both of them, however, lead their lives according to the principles of the *Vedas.* Without following the principles of the scriptures, one cannot elevate himself to the perfectional stage. One who actually, therefore, understands the purport of the *śāstras* is considered fortunate.

In human society, aversion to the principles of understanding the Supreme Personality of Godhead is the cause of all falldowns. That is the greatest offense of human life. Therefore, *māyā,* the material energy of the Supreme Personality of Godhead, is always giving us trouble in the shape of the threefold miseries. This material energy is constituted of the three modes of material nature. One has to raise himself at least to the mode of goodness before the path to understanding the Supreme Lord can be opened. Without raising oneself to the standard of the mode of goodness, one remains in ignorance and passion, which are the cause of demoniac life. Those in the modes of passion and ignorance deride the scriptures, deride the holy man, and deride the proper understanding of the Supreme Personality of Godhead. They disobey the instructions of the spiritual master, and they do not care for the regulations of the scriptures. In spite of hearing the glories of devotional service, they are not attracted. Thus they manufacture their own way of elevation. These are some of the defects of human society which lead to the demoniac status of life. If, however, one is able to be guided by a proper and bona fide spiritual master, who can lead one to the path of elevation, to the higher stage, then one's life becomes successful.

Thus end the Bhaktivedanta Purports to the Sixteenth Chapter of the Śrīmad Bhagavad-gītā *in the matter of the Divine and Demoniac Natures.*

CHAPTER SEVENTEEN

The Divisions of Faith

Text 1 अर्जुन उवाच
ये शास्त्रविधिमुत्सृज्य यजन्ते श्रद्धयान्विताः ।
तेषां निष्ठा तु का कृष्ण सत्त्वमाहो रजस्तमः ॥ १ ॥

arjuna uvāca
ye śāstra-vidhim utsṛjya, yajante śraddhayānvitāḥ
teṣāṁ niṣṭhā tu kā kṛṣṇa, sattvam āho rajas tamaḥ

arjunaḥ uvāca – Arjuna said; *ye* – those who; *śāstra-vidhim* – the regulations of scripture; *utsṛjya* – giving up; *yajante* – worship; *śraddhayā* – full faith; *anvitāḥ* – possessed of; *teṣām* – of them; *niṣṭhā* – the faith; *tu* – but; *kā* – what; *kṛṣṇa* – O Kṛṣṇa; *sattvam* – in goodness; *āho* – or else; *rajaḥ* – in passion; *tamaḥ* – in ignorance.

Arjuna inquired: O Kṛṣṇa, what is the situation of those who do not follow the principles of scripture but worship according to their own imagination? Are they in goodness, in passion or in ignorance?

PURPORT: In the Fourth Chapter, thirty-ninth verse, it is said that a person faithful to a particular type of worship gradually becomes elevated to the stage of knowledge and attains the highest perfectional stage of peace and prosperity. In the Sixteenth Chapter, it is concluded that one who does not follow the principles laid down in the scriptures is called an *asura,* demon, and one who follows the scriptural injunctions faithfully is called a *deva,* or demigod. Now, if one, with faith, follows some rules which are not mentioned in the scriptural injunctions, what is his position? This doubt of Arjuna's is to be cleared by Kṛṣṇa. Are those who create some sort of God by selecting a human being and placing their faith in him worshiping in goodness, passion or ignorance? Do such persons attain the perfectional stage of life? Is it possible for them to be situated in real knowledge and elevate themselves to the highest perfectional stage? Do those who do not follow the rules and regulations of the scriptures but who have faith in something and worship gods and demigods and men attain success in their effort? Arjuna is putting these questions to Kṛṣṇa.

Text 2 श्रीभगवानुवाच
त्रिविधा भवति श्रद्धा देहिनां सा स्वभावजा ।
सात्त्विकी राजसी चैव तामसी चेति तां शृणु ॥ २ ॥

śrī-bhagavān uvāca
tri-vidhā bhavati śraddhā, dehināṁ sā svabhāva-jā
sāttvikī rājasī caiva, tāmasī ceti tāṁ śṛṇu

śrī-bhagavān uvāca – the Supreme Personality of Godhead said; *tri-vidhā* – of three kinds; *bhavati* – becomes; *śraddhā* – the faith; *dehinām* – of the embodied; *sā* – that; *sva-bhāva-jā* – according to his mode of material nature; *sāttvikī* – in the mode of goodness; *rājasī* – in the mode of passion; *ca* – also; *eva* – certainly; *tāmasī* – in the mode of ignorance; *ca* – and; *iti* – thus; *tām* – that; *śṛṇu* – hear from Me.

The Supreme Personality of Godhead said: According to the modes of nature acquired by the embodied soul, one's faith can be of three kinds – in goodness, in passion or in ignorance. Now hear about this.

PURPORT: Those who know the rules and regulations of the scriptures but out of laziness or indolence give up following these rules and regulations are governed by the modes of material nature. According to their previous activities in the mode of goodness, passion or ignorance, they acquire a nature which is of a specific quality. The association of the living entity with the different modes of nature has been going on perpetually; since the living entity is in contact with material nature, he acquires different types of mentality according to his association with the material modes. But this nature can be changed if one associates with a bona fide spiritual master and abides by his rules and the scriptures. Gradually, one can change his position from ignorance to goodness, or from passion to goodness. The conclusion is that blind faith in a particular mode of nature cannot help a person become elevated to the perfectional stage. One has to consider things carefully, with intelligence, in the association of a bona fide spiritual master. Thus one can change his position to a higher mode of nature.

Text 3 सत्त्वानुरूपा सर्वस्य श्रद्धा भवति भारत ।
श्रद्धामयोऽयं पुरुषो यो यच्छ्रद्धः स एव सः ॥ ३ ॥

sattvānurūpā sarvasya, śraddhā bhavati bhārata
śraddhā-mayo 'yaṁ puruṣo, yo yac-chraddhaḥ sa eva saḥ

sattva-anurūpā – according to the existence; *sarvasya* – of everyone; *śraddhā* – faith; *bhavati* – becomes; *bhārata* – O son of Bharata; *śraddhā* – faith; *mayaḥ* – full of; *ayam* – this; *puruṣaḥ* – living entity; *yaḥ* – who; *yat* – having which; *śraddhaḥ* – faith; *saḥ* – thus; *eva* – certainly; *saḥ* – he.

O son of Bharata, according to one's existence under the various modes of nature, one evolves a particular kind of faith. The living being is said to be of a particular faith according to the modes he has acquired.

PURPORT: Everyone has a particular type of faith, regardless of what he is. But his faith is considered good, passionate or ignorant according to the nature he has acquired. Thus, according to his particular type of faith, one associates with certain persons. Now the real fact is that every living being, as is stated in the Fifteenth Chapter, is originally a fragmental part and parcel of the Supreme Lord. Therefore one is originally transcendental to all the modes of material nature. But when one forgets his relationship with the Supreme Personality of Godhead and comes into contact with the material nature in conditional life, he generates his own position by association with the different varieties of material nature. The resultant artificial faith and existence are only material. Although one may be conducted by some impression, or some conception of life, originally he is *nirguṇa,* or transcendental. Therefore one has to become cleansed of the material contamination that he has acquired, in order to regain his relationship with the Supreme Lord. That is the only path back without fear: Kṛṣṇa consciousness. If one is situated in Kṛṣṇa consciousness, then that path is guaranteed for his elevation to the perfectional stage. If one does not take to this path of self-realization, then he is surely to be conducted by the influence of the modes of nature.

The word *śraddhā,* or "faith," is very significant in this verse. *Śraddhā,* or faith, originally comes out of the mode of goodness. One's faith may be in a demigod or some created God or some mental concoction. One's strong faith is supposed to be productive of works of material goodness. But in material conditional life, no works are completely purified. They are mixed. They are not in pure goodness. Pure goodness is transcendental; in purified goodness one can understand the real nature of the Supreme Personality of Godhead. As long as one's faith is not completely in purified goodness, the faith is subject to contamination by any of the modes of material nature. The contaminated modes of material nature expand to the heart. Therefore according to the position of the heart in contact with a particular mode of material nature, one's faith is established. It should be understood that if one's heart is in the mode of goodness his faith is also in the mode of goodness. If his heart is in the mode of passion, his faith is also in the mode of passion. And if his heart is in the mode of darkness, illusion, his faith is also thus contaminated. Thus we find different types of faith in this world, and there are different types of religions due to different types of faith. The real principle of religious faith is situated in the mode of pure goodness, but because the heart is tainted we find different types of religious principles. Thus according to different types of faith, there are different kinds of worship.

Text 4 यजन्ते सात्त्विका देवान् यक्षरक्षांसि राजसाः ।
प्रेतान् भूतगणांश्चान्ये यजन्ते तामसा जनाः ॥ ४ ॥

yajante sāttvikā devān, yakṣa-rakṣāṁsi rājasāḥ
pretān bhūta-gaṇāṁś cānye, yajante tāmasā janāḥ

yajante – worship; *sāttvikāḥ* – those who are in the mode of goodness; *devān* – demigods; *yakṣa-rakṣāṁsi* – demons; *rājasāḥ* – those who are in the mode of passion; *pretān* – spirits of the dead; *bhūta-gaṇān* – ghosts; *ca* – and; *anye* – others; *yajante* – worship; *tāmasāḥ* – in the mode of ignorance; *janāḥ* – people.

Men in the mode of goodness worship the demigods; those in the mode of passion worship the demons; and those in the mode of ignorance worship ghosts and spirits.

PURPORT: In this verse the Supreme Personality of Godhead describes different kinds of worshipers according to their external activities. According to scriptural injunction, only the Supreme Personality of Godhead is worshipable, but those who are not very conversant with, or faithful to, the scriptural injunctions worship different objects, according to their specific situations in the modes of material nature. Those who are situated in goodness generally worship the demigods. The demigods include Brahmā, Śiva and others such as Indra, Candra and the sun-god. There are various demigods. Those in goodness worship a particular demigod for a particular purpose. Similarly, those who are in the mode of passion worship the demons. We recall that during the Second World War a man in Calcutta worshiped Hitler because thanks to that war he had amassed a large amount of wealth by dealing in the black market. Similarly, those in the modes of passion and ignorance generally select a powerful man to be God. They think that anyone can be worshiped as God and that the same results will be obtained.

Now, it is clearly described here that those who are in the mode of passion worship and create such gods, and those who are in the mode of ignorance, in darkness, worship dead spirits. Sometimes people worship at the tomb of some dead man. Sexual service is also considered to be in the mode of darkness. Similarly, in remote villages in India there are worshipers of ghosts. We have seen that in India the lower-class people sometimes go to the forest, and if they have knowledge that a ghost lives in a tree, they worship that tree and offer sacrifices. These different kinds of worship are not actually God worship. God worship is for persons who are transcendentally situated in pure goodness. In the *Śrīmad-Bhāgavatam* (4.3.23) it is said, *sattvaṁ viśuddhaṁ vasudeva-śabditam:* "When a man is situated in pure goodness, he worships Vāsudeva." The purport is that those who are completely purified of the material modes of nature and who are transcendentally situated can worship the Supreme Personality of Godhead.

The impersonalists are supposed to be situated in the mode of goodness, and they worship five kinds of demigods. They worship the impersonal Viṣṇu form in the material world, which is known as philosophized Viṣṇu. Viṣṇu is the expansion of the Supreme Personality of Godhead, but the impersonalists, because they do not ultimately believe in the Supreme Personality of Godhead, imagine that the Viṣṇu form is just another aspect of the impersonal Brahman; similarly, they imagine that Lord Brahmā is the impersonal form in the material mode of passion. Thus they sometimes describe five kinds of gods that are worshipable, but because they think that the actual truth is impersonal Brahman, they dispose of all worshipable objects at the ultimate end. In conclusion, the different qualities of the material modes of nature can be purified through association with persons who are of transcendental nature.

Texts 5–6

अशास्त्रविहितं घोरं तप्यन्ते ये तपो जनाः ।
दम्भाहङ्कारसंयुक्ताः कामरागबलान्विताः ॥ ५ ॥
कर्षयन्तः शरीरस्थं भूतग्राममचेतसः ।
मां चैवान्तः शरीरस्थं तान् विद्ध्यासुरनिश्चयान् ॥ ६ ॥

aśāstra-vihitaṁ ghoraṁ, tapyante ye tapo janāḥ
dambhāhaṅkāra-saṁyuktāḥ, kāma-rāga-balānvitāḥ

karṣayantaḥ śarīra-sthaṁ, bhūta-grāmam acetasaḥ
māṁ caivāntaḥ śarīra-sthaṁ, tān viddhy āsura-niścayān

aśāstra – not in the scriptures; *vihitam* – directed; *ghoram* – harmful to others; *tapyante* – undergo; *ye* – those who; *tapaḥ* – austerities; *janāḥ* – persons; *dambha* – with pride; *ahaṅkāra* – and egoism; *saṁyuktāḥ* – engaged; *kāma* – of lust; *rāga* – and attachment; *bala* – by the force; *anvitāḥ* – impelled; *karṣayantaḥ* – tormenting; *śarīra-stham* – situated within the body; *bhūta-grāmam* – the combination of material elements; *acetasaḥ* – having a misled mentality; *mām* – Me; *ca* – also; *eva* – certainly; *antaḥ* – within; *śarīra-stham* – situated in the body; *tān* – them; *viddhi* – understand; *āsura-niścayān* – demons.

Those who undergo severe austerities and penances not recommended in the scriptures, performing them out of pride and egoism, who are impelled by lust and attachment, who are foolish and who torture the material elements of the body as well as the Supersoul dwelling within, are to be known as demons.

PURPORT: There are persons who manufacture modes of austerity and penance which are not mentioned in the scriptural injunctions. For instance, fasting for some ulterior purpose, such as to promote a purely political end, is not mentioned in the scriptural directions. The scriptures recommend fasting for spiritual advancement, not for some political end or social purpose. Persons who take to such austerities are, according to *Bhagavad-gītā,* certainly demoniac. Their acts are against the scriptural injunctions and are not beneficial for the people in general. Actually, they act out of pride, false ego, lust and attachment for material enjoyment. By such activities, not only is the combination of material elements of which the body is constructed disturbed, but also the Supreme Personality of Godhead Himself living within the body. Such unauthorized fasting or austerities for some political end are certainly very disturbing to others. They are not mentioned in the Vedic literature. A demoniac person may think that he can force his enemy or other parties to comply with his desire by this method, but sometimes one dies by such fasting. These acts are not approved by the Supreme Personality of Godhead, and He says that those who engage in them are demons. Such demonstrations are insults to the Supreme Personality of Godhead because they are enacted in disobedience to the Vedic scriptural injunctions. The word *acetasaḥ* is significant in this connection. Persons of normal mental condition must obey the scriptural injunctions. Those who are not in such a position neglect and disobey the scriptures and manufacture their own way of austerities and penances. One should always remember the ultimate end of the demoniac people, as described in the previous chapter. The Lord forces them to take birth in the wombs of demoniac persons. Consequently they will live by demoniac principles life after life without knowing their relationship with the Supreme Personality of Godhead. If, however, such persons are fortunate enough to be guided by a spiritual master who can direct them to the path of Vedic wisdom, they can get out of this entanglement and ultimately achieve the supreme goal.

Text 7 आहारस्त्वपि सर्वस्य त्रिविधो भवति प्रियः ।
यज्ञस्तपस्तथा दानं तेषां भेदमिमं शृणु ॥ ७ ॥

āhāras tv api sarvasya, tri-vidho bhavati priyaḥ
yajñas tapas tathā dānaṁ, teṣāṁ bhedam imaṁ śṛṇu

āhāraḥ – eating; *tu* – certainly; *api* – also; *sarvasya* – of everyone; *tri-vidhaḥ* – of three kinds; *bhavati* – there is; *priyaḥ* – dear; *yajñaḥ* – sacrifice; *tapaḥ* – austerity; *tathā* – also; *dānam* – charity; *teṣām* – of them; *bhedam* – the differences; *imam* – this; *śṛṇu* – hear.

Even the food each person prefers is of three kinds, according to the three modes of material nature. The same is true of sacrifices, austerities and charity. Now hear of the distinctions between them.

PURPORT: In terms of different situations in the modes of material nature, there are differences in the manner of eating and performing sacrifices, austerities and charities. They are not all conducted on the same level. Those who can understand analytically what kind of performances are in what modes of material nature are actually wise; those who consider all kinds of sacrifice or food or charity to be the same cannot discriminate, and they are foolish. There are missionary workers who advocate that one can do whatever he likes and attain perfection. But these foolish guides are not acting according to the direction of the scripture. They are manufacturing ways and misleading the people in general.

Text 8 आयुःसत्त्वबलारोग्यसुखप्रीतिविवर्धनाः ।
रस्याः स्निग्धाः स्थिरा हृद्या आहाराः सात्त्विकप्रियाः ॥ ८ ॥

āyuḥ-sattva-balārogya-, sukha-prīti-vivardhanāḥ
rasyāḥ snigdhāḥ sthirā hṛdyā, āhārāḥ sāttvika-priyāḥ

āyuḥ – duration of life; *sattva* – existence; *bala* – strength; *ārogya* – health; *sukha* – happiness; *prīti* – and satisfaction; *vivardhanāḥ* – increasing; *rasyāḥ* – juicy; *snigdhāḥ* – fatty; *sthirāḥ* – enduring; *hṛdyāḥ* – pleasing to the heart; *āhārāḥ* – food; *sāttvika* – to one in goodness; *priyāḥ* – palatable.

Foods dear to those in the mode of goodness increase the duration of life, purify one's existence and give strength, health, happiness and satisfaction. Such foods are juicy, fatty, wholesome, and pleasing to the heart.

Text 9 कट्वम्ललवणात्युष्णतीक्ष्णरूक्षविदाहिनः ।
आहारा राजसस्येष्टा दुःखशोकामयप्रदाः ॥ ९ ॥

kaṭv-amla-lavaṇāty-uṣṇa-, tīkṣṇa-rūkṣa-vidāhinaḥ
āhārā rājasasyeṣṭā, duḥkha-śokāmaya-pradāḥ

kaṭu – bitter; *amla* – sour; *lavaṇa* – salty; *ati-uṣṇa* – very hot; *tīkṣṇa* – pungent; *rūkṣa* – dry; *vidāhinaḥ* – burning; *āhārāḥ* – food; *rājasasya* – to one in the mode of passion; *iṣṭāḥ* – palatable; *duḥkha* – distress; *śoka* – misery; *āmaya* – disease; *pradāḥ* – causing.

Foods that are too bitter, too sour, salty, hot, pungent, dry and burning are dear to those in the mode of passion. Such foods cause distress, misery and disease.

Text 10 यातयामं गतरसं पूति पर्युषितं च यत् ।
उच्छिष्टमपि चामेध्यं भोजनं तामसप्रियम् ॥१०॥

yāta-yāmaṁ gata-rasaṁ, pūti paryuṣitaṁ ca yat
ucchiṣṭam api cāmedhyaṁ, bhojanaṁ tāmasa-priyam

yāta-yāmam – food cooked three hours before being eaten; *gata-rasam* – tasteless; *pūti* – bad-smelling; *paryuṣitam* – decomposed; *ca* – also; *yat* – that which; *ucchiṣṭam* – remnants of food eaten by others; *api* – also; *ca* – and; *amedhyam* – untouchable; *bhojanam* – eating; *tāmasa* – to one in the mode of darkness; *priyam* – dear.

Food prepared more than three hours before being eaten, food that is tasteless, decomposed and putrid, and food consisting of remnants and untouchable things is dear to those in the mode of darkness.

PURPORT: The purpose of food is to increase the duration of life, purify the mind and aid bodily strength. This is its only purpose. In the past, great authorities selected those foods that best aid health and increase life's duration, such as milk products, sugar, rice, wheat, fruits and vegetables. These foods are very dear to those in the mode of goodness. Some other foods, such as baked corn and molasses, while not very palatable in themselves, can be made pleasant when mixed with milk or other foods. They are then in the mode of goodness. All these foods are pure by nature. They are quite distinct from untouchable things like meat and liquor. Fatty foods, as mentioned in the eighth verse, have no connection with animal fat obtained by slaughter. Animal fat is available in the form of milk, which is the most wonderful of all foods. Milk, butter, cheese and similar products give animal fat in a form which rules out any need for the killing of innocent creatures. It is only through brute mentality that this killing goes on. The civilized method of obtaining needed fat is by milk. Slaughter is the way of subhumans. Protein is amply available through split peas, *dāl,* whole wheat, etc.

Foods in the mode of passion, which are bitter, too salty, or too hot or overly mixed with red pepper, cause misery by reducing the mucus in the stomach, leading to disease. Foods in the mode of ignorance or darkness are essentially those that are not fresh. Any food cooked more than three hours before it is eaten (except *prasādam,* food offered to the Lord) is considered to be in the mode of darkness. Because they are decomposing, such foods give a bad odor, which often attracts people in this mode but repulses those in the mode of goodness.

Remnants of food may be eaten only when they are part of a meal that was first offered to the Supreme Lord or first eaten by saintly persons, especially the spiritual master. Otherwise the remnants of food are considered to be in the mode of darkness, and they increase infection or disease. Such foodstuffs, although very palatable to persons in the mode of darkness, are neither liked nor even touched by those in the mode of goodness. The best food is the remnants of what is offered to the Supreme Personality of Godhead. In *Bhagavad-gītā* the Supreme Lord says that He accepts preparations of vegetables, flour and milk when offered with devotion. *Patraṁ puṣpaṁ phalaṁ toyam.* Of course, devotion and love are the chief things which the Supreme Personality of Godhead accepts. But it is also mentioned that the *prasādam* should be prepared in a particular way. Any food prepared by the injunctions of the scripture and offered to the Supreme Personality of Godhead can be taken even if prepared long, long ago, because such food is transcendental. Therefore to make food antiseptic, eatable and palatable for all persons, one should offer food to the Supreme Personality of Godhead.

Text 11 अफलाकाङ्क्षिभिर्यज्ञो विधिदिष्टो य इज्यते ।
यष्टव्यमेवेति मनः समाधाय स सात्त्विकः ॥११॥

aphalākāṅkṣibhir yajño, vidhi-diṣṭo ya ijyate
yaṣṭavyam eveti manaḥ, samādhāya sa sāttvikaḥ

aphala-ākāṅkṣibhiḥ – by those devoid of desire for result; *yajñaḥ* – sacrifice; *vidhi-diṣṭaḥ* – according to the direction of scripture; *yaḥ* – which; *ijyate* – is performed; *yaṣṭavyam* – must be performed; *eva* – certainly; *iti* – thus; *manaḥ* – mind; *samādhāya* – fixing; *saḥ* – it; *sāttvikaḥ* – in the mode of goodness.

Of sacrifices, the sacrifice performed according to the directions of scripture, as a matter of duty, by those who desire no reward, is of the nature of goodness.

PURPORT: The general tendency is to offer sacrifice with some purpose in mind, but here it is stated that sacrifice should be performed without any such desire. It should be done as a matter of duty. Take, for example, the performance of rituals in temples or in churches. Generally they are performed with the purpose of material benefit, but that is not in the mode of goodness. One should go to a temple or church as a matter of duty, offer respect to the Supreme Personality of Godhead and offer flowers and eatables without any purpose of obtaining material benefit. Everyone thinks that there is no use in going to the temple just to worship God. But worship for economic benefit is not recommended in the scriptural injunctions. One should go simply to offer respect to the Deity. That will place one in the mode of goodness. It is the duty of every civilized man to obey the injunctions of the scriptures and offer respect to the Supreme Personality of Godhead.

Text 12 अभिसन्धाय तु फलं दम्भार्थमपि चैव यत् ।
इज्यते भरतश्रेष्ठ तं यज्ञं विद्धि राजसम् ॥१२॥

abhisandhāya tu phalaṁ, dambhārtham api caiva yat
ijyate bharata-śreṣṭha, taṁ yajñaṁ viddhi rājasam

abhisandhāya – desiring; *tu* – but; *phalam* – the result; *dambha* – pride; *artham* – for the sake of; *api* – also; *ca* – and; *eva* – certainly; *yat* – that which; *ijyate* – is performed; *bharata-śreṣṭha* – O chief of the Bhāratas; *tam* – that; *yajñam* – sacrifice; *viddhi* – know; *rājasam* – in the mode of passion.

But the sacrifice performed for some material benefit, or for the sake of pride, O chief of the Bhāratas, you should know to be in the mode of passion.

PURPORT: Sometimes sacrifices and rituals are performed for elevation to the heavenly kingdom or for some material benefits in this world. Such sacrifices or ritualistic performances are considered to be in the mode of passion.

Text 13 विधिहीनमसृष्टान्नं मन्त्रहीनमदक्षिणम् ।
श्रद्धाविरहितं यज्ञं तामसं परिचक्षते ॥१३॥

vidhi-hīnam asṛṣṭānnaṁ, mantra-hīnam adakṣiṇam
śraddhā-virahitaṁ yajñaṁ, tāmasaṁ paricakṣate

vidhi-hīnam – without scriptural direction; *asṛṣṭa-annam* – without distribution of *prasādam; mantra-hīnam* – with no chanting of the Vedic hymns; *adakṣiṇam* – with no remunerations to the priests; *śraddhā* – faith; *virahitam* – without; *yajñam* – sacrifice; *tāmasam* – in the mode of ignorance; *paricakṣate* – is to be considered.

Any sacrifice performed without regard for the directions of scripture, without distribution of prasādam [spiritual food], without chanting of

Vedic hymns and remunerations to the priests, and without faith is considered to be in the mode of ignorance.

PURPORT: Faith in the mode of darkness or ignorance is actually faithlessness. Sometimes people worship some demigod just to make money and then spend the money for recreation, ignoring the scriptural injunctions. Such ceremonial shows of religiosity are not accepted as genuine. They are all in the mode of darkness; they produce a demoniac mentality and do not benefit human society.

Text 14 देवद्विजगुरुप्राज्ञपूजनं शौचमार्जवम् ।
ब्रह्मचर्यमहिंसा च शारीरं तप उच्यते ॥१४॥

deva-dvija-guru-prājña-, pūjanaṁ śaucam ārjavam
brahmacaryam ahiṁsā ca, śārīraṁ tapa ucyate

deva – of the Supreme Lord; *dvija* – the *brāhmaṇas; guru* – the spiritual master; *prājña* – and worshipable personalities; *pūjanam* – worship; *śaucam* – cleanliness; *ārjavam* – simplicity; *brahmacaryam* – celibacy; *ahiṁsā* – nonviolence; *ca* – also; *śārīram* – pertaining to the body; *tapaḥ* – austerity; *ucyate* – is said to be.

Austerity of the body consists in worship of the Supreme Lord, the brāhmaṇas, the spiritual master, and superiors like the father and mother, and in cleanliness, simplicity, celibacy and nonviolence.

PURPORT: The Supreme Godhead here explains the different kinds of austerity and penance. First He explains the austerities and penances practiced by the body. One should offer, or learn to offer, respect to God or to the demigods, the perfect, qualified *brāhmaṇas* and the spiritual master and superiors like father, mother or any person who is conversant with Vedic knowledge. These should be given proper respect. One should practice cleansing oneself externally and internally, and he should learn to become simple in behavior. He should not do anything which is not sanctioned by the scriptural injunctions. He should not indulge in sex outside of married life, for sex is sanctioned in the scripture only in marriage, not otherwise. This is called celibacy. These are penances and austerities as far as the body is concerned.

Text 15 अनुद्वेगकरं वाक्यं सत्यं प्रियहितं च यत् ।
स्वाध्यायाभ्यसनं चैव वाङ्मयं तप उच्यते ॥१५॥

anudvega-karaṁ vākyaṁ, satyaṁ priya-hitaṁ ca yat
svādhyāyābhyasanaṁ caiva, vāṅ-mayaṁ tapa ucyate

anudvega-karam – not agitating; *vākyam* – words; *satyam* – truthful; *priya* – dear; *hitam* – beneficial; *ca* – also; *yat* – which; *svādhyāya* – of Vedic study; *abhyasanam* – practice; *ca* – also; *eva* – certainly; *vāk-mayam* – of the voice; *tapah* – austerity; *ucyate* – is said to be.

Austerity of speech consists in speaking words that are truthful, pleasing, beneficial, and not agitating to others, and also in regularly reciting Vedic literature.

PURPORT: One should not speak in such a way as to agitate the minds of others. Of course, when a teacher speaks, he can speak the truth for the instruction of his students, but such a teacher should not speak to those who are not his students if he will agitate their minds. This is penance as far as talking is concerned. Besides that, one should not talk nonsense. The process of speaking in spiritual circles is to say something upheld by the scriptures. One should at once quote from scriptural authority to back up what he is saying. At the same time, such talk should be very pleasurable to the ear. By such discussions, one may derive the highest benefit and elevate human society. There is a limitless stock of Vedic literature, and one should study this. This is called penance of speech.

Text 16 मनःप्रसादः सौम्यत्वं मौनमात्मविनिग्रहः ।
भावसंशुद्धिरित्येतत्तपो मानसमुच्यते ॥१६॥

manaḥ-prasādaḥ saumyatvaṁ, maunam ātma-vinigrahaḥ
bhāva-saṁśuddhir ity etat, tapo mānasam ucyate

manaḥ-prasādaḥ – satisfaction of the mind; *saumyatvam* – being without duplicity towards others; *maunam* – gravity; *ātma* – of the self; *vinigrahaḥ* – control; *bhāva* – of one's nature; *saṁśuddhiḥ* – purification; *iti* – thus; *etat* – this; *tapaḥ* – austerity; *mānasam* – of the mind; *ucyate* – is said to be.

And satisfaction, simplicity, gravity, self-control and purification of one's existence are the austerities of the mind.

PURPORT: To make the mind austere is to detach it from sense gratification. It should be so trained that it can be always thinking of doing good for others. The best training for the mind is gravity in thought.

One should not deviate from Kṛṣṇa consciousness and must always avoid sense gratification. To purify one's nature is to become Kṛṣṇa conscious. Satisfaction of the mind can be obtained only by taking the mind away from thoughts of sense enjoyment. The more we think of sense enjoyment, the more the mind becomes dissatisfied. In the present age we unnecessarily engage the mind in so many different ways for sense gratification, and so there is no possibility of the mind's becoming satisfied. The best course is to divert the mind to the Vedic literature, which is full of satisfying stories, as in the *Purāṇas* and the *Mahābhārata.* One can take advantage of this knowledge and thus become purified. The mind should be devoid of duplicity, and one should think of the welfare of all. Silence means that one is always thinking of self-realization. The person in Kṛṣṇa consciousness observes perfect silence in this sense. Control of the mind means detaching the mind from sense enjoyment. One should be straightforward in his dealings and thereby purify his existence. All these qualities together constitute austerity in mental activities.

Text 17 श्रद्धया परया तप्तं तपस्तत्त्रिविधं नरैः ।
अफलाकाङ्क्षिभिर्युक्तैः सात्त्विकं परिचक्षते ॥१७॥

śraddhayā parayā taptaṁ, tapas tat tri-vidhaṁ naraiḥ
aphalākāṅkṣibhir yuktaiḥ, sāttvikaṁ paricakṣate

śraddhayā – with faith; *parayā* – transcendental; *taptam* – executed; *tapaḥ* – austerity; *tat* – that; *tri-vidham* – of three kinds; *naraiḥ* – by men; *aphala-ākāṅkṣibhiḥ* – who are without desires for fruits; *yuktaiḥ* – engaged; *sāttvikam* – in the mode of goodness; *paricakṣate* – is called.

This threefold austerity, performed with transcendental faith by men not expecting material benefits but engaged only for the sake of the Supreme, is called austerity in goodness.

Text 18 सत्कारमानपूजार्थं तपो दम्भेन चैव यत् ।
क्रियते तदिह प्रोक्तं राजसं चलमध्रुवम् ॥१८॥

satkāra-māna-pūjārthaṁ, tapo dambhena caiva yat
kriyate tad iha proktaṁ, rājasaṁ calam adhruvam

sat-kāra – respect; *māna* – honor; *pūjā* – and worship; *artham* – for the sake of; *tapaḥ* – austerity; *dambhena* – with pride; *ca* – also; *eva* – certainly; *yat* – which; *kriyate* – is performed; *tat* – that; *iha* – in this world; *proktam* – is said; *rājasam* – in the mode of passion; *calam* – flickering; *adhruvam* – temporary.

Penance performed out of pride and for the sake of gaining respect, honor and worship is said to be in the mode of passion. It is neither stable nor permanent.

PURPORT: Sometimes penance and austerity are executed to attract people and receive honor, respect and worship from others. Persons in the mode of passion arrange to be worshiped by subordinates and let them wash their feet and offer riches. Such arrangements artificially made by the performance of penances are considered to be in the mode of passion. The results are temporary; they can be continued for some time, but they are not permanent.

Text 19 मूढग्राहेणात्मनो यत्पीडया क्रियते तपः ।
परस्योत्सादनार्थं वा तत्तामसमुदाहृतम् ॥१९॥

mūḍha-grāheṇātmano yat, pīḍayā kriyate tapaḥ
parasyotsādanārthaṁ vā, tat tāmasam udāhṛtam

mūḍha – foolish; *grāheṇa* – with endeavor; *ātmanaḥ* – of one's own self; *yat* – which; *pīḍayā* – by torture; *kriyate* – is performed; *tapaḥ* – penance; *parasya* – to others; *utsādana-artham* – for the sake of causing annihilation; *vā* – or; *tat* – that; *tāmasam* – in the mode of darkness; *udāhṛtam* – is said to be.

Penance performed out of foolishness, with self-torture or to destroy or injure others, is said to be in the mode of ignorance.

PURPORT: There are instances of foolish penance undertaken by demons like Hiraṇyakaśipu, who performed austere penances to become immortal and kill the demigods. He prayed to Brahmā for such things, but ultimately he was killed by the Supreme Personality of Godhead. To undergo penances for something which is impossible is certainly in the mode of ignorance.

Text 20 दातव्यमिति यद्दानं दीयतेऽनुपकारिणे ।
देशे काले च पात्रे च तद्दानं सात्त्विकं स्मृतम् ॥२०॥

dātavyam iti yad dānaṁ, dīyate 'nupakāriṇe
deśe kāle ca pātre ca, tad dānaṁ sāttvikaṁ smṛtam

dātavyam – worth giving; *iti* – thus; *yat* – that which; *dānam* – charity; *dīyate* – is given; *anupakāriṇe* – irrespective of return; *deśe* – in a proper place; *kāle* – at a proper time; *ca* – also; *pātre* – to a suitable person; *ca* – and; *tat* – that; *dānam* – charity; *sāttvikam* – in the mode of goodness; *smṛtam* – is considered.

Charity given out of duty, without expectation of return, at the proper time and place, and to a worthy person is considered to be in the mode of goodness.

PURPORT: In the Vedic literature, charity given to a person engaged in spiritual activities is recommended. There is no recommendation for giving charity indiscriminately. Spiritual perfection is always a consideration. Therefore charity is recommended to be given at a place of pilgrimage and at lunar or solar eclipses or at the end of the month or to a qualified *brāhmaṇa* or a Vaiṣṇava (devotee) or in temples. Such charities should be given without any consideration of return. Charity to the poor is sometimes given out of compassion, but if a poor man is not worth giving charity to, then there is no spiritual advancement. In other words, indiscriminate charity is not recommended in the Vedic literature.

Text 21 यत्तु प्रत्युपकारार्थं फलमुद्दिश्य वा पुनः ।
दीयते च परिक्लिष्टं तद्दानं राजसं स्मृतम् ॥२१॥

yat tu pratyupakārārthaṁ, phalam uddiśya vā punaḥ
dīyate ca parikliṣṭaṁ, tad dānaṁ rājasaṁ smṛtam

yat – that which; *tu* – but; *prati-upakāra-artham* – for the sake of getting some return; *phalam* – a result; *uddiśya* – desiring; *vā* – or; *punaḥ* – again; *dīyate* – is given; *ca* – also; *parikliṣṭam* – grudgingly; *tat* – that; *dānam* – charity; *rājasam* – in the mode of passion; *smṛtam* – is understood to be.

But charity performed with the expectation of some return, or with a desire for fruitive results, or in a grudging mood, is said to be charity in the mode of passion.

PURPORT: Charity is sometimes performed for elevation to the heavenly kingdom and sometimes with great trouble and with repentance afterwards: "Why have I spent so much in this way?" Charity is also sometimes given under some obligation, at the request of a superior. These kinds of charity are said to be given in the mode of passion.

There are many charitable foundations which offer their gifts to institutions where sense gratification goes on. Such charities are not recommended in the Vedic scripture. Only charity in the mode of goodness is recommended.

Text 22 अदेशकाले यद्दानमपात्रेभ्यश्च दीयते ।
असत्कृतमवज्ञातं तत्तामसमुदाहृतम् ॥२२॥

adeśa-kāle yad dānam, apātrebhyaś ca dīyate
asat-kṛtam avajñātaṁ, tat tāmasam udāhṛtam

adeśa – at an unpurified place; *kāle* – and unpurified time; *yat* – that which; *dānam* – charity; *apātrebhyaḥ* – to unworthy persons; *ca* – also; *dīyate* – is given; *asat-kṛtam* – without respect; *avajñātam* – without proper attention; *tat* – that; *tāmasam* – in the mode of darkness; *udāhṛtam* – is said to be.

And charity performed at an impure place, at an improper time, to unworthy persons, or without proper attention and respect is said to be in the mode of ignorance.

PURPORT: Contributions for indulgence in intoxication and gambling are not encouraged here. That sort of contribution is in the mode of ignorance. Such charity is not beneficial; rather, sinful persons are encouraged. Similarly, if a person gives charity to a suitable person but without respect and without attention, that sort of charity is also said to be in the mode of darkness.

Text 23 ॐ तत्सदिति निर्देशो ब्रह्मणस्त्रिविधः स्मृतः ।
ब्राह्मणास्तेन वेदाश्च यज्ञाश्च विहिताः पुरा ॥२३॥

oṁ tat sad iti nirdeśo, brahmaṇas tri-vidhaḥ smṛtaḥ
brāhmaṇās tena vedāś ca, yajñāś ca vihitāḥ purā

oṁ – indication of the Supreme; *tat* – that; *sat* – eternal; *iti* – thus; *nirdeśaḥ* – indication; *brahmaṇaḥ* – of the Supreme; *tri-vidhaḥ* – threefold; *smṛtaḥ* – is considered; *brāhmaṇāḥ* – the *brāhmaṇas; tena* – with that; *vedāḥ* – the Vedic literature; *ca* – also; *yajñāḥ* – sacrifice; *ca* – also; *vihitāḥ* – used; *purā* – formerly.

From the beginning of creation, the three words oṁ tat sat were used to indicate the Supreme Absolute Truth. These three symbolic representations were used by brāhmaṇas while chanting the hymns of the Vedas and during sacrifices for the satisfaction of the Supreme.

PURPORT: It has been explained that penance, sacrifice, charity and foods are divided into three categories: the modes of goodness, passion and ignorance. But whether first class, second class or third class, they are all conditioned, contaminated by the material modes of nature. When they are aimed at the Supreme – *oṁ tat sat,* the Supreme Personality of Godhead, the eternal – they become means for spiritual elevation. In the scriptural injunctions such an objective is indicated. These three words, *oṁ tat sat,* particularly indicate the Absolute Truth, the Supreme Personality of Godhead. In the Vedic hymns, the word *oṁ* is always found.

One who acts without following the regulations of the scriptures will not attain the Absolute Truth. He will get some temporary result, but not the ultimate end of life. The conclusion is that the performance of charity, sacrifice and penance must be done in the mode of goodness. Performed in the mode of passion or ignorance, they are certainly inferior in quality. The three words *oṁ tat sat* are uttered in conjunction with the holy name of the Supreme Lord, e.g., *oṁ tad viṣṇoḥ.* Whenever a Vedic hymn or the holy name of the Supreme Lord is uttered, *oṁ* is added. This is the indication of Vedic literature. These three words are taken from Vedic hymns. *Oṁ ity etad brahmaṇo nediṣṭhaṁ nāma* indicates the first goal. Then *tat tvam asi* (*Chāndogya Upaniṣad* 6.8.7) indicates the second goal. And *sad eva saumya* (*Chāndogya Upaniṣad* 6.2.1) indicates the third goal. Combined they become *oṁ tat sat.* Formerly when Brahmā, the first created living entity, performed sacrifices, he indicated by these three words the Supreme Personality of Godhead. Therefore the same principle has always been followed by disciplic succession. So this hymn has great significance. *Bhagavad-gītā* recommends, therefore, that any work done should be done for *oṁ tat sat,* or for the Supreme Personality of Godhead. When one performs penance, charity and sacrifice with these three words, he is acting in Kṛṣṇa consciousness. Kṛṣṇa consciousness is a scientific execution of transcendental activities which enables one to return home, back to Godhead. There is no loss of energy in acting in such a transcendental way.

Text 24 तस्मादों इत्युदाहृत्य यज्ञदानतपःक्रियाः ।
प्रवर्तन्ते विधानोक्ताः सततं ब्रह्मवादिनाम् ॥२४॥

tasmād oṁ ity udāhṛtya, yajña-dāna-tapaḥ-kriyāḥ
pravartante vidhānoktāḥ, satataṁ brahma-vādinām

tasmāt – therefore; *oṁ* – beginning with *oṁ; iti* – thus; *udāhṛtya* – indicating; *yajña* – of sacrifice; *dāna* – charity; *tapaḥ* – and penance; *kriyāḥ* – performances; *pravartante* – begin; *vidhāna-uktāḥ* – according to scriptural regulation; *satatam* – always; *brahma-vādinām* – of the transcendentalists.

Therefore, transcendentalists undertaking performances of sacrifice, charity and penance in accordance with scriptural regulations begin always with oṁ, to attain the Supreme.

PURPORT: *Oṁ tad viṣṇoḥ paramaṁ padam* (*Ṛg Veda* 1.22.20). The lotus feet of Viṣṇu are the supreme devotional platform. The performance of everything on behalf of the Supreme Personality of Godhead assures the perfection of all activity.

Text 25 तदित्यनभिसन्धाय फलं यज्ञतपःक्रियाः ।
दानक्रियाश्च विविधाः क्रियन्ते मोक्षकाङ्क्षिभिः ॥२५॥

tad ity anabhisandhāya, phalaṁ yajña-tapaḥ-kriyāḥ
dāna-kriyāś ca vividhāḥ, kriyante mokṣa-kāṅkṣibhiḥ

tat – that; *iti* – thus; *anabhisandhāya* – without desiring; *phalam* – the fruitive result; *yajña* – of sacrifice; *tapaḥ* – and penance; *kriyāḥ* – activities; *dāna* – of charity; *kriyāḥ* – activities; *ca* – also; *vividhāḥ* – various; *kriyante* – are done; *mokṣa-kāṅkṣibhiḥ* – by those who actually desire liberation.

Without desiring fruitive results, one should perform various kinds of sacrifice, penance and charity with the word tat. The purpose of such transcendental activities is to get free from material entanglement.

PURPORT: To be elevated to the spiritual position, one should not act for any material gain. Acts should be performed for the ultimate gain of being transferred to the spiritual kingdom, back to home, back to Godhead.

Texts 26–27

सद्भावे साधुभावे च सदित्येतत्प्रयुज्यते ।
प्रशस्ते कर्मणि तथा सच्छब्दः पार्थ युज्यते ॥२६॥
यज्ञे तपसि दाने च स्थितिः सदिति चोच्यते ।
कर्म चैव तदर्थीयं सदित्येवाभिधीयते ॥२७॥

sad-bhāve sādhu-bhāve ca, sad ity etat prayujyate
praśaste karmaṇi tathā, sac-chabdaḥ pārtha yujyate

yajñe tapasi dāne ca, sthitiḥ sad iti cocyate
karma caiva tad-arthīyaṁ, sad ity evābhidhīyate

sat-bhāve – in the sense of the nature of the Supreme; *sādhu-bhāve* – in the sense of the nature of the devotee; *ca* – also; *sat* – the word *sat; iti* – thus; *etat* – this; *prayujyate* – is used; *praśaste* – in bona fide; *karmaṇi* – activities; *tathā* – also; *sat-śabdaḥ* – the sound *sat; pārtha* – O son of Pṛthā; *yujyate* – is used; *yajñe* – in sacrifice; *tapasi* – in penance; *dāne* – in charity; *ca* – also; *sthitiḥ* – the situation; *sat* – the Supreme; *iti* – thus; *ca* – and; *ucyate* – is pronounced; *karma* – work; *ca* – also; *eva* – certainly; *tat* – for that; *arthīyam* – meant; *sat* – the Supreme; *iti* – thus; *eva* – certainly; *abhidhīyate* – is indicated.

The Absolute Truth is the objective of devotional sacrifice, and it is indicated by the word sat. The performer of such sacrifice is also called sat, as are all works of sacrifice, penance and charity which, true to the absolute nature, are performed to please the Supreme Person, O son of Pṛthā.

PURPORT: The words *praśaste karmaṇi,* or "prescribed duties," indicate that there are many activities prescribed in the Vedic literature which are purificatory processes, beginning from the time of conception up to the end of one's life. Such purificatory processes are adopted for the ultimate liberation of the living entity. In all such activities it is recommended that one vibrate *oṁ tat sat.* The words *sad-bhāve* and *sādhu-bhāve* indicate the transcendental situation. Acting in Kṛṣṇa consciousness is called *sattva,* and one who is fully conscious of the activities of Kṛṣṇa consciousness is called a *sādhu.* In the *Śrīmad-Bhāgavatam* (3.25.25) it is said that the transcendental subject matter becomes clear in the association of the devotees. The words used are *satāṁ prasaṅgāt.* Without good association, one cannot achieve transcendental knowledge. When initiating a person or offering the sacred thread, one vibrates the words *oṁ tat sat.* Similarly, in all kinds of performance of *yajña* the object is the Supreme, *oṁ tat sat.*

The word *tad-arthīyam* further means offering service to anything which represents the Supreme, including such service as cooking and helping in the Lord's temple, or any other kind of work for broadcasting the glories of the Lord. These supreme words *oṁ tat sat* are thus used in many ways to perfect all activities and make everything complete.

Text 28 अश्रद्धया हुतं दत्तं तपस्तप्तं कृतं च यत् ।
असदित्युच्यते पार्थ न च तत्प्रेत्य नो इह ॥२८॥

aśraddhayā hutaṁ dattaṁ, tapas taptaṁ kṛtaṁ ca yat
asad ity ucyate pārtha, na ca tat pretya no iha

aśraddhayā – without faith; *hutam* – offered in sacrifice; *dattam* – given; *tapaḥ* – penance; *taptam* – executed; *kṛtam* – performed; *ca* – also; *yat* – that which; *asat* – false; *iti* – thus; *ucyate* – is said to be; *pārtha* – O son of Pṛthā; *na* – never; *ca* – also; *tat* – that; *pretya* – after death; *na u* – nor; *iha* – in this life.

Anything done as sacrifice, charity or penance without faith in the Supreme, O son of Pṛthā, is impermanent. It is called asat and is useless both in this life and the next.

PURPORT: Anything done without the transcendental objective – whether it be sacrifice, charity or penance – is useless. Therefore in this verse it is declared that such activities are abominable. Everything should be done for the Supreme in Kṛṣṇa consciousness. Without such faith, and without the proper guidance, there can never be any fruit. In all the Vedic scriptures, faith in the Supreme is advised. In the pursuit of all Vedic instructions, the ultimate goal is the understanding of Kṛṣṇa. No one can obtain success without following this principle. Therefore, the best course is to work from the very beginning in Kṛṣṇa consciousness under the guidance of a bona fide spiritual master. That is the way to make everything successful.

In the conditional state, people are attracted to worshiping demigods, ghosts, or Yakṣas like Kuvera. The mode of goodness is better than the modes of passion and ignorance, but one who takes directly to Kṛṣṇa consciousness is transcendental to all three modes of material nature. Although there is a process of gradual elevation, if one, by the association of pure devotees, takes directly to Kṛṣṇa consciousness, that is the best way. And that is recommended in this chapter. To achieve success in this way, one must first find the proper spiritual master and receive training under his direction. Then one can achieve faith in the Supreme. When that faith matures, in course of time, it is called love of God. This love is the ultimate goal of the living entities. One should therefore take to Kṛṣṇa consciousness directly. That is the message of this Seventeenth Chapter.

Thus end the Bhaktivedanta Purports to the Seventeenth Chapter of the Śrīmad Bhagavad-gītā *in the matter of the Divisions of Faith.*

CHAPTER EIGHTEEN

Conclusion – The Perfection of Renunciation

Text 1 अर्जुन उवाच
सन्न्यासस्य महाबाहो तत्त्वमिच्छामि वेदितुम् ।
त्यागस्य च हृषीकेश पृथक्केशिनिषूदन ॥ १ ॥

arjuna uvāca
sannyāsasya mahā-bāho, tattvam icchāmi veditum
tyāgasya ca hṛṣīkeśa, pṛthak keśi-niṣūdana

arjunaḥ uvāca – Arjuna said; *sannyāsasya* – of renunciation; *mahā-bāho* – O mighty-armed one; *tattvam* – the truth; *icchāmi* – I wish; *veditum* – to understand; *tyāgasya* – of renunciation; *ca* – also; *hṛṣīkeśa* – O master of the senses; *pṛthak* – differently; *keśi-niṣūdana* – O killer of the Keśī demon.

Arjuna said: O mighty-armed one, I wish to understand the purpose of renunciation [tyāga] and of the renounced order of life [sannyāsa], O killer of the Keśī demon, master of the senses.

PURPORT: Actually the *Bhagavad-gītā* is finished in seventeen chapters. The Eighteenth Chapter is a supplementary summarization of the topics discussed before. In every chapter of *Bhagavad-gītā,* Lord Kṛṣṇa stresses that devotional service unto the Supreme Personality of Godhead is the ultimate goal of life. This same point is summarized in the Eighteenth Chapter as the most confidential path of knowledge. In the first six chapters, stress was given to devotional service: *yoginām api sarveṣām* . . . "Of all *yogīs* or transcendentalists, one who always thinks of Me within himself is best." In the next six chapters, pure devotional service and its nature and activity were discussed. In the third six chapters, knowledge, renunciation, the activities of material nature and transcendental nature, and devotional service were described. It was concluded that all acts should be performed in conjunction with the Supreme Lord, represented by the words *oṁ tat sat,* which indicate Viṣṇu, the Supreme Person. The third part of *Bhagavad-gītā* has shown that devotional service, and nothing else, is the ultimate purpose of life. This has been established by citing past *ācāryas* and the *Brahma-sūtra,* the *Vedānta-sūtra*. Certain impersonalists consider themselves to have a monopoly on the knowledge of *Vedānta-sūtra,* but actually the *Vedānta-sūtra* is meant for understanding devotional service, for the Lord Himself is the composer of the *Vedānta-sūtra* and He is its knower. That is described in the Fifteenth Chapter. In every scripture, every *Veda,* devotional service is the objective. That is explained in *Bhagavad-gītā*.

As in the Second Chapter a synopsis of the whole subject matter was described, in the Eighteenth Chapter also the summary of all instruction is given. The purpose of life is indicated to be renunciation and attainment of the transcendental position above the three material modes of nature. Arjuna wants to clarify the two distinct subject matters of *Bhagavad-gītā,* namely renunciation (*tyāga*) and the renounced order of life (*sannyāsa*). Thus he is asking the meaning of these two words.

Two words used in this verse to address the Supreme Lord – Hṛṣīkeśa and Keśi-niṣūdana – are significant. Hṛṣīkeśa is Kṛṣṇa, the master of all senses, who can always help us attain mental serenity. Arjuna requests Him to summarize everything in such a way that he can remain equipoised. Yet he has some doubts, and doubts are always compared to demons. He therefore addresses Kṛṣṇa as Keśi-niṣūdana. Keśī was a most formidable demon who was killed by the Lord; now Arjuna is expecting Kṛṣṇa to kill the demon of doubt.

Text 2 श्रीभगवानुवाच
काम्यानां कर्मणां न्यासं सन्न्यासं कवयो विदुः ।
सर्वकर्मफलत्यागं प्राहुस्त्यागं विचक्षणाः ॥ २ ॥

śrī-bhagavān uvāca
kāmyānāṁ karmaṇāṁ nyāsaṁ, sannyāsaṁ kavayo viduḥ
sarva-karma-phala-tyāgaṁ, prāhus tyāgaṁ vicakṣaṇāḥ

śrī-bhagavān uvāca – the Supreme Personality of Godhead said; *kāmyānām* – with desire; *karmaṇām* – of activities; *nyāsam* – renunciation; *sannyāsam* – the renounced order of life; *kavayaḥ* – the learned; *viduḥ* – know; *sarva* – of all; *karma* – activities; *phala* – of results; *tyāgam* – renunciation; *prāhuḥ* – call; *tyāgam* – renunciation; *vicakṣaṇāḥ* – the experienced.

The Supreme Personality of Godhead said: The giving up of activities that are based on material desire is what great learned men call the renounced order of life [sannyāsa]. And giving up the results of all activities is what the wise call renunciation [tyāga].

PURPORT: The performance of activities for results has to be given up. This is the instruction of *Bhagavad-gītā*. But activities leading to advanced spiritual knowledge are not to be given up. This will be made clear in the next verses. In the Vedic literature there are many prescriptions of methods for performing sacrifice for some particular purpose. There are certain sacrifices to perform to attain a good son or to attain elevation to the higher planets, but sacrifices prompted by desires should be stopped. However, sacrifice for the purification of one's heart or for advancement in the spiritual science should not be given up.

Text 3 त्याज्यं दोषवदित्येके कर्म प्राहुर्मनीषिणः ।
यज्ञदानतपःकर्म न त्याज्यमिति चापरे ॥ ३ ॥

tyājyaṁ doṣa-vad ity eke, karma prāhur manīṣiṇaḥ
yajña-dāna-tapaḥ-karma, na tyājyam iti cāpare

tyājyam – must be given up; *doṣa-vat* – as an evil; *iti* – thus; *eke* – one group; *karma* – work; *prāhuḥ* – they say; *manīṣiṇaḥ* – great thinkers; *yajña* – of sacrifice; *dāna* – charity; *tapaḥ* – and penance; *karma* – works; *na* – never; *tyājyam* – are to be given up; *iti* – thus; *ca* – and; *apare* – others.

Some learned men declare that all kinds of fruitive activities should be given up as faulty, yet other sages maintain that acts of sacrifice, charity and penance should never be abandoned.

PURPORT: There are many activities in the Vedic literature which are subjects of contention. For instance, it is said that an animal can be killed in a sacrifice, yet some maintain that animal killing is completely abominable. Although animal killing in a sacrifice is recommended in the Vedic literature, the animal is not considered to be killed. The sacrifice is to give a new life to the animal. Sometimes the animal is given a new animal life after being killed in the sacrifice, and sometimes the animal is promoted immediately to the human form of life. But there are different opinions among the sages. Some say that animal killing should always be avoided, and others say that for a specific sacrifice it is good. All these different opinions on sacrificial activity are now being clarified by the Lord Himself.

Text 4 निश्चयं शृणु मे तत्र त्यागे भरतसत्तम ।
त्यागो हि पुरुषव्याघ्र त्रिविधः सम्प्रकीर्तितः ॥ ४ ॥

niścayaṁ śṛṇu me tatra, tyāge bharata-sattama
tyāgo hi puruṣa-vyāghra, tri-vidhaḥ samprakīrtitaḥ

niścayam - certainty; *śṛṇu* – hear; *me* – from Me; *tatra* – therein; *tyāge* – in the matter of renunciation; *bharata-sat-tama* – O best of the Bhāratas; *tyāgaḥ* – renunciation; *hi* – certainly; *puruṣa-vyāghra* – O tiger among human beings; *tri-vidhaḥ* – of three kinds; *samprakīrtitaḥ* – is declared.

O best of the Bhāratas, now hear My judgment about renunciation. O tiger among men, renunciation is declared in the scriptures to be of three kinds.

PURPORT: Although there are differences of opinion about renunciation, here the Supreme Personality of Godhead, Śrī Kṛṣṇa, gives His judgment, which should be taken as final. After all, the *Vedas* are different laws given by the Lord. Here the Lord is personally present, and His word should be taken as final. The Lord says that the process of renunciation should be considered in terms of the modes of material nature in which it is performed.

Text 5 यज्ञदानतपःकर्म न त्याज्यं कार्यमेव तत् ।
यज्ञो दानं तपश्चैव पावनानि मनीषिणाम् ॥ ५ ॥

yajña-dāna-tapaḥ-karma, na tyājyaṁ kāryam eva tat
yajño dānaṁ tapaś caiva, pāvanāni manīṣiṇām

yajña – of sacrifice; *dāna* – charity; *tapaḥ* – and penance; *karma* – activity; *na* – never; *tyājyam* – to be given up; *kāryam* – must be done; *eva* – certainly; *tat* – that; *yajñaḥ* – sacrifice; *dānam* – charity; *tapaḥ* – penance; *ca* – also; *eva* – certainly; *pāvanāni* – purifying; *manīṣiṇām* – even for the great souls.

Acts of sacrifice, charity and penance are not to be given up; they must be performed. Indeed, sacrifice, charity and penance purify even the great souls.

PURPORT: The *yogīs* should perform acts for the advancement of human society. There are many purificatory processes for advancing a human being to spiritual life. The marriage ceremony, for example, is considered to be one of these sacrifices. It is called *vivāha-yajña.* Should a *sannyāsī,* who is in the renounced order of life and who has given up his family relations, encourage the marriage ceremony? The Lord says here that any sacrifice which is meant for human welfare should never be given up. *Vivāha-yajña,* the marriage ceremony, is meant to regulate the human mind so that it may become peaceful for spiritual advancement. For most men, this *vivāha-yajña* should be encouraged even by persons in the renounced order of life. *Sannyāsīs* should never associate with women, but that does not mean that one who is in the lower stages of life, a young man, should not accept a wife in the marriage ceremony. All prescribed sacrifices are meant for achieving the Supreme Lord. Therefore, in the lower stages, they should not be given up. Similarly, charity is for the purification of the heart. If charity is given to suitable persons, as described previously, it leads one to advanced spiritual life.

Text 6 एतान्यपि तु कर्माणि सङ्गं त्यक्त्वा फलानि च ।
कर्तव्यानीति मे पार्थ निश्चितं मतमुत्तमम् ॥ ६ ॥

etāny api tu karmāṇi, saṅgaṁ tyaktvā phalāni ca
kartavyānīti me pārtha, niścitaṁ matam uttamam

etāni – all these; *api* – certainly; *tu* – but; *karmāṇi* – activities; *saṅgam* – association; *tyaktvā* – renouncing; *phalāni* – results; *ca* – also; *kartavyāni* – should be done as duty; *iti* – thus; *me* – My; *pārtha* – O son of Pṛthā; *niścitam* – definite; *matam* – opinion; *uttamam* – the best.

All these activities should be performed without attachment or any expectation of result. They should be performed as a matter of duty, O son of Pṛthā. That is My final opinion.

PURPORT: Although all sacrifices are purifying, one should not expect any result by such performances. In other words, all sacrifices which are meant for material advancement in life should be given up, but sacrifices that purify one's existence and elevate one to the spiritual plane should not be stopped. Everything that leads to Kṛṣṇa consciousness must be encouraged. In the *Śrīmad-Bhāgavatam* also it is said that any activity which leads to devotional service to the Lord should be accepted. That is the highest criterion of religion. A devotee of the Lord should accept any kind of work, sacrifice or charity which will help him in the discharge of devotional service to the Lord.

Text 7 नियतस्य तु सन्न्यासः कर्मणो नोपपद्यते ।
मोहात्तस्य परित्यागस्तामसः परिकीर्तितः ॥ ७ ॥

niyatasya tu sannyāsaḥ, karmaṇo nopapadyate
mohāt tasya parityāgas, tāmasaḥ parikīrtitaḥ

niyatasya – prescribed; *tu* – but; *sannyāsaḥ* – renunciation; *karmaṇaḥ* – of activities; *na* – never; *upapadyate* – is deserved; *mohāt* – by illusion; *tasya* – of them; *parityāgaḥ* – renunciation; *tāmasaḥ* – in the mode of ignorance; *parikīrtitaḥ* – is declared.

Prescribed duties should never be renounced. If one gives up his prescribed duties because of illusion, such renunciation is said to be in the mode of ignorance.

PURPORT: Work for material satisfaction must be given up, but activities which promote one to spiritual activity, like cooking for the Supreme Lord and offering the food to the Lord and then accepting the food, are recommended. It is said that a person in the renounced order of life should not cook for himself. Cooking for oneself is prohibited, but cooking for the Supreme Lord is not prohibited. Similarly, a *sannyāsī* may perform a marriage ceremony to help his disciple in the advancement of Kṛṣṇa consciousness. If one renounces such activities, it is to be understood that he is acting in the mode of darkness.

Text 8 दुःखमित्येव यत्कर्म कायक्लेशभयात्त्यजेत् ।
स कृत्वा राजसं त्यागं नैव त्यागफलं लभेत् ॥ ८ ॥

duḥkham ity eva yat karma, kāya-kleśa-bhayāt tyajet
sa kṛtvā rājasaṁ tyāgaṁ, naiva tyāga-phalaṁ labhet

duḥkham – unhappy; *iti* – thus; *eva* – certainly; *yat* – which; *karma* – work; *kāya* – for the body; *kleśa* – trouble; *bhayāt* – out of fear; *tyajet* – gives up; *saḥ* – he; *kṛtvā* – after doing; *rājasam* – in the mode of passion; *tyāgam* – renunciation; *na* – not; *eva* – certainly; *tyāga* – of renunciation; *phalam* – the results; *labhet* – gains.

Anyone who gives up prescribed duties as troublesome or out of fear of bodily discomfort is said to have renounced in the mode of passion. Such action never leads to the elevation of renunciation.

PURPORT: One who is in Kṛṣṇa consciousness should not give up earning money out of fear that he is performing fruitive activities. If by working one can engage his money in Kṛṣṇa consciousness, or if by rising early in the morning one can advance his transcendental Kṛṣṇa consciousness, one should not desist out of fear or because such activities are considered troublesome. Such renunciation is in the mode of passion. The result of passionate work is always miserable. If a person renounces work in that spirit, he never gets the result of renunciation.

Text 9 कार्यमित्येव यत्कर्म नियतं क्रियतेऽर्जुन ।
सङ्गं त्यक्त्वा फलं चैव स त्यागः सात्त्विको मतः ॥ ९ ॥

kāryam ity eva yat karma, niyataṁ kriyate 'rjuna
saṅgaṁ tyaktvā phalaṁ caiva, sa tyāgaḥ sāttviko mataḥ

kāryam – it must be done; *iti* – thus; *eva* – indeed; *yat* – which; *karma* – work; *niyatam* – prescribed; *kriyate* – is performed; *arjuna* – O Arjuna; *saṅgam* – association; *tyaktvā* – giving up; *phalam* – the result; *ca* – also; *eva* – certainly; *saḥ* – that; *tyāgaḥ* – renunciation; *sāttvikaḥ* – in the mode of goodness; *mataḥ* – in My opinion.

O Arjuna, when one performs his prescribed duty only because it ought to be done, and renounces all material association and all attachment to the fruit, his renunciation is said to be in the mode of goodness.

PURPORT: Prescribed duties must be performed with this mentality. One should act without attachment for the result; he should be disassociated from the modes of work. A man working in Kṛṣṇa consciousness in a factory does not associate himself with the work of the factory, nor with the workers of the factory. He simply works for Kṛṣṇa. And when he gives up the result for Kṛṣṇa, he is acting transcendentally.

Text 10 न द्वेष्ट्यकुशलं कर्म कुशले नानुषज्जते ।
त्यागी सत्त्वसमाविष्टो मेधावी छिन्नसंशयः ॥१०॥

na dveṣṭy akuśalaṁ karma, kuśale nānuṣajjate
tyāgī sattva-samāviṣṭo, medhāvī chinna-saṁśayaḥ

na – never; *dveṣṭi* – hates; *akuśalam* – inauspicious; *karma* – work; *kuśale* – in the auspicious; *na* – nor; *anuṣajjate* – becomes attached; *tyāgī* – the renouncer; *sattva* – in goodness; *samāviṣṭaḥ* – absorbed; *medhāvī* – intelligent; *chinna* – having cut off; *saṁśayaḥ* – all doubts.

The intelligent renouncer situated in the mode of goodness, neither hateful of inauspicious work nor attached to auspicious work, has no doubts about work.

PURPORT: A person in Kṛṣṇa consciousness or in the mode of goodness does not hate anyone or anything which troubles his body. He does work in the proper place and at the proper time without fearing the troublesome effects of his duty. Such a person situated in transcendence should be understood to be most intelligent and beyond all doubts in his activities.

Text 11 न हि देहभृता शक्यं त्यक्तुं कर्माण्यशेषतः ।
यस्तु कर्मफलत्यागी स त्यागीत्यभिधीयते ॥११॥

na hi deha-bhṛtā śakyaṁ, tyaktuṁ karmāṇy aśeṣataḥ
yas tu karma-phala-tyāgī, sa tyāgīty abhidhīyate

na – never; *hi* – certainly; *deha-bhṛtā* – by the embodied; *śakyam* – is possible; *tyaktum* – to be renounced; *karmāṇi* – activities; *aśeṣataḥ* – altogether; *yaḥ* – anyone who; *tu* – but; *karma* – of work; *phala* – of the result; *tyāgī* – the renouncer; *saḥ* – he; *tyāgī* – the renouncer; *iti* – thus; *abhidhīyate* – is said.

It is indeed impossible for an embodied being to give up all activities. But he who renounces the fruits of action is called one who has truly renounced.

PURPORT: It is said in *Bhagavad-gītā* that one can never give up work at any time. Therefore he who works for Kṛṣṇa and does not enjoy the fruitive results, who offers everything to Kṛṣṇa, is actually a renouncer. There are many members of the International Society for Krishna Consciousness who work very hard in their office or in the factory or some other place, and whatever they earn they give to the Society. Such highly elevated souls are actually *sannyāsīs* and are situated in the renounced order of life. It is clearly outlined here how to renounce the fruits of work and for what purpose fruits should be renounced.

Text 12 अनिष्टमिष्टं मिश्रं च त्रिविधं कर्मणः फलम् ।
भवत्यत्यागिनां प्रेत्य न तु सन्न्यासिनां क्वचित् ॥१२॥

aniṣṭam iṣṭaṁ miśraṁ ca, tri-vidhaṁ karmaṇaḥ phalam
bhavaty atyāginām pretya, na tu sannyāsinām kvacit

aniṣṭam – leading to hell; *iṣṭam* – leading to heaven; *miśram* – mixed; *ca* – and; *tri-vidham* – of three kinds; *karmaṇaḥ* – of work; *phalam* – the result; *bhavati* – comes; *atyāginām* – for those who are not renounced; *pretya* – after death; *na* – not; *tu* – but; *sannyāsinām* – for the renounced order; *kvacit* – at any time.

For one who is not renounced, the threefold fruits of action – desirable, undesirable and mixed – accrue after death. But those who are in the renounced order of life have no such result to suffer or enjoy.

PURPORT: A person in Kṛṣṇa consciousness acting in knowledge of his relationship with Kṛṣṇa is always liberated. Therefore he does not have to enjoy or suffer the results of his acts after death.

Text 13 पञ्चैतानि महाबाहो कारणानि निबोध मे ।
साङ्ख्ये कृतान्ते प्रोक्तानि सिद्धये सर्वकर्मणाम् ॥१३॥

pañcaitāni mahā-bāho, kāraṇāni nibodha me
sāṅkhye kṛtānte proktāni, siddhaye sarva-karmaṇām

pañca – five; *etāni* – these; *mahā-bāho* – O mighty-armed one; *kāraṇāni* – causes; *nibodha* – just understand; *me* – from Me; *sāṅkhye* – in the *Vedānta; kṛta-ante* – in the conclusion; *proktāni* – said; *siddhaye* – for the perfection; *sarva* – of all; *karmaṇām* – activities.

O mighty-armed Arjuna, according to the Vedānta there are five causes for the accomplishment of all action. Now learn of these from Me.

PURPORT: A question may be raised that since any activity performed must have some reaction, how is it that the person in Kṛṣṇa consciousness does not suffer or enjoy the reactions of work? The Lord is citing *Vedānta* philosophy to show how this is possible. He says that there are five causes for all activities, and for success in all activity one should consider these five causes. *Sāṅkhya* means the stock of knowledge, and *Vedānta* is the final stock of knowledge accepted by all leading *ācāryas.* Even Śaṅkara accepts *Vedānta-sūtra* as such. Therefore such authority should be consulted.

The ultimate control is invested in the Supersoul. As it is stated in the *Bhagavad-gītā, sarvasya cāhaṁ hṛdi sanniviṣṭaḥ.* He is engaging everyone in certain activities by reminding him of his past actions. And Kṛṣṇa conscious acts done under His direction from within yield no reaction, either in this life or in the life after death.

Text 14 अधिष्ठानं तथा कर्ता करणं च पृथग्विधम् ।
विविधाश्च पृथक्चेष्टा दैवं चैवात्र पञ्चमम् ॥१४॥

adhiṣṭhānaṁ tathā kartā, karaṇaṁ ca pṛthag-vidham
vividhāś ca pṛthak ceṣṭā, daivaṁ caivātra pañcamam

adhiṣṭhānam – the place; *tathā* – also; *kartā* – the worker; *karaṇam* – instruments; *ca* – and; *pṛthak-vidham* – of different kinds; *vividhāḥ* – various; *ca* – and; *pṛthak* – separate; *ceṣṭāḥ* – the endeavors; *daivam* – the Supreme; *ca* – also; *eva* – certainly; *atra* – here; *pañcamam* – the fifth.

The place of action [the body], the performer, the various senses, the many different kinds of endeavor, and ultimately the Supersoul – these are the five factors of action.

PURPORT: The word *adhiṣṭhānam* refers to the body. The soul within the body is acting to bring about the results of activity and is therefore known as *kartā,* "the doer." That the soul is the knower and the doer is stated in the *śruti. Eṣa hi draṣṭā sraṣṭā* (*Praśna Upaniṣad* 4.9). It is also confirmed in the *Vedānta-sūtra* by the verses *jño 'ta eva* (2.3.18) and *kartā śāstrārthavattvāt* (2.3.33). The instruments of action are the senses, and by the senses the soul acts in various ways. For each and every action there is a different endeavor. But all one's activities depend on the will of the Supersoul, who is seated within the heart as a friend. The Supreme Lord is the supercause. Under these circumstances, he who is acting in Kṛṣṇa consciousness under the direction of the Supersoul situated within the heart is naturally not bound by any activity. Those in complete Kṛṣṇa consciousness are not ultimately responsible for their actions. Everything is dependent on the supreme will, the Supersoul, the Supreme Personality of Godhead.

Text 15 शरीरवाङ्मनोभिर्यत्कर्म प्रारभते नरः ।
न्याय्यं वा विपरीतं वा पञ्चैते तस्य हेतवः ॥१५॥

śarīra-vāṅ-manobhir yat, karma prārabhate naraḥ
nyāyyaṁ vā viparītaṁ vā, pañcaite tasya hetavaḥ

śarīra – by the body; *vāk* – speech; *manobhiḥ* – and mind; *yat* – which; *karma* – work; *prārabhate* – begins; *naraḥ* – a person; *nyāyyam* – right; *vā* – or; *viparītam* – the opposite; *vā* – or; *pañca* – five; *ete* – all these; *tasya* – its; *hetavaḥ* – causes.

Whatever right or wrong action a man performs by body, mind or speech is caused by these five factors.

PURPORT: The words "right" and "wrong" are very significant in this verse. Right work is work done in terms of the prescribed directions in the scriptures, and wrong work is work done against the principles of the scriptural injunctions. But whatever is done requires these five factors for its complete performance.

Text 16 तत्रैवं सति कर्तारमात्मानं केवलं तु यः ।
पश्यत्यकृतबुद्धित्वान्न स पश्यति दुर्मतिः ॥१६॥

tatraivaṁ sati kartāram, ātmānaṁ kevalaṁ tu yaḥ
paśyaty akṛta-buddhitvān, na sa paśyati durmatiḥ

tatra – there; *evam* – thus; *sati* – being; *kartāram* – the worker; *ātmānam* – himself; *kevalam* – only; *tu* – but; *yaḥ* – anyone who; *paśyati* – sees; *akṛta-buddhitvāt* – due to unintelligence; *na* – never; *saḥ* – he; *paśyati* – sees; *durmatiḥ* – foolish.

Therefore one who thinks himself the only doer, not considering the five factors, is certainly not very intelligent and cannot see things as they are.

PURPORT: A foolish person cannot understand that the Supersoul is sitting as a friend within and conducting his actions. Although the material causes are the place, the worker, the endeavor and the senses, the final cause is the Supreme, the Personality of Godhead. Therefore, one should see not only the four material causes but the supreme efficient cause as well. One who does not see the Supreme thinks himself to be the doer.

Text 17 यस्य नाहङ्कृतो भावो बुद्धिर्यस्य न लिप्यते ।
हत्वापि स इमाँल्लोकान्न हन्ति न निबध्यते ॥१७॥

yasya nāhaṅkṛto bhāvo, buddhir yasya na lipyate
hatvāpi sa imāl̐ lokān, na hanti na nibadhyate

yasya – one whose; *na* – never; *ahaṅkṛtaḥ* – of false ego; *bhāvaḥ* – nature; *buddhiḥ* – intelligence; *yasya* – one whose; *na* – never; *lipyate* – is attached; *hatvā* – killing; *api* – even; *saḥ* – he; *imān* – this; *lokān* – world; *na* – never; *hanti* – kills; *na* – never; *nibadhyate* – becomes entangled.

One who is not motivated by false ego, whose intelligence is not entangled, though he kills men in this world, does not kill. Nor is he bound by his actions.

PURPORT: In this verse the Lord informs Arjuna that the desire not to fight arises from false ego. Arjuna thought himself to be the doer of action, but he did not consider the supreme sanction within and without. If one does not know that a supersanction is there, why should he act? But one who knows the instruments of work, himself as the worker, and the Supreme Lord as the supreme sanctioner is perfect in doing everything. Such a person is never in illusion. Personal activity and responsibility arise from false ego and godlessness, or a lack of Kṛṣṇa consciousness. Anyone who is acting in Kṛṣṇa consciousness under the direction of the Supersoul or the Supreme Personality of Godhead, even though killing, does not kill. Nor is he ever affected by the reaction of such killing. When a soldier kills under the command of a superior officer, he is not subject to be judged. But if a soldier kills on his own personal account, then he is certainly judged by a court of law.

Text 18 ज्ञानं ज्ञेयं परिज्ञाता त्रिविधा कर्मचोदना ।
करणं कर्म कर्तेति त्रिविधः कर्मसङ्ग्रहः ॥१८॥

jñānaṁ jñeyaṁ parijñātā, tri-vidhā karma-codanā
karaṇaṁ karma karteti, tri-vidhaḥ karma-saṅgrahaḥ

jñānam – knowledge; *jñeyam* – the objective of knowledge; *parijñātā* – the knower; *tri-vidhā* – of three kinds; *karma* – of work; *codanā* – the impetus; *karaṇam* – the senses; *karma* – the work; *kartā* – the doer;

iti – thus; *tri-vidhaḥ* – of three kinds; *karma* – of work; *saṅgrahaḥ* – the accumulation.

Knowledge, the object of knowledge, and the knower are the three factors that motivate action; the senses, the work and the doer are the three constituents of action.

PURPORT: There are three kinds of impetus for daily work: knowledge, the object of knowledge, and the knower. The instruments of work, the work itself and the worker are called the constituents of work. Any work done by any human being has these elements. Before one acts, there is some impetus, which is called inspiration. Any solution arrived at before work is actualized is a subtle form of work. Then work takes the form of action. First one has to undergo the psychological processes of thinking, feeling and willing, and that is called impetus. The inspiration to work is the same if it comes from the scripture or from the instruction of the spiritual master. When the inspiration is there and the worker is there, then actual activity takes place by the help of the senses, including the mind, which is the center of all the senses. The sum total of all the constituents of an activity are called the accumulation of work.

Text 19 ज्ञानं कर्म च कर्ता च त्रिधैव गुणभेदतः ।
प्रोच्यते गुणसङ्ख्याने यथावच्छृणु तान्यपि ॥१९॥

jñānaṁ karma ca kartā ca, tridhaiva guṇa-bhedataḥ
procyate guṇa-saṅkhyāne, yathāvac chṛṇu tāny api

jñānam – knowledge; *karma* – work; *ca* – also; *kartā* – worker; *ca* – also; *tridhā* – of three kinds; *eva* – certainly; *guṇa-bhedataḥ* – in terms of different modes of material nature; *procyate* – are said; *guṇa-saṅkhyāne* – in terms of different modes; *yathā-vat* – as they are; *śṛṇu* – hear; *tāni* – all of them; *api* – also.

According to the three different modes of material nature, there are three kinds of knowledge, action and performer of action. Now hear of them from Me.

PURPORT: In the Fourteenth Chapter the three divisions of the modes of material nature were elaborately described. In that chapter it was said that the mode of goodness is illuminating, the mode of passion materialistic, and the mode of ignorance conducive to laziness and indolence. All the modes of material nature are binding; they are not sources of liberation. Even in the mode of goodness one is conditioned. In the Seventeenth Chapter, the different types of worship by different types of men in different modes of material nature were described. In this verse, the Lord says that He wishes to speak about the different types of knowledge, workers and work itself according to the three material modes.

Text 20 सर्वभूतेषु येनैकं भावमव्ययमीक्षते ।
अविभक्तं विभक्तेषु तज्ज्ञानं विद्धि सात्त्विकम् ॥२०॥

sarva-bhūteṣu yenaikaṁ, bhāvam avyayam īkṣate
avibhaktaṁ vibhakteṣu, taj jñānaṁ viddhi sāttvikam

sarva-bhūteṣu – in all living entities; *yena* – by which; *ekam* – one; *bhāvam* – situation; *avyayam* – imperishable; *īkṣate* – one sees; *avibhaktam* – undivided; *vibhakteṣu* – in the numberless divided; *tat* – that; *jñānam* – knowledge; *viddhi* – know; *sāttvikam* – in the mode of goodness.

That knowledge by which one undivided spiritual nature is seen in all living entities, though they are divided into innumerable forms, you should understand to be in the mode of goodness.

PURPORT: A person who sees one spirit soul in every living being, whether a demigod, human being, animal, bird, beast, aquatic or plant, possesses knowledge in the mode of goodness. In all living entities, one spirit soul is there, although they have different bodies in terms of their previous work. As described in the Seventh Chapter, the manifestation of the living force in every body is due to the superior nature of the Supreme Lord. Thus to see that one superior nature, that living force, in every body is to see in the mode of goodness. That living energy is imperishable, although the bodies are perishable. Differences are perceived in terms of the body; because there are many forms of material existence in conditional life, the living force appears to be divided. Such impersonal knowledge is an aspect of self-realization.

Text 21 पृथक्त्वेन तु यज्ज्ञानं नानाभावान् पृथग्विधान् ।
वेत्ति सर्वेषु भूतेषु तज्ज्ञानं विद्धि राजसम् ॥२१॥

pṛthaktvena tu yaj jñānaṁ, nānā-bhāvān pṛthag-vidhān
vetti sarveṣu bhūteṣu, taj jñānaṁ viddhi rājasam

pṛthaktvena – because of division; *tu* – but; *yat* – which; *jñānam* – knowledge; *nānā-bhāvān* – multifarious situations; *pṛthak-vidhān* – different; *vetti* – knows; *sarveṣu* – in all; *bhūteṣu* – living entities; *tat* – that; *jñānam* – knowledge; *viddhi* – must be known; *rājasam* – in terms of passion.

That knowledge by which one sees that in every different body there is a different type of living entity you should understand to be in the mode of passion.

PURPORT: The concept that the material body is the living entity and that with the destruction of the body the consciousness is also destroyed is called knowledge in the mode of passion. According to that knowledge, bodies differ from one another because of the development of different types of consciousness, otherwise there is no separate soul which manifests consciousness. The body is itself the soul, and there is no separate soul beyond the body. According to such knowledge, consciousness is temporary. Or else there are no individual souls, but there is an all-pervading soul, which is full of knowledge, and this body is a manifestation of temporary ignorance. Or beyond this body there is no special individual or supreme soul. All such conceptions are considered products of the mode of passion.

Text 22 यत्तु कृत्स्नवदेकस्मिन् कार्ये सक्तमहैतुकम् ।
अतत्त्वार्थवदल्पं च तत्तामसमुदाहृतम् ॥२२॥

yat tu kṛtsna-vad ekasmin, kārye saktam ahaitukam
atattvārtha-vad alpaṁ ca, tat tāmasam udāhṛtam

yat – that which; *tu* – but; *kṛtsna-vat* – as all in all; *ekasmin* – in one; *kārye* – work; *saktam* – attached; *ahaitukam* – without cause; *atattva-artha-vat* – without knowledge of reality; *alpam* – very meager; *ca* – and; *tat* – that; *tāmasam* – in the mode of darkness; *udāhṛtam* – is said to be.

And that knowledge by which one is attached to one kind of work as the all in all, without knowledge of the truth, and which is very meager, is said to be in the mode of darkness.

PURPORT: The "knowledge" of the common man is always in the mode of darkness or ignorance because every living entity in conditional life is born into the mode of ignorance. One who does not develop knowledge through the authorities or scriptural injunctions has knowledge that is limited to the body. He is not concerned about acting in terms of the directions of scripture. For him God is money, and knowledge means the satisfaction of bodily demands. Such knowledge has no connection with the Absolute Truth. It is more or less like the knowledge of the ordinary animals: the knowledge of eating, sleeping, defending and mating. Such knowledge is described here as the product of the mode of darkness. In other words, knowledge concerning the spirit soul beyond this body is called knowledge in the mode of goodness, knowledge producing many theories and doctrines by dint of mundane logic and mental speculation is the product of the mode of passion, and knowledge concerned only with keeping the body comfortable is said to be in the mode of ignorance.

Text 23 नियतं सङ्गरहितमरागद्वेषतः कृतम् ।
अफलप्रेप्सुना कर्म यत्तत्सात्त्विकमुच्यते ॥२३॥

niyataṁ saṅga-rahitam, arāga-dveṣataḥ kṛtam
aphala-prepsunā karma, yat tat sāttvikam ucyate

niyatam – regulated; *saṅga-rahitam* – without attachment; *arāga-dveṣataḥ* – without love or hatred; *kṛtam* – done; *aphala-prepsunā* – by one without desire for fruitive result; *karma* – action; *yat* – which; *tat* – that; *sāttvikam* – in the mode of goodness; *ucyate* – is called.

That action which is regulated and which is performed without attachment, without love or hatred, and without desire for fruitive results is said to be in the mode of goodness.

PURPORT: Regulated occupational duties, as prescribed in the scriptures in terms of the different orders and divisions of society, performed without attachment or proprietary rights and therefore without any love or hatred, and performed in Kṛṣṇa consciousness for the satisfaction of the Supreme, without self-satisfaction or self-gratification, are called actions in the mode of goodness.

Text 24 यत्तु कामेप्सुना कर्म साहङ्कारेण वा पुनः ।
क्रियते बहुलायासं तद्राजसमुदाहृतम् ॥२४॥

yat tu kāmepsunā karma, sāhaṅkāreṇa vā punaḥ
kriyate bahulāyāsaṁ, tad rājasam udāhṛtam

yat – that which; *tu* – but; *kāma-īpsunā* – by one with desires for fruitive results; *karma* – work; *sa-ahaṅkāreṇa* – with ego; *vā* – or; *punaḥ* – again; *kriyate* – is performed; *bahula-āyāsam* – with great labor; *tat* – that; *rājasam* – in the mode of passion; *udāhṛtam* – is said to be.

But action performed with great effort by one seeking to gratify his desires, and enacted from a sense of false ego, is called action in the mode of passion.

Text 25 अनुबन्धं क्षयं हिंसामनपेक्ष्य च पौरुषम् ।
मोहादारभ्यते कर्म यत्तत्तामसमुच्यते ॥२५॥

anubandhaṁ kṣayaṁ hiṁsām, anapekṣya ca pauruṣam
mohād ārabhyate karma, yat tat tāmasam ucyate

anubandham – of future bondage; *kṣayam* – destruction; *hiṁsām* – and distress to others; *anapekṣya* – without considering the consequences; *ca* – also; *pauruṣam* – self-sanctioned; *mohāt* – by illusion; *ārabhyate* – is begun; *karma* – work; *yat* – which; *tat* – that; *tāmasam* – in the mode of ignorance; *ucyate* – is said to be.

That action performed in illusion, in disregard of scriptural injunctions, and without concern for future bondage or for violence or distress caused to others is said to be in the mode of ignorance.

PURPORT: One has to give account of one's actions to the state or to the agents of the Supreme Lord called the Yamadūtas. Irresponsible work is destructive because it destroys the regulative principles of scriptural injunction. It is often based on violence and is distressing to other living entities. Such irresponsible work is carried out in the light of one's personal experience. This is called illusion. And all such illusory work is a product of the mode of ignorance.

Text 26 मुक्तसङ्गोऽनहंवादी धृत्युत्साहसमन्वितः ।
सिद्ध्यसिद्ध्योर्निर्विकारः कर्ता सात्त्विक उच्यते ॥२६॥

mukta-saṅgo 'nahaṁ-vādī, dhṛty-utsāha-samanvitaḥ
siddhy-asiddhyor nirvikāraḥ, kartā sāttvika ucyate

mukta-saṅgaḥ – liberated from all material association; *anaham-vādī* – without false ego; *dhṛti* – with determination; *utsāha* – and great enthusiasm; *samanvitaḥ* – qualified; *siddhi* – in perfection; *asiddhyoḥ* – and failure; *nirvikāraḥ* – without change; *kartā* – worker; *sāttvikaḥ* – in the mode of goodness; *ucyate* – is said to be.

One who performs his duty without association with the modes of material nature, without false ego, with great determination and enthusiasm, and without wavering in success or failure is said to be a worker in the mode of goodness.

PURPORT: A person in Kṛṣṇa consciousness is always transcendental to the material modes of nature. He has no expectations for the result of the work entrusted to him, because he is above false ego and pride. Still, he is always enthusiastic till the completion of such work. He does not worry about the distress undertaken; he is always enthusiastic. He does not care for success or failure; he is equal in both distress and happiness. Such a worker is situated in the mode of goodness.

Text 27 रागी कर्मफलप्रेप्सुर्लुब्धो हिंसात्मकोऽशुचिः ।
हर्षशोकान्वितः कर्ता राजसः परिकीर्तितः ॥२७॥

rāgī karma-phala-prepsur, lubdho hiṁsātmako 'śuciḥ
harṣa-śokānvitaḥ kartā, rājasaḥ parikīrtitaḥ

rāgī – very much attached; *karma-phala* – the fruit of the work; *prepsuḥ* – desiring; *lubdhaḥ* – greedy; *hiṁsā-ātmakaḥ* – always envious; *aśuciḥ* – unclean; *harṣa-śoka-anvitaḥ* – subject to joy and sorrow; *kartā* – such a worker; *rājasaḥ* – in the mode of passion; *parikīrtitaḥ* – is declared.

The worker who is attached to work and the fruits of work, desiring to enjoy those fruits, and who is greedy, always envious, impure, and moved by joy and sorrow, is said to be in the mode of passion.

PURPORT: A person is too much attached to a certain kind of work or to the result because he has too much attachment for materialism or hearth and home, wife and children. Such a person has no desire for higher elevation in life. He is simply concerned with making this world as materially comfortable as possible. He is generally very greedy, and he thinks that anything attained by him is permanent and never to be lost. Such a person is envious of others and prepared to do anything wrong for sense gratification. Therefore such a person is unclean, and he does not care whether his earning is pure or impure. He is very happy if his work is successful and very much distressed when his work is not successful. Such is the worker in the mode of passion.

Text 28 अयुक्तः प्राकृतः स्तब्धः शठो नैष्कृतिकोऽलसः ।
विषादी दीर्घसूत्री च कर्ता तामस उच्यते ॥२८॥

ayuktaḥ prākṛtaḥ stabdhaḥ, śaṭho naiṣkṛtiko 'lasaḥ
viṣādī dīrgha-sūtrī ca, kartā tāmasa ucyate

ayuktaḥ – not referring to the scriptural injunctions; *prākṛtaḥ* – materialistic; *stabdhaḥ* – obstinate; *śaṭhaḥ* – deceitful; *naiṣkṛtikaḥ* – expert in insulting others; *alasaḥ* – lazy; *viṣādī* – morose; *dīrgha-sūtrī* – procrastinating; *ca* – also; *kartā* – worker; *tāmasaḥ* – in the mode of ignorance; *ucyate* – is said to be.

The worker who is always engaged in work against the injunctions of the scripture, who is materialistic, obstinate, cheating and expert in insulting others, and who is lazy, always morose and procrastinating is said to be a worker in the mode of ignorance.

PURPORT: In the scriptural injunctions we find what sort of work should be performed and what sort of work should not be performed. Those who do not care for those injunctions engage in work not to be done, and such persons are generally materialistic. They work according to the modes of nature, not according to the injunctions of the scripture. Such workers are not very gentle, and generally they are always cunning and expert in insulting others. They are very lazy; even though they have some duty, they do not do it properly, and they put it aside to be done later on. Therefore they appear to be morose. They procrastinate; anything which can be done in an hour they drag on for years. Such workers are situated in the mode of ignorance.

Text 29 बुद्धेर्भेदं धृतेश्चैव गुणतस्त्रिविधं शृणु ।
प्रोच्यमानमशेषेण पृथक्त्वेन धनञ्जय ॥२९॥

buddher bhedaṁ dhṛteś caiva, guṇatas tri-vidhaṁ śṛṇu
procyamānam aśeṣeṇa, pṛthaktvena dhanañ-jaya

buddheḥ – of intelligence; *bhedam* – the differences; *dhṛteḥ* – of steadiness; *ca* – also; *eva* – certainly; *guṇataḥ* – by the modes of material nature; *tri-vidham* – of three kinds; *śṛṇu* – just hear; *procyamānam* –

as described by Me; *aśeṣeṇa* – in detail; *pṛthaktvena* – differently; *dhanam-jaya* – O winner of wealth.

O winner of wealth, now please listen as I tell you in detail of the different kinds of understanding and determination, according to the three modes of material nature.

PURPORT: Now after explaining knowledge, the object of knowledge, and the knower, in three different divisions according to the modes of material nature, the Lord is explaining the intelligence and determination of the worker in the same way.

Text 30 प्रवृत्तिं च निवृत्तिं च कार्याकार्ये भयाभये ।
बन्धं मोक्षं च या वेत्ति बुद्धिः सा पार्थ सात्त्विकी ॥३०॥

pravṛttiṁ ca nivṛttiṁ ca, kāryākārye bhayābhaye
bandhaṁ mokṣaṁ ca yā vetti, buddhiḥ sā pārtha sāttvikī

pravṛttim – doing; *ca* – also; *nivṛttim* – not doing; *ca* – and; *kārya* – what ought to be done; *akārye* – and what ought not to be done; *bhaya* – fear; *abhaye* – and fearlessness; *bandham* – bondage; *mokṣam* – liberation; *ca* – and; *yā* – that which; *vetti* – knows; *buddhiḥ* – understanding; *sā* – that; *pārtha* – O son of Pṛthā; *sāttvikī* – in the mode of goodness.

O son of Pṛthā, that understanding by which one knows what ought to be done and what ought not to be done, what is to be feared and what is not to be feared, what is binding and what is liberating, is in the mode of goodness.

PURPORT: Performing actions in terms of the directions of the scriptures is called *pravṛtti,* or executing actions that deserve to be performed. And actions which are not so directed are not to be performed. One who does not know the scriptural directions becomes entangled in the actions and reactions of work. Understanding which discriminates by intelligence is situated in the mode of goodness.

Text 31 यया धर्ममधर्मं च कार्यं चाकार्यमेव च ।
अयथावत्प्रजानाति बुद्धिः सा पार्थ राजसी ॥३१॥

yayā dharmam adharmaṁ ca, kāryaṁ cākāryam eva ca
ayathāvat prajānāti, buddhiḥ sā pārtha rājasī

yayā – by which; *dharmam* – the principles of religion; *adharmam* – irreligion; *ca* – and; *kāryam* – what ought to be done; *ca* – also; *akāryam* – what ought not to be done; *eva* – certainly; *ca* – also; *ayathā-vat* – imperfectly; *prajānāti* – knows; *buddhiḥ* – intelligence; *sā* – that; *pārtha* – O son of Pṛthā; *rājasī* – in the mode of passion.

O son of Pṛthā, that understanding which cannot distinguish between religion and irreligion, between action that should be done and action that should not be done, is in the mode of passion.

Text 32 अधर्मं धर्ममिति या मन्यते तमसावृता ।
सर्वार्थान् विपरीतांश्च बुद्धिः सा पार्थ तामसी ॥३२॥

adharmaṁ dharmam iti yā, manyate tamasāvṛtā
sarvārthān viparītāṁś ca, buddhiḥ sā pārtha tāmasī

adharmam – irreligion; *dharmam* – religion; *iti* – thus; *yā* – which; *manyate* – thinks; *tamasā* – by illusion; *āvṛtā* – covered; *sarva-arthān* – all things; *viparītān* – in the wrong direction; *ca* – also; *buddhiḥ* – intelligence; *sā* – that; *pārtha* – O son of Pṛthā; *tāmasī* – in the mode of ignorance.

That understanding which considers irreligion to be religion and religion to be irreligion, under the spell of illusion and darkness, and strives always in the wrong direction, O Pārtha, is in the mode of ignorance.

PURPORT: Intelligence in the mode of ignorance is always working the opposite of the way it should. It accepts religions which are not actually religions and rejects actual religion. Men in ignorance understand a great soul to be a common man and accept a common man as a great soul. They think truth to be untruth and accept untruth as truth. In all activities they simply take the wrong path; therefore their intelligence is in the mode of ignorance.

Text 33 धृत्या यया धारयते मनःप्राणेन्द्रियक्रियाः ।
योगेनाव्यभिचारिण्या धृतिः सा पार्थ सात्त्विकी ॥३३॥

dhṛtyā yayā dhārayate, manaḥ-prāṇendriya-kriyāḥ
yogenāvyabhicāriṇyā, dhṛtiḥ sā pārtha sāttvikī

dhṛtyā – determination; *yayā* – by which; *dhārayate* – one sustains; *manaḥ* – of the mind; *prāṇa* – life; *indriya* – and senses; *kriyāḥ* – the activities; *yogena* – by *yoga* practice; *avyabhicāriṇyā* – without any break; *dhṛtiḥ* – determination; *sā* – that; *pārtha* – O son of Pṛthā; *sāttvikī* – in the mode of goodness.

O son of Pṛthā, that determination which is unbreakable, which is sustained with steadfastness by yoga practice, and which thus controls the activities of the mind, life and senses is determination in the mode of goodness.

PURPORT: *Yoga* is a means to understand the Supreme Soul. One who is steadily fixed in the Supreme Soul with determination, concentrating one's mind, life and sensory activities on the Supreme, engages in Kṛṣṇa consciousness. That sort of determination is in the mode of goodness. The word *avyabhicāriṇyā* is very significant, for it indicates that persons who are engaged in Kṛṣṇa consciousness are never deviated by any other activity.

Text 34 यया तु धर्मकामार्थान्धृत्या धारयतेऽर्जुन ।
प्रसङ्गेन फलाकाङ्क्षी धृतिः सा पार्थ राजसी ॥३४॥

yayā tu dharma-kāmārthān, dhṛtyā dhārayate 'rjuna
prasaṅgena phalākāṅkṣī, dhṛtiḥ sā pārtha rājasī

yayā – by which; *tu* – but; *dharma* – religiosity; *kāma* – sense gratification; *arthān* – and economic development; *dhṛtyā* – by determination; *dhārayate* – one sustains; *arjuna* – O Arjuna; *prasaṅgena* – because of attachment; *phala-ākāṅkṣī* – desiring fruitive results; *dhṛtiḥ* – determination; *sā* – that; *pārtha* – O son of Pṛthā; *rājasī* – in the mode of passion.

But that determination by which one holds fast to fruitive results in religion, economic development and sense gratification is of the nature of passion, O Arjuna.

PURPORT: Any person who is always desirous of fruitive results in religious or economic activities, whose only desire is sense gratification, and whose mind, life and senses are thus engaged is in the mode of passion.

Text 35 यया स्वप्नं भयं शोकं विषादं मदमेव च ।
न विमुञ्चति दुर्मेधा धृतिः सा पार्थ तामसी ॥३५॥

yayā svapnaṁ bhayaṁ śokaṁ, viṣādaṁ madam eva ca
na vimuñcati durmedhā, dhṛtiḥ sā pārtha tāmasī

yayā – by which; *svapnam* – dreaming; *bhayam* – fearfulness; *śokam* – lamentation; *viṣādam* – moroseness; *madam* – illusion; *eva* – certainly; *ca* – also; *na* – never; *vimuñcati* – one gives up; *durmedhā* – unintelligent; *dhṛtiḥ* – determination; *sā* – that; *pārtha* – O son of Pṛthā; *tāmasī* – in the mode of ignorance.

And that determination which cannot go beyond dreaming, fearfulness, lamentation, moroseness and illusion – such unintelligent determination, O son of Pṛthā, is in the mode of darkness.

PURPORT: It should not be concluded that a person in the mode of goodness does not dream. Here "dream" means too much sleep. Dreaming is always present; either in the mode of goodness, passion or ignorance, dreaming is a natural occurrence. But those who cannot avoid oversleeping, who cannot avoid the pride of enjoying material objects, who are always dreaming of lording it over the material world, and whose life, mind and senses are thus engaged, are considered to have determination in the mode of ignorance.

Text 36 सुखं त्विदानीं त्रिविधं शृणु मे भरतर्षभ ।
अभ्यासाद्रमते यत्र दुःखान्तं च निगच्छति ॥३६॥

sukhaṁ tv idānīṁ tri-vidhaṁ, śṛnu me bharatarṣabha
abhyāsād ramate yatra, duḥkhāntaṁ ca nigacchati

sukham – happiness; *tu* – but; *idānīm* – now; *tri-vidham* – of three kinds; *śṛṇu* – hear; *me* – from Me; *bharata-ṛṣabha* – O best amongst the Bhāratas; *abhyāsāt* – by practice; *ramate* – one enjoys; *yatra* – where; *duḥkha* – of distress; *antam* – the end; *ca* – also; *nigacchati* – gains.

O best of the Bhāratas, now please hear from Me about the three kinds of happiness by which the conditioned soul enjoys, and by which he sometimes comes to the end of all distress.

PURPORT: A conditioned soul tries to enjoy material happiness again and again. Thus he chews the chewed. But sometimes, in the course of such enjoyment, he becomes relieved from material entanglement by association with a great soul. In other words, a conditioned soul is always engaged in some type of sense gratification, but when he understands by good association that it is only a repetition of the same thing, and he is awakened to his real Kṛṣṇa consciousness, he is sometimes relieved from such repetitive so-called happiness.

Text 37 यत्तदग्रे विषमिव परिणामेऽमृतोपमम् ।
तत्सुखं सात्त्विकं प्रोक्तमात्मबुद्धिप्रसादजम् ॥३७॥

yat tad agre viṣam iva, pariṇāme 'mṛtopamam
tat sukhaṁ sāttvikaṁ proktam, ātma-buddhi-prasāda-jam

yat – which; *tat* – that; *agre* – in the beginning; *viṣam iva* – like poison; *pariṇāme* – at the end; *amṛta* – nectar; *upamam* – compared to; *tat* – that; *sukham* – happiness; *sāttvikam* – in the mode of goodness; *proktam* – is said; *ātma* – in the self; *buddhi* – of intelligence; *prasāda-jam* – born of the satisfaction.

That which in the beginning may be just like poison but at the end is just like nectar and which awakens one to self-realization is said to be happiness in the mode of goodness.

PURPORT: In the pursuit of self-realization, one has to follow many rules and regulations to control the mind and the senses and to concentrate the mind on the self. All these procedures are very difficult, bitter like poison, but if one is successful in following the regulations and comes to the transcendental position, he begins to drink real nectar, and he enjoys life.

Text 38 विषयेन्द्रियसंयोगाद्यत्तदग्रेऽमृतोपमम् ।
परिणामे विषमिव तत्सुखं राजसं स्मृतम् ॥३८॥

viṣayendriya-saṁyogād, yat tad agre 'mṛtopamam
pariṇāme viṣam iva, tat sukhaṁ rājasaṁ smṛtam

viṣaya – of the objects of the senses; *indriya* – and the senses; *saṁyogāt* – from the combination; *yat* – which; *tat* – that; *agre* – in the beginning; *amṛta-upamam* – just like nectar; *pariṇāme* – at the end; *viṣam iva* – like poison; *tat* – that; *sukham* – happiness; *rājasam* – in the mode of passion; *smṛtam* – is considered.

That happiness which is derived from contact of the senses with their objects and which appears like nectar at first but poison at the end is said to be of the nature of passion.

PURPORT: A young man and a young woman meet, and the senses drive the young man to see her, to touch her and to have sexual intercourse. In the beginning this may be very pleasing to the senses, but at the end, or after some time, it becomes just like poison. They are separated or there is divorce, there is lamentation, there is sorrow, etc. Such happiness is always in the mode of passion. Happiness derived from a combination of the senses and the sense objects is always a cause of distress and should be avoided by all means.

Text 39 यदग्रे चानुबन्धे च सुखं मोहनमात्मनः ।
निद्रालस्यप्रमादोत्थं तत्तामसमुदाहृतम् ॥३९॥

yad agre cānubandhe ca, sukhaṁ mohanam ātmanaḥ
nidrālasya-pramādotthaṁ, tat tāmasam udāhṛtam

yat – that which; *agre* – in the beginning; *ca* – also; *anubandhe* – at the end; *ca* – also; *sukham* – happiness; *mohanam* – illusory; *ātmanaḥ* – of the self; *nidrā* – sleep; *ālasya* – laziness; *pramāda* – and illusion; *uttham* – produced of; *tat* – that; *tāmasam* – in the mode of ignorance; *udāhṛtam* – is said to be.

And that happiness which is blind to self-realization, which is delusion from beginning to end and which arises from sleep, laziness and illusion is said to be of the nature of ignorance.

PURPORT: One who takes pleasure in laziness and in sleep is certainly in the mode of darkness, ignorance, and one who has no idea how to act and how not to act is also in the mode of ignorance. For the person in the mode of ignorance, everything is illusion. There is no happiness either in the beginning or at the end. For the person in the mode of passion there might be some kind of ephemeral happiness in the beginning and at the end distress, but for the person in the mode of ignorance there is only distress both in the beginning and at the end.

Text 40 न तदस्ति पृथिव्यां वा दिवि देवेषु वा पुनः ।
सत्त्वं प्रकृतिजैर्मुक्तं यदेभिः स्यात्त्रिभिर्गुणैः ॥४०॥

na tad asti pṛthivyāṁ vā, divi deveṣu vā punaḥ
sattvaṁ prakṛti-jair muktaṁ, yad ebhiḥ syāt tribhir guṇaiḥ

na – not; *tat* – that; *asti* – there is; *pṛthivyām* – on the earth; *vā* – or; *divi* – in the higher planetary system; *deveṣu* – amongst the demigods; *vā* – or; *punaḥ* – again; *sattvam* – existence; *prakṛti-jaiḥ* – born of material nature; *muktam* – liberated; *yat* – that; *ebhiḥ* – from the influence of these; *syāt* – is; *tribhiḥ* – three; *guṇaiḥ* – modes of material nature.

There is no being existing, either here or among the demigods in the higher planetary systems, which is freed from these three modes born of material nature.

PURPORT: The Lord here summarizes the total influence of the three modes of material nature all over the universe.

Text 41 ब्राह्मणक्षत्रियविशां शूद्राणां च परन्तप ।
कर्माणि प्रविभक्तानि स्वभावप्रभवैर्गुणैः ॥४१॥

brāhmaṇa-kṣatriya-viśāṁ, śūdrāṇāṁ ca paran-tapa
karmāṇi pravibhaktāni, svabhāva-prabhavair guṇaiḥ

brāhmaṇa – of the *brāhmaṇas; kṣatriya* – the *kṣatriyas; viśām* – and the *vaiśyas; śūdrāṇām* – of the *śūdras; ca* – and; *param-tapa* – O subduer of the enemies; *karmāṇi* – the activities; *pravibhaktāni* – are divided; *svabhāva* – their own nature; *prabhavaiḥ* – born of; *guṇaiḥ* – by the modes of material nature.

Brāhmaṇas, kṣatriyas, vaiśyas and śūdras are distinguished by the qualities born of their own natures in accordance with the material modes, O chastiser of the enemy.

Text 42 शमो दमस्तपः शौचं क्षान्तिरार्जवमेव च ।
ज्ञानं विज्ञानमास्तिक्यं ब्रह्मकर्म स्वभावजम् ॥४२॥

śamo damas tapaḥ śaucaṁ, kṣāntir ārjavam eva ca
jñānaṁ vijñānam āstikyaṁ, brahma-karma svabhāva-jam

śamaḥ – peacefulness; *damaḥ* – self-control; *tapaḥ* – austerity; *śaucam* – purity; *kṣāntiḥ* – tolerance; *ārjavam* – honesty; *eva* – certainly; *ca* – and; *jñānam* – knowledge; *vijñānam* – wisdom; *āstikyam* – religiousness;

brahma – of a *brāhmaṇa; karma* – duty; *svabhāva-jam* – born of his own nature.

Peacefulness, self-control, austerity, purity, tolerance, honesty, knowledge, wisdom and religiousness – these are the natural qualities by which the brāhmaṇas work.

Text 43 शौर्यं तेजो धृतिर्दाक्ष्यं युद्धे चाप्यपलायनम् ।
दानमीश्वरभावश्च क्षात्रं कर्म स्वभावजम् ॥४३॥

śauryaṁ tejo dhṛtir dākṣyaṁ, yuddhe cāpy apalāyanam
dānam īśvara-bhāvaś ca, kṣātraṁ karma svabhāva-jam

śauryam – heroism; *tejaḥ* – power; *dhṛtiḥ* – determination; *dākṣyam* – resourcefulness; *yuddhe* – in battle; *ca* – and; *api* – also; *apalāyanam* – not fleeing; *dānam* – generosity; *īśvara* – of leadership; *bhāvaḥ* – the nature; *ca* – and; *kṣātram* – of a *kṣatriya; karma* – duty; *svabhāva-jam* – born of his own nature.

Heroism, power, determination, resourcefulness, courage in battle, generosity and leadership are the natural qualities of work for the kṣatriyas.

Text 44 कृषिगोरक्ष्यवाणिज्यं वैश्यकर्म स्वभावजम् ।
परिचर्यात्मकं कर्म शूद्रस्यापि स्वभावजम् ॥४४॥

kṛṣi-go-rakṣya-vāṇijyaṁ, vaiśya-karma svabhāva-jam
paricaryātmakaṁ karma, śūdrasyāpi svabhāva-jam

kṛṣi – plowing; *go* – of cows; *rakṣya* – protection; *vāṇijyam* – trade; *vaiśya* – of a *vaiśya; karma* – duty; *svabhāva-jam* – born of his own nature; *paricaryā* – service; *ātmakam* – consisting of; *karma* – duty; *śūdrasya* – of the *śūdra; api* – also; *svabhāva-jam* – born of his own nature.

Farming, cow protection and business are the natural work for the vaiśyas, and for the śūdras there are labor and service to others.

Text 45 स्वे स्वे कर्मण्यभिरतः संसिद्धिं लभते नरः ।
स्वकर्मनिरतः सिद्धिं यथा विन्दति तच्छृणु ॥४५॥

sve sve karmaṇy abhirataḥ, saṁsiddhiṁ labhate naraḥ
sva-karma-nirataḥ siddhiṁ, yathā vindati tac chṛṇu

sve sve – each his own; *karmaṇi* – work; *abhirataḥ* – following; *saṁsiddhim* – perfection; *labhate* – achieves; *naraḥ* – a man; *sva-karma* – in his own duty; *nirataḥ* – engaged; *siddhim* – perfection; *yathā* – as; *vindati* – attains; *tat* – that; *śṛṇu* – listen.

By following his qualities of work, every man can become perfect. Now please hear from Me how this can be done.

Text 46 यतः प्रवृत्तिर्भूतानां येन सर्वमिदं ततम् ।
स्वकर्मणा तमभ्यर्च्य सिद्धिं विन्दति मानवः ॥४६॥

yataḥ pravṛttir bhūtānāṁ, yena sarvam idaṁ tatam
sva-karmaṇā tam abhyarcya, siddhiṁ vindati mānavaḥ

yataḥ – from whom; *pravṛttiḥ* – the emanation; *bhūtānām* – of all living entities; *yena* – by whom; *sarvam* – all; *idam* – this; *tatam* – is pervaded; *sva-karmaṇā* – by his own duties; *tam* – Him; *abhyarcya* – by worshiping; *siddhim* – perfection; *vindati* – achieves; *mānavaḥ* – a man.

By worship of the Lord, who is the source of all beings and who is all-pervading, a man can attain perfection through performing his own work.

PURPORT: As stated in the Fifteenth Chapter, all living beings are fragmental parts and parcels of the Supreme Lord. Thus the Supreme Lord is the beginning of all living entities. This is confirmed in the *Vedānta-sūtra – janmādy asya yataḥ.* The Supreme Lord is therefore the beginning of life of every living entity. And as stated in the Seventh Chapter of *Bhagavad-gītā,* the Supreme Lord, by His two energies, His external energy and internal energy, is all-pervading. Therefore one should worship the Supreme Lord with His energies. Generally the Vaiṣṇava devotees worship the Supreme Lord with His internal energy. His external energy is a perverted reflection of the internal energy. The external energy is a background, but the Supreme Lord by the expansion of His plenary portion as Paramātmā is situated everywhere. He is the Supersoul of all demigods, all human beings, all animals, everywhere. One should therefore know that as part and parcel of the Supreme Lord one has his duty to render service unto the Supreme. Everyone should be engaged in devotional service to the Lord in full Kṛṣṇa consciousness. That is recommended in this verse.

Everyone should think that he is engaged in a particular type of occupation by Hṛṣīkeśa, the master of the senses. And by the result of the work in which one is engaged, the Supreme Personality of Godhead, Śrī Kṛṣṇa, should be worshiped. If one thinks always in this way, in full Kṛṣṇa consciousness, then, by the grace of the Lord, he becomes fully aware of everything. That is the perfection of life. The Lord says in *Bhagavad-gītā* (12.7), *teṣām ahaṁ samuddhartā.* The Supreme Lord Himself takes charge of delivering such a devotee. That is the highest perfection of life. In whatever occupation one may be engaged, if he serves the Supreme Lord he will achieve the highest perfection.

Text 47 श्रेयान् स्वधर्मो विगुणः परधर्मात्स्वनुष्ठितात् ।
स्वभावनियतं कर्म कुर्वन्नाप्नोति किल्बिषम् ॥४७॥

śreyān sva-dharmo viguṇaḥ, para-dharmāt sv-anuṣṭhitāt
svabhāva-niyataṁ karma, kurvan nāpnoti kilbiṣam

śreyān – better; *sva-dharmaḥ* – one's own occupation; *viguṇaḥ* – imperfectly performed; *para-dharmāt* – than another's occupation; *su-anuṣṭhitāt* – perfectly done; *svabhāva-niyatam* – prescribed according to one's nature; *karma* – work; *kurvan* – performing; *na* – never; *āpnoti* – achieves; *kilbiṣam* – sinful reactions.

It is better to engage in one's own occupation, even though one may perform it imperfectly, than to accept another's occupation and perform it perfectly. Duties prescribed according to one's nature are never affected by sinful reactions.

PURPORT: One's occupational duty is prescribed in *Bhagavad-gītā.* As already discussed in previous verses, the duties of a *brāhmaṇa, kṣatriya, vaiśya* and *śūdra* are prescribed according to their particular modes of nature. One should not imitate another's duty. A man who is by nature attracted to the kind of work done by *śūdras* should not artificially claim to be a *brāhmaṇa,* although he may have been born into a *brāhmaṇa* family. In this way one should work according to his own nature; no work is abominable, if performed in the service of the Supreme Lord. The occupational duty of a *brāhmaṇa* is certainly in the mode of goodness, but if a person is not by nature in the mode of goodness, he should not imitate the occupational duty of a *brāhmaṇa.* For a *kṣatriya,* or administrator, there are so many abominable things; a *kṣatriya* has to be violent to kill his enemies, and sometimes a *kṣatriya* has to tell lies for the sake of diplomacy. Such violence and duplicity accompany political affairs, but a *kṣatriya* is not supposed to give up his occupational duty and try to perform the duties of a *brāhmaṇa.*

One should act to satisfy the Supreme Lord. For example, Arjuna was a *kṣatriya.* He was hesitating to fight the other party. But if such fighting is performed for the sake of Kṛṣṇa, the Supreme Personality of Godhead, there need be no fear of degradation. In the business field also, sometimes a merchant has to tell so many lies to make a profit. If he does not do so, there can be no profit. Sometimes a merchant says, "Oh, my dear customer, for you I am making no profit," but one should know that without profit the merchant cannot exist. Therefore it should be taken as a simple lie if a merchant says that he is not making a profit. But the merchant should not think that because he is engaged in an occupation in which the telling of lies is compulsory, he should give up his profession and pursue the profession of a *brāhmaṇa.* That is not recommended. Whether one is a *kṣatriya,* a *vaiśya,* or a *śūdra* doesn't matter, if he serves, by his work, the Supreme Personality of Godhead. Even *brāhmaṇas,* who perform different types of sacrifice, sometimes must kill animals because sometimes animals are sacrificed in such ceremonies. Similarly, if a *kṣatriya* engaged in his own occupation kills an enemy, there is no sin incurred. In the Third Chapter these matters have been clearly and elaborately explained; every man should work for the purpose of Yajña, or for Viṣṇu, the Supreme Personality of Godhead. Anything done for personal sense gratification is a cause of bondage. The conclusion is that everyone should be engaged according to the particular mode of nature he has acquired, and he should decide to work only to serve the supreme cause of the Supreme Lord.

Text 48 सहजं कर्म कौन्तेय सदोषमपि न त्यजेत् ।
सर्वारम्भा हि दोषेण धूमेनाग्निरिवावृताः ॥४८॥

saha-jaṁ karma kaunteya, sa-doṣam api na tyajet
sarvārambhā hi doṣeṇa, dhūmenāgnir ivāvṛtāḥ

saha-jam – born simultaneously; *karma* – work; *kaunteya* – O son of Kuntī; *sa-doṣam* – with fault; *api* – although; *na* – never; *tyajet* – one should give up; *sarva-ārambhāḥ* – all ventures; *hi* – certainly; *doṣeṇa* – with fault; *dhūmena* – with smoke; *agniḥ* – fire; *iva* – as; *āvṛtāḥ* – covered.

Every endeavor is covered by some fault, just as fire is covered by smoke. Therefore one should not give up the work born of his nature, O son of Kuntī, even if such work is full of fault.

PURPORT: In conditioned life, all work is contaminated by the material modes of nature. Even if one is a *brāhmaṇa,* he has to perform sacrifices in which animal killing is necessary. Similarly, a *kṣatriya,* however pious he may be, has to fight enemies. He cannot avoid it. Similarly, a merchant, however pious he may be, must sometimes hide his profit to stay in business, or he may sometimes have to do business on the black market. These things are necessary; one cannot avoid them. Similarly, even though a man is a *śūdra* serving a bad master, he has to carry out the order of the master, even though it should not be done. Despite these flaws, one should continue to carry out his prescribed duties, for they are born out of his own nature.

A very nice example is given herein. Although fire is pure, still there is smoke. Yet smoke does not make the fire impure. Even though there is smoke in the fire, fire is still considered to be the purest of all elements. If one prefers to give up the work of a *kṣatriya* and take up the occupation of a *brāhmaṇa,* he is not assured that in the occupation of a *brāhmaṇa* there are no unpleasant duties. One may then conclude that in the material world no one can be completely free from the contamination of material nature. This example of fire and smoke is very appropriate in this connection. When in wintertime one takes a stone from the fire, sometimes smoke disturbs the eyes and other parts of the body, but still one must make use of the fire despite disturbing conditions. Similarly, one should not give up his natural occupation because there are some disturbing elements. Rather, one should be determined to serve the Supreme Lord by his occupational duty in Kṛṣṇa consciousness. That is the perfectional point. When a particular type of occupation is performed for the satisfaction of the Supreme Lord, all the defects in that particular occupation are purified. When the results of work are purified, when connected with devotional service, one becomes perfect in seeing the self within, and that is self-realization.

Text 49 असक्तबुद्धिः सर्वत्र जितात्मा विगतस्पृहः ।
नैष्कर्म्यसिद्धिं परमां सन्न्यासेनाधिगच्छति ॥४९॥

asakta-buddhiḥ sarvatra, jitātmā vigata-spṛhaḥ
naiṣkarmya-siddhiṁ paramāṁ, sannyāsenādhigacchati

asakta-buddhiḥ – having unattached intelligence; *sarvatra* – everywhere; *jita-ātmā* – having control of the mind; *vigata-spṛhaḥ* – without material desires; *naiṣkarmya-siddhim* – the perfection of nonreaction; *paramām* – supreme; *sannyāsena* – by the renounced order of life; *adhigacchati* – one attains.

One who is self-controlled and unattached and who disregards all material enjoyments can obtain, by practice of renunciation, the highest perfect stage of freedom from reaction.

PURPORT: Real renunciation means that one should always think himself part and parcel of the Supreme Lord and therefore think that he has no right to enjoy the results of his work. Since he is part and parcel of the Supreme Lord, the results of his work must be enjoyed by the Supreme Lord. This is actually Kṛṣṇa consciousness. The person acting in Kṛṣṇa consciousness is really a *sannyāsī,* one in the renounced order of life. By such a mentality, one is satisfied because he is actually acting for the Supreme. Thus he is not attached to anything material; he becomes accustomed to not taking pleasure in anything beyond the transcendental happiness derived from the service of the Lord. A *sannyāsī* is supposed to be free from the reactions of his past activities, but a person who is in Kṛṣṇa consciousness automatically attains this perfection without even accepting the so-called order of renunciation. This state of mind is called *yogārūḍha,* or the perfectional stage of *yoga.* As confirmed in the Third Chapter, *yas tv ātma-ratir eva syāt:* one who is satisfied in himself has no fear of any kind of reaction from his activity.

Text 50 सिद्धिं प्राप्तो यथा ब्रह्म तथाप्नोति निबोध मे ।
समासेनैव कौन्तेय निष्ठा ज्ञानस्य या परा ॥५०॥

siddhiṁ prāpto yathā brahma, tathāpnoti nibodha me
samāsenaiva kaunteya, niṣṭhā jñānasya yā parā

siddhim – perfection; *prāptaḥ* – achieving; *yathā* – as; *brahma* – the Supreme; *tathā* – so; *āpnoti* – one achieves; *nibodha* – try to understand; *me* – from Me; *samāsena* – summarily; *eva* – certainly; *kaunteya* – O son of Kuntī; *niṣṭhā* – the stage; *jñānasya* – of knowledge; *yā* – which; *parā* – transcendental.

O son of Kuntī, learn from Me how one who has achieved this perfection can attain to the supreme perfectional stage, Brahman, the stage of highest knowledge, by acting in the way I shall now summarize.

PURPORT: The Lord describes for Arjuna how one can achieve the highest perfectional stage simply by being engaged in his occupational duty, performing that duty for the Supreme Personality of Godhead. One attains the supreme stage of Brahman simply by renouncing the result of his work for the satisfaction of the Supreme Lord. That is the process of self-realization. The actual perfection of knowledge is in attaining pure Kṛṣṇa consciousness; that is described in the following verses.

Texts 51–53

बुद्ध्या विशुद्धया युक्तो धृत्यात्मानं नियम्य च ।
शब्दादीन् विषयांस्त्यक्त्वा रागद्वेषौ व्युदस्य च ॥५१॥
विविक्तसेवी लघ्वाशी यतवाक्कायमानसः ।
ध्यानयोगपरो नित्यं वैराग्यं समुपाश्रितः ॥५२॥
अहङ्कारं बलं दर्पं कामं क्रोधं परिग्रहम् ।
विमुच्य निर्ममः शान्तो ब्रह्मभूयाय कल्पते ॥५३॥

buddhyā viśuddhayā yukto, dhṛtyātmānaṁ niyamya ca
śabdādīn viṣayāṁs tyaktvā, rāga-dveṣau vyudasya ca
vivikta-sevī laghv-āśī, yata-vāk-kāya-mānasaḥ
dhyāna-yoga-paro nityaṁ, vairāgyaṁ samupāśritaḥ

ahaṅkāraṁ balaṁ darpaṁ, kāmaṁ krodhaṁ parigraham
vimucya nirmamaḥ śānto, brahma-bhūyāya kalpate

buddhyā – with the intelligence; *viśuddhayā* – fully purified; *yuktaḥ* – engaged; *dhṛtyā* – by determination; *ātmānam* – the self; *niyamya* – regulating; *ca* – also; *śabda-ādīn* – such as sound; *viṣayān* – the sense objects; *tyaktvā* – giving up; *rāga* – attachment; *dveṣau* – and hatred; *vyudasya* – laying aside; *ca* – also; *vivikta-sevī* – living in a secluded place; *laghu-āśī* – eating a small quantity; *yata* – having controlled; *vāk* – speech; *kāya* – body; *mānasaḥ* – and mind; *dhyāna-yoga-paraḥ* – absorbed in trance; *nityam* – twenty-four hours a day; *vairāgyam* – detachment; *samupāśritaḥ* – having taken shelter of; *ahaṅkāram* – false ego; *balam* – false strength; *darpam* – false pride; *kāmam* – lust; *krodham* – anger; *parigraham* – and acceptance of material things; *vimucya* – being delivered from; *nirmamaḥ* – without a sense of proprietorship; *śāntaḥ* – peaceful; *brahma-bhūyāya* – for self-realization; *kalpate* – is qualified.

Being purified by his intelligence and controlling the mind with determination, giving up the objects of sense gratification, being freed from attachment and hatred, one who lives in a secluded place, who eats

little, who controls his body, mind and power of speech, who is always in trance and who is detached, free from false ego, false strength, false pride, lust, anger, and acceptance of material things, free from false proprietorship, and peaceful – such a person is certainly elevated to the position of self-realization.

PURPORT: When one is purified by intelligence, he keeps himself in the mode of goodness. Thus one becomes the controller of the mind and is always in trance. He is not attached to the objects of sense gratification, and he is free from attachment and hatred in his activities. Such a detached person naturally prefers to live in a secluded place, he does not eat more than what he requires, and he controls the activities of his body and mind. He has no false ego because he does not accept the body as himself. Nor has he a desire to make the body fat and strong by accepting so many material things. Because he has no bodily concept of life, he is not falsely proud. He is satisfied with everything that is offered to him by the grace of the Lord, and he is never angry in the absence of sense gratification. Nor does he endeavor to acquire sense objects. Thus when he is completely free from false ego, he becomes nonattached to all material things, and that is the stage of self-realization of Brahman. That stage is called the *brahma-bhūta* stage. When one is free from the material conception of life, he becomes peaceful and cannot be agitated. This is described in *Bhagavad-gītā* (2.70):

āpūryamāṇam acala-pratiṣṭhaṁ, samudram āpaḥ praviśanti yadvat
tadvat kāmā yaṁ praviśanti sarve, sa śāntim āpnoti na kāma-kāmī

"A person who is not disturbed by the incessant flow of desires – that enter like rivers into the ocean, which is ever being filled but is always still – can alone achieve peace, and not the man who strives to satisfy such desires."

Text 54 ब्रह्मभूतः प्रसन्नात्मा न शोचति न काङ्क्षति ।
समः सर्वेषु भूतेषु मद्भक्तिं लभते पराम् ॥५४॥

brahma-bhūtaḥ prasannātmā, na śocati na kāṅkṣati
samaḥ sarveṣu bhūteṣu, mad-bhaktiṁ labhate parām

brahma-bhūtaḥ – being one with the Absolute; *prasanna-ātmā* – fully joyful; *na* – never; *śocati* – laments; *na* – never; *kāṅkṣati* – desires; *samaḥ* – equally disposed; *sarveṣu* – to all; *bhūteṣu* – living entities;

mat-bhaktim – My devotional service; *labhate* – gains; *parām* – transcendental.

One who is thus transcendentally situated at once realizes the Supreme Brahman and becomes fully joyful. He never laments or desires to have anything. He is equally disposed toward every living entity. In that state he attains pure devotional service unto Me.

PURPORT: To the impersonalist, achieving the *brahma-bhūta* stage, becoming one with the Absolute, is the last word. But for the personalist, or pure devotee, one has to go still further, to become engaged in pure devotional service. This means that one who is engaged in pure devotional service to the Supreme Lord is already in a state of liberation, called *brahma-bhūta,* oneness with the Absolute. Without being one with the Supreme, the Absolute, one cannot render service unto Him. In the absolute conception, there is no difference between the served and the servitor; yet the distinction is there, in a higher spiritual sense.

In the material concept of life, when one works for sense gratification, there is misery, but in the absolute world, when one is engaged in pure devotional service, there is no misery. The devotee in Kṛṣṇa consciousness has nothing for which to lament or desire. Since God is full, a living entity who is engaged in God's service, in Kṛṣṇa consciousness, becomes also full in himself. He is just like a river cleansed of all dirty water. Because a pure devotee has no thought other than Kṛṣṇa, he is naturally always joyful. He does not lament for any material loss or aspire for gain, because he is full in the service of the Lord. He has no desire for material enjoyment, because he knows that every living entity is a fragmental part and parcel of the Supreme Lord and therefore eternally a servant. He does not see, in the material world, someone as higher and someone as lower; higher and lower positions are ephemeral, and a devotee has nothing to do with ephemeral appearances or disappearances. For him stone and gold are of equal value. This is the *brahma-bhūta* stage, and this stage is attained very easily by the pure devotee. In that stage of existence, the idea of becoming one with the Supreme Brahman and annihilating one's individuality becomes hellish, the idea of attaining the heavenly kingdom becomes phantasmagoria, and the senses are like serpents whose poison teeth are broken. As there is no fear of a serpent with broken teeth, there is no fear from the senses when they are automatically controlled. The world is miserable for the materially infected person, but for a devotee the entire world is as good as Vaikuṇṭha, or the spiritual sky. The highest personality in this material universe is no more significant than an ant for a devotee. Such a stage can be achieved by the mercy of Lord Caitanya, who preached pure devotional service in this age.

Text 55 भक्त्या मामभिजानाति यावान् यश्चास्मि तत्त्वतः ।
ततो मां तत्त्वतो ज्ञात्वा विशते तदनन्तरम् ॥५५॥

bhaktyā mām abhijānāti, yāvān yaś cāsmi tattvataḥ
tato māṁ tattvato jñātvā, viśate tad-anantaram

bhaktyā – by pure devotional service; *mām* – Me; *abhijānāti* – one can know; *yāvān* – as much as; *yaḥ ca asmi* – as I am; *tattvataḥ* – in truth; *tataḥ* – thereafter; *mām* – Me; *tattvataḥ* – in truth; *jñātvā* – knowing; *viśate* – he enters; *tat-anantaram* – thereafter.

One can understand Me as I am, as the Supreme Personality of Godhead, only by devotional service. And when one is in full consciousness of Me by such devotion, he can enter into the kingdom of God.

PURPORT: The Supreme Personality of Godhead, Kṛṣṇa, and His plenary portions cannot be understood by mental speculation nor by the nondevotees. If anyone wants to understand the Supreme Personality of Godhead, he has to take to pure devotional service under the guidance of a pure devotee. Otherwise, the truth of the Supreme Personality of Godhead will always be hidden. As already stated in *Bhagavad-gītā* (7.25), *nāhaṁ prakāśaḥ sarvasya:* He is not revealed to everyone. No one can understand God simply by erudite scholarship or mental speculation. Only one who is actually engaged in Kṛṣṇa consciousness and devotional service can understand what Kṛṣṇa is. University degrees are not helpful.

One who is fully conversant with the Kṛṣṇa science becomes eligible to enter into the spiritual kingdom, the abode of Kṛṣṇa. Becoming Brahman does not mean that one loses his identity. Devotional service is there, and as long as devotional service exists, there must be God, the devotee, and the process of devotional service. Such knowledge is never vanquished, even after liberation. Liberation involves getting free from the concept of material life; in spiritual life the same distinction is there, the same individuality is there, but in pure Kṛṣṇa consciousness. One should not mistakenly think that the word *viśate,* "enters into Me," supports the monist theory that one becomes homogeneous with the impersonal Brahman. No. *Viśate* means that one can enter into the abode of the Supreme Lord in one's individuality to engage in His association and render service unto Him. For instance, a green bird enters a green tree not to become one with the tree but to enjoy the fruits of the tree. Impersonalists generally give the example of a river flowing into the ocean and merging. This may be a source of happiness for the impersonalist, but the personalist keeps his personal individuality like an aquatic in the ocean. We find so many living entities within the ocean, if we go deep. Surface acquaintance with the ocean is not sufficient; one must have complete knowledge of the aquatics living in the ocean depths.

Because of his pure devotional service, a devotee can understand the transcendental qualities and the opulences of the Supreme Lord in truth. As it is stated in the Eleventh Chapter, only by devotional service can one understand. The same is confirmed here; one can understand the Supreme Personality of Godhead by devotional service and enter into His kingdom.

After attainment of the *brahma-bhūta* stage of freedom from material conceptions, devotional service begins by one's hearing about the Lord. When one hears about the Supreme Lord, automatically the *brahma-bhūta* stage develops, and material contamination – greediness and lust for sense enjoyment – disappears. As lust and desires disappear from the heart of a devotee, he becomes more attached to the service of the Lord, and by such attachment he becomes free from material contamination. In that state of life he can understand the Supreme Lord. This is the statement of *Śrīmad-Bhāgavatam* also. After liberation the process of *bhakti,* or transcendental service, continues. The *Vedānta-sūtra* (4.1.12) confirms this: *ā-prāyaṇāt tatrāpi hi dṛṣṭam.* This means that after liberation the process of devotional service continues. In the *Śrīmad-Bhāgavatam,* real devotional liberation is defined as the reinstatement of the living entity in his own identity, his own constitutional position. The constitutional position is already explained: every living entity is a part-and-parcel fragmental portion of the Supreme Lord. Therefore his constitutional position is to serve. After liberation, this service is never stopped. Actual liberation is getting free from misconceptions of life.

Text 56 सर्वकर्माण्यपि सदा कुर्वाणो मद्व्यपाश्रयः ।
मत्प्रसादादवाप्नोति शाश्वतं पदमव्ययम् ॥५६॥

sarva-karmāṇy api sadā, kurvāṇo mad-vyapāśrayaḥ
mat-prasādād avāpnoti, śāśvataṁ padam avyayam

sarva – all; *karmāṇi* – activities; *api* – although; *sadā* – always; *kurvāṇaḥ* – performing; *mat-vyapāśrayaḥ* – under My protection; *mat-*

prasādāt – by My mercy; *avāpnoti* – one achieves; *śāśvatam* – the eternal; *padam* – abode; *avyayam* – imperishable.

Though engaged in all kinds of activities, My pure devotee, under My protection, reaches the eternal and imperishable abode by My grace.

PURPORT: The word *mad-vyapāśrayaḥ* means under the protection of the Supreme Lord. To be free from material contamination, a pure devotee acts under the direction of the Supreme Lord or His representative, the spiritual master. There is no time limitation for a pure devotee. He is always, twenty-four hours a day, one hundred percent engaged in activities under the direction of the Supreme Lord. To a devotee who is thus engaged in Kṛṣṇa consciousness the Lord is very, very kind. In spite of all difficulties, he is eventually placed in the transcendental abode, or Kṛṣṇaloka. He is guaranteed entrance there; there is no doubt about it. In that supreme abode, there is no change; everything is eternal, imperishable and full of knowledge.

Text 57 चेतसा सर्वकर्माणि मयि सन्न्यस्य मत्परः ।
बुद्धियोगमुपाश्रित्य मच्चित्तः सततं भव ॥५७॥

cetasā sarva-karmāṇi, mayi sannyasya mat-paraḥ
buddhi-yogam upāśritya, mac-cittaḥ satataṁ bhava

cetasā – by intelligence; *sarva-karmāṇi* – all kinds of activities; *mayi* – unto Me; *sannyasya* – giving up; *mat-paraḥ* – under My protection; *buddhi-yogam* – devotional activities; *upāśritya* – taking shelter of; *mat-cittaḥ* – in consciousness of Me; *satatam* – twenty-four hours a day; *bhava* – just become.

In all activities just depend upon Me and work always under My protection. In such devotional service, be fully conscious of Me.

PURPORT: When one acts in Kṛṣṇa consciousness, he does not act as the master of the world. Just like a servant, one should act fully under the direction of the Supreme Lord. A servant has no individual independence. He acts only on the order of the master. A servant acting on behalf of the supreme master is unaffected by profit and loss. He simply discharges his duty faithfully in terms of the order of the Lord. Now, one may argue that Arjuna was acting under the personal direction of Kṛṣṇa, but when Kṛṣṇa is not present how should one act? If one acts according to the direction of Kṛṣṇa in this book, as well as under the guidance of the representative of Kṛṣṇa, then the result will be the same. The Sanskrit word *mat-paraḥ* is very important in this verse. It indicates that one has no goal in life save and except acting in Kṛṣṇa consciousness just to satisfy Kṛṣṇa. And while working in that way, one should think of Kṛṣṇa only: "I have been appointed to discharge this particular duty by Kṛṣṇa." While acting in such a way, one naturally has to think of Kṛṣṇa. This is perfect Kṛṣṇa consciousness. One should, however, note that after doing something whimsically he should not offer the result to the Supreme Lord. That sort of duty is not in the devotional service of Kṛṣṇa consciousness. One should act according to the order of Kṛṣṇa. This is a very important point. That order of Kṛṣṇa comes through disciplic succession from the bona fide spiritual master. Therefore the spiritual master's order should be taken as the prime duty of life. If one gets a bona fide spiritual master and acts according to his direction, then one's perfection of life in Kṛṣṇa consciousness is guaranteed.

Text 58 मच्चित्तः सर्वदुर्गाणि मत्प्रसादात्तरिष्यसि ।
अथ चेत्त्वमहङ्कारान्न श्रोष्यसि विनङ्क्ष्यसि ॥५८॥

mac-cittaḥ sarva-durgāṇi, mat-prasādāt tariṣyasi
atha cet tvam ahaṅkārān, na śroṣyasi vinaṅkṣyasi

mat – of Me; *cittaḥ* – being in consciousness; *sarva* – all; *durgāṇi* – impediments; *mat-prasādāt* – by My mercy; *tariṣyasi* – you will overcome; *atha* – but; *cet* – if; *tvam* – you; *ahaṅkārāt* – by false ego; *na śroṣyasi* – do not hear; *vinaṅkṣyasi* – you will be lost.

If you become conscious of Me, you will pass over all the obstacles of conditioned life by My grace. If, however, you do not work in such consciousness but act through false ego, not hearing Me, you will be lost.

PURPORT: A person in full Kṛṣṇa consciousness is not unduly anxious about executing the duties of his existence. The foolish cannot understand this great freedom from all anxiety. For one who acts in Kṛṣṇa consciousness, Lord Kṛṣṇa becomes the most intimate friend. He always looks after His friend's comfort, and He gives Himself to His friend, who is so devotedly engaged working twenty-four hours a day to please the Lord. Therefore, no one should be carried away by the false ego of the bodily concept of life. One should not falsely think himself independent of the laws of material nature or free to act. He is already under strict material laws. But as soon as he acts in Kṛṣṇa consciousness, he is liberated, free from the material perplexities. One should note very carefully that one who is not active in Kṛṣṇa consciousness is losing himself in the material whirlpool, in the ocean of birth and death. No conditioned soul actually knows what is to be done and what is not to be done, but a person who acts in Kṛṣṇa consciousness is free to act because everything is prompted by Kṛṣṇa from within and confirmed by the spiritual master.

Text 59 यदहङ्कारमाश्रित्य न योत्स्य इति मन्यसे ।
मिथ्यैष व्यवसायस्ते प्रकृतिस्त्वां नियोक्ष्यति ॥५९॥

yad ahaṅkāram āśritya, na yotsya iti manyase
mithyaiṣa vyavasāyas te, prakṛtis tvāṁ niyokṣyati

yat – if; *ahaṅkāram* – of false ego; *āśritya* – taking shelter; *na yotsye* – I shall not fight; *iti* – thus; *manyase* – you think; *mithyā eṣaḥ* – this is all false; *vyavasāyaḥ* – determination; *te* – your; *prakṛtiḥ* – material nature; *tvām* – you; *niyokṣyati* – will engage.

If you do not act according to My direction and do not fight, then you will be falsely directed. By your nature, you will have to be engaged in warfare.

PURPORT: Arjuna was a military man, and born of the nature of the *kṣatriya.* Therefore his natural duty was to fight. But due to false ego he was fearing that by killing his teacher, grandfather and friends he would incur sinful reactions. Actually he was considering himself master of his actions, as if he were directing the good and bad results of such work. He forgot that the Supreme Personality of Godhead was present there, instructing him to fight. That is the forgetfulness of the conditioned soul. The Supreme Personality gives directions as to what is good and what is bad, and one simply has to act in Kṛṣṇa consciousness to attain the perfection of life. No one can ascertain his destiny as the Supreme Lord can; therefore the best course is to take direction from the Supreme Lord and act. No one should neglect the order of the Supreme Personality of Godhead or the order of the spiritual master, who is the representative of God. One should act unhesitatingly to execute the order of the Supreme Personality of Godhead – that will keep one safe under all circumstances.

Text 60 स्वभावजेन कौन्तेय निबद्धः स्वेन कर्मणा ।
कर्तुं नेच्छसि यन्मोहात्करिष्यस्यवशोऽपि तत् ॥६०॥

svabhāva-jena kaunteya, nibaddhaḥ svena karmaṇā
kartuṁ necchasi yan mohāt, kariṣyasy avaśo 'pi tat

svabhāva-jena – born of your own nature; *kaunteya* – O son of Kuntī; *nibaddhaḥ* – conditioned; *svena* – by your own; *karmaṇā* – activities; *kartum* – to do; *na* – not; *icchasi* – you like; *yat* – that which; *mohāt* – by illusion; *kariṣyasi* – you will do; *avaśaḥ* – involuntarily; *api* – even; *tat* – that.

Under illusion you are now declining to act according to My direction. But, compelled by the work born of your own nature, you will act all the same, O son of Kuntī.

PURPORT: If one refuses to act under the direction of the Supreme Lord, then he is compelled to act by the modes in which he is situated. Everyone is under the spell of a particular combination of the modes of nature and is acting in that way. But anyone who voluntarily engages himself under the direction of the Supreme Lord becomes glorious.

Text 61 ईश्वरः सर्वभूतानां हृद्देशेऽर्जुन तिष्ठति ।
भ्रामयन् सर्वभूतानि यन्त्रारूढानि मायया ॥६१॥

īśvaraḥ sarva-bhūtānāṁ, hṛd-deśe 'rjuna tiṣṭhati
bhrāmayan sarva-bhūtāni, yantrārūḍhāni māyayā

īśvaraḥ – the Supreme Lord; *sarva-bhūtānām* – of all living entities; *hṛt-deśe* – in the location of the heart; *arjuna* – O Arjuna; *tiṣṭhati* – resides; *bhrāmayan* – causing to travel; *sarva-bhūtāni* – all living entities; *yantra* – on a machine; *ārūḍhani* – being placed; *māyayā* – under the spell of material energy.

The Supreme Lord is situated in everyone's heart, O Arjuna, and is directing the wanderings of all living entities, who are seated as on a machine, made of the material energy.

PURPORT: Arjuna was not the supreme knower, and his decision to fight or not to fight was confined to his limited discretion. Lord Kṛṣṇa instructed that the individual is not all in all. The Supreme Personality of Godhead, or He Himself, Kṛṣṇa, as the localized Supersoul, sits in the heart directing the living being. After changing bodies, the living entity forgets his past deeds, but the Supersoul, as the knower of the past, present and future, remains the witness of all his activities. Therefore all the activities of living entities are directed by this Supersoul. The living entity gets what he deserves and is carried by the material body, which is created in the material energy under the direction of the Supersoul. As soon as a living entity is placed in a particular type of body, he has to work under the spell of that bodily situation. A person seated in a high-speed motorcar goes faster than one seated in a slower car, though the living entities, the drivers, may be the same. Similarly, by the order of the Supreme Soul, material nature fashions a particular type of body to a particular type of living entity so that he may work according to his past desires. The living entity is not independent. One should not think himself independent of the Supreme Personality of Godhead. The individual is always under the Lord's control. Therefore one's duty is to surrender, and that is the injunction of the next verse.

Text 62 तमेव शरणं गच्छ सर्वभावेन भारत ।
तत्प्रसादात्परां शान्तिं स्थानं प्राप्स्यसि शाश्वतम् ॥६२॥

tam eva śaraṇaṁ gaccha, sarva-bhāvena bhārata
tat-prasādāt parāṁ śāntiṁ, sthānaṁ prāpsyasi śāśvatam

tam – unto Him; *eva* – certainly; *śaraṇam gaccha* – surrender; *sarva-bhāvena* – in all respects; *bhārata* – O son of Bharata; *tat-prasādāt* – by His grace; *parām* – transcendental; *śāntim* – peace; *sthānam* – the abode; *prāpsyasi* – you will get; *śāśvatam* – eternal.

O scion of Bharata, surrender unto Him utterly. By His grace you will attain transcendental peace and the supreme and eternal abode.

PURPORT: A living entity should therefore surrender unto the Supreme Personality of Godhead, who is situated in everyone's heart, and that will relieve him from all kinds of miseries of this material existence. By such surrender, not only will one be released from all miseries in this life, but at the end he will reach the Supreme God. The transcendental world is described in the Vedic literature (*Ṛg Veda* 1.22.20) as *tad viṣṇoḥ paramaṁ padam.* Since all of creation is the kingdom of God, everything material is actually spiritual, but *paramaṁ padam* specifically refers to the eternal abode, which is called the spiritual sky or Vaikuṇṭha.

In the Fifteenth Chapter of *Bhagavad-gītā* it is stated, *sarvasya cāhaṁ hṛdi sanniviṣṭaḥ:* the Lord is seated in everyone's heart. So this recommendation that one should surrender unto the Supersoul sitting within means that one should surrender unto the Supreme Personality of Godhead, Kṛṣṇa. Kṛṣṇa has already been accepted by Arjuna as the Supreme. He was accepted in the Tenth Chapter as *paraṁ brahma paraṁ dhāma.* Arjuna has accepted Kṛṣṇa as the Supreme Personality of Godhead and the supreme abode of all living entities, not only because of his personal experience but also because of the evidence of great authorities like Nārada, Asita, Devala and Vyāsa.

Text 63 इति ते ज्ञानमाख्यातं गुह्याद्गुह्यतरं मया ।
विमृश्यैतदशेषेण यथेच्छसि तथा कुरु ॥६३॥

iti te jñānam ākhyātaṁ, guhyād guhya-taraṁ mayā
vimṛśyaitad aśeṣeṇa, yathecchasi tathā kuru

iti – thus; *te* – unto you; *jñānam* – knowledge; *ākhyātam* – described; *guhyāt* – than confidential; *guhya-taram* – still more confidential; *mayā* – by Me; *vimṛśya* – deliberating; *etat* – on this; *aśeṣeṇa* – fully; *yathā* – as; *icchasi* – you like; *tathā* – that; *kuru* – perform.

Thus I have explained to you knowledge still more confidential. Deliberate on this fully, and then do what you wish to do.

PURPORT: The Lord has already explained to Arjuna the knowledge of *brahma-bhūta.* One who is in the *brahma-bhūta* condition is joyful; he never laments, nor does he desire anything. That is due to confidential knowledge. Kṛṣṇa also discloses knowledge of the Supersoul. This is also Brahman knowledge, knowledge of Brahman, but it is superior.

Here the words *yathecchasi tathā kuru* – "As you like, you may act" – indicate that God does not interfere with the little independence of the living entity. In *Bhagavad-gītā,* the Lord has explained in all respects how one can elevate his living condition. The best advice imparted to Arjuna is to surrender unto the Supersoul seated within his heart. By right discrimination, one should agree to act according to the order of the Supersoul. That will help one become situated constantly in Kṛṣṇa consciousness, the highest perfectional stage of human life. Arjuna is being directly ordered by the Personality of Godhead to fight. Surrender to the Supreme Personality of Godhead is in the best interest of the living entities. It is not for the interest of the Supreme. Before surrendering, one is free to deliberate on this subject as far as the intelligence goes; that is the best way to accept the instruction of the Supreme Personality of Godhead. Such instruction comes also through the spiritual master, the bona fide representative of Kṛṣṇa.

Text 64 सर्वगुह्यतमं भूयः शृणु मे परमं वचः ।
इष्टोऽसि मे दृढमिति ततो वक्ष्यामि ते हितम् ॥६४॥

sarva-guhyatamaṁ bhūyaḥ, śṛṇu me paramaṁ vacaḥ
iṣṭo 'si me dṛḍham iti, tato vakṣyāmi te hitam

sarva-guhya-tamam – the most confidential of all; *bhūyaḥ* – again; *śṛṇu* – just hear; *me* – from Me; *paramam* – the supreme; *vacaḥ* – instruction; *iṣṭaḥ asi* – you are dear; *me* – to Me; *dṛḍham* – very; *iti* – thus; *tataḥ* – therefore; *vakṣyāmi* – I am speaking; *te* – for your; *hitam* – benefit.

Because you are My very dear friend, I am speaking to you My supreme instruction, the most confidential knowledge of all. Hear this from Me, for it is for your benefit.

PURPORT: The Lord has given Arjuna knowledge that is confidential (knowledge of Brahman) and still more confidential (knowledge of the Supersoul within everyone's heart), and now He is giving the most confidential part of knowledge: just surrender unto the Supreme Personality of Godhead. At the end of the Ninth Chapter He has said, *man-manāḥ:* "Just always think of Me." The same instruction is repeated here to stress the essence of the teachings of *Bhagavad-gītā.* This essence is not understood by a common man, but by one who is actually very dear to Kṛṣṇa, a pure devotee of Kṛṣṇa. This is the most important instruction in all Vedic literature. What Kṛṣṇa is saying in this connection is the most essential part of knowledge, and it should be carried out not only by Arjuna but by all living entities.

Text 65 मन्मना भव मद्भक्तो मद्याजी मां नमस्कुरु ।
मामेवैष्यसि सत्यं ते प्रतिजाने प्रियोऽसि मे ॥६५॥

man-manā bhava mad-bhakto, mad-yājī māṁ namaskuru
mām evaiṣyasi satyaṁ te, pratijāne priyo 'si me

mat-manāḥ – thinking of Me; *bhava* – just become; *mat-bhaktaḥ* – My devotee; *mat-yājī* – My worshiper; *mām* – unto Me; *namaskuru* – offer your obeisances; *mām* – unto Me; *eva* – certainly; *eṣyasi* – you will come; *satyam* – truly; *te* – to you; *pratijāne* – I promise; *priyaḥ* – dear; *asi* – you are; *me* – to Me.

Always think of Me, become My devotee, worship Me and offer your homage unto Me. Thus you will come to Me without fail. I promise you this because you are My very dear friend.

PURPORT: The most confidential part of knowledge is that one should become a pure devotee of Kṛṣṇa and always think of Him and act for Him. One should not become an official meditator. Life should be so molded that one will always have the chance to think of Kṛṣṇa. One should always act in such a way that all his daily activities are in connection with Kṛṣṇa. He should arrange his life in such a way that throughout the twenty-four hours he cannot but think of Kṛṣṇa. And the Lord's promise is that anyone who is in such pure Kṛṣṇa consciousness will certainly return to the abode of Kṛṣṇa, where he will be engaged in the association of Kṛṣṇa face to face. This most confidential part of knowledge is spoken to Arjuna because he is the dear friend of Kṛṣṇa. Everyone who follows the path of Arjuna can become a dear friend to Kṛṣṇa and obtain the same perfection as Arjuna.

These words stress that one should concentrate his mind upon Kṛṣṇa – the very form with two hands carrying a flute, the bluish boy with a beautiful face and peacock feathers in His hair. There are descriptions of Kṛṣṇa found in the *Brahma-saṁhitā* and other literatures. One should fix his mind on this original form of Godhead, Kṛṣṇa. One should not even divert his attention to other forms of the Lord. The Lord has multiforms as Viṣṇu, Nārāyaṇa, Rāma, Varāha, etc., but a devotee should concentrate his mind on the form that was present before Arjuna. Concentration of the mind on the form of Kṛṣṇa constitutes the most confidential part of knowledge, and this is disclosed to Arjuna because Arjuna is the most dear friend of Kṛṣṇa's.

Text 66 सर्वधर्मान् परित्यज्य मामेकं शरणं व्रज ।
अहं त्वां सर्वपापेभ्यो मोक्षयिष्यामि मा शुचः ॥६६॥

sarva-dharmān parityajya, mām ekaṁ śaraṇaṁ vraja
ahaṁ tvāṁ sarva-pāpebhyo, mokṣayiṣyāmi mā śucaḥ

sarva-dharmān – all varieties of religion; *parityajya* – abandoning; *mām* – unto Me; *ekam* – only; *śaraṇam* – for surrender; *vraja* – go; *aham* – I;

tvām – you; *sarva* – all; *pāpebhyaḥ* – from sinful reactions; *mokṣayiṣyāmi* – will deliver; *mā* – do not; *śucaḥ* – worry.

Abandon all varieties of religion and just surrender unto Me. I shall deliver you from all sinful reactions. Do not fear.

PURPORT: The Lord has described various kinds of knowledge and processes of religion – knowledge of the Supreme Brahman, knowledge of the Supersoul, knowledge of the different types of orders and statuses of social life, knowledge of the renounced order of life, knowledge of nonattachment, sense and mind control, meditation, etc. He has described in so many ways different types of religion. Now, in summarizing *Bhagavad-gītā,* the Lord says that Arjuna should give up all the processes that have been explained to him; he should simply surrender to Kṛṣṇa. That surrender will save him from all kinds of sinful reactions, for the Lord personally promises to protect him.

In the Seventh Chapter it was said that only one who has become free from all sinful reactions can take to the worship of Lord Kṛṣṇa. Thus one may think that unless he is free from all sinful reactions he cannot take to the surrendering process. To such doubts it is here said that even if one is not free from all sinful reactions, simply by the process of surrendering to Śrī Kṛṣṇa he is automatically freed. There is no need of strenuous effort to free oneself from sinful reactions. One should unhesitatingly accept Kṛṣṇa as the supreme savior of all living entities. With faith and love, one should surrender unto Him.

The process of surrender to Kṛṣṇa is described in the *Hari-bhakti-vilāsa* (11.676):

ānukūlyasya saṅkalpaḥ, prātikūlyasya varjanam
rakṣiṣyatīti viśvāso, goptṛtve varaṇaṁ tathā
ātma-nikṣepa-kārpaṇye, ṣaḍ-vidhā śaraṇāgatiḥ

According to the devotional process, one should simply accept such religious principles that will lead ultimately to the devotional service of the Lord. One may perform a particular occupational duty according to his position in the social order, but if by executing his duty one does not come to the point of Kṛṣṇa consciousness, all his activities are in vain. Anything that does not lead to the perfectional stage of Kṛṣṇa consciousness should be avoided. One should be confident that in all circumstances Kṛṣṇa will protect him from all difficulties. There is no need of thinking how one should keep the body and soul together. Kṛṣṇa will see to that. One should always think himself helpless and should consider Kṛṣṇa the only basis for his progress in life. As soon as one seriously engages himself in devotional service to the Lord in full Kṛṣṇa consciousness, at once he becomes freed from all contamination of material nature. There are different processes of religion and purificatory processes by cultivation of knowledge, meditation in the mystic *yoga* system, etc., but one who surrenders unto Kṛṣṇa does not have to execute so many methods. That simple surrender unto Kṛṣṇa will save him from unnecessarily wasting time. One can thus make all progress at once and be freed from all sinful reactions.

One should be attracted by the beautiful vision of Kṛṣṇa. His name is Kṛṣṇa because He is all-attractive. One who becomes attracted by the beautiful, all-powerful, omnipotent vision of Kṛṣṇa is fortunate. There are different kinds of transcendentalists – some of them are attached to the impersonal Brahman vision, some of them are attracted by the Supersoul feature, etc., but one who is attracted to the personal feature of the Supreme Personality of Godhead, and, above all, one who is attracted by the Supreme Personality of Godhead as Kṛṣṇa Himself, is the most perfect transcendentalist. In other words, devotional service to Kṛṣṇa, in full consciousness, is the most confidential part of knowledge, and this is the essence of the whole *Bhagavad-gītā. Karma-yogīs,* empiric philosophers, mystics and devotees are all called transcendentalists, but one who is a pure devotee is the best of all. The particular words used here, *mā śucaḥ,* "Don't fear, don't hesitate, don't worry," are very significant. One may be perplexed as to how one can give up all kinds of religious forms and simply surrender unto Kṛṣṇa, but such worry is useless.

Text 67 इदं ते नातपस्काय नाभक्ताय कदाचन ।
न चाशुश्रूषवे वाच्यं न च मां योऽभ्यसूयति ॥६७॥

idaṁ te nātapaskāya, nābhaktāya kadācana
na cāśuśrūṣave vācyaṁ, na ca māṁ yo 'bhyasūyati

idam – this; *te* – by you; *na* – never; *atapaskāya* – to one who is not austere; *na* – never; *abhaktāya* – to one who is not a devotee; *kadācana* – at any time; *na* – never; *ca* – also; *aśuśrūṣave* – to one who is not engaged in devotional service; *vācyam* – to be spoken; *na* – never; *ca* – also; *mām* – toward Me; *yaḥ* – anyone who; *abhyasūyati* – is envious.

This confidential knowledge may never be explained to those who are not austere, or devoted, or engaged in devotional service, nor to one who is envious of Me.

PURPORT: Persons who have not undergone the austerities of the religious process, who have never attempted devotional service in Kṛṣṇa consciousness, who have not tended a pure devotee, and especially those who are conscious of Kṛṣṇa only as a historical personality or who are envious of the greatness of Kṛṣṇa should not be told this most confidential part of knowledge. It is, however, sometimes found that even demoniac persons who are envious of Kṛṣṇa, worshiping Kṛṣṇa in a different way, take to the profession of explaining *Bhagavad-gītā* in a different way to make business, but anyone who desires actually to understand Kṛṣṇa must avoid such commentaries on *Bhagavad-gītā.* Actually the purpose of *Bhagavad-gītā* is not understandable to those who are sensuous. Even if one is not sensuous but is strictly following the disciplines enjoined in the Vedic scripture, if he is not a devotee he also cannot understand Kṛṣṇa. And even when one poses himself as a devotee of Kṛṣṇa but is not engaged in Kṛṣṇa conscious activities, he also cannot understand Kṛṣṇa. There are many persons who envy Kṛṣṇa because He has explained in *Bhagavad-gītā* that He is the Supreme and that nothing is above Him or equal to Him. There are many persons who are envious of Kṛṣṇa. Such persons should not be told of *Bhagavad-gītā,* for they cannot understand. There is no possibility of faithless persons' understanding *Bhagavad-gītā* and Kṛṣṇa. Without understanding Kṛṣṇa from the authority of a pure devotee, one should not try to comment upon *Bhagavad-gītā.*

Text 68 य इदं परमं गुह्यं मद्भक्तेष्वभिधास्यति ।
भक्तिं मयि परां कृत्वा मामेवैष्यत्यसंशयः ॥६८॥

ya idaṁ paramaṁ guhyaṁ, mad-bhakteṣv abhidhāsyati
bhaktiṁ mayi parāṁ kṛtvā, mām evaiṣyaty asaṁśayaḥ

yaḥ – anyone who; *idam* – this; *paramam* – most; *guhyam* – confidential secret; *mat* – of Mine; *bhakteṣu* – amongst devotees; *abhidhāsyati* – explains; *bhaktim* – devotional service; *mayi* – unto Me; *parām* – transcendental; *kṛtvā* – doing; *mām* – unto Me; *eva* – certainly; *eṣyati* – comes; *asaṁśayaḥ* – without doubt.

For one who explains this supreme secret to the devotees, pure devotional service is guaranteed, and at the end he will come back to Me.

PURPORT: Generally it is advised that *Bhagavad-gītā* be discussed amongst the devotees only, for those who are not devotees will understand neither Kṛṣṇa nor *Bhagavad-gītā*. Those who do not accept Kṛṣṇa as He is and *Bhagavad-gītā* as it is should not try to explain *Bhagavad-gītā* whimsically and become offenders. *Bhagavad-gītā* should be explained to persons who are ready to accept Kṛṣṇa as the Supreme Personality of Godhead. It is a subject matter for the devotees only and not for philosophical speculators. Anyone, however, who tries sincerely to present *Bhagavad-gītā* as it is will advance in devotional activities and reach the pure devotional state of life. As a result of such pure devotion, he is sure to go back home, back to Godhead.

Text 69 न च तस्मान्मनुष्येषु कश्चिन्मे प्रियकृत्तमः ।
भविता न च मे तस्मादन्यः प्रियतरो भुवि ॥६९॥

na ca tasmān manusyeṣu, kaścin me priya-kṛttamaḥ
bhavitā na ca me tasmād, anyaḥ priya-taro bhuvi

na – never; *ca* – and; *tasmāt* – than him; *manuṣyeṣu* – among men; *kaścit* – anyone; *me* – to Me; *priya-kṛt-tamaḥ* – more dear; *bhavitā* – will become; *na* – nor; *ca* – and; *me* – to Me; *tasmāt* – than him; *anyaḥ* – another; *priya-taraḥ* – dearer; *bhuvi* – in this world.

There is no servant in this world more dear to Me than he, nor will there ever be one more dear.

Text 70 अध्येष्यते च य इमं धर्म्यं संवादमावयोः ।
ज्ञानयज्ञेन तेनाहमिष्टः स्यामिति मे मतिः ॥७०॥

adhyeṣyate ca ya imaṁ, dharmyaṁ saṁvādam āvayoḥ
jñāna-yajñena tenāham, iṣṭaḥ syām iti me matiḥ

adhyeṣyate – will study; *ca* – also; *yaḥ* – he who; *imam* – this; *dharmyam* – sacred; *saṁvādam* – conversation; *āvayoḥ* – of ours; *jñāna* – of knowledge; *yajñena* – by the sacrifice; *tena* – by him; *aham* – I; *iṣṭaḥ* – worshiped; *syām* – shall be; *iti* – thus; *me* – My; *matiḥ* – opinion.

And I declare that he who studies this sacred conversation of ours worships Me by his intelligence.

Text 71 श्रद्धावाननसूयश्च शृणुयादपि यो नरः ।
सोऽपि मुक्तः शुभाँल्लोकान् प्राप्नुयात्पुण्यकर्मणाम् ॥७१॥

śraddhāvān anasūyaś ca, śṛṇuyād api yo naraḥ
so 'pi muktaḥ śubhāl̐ lokān, prāpnuyāt puṇya-karmaṇām

śraddhā-vān – faithful; *anasūyaḥ* – not envious; *ca* – and; *śṛṇuyāt* – does hear; *api* – certainly; *yaḥ* – who; *naraḥ* – a man; *saḥ* – he; *api* – also; *muktaḥ* – being liberated; *śubhān* – the auspicious; *lokān* – planets; *prāpnuyāt* – he attains; *puṇya-karmaṇām* – of the pious.

And one who listens with faith and without envy becomes free from sinful reactions and attains to the auspicious planets where the pious dwell.

PURPORT: In the sixty-seventh verse of this chapter, the Lord explicitly forbade the *Gītā's* being spoken to those who are envious of the Lord. In other words, *Bhagavad-gītā* is for the devotees only. But it so happens that sometimes a devotee of the Lord will hold open class, and in that class not all the students are expected to be devotees. Why do such persons hold open class? It is explained here that although not everyone is a devotee, still there are many men who are not envious of Kṛṣṇa. They have faith in Him as the Supreme Personality of Godhead. If such persons hear from a bona fide devotee about the Lord, the result is that they become at once free from all sinful reactions and after that attain to the planetary system where all righteous persons are situated. Therefore simply by hearing *Bhagavad-gītā,* even a person who does not try to be a pure devotee attains the result of righteous activities. Thus a pure devotee of the Lord gives everyone a chance to become free from all sinful reactions and to become a devotee of the Lord.

Generally those who are free from sinful reactions, those who are righteous, very easily take to Kṛṣṇa consciousness. The word *puṇya-karmaṇām* is very significant here. This refers to the performance of great sacrifices, like the *aśvamedha-yajña,* mentioned in the Vedic literature. Those who are righteous in performing devotional service but who are not pure can attain the planetary system of the polestar, or Dhruvaloka, where Dhruva Mahārāja is presiding. He is a great devotee of the Lord, and he has a special planet, which is called the polestar.

Text 72 कच्चिदेतच्छ्रुतं पार्थ त्वयैकाग्रेण चेतसा ।
कच्चिदज्ञानसम्मोहः प्रणष्टस्ते धनञ्जय ॥७२॥

kaccid etac chrutaṁ pārtha, tvayaikāgreṇa cetasā
kaccid ajñāna-sammohaḥ, praṇaṣṭas te dhanañ-jaya

kaccit – whether; *etat* – this; *śrutam* – heard; *pārtha* – O son of Pṛthā; *tvayā* – by you; *eka-agreṇa* – with full attention; *cetasā* – by the mind;

kaccit – whether; *ajñāna* – of ignorance; *sammohaḥ* – the illusion; *praṇaṣṭaḥ* – dispelled; *te* – of you; *dhanam-jaya* – O conqueror of wealth (Arjuna).

O son of Pṛthā, O conqueror of wealth, have you heard this with an attentive mind? And are your ignorance and illusions now dispelled?

PURPORT: The Lord was acting as the spiritual master of Arjuna. Therefore it was His duty to inquire from Arjuna whether he understood the whole *Bhagavad-gītā* in its proper perspective. If not, the Lord was ready to re-explain any point, or the whole *Bhagavad-gītā* if so required. Actually, anyone who hears *Bhagavad-gītā* from a bona fide spiritual master like Kṛṣṇa or His representative will find that all his ignorance is dispelled. *Bhagavad-gītā* is not an ordinary book written by a poet or fiction writer; it is spoken by the Supreme Personality of Godhead. Any person fortunate enough to hear these teachings from Kṛṣṇa or from His bona fide spiritual representative is sure to become a liberated person and get out of the darkness of ignorance.

Text 73 अर्जुन उवाच
नष्टो मोहः स्मृतिर्लब्धा त्वत्प्रसादान्मयाच्युत ।
स्थितोऽस्मि गतसन्देहः करिष्ये वचनं तव ॥७३॥

arjuna uvāca
naṣṭo mohaḥ smṛtir labdhā, tvat-prasādān mayācyuta
sthito 'smi gata-sandehaḥ, kariṣye vacanaṁ tava

arjunaḥ uvāca – Arjuna said; *naṣṭaḥ* – dispelled; *mohaḥ* – illusion; *smṛtiḥ* – memory; *labdhā* – regained; *tvat-prasādāt* – by Your mercy; *mayā* – by me; *acyuta* – O infallible Kṛṣṇa; *sthitaḥ* – situated; *asmi* – I am; *gata* – removed; *sandehaḥ* – all doubts; *kariṣye* – I shall execute; *vacanam* – order; *tava* – Your.

Arjuna said: My dear Kṛṣṇa, O infallible one, my illusion is now gone. I have regained my memory by Your mercy. I am now firm and free from doubt and am prepared to act according to Your instructions.

PURPORT: The constitutional position of a living entity, represented by Arjuna, is that he has to act according to the order of the Supreme Lord. He is meant for self-discipline. Śrī Caitanya Mahāprabhu says that the actual position of the living entity is that of eternal servant of the

Supreme Lord. Forgetting this principle, the living entity becomes conditioned by material nature, but in serving the Supreme Lord he becomes the liberated servant of God. The living entity's constitutional position is to be a servitor; he has to serve either the illusory *māyā* or the Supreme Lord. If he serves the Supreme Lord he is in his normal condition, but if he prefers to serve the illusory, external energy, then certainly he will be in bondage. In illusion the living entity is serving in this material world. He is bound by his lust and desires, yet he thinks of himself as the master of the world. This is called illusion. When a person is liberated, his illusion is over, and he voluntarily surrenders unto the Supreme to act according to His desires. The last illusion, the last snare of *māyā* to trap the living entity, is the proposition that he is God. The living entity thinks that he is no longer a conditioned soul, but God. He is so unintelligent that he does not think that if he were God, then how could he be in doubt? That he does not consider. So that is the last snare of illusion. Actually to become free from the illusory energy is to understand Kṛṣṇa, the Supreme Personality of Godhead, and agree to act according to His order.

The word *moha* is very important in this verse. *Moha* refers to that which is opposed to knowledge. Actually real knowledge is the understanding that every living being is eternally a servitor of the Lord, but instead of thinking oneself in that position, the living entity thinks that he is not a servant, that he is the master of this material world, for he wants to lord it over the material nature. That is his illusion. This illusion can be overcome by the mercy of the Lord or by the mercy of a pure devotee. When that illusion is over, one agrees to act in Kṛṣṇa consciousness.

Kṛṣṇa consciousness is acting according to Kṛṣṇa's order. A conditioned soul, illusioned by the external energy of matter, does not know that the Supreme Lord is the master who is full of knowledge and who is the proprietor of everything. Whatever He desires He can bestow upon His devotees; He is the friend of everyone, and He is especially inclined to His devotee. He is the controller of this material nature and of all living entities. He is also the controller of inexhaustible time, and He is full of all opulences and all potencies. The Supreme Personality of Godhead can even give Himself to the devotee. One who does not know Him is under the spell of illusion; he does not become a devotee, but a servitor of *māyā*. Arjuna, however, after hearing *Bhagavad-gītā* from the Supreme Personality of Godhead, became free from all illusion. He could understand that Kṛṣṇa was not only his friend but the Supreme Personality of Godhead. And he understood Kṛṣṇa factually. So to study *Bhagavad-gītā* is to understand Kṛṣṇa factually. When a person is in full knowledge, he naturally surrenders to Kṛṣṇa. When Arjuna understood that it was Kṛṣṇa's plan to reduce the unnecessary increase of population, he agreed to fight according to Kṛṣṇa's desire. He again took up his weapons – his arrows and bow – to fight under the order of the Supreme Personality of Godhead.

Text 74 सञ्जय उवाच
इत्यहं वासुदेवस्य पार्थस्य च महात्मनः ।
संवादमिममश्रौषमद्भुतं रोमहर्षणम् ॥७४॥

sañjaya uvāca
ity ahaṁ vāsudevasya, pārthasya ca mahātmanaḥ
saṁvādam imam aśrauṣam, adbhutaṁ roma-harṣaṇam

sañjayaḥ uvāca – Sañjaya said; *iti* – thus; *aham* – I; *vāsudevasya* – of Kṛṣṇa; *pārthasya* – and Arjuna; *ca* – also; *mahā-ātmanaḥ* – of the great soul; *saṁvādam* – discussion; *imam* – this; *aśrauṣam* – have heard; *adbhutam* – wonderful; *roma-harṣaṇam* – making the hair stand on end.

Sañjaya said: Thus have I heard the conversation of two great souls, Kṛṣṇa and Arjuna. And so wonderful is that message that my hair is standing on end.

PURPORT: In the beginning of *Bhagavad-gītā,* Dhṛtarāṣṭra inquired from his secretary Sañjaya, "What happened on the Battlefield of Kurukṣetra?" The entire study was related to the heart of Sañjaya by the grace of his spiritual master, Vyāsa. He thus explained the theme of the battlefield. The conversation was wonderful because such an important conversation between two great souls had never taken place before and would not take place again. It was wonderful because the Supreme Personality of Godhead was speaking about Himself and His energies to the living entity, Arjuna, a great devotee of the Lord. If we follow in the footsteps of Arjuna to understand Kṛṣṇa, then our life will be happy and successful. Sañjaya realized this, and as he began to understand it, he related the conversation to Dhṛtarāṣṭra. Now it is concluded that wherever there is Kṛṣṇa and Arjuna, there is victory.

Text 75 व्यासप्रसादाच्छ्रुतवानेतद्गुह्यमहं परम् ।
योगं योगेश्वरात्कृष्णात्साक्षात्कथयतः स्वयम् ॥७५॥

vyāsa-prasādāc chrutavān, etad guhyam ahaṁ param
yogaṁ yogeśvarāt kṛṣṇāt, sākṣāt kathayataḥ svayam

vyāsa-prasādāt – by the mercy of Vyāsadeva; *śrutavān* – have heard; *etat* – this; *guhyam* – confidential; *aham* – I; *param* – the supreme; *yogam* – mysticism; *yoga-īśvarāt* – from the master of all mysticism; *kṛṣṇāt* – from Kṛṣṇa; *sākṣāt* – directly; *kathayataḥ* – speaking; *svayam* – personally.

By the mercy of Vyāsa, I have heard these most confidential talks directly from the master of all mysticism, Kṛṣṇa, who was speaking personally to Arjuna.

PURPORT: Vyāsa was the spiritual master of Sañjaya, and Sañjaya admits that it was by Vyāsa's mercy that he could understand the Supreme Personality of Godhead. This means that one has to understand Kṛṣṇa not directly but through the medium of the spiritual master. The spiritual master is the transparent medium, although it is true that the experience is still direct. This is the mystery of the disciplic succession. When the spiritual master is bona fide, then one can hear *Bhagavad-gītā* directly, as Arjuna heard it. There are many mystics and *yogīs* all over the world, but Kṛṣṇa is the master of all *yoga* systems. Kṛṣṇa's instruction is explicitly stated in *Bhagavad-gītā* – surrender unto Kṛṣṇa. One who does so is the topmost *yogī.* This is confirmed in the last verse of the Sixth Chapter. *Yoginām api sarveṣām.*

Nārada is the direct disciple of Kṛṣṇa and the spiritual master of Vyāsa. Therefore Vyāsa is as bona fide as Arjuna because he comes in the disciplic succession, and Sañjaya is the direct disciple of Vyāsa. Therefore by the grace of Vyāsa, Sañjaya's senses were purified, and he could see and hear Kṛṣṇa directly. One who directly hears Kṛṣṇa can understand this confidential knowledge. If one does not come to the disciplic succession, he cannot hear Kṛṣṇa; therefore his knowledge is always imperfect, at least as far as understanding *Bhagavad-gītā* is concerned.

In *Bhagavad-gītā,* all the *yoga* systems – *karma-yoga, jñāna-yoga* and *bhakti-yoga* – are explained. Kṛṣṇa is the master of all such mysticism. It is to be understood, however, that as Arjuna was fortunate enough to understand Kṛṣṇa directly, so, by the grace of Vyāsa, Sañjaya was also able to hear Kṛṣṇa directly. Actually there is no difference between hearing directly from Kṛṣṇa and hearing directly from Kṛṣṇa via a bona fide spiritual master like Vyāsa. The spiritual master is the representative of Vyāsadeva also. Therefore, according to the Vedic system, on the birth-

predicted here that Yudhiṣṭhira, after gaining victory in this battle, would flourish more and more because not only was he righteous and pious but he was also a strict moralist. He never spoke a lie during his life.

There are many less intelligent persons who take *Bhagavad-gītā* to be a discussion of topics between two friends on a battlefield. But such a book cannot be scripture. Some may protest that Kṛṣṇa incited Arjuna to fight, which is immoral, but the reality of the situation is clearly stated: *Bhagavad-gītā* is the supreme instruction in morality. The supreme instruction of morality is stated in the Ninth Chapter, in the thirty-fourth verse: *man-manā bhava mad-bhaktaḥ.* One must become a devotee of Kṛṣṇa, and the essence of all religion is to surrender unto Kṛṣṇa (*sarva-dharmān parityajya mām ekaṁ śaraṇaṁ vraja*). The instructions of *Bhagavad-gītā* constitute the supreme process of religion and of morality. All other processes may be purifying and may lead to this process, but the last instruction of the *Gītā* is the last word in all morality and religion: surrender unto Kṛṣṇa. This is the verdict of the Eighteenth Chapter.

From *Bhagavad-gītā* we can understand that to realize oneself by philosophical speculation and by meditation is one process, but to fully surrender unto Kṛṣṇa is the highest perfection. This is the essence of the teachings of *Bhagavad-gītā.* The path of regulative principles according to the orders of social life and according to the different courses of religion may be a confidential path of knowledge. But although the rituals of religion are confidential, meditation and cultivation of knowledge are still more confidential. And surrender unto Kṛṣṇa in devotional service in full Kṛṣṇa consciousness is the most confidential instruction. That is the essence of the Eighteenth Chapter.

Another feature of *Bhagavad-gītā* is that the actual truth is the Supreme Personality of Godhead, Kṛṣṇa. The Absolute Truth is realized in three features – impersonal Brahman, localized Paramātmā, and ultimately the Supreme Personality of Godhead, Kṛṣṇa. Perfect knowledge of the Absolute Truth means perfect knowledge of Kṛṣṇa. If one understands Kṛṣṇa, then all the departments of knowledge are part and parcel of that understanding. Kṛṣṇa is transcendental, for He is always situated in His eternal internal potency. The living entities are manifested of His energy and are divided into two classes, eternally conditioned and eternally liberated. Such living entities are innumerable, and they are considered fundamental parts of Kṛṣṇa. Material energy is manifested into twenty-four divisions. The creation is effected by eternal time, and it is created and dissolved by external energy. This manifestation of the cosmic world repeatedly becomes visible and invisible.

In *Bhagavad-gītā* five principal subject matters have been discussed: the Supreme Personality of Godhead, material nature, the living entities, eternal time and all kinds of activities. All is dependent on the Supreme Personality of Godhead, Kṛṣṇa. All conceptions of the Absolute Truth – impersonal Brahman, localized Paramātmā and any other transcendental conception – exist within the category of understanding the Supreme Personality of Godhead. Although superficially the Supreme Personality of Godhead, the living entity, material nature and time appear to be different, nothing is different from the Supreme. But the Supreme is always different from everything. Lord Caitanya's philosophy is that of "inconceivable oneness and difference." This system of philosophy constitutes perfect knowledge of the Absolute Truth.

The living entity in his original position is pure spirit. He is just like an atomic particle of the Supreme Spirit. Thus Lord Kṛṣṇa may be compared to the sun, and the living entities to sunshine. Because the living entities are the marginal energy of Kṛṣṇa, they have a tendency to be in contact either with the material energy or with the spiritual energy. In other words, the living entity is situated between the two energies of the Lord, and because he belongs to the superior energy of the Lord, he has a particle of independence. By proper use of that independence he comes under the direct order of Kṛṣṇa. Thus he attains his normal condition in the pleasure-giving potency.

Thus end the Bhaktivedanta Purports to the Eighteenth Chapter of the Śrīmad Bhagavad-gītā *in the matter of its Conclusion – the Perfection of Renunciation.*

Appendixes

A Note About the Second Edition

For the benefit of readers who have become familiar with the first edition of the *Bhagavad-gītā As It Is,* a few words about this second edition seem in order.

Although in most respects the two editions are the same, the editors of the Bhaktivedanta Book Trust have gone back to the oldest manuscripts in their archives to make this second edition even more faithful to Śrīla Prabhupāda's original work.

Śrīla Prabhupāda finished *Bhagavad-gītā As It Is* in 1967, two years after he came from India to America. The Macmillan Company published an abridged edition in 1968 and the first unabridged edition in 1972.

The new American disciples who helped Śrīla Prabhupāda ready the manuscript for publication struggled with several difficulties. Those who transcribed his taped dictation sometimes found his heavily accented English hard to follow and his Sanskrit quotations strange to their ears. The Sanskrit editors had to do their best with a manuscript spotted with gaps and phonetic approximations. Yet their effort to publish Śrīla Prabhupāda's work was a success, and *Bhagavad-gītā As It Is* has become the standard edition for scholars and devotees around the world.

For this second edition, however, Śrīla Prabhupāda's disciples had the benefit of having worked with his books for fifteen years. The English editors were familiar with his philosophy and language, and the Sanskrit editors were by now accomplished scholars. And now they were able to see their way through perplexities in the manuscript by consulting the same Sanskrit commentaries Śrīla Prabhupāda consulted when writing *Bhagavad-gītā As It Is.*

The result is a work of even greater richness and authenticity. The word-for-word Sanskrit-English equivalents now follow more closely the standard of Śrīla Prabhupāda's other books and are therefore more clear and precise. In places the translations, though already correct, have been revised to come closer to the original Sanskrit and to Śrīla Prabhupāda's original dictation. In the Bhaktivedanta purports, many passages lost to the original edition have been restored to their places. And Sanskrit quotations whose sources were unnamed in the first edition now appear with full references to chapter and verse.

The Publishers

The Author

His Divine Grace A. C. Bhaktivedanta Swami Prabhupāda appeared in this world in 1896 in Calcutta, India. He first met his spiritual master, Śrīla Bhaktisiddhānta Sarasvatī Gosvāmī, in Calcutta in 1922. Bhaktisiddhānta Sarasvatī, a prominent religious scholar and the founder of sixty-four Gauḍīya Maṭhas (Vedic institutes), liked this educated young man and convinced him to dedicate his life to teaching Vedic knowledge. Śrīla Prabhupāda became his student and, in 1933, his formally initiated disciple.

At their first meeting, in 1922, Śrīla Bhaktisiddhānta Sarasvatī requested Śrīla Prabhupāda to broadcast Vedic knowledge in English. In the years that followed, Śrīla Prabhupāda wrote a commentary on the *Bhagavad-gītā,* assisted the Gauḍīya Maṭha in its work and, in 1944, started *Back to Godhead,* an English fortnightly magazine. Single-handedly, Śrīla Prabhupāda edited it, typed the manuscripts, checked the galley proofs and even distributed the individual copies. The magazine is now being continued by his disciples.

In 1950 Śrīla Prabhupāda retired from married life, adopting the *vānaprastha* (retired) order to devote more time to his studies and writing. He traveled to the holy city of Vṛndāvana, where he lived in humble circumstances in the historic temple of Rādhā-Dāmodara. There he engaged for several years in deep study and writing. He accepted the renounced order of life (*sannyāsa*) in 1959. At Rādhā-Dāmodara, Śrīla Prabhupāda began work on his life's masterpiece: a multivolume commentated translation of the eighteen-thousand-verse *Śrīmad-Bhāgavatam (Bhāgavata Purāṇa).* He also wrote *Easy Journey to Other Planets.*

After publishing three volumes of the *Bhāgavatam,* Śrīla Prabhupāda came to the United States, in September 1965, to fulfill the mission of his spiritual master. Subsequently, His Divine Grace wrote more than fifty volumes of authoritative commentated translations and summary studies of the philosophical and religious classics of India.

When he first arrived by freighter in New York City, Śrīla Prabhupāda was practically penniless. Only after almost a year of great difficulty did he establish the International Society for Krishna Consciousness, in July of 1966. Before he passed away on November 14, 1977, he had guided the Society and seen it grow to a worldwide confederation of more than one hundred *āśramas,* schools, temples, institutes and farm communities.

In 1972 His Divine Grace introduced the Vedic system of primary and secondary education in the West by founding the *gurukula* school in Dallas, Texas. Since then his disciples have established similar schools throughout the United States and the rest of the world.

Śrīla Prabhupāda also inspired the construction of several large international cultural centers in India. At Śrīdhāma Māyāpur, in West Bengal, devotees are building a spiritual city centered on a magnificent temple – an ambitious project for which construction will extend over many years to come. In Vṛndāvana are the Krishna-Balaram Temple and International Guesthouse, *gurukula* school and Śrīla Prabhupāda Memorial and Museum. There are also major temples and cultural centers in Mumbai, New Delhi, Ahmedabad, Siliguri and Ujjain. Other centers are planned in many important locations on the Indian subcontinent.

Śrīla Prabhupāda's most significant contribution, however, is his books. Highly respected by scholars for their authority, depth and clarity, they are used as textbooks in numerous college courses. His writings have been translated into over fifty languages. The Bhaktivedanta Book Trust, established in 1972 to publish the works of His Divine Grace, has thus become the world's largest publisher of books in the field of Indian religion and philosophy.

In just twelve years, despite his advanced age, Śrīla Prabhupāda circled the globe fourteen times on lecture tours that took him to six continents. In spite of such a vigorous schedule, Śrīla Prabhupāda continued to write prolifically. His writings constitute a veritable library of Vedic philosophy, religion, literature and culture.

A Summary of the Bhagavad-gītā

Bhūrijana Dāsa

The *Bhagavad-gītā* opens with the blind King Dhṛtarāṣṭra requesting his secretary Sañjaya to tell him about the battle between his sons (the Kauravas) and nephews (the Pāṇḍavas). Sañjaya has been blessed by his guru to be able to see the battlefield even from his seat in the court, at Dhṛtarāṣṭra's side, and he begins by describing both armies. Sañjaya then indicates to Dhṛtarāṣṭra that Lord Kṛṣṇa, the Supreme Personality of Godhead, out of affection for His devotee the Pāṇḍava prince Arjuna is driving Arjuna's chariot.

As the action opens, conches blow and Arjuna takes up his bow and prepares himself for the fight. He then turns to the infallible Kṛṣṇa and asks Him to draw their chariot between the two fighting forces. Arjuna wants to identify his opponents in the battle. Kṛṣṇa complies, and Arjuna looks across the field to see family and friends, teachers and respected elders on the other side. His mind reels. How can he kill persons so dear to him, even in a righteous battle? He throws down his bow and arrows and decides not to fight.

In the balance of Chapter One and at the beginning of Chapter Two, Arjuna presents his arguments for refusing to fight. Although his reasons are many, he mostly fears the sinful reaction (*karma*) he will receive from killing his kinsmen and the other warriors. Arjuna, lost in an ocean of fears, doubts, and ambivalence, chooses to surrender to Lord Kṛṣṇa, and requests His instruction.

Kṛṣṇa's initial response is philosophical, pointing out that no killing will actually take place in this battle because the eternal soul cannot die. Besides that, as a *kṣatriya* (warrior), Arjuna has a duty to fight; dutiful fighting does not incur sinful reactions. Kṛṣṇa also explains that the purpose of the *Vedas* (spiritual books of knowledge) is to inspire the gradual elevation of souls from bodily consciousness to Kṛṣṇa consciousness. Ultimately, Kṛṣṇa encourages Arjuna to remain fixed as His servant – and Kṛṣṇa wants him to serve by fighting – and ignore his mind's fears.

Because Kṛṣṇa has quickly offered Arjuna many reasons why he should fight, and has glorified both *buddhi-yoga* (the application of one's intelligence to avoid unfavorable results) and *karma-yoga* (work without attachment to the results [2.47–48, 2.50]), Arjuna becomes confused. Then, citing Kṛṣṇa's instruction that he perform *buddhi-yoga,* he tries to excuse himself from the battlefield for a life of contemplation. He is certain that fighting will cause him to suffer both now and in the future. Arjuna therefore opens Chapter Three with a question: "O Kṛṣṇa, why do You encourage me to fight if using intelligence [*buddhi*] is better than performing work that brings *karma*?"

Kṛṣṇa responds by describing *karma-yoga* – work free of karmic reactions – and clears up Arjuna's mistaken idea that all work is by definition fruitive and thus leads to bondage. Kṛṣṇa explains that Arjuna should fight because avoiding sinful reactions by working in devotion is better than attempting to escape reactions through renouncing work. Kṛṣṇa also instructs Arjuna to fight simply to set a proper example of dutifulness. Arjuna should enter the battle as an act of *yoga* – with knowledge and detachment (3.29–30) and without falling victim to his own attractions and aversions.

Arjuna then wonders why people are impelled to act sinfully. Kṛṣṇa names the enemy: lust. He recommends that Arjuna conquer this forceful and degrading enemy by regulating his senses and becoming fixed in his pure identity as Kṛṣṇa's servant. Such spiritual strength and deliberate use of intelligence will award him true freedom and success.

In Chapter Three Kṛṣṇa recommended that Arjuna fight in full knowledge of Him (3.30), so in Chapter Four Kṛṣṇa discusses different aspects of transcendental knowledge. First Kṛṣṇa explains that knowledge descends through the disciplic succession of spiritual masters stemming from Kṛṣṇa Himself. To answer the obvious question "Who is Kṛṣṇa?" He explains His own advent and mission and then discusses how devotional service to Him is the goal of all sacrifices. (Kṛṣṇa has already referred to the importance of performing *yajña,* sacrifice, in the third chapter, texts 9–16). Next Kṛṣṇa explains the soul's "part and parcel" relationship with Him. All this knowledge, He says, one can gain by approaching a bona fide spiritual master – one who represents the chain of true teachers and can speak realized truth. Chapter Four ends with

Kṛṣṇa glorifying transcendental knowledge, which has the power to burn to ashes all the sinful reactions Arjuna fears. Kṛṣṇa encourages Arjuna to "slash" his doubts with the "weapon of knowledge" and fight.

But Arjuna again becomes perplexed. Kṛṣṇa has impressed on him both the importance of working (which requires activity) and of seeking knowledge (which appears to keep one inactive). Aren't these two contradictory? Arjuna opens Chapter Five by asking Kṛṣṇa to say definitivelywhich is superior: to renounce work by cultivating philosophical speculation (the path of Sāṅkhya, *jñāna,* inaction-in-knowledge) or to work in devotion. Kṛṣṇa answers that those who are detached from the results of their work are truly renounced. Such persons know that while the body acts, they, the soul, actually do nothing. Arjuna should therefore do his duty and steadily act for Kṛṣṇa's satisfaction. Viewing the external world impartially, he should live in his body, conscious of his true self, and remain aloof from his bodily activities. By fixing his consciousness on the Supreme and recognizing Kṛṣṇa as the true enjoyer of His own creation as well as the goal of all sacrifice and austerity and the Lord of all planets, he, the pure soul, will find true peace, because he will be liberated from the pains of this material world.

In the first five chapters Kṛṣṇa has explained *buddhi-yoga,* working with one's consciousness focused on Kṛṣṇa without the desire to taste the fruits of one's own actions. The Lord has also explained *sāṅkhya-yoga, karma-yoga* and *jñāna-yoga* as processes to obtain liberation and as steppingstones to Kṛṣṇa consciousness. At the end of the fifth chapter (texts 27–28) and continuing on into the sixth (where Kṛṣṇa explains the practice of *yoga* in more detail), Kṛṣṇa discusses *dhyāna-yoga* (meditation) and concludes that fixing the mind on Him is the goal of both *yoga* and meditation.

Kṛṣṇa begins the sixth chapter by explaining that the neophyte *yogī* remains aloof from the world, practicing sitting postures, while the advanced *yogī,* the true *sannyāsī,* is detached, acting without material motivation. Such advanced *yogīs* liberate themselves and are not degraded by their mind's activities. Carefully controlling the mind, body, and self, these *yogīs* strictly practice *dhyāna-yoga* in a secluded place. Fixing the mind on Kṛṣṇa, they attain transcendental happiness in the kingdom of God.

Arjuna points out the main difficulty people experience while practicing *yoga:* controlling the mind. Kṛṣṇa responds that one can overcome the obstinate mind by constant practice and determination. Arjuna then asks about the fate of *yogīs* who are unable to sustain determined practice, and Kṛṣṇa says that such persons will be reborn in the families of prosperous people, intellectuals, or wise transcendentalists and again become attracted to yogic principles.

In conclusion, Kṛṣṇa tells Arjuna in the last two verses of the chapter that *yogīs* are greater than ascetics, *jñānīs* and *karmīs,* and that the greatest of all *yogīs* are those who always think of Him and with great faith worship Him in loving service.

With Kṛṣṇa's instruction at the end of Chapter Six in mind, one should initiate one's *yoga* practice from the point of concentration on Kṛṣṇa. Therefore Chapter Seven opens with Kṛṣṇa describing His opulence and energies. This provides Arjuna with the needed content for him to fully meditate on and worship Kṛṣṇa, and also to think of Kṛṣṇa with devotion as he fights.

Kṛṣṇa first explains that He is the Supreme Truth and that all in existence is a combination of His material and spiritual energies; He is the active principle in everything, and His diverse material and spiritual energies pervade all existence. Because the modes of nature – which emanate from Kṛṣṇa but do not affect Him – control the world's activities, only a person who surrenders to Him can cross beyond these modes and come to know Him. Four categories of pious souls surrender and four categories of impious souls do not. Kṛṣṇa does not reveal Himself to the impious, nor to the impersonalists (those who deny His personhood or think that He is simply an amalgamation of all souls), nor to those who surrender to demigods instead of the Supreme. Those who are truly pious, the "undeluded," serve Kṛṣṇa with determination and practice their devotional service on the Brahman platform, where they experience the oneness of everything in existence.* Those souls who know that Kṛṣṇa governs the material manifestation, that He is the master of the demigods and the Lord of sacrifice, can know and understand Him – even at the time of death. Arjuna is particularly concerned with this information because he is standing on a battlefield, with the obvious possibility of death before him.

Chapter Eight begins with Arjuna asking Kṛṣṇa about Brahman, *karma,* the demigods, the material world and how to know God at the time of death. Kṛṣṇa answers Arjuna's first five questions briefly, and then explains in detail how to know Him while leaving the body. Since one's consciousness at the moment of death determines one's next body, one who remembers Kṛṣṇa goes to Kṛṣṇa. Kṛṣṇa further explains

* This realization is the final goal of the impersonalists.

how one can think of Him constantly: as the transcendental person who knows everything, as the oldest, the controller, the smallest and the maintainer. Thus by practicing *yoga* and remembering Him, Kṛṣṇa explains, one will go to the eternal spiritual world and never return to this temporary, miserable material world.

After describing the different yogic ways in which one can leave this world, Kṛṣṇa advises Arjuna not to worry about the practices that comprise the many existing paths – whether Vedic study, *aṣṭāṅga-yoga,* penance, sacrifice, charity, *jñāna* or *karma.* He should focus himself on devotional remembrance of Kṛṣṇa, because the results of all other practices and more are automatically obtained when one performs devotional service. And, Kṛṣṇa notes, those other paths take one to different destinations but not usually to the supreme goal of the soul; *yogīs* who practice devotion reach the supreme abode.

After Kṛṣṇa answers Arjuna's questions in Chapter Eight, in Chapter Nine He continues to give knowledge about Himself similar to what He offered in Chapter Seven. Kṛṣṇa prefaces Chapter Nine with an important statement: The knowledge He will now reveal is most confidential, for He is explaining His actual position, which only the nonenvious and faithful can understand. Then Kṛṣṇa explains that although He is independent and aloof, He pervades, creates and annihilates the entire cosmos through His material energies. Those *mahātmās,* great souls, who know Kṛṣṇa as the Supreme Personality of Godhead take shelter of and serve Him as the one true enjoyer and the supreme object of worship.

Kṛṣṇa next describes the fortunate position of such *mahātmās:* if one worships Kṛṣṇa, Kṛṣṇa cares for him, compensates for his deficiencies and preserves his strengths. And all Kṛṣṇa asks for as an expression of the devotee's love is a simple leaf, flower or a little water offered with devotion. Through this loving exchange Kṛṣṇa's devotees go to Him. Even if a devotee unintentionally commits a horrendous act, he or she will be purified and excused, for Kṛṣṇa promises that His devotee will never perish.

In chapters Seven and Nine, Kṛṣṇa explained His energies. In Chapter Ten Kṛṣṇa explains His opulences more specifically and reveals Himself through them as the Supreme Personality of Godhead, the source of everything. Kṛṣṇa also tells how His pure devotees recognize Him as the unborn Supreme Lord, the source of all sages, the source of the material and spiritual worlds and the source of all qualities and attitudes. Pure and wise devotees worship Kṛṣṇa and converse about Him. Their thoughts dwelling on Him, undeluded and free from sin, they engage in

His service. Kṛṣṇa feels such compassion for these dedicated souls that He destroys whatever ignorance remains in their hearts and thus frees them from any obstacles blocking their spiritual progress. After hearing of Kṛṣṇa's opulences, Arjuna confirms that Kṛṣṇa is the Supreme Lord by quoting Vedic authorities and expressing that only Kṛṣṇa can truly know Himself. Kṛṣṇa then tells of His divine manifestations in this world – as the Supersoul, the ocean, the Himalayas – all of which merely indicate His limitless opulence, for a single fragment of His energy pervades and supports the entire universe.

Although Arjuna acknowledges the two-armed form of Kṛṣṇa before him as supreme, Arjuna asks Kṛṣṇa to reveal the all-pervading universal form – the form that supports the universe. Thus in Chapter Eleven Kṛṣṇa proves His claim that He is the Supreme Lord and establishes the criterion by which anyone who claims to be God must also prove himself: He reveals to Arjuna His wondrous, effulgent, all-expansive form as the universe, and Arjuna sees all the soldiers on both sides dying within it. Kṛṣṇa tells Arjuna that He is time, destroyer of all the worlds, and He assures Arjuna that He has already killed the warriors on both sides. Kṛṣṇa expresses that Arjuna, now aware that these deaths are inevitable, should become His instrument and fight in the battle.

Arjuna is overwhelmed by the universal form and begins to pray fearfully. In answer to his prayerful request, Kṛṣṇa changes the revelation, first showing His four-armed form before again returning to the two-armed form Arjuna knows and loves. Kṛṣṇa then states that He empowers only pure devotees to view His two-armed form, and that such pure souls, working for Him without desire to attain anything from their endeavor, make Him the supreme goal of their lives. Thus they ultimately come to Him.

In Chapter Twelve, an awed Arjuna wishes to confirm his own position as a devotee, a person practicing the highest worship of the Supreme, so he asks Kṛṣṇa which is superior – worshiping Him through devotional service or worshiping the impersonal feature of the Absolute. Kṛṣṇa responds emphatically that one engaged in His personal service is topmost. One's mind and intelligence should therefore be fixed on Him exclusively. If one is unable to be so fixed, one should follow the rules and regulations of *bhakti-yoga,* which will purify one so that he or she can later surrender fully. Kṛṣṇa then describes other processes that eventually lead to His pure devotional service.

The qualities that endear a devotee to Kṛṣṇa, such as equanimity in both happiness and distress, not becoming enamored with the ordinary course of activities, satisfaction in life with no hankering for what one doesn't have, and the faithful following of the path of devotional service, are also mentioned as part of the process of worshiping Kṛṣṇa in devotional service.

Arjuna opens Chapter Thirteen by inquiring about the "field of activities" and the "knower of that field." Kṛṣṇa answers that the conditioned soul's body and its interactions with the material world are the soul's limited field of activities. By understanding the difference between the body, soul and Supersoul, and by studying spiritual knowledge, the soul can transcend duality, realize his eternal subordination to Kṛṣṇa, and attain the supreme destination.

The thirteenth chapter clearly explains that by humbly developing knowledge one can free oneself from material entanglement. Material entanglement, Kṛṣṇa tells us (13.20–22), is caused by association with the modes of material nature. Therefore in Chapter Fourteen Kṛṣṇa explains the three modes – goodness, passion and ignorance – in detail, describing them as the forces that control and bind all conditioned souls to this world. Since all other processes of spiritual elevation are tinged by the three modes, a soul can transcend the modes only by practicing devotional service to Kṛṣṇa, who both controls the modes and exists beyond them. Thus the limitations imposed by the conditioned soul's field of activities can be overcome, and the purified soul can be elevated to the Brahman platform, the constitutional position of purity and happiness – a platform of which Kṛṣṇa is the basis.

Because one must be detached from the modes and their results to become attached to Kṛṣṇa's service, in Chapter Fifteen Kṛṣṇa describes how to free oneself from the grip of the material modes. He begins by comparing the material world to a gigantic, inverted banyan tree, a reflection of the spiritual realm, with its roots upward and its branches downward, and then instructs Arjuna to detach himself from this tree through surrender to Him. Those who surrender to Kṛṣṇa can end the cycle of transmigration and return to Him in the spiritual world.

Although the ignorant cannot understand that the soul transmigrates from one body to another according to the mind's desires, transcendentalists see this clearly. The ignorant can attain proper vision by seeing Kṛṣṇa's potency in all things – for example, recognizing Kṛṣṇa as the splendor of the sun, moon and fire; as the one keeping the planets in orbit and making the vegetables succulent; as the fire of digestion; as the Paramātmā in everyone's heart; as the giver of remembrance, knowledge and forgetfulness; and as both the goal of the *Vedas* and the compiler of *Vedānta.* Kṛṣṇa reveals that knowing Him as the Supreme Personality of Godhead and engaging in His service is the ultimate purpose of the *Vedānta* and the most confidential instruction in the *Vedas.*

In Chapter Fifteen, auspicious, elevating activities are described as part of the banyan tree. In Chapter Sixteen, after mentioning twenty-six godly qualities, Kṛṣṇa explains the demonic nature, which degrades the soul through arrogant, ignorant and conceited self-centered pursuits of sense gratification and power.

Kṛṣṇa explains the demonic mentality: the world is unreal and produced only from sexual desire. Taking shelter of lust, those with a demonic mentality think sense gratification the goal of life and scheme to illegally increase their wealth. While plotting to kill their enemies, they think themselves powerful and happy, and surrounded by their relatives they use sacrifices and charity only to further their own happiness. Perplexed by anxieties that are based on misunderstandings, bewildered by complacency, impudence, and wealth, and envying the Supersoul in their own bodies and in the bodies of others, such persons blaspheme real religion and are repeatedly cast by Kṛṣṇa into the lower species and so gradually sink into the most abominable forms of existence.

Kṛṣṇa ends the chapter by explaining that since lust, anger, and greed are the beginning of demonic life, all sane people should eradicate these qualities from their hearts and instead understand and perform their duties by faithfully following the scriptures. Kṛṣṇa concludes Chapter Sixteen with a declaration that the ultimate difference between the divine and the demonic is that the divine follow the scriptures and the demonic do not.

At the beginning of Chapter Seventeen, Arjuna inquires more about those who don't follow scriptures but who worship according to personal whims. Kṛṣṇa answers by describing how the particular combination of modes that controls each person dictates his faith, his method of worship, what he eats and what types of sacrifice, charity and penance he performs. The chapter ends with Kṛṣṇa explaining the syllables *oṁ tat sat,* which indicate that any sacrifice, austerity, or charity dictated by the modes and performed without devotional service is useless both in this life and the next. One should therefore serve Kṛṣṇa directly in Kṛṣṇa consciousness.

The topics of the *Bhagavad-gītā* are completed in seventeen chapters. In the eighteenth chapter Kṛṣṇa reviews the knowledge He has presented. His conclusion, as He has stated all along, is that one should practice devotional service in Kṛṣṇa consciousness.

Since Arjuna's intrinsic reason for desiring to renounce his duty as a warrior was his fear of sinful reaction, Kṛṣṇa explains true renunciation and how to transcend sinful reaction by (1) renouncing the fruits of activities, (2) abiding by the order of the Supersoul, and (3) worshiping the Lord with the fruit of one's work while acting either as a *brāhmaṇa, kṣatriya, vaiśya* or *śūdra,* according to the central mode of nature by which one is controlled. Each of these three should lead Arjuna to fight. Thus one can become self-realized and, from there, detach himself from matter and practice pure devotional service.

Kṛṣṇa can be known only by one who surrenders to Him in devotional service. If Arjuna takes to the direct devotional process – free of *karma* and *jñāna* – he need not fear any sinful reaction, because Kṛṣṇa will protect him. Under Kṛṣṇa's protection, the pure devotee reaches Kṛṣṇa's shelter. Kṛṣṇa again instructs Arjuna in surrender and encourages him to attain peace in the supreme eternal abode. Kṛṣṇa then repeats the confidential knowledge He previously spoke in Chapter Nine: "Become My devotee, always think of Me, act for Me, worship Me and offer all homage unto Me. Surrender to Me alone. Do not fear sinful reactions."

After hearing Śrī Kṛṣṇa's instructions, Arjuna is fixed and ready to fight. Sañjaya, now at the end of his narration, speaks ecstatically to Dhṛtarāṣṭra of Kṛṣṇa's wondrous universal form and predicts victory for Arjuna, the supreme archer, for Arjuna has surrendered to Kṛṣṇa, the master of all mystics.

The Ascending Stages of Yoga

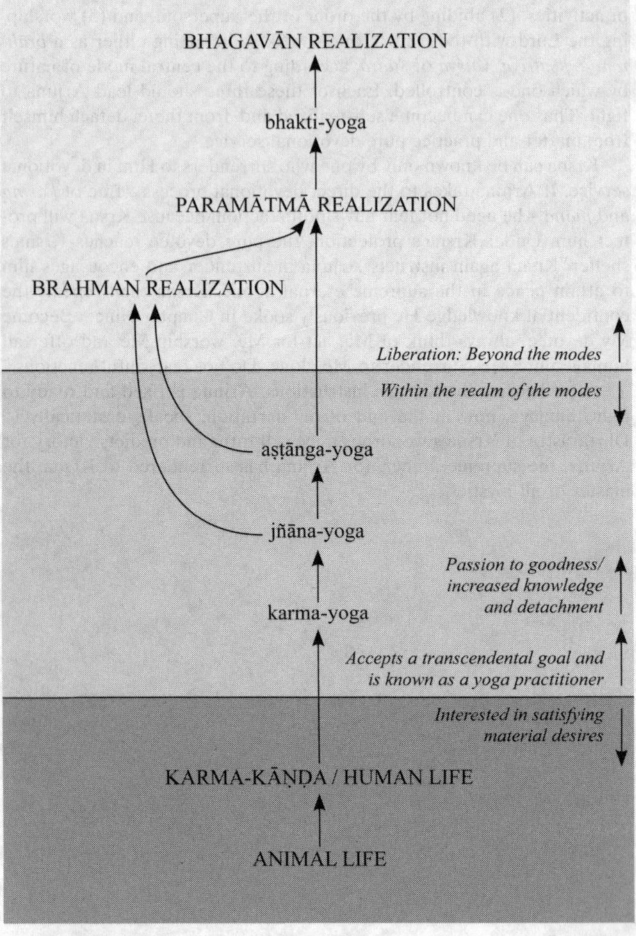

Notes on the Stages of Yoga

Bhagavān realization: The goal of the yoga system. Realization by the *bhakti-yogī* of Kṛṣṇa, the Supreme Personality of Godhead, in full spiritual consciousness.
Bhakti-yoga: Linking with the Supreme Lord through devotional service. By the practice of *bhakti-yoga,* the *yogī* is elevated to full Kṛṣṇa consciousness, also known as Bhagavān realization.
Paramātmā realization: Realization of the localized aspect of Kṛṣṇa, also known as the Supersoul, within the heart of all living entities. Since Kṛṣṇa's manifestation of Paramātmā exists only in the material world, Paramātmā-realized *yogīs* will either merge with Brahman or transfer themselves to higher realms through *bhakti-yoga*. For a further explanation, see *Bhagavad-gītā* 2.2, purport.
Brahman realization: Realization of the impersonal, all-pervasive aspect of the Supreme.
Aṣṭāṅga-yoga: Also known as *dhyāna-yoga.* An eight-stage mechanical practice that includes controlling the mind and senses and focusing one's concentration on the Supreme Lord. See the sixth chapter of *Bhagavad-gītā* for a detailed description.
Jñāna-yoga: The path of spiritual realization through a speculative philosophical search for the Absolute Truth. *Jñānīs* are fixed in goodness and realize they are not the body but eternal souls.
Karma-yoga: There are two levels of *karma-yoga:* (1) Detached work in goodness wherein the *yogīs* remain attached to their duty but detached from the fruits of their work. They attain knowledge and realize they are not the body. (2) Attached work influenced by passion wherein the *yogīs* remain attached to the fruit of their work but nevertheless renounce some of the fruit, gradually increase in knowledge, are purified of passion, and become elevated to goodness.
Karma-kāṇḍa: Fulfilling one's material desires by following the ritualistic activities recommended in the Vedic literature. The follower of *karma-kāṇḍa* is gradually elevated.

Animal Life: Human beings who try to fulfill their material desires without having a higher, spiritual purpose are considered to be acting on the level of animals.

Further notes: Bhakti-yoga

To achieve any realization, one needs at least some degree of *bhakti* in one's practice.

At any stage, the practitioner who attains the association of *bhakti-yogīs* can begin to engage directly in *bhakti-yoga*.

On the path of *bhakti*, those who perform devotional service are purified in the same way as those following the ascending stages of *yoga*. Their passion decreases and their goodness and transcendental knowledge increase. They become less attached to the fruits of their work and more attached to Kṛṣṇa's service. Thus it may be said that *bhakti-yogīs* have also the two stages of *karma-yoga* included in their practice.

In the *Bhagavad-gītā* Kṛṣṇa many times recommends *bhakti-yoga* practiced on the level of detached work in goodness.

Kṛṣṇa's ultimate instructions on yoga are given at the end of the *Gītā* (18.65–18.66): Pure *bhakti-yoga* begins when one surrenders and agrees to serve Kṛṣṇa with no desire other than to please Him.

One at any stage may transcend the modes through full surrender to Kṛṣṇa.

Glossary

Ācārya – one who teaches by his own example; a spiritual master.

Acintya-bhedābheda-tattva – Lord Caitanya's doctrine of the "inconceivable oneness and difference" of God and His energies.

Agni – the demigod of fire.

Agnihotra-yajña – the ceremonial fire sacrifice performed in Vedic rituals.

Ahaṅkāra – false ego, by which the soul misidentifies with the material body.

Ahiṁsā – nonviolence.

Akarma – "nonaction"; devotional activity, for which one suffers no reaction.

Ānanda – spiritual bliss.

Aparā-prakṛti – the inferior, material energy of the Lord (matter).

Arcana – the procedures followed for worshiping the *arcā-vigraha.*

Arcā-vigraha – the form of God manifested through material elements, as in a painting or statue of Kṛṣṇa worshiped in a home or temple. Present in this form, the Lord personally accepts worship from His devotees.

Arjuna – the third son of Pāṇḍu and an intimate friend of Lord Kṛṣṇa's. Kṛṣṇa became his chariot driver and spoke the *Bhagavad-gītā* to him on the battlefield of Kurukṣetra.

Āryan – a civilized follower of Vedic culture; one whose goal is spiritual advancement.

Asat – not eternal; temporary.

Āśramas – the four spiritual orders according to the Vedic social system: *brahmacarya* (student life), *gṛhastha* (householder life), *vānaprastha* (retirement) and *sannyāsa* (renunciation).

Aṣṭāṅga-yoga – the "eightfold path" of mystic yoga, propounded by Patañjali, consisting of *yama* and *niyama* (moral practices), *āsana* (bodily postures), *prāṇāyāma* (breath control), *pratyāhāra* (sensory withdrawal), *dhāraṇā* (steadying the mind), *dhyāna* (meditation) and *samādhi* (deep contemplation on Viṣṇu within the heart).

Asura – a person opposed to the service and supremacy of the Supreme Lord; one who does not follow the scriptural principles and tends toward gross materialism.

Ātmā – the self. *Ātmā* may refer to the body, the mind, the intellect or the Supreme Self. Usually, however, it indicates the individual soul.

Avatāra – "one who descends"; a fully or partially empowered incarnation of God who descends from the spiritual realm for a particular mission.

Avidyā – ignorance.

Bhagavān – "He who possesses all opulences"; the Supreme Lord, who is the reservoir of all beauty, strength, fame, wealth, knowledge and renunciation.

Bhakta – devotee.

Bhakti – devotional service to the Supreme Lord. The formal systemization of devotional service is called *bhakti-yoga.*

Bhakti-rasāmṛta-sindhu – a manual on devotional service written in Sanskrit in the sixteenth century by Śrīla Rūpa Gosvāmī.

Bhakti-yoga – linking with the Supreme Lord through devotional service; untinged by *jñāna* or *karma.*

Bharata – an ancient king of India from whom the Pāṇḍavas descended.

Bhāva – ecstasy; the stage of *bhakti* just prior to pure love for God.

Bhīma – the second son of Pāṇḍu and Kuntī. He was known for his great strength and prodigious appetite.

Bhīṣma – the noble general respected as the "grandfather" of the Kuru dynasty.

Brahmā – the first created being of the universe and secondary creator of the universe. Directed by Lord Viṣṇu, he creates all life forms in the universe and rules the mode of passion. His life span is more than 311 trillion of our years. He is the forefather and guru of the demigods, the giver of the *Vedas,* and the director of the secondary phase of cosmic creation by which all species of plants, animals, human beings and demigods come into existence.

Brahma-bhūta – oneness with the Supreme; the joyful state of being freed from material contamination. One in this state is characterized by transcendental happiness, and engages in the service of the Supreme Lord; liberation.

Brahmacārī – a celibate student under the care of a spiritual master. One in the first order of spiritual life according to the Vedic social system (see *āśramas*).

Brahma-jijñāsā – inquiry into spiritual knowledge.

Brahma-jyotir – the spiritual effulgence emanating from the transcendental body of Lord Kṛṣṇa and illuminating the spiritual world. The material *prakṛti,* the *jīvas* who desire to enjoy matter, and *kāla* (time), are situated in this *brahma-jyotir,* which is pure existence devoid of difference and activity. The *brahma-jyotir* is Kṛṣṇa's feature of *sat* (eternality) separated from *cit* (knowledge) and *ānanda* (bliss).

Brahmaloka – the abode of Lord Brahmā; the highest planet in this world.

Brahman – (1) the individual soul; (2) the impersonal, all-pervasive aspect of the Supreme; (3) the Supreme Personality of Godhead; (4) the *mahat-tattva,* or total material substance.

Brāhmaṇa – a member of the intellectual or priestly class, according to the Vedic social system; a person wise in Vedic knowledge, fixed in the mode of goodness, and knowledgeable of Brahman.

Brahma-saṁhitā – a very ancient text recording prayers offered by Lord Brahmā to Lord Kṛṣṇa; discovered by Caitanya Mahāprabhu in South India.

Buddhi-yoga – another term for *bhakti-yoga* (devotional service to Kṛṣṇa), indicating that it represents the highest use of intelligence (*buddhi*).

Caitanya-caritāmṛta – the biography of Śrī Caitanya Mahāprabhu composed in Bengali in the late sixteenth century by Śrīla Kṛṣṇadāsa Kavirāja.

Caitanya Mahāprabhu – Lord Kṛṣṇa's incarnation in the Age of Kali. He appeared in Navadvīpa, West Bengal, in the late fifteenth century and inaugurated the *yuga-dharma* (prime religious dispensation for the age) – the congregational chanting of the divine names of God.

Caṇḍāla – a dog-eater; an outcaste.

Candra – the presiding demigod of the moon (Candraloka).

Cāturmāsya – the four months of the rainy season in India, during which devotees of Viṣṇu observe special austerities.

Daivī prakṛti – lit., "divine nature." Refers to the original spiritual nature, out of which matter (*guṇa-māyā*), personified as Goddess Durgā, manifests. *Daivī prakṛti* is not separate from God.

Deva – a demigod or godly person.

Dhanañ-jaya – a name for Arjuna meaning "he who attains great wealth by conquest."

Dharma – (1) religious principles; (2) one's eternal, natural occupation (i.e., devotional service to the Lord). (3) the nature of anything, regarded as inseparable from itself. The Sanskrit term *dharma* is variously translated as duty, virtue, morality, righteousness or religion, but there is no single English equivalent.

Dhṛṣṭadyumna – the fire-born son of King Drupada, who arranged the military phalanx of the Pāṇḍavas on the Battlefield of Kurukṣetra, and the brother of the Pāṇḍavas' queen, Draupadī. He was born to kill Droṇa.

Dhṛtarāṣṭra – the father of the Kauravas, born blind because his mother closed her eyes out of fear during conception. The uncle of the Pāṇḍavas, whose attempt to usurp their kingdom for the sake of his own sons resulted in the Kurukṣetra war. The *Bhagavad-gītā* was related to Dhṛtarāṣṭra by his secretary as it was being spoken by Kṛṣṇa to Arjuna on the Battlefield of Kurukṣetra.

Dhyāna – meditation.

Droṇa – the martial preceptor of the Pāṇḍavas and the Kauravas. The military teacher of Arjuna and the other Pāṇḍavas and the commander-in-chief of the Kurus, who was obliged to fight the Pāṇḍavas on the Battlefield of Kurukṣetra. He was killed by Dhṛṣṭadyumna during the great Kurukṣetra war.

Duryodhana – the first-born and chief of the evil-minded one hundred sons of Dhṛtarāṣṭra, and chief rival of the Pāṇḍavas. He was a wicked *asura* by birth. He became envious of the Pāṇḍavas and tried in many ways to kill them. It was for the sake of establishing Duryodhana as king of the world that the Kurus fought the Battle of Kurukṣetra. He was killed by Bhīma when the latter broke his thighs on the last day of the battle of Kurukṣetra.

Dvāpara-yuga – see *Yuga.*

Gandharvas – the celestial singers and musicians among the demigods.

Gāṇḍīva – the famous bow of Arjuna, gifted to him by Varuṇa, demigod ruling the waters.

Garbhodaka-śāyī Viṣṇu – see *Puruṣa-avatāras.*
Garuḍa – the bird carrier of Lord Viṣṇu.
Godhead – the ultimate source of all energies.
Goloka – Kṛṣṇaloka, the eternal abode of Lord Kṛṣṇa and the highest planet in the spiritual abode.
Gosvāmī – a *svāmī,* one fully able to control his senses.
Govinda – a name of the Supreme Lord Kṛṣṇa meaning "One who gives pleasure to the land, cows, and senses."
Gṛhastha – a married person living according to the Vedic social system. The second order of the Vedic social system.
Guṇas – the three "modes," or qualities, of the material world: goodness, passion and ignorance.
Guru – lit., "heavy" [with knowledge]; a spiritual master.

Hanumān – the famous monkey devotee of Lord Rāmacandra and half-brother of Bhīma. Hanumān promised Bhīma that he would ride on Arjuna's flag and strike terror into the Kaurava troops during the Battle of Kurukṣetra.
Hare Kṛṣṇa mantra – a sixteen-word prayer composed of the names *Hare, Kṛṣṇa* and *Rāma:* Hare Kṛṣṇa, Hare Kṛṣṇa, Kṛṣṇa Kṛṣṇa, Hare Hare, Hare Rāma, Hare Rāma, Rāma Rāma, Hare Hare. *Hare,* the vocative form of Harā, is the personal form of God's own happiness, His eternal consort, Śrīmatī Rādhārāṇī; Kṛṣṇa is "the all-attractive one"; and Rāma is "the all-pleasing one." It is a prayer to be engaged in Kṛṣṇa's devotional service.
Heavenly planets – the higher planets of the universe, residences of the demigods.
Hṛṣīkeśa – a name of Kṛṣṇa meaning "master of the senses."

Ikṣvāku – the son of Manu who was king of the earth in ancient times and to whom Manu spoke the *Bhagavad-gītā.*
Indra – the chief sovereign of heaven and presiding deity of rain.
Īśvara – lit., "controller." One of the five *tattvas,* or ontological truths discussed in the *Gītā*. The *īśvara* (Kṛṣṇa) has full control over the other four truths: the *jīva* (living entity), *prakṛti* (material nature), *kāla* (time factor) and *karma* (actions).

Janārdana – a name for the Supreme Personality of Godhead meaning "He who is the original abode and protector of all living beings."
Jīva (Jīvātmā) – the eternal individual soul.

Jñāna – lit., "knowledge." This Sanskrit term is related in both form and meaning to the Greek word *gnosis*. Material *jñāna* does not go beyond knowledge of the material body and the material world; transcendental *jñāna* discriminates between matter and spirit. Perfect *jñāna* is knowledge of the body, the soul, and the Supreme Lord.

Jñāna-yoga – the path of spiritual realization through a speculative philosophical search for truth; the process of approaching the Supreme through the empiric process.

Jñānī – one adhering to the path of *jñāna-yoga.*

Kāla – time.

Kali-yuga – the age of quarrel and hypocrisy, which began five thousand years ago and lasts a total of 432,000 years. *See also: Yuga.*

Kalpa – the length of Brahmā's day, which lasts 4,320,000,000 years.

Karaṇadaka-śāyī Viṣṇu – see *Puruṣa-avatāras.*

Karma – material activities, for which one incurs subsequent reactions.

Karma-yoga – the path of God realization through dedicating the fruits of one's work to God.

Karmī – one engaged in *karma* (fruitive activity); a materialist.

Kṛpana – a miser who wastes his or her time in material instead of spiritual pursuits.

Kṛṣṇaloka – the supreme abode of Lord Kṛṣṇa.

Kṣatriya – a member of the warrior and administrative class; a member of the third of the four orders of the Vedic social system.

Kṣīrodaka-śāyī Viṣṇu – see *Puruṣa-avatāras.*

Kuntī – the mother of the Pāṇḍavas and Lord Kṛṣṇa's aunt. Her other name is Pṛthā.

Kurus – the descendants of Kuru, in particular the sons of Dhṛtarāṣṭra who opposed the Pāṇḍavas.

Līlā – a transcendental "pastime," or activity, performed by the Supreme Lord.

Loka – a planet.

Mahābhārata – an important and famous historical scripture belonging to the *smṛti* section of the Vedic literature. The *Mahābhārata* narrates the history of the Kuru dynasty of *kṣatriyas,* which was annihilated during the Kurukṣetra war. Contained within the *Mahābhārata* is the *Bhagavad-gītā*.

Mahā-mantra – the "great *mantra*": Hare Kṛṣṇa, Hare Kṛṣṇa, Kṛṣṇa Kṛṣṇa, Hare Hare/ Hare Rāma, Hare Rāma, Rāma Rāma, Hare Hare.

Mahātmā – a "great soul"; a liberated person who is fully Kṛṣṇa conscious.

Mahat-tattva – the total material energy.

Mantra – lit., *man* – "mind" + *tra* – deliverance: a transcendental sound or Vedic hymn that when repeated over and over delivers the mind or consciousness from material inclinations and illusion. The Vedic literatures contain thousands of mantras, including the *mahā-mantra,* or "great chant for deliverance," the Hare Kṛṣṇa mantra.

Manu – the demigod who is the father of mankind.

Māyā – illusion; the energy of the Supreme Lord that deludes living entities into forgetfulness of their spiritual nature and of God.

Māyāvādī – an impersonalist.

Mukti – liberation from material existence.

Muni – a sage.

Naiṣkarmya – another term for *akarma.*

Nārāyaṇa – the four-armed form of Lord Kṛṣṇa who presides over the Vaikuṇṭha planets; Lord Viṣṇu.

Nirguṇa – without attributes or qualities. In reference to the Supreme Lord, the term signifies that He is beyond material qualities.

Nirvāṇa – freedom from material existence.

Oṁ (Oṁ-kāra) – the sacred syllable that represents the Absolute Truth.

Pāṇḍavas – the five sons of King Pāṇḍu: Yudhiṣṭhira, Bhīma, Arjuna, Nakula and Sahadeva.

Pāṇḍu – the brother of Dhṛtarāṣṭra and father of the Pāṇḍava brothers.

Paramātmā – the Supersoul; the localized aspect of the Supreme Lord; the indwelling witness and guide who accompanies every conditioned soul.

Paramparā – a disciplic succession.

Prakṛti – energy or nature.

Prāṇāyāma – breath control, as a means of advancement in *yoga.*

Prasādam – sanctified food; food offered in devotion to Lord Kṛṣṇa.
Pratyāhāra – sensory withdrawal, as a means of advancement in *yoga.*
Prema – pure, spontaneous devotional love for God.
Pṛthā – Kuntī, the wife of King Pāṇḍu and mother of the Pāṇḍavas.
Purāṇas – the eighteen historical supplements to the *Vedas.*
Puruṣa – "the enjoyer"; the individual soul or the Supreme Lord.
Puruṣa-avatāras – the primary expansions of Lord Viṣṇu who effect the creation, maintenance and destruction of the material universes. Kāraṇodaka-śāyī Viṣṇu (Mahā-viṣṇu) lies within the Causal Ocean and breathes out innumerable universes; Garbhodaka-śāyī Viṣṇu enters each universe and creates diversity; Kṣīrodaka-śāyī Viṣṇu (the Supersoul) enters into the heart of every created being and into every atom.

Rajo-guṇa – the mode of passion.
Rākṣasas – a race of man-eating demons.
Rāma – (1) a name of Lord Kṛṣṇa meaning "the source of all pleasure"; (2) Lord Rāmacandra, an incarnation of Kṛṣṇa as a perfect righteous king.
Rūpa Gosvāmī – the leader of the six Gosvāmīs of Vṛndāvana, principal followers of Śrī Caitanya Mahāprabhu.

Sac-cid-ānanda – eternal, blissful and full of knowledge.
Sādhu – a saint or Kṛṣṇa conscious person.
Saguṇa – "possessing attributes or qualities." In reference to the Supreme Lord, the term signifies that He has spiritual, transcendental qualities.
Samādhi – trance; complete absorption in God consciousness.
Saṁsāra – the cycle of repeated birth and death in the material world.
Sanātana-dharma – the eternal religion: devotional service.
Śaṅkara (Śaṅkarācārya) – the great philosopher who established the doctrine of *advaita* (nondualism), stressing the nonpersonal nature of God and the identity of all souls with the undifferentiated Brahman.
Sāṅkhya – (1) analytical discrimination between spirit and matter; (2) the path of devotional service as described by Lord Kapila, the son of Devahūti.
Saṅkīrtana – congregational glorification of God, especially through chanting of His holy name.
Sannyāsa – the renounced order of life for spiritual culture.

Sannyāsī – a person in the renounced order.
Śāstra – revealed scripture; Vedic literature.
Sattva-guṇa – the mode of goodness.
Satya-yuga – see *Yuga.*
Śiva – the demigod who supervises the material mode of ignorance (*tamo-guṇa*) and who annihilates the material cosmos.
Smaraṇam – devotional remembrance (of Lord Kṛṣṇa); one of the nine basic forms of *bhakti-yoga.*
Smṛti – revealed scriptures supplementary to the *Vedas,* such as the *Purāṇas.*
Soma-rasa – a celestial beverage imbibed by the demigods.
Śravaṇam – hearing about the Lord; one of the nine basic forms of devotional service.
Śrīmad-Bhāgavatam – the *Purāṇa,* or history, written by Vyāsadeva specifically to give a deep understanding of Lord Śrī Kṛṣṇa.
Śruti – the *Vedas.*
Śūdra – a member of the laborer class of men, according to the four Vedic occupational divisions of society.
Svāmī – one fully able to control his senses; a person in the renounced order.
Svargaloka – the heavenly material planets, the abodes of the demigods.
Svarūpa – the original spiritual form, or constitutional position, of the soul.

Tamo-guṇa – the mode of ignorance.
Tretā-yuga – see *Yuga.*

Upaniṣads – 108 philosophical treatises that appear within the *Vedas.*

Vaikuṇṭhas – the eternal planets of the spiritual world.
Vaiṣṇava – a devotee of the Supreme Lord.
Vaiśya – a member of the mercantile and agricultural class, according to the four Vedic occupational divisions of society.
Vānaprastha – a man who has retired from householder life to cultivate greater renunciation, according to the Vedic social system.
Varṇāśrama-dharma – the Vedic social system, which organizes society into four occupational and four spiritual divisions (*varṇas* and *āśramas*).
Vasudeva – the father of Lord Kṛṣṇa.

Vāsudeva – Kṛṣṇa, the son of Vasudeva.
Vedānta-sūtra – the philosophical treatise written by Vyāsadeva, consisting of succinct aphorisms that embody the essential meaning of the *Upaniṣads.*
Vedas – the four original scriptures (*Ṛg, Sāma, Atharva* and *Yajur*).
Vidyā – knowledge.
Vikarma – work performed against scriptural directions; sinful action.
Virāṭ-rūpa – the universal form of the Supreme Lord.
Viṣṇu – the Personality of Godhead.
Viṣṇu-tattva – the status or category of Godhead.
Viśva-rūpa – the universal form of the Supreme Lord.
Vṛndāvana – the transcendental abode of Lord Kṛṣṇa. It is also called Goloka Vṛndāvana or Kṛṣṇaloka. The town of Vṛndāvana in the Mathurā District of Uttar Pradesh, India, where Kṛṣṇa enacted His childhood pastimes five thousand years ago, is a manifestation on earth of Kṛṣṇa's abode in the spiritual world.
Vyāsadeva – the compiler of the *Vedas* and author of the *Purāṇas, Mahābhārata* and *Vedānta-sūtra.*

Yajña – sacrifice.
Yakṣas – the ghostly followers of the demigod Kuvera.
Yamarāja – the demigod who punishes the sinful after death.
Yoga – spiritual discipline to link oneself with the Supreme.
Yoga-māyā – the internal, spiritual energy of the Lord.
Yuga – an "age." There are four *yugas,* which cycle perpetually: Satya-yuga, Tretā-yuga, Dvāpara-yuga and Kali-yuga. As the ages proceed from Satya to Kali, religion and the good qualities of men gradually decline.

References

The purports of *Bhagavad-gītā* are all confirmed by standard Vedic authorities. The following authentic scriptures are specifically cited in this volume. For specific page references, consult the general index.

Amṛta-bindu Upaniṣad
Atharva Veda
Bhagavad-gītā
Bhakti-rasāmṛta-sindhu
Brahma-saṁhitā
Brahma-sūtra
Bṛhad-āraṇyaka Upaniṣad
Bṛhad-viṣṇu-smṛti
Bṛhan-nāradīya Purāṇa
Caitanya-caritāmṛta
Chāndogya Upaniṣad
Garga Upaniṣad
Gītā-māhātmya
Gopāla-tāpanī Upaniṣad
Hari-bhakti-vilāsa
Īśopaniṣad
Kaṭha Upaniṣad
Kauṣītakī Upaniṣad
Kūrma Purāṇa
Mādhyandināyana-śruti
Mahābhārata
Mahā Upaniṣad
Māṇḍūkya Upaniṣad
Muṇḍaka Upaniṣad
Nārada Pañcarātra
Nārāyaṇa Upaniṣad
Nārāyaṇīya
Nirukti (dictionary)
Nṛsiṁha Purāṇa
Padma Purāṇa
Parāśara-smṛti
Praśna Upaniṣad
Puruṣa-bodhinī Upaniṣad
Ṛg Veda
Śrīmad-Bhāgavatam
Stotra-ratna
Subāla Upaniṣad
Śvetāśvatara Upaniṣad
Taittirīya Upaniṣad
Upadeśāmṛta
Varāha Purāṇa
Vedānta-sūtra
Viṣṇu Purāṇa
Yoga-sūtra

Sanskrit Pronunciation Guide

Throughout the centuries, the Sanskrit language has been written in a variety of alphabets. The mode of writing most widely used throughout India, however, is called *devanāgarī,* which means, literally, the writing used in "the cities of the demigods." The *devanāgarī* alphabet consists of forty-eight characters: thirteen vowels and thirty-five consonants. Ancient Sanskrit grammarians arranged this alphabet according to practical linguistic principles, and this order has been accepted by all Western scholars. The system of transliteration used in this book conforms to a system that scholars have accepted to indicate the pronunciation of each Sanskrit sound.

Vowels

अ **a** आ **ā** इ **i** ई **ī** उ **u** ऊ **ū** ऋ **ṛ**

ॠ **ṝ** ॡ **ḹ** ए **e** ऐ **ai** ओ **o** औ **au**

Consonants

Gutturals:	क **ka**	ख **kha**	ग **ga**	घ **gha**	ङ **ṅa**
Palatals:	च **ca**	छ **cha**	ज **ja**	झ **jha**	ञ **ña**
Cerebrals:	ट **ṭa**	ठ **ṭha**	ड **ḍa**	ढ **ḍha**	ण **ṇa**
Dentals:	त **ta**	थ **tha**	द **da**	ध **dha**	न **na**
Labials:	प **pa**	फ **pha**	ब **ba**	भ **bha**	म **ma**
Semivowels:	य **ya**	र **ra**	ल **la**	व **va**	
Sibilants:	श **śa**	ष **ṣa**	स **sa**		
Aspirate:	ह **ha**	Anusvāra: ं **ṁ**		Visarga: ः **ḥ**	

Numerals

०-0 १-1 २-2 ३-3 ४-4 ५-5 ६-6 ७-7 ८-8 ९-9

The vowels are written as follows after a consonant:

ा ā ि i ी ī ु u ू ū ृ ṛ ॄ ṝ े e ै ai ो o ौ au

For example: क **ka** का **kā** कि **ki** की **kī** कु **ku** कू **kū**

कृ **kṛ** कॄ **kṝ** कॢ **kḷ** के **ke** कै **kai** को **ko** कौ **kau**

Generally two or more consonants in conjunction are written together in a special form, as for example: क्ष **kṣa** त्र **tra**

The vowel "**a**" is implied after a consonant with no vowel symbol.

The symbol *virāma* (्) indicates that there is no final vowel: क्

The vowels are pronounced as follows:

a – as in b**u**t
ā – as in f**a**r but held twice as long as **a**
i – as in p**i**n
ī – as in p**i**que but held twice as long as **i**
u – as in p**u**sh
ū – as in r**u**le but held twice as long as **u**
ṛ – as in **ri**m
ṝ – as in **ree**d but held twice as long as **ṛ**
ḷ – as in happi**ly**
e – as in th**ey**
ai – as in **ai**sle
o – as in g**o**
au – as in h**ow**

The consonants are pronounced as follows:

Gutturals
(pronounced from the throat)
k – as in **k**ite
kh – as in Ec**kh**art
g – as in **g**ive
gh – as in di**g-h**ard
ṅ – as in si**ng**

Palatals
(Pronounced with the middle of the tongue against the palate)
c – as in **ch**air
ch – as in staun**ch-h**eart
j – as in **j**oy
jh – as in he**dgeh**og
ñ – as in ca**ny**on

Cerebrals
(pronounced with the tip of the tongue against the roof of the mouth)

ṭ	– as in **t**ub
ṭh	– as in ligh**t-h**eart
ḍ	– as in **d**ove
ḍh	– as in re**d-h**ot
ṇ	– as in si**ng**

Dentals
(pronounced like cerebrals but with the tongue against the teeth)

t	– as in **t**ub
th	– as in ligh**t-h**eart
d	– as in **d**ove
dh	– as in re**d-h**ot
n	– as in **n**ut

Labials
(pronounced with the lips)

p	– as in **p**ine
ph	– as in u**p-h**ill
b	– as in **b**ird
bh	– as in ru**b-h**ard
m	– as in **m**other

Semivowels

y	– as in **y**es
r	– as in **r**un
l	– as in **l**ight
v	– as in **v**ine, except when preceded in the same syllable by a consonant, as in s**w**an

Sibilants

ś	– as in the German word *sprechen*
ṣ	– as in **sh**ine
s	– as in **s**un

Aspirate

h	– as in **h**ome

Anusvāra

ṁ	– a resonant nasal sound as in the French word *bon*

Visarga

ḥ	– a final h-sound: **aḥ** is pronounced like **aha; iḥ** like **ihi**

There is no strong accentuation of syllables in Sanskrit, or pausing between words in a line, only a flowing of short and long syllables (the long twice as long as the short). A long syllable is one whose vowel is long (**ā, ī, ū, ṝ, e, ai, o, au**) or whose short vowel is followed by more than one consonant. Aspirated consonants (consonants followed by an **h**) count as single consonants.

Index of Sanskrit Verses

This index gives a listing of the first and third lines of each four-line Sanskrit verse of the *Bhagavad-gītā,* and both lines of each two-line verse. The references are to chapter and text.

Index of Verses Quoted

This index lists the verses quoted in the Introduction and purports of the *Bhagavad-gītā*. Numerals in boldface refer to the first or third lines of four-line verses quoted in full, or the first or second lines of two-line verses; numerals in lightface refer to partially quoted verses. Page numbers refer to the Introduction, and the numbers in parentheses refer to the paragraph in which the quoted verse appears.

General Index

The following is an index to the translations of the verses of *Bhagavad-gītā As It Is*. Further information on a given topic is likely to be found in the purport following the referenced translation.

Centres of the International Society for Krishna Consciousness

For further information on classes, programmes, festivals, residential courses, and local meetings please contact the centre nearest you.

United Kingdom and Ireland

Belfast – Sri Sri Radha-Madhava Mandir, Brooklands, 140 Upper Dunmurry Lane, Belfast, BT17 0HE, Northern Ireland; Tel. +44 (0)28 9062 0530 belfast@iskcon.org.uk; www.iskconuk.com/belfast

Birmingham – 84 Stanmore Rd, Edgbaston, Birmingham, B16 9TB Tel. +44 (0)121 420 4999; birmingham@iskcon.org.uk/ nitaicharan@fsmail.net www.iskconbirmingham.org

Coventry – Radha Krishna Centre, Kingfield Rd, Coventry (mail: 19 Gloucester St, Coventry CV1 3BZ); Tel. +44 (0)2476 552822; kov@krishnaofvrindavan.com www.krishnaofvrindavan.com

Dublin – Govinda's Kirtan Centre, 83 Middle Abbey St, Dublin 1, Irish Republic Tel. +353 (0)87 992 1332; syamananda@govindas.ie; www.govindas.ie

Lanarkshire – Karuna Bhavan, Bankhouse Rd, Lesmahagow, Lanarkshire, ML11 0ES Tel. +44 (0)1555 894790; karunabhavan@aol.com; www.iskcon.org.uk/scotland

Leicester – 31 Granby Street, Leicester, LE1 6EP; Tel. +44 (0)116 276 2587/ +44 (0)7597 786676; info@iskconleicester.org; www.iskconleicester.org

London (Kings Cross) – Matchless Gifts, 102 Caledonian Road, Kings Cross, London N1 Tel. +44 (0)20 7168 5732; foodforalluk@gmail.com; www.matchlessgifts.org.uk

London (city) – 10 Soho Street, London W1D 3DL; Tel. +44-20-74373662 shop: 72870269; Govinda's Restaurant: 74374928; london@pamho.net www.iskcon-london.org

London (south) – 42 Enmore Rd, South Norwood, London, SE25 5NG Tel. +44 (0)20 8656 4296

Manchester – 20 Mayfield Rd, Whalley Range, Manchester, M16 8FT Tel. +44 (0)161 226 4416; contact@iskconmanchester.com www.iskconmanchester.com

Swansea – The Hare Krishna Temple, 8 Craddock St, Swansea, SA1 3EN Tel. +44 (0)1792 468469; iskcon.swansea@pamho.net; www.iskconwales.org.uk

Newcastle-upon-Tyne – 304 Westgate Rd, Newcastle-upon-Tyne, NE4 6AR Tel. +44 (0)191 272 2620; newcastle@iskcon.org.uk www.iskconnewcastle.wordpress.com

Watford – Bhaktivedanta Manor, Hilfield Lane, Watford, WD25 8EZ Tel. +44 (0)1923 851000; info@krishnatemple.com; www.krishnatemple.com

Rural Community

Upper Lough Erne (Govindadwipa) – Hare Krishna Temple, Inis Rath Island, Derrylin, Co. Fermanagh, BT92 0BY Northern Ireland; Tel. +44 (0)28 677 23878 tp@krishnaisland.com; www.krishnaisland.com

Restaurants

Cardiff – Tel. +44 (0)2920 390391; iskcon.wales@pamho.net www.iskconwales.org.uk

Dublin - Govinda's, 4 Aungier St, Dublin 2, Rep. of Ireland; Tel. +353 (0)1 475 0309 nicola@govindas.ie; www.govindas.ie

Dublin – Govinda's, 83 Middle Abbey, Dublin 1, Rep. of Ireland mark@govindas.ie; www.govindas.ie

Dublin – Govinda's, 18 Merrion Row, Dublin 2, Rep. of Ireland Tel. +353 (0)1 661 5095; praghosa.sdg@pamho.net; www.govindas.ie

Hare Krishna meetings are held regularly in more than forty towns in the UK.

For more information, contact:
ISKCON Reader Services, P.O. Box 730, Watford, WD25 8EZ.

Visit us on the web at www.iskcon.org and for UK info and projects at www.iskconuk.com

Hungary

Budapest – Hungarian Society for Krishna Consciousness, Lehel str. 15-17, 1039 Budapest; Tel. +36-1-212-6270; info@krisna.hu; www.krisna.hu

Debrecen — Péterfia u. 57., 4024 Debrecen; Tel. +36-52-458092; debrecen@pamho.net; www.krisna.hu

Eger — Szechenyi u. 64., 3300 Eger; Tel. +36-36-313761; eger@pamho.net www.krisna.hu

Kecskemét — Felsöcsalános 116, 6000 Kecskemét (mail: Pf. 546, 6001 Kecskemét); Tel. +36-76-480920; kecskemet@pamho.net www.krisna.hu

Pécs — Damjanich u. 22., 7624 Pécs; Tel. +36-72-515991; Fax +36-72-313771 pecs@pamho.net; www.krisna.hu

Rural Community

Somogyvámos — Krisna-völgy, Fö u. 38., 8699 Somogyvámos Tel. +36-85-540002; krisna-volgy@pamho.net; www.krisna-volgy.hu

Restaurant

Budapest — Govinda Restaurant, Vigyázó Ferenc utca 4., 1051 Budapest Tel. +36-1-2691625; govinda@invitel.hu

Sweden

Gothenburg — Karl Johansgatan 57, 41455 Göteborg; Tel. +46-31-879648 restaurant: +46-31-421462; info@harekrishnagoteborg.com www.harekrishnagoteborg.com; restaurant: govindas.gothenburg@pamho.net www.govindas.gastrogate.com

Lund — Bredgatan 28, 22221 Lund; Tel. +46-46-399500, +46-46-120413 (restaurant); Fax +46-46-188804; vedicstudieslund@pamho.net.

Malmö — Box 8119, 20041 Malmö; info@harekrishna.nu; www.harekrishna.nu

Stockholm (country) — New Radhakund, Korsnäs Gård, 14792 Grödinge Tel. +46-8-53029800; Fax +46-8-53025062; info@pamho.net; www.krishna.se

Rural Community

Järna — Almviks Gård, 15395 Järna; Tel. +46-8-55152050 Fax +46-8-55152060; almviks.gard@pamho.net; www.almviksgard.se

Restaurant

Malmö — Govindas, Brogatan 11, 21144 Malmö; Tel. +46-40-308108

Canada

Montreal, Quebec – 1626 Pie-IX Boulevard, H1V 2C5; Tel. +1 (514) 521-1301 Fax +1 (514) 596-1423; iskconmontreal@gmail.com; www.iskconmontreal.ca

Vancouver, B.C — 5462 S.E. Marine Dr., Burnaby V5J 3G8; Tel. +1 (604) 433-9728 Fax +1 (604) 648-8715; vancouver@iskcon.ca; www.vancouver.iskcon.ca

Toronto, Ontario — 243 Avenue Rd., M5R 2J6; Tel. +1 (416) 922-5415 Fax +1 (416) 922-1021; www.toronto.iskcon.ca

USA

Boston, Massachusetts — 72 Commonwealth Ave., 02116; Tel. (617) 247-8611 www.iskconboston.org

Chicago, Illinois — 1716 W. Lunt Ave., 60626; Tel. (773) 973-0900 Fax (773) 973-0526; chicago@iskcon.net

Los Angeles, California — 3764 Watseka Ave., 90034; Tel. (310) 836-2676 Fax (310) 839-2715; nirantara@juno.com; restaurant: arcita@webcom.com

New York, New York — 305 Schermerhorn St., Brooklyn 11217 Tel. (718) 855-6714; Fax (718) 875-6127; ramabhadra@aol.com

Rural community

Alachua, Florida — New Raman Reti, 17306 N.W., 112th Blvd., 32615 (mail: P.O. Box 819, 32616); Tel. (386) 462-2017; alachuatemple@gmail.com